BIG IDEAS
MATH®

INTEGRATED MATHEMATICS II

Ron Larson
Laurie Boswell

BIG IDEAS LEARNING®

Erie, Pennsylvania
BigIdeasLearning.com

Big Ideas Learning, LLC
1762 Norcross Road
Erie, PA 16510-3838
USA

For product information and customer support, contact Big Ideas Learning
at **1-877-552-7766** or visit us at ***BigIdeasLearning.com***.

Cover Image
Mopic/Shutterstock.com, © Abidal | Dreamstime.com

Printed in the U.S.A.

ISBN 13: 978-1-68033-068-7
ISBN 10: 1-68033-068-3

3 4 5 6 7 8 9 10 WEB 19 18 17 16

Authors

Ron Larson, Ph.D., is well known as the lead author of a comprehensive program for mathematics that spans middle school, high school, and college courses. He holds the distinction of Professor Emeritus from Penn State Erie, The Behrend College, where he taught for nearly 40 years. He received his Ph.D. in mathematics from the University of Colorado. Dr. Larson's numerous professional activities keep him actively involved in the mathematics education community and allow him to fully understand the needs of students, teachers, supervisors, and administrators.

Ron Larson

Laurie Boswell, Ed.D., is the Head of School and a mathematics teacher at the Riverside School in Lyndonville, Vermont. Dr. Boswell is a recipient of the Presidential Award for Excellence in Mathematics Teaching and has taught mathematics to students at all levels, from elementary through college. Dr. Boswell was a Tandy Technology Scholar and served on the NCTM Board of Directors from 2002 to 2005. She currently serves on the board of NCSM and is a popular national speaker.

Laurie Boswell

Dr. Ron Larson and **Dr. Laurie Boswell** began writing together in 1992. Since that time, they have authored over two dozen textbooks. In their collaboration, Ron is primarily responsible for the student edition while Laurie is primarily responsible for the teaching edition.

For the Student

Welcome to *Big Ideas Math Integrated Mathematics II*. From start to finish, this program was designed with you, the learner, in mind.

As you work through the chapters in your Integrated Mathematics II course, you will be encouraged to think and to make conjectures while you persevere through challenging problems and exercises. You will make errors—and that is ok! Learning and understanding occur when you make errors and push through mental roadblocks to comprehend and solve new and challenging problems.

In this program, you will also be required to explain your thinking and your analysis of diverse problems and exercises. You will master content through engaging explorations that will provide deeper understanding, concise stepped-out examples and rich thought-provoking exercises. Being actively involved in learning will help you develop mathematical reasoning and use it to solve math problems and work through other everyday challenges. We wish you the best of luck as you explore Integrated Mathematics II. We are excited to be a part of your preparation for the challenges you will face in the remainder of your high school career and beyond.

Big Ideas Math High School Research

Big Ideas Math Integrated Mathematics I, II, and *III* is a research-based program providing a rigorous, focused, and coherent curriculum for high school students. Ron Larson and Laurie Boswell utilized their expertise as well as the body of knowledge collected by additional expert mathematicians and researchers to develop each course.

The pedagogical approach to this program follows the best practices outlined in the most prominent and widely-accepted educational research and standards, including:

Achieve, ACT, and The College Board

Adding It Up: Helping Children Learn Mathematics
National Research Council ©2001

Common Core State Standards for Mathematics
National Governors Association Center for Best Practices and the Council of Chief State
    School Officers ©2010

Curriculum Focal Points and the *Principles and Standards for School Mathematics* ©2000
National Council of Teachers of Mathematics (NCTM)

Project Based Learning
The Buck Institute

Rigor/Relevance Framework™
International Center for Leadership in Education

Universal Design for Learning Guidelines
CAST ©2011

Big Ideas Math would like to express our gratitude to the mathematics education and instruction experts who served as consultants during the writing of *Big Ideas Math Integrated Mathematics I, II,* and *III*. Their input was an invaluable asset during the development of this program.

Kristen Karbon
Curriculum and Assessment Coordinator
Troy School District
Troy, Michigan

Jean Carwin
Math Specialist/TOSA
Snohomish School District
Snohomish, Washington

Carolyn Briles
Performance Tasks Consultant
Mathematics Teacher, Loudoun County Public Schools
Leesburg, Virginia

Bonnie Spence
Differentiated Instruction Consultant
Mathematics Lecturer, The University of Montana
Missoula, Montana

Connie Schrock, Ph.D.
Performance Tasks Consultant
Mathematics Professor, Emporia State University
Emporia, Kansas

We would also like to thank all of our reviewers who took the time to provide feedback during the final development phases. For a complete list of the *Big Ideas Math* program reviewers, please visit *www.BigIdeasLearning.com*.

Mathematical Practices

Make sense of problems and persevere in solving them.
- *Essential Questions* help students focus on core concepts as they analyze and work through each *Exploration*.
- Section opening *Explorations* allow students to struggle with new mathematical concepts and explain their reasoning in the *Communicate Your Answer* questions.

Reason abstractly and quantitatively.
- *Reasoning*, *Critical Thinking*, *Abstract Reasoning*, and *Problem Solving* exercises challenge students to apply their acquired knowledge and reasoning skills to solve each problem.
- *Thought Provoking* exercises test the reasoning skills of students as they analyze and interpret perplexing scenarios.

Construct viable arguments and critique the reasoning of others.
- Students must justify their responses to each *Essential Question* in the *Communicate Your Answer* questions at the end of each *Exploration* set.
- Students are asked to construct arguments and critique the reasoning of others in specialized exercises, including *Making an Argument, How Do You See It?, Drawing Conclusions, Reasoning, Error Analysis, Problem Solving*, and *Writing*.

Model with mathematics.
- Real-life scenarios are utilized in *Explorations, Examples, Exercises*, and *Assessments* so students have opportunities to apply the mathematical concepts they have learned to realistic situations.
- *Modeling with Mathematics* exercises allow students to interpret a problem in the context of a real-life situation, often utilizing tables, graphs, visual representations, and formulas.

Use appropriate tools strategically.
- Students are provided opportunities for selecting and utilizing the appropriate mathematical tool in *Using Tools* exercises. Students work with graphing calculators, dynamic geometry software, models, and more.
- A variety of tool papers and manipulatives are available for students to use in problems as strategically appropriate.

Attend to precision.
- *Vocabulary and Core Concept Check* exercises require students to use clear, precise mathematical language in their solutions and explanations.
- The many opportunities for cooperative learning in this program, including working with partners for each *Exploration*, support precise, explicit mathematical communication.

Look for and make use of structure.
- *Using Structure* exercises provide students with the opportunity to explore patterns and structure in mathematics.
- Students analyze structure in problems through *Justifying Steps* and *Analyzing Equations* exercises.

Look for and express regularity in repeated reasoning.
- Students are continually encouraged to evaluate the reasonableness of their solutions and their steps in the problem-solving process.
- Stepped-out *Examples* encourage students to maintain oversight of their problem-solving process and pay attention to the relevant details in each step.

Course Overview

Big Ideas Math Integrated Mathematics I, II, and *III* were developed using the consistent, dependable learning and instructional theory that have become synonymous with *Big Ideas Math*. Students will gain a deeper understanding of mathematics by narrowing their focus to fewer topics at each grade level. They will also master content through inductive reasoning opportunities, engaging explorations, concise stepped-out examples, and rich thought-provoking exercises.

The research-based curriculum features a continual development of concepts that have been previously taught while integrating algebra, geometry, probability, and statistics topics throughout each course.

In *Integrated Mathematics I*, students will study linear and exponential equations and functions. Students will use linear regression and perform data analysis. They will also learn about geometry topics such as simple proofs, congruence, and transformations.

Integrated Mathematics II expands into quadratic, absolute value, and other functions. Students will also explore polynomial equations and factoring, and probability and its applications. Coverage of geometry topics extends to polygon relationships, proofs, similarity, trigonometry, circles, and three-dimensional figures.

In *Integrated Mathematics III*, students will expand their understanding of area and volume with geometric modeling, which students will apply throughout the course as they learn new types of functions. Students will study polynomial, radical, logarithmic, rational, and trigonometric functions. They will also learn how visual displays and statistics relate to different types of data and probability distributions.

1 Functions and Exponents

See the Big Idea
Learn how to make bank shots on a pool table using the reflection of a line.

2 Polynomial Equations and Factoring

See the Big Idea
Explore whether seagulls and crows use the optimal
height while dropping hard-shelled food to crack it open.

3 Graphing Quadratic Functions

See the Big Idea
Learn how to build your own parabolic mirror that uses sunlight to generate electricity.

4 Solving Quadratic Equations

See the Big Idea
Explore the Parthenon and investigate how the use of the golden rectangle has evolved since its discovery.

5 Probability

See the Big Idea
Learn about caring for trees at an arboretum.

6 Relationships Within Triangles

See the Big Idea
Discover why triangles are used in building for strength.

7 Quadrilaterals and Other Polygons

See the Big Idea
Explore what the refractive index, reflected light, and light dispersion have to do with diamonds.

8 Similarity

See the Big Idea
Discover how many different ways you can scale a model.

9 Right Triangles and Trigonometry

See the Big Idea
Test the accuracy of two measurement
methods and discover which one prevails.

10 Circles

See the Big Idea
Utilize trilateration to find the epicenters of historical earthquakes and discover where they lie on known fault lines.

11 Circumference, Area, and Volume

See the Big Idea
Learn how to cover a decagon-shaped
tabletop using Penrose tiling.

How to Use Your Math Book

Get ready for each chapter by **Maintaining Mathematical Proficiency** and reviewing the **Mathematical Practices**. Begin each section by working through the **EXPLORATIONS** to **Communicate Your Answer** to the **Essential Question**. Each **Lesson** will explain **What You Will Learn** through **EXAMPLES**, **Core Concepts**, and **Core Vocabulary**. Answer the **Monitoring Progress** questions as you work through each lesson. Look for STUDY TIPS, COMMON ERRORS, and suggestions for looking at a problem ANOTHER WAY throughout the lessons. Take note of **CONNECTIONS TO ALGEBRA** and **CONNECTIONS TO GEOMETRY** which will inform you that the current concept can be applied to other topics throughout the program. We will also provide you with guidance for accurate mathematical READING and concept details you should REMEMBER.

Sharpen your newly acquired skills with **Exercises** at the end of every section. Halfway through each chapter you will be asked **What Did You Learn?** and you can use the Mid-Chapter **Quiz** to check your progress. You can also use the **Chapter Review** and **Chapter Test** to review and assess yourself after you have completed a chapter.

Apply what you learned in each chapter to a **Performance Task** and build your confidence for taking standardized tests with each chapter's **Cumulative Assessment**. For extra practice in any chapter, use your *Online Resources*, *Skills Review Handbook*, or your *Student Journal*.

1 Functions and Exponents

Duckweed *(p. 49)*

Jellyfish *(p. 31)*

Miniature Golf *(p. 18)*

Karaoke Machine *(p. 14)*

SEE the Big Idea

Pool *(p. 9)*

Maintaining Mathematical Proficiency

Transforming Graphs of Linear Functions

Example 1 Graph $f(x) = x$ and $g(x) = -3x - 2$. Describe the transformations from the graph of f to the graph of g.

Note that you can rewrite g as $g(x) = -3f(x) - 2$.

Step 1 There is no horizontal translation from the graph of f to the graph of g.

Step 2 Stretch the graph of f vertically by a factor of 3 to get the graph of $h(x) = 3x$.

Step 3 Reflect the graph of h in the x-axis to get the graph of $r(x) = -3x$.

Step 4 Translate the graph of r vertically 2 units down to get the graph of $g(x) = -3x - 2$.

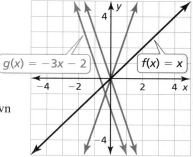

Let $f(x) = x + 1$. Graph f and g. Describe the transformation from the graph of f to the graph of g.

1. $g(x) = f(x - 4)$ **2.** $g(x) = f(x) + 5$ **3.** $g(x) = f(2x)$ **4.** $g(x) = -\frac{1}{2}f(x)$

Reflecting Figures in the Line $y = x$

Example 2 Graph $\overline{PQ}$ with endpoints $P(-3, 1)$ and $Q(2, 4)$ and its image after a reflection in the line $y = x$.

Graph $\overline{PQ}$ and the line $y = x$. Use the coordinate rule for reflecting in the line $y = x$ to find the coordinates of the endpoints of the image. Then graph the image $\overline{P'Q'}$.

$$(a, b) \rightarrow (b, a)$$
$$P(-3, 1) \rightarrow P'(1, -3)$$
$$Q(2, 4) \rightarrow Q'(4, 2)$$

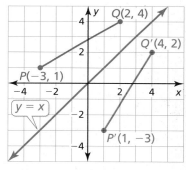

Graph the figure and its image after a reflection in the line $y = x$.

5. $\overline{AB}$ with endpoints $A(0, 0)$ and $B(0, -3.5)$

6. $\overline{CD}$ with endpoints $C(1, -2)$ and $D(-4, -1)$

7. $\triangle LMN$ with vertices $L(5, 3)$, $M(5, -3)$, and $N(0, -3)$

8. $\square STUV$ with vertices $S(-4, 6)$, $T(-1, 7)$, $U(-1, -4)$, and $V(-4, -5)$

9. Give an example of a line segment that when reflected in the line $y = x$, has the same endpoints as the original figure.

10. ABSTRACT REASONING Describe the relationship between the possible input and output values of the graph of $f(x) = a$ and its reflection in the line $y = x$.

Mathematical Practices

Mathematically proficient students use technological tools to explore concepts.

Using a Graphing Calculator

⑤ Core Concept

Restricting the Domain of a Function

You can use a graphing calculator to graph a function with a restricted domain.

1. Enter the function, in parentheses, into a graphing calculator.
2. Press the division symbol key.
3. Enter the specified domain, in parentheses.
4. Graph the function in an appropriate viewing window.

EXAMPLE 1 **Using a Graphing Calculator**

Use a graphing calculator to graph (a) $y = -2x + 7$, $x \geq 2$, and (b) $y = \frac{3}{4}x - 1$, $-3 < x < 4$.

SOLUTION

a. Enter the function $y = -2x + 7$ and the domain $x \geq 2$ into a graphing calculator, as shown. Then graph the function in an appropriate viewing window.

b. Enter the function $y = \frac{3}{4}x - 1$ and the domain $-3 < x < 4$ into a graphing calculator. In this case, you must enter the inequality using "and," as shown. Then graph the function in an appropriate viewing window.

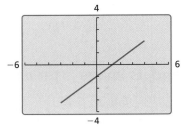

Notice that the graphing calculator does not distinguish between domains such as $x \geq 2$ and $x > 2$. You must distinguish between these yourself, based on the inequality symbol in the problem statement.

Monitoring Progress

Use a graphing calculator to graph the function with the specified domain. Describe the range of the function.

1. $y = 3x + 2$, $x \leq -1$
2. $y = -x - 4$, $x > 0$
3. $-\frac{1}{2}x + y = 1$, $-4 \leq x \leq 1$

Essential Question
How do the values of a, h, and k affect the graph of the absolute value function $g(x) = a|x - h| + k$?

The parent absolute value function is

$f(x) = |x|$.　　Parent absolute value function

The graph of f is V-shaped.

EXPLORATION 1　Identifying Graphs of Absolute Value Functions

Work with a partner. Match each absolute value function with its graph. Then use a graphing calculator to verify your answers.

a. $g(x) = -|x - 2|$

b. $g(x) = |x - 2| + 2$

c. $g(x) = -|x + 2| - 2$

d. $g(x) = |x - 2| - 2$

e. $g(x) = 2|x - 2|$

f. $g(x) = -|x + 2| + 2$

A.

B.

C.

D.

E.

F.

LOOKING FOR STRUCTURE

To be proficient in math, you need to look closely to discern a pattern or structure.

Communicate Your Answer

2. How do the values of a, h, and k affect the graph of the absolute value function

$g(x) = a|x - h| + k$?

3. Write the equation of the absolute value function whose graph is shown. Use a graphing calculator to verify your equation.

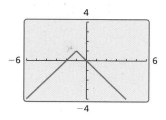

What You Will Learn

▶ Translate graphs of absolute value functions.

▶ Stretch, shrink, and reflect graphs of absolute value functions.

▶ Combine transformations of graphs of absolute value functions.

Core Vocabulary

absolute value function, *p. 4*
vertex, *p. 4*
vertex form, *p. 6*

Previous
domain
range

Translating Graphs of Absolute Value Functions

🌀 Core Concept

Absolute Value Function

An **absolute value function** is a function that contains an absolute value expression. The parent absolute value function is $f(x) = |x|$. The graph of $f(x) = |x|$ is V-shaped and symmetric about the y-axis. The **vertex** is the point where the graph changes direction. The vertex of the graph of $f(x) = |x|$ is $(0, 0)$.

The domain of $f(x) = |x|$ is all real numbers. The range is $y \geq 0$.

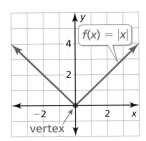

The graphs of all other absolute value functions are transformations of the graph of the parent function $f(x) = |x|$. The transformations of graphs of linear functions that you learned in a previous course also apply to absolute value functions.

REMEMBER

The graph of $y = f(x - h)$ is a horizontal translation and $y = f(x) + k$ is a vertical translation of the graph of $y = f(x)$, where $h, k \neq 0$.

EXAMPLE 1 Graphing $g(x) = |x| + k$ and $g(x) = |x - h|$

Graph each function. Compare each graph to the graph of $f(x) = |x|$. Describe the domain and range.

a. $g(x) = |x| + 3$

b. $m(x) = |x - 2|$

SOLUTION

a. Step 1 Make a table of values.

x	−2	−1	0	1	2
g(x)	5	4	3	4	5

Step 2 Plot the ordered pairs.

Step 3 Draw the V-shaped graph.

▶ The function g is of the form $y = f(x) + k$, where $k = 3$. So, the graph of g is a vertical translation 3 units up of the graph of f. The domain is all real numbers. The range is $y \geq 3$.

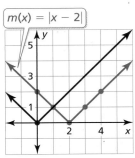

b. Step 1 Make a table of values.

x	0	1	2	3	4
m(x)	2	1	0	1	2

Step 2 Plot the ordered pairs.

Step 3 Draw the V-shaped graph.

▶ The function m is of the form $y = f(x - h)$, where $h = 2$. So, the graph of m is a horizontal translation 2 units right of the graph of f. The domain is all real numbers. The range is $y \geq 0$.

Monitoring Progress   Help in English and Spanish at *BigIdeasMath.com*

Graph the function. Compare the graph to the graph of $f(x) = |x|$. Describe the domain and range.

1. $h(x) = |x| - 1$

2. $n(x) = |x + 4|$

Stretching, Shrinking, and Reflecting

EXAMPLE 2 **Graphing** $g(x) = a|x|$

Graph each function. Compare each graph to the graph of $f(x) = |x|$. Describe the domain and range.

a. $q(x) = 2|x|$ **b.** $p(x) = -\frac{1}{2}|x|$

SOLUTION

a. Step 1 Make a table of values.

x	-2	-1	0	1	2
$q(x)$	4	2	0	2	4

Step 2 Plot the ordered pairs.

Step 3 Draw the V-shaped graph.

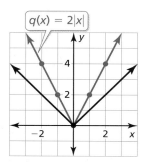

▶ The function q is of the form $y = a \cdot f(x)$, where $a = 2$. So, the graph of q is a vertical stretch of the graph of f by a factor of 2. The domain is all real numbers. The range is $y \geq 0$.

b. Step 1 Make a table of values.

x	-2	-1	0	1	2
$p(x)$	-1	$-\frac{1}{2}$	0	$-\frac{1}{2}$	-1

Step 2 Plot the ordered pairs.

Step 3 Draw the V-shaped graph.

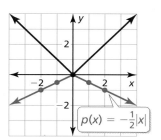

▶ The function p is of the form $y = -a \cdot f(x)$, where $a = \frac{1}{2}$. So, the graph of p is a vertical shrink of the graph of f by a factor of $\frac{1}{2}$ and a reflection in the x-axis. The domain is all real numbers. The range is $y \leq 0$.

REMEMBER

Recall the following transformations of the graph of $y = f(x)$.

$y = -f(x)$: reflection in the x-axis

$y = f(-x)$: reflection in the y-axis

$y = f(ax)$: horizontal stretch or shrink by a factor of $\frac{1}{a}$, where $a > 0$ and $a \neq 1$

$y = a \cdot f(x)$: vertical stretch or shrink by a factor of a, where $a > 0$ and $a \neq 1$

STUDY TIP

A vertical stretch of the graph of $f(x) = |x|$ is *narrower* than the graph of $f(x) = |x|$.

STUDY TIP

A vertical shrink of the graph of $f(x) = |x|$ is *wider* than the graph of $f(x) = |x|$.

Monitoring Progress Help in English and Spanish at *BigIdeasMath.com*

Graph the function. Compare the graph to the graph of $f(x) = |x|$. Describe the domain and range.

3. $t(x) = -3|x|$ **4.** $v(x) = \frac{1}{4}|x|$

Core Concept

Vertex Form of an Absolute Value Function

An absolute value function written in the form $g(x) = a|x - h| + k$, where $a \neq 0$, is in **vertex form**. The vertex of the graph of g is (h, k).

Any absolute value function can be written in vertex form, and its graph is symmetric about the line $x = h$.

STUDY TIP

The function g is *not* in vertex form because the x variable does not have a coefficient of 1.

EXAMPLE 3 Graphing $f(x) = |x - h| + k$ and $g(x) = f(ax)$

Graph $f(x) = |x + 2| - 3$ and $g(x) = |2x + 2| - 3$. Compare the graph of g to the graph of f.

SOLUTION

Step 1 Make a table of values for each function.

x	−4	−3	−2	−1	0	1	2
f(x)	−1	−2	−3	−2	−1	0	1

x	−2	−1.5	−1	−0.5	0	0.5	1
g(x)	−1	−2	−3	−2	−1	0	1

Step 2 Plot the ordered pairs.

Step 3 Draw the V-shaped graph of each function. Notice that the vertex of the graph of f is $(-2, -3)$ and the graph is symmetric about $x = -2$.

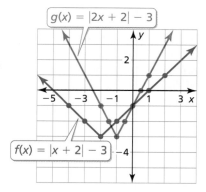

Note that you can rewrite g as $g(x) = f(2x)$, which is of the form $y = f(ax)$, where $a = 2$. So, the graph of g is a horizontal shrink of the graph of f by a factor of $\frac{1}{2}$. The y-intercept is the same for both graphs. The points on the graph of f move halfway closer to the y-axis, resulting in the graph of g. When the input values of f are 2 times the input values of g, the output values of f and g are the same.

Monitoring Progress Help in English and Spanish at *BigIdeasMath.com*

5. Graph $f(x) = |x - 1|$ and $g(x) = \left|\frac{1}{2}x - 1\right|$. Compare the graph of g to the graph of f.

6. Graph $f(x) = |x + 2| + 2$ and $g(x) = |-4x + 2| + 2$. Compare the graph of g to the graph of f.

Combining Transformations

EXAMPLE 4 **Graphing $g(x) = a|x - h| + k$**

Let $g(x) = -2|x - 1| + 3$. (a) Describe the transformations from the graph of $f(x) = |x|$ to the graph of g. (b) Graph g.

SOLUTION

a. Step 1 Translate the graph of f horizontally 1 unit right to get the graph of $t(x) = |x - 1|$.

Step 2 Stretch the graph of t vertically by a factor of 2 to get the graph of $h(x) = 2|x - 1|$.

Step 3 Reflect the graph of h in the x-axis to get the graph of $r(x) = -2|x - 1|$.

Step 4 Translate the graph of r vertically 3 units up to get the graph of $g(x) = -2|x - 1| + 3$.

b. Method 1

Step 1 Make a table of values.

x	−1	0	1	2	3
g(x)	−1	1	3	1	−1

Step 2 Plot the ordered pairs.

Step 3 Draw the V-shaped graph.

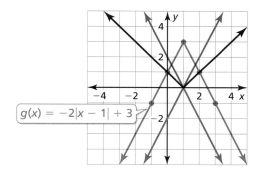

$g(x) = -2|x - 1| + 3$

Method 2

Step 1 Identify and plot the vertex. $(h, k) = (1, 3)$

Step 2 Plot another point on the graph, such as $(2, 1)$. Because the graph is symmetric about the line $x = 1$, you can use symmetry to plot a third point, $(0, 1)$.

Step 3 Draw the V-shaped graph.

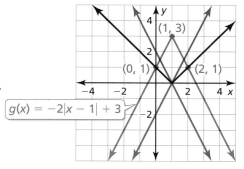

$g(x) = -2|x - 1| + 3$

Monitoring Progress

Help in English and Spanish at *BigIdeasMath.com*

7. Let $g(x) = \left|-\frac{1}{2}x + 2\right| + 1$. (a) Describe the transformations from the graph of $f(x) = |x|$ to the graph of g. (b) Graph g.

Vocabulary and Core Concept Check

1. **COMPLETE THE SENTENCE** The point $(1, -4)$ is the _____ of the graph of $f(x) = -3|x - 1| - 4$.

2. **USING STRUCTURE** How do you know whether the graph of $f(x) = a|x - h| + k$ is a vertical stretch or a vertical shrink of the graph of $f(x) = |x|$?

3. **WRITING** Describe three different types of transformations of the graph of an absolute value function.

4. **REASONING** The graph of which function has the same y-intercept as the graph of $f(x) = |x - 2| + 5$? Explain.

$$g(x) = |3x - 2| + 5 \qquad h(x) = 3|x - 2| + 5$$

Monitoring Progress and Modeling with Mathematics

In Exercises 5–12, graph the function. Compare the graph to the graph of $f(x) = |x|$. Describe the domain and range. *(See Examples 1 and 2.)*

5. $d(x) = |x| - 4$

6. $r(x) = |x| + 5$

7. $m(x) = |x + 1|$

8. $v(x) = |x - 3|$

9. $p(x) = \frac{1}{3}|x|$

10. $j(x) = 3|x|$

11. $a(x) = -5|x|$

12. $q(x) = -\frac{3}{2}|x|$

In Exercises 13–16, graph the function. Compare the graph to the graph of $f(x) = |x - 6|$.

13. $h(x) = |x - 6| + 2$

14. $n(x) = \frac{1}{2}|x - 6|$

15. $k(x) = -3|x - 6|$

16. $g(x) = |x - 1|$

In Exercises 17 and 18, graph the function. Compare the graph to the graph of $f(x) = |x + 3| - 2$.

17. $y(x) = |x + 4| - 2$

18. $b(x) = |x + 3| + 3$

In Exercises 19–22, compare the graphs. Find the value of h, k, or a.

19.

20.

21.

22.

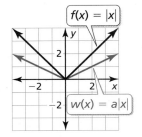

In Exercises 23–26, write an equation that represents the given transformation(s) of the graph of $g(x) = |x|$.

23. vertical translation 7 units down

24. horizontal translation 10 units left

25. vertical shrink by a factor of $\frac{1}{4}$

26. vertical stretch by a factor of 3 and a reflection in the x-axis

In Exercises 27–32, graph and compare the two functions. *(See Example 3.)*

27. $f(x) = |x - 4|$; $g(x) = |3x - 4|$

28. $h(x) = |x + 5|$; $t(x) = |2x + 5|$

29. $p(x) = |x + 1| - 2$; $q(x) = \left|\frac{1}{4}x + 1\right| - 2$

30. $w(x) = |x - 3| + 4$; $y(x) = |5x - 3| + 4$

31. $a(x) = |x + 2| + 3$; $b(x) = |-4x + 2| + 3$

32. $u(x) = |x - 1| + 2$; $v(x) = \left|-\frac{1}{2}x - 1\right| + 2$

In Exercises 33–40, describe the transformations from the graph of $f(x) = |x|$ to the graph of the given function. Then graph the given function. *(See Example 4.)*

33. $r(x) = |x + 2| - 6$ **34.** $c(x) = |x + 4| + 4$

35. $d(x) = -|x - 3| + 5$ **36.** $v(x) = -3|x + 1| + 4$

37. $m(x) = \frac{1}{2}|x + 4| - 1$ **38.** $s(x) = |2x - 2| - 3$

39. $j(x) = |-x + 1| - 5$ **40.** $n(x) = \left|-\frac{1}{3}x + 1\right| + 2$

41. MODELING WITH MATHEMATICS The number of pairs of shoes sold s (in thousands) increases and then decreases as described by the function $s(t) = -2|t - 15| + 50$, where t is the time (in weeks).

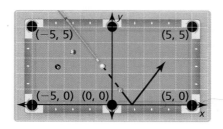

    a. Graph the function.

    b. What is the greatest number of pairs of shoes sold in 1 week?

42. MODELING WITH MATHEMATICS On the pool table shown, you bank the five ball off the side represented by the x-axis. The path of the ball is described by the function $p(x) = \frac{4}{3}\left|x - \frac{5}{4}\right|$.

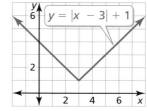

    a. At what point does the five ball bank off the side?

    b. Do you make the shot? Explain your reasoning.

43. USING TRANSFORMATIONS The points $A\left(-\frac{1}{2}, 3\right)$, $B(1, 0)$, and $C(-4, -2)$ lie on the graph of the absolute value function f. Find the coordinates of the points corresponding to A, B, and C on the graph of each function.

    a. $g(x) = f(x) - 5$ **b.** $h(x) = f(x - 3)$

    c. $j(x) = -f(x)$ **d.** $k(x) = 4f(x)$

44. USING STRUCTURE Explain how the graph of each function compares to the graph of $y = |x|$ for positive and negative values of k, h, and a.

    a. $y = |x| + k$

    b. $y = |x - h|$

    c. $y = a|x|$

    d. $y = |ax|$

ERROR ANALYSIS In Exercises 45 and 46, describe and correct the error in graphing the function.

45.

46.

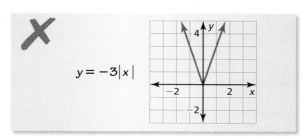

MATHEMATICAL CONNECTIONS In Exercises 47 and 48, write an absolute value function whose graph forms a square with the given graph.

47.

48.

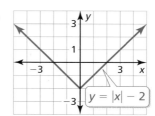

49. WRITING Compare the graphs of $p(x) = |x - 6|$ and $q(x) = |x| - 6$.

50. HOW DO YOU SEE IT? The object of a computer game is to break bricks by deflecting a ball toward them using a paddle. The graph shows the current path of the ball and the location of the last brick.

a. You can move the paddle up, down, left, and right. At what coordinates should you place the paddle to break the last brick? Assume the ball deflects at a right angle.

b. You move the paddle to the coordinates in part (a), and the ball is deflected. How can you write an absolute value function that describes the path of the ball?

In Exercises 51–54, graph the function. Then rewrite the absolute value function as two linear functions, one that has the domain $x < 0$ and one that has the domain $x \geq 0$.

51. $y = |x|$

52. $y = |x| - 3$

53. $y = -|x| + 9$

54. $y = -4|x|$

In Exercises 55–58, graph and compare the two functions.

55. $f(x) = |x - 1| + 2$; $g(x) = 4|x - 1| + 8$

56. $s(x) = |2x - 5| - 6$; $t(x) = \frac{1}{2}|2x - 5| - 3$

57. $v(x) = -2|3x + 1| + 4$; $w(x) = 3|3x + 1| - 6$

58. $c(x) = 4|x + 3| - 1$; $d(x) = -\frac{4}{3}|x + 3| + \frac{1}{3}$

59. REASONING Describe the transformations from the graph of $g(x) = -2|x + 1| + 4$ to the graph of $h(x) = |x|$. Explain your reasoning.

60. THOUGHT PROVOKING Graph an absolute value function f that represents the route a wide receiver runs in a football game. Let the x-axis represent distance (in yards) across the field horizontally. Let the y-axis represent distance (in yards) down the field. Be sure to limit the domain so the route is realistic.

61. SOLVING BY GRAPHING Graph $y = 2|x + 2| - 6$ and $y = -2$ in the same coordinate plane. Use the graph to solve the equation $2|x + 2| - 6 = -2$. Check your solutions.

62. MAKING AN ARGUMENT Let p be a positive constant. Your friend says that because the graph of $y = |x| + p$ is a *positive* vertical translation of the graph of $y = |x|$, the graph of $y = |x + p|$ is a *positive* horizontal translation of the graph of $y = |x|$. Is your friend correct? Explain.

63. ABSTRACT REASONING Write the vertex of the absolute value function $f(x) = |ax - h| + k$ in terms of a, h, and k.

Maintaining Mathematical Proficiency
Reviewing what you learned in previous grades and lessons

Solve the formula for the indicated variable. *(Skills Review Handbook)*

64. Solve for h.

$V = \pi r^2 h$

65. Solve for w.

$P = 2\ell + 2w$

Write an equation of the line that passes through the points. *(Skills Review Handbook)*

66. $(1, -4), (2, -1)$

67. $(-3, 12), (0, 6)$

68. $(3, 1), (-5, 5)$

69. $(2, -1), (0, 1)$

1.2 Piecewise Functions

Essential Question How can you describe a function that is represented by more than one equation?

EXPLORATION 1 **Writing Equations for a Function**

Work with a partner.

CONSTRUCTING VIABLE ARGUMENTS

To be proficient in math, you need to justify your conclusions and communicate them to others.

a. Does the graph represent y as a function of x? Justify your conclusion.

b. What is the value of the function when $x = 0$? How can you tell?

c. Write an equation that represents the values of the function when $x \leq 0$.

$$f(x) = \boxed{}, \text{ if } x \leq 0$$

d. Write an equation that represents the values of the function when $x > 0$.

$$f(x) = \boxed{}, \text{ if } x > 0$$

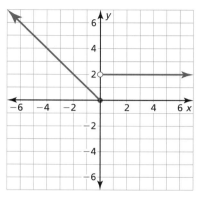

e. Combine the results of parts (c) and (d) to write a single description of the function.

$$f(x) = \begin{cases} \boxed{}, \text{ if } x \leq 0 \\ \boxed{}, \text{ if } x > 0 \end{cases}$$

EXPLORATION 2 **Writing Equations for a Function**

Work with a partner.

a. Does the graph represent y as a function of x? Justify your conclusion.

b. Describe the values of the function for the following intervals.

$$f(x) = \begin{cases} \boxed{}, \text{ if } -6 \leq x < -3 \\ \boxed{}, \text{ if } -3 \leq x < 0 \\ \boxed{}, \text{ if } 0 \leq x < 3 \\ \boxed{}, \text{ if } 3 \leq x < 6 \end{cases}$$

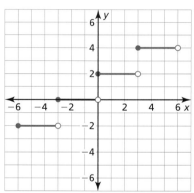

Communicate Your Answer

3. How can you describe a function that is represented by more than one equation?

4. Use two equations to describe the function represented by the graph.

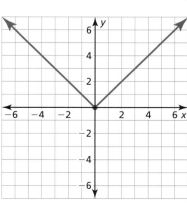

What You Will Learn

▶ Evaluate piecewise functions.

▶ Graph and write piecewise functions.

▶ Graph and write step functions.

▶ Write absolute value functions.

Core Vocabulary

piecewise function, *p. 12*
step function, *p. 14*

Previous
absolute value function
vertex form
vertex

Evaluating Piecewise Functions

Core Concept

Piecewise Function

A **piecewise function** is a function defined by two or more equations. Each "piece" of the function applies to a different part of its domain. An example is shown below.

$$f(x) = \begin{cases} x - 2, & \text{if } x \le 0 \\ 2x + 1, & \text{if } x > 0 \end{cases}$$

- The expression $x - 2$ represents the value of f when x is less than or equal to 0.

- The expression $2x + 1$ represents the value of f when x is greater than 0.

$f(x) = 2x + 1, x > 0$

$f(x) = x - 2, x \le 0$

EXAMPLE 1 **Evaluating a Piecewise Function**

Evaluate the function f above when (a) $x = 0$ and (b) $x = 4$.

SOLUTION

a. $f(x) = x - 2$ Because $0 \le 0$, use the first equation.

$f(0) = 0 - 2$ Substitute 0 for x.

$f(0) = -2$ Simplify.

▶ The value of f is -2 when $x = 0$.

b. $f(x) = 2x + 1$ Because $4 > 0$, use the second equation.

$f(4) = 2(4) + 1$ Substitute 4 for x.

$f(4) = 9$ Simplify.

▶ The value of f is 9 when $x = 4$.

Monitoring Progress Help in English and Spanish at *BigIdeasMath.com*

Evaluate the function.

$$f(x) = \begin{cases} 3, & \text{if } x < -2 \\ x + 2, & \text{if } -2 \le x \le 5 \\ 4x, & \text{if } x > 5 \end{cases}$$

1. $f(-8)$ **2.** $f(-2)$

3. $f(0)$ **4.** $f(3)$

5. $f(5)$ **6.** $f(10)$

Graphing and Writing Piecewise Functions

EXAMPLE 2   **Graphing a Piecewise Function**

Graph $y = \begin{cases} -x - 4, & \text{if } x < 0 \\ x, & \text{if } x \geq 0 \end{cases}$. Describe the domain and range.

SOLUTION

Step 1 Graph $y = -x - 4$ for $x < 0$. Because x is not equal to 0, use an open circle at $(0, -4)$.

Step 2 Graph $y = x$ for $x \geq 0$. Because x is greater than or equal to 0, use a closed circle at $(0, 0)$.

▶ The domain is all real numbers. The range is $y > -4$.

Monitoring Progress Help in English and Spanish at *BigIdeasMath.com*

Graph the function. Describe the domain and range.

7. $y = \begin{cases} x + 1, & \text{if } x \leq 0 \\ -x, & \text{if } x > 0 \end{cases}$

8. $y = \begin{cases} x - 2, & \text{if } x < 0 \\ 4x, & \text{if } x \geq 0 \end{cases}$

EXAMPLE 3   **Writing a Piecewise Function**

Write a piecewise function for the graph.

SOLUTION

Each "piece" of the function is linear.

Left Piece When $x < 0$, the graph is the line given by $y = x + 3$.

Right Piece When $x \geq 0$, the graph is the line given by $y = 2x - 1$.

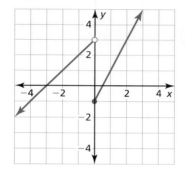

▶ So, a piecewise function for the graph is

$$f(x) = \begin{cases} x + 3, & \text{if } x < 0 \\ 2x - 1, & \text{if } x \geq 0 \end{cases}.$$

Monitoring Progress Help in English and Spanish at *BigIdeasMath.com*

Write a piecewise function for the graph.

9.

10.

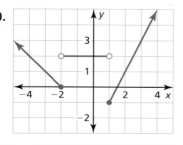

Graphing and Writing Step Functions

A **step function** is a piecewise function defined by a constant value over each part of its domain. The graph of a step function consists of a series of line segments.

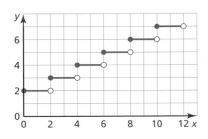

$$f(x) = \begin{cases} 2, & \text{if } 0 \le x < 2 \\ 3, & \text{if } 2 \le x < 4 \\ 4, & \text{if } 4 \le x < 6 \\ 5, & \text{if } 6 \le x < 8 \\ 6, & \text{if } 8 \le x < 10 \\ 7, & \text{if } 10 \le x < 12 \end{cases}$$

EXAMPLE 4   Graphing and Writing a Step Function

You rent a karaoke machine for 5 days. The rental company charges $50 for the first day and $25 for each additional day. Write and graph a step function that represents the relationship between the number x of days and the total cost y (in dollars) of renting the karaoke machine.

SOLUTION

Step 1 Use a table to organize the information.

Number of days	Total cost (dollars)
$0 < x \le 1$	50
$1 < x \le 2$	75
$2 < x \le 3$	100
$3 < x \le 4$	125
$4 < x \le 5$	150

Step 2 Write the step function.

$$f(x) = \begin{cases} 50, & \text{if } 0 < x \le 1 \\ 75, & \text{if } 1 < x \le 2 \\ 100, & \text{if } 2 < x \le 3 \\ 125, & \text{if } 3 < x \le 4 \\ 150, & \text{if } 4 < x \le 5 \end{cases}$$

Step 3 Graph the step function.

Karaoke Machine Rental

Monitoring Progress Help in English and Spanish at *BigIdeasMath.com*

11. A landscaper rents a wood chipper for 4 days. The rental company charges $100 for the first day and $50 for each additional day. Write and graph a step function that represents the relationship between the number x of days and the total cost y (in dollars) of renting the chipper.

Writing Absolute Value Functions

The absolute value function $f(x) = |x|$ can be written as a piecewise function.

$$f(x) = \begin{cases} -x, & \text{if } x < 0 \\ x, & \text{if } x \geq 0 \end{cases}$$

Similarly, the vertex form of an absolute value function $g(x) = a|x - h| + k$ can be written as a piecewise function.

$$g(x) = \begin{cases} a[-(x - h)] + k, & \text{if } x - h < 0 \\ a(x - h) + k, & \text{if } x - h \geq 0 \end{cases}$$

EXAMPLE 5   **Writing an Absolute Value Function**

In holography, light from a laser beam is split into two beams, a reference beam and an object beam. Light from the object beam reflects off an object and is recombined with the reference beam to form images on film that can be used to create three-dimensional images.

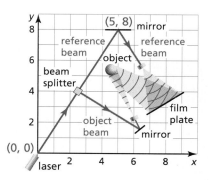

a. Write an absolute value function that represents the path of the reference beam.

b. Write the function in part (a) as a piecewise function.

SOLUTION

a. The vertex of the path of the reference beam is (5, 8). So, the function has the form $g(x) = a|x - 5| + 8$. Substitute the coordinates of the point (0, 0) into the equation and solve for a.

$$g(x) = a|x - 5| + 8 \qquad \text{Vertex form of the function}$$
$$0 = a|0 - 5| + 8 \qquad \text{Substitute 0 for } x \text{ and 0 for } g(x).$$
$$-1.6 = a \qquad \text{Solve for } a.$$

▶ So, the function $g(x) = -1.6|x - 5| + 8$ represents the path of the reference beam.

b. Write $g(x) = -1.6|x - 5| + 8$ as a piecewise function.

$$g(x) = \begin{cases} -1.6[-(x - 5)] + 8, & \text{if } x - 5 < 0 \\ -1.6(x - 5) + 8, & \text{if } x - 5 \geq 0 \end{cases}$$

Simplify each expression and solve the inequalities.

▶ So, a piecewise function for $g(x) = -1.6|x - 5| + 8$ is

$$g(x) = \begin{cases} 1.6x, & \text{if } x < 5 \\ -1.6x + 16, & \text{if } x \geq 5 \end{cases}.$$

STUDY TIP

The graph of an absolute value function is symmetric about the line $x = h$. So, it makes sense that the piecewise definition "splits" the function at $x = 5$.

Monitoring Progress Help in English and Spanish at *BigIdeasMath.com*

12. **WHAT IF?** The reference beam originates at (3, 0) and reflects off a mirror at (5, 4).

    a. Write an absolute value function that represents the path of the reference beam.

    b. Write the function in part (a) as a piecewise function.

Vocabulary and Core Concept Check

1. **VOCABULARY** Compare piecewise functions and step functions.

2. **WRITING** Use a graph to explain why you can write the absolute value function $y = |x|$ as a piecewise function.

Monitoring Progress and Modeling with Mathematics

In Exercises 3–12, evaluate the function. *(See Example 1.)*

$$f(x) = \begin{cases} 5x - 1, & \text{if } x < -2 \\ x + 3, & \text{if } x \geq -2 \end{cases}$$

$$g(x) = \begin{cases} -x + 4, & \text{if } x \leq -1 \\ 3, & \text{if } -1 < x < 2 \\ 2x - 5, & \text{if } x \geq 2 \end{cases}$$

3. $f(-3)$

4. $f(-2)$

5. $f(0)$

6. $f(5)$

7. $g(-4)$

8. $g(-1)$

9. $g(0)$

10. $g(1)$

11. $g(2)$

12. $g(5)$

13. **MODELING WITH MATHEMATICS** On a trip, the total distance (in miles) you travel in x hours is represented by the piecewise function

$$d(x) = \begin{cases} 55x, & \text{if } 0 \leq x \leq 2 \\ 65x - 20, & \text{if } 2 < x \leq 5 \end{cases}.$$

How far do you travel in 4 hours?

14. **MODELING WITH MATHEMATICS** The total cost (in dollars) of ordering x custom shirts is represented by the piecewise function

$$c(x) = \begin{cases} 17x + 20, & \text{if } 0 \leq x < 25 \\ 15.80x + 20, & \text{if } 25 \leq x < 50 \\ 14x + 20, & \text{if } x \geq 50 \end{cases}.$$

Determine the total cost of ordering 26 shirts.

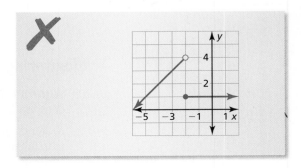

In Exercises 15–20, graph the function. Describe the domain and range. *(See Example 2.)*

15. $y = \begin{cases} -x, & \text{if } x < 2 \\ x - 6, & \text{if } x \geq 2 \end{cases}$

16. $y = \begin{cases} 2x, & \text{if } x \leq -3 \\ -2x, & \text{if } x > -3 \end{cases}$

17. $y = \begin{cases} -3x - 2, & \text{if } x \leq -1 \\ x + 2, & \text{if } x > -1 \end{cases}$

18. $y = \begin{cases} x + 8, & \text{if } x < 4 \\ 4x - 4, & \text{if } x \geq 4 \end{cases}$

19. $y = \begin{cases} 1, & \text{if } x < -3 \\ x - 1, & \text{if } -3 \leq x \leq 3 \\ -2x + 4, & \text{if } x > 3 \end{cases}$

20. $y = \begin{cases} 2x + 1, & \text{if } x \leq -1 \\ -x + 2, & \text{if } -1 < x < 2 \\ -3, & \text{if } x \geq 2 \end{cases}$

21. **ERROR ANALYSIS** Describe and correct the error in finding $f(5)$ when $f(x) = \begin{cases} 2x - 3, & \text{if } x < 5 \\ x + 8, & \text{if } x \geq 5 \end{cases}$.

$$f(5) = 2(5) - 3$$
$$= 7$$

22. **ERROR ANALYSIS** Describe and correct the error in graphing $y = \begin{cases} x + 6, & \text{if } x \leq -2 \\ 1, & \text{if } x > -2 \end{cases}$.

In Exercises 23–30, write a piecewise function for the graph. (*See Example 3.*)

23.

24.

25.

26.

27.

28.

29.

30.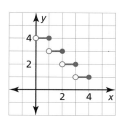

In Exercises 31–34, graph the step function. Describe the domain and range.

31. $f(x) = \begin{cases} 3, & \text{if } 0 \le x < 2 \\ 4, & \text{if } 2 \le x < 4 \\ 5, & \text{if } 4 \le x < 6 \\ 6, & \text{if } 6 \le x < 8 \end{cases}$

32. $f(x) = \begin{cases} -4, & \text{if } 1 < x \le 2 \\ -6, & \text{if } 2 < x \le 3 \\ -8, & \text{if } 3 < x \le 4 \\ -10, & \text{if } 4 < x \le 5 \end{cases}$

33. $f(x) = \begin{cases} 9, & \text{if } 1 < x \le 2 \\ 6, & \text{if } 2 < x \le 4 \\ 5, & \text{if } 4 < x \le 9 \\ 1, & \text{if } 9 < x \le 12 \end{cases}$

34. $f(x) = \begin{cases} -2, & \text{if } -6 \le x < -5 \\ -1, & \text{if } -5 \le x < -3 \\ 0, & \text{if } -3 \le x < -2 \\ 1, & \text{if } -2 \le x < 0 \end{cases}$

35. **MODELING WITH MATHEMATICS** The cost to join an intramural sports league is $180 per team and includes the first five team members. For each additional team member, there is a $30 fee. You plan to have nine people on your team. Write and graph a step function that represents the relationship between the number p of people on your team and the total cost of joining the league. (*See Example 4.*)

36. **MODELING WITH MATHEMATICS** The rates for a parking garage are shown. Write and graph a step function that represents the relationship between the number x of hours a car is parked in the garage and the total cost of parking in the garage for 1 day.

In Exercises 37–46, write the absolute value function as a piecewise function.

37. $y = |x| + 1$

38. $y = |x| - 3$

39. $y = |x - 2|$

40. $y = |x + 5|$

41. $y = 2|x + 3|$

42. $y = 4|x - 1|$

43. $y = -5|x - 8|$

44. $y = -3|x + 6|$

45. $y = -|x - 3| + 2$

46. $y = 7|x + 1| - 5$

47. **MODELING WITH MATHEMATICS** You are sitting on a boat on a lake. You can get a sunburn from the sunlight that hits you directly and also from the sunlight that reflects off the water. (*See Example 5.*)

a. Write an absolute value function that represents the path of the sunlight that reflects off the water.

b. Write the function in part (a) as a piecewise function.

48. MODELING WITH MATHEMATICS You are trying to make a hole in one on the miniature golf green.

a. Write an absolute value function that represents the path of the golf ball.

b. Write the function in part (a) as a piecewise function.

49. REASONING The piecewise function f consists of two linear "pieces." The graph of f is shown.

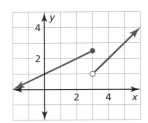

a. What is the value of $f(-10)$?

b. What is the value of $f(8)$?

50. CRITICAL THINKING Describe how the graph of each piecewise function changes when $<$ is replaced with $\leq$ and $\geq$ is replaced with $>$. Do the domain and range change? Explain.

a. $f(x) = \begin{cases} x + 2, & \text{if } x < 2 \\ -x - 1, & \text{if } x \geq 2 \end{cases}$

b. $f(x) = \begin{cases} \frac{1}{2}x + \frac{3}{2}, & \text{if } x < 1 \\ -x + 3, & \text{if } x \geq 1 \end{cases}$

51. USING STRUCTURE Graph

$$y = \begin{cases} -x + 2, & \text{if } x \leq -2 \\ |x|, & \text{if } x > -2 \end{cases}.$$

Describe the domain and range.

52. HOW DO YOU SEE IT? The graph shows the total cost C of making x photocopies at a copy shop.

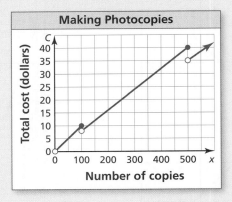

a. Does it cost more money to make 100 photocopies or 101 photocopies? Explain.

b. You have \$40 to make photocopies. Can you buy more than 500 photocopies? Explain.

53. USING STRUCTURE The output y of the *greatest integer function* is the greatest integer less than or equal to the input value x. This function is written as $f(x) = [\![x]\!]$. Graph the function for $-4 \leq x < 4$. Is it a piecewise function? a step function? Explain.

54. THOUGHT PROVOKING Explain why

$$y = \begin{cases} 2x - 2, & \text{if } x \leq 3 \\ -3, & \text{if } x \geq 3 \end{cases}$$

does not represent a function. How can you redefine y so that it does represent a function?

55. MAKING AN ARGUMENT During a 9-hour snowstorm, it snows at a rate of 1 inch per hour for the first 2 hours, 2 inches per hour for the next 6 hours, and 1 inch per hour for the final hour.

a. Write and graph a piecewise function that represents the depth of the snow during the snowstorm.

b. Your friend says 12 inches of snow accumulated during the storm. Is your friend correct? Explain.

Maintaining Mathematical Proficiency
Reviewing what you learned in previous grades and lessons

Write the sentence as an inequality. Graph the inequality. *(Skills Review Handbook)*

56. A number r is greater than -12 and no more than 13.

57. A number t is less than or equal to 4 or no less than 18.

Describe the transformation(s) from the graph of $f(x) = |x|$ to the graph of the given function. *(Section 1.1)*

58. $g(x) = |x - 5|$ **59.** $h(x) = -2.5|x|$ **60.** $p(x) = |x + 1| + 6$ **61.** $v(x) = 4|x + 3|$

1.3 Inverse of a Function

Essential Question How are a function and its inverse related?

EXPLORATION 1 Exploring Inverse Functions

Work with a partner. The functions *f* and *g* are *inverses* of each other. Compare the tables of values of the two functions. How are the functions related?

x	0	0.5	1	1.5	2	2.5	3	3.5
f(x)	−2	−0.75	0.5	1.75	3	4.25	5.5	6.75

x	−2	−0.75	0.5	1.75	3	4.25	5.5	6.75
g(x)	0	0.5	1	1.5	2	2.5	3	3.5

EXPLORATION 2 Exploring Inverse Functions

Work with a partner.

a. Use the coordinate plane below to plot the two sets of points represented by the tables in Exploration 1. Then draw a line through each set of points.

b. Describe the relationship between the two graphs.

c. Write an equation for each function.

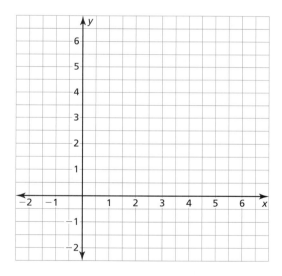

Communicate Your Answer

3. How are a function and its inverse related?

4. A table of values for a function *f* is given. Create a table of values for a function *g*, the inverse of *f*.

x	0	1	2	3	4	5	6	7
f(x)	1	2	3	4	5	6	7	8

ATTENDING TO PRECISION

To be proficient in math, you need to communicate precisely with others.

5. Sketch the graphs of $f(x) = x + 4$ and its inverse in the same coordinate plane. Then write an equation of the inverse of *f*. Explain your reasoning.

1.3 Lesson

Core Vocabulary

inverse relation, *p. 20*
inverse function, *p. 21*

Previous
input
output
inverse operations
reflection
line of reflection

What You Will Learn

▶ Find inverses of relations.
▶ Explore inverses of functions.
▶ Find inverses of functions algebraically.

Finding Inverses of Relations

Recall that a relation pairs inputs with outputs. An **inverse relation** switches the input and output values of the original relation.

 Core Concept

Inverse Relation

When a relation contains (a, b), the inverse relation contains (b, a).

EXAMPLE 1   **Finding Inverses of Relations**

Find the inverse of each relation.

a. $(-4, 7), (-2, 4), (0, 1), (2, -2), (4, -5)$ Switch the coordinates of each ordered pair.

$(7, -4), (4, -2), (1, 0), (-2, 2), (-5, 4)$ Inverse relation

b.

Input	−1	0	1	2	3	4
Output	5	10	15	20	25	30

Inverse relation:

Input	5	10	15	20	25	30
Output	−1	0	1	2	3	4

Switch the inputs and outputs.

Monitoring Progress Help in English and Spanish at *BigIdeasMath.com*

Find the inverse of the relation.

1. $(-3, -4), (-2, 0), (-1, 4), (0, 8), (1, 12), (2, 16), (3, 20)$

2.

Input	−2	−1	0	1	2
Output	4	1	0	1	4

Exploring Inverses of Functions

You have previously used given inputs to find corresponding outputs of $y = f(x)$ for various types of functions. You have also used given outputs to find corresponding inputs. Now you will solve equations of the form $y = f(x)$ for x to obtain a formula for finding the input given a specific output of the function f.

EXAMPLE 2   Writing a Formula for the Input of a Function

Let $f(x) = 2x + 1$. Solve $y = f(x)$ for x. Then find the input when the output is -3.

SOLUTION

$y = 2x + 1$ Set y equal to $f(x)$.

$y - 1 = 2x$ Subtract 1 from each side.

$\dfrac{y - 1}{2} = x$ Divide each side by 2.

Find the input when $y = -3$.

$x = \dfrac{-3 - 1}{2}$ Substitute -3 for y.

$= \dfrac{-4}{2}$ Subtract.

$= -2$ Divide.

▶ So, the input is -2 when the output is -3.

Check

$f(-2) = 2(-2) + 1$

$= -4 + 1$

$= -3$ ✓

Monitoring Progress Help in English and Spanish at *BigIdeasMath.com*

Solve $y = f(x)$ for x. Then find the input when the output is 4.

3. $f(x) = x - 6$ **4.** $f(x) = \frac{1}{2}x + 3$ **5.** $f(x) = 10 - x$

UNDERSTANDING MATHEMATICAL TERMS

The term *inverse functions* does not refer to a new type of function. Rather, it describes any pair of functions that are inverses.

In Example 2, notice the steps involved after substituting for x in $y = 2x + 1$ and after substituting for y in $x = \dfrac{y - 1}{2}$.

$y = 2x + 1$ $x = \dfrac{y - 1}{2}$

Step 1 Multiply by 2.   **Step 1** Subtract 1.

Step 2 Add 1.   inverse operations in the reverse order   **Step 2** Divide by 2.

Notice that these steps *undo* each other. **Inverse functions** are functions that undo each other. In Example 2, you can use the equation solved for x to write the inverse of f by switching the roles of x and y.

$f(x) = 2x + 1$ original function $g(x) = \dfrac{x - 1}{2}$ inverse function

Because an inverse function interchanges the input and output values of the original function, the domain and range are also interchanged.

LOOKING FOR A PATTERN

Notice that the graph of the inverse function g is a reflection of the graph of the original function f. The line of reflection is $y = x$.

Original function: $f(x) = 2x + 1$

x	−2	−1	0	1	2
y	−3	−1	1	3	5

Inverse function: $g(x) = \dfrac{x - 1}{2}$

x	−3	−1	1	3	5
y	−2	−1	0	1	2

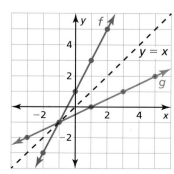

Finding Inverses of Functions Algebraically

🌀 Core Concept

Finding Inverses of Functions Algebraically

Step 1 Set y equal to $f(x)$.

Step 2 Switch x and y in the equation.

Step 3 Solve the equation for y.

STUDY TIP

On the previous page, you solved a function for x and switched the roles of x and y to find the inverse function. You can also find the inverse function by switching x and y first, and then solving for y.

EXAMPLE 3 **Finding the Inverse of a Function**

Find the inverse of $f(x) = 4x - 9$.

SOLUTION

Method 1 Use the method above.

Step 1	$f(x) = 4x - 9$	Write the function.
	$y = 4x - 9$	Set y equal to $f(x)$.
Step 2	$x = 4y - 9$	Switch x and y in the equation.
Step 3	$x + 9 = 4y$	Add 9 to each side.
	$\dfrac{x + 9}{4} = y$	Divide each side by 4.

▶ The inverse of f is $g(x) = \dfrac{x + 9}{4}$, or $g(x) = \dfrac{1}{4}x + \dfrac{9}{4}$.

Method 2 Use inverse operations in the reverse order.

$$f(x) = 4x - 9 \qquad \text{Multiply the input } x \text{ by 4 and then subtract 9.}$$

To find the inverse, apply inverse operations in the reverse order.

$$g(x) = \dfrac{x + 9}{4} \qquad \text{Add 9 to the input } x \text{ and then divide by 4.}$$

▶ The inverse of f is $g(x) = \dfrac{x + 9}{4}$, or $g(x) = \dfrac{1}{4}x + \dfrac{9}{4}$.

Check

The graph of g appears to be a reflection of the graph of f in the line $y = x$. ✔

Monitoring Progress   Help in English and Spanish at *BigIdeasMath.com*

Find the inverse of the function. Then graph the function and its inverse.

6. $f(x) = 6x$ **7.** $f(x) = -x + 5$ **8.** $f(x) = \frac{1}{4}x - 1$

Vocabulary and Core Concept Check

1. **COMPLETE THE SENTENCE** A relation contains the point $(-3, 10)$. The _____ contains the point $(10, -3)$.

2. **DIFFERENT WORDS, SAME QUESTION** Consider the function f represented by the graph. Which is different? Find "both" answers.

   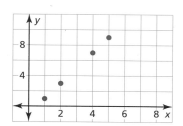

   Graph the inverse of the function.

   Reflect the graph of the function in the x-axis.

   Reflect the graph of the function in the line $y = x$.

   Switch the inputs and outputs of the function and graph the resulting function.

Monitoring Progress and Modeling with Mathematics

In Exercises 3–8, find the inverse of the relation.
(See Example 1.)

3. $(1, 0), (3, -8), (4, -3), (7, -5), (9, -1)$

4. $(2, 1), (4, -3), (6, 7), (8, 1), (10, -4)$

5.
Input	−5	−5	0	5	10
Output	8	6	0	6	8

6.
Input	−12	−8	−5	−3	−2
Output	2	5	−1	10	−2

7.

8.
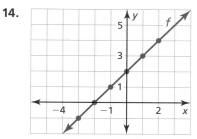

In Exercises 9–12, solve $y = f(x)$ for x. Then find the input when the output is 2. *(See Example 2.)*

9. $f(x) = x + 5$

10. $f(x) = 2x - 3$

11. $f(x) = \frac{1}{4}x - 1$

12. $f(x) = \frac{2}{3}x + 4$

In Exercises 13 and 14, graph the inverse of the function by reflecting the graph in the line $y = x$. Describe the domain and range of the inverse.

13.
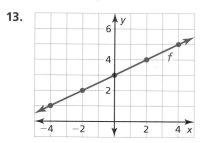

14.

In Exercises 15–22, find the inverse of the function. Then graph the function and its inverse. *(See Example 3.)*

15. $f(x) = 3x$

16. $f(x) = -5x$

17. $f(x) = 4x - 1$

18. $f(x) = -2x + 5$

19. $f(x) = -3x - 2$

20. $f(x) = 2x + 3$

21. $f(x) = \frac{1}{3}x + 8$

22. $f(x) = -\frac{3}{2}x + \frac{7}{2}$

23. **ERROR ANALYSIS** Describe and correct the error in finding the inverse of the function $f(x) = 3x + 5$.

$$y = 3x + 5$$
$$y - 5 = 3x$$
$$\frac{y - 5}{3} = x$$

The inverse of f is $g(x) = \frac{y - 5}{3}$, or $g(x) = \frac{y}{3} - \frac{5}{3}$.

24. **ERROR ANALYSIS** Describe and correct the error in graphing the inverse g of the function f.

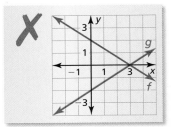

25. **MODELING WITH MATHEMATICS** The euro is the unit of currency for the European Union. On a certain day, the number E of euros that could be obtained for D U.S. dollars was represented by the formula shown.

$$E = 0.74683D$$

Solve the formula for D. Then find the number of U.S. dollars that could be obtained for 250 euros on that day.

26. **MODELING WITH MATHEMATICS** You work at a manufacturing plant and earn $11 per hour plus $0.50 for each unit you produce per hour.

   a. Write a linear model that represents your hourly wage as a function of the number of units you produce per hour.

   b. Find the inverse of the function you wrote in part (a). What does each variable in the inverse function represent?

   c. What is your hourly wage when you produce 8 units per hour?

   d. How many units must you produce per hour to double your hourly wage in part (c)?

27. **OPEN-ENDED** Write a function such that the graph of its inverse is a line with a slope of 4.

28. **HOW DO YOU SEE IT?** Pair the graph of each function with the graph of its inverse.

   A.

   B.

   C.

   D.

   E.

   F.

29. **CRITICAL THINKING** Consider the function $g(x) = -x$.

   a. Graph $g(x) = -x$ and explain why it is its own inverse.

   b. Graph other linear functions that are their own inverses. Write equations of the lines you graph.

   c. Use your results from part (b) to write a general equation that describes the family of linear functions that are their own inverses.

30. **THOUGHT PROVOKING** Find a formula (for instance, from geometry or physics) that has an inverse function. Explain what the variables in your formula represent.

31. **REASONING** Show that the inverse of any linear function $f(x) = mx + b$, where $m \neq 0$, is also a linear function. Write the slope and y-intercept of the graph of the inverse in terms of m and b.

Maintaining Mathematical Proficiency
Reviewing what you learned in previous grades and lessons

Evaluate the expression. *(Skills Review Handbook)*

32. 12^5

33. -11^3

34. $\left(\frac{5}{6}\right)^4$

35. $-\left(\frac{1}{3}\right)^6$

Write the number in scientific notation. *(Skills Review Handbook)*

36. 84,375

37. 0.00944

38. 400,700,000

39. 0.000000082

Core Vocabulary

absolute value function, *p. 4*
vertex, *p. 4*
vertex form, *p. 6*

piecewise function, *p. 12*
step function, *p. 14*

inverse relation, *p. 20*
inverse function, *p. 21*

Core Concepts

Section 1.1

Absolute Value Function, *p. 4*

Vertex Form of an Absolute Value Function, *p. 6*

Section 1.2

Piecewise Function, *p. 12*
Step Function, *p. 14*

Writing Absolute Value Functions, *p. 15*

Section 1.3

Inverse Relation, *p. 20*

Finding Inverses of Functions Algebraically, *p. 22*

Mathematical Practices

1. Describe the definitions you used when you explained your answer in Exercise 53 on page 18.

2. What external resources could you use to check the reasonableness of your answer in Exercise 25 on page 24?

Making Note Cards

Invest in three different colors of note cards. Use one color for each of the following: vocabulary words, rules, and calculator keystrokes.

- Using the first color of note cards, write a vocabulary word on one side of a card. On the other side, write the definition and an example. If possible, put the definition in your own words.

- Using the second color of note cards, write a rule on one side of a card. On the other side, write an explanation and an example.

- Using the third color of note cards, write a calculation on one side of a card. On the other side, write the keystrokes required to perform the calculation.

Use the note cards as references while completing your homework. Quiz yourself once a day.

STUDY SKILLS

Describe the transformations from the graph of $f(x) = |x|$ to the graph of the given function. Then graph the given function. *(Section 1.1)*

1. $f(x) = |x + 5| + 4$

2. $g(x) = -\frac{1}{2}|x - 3| - 6$

3. $h(x) = |-x + 2| - 4$

Write an equation that represents the given transformation(s) of the graph of $f(x) = |x|$. *(Section 1.1)*

4. horizontal translation 9 units right

5. vertical translation 4.5 units up

6. horizontal stretch by a factor of 5

7. vertical shrink by a factor of $\frac{1}{4}$ and a reflection in the x-axis

Graph the function. Describe the domain and range. *(Section 1.2)*

8. $y = \begin{cases} \frac{3}{4}x + 1, & \text{if } x < -4 \\ -2x - 3, & \text{if } x \geq -4 \end{cases}$

9. $y = \begin{cases} -3, & \text{if } -4 \leq x < -2 \\ -2, & \text{if } -2 \leq x < -1 \\ -1, & \text{if } -1 \leq x < 1 \\ 0, & \text{if } 1 \leq x < 2 \end{cases}$

10. Write a piecewise function represented by the graph shown. *(Section 1.2)*

11. Write the function $y = -4|x + 1|$ as a piecewise function. *(Section 1.2)*

12. Find the inverse of the relation shown in the table. *(Section 1.3)*

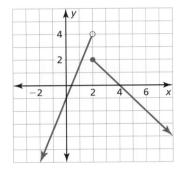

Input	−4	−2	0	2	4
Output	6	3	0	−3	−6

Find the inverse of the function. Then graph the function and its inverse. *(Section 1.3)*

13. $k(x) = -\frac{1}{2}x$

14. $p(x) = 3x - 5$

15. $r(x) = 6 - 0.2x$

16. Write two absolute value functions whose graphs form a square in a coordinate plane. *(Section 1.1)*

17. Describe a real-life situation that can be represented by the graph shown. *(Section 1.2)*

18. You are ordering customized bracelets for a fundraiser. The total cost (in dollars) of ordering x bracelets is represented by the function below. *(Section 1.2)*

$$f(x) = \begin{cases} 0.9x + 25, & \text{if } 0 \leq x < 100 \\ 0.65x + 25, & \text{if } 100 \leq x < 500 \\ 0.4x + 25, & \text{if } 500 \leq x < 1000 \\ 0.1x + 25, & \text{if } x \geq 1000 \end{cases}$$

a. Find and interpret $f(35)$.

b. Determine the costs of ordering 100, 500, and 2500 bracelets.

c. What do you think the 25s in the function represent?

1.4 Properties of Exponents

Essential Question How can you write general rules involving properties of exponents?

Writing Rules for Properties of Exponents

Work with a partner.

WRITING GENERAL RULES

To be proficient in math, you need to understand and use stated assumptions, definitions, and previously established results in writing general rules.

a. What happens when you multiply two powers with the same base? Write the product of the two powers as a single power. Then write a *general rule* for finding the product of two powers with the same base.

i. $(2^2)(2^3) = $

ii. $(4^1)(4^5) = $

iii. $(5^3)(5^5) = $

iv. $(x^2)(x^6) = $

b. What happens when you divide two powers with the same base? Write the quotient of the two powers as a single power. Then write a *general rule* for finding the quotient of two powers with the same base.

i. $\dfrac{4^3}{4^2} = $

ii. $\dfrac{2^5}{2^2} = $

iii. $\dfrac{x^6}{x^3} = $

iv. $\dfrac{3^4}{3^4} = $

c. What happens when you find a power of a power? Write the expression as a single power. Then write a *general rule* for finding a power of a power.

i. $(2^2)^4 = $

ii. $(7^3)^2 = $

iii. $(y^3)^3 = $

iv. $(x^4)^2 = $

d. What happens when you find a power of a product? Write the expression as the product of two powers. Then write a *general rule* for finding a power of a product.

i. $(2 \cdot 5)^2 = $

ii. $(5 \cdot 4)^3 = $

iii. $(6a)^2 = $

iv. $(3x)^2 = $

e. What happens when you find a power of a quotient? Write the expression as the quotient of two powers. Then write a *general rule* for finding a power of a quotient.

i. $\left(\dfrac{2}{3}\right)^2 = $

ii. $\left(\dfrac{4}{3}\right)^3 = $

iii. $\left(\dfrac{x}{2}\right)^3 = $

iv. $\left(\dfrac{a}{b}\right)^4 = $

Communicate Your Answer

2. How can you write general rules involving properties of exponents?

3. There are 3^3 small cubes in the cube below. Write an expression for the number of small cubes in the large cube at the right.

What You Will Learn

▶ Use zero and negative exponents.
▶ Use the properties of exponents.
▶ Solve real-life problems involving exponents.

Using Zero and Negative Exponents

🌀 Core Concept

Zero Exponent

Words For any nonzero number a, $a^0 = 1$. The power 0^0 is undefined.

Numbers $4^0 = 1$ **Algebra** $a^0 = 1$, where $a \neq 0$

Negative Exponents

Words For any integer n and any nonzero number a, a^{-n} is the reciprocal of a^n.

Numbers $4^{-2} = \dfrac{1}{4^2}$ **Algebra** $a^{-n} = \dfrac{1}{a^n}$, where $a \neq 0$

EXAMPLE 1 **Using Zero and Negative Exponents**

Evaluate each expression.

a. 6.7^0 **b.** $(-2)^{-4}$

SOLUTION

a. $6.7^0 = 1$ Definition of zero exponent

b. $(-2)^{-4} = \dfrac{1}{(-2)^4}$ Definition of negative exponent

   $= \dfrac{1}{16}$ Simplify.

EXAMPLE 2 **Simplifying an Expression**

Simplify the expression $\dfrac{4x^0}{y^{-3}}$. Write your answer using only positive exponents.

SOLUTION

$\dfrac{4x^0}{y^{-3}} = 4x^0 y^3$ Definition of negative exponent

   $= 4y^3$ Definition of zero exponent

Monitoring Progress Help in English and Spanish at *BigIdeasMath.com*

Evaluate the expression.

1. $(-9)^0$ **2.** 3^{-3} **3.** $\dfrac{-5^0}{2^{-2}}$

4. Simplify the expression $\dfrac{3^{-2}x^{-5}}{y^0}$. Write your answer using only positive exponents.

Using the Properties of Exponents

REMEMBER

The expression x^3 is called a *power*. The *base*, x, is used as a factor 3 times because the *exponent* is 3.

Core Concept

Product of Powers Property

Let a be a real number, and let m and n be integers.

Words To multiply powers with the same base, add their exponents.

Numbers $4^6 \cdot 4^3 = 4^{6+3} = 4^9$ **Algebra** $a^m \cdot a^n = a^{m+n}$

Quotient of Powers Property

Let a be a nonzero real number, and let m and n be integers.

Words To divide powers with the same base, subtract their exponents.

Numbers $\dfrac{4^6}{4^3} = 4^{6-3} = 4^3$ **Algebra** $\dfrac{a^m}{a^n} = a^{m-n}$, where $a \neq 0$

Power of a Power Property

Let a be a real number, and let m and n be integers.

Words To find a power of a power, multiply the exponents.

Numbers $(4^6)^3 = 4^{6 \cdot 3} = 4^{18}$ **Algebra** $(a^m)^n = a^{mn}$

EXAMPLE 3   **Using Properties of Exponents**

Simplify each expression. Write your answer using only positive exponents.

a. $3^2 \cdot 3^6$

b. $\dfrac{(-4)^2}{(-4)^7}$

c. $(z^4)^{-3}$

SOLUTION

a. $3^2 \cdot 3^6 = 3^{2+6}$ Product of Powers Property

$\qquad\quad = 3^8 = 6561$ Simplify.

b. $\dfrac{(-4)^2}{(-4)^7} = (-4)^{2-7}$ Quotient of Powers Property

$\qquad\quad = (-4)^{-5}$ Simplify.

$\qquad\quad = \dfrac{1}{(-4)^5} = -\dfrac{1}{1024}$ Definition of negative exponent

c. $(z^4)^{-3} = z^{4 \cdot (-3)}$ Power of a Power Property

$\qquad\quad = z^{-12}$ Simplify.

$\qquad\quad = \dfrac{1}{z^{12}}$ Definition of negative exponent

Monitoring Progress   Help in English and Spanish at *BigIdeasMath.com*

Simplify the expression. Write your answer using only positive exponents.

5. $10^4 \cdot 10^{-6}$

6. $x^9 \cdot x^{-9}$

7. $\dfrac{-5^8}{-5^4}$

8. $\dfrac{y^6}{y^7}$

9. $(6^{-2})^{-1}$

10. $(w^{12})^5$

Core Concept

Power of a Product Property

Let a and b be real numbers, and let m be an integer.

Words To find a power of a product, find the power of each factor and multiply.

Numbers $(3 \cdot 2)^5 = 3^5 \cdot 2^5$ **Algebra** $(ab)^m = a^m b^m$

Power of a Quotient Property

Let a and b be real numbers with $b \neq 0$, and let m be an integer.

Words To find the power of a quotient, find the power of the numerator and the power of the denominator and divide.

Numbers $\left(\dfrac{3}{2}\right)^5 = \dfrac{3^5}{2^5}$ **Algebra** $\left(\dfrac{a}{b}\right)^m = \dfrac{a^m}{b^m}$, where $b \neq 0$

EXAMPLE 4 Using Properties of Exponents

Simplify each expression. Write your answer using only positive exponents.

a. $(-1.5y)^2$ **b.** $\left(\dfrac{a}{-10}\right)^3$ **c.** $\left(\dfrac{3d}{2}\right)^4$ **d.** $\left(\dfrac{2x}{3}\right)^{-5}$

SOLUTION

a. $(-1.5y)^2 = (-1.5)^2 \cdot y^2$ Power of a Product Property

           $= 2.25y^2$ Simplify.

b. $\left(\dfrac{a}{-10}\right)^3 = \dfrac{a^3}{(-10)^3}$ Power of a Quotient Property

           $= -\dfrac{a^3}{1000}$ Simplify.

ANOTHER WAY

Because the exponent is negative, you could find the reciprocal of the base first. Then simplify.

$\left(\dfrac{2x}{3}\right)^{-5} = \left(\dfrac{3}{2x}\right)^{5} = \dfrac{243}{32x^5}$

c. $\left(\dfrac{3d}{2}\right)^4 = \dfrac{(3d)^4}{2^4}$ Power of a Quotient Property

           $= \dfrac{3^4 d^4}{2^4}$ Power of a Product Property

           $= \dfrac{81d^4}{16}$ Simplify.

d. $\left(\dfrac{2x}{3}\right)^{-5} = \dfrac{(2x)^{-5}}{3^{-5}}$ Power of a Quotient Property

           $= \dfrac{3^5}{(2x)^5}$ Definition of negative exponent

           $= \dfrac{3^5}{2^5 x^5}$ Power of a Product Property

           $= \dfrac{243}{32x^5}$ Simplify.

Monitoring Progress Help in English and Spanish at *BigIdeasMath.com*

Simplify the expression. Write your answer using only positive exponents.

11. $(10y)^{-3}$ **12.** $\left(-\dfrac{4}{n}\right)^5$ **13.** $\left(\dfrac{1}{2k^2}\right)^5$ **14.** $\left(\dfrac{6c}{7}\right)^{-2}$

Solving Real-Life Problems

EXAMPLE 5 **Simplifying a Real-Life Expression**

Which of the expressions shown represent the volume of the cylinder, where r is the radius and h is the height?

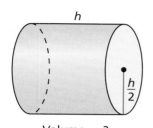

Volume = ?

$$2\pi r^3 \qquad \pi h^3 2^{-2} \qquad \pi h 4^{-1}$$

$$\frac{\pi h^2}{4} \qquad \frac{\pi h^3}{4} \qquad \frac{\pi h^3}{2}$$

SOLUTION

$$V = \pi r^2 h \qquad \text{Formula for the volume of a cylinder}$$

$$= \pi\left(\frac{h}{2}\right)^2 (h) \qquad \text{Substitute } \frac{h}{2} \text{ for } r.$$

$$= \pi\left(\frac{h^2}{2^2}\right)(h) \qquad \text{Power of a Quotient Property}$$

$$= \frac{\pi h^3}{4} \qquad \text{Simplify.}$$

Any expression equivalent to $\frac{\pi h^3}{4}$ represents the volume of the cylinder.

- You can use the properties of exponents to write $\pi h^3 2^{-2}$ as $\frac{\pi h^3}{4}$.

- Note $h = 2r$. When you substitute $2r$ for h in $\frac{\pi h^3}{4}$, you can write $\frac{\pi (2r)^3}{4}$ as $2\pi r^3$.

- None of the other expressions are equivalent to $\frac{\pi h^3}{4}$.

▶ The expressions $2\pi r^3$, $\pi h^3 2^{-2}$, and $\frac{\pi h^3}{4}$ represent the volume of the cylinder.

EXAMPLE 6 **Solving a Real-Life Problem**

A jellyfish emits about 1.25×10^8 particles of light, or photons, in 6.25×10^{-4} second. How many photons does the jellyfish emit each second? Write your answer in scientific notation and in standard form.

SOLUTION

Divide to find the unit rate.

$$\frac{1.25 \times 10^8}{6.25 \times 10^{-4}} \leftarrow \text{photons} \atop \leftarrow \text{seconds} \qquad \text{Write the rate.}$$

$$= \frac{1.25}{6.25} \times \frac{10^8}{10^{-4}} \qquad \text{Rewrite.}$$

$$= 0.2 \times 10^{12} \qquad \text{Simplify.}$$

$$= 2 \times 10^{11} \qquad \text{Write in scientific notation.}$$

▶ The jellyfish emits 2×10^{11}, or 200,000,000,000 photons per second.

REMEMBER

A number is written in scientific notation when it is of the form $a \times 10^b$, where $1 \le a < 10$ and b is an integer.

Monitoring Progress ◆)) Help in English and Spanish at *BigIdeasMath.com*

15. Write two expressions that represent the area of a base of the cylinder in Example 5.

16. It takes the Sun about 2.3×10^8 years to orbit the center of the Milky Way. It takes Pluto about 2.5×10^2 years to orbit the Sun. How many times does Pluto orbit the Sun while the Sun completes one orbit around the center of the Milky Way? Write your answer in scientific notation.

Vocabulary and Core Concept Check

1. **VOCABULARY** Which definitions or properties would you use to simplify the expression $(4^8 \cdot 4^{-4})^{-2}$? Explain.

2. **WRITING** Explain when and how to use the Power of a Product Property.

3. **WRITING** Explain when and how to use the Quotient of Powers Property.

4. **DIFFERENT WORDS, SAME QUESTION** Which is different? Find "both" answers.

   Simplify $3^3 \cdot 3^6$.   Simplify 3^{3+6}.   Simplify $3^{6 \cdot 3}$.   Simplify $3^6 \cdot 3^3$.

Monitoring Progress and Modeling with Mathematics

In Exercises 5–12, evaluate the expression.
(See Example 1.)

5. $(-7)^0$

6. 4^0

7. 5^{-4}

8. $(-2)^{-5}$

9. $\dfrac{2^{-4}}{4^0}$

10. $\dfrac{5^{-1}}{-9^0}$

11. $\dfrac{-3^{-3}}{6^{-2}}$

12. $\dfrac{(-8)^{-2}}{3^{-4}}$

In Exercises 13–22, simplify the expression. Write your answer using only positive exponents. *(See Example 2.)*

13. x^{-7}

14. y^0

15. $9x^0y^{-3}$

16. $15c^{-8}d^0$

17. $\dfrac{2^{-2}m^{-3}}{n^0}$

18. $\dfrac{10^0r^{-11}s}{3^2}$

19. $\dfrac{4^{-3}a^0}{b^{-7}}$

20. $\dfrac{p^{-8}}{7^{-2}q^{-9}}$

21. $\dfrac{2^2y^{-6}}{8^{-1}z^0x^{-7}}$

22. $\dfrac{13x^{-5}y^0}{5^{-3}z^{-10}}$

In Exercises 23–32, simplify the expression. Write your answer using only positive exponents. *(See Example 3.)*

23. $\dfrac{5^6}{5^2}$

24. $\dfrac{(-6)^8}{(-6)^5}$

25. $(-9)^2 \cdot (-9)^2$

26. $4^{-5} \cdot 4^5$

27. $(p^6)^4$

28. $(s^{-5})^3$

29. $6^{-8} \cdot 6^5$

30. $-7 \cdot (-7)^{-4}$

31. $\dfrac{x^5}{x^4} \cdot x$

32. $\dfrac{z^8 \cdot z^2}{z^5}$

33. **USING PROPERTIES** A microscope magnifies an object 10^5 times. The length of an object is 10^{-7} meter. What is its magnified length?

34. **USING PROPERTIES** The area of the rectangular computer chip is $112a^3b^2$ square microns. What is the length?

width = $8ab$ microns

ERROR ANALYSIS In Exercises 35 and 36, describe and correct the error in simplifying the expression.

35.

$2^4 \cdot 2^5 = (2 \cdot 2)^{4+5}$
$= 4^9$

36.

$\dfrac{x^5 \cdot x^3}{x^4} = \dfrac{x^8}{x^4}$
$= x^{8/4}$
$= x^2$

In Exercises 37–44, simplify the expression. Write your answer using only positive exponents. *(See Example 4.)*

37. $(-5z)^3$

38. $(4x)^{-4}$

39. $\left(\dfrac{6}{n}\right)^{-2}$

40. $\left(\dfrac{-t}{3}\right)^{2}$

41. $(3s^8)^{-5}$

42. $(-5p^3)^3$

43. $\left(-\dfrac{w^3}{6}\right)^{-2}$

44. $\left(\dfrac{1}{2r^6}\right)^{-6}$

45. **USING PROPERTIES**
Which of the expressions represent the volume of the sphere? Explain. *(See Example 5.)*

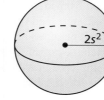

$2s^2$

Ⓐ $\left(\dfrac{3s^2}{2^4\pi s^8}\right)^{-1}$

Ⓑ $(2^5\pi s^6)(3^{-1})$

Ⓒ $\dfrac{32\pi s^6}{3}$

Ⓓ $(2s)^5 \cdot \dfrac{\pi s}{3}$

Ⓔ $\left(\dfrac{3\pi s^6}{32}\right)^{-1}$

Ⓕ $\dfrac{32}{3}\pi s^5$

46. **MODELING WITH MATHEMATICS** Diffusion is the movement of molecules from one location to another. The time t (in seconds) it takes molecules to diffuse a distance of x centimeters is given by $t = \dfrac{x^2}{2D}$, where D is the diffusion coefficient. The diffusion coefficient for a drop of ink in water is about 10^{-5} square centimeters per second. How long will it take the ink to diffuse 1 micrometer (10^{-4} centimeter)?

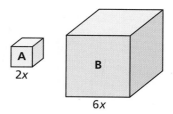

In Exercises 47–50, simplify the expression. Write your answer using only positive exponents.

47. $\left(\dfrac{2x^{-2}y^3}{3xy^{-4}}\right)^4$

48. $\left(\dfrac{4s^5t^{-7}}{-2s^{-2}t^4}\right)^3$

49. $\left(\dfrac{3m^{-5}n^2}{4m^{-2}n^0}\right)^2 \cdot \left(\dfrac{mn^4}{9n}\right)^2$

50. $\left(\dfrac{3x^3y^0}{x^{-2}}\right)^4 \cdot \left(\dfrac{y^2x^{-4}}{5xy^{-8}}\right)^3$

In Exercises 51–54, evaluate the expression. Write your answer in scientific notation and standard form.

51. $(3 \times 10^2)(1.5 \times 10^{-5})$

52. $(6.1 \times 10^{-3})(8 \times 10^9)$

53. $\dfrac{(6.4 \times 10^7)}{(1.6 \times 10^5)}$

54. $\dfrac{(3.9 \times 10^{-5})}{(7.8 \times 10^{-8})}$

55. **PROBLEM SOLVING** In 2012, on average, about 9.46×10^{-1} pound of potatoes was produced for every 2.3×10^{-5} acre harvested. How many pounds of potatoes on average were produced for each acre harvested? Write your answer in scientific notation and in standard form. *(See Example 6.)*

56. **PROBLEM SOLVING** The speed of light is approximately 3×10^5 kilometers per second. How long does it take sunlight to reach Jupiter? Write your answer in scientific notation and in standard form.

OUR SOLAR SYSTEM

NEPTUNE
URANUS
SATURN
JUPITER
MARS
EARTH
VENUS
MERCURY
SUN

Average Distance: 7.8×10^8 kilometers

57. **MATHEMATICAL CONNECTIONS** Consider Cube A and Cube B.

A
$2x$

B
$6x$

a. Which property of exponents should you use to simplify an expression for the volume of each cube?

b. How can you use the Power of a Quotient Property to find how many times greater the volume of Cube B is than the volume of Cube A?

58. **PROBLEM SOLVING** A byte is a unit used to measure a computer's memory. The table shows the numbers of bytes in several units of measure.

Unit	kilobyte	megabyte	gigabyte	terabyte
Number of bytes	2^{10}	2^{20}	2^{30}	2^{40}

a. How many kilobytes are in 1 terabyte?

b. How many megabytes are in 16 gigabytes?

c. Another unit used to measure a computer's memory is a bit. There are 8 bits in a byte. How can you convert the number of bytes in each unit of measure given in the table to bits? Can you still use a base of 2? Explain.

REWRITING EXPRESSIONS In Exercises 59–62, rewrite the expression as a power of a product.

59. $8a^3b^3$

60. $16r^2s^2$

61. $64w^{18}z^{12}$

62. $81x^4y^8$

63. USING STRUCTURE The probability of rolling a 6 on a number cube is $\frac{1}{6}$. The probability of rolling a 6 twice in a row is $\left(\frac{1}{6}\right)^2 = \frac{1}{36}$.

   a. Write an expression that represents the probability of rolling a 6 n times in a row.

   b. What is the probability of rolling a 6 four times in a row?

   c. What is the probability of flipping heads on a coin five times in a row? Explain.

64. HOW DO YOU SEE IT? The shaded part of Figure n represents the portion of a piece of paper visible after folding the paper in half n times.

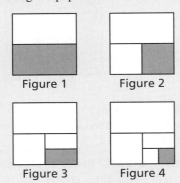

Figure 1   Figure 2

Figure 3   Figure 4

   a. What fraction of the original piece of paper is each shaded part?

   b. Rewrite each fraction from part (a) in the form 2^x.

65. REASONING Find x and y when $\dfrac{b^x}{b^y} = b^9$ and $\dfrac{b^x \cdot b^2}{b^{3y}} = b^{13}$. Explain how you found your answer.

66. THOUGHT PROVOKING Write expressions for r and h so that the volume of the cone can be represented by the expression $27\pi x^8$. Find r and h.

67. MAKING AN ARGUMENT One of the smallest plant seeds comes from an orchid, and one of the largest plant seeds comes from a double coconut palm. A seed from an orchid has a mass of 10^{-6} gram. The mass of a seed from a double coconut palm is 10^{10} times the mass of the seed from the orchid. Your friend says that the seed from the double coconut palm has a mass of about 1 kilogram. Is your friend correct? Explain.

68. CRITICAL THINKING Your school is conducting a survey. Students can answer the questions in either part with "agree" or "disagree."

Part 1: 13 questions		
Part 2: 10 questions		
Part 1: Classroom	Agree	Disagree
1. I come prepared for class.	○	○
2. I enjoy my assignments.	○	○

   a. What power of 2 represents the number of different ways that a student can answer all the questions in Part 1?

   b. What power of 2 represents the number of different ways that a student can answer all the questions on the entire survey?

   c. The survey changes, and students can now answer "agree," "disagree," or "no opinion." How does this affect your answers in parts (a) and (b)?

69. ABSTRACT REASONING Compare the values of a^n and a^{-n} when $n < 0$, when $n = 0$, and when $n > 0$ for (a) $a > 1$ and (b) $0 < a < 1$. Explain your reasoning.

Maintaining Mathematical Proficiency

Reviewing what you learned in previous grades and lessons

Find the square root(s). *(Skills Review Handbook)*

70. $\sqrt{25}$

71. $-\sqrt{100}$

72. $\pm\sqrt{\dfrac{1}{64}}$

Classify the real number in as many ways as possible. *(Skills Review Handbook)*

73. 12

74. $\dfrac{65}{9}$

75. $\dfrac{\pi}{4}$

1.5 Radicals and Rational Exponents

Essential Question   How can you write and evaluate an *n*th root of a number?

Recall that you cube a number as follows.

3rd power

$$2^3 = 2 \cdot 2 \cdot 2 = 8 \qquad \text{2 cubed is 8.}$$

To "undo" cubing a number, take the cube root of the number.

Symbol for cube root is $\sqrt[3]{}$.

$$\sqrt[3]{8} = \sqrt[3]{2^3} = 2 \qquad \text{The cube root of 8 is 2.}$$

EXPLORATION 1   Finding Cube Roots

Work with a partner. Use a cube root symbol to write the side length of each cube. Then find the cube root. Check your answers by multiplying. Which cube is the largest? Which two cubes are the same size? Explain your reasoning.

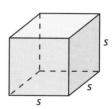

a. Volume = 27 ft³

b. Volume = 125 cm³

c. Volume = 3375 in.³

d. Volume = 3.375 m³

e. Volume = 1 yd³

f. Volume = $\dfrac{125}{8}$ mm³

JUSTIFYING CONCLUSIONS

To be proficient in math, you need to justify your conclusions and communicate them to others.

EXPLORATION 2   Estimating *n*th Roots

Work with a partner. Estimate each positive *n*th root. Then match each *n*th root with the point on the number line. Justify your answers.

a. $\sqrt[4]{25}$

b. $\sqrt{0.5}$

c. $\sqrt[5]{2.5}$

d. $\sqrt[3]{65}$

e. $\sqrt[3]{55}$

f. $\sqrt[6]{20,000}$

Communicate Your Answer

3. How can you write and evaluate an *n*th root of a number?

4. The body mass *m* (in kilograms) of a dinosaur that walked on two feet can be modeled by

$$m = (0.00016)C^{2.73}$$

where *C* is the circumference (in millimeters) of the dinosaur's femur. The mass of a *Tyrannosaurus rex* was 4000 kilograms. Use a calculator to approximate the circumference of its femur.

Core Vocabulary

*n*th root of *a, p. 36*
radical, *p. 36*
index of a radical, *p. 36*

Previous
square root

What You Will Learn

▶ Find *n*th roots.

▶ Evaluate expressions with rational exponents.

▶ Solve real-life problems involving rational exponents.

Finding *n*th Roots

You can extend the concept of a square root to other types of roots. For example, 2 is a cube root of 8 because $2^3 = 8$, and 3 is a fourth root of 81 because $3^4 = 81$. In general, for an integer *n* greater than 1, if $b^n = a$, then *b* is an **nth root of a**. An *n*th root of *a* is written as $\sqrt[n]{a}$, where the expression $\sqrt[n]{a}$ is called a **radical** and *n* is the **index** of the radical.

You can also write an *n*th root of *a* as a power of *a*. If you assume the Power of a Power Property applies to rational exponents, then the following is true.

$$(a^{1/2})^2 = a^{(1/2) \cdot 2} = a^1 = a$$
$$(a^{1/3})^3 = a^{(1/3) \cdot 3} = a^1 = a$$
$$(a^{1/4})^4 = a^{(1/4) \cdot 4} = a^1 = a$$

Because $a^{1/2}$ is a number whose square is *a*, you can write $\sqrt{a} = a^{1/2}$. Similarly, $\sqrt[3]{a} = a^{1/3}$ and $\sqrt[4]{a} = a^{1/4}$. In general, $\sqrt[n]{a} = a^{1/n}$ for any integer *n* greater than 1.

Core Concept

READING

$\pm \sqrt[n]{a}$ represents both the positive and negative *n*th roots of *a*.

Real *n*th Roots of *a*

Let *n* be an integer greater than 1, and let *a* be a real number.

- If *n* is odd, then *a* has one real *n*th root: $\sqrt[n]{a} = a^{1/n}$

- If *n* is even and $a > 0$, then *a* has two real *n*th roots: $\pm\sqrt[n]{a} = \pm a^{1/n}$

- If *n* is even and $a = 0$, then *a* has one real *n*th root: $\sqrt[n]{0} = 0$

- If *n* is even and $a < 0$, then *a* has no real *n*th roots.

The *n*th roots of a number may be real numbers or *imaginary numbers*. You will study imaginary numbers in Chapter 4.

EXAMPLE 1 **Finding *n*th Roots**

Find the indicated real *n*th root(s) of *a*.

a. $n = 3, a = -27$ **b.** $n = 4, a = 16$

SOLUTION

a. The index $n = 3$ is odd, so -27 has one real cube root. Because $(-3)^3 = -27$, the cube root of -27 is $\sqrt[3]{-27} = -3$, or $(-27)^{1/3} = -3$.

b. The index $n = 4$ is even, and $a > 0$. So, 16 has two real fourth roots. Because $2^4 = 16$ and $(-2)^4 = 16$, the fourth roots of 16 are $\pm\sqrt[4]{16} = \pm 2$, or $\pm 16^{1/4} = \pm 2$.

Monitoring Progress Help in English and Spanish at *BigIdeasMath.com*

Find the indicated real *n*th root(s) of *a*.

1. $n = 3, a = -125$ **2.** $n = 6, a = 64$

Evaluating Expressions with Rational Exponents

Recall that the radical $\sqrt{a}$ indicates the positive square root of a. Similarly, an nth root of a, $\sqrt[n]{a}$, with an *even* index indicates the positive nth root of a.

REMEMBER

The expression under the radical sign is the radicand.

EXAMPLE 2 **Evaluating nth Root Expressions**

Evaluate each expression.

a. $\sqrt[3]{-8}$ b. $-\sqrt[3]{8}$ c. $16^{1/4}$ d. $(-16)^{1/4}$

SOLUTION

a. $\sqrt[3]{-8} = \sqrt[3]{(-2) \cdot (-2) \cdot (-2)}$ Rewrite the expression showing factors.

       $= -2$ Evaluate the cube root.

b. $-\sqrt[3]{8} = -\left(\sqrt[3]{2 \cdot 2 \cdot 2}\right)$ Rewrite the expression showing factors.

       $= -(2)$ Evaluate the cube root.

       $= -2$ Simplify.

c. $16^{1/4} = \sqrt[4]{16}$ Rewrite the expression in radical form.

       $= \sqrt[4]{2 \cdot 2 \cdot 2 \cdot 2}$ Rewrite the expression showing factors.

       $= 2$ Evaluate the fourth root.

d. $(-16)^{1/4}$ is not a real number because there is no real number that can be multiplied by itself four times to produce -16.

A rational exponent does not have to be of the form $1/n$. Other rational numbers such as $3/2$ can also be used as exponents. You can use the properties of exponents to evaluate or simplify expressions involving rational exponents.

STUDY TIP

You can rewrite $27^{2/3}$ as $27^{(1/3) \cdot 2}$ and then use the Power of a Power Property to show that

$27^{(1/3) \cdot 2} = (27^{1/3})^2$.

Core Concept

Rational Exponents

Let $a^{1/n}$ be an nth root of a, and let m be a positive integer.

Algebra $a^{m/n} = (a^{1/n})^m = \left(\sqrt[n]{a}\right)^m$

Numbers $27^{2/3} = (27^{1/3})^2 = \left(\sqrt[3]{27}\right)^2$

EXAMPLE 3 **Evaluating Expressions with Rational Exponents**

Evaluate (a) $16^{3/4}$ and (b) $27^{4/3}$.

SOLUTION

a. $16^{3/4} = (16^{1/4})^3$ Rational exponents   b. $27^{4/3} = (27^{1/3})^4$

     $= 2^3$ Evaluate the nth root. $= 3^4$

     $= 8$ Evaluate the power. $= 81$

Monitoring Progress Help in English and Spanish at *BigIdeasMath.com*

Evaluate the expression.

3. $\sqrt[3]{-125}$ 4. $(-64)^{2/3}$ 5. $9^{5/2}$ 6. $256^{3/4}$

Solving Real-Life Problems

EXAMPLE 4   Solving a Real-Life Problem

Volume = 113 cubic feet

The radius r of a sphere is given by the equation $r = \left(\dfrac{3V}{4\pi}\right)^{1/3}$, where V is the volume of the sphere. Find the radius of the beach ball to the nearest foot. Use 3.14 for π.

SOLUTION

1. **Understand the Problem** You know the equation that represents the radius of a sphere in terms of its volume. You are asked to find the radius for a given volume.

2. **Make a Plan** Substitute the given volume into the equation. Then evaluate to find the radius.

3. **Solve the Problem**

$$r = \left(\frac{3V}{4\pi}\right)^{1/3} \qquad \text{Write the equation.}$$

$$= \left(\frac{3(113)}{4(3.14)}\right)^{1/3} \qquad \text{Substitute 113 for } V \text{ and 3.14 for } \pi.$$

$$= \left(\frac{339}{12.56}\right)^{1/3} \qquad \text{Multiply.}$$

$$\approx 3 \qquad \text{Use a calculator.}$$

▶ The radius of the beach ball is about 3 feet.

4. **Look Back** To check that your answer is reasonable, compare the size of the ball to the size of the woman pushing the ball. The ball appears to be slightly taller than the woman. The average height of a woman is between 5 and 6 feet. So, a radius of 3 feet, or height of 6 feet, seems reasonable for the beach ball.

EXAMPLE 5   Solving a Real-Life Problem

To calculate the annual inflation rate r (in decimal form) of an item that increases in value from P to F over a period of n years, you can use the equation $r = \left(\dfrac{F}{P}\right)^{1/n} - 1$.

Find the annual inflation rate to the nearest tenth of a percent of a house that increases in value from \$200,000 to \$235,000 over a period of 5 years.

SOLUTION

$$r = \left(\frac{F}{P}\right)^{1/n} - 1 \qquad \text{Write the equation.}$$

$$= \left(\frac{235,000}{200,000}\right)^{1/5} - 1 \qquad \text{Substitute 235,000 for } F, \text{ 200,000 for } P, \text{ and 5 for } n.$$

$$= 1.175^{1/5} - 1 \qquad \text{Divide.}$$

$$\approx 0.03278 \qquad \text{Use a calculator.}$$

REMEMBER

To write a decimal as a percent, move the decimal point two places to the right. Then add a percent symbol.

▶ The annual inflation rate is about 3.3%.

Monitoring Progress   Help in English and Spanish at *BigIdeasMath.com*

7. **WHAT IF?** In Example 4, the volume of the beach ball is 17,000 cubic inches. Find the radius to the nearest inch. Use 3.14 for π.

8. The average cost of college tuition increases from \$8500 to \$13,500 over a period of 8 years. Find the annual inflation rate to the nearest tenth of a percent.

Vocabulary and Core Concept Check

1. WRITING Explain how to evaluate $81^{1/4}$.

2. WHICH ONE DOESN'T BELONG? Which expression does *not* belong with the other three? Explain your reasoning.

$$\left(\sqrt[3]{27}\right)^2 \qquad 27^{2/3} \qquad 3^2 \qquad \left(\sqrt[2]{27}\right)^3$$

Monitoring Progress and Modeling with Mathematics

In Exercises 3 and 4, rewrite the expression in rational exponent form.

3. $\sqrt{10}$

4. $\sqrt[5]{34}$

In Exercises 5 and 6, rewrite the expression in radical form.

5. $15^{1/3}$

6. $140^{1/8}$

In Exercises 7–10, find the indicated real *n*th root(s) of *a*. *(See Example 1.)*

7. $n = 2, a = 36$

8. $n = 4, a = 81$

9. $n = 3, a = 1000$

10. $n = 9, a = -512$

MATHEMATICAL CONNECTIONS In Exercises 11 and 12, find the dimensions of the cube. Check your answer.

11. Volume = 64 in.^{3}

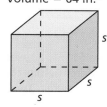

12. Volume = 216 cm^3

In Exercises 13–18, evaluate the expression. *(See Example 2.)*

13. $\sqrt[4]{256}$

14. $\sqrt[3]{-216}$

15. $\sqrt[3]{-343}$

16. $-\sqrt[5]{1024}$

17. $128^{1/7}$

18. $(-64)^{1/2}$

In Exercises 19 and 20, rewrite the expression in rational exponent form.

19. $\left(\sqrt[5]{8}\right)^4$

20. $\left(\sqrt[5]{-21}\right)^6$

In Exercises 21 and 22, rewrite the expression in radical form.

21. $(-4)^{2/7}$

22. $9^{5/2}$

In Exercises 23–28, evaluate the expression. *(See Example 3.)*

23. $32^{3/5}$

24. $125^{2/3}$

25. $(-36)^{3/2}$

26. $(-243)^{2/5}$

27. $(-128)^{5/7}$

28. $343^{4/3}$

29. ERROR ANALYSIS Describe and correct the error in rewriting the expression in rational exponent form.

$$\left(\sqrt[3]{2}\right)^4 = 2^{3/4}$$

30. ERROR ANALYSIS Describe and correct the error in evaluating the expression.

$$(-81)^{3/4} = [(-81)^{1/4}]^3$$
$$= (-3)^3$$
$$= -27$$

In Exercises 31–34, evaluate the expression.

31. $\left(\dfrac{1}{1000}\right)^{1/3}$

32. $\left(\dfrac{1}{64}\right)^{1/6}$

33. $(27)^{-2/3}$

34. $(9)^{-5/2}$

35. PROBLEM SOLVING A math club is having a bake sale. Find the area of the bake sale sign.

$4^{1/2}$ ft

$\sqrt[6]{729}$ ft

36. PROBLEM SOLVING The volume of a cube-shaped box is 27^5 cubic millimeters. Find the length of one side of the box.

37. MODELING WITH MATHEMATICS The radius r of the base of a cone is given by the equation

$$r = \left(\frac{3V}{\pi h}\right)^{1/2}$$

where V is the volume of the cone and h is the height of the cone. Find the radius of the paper cup to the nearest inch. Use 3.14 for π. *(See Example 4.)*

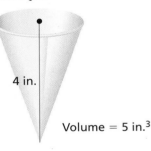

4 in.

Volume = 5 in.^{3}

38. MODELING WITH MATHEMATICS The volume of a sphere is given by the equation $V = \dfrac{1}{6\sqrt{\pi}}S^{3/2}$, where S is the surface area of the sphere. Find the volume of a sphere, to the nearest cubic meter, that has a surface area of 60 square meters. Use 3.14 for π.

39. WRITING Explain how to write $(\sqrt[n]{a})^m$ in rational exponent form.

40. HOW DO YOU SEE IT? Write an expression in rational exponent form that represents the side length of the square.

Area = x in.^{2}

In Exercises 41 and 42, use the formula $r = \left(\dfrac{F}{P}\right)^{1/n} - 1$ to find the annual inflation rate to the nearest tenth of a percent. *(See Example 5.)*

41. A farm increases in value from \$800,000 to \$1,100,000 over a period of 6 years.

42. The cost of a gallon of gas increases from \$1.46 to \$3.53 over a period of 10 years.

43. REASONING For what values of x is $x = x^{1/5}$?

44. MAKING AN ARGUMENT Your friend says that for a real number a and a positive integer n, the value of $\sqrt[n]{a}$ is always positive and the value of $-\sqrt[n]{a}$ is always negative. Is your friend correct? Explain.

In Exercises 45–48, simplify the expression.

45. $(y^{1/6})^3 \cdot \sqrt{x}$

46. $(y \cdot y^{1/3})^{3/2}$

47. $x \cdot \sqrt[3]{y^6} + y^2 \cdot \sqrt[3]{x^3}$

48. $(x^{1/3} \cdot y^{1/2})^9 \cdot \sqrt{y}$

49. PROBLEM SOLVING The formula for the volume of a regular dodecahedron is $V \approx 7.66\,\ell^3$, where ℓ is the length of an edge. The volume of the dodecahedron is 20 cubic feet. Estimate the edge length.

ℓ

50. THOUGHT PROVOKING To find the arithmetic mean of n numbers, divide the sum of the numbers by n. To find the geometric mean of n numbers $a_1, a_2, a_3, \ldots, a_n$, take the nth root of the product of the numbers.

$$\text{geometric mean} = \sqrt[n]{a_1 \cdot a_2 \cdot a_3 \cdot \ldots \cdot a_n}$$

Compare the arithmetic mean to the geometric mean of n numbers.

ABSTRACT REASONING In Exercises 51–56, let x be a nonnegative real number. Determine whether the statement is *always*, *sometimes*, or *never* true. Justify your answer.

51. $(x^{1/3})^3 = x$

52. $x^{1/3} = x^{-3}$

53. $x^{1/3} = \sqrt[3]{x}$

54. $x^{1/3} = x^3$

55. $\dfrac{x^{2/3}}{x^{1/3}} = \sqrt[3]{x}$

56. $x = x^{1/3} \cdot x^3$

Maintaining Mathematical Proficiency   Reviewing what you learned in previous grades and lessons

Evaluate the function when $x = -3, 0,$ and 8.   *(Skills Review Handbook)*

57. $f(x) = 2x - 10$ **58.** $w(x) = -5x - 1$ **59.** $h(x) = 13 - x$ **60.** $g(x) = 8x + 16$

1.6 Exponential Functions

Essential Question
What are some of the characteristics of the graph of an exponential function?

You can use a graphing calculator to evaluate an exponential function. For example, consider the exponential function $f(x) = 2^x$.

Function Value	Graphing Calculator Keystrokes	Display
$f(-3.1) = 2^{-3.1}$	2 ^ (−) 3.1 ENTER	0.1166291
$f\left(\frac{2}{3}\right) = 2^{2/3}$	2 ^ (2 ÷ 3) ENTER	1.5874011

EXPLORATION 1 Identifying Graphs of Exponential Functions

Work with a partner. Match each exponential function with its graph. Use a table of values to sketch the graph of the function, if necessary.

a. $f(x) = 2^x$

b. $f(x) = 3^x$

c. $f(x) = 4^x$

d. $f(x) = \left(\frac{1}{2}\right)^x$

e. $f(x) = \left(\frac{1}{3}\right)^x$

f. $f(x) = \left(\frac{1}{4}\right)^x$

A.

B.

C.

D.

E.

F.

EXPLORATION 2 Characteristics of Graphs of Exponential Functions

CONSTRUCTING VIABLE ARGUMENTS

To be proficient in math, you need to justify your conclusions and communicate them to others.

Work with a partner. Use the graphs in Exploration 1 to determine the domain, range, and y-intercept of the graph of $f(x) = b^x$, where b is a positive real number other than 1. Explain your reasoning.

Communicate Your Answer

3. What are some of the characteristics of the graph of an exponential function?

4. In Exploration 2, is it possible for the graph of $f(x) = b^x$ to have an x-intercept? Explain your reasoning.

1.6 Lesson

Core Vocabulary

exponential function, *p. 42*
exponential growth function,
     p. 42
growth factor, *p. 42*
asymptote, *p. 42*
exponential decay function,
     p. 42
decay factor, *p. 42*
recursive rule for an
     exponential function, *p. 44*

Previous
sequences
properties of exponents

What You Will Learn

▶ Graph exponential growth and decay functions.
▶ Write exponential models and recursive rules.
▶ Rewrite exponential functions.

Exponential Growth and Decay Functions

An **exponential function** has the form $y = ab^x$, where $a \neq 0$ and the base b is a positive real number other than 1. If $a > 0$ and $b > 1$, then $y = ab^x$ is an **exponential growth function**, and b is called the **growth factor**. The simplest type of exponential growth function has the form $y = b^x$.

Core Concept

Parent Function for Exponential Growth Functions

The function $f(x) = b^x$, where $b > 1$, is the parent function for the family of exponential growth functions with base b. The graph shows the general shape of an exponential growth function.

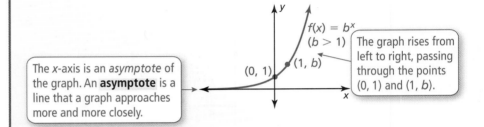

The *x*-axis is an *asymptote* of the graph. An **asymptote** is a line that a graph approaches more and more closely.

$f(x) = b^x$
$(b > 1)$ The graph rises from left to right, passing through the points $(0, 1)$ and $(1, b)$.

$(0, 1)$ $(1, b)$

The domain of $f(x) = b^x$ is all real numbers. The range is $y > 0$.

If $a > 0$ and $0 < b < 1$, then $y = ab^x$ is an **exponential decay function**, and b is called the **decay factor**.

Core Concept

Parent Function for Exponential Decay Functions

The function $f(x) = b^x$, where $0 < b < 1$, is the parent function for the family of exponential decay functions with base b. The graph shows the general shape of an exponential decay function.

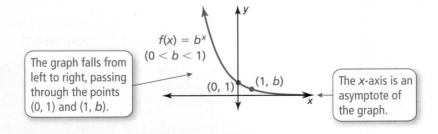

The graph falls from left to right, passing through the points $(0, 1)$ and $(1, b)$.

$f(x) = b^x$
$(0 < b < 1)$

$(0, 1)$ $(1, b)$

The *x*-axis is an asymptote of the graph.

The domain of $f(x) = b^x$ is all real numbers. The range is $y > 0$.

EXAMPLE 1 Graphing Exponential Growth and Decay Functions

Determine whether each function represents *exponential growth* or *exponential decay*. Then graph the function.

a. $y = 2^x$

b. $y = \left(\frac{1}{2}\right)^x$

SOLUTION

a. Step 1 Identify the value of the base. The base, 2, is greater than 1, so the function represents exponential growth.

STUDY TIP

When graphing exponential functions, you connect the points with a smooth curve because $y = ab^x$ is defined for rational *x*-values. This should make sense from your study of rational exponents. For instance, in Example 1(a), when $x = \frac{1}{2}$,

$$y = 2^{1/2} = \sqrt{2} \approx 1.4.$$

Step 2 Make a table of values.

x	−2	−1	0	1	2	3
y	$\frac{1}{4}$	$\frac{1}{2}$	1	2	4	8

Step 3 Plot the points from the table.

Step 4 Draw, from *left to right*, a smooth curve that begins just above the *x*-axis, passes through the plotted points, and moves up to the right.

b. Step 1 Identify the value of the base. The base, $\frac{1}{2}$, is greater than 0 and less than 1, so the function represents exponential decay.

Step 2 Make a table of values.

x	−3	−2	−1	0	1	2
y	8	4	2	1	$\frac{1}{2}$	$\frac{1}{4}$

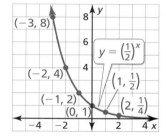

Step 3 Plot the points from the table.

Step 4 Draw, from *right to left*, a smooth curve that begins just above the *x*-axis, passes through the plotted points, and moves up to the left.

Monitoring Progress   Help in English and Spanish at *BigIdeasMath.com*

Determine whether the function represents *exponential growth* or *exponential decay*. Then graph the function.

1. $y = 4^x$

2. $y = \left(\frac{2}{3}\right)^x$

3. $f(x) = (0.25)^x$

4. $f(x) = (1.5)^x$

Writing Exponential Models and Recursive Rules

Some real-life quantities increase or decrease by a fixed percent each year (or some other time period). The amount *y* of such a quantity after *t* years can be modeled by one of these equations.

Exponential Growth Model	**Exponential Decay Model**
$y = a(1 + r)^t$	$y = a(1 - r)^t$

Note that *a* is the initial amount and *r* is the percent increase or decrease written as a decimal. The quantity $1 + r$ is the growth factor, and $1 - r$ is the decay factor.

EXAMPLE 2   Writing an Exponential Model

The population of a country was about 6.09 million on January 1, 2000. The population at the beginning of each subsequent year increased by about 1.18%.

a. Write an exponential growth model that represents the population y (in millions) t years after January 1, 2000. Find and interpret the y-value when $t = 7.5$.

b. Estimate when the population was 7 million.

SOLUTION

a. The initial amount is $a = 6.09$, and the percent increase is $r = 0.0118$. So, the exponential growth model is

X	Y1
11.4	6.9614
11.5	6.9696
11.6	6.9778
11.7	6.9859
11.8	6.9941
11.9	**7.0024**
12	7.0106

X=11.9

$$y = a(1 + r)^t \qquad \text{Write exponential growth model.}$$
$$= 6.09(1 + 0.0118)^t \qquad \text{Substitute 6.09 for } a \text{ and 0.0118 for } r.$$
$$= 6.09(1.0118)^t. \qquad \text{Simplify.}$$

Using this model, you can estimate the *midyear* population in 2007 ($t = 7.5$) to be $y = 6.09(1.0118)^{7.5} \approx 6.65$ million.

b. Use the *table* feature of a graphing calculator to determine that $y \approx 7$ when $t \approx 11.9$. So, the population was about 7 million near the end of 2011.

Monitoring Progress   Help in English and Spanish at *BigIdeasMath.com*

5. WHAT IF? Assume the population increased by 1.5% each year. Write an equation to model this situation. Estimate when the population was 7 million.

In real-life situations, you can also show exponential relationships using *recursive rules*.

A **recursive rule** for an exponential function gives the initial value of the function $f(0)$, and a recursive equation that tells how a value $f(n)$ is related to a preceding value $f(n - 1)$.

REMEMBER

Recall that for a sequence, a recursive rule gives the beginning term(s) of the sequence and a recursive equation that tells how a_n is related to one or more preceding terms.

Core Concept

Writing Recursive Rules for Exponential Functions

An exponential function of the form $f(x) = ab^x$ is written using a recursive rule as follows.

Recursive Rule $f(0) = a, \ f(n) = r \cdot f(n - 1)$

where $a \neq 0$, r is the common ratio, and n is a natural number

Example $y = 6(3)^x$ can be written as $f(0) = 6, \ f(n) = 3 \cdot f(n - 1)$

— initial value —

— common ratio —

Notice that the base b of the exponential function is the common ratio r in the recursive equation. Also, notice the value of a in the exponential function is the initial value of the recursive rule.

EXAMPLE 3 Writing a Recursive Rule for an Exponential Function

STUDY TIP

Notice that the domain consists of the natural numbers when written recursively.

Write a recursive rule for the function you wrote in Example 2.

SOLUTION

The function $y = 6.09(1.0118)^t$ is exponential with initial value $f(0) = 6.09$ and common ratio $r = 1.0118$. So, a recursive equation is

$$f(n) = r \cdot f(n - 1) \qquad \text{Recursive equation for exponential functions}$$
$$= 1.0118 \cdot f(n - 1). \qquad \text{Substitute 1.0118 for } r.$$

▶ A recursive rule for the exponential function is $f(0) = 6.09$, $f(n) = 1.0118 \cdot f(n - 1)$.

Monitoring Progress Help in English and Spanish at *BigIdeasMath.com*

Write an recursive rule for the exponential function.

6. $f(x) = 4(7)^x$

7. $y = 9\left(\frac{1}{3}\right)^t$

Rewriting Exponential Functions

EXAMPLE 4 Rewriting Exponential Functions

STUDY TIP

You can rewrite exponential expressions and functions using the properties of exponents. Changing the form of an exponential function can reveal important attributes of the function.

Rewrite each function to determine whether it represents *exponential growth* or *exponential decay*. Then identify the percent rate of change.

a. $y = 100(0.96)^{t/4}$

b. $f(t) = (1.1)^{t-3}$

SOLUTION

a. $y = 100(0.96)^{t/4}$ Write the function.

$= 100(0.96^{1/4})^t$ Power of a Power Property

$\approx 100(0.99)^t$ Evaluate the power.

▶ So, the function represents exponential decay. Use the decay factor $1 - r \approx 0.99$ to find the rate of decay $r \approx 0.01$, or about 1%.

b. $f(t) = (1.1)^{t-3}$ Write the function.

$= \dfrac{(1.1)^t}{(1.1)^3}$ Quotient of Powers Property

$\approx 0.75(1.1)^t$ Evaluate the power and simplify.

▶ So, the function represents exponential growth. Use the growth factor $1 + r = 1.1$ to find the rate of growth $r = 0.1$, or 10%.

Monitoring Progress Help in English and Spanish at *BigIdeasMath.com*

Rewrite the function to determine whether it represents *exponential growth* or *exponential decay*. Then identify the percent rate of change.

8. $f(t) = 3(1.02)^{10t}$

9. $y = (0.95)^{t+2}$

EXAMPLE 5 **Solving a Real-Life Problem**

The value of a car is $21,500. It loses 12% of its value every year. (a) Write a function that represents the value y (in dollars) of the car after t years. (b) Find the approximate monthly percent decrease in value. (c) Graph the function from part (a). Use the graph to estimate the value of the car after 6 years.

SOLUTION

1. **Understand the Problem** You know the value of the car and its annual percent decrease in value. You are asked to write a function that represents the value of the car over time and approximate the monthly percent decrease in value. Then graph the function and use the graph to estimate the value of the car in the future.

2. **Make a Plan** Use the initial amount and the annual percent decrease in value to write an exponential decay function. Note that the annual percent decrease represents the rate of decay. Rewrite the function using the properties of exponents to approximate the monthly percent decrease (rate of decay). Then graph the original function and use the graph to estimate the y-value when the t-value is 6.

3. **Solve the Problem**

   a. The initial value is $21,500, and the rate of decay is 12%, or 0.12.

$y = a(1 - r)^t$	Write exponential decay model.
$= 21,500(1 - 0.12)^t$	Substitute 21,500 for a and 0.12 for r.
$= 21,500(0.88)^t$	Simplify.

   ▶ The value of the car can be represented by $y = 21,500(0.88)^t$.

   b. Use the fact that $t = \frac{1}{12}(12t)$ and the properties of exponents to rewrite the function in a form that reveals the monthly rate of decay.

$y = 21,500(0.88)^t$	Write the original function.
$= 21,500(0.88)^{(1/12)(12t)}$	Rewrite the exponent.
$= 21,500(0.88^{1/12})^{12t}$	Power of a Power Property
$\approx 21,500(0.989)^{12t}$	Evaluate the power.

   Use the decay factor $1 - r \approx 0.989$ to find the rate of decay $r \approx 0.011$.

   ▶ So, the monthly percent decrease is about 1.1%.

   c. From the graph, you can see that the y-value is about 10,000 when $t = 6$.

   ▶ So, the value of the car is about $10,000 after 6 years.

4. **Look Back** To check that the monthly percent decrease is reasonable, multiply it by 12 to see if it is close in value to the annual percent decrease of 12%.

   $1.1\% \times 12 = 13.2\%$ 13.2% is close to 12%, so 1.1% is reasonable.

   When you evaluate $y = 21,500(0.88)^t$ for $t = 6$, you get about $9985. So, $10,000 is a reasonable estimation.

REASONING QUANTITATIVELY

The decay factor, 0.88, tells you what fraction of the car's value *remains* each year. The rate of decay, 12%, tells you how much value the car *loses* each year. In real life, the percent decrease in value of an asset is the *depreciation rate*.

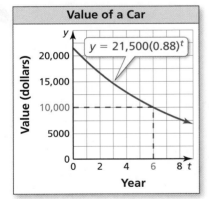

Value of a Car

$y = 21,500(0.88)^t$

Value (dollars): 0, 5000, 10,000, 15,000, 20,000
Year: 0, 2, 4, 6, 8 t

Monitoring Progress Help in English and Spanish at *BigIdeasMath.com*

10. **WHAT IF?** The car loses 9% of its value every year. (a) Write a function that represents the value y (in dollars) of the car after t years. (b) Find the approximate monthly percent decrease in value. (c) Graph the function from part (a). Use the graph to estimate the value of the car after 12 years. Round your answer to the nearest thousand.

Vocabulary and Core Concept Check

1. **VOCABULARY** In the exponential growth model $y = 2.4(1.5)^x$, identify the initial amount, the growth factor, and the percent increase.

2. **WHICH ONE DOESN'T BELONG?** Which characteristic of an exponential decay function does *not* belong with the other three? Explain your reasoning.

base of 0.8	decay factor of 0.8
decay rate of 20%	80% decrease

Monitoring Progress and Modeling with Mathematics

In Exercises 3–8, evaluate the expression for (a) $x = -2$ and (b) $x = 3$.

3. 2^x

4. 4^x

5. $8 \cdot 3^x$

6. $6 \cdot 2^x$

7. $5 + 3^x$

8. $2^x - 2$

In Exercises 9–18, determine whether the function represents *exponential growth* or *exponential decay*. Then graph the function. *(See Example 1.)*

9. $y = 6^x$

10. $y = 7^x$

11. $y = \left(\dfrac{1}{6}\right)^x$

12. $y = \left(\dfrac{1}{8}\right)^x$

13. $y = \left(\dfrac{4}{3}\right)^x$

14. $y = \left(\dfrac{2}{5}\right)^x$

15. $y = (1.2)^x$

16. $y = (0.75)^x$

17. $y = (0.6)^x$

18. $y = (1.8)^x$

ANALYZING RELATIONSHIPS In Exercises 19 and 20, use the graph of $f(x) = b^x$ to identify the value of the base b.

19.

20.
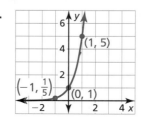

21. **MODELING WITH MATHEMATICS** The population of Austin, Texas, was about 494,000 at the beginning of a decade. The population increased by about 3% each year. *(See Example 2.)*

    a. Write an exponential growth model that represents the population y (in thousands) t years after the beginning of the decade. Find and interpret the y-value when $t = 10$.

    b. Estimate when the population was about 590,000.

22. **MODELING WITH MATHEMATICS** You take a 325 milligram dosage of ibuprofen. During each subsequent hour, the amount of medication in your bloodstream decreases by about 29% each hour.

    a. Write an exponential decay model giving the amount y (in milligrams) of ibuprofen in your bloodstream t hours after the initial dose. Find and interpret the y-value when $t = 1.5$.

    b. Estimate how long it takes for you to have 100 milligrams of ibuprofen in your bloodstream.

23. **ERROR ANALYSIS** You invest $500 in the stock of a company. The value of the stock decreases 2% each year. Describe and correct the error in writing a model for the value of the stock after t years.

$$y = \begin{pmatrix} \text{Initial} \\ \text{amount} \end{pmatrix} \begin{pmatrix} \text{Decay} \\ \text{factor} \end{pmatrix}^t$$

$$y = 500(0.02)^t$$

24. USING EQUATIONS Complete a table of values for $0 \le n \le 5$ using the given recursive rule of an exponential function.

$$f(0) = 4, \; f(n) = 3 \cdot f(n-1)$$

In Exercises 25–32, write a recursive rule for the exponential function. *(See Example 3.)*

25. $y = 3(7)^x$

26. $y = 25(0.2)^x$

27. $y = 12(0.5)^t$

28. $y = 19(4)^t$

29. $g(x) = 0.5(3)^x$

30. $m(t) = \frac{1}{3}(2)^t$

31. $f(x) = 4\left(\frac{1}{6}\right)^x$

32. $f(t) = 0.25\left(\frac{2}{3}\right)^t$

In Exercises 33–36, show that an exponential model fits the data. Then write a recursive rule that models the data.

33.

n	0	1	2	3	4	5
f(n)	0.75	1.5	3	6	12	24

34.

n	0	1	2	3	4
f(n)	2	8	32	128	512

35.

n	0	1	2	3	4	5
f(n)	96	48	24	12	6	3

36.

n	0	1	2	3	4	5
f(n)	162	54	18	6	2	$\frac{2}{3}$

In Exercises 37 and 38, write an exponential function for the recursive rule.

37. $f(0) = 24, f(n) = 0.1 \cdot f(n-1)$

38. $f(0) = \frac{1}{2}, f(n) = \frac{5}{2} \cdot f(n-1)$

39. PROBLEM SOLVING Describe a real-life situation that can be represented by the graph. Write a recursive rule that models the data. Then find and interpret $f(6)$.

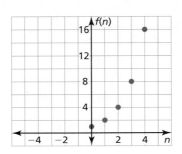

40. PROBLEM SOLVING The cross-sectional area of a tree 4.5 feet from the ground is called its *basal area*. The table shows the basal areas (in square inches) of Tree A over time.

Year	0	1	2	3	4
Basal area	120	132	145.2	159.7	175.7

Tree B

Growth rate: 6%

Initial basal area: 154 in.²

a. Write recursive rules that represent the basal areas of the trees after t years.

b. Which tree has a greater initial basal area? a greater basal area growth rate? Use the recursive rules you wrote in part (a) to justify your answers.

c. Use a graph to represent the growth of the trees over the interval $0 \le t \le 10$. Does the graph support your answers in part (b)? Explain. Then make an additional observation from the graph.

In Exercises 41–44, determine whether the function represents *exponential growth* or *exponential decay*. Then identify the percent rate of change.

41. $y = 5(0.6)^t$

42. $y = 10(1.07)^t$

43. $f(t) = 200\left(\frac{4}{3}\right)^t$

44. $f(t) = 0.8\left(\frac{1}{4}\right)^t$

45. PROBLEM SOLVING A website recorded the number y of referrals it received from social media websites over a 10-year period. The results can be modeled by $y = 2500(1.50)^t$, where t is the year and $0 \le t \le 9$.

a. Describe the real-life meaning of 2500 and 1.50 in the model.

b. What is the annual percent increase? Explain.

46. PROBLEM SOLVING The population p of a small town after x years can be modeled by the function $p = 6850(0.97)^x$.

a. What is the annual percent decrease? Explain.

b. What is the average rate of change in the population over the first 6 years? Justify your answer.

JUSTIFYING STEPS In Exercises 47 and 48, justify each step in rewriting the exponential function.

47. $y = a(3)^{t/14}$ Write original function.

$= a[(3)^{1/14}]^t$

$\approx a(1.0816)^t$

$= a(1 + 0.0816)^t$

48. $y = a(0.1)^{t/3}$ Write original function.

$= a[(0.1)^{1/3}]^t$

$\approx a(0.4642)^t$

$= a(1 - 0.5358)^t$

In Exercises 49–56, rewrite the function to determine whether it represents *exponential growth* or *exponential decay*. Then identify the percent rate of change. (*See Example 4.*)

49. $y = (0.9)^{t-4}$ **50.** $y = (1.4)^{t+8}$

51. $y = 2(1.06)^{9t}$ **52.** $y = 5(0.82)^{t/5}$

53. $x(t) = (1.45)^{t/2}$ **54.** $f(t) = 0.4(1.16)^{t-1}$

55. $b(t) = 4(0.55)^{t+3}$ **56.** $r(t) = (0.88)^{4t}$

In Exercises 57–62, rewrite the function in the form $y = a(1 + r)^t$ or $y = a(1 - r)^t$. Then state the growth or decay rate.

57. $y = a(2)^{t/3}$ **58.** $y = a(0.5)^{t/12}$

59. $y = a\left(\dfrac{2}{3}\right)^{t/10}$ **60.** $y = a\left(\dfrac{5}{4}\right)^{t/22}$

61. $y = a(2)^{8t}$ **62.** $y = a\left(\dfrac{1}{3}\right)^{3t}$

63. PROBLEM SOLVING When a plant or animal dies, it stops acquiring carbon-14 from the atmosphere. The amount y (in grams) of carbon-14 in the body of an organism after t years is $y = a(0.5)^{t/5730}$, where a is the initial amount (in grams). What percent of the carbon-14 is released each year?

64. PROBLEM SOLVING The number y of duckweed fronds in a pond after t days is $y = a(1230.25)^{t/16}$, where a is the initial number of fronds. By what percent does the duckweed increase each day?

65. PROBLEM SOLVING A city has a population of 25,000. The population is expected to increase by 5.5% annually for the next decade. (*See Example 5.*)

a. Write a function that represents the population y after t years.

b. Find the approximate monthly percent increase in population.

c. Graph the function from part (a). Use the graph to estimate the population after 4 years.

66. PROBLEM SOLVING Plutonium-238 is a material that generates steady heat due to decay and is used in power systems for some spacecraft. The function $y = a(0.5)^{t/x}$ represents the amount y of a substance remaining after t years, where a is the initial amount and x is the length of the half-life (in years).

Plutonium-238
Half-life ≈ 88 years

a. A scientist is studying a 3-gram sample. Write a function that represents the amount y of plutonium-238 after t years.

b. What is the yearly percent decrease of plutonium-238?

c. Graph the function from part (a). Use the graph to estimate the amount remaining after 12 years.

67. MAKING AN ARGUMENT Your friend says the graph of $f(x) = 2^x$ increases at a faster rate than the graph of $g(x) = 4x$ when $x \geq 0$. Is your friend correct? Explain your reasoning.

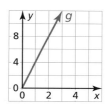

68. HOW DO YOU SEE IT? Consider the graph of an exponential function of the form $f(x) = ab^x$.

(−1, 4)

(0, 1) $\left(1, \frac{1}{4}\right)$

$\left(2, \frac{1}{16}\right)$

a. Determine whether the graph of f represents exponential growth or exponential decay.

b. What are the domain and range of the function? Explain.

69. COMPARING FUNCTIONS The two given functions describe the amount y of ibuprofen (in milligrams) in a person's bloodstream t hours after taking the dosage.

$$y \approx 325(0.9943)^{60t} \qquad y \approx 325(0.843)^{2t}$$

a. Show that these models are approximately equivalent to the model you wrote in Exercise 22.

b. Describe the information given by each of the models above.

70. DRAWING CONCLUSIONS The amount A in an account after t years with principal P, annual interest rate r (expressed as a decimal), and compounded n times per year is given by

$$A = P\left(1 + \frac{r}{n}\right)^{nt}.$$

You deposit $1000 into three separate bank accounts that each pay 3% annual interest. For each account, evaluate $\left(1 + \frac{r}{n}\right)^n$. Interpret this quantity in the context of the problem. Then complete the table.

Account	Compounding	Balance after 1 year
1	quarterly	
2	monthly	
3	daily	

71. REASONING Consider the exponential function $f(x) = ab^x$.

a. Show that $\dfrac{f(x + 1)}{f(x)} = b$.

b. Use the equation in part (a) to explain why there is no exponential function of the form $f(x) = ab^x$ whose graph passes through the points in the table below.

x	0	1	2	3	4
y	4	4	8	24	72

72. THOUGHT PROVOKING The function $f(x) = b^x$ represents an exponential decay function. Write a second exponential decay function in terms of b and x.

73. PROBLEM SOLVING The number E of eggs a Leghorn chicken produces per year can be modeled by the equation $E = 179.2(0.89)^{w/52}$, where w is the age (in weeks) of the chicken and $w \geq 22$.

a. Identify the decay factor and the percent decrease.

b. Graph the model.

c. Estimate the egg production of a chicken that is 2.5 years old.

d. Explain how you can rewrite the model so that time is measured in years rather than in weeks.

74. CRITICAL THINKING You buy a new stereo for $1300 and are able to sell it 4 years later for $275. Assume that the resale value of the stereo decays exponentially with time. Write an equation giving the resale value V (in dollars) of the stereo as a function of the time t (in years) since you bought it.

Maintaining Mathematical Proficiency
Reviewing what you learned in previous grades and lessons

Simplify the expression. *(Skills Review Handbook)*

75. $x + 3x$

76. $8y - 21y$

77. $13z + 9 - 8z$

78. $-9w + w - 5$

Simplify the expression. Write your answer using only positive exponents. *(Section 1.4)*

79. $x^{-9} \cdot x^2$

80. $\dfrac{x^4}{x^3}$

81. $(-6x)^2$

82. $\left(\dfrac{4x^8}{2x^6}\right)^4$

1.4–1.6 What Did You Learn?

Core Vocabulary

nth root of a, *p. 36*
radical, *p. 36*
index of a radical, *p. 36*
exponential function, *p. 42*

exponential growth function, *p. 42*
growth factor, *p. 42*
asymptote, *p. 42*
exponential decay function, *p. 42*

decay factor, *p. 42*
recursive rule for an exponential
    function, *p. 44*

Core Concepts

Section 1.4

Zero Exponent, *p. 28*
Negative Exponents, *p. 28*
Product of Powers Property, *p. 29*
Quotient of Powers Property, *p. 29*

Power of a Power Property, *p. 29*
Power of a Product Property, *p. 30*
Power of a Quotient Property, *p. 30*

Section 1.5

Real nth Roots of a, *p. 36*

Rational Exponents, *p. 37*

Section 1.6

Parent Function for Exponential Growth
    Functions, *p. 42*
Parent Function for Exponential Decay
    Functions, *p. 42*

Exponential Growth and Decay Models, *p. 43*
Writing Recursive Rules for Exponential
    Functions, *p. 44*

Mathematical Practices

1. How did you apply what you know to simplify the complicated situation in Exercise 56 on page 33?

2. How can you use previously established results to construct an argument in Exercise 44 on page 40?

Performance Task:

Pool Shots

How can mathematics help you become a better pool player? What type of function could you use to sink a pool ball? What aspects of the function will help the shot be successful?

To explore the answers to these questions and more, check out the Performance Task and Real-Life STEM video at *BigIdeasMath.com*.

1.1 Absolute Value Functions *(pp. 3–10)*

Let $g(x) = -3|x + 1| + 2$. (a) Describe the transformations from the graph of $f(x) = |x|$ to the graph of g. (b) Graph g.

a. **Step 1** Translate the graph of f horizontally 1 unit left to get the graph of $t(x) = |x + 1|$.

   Step 2 Stretch the graph of t vertically by a factor of 3 to get the graph of $h(x) = 3|x + 1|$.

   Step 3 Reflect the graph of h in the x-axis to get the graph of $r(x) = -3|x + 1|$.

   Step 4 Translate the graph of r vertically 2 units up to get the graph of $g(x) = -3|x + 1| + 2$.

b. **Step 1** Make a table of values.

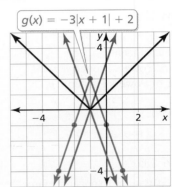

$g(x) = -3|x + 1| + 2$

x	−3	−2	−1	0	1
g(x)	−4	−1	2	−1	−4

   Step 2 Plot the ordered pairs.

   Step 3 Draw the V-shaped graph.

Graph the function. Compare the graph to the graph of $f(x) = |x|$. Describe the domain and range.

1. $m(x) = |x| + 6$ 2. $p(x) = |x - 4|$ 3. $q(x) = 4|x|$ 4. $r(x) = -\frac{1}{4}|x|$

5. Graph $f(x) = |x - 2| + 4$ and $g(x) = |3x - 2| + 4$. Compare the graph of g to the graph of f.

6. Describe another method you can use to graph g in the example above.

7. Let $g(x) = \frac{1}{3}|x - 1| - 2$. (a) Describe the transformations from the graph of $f(x) = |x|$ to the graph of g. (b) Graph g.

1.2 Piecewise Functions *(pp. 11–18)*

Graph $y = \begin{cases} \frac{3}{2}x + 3, & \text{if } x \le 0 \\ -2x, & \text{if } x > 0 \end{cases}$. **Describe the domain and range.**

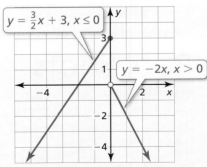

$y = \frac{3}{2}x + 3, x \le 0$

$y = -2x, x > 0$

Step 1 Graph $y = \frac{3}{2}x + 3$ for $x \le 0$. Because x is less than or equal to 0, use a closed circle at $(0, 3)$.

Step 2 Graph $y = -2x$ for $x > 0$. Because x is not equal to 0, use an open circle at $(0, 0)$.

▶ The domain is all real numbers. The range is $y \le 3$.

8. Evaluate the function in the example when (a) $x = 0$ and (b) $x = 5$.

Graph the function. Describe the domain and range.

9. $y = \begin{cases} x + 6, & \text{if } x \le 0 \\ -3x, & \text{if } x > 0 \end{cases}$

10. $y = \begin{cases} 4x + 2, & \text{if } x < -4 \\ 2x - 6, & \text{if } x \ge -4 \end{cases}$

Write the absolute value function as a piecewise function.

11. $y = |x| + 15$

12. $y = 4|x + 5|$

13. $y = 2|x + 2| - 3$

14. You are organizing a school fair and rent a popcorn machine for 3 days. The rental company charges $65 for the first day and $35 for each additional day. Write and graph a step function that represents the relationship between the number x of days and the total cost y (in dollars) of renting the popcorn machine.

1.3   **Inverse of a Function**   *(pp. 19–24)*

Find the inverse of $f(x) = \frac{1}{3}x - 2$. Then graph the function and its inverse.

$y = \frac{1}{3}x - 2$ Set y equal to $f(x)$.

$x = \frac{1}{3}y - 2$ Switch x and y in the equation.

$x + 2 = \frac{1}{3}y$ Add 2 to each side.

$3x + 6 = y$ Multiply each side by 3.

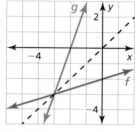

▶   The inverse of f is $g(x) = 3x + 6$.

15. Find the inverse of the relation: $(1, -10)$, $(3, -4)$, $(5, 4)$, $(7, 14)$, $(9, 26)$.

Find the inverse of the function. Then graph the function and its inverse.

16. $f(x) = \frac{3}{4}x$

17. $f(x) = -5x + 10$

18. $f(x) = -\frac{2}{5}x + 6$

19. In bowling, a handicap is an adjustment to a bowler's score to even out differences in ability levels. In a particular league, you can find a bowler's handicap h by using the formula $h = 0.8(210 - a)$, where a is the bowler's average. Solve the formula for a. Then find a bowler's average when the bowler's handicap is 28.

1.4   **Properties of Exponents**   *(pp. 27–34)*

Simplify $\left(\dfrac{x}{4}\right)^{-4}$. Write your answer using only positive exponents.

$\left(\dfrac{x}{4}\right)^{-4} = \dfrac{x^{-4}}{4^{-4}}$ Power of a Quotient Property

$= \dfrac{4^4}{x^4}$ Definition of negative exponent

$= \dfrac{256}{x^4}$ Simplify.

Simplify the expression. Write your answer using only positive exponents.

20. $y^3 \cdot y^{-5}$

21. $\dfrac{x^4}{x^7}$

22. $(x^0 y^2)^3$

23. $\left(\dfrac{2x^2}{5y^4}\right)^{-2}$

1.5　Radicals and Rational Exponents　*(pp. 35–40)*

Evaluate $512^{1/3}$.

$$512^{1/3} = \sqrt[3]{512}$$　　Rewrite the expression in radical form.

$$= \sqrt[3]{8 \cdot 8 \cdot 8}$$　　Rewrite the expression showing factors.

$$= 8$$　　Evaluate the cube root.

Evaluate the expression.

24. $\sqrt[3]{8}$ **25.** $\sqrt[5]{-243}$ **26.** $625^{3/4}$ **27.** $(-25)^{1/2}$

1.6　Exponential Functions　*(pp. 41–50)*

a. Determine whether the function $y = 3^x$ represents *exponential growth* or *exponential decay*. Then graph the function.

Step 1　Identify the value of the base. The base, 3, is greater than 1, so the function represents exponential growth.

Step 2　Make a table of values.

x	-2	-1	0	1	2
y	$\frac{1}{9}$	$\frac{1}{3}$	1	3	9

Step 3　Plot the points from the table.

Step 4　Draw, from *left to right*, a smooth curve that begins just above the x-axis, passes through the plotted points, and moves up to the right.

b. Rewrite the function $y = 10(0.65)^{t/8}$ to determine whether it represents *exponential growth* or *exponential decay*. Then identify the percent rate of change.

$$y = 10(0.65)^{t/8}$$　　Write the function.

$$= 10(0.65^{1/8})^t$$　　Power of a Power Property

$$\approx 10(0.95)^t$$　　Evaluate the power.

▶　So, the function represents exponential decay. Use the decay factor $1 - r \approx 0.95$ to find the rate of decay $r \approx 0.05$, or about 5%.

Determine whether the function represents exponential growth or exponential decay. Identify the percent rate of change. Then graph the function.

28. $f(x) = \left(\frac{1}{3}\right)^x$ **29.** $y = 5^x$ **30.** $f(x) = (0.2)^x$

Rewrite the function to determine whether it represents *exponential growth* or *exponential decay*. Then identify the percent rate of change.

31. $f(t) = 4(1.25)^{t+3}$ **32.** $y = (1.06)^{8t}$ **33.** $f(t) = 6(0.84)^{t-4}$

1 Chapter Test

Evaluate the expression.

1. $-\sqrt[4]{16}$

2. $729^{1/6}$

3. $(-32)^{7/5}$

Simplify the expression. Write your answer using only positive exponents.

4. $z^{-2} \cdot z^4$

5. $\dfrac{b^{-5}}{a^0 b^{-8}}$

6. $\left(\dfrac{2c^4}{5}\right)^{-3}$

Graph the function. Describe the domain and range.

7. $h(x) = -|x - 1| - 4$

8. $p(x) = \left|\dfrac{1}{2}x + 3\right| + 2$

9. $y = \begin{cases} 2x + 4, & \text{if } x \le -1 \\ \frac{1}{3}x - 1, & \text{if } x > -1 \end{cases}$

10. $y = \begin{cases} 1, & \text{if } 0 \le x < 3 \\ 0, & \text{if } 3 \le x < 6 \\ -1, & \text{if } 6 \le x < 9 \\ -2, & \text{if } 9 \le x < 12 \end{cases}$

Find the inverse of the function. Then graph the function and its inverse.

11. $g(x) = -4x$

12. $r(x) = 3x + 5$

13. $v(x) = -\dfrac{3}{4}x - \dfrac{1}{3}$

Use the equation to complete the statement "a ▢ b" with the symbol <, >, or =. Do not attempt to solve the equation.

14. $\dfrac{5^a}{5^b} = 5^{-3}$

15. $9^a \cdot 9^{-b} = 1$

16. Write a piecewise function defined by three equations that has a domain of all real numbers and a range of $-3 < y \le 1$.

17. A rock band releases a new single. Weekly sales s (in thousands of dollars) increase and then decrease as described by the function $s(t) = -2|t - 20| + 40$, where t is the time (in weeks).

    a. Graph s. Describe the transformations from the graph of $f(x) = |x|$ to the graph of s.

    b. Identify and interpret the vertex of the graph of s in the context of the problem.

18. The speed of light is approximately 3×10^5 kilometers per second. The average distance from the Sun to Neptune is about 4.5 billion kilometers. How long does it take sunlight to reach Neptune? Write your answer in scientific notation and in standard form.

19. The value of a mountain bike y (in dollars) can be approximated by the model $y = 200(0.75)^t$, where t is the number of years since the bike was new.

    a. Determine whether the model represents exponential growth or exponential decay.

    b. Identify the annual percent increase or decrease in the value of the bike.

    c. Estimate when the value of the bike will be $50.

20. The amount y (in grams) of the radioactive isotope iodine-123 remaining after t hours is $y = a(0.5)^{t/13}$, where a is the initial amount (in grams). What percent of the iodine-123 decays each hour?

1. Fill in the exponent of x with a number to simplify the expression.

$$\frac{x^{5/3} \cdot x^{-1} \cdot \sqrt[3]{x}}{x^{-2} \cdot x^0} = x^{\boxed{}}$$

2. Fill in the piecewise function with $-$, $+$, $<$, $\le$, $>$, or $\ge$ so that the function is represented by the graph.

$$y = \begin{cases} 2x \;\boxed{}\; 3, & \text{if } x \;\boxed{}\; 0 \\ 2x \;\boxed{}\; 3, & \text{if } x \;\boxed{}\; 0 \end{cases}$$

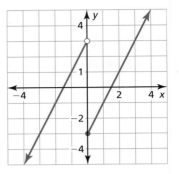

3. Which graph represents the inverse of the function $f(x) = 2x + 4$?

Ⓐ

Ⓑ

Ⓒ

Ⓓ

4. Let $f(x) = |x|$ and $g(x) = -4|x + 11|$. Select the possible transformations of the graph of f represented by the function g.

Ⓐ reflection in the x-axis

Ⓑ reflection in the y-axis

Ⓒ horizontal translation 11 units right

Ⓓ horizontal translation 11 units left

Ⓔ horizontal shrink by a factor of $\frac{1}{4}$

Ⓕ vertical stretch by a factor of 4

5. Select all the numbers that are in the range of the function shown.

$$y = \begin{cases} |x + 2| + 3, & \text{if } x \le -2 \\ \frac{1}{2}x + 3, & \text{if } x > -2 \end{cases}$$

| 0 | $\frac{1}{2}$ | 1 | $1\frac{1}{2}$ | 2 | $2\frac{1}{2}$ | 3 | $3\frac{1}{2}$ | 4 |

6. Select every value of b for the equation $y = b^x$ that could result in the graph shown.

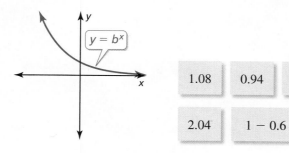

| 1.08 | 0.94 | $1 + 0.85$ |

| 2.04 | $1 - 0.6$ | $\dfrac{5}{4}$ |

7. Pair each function with its inverse.

| $y = -\dfrac{1}{3}x$ | $y = -x + 3$ | $y = 3x - 12$ | $y = 3x + 3$ |

| $y = \dfrac{1}{3}x + 4$ | $y = -3x$ | $y = \dfrac{1}{3}x - 1$ | $y = -x + 3$ |

8. Describe the transformation of the graph of $f(x) = |x|$ represented in each graph.

a.

b.

c.

d.

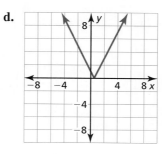

9. Which of the expressions are equivalent?

| $32^{3/5}$ | $(32^{1/5})^3$ | 2^5 | $(32^{1/3})^5$ | 8 | $\sqrt[3]{32^5}$ |

2 Polynomial Equations and Factoring

SEE the Big Idea

Height of a Falling Object *(p. 104)*

Game Reserve *(p. 98)*

Photo Cropping *(p. 94)*

Framing a Photo *(p. 74)*

Gateway Arch *(p. 86)*

Maintaining Mathematical Proficiency

Simplifying Algebraic Expressions

Example 1   Simplify $6x + 5 - 3x - 4$.

$$6x + 5 - 3x - 4 = 6x - 3x + 5 - 4 \qquad \text{Commutative Property of Addition}$$

$$= (6 - 3)x + 5 - 4 \qquad \text{Distributive Property}$$

$$= 3x + 1 \qquad \text{Simplify.}$$

Example 2   Simplify $-8(y - 3) + 2y$.

$$-8(y - 3) + 2y = -8(y) - (-8)(3) + 2y \qquad \text{Distributive Property}$$

$$= -8y + 24 + 2y \qquad \text{Multiply.}$$

$$= -8y + 2y + 24 \qquad \text{Commutative Property of Addition}$$

$$= (-8 + 2)y + 24 \qquad \text{Distributive Property}$$

$$= -6y + 24 \qquad \text{Simplify.}$$

Simplify the expression.

1. $3x - 7 + 2x$ **2.** $4r + 6 - 9r - 1$ **3.** $-5t + 3 - t - 4 + 8t$

4. $3(s - 1) + 5$ **5.** $2m - 7(3 - m)$ **6.** $4(h + 6) - (h - 2)$

Finding the Greatest Common Factor

Example 3   **Find the greatest common factor (GCF) of 42 and 70.**

To find the GCF of two numbers, first write the prime factorization of each number. Then find the product of the common prime factors.

$$42 = 2 \cdot 3 \cdot 7$$
$$70 = 2 \cdot 5 \cdot 7$$

▶   The GCF of 42 and 70 is $2 \cdot 7 = 14$.

Find the greatest common factor.

7. 20, 36   **8.** 42, 63   **9.** 54, 81

10. 72, 84   **11.** 28, 64   **12.** 30, 77

13. **ABSTRACT REASONING** Is it possible for two integers to have no common factors? Explain your reasoning.

Mathematical Practices

Mathematically proficient students consider concrete models when solving a mathematics problem.

Using Models

Core Concept

Using Algebra Tiles

When solving a problem, it can be helpful to use a model. For instance, you can use algebra tiles to model algebraic expressions and operations with algebraic expressions.

EXAMPLE 1 **Writing Expressions Modeled by Algebra Tiles**

Write the algebraic expression modeled by the algebra tiles.

a.   b.   c.

SOLUTION

a. The algebraic expression is x^2.

b. The algebraic expression is $3x + 4$.

c. The algebraic expression is $x^2 - x + 2$.

Monitoring Progress

Write the algebraic expression modeled by the algebra tiles.

1.   2.   3.

4.   5.   6.

7.   8.   9.

2.1 Adding and Subtracting Polynomials

Essential Question How can you add and subtract polynomials?

EXPLORATION 1 Adding Polynomials

Work with a partner. Write the expression modeled by the algebra tiles in each step.

Step 1 $(3x + 2) + (x - 5)$

Step 2

Step 3

Step 4

EXPLORATION 2 Subtracting Polynomials

Work with a partner. Write the expression modeled by the algebra tiles in each step.

Step 1 $(x^2 + 2x + 2) - (x - 1)$

Step 2

Step 3

Step 4

REASONING ABSTRACTLY

To be proficient in math, you need to represent a given situation using symbols.

Step 5

Communicate Your Answer

3. How can you add and subtract polynomials?

4. Use your methods in Question 3 to find each sum or difference.

  a. $(x^2 + 2x - 1) + (2x^2 - 2x + 1)$ **b.** $(4x + 3) + (x - 2)$

  c. $(x^2 + 2) - (3x^2 + 2x + 5)$ **d.** $(2x - 3x) - (x^2 - 2x + 4)$

What You Will Learn

▶ Find the degrees of monomials.

▶ Classify polynomials.

▶ Add and subtract polynomials.

▶ Solve real-life problems.

Core Vocabulary

monomial, *p. 62*
degree of a monomial, *p. 62*
polynomial, *p. 63*
binomial, *p. 63*
trinomial, *p. 63*
degree of a polynomial, *p. 63*
standard form, *p. 63*
leading coefficient, *p. 63*
closed, *p. 64*

Finding the Degrees of Monomials

A **monomial** is a number, a variable, or the product of a number and one or more variables with whole number exponents.

The **degree of a monomial** is the sum of the exponents of the variables in the monomial. The degree of a nonzero constant term is 0. The constant 0 does not have a degree.

Monomial	Degree		Not a monomial	Reason
10	0		$5 + x$	A sum is not a monomial.
$3x$	1		$\dfrac{2}{n}$	A monomial cannot have a variable in the denominator.
$\frac{1}{2}ab^2$	$1 + 2 = 3$		4^a	A monomial cannot have a variable exponent.
$-1.8m^5$	5		x^{-1}	The variable must have a whole number exponent.

EXAMPLE 1 **Finding the Degrees of Monomials**

Find the degree of each monomial.

a. $5x^2$ **b.** $-\frac{1}{2}xy^3$ **c.** $8x^3y^3$ **d.** -3

SOLUTION

a. The exponent of x is 2.

▶ So, the degree of the monomial is 2.

b. The exponent of x is 1, and the exponent of y is 3.

▶ So, the degree of the monomial is $1 + 3$, or 4.

c. The exponent of x is 3, and the exponent of y is 3.

▶ So, the degree of the monomial is $3 + 3$, or 6.

d. You can rewrite -3 as $-3x^0$.

▶ So, the degree of the monomial is 0.

Monitoring Progress Help in English and Spanish at *BigIdeasMath.com*

Find the degree of the monomial.

1. $-3x^4$ **2.** $7c^3d^2$ **3.** $\frac{5}{3}y$ **4.** -20.5

Classifying Polynomials

 Core Concept

Polynomials

A **polynomial** is a monomial or a sum of monomials. Each monomial is called a *term* of the polynomial. A polynomial with two terms is a **binomial**. A polynomial with three terms is a **trinomial**.

Binomial	Trinomial
$5x + 2$	$x^2 + 5x + 2$

The **degree of a polynomial** is the greatest degree of its terms. A polynomial in one variable is in **standard form** when the exponents of the terms decrease from left to right. When you write a polynomial in standard form, the coefficient of the first term is the **leading coefficient**.

$$2x^3 + x^2 - 5x + 12$$

leading coefficient   degree   constant term

EXAMPLE 2 **Writing a Polynomial in Standard Form**

Write $15x - x^3 + 3$ in standard form. Identify the degree and leading coefficient of the polynomial.

SOLUTION

Consider the degree of each term of the polynomial.

Degree is 1. → $15x - x^3 + 3$ ← Degree is 0.

Degree is 3.

▶ You can write the polynomial in standard form as $-x^3 + 15x + 3$. The greatest degree is 3, so the degree of the polynomial is 3, and the leading coefficient is -1.

EXAMPLE 3 **Classifying Polynomials**

Write each polynomial in standard form. Identify the degree and classify each polynomial by the number of terms.

a. $-3z^4$ **b.** $4 + 5x^2 - x$ **c.** $8q + q^5$

SOLUTION

Polynomial	Standard Form	Degree	Type of Polynomial
a. $-3z^4$	$-3z^4$	4	monomial
b. $4 + 5x^2 - x$	$5x^2 - x + 4$	2	trinomial
c. $8q + q^5$	$q^5 + 8q$	5	binomial

Monitoring Progress Help in English and Spanish at *BigIdeasMath.com*

Write the polynomial in standard form. Identify the degree and leading coefficient of the polynomial. Then classify the polynomial by the number of terms.

5. $4 - 9z$ **6.** $t^2 - t^3 - 10t$ **7.** $2.8x + x^3$

Adding and Subtracting Polynomials

A set of numbers is **closed** under an operation when the operation performed on any two numbers in the set results in a number that is also in the set. For example, the set of integers is closed under addition, subtraction, and multiplication. This means that if a and b are two integers, then $a + b$, $a - b$, and ab are also integers.

The set of polynomials is closed under addition and subtraction. So, the sum or difference of any two polynomials is also a polynomial.

To add polynomials, add like terms. You can use a vertical or a horizontal format.

EXAMPLE 4 Adding Polynomials

Find the sum.

a. $(2x^3 - 5x^2 + x) + (2x^2 + x^3 - 1)$ **b.** $(3x^2 + x - 6) + (x^2 + 4x + 10)$

SOLUTION

a. Vertical format: Align like terms vertically and add.

$$
\begin{array}{r}
2x^3 - 5x^2 + x \\
+ \quad x^3 + 2x^2 \qquad - 1 \\
\hline
3x^3 - 3x^2 + x - 1
\end{array}
$$

▶ The sum is $3x^3 - 3x^2 + x - 1$.

b. Horizontal format: Group like terms and simplify.

$$(3x^2 + x - 6) + (x^2 + 4x + 10) = (3x^2 + x^2) + (x + 4x) + (-6 + 10)$$
$$= 4x^2 + 5x + 4$$

▶ The sum is $4x^2 + 5x + 4$.

To subtract a polynomial, add its opposite. To find the opposite of a polynomial, multiply each of its terms by -1.

EXAMPLE 5 Subtracting Polynomials

Find the difference.

a. $(4n^2 + 5) - (-2n^2 + 2n - 4)$ **b.** $(4x^2 - 3x + 5) - (3x^2 - x - 8)$

SOLUTION

a. Vertical format: Align like terms vertically and subtract.

$$
\begin{array}{r}
4n^2 \qquad + 5 \\
- \ (-2n^2 + 2n - 4)
\end{array}
\quad \Longrightarrow \quad
\begin{array}{r}
4n^2 \qquad + 5 \\
+ \ 2n^2 - 2n + 4 \\
\hline
6n^2 - 2n + 9
\end{array}
$$

▶ The difference is $6n^2 - 2n + 9$.

b. Horizontal format: Group like terms and simplify.

$$(4x^2 - 3x + 5) - (3x^2 - x - 8) = 4x^2 - 3x + 5 - 3x^2 + x + 8$$
$$= (4x^2 - 3x^2) + (-3x + x) + (5 + 8)$$
$$= x^2 - 2x + 13$$

▶ The difference is $x^2 - 2x + 13$.

STUDY TIP

When a power of the variable appears in one polynomial but not the other, leave a space in that column, or write the term with a coefficient of 0.

COMMON ERROR

Remember to multiply *each* term of the polynomial by -1 when you write the subtraction as addition.

Find the sum or difference.

8. $(b - 10) + (4b - 3)$

9. $(x^2 - x - 2) + (7x^2 - x)$

10. $(p^2 + p + 3) - (-4p^2 - p + 3)$

11. $(-k + 5) - (3k^2 - 6)$

Solving Real-Life Problems

EXAMPLE 6   Solving a Real-Life Problem

A penny is thrown straight down from a height of 200 feet. At the same time, a paintbrush is dropped from a height of 100 feet. The polynomials represent the heights (in feet) of the objects after t seconds.

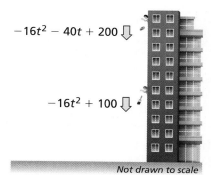

$-16t^2 - 40t + 200$

$-16t^2 + 100$

Not drawn to scale

a. Write a polynomial that represents the distance between the penny and the paintbrush after t seconds.

b. Interpret the coefficients of the polynomial in part (a).

SOLUTION

a. To find the distance between the objects after t seconds, subtract the polynomials.

Penny	$-16t^2 - 40t + 200$	$-16t^2 - 40t + 200$
Paintbrush	$- (-16t^2 \qquad + 100)$	$+ \quad 16t^2 \qquad - 100$
		$\overline{ -40t + 100}$

▶ The polynomial $-40t + 100$ represents the distance between the objects after t seconds.

b. When $t = 0$, the distance between the objects is $-40(0) + 100 = 100$ feet. So, the constant term 100 represents the distance between the penny and the paintbrush when both objects begin to fall.

As the value of t increases by 1, the value of $-40t + 100$ decreases by 40. This means that the objects become 40 feet closer to each other each second. So, -40 represents the amount that the distance between the objects changes each second.

INTERPRETING EXPRESSIONS

Notice that each term of the resulting expression has special meaning in the context of the problem. Analyzing the terms helps you understand the problem in more depth.

12. **WHAT IF?** The polynomial $-16t^2 - 25t + 200$ represents the height of the penny after t seconds.

   a. Write a polynomial that represents the distance between the penny and the paintbrush after t seconds.

   b. Interpret the coefficients of the polynomial in part (a).

Vocabulary and Core Concept Check

1. **VOCABULARY** When is a polynomial in one variable in standard form?

2. **OPEN-ENDED** Write a trinomial in one variable of degree 5 in standard form.

3. **VOCABULARY** How can you determine whether a set of numbers is closed under an operation?

4. **WHICH ONE DOESN'T BELONG?** Which expression does *not* belong with the other three? Explain your reasoning.

$$a^3 + 4a \qquad x^2 - 8^x \qquad b - 2^{-1} \qquad -\frac{\pi}{3} + 6y^8z$$

Monitoring Progress and Modeling with Mathematics

In Exercises 5–12, find the degree of the monomial.
(See Example 1.)

5. $4g$

6. $23x^4$

7. $-1.75k^2$

8. $-\frac{4}{9}$

9. s^8t

10. $8m^2n^4$

11. $9xy^3z^7$

12. $-3q^4rs^6$

In Exercises 13–20, write the polynomial in standard form. Identify the degree and leading coefficient of the polynomial. Then classify the polynomial by the number of terms. *(See Examples 2 and 3.)*

13. $6c^2 + 2c^4 - c$

14. $4w^{11} - w^{12}$

15. $7 + 3p^2$

16. $8d - 2 - 4d^3$

17. $3t^8$

18. $5z + 2z^3 + 3z^4$

19. $\pi r^2 - \frac{5}{7}r^8 + 2r^5$

20. $\sqrt{7}n^4$

21. **MODELING WITH MATHEMATICS** The expression $\frac{4}{3}\pi r^3$ represents the volume of a sphere with radius r. Why is this expression a monomial? What is its degree?

22. **MODELING WITH MATHEMATICS** The amount of money you have after investing $400 for 8 years and $600 for 6 years at the same interest rate is represented by $400x^8 + 600x^6$, where x is the growth factor. Classify the polynomial by the number of terms. What is its degree?

In Exercises 23–30, find the sum. *(See Example 4.)*

23. $(5y + 4) + (-2y + 6)$

24. $(-8x - 12) + (9x + 4)$

25. $(2n^2 - 5n - 6) + (-n^2 - 3n + 11)$

26. $(-3p^3 + 5p^2 - 2p) + (-p^3 - 8p^2 - 15p)$

27. $(3g^2 - g) + (3g^2 - 8g + 4)$

28. $(9r^2 + 4r - 7) + (3r^2 - 3r)$

29. $(4a - a^3 - 3) + (2a^3 - 5a^2 + 8)$

30. $(s^3 - 2s - 9) + (2s^2 - 6s^3 + s)$

In Exercises 31–38, find the difference. *(See Example 5.)*

31. $(d - 9) - (3d - 1)$

32. $(6x + 9) - (7x + 1)$

33. $(y^2 - 4y + 9) - (3y^2 - 6y - 9)$

34. $(4m^2 - m + 2) - (-3m^2 + 10m + 4)$

35. $(k^3 - 7k + 2) - (k^2 - 12)$

36. $(-r - 10) - (-4r^3 + r^2 + 7r)$

37. $(t^4 - t^2 + t) - (12 - 9t^2 - 7t)$

38. $(4d - 6d^3 + 3d^2) - (10d^3 + 7d - 2)$

ERROR ANALYSIS In Exercises 39 and 40, describe and correct the error in finding the sum or difference.

39.

> ✗ $(x^2 + x) - (2x^2 - 3x) = x^2 + x - 2x^2 - 3x$
> $= (x^2 - 2x^2) + (x - 3x)$
> $= -x^2 - 2x$

40.

> ✗
> $\qquad x^3 - 4x^2 + 3$
> $+ \ -3x^3 + 8x \ - 2$
> $\overline{\qquad -2x^3 + 4x^2 + 1}$

41. MODELING WITH MATHEMATICS The cost (in dollars) of making b bracelets is represented by $4 + 5b$. The cost (in dollars) of making b necklaces is represented by $8b + 6$. Write a polynomial that represents how much more it costs to make b necklaces than b bracelets.

42. MODELING WITH MATHEMATICS The number of individual memberships at a fitness center in m months is represented by $142 + 12m$. The number of family memberships at the fitness center in m months is represented by $52 + 6m$. Write a polynomial that represents the total number of memberships at the fitness center.

In Exercises 43–46, find the sum or difference.

43. $(2s^2 - 5st - t^2) - (s^2 + 7st - t^2)$

44. $(a^2 - 3ab + 2b^2) + (-4a^2 + 5ab - b^2)$

45. $(c^2 - 6d^2) + (c^2 - 2cd + 2d^2)$

46. $(-x^2 + 9xy) - (x^2 + 6xy - 8y^2)$

REASONING In Exercises 47–50, complete the statement with *always*, *sometimes*, or *never*. Explain your reasoning.

47. The terms of a polynomial are _____ monomials.

48. The difference of two trinomials is _____ a trinomial.

49. A binomial is _____ a polynomial of degree 2.

50. The sum of two polynomials is _____ a polynomial.

MODELING WITH MATHEMATICS The polynomial $-16t^2 + v_0 t + s_0$ represents the height (in feet) of an object, where v_0 is the initial vertical velocity (in feet per second), s_0 is the initial height of the object (in feet), and t is the time (in seconds). In Exercises 51 and 52, write a polynomial that represents the height of the object. Then find the height of the object after 1 second.

51. You throw a water balloon from a building.

$v_0 = -45$ ft/sec

$s_0 = 200$ ft

Not drawn to scale

52. You bounce a tennis ball on a racket.

$v_0 = 16$ ft/sec

$s_0 = 3$ ft

53. MODELING WITH MATHEMATICS You drop a ball from a height of 98 feet. At the same time, your friend throws a ball upward. The polynomials represent the heights (in feet) of the balls after t seconds. *(See Example 6.)*

$-16t^2 + 98$

$-16t^2 + 46t + 6$

Not drawn to scale

a. Before the balls reach the same height, write a polynomial that represents the distance between your ball and your friend's ball after t seconds.

b. Interpret the coefficients of the polynomial in part (a).

54. MODELING WITH MATHEMATICS During a 7-year period, the amounts (in millions of dollars) spent each year on buying new vehicles N and used vehicles U by United States residents are modeled by the equations

$$N = -0.028t^3 + 0.06t^2 + 0.1t + 17$$
$$U = -0.38t^2 + 1.5t + 42$$

where $t = 1$ represents the first year in the 7-year period.

a. Write a polynomial that represents the total amount spent each year on buying new and used vehicles in the 7-year period.

b. How much is spent on buying new and used vehicles in the fifth year?

55. MATHEMATICAL CONNECTIONS

Write the polynomial in standard form that represents the perimeter of the quadrilateral.

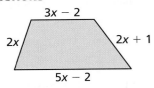

56. HOW DO YOU SEE IT? The right side of the equation of each line is a polynomial.

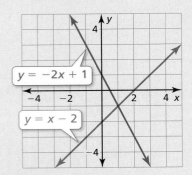

$y = -2x + 1$
$y = x - 2$

a. The absolute value of the difference of the two polynomials represents the vertical distance between points on the lines with the same x-value. Write this expression.

b. When does the expression in part (a) equal 0? How does this value relate to the graph?

57. MAKING AN ARGUMENT Your friend says that when adding polynomials, the order in which you add does not matter. Is your friend correct? Explain.

58. THOUGHT PROVOKING Write two polynomials whose sum is x^2 and whose difference is 1.

59. REASONING Determine whether the set is closed under the given operation. Explain.

a. the set of negative integers; multiplication

b. the set of whole numbers; addition

60. PROBLEM SOLVING You are building a multi-level deck.

a. For each level, write a polynomial in standard form that represents the area of that level. Then write the polynomial in standard form that represents the total area of the deck.

b. What is the total area of the deck when $x = 20$?

c. A gallon of deck sealant covers 400 square feet. How many gallons of sealant do you need to cover the deck in part (b) once? Explain.

61. PROBLEM SOLVING A hotel installs a new swimming pool and a new hot tub.

a. Write the polynomial in standard form that represents the area of the patio.

b. The patio will cost $10 per square foot. Determine the cost of the patio when $x = 9$.

Maintaining Mathematical Proficiency
Reviewing what you learned in previous grades and lessons

Simplify the expression. *(Skills Review Handbook)*

62. $2(x - 1) + 3(x + 2)$

63. $8(4y - 3) + 2(y - 5)$

64. $5(2r + 1) - 3(-4r + 2)$

2.2 Multiplying Polynomials

Essential Question How can you multiply two polynomials?

EXPLORATION 1 **Multiplying Monomials Using Algebra Tiles**

Work with a partner. Write each product. Explain your reasoning.

a. $\boxed{+} \cdot \boxed{+} =$ ▭

b. $\boxed{+} \cdot \boxed{-} =$ ▭

c. $\boxed{-} \cdot \boxed{-} =$ ▭

d. $\boxed{+} \cdot \boxed{+} =$ ▭

e. $\boxed{+} \cdot \boxed{-} =$ ▭

f. $\boxed{-} \cdot \boxed{+} =$ ▭

g. $\boxed{-} \cdot \boxed{-} =$ ▭

h. $\boxed{+} \cdot \boxed{+} =$ ▭

i. $\boxed{+} \cdot \boxed{-} =$ ▭

j. $\boxed{-} \cdot \boxed{-} =$ ▭

REASONING ABSTRACTLY

To be proficient in math, you need to reason abstractly and quantitatively. You need to pause as needed to recall the meanings of the symbols, operations, and quantities involved.

EXPLORATION 2 **Multiplying Binomials Using Algebra Tiles**

Work with a partner. Write the product of two binomials modeled by each rectangular array of algebra tiles. In parts (c) and (d), first draw the rectangular array of algebra tiles that models each product.

a. $(x + 3)(x - 2) =$ ▭

b. $(2x - 1)(2x + 1) =$ ▭

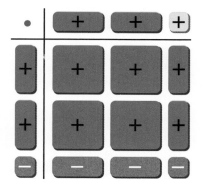

c. $(x + 2)(2x - 1) =$ ▭

d. $(-x - 2)(x - 3) =$ ▭

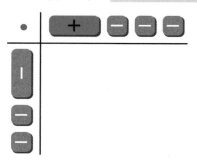

Communicate Your Answer

3. How can you multiply two polynomials?

4. Give another example of multiplying two binomials using algebra tiles that is similar to those in Exploration 2.

Core Vocabulary

FOIL Method, *p. 71*

Previous
polynomial
closed
binomial
trinomial

What You Will Learn

▶ Multiply binomials.
▶ Use the FOIL Method.
▶ Multiply binomials and trinomials.

Multiplying Binomials

The product of two polynomials is always a polynomial. So, like the set of integers, the set of polynomials is closed under multiplication. You can use the Distributive Property to multiply two binomials.

EXAMPLE 1 **Multiplying Binomials Using the Distributive Property**

Find (a) $(x + 2)(x + 5)$ and (b) $(x + 3)(x - 4)$.

SOLUTION

a. Use the horizontal method.

$$(x + 2)(x + 5) = x(x + 5) + 2(x + 5)$$ Distribute $(x + 5)$ to each term of $(x + 2)$.

$$= x(x) + x(5) + 2(x) + 2(5)$$ Distributive Property

$$= x^2 + 5x + 2x + 10$$ Multiply.

$$= x^2 + 7x + 10$$ Combine like terms.

▶ The product is $x^2 + 7x + 10$.

b. Use the vertical method.

$$\begin{array}{r} x + 3 \\ \times \quad x - 4 \\ \hline \end{array}$$ Align like terms vertically.

Multiply $-4(x + 3)$. $\longrightarrow -4x - 12$ Distributive Property

Multiply $x(x + 3)$. $\longrightarrow \dfrac{x^2 + 3x}{x^2 - x - 12}$ Distributive Property / Combine like terms.

▶ The product is $x^2 - x - 12$.

EXAMPLE 2 **Multiplying Binomials Using a Table**

Find $(2x - 3)(x + 5)$.

SOLUTION

Step 1 Write each binomial as a sum of terms.

$$(2x - 3)(x + 5) = [2x + (-3)](x + 5)$$

Step 2 Make a table of products.

	2x	**−3**
x	$2x^2$	$-3x$
5	$10x$	-15

▶ The product is $2x^2 - 3x + 10x - 15$, or $2x^2 + 7x - 15$.

Monitoring Progress 🔊 Help in English and Spanish at *BigIdeasMath.com*

Use the Distributive Property to find the product.

1. $(y + 4)(y + 1)$ **2.** $(z - 2)(z + 6)$

Use a table to find the product.

3. $(p + 3)(p - 8)$ **4.** $(r - 5)(2r - 1)$

Using the FOIL Method

The **FOIL Method** is a shortcut for multiplying two binomials.

Core Concept

FOIL Method

To multiply two binomials using the FOIL Method, find the sum of the products of the

First terms, $(x + 1)(x + 2)$ ➡ $x(x) = x^2$

Outer terms, $(x + 1)(x + 2)$ ➡ $x(2) = 2x$

Inner terms, and $(x + 1)(x + 2)$ ➡ $1(x) = x$

Last terms. $(x + 1)(x + 2)$ ➡ $1(2) = 2$

$$(x + 1)(x + 2) = x^2 + 2x + x + 2 = x^2 + 3x + 2$$

EXAMPLE 3 **Multiplying Binomials Using the FOIL Method**

Find each product.

a. $(x - 3)(x - 6)$ **b.** $(2x + 1)(3x - 5)$

SOLUTION

a. Use the FOIL Method.

$$\begin{array}{cccc} \text{First} & \text{Outer} & \text{Inner} & \text{Last} \end{array}$$

$(x - 3)(x - 6) = x(x) + x(-6) + (-3)(x) + (-3)(-6)$ FOIL Method

$\qquad\qquad = x^2 + (-6x) + (-3x) + 18$ Multiply.

$\qquad\qquad = x^2 - 9x + 18$ Combine like terms.

▶ The product is $x^2 - 9x + 18$.

b. Use the FOIL Method.

$$\begin{array}{cccc} \text{First} & \text{Outer} & \text{Inner} & \text{Last} \end{array}$$

$(2x + 1)(3x - 5) = 2x(3x) + 2x(-5) + 1(3x) + 1(-5)$ FOIL Method

$\qquad\qquad = 6x^2 + (-10x) + 3x + (-5)$ Multiply.

$\qquad\qquad = 6x^2 - 7x - 5$ Combine like terms.

▶ The product is $6x^2 - 7x - 5$.

Monitoring Progress Help in English and Spanish at *BigIdeasMath.com*

Use the FOIL Method to find the product.

5. $(m - 3)(m - 7)$ **6.** $(x - 4)(x + 2)$

7. $\left(2u + \frac{1}{2}\right)\left(u - \frac{3}{2}\right)$ **8.** $(n + 2)(n^2 + 3)$

Multiplying Binomials and Trinomials

EXAMPLE 4   Multiplying a Binomial and a Trinomial

Find $(x + 5)(x^2 - 3x - 2)$.

SOLUTION

$$
\begin{array}{r}
x^2 - 3x - 2 \\
\times \qquad x + 5 \\
\hline
5x^2 - 15x - 10 \\
x^3 - 3x^2 - 2x \qquad \\
\hline
x^3 + 2x^2 - 17x - 10
\end{array}
$$

Multiply $5(x^2 - 3x - 2)$.

Multiply $x(x^2 - 3x - 2)$.

Align like terms vertically.
Distributive Property
Distributive Property
Combine like terms.

▶   The product is $x^3 + 2x^2 - 17x - 10$.

EXAMPLE 5   Solving a Real-Life Problem

In hockey, a goalie behind the goal line can only play a puck in the trapezoidal region.

a. Write a polynomial that represents the area of the trapezoidal region.

b. Find the area of the trapezoidal region when the shorter base is 18 feet.

SOLUTION

CONNECTIONS TO GEOMETRY

Recall that the formula for the area A of a trapezoid with height h and bases b_1 and b_2 is

$$A = \tfrac{1}{2}h(b_1 + b_2).$$

a.
$$
\begin{aligned}
\tfrac{1}{2}h(b_1 + b_2) &= \tfrac{1}{2}(x - 7)[x + (x + 10)] \\
&= \tfrac{1}{2}(x - 7)(2x + 10). \\
&\qquad \text{F} \qquad \text{O} \qquad \text{I} \qquad \text{L} \\
&= \tfrac{1}{2}[2x^2 + 10x + (-14x) + (-70)] \\
&= \tfrac{1}{2}(2x^2 - 4x - 70) \\
&= x^2 - 2x - 35
\end{aligned}
$$

▶   A polynomial that represents the area of the trapezoidal region is $x^2 - 2x - 35$.

b. Find the value of $x^2 - 2x - 35$ when $x = 18$.

$$
\begin{aligned}
x^2 - 2x - 35 &= 18^2 - 2(18) - 35 \\
&= 324 - 36 - 35 \\
&= 253
\end{aligned}
$$

Substitute 18 for x.

Simplify.

Subtract.

▶   The area of the trapezoidal region is 253 square feet.

Monitoring Progress Help in English and Spanish at *BigIdeasMath.com*

Find the product.

9. $(x + 1)(x^2 + 5x + 8)$

10. $(n - 3)(n^2 - 2n + 4)$

11. WHAT IF? In Example 5(a), how does the polynomial change when the longer base is extended by 1 foot? Explain.

Vocabulary and Core Concept Check

1. **VOCABULARY** Describe two ways to find the product of two binomials.

2. **WRITING** Explain how the letters of the word FOIL can help you to remember how to multiply two binomials.

Monitoring Progress and Modeling with Mathematics

In Exercises 3–10, use the Distributive Property to find the product. *(See Example 1.)*

3. $(x + 1)(x + 3)$ 　　4. $(y + 6)(y + 4)$

5. $(z - 5)(z + 3)$ 　　6. $(a + 8)(a - 3)$

7. $(g - 7)(g - 2)$ 　　8. $(n - 6)(n - 4)$

9. $(3m + 1)(m + 9)$ 　　10. $(5s + 6)(s - 2)$

In Exercises 11–18, use a table to find the product. *(See Example 2.)*

11. $(x + 3)(x + 2)$ 　　12. $(y + 10)(y - 5)$

13. $(h - 8)(h - 9)$ 　　14. $(c - 6)(c - 5)$

15. $(3k - 1)(4k + 9)$ 　　16. $(5g + 3)(g + 8)$

17. $(-3 + 2j)(4j - 7)$ 　　18. $(5d - 12)(-7 + 3d)$

ERROR ANALYSIS In Exercises 19 and 20, describe and correct the error in finding the product of the binomials.

19.

$$(t - 2)(t + 5) = t - 2(t + 5)$$
$$= t - 2t - 10$$
$$= -t - 10$$

20.

$(x - 5)(3x + 1)$

	$3x$	1
x	$3x^2$	x
5	$15x$	5

$(x - 5)(3x + 1) = 3x^2 + 16x + 5$

In Exercises 21–30, use the FOIL Method to find the product. *(See Example 3.)*

21. $(b + 3)(b + 7)$ 　　22. $(w + 9)(w + 6)$

23. $(k + 5)(k - 1)$ 　　24. $(x - 4)(x + 8)$

25. $\left(q - \frac{3}{4}\right)\left(q + \frac{1}{4}\right)$ 　　26. $\left(z - \frac{5}{3}\right)\left(z - \frac{2}{3}\right)$

27. $(9 - r)(2 - 3r)$ 　　28. $(8 - 4x)(2x + 6)$

29. $(w + 5)(w^2 + 3w)$ 　　30. $(v - 3)(v^2 + 8v)$

MATHEMATICAL CONNECTIONS In Exercises 31–34, write a polynomial that represents the area of the shaded region.

31.
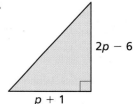
$x + 5$
$2x - 9$

32.

$2p - 6$
$p + 1$

33.

$x + 5$
$x + 6$

34.

$x + 1$
$x - 7$
5
$x + 1$

In Exercises 35–42, find the product. *(See Example 4.)*

35. $(x + 4)(x^2 + 3x + 2)$ 　　36. $(f + 1)(f^2 + 4f + 8)$

37. $(y + 3)(y^2 + 8y - 2)$ 　　38. $(t - 2)(t^2 - 5t + 1)$

39. $(4 - b)(5b^2 + 5b - 4)$ 　　40. $(d + 6)(2d^2 - d + 7)$

41. $(3e^2 - 5e + 7)(6e + 1)$

42. $(6v^2 + 2v - 9)(4 - 5v)$

43. MODELING WITH MATHEMATICS The football field is rectangular. *(See Example 5.)*

(10x + 10) ft

(4x + 20) ft

a. Write a polynomial that represents the area of the football field.

b. Find the area of the football field when the width is 160 feet.

44. MODELING WITH MATHEMATICS You design a frame to surround a rectangular photo. The width of the frame is the same on every side, as shown.

x in.

20 in.

x in.

22 in.

x in.   x in.

a. Write a polynomial that represents the combined area of the photo and the frame.

b. Find the combined area of the photo and the frame when the width of the frame is 4 inches.

45. WRITING When multiplying two binomials, explain how the degree of the product is related to the degree of each binomial.

46. THOUGHT PROVOKING Write two polynomials that are not monomials whose product is a trinomial of degree 3.

47. MAKING AN ARGUMENT Your friend says the FOIL Method can be used to multiply two trinomials. Is your friend correct? Explain your reasoning.

48. HOW DO YOU SEE IT? The table shows one method of finding the product of two binomials.

	$-4x$	3
$-8x$	a	b
-9	c	d

a. Write the two binomials being multiplied.

b. Determine whether a, b, c, and d will be positive or negative when $x > 0$.

49. COMPARING METHODS You use the Distributive Property to multiply $(x + 3)(x - 5)$. Your friend uses the FOIL Method to multiply $(x - 5)(x + 3)$. Should your answers be equivalent? Justify your answer.

50. USING STRUCTURE The shipping container is a rectangular prism. Write a polynomial that represents the volume of the container.

(x + 2) ft

(4x − 3) ft

(x + 1) ft

51. ABSTRACT REASONING The product of $(x + m)(x + n)$ is $x^2 + bx + c$.

a. What do you know about m and n when $c > 0$?

b. What do you know about m and n when $c < 0$?

Maintaining Mathematical Proficiency
Reviewing what you learned in previous grades and lessons

Write the absolute value function as a piecewise function. *(Section 1.2)*

52. $y = |x| + 4$

53. $y = 6|x - 3|$

54. $y = -4|x + 2|$

Simplify the expression. Write your answer using only positive exponents. *(Section 1.4)*

55. $10^2 \cdot 10^9$

56. $\dfrac{x^5 \cdot x}{x^8}$

57. $(3z^6)^{-3}$

58. $\left(\dfrac{2y^4}{y^3}\right)^{-2}$

2.3 Special Products of Polynomials

Essential Question What are the patterns in the special products $(a + b)(a - b)$, $(a + b)^2$, and $(a - b)^2$?

EXPLORATION 1 **Finding a Sum and Difference Pattern**

Work with a partner. Write the product of two binomials modeled by each rectangular array of algebra tiles.

a. $(x + 2)(x - 2) = $ ▦

b. $(2x - 1)(2x + 1) = $ ▦

EXPLORATION 2 **Finding the Square of a Binomial Pattern**

Work with a partner. Draw the rectangular array of algebra tiles that models each product of two binomials. Write the product.

a. $(x + 2)^2 = $ ▦

b. $(2x - 1)^2 = $ ▦

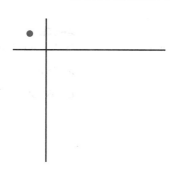

LOOKING FOR STRUCTURE

To be proficient in math, you need to look closely to discern a pattern or structure.

Communicate Your Answer

3. What are the patterns in the special products $(a + b)(a - b)$, $(a + b)^2$, and $(a - b)^2$?

4. Use the appropriate special product pattern to find each product. Check your answers using algebra tiles.

a. $(x + 3)(x - 3)$ **b.** $(x - 4)(x + 4)$ **c.** $(3x + 1)(3x - 1)$

d. $(x + 3)^2$ **e.** $(x - 2)^2$ **f.** $(3x + 1)^2$

What You Will Learn

▶ Use the square of a binomial pattern.
▶ Use the sum and difference pattern.
▶ Use special product patterns to solve real-life problems.

Using the Square of a Binomial Pattern

The diagram shows a square with a side length of $(a + b)$ units. You can see that the area of the square is

$$(a + b)^2 = a^2 + 2ab + b^2.$$

This is one version of a pattern called the square of a binomial. To find another version of this pattern, use algebra: replace b with $-b$.

	a	b
a	a^2	ab
b	ab	b^2

$(a + (-b))^2 = a^2 + 2a(-b) + (-b)^2$ Replace b with $-b$ in the pattern above.

$(a - b)^2 = a^2 - 2ab + b^2$ Simplify.

🅢 Core Concept

Square of a Binomial Pattern

Algebra

$(a + b)^2 = a^2 + 2ab + b^2$

$(a - b)^2 = a^2 - 2ab + b^2$

Example

$(x + 5)^2 = (x)^2 + 2(x)(5) + (5)^2$
$= x^2 + 10x + 25$

$(2x - 3)^2 = (2x)^2 - 2(2x)(3) + (3)^2$
$= 4x^2 - 12x + 9$

LOOKING FOR STRUCTURE

When you use special product patterns, remember that a and b can be numbers, variables, or variable expressions.

EXAMPLE 1   Using the Square of a Binomial Pattern

Find each product.

a. $(3x + 4)^2$

b. $(5x - 2y)^2$

SOLUTION

a. $(3x + 4)^2 = (3x)^2 + 2(3x)(4) + 4^2$ Square of a binomial pattern

             $= 9x^2 + 24x + 16$ Simplify.

▶ The product is $9x^2 + 24x + 16$.

b. $(5x - 2y)^2 = (5x)^2 - 2(5x)(2y) + (2y)^2$ Square of a binomial pattern

               $= 25x^2 - 20xy + 4y^2$ Simplify.

▶ The product is $25x^2 - 20xy + 4y^2$.

Monitoring Progress Help in English and Spanish at *BigIdeasMath.com*

Find the product.

1. $(x + 7)^2$ **2.** $(7x - 3)^2$ **3.** $(4x - y)^2$ **4.** $(3m + n)^2$

Using the Sum and Difference Pattern

To find the product $(x + 2)(x - 2)$, you can multiply the two binomials using the FOIL Method.

$$(x + 2)(x - 2) = x^2 - 2x + 2x - 4 \qquad \text{FOIL Method}$$
$$= x^2 - 4 \qquad \text{Combine like terms.}$$

This suggests a pattern for the product of the sum and difference of two terms.

Core Concept

Sum and Difference Pattern

Algebra

$(a + b)(a - b) = a^2 - b^2$

Example

$(x + 3)(x - 3) = x^2 - 9$

EXAMPLE 2 Using the Sum and Difference Pattern

Find each product.

a. $(t + 5)(t - 5)$ 　　　　　　　　**b.** $(3x + y)(3x - y)$

SOLUTION

a. $(t + 5)(t - 5) = t^2 - 5^2$ 　　　　Sum and difference pattern
$= t^2 - 25$ 　　　　Simplify.

▶ The product is $t^2 - 25$.

b. $(3x + y)(3x - y) = (3x)^2 - y^2$ 　　　　Sum and difference pattern
$= 9x^2 - y^2$ 　　　　Simplify.

▶ The product is $9x^2 - y^2$.

The special product patterns can help you use mental math to find certain products of numbers.

EXAMPLE 3 Using Special Product Patterns and Mental Math

Use special product patterns to find the product $26 \cdot 34$.

SOLUTION

Notice that 26 is 4 less than 30, while 34 is 4 more than 30.

$26 \cdot 34 = (30 - 4)(30 + 4)$ 　　　　Write as product of difference and sum.
$= 30^2 - 4^2$ 　　　　Sum and difference pattern
$= 900 - 16$ 　　　　Evaluate powers.
$= 884$ 　　　　Simplify.

▶ The product is 884.

Monitoring Progress Help in English and Spanish at *BigIdeasMath.com*

Find the product.

5. $(x + 10)(x - 10)$ 　　　**6.** $(2x + 1)(2x - 1)$ 　　　**7.** $(x + 3y)(x - 3y)$

8. Describe how to use special product patterns to find 21^2.

Solving Real-Life Problems

EXAMPLE 4   **Modeling with Mathematics**

A combination of two genes determines the color of the dark patches of a border collie's coat. An offspring inherits one patch color gene from each parent. Each parent has two color genes, and the offspring has an equal chance of inheriting either one.

The gene B is for black patches, and the gene r is for red patches. Any gene combination with a B results in black patches. Suppose each parent has the same gene combination Br. The Punnett square shows the possible gene combinations of the offspring and the resulting patch colors.

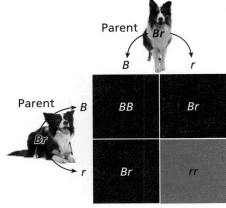

a. What percent of the possible gene combinations result in black patches?

b. Show how you could use a polynomial to model the possible gene combinations.

SOLUTION

a. Notice that the Punnett square shows four possible gene combinations of the offspring. Of these combinations, three result in black patches.

▶   So, 75% of the possible gene combinations result in black patches.

b. Model the gene from each parent with $0.5B + 0.5r$. There is an equal chance that the offspring inherits a black or a red gene from each parent.

You can model the possible gene combinations of the offspring with $(0.5B + 0.5r)^2$. Notice that this product also represents the area of the Punnett square.

Expand the product to find the possible patch colors of the offspring.

$$(0.5B + 0.5r)^2 = (0.5B)^2 + 2(0.5B)(0.5r) + (0.5r)^2$$
$$= 0.25B^2 + 0.5Br + 0.25r^2$$

Consider the coefficients in the polynomial.

$$0.25B^2 + 0.5Br + 0.25r^2$$

| 25% BB, black patches | 50% Br, black patches | 25% rr, red patches |

The coefficients show that $25\% + 50\% = 75\%$ of the possible gene combinations result in black patches.

Monitoring Progress Help in English and Spanish at *BigIdeasMath.com*

9. Each of two dogs has one black gene (B) and one white gene (W). The Punnett square shows the possible gene combinations of an offspring and the resulting colors.

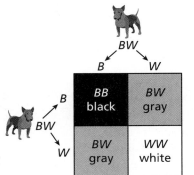

    a. What percent of the possible gene combinations result in black?

    b. Show how you could use a polynomial to model the possible gene combinations of the offspring.

Vocabulary and Core Concept Check

1. **WRITING** Explain how to use the square of a binomial pattern.

2. **WHICH ONE DOESN'T BELONG?** Which expression does *not* belong with the other three? Explain your reasoning.

   | $(x + 1)(x - 1)$ | $(3x + 2)(3x - 2)$ | $(x + 2)(x - 3)$ | $(2x + 5)(2x - 5)$ |

Monitoring Progress and Modeling with Mathematics

In Exercises 3–10, find the product. *(See Example 1.)*

3. $(x + 8)^2$

4. $(a - 6)^2$

5. $(2f - 1)^2$

6. $(5p + 2)^2$

7. $(-7t + 4)^2$

8. $(-12 - n)^2$

9. $(2a + b)^2$

10. $(6x - 3y)^2$

MATHEMATICAL CONNECTIONS In Exercises 11–14, write a polynomial that represents the area of the square.

11.

12.

13.
    $7n - 5$

14.
    $4c + 4d$

In Exercises 15–24, find the product. *(See Example 2.)*

15. $(t - 7)(t + 7)$

16. $(m + 6)(m - 6)$

17. $(4x + 1)(4x - 1)$

18. $(2k - 4)(2k + 4)$

19. $(8 + 3a)(8 - 3a)$

20. $\left(\frac{1}{2} - c\right)\left(\frac{1}{2} + c\right)$

21. $(p - 10q)(p + 10q)$

22. $(7m + 8n)(7m - 8n)$

23. $(-y + 4)(-y - 4)$

24. $(-5g - 2h)(-5g + 2h)$

In Exercises 25–30, use special product patterns to find the product. *(See Example 3.)*

25. $16 \cdot 24$

26. $33 \cdot 27$

27. 42^2

28. 29^2

29. 30.5^2

30. $10\frac{1}{3} \cdot 9\frac{2}{3}$

ERROR ANALYSIS In Exercises 31 and 32, describe and correct the error in finding the product.

31.

$$(k + 4)^2 = k^2 + 4^2$$
$$= k^2 + 16$$

32.
$$(s + 5)(s - 5) = s^2 + 2(s)(5) - 5^2$$
$$= s^2 + 10s - 25$$

33. **MODELING WITH MATHEMATICS** A contractor extends a house on two sides.

a. The area of the house after the renovation is represented by $(x + 50)^2$. Find this product.

b. Use the polynomial in part (a) to find the area when $x = 15$. What is the area of the extension?

34. MODELING WITH MATHEMATICS A square-shaped parking lot with 100-foot sides is reduced by x feet on one side and extended by x feet on an adjacent side.

  a. The area of the new parking lot is represented by $(100 - x)(100 + x)$. Find this product.

  b. Does the area of the parking lot increase, decrease, or stay the same? Explain.

  c. Use the polynomial in part (a) to find the area of the new parking lot when $x = 21$.

35. MODELING WITH MATHEMATICS In deer, the gene N is for normal coloring and the gene a is for no coloring, or albino. Any gene combination with an N results in normal coloring. The Punnett square shows the possible gene combinations of an offspring and the resulting colors from parents that both have the gene combination Na. *(See Example 4.)*

  a. What percent of the possible gene combinations result in albino coloring?

  b. Show how you could use a polynomial to model the possible gene combinations of the offspring.

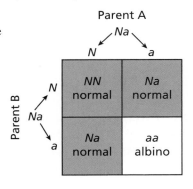

Parent A

36. MODELING WITH MATHEMATICS Your iris controls the amount of light that enters your eye by changing the size of your pupil.

iris

pupil

  a. Write a polynomial that represents the area of your pupil. Write your answer in terms of π.

  b. The width x of your iris decreases from 4 millimeters to 2 millimeters when you enter a dark room. How many times greater is the area of your pupil after entering the room than before entering the room? Explain.

37. CRITICAL THINKING Write two binomials that have the product $x^2 - 121$. Explain.

38. HOW DO YOU SEE IT? In pea plants, any gene combination with a green gene (G) results in a green pod. The Punnett square shows the possible gene combinations of the offspring of two Gy pea plants and the resulting pod colors.

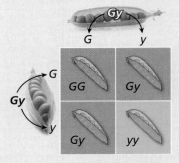

G = Green gene
y = Yellow gene

A polynomial that models the possible gene combinations of the offspring is

$$(0.5G + 0.5y)^2 = 0.25G^2 + 0.5Gy + 0.25y^2.$$

Describe two ways to determine the percent of possible gene combinations that result in green pods.

In Exercises 39–42, find the product.

39. $(x^2 + 1)(x^2 - 1)$ **40.** $(y^3 + 4)^2$

41. $(2m^2 - 5n^2)^2$ **42.** $(r^3 - 6t^4)(r^3 + 6t^4)$

43. MAKING AN ARGUMENT Your friend claims to be able to use a special product pattern to determine that $\left(4\frac{1}{3}\right)^2$ is equal to $16\frac{1}{9}$. Is your friend correct? Explain.

44. THOUGHT PROVOKING Modify the dimensions of the original parking lot in Exercise 34 so that the area can be represented by two other types of special product patterns discussed in this section. Is there a positive x-value for which the three area expressions are equivalent? Explain.

45. REASONING Find k so that $9x^2 - 48x + k$ is the square of a binomial.

46. REPEATED REASONING Find $(x + 1)^3$ and $(x + 2)^3$. Find a pattern in the terms and use it to write a pattern for the cube of a binomial $(a + b)^3$.

47. PROBLEM SOLVING Find two numbers a and b such that $(a + b)(a - b) < (a - b)^2 < (a + b)^2$.

Maintaining Mathematical Proficiency
Reviewing what you learned in previous grades and lessons

Factor the expression using the GCF. *(Skills Review Handbook)*

48. $12y - 18$ **49.** $9r + 27$ **50.** $49s + 35t$ **51.** $15x - 10y$

2.4 Solving Polynomial Equations in Factored Form

Essential Question How can you solve a polynomial equation?

EXPLORATION 1   Matching Equivalent Forms of an Equation

Work with a partner. An equation is considered to be in *factored form* when the product of the factors is equal to 0. Match each factored form of the equation with its equivalent standard form and nonstandard form.

	Factored Form		Standard Form		Nonstandard Form
a.	$(x-1)(x-3)=0$	**A.**	$x^2-x-2=0$	**1.**	$x^2-5x=-6$
b.	$(x-2)(x-3)=0$	**B.**	$x^2+x-2=0$	**2.**	$(x-1)^2=4$
c.	$(x+1)(x-2)=0$	**C.**	$x^2-4x+3=0$	**3.**	$x^2-x=2$
d.	$(x-1)(x+2)=0$	**D.**	$x^2-5x+6=0$	**4.**	$x(x+1)=2$
e.	$(x+1)(x-3)=0$	**E.**	$x^2-2x-3=0$	**5.**	$x^2-4x=-3$

USING TOOLS STRATEGICALLY

To be proficient in math, you need to consider using tools such as a table or a spreadsheet to organize your results.

EXPLORATION 2   Writing a Conjecture

Work with a partner. Substitute 1, 2, 3, 4, 5, and 6 for x in each equation and determine whether the equation is true. Organize your results in a table. Write a conjecture describing what you discovered.

a. $(x-1)(x-2)=0$ **b.** $(x-2)(x-3)=0$

c. $(x-3)(x-4)=0$ **d.** $(x-4)(x-5)=0$

e. $(x-5)(x-6)=0$ **f.** $(x-6)(x-1)=0$

EXPLORATION 3   Special Properties of 0 and 1

Work with a partner. The numbers 0 and 1 have special properties that are shared by no other numbers. For each of the following, decide whether the property is true for 0, 1, both, or neither. Explain your reasoning.

a. When you add   to a number n, you get n.

b. If the product of two numbers is   , then at least one of the numbers is 0.

c. The square of   is equal to itself.

d. When you multiply a number n by   , you get n.

e. When you multiply a number n by   , you get 0.

f. The opposite of   is equal to itself.

Communicate Your Answer

4. How can you solve a polynomial equation?

5. One of the properties in Exploration 3 is called the Zero-Product Property. It is one of the most important properties in all of algebra. Which property is it? Why do you think it is called the Zero-Product Property? Explain how it is used in algebra and why it is so important.

Core Vocabulary

factored form, *p. 82*
Zero-Product Property, *p. 82*
roots, *p. 82*
repeated roots, *p. 83*

Previous
polynomial
standard form
greatest common factor (GCF)
monomial

What You Will Learn

▶ Use the Zero-Product Property.
▶ Factor polynomials using the GCF.
▶ Use the Zero-Product Property to solve real-life problems.

Using the Zero-Product Property

A polynomial is in **factored form** when it is written as a product of factors.

Standard form	**Factored form**
$x^2 + 2x$	$x(x + 2)$
$x^2 + 5x - 24$	$(x - 3)(x + 8)$

When one side of an equation is a polynomial in factored form and the other side is 0, use the **Zero-Product Property** to solve the polynomial equation. The solutions of a polynomial equation are also called **roots**.

Core Concept

Zero-Product Property

Words If the product of two real numbers is 0, then at least one of the numbers is 0.

Algebra If a and b are real numbers and $ab = 0$, then $a = 0$ or $b = 0$.

EXAMPLE 1 **Solving Polynomial Equations**

Solve each equation.

a. $2x(x - 4) = 0$ **b.** $(x - 3)(x - 9) = 0$

SOLUTION

a. $2x(x - 4) = 0$ Write equation.

$\qquad 2x = 0 \quad or \quad x - 4 = 0$ Zero-Product Property

$\qquad x = 0 \quad or \qquad x = 4$ Solve for x.

▶ The roots are $x = 0$ and $x = 4$.

b. $(x - 3)(x - 9) = 0$ Write equation.

$\qquad x - 3 = 0 \quad or \quad x - 9 = 0$ Zero-Product Property

$\qquad x = 3 \quad or \qquad x = 9$ Solve for x.

▶ The roots are $x = 3$ and $x = 9$.

Check

To check the solutions of Example 1(a), substitute each solution in the original equation.

$2(0)(0 - 4) \overset{?}{=} 0$

$0(-4) \overset{?}{=} 0$

$0 = 0 \checkmark$

$2(4)(4 - 4) \overset{?}{=} 0$

$8(0) \overset{?}{=} 0$

$0 = 0 \checkmark$

Monitoring Progress Help in English and Spanish at *BigIdeasMath.com*

Solve the equation. Check your solutions.

1. $x(x - 1) = 0$

2. $3t(t + 2) = 0$

3. $(z - 4)(z - 6) = 0$

When two or more roots of an equation are the same number, the equation has **repeated roots**.

EXAMPLE 2 **Solving Polynomial Equations**

Solve each equation.

a. $(2x + 7)(2x - 7) = 0$ **b.** $(x - 1)^2 = 0$ **c.** $(x + 1)(x - 3)(x - 2) = 0$

SOLUTION

a. $(2x + 7)(2x - 7) = 0$ Write equation.

$\qquad 2x + 7 = 0 \quad or \quad 2x - 7 = 0$ Zero-Product Property

$\qquad\qquad x = -\frac{7}{2} \quad or \qquad x = \frac{7}{2}$ Solve for x.

▶ The roots are $x = -\frac{7}{2}$ and $x = \frac{7}{2}$.

b. $\qquad (x - 1)^2 = 0$ Write equation.

$\quad (x - 1)(x - 1) = 0$ Expand equation.

$\qquad x - 1 = 0 \quad or \quad x - 1 = 0$ Zero-Product Property

$\qquad\qquad x = 1 \quad or \qquad x = 1$ Solve for x.

▶ The equation has repeated roots of $x = 1$.

c. $(x + 1)(x - 3)(x - 2) = 0$ Write equation.

$\quad x + 1 = 0 \quad or \quad x - 3 = 0 \quad or \quad x - 2 = 0$ Zero-Product Property

$\qquad x = -1 \ or \qquad x = 3 \quad or \qquad x = 2$ Solve for x.

▶ The roots are $x = -1$, $x = 3$, and $x = 2$.

Monitoring Progress Help in English and Spanish at *BigIdeasMath.com*

Solve the equation. Check your solutions.

4. $(3s + 5)(5s + 8) = 0$ **5.** $(b + 7)^2 = 0$ **6.** $(d - 2)(d + 6)(d + 8) = 0$

Factoring Polynomials Using the GCF

To solve a polynomial equation using the Zero-Product Property, you may need to *factor* the polynomial, or write it as a product of other polynomials. Look for the *greatest common factor* (GCF) of the terms of the polynomial. This is a monomial that divides evenly into each term.

EXAMPLE 3 **Finding the Greatest Common Monomial Factor**

Factor out the greatest common monomial factor from $4x^4 + 24x^3$.

SOLUTION

The GCF of 4 and 24 is 4. The GCF of x^4 and x^3 is x^3. So, the greatest common monomial factor of the terms is $4x^3$.

▶ So, $4x^4 + 24x^3 = 4x^3(x + 6)$.

Monitoring Progress Help in English and Spanish at *BigIdeasMath.com*

7. Factor out the greatest common monomial factor from $8y^2 - 24y$.

EXAMPLE 4   Solving Equations by Factoring

Solve (a) $2x^2 + 8x = 0$ and (b) $6n^2 = 15n$.

SOLUTION

a.

$2x^2 + 8x = 0$	Write equation.
$2x(x + 4) = 0$	Factor left side.
$2x = 0 \quad or \quad x + 4 = 0$	Zero-Product Property
$x = 0 \quad or \qquad x = -4$	Solve for x.

▶ The roots are $x = 0$ and $x = -4$.

b.

$6n^2 = 15n$	Write equation.
$6n^2 - 15n = 0$	Subtract $15n$ from each side.
$3n(2n - 5) = 0$	Factor left side.
$3n = 0 \quad or \quad 2n - 5 = 0$	Zero-Product Property
$n = 0 \quad or \qquad n = \frac{5}{2}$	Solve for n.

▶ The roots are $n = 0$ and $n = \frac{5}{2}$.

Monitoring Progress Help in English and Spanish at *BigIdeasMath.com*

Solve the equation. Check your solutions.

8. $a^2 + 5a = 0$ **9.** $3s^2 - 9s = 0$ **10.** $4x^2 = 2x$

Solving Real-Life Problems

EXAMPLE 5   Modeling with Mathematics

You can model the arch of a fireplace using the equation $y = -\frac{1}{9}(x + 18)(x - 18)$, where x and y are measured in inches. The x-axis represents the floor. Find the width of the arch at floor level.

SOLUTION

Use the x-coordinates of the points where the arch meets the floor to find the width. At floor level, $y = 0$. So, substitute 0 for y and solve for x.

$y = -\frac{1}{9}(x + 18)(x - 18)$	Write equation.
$0 = -\frac{1}{9}(x + 18)(x - 18)$	Substitute 0 for y.
$0 = (x + 18)(x - 18)$	Multiply each side by -9.
$x + 18 = 0 \qquad or \quad x - 18 = 0$	Zero-Product Property
$x = -18 \quad or \qquad x = 18$	Solve for x.

The width is the distance between the x-coordinates, -18 and 18.

▶ So, the width of the arch at floor level is $|-18 - 18| = 36$ inches.

Monitoring Progress Help in English and Spanish at *BigIdeasMath.com*

11. You can model the entrance to a mine shaft using the equation $y = -\frac{1}{2}(x + 4)(x - 4)$, where x and y are measured in feet. The x-axis represents the ground. Find the width of the entrance at ground level.

Vocabulary and Core Concept Check

1. **WRITING** Explain how to use the Zero-Product Property to find the solutions of the equation $3x(x - 6) = 0$.

2. **DIFFERENT WORDS, SAME QUESTION** Which is different? Find *both* answers.

Solve the equation
$(2k + 4)(k - 3) = 0$.

Find the values of k for which
$2k + 4 = 0 \ or \ k - 3 = 0$.

Find the value of k for which
$(2k + 4) + (k - 3) = 0$.

Find the roots of the equation
$(2k + 4)(k - 3) = 0$.

Monitoring Progress and Modeling with Mathematics

In Exercises 3–8, solve the equation. *(See Example 1.)*

3. $x(x + 7) = 0$

4. $r(r - 10) = 0$

5. $12t(t - 5) = 0$

6. $-2v(v + 1) = 0$

7. $(s - 9)(s - 1) = 0$

8. $(y + 2)(y - 6) = 0$

In Exercises 9–20, solve the equation. *(See Example 2.)*

9. $(2a - 6)(3a + 15) = 0$

10. $(4q + 3)(q + 2) = 0$

11. $(5m + 4)^2 = 0$

12. $(h - 8)^2 = 0$

13. $(3 - 2g)(7 - g) = 0$

14. $(2 - 4d)(2 + 4d) = 0$

15. $z(z + 2)(z - 1) = 0$

16. $5p(2p - 3)(p + 7) = 0$

17. $(r - 4)^2(r + 8) = 0$

18. $w(w - 6)^2 = 0$

19. $(15 - 5c)(5c + 5)(-c + 6) = 0$

20. $(2 - n)\left(6 + \frac{2}{3}n\right)(n - 2) = 0$

In Exercises 21–24, find the x-coordinates of the points where the graph crosses the x-axis.

21.

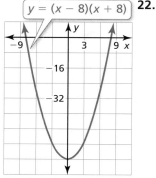

$y = (x - 8)(x + 8)$

22.

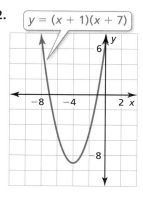

$y = (x + 1)(x + 7)$

23.

$y = -(x - 14)(x - 5)$

24.

$y = -0.2(x + 22)(x - 15)$

In Exercises 25–30, factor the polynomial. *(See Example 3.)*

25. $5z^2 + 45z$

26. $6d^2 - 21d$

27. $3y^3 - 9y^2$

28. $20x^3 + 30x^2$

29. $5n^6 + 2n^5$

30. $12a^4 + 8a$

In Exercises 31–36, solve the equation. *(See Example 4.)*

31. $4p^2 - p = 0$

32. $6m^2 + 12m = 0$

33. $25c + 10c^2 = 0$

34. $18q - 2q^2 = 0$

35. $3n^2 = 9n$

36. $-28r = 4r^2$

37. **ERROR ANALYSIS** Describe and correct the error in solving the equation.

$6x(x + 5) = 0$
$x + 5 = 0$
$x = -5$
The root is $x = -5$.

38. ERROR ANALYSIS Describe and correct the error in solving the equation.

$$3y^2 = 21y$$
$$3y = 21$$
$$y = 7$$
The root is $y = 7$.

39. MODELING WITH MATHEMATICS The entrance of a tunnel can be modeled by $y = -\frac{11}{50}(x - 4)(x - 24)$, where x and y are measured in feet. The x-axis represents the ground. Find the width of the tunnel at ground level. *(See Example 5.)*

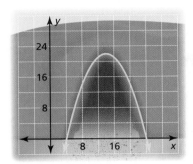

40. MODELING WITH MATHEMATICS The Gateway Arch in St. Louis can be modeled by $y = -\frac{2}{315}(x + 315)(x - 315)$, where x and y are measured in feet. The x-axis represents the ground.

a. Find the width of the arch at ground level.

b. How tall is the arch?

41. MODELING WITH MATHEMATICS A penguin leaps out of the water while swimming. This action is called porpoising. The height y (in feet) of a porpoising penguin can be modeled by $y = -16x^2 + 4.8x$, where x is the time (in seconds) since the penguin leaped out of the water. Find the roots of the equation when $y = 0$. Explain what the roots mean in this situation.

42. HOW DO YOU SEE IT? Use the graph to fill in each blank in the equation with the symbol $+$ or $-$. Explain your reasoning.

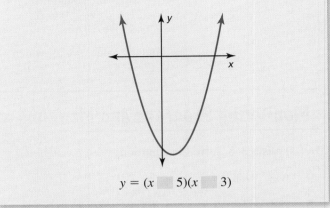

$$y = (x \quad 5)(x \quad 3)$$

43. CRITICAL THINKING How many x-intercepts does the graph of $y = (2x + 5)(x - 9)^2$ have? Explain.

44. MAKING AN ARGUMENT Your friend says that the graph of the equation $y = (x - a)(x - b)$ always has two x-intercepts for any values of a and b. Is your friend correct? Explain.

45. CRITICAL THINKING Does the equation $(x^2 + 3)(x^4 + 1) = 0$ have any real roots? Explain.

46. THOUGHT PROVOKING Write a polynomial equation of degree 4 whose only roots are $x = 1$, $x = 2$, and $x = 3$.

47. REASONING Find the values of x in terms of y that are solutions of each equation.

a. $(x + y)(2x - y) = 0$

b. $(x^2 - y^2)(4x + 16y) = 0$

48. PROBLEM SOLVING Solve the equation $(4^{x-5} - 16)(3^x - 81) = 0$.

Maintaining Mathematical Proficiency
Reviewing what you learned in previous grades and lessons

List the factor pairs of the number. *(Skills Review Handbook)*

49. 10

50. 18

51. 30

52. 48

Core Vocabulary

monomial, *p. 62*
degree of a monomial, *p. 62*
polynomial, *p. 63*
binomial, *p. 63*
trinomial, *p. 63*

degree of a polynomial, *p. 63*
standard form, *p. 63*
leading coefficient, *p. 63*
closed, *p. 64*
FOIL Method, *p. 71*

factored form, *p. 82*
Zero-Product Property, *p. 82*
roots, *p. 82*
repeated roots, *p. 83*

Core Concepts

Section 2.1

Polynomials, *p. 63*
Adding Polynomials, *p. 64*

Subtracting Polynomials, *p. 64*

Section 2.2

Multiplying Binomials, *p. 70*
FOIL Method, *p. 71*

Multiplying Binomials and Trinomials, *p. 72*

Section 2.3

Square of a Binomial Pattern, *p. 76*

Sum and Difference Pattern, *p. 77*

Section 2.4

Zero-Product Property, *p. 82*

Factoring Polynomials Using the GCF, *p. 83*

Mathematical Practices

1. Explain how you wrote the polynomial in Exercise 11 on page 79. Is there another method you can use to write the same polynomial?

2. Find a shortcut for exercises like Exercise 7 on page 85 when the variable has a coefficient of 1. Does your shortcut work when the coefficient is *not* 1?

Preparing for a Test

- Review examples of each type of problem that could appear on the test. Use the tutorials at *BigIdeasMath.com* for additional help.
- Review the homework problems your teacher assigned.
- Take a practice test.

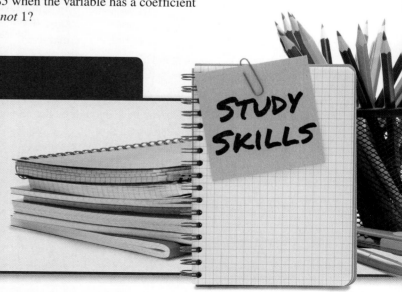

STUDY SKILLS

Write the polynomial in standard form. Identify the degree and leading coefficient of the polynomial. Then classify the polynomial by the number of terms. *(Section 2.1)*

1. $-8q^3$

2. $9 + d^2 - 3d$

3. $\frac{2}{3}m^4 - \frac{5}{6}m^6$

4. $-1.3z + 3z^4 + 7.4z^2$

Find the sum or difference. *(Section 2.1)*

5. $(2x^2 + 5) + (-x^2 + 4)$

6. $(-3n^2 + n) - (2n^2 - 7)$

7. $(-p^2 + 4p) - (p^2 - 3p + 15)$

8. $(a^2 - 3ab + b^2) + (-a^2 + ab + b^2)$

Find the product. *(Section 2.2 and Section 2.3)*

9. $(w + 6)(w + 7)$

10. $(3 - 4d)(2d - 5)$

11. $(y + 9)(y^2 + 2y - 3)$

12. $(3z - 5)(3z + 5)$

13. $(t + 5)^2$

14. $(2q - 6)^2$

Solve the equation. *(Section 2.4)*

15. $5x^2 - 15x = 0$

16. $(8 - g)(8 - g) = 0$

17. $(3p + 7)(3p - 7)(p + 8) = 0$

18. $-3y(y - 8)(2y + 1) = 0$

19. You are making a blanket with a fringe border of equal width on each side. *(Section 2.1 and Section 2.2)*

   a. Write a polynomial that represents the perimeter of the blanket including the fringe.

   b. Write a polynomial that represents the area of the blanket including the fringe.

   c. Find the perimeter and the area of the blanket including the fringe when the width of the fringe is 4 inches.

20. You are saving money to buy an electric guitar. You deposit $1000 in an account that earns interest compounded annually. The expression $1000(1 + r)^2$ represents the balance after 2 years, where r is the annual interest rate in decimal form. *(Section 2.3)*

   a. Write the polynomial in standard form that represents the balance of your account after 2 years.

   b. The interest rate is 3%. What is the balance of your account after 2 years?

   c. The guitar costs $1100. Do you have enough money in your account *after 3 years*? Explain.

21. The front of a storage bunker can be modeled by $y = -\frac{5}{216}(x - 72)(x + 72)$, where x and y are measured in inches. The x-axis represents the ground. Find the width of the bunker at ground level. *(Section 2.4)*

2.5 Factoring $x^2 + bx + c$

Essential Question
How can you use algebra tiles to factor the trinomial $x^2 + bx + c$ into the product of two binomials?

EXPLORATION 1 Finding Binomial Factors

Work with a partner. Use algebra tiles to write each polynomial as the product of two binomials. Check your answer by multiplying.

Sample $x^2 + 5x + 6$

Step 1 Arrange algebra tiles that model $x^2 + 5x + 6$ into a rectangular array.

Step 2 Use additional algebra tiles to model the dimensions of the rectangle.

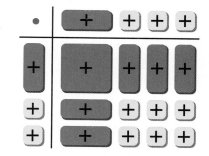

Step 3 Write the polynomial in factored form using the dimensions of the rectangle.

width   length

$$\text{Area} = x^2 + 5x + 6 = (x + 2)(x + 3)$$

a. $x^2 - 3x + 2 = \underline{}$

b. $x^2 + 5x + 4 = \underline{}$

c. $x^2 - 7x + 12 = \underline{}$

d. $x^2 + 7x + 12 = \underline{}$

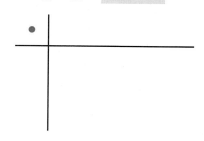

REASONING ABSTRACTLY

To be proficient in math, you need to understand a situation abstractly and represent it symbolically.

Communicate Your Answer

2. How can you use algebra tiles to factor the trinomial $x^2 + bx + c$ into the product of two binomials?

3. Describe a strategy for factoring the trinomial $x^2 + bx + c$ that does not use algebra tiles.

What You Will Learn

▶ Factor $x^2 + bx + c$.

▶ Use factoring to solve real-life problems.

Factoring $x^2 + bx + c$

Writing a polynomial as a product of factors is called *factoring*. To factor $x^2 + bx + c$ as $(x + p)(x + q)$, you need to find p and q such that $p + q = b$ and $pq = c$.

$$(x + p)(x + q) = x^2 + px + qx + pq$$
$$= x^2 + (p + q)x + pq$$

Core Concept

Factoring $x^2 + bx + c$ When c Is Positive

Algebra $x^2 + bx + c = (x + p)(x + q)$ when $p + q = b$ and $pq = c$.

When c is positive, p and q have the same sign as b.

Examples $x^2 + 6x + 5 = (x + 1)(x + 5)$

$x^2 - 6x + 5 = (x - 1)(x - 5)$

EXAMPLE 1   **Factoring $x^2 + bx + c$ When b and c Are Positive**

Factor $x^2 + 10x + 16$.

SOLUTION

Notice that $b = 10$ and $c = 16$.

- Because c is positive, the factors p and q must have the same sign so that pq is positive.

- Because b is also positive, p and q must each be positive so that $p + q$ is positive.

Find two positive integer factors of 16 whose sum is 10.

Check

Use the FOIL Method.

$(x + 2)(x + 8)$

$\qquad = x^2 + 8x + 2x + 16$

$\qquad = x^2 + 10x + 16$ ✔

Factors of 16	Sum of factors
1, 16	17
2, 8	10
4, 4	8

The values of p and q are 2 and 8.

▶ So, $x^2 + 10x + 16 = (x + 2)(x + 8)$.

Monitoring Progress Help in English and Spanish at *BigIdeasMath.com*

Factor the polynomial.

   1. $x^2 + 7x + 6$

   2. $x^2 + 9x + 8$

EXAMPLE 2 **Factoring $x^2 + bx + c$ When b Is Negative and c Is Positive**

Factor $x^2 - 8x + 12$.

SOLUTION

Notice that $b = -8$ and $c = 12$.

- Because c is positive, the factors p and q must have the same sign so that pq is positive.

- Because b is negative, p and q must each be negative so that $p + q$ is negative.

Find two negative integer factors of 12 whose sum is -8.

Factors of 12	$-1, -12$	$-2, -6$	$-3, -4$
Sum of factors	-13	-8	-7

The values of p and q are -2 and -6.

▶ So, $x^2 - 8x + 12 = (x - 2)(x - 6)$.

Check

Use the FOIL Method.

$(x - 2)(x - 6)$

$\quad = x^2 - 6x - 2x + 12$

$\quad = x^2 - 8x + 12$ ✓

⟳ Core Concept

Factoring $x^2 + bx + c$ When c Is Negative

Algebra $\quad x^2 + bx + c = (x + p)(x + q)$ when $p + q = b$ and $pq = c$.

When c is negative, p and q have different signs.

Example $\quad x^2 - 4x - 5 = (x + 1)(x - 5)$

EXAMPLE 3 **Factoring $x^2 + bx + c$ When c Is Negative**

Factor $x^2 + 4x - 21$.

SOLUTION

Notice that $b = 4$ and $c = -21$. Because c is negative, the factors p and q must have different signs so that pq is negative.

Find two integer factors of -21 whose sum is 4.

Factors of −21	$-21, 1$	$-1, 21$	$-7, 3$	$-3, 7$
Sum of factors	-20	20	-4	4

The values of p and q are -3 and 7.

▶ So, $x^2 + 4x - 21 = (x - 3)(x + 7)$.

Check

Use the FOIL Method.

$(x - 3)(x + 7)$

$\quad = x^2 + 7x - 3x - 21$

$\quad = x^2 + 4x - 21$ ✓

Monitoring Progress Help in English and Spanish at *BigIdeasMath.com*

Factor the polynomial.

3. $w^2 - 4w + 3$

4. $n^2 - 12n + 35$

5. $x^2 - 14x + 24$

6. $x^2 + 2x - 15$

7. $y^2 + 13y - 30$

8. $v^2 - v - 42$

Solving Real-Life Problems

EXAMPLE 4 Solving a Real-Life Problem

A farmer plants a rectangular pumpkin patch in the northeast corner of a square plot of land. The area of the pumpkin patch is 600 square meters. What is the area of the square plot of land?

SOLUTION

1. **Understand the Problem** You are given the area of the pumpkin patch, the difference of the side length of the square plot and the length of the pumpkin patch, and the difference of the side length of the square plot and the width of the pumpkin patch.

2. **Make a Plan** The length of the pumpkin patch is $(s - 30)$ meters and the width is $(s - 40)$ meters. Write and solve an equation to find the side length s. Then use the solution to find the area of the square plot of land.

3. **Solve the Problem** Use the equation for the area of a rectangle to write and solve an equation to find the side length s of the square plot of land.

$600 = (s - 30)(s - 40)$	Write an equation.
$600 = s^2 - 70s + 1200$	Multiply.
$0 = s^2 - 70s + 600$	Subtract 600 from each side.
$0 = (s - 10)(s - 60)$	Factor the polynomial.
$s - 10 = 0 \quad or \quad s - 60 = 0$	Zero-Product Property
$s = 10 \quad or \quad s = 60$	Solve for s.

 So, the area of the square plot of land is $60(60) = 3600$ square meters.

4. **Look Back** Use the diagram to check that you found the correct side length. Using $s = 60$, the length of the pumpkin patch is $60 - 30 = 30$ meters and the width is $60 - 40 = 20$ meters. So, the area of the pumpkin patch is 600 square meters. This matches the given information and confirms the side length is 60 meters, which gives an area of 3600 square meters.

STUDY TIP

The diagram shows that the side length is more than 40 meters, so a side length of 10 meters does not make sense in this situation. The side length is 60 meters.

Monitoring Progress 🔊 Help in English and Spanish at *BigIdeasMath.com*

9. **WHAT IF?** The area of the pumpkin patch is 200 square meters. What is the area of the square plot of land?

Concept Summary

Factoring $x^2 + bx + c$ as $(x + p)(x + q)$

The diagram shows the relationships between the signs of b and c and the signs of p and q.

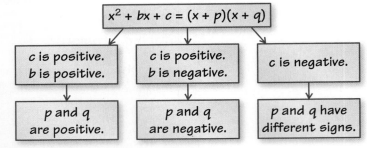

Vocabulary and Core Concept Check

1. **WRITING** You are factoring $x^2 + 11x - 26$. What do the signs of the terms tell you about the factors? Explain.

2. **OPEN-ENDED** Write a trinomial that can be factored as $(x + p)(x + q)$, where p and q are positive.

Monitoring Progress and Modeling with Mathematics

In Exercises 3–8, factor the polynomial. *(See Example 1.)*

3. $x^2 + 8x + 7$

4. $z^2 + 10z + 21$

5. $n^2 + 9n + 20$

6. $s^2 + 11s + 30$

7. $h^2 + 11h + 18$

8. $y^2 + 13y + 40$

In Exercises 9–14, factor the polynomial.
(See Example 2.)

9. $v^2 - 5v + 4$

10. $x^2 - 13x + 22$

11. $d^2 - 5d + 6$

12. $k^2 - 10k + 24$

13. $w^2 - 17w + 72$

14. $j^2 - 13j + 42$

In Exercises 15–24, factor the polynomial.
(See Example 3.)

15. $x^2 + 3x - 4$

16. $z^2 + 7z - 18$

17. $n^2 + 4n - 12$

18. $s^2 + 3s - 40$

19. $y^2 + 2y - 48$

20. $h^2 + 6h - 27$

21. $x^2 - x - 20$

22. $m^2 - 6m - 7$

23. $-6t - 16 + t^2$

24. $-7y + y^2 - 30$

25. **MODELING WITH MATHEMATICS** A projector displays an image on a wall. The area (in square feet) of the projection is represented by $x^2 - 8x + 15$.

a. Write a binomial that represents the height of the projection.

b. Find the perimeter of the projection when the height of the wall is 8 feet.

(x − 3) ft

x ft

26. **MODELING WITH MATHEMATICS** A dentist's office and parking lot are on a rectangular piece of land. The area (in square meters) of the land is represented by $x^2 + x - 30$.

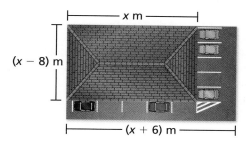

x m

(x − 8) m

(x + 6) m

a. Write a binomial that represents the width of the land.

b. Find the area of the land when the length of the dentist's office is 20 meters.

ERROR ANALYSIS In Exercises 27 and 28, describe and correct the error in factoring the polynomial.

27.

$x^2 + 14x + 48 = (x + 4)(x + 12)$

28.

$s^2 - 17s - 60 = (s - 5)(s - 12)$

In Exercises 29–38, solve the equation.

29. $m^2 + 3m + 2 = 0$

30. $n^2 - 9n + 18 = 0$

31. $x^2 + 5x - 14 = 0$

32. $v^2 + 11v - 26 = 0$

33. $t^2 + 15t = -36$

34. $n^2 - 5n = 24$

35. $a^2 + 5a - 20 = 30$

36. $y^2 - 2y - 8 = 7$

37. $m^2 + 10 = 15m - 34$

38. $b^2 + 5 = 8b - 10$

39. MODELING WITH MATHEMATICS You trimmed a large square picture so that you could fit it into a frame. The area of the cut picture is 20 square inches. What is the area of the original picture? *(See Example 4.)*

40. MODELING WITH MATHEMATICS A web browser is open on your computer screen.

a. The area of the browser window is 24 square inches. Find the length of the browser window x.

b. The browser covers $\frac{3}{13}$ of the screen. What are the dimensions of the screen?

41. MAKING AN ARGUMENT Your friend says there are six integer values of b for which the trinomial $x^2 + bx - 12$ has two binomial factors of the form $(x + p)$ and $(x + q)$. Is your friend correct? Explain.

42. THOUGHT PROVOKING Use algebra tiles to factor each polynomial modeled by the tiles. Show your work.

a.

b.

MATHEMATICAL CONNECTIONS In Exercises 43 and 44, find the dimensions of the polygon with the given area.

43. Area = 44 ft^2 **44.** Area = 35 m^2

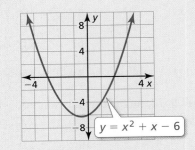

45. REASONING Write an equation of the form $x^2 + bx + c = 0$ that has the solutions $x = -4$ and $x = 6$. Explain how you found your answer.

46. HOW DO YOU SEE IT? The graph of $y = x^2 + x - 6$ is shown.

a. Explain how you can use the graph to factor the polynomial $x^2 + x - 6$.

b. Factor the polynomial.

47. PROBLEM SOLVING Road construction workers are paving the area shown.

a. Write an expression that represents the area being paved.

b. The area being paved is 280 square meters. Write and solve an equation to find the width of the road x.

USING STRUCTURE In Exercises 48–51, factor the polynomial.

48. $x^2 + 6xy + 8y^2$ **49.** $r^2 + 7rs + 12s^2$

50. $a^2 + 11ab - 26b^2$ **51.** $x^2 - 2xy - 35y^2$

Maintaining Mathematical Proficiency

Reviewing what you learned in previous grades and lessons

Solve the equation. Check your solution. *(Skills Review Handbook)*

52. $p - 9 = 0$ **53.** $z + 12 = -5$ **54.** $6 = \dfrac{c}{-7}$ **55.** $4k = 0$

2.6 Factoring $ax^2 + bx + c$

Essential Question How can you use algebra tiles to factor the trinomial $ax^2 + bx + c$ into the product of two binomials?

EXPLORATION 1 Finding Binomial Factors

Work with a partner. Use algebra tiles to write each polynomial as the product of two binomials. Check your answer by multiplying.

Sample $2x^2 + 5x + 2$

Step 1 Arrange algebra tiles that model $2x^2 + 5x + 2$ into a rectangular array.

Step 2 Use additional algebra tiles to model the dimensions of the rectangle.

 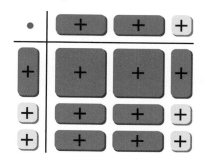

Step 3 Write the polynomial in factored form using the dimensions of the rectangle.

(width) (length)

$$\text{Area} = 2x^2 + 5x + 2 = (x + 2)(2x + 1)$$

a. $3x^2 + 5x + 2 =$ ▢

b. $4x^2 + 4x - 3 =$ ▢

c. $2x^2 - 11x + 5 =$ ▢

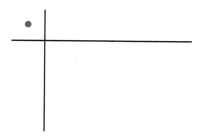

USING TOOLS STRATEGICALLY

To be proficient in math, you need to consider the available tools, including concrete models, when solving a mathematical problem.

Communicate Your Answer

2. How can you use algebra tiles to factor the trinomial $ax^2 + bx + c$ into the product of two binomials?

3. Is it possible to factor the trinomial $2x^2 + 2x + 1$? Explain your reasoning.

What You Will Learn

▶ Factor $ax^2 + bx + c$.

▶ Use factoring to solve real-life problems.

Factoring $ax^2 + bx + c$

In Section 2.5, you factored polynomials of the form $ax^2 + bx + c$, where $a = 1$. To factor polynomials of the form $ax^2 + bx + c$, where $a \neq 1$, first look for the GCF of the terms of the polynomial and then factor further if possible.

EXAMPLE 1 Factoring Out the GCF

Factor $5x^2 + 15x + 10$.

SOLUTION

Notice that the GCF of the terms $5x^2$, $15x$, and 10 is 5.

$5x^2 + 15x + 10 = 5(x^2 + 3x + 2)$ Factor out GCF.

$ = 5(x + 1)(x + 2)$ Factor $x^2 + 3x + 2$.

▶ So, $5x^2 + 15x + 10 = 5(x + 1)(x + 2)$.

When there is no GCF, consider the possible factors of a and c.

EXAMPLE 2 Factoring $ax^2 + bx + c$ When ac Is Positive

Factor each polynomial.

a. $4x^2 + 13x + 3$ **b.** $3x^2 - 7x + 2$

STUDY TIP

You must consider the order of the factors of 3, because the middle terms formed by the possible factorizations are different.

SOLUTION

a. There is no GCF, so you need to consider the possible factors of a and c. Because b and c are both positive, the factors of c must be positive. Use a table to organize information about the factors of a and c.

Factors of 4	Factors of 3	Possible factorization	Middle term	
1, 4	1, 3	$(x + 1)(4x + 3)$	$3x + 4x = 7x$	✗
1, 4	3, 1	$(x + 3)(4x + 1)$	$x + 12x = 13x$	✓
2, 2	1, 3	$(2x + 1)(2x + 3)$	$6x + 2x = 8x$	✗

▶ So, $4x^2 + 13x + 3 = (x + 3)(4x + 1)$.

b. There is no GCF, so you need to consider the possible factors of a and c. Because b is negative and c is positive, both factors of c must be negative. Use a table to organize information about the factors of a and c.

Factors of 3	Factors of 2	Possible factorization	Middle term	
1, 3	$-1, -2$	$(x - 1)(3x - 2)$	$-2x - 3x = -5x$	✗
1, 3	$-2, -1$	$(x - 2)(3x - 1)$	$-x - 6x = -7x$	✓

▶ So, $3x^2 - 7x + 2 = (x - 2)(3x - 1)$.

EXAMPLE 3 **Factoring $ax^2 + bx + c$ When ac Is Negative**

Factor $2x^2 - 5x - 7$.

SOLUTION

There is no GCF, so you need to consider the possible factors of a and c. Because c is negative, the factors of c must have different signs. Use a table to organize information about the factors of a and c.

Factors of 2	Factors of −7	Possible factorization	Middle term	
1, 2	1, −7	$(x + 1)(2x - 7)$	$-7x + 2x = -5x$	✓
1, 2	7, −1	$(x + 7)(2x - 1)$	$-x + 14x = 13x$	✗
1, 2	−1, 7	$(x - 1)(2x + 7)$	$7x - 2x = 5x$	✗
1, 2	−7, 1	$(x - 7)(2x + 1)$	$x - 14x = -13x$	✗

▶ So, $2x^2 - 5x - 7 = (x + 1)(2x - 7)$.

STUDY TIP

When a is negative, factor −1 from each term of $ax^2 + bx + c$. Then factor the resulting trinomial as in the previous examples.

EXAMPLE 4 **Factoring $ax^2 + bx + c$ When a Is Negative**

Factor $-4x^2 - 8x + 5$.

SOLUTION

Step 1 Factor −1 from each term of the trinomial.

$$-4x^2 - 8x + 5 = -(4x^2 + 8x - 5)$$

Step 2 Factor the trinomial $4x^2 + 8x - 5$. Because c is negative, the factors of c must have different signs. Use a table to organize information about the factors of a and c.

Factors of 4	Factors of −5	Possible factorization	Middle term	
1, 4	1, −5	$(x + 1)(4x - 5)$	$-5x + 4x = -x$	✗
1, 4	5, −1	$(x + 5)(4x - 1)$	$-x + 20x = 19x$	✗
1, 4	−1, 5	$(x - 1)(4x + 5)$	$5x - 4x = x$	✗
1, 4	−5, 1	$(x - 5)(4x + 1)$	$x - 20x = -19x$	✗
2, 2	1, −5	$(2x + 1)(2x - 5)$	$-10x + 2x = -8x$	✗
2, 2	−1, 5	$(2x - 1)(2x + 5)$	$10x - 2x = 8x$	✓

▶ So, $-4x^2 - 8x + 5 = -(2x - 1)(2x + 5)$.

Monitoring Progress Help in English and Spanish at *BigIdeasMath.com*

Factor the polynomial.

1. $8x^2 - 56x + 48$ **2.** $14x^2 + 31x + 15$ **3.** $2x^2 - 7x + 5$

4. $3x^2 - 14x + 8$ **5.** $4x^2 - 19x - 5$ **6.** $6x^2 + x - 12$

7. $-2y^2 - 5y - 3$ **8.** $-5m^2 + 6m - 1$ **9.** $-3x^2 - x + 2$

Solving Real-Life Problems

EXAMPLE 5   **Solving a Real-Life Problem**

The length of a rectangular game reserve is 1 mile longer than twice the width. The area of the reserve is 55 square miles. What is the width of the reserve?

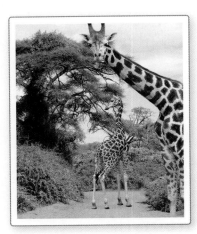

SOLUTION

Use the formula for the area of a rectangle to write an equation for the area of the reserve. Let w represent the width. Then $2w + 1$ represents the length. Solve for w.

$w(2w + 1) = 55$	Area of the reserve
$2w^2 + w = 55$	Distributive Property
$2w^2 + w - 55 = 0$	Subtract 55 from each side.

Factor the left side of the equation. There is no GCF, so you need to consider the possible factors of a and c. Because c is negative, the factors of c must have different signs. Use a table to organize information about the factors of a and c.

Factors of 2	Factors of -55	Possible factorization	Middle term	
1, 2	1, -55	$(w + 1)(2w - 55)$	$-55w + 2w = -53w$	✗
1, 2	55, -1	$(w + 55)(2w - 1)$	$-w + 110w = 109w$	✗
1, 2	$-1, 55$	$(w - 1)(2w + 55)$	$55w - 2w = 53w$	✗
1, 2	$-55, 1$	$(w - 55)(2w + 1)$	$w - 110w = -109w$	✗
1, 2	5, -11	$(w + 5)(2w - 11)$	$-11w + 10w = -w$	✗
1, 2	11, -5	$(w + 11)(2w - 5)$	$-5w + 22w = 17w$	✗
1, 2	$-5, 11$	$(w - 5)(2w + 11)$	$11w - 10w = w$	✓
1, 2	$-11, 5$	$(w - 11)(2w + 5)$	$5w - 22w = -17w$	✗

So, you can rewrite $2w^2 + w - 55$ as $(w - 5)(2w + 11)$. Write the equation with the left side factored and continue solving for w.

$(w - 5)(2w + 11) = 0$	Rewrite equation with left side factored.
$w - 5 = 0 \quad or \quad 2w + 11 = 0$	Zero-Product Property
$w = 5 \quad or \quad w = -\frac{11}{2}$	Solve for w.

A negative width does not make sense, so you should use the positive solution.

▶   So, the width of the reserve is 5 miles.

> **Check**
>
> Use mental math.
>
> The width is 5 miles, so the length is $5(2) + 1 = 11$ miles and the area is $5(11) = 55$ square miles. ✔

Monitoring Progress Help in English and Spanish at *BigIdeasMath.com*

10. WHAT IF? The area of the reserve is 136 square miles. How wide is the reserve?

Vocabulary and Core Concept Check

1. **REASONING** What is the greatest common factor of the terms of $3y^2 - 21y + 36$?

2. **WRITING** Compare factoring $6x^2 - x - 2$ with factoring $x^2 - x - 2$.

Monitoring Progress and Modeling with Mathematics

In Exercises 3–8, factor the polynomial. *(See Example 1.)*

3. $3x^2 + 3x - 6$

4. $8v^2 + 8v - 48$

5. $4k^2 + 28k + 48$

6. $6y^2 - 24y + 18$

7. $7b^2 - 63b + 140$

8. $9r^2 - 36r - 45$

In Exercises 9–16, factor the polynomial.
(See Examples 2 and 3.)

9. $3h^2 + 11h + 6$

10. $8m^2 + 30m + 7$

11. $6x^2 - 5x + 1$

12. $10w^2 - 31w + 15$

13. $3n^2 + 5n - 2$

14. $4z^2 + 4z - 3$

15. $8g^2 - 10g - 12$

16. $18v^2 - 15v - 18$

In Exercises 17–22, factor the polynomial.
(See Example 4.)

17. $-3t^2 + 11t - 6$

18. $-7v^2 - 25v - 12$

19. $-4c^2 + 19c + 5$

20. $-8h^2 - 13h + 6$

21. $-15w^2 - w + 28$

22. $-22d^2 + 29d - 9$

ERROR ANALYSIS In Exercises 23 and 24, describe and correct the error in factoring the polynomial.

23.

$$2x^2 - 2x - 24 = 2(x^2 - 2x - 24)$$
$$= 2(x - 6)(x + 4)$$

24.

$$6x^2 - 7x - 3 = (3x - 3)(2x + 1)$$

In Exercises 25–28, solve the equation.

25. $5x^2 - 5x - 30 = 0$

26. $2k^2 - 5k - 18 = 0$

27. $-12n^2 - 11n = -15$

28. $14b^2 - 2 = -3b$

In Exercises 29–32, find the *x*-coordinates of the points where the graph crosses the *x*-axis.

29.

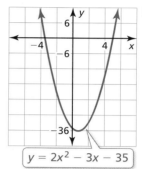

$y = 2x^2 - 3x - 35$

30.

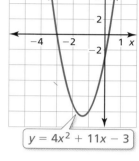

$y = 4x^2 + 11x - 3$

31.

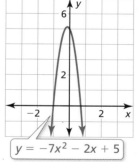

$y = -7x^2 - 2x + 5$

32.

$y = -3x^2 + 14x + 5$

33. **MODELING WITH MATHEMATICS** The area (in square feet) of the school sign can be represented by $15x^2 - x - 2$.

   a. Write an expression that represents the length of the sign.

   b. Describe two ways to find the area of the sign when $x = 3$.

$(3x + 1)$ ft

34. MODELING WITH MATHEMATICS The height h (in feet) above the water of a cliff diver is modeled by $h = -16t^2 + 8t + 80$, where t is the time (in seconds). What does the constant term represent? How long is the diver in the air?

35. MODELING WITH MATHEMATICS The Parthenon in Athens, Greece, is an ancient structure that has a rectangular base. The length of the base of the Parthenon is 8 meters more than twice its width. The area of the base is about 2170 square meters. Find the length and width of the base. *(See Example 5.)*

36. MODELING WITH MATHEMATICS The length of a rectangular birthday party invitation is 1 inch less than twice its width. The area of the invitation is 15 square inches. Will the invitation fit in the envelope shown without being folded? Explain.

$3\frac{5}{8}$ in.

$5\frac{1}{8}$ in.

37. OPEN-ENDED Write a binomial whose terms have a GCF of $3x$.

38. HOW DO YOU SEE IT? Without factoring, determine which of the graphs represents the function $g(x) = 21x^2 + 37x + 12$ and which represents the function $h(x) = 21x^2 - 37x + 12$. Explain your reasoning.

39. REASONING When is it not possible to factor $ax^2 + bx + c$, where $a \neq 1$? Give an example.

40. MAKING AN ARGUMENT Your friend says that to solve the equation $5x^2 + x - 4 = 2$, you should start by factoring the left side as $(5x - 4)(x + 1)$. Is your friend correct? Explain.

41. REASONING For what values of t can $2x^2 + tx + 10$ be written as the product of two binomials?

42. THOUGHT PROVOKING Use algebra tiles to factor each polynomial modeled by the tiles. Show your work.

43. MATHEMATICAL CONNECTIONS The length of a rectangle is 1 inch more than twice its width. The value of the area of the rectangle (in square inches) is 5 more than the value of the perimeter of the rectangle (in inches). Find the width.

44. PROBLEM SOLVING A rectangular swimming pool is bordered by a concrete patio. The width of the patio is the same on every side. The area of the surface of the pool is equal to the area of the patio. What is the width of the patio?

16 ft

24 ft

In Exercises 45–48, factor the polynomial.

45. $4k^2 + 7jk - 2j^2$

46. $6x^2 + 5xy - 4y^2$

47. $-6a^2 + 19ab - 14b^2$

48. $18m^3 + 39m^2n - 15mn^2$

Maintaining Mathematical Proficiency
Reviewing what you learned in previous grades and lessons

Graph the function. Compare the graph to the graph of $f(x) = |x|$. Describe the domain and range. *(Section 1.1)*

49. $h(x) = 3|x|$

50. $v(x) = |x - 5|$

51. $g(x) = |x| + 1$

52. $r(x) = -2|x|$

Evaluate the expression. *(Section 1.5)*

53. $-\sqrt[3]{216}$

54. $\sqrt[5]{-32}$

55. $16^{5/4}$

56. $(-27)^{2/3}$

2.7 Factoring Special Products

Essential Question How can you recognize and factor special products?

EXPLORATION 1   Factoring Special Products

Work with a partner. Use algebra tiles to write each polynomial as the product of two binomials. Check your answer by multiplying. State whether the product is a "special product" that you studied in Section 2.3.

LOOKING FOR STRUCTURE

To be proficient in math, you need to see complicated things as single objects or as being composed of several objects.

a. $4x^2 - 1 =$

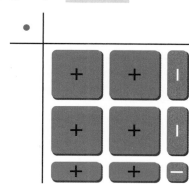

b. $4x^2 - 4x + 1 =$

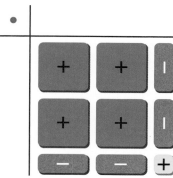

c. $4x^2 + 4x + 1 =$

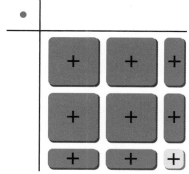

d. $4x^2 - 6x + 2 =$

EXPLORATION 2   Factoring Special Products

Work with a partner. Use algebra tiles to complete the rectangular array at the left in three different ways, so that each way represents a different special product. Write each special product in standard form and in factored form.

Communicate Your Answer

3. How can you recognize and factor special products? Describe a strategy for recognizing which polynomials can be factored as special products.

4. Use the strategy you described in Question 3 to factor each polynomial.

    a. $25x^2 + 10x + 1$ **b.** $25x^2 - 10x + 1$ **c.** $25x^2 - 1$

2.7 Lesson

Core Vocabulary

Previous
polynomial
trinomial

What You Will Learn

▶ Factor the difference of two squares.
▶ Factor perfect square trinomials.
▶ Use factoring to solve real-life problems.

Factoring the Difference of Two Squares

You can use special product patterns to factor polynomials.

Core Concept

Difference of Two Squares Pattern

Algebra

$a^2 - b^2 = (a + b)(a - b)$

Example

$x^2 - 9 = x^2 - 3^2 = (x + 3)(x - 3)$

EXAMPLE 1 **Factoring the Difference of Two Squares**

Factor (a) $x^2 - 25$ and (b) $4z^2 - 1$.

SOLUTION

a. $x^2 - 25 = x^2 - 5^2$ .... Write as $a^2 - b^2$.

$\qquad = (x + 5)(x - 5)$ .... Difference of two squares pattern

▶ So, $x^2 - 25 = (x + 5)(x - 5)$.

b. $4z^2 - 1 = (2z)^2 - 1^2$ .... Write as $a^2 - b^2$.

$\qquad = (2z + 1)(2z - 1)$ .... Difference of two squares pattern

▶ So, $4z^2 - 1 = (2z + 1)(2z - 1)$.

EXAMPLE 2 **Evaluating a Numerical Expression**

Use a special product pattern to evaluate the expression $54^2 - 48^2$.

SOLUTION

Notice that $54^2 - 48^2$ is a difference of two squares. So, you can rewrite the expression in a form that it is easier to evaluate using the difference of two squares pattern.

$54^2 - 48^2 = (54 + 48)(54 - 48)$ .... Difference of two squares pattern

$\qquad = 102(6)$ .... Simplify.

$\qquad = 612$ .... Multiply.

▶ So, $54^2 - 48^2 = 612$.

Monitoring Progress Help in English and Spanish at *BigIdeasMath.com*

Factor the polynomial.

1. $x^2 - 36$ .... **2.** $100 - m^2$ .... **3.** $9n^2 - 16$ .... **4.** $16h^2 - 49$

Use a special product pattern to evaluate the expression.

5. $36^2 - 34^2$ .... **6.** $47^2 - 44^2$ .... **7.** $55^2 - 50^2$ .... **8.** $28^2 - 24^2$

Factoring Perfect Square Trinomials

 Core Concept

Perfect Square Trinomial Pattern

Algebra	Example
$a^2 + 2ab + b^2 = (a + b)^2$	$x^2 + 6x + 9 = x^2 + 2(x)(3) + 3^2$
	$= (x + 3)^2$
$a^2 - 2ab + b^2 = (a - b)^2$	$x^2 - 6x + 9 = x^2 - 2(x)(3) + 3^2$
	$= (x - 3)^2$

EXAMPLE 3   **Factoring Perfect Square Trinomials**

Factor each polynomial.

a. $n^2 + 8n + 16$
            b. $4x^2 - 12x + 9$

SOLUTION

a. $n^2 + 8n + 16 = n^2 + 2(n)(4) + 4^2$ Write as $a^2 + 2ab + b^2$.

$\qquad\qquad\qquad = (n + 4)^2$ Perfect square trinomial pattern

▶   So, $n^2 + 8n + 16 = (n + 4)^2$.

b. $4x^2 - 12x + 9 = (2x)^2 - 2(2x)(3) + 3^2$ Write as $a^2 - 2ab + b^2$.

$\qquad\qquad\qquad = (2x - 3)^2$ Perfect square trinomial pattern

▶   So, $4x^2 - 12x + 9 = (2x - 3)^2$.

EXAMPLE 4   **Solving a Polynomial Equation**

Solve $x^2 + \frac{2}{3}x + \frac{1}{9} = 0$.

SOLUTION

$$x^2 + \tfrac{2}{3}x + \tfrac{1}{9} = 0 \qquad \text{Write equation.}$$

$$9x^2 + 6x + 1 = 0 \qquad \text{Multiply each side by 9.}$$

$$(3x)^2 + 2(3x)(1) + 1^2 = 0 \qquad \text{Write left side as } a^2 + 2ab + b^2.$$

$$(3x + 1)^2 = 0 \qquad \text{Perfect square trinomial pattern}$$

$$3x + 1 = 0 \qquad \text{Zero-Product Property}$$

$$x = -\tfrac{1}{3} \qquad \text{Solve for } x.$$

▶   The solution is $x = -\frac{1}{3}$.

LOOKING FOR STRUCTURE

Equations of the form $(x + a)^2 = 0$ always have repeated roots of $x = -a$.

Monitoring Progress Help in English and Spanish at *BigIdeasMath.com*

Factor the polynomial.

9. $m^2 - 2m + 1$ **10.** $d^2 - 10d + 25$ **11.** $9z^2 + 36z + 36$

Solve the equation.

12. $a^2 + 6a + 9 = 0$ **13.** $w^2 - \frac{7}{3}w + \frac{49}{36} = 0$ **14.** $n^2 - 81 = 0$

Solving Real-Life Problems

> **EXAMPLE 5** **Modeling with Mathematics**

A bird picks up a golf ball and drops it while flying. The function represents the height y (in feet) of the golf ball t seconds after it is dropped. The ball hits the top of a 32-foot-tall pine tree. After how many seconds does the ball hit the tree?

$y = 81 - 16t^2$

SOLUTION

1. **Understand the Problem** You are given the height of the golf ball as a function of the amount of time after it is dropped and the height of the tree that the golf ball hits. You are asked to determine how many seconds it takes for the ball to hit the tree.

2. **Make a Plan** Use the function for the height of the golf ball. Substitute the height of the tree for y and solve for the time t.

3. **Solve the Problem** Substitute 32 for y and solve for t.

$y = 81 - 16t^2$	Write equation.
$32 = 81 - 16t^2$	Substitute 32 for y.
$0 = 49 - 16t^2$	Subtract 32 from each side.
$0 = 7^2 - (4t)^2$	Write as $a^2 - b^2$.
$0 = (7 + 4t)(7 - 4t)$	Difference of two squares pattern
$7 + 4t = 0 \quad or \quad 7 - 4t = 0$	Zero-Product Property
$t = -\frac{7}{4} \quad or \quad t = \frac{7}{4}$	Solve for t.

A negative time does not make sense in this situation.

▶ So, the golf ball hits the tree after $\frac{7}{4}$, or 1.75 seconds.

4. **Look Back** Check your solution, as shown, by substituting $t = \frac{7}{4}$ into the equation $32 = 81 - 16t^2$. Then verify that a time of $\frac{7}{4}$ seconds gives a height of 32 feet.

Check

$$32 = 81 - 16t^2$$
$$32 \overset{?}{=} 81 - 16\left(\tfrac{7}{4}\right)^2$$
$$32 \overset{?}{=} 81 - 16\left(\tfrac{49}{16}\right)$$
$$32 \overset{?}{=} 81 - 49$$
$$32 = 32 \ \checkmark$$

Monitoring Progress   Help in English and Spanish at *BigIdeasMath.com*

15. **WHAT IF?** The golf ball does not hit the pine tree. After how many seconds does the ball hit the ground?

Vocabulary and Core Concept Check

1. **REASONING** Can you use the perfect square trinomial pattern to factor $y^2 + 16y + 64$? Explain.

2. **WHICH ONE DOESN'T BELONG?** Which polynomial does *not* belong with the other three? Explain your reasoning.

$$n^2 - 4 \qquad g^2 - 6g + 9 \qquad r^2 + 12r + 36 \qquad k^2 + 25$$

Monitoring Progress and Modeling with Mathematics

In Exercises 3–8, factor the polynomial. *(See Example 1.)*

3. $m^2 - 49$

4. $z^2 - 81$

5. $64 - 81d^2$

6. $25 - 4x^2$

7. $225a^2 - 36b^2$

8. $16x^2 - 169y^2$

In Exercises 9–14, use a special product pattern to evaluate the expression. *(See Example 2.)*

9. $12^2 - 9^2$

10. $19^2 - 11^2$

11. $78^2 - 72^2$

12. $54^2 - 52^2$

13. $53^2 - 47^2$

14. $39^2 - 36^2$

In Exercises 15–22, factor the polynomial. *(See Example 3.)*

15. $h^2 + 12h + 36$

16. $p^2 + 30p + 225$

17. $y^2 - 22y + 121$

18. $x^2 - 4x + 4$

19. $a^2 - 28a + 196$

20. $m^2 + 24m + 144$

21. $25n^2 + 20n + 4$

22. $49a^2 - 14a + 1$

ERROR ANALYSIS In Exercises 23 and 24, describe and correct the error in factoring the polynomial.

23.

$$n^2 - 64 = n^2 - 8^2$$
$$= (n - 8)^2$$

24.

$$y^2 - 6y + 9 = y^2 - 2(y)(3) + 3^2$$
$$= (y - 3)(y + 3)$$

25. **MODELING WITH MATHEMATICS** The area (in square centimeters) of a square coaster can be represented by $d^2 + 8d + 16$.

   a. Write an expression that represents the side length of the coaster.

   b. Write an expression for the perimeter of the coaster.

26. **MODELING WITH MATHEMATICS** The polynomial represents the area (in square feet) of the square playground.

   a. Write a polynomial that represents the side length of the playground.

$$A = x^2 - 30x + 225$$

   b. Write an expression for the perimeter of the playground.

In Exercises 27–34, solve the equation. *(See Example 4.)*

27. $z^2 - 4 = 0$

28. $4x^2 = 49$

29. $k^2 - 16k + 64 = 0$

30. $s^2 + 20s + 100 = 0$

31. $n^2 + 9 = 6n$

32. $y^2 = 12y - 36$

33. $y^2 + \frac{1}{2}y = -\frac{1}{16}$

34. $-\frac{4}{3}x + \frac{4}{9} = -x^2$

In Exercises 35–40, factor the polynomial.

35. $3z^2 - 27$

36. $2m^2 - 50$

37. $4y^2 - 16y + 16$

38. $8k^2 + 80k + 200$

39. $50y^2 + 120y + 72$

40. $27m^2 - 36m + 12$

41. MODELING WITH MATHEMATICS While standing on a ladder, you drop a paintbrush. The function represents the height y (in feet) of the paintbrush t seconds after it is dropped. After how many seconds does the paintbrush land on the ground? *(See Example 5.)*

$y = 25 - 16t^2$

42. MODELING WITH MATHEMATICS
The function represents the height y (in feet) of a grasshopper jumping straight up from the ground t seconds after the start of the jump. After how many seconds is the grasshopper 1 foot off the ground?

$y = -16t^2 + 8t$

43. REASONING Tell whether the polynomial can be factored. If not, change the constant term so that the polynomial is a perfect square trinomial.

    a. $w^2 + 18w + 84$ **b.** $y^2 - 10y + 23$

44. THOUGHT PROVOKING Use algebra tiles to factor each polynomial modeled by the tiles. Show your work.

45. COMPARING METHODS Describe two methods you can use to simplify $(2x - 5)^2 - (x - 4)^2$. Which one would you use? Explain.

46. HOW DO YOU SEE IT? The figure shows a large square with an area of a^2 that contains a smaller square with an area of b^2.

    a. Describe the regions that represent $a^2 - b^2$. How can you rearrange these regions to show that $a^2 - b^2 = (a + b)(a - b)$?

    b. How can you use the figure to show that $(a - b)^2 = a^2 - 2ab + b^2$?

47. PROBLEM SOLVING You hang nine identical square picture frames on a wall.

    a. Write a polynomial that represents the area of the picture frames, not including the pictures.

    b. The area in part (a) is 81 square inches. What is the side length of one of the picture frames? Explain your reasoning.

48. MATHEMATICAL CONNECTIONS The composite solid is made up of a cube and a rectangular prism.

    a. Write a polynomial that represents the volume of the composite solid.

    b. The volume of the composite solid is equal to $25x$. What is the value of x? Explain your reasoning.

Maintaining Mathematical Proficiency
Reviewing what you learned in previous grades and lessons

Write the prime factorization of the number. *(Skills Review Handbook)*

49. 50   **50.** 44   **51.** 85   **52.** 96

Find the inverse of the function. Then graph the function and its inverse. *(Section 1.3)*

53. $f(x) = x - 3$ **54.** $f(x) = -2x + 5$ **55.** $f(x) = \frac{1}{2}x - 1$

2.8 Factoring Polynomials Completely

Essential Question How can you factor a polynomial completely?

EXPLORATION 1 Writing a Product of Linear Factors

Work with a partner. Write the product represented by the algebra tiles. Then multiply to write the polynomial in standard form.

a. $(+ \ +)(+ \ +)(- \ -)$

b. $(+ \ + \ +)(+ \ +)(-)$

c. $(+ \ + \ + \ +)(+)(+ \ +)$

d. $(+ \ +)(+ \ -)(+)$

e. $(- \ +)(+ \ +)(-)$

f. $(- \ -)(+ \ +)(- \ -)$

REASONING ABSTRACTLY

To be proficient in math, you need to know and flexibly use different properties of operations and objects.

EXPLORATION 2 Matching Standard and Factored Forms

Work with a partner. Match the standard form of the polynomial with the equivalent factored form. Explain your strategy.

a. $x^3 + x^2$ **A.** $x(x + 1)(x - 1)$

b. $x^3 - x$ **B.** $x(x - 1)^2$

c. $x^3 + x^2 - 2x$ **C.** $x(x + 1)^2$

d. $x^3 - 4x^2 + 4x$ **D.** $x(x + 2)(x - 1)$

e. $x^3 - 2x^2 - 3x$ **E.** $x(x - 1)(x - 2)$

f. $x^3 - 2x^2 + x$ **F.** $x(x + 2)(x - 2)$

g. $x^3 - 4x$ **G.** $x(x - 2)^2$

h. $x^3 + 2x^2$ **H.** $x(x + 2)^2$

i. $x^3 - x^2$ **I.** $x^2(x - 1)$

j. $x^3 - 3x^2 + 2x$ **J.** $x^2(x + 1)$

k. $x^3 + 2x^2 - 3x$ **K.** $x^2(x - 2)$

l. $x^3 - 4x^2 + 3x$ **L.** $x^2(x + 2)$

m. $x^3 - 2x^2$ **M.** $x(x + 3)(x - 1)$

n. $x^3 + 4x^2 + 4x$ **N.** $x(x + 1)(x - 3)$

o. $x^3 + 2x^2 + x$ **O.** $x(x - 1)(x - 3)$

Communicate Your Answer

3. How can you factor a polynomial completely?

4. Use your answer to Question 3 to factor each polynomial completely.

     a. $x^3 + 4x^2 + 3x$ b. $x^3 - 6x^2 + 9x$ c. $x^3 + 6x^2 + 9x$

Core Vocabulary

factoring by grouping, *p. 108*
factored completely, *p. 108*

Previous
polynomial
binomial

What You Will Learn

▶ Factor polynomials by grouping.
▶ Factor polynomials completely.
▶ Use factoring to solve real-life problems.

Factoring Polynomials by Grouping

You have used the Distributive Property to factor out a greatest common monomial from a polynomial. Sometimes, you can factor out a common binomial. You may be able to use the Distributive Property to factor polynomials with four terms, as described below.

⟳ Core Concept

Factoring by Grouping

To factor a polynomial with four terms, group the terms into pairs. Factor the GCF out of each pair of terms. Look for and factor out the common binomial factor. This process is called **factoring by grouping**.

EXAMPLE 1   **Factoring by Grouping**

Factor each polynomial by grouping.

a. $x^3 + 3x^2 + 2x + 6$ **b.** $x^2 + y + x + xy$

SOLUTION

a. $x^3 + 3x^2 + 2x + 6 = (x^3 + 3x^2) + (2x + 6)$ Group terms with common factors.

⎡ Common binomial factor is $x + 3$. ⎤ ⟶ $= x^2(x + 3) + 2(x + 3)$ Factor out GCF of each pair of terms.

$= (x + 3)(x^2 + 2)$ Factor out $(x + 3)$.

▶ So, $x^3 + 3x^2 + 2x + 6 = (x + 3)(x^2 + 2)$.

b. $x^2 + y + x + xy = x^2 + x + xy + y$ Rewrite polynomial.

$= (x^2 + x) + (xy + y)$ Group terms with common factors.

⎡ Common binomial factor is $x + 1$. ⎤ ⟶ $= x(x + 1) + y(x + 1)$ Factor out GCF of each pair of terms.

$= (x + 1)(x + y)$ Factor out $(x + 1)$.

▶ So, $x^2 + y + x + xy = (x + 1)(x + y)$.

Monitoring Progress Help in English and Spanish at *BigIdeasMath.com*

Factor the polynomial by grouping.

1. $a^3 + 3a^2 + a + 3$ **2.** $y^2 + 2x + yx + 2y$

Factoring Polynomials Completely

You have seen that the polynomial $x^2 - 1$ can be factored as $(x + 1)(x - 1)$. This polynomial is factorable. Notice that the polynomial $x^2 + 1$ cannot be written as the product of polynomials with integer coefficients. This polynomial is unfactorable. A factorable polynomial with integer coefficients is **factored completely** when it is written as a product of unfactorable polynomials with integer coefficients.

Concept Summary

Guidelines for Factoring Polynomials Completely

To factor a polynomial completely, you should try each of these steps.

1. Factor out the greatest common monomial factor. $\qquad 3x^2 + 6x = 3x(x + 2)$

2. Look for a difference of two squares or a perfect square trinomial. $\qquad x^2 + 4x + 4 = (x + 2)^2$

3. Factor a trinomial of the form $ax^2 + bx + c$ into a product of binomial factors. $\qquad 3x^2 - 5x - 2 = (3x + 1)(x - 2)$

4. Factor a polynomial with four terms by grouping. $\qquad x^3 + x - 4x^2 - 4 = (x^2 + 1)(x - 4)$

EXAMPLE 2 **Factoring Completely**

Factor (a) $3x^3 + 6x^2 - 18x$ and (b) $7x^4 - 28x^2$.

SOLUTION

a. $3x^3 + 6x^2 - 18x = 3x(x^2 + 2x - 6)$ $\qquad$ Factor out $3x$.

$x^2 + 2x - 6$ is unfactorable, so the polynomial is factored completely.

▶ So, $3x^3 + 6x^2 - 18x = 3x(x^2 + 2x - 6)$.

b. $7x^4 - 28x^2 = 7x^2(x^2 - 4)$ $\qquad$ Factor out $7x^2$.

$\qquad\qquad\quad = 7x^2(x^2 - 2^2)$ $\qquad$ Write as $a^2 - b^2$.

$\qquad\qquad\quad = 7x^2(x + 2)(x - 2)$ $\qquad$ Difference of two squares pattern

▶ So, $7x^4 - 28x^2 = 7x^2(x + 2)(x - 2)$.

EXAMPLE 3 **Solving an Equation by Factoring Completely**

Solve $2x^3 + 8x^2 = 10x$.

SOLUTION

$\qquad\qquad 2x^3 + 8x^2 = 10x$ $\qquad$ Original equation

$\qquad\quad 2x^3 + 8x^2 - 10x = 0$ $\qquad$ Subtract $10x$ from each side.

$\qquad\qquad 2x(x^2 + 4x - 5) = 0$ $\qquad$ Factor out $2x$.

$\qquad\qquad 2x(x + 5)(x - 1) = 0$ $\qquad$ Factor $x^2 + 4x - 5$.

$2x = 0 \quad or \quad x + 5 = 0 \quad or \quad x - 1 = 0$ $\qquad$ Zero-Product Property

$x = 0 \quad or \qquad x = -5 \quad or \qquad x = 1$ $\qquad$ Solve for x.

▶ The roots are $x = -5$, $x = 0$, and $x = 1$.

Monitoring Progress Help in English and Spanish at *BigIdeasMath.com*

Factor the polynomial completely.

3. $3x^3 - 12x$ $\qquad$ **4.** $2y^3 - 12y^2 + 18y$ $\qquad$ **5.** $m^3 - 2m^2 - 8m$

Solve the equation.

6. $w^3 - 8w^2 + 16w = 0$ $\qquad$ **7.** $x^3 - 25x = 0$ $\qquad$ **8.** $c^3 - 7c^2 + 12c = 0$

Solving Real-Life Problems

(w + 4) in.

(36 − w) in.   w in.

EXAMPLE 4   **Modeling with Mathematics**

A terrarium in the shape of a rectangular prism has a volume of 4608 cubic inches. Its length is more than 10 inches. The dimensions of the terrarium in terms of its width are shown. Find the length, width, and height of the terrarium.

SOLUTION

1. **Understand the Problem** You are given the volume of a terrarium in the shape of a rectangular prism and a description of the length. The dimensions are written in terms of its width. You are asked to find the length, width, and height of the terrarium.

2. **Make a Plan** Use the formula for the volume of a rectangular prism to write and solve an equation for the width of the terrarium. Then substitute that value in the expressions for the length and height of the terrarium.

3. **Solve the Problem**

Volume = length • width • height	Volume of a rectangular prism
$4608 = (36 − w)(w)(w + 4)$	Write equation.
$4608 = 32w^2 + 144w − w^3$	Multiply.
$0 = 32w^2 + 144w − w^3 − 4608$	Subtract 4608 from each side.
$0 = (−w^3 + 32w^2) + (144w − 4608)$	Group terms with common factors.
$0 = −w^2(w − 32) + 144(w − 32)$	Factor out GCF of each pair of terms.
$0 = (w − 32)(−w^2 + 144)$	Factor out $(w − 32)$.
$0 = −1(w − 32)(w^2 − 144)$	Factor −1 from $−w^2 + 144$.
$0 = −1(w − 32)(w − 12)(w + 12)$	Difference of two squares pattern
$w − 32 = 0$ *or* $w − 12 = 0$ *or* $w + 12 = 0$	Zero-Product Property
$w = 32$ *or* $w = 12$ *or* $w = −12$	Solve for w.

Disregard $w = −12$ because a negative width does not make sense. You know that the length is more than 10 inches. Test the solutions of the equation, 12 and 32, in the expression for the length.

length = $36 − w = 36 − 12 = 24$ ✓ *or* length = $36 − w = 36 − 32 = 4$ ✗

The solution 12 gives a length of 24 inches, so 12 is the correct value of w.

Use $w = 12$ to find the height, as shown.

height = $w + 4 = 12 + 4 = 16$

▶ The width is 12 inches, the length is 24 inches, and the height is 16 inches.

Check

$V = \ell w h$

$4608 \overset{?}{=} 24(12)(16)$

$4608 = 4608$ ✓

4. **Look Back** Check your solution. Substitute the values for the length, width, and height when the width is 12 inches into the formula for volume. The volume of the terrarium should be 4608 cubic inches.

Monitoring Progress   Help in English and Spanish at *BigIdeasMath.com*

9. A box in the shape of a rectangular prism has a volume of 72 cubic feet. The box has a length of x feet, a width of $(x − 1)$ feet, and a height of $(x + 9)$ feet. Find the dimensions of the box.

Vocabulary and Core Concept Check

1. VOCABULARY What does it mean for a polynomial to be factored completely?

2. WRITING Explain how to choose which terms to group together when factoring by grouping.

Monitoring Progress and Modeling with Mathematics

In Exercises 3–10, factor the polynomial by grouping.
(See Example 1.)

3. $x^3 + x^2 + 2x + 2$ **4.** $y^3 - 9y^2 + y - 9$

5. $3z^3 + 2z - 12z^2 - 8$ **6.** $2s^3 - 27 - 18s + 3s^2$

7. $x^2 + xy + 8x + 8y$ **8.** $q^2 + q + 5pq + 5p$

9. $m^2 - 3m + mn - 3n$ **10.** $2a^2 + 8ab - 3a - 12b$

In Exercises 11–22, factor the polynomial completely.
(See Example 2.)

11. $2x^3 - 2x$ **12.** $36a^4 - 4a^2$

13. $2c^2 - 7c + 19$ **14.** $m^2 - 5m - 35$

15. $6g^3 - 24g^2 + 24g$ **16.** $-15d^3 + 21d^2 - 6d$

17. $3r^5 + 3r^4 - 90r^3$ **18.** $5w^4 - 40w^3 + 80w^2$

19. $-4c^4 + 8c^3 - 28c^2$ **20.** $8t^2 + 8t - 72$

21. $b^3 - 5b^2 - 4b + 20$ **22.** $h^3 + 4h^2 - 25h - 100$

In Exercises 23–28, solve the equation. *(See Example 3.)*

23. $5n^3 - 30n^2 + 40n = 0$ **24.** $k^4 - 100k^2 = 0$

25. $x^3 + x^2 = 4x + 4$ **26.** $2t^5 + 2t^4 - 144t^3 = 0$

27. $12s - 3s^3 = 0$ **28.** $4y^3 - 7y^2 + 28 = 16y$

In Exercises 29–32, find the *x*-coordinates of the points where the graph crosses the *x*-axis.

29.

$y = x^3 - 81x$

30.

$y = -3x^4 - 24x^3 - 45x^2$

31.

$y = -2x^4 + 16x^3 - 32x^2$

32.

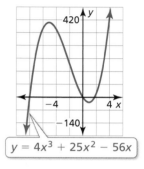

$y = 4x^3 + 25x^2 - 56x$

ERROR ANALYSIS In Exercises 33 and 34, describe and correct the error in factoring the polynomial completely.

33.

$$a^3 + 8a^2 - 6a - 48 = a^2(a + 8) + 6(a + 8)$$
$$= (a + 8)(a^2 + 6)$$

34.

$$x^3 - 6x^2 - 9x + 54 = x^2(x - 6) - 9(x - 6)$$
$$= (x - 6)(x^2 - 9)$$

35. MODELING WITH MATHEMATICS
You are building a birdhouse in the shape of a rectangular prism that has a volume of 128 cubic inches. The dimensions of the birdhouse in terms of its width are shown.
(See Example 4.)

$(w + 4)$ in.

w in.   4 in.

a. Write a polynomial that represents the volume of the birdhouse.

b. What are the dimensions of the birdhouse?

36. MODELING WITH MATHEMATICS A gift bag shaped like a rectangular prism has a volume of 1152 cubic inches. The dimensions of the gift bag in terms of its width are shown. The height is greater than the width. What are the dimensions of the gift bag?

$(18 - w)$ in.

$(2w + 4)$ in. w in.

In Exercises 37–40, factor the polynomial completely.

37. $x^3 + 2x^2y - x - 2y$ **38.** $8b^3 - 4b^2a - 18b + 9a$

39. $4s^2 - s + 12st - 3t$

40. $6m^3 - 12mn + m^2n - 2n^2$

41. WRITING Is it possible to find three real solutions of the equation $x^3 + 2x^2 + 3x + 6 = 0$? Explain your reasoning.

42. HOW DO YOU SEE IT? How can you use the factored form of the polynomial
$x^4 - 2x^3 - 9x^2 + 18x = x(x - 3)(x + 3)(x - 2)$
to find the x-intercepts of the graph of the function?

$y = x^4 - 2x^3 - 9x^2 + 18x$

43. OPEN-ENDED Write a polynomial of degree 3 that satisfies each of the given conditions.

  a. is not factorable   **b.** can be factored by grouping

44. MAKING AN ARGUMENT Your friend says that if a trinomial cannot be factored as the product of two binomials, then the trinomial is factored completely. Is your friend correct? Explain.

45. PROBLEM SOLVING The volume (in cubic feet) of a room in the shape of a rectangular prism is represented by $12z^3 - 27z$. Find expressions that could represent the dimensions of the room.

46. MATHEMATICAL CONNECTIONS The width of a box in the shape of a rectangular prism is 4 inches more than the height h. The length is the difference of 9 inches and the height.

  a. Write a polynomial that represents the volume of the box in terms of its height (in inches).

  b. The volume of the box is 180 cubic inches. What are the possible dimensions of the box?

  c. Which dimensions result in a box with the least possible surface area? Explain your reasoning.

47. MATHEMATICAL CONNECTIONS The volume of a cylinder is given by $V = \pi r^2 h$, where r is the radius of the base of the cylinder and h is the height of the cylinder. Find the dimensions of the cylinder.

Volume $= 25h\pi$ h

$h - 3$

48. THOUGHT PROVOKING Factor the polynomial
$x^5 - x^4 - 5x^3 + 5x^2 + 4x - 4$ completely.

49. REASONING Find a value for w so that the equation has (a) two solutions and (b) three solutions. Explain your reasoning.

$$5x^3 + wx^2 + 80x = 0$$

Maintaining Mathematical Proficiency   Reviewing what you learned in previous grades and lessons

Solve the system of linear equations by graphing. *(Skills Review Handbook)*

50. $y = x - 4$
    $y = -2x + 2$

51. $y = \frac{1}{2}x + 2$
    $y = 3x - 3$

52. $5x - y = 12$
    $\frac{1}{4}x + y = 9$

53. $x = 3y$
    $y - 10 = 2x$

Determine whether the function represents *exponential growth* or *exponential decay*. *(Section 1.6)*

54. $y = \left(\frac{4}{3}\right)^x$

55. $y = 5(0.95)^x$

56. $f(x) = (2.3)^{x-2}$

57. $f(x) = 50(1.1)^{3x}$

Core Vocabulary

factoring by grouping, *p. 108*
factored completely, *p. 108*

Core Concepts

Section 2.5

Factoring $x^2 + bx + c$ When c Is Positive, *p. 90*
Factoring $x^2 + bx + c$ When c Is Negative, *p. 91*

Section 2.6

Factoring $ax^2 + bx + c$ When ac Is Positive, *p. 96*
Factoring $ax^2 + bx + c$ When ac Is Negative, *p. 97*

Section 2.7

Difference of Two Squares Pattern, *p. 102*
Perfect Square Trinomial Pattern, *p. 103*

Section 2.8

Factoring by Grouping, *p. 108*
Factoring Polynomials Completely, *p. 108*

Mathematical Practices

1. How are the solutions of Exercise 29 on page 93 related to the graph
   of $y = m^2 + 3m + 2$?

2. The equation in part (b) of Exercise 47 on page 94 has two solutions. Are both solutions
   of the equation reasonable in the context of the problem? Explain your reasoning.

Performance Task:

Flight Path of a Bird

Some birds, like parrots, have strong, large beaks to break
open nuts and shells. But other birds, like crows, crack open
their food by dropping it to the ground. How can a bird
change its flight path to protect its falling food from
other hungry birds?

To explore the answer to this question and
more, check out the Performance Task and
Real-Life STEM video at *BigIdeasMath.com*.

2.1 Adding and Subtracting Polynomials *(pp. 61–68)*

Find $(2x^3 + 6x^2 - x) - (-3x^3 - 2x^2 - 9x)$.

$$(2x^3 + 6x^2 - x) - (-3x^3 - 2x^2 - 9x) = (2x^3 + 6x^2 - x) + (3x^3 + 2x^2 + 9x)$$
$$= (2x^3 + 3x^3) + (6x^2 + 2x^2) + (-x + 9x)$$
$$= 5x^3 + 8x^2 + 8x$$

Write the polynomial in standard form. Identify the degree and leading coefficient of the polynomial. Then classify the polynomial by the number of terms.

1. $6 + 2x^2$ **2.** $-3p^3 + 5p^6 - 4$ **3.** $9x^7 - 6x^2 + 13x^5$ **4.** $-12y + 8y^3$

Find the sum or difference.

5. $(3a + 7) + (a - 1)$ **6.** $(x^2 + 6x - 5) + (2x^2 + 15)$

7. $(-y^2 + y + 2) - (y^2 - 5y - 2)$ **8.** $(p + 7) - (6p^2 + 13p)$

2.2 Multiplying Polynomials *(pp. 69–74)*

Find $(x + 7)(x - 9)$.

$$(x + 7)(x - 9) = x(x - 9) + 7(x - 9)$$ Distribute $(x - 9)$ to each term of $(x + 7)$.
$$= x(x) + x(-9) + 7(x) + 7(-9)$$ Distributive Property
$$= x^2 + (-9x) + 7x + (-63)$$ Multiply.
$$= x^2 - 2x - 63$$ Combine like terms.

Find the product.

9. $(x + 6)(x - 4)$ **10.** $(y - 5)(3y + 8)$ **11.** $(x + 4)(x^2 + 7x)$ **12.** $(-3y + 1)(4y^2 - y - 7)$

2.3 Special Products of Polynomials *(pp. 75–80)*

Find each product.

a. $(6x + 4y)^2$

$$(6x + 4y)^2 = (6x)^2 + 2(6x)(4y) + (4y)^2$$ Square of a binomial pattern
$$= 36x^2 + 48xy + 16y^2$$ Simplify.

b. $(2x + 3y)(2x - 3y)$

$$(2x + 3y)(2x - 3y) = (2x)^2 - (3y)^2$$ Sum and difference pattern
$$= 4x^2 - 9y^2$$ Simplify.

Find the product.

13. $(x + 9)(x - 9)$ **14.** $(2y + 4)(2y - 4)$ **15.** $(p + 4)^2$ **16.** $(-1 + 2d)^2$

2.4 Solving Polynomial Equations in Factored Form *(pp. 81–86)*

Solve $(x + 6)(x - 8) = 0$.

$(x + 6)(x - 8) = 0$	Write equation.
$x + 6 = 0 \quad or \quad x - 8 = 0$	Zero-Product Property
$x = -6 \quad or \quad x = 8$	Solve for x.

Solve the equation.

17. $x^2 + 5x = 0$ **18.** $(z + 3)(z - 7) = 0$ **19.** $(b + 13)^2 = 0$ **20.** $2y(y - 9)(y + 4) = 0$

2.5 Factoring $x^2 + bx + c$ *(pp. 89–94)*

Factor $x^2 + 6x - 27$.

Notice that $b = 6$ and $c = -27$. Because c is negative, the factors p and q must have different signs so that pq is negative.

Find two integer factors of -27 whose sum is 6.

Factors of −27	−27, 1	−1, 27	−9, 3	−3, 9
Sum of factors	−26	26	−6	6

The values of p and q are -3 and 9.

▶ So, $x^2 + 6x - 27 = (x - 3)(x + 9)$.

Factor the polynomial.

21. $p^2 + 2p - 35$ **22.** $b^2 + 18b + 80$ **23.** $z^2 - 4z - 21$ **24.** $x^2 - 11x + 28$

2.6 Factoring $ax^2 + bx + c$ *(pp. 95–100)*

Factor $5x^2 + 36x + 7$.

There is no GCF, so you need to consider the possible factors of a and c. Because b and c are both positive, the factors of c must be positive. Use a table to organize information about the factors of a and c.

Factors of 5	Factors of 7	Possible factorization	Middle term	
1, 5	1, 7	$(x + 1)(5x + 7)$	$7x + 5x = 12x$	✗
1, 5	7, 1	$(x + 7)(5x + 1)$	$x + 35x = 36x$	✓

▶ So, $5x^2 + 36x + 7 = (x + 7)(5x + 1)$.

Factor the polynomial.

25. $3t^2 + 16t - 12$ **26.** $-5y^2 - 22y - 8$ **27.** $6x^2 + 17x + 7$

28. $-2y^2 + 7y - 6$ **29.** $3z^2 + 26z - 9$ **30.** $10a^2 - 13a - 3$

2.7 **Factoring Special Products** *(pp. 101–106)*

Factor each polynomial.

a. $x^2 - 16$

$$x^2 - 16 = x^2 - 4^2 \qquad \text{Write as } a^2 - b^2.$$
$$= (x + 4)(x - 4) \qquad \text{Difference of two squares pattern}$$

b. $25x^2 - 30x + 9$

$$25x^2 - 30x + 9 = (5x)^2 - 2(5x)(3) + 3^2 \qquad \text{Write as } a^2 - 2ab + b^2.$$
$$= (5x - 3)^2 \qquad \text{Perfect square trinomial pattern}$$

Factor the polynomial.

31. $x^2 - 9$ **32.** $y^2 - 100$ **33.** $z^2 - 6z + 9$ **34.** $m^2 + 16m + 64$

2.8 **Factoring Polynomials Completely** *(pp. 107–112)*

Factor each polynomial completely.

a. $x^3 + 4x^2 - 3x - 12$

$$x^3 + 4x^2 - 3x - 12 = (x^3 + 4x^2) + (-3x - 12) \qquad \text{Group terms with common factors.}$$
$$= x^2(x + 4) + (-3)(x + 4) \qquad \text{Factor out GCF of each pair of terms.}$$
$$= (x + 4)(x^2 - 3) \qquad \text{Factor out } (x + 4).$$

b. $2x^4 - 8x^2$

$$2x^4 - 8x^2 = 2x^2(x^2 - 4) \qquad \text{Factor out } 2x^2.$$
$$= 2x^2(x^2 - 2^2) \qquad \text{Write as } a^2 - b^2.$$
$$= 2x^2(x + 2)(x - 2) \qquad \text{Difference of two squares pattern}$$

c. $2x^3 + 18x^2 - 72x$

$$2x^3 + 18x^2 - 72x = 2x(x^2 + 9x - 36) \qquad \text{Factor out } 2x.$$
$$= 2x(x + 12)(x - 3) \qquad \text{Factor } x^2 + 9x - 36.$$

Factor the polynomial completely.

35. $n^3 - 9n$ **36.** $x^2 - 3x + 4ax - 12a$ **37.** $2x^4 + 2x^3 - 20x^2$

Solve the equation.

38. $3x^3 - 9x^2 - 54x = 0$ **39.** $16x^2 - 36 = 0$ **40.** $z^3 + 3z^2 - 25z - 75 = 0$

41. A box in the shape of a rectangular prism has a volume of 96 cubic feet. The box has a length of $(x + 8)$ feet, a width of x feet, and a height of $(x - 2)$ feet. Find the dimensions of the box.

Find the sum or difference. Then identify the degree of the sum or difference and classify it by the number of terms.

1. $(-2p + 4) - (p^2 - 6p + 8)$

2. $(9c^6 - 5b^4) - (4c^6 - 5b^4)$

3. $(4s^4 + 2st + t) + (2s^4 - 2st - 4t)$

Find the product.

4. $(h - 5)(h - 8)$

5. $(2w - 3)(3w + 5)$

6. $(z + 11)(z - 11)$

7. Explain how you can determine whether a polynomial is a perfect square trinomial.

8. Is 18 a polynomial? Explain your reasoning.

Factor the polynomial completely.

9. $s^2 - 15s + 50$

10. $h^3 + 2h^2 - 9h - 18$

11. $-5k^2 - 22k + 15$

Solve the equation.

12. $(n - 1)(n + 6)(n + 5) = 0$

13. $d^2 + 14d + 49 = 0$

14. $6x^4 + 8x^2 = 26x^3$

15. The expression $\pi(r - 3)^2$ represents the area covered by the hour hand on a clock in one rotation, where r is the radius of the entire clock. Write a polynomial in standard form that represents the area covered by the hour hand in one rotation.

16. A magician's stage has a trapdoor.

    a. The total area (in square feet) of the stage can be represented by $x^2 + 27x + 176$. Write an expression for the width of the stage.

    b. Write an expression for the perimeter of the stage.

    c. The area of the trapdoor is 10 square feet. Find the value of x.

    d. The magician wishes to have the area of the stage be at least 20 times the area of the trapdoor. Does this stage satisfy his requirement? Explain.

$\left(x + \frac{1}{2}\right)$ ft

2x ft

(x + 16) ft

17. Write a polynomial equation in factored form that has three positive roots.

18. You are jumping on a trampoline. For one jump, your height y (in feet) above the trampoline after t seconds can be represented by $y = -16t^2 + 24t$. How many seconds are you in the air?

19. A cardboard box in the shape of a rectangular prism has the dimensions shown.

    a. Write a polynomial that represents the volume of the box.

    b. The volume of the box is 60 cubic inches. What are the length, width, and height of the box?

(x − 1) in.

(x − 2) in.

(x + 6) in.

1. Classify each polynomial by the number of terms. Then order the polynomials by degree from least to greatest.

   a. $-4x^3$

   b. $6y - 3y^5$

   c. $c^2 + 2 + c$

   d. $-10d^4 + 7d^2$

   e. $-5z^{11} + 8z^{12}$

   f. $3b^6 - 12b^8 + 4b^4$

2. Which exponential function has the greatest percent rate of change?

   (A) $f(x) = 4(2.5)^{x/3}$

   (B)

x	0	1	2	3	4
g(x)	8	12	18	27	40.5

   (C)

   (D) An exponential function j models a relationship in which the dependent variable is multiplied by 6 for every 1 unit the independent variable increases. The value of the function at 0 is 2.

3. Find the x-coordinates of the points where the graph of $f(x) = x^2 - 2x - 24$ crosses the x-axis.

   | -24 | -6 | -4 | -2 | -1 | 0 | 1 | 2 | 4 | 6 | 24 |

4. The table shows your distances from a national park over time.

   a. Write and graph an absolute value function that represents the distance as a function of the number of hours.

   b. When do you reach the national park? Explain.

   c. Write the function in part (a) as a piecewise function.

Hours, x	Distance (miles), y
1	195
2	130
3	65
4	0
5	65
6	130
7	195

5. Which function has a steeper graph, $f(x) = 2x - 3$ or the inverse of f? Explain your reasoning.

6. Which expressions are equivalent to $-2x + 15x^2 - 8$?

$15x^2 - 2x - 8$	$(5x + 4)(3x + 2)$
$(5x - 4)(3x + 2)$	$15x^2 + 2x - 8$
$(3x - 2)(5x - 4)$	$(3x + 2)(5x - 4)$

7. The graph represents an exponential function.

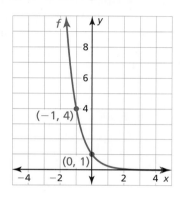

a. Write the function.

b. Find $f\left(\frac{1}{2}\right)$ and $f\left(-\frac{5}{2}\right)$.

8. Which polynomial represents the product of $3x + 1$ and $4x - 1$?

A $7x - 1$

B $12x^2 - 1$

C $12x^2 - x - 1$

D $12x^2 + x - 1$

9. You are playing miniature golf on the hole shown.

a. Write a polynomial that represents the area of the golf hole.

b. Write a polynomial that represents the perimeter of the golf hole.

c. Find the perimeter of the golf hole when the area is 216 square feet.

3 Graphing Quadratic Functions

Breathing Rates *(p. 177)*

SEE the Big Idea

Electricity-Generating Dish *(p. 165)*

Roller Coaster *(p. 152)*

Firework Explosion *(p. 141)*

Garden Waterfalls *(p. 134)*

Maintaining Mathematical Proficiency

Graphing Linear Equations

Example 1 Graph $y = -x - 1$.

Step 1 Make a table of values.

x	$y = -x - 1$	y	(x, y)
-1	$y = -(-1) - 1$	0	$(-1, 0)$
0	$y = -(0) - 1$	-1	$(0, -1)$
1	$y = -(1) - 1$	-2	$(1, -2)$
2	$y = -(2) - 1$	-3	$(2, -3)$

Step 2 Plot the ordered pairs.

Step 3 Draw a line through the points.

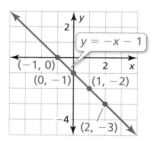

Graph the linear equation.

1. $y = 2x - 3$

2. $y = -3x + 4$

3. $y = -\frac{1}{2}x - 2$

4. $y = x + 5$

Evaluating Expressions

Example 2 Evaluate $2x^2 + 3x - 5$ when $x = -1$.

$$2x^2 + 3x - 5 = 2(-1)^2 + 3(-1) - 5 \qquad \text{Substitute } -1 \text{ for } x.$$
$$= 2(1) + 3(-1) - 5 \qquad \text{Evaluate the power.}$$
$$= 2 - 3 - 5 \qquad \text{Multiply.}$$
$$= -6 \qquad \text{Subtract.}$$

Evaluate the expression when $x = -2$.

5. $5x^2 - 9$

6. $3x^2 + x - 2$

7. $-x^2 + 4x + 1$

8. $x^2 + 8x + 5$

9. $-2x^2 - 4x + 3$

10. $-4x^2 + 2x - 6$

11. ABSTRACT REASONING Complete the table. Find a pattern in the differences of consecutive y-values. Use the pattern to write an expression for y when $x = 6$.

x	1	2	3	4	5
$y = ax^2$					

Mathematical Practices

Mathematically proficient students try special cases of the original problem to gain insight into its solution.

Problem-Solving Strategies

⑤ Core Concept

Trying Special Cases

When solving a problem in mathematics, it can be helpful to try special cases of the original problem. For instance, in this chapter, you will learn to graph a quadratic function of the form $f(x) = ax^2 + bx + c$. The problem-solving strategy used is to first graph quadratic functions of the form $f(x) = ax^2$. From there, you progress to other forms of quadratic functions.

$f(x) = ax^2$	Section 3.1
$f(x) = ax^2 + c$	Section 3.2
$f(x) = ax^2 + bx + c$	Section 3.3
$f(x) = a(x - h)^2 + k$	Section 3.4
$f(x) = a(x - p)(x - q)$	Section 3.5

EXAMPLE 1   Graphing the Parent Quadratic Function

Graph the parent quadratic function $y = x^2$. Then describe its graph.

SOLUTION

The function is of the form $y = ax^2$, where $a = 1$. By plotting several points, you can see that the graph is U-shaped, as shown.

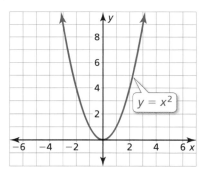

▶ The graph opens up, and the lowest point is at the origin.

Monitoring Progress

Graph the quadratic function. Then describe its graph.

1. $y = -x^2$
2. $y = 2x^2$
3. $f(x) = 2x^2 + 1$
4. $f(x) = 2x^2 - 1$

5. $f(x) = \frac{1}{2}x^2 + 4x + 3$
6. $f(x) = \frac{1}{2}x^2 - 4x + 3$
7. $y = -2(x + 1)^2 + 1$
8. $y = -2(x - 1)^2 + 1$

9. How are the graphs in Monitoring Progress Questions 1−8 similar? How are they different?

3.1 Graphing $f(x) = ax^2$

Essential Question What are some of the characteristics of the graph of a quadratic function of the form $f(x) = ax^2$?

> **EXPLORATION 1** Graphing Quadratic Functions

Work with a partner. Graph each quadratic function. Compare each graph to the graph of $f(x) = x^2$.

a. $g(x) = 3x^2$

b. $g(x) = -5x^2$

c. $g(x) = -0.2x^2$

d. $g(x) = \frac{1}{10}x^2$

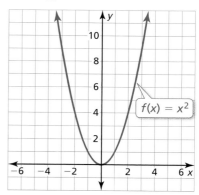

REASONING QUANTITATIVELY

To be proficient in math, you need to make sense of quantities and their relationships in problem situations.

Communicate Your Answer

2. What are some of the characteristics of the graph of a quadratic function of the form $f(x) = ax^2$?

3. How does the value of a affect the graph of $f(x) = ax^2$? Consider $0 < a < 1$, $a > 1$, $-1 < a < 0$, and $a < -1$. Use a graphing calculator to verify your answers.

4. The figure shows the graph of a quadratic function of the form $y = ax^2$. Which of the intervals in Question 3 describes the value of a? Explain your reasoning.

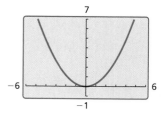

What You Will Learn

▶ Identify characteristics of quadratic functions.

▶ Graph and use quadratic functions of the form $f(x) = ax^2$.

Core Vocabulary

quadratic function, *p. 124*
parabola, *p. 124*
vertex, *p. 124*
axis of symmetry, *p. 124*

Previous
domain
range
vertical shrink
vertical stretch
reflection

Identifying Characteristics of Quadratic Functions

A **quadratic function** is a nonlinear function that can be written in the standard form $y = ax^2 + bx + c$, where $a \neq 0$. The U-shaped graph of a quadratic function is called a **parabola**. In this lesson, you will graph quadratic functions, where b and c equal 0.

🔄 Core Concept

Characteristics of Quadratic Functions

The *parent quadratic function* is $f(x) = x^2$. The graphs of all other quadratic functions are *transformations* of the graph of the parent quadratic function.

REMEMBER

The notation $f(x)$ is another name for y.

The lowest point on a parabola that opens up or the highest point on a parabola that opens down is the **vertex**. The vertex of the graph of $f(x) = x^2$ is (0, 0).

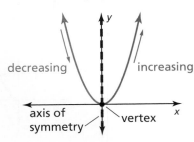

The vertical line that divides the parabola into two symmetric parts is the **axis of symmetry**. The axis of symmetry passes through the vertex. For the graph of $f(x) = x^2$, the axis of symmetry is the y-axis, or $x = 0$.

EXAMPLE 1   **Identifying Characteristics of a Quadratic Function**

Consider the graph of the quadratic function.

Using the graph, you can identify characteristics such as the vertex, axis of symmetry, and the behavior of the graph, as shown.

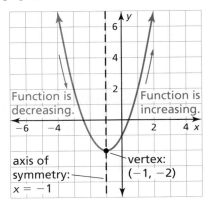

You can also determine the following:

• The domain is all real numbers.

• The range is all real numbers greater than or equal to -2.

• When $x < -1$, y increases as x decreases.

• When $x > -1$, y increases as x increases.

Identify characteristics of the quadratic function and its graph.

1.

2.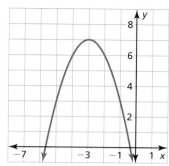

REMEMBER

The graph of $y = a \cdot f(x)$ is a vertical stretch or shrink by a factor of a of the graph of $y = f(x)$.

The graph of $y = -f(x)$ is a reflection in the x-axis of the graph of $y = f(x)$.

Graphing and Using $f(x) = ax^2$

Core Concept

Graphing $f(x) = ax^2$ When $a > 0$

- When $0 < a < 1$, the graph of $f(x) = ax^2$ is a vertical shrink of the graph of $f(x) = x^2$.

- When $a > 1$, the graph of $f(x) = ax^2$ is a vertical stretch of the graph of $f(x) = x^2$.

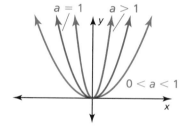

Graphing $f(x) = ax^2$ When $a < 0$

- When $-1 < a < 0$, the graph of $f(x) = ax^2$ is a vertical shrink with a reflection in the x-axis of the graph of $f(x) = x^2$.

- When $a < -1$, the graph of $f(x) = ax^2$ is a vertical stretch with a reflection in the x-axis of the graph of $f(x) = x^2$.

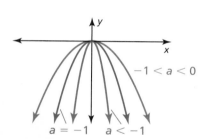

EXAMPLE 2 Graphing $y = ax^2$ When $a > 0$

Graph $g(x) = 2x^2$. Compare the graph to the graph of $f(x) = x^2$.

SOLUTION

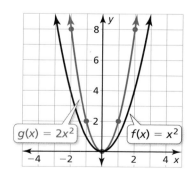

Step 1 Make a table of values.

x	-2	-1	0	1	2
$g(x)$	8	2	0	2	8

Step 2 Plot the ordered pairs.

Step 3 Draw a smooth curve through the points.

▶ Both graphs open up and have the same vertex, $(0, 0)$, and the same axis of symmetry, $x = 0$. The graph of g is narrower than the graph of f because the graph of g is a vertical stretch by a factor of 2 of the graph of f.

EXAMPLE 3 Graphing $y = ax^2$ When $a < 0$

Graph $h(x) = -\frac{1}{3}x^2$. Compare the graph to the graph of $f(x) = x^2$.

SOLUTION

Step 1 Make a table of values.

x	-6	-3	0	3	6
$h(x)$	-12	-3	0	-3	-12

Step 2 Plot the ordered pairs.

Step 3 Draw a smooth curve through the points.

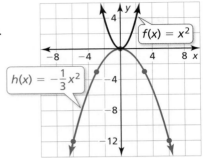

▶ The graphs have the same vertex, $(0, 0)$, and the same axis of symmetry, $x = 0$, but the graph of h opens down and is wider than the graph of f. So, the graph of h is a vertical shrink by a factor of $\frac{1}{3}$ and a reflection in the x-axis of the graph of f.

Monitoring Progress Help in English and Spanish at *BigIdeasMath.com*

Graph the function. Compare the graph to the graph of $f(x) = x^2$.

3. $g(x) = 5x^2$

4. $h(x) = \frac{1}{3}x^2$

5. $n(x) = \frac{3}{2}x^2$

6. $p(x) = -3x^2$

7. $q(x) = -0.1x^2$

8. $g(x) = -\frac{1}{4}x^2$

EXAMPLE 4 Solving a Real-Life Problem

The diagram at the left shows the cross section of a satellite dish, where x and y are measured in meters. Find the width and depth of the dish.

SOLUTION

Use the domain of the function to find the width of the dish. Use the range to find the depth.

The leftmost point on the graph is $(-2, 1)$, and the rightmost point is $(2, 1)$. So, the domain is $-2 \leq x \leq 2$, which represents 4 meters.

The lowest point on the graph is $(0, 0)$, and the highest points on the graph are $(-2, 1)$ and $(2, 1)$. So, the range is $0 \leq y \leq 1$, which represents 1 meter.

▶ So, the satellite dish is 4 meters wide and 1 meter deep.

Monitoring Progress Help in English and Spanish at *BigIdeasMath.com*

9. The cross section of a spotlight can be modeled by the graph of $y = 0.5x^2$, where x and y are measured in inches and $-2 \leq x \leq 2$. Find the width and depth of the spotlight.

Vocabulary and Core Concept Check

1. **VOCABULARY** What is the U-shaped graph of a quadratic function called?

2. **WRITING** When does the graph of a quadratic function open up? open down?

Monitoring Progress and Modeling with Mathematics

In Exercises 3 and 4, identify characteristics of the quadratic function and its graph. *(See Example 1.)*

3.

4.

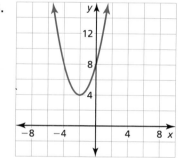

In Exercises 5–12, graph the function. Compare the graph to the graph of $f(x) = x^2$. *(See Examples 2 and 3.)*

5. $g(x) = 6x^2$

6. $b(x) = 2.5x^2$

7. $h(x) = \frac{1}{4}x^2$

8. $j(x) = 0.75x^2$

9. $m(x) = -2x^2$

10. $q(x) = -\frac{9}{2}x^2$

11. $k(x) = -0.2x^2$

12. $p(x) = -\frac{2}{3}x^2$

In Exercises 13–16, use a graphing calculator to graph the function. Compare the graph to the graph of $y = -4x^2$.

13. $y = 4x^2$

14. $y = -0.4x^2$

15. $y = -0.04x^2$

16. $y = -0.004x^2$

17. **ERROR ANALYSIS** Describe and correct the error in graphing and comparing $y = x^2$ and $y = 0.5x^2$.

The graphs have the same vertex and the same axis of symmetry. The graph of $y = 0.5x^2$ is narrower than the graph of $y = x^2$.

18. **MODELING WITH MATHEMATICS** The arch support of a bridge can be modeled by $y = -0.0012x^2$, where x and y are measured in feet. Find the height and width of the arch. *(See Example 4.)*

19. **PROBLEM SOLVING** The breaking strength z (in pounds) of a manila rope can be modeled by $z = 8900d^2$, where d is the diameter (in inches) of the rope.

   a. Describe the domain and range of the function.

   b. Graph the function using the domain in part (a).

   c. A manila rope has four times the breaking strength of another manila rope. Does the stronger rope have four times the diameter? Explain.

20. HOW DO YOU SEE IT? Describe the possible values of a.

a.

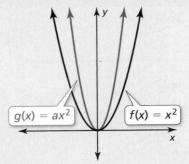

$g(x) = ax^2$ $f(x) = x^2$

b.

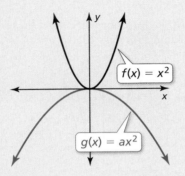

$f(x) = x^2$

$g(x) = ax^2$

ANALYZING GRAPHS In Exercises 21–23, use the graph.

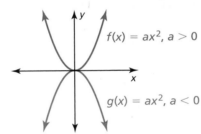

$f(x) = ax^2, a > 0$

$g(x) = ax^2, a < 0$

21. When is each function increasing?

22. When is each function decreasing?

23. Which function could include the point $(-2, 3)$? Find the value of a when the graph passes through $(-2, 3)$.

24. REASONING Is the x-intercept of the graph of $y = ax^2$ always 0? Justify your answer.

25. REASONING A parabola opens up and passes through $(-4, 2)$ and $(6, -3)$. How do you know that $(-4, 2)$ is not the vertex?

ABSTRACT REASONING In Exercises 26–29, determine whether the statement is *always*, *sometimes*, or *never* true. Explain your reasoning.

26. The graph of $f(x) = ax^2$ is narrower than the graph of $g(x) = x^2$ when $a > 0$.

27. The graph of $f(x) = ax^2$ is narrower than the graph of $g(x) = x^2$ when $|a| > 1$.

28. The graph of $f(x) = ax^2$ is wider than the graph of $g(x) = x^2$ when $0 < |a| < 1$.

29. The graph of $f(x) = ax^2$ is wider than the graph of $g(x) = dx^2$ when $|a| > |d|$.

30. THOUGHT PROVOKING Draw the isosceles triangle shown. Divide each leg into eight congruent segments. Connect the highest point of one leg with the lowest point of the other leg. Then connect the second highest point of one leg to the second lowest point of the other leg. Continue this process. Write a quadratic function whose graph models the shape that appears.

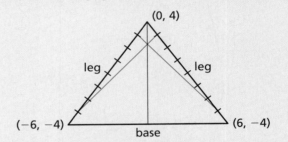

(0, 4)

leg   leg

$(-6, -4)$ base $(6, -4)$

31. MAKING AN ARGUMENT The diagram shows the parabolic cross section of a swirling glass of water, where x and y are measured in centimeters.

$(-4, 3.2)$ $(4, 3.2)$

$(0, 0)$

a. About how wide is the mouth of the glass?

b. Your friend claims that the rotational speed of the water would have to increase for the cross section to be modeled by $y = 0.1x^2$. Is your friend correct? Explain your reasoning.

Maintaining Mathematical Proficiency Reviewing what you learned in previous grades and lessons

Evaluate the expression when $n = 3$ and $x = -2$. *(Skills Review Handbook)*

32. $n^2 + 5$ **33.** $3x^2 - 9$ **34.** $-4n^2 + 11$ **35.** $n + 2x^2$

Essential Question How does the value of c affect the graph of $f(x) = ax^2 + c$?

EXPLORATION 1 Graphing $y = ax^2 + c$

Work with a partner. Sketch the graphs of the functions in the same coordinate plane. What do you notice?

a. $f(x) = x^2$ and $g(x) = x^2 + 2$

b. $f(x) = 2x^2$ and $g(x) = 2x^2 - 2$

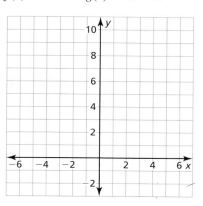

EXPLORATION 2 Finding x-Intercepts of Graphs

Work with a partner. Graph each function. Find the x-intercepts of the graph. Explain how you found the x-intercepts.

a. $y = x^2 - 7$

b. $y = -x^2 + 1$

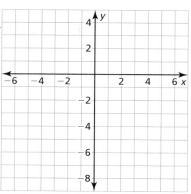

USING TOOLS STRATEGICALLY

To be proficient in math, you need to consider the available tools, such as a graphing calculator, when solving a mathematical problem.

Communicate Your Answer

3. How does the value of c affect the graph of $f(x) = ax^2 + c$?

4. Use a graphing calculator to verify your answers to Question 3.

5. The figure shows the graph of a quadratic function of the form $y = ax^2 + c$. Describe possible values of a and c. Explain your reasoning.

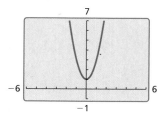

What You Will Learn

▶ Graph quadratic functions of the form $f(x) = ax^2 + c$.

▶ Solve real-life problems involving functions of the form $f(x) = ax^2 + c$.

Core Vocabulary

zero of a function, *p. 132*

Previous
translation
vertex of a parabola
axis of symmetry
vertical stretch
vertical shrink

Graphing $f(x) = ax^2 + c$

🌀 Core Concept

Graphing $f(x) = ax^2 + c$

- When $c > 0$, the graph of $f(x) = ax^2 + c$ is a vertical translation c units up of the graph of $f(x) = ax^2$.

- When $c < 0$, the graph of $f(x) = ax^2 + c$ is a vertical translation $|c|$ units down of the graph of $f(x) = ax^2$.

The vertex of the graph of $f(x) = ax^2 + c$ is $(0, c)$, and the axis of symmetry is $x = 0$.

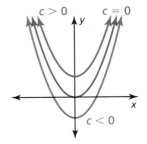

EXAMPLE 1   Graphing $y = x^2 + c$

Graph $g(x) = x^2 - 2$. Compare the graph to the graph of $f(x) = x^2$.

SOLUTION

Step 1   Make a table of values.

x	−2	−1	0	1	2
g(x)	2	−1	−2	−1	2

Step 2   Plot the ordered pairs.

Step 3   Draw a smooth curve through the points.

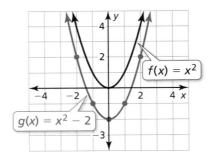

REMEMBER

The graph of $y = f(x) + k$ is a vertical translation, and the graph of $y = f(x - h)$ is a horizontal translation of the graph of f.

▶ Both graphs open up and have the same axis of symmetry, $x = 0$. The vertex of the graph of g, $(0, -2)$, is below the vertex of the graph of f, $(0, 0)$, because the graph of g is a vertical translation 2 units down of the graph of f.

Monitoring Progress Help in English and Spanish at *BigIdeasMath.com*

Graph the function. Compare the graph to the graph of $f(x) = x^2$.

1. $g(x) = x^2 - 5$

2. $h(x) = x^2 + 3$

EXAMPLE 2 Graphing $y = ax^2 + c$

Graph $g(x) = 4x^2 + 1$. Compare the graph to the graph of $f(x) = x^2$.

SOLUTION

Step 1 Make a table of values.

x	−2	−1	0	1	2
g(x)	17	5	1	5	17

Step 2 Plot the ordered pairs.

Step 3 Draw a smooth curve through the points.

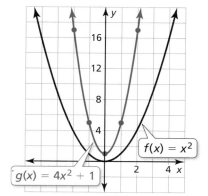

▶ Both graphs open up and have the same axis of symmetry, $x = 0$. The graph of g is narrower, and its vertex, $(0, 1)$, is above the vertex of the graph of f, $(0, 0)$. So, the graph of g is a vertical stretch by a factor of 4 and a vertical translation 1 unit up of the graph of f.

EXAMPLE 3 Translating the Graph of $y = ax^2 + c$

Let $f(x) = -0.5x^2 + 2$ and $g(x) = f(x) - 7$.

a. Describe the transformation from the graph of f to the graph of g. Then graph f and g in the same coordinate plane.

b. Write an equation that represents g in terms of x.

SOLUTION

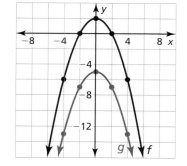

a. The function g is of the form $y = f(x) + k$, where $k = -7$. So, the graph of g is a vertical translation 7 units down of the graph of f.

x	−4	−2	0	2	4
f(x)	−6	0	2	0	−6
g(x)	−13	−7	−5	−7	−13

$-0.5x^2 + 2$

$f(x) - 7$

b. $g(x) = f(x) - 7$ Write the function g.

$\quad\quad = -0.5x^2 + 2 - 7$ Substitute for $f(x)$.

$\quad\quad = -0.5x^2 - 5$ Subtract.

▶ So, the equation $g(x) = -0.5x^2 - 5$ represents g in terms of x.

Monitoring Progress Help in English and Spanish at *BigIdeasMath.com*

Graph the function. Compare the graph to the graph of $f(x) = x^2$.

3. $g(x) = 2x^2 - 5$

4. $h(x) = -\frac{1}{4}x^2 + 4$

5. Let $f(x) = 3x^2 - 1$ and $g(x) = f(x) + 3$.

    a. Describe the transformation from the graph of f to the graph of g. Then graph f and g in the same coordinate plane.

    b. Write an equation that represents g in terms of x.

Solving Real-Life Problems

A **zero of a function** f is an x-value for which $f(x) = 0$. A zero of a function is an x-intercept of the graph of the function.

EXAMPLE 4 Solving a Real-Life Problem

64 ft

The function $f(t) = 16t^2$ represents the distance (in feet) a dropped object falls in t seconds. The function $g(t) = s_0$ represents the initial height (in feet) of the object.

a. Find and interpret $h(t) = -f(t) + g(t)$.

b. An egg is dropped from a height of 64 feet. After how many seconds does the egg hit the ground?

c. Suppose the initial height is adjusted by k feet. How will this affect part (b)?

SOLUTION

a. $h(t) = -f(t) + g(t)$ Write the function h.

     $= -(16t^2) + s_0$ Substitute for $f(t)$ and $g(t)$.

     $= -16t^2 + s_0$ Simplify.

▶ The function $h(t) = -16t^2 + s_0$ represents the height (in feet) of a falling object t seconds after it is dropped from an initial height s_0 (in feet).

COMMON ERROR

The graph in Step 1 shows the height of the object over time, not the path of the object.

b. The initial height is 64 feet. So, the function $h(t) = -16t^2 + 64$ represents the height of the egg t seconds after it is dropped. The egg hits the ground when $h(t) = 0$.

Step 1 Make a table of values and sketch the graph.

t	0	1	2
$h(t)$	64	48	0

$h(t) = -16t^2 + 64$

Step 2 Find the positive zero of the function. When $t = 2$, $h(t) = 0$. So, the zero is 2.

▶ The egg hits the ground 2 seconds after it is dropped.

c. When the initial height is adjusted by k feet, the graph of h is translated up k units when $k > 0$ or down $|k|$ units when $k < 0$. So, the x-intercept of the graph of h will move right when $k > 0$ or left when $k < 0$.

▶ When $k > 0$, the egg will take more than 2 seconds to hit the ground. When $k < 0$, the egg will take less than 2 seconds to hit the ground.

Monitoring Progress Help in English and Spanish at *BigIdeasMath.com*

6. Explain why only nonnegative values of t are used in Example 4.

7. WHAT IF? The egg is dropped from a height of 100 feet. After how many seconds does the egg hit the ground?

Vocabulary and Core Concept Check

1. **VOCABULARY** State the vertex and axis of symmetry of the graph of $y = ax^2 + c$.

2. **WRITING** How does the graph of $y = ax^2 + c$ compare to the graph of $y = ax^2$?

Monitoring Progress and Modeling with Mathematics

In Exercises 3–6, graph the function. Compare the graph to the graph of $f(x) = x^2$. *(See Example 1.)*

3. $g(x) = x^2 + 6$

4. $h(x) = x^2 + 8$

5. $p(x) = x^2 - 3$

6. $q(x) = x^2 - 1$

In Exercises 7–12, graph the function. Compare the graph to the graph of $f(x) = x^2$. *(See Example 2.)*

7. $g(x) = -x^2 + 3$

8. $h(x) = -x^2 - 7$

9. $s(x) = 2x^2 - 4$

10. $t(x) = -3x^2 + 1$

11. $p(x) = -\frac{1}{3}x^2 - 2$

12. $q(x) = \frac{1}{2}x^2 + 6$

In Exercises 13–16, describe the transformation from the graph of f to the graph of g. Then graph f and g in the same coordinate plane. Write an equation that represents g in terms of x. *(See Example 3.)*

13. $f(x) = 3x^2 + 4$
    $g(x) = f(x) + 2$

14. $f(x) = \frac{1}{2}x^2 + 1$
    $g(x) = f(x) - 4$

15. $f(x) = -\frac{1}{4}x^2 - 6$
    $g(x) = f(x) - 3$

16. $f(x) = 4x^2 - 5$
    $g(x) = f(x) + 7$

17. **ERROR ANALYSIS** Describe and correct the error in comparing the graphs.

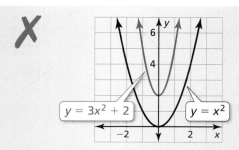

The graph of $y = 3x^2 + 2$ is a vertical shrink by a factor of 3 and a translation 2 units up of the graph of $y = x^2$.

18. **ERROR ANALYSIS** Describe and correct the error in graphing and comparing $f(x) = x^2$ and $g(x) = x^2 - 10$.

Both graphs open up and have the same axis of symmetry. However, the vertex of the graph of g, $(0, 10)$, is 10 units above the vertex of the graph of f, $(0, 0)$.

In Exercises 19–26, find the zeros of the function.

19. $y = x^2 - 1$

20. $y = x^2 - 36$

21. $f(x) = -x^2 + 25$

22. $f(x) = -x^2 + 49$

23. $f(x) = 4x^2 - 16$

24. $f(x) = 3x^2 - 27$

25. $f(x) = -12x^2 + 3$

26. $f(x) = -8x^2 + 98$

27. **MODELING WITH MATHEMATICS** A water balloon is dropped from a height of 144 feet. *(See Example 4.)*

    a. What does the function $h(t) = -16t^2 + 144$ represent in this situation?

    b. After how many seconds does the water balloon hit the ground?

    c. Suppose the initial height is adjusted by k feet. How does this affect part (b)?

28. **MODELING WITH MATHEMATICS** The function $y = -16x^2 + 36$ represents the height y (in feet) of an apple x seconds after falling from a tree. Find and interpret the x- and y-intercepts.

In Exercises 29–32, sketch a parabola with the given characteristics.

29. The parabola opens up, and the vertex is (0, 3).

30. The vertex is (0, 4), and one of the x-intercepts is 2.

31. The related function is increasing when $x < 0$, and the zeros are -1 and 1.

32. The highest point on the parabola is (0, -5).

33. **DRAWING CONCLUSIONS** You and your friend both drop a ball at the same time. The function $h(x) = -16x^2 + 256$ represents the height (in feet) of your ball after x seconds. The function $g(x) = -16x^2 + 300$ represents the height (in feet) of your friend's ball after x seconds.

    a. Write the function $T(x) = h(x) - g(x)$. What does $T(x)$ represent?

    b. When your ball hits the ground, what is the height of your friend's ball? Use a graph to justify your answer.

34. **MAKING AN ARGUMENT** Your friend claims that in the equation $y = ax^2 + c$, the vertex changes when the value of a changes. Is your friend correct? Explain your reasoning.

35. **MATHEMATICAL CONNECTIONS** The area A (in square feet) of a square patio is represented by $A = x^2$, where x is the length of one side of the patio. You add 48 square feet to the patio, resulting in a total area of 192 square feet. What are the dimensions of the original patio? Use a graph to justify your answer.

36. **HOW DO YOU SEE IT?** The graph of $f(x) = ax^2 + c$ is shown. Points A and B are the same distance from the vertex of the graph of f. Which point is closer to the vertex of the graph of f as c increases?

37. **REASONING** Describe two methods you can use to find the zeros of the function $f(t) = -16t^2 + 400$. Check your answer by graphing.

38. **PROBLEM SOLVING** The paths of water from three different garden waterfalls are given below. Each function gives the height h (in feet) and the horizontal distance d (in feet) of the water.

    Waterfall 1 $h = -3.1d^2 + 4.8$

    Waterfall 2 $h = -3.5d^2 + 1.9$

    Waterfall 3 $h = -1.1d^2 + 1.6$

    a. Which waterfall drops water from the highest point?

    b. Which waterfall follows the narrowest path?

    c. Which waterfall sends water the farthest?

39. **WRITING EQUATIONS** Two acorns fall to the ground from an oak tree. One falls 45 feet, while the other falls 32 feet.

    a. For each acorn, write an equation that represents the height h (in feet) as a function of the time t (in seconds).

    b. Describe how the graphs of the two equations are related.

40. **THOUGHT PROVOKING** One of two classic problems in calculus is to find the area under a curve. Approximate the area of the region bounded by the parabola and the x-axis. Show your work.

41. **CRITICAL THINKING** A cross section of the parabolic surface of the antenna shown can be modeled by $y = 0.012x^2$, where x and y are measured in feet. The antenna is moved up so that the outer edges of the dish are 25 feet above the x-axis. Where is the vertex of the cross section located? Explain.

Maintaining Mathematical Proficiency   Reviewing what you learned in previous grades and lessons

Evaluate the expression when $a = 4$ and $b = -3$. *(Skills Review Handbook)*

42. $\dfrac{a}{4b}$

43. $-\dfrac{b}{2a}$

44. $\dfrac{a - b}{3a + b}$

45. $-\dfrac{b + 2a}{ab}$

Essential Question How can you find the vertex of the graph of $f(x) = ax^2 + bx + c$?

EXPLORATION 1 Comparing *x*-Intercepts with the Vertex

Work with a partner.

a. Sketch the graphs of $y = 2x^2 - 8x$ and $y = 2x^2 - 8x + 6$.

b. What do you notice about the *x*-coordinate of the vertex of each graph?

c. Use the graph of $y = 2x^2 - 8x$ to find its *x*-intercepts. Verify your answer by solving $0 = 2x^2 - 8x$.

d. Compare the value of the *x*-coordinate of the vertex with the values of the *x*-intercepts.

EXPLORATION 2 Finding *x*-Intercepts

Work with a partner.

a. Solve $0 = ax^2 + bx$ for *x* by factoring.

b. What are the *x*-intercepts of the graph of $y = ax^2 + bx$?

c. Copy and complete the table to verify your answer.

x	$y = ax^2 + bx$
0	
$-\dfrac{b}{a}$	

CONSTRUCTING VIABLE ARGUMENTS

To be proficient in math, you need to make conjectures and build a logical progression of statements.

EXPLORATION 3 Deductive Reasoning

Work with a partner. Complete the following logical argument.

The *x*-intercepts of the graph of $y = ax^2 + bx$ are 0 and $-\dfrac{b}{a}$.

The vertex of the graph of $y = ax^2 + bx$ occurs when $x = $ [____].

The vertices of the graphs of $y = ax^2 + bx$ and $y = ax^2 + bx + c$ have the same *x*-coordinate.

The vertex of the graph of $y = ax^2 + bx + c$ occurs when $x = $ [____].

Communicate Your Answer

4. How can you find the vertex of the graph of $f(x) = ax^2 + bx + c$?

5. Without graphing, find the vertex of the graph of $f(x) = x^2 - 4x + 3$. Check your result by graphing.

What You Will Learn

▶ Graph quadratic functions of the form $f(x) = ax^2 + bx + c$.

▶ Find maximum and minimum values of quadratic functions.

Graphing $f(x) = ax^2 + bx + c$

Core Concept

Graphing $f(x) = ax^2 + bx + c$

- The graph opens up when $a > 0$, and the graph opens down when $a < 0$.

- The y-intercept is c.

- The x-coordinate of the vertex is $-\dfrac{b}{2a}$.

- The axis of symmetry is $x = -\dfrac{b}{2a}$.

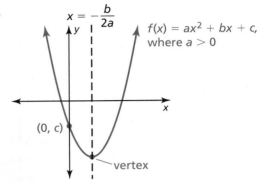

EXAMPLE 1 **Finding the Axis of Symmetry and the Vertex**

Find (a) the axis of symmetry and (b) the vertex of the graph of $f(x) = 2x^2 + 8x - 1$.

SOLUTION

a. Find the axis of symmetry when $a = 2$ and $b = 8$.

$$x = -\frac{b}{2a}$$ Write the equation for the axis of symmetry.

$$x = -\frac{8}{2(2)}$$ Substitute 2 for a and 8 for b.

$$x = -2$$ Simplify.

▶ The axis of symmetry is $x = -2$.

b. The axis of symmetry is $x = -2$, so the x-coordinate of the vertex is -2. Use the function to find the y-coordinate of the vertex.

$$f(x) = 2x^2 + 8x - 1$$ Write the function.

$$f(-2) = 2(-2)^2 + 8(-2) - 1$$ Substitute -2 for x.

$$= -9$$ Simplify.

▶ The vertex is $(-2, -9)$.

Check

Monitoring Progress

Help in English and Spanish at *BigIdeasMath.com*

Find (a) the axis of symmetry and (b) the vertex of the graph of the function.

1. $f(x) = 3x^2 - 2x$ **2.** $g(x) = x^2 + 6x + 5$ **3.** $h(x) = -\frac{1}{2}x^2 + 7x - 4$

EXAMPLE 2 **Graphing $f(x) = ax^2 + bx + c$**

Graph $f(x) = 3x^2 - 6x + 5$. Describe the domain and range.

SOLUTION

Step 1 Find and graph the axis of symmetry.

$$x = -\frac{b}{2a} = -\frac{(-6)}{2(3)} = 1 \qquad \text{Substitute and simplify.}$$

Step 2 Find and plot the vertex.

The axis of symmetry is $x = 1$, so the x-coordinate of the vertex is 1. Use the function to find the y-coordinate of the vertex.

$$f(x) = 3x^2 - 6x + 5 \qquad \text{Write the function.}$$

$$f(1) = 3(1)^2 - 6(1) + 5 \qquad \text{Substitute 1 for } x.$$

$$= 2 \qquad \text{Simplify.}$$

So, the vertex is $(1, 2)$.

Step 3 Use the y-intercept to find two more points on the graph.

Because $c = 5$, the y-intercept is 5. So, $(0, 5)$ lies on the graph. Because the axis of symmetry is $x = 1$, the point $(2, 5)$ also lies on the graph.

Step 4 Draw a smooth curve through the points.

▶ The domain is all real numbers. The range is $y \geq 2$.

Monitoring Progress Help in English and Spanish at *BigIdeasMath.com*

Graph the function. Describe the domain and range.

4. $h(x) = 2x^2 + 4x + 1$ **5.** $k(x) = x^2 - 8x + 7$ **6.** $p(x) = -5x^2 - 10x - 2$

Finding Maximum and Minimum Values

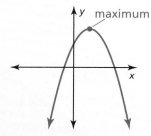 **Core Concept**

Maximum and Minimum Values

The y-coordinate of the vertex of the graph of $f(x) = ax^2 + bx + c$ is the **maximum value** of the function when $a < 0$ or the **minimum value** of the function when $a > 0$.

$$f(x) = ax^2 + bx + c, a < 0 \qquad\qquad f(x) = ax^2 + bx + c, a > 0$$

COMMON ERROR

Be sure to include the negative sign before the fraction when finding the axis of symmetry.

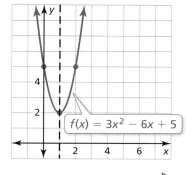

$f(x) = 3x^2 - 6x + 5$

REMEMBER

The domain is the set of all possible input values of the independent variable x. The range is the set of all possible output values of the dependent variable y.

EXAMPLE 3 **Finding a Maximum or Minimum Value**

Tell whether the function $f(x) = -4x^2 - 24x - 19$ has a minimum value or a maximum value. Then find the value.

SOLUTION

For $f(x) = -4x^2 - 24x - 19$, $a = -4$ and $-4 < 0$. So, the parabola opens down and the function has a maximum value. To find the maximum value, find the y-coordinate of the vertex.

First, find the x-coordinate of the vertex. Use $a = -4$ and $b = -24$.

$$x = -\frac{b}{2a} = -\frac{(-24)}{2(-4)} = -3 \qquad \text{Substitute and simplify.}$$

Then evaluate the function when $x = -3$ to find the y-coordinate of the vertex.

$$f(-3) = -4(-3)^2 - 24(-3) - 19 \qquad \text{Substitute } -3 \text{ for } x.$$
$$= 17 \qquad \text{Simplify.}$$

▶ The maximum value is 17.

EXAMPLE 4 **Finding a Minimum Value**

The suspension cables between the two towers of the Mackinac Bridge in Michigan form a parabola that can be modeled by $y = 0.000098x^2 - 0.37x + 552$, where x and y are measured in feet. What is the height of the cable above the water at its lowest point?

SOLUTION

The lowest point of the cable is at the vertex of the parabola. Find the x-coordinate of the vertex. Use $a = 0.000098$ and $b = -0.37$.

$$x = -\frac{b}{2a} = -\frac{(-0.37)}{2(0.000098)} \approx 1888 \qquad \text{Substitute and use a calculator.}$$

Substitute 1888 for x in the equation to find the y-coordinate of the vertex.

$$y = 0.000098(1888)^2 - 0.37(1888) + 552 \approx 203$$

▶ The cable is about 203 feet above the water at its lowest point.

Monitoring Progress ◀)) Help in English and Spanish at *BigIdeasMath.com*

Tell whether the function has a minimum value or a maximum value. Then find the value.

7. $g(x) = 8x^2 - 8x + 6$

8. $h(x) = -\frac{1}{4}x^2 + 3x + 1$

9. The cables between the two towers of the Tacoma Narrows Bridge in Washington form a parabola that can be modeled by $y = 0.00016x^2 - 0.46x + 507$, where x and y are measured in feet. What is the height of the cable above the water at its lowest point?

EXAMPLE 5   **Modeling with Mathematics**

A group of friends is launching water balloons. The function $f(t) = -16t^2 + 80t + 5$ represents the height (in feet) of the first water balloon t seconds after it is launched. The height of the second water balloon t seconds after it is launched is shown in the graph. Which water balloon went higher?

SOLUTION

MODELING WITH MATHEMATICS

Because time cannot be negative, use only nonnegative values of t.

1. **Understand the Problem** You are given a function that represents the height of the first water balloon. The height of the second water balloon is represented graphically. You need to find and compare the maximum heights of the water balloons.

2. **Make a Plan** To compare the maximum heights, represent both functions graphically. Use a graphing calculator to graph $f(t) = -16t^2 + 80t + 5$ in an appropriate viewing window. Then visually compare the heights of the water balloons.

3. **Solve the Problem** Enter the function $f(t) = -16t^2 + 80t + 5$ into your calculator and graph it. Compare the graphs to determine which function has a greater maximum value.

You can see that the second water balloon reaches a height of about 125 feet, while the first water balloon reaches a height of only about 100 feet.

▶ So, the second water balloon went higher.

4. **Look Back** Use the *maximum* feature to determine that the maximum value of $f(t) = -16t^2 + 80t + 5$ is 105. Use a straightedge to represent a height of 105 feet on the graph that represents the second water balloon to clearly see that the second water balloon went higher.

Monitoring Progress 🔊 Help in English and Spanish at *BigIdeasMath.com*

10. Which balloon is in the air longer? Explain your reasoning.

11. Which balloon reaches its maximum height faster? Explain your reasoning.

Vocabulary and Core Concept Check

1. **VOCABULARY** Explain how you can tell whether a quadratic function has a maximum value or a minimum value without graphing the function.

2. **DIFFERENT WORDS, SAME QUESTION** Consider the quadratic function $f(x) = -2x^2 + 8x + 24$. Which is different? Find "both" answers.

> What is the maximum value of the function?

> What is the greatest number in the range of the function?

> What is the y-coordinate of the vertex of the graph of the function?

> What is the axis of symmetry of the graph of the function?

Monitoring Progress and Modeling with Mathematics

In Exercises 3–6, find the vertex, the axis of symmetry, and the y-intercept of the graph.

3.

4.

5.

6.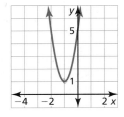

In Exercises 7–12, find (a) the axis of symmetry and (b) the vertex of the graph of the function. *(See Example 1.)*

7. $f(x) = 2x^2 - 4x$

8. $y = 3x^2 + 2x$

9. $y = -9x^2 - 18x - 1$

10. $f(x) = -6x^2 + 24x - 20$

11. $f(x) = \frac{2}{5}x^2 - 4x + 14$

12. $y = -\frac{3}{4}x^2 + 9x - 18$

In Exercises 13–18, graph the function. Describe the domain and range. *(See Example 2.)*

13. $f(x) = 2x^2 + 12x + 4$

14. $y = 4x^2 + 24x + 13$

15. $y = -8x^2 - 16x - 9$

16. $f(x) = -5x^2 + 20x - 7$

17. $y = \frac{2}{3}x^2 - 6x + 5$

18. $f(x) = -\frac{1}{2}x^2 - 3x - 4$

19. **ERROR ANALYSIS** Describe and correct the error in finding the axis of symmetry of the graph of $y = 3x^2 - 12x + 11$.

> $x = -\frac{b}{2a} = \frac{-12}{2(3)} = -2$
>
> The axis of symmetry is $x = -2$.

20. **ERROR ANALYSIS** Describe and correct the error in graphing the function $f(x) = x^2 + 4x + 3$.

> The axis of symmetry is $x = \frac{b}{2a} = \frac{4}{2(1)} = 2$.
>
> $f(2) = 2^2 + 4(2) + 3 = 15$
>
> So, the vertex is $(2, 15)$.
>
> The y-intercept is 3. So, the points $(0, 3)$ and $(4, 3)$ lie on the graph.

In Exercises 21–26, tell whether the function has a minimum value or a maximum value. Then find the value. *(See Example 3.)*

21. $y = 3x^2 - 18x + 15$

22. $f(x) = -5x^2 + 10x + 7$

23. $f(x) = -4x^2 + 4x - 2$

24. $y = 2x^2 - 10x + 13$

25. $y = -\frac{1}{2}x^2 - 11x + 6$

26. $f(x) = \frac{1}{5}x^2 - 5x + 27$

27. MODELING WITH MATHEMATICS The function shown represents the height h (in feet) of a firework t seconds after it is launched. The firework explodes at its highest point. *(See Example 4.)*

$h = -16t^2 + 128t$

a. When does the firework explode?

b. At what height does the firework explode?

28. MODELING WITH MATHEMATICS The function $h(t) = -16t^2 + 16t$ represents the height (in feet) of a horse t seconds after it jumps during a steeplechase.

a. When does the horse reach its maximum height?

b. Can the horse clear a fence that is 3.5 feet tall? If so, by how much?

c. How long is the horse in the air?

29. MODELING WITH MATHEMATICS The cable between two towers of a suspension bridge can be modeled by the function shown, where x and y are measured in feet. The cable is at road level midway between the towers.

$y = \frac{1}{400}x^2 - x + 150$

a. How far from each tower shown is the lowest point of the cable?

b. How high is the road above the water?

c. Describe the domain and range of the function shown.

30. REASONING Find the axis of symmetry of the graph of the equation $y = ax^2 + bx + c$ when $b = 0$. Can you find the axis of symmetry when $a = 0$? Explain.

31. ATTENDING TO PRECISION The vertex of a parabola is $(3, -1)$. One point on the parabola is $(6, 8)$. Find another point on the parabola. Justify your answer.

32. MAKING AN ARGUMENT Your friend claims that it is possible to draw a parabola through any two points with different x-coordinates. Is your friend correct? Explain.

USING TOOLS In Exercises 33–36, use the *minimum* or *maximum* feature of a graphing calculator to approximate the vertex of the graph of the function.

33. $y = 0.5x^2 + \sqrt{2}x - 3$

34. $y = -6.2x^2 + 4.8x - 1$

35. $y = -\pi x^2 + 3x$

36. $y = 0.25x^2 - 5^{2/3}x + 2$

37. MODELING WITH MATHEMATICS The opening of one aircraft hangar is a parabolic arch that can be modeled by the equation $y = -0.006x^2 + 1.5x$, where x and y are measured in feet. The opening of a second aircraft hangar is shown in the graph. *(See Example 5.)*

a. Which aircraft hangar is taller?

b. Which aircraft hangar is wider?

38. MODELING WITH MATHEMATICS An office supply store sells about 80 graphing calculators per month for $120 each. For each $6 decrease in price, the store expects to sell eight more calculators. The revenue from calculator sales is given by the function $R(n) = $ (unit price)(units sold), or $R(n) = (120 - 6n)(80 + 8n)$, where n is the number of $6 price decreases.

a. How much should the store charge to maximize monthly revenue?

b. Using a different revenue model, the store expects to sell five more calculators for each $4 decrease in price. Which revenue model results in a greater maximum monthly revenue? Explain.

MATHEMATICAL CONNECTIONS In Exercises 39 and 40, (a) find the value of x that maximizes the area of the figure and (b) find the maximum area.

39.

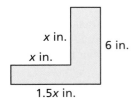

x in.
x in.
6 in.
1.5x in.

40.

$(12 - 4x)$ ft
$(x + 2)$ ft
12 ft

41. WRITING Compare the graph of $g(x) = x^2 + 4x + 1$ with the graph of $h(x) = x^2 - 4x + 1$.

42. HOW DO YOU SEE IT? During an archery competition, an archer shoots an arrow. The arrow follows the parabolic path shown, where x and y are measured in meters.

a. What is the initial height of the arrow?

b. Estimate the maximum height of the arrow.

c. How far does the arrow travel?

43. USING TOOLS The graph of a quadratic function passes through $(3, 2)$, $(4, 7)$, and $(9, 2)$. Does the graph open up or down? Explain your reasoning.

44. REASONING For a quadratic function f, what does $f\left(-\dfrac{b}{2a}\right)$ represent? Explain your reasoning.

45. PROBLEM SOLVING Write a function of the form $y = ax^2 + bx$ whose graph contains the points $(1, 6)$ and $(3, 6)$.

46. CRITICAL THINKING Parabolas A and B contain the points shown. Identify characteristics of each parabola, if possible. Explain your reasoning.

Parabola A	
x	y
2	3
6	4

Parabola B	
x	y
1	4
3	-4
5	4

47. MODELING WITH MATHEMATICS At a basketball game, an air cannon launches T-shirts into the crowd. The function $y = -\frac{1}{8}x^2 + 4x$ represents the path of a T-shirt. The function $3y = 2x - 14$ represents the height of the bleachers. In both functions, y represents vertical height (in feet) and x represents horizontal distance (in feet). At what height does the T-shirt land in the bleachers?

48. THOUGHT PROVOKING One of two classic problems in calculus is finding the slope of a *tangent line* to a curve. An example of a tangent line, which just touches the parabola at one point, is shown.

Approximate the slope of the tangent line to the graph of $y = x^2$ at the point $(1, 1)$. Explain your reasoning.

49. PROBLEM SOLVING The owners of a dog shelter want to enclose a rectangular play area on the side of their building. They have k feet of fencing. What is the maximum area of the outside enclosure in terms of k? (*Hint:* Find the y-coordinate of the vertex of the graph of the area function.)

ℓ
w
play area
w
dog shelter building

Maintaining Mathematical Proficiency
Reviewing what you learned in previous grades and lessons

Describe the transformation(s) from the graph of $f(x) = |x|$ to the graph of the given function. (*Section 1.1*)

50. $q(x) = |x + 6|$ **51.** $h(x) = -0.5|x|$ **52.** $g(x) = |x - 2| + 5$ **53.** $p(x) = 3|x + 1|$

Core Vocabulary

quadratic function, *p. 124*
parabola, *p. 124*
vertex, *p. 124*

axis of symmetry, *p. 124*
zero of a function, *p. 132*

maximum value, *p. 137*
minimum value, *p. 137*

Core Concepts

Section 3.1

Characteristics of Quadratic Functions, *p. 124*
Graphing $f(x) = ax^2$ When $a > 0$, *p. 125*
Graphing $f(x) = ax^2$ When $a < 0$, *p. 125*

Section 3.2

Graphing $f(x) = ax^2 + c$, *p. 130*

Section 3.3

Graphing $f(x) = ax^2 + bx + c$, *p. 136*
Maximum and Minimum Values, *p. 137*

Mathematical Practices

1. Explain your plan for solving Exercise 18 on page 127.

2. How does graphing the function in Exercise 27 on page 133 help you answer the questions?

3. What definition and characteristics of the graph of a quadratic function did you use to answer Exercise 44 on page 142?

Learning Visually

- Draw a picture of a word problem before writing a verbal model. You do not have to be an artist.

- When making a review card for a word problem, include a picture. This will help you recall the information while taking a test.

- Make sure your notes are visually neat for easy recall.

STUDY SKILLS

Identify characteristics of the quadratic function and its graph. *(Section 3.1)*

1.

2.
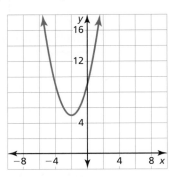

Graph the function. Compare the graph to the graph of $f(x) = x^2$. *(Section 3.1 and Section 3.2)*

3. $h(x) = -x^2$

4. $p(x) = 2x^2 + 2$

5. $r(x) = 4x^2 - 16$

6. $b(x) = 8x^2$

7. $g(x) = \frac{2}{5}x^2$

8. $m(x) = -\frac{1}{2}x^2 - 4$

Describe the transformation from the graph of f to the graph of g. Then graph f and g in the same coordinate plane. Write an equation that represents g in terms of x. *(Section 3.2)*

9. $f(x) = 2x^2 + 1;\ g(x) = f(x) + 2$

10. $f(x) = -3x^2 + 12;\ g(x) = f(x) - 9$

11. $f(x) = \frac{1}{2}x^2 - 2;\ g(x) = f(x) - 6$

12. $f(x) = 5x^2 - 3;\ g(x) = f(x) + 1$

Graph the function. Describe the domain and range. *(Section 3.3)*

13. $f(x) = -4x^2 - 4x + 7$

14. $f(x) = 2x^2 + 12x + 5$

15. $y = x^2 + 4x - 5$

16. $y = -3x^2 + 6x + 9$

Tell whether the function has a minimum value or a maximum value. Then find the value. *(Section 3.3)*

17. $f(x) = 5x^2 + 10x - 3$

18. $f(x) = -\frac{1}{2}x^2 + 2x + 16$

19. $y = -x^2 + 4x + 12$

20. $y = 2x^2 + 8x + 3$

21. The distance y (in feet) that a coconut falls after t seconds is given by the function $y = 16t^2$. Use a graph to determine how many seconds it takes for the coconut to fall 64 feet. *(Section 3.1)*

22. The function $y = -16t^2 + 25$ represents the height y (in feet) of a pinecone t seconds after falling from a tree. *(Section 3.2)*

    a. After how many seconds does the pinecone hit the ground?

    b. A second pinecone falls from a height of 36 feet. Which pinecone hits the ground in the least amount of time? Explain.

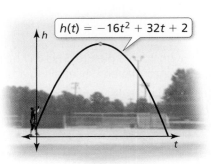

$h(t) = -16t^2 + 32t + 2$

23. The function shown models the height (in feet) of a softball t seconds after it is pitched in an underhand motion. Describe the domain and range. Find the maximum height of the softball. *(Section 3.3)*

Essential Question How can you describe the graph of $f(x) = a(x - h)^2$?

EXPLORATION 1 **Graphing** $y = a(x - h)^2$ **When** $h > 0$

Work with a partner. Sketch the graphs of the functions in the same coordinate plane. How does the value of h affect the graph of $y = a(x - h)^2$?

a. $f(x) = x^2$ and $g(x) = (x - 2)^2$

b. $f(x) = 2x^2$ and $g(x) = 2(x - 2)^2$

 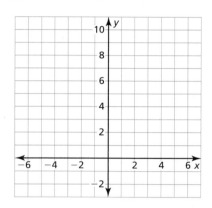

EXPLORATION 2 **Graphing** $y = a(x - h)^2$ **When** $h < 0$

Work with a partner. Sketch the graphs of the functions in the same coordinate plane. How does the value of h affect the graph of $y = a(x - h)^2$?

a. $f(x) = -x^2$ and $g(x) = -(x + 2)^2$

b. $f(x) = -2x^2$ and $g(x) = -2(x + 2)^2$

 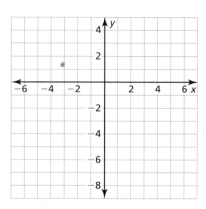

USING TOOLS STRATEGICALLY

To be proficient in math, you need to consider the available tools, such as a graphing calculator, when solving a mathematical problem.

Communicate Your Answer

3. How can you describe the graph of $f(x) = a(x - h)^2$?

4. Without graphing, describe the graph of each function. Use a graphing calculator to check your answer.

a. $y = (x - 3)^2$

b. $y = (x + 3)^2$

c. $y = -(x - 3)^2$

> **STUDY TIP**
> The graph of an odd function looks the same after a 180° rotation about the origin.

> **STUDY TIP**
> Most functions are neither even nor odd.

What You Will Learn

▶ Identify even and odd functions.
▶ Graph quadratic functions of the form $f(x) = a(x - h)^2$.
▶ Graph quadratic functions of the form $f(x) = a(x - h)^2 + k$.
▶ Model real-life problems using $f(x) = a(x - h)^2 + k$.

Identifying Even and Odd Functions

Core Concept

Even and Odd Functions

A function $y = f(x)$ is **even** when $f(-x) = f(x)$ for each x in the domain of f. The graph of an even function is symmetric about the y-axis.

A function $y = f(x)$ is **odd** when $f(-x) = -f(x)$ for each x in the domain of f. The graph of an odd function is symmetric about the origin. A graph is *symmetric about the origin* when it looks the same after reflections in the x-axis and then in the y-axis.

EXAMPLE 1   Identifying Even and Odd Functions

Determine whether each function is *even*, *odd*, or *neither*.

a. $f(x) = 2x$ **b.** $g(x) = x^2 - 2$ **c.** $h(x) = 2x^2 + x - 2$

SOLUTION

a.
$f(x) = 2x$	Write the original function.
$f(-x) = 2(-x)$	Substitute $-x$ for x.
$= -2x$	Simplify.
$= -f(x)$	Substitute $f(x)$ for $2x$.

▶ Because $f(-x) = -f(x)$, the function is odd.

b.
$g(x) = x^2 - 2$	Write the original function.
$g(-x) = (-x)^2 - 2$	Substitute $-x$ for x.
$= x^2 - 2$	Simplify.
$= g(x)$	Substitute $g(x)$ for $x^2 - 2$.

▶ Because $g(-x) = g(x)$, the function is even.

c.
$h(x) = 2x^2 + x - 2$	Write the original function.
$h(-x) = 2(-x)^2 + (-x) - 2$	Substitute $-x$ for x.
$= 2x^2 - x - 2$	Simplify.

▶ Because $h(x) = 2x^2 + x - 2$ and $-h(x) = -2x^2 - x + 2$, you can conclude that $h(-x) \neq h(x)$ and $h(-x) \neq -h(x)$. So, the function is neither even nor odd.

Monitoring Progress Help in English and Spanish at *BigIdeasMath.com*

Determine whether the function is *even*, *odd*, or *neither*.

1. $f(x) = 5x$ **2.** $g(x) = 2^x$ **3.** $h(x) = 2x^2 + 3$

Graphing $f(x) = a(x - h)^2$

Core Concept

Graphing $f(x) = a(x - h)^2$

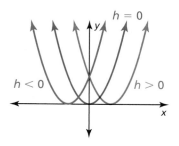

- When $h > 0$, the graph of $f(x) = a(x - h)^2$ is a horizontal translation h units right of the graph of $f(x) = ax^2$.

- When $h < 0$, the graph of $f(x) = a(x - h)^2$ is a horizontal translation $|h|$ units left of the graph of $f(x) = ax^2$.

The vertex of the graph of $f(x) = a(x - h)^2$ is $(h, 0)$, and the axis of symmetry is $x = h$.

EXAMPLE 2 Graphing $y = a(x - h)^2$

ANOTHER WAY

In Step 3, you could instead choose two x-values greater than the x-coordinate of the vertex.

Graph $g(x) = \frac{1}{2}(x - 4)^2$. Compare the graph to the graph of $f(x) = x^2$.

SOLUTION

Step 1 Graph the axis of symmetry. Because $h = 4$, graph $x = 4$.

Step 2 Plot the vertex. Because $h = 4$, plot $(4, 0)$.

Step 3 Find and plot two more points on the graph. Choose two x-values less than the x-coordinate of the vertex. Then find $g(x)$ for each x-value.

When $x = 0$:

$g(0) = \frac{1}{2}(0 - 4)^2$

$= 8$

When $x = 2$:

$g(2) = \frac{1}{2}(2 - 4)^2$

$= 2$

So, plot $(0, 8)$ and $(2, 2)$.

Step 4 Reflect the points plotted in Step 3 in the axis of symmetry. So, plot $(8, 8)$ and $(6, 2)$.

Step 5 Draw a smooth curve through the points.

STUDY TIP

From the graph, you can see that $f(x) = x^2$ is an even function. However, $g(x) = \frac{1}{2}(x - 4)^2$ is neither even nor odd.

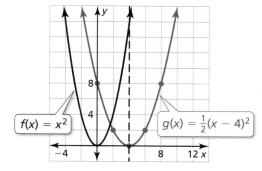

$f(x) = x^2$

$g(x) = \frac{1}{2}(x - 4)^2$

▶ Both graphs open up. The graph of g is wider than the graph of f. The axis of symmetry $x = 4$ and the vertex $(4, 0)$ of the graph of g are 4 units right of the axis of symmetry $x = 0$ and the vertex $(0, 0)$ of the graph of f. So, the graph of g is a translation 4 units right and a vertical shrink by a factor of $\frac{1}{2}$ of the graph of f.

Monitoring Progress Help in English and Spanish at *BigIdeasMath.com*

Graph the function. Compare the graph to the graph of $f(x) = x^2$.

4. $g(x) = 2(x + 5)^2$

5. $h(x) = -(x - 2)^2$

Graphing $f(x) = a(x - h)^2 + k$

Core Concept

Graphing $f(x) = a(x - h)^2 + k$

The **vertex form** of a quadratic function is $f(x) = a(x - h)^2 + k$, where $a \neq 0$. The graph of $f(x) = a(x - h)^2 + k$ is a translation h units horizontally and k units vertically of the graph of $f(x) = ax^2$.

The vertex of the graph of $f(x) = a(x - h)^2 + k$ is (h, k), and the axis of symmetry is $x = h$.

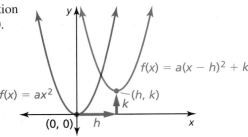

EXAMPLE 3   Graphing $y = a(x - h)^2 + k$

Graph $g(x) = -2(x + 2)^2 + 3$. Compare the graph to the graph of $f(x) = x^2$.

SOLUTION

Step 1 Graph the axis of symmetry. Because $h = -2$, graph $x = -2$.

Step 2 Plot the vertex. Because $h = -2$ and $k = 3$, plot $(-2, 3)$.

Step 3 Find and plot two more points on the graph. Choose two x-values less than the x-coordinate of the vertex. Then find $g(x)$ for each x-value. So, plot $(-4, -5)$ and $(-3, 1)$.

x	-4	-3
$g(x)$	-5	1

Step 4 Reflect the points plotted in Step 3 in the axis of symmetry. So, plot $(-1, 1)$ and $(0, -5)$.

Step 5 Draw a smooth curve through the points.

▶ The graph of g opens down and is narrower than the graph of f. The vertex of the graph of g, $(-2, 3)$, is 2 units left and 3 units up of the vertex of the graph of f, $(0, 0)$. So, the graph of g is a vertical stretch by a factor of 2, a reflection in the x-axis, and a translation 2 units left and 3 units up of the graph of f.

EXAMPLE 4   Transforming the Graph of $y = a(x - h)^2 + k$

Consider function g in Example 3. Graph $f(x) = g(x + 5)$.

SOLUTION

The function f is of the form $y = g(x - h)$, where $h = -5$. So, the graph of f is a horizontal translation 5 units left of the graph of g. To graph f, subtract 5 from the x-coordinates of the points on the graph of g.

Monitoring Progress Help in English and Spanish at *BigIdeasMath.com*

Graph the function. Compare the graph to the graph of $f(x) = x^2$.

6. $g(x) = 3(x - 1)^2 + 6$

7. $h(x) = \frac{1}{2}(x + 4)^2 - 2$

8. Consider function g in Example 3. Graph $f(x) = g(x) - 3$.

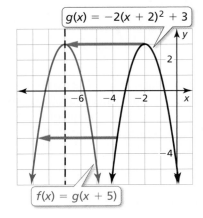

Modeling Real-Life Problems

EXAMPLE 5 **Modeling with Mathematics**

Water fountains are usually designed to give a specific visual effect. For example, the water fountain shown consists of streams of water that are shaped like parabolas. Notice how the streams are designed to land on the underwater spotlights. Write and graph a quadratic function that models the path of a stream of water with a maximum height of 5 feet, represented by a vertex of (3, 5), landing on a spotlight 6 feet from the water jet, represented by (6, 0).

SOLUTION

1. **Understand the Problem** You know the vertex and another point on the graph that represents the parabolic path. You are asked to write and graph a quadratic function that models the path.

2. **Make a Plan** Use the given points and the vertex form to write a quadratic function. Then graph the function.

3. **Solve the Problem**
Use the vertex form, vertex (3, 5), and point (6, 0) to find the value of a.

$f(x) = a(x - h)^2 + k$ Write the vertex form of a quadratic function.

$f(x) = a(x - 3)^2 + 5$ Substitute 3 for h and 5 for k.

$0 = a(6 - 3)^2 + 5$ Substitute 6 for x and 0 for $f(x)$.

$0 = 9a + 5$ Simplify.

$-\frac{5}{9} = a$ Solve for a.

So, $f(x) = -\frac{5}{9}(x - 3)^2 + 5$ models the path of a stream of water. Now graph the function.

Step 1 Graph the axis of symmetry. Because $h = 3$, graph $x = 3$.

Step 2 Plot the vertex, (3, 5).

Step 3 Find and plot two more points on the graph. Because the x-axis represents the water surface, the graph should only contain points with nonnegative values of $f(x)$. You know that (6, 0) is on the graph. To find another point, choose an x-value between $x = 3$ and $x = 6$. Then find the corresponding value of $f(x)$.

$f(4.5) = -\frac{5}{9}(4.5 - 3)^2 + 5 = 3.75$

So, plot (6, 0) and (4.5, 3.75).

Step 4 Reflect the points plotted in Step 3 in the axis of symmetry. So, plot (0, 0) and (1.5, 3.75).

Step 5 Draw a smooth curve through the points.

4. **Look Back** Use a graphing calculator to graph $f(x) = -\frac{5}{9}(x - 3)^2 + 5$. Use the *maximum* feature to verify that the maximum value is 5. Then use the *zero* feature to verify that $x = 6$ is a zero of the function.

Monitoring Progress

Help in English and Spanish at *BigIdeasMath.com*

9. **WHAT IF?** The vertex is (3, 6). Write and graph a quadratic function that models the path.

Vocabulary and Core Concept Check

1. **VOCABULARY** Compare the graph of an even function with the graph of an odd function.

2. **OPEN-ENDED** Write a quadratic function whose graph has a vertex of $(1, 2)$.

3. **WRITING** Describe the transformation from the graph of $f(x) = ax^2$ to the graph of $g(x) = a(x - h)^2 + k$.

4. **WHICH ONE DOESN'T BELONG?** Which function does *not* belong with the other three? Explain your reasoning.

$$f(x) = 8(x + 4)^2 \qquad f(x) = (x - 2)^2 + 4 \qquad f(x) = 2(x + 0)^2 \qquad f(x) = 3(x + 1)^2 + 1$$

Monitoring Progress and Modeling with Mathematics

In Exercises 5–12, determine whether the function is *even*, *odd*, or *neither*. *(See Example 1.)*

5. $f(x) = 4x + 3$

6. $g(x) = 3x^2$

7. $h(x) = 5^x + 2$

8. $m(x) = 2x^2 - 7x$

9. $p(x) = -x^2 + 8$

10. $f(x) = -\frac{1}{2}x$

11. $n(x) = 2x^2 - 7x + 3$

12. $r(x) = -6x^2 + 5$

In Exercises 13–18, determine whether the function represented by the graph is *even*, *odd*, or *neither*.

13.

14.

15.

16.

17.

18.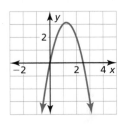

In Exercises 19–22, find the vertex and the axis of symmetry of the graph of the function.

19. $f(x) = 3(x + 1)^2$

20. $f(x) = \frac{1}{4}(x - 6)^2$

21. $y = -\frac{1}{8}(x - 4)^2$

22. $y = -5(x + 9)^2$

In Exercises 23–28, graph the function. Compare the graph to the graph of $f(x) = x^2$. *(See Example 2.)*

23. $g(x) = 2(x + 3)^2$

24. $p(x) = 3(x - 1)^2$

25. $r(x) = \frac{1}{4}(x + 10)^2$

26. $n(x) = \frac{1}{3}(x - 6)^2$

27. $d(x) = \frac{1}{5}(x - 5)^2$

28. $q(x) = 6(x + 2)^2$

29. **ERROR ANALYSIS** Describe and correct the error in determining whether the function $f(x) = x^2 + 3$ is even, odd, or neither.

> ✗
> $$f(x) = x^2 + 3$$
> $$f(-x) = (-x)^2 + 3$$
> $$= x^2 + 3$$
> $$= f(x)$$
> So, $f(x)$ is an odd function.

30. **ERROR ANALYSIS** Describe and correct the error in finding the vertex of the graph of the function.

> ✗
> $$y = -(x + 8)^2$$
> Because $h = -8$, the vertex is $(0, -8)$.

In Exercises 31–34, find the vertex and the axis of symmetry of the graph of the function.

31. $y = -6(x + 4)^2 - 3$ **32.** $f(x) = 3(x - 3)^2 + 6$

33. $f(x) = -4(x + 3)^2 + 1$ **34.** $y = -(x - 6)^2 - 5$

In Exercises 35–38, match the function with its graph.

35. $y = -(x + 1)^2 - 3$ **36.** $y = -\frac{1}{2}(x - 1)^2 + 3$

37. $y = \frac{1}{3}(x - 1)^2 + 3$ **38.** $y = 2(x + 1)^2 - 3$

A.

B.

C.

D.
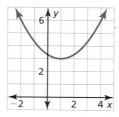

In Exercises 39–44, graph the function. Compare the graph to the graph of $f(x) = x^2$. *(See Example 3.)*

39. $h(x) = (x - 2)^2 + 4$ **40.** $g(x) = (x + 1)^2 - 7$

41. $r(x) = 4(x - 1)^2 - 5$ **42.** $n(x) = -(x + 4)^2 + 2$

43. $g(x) = -\frac{1}{3}(x + 3)^2 - 2$ **44.** $r(x) = \frac{1}{2}(x - 2)^2 - 4$

In Exercises 45–48, let $f(x) = (x - 2)^2 + 1$. Match the function with its graph.

45. $g(x) = f(x - 1)$ **46.** $r(x) = f(x + 2)$

47. $h(x) = f(x) + 2$ **48.** $p(x) = f(x) - 3$

A.

B.

C.

D.
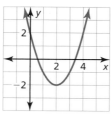

In Exercises 49–54, graph g. *(See Example 4.)*

49. $f(x) = 2(x - 1)^2 + 1; g(x) = f(x + 3)$

50. $f(x) = -(x + 1)^2 + 2; g(x) = \frac{1}{2}f(x)$

51. $f(x) = -3(x + 5)^2 - 6; g(x) = 2f(x)$

52. $f(x) = 5(x - 3)^2 - 1; g(x) = f(x) - 6$

53. $f(x) = (x + 3)^2 + 5; g(x) = f(x - 4)$

54. $f(x) = -2(x - 4)^2 - 8; g(x) = -f(x)$

55. MODELING WITH MATHEMATICS The height (in meters) of a bird diving to catch a fish is represented by $h(t) = 5(t - 2.5)^2$, where t is the number of seconds after beginning the dive.

   a. Graph h.

   b. Another bird's dive is represented by $r(t) = 2h(t)$. Graph r.

   c. Compare the graphs. Which bird starts its dive from a greater height? Explain.

56. MODELING WITH MATHEMATICS A kicker punts a football. The height (in yards) of the football is represented by $f(x) = -\frac{1}{9}(x - 30)^2 + 25$, where x is the horizontal distance (in yards) from the kicker's goal line.

   a. Graph f. Describe the domain and range.

   b. On the next possession, the kicker punts the football. The height of the football is represented by $g(x) = f(x + 5)$. Graph g. Describe the domain and range.

   c. Compare the graphs. On which possession does the kicker punt closer to his goal line? Explain.

In Exercises 57–62, write a quadratic function in vertex form whose graph has the given vertex and passes through the given point.

57. vertex: $(1, 2)$; passes through $(3, 10)$

58. vertex: $(-3, 5)$; passes through $(0, -14)$

59. vertex: $(-2, -4)$; passes through $(-1, -6)$

60. vertex: $(1, 8)$; passes through $(3, 12)$

61. vertex: $(5, -2)$; passes through $(7, 0)$

62. vertex: $(-5, -1)$; passes through $(-2, 2)$

63. MODELING WITH MATHEMATICS A portion of a roller coaster track is in the shape of a parabola. Write and graph a quadratic function that models this portion of the roller coaster with a maximum height of 90 feet, represented by a vertex of $(25, 90)$, passing through the point $(50, 0)$. *(See Example 5.)*

64. MODELING WITH MATHEMATICS A flare is launched from a boat and travels in a parabolic path until reaching the water. Write and graph a quadratic function that models the path of the flare with a maximum height of 300 meters, represented by a vertex of $(59, 300)$, landing in the water at the point $(119, 0)$.

In Exercises 65–68, rewrite the quadratic function in vertex form.

65. $y = 2x^2 - 8x + 4$ **66.** $y = 3x^2 + 6x - 1$

67. $f(x) = -5x^2 + 10x + 3$

68. $f(x) = -x^2 - 4x + 2$

69. REASONING Can a function be symmetric about the x-axis? Explain.

70. HOW DO YOU SEE IT? The graph of a quadratic function is shown. Determine which symbols to use to complete the vertex form of the quadratic function. Explain your reasoning.

$y = a(x \quad 2)^2 \quad 3$

In Exercises 71–74, describe the transformation from the graph of f to the graph of h. Write an equation that represents h in terms of x.

71. $f(x) = -(x + 1)^2 - 2$
$h(x) = f(x) + 4$

72. $f(x) = 2(x - 1)^2 + 1$
$h(x) = f(x - 5)$

73. $f(x) = 4(x - 2)^2 + 3$
$h(x) = 2f(x)$

74. $f(x) = -(x + 5)^2 - 6$
$h(x) = \frac{1}{3}f(x)$

75. REASONING The graph of $y = x^2$ is translated 2 units right and 5 units down. Write an equation for the function in vertex form and in standard form. Describe advantages of writing the function in each form.

76. THOUGHT PROVOKING Which of the following are true? Justify your answers.

  a. Any constant multiple of an even function is even.

  b. Any constant multiple of an odd function is odd.

  c. The sum or difference of two even functions is even.

  d. The sum or difference of two odd functions is odd.

  e. The sum or difference of an even function and an odd function is odd.

77. COMPARING FUNCTIONS A cross section of a birdbath can be modeled by $y = \frac{1}{81}(x - 18)^2 - 4$, where x and y are measured in inches. The graph shows the cross section of another birdbath.

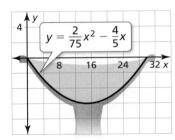

$y = \frac{2}{75}x^2 - \frac{4}{5}x$

  a. Which birdbath is deeper? Explain.

  b. Which birdbath is wider? Explain.

78. REASONING Compare the graphs of $y = 2x^2 + 8x + 8$ and $y = x^2$ without graphing the functions. How can factoring help you compare the parabolas? Explain.

79. MAKING AN ARGUMENT Your friend says all absolute value functions are even because of their symmetry. Is your friend correct? Explain.

Maintaining Mathematical Proficiency
   Reviewing what you learned in previous grades and lessons

Solve the equation. *(Section 2.4)*

80. $x(x - 1) = 0$ **81.** $(x + 3)(x - 8) = 0$ **82.** $(3x - 9)(4x + 12) = 0$

3.5 Graphing $f(x) = a(x - p)(x - q)$

Essential Question
What are some of the characteristics of the graph of $f(x) = a(x - p)(x - q)$?

EXPLORATION 1 **Using Zeros to Write Functions**

Work with a partner. Each graph represents a function of the form $f(x) = (x - p)(x - q)$ or $f(x) = -(x - p)(x - q)$. Write the function represented by each graph. Explain your reasoning.

a.

b.

c.

d.

e.

f.

g.

h.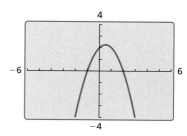

CONSTRUCTING VIABLE ARGUMENTS

To be proficient in math, you need to justify your conclusions and communicate them to others.

Communicate Your Answer

2. What are some of the characteristics of the graph of $f(x) = a(x - p)(x - q)$?

3. Consider the graph of $f(x) = a(x - p)(x - q)$.

   a. Does changing the sign of a change the x-intercepts? Does changing the sign of a change the y-intercept? Explain your reasoning.

   b. Does changing the value of p change the x-intercepts? Does changing the value of p change the y-intercept? Explain your reasoning.

What You Will Learn

▶ Graph quadratic functions of the form $f(x) = a(x - p)(x - q)$.

▶ Use intercept form to find zeros of functions.

▶ Use characteristics to graph and write quadratic functions.

Graphing $f(x) = a(x - p)(x - q)$

You have already graphed quadratic functions written in several different forms, such as $f(x) = ax^2 + bx + c$ (standard form) and $g(x) = a(x - h)^2 + k$ (vertex form). Quadratic functions can also be written in **intercept form**, $f(x) = a(x - p)(x - q)$, where $a \neq 0$. In this form, the polynomial that defines a function is in factored form and the x-intercepts of the graph can be easily determined.

Core Concept

Graphing $f(x) = a(x - p)(x - q)$

- The x-intercepts are p and q.

- The axis of symmetry is halfway between $(p, 0)$ and $(q, 0)$. So, the axis of symmetry is $x = \dfrac{p + q}{2}$.

- The graph opens up when $a > 0$, and the graph opens down when $a < 0$.

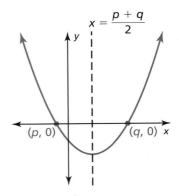

EXAMPLE 1 **Graphing $f(x) = a(x - p)(x - q)$**

Graph $f(x) = -(x + 1)(x - 5)$. Describe the domain and range.

SOLUTION

Step 1 Identify the x-intercepts. Because the x-intercepts are $p = -1$ and $q = 5$, plot $(-1, 0)$ and $(5, 0)$.

Step 2 Find and graph the axis of symmetry.

$$x = \frac{p + q}{2} = \frac{-1 + 5}{2} = 2$$

Step 3 Find and plot the vertex.

The x-coordinate of the vertex is 2. To find the y-coordinate of the vertex, substitute 2 for x and simplify.

$$f(2) = -(2 + 1)(2 - 5) = 9$$

So, the vertex is $(2, 9)$.

Step 4 Draw a parabola through the vertex and the points where the x-intercepts occur.

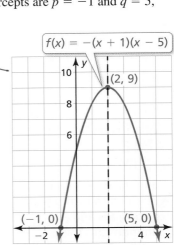

▶ The domain is all real numbers. The range is $y \leq 9$.

EXAMPLE 2 **Graphing a Quadratic Function**

Graph $f(x) = 2x^2 - 8$. Describe the domain and range.

SOLUTION

Step 1 Rewrite the quadratic function in intercept form.

$$f(x) = 2x^2 - 8 \qquad \text{Write the function.}$$
$$= 2(x^2 - 4) \qquad \text{Factor out common factor.}$$
$$= 2(x + 2)(x - 2) \qquad \text{Difference of two squares pattern}$$

Step 2 Identify the x-intercepts. Because the x-intercepts are $p = -2$ and $q = 2$, plot $(-2, 0)$ and $(2, 0)$.

Step 3 Find and graph the axis of symmetry.

$$x = \frac{p + q}{2} = \frac{-2 + 2}{2} = 0$$

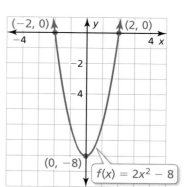

Step 4 Find and plot the vertex.

The x-coordinate of the vertex is 0.
The y-coordinate of the vertex is

$$f(0) = 2(0)^2 - 8 = -8.$$

So, the vertex is $(0, -8)$.

Step 5 Draw a parabola through the vertex and the points where the x-intercepts occur.

▶ The domain is all real numbers. The range is $y \geq -8$.

Monitoring Progress 🔊 Help in English and Spanish at *BigIdeasMath.com*

Graph the quadratic function. Label the vertex, axis of symmetry, and x-intercepts. Describe the domain and range of the function.

1. $f(x) = (x + 2)(x - 3)$ **2.** $g(x) = -2(x - 4)(x + 1)$ **3.** $h(x) = 4x^2 - 36$

REMEMBER

Functions have zeros, and *graphs* have x-intercepts.

Using Intercept Form to Find Zeros of Functions

In Section 3.2, you learned that a zero of a function is an x-value for which $f(x) = 0$. You can use the intercept form of a function to find the zeros of the function.

EXAMPLE 3 **Finding Zeros of a Function**

Find the zeros of $f(x) = (x - 1)(x + 2)$.

Check

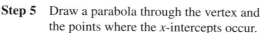

SOLUTION

To find the zeros, determine the x-values for which $f(x)$ is 0.

$$f(x) = (x - 1)(x + 2) \qquad \text{Write the function.}$$
$$0 = (x - 1)(x + 2) \qquad \text{Substitute 0 for } f(x).$$
$$x - 1 = 0 \quad or \quad x + 2 = 0 \qquad \text{Zero-Product Property}$$
$$x = 1 \quad or \qquad x = -2 \qquad \text{Solve for } x.$$

▶ So, the zeros of the function are -2 and 1.

Core Concept

Factors and Zeros

For any factor $x - n$ of a polynomial, n is a zero of the function defined by the polynomial.

EXAMPLE 4 **Finding Zeros of Functions**

Find the zeros of each function.

a. $h(x) = x^2 - 16$ **b.** $f(x) = -2x^2 - 10x - 12$

SOLUTION

Write each function in intercept form to identify the zeros.

a. $h(x) = x^2 - 16$ Write the function.

$\quad\quad = (x + 4)(x - 4)$ Difference of two squares pattern

▶ So, the zeros of the function are -4 and 4.

b. $f(x) = -2x^2 - 10x - 12$ Write the function.

$\quad\quad = -2(x^2 + 5x + 6)$ Factor out common factor.

$\quad\quad = -2(x + 3)(x + 2)$ Factor the trinomial.

▶ So, the zeros of the function are -3 and -2.

Monitoring Progress Help in English and Spanish at *BigIdeasMath.com*

Find the zero(s) of the function.

4. $f(x) = (x - 6)(x - 1)$ **5.** $h(x) = x^2 - 1$ **6.** $g(x) = 3x^2 - 12x + 12$

Using Characteristics to Graph and Write Quadratic Functions

EXAMPLE 5 **Graphing a Quadratic Function Using Zeros**

Use zeros to graph $h(x) = x^2 - 2x - 3$.

SOLUTION

The function is in standard form. You know that the parabola opens up ($a > 0$) and the y-intercept is -3. So, begin by plotting $(0, -3)$.

ATTENDING TO PRECISION

To sketch a more precise graph, make a table of values and plot other points on the graph.

Notice that the polynomial that defines the function is factorable. So, write the function in intercept form and identify the zeros.

$\quad h(x) = x^2 - 2x - 3$ Write the function.

$\quad\quad = (x + 1)(x - 3)$ Factor the trinomial.

The zeros of the function are -1 and 3. So, plot $(-1, 0)$ and $(3, 0)$. Draw a parabola through the points.

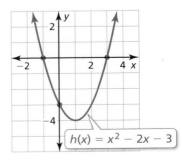

$h(x) = x^2 - 2x - 3$

EXAMPLE 6 **Writing Quadratic Functions**

STUDY TIP

In part (a), many possible functions satisfy the given condition. The value *a* can be *any* nonzero number. To allow easier calculations, let *a* = 1. By letting *a* = 2, the resulting function would be
$f(x) = 2x^2 + 12x + 22$.

Write a quadratic function in standard form whose graph satisfies the given condition(s).

a. vertex: $(-3, 4)$

b. passes through $(-9, 0)$, $(-2, 0)$, and $(-4, 20)$

SOLUTION

a. Because you know the vertex, use vertex form to write a function.

$$f(x) = a(x - h)^2 + k \qquad \text{Vertex form}$$
$$= 1(x + 3)^2 + 4 \qquad \text{Substitute for } a, h, \text{ and } k.$$
$$= x^2 + 6x + 9 + 4 \qquad \text{Find the product } (x + 3)^2.$$
$$= x^2 + 6x + 13 \qquad \text{Combine like terms.}$$

b. The given points indicate that the *x*-intercepts are -9 and -2. So, use intercept form to write a function.

$$f(x) = a(x - p)(x - q) \qquad \text{Intercept form}$$
$$= a(x + 9)(x + 2) \qquad \text{Substitute for } p \text{ and } q.$$

Use the other given point, $(-4, 20)$, to find the value of *a*.

$$20 = a(-4 + 9)(-4 + 2) \qquad \text{Substitute } -4 \text{ for } x \text{ and } 20 \text{ for } f(x).$$
$$20 = a(5)(-2) \qquad \text{Simplify.}$$
$$-2 = a \qquad \text{Solve for } a.$$

Use the value of *a* to write the function.

$$f(x) = -2(x + 9)(x + 2) \qquad \text{Substitute } -2 \text{ for } a.$$
$$= -2x^2 - 22x - 36 \qquad \text{Simplify.}$$

Check

Monitoring Progress Help in English and Spanish at *BigIdeasMath.com*

Use zeros to graph the function.

7. $f(x) = (x - 1)(x - 4)$

8. $g(x) = x^2 + x - 12$

Write a quadratic function in standard form whose graph satisfies the given condition(s).

9. *x*-intercepts: -1 and 1

10. vertex: $(8, 8)$

11. passes through $(0, 0)$, $(10, 0)$, and $(4, 12)$

12. passes through $(-5, 0)$, $(4, 0)$, and $(3, -16)$

Vocabulary and Core Concept Check

1. **COMPLETE THE SENTENCE** The values p and q are _____ of the graph of the function $f(x) = a(x - p)(x - q)$.

2. **WRITING** Explain how to find the maximum value or minimum value of a quadratic function when the function is given in intercept form.

Monitoring Progress and Modeling with Mathematics

In Exercises 3–6, find the *x*-intercepts and axis of symmetry of the graph of the function.

3.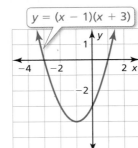
$y = (x - 1)(x + 3)$

4.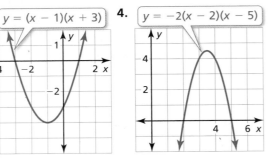
$y = -2(x - 2)(x - 5)$

5. $f(x) = -5(x + 7)(x - 5)$ 6. $g(x) = \frac{2}{3}x(x + 8)$

In Exercises 7–12, graph the quadratic function. Label the vertex, axis of symmetry, and *x*-intercepts. Describe the domain and range of the function. *(See Example 1.)*

7. $f(x) = (x + 4)(x + 1)$ 8. $y = (x - 2)(x + 2)$

9. $y = -(x + 6)(x - 4)$ 10. $h(x) = -4(x - 7)(x - 3)$

11. $g(x) = 5(x + 1)(x + 2)$ 12. $y = -2(x - 3)(x + 4)$

In Exercises 13–20, graph the quadratic function. Label the vertex, axis of symmetry, and *x*-intercepts. Describe the domain and range of the function. *(See Example 2.)*

13. $y = x^2 - 9$ 14. $f(x) = x^2 - 8x$

15. $h(x) = -5x^2 + 5x$ 16. $y = 3x^2 - 48$

17. $q(x) = x^2 + 9x + 14$ 18. $p(x) = x^2 + 6x - 27$

19. $y = 4x^2 - 36x + 32$ 20. $y = -2x^2 - 4x + 30$

In Exercises 21–28, find the zero(s) of the function. *(See Examples 3 and 4.)*

21. $y = -2(x - 2)(x - 10)$ 22. $f(x) = \frac{1}{3}(x + 5)(x - 1)$

23. $f(x) = x^2 - 4$ 24. $h(x) = x^2 - 36$

25. $g(x) = x^2 + 5x - 24$ 26. $y = x^2 - 17x + 52$

27. $y = 3x^2 - 15x - 42$ 28. $g(x) = -4x^2 - 8x - 4$

In Exercises 29–34, match the function with its graph.

29. $y = (x + 5)(x + 3)$ 30. $y = (x + 5)(x - 3)$

31. $y = (x - 5)(x + 3)$ 32. $y = (x - 5)(x - 3)$

33. $y = (x + 5)(x - 5)$ 34. $y = (x + 3)(x - 3)$

A.

B.

C.

D.

E.

F.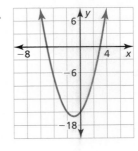

In Exercises 35–40, use zeros to graph the function. (*See Example 5.*)

35. $f(x) = (x + 2)(x - 6)$ **36.** $g(x) = -3(x + 1)(x + 7)$

37. $y = x^2 - 11x + 18$ **38.** $y = x^2 - x - 30$

39. $y = -5x^2 - 10x + 40$ **40.** $h(x) = 8x^2 - 8$

ERROR ANALYSIS In Exercises 41 and 42, describe and correct the error in finding the zeros of the function.

41.

✗ $y = 5(x + 3)(x - 2)$

The zeros of the function are 3 and −2.

42.

✗ $y = x^2 - 9$

The zero of the function is 9.

In Exercises 43–54, write a quadratic function in standard form whose graph satisfies the given condition(s). (*See Example 6.*)

43. vertex: $(7, -3)$ **44.** vertex: $(4, 8)$

45. x-intercepts: 1 and 9   **46.** x-intercepts: -2 and -5

47. passes through $(-4, 0)$, $(3, 0)$, and $(2, -18)$

48. passes through $(-5, 0)$, $(-1, 0)$, and $(-4, 3)$

49. passes through $(7, 0)$

50. passes through $(0, 0)$ and $(6, 0)$

51. axis of symmetry: $x = -5$

52. y increases as x increases when $x < 4$; y decreases as x increases when $x > 4$.

53. range: $y \geq -3$ **54.** range: $y \leq 10$

In Exercises 55–58, write the quadratic function represented by the graph.

55.

56.

57.

58.
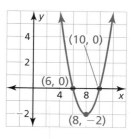

In Exercises 59 and 60, all the zeros of a function are given. Use the zeros and the other point given to write a quadratic function represented by the table.

59.

x	y
0	0
2	30
7	0

60.

x	y
−3	0
1	−72
4	0

In Exercises 61–64, sketch a parabola that satisfies the given conditions.

61. x-intercepts: -4 and 2; range: $y \geq -3$

62. axis of symmetry: $x = 6$; passes through $(4, 15)$

63. range: $y \leq 5$; passes through $(0, 2)$

64. x-intercept: 6; y-intercept: 1; range: $y \geq -4$

65. MODELING WITH MATHEMATICS Satellite dishes are shaped like parabolas to optimally receive signals. The cross section of a satellite dish can be modeled by the function shown, where x and y are measured in feet. The x-axis represents the top of the opening of the dish.

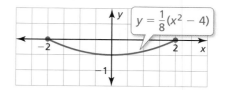

$y = \frac{1}{8}(x^2 - 4)$

a. How wide is the satellite dish?

b. How deep is the satellite dish?

c. Write a quadratic function in standard form that models the cross section of a satellite dish that is 6 feet wide and 1.5 feet deep.

66. **MODELING WITH MATHEMATICS** A professional basketball player's shot is modeled by the function shown, where x and y are measured in feet.

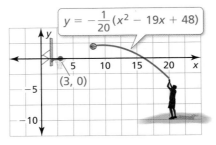

$$y = -\frac{1}{20}(x^2 - 19x + 48)$$

(3, 0)

a. Does the player make the shot? Explain.

b. The basketball player releases another shot from the point (13, 0) and makes the shot. The shot also passes through the point (10, 1.4). Write a quadratic function in standard form that models the path of the shot.

USING STRUCTURE In Exercises 67–70, match the function with its graph.

67. $y = -x^2 + 5x$

68. $y = x^2 - x - 12$

69. $y = -2x^2 - 8$

70. $y = 3x^2 + 6$

A.

B.

C.

D.
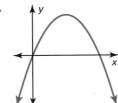

71. **CRITICAL THINKING** Write a quadratic function represented by the table, if possible. If not, explain why.

x	−5	−3	−1	1
y	0	12	4	0

72. **HOW DO YOU SEE IT?** The graph shows the parabolic arch that supports the roof of a convention center, where x and y are measured in feet.

a. The arch can be represented by a function of the form $f(x) = a(x - p)(x - q)$. Estimate the values of p and q.

b. Estimate the width and height of the arch. Explain how you can use your height estimate to calculate a.

ANALYZING EQUATIONS In Exercises 73 and 74, (a) rewrite the quadratic function in intercept form and (b) graph the function using any method. Explain the method you used.

73. $f(x) = -3(x + 1)^2 + 27$

74. $g(x) = 2(x - 1)^2 - 2$

75. **WRITING** Can a quadratic function with exactly one real zero be written in intercept form? Explain.

76. **MAKING AN ARGUMENT** Your friend claims that any quadratic function can be written in standard form and in vertex form. Is your friend correct? Explain.

77. **REASONING** Let k be a constant. Find the zeros of the function $f(x) = kx^2 - k^2x - 2k^3$ in terms of k.

78. **THOUGHT PROVOKING** Sketch the graph of each function. Explain your procedure.

   a. $f(x) = (x^2 - 1)(x^2 - 4)$

   b. $g(x) = x(x^2 - 1)(x^2 - 4)$

PROBLEM SOLVING In Exercises 79 and 80, write two quadratic functions whose graphs intersect at the given points. Explain your reasoning.

79. $(-4, 0)$ and $(2, 0)$ 80. $(3, 6)$ and $(7, 6)$

Maintaining Mathematical Proficiency
Reviewing what you learned in previous grades and lessons

Find the distance between the two points. *(Skills Review Handbook)*

81. $(2, 1)$ and $(3, 0)$

82. $(-1, 8)$ and $(-9, 2)$

83. $(-1, -6)$ and $(-3, -5)$

3.6 Focus of a Parabola

Essential Question What is the focus of a parabola?

EXPLORATION 1 Analyzing Satellite Dishes

Work with a partner. Vertical rays enter a satellite dish whose cross section is a parabola. When the rays hit the parabola, they reflect at the same angle at which they entered. (See Ray 1 in the figure.)

a. Draw the reflected rays so that they intersect the y-axis.

b. What do the reflected rays have in common?

c. The optimal location for the receiver of the satellite dish is at a point called the *focus* of the parabola. Determine the location of the focus. Explain why this makes sense in this situation.

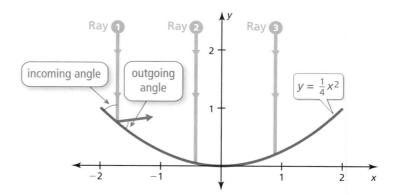

CONSTRUCTING VIABLE ARGUMENTS

To be proficient in math, you need to make conjectures and build logical progressions of statements to explore the truth of your conjectures.

EXPLORATION 2 Analyzing Spotlights

Work with a partner. Beams of light are coming from the bulb in a spotlight, located at the focus of the parabola. When the beams hit the parabola, they reflect at the same angle at which they hit. (See Beam 1 in the figure.) Draw the reflected beams. What do they have in common? Would you consider this to be the optimal result? Explain.

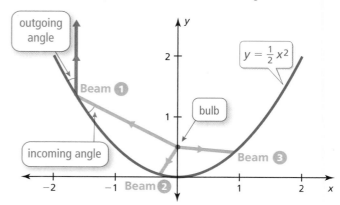

Communicate Your Answer

3. What is the focus of a parabola?

4. Describe some of the properties of the focus of a parabola.

What You Will Learn

▶ Explore the focus and the directrix of a parabola.

▶ Write equations of parabolas.

▶ Solve real-life problems.

Core Vocabulary

focus, *p. 162*
directrix, *p. 162*

Previous
perpendicular
Distance Formula
congruent

Exploring the Focus and Directrix

Previously, you learned that the graph of a quadratic function is a parabola that opens up or down. A parabola can also be defined as the set of all points (x, y) in a plane that are equidistant from a fixed point called the **focus** and a fixed line called the **directrix**.

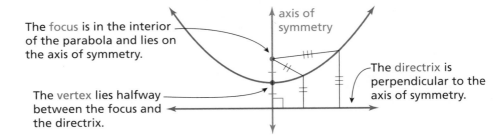

The **focus** is in the interior of the parabola and lies on the axis of symmetry.

axis of symmetry

The **directrix** is perpendicular to the axis of symmetry.

The **vertex** lies halfway between the focus and the directrix.

EXAMPLE 1 **Using the Distance Formula to Write an Equation**

REMEMBER

The distance from a point to a line is defined as the length of the perpendicular segment from the point to the line.

Use the Distance Formula to write an equation of the parabola with focus $F(0, 2)$ and directrix $y = -2$.

SOLUTION

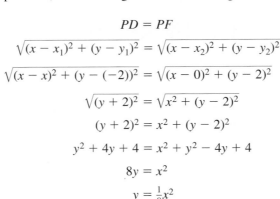

Notice the line segments drawn from point F to point P and from point P to point D. By the definition of a parabola, these line segments must be congruent.

$PD = PF$	Definition of a parabola
$\sqrt{(x - x_1)^2 + (y - y_1)^2} = \sqrt{(x - x_2)^2 + (y - y_2)^2}$	Distance Formula
$\sqrt{(x - x)^2 + (y - (-2))^2} = \sqrt{(x - 0)^2 + (y - 2)^2}$	Substitute for x_1, y_1, x_2, and y_2.
$\sqrt{(y + 2)^2} = \sqrt{x^2 + (y - 2)^2}$	Simplify.
$(y + 2)^2 = x^2 + (y - 2)^2$	Square each side.
$y^2 + 4y + 4 = x^2 + y^2 - 4y + 4$	Expand.
$8y = x^2$	Combine like terms.
$y = \frac{1}{8}x^2$	Divide each side by 8.

REMEMBER

Squaring a positive number and finding a square root are inverse operations. So, you can square each side of the equation to eliminate the radicals.

Monitoring Progress Help in English and Spanish at *BigIdeasMath.com*

1. Use the Distance Formula to write an equation of the parabola with focus $F(0, -3)$ and directrix $y = 3$.

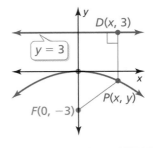

You can derive the equation of a parabola that opens up or down with vertex $(0, 0)$, focus $(0, p)$, and directrix $y = -p$ using the procedure in Example 1.

$$\sqrt{(x - x)^2 + (y - (-p))^2} = \sqrt{(x - 0)^2 + (y - p)^2}$$

$$(y + p)^2 = x^2 + (y - p)^2$$

$$y^2 + 2py + p^2 = x^2 + y^2 - 2py + p^2$$

$$4py = x^2$$

$$y = \frac{1}{4p}x^2$$

The focus and directrix each lie $|p|$ units from the vertex. Parabolas can also open left or right, in which case the equation has the form $x = \frac{1}{4p}y^2$ when the vertex is $(0, 0)$.

LOOKING FOR STRUCTURE

Notice that $y = \frac{1}{4p}x^2$ is of the form $y = ax^2$. So, changing the value of p vertically stretches or shrinks the parabola.

STUDY TIP

Notice that parabolas opening left or right do *not* represent functions.

⑤ Core Concept

Standard Equations of a Parabola with Vertex at the Origin

Vertical axis of symmetry ($x = 0$)

Equation: $y = \frac{1}{4p}x^2$

Focus: $(0, p)$

Directrix: $y = -p$

$p > 0$

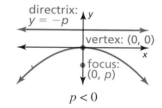

$p < 0$

Horizontal axis of symmetry ($y = 0$)

Equation: $x = \frac{1}{4p}y^2$

Focus: $(p, 0)$

Directrix: $x = -p$

$p > 0$

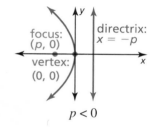

$p < 0$

EXAMPLE 2 Graphing an Equation of a Parabola

Identify the focus, directrix, and axis of symmetry of $-4x = y^2$. Graph the equation.

SOLUTION

Step 1 Rewrite the equation in standard form.

$$-4x = y^2 \qquad \text{Write the original equation.}$$

$$x = -\frac{1}{4}y^2 \qquad \text{Divide each side by } -4.$$

Step 2 Identify the focus, directrix, and axis of symmetry. The equation has the form $x = \frac{1}{4p}y^2$, where $p = -1$. The focus is $(p, 0)$, or $(-1, 0)$. The directrix is $x = -p$, or $x = 1$. Because y is squared, the axis of symmetry is the x-axis.

Step 3 Use a table of values to graph the equation. Notice that it is easier to substitute y-values and solve for x. Opposite y-values result in the same x-value.

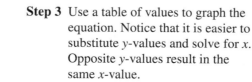

y	0	±1	±2	±3	±4
x	0	−0.25	−1	−2.25	−4

Writing Equations of Parabolas

EXAMPLE 3 **Writing an Equation of a Parabola**

Write an equation of the parabola shown.

SOLUTION

Because the vertex is at the origin and the axis of symmetry is vertical, the equation has the form $y = \frac{1}{4p}x^2$. The directrix is $y = -p = 3$, so $p = -3$. Substitute -3 for p to write an equation of the parabola.

$$y = \frac{1}{4(-3)}x^2 = -\frac{1}{12}x^2$$

▶ So, an equation of the parabola is $y = -\frac{1}{12}x^2$.

Monitoring Progress Help in English and Spanish at *BigIdeasMath.com*

Identify the focus, directrix, and axis of symmetry of the parabola. Then graph the equation.

2. $y = 0.5x^2$ **3.** $-y = x^2$ **4.** $y^2 = 6x$

Write an equation of the parabola with vertex at (0, 0) and the given directrix or focus.

5. directrix: $x = -3$ **6.** focus: $(-2, 0)$ **7.** focus: $\left(0, \frac{3}{2}\right)$

The vertex of a parabola is not always at the origin. As in previous transformations, adding a value to the input or output of a function translates its graph.

🔄 Core Concept

Standard Equations of a Parabola with Vertex at (*h*, *k*)

Vertical axis of symmetry (*x* = *h*)

Equation: $y = \frac{1}{4p}(x - h)^2 + k$

Focus: $(h, k + p)$

Directrix: $y = k - p$

$p > 0$

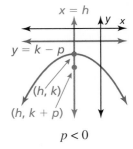

$p < 0$

STUDY TIP

The standard form for a vertical axis of symmetry looks like vertex form. To remember the standard form for a horizontal axis of symmetry, switch *x* and *y*, and *h* and *k*.

Horizontal axis of symmetry (*y* = *k*)

Equation: $x = \frac{1}{4p}(y - k)^2 + h$

Focus: $(h + p, k)$

Directrix: $x = h - p$

$p > 0$

$p < 0$

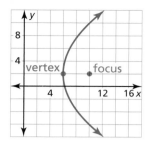

EXAMPLE 4 **Writing an Equation of a Translated Parabola**

Write an equation of the parabola shown.

SOLUTION

Because the vertex is not at the origin and the axis of symmetry is horizontal, the equation has the form $x = \frac{1}{4p}(y - k)^2 + h$. The vertex (h, k) is $(6, 2)$ and the focus $(h + p, k)$ is $(10, 2)$, so $h = 6$, $k = 2$, and $p = 4$. Substitute these values to write an equation of the parabola.

$$x = \frac{1}{4(4)}(y - 2)^2 + 6 = \frac{1}{16}(y - 2)^2 + 6$$

▶ So, an equation of the parabola is $x = \frac{1}{16}(y - 2)^2 + 6$.

Solving Real-Life Problems

Parabolic reflectors have cross sections that are parabolas. Incoming sound, light, or other energy that arrives at a parabolic reflector parallel to the axis of symmetry is directed to the focus (Diagram 1). Similarly, energy that is emitted from the focus of a parabolic reflector and then strikes the reflector is directed parallel to the axis of symmetry (Diagram 2).

Diagram 1   Diagram 2

EXAMPLE 5 **Solving a Real-Life Problem**

An electricity-generating dish uses a parabolic reflector to concentrate sunlight onto a high-frequency engine located at the focus of the reflector. The sunlight heats helium to 650°C to power the engine. Write an equation that represents the cross section of the dish shown with its vertex at $(0, 0)$. What is the depth of the dish?

SOLUTION

Because the vertex is at the origin, and the axis of symmetry is vertical, the equation has the form $y = \frac{1}{4p}x^2$. The engine is at the focus, which is 4.5 meters above the vertex. So, $p = 4.5$. Substitute 4.5 for p to write the equation.

$$y = \frac{1}{4(4.5)}x^2 = \frac{1}{18}x^2$$

The depth of the dish is the y-value at the dish's outside edge. The dish extends $\frac{8.5}{2} = 4.25$ meters to either side of the vertex $(0, 0)$, so find y when $x = 4.25$.

$$y = \frac{1}{18}(4.25)^2 \approx 1$$

▶ The depth of the dish is about 1 meter.

Monitoring Progress Help in English and Spanish at *BigIdeasMath.com*

8. Write an equation of a parabola with vertex $(-1, 4)$ and focus $(-1, 2)$.

9. A parabolic microwave antenna is 16 feet in diameter. Write an equation that represents the cross section of the antenna with its vertex at $(0, 0)$ and its focus 10 feet to the right of the vertex. What is the depth of the antenna?

Vocabulary and Core Concept Check

1. **COMPLETE THE SENTENCE** A parabola is the set of all points in a plane equidistant from a fixed point called the _____ and a fixed line called the _____ .

2. **WRITING** Explain how to find the coordinates of the focus of a parabola with vertex $(0, 0)$ and directrix $y = 5$.

Monitoring Progress and Modeling with Mathematics

In Exercises 3–10, use the Distance Formula to write an equation of the parabola. *(See Example 1.)*

3.

4.
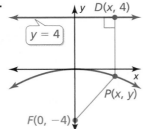

5. focus: $(0, -2)$
   directrix: $y = 2$

6. directrix: $y = 7$
   focus: $(0, -7)$

7. vertex: $(0, 0)$
   directrix: $y = -6$

8. vertex: $(0, 0)$
   focus: $(0, 5)$

9. vertex: $(0, 0)$
   focus: $(0, -10)$

10. vertex: $(0, 0)$
    directrix: $y = -9$

11. **ANALYZING RELATIONSHIPS** Which of the given characteristics describe parabolas that open down? Explain your reasoning.

    Ⓐ focus: $(0, -6)$
       directrix: $y = 6$

    Ⓑ focus: $(0, -2)$
       directrix: $y = 2$

    Ⓒ focus: $(0, 6)$
       directrix: $y = -6$

    Ⓓ focus: $(0, -1)$
       directrix: $y = 1$

12. **REASONING** Which of the following are possible coordinates of the point P in the graph shown? Explain.

    Ⓐ $(-6, -1)$ Ⓑ $\left(3, -\frac{1}{4}\right)$ Ⓒ $\left(4, -\frac{4}{9}\right)$

    Ⓓ $\left(1, \frac{1}{36}\right)$ Ⓔ $(6, -1)$ Ⓕ $\left(2, -\frac{1}{18}\right)$

In Exercises 13–20, identify the focus, directrix, and axis of symmetry of the parabola. Graph the equation. *(See Example 2.)*

13. $y = \frac{1}{8}x^2$

14. $y = -\frac{1}{12}x^2$

15. $x = -\frac{1}{20}y^2$

16. $x = \frac{1}{24}y^2$

17. $y^2 = 16x$

18. $-x^2 = 48y$

19. $6x^2 + 3y = 0$

20. $8x^2 - y = 0$

ERROR ANALYSIS In Exercises 21 and 22, describe and correct the error in graphing the parabola.

21.

22.

23. **ANALYZING EQUATIONS** The cross section (with units in inches) of a parabolic satellite dish can be modeled by the equation $y = \frac{1}{38}x^2$. How far is the receiver from the vertex of the cross section? Explain.

24. ANALYZING EQUATIONS The cross section (with units in inches) of a parabolic spotlight can be modeled by the equation $x = \frac{1}{20}y^2$. How far is the bulb from the vertex of the cross section? Explain.

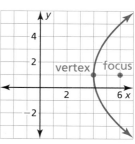

In Exercises 25–28, write an equation of the parabola shown. *(See Example 3.)*

25.

$y = -8$

26.

$y = \frac{3}{4}$

directrix

vertex

27.

$x = \frac{5}{2}$

vertex

directrix

28.

$x = -2$

vertex

directrix

In Exercises 29–36, write an equation of the parabola with the given characteristics.

29. focus: $(3, 0)$

directrix: $x = -3$

30. focus: $\left(\frac{2}{3}, 0\right)$

directrix: $x = -\frac{2}{3}$

31. directrix: $x = -10$

vertex: $(0, 0)$

32. directrix: $y = \frac{8}{3}$

vertex: $(0, 0)$

33. focus: $\left(0, -\frac{5}{3}\right)$

directrix: $y = \frac{5}{3}$

34. focus: $\left(0, \frac{5}{4}\right)$

directrix: $y = -\frac{5}{4}$

35. focus: $\left(0, \frac{6}{7}\right)$

vertex: $(0, 0)$

36. focus: $\left(-\frac{4}{5}, 0\right)$

vertex: $(0, 0)$

In Exercises 37–40, write an equation of the parabola shown. *(See Example 4.)*

37.

focus

vertex

38.

vertex focus

39.

focus

vertex

40.

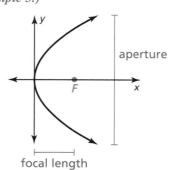

vertex

focus

In Exercises 41–46, identify the vertex, focus, directrix, and axis of symmetry of the parabola. Describe the transformations of the graph of the standard equation with $p = 1$ and vertex $(0, 0)$.

41. $y = \frac{1}{8}(x - 3)^2 + 2$

42. $y = -\frac{1}{4}(x + 2)^2 + 1$

43. $x = \frac{1}{16}(y - 3)^2 + 1$

44. $y = (x + 3)^2 - 5$

45. $x = -3(y + 4)^2 + 2$

46. $x = 4(y + 5)^2 - 1$

47. MODELING WITH MATHEMATICS Scientists studying dolphin echolocation simulate the projection of a bottlenose dolphin's clicking sounds using computer models. The models originate the sounds at the focus of a parabolic reflector. The parabola in the graph shows the cross section of the reflector with focal length of 1.3 inches and aperture width of 8 inches. Write an equation to represent the cross section of the reflector. What is the depth of the reflector? *(See Example 5.)*

aperture

F

focal length

48. MODELING WITH MATHEMATICS Solar energy can be concentrated using long troughs that have a parabolic cross section as shown in the figure. Write an equation to represent the cross section of the trough. What are the domain and range in this situation? What do they represent?

—5.8 m—

1.7 m

49. ABSTRACT REASONING As $|p|$ increases, how does the width of the graph of the equation $y = \dfrac{1}{4p}x^2$ change? Explain your reasoning.

50. HOW DO YOU SEE IT? The graph shows the path of a volleyball served from an initial height of 6 feet as it travels over a net.

a. Label the vertex, focus, and a point on the directrix.

b. An underhand serve follows the same parabolic path but is hit from a height of 3 feet. How does this affect the focus? the directrix?

51. CRITICAL THINKING The distance from point P to the directrix is 2 units. Write an equation of the parabola.

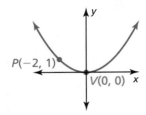

52. THOUGHT PROVOKING Two parabolas have the same focus (a, b) and focal length of 2 units. Write an equation of each parabola. Identify the directrix of each parabola.

53. REPEATED REASONING Use the Distance Formula to derive the equation of a parabola that opens to the right with vertex $(0, 0)$, focus $(p, 0)$, and directrix $x = -p$.

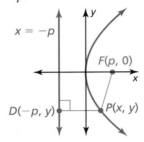

54. PROBLEM SOLVING The *latus rectum* of a parabola is the line segment that is parallel to the directrix, passes through the focus, and has endpoints that lie on the parabola. Find the length of the latus rectum of the parabola shown.

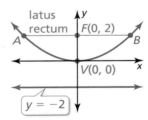

Maintaining Mathematical Proficiency
Reviewing what you learned in previous grades and lessons

Show that an exponential model fits the data. Then write a recursive rule that models the data. (Section 1.6)

55.

n	0	1	2	3	4	5
f(n)	0.25	0.5	1	2	4	8

56.

n	0	1	2	3	4	5
f(n)	2	6	18	54	162	486

57.

n	0	1	2	3	4	5
f(n)	144	72	36	18	9	4.5

58.

n	0	1	2	3	4	5
f(n)	1250	250	50	10	2	$\frac{2}{5}$

Essential Question How can you compare the growth rates of linear, exponential, and quadratic functions?

EXPLORATION 1 Comparing Speeds

Work with a partner. Three cars start traveling at the same time. The distance traveled in t minutes is y miles. Complete each table and sketch all three graphs in the same coordinate plane. Compare the speeds of the three cars. Which car has a constant speed? Which car is accelerating the most? Explain your reasoning.

COMPARING PREDICTIONS

To be proficient in math, you need to visualize the results of varying assumptions, explore consequences, and compare predictions with data.

t	$y = t$
0	
0.2	
0.4	
0.6	
0.8	
1.0	

t	$y = 2^t - 1$
0	
0.2	
0.4	
0.6	
0.8	
1.0	

t	$y = t^2$
0	
0.2	
0.4	
0.6	
0.8	
1.0	

EXPLORATION 2 Comparing Speeds

Work with a partner. Analyze the speeds of the three cars over the given time periods. The distance traveled in t minutes is y miles. Which car eventually overtakes the others?

t	$y = t$
1.0	
1.5	
2.0	
2.5	
3.0	
3.5	
4.0	
4.5	
5.0	

t	$y = 2^t - 1$
1.0	
1.5	
2.0	
2.5	
3.0	
3.5	
4.0	
4.5	
5.0	

t	$y = t^2$
1.0	
1.5	
2.0	
2.5	
3.0	
3.5	
4.0	
4.5	
5.0	

Communicate Your Answer

3. How can you compare the growth rates of linear, exponential, and quadratic functions?

4. Which function has a growth rate that is eventually much greater than the growth rates of the other two functions? Explain your reasoning.

What You Will Learn

▶ Choose functions to model data.

▶ Write functions to model data.

▶ Compare functions using average rates of change.

Core Vocabulary

Previous
average rate of change
slope

Choosing Functions to Model Data

So far, you have studied linear functions, exponential functions, and quadratic functions. You can use these functions to model data.

Core Concept

Linear, Exponential, and Quadratic Functions

Linear Function	Exponential Function	Quadratic Function
$y = mx + b$	$y = ab^x$	$y = ax^2 + bx + c$

 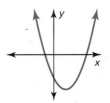

EXAMPLE 1 **Using Graphs to Identify Functions**

Plot the points. Tell whether the points appear to represent a *linear*, an *exponential*, or a *quadratic* function.

a. $(4, 4), (2, 0), (0, 0),$
$\left(1, -\frac{1}{2}\right), (-2, 4)$

b. $(0, 1), (2, 4), (4, 7),$
$(-2, -2), (-4, -5)$

c. $(0, 2), (2, 8), (1, 4),$
$(-1, 1), \left(-2, \frac{1}{2}\right)$

SOLUTION

a.

▶ quadratic

b.

▶ linear

c.

▶ exponential

Monitoring Progress Help in English and Spanish at *BigIdeasMath.com*

Plot the points. Tell whether the points appear to represent a *linear*, an *exponential*, or a *quadratic* function.

1. $(-1, 5), (2, -1), (0, -1), (3, 5), (1, -3)$

2. $(-1, 2), (-2, 8), (-3, 32), \left(0, \frac{1}{2}\right), \left(1, \frac{1}{8}\right)$

3. $(-3, 5), (0, -1), (2, -5), (-4, 7), (1, -3)$

Core Concept

Differences and Ratios of Functions

You can use patterns between consecutive data pairs to determine which type of function models the data. The differences of consecutive y-values are called *first differences*. The differences of consecutive first differences are called *second differences*.

- **Linear Function** The first differences are constant.
- **Exponential Function** Consecutive y-values have a common *ratio*.
- **Quadratic Function** The second differences are constant.

In all cases, the differences of consecutive x-values need to be constant.

STUDY TIP

The first differences for exponential and quadratic functions are *not* constant.

STUDY TIP

First determine that the differences of consecutive x-values are constant. Then check whether the first differences are constant or consecutive y-values have a common ratio. If neither of these is true, check whether the second differences are constant.

EXAMPLE 2   Using Differences or Ratios to Identify Functions

Tell whether each table of values represents a *linear*, an *exponential*, or a *quadratic* function.

a.

x	−3	−2	−1	0	1
y	11	8	5	2	−1

b.

x	−2	−1	0	1	2
y	1	2	4	8	16

c.

x	−2	−1	0	1	2
y	−1	−2	−1	2	7

SOLUTION

a.

$$\begin{array}{c|ccccc} x & -3 & -2 & -1 & 0 & 1 \\ \hline y & 11 & 8 & 5 & 2 & -1 \end{array}$$

first differences: $+1$ each ; $-3 \quad -3 \quad -3 \quad -3$

▶ The first differences are constant. So, the table represents a linear function.

b.

$$\begin{array}{c|ccccc} x & -2 & -1 & 0 & 1 & 2 \\ \hline y & 1 & 2 & 4 & 8 & 16 \end{array}$$

$+1$ each ; $\times 2 \quad \times 2 \quad \times 2 \quad \times 2$

▶ Consecutive y-values have a common ratio. So, the table represents an exponential function.

c.

$$\begin{array}{c|ccccc} x & -2 & -1 & 0 & 1 & 2 \\ \hline y & -1 & -2 & -1 & 2 & 7 \end{array}$$

$+1$ each

first differences $\longrightarrow$ $-1 \quad +1 \quad +3 \quad +5$

second differences $\longrightarrow$ $+2 \quad +2 \quad +2$

▶ The second differences are constant. So, the table represents a quadratic function.

Monitoring Progress Help in English and Spanish at *BigIdeasMath.com*

4. Tell whether the table of values represents a *linear*, an *exponential*, or a *quadratic* function.

x	−1	0	1	2	3
y	1	3	9	27	81

Writing Functions to Model Data

EXAMPLE 3 **Writing a Function to Model Data**

x	0	1	2	3	4
f(x)	12	0	−4	0	12

Tell whether the table of values represents a *linear*, an *exponential*, or a *quadratic* function. Then write the function.

SOLUTION

Step 1 Determine which type of function the table of values represents.

The second differences are constant. So, the table represents a quadratic function.

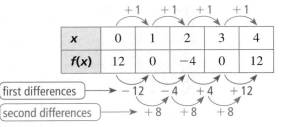

Step 2 Write an equation of the quadratic function. Using the table, notice that the x-intercepts are 1 and 3. So, use intercept form to write a function.

$$f(x) = a(x - 1)(x - 3)$$ Substitute for p and q in intercept form.

Use another point from the table, such as (0, 12), to find a.

$$12 = a(0 - 1)(0 - 3)$$ Substitute 0 for x and 12 for f(x).

$$4 = a$$ Solve for a.

Use the value of a to write the function.

$$f(x) = 4(x - 1)(x - 3)$$ Substitute 4 for a.

$$= 4x^2 - 16x + 12$$ Use the FOIL Method and combine like terms.

STUDY TIP

To check your function in Example 3, substitute the other points from the table to verify that they satisfy the function.

▶ So, the quadratic function is $f(x) = 4x^2 - 16x + 12$.

Previously, you wrote recursive rules for linear and exponential functions. You can use the pattern in the first differences to write recursive rules for quadratic functions.

EXAMPLE 4 **Writing a Recursive Rule**

Write a recursive rule for the quadratic function f in Example 3.

SOLUTION

An expression for the nth term of the sequence of first differences is $-12 + 8(n - 1)$, or $8n - 20$. Notice that $f(n) - f(n - 1) = 8n - 20$.

▶ So, a recursive rule for the quadratic function is $f(0) = 12$, $f(n) = f(n - 1) + 8n - 20$.

Monitoring Progress

Help in English and Spanish at *BigIdeasMath.com*

5. Tell whether the table of values represents a *linear*, an *exponential*, or a *quadratic* function. Then write the function.

x	−1	0	1	2	3
y	16	8	4	2	1

6. Write a recursive rule for the function represented by the table of values.

x	0	1	2	3	4
f(x)	−8	−1	10	25	44

Comparing Functions Using Average Rates of Change

For nonlinear functions, the rate of change is not constant. You can compare two nonlinear functions over the same interval using their average rates of change. Recall that the average rate of change of a function $y = f(x)$ between $x = a$ and $x = b$ is the slope of the line through $(a, f(a))$ and $(b, f(b))$.

$$\text{average rate of change} = \frac{\text{change in } y}{\text{change in } x} = \frac{f(b) - f(a)}{b - a}$$

Exponential Function

Quadratic Function

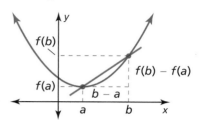

EXAMPLE 5   **Using and Interpreting Average Rates of Change**

The table and graph show the populations of two species of fish introduced into a lake. Compare the populations by calculating and interpreting the average rates of change from Year 0 to Year 4.

Species A	
Year, *x*	Population, *y*
0	100
2	264
4	428
6	592
8	756
10	920

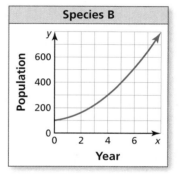

SOLUTION

Calculate the average rates of change by using the points whose *x*-coordinates are 0 and 4.

Species A: Use (0, 100) and (4, 428).

$$\text{average rate of change} = \frac{f(b) - f(a)}{b - a} = \frac{428 - 100}{4 - 0} = 82$$

Species B: Use the graph to estimate the points when $x = 0$ and $x = 4$. Use (0, 100) and (4, 300).

$$\text{average rate of change} = \frac{f(b) - f(a)}{b - a} \approx \frac{300 - 100}{4 - 0} = 50$$

> From Year 0 to Year 4, the population of Species A increases at an average rate of 82 fish per year, and the population of Species B increases at an average rate of about 50 fish per year. So, the population of Species A is growing faster.

Monitoring Progress Help in English and Spanish at *BigIdeasMath.com*

7. Compare the populations by calculating and interpreting the average rates of change from Year 4 to Year 8.

Core Concept

Comparing Functions Using Average Rates of Change

- As a and b increase, the average rate of change between $x = a$ and $x = b$ of an increasing exponential function $y = f(x)$ will eventually exceed the average rate of change between $x = a$ and $x = b$ of an increasing quadratic function $y = g(x)$ or an increasing linear function $y = h(x)$. So, as x increases, $f(x)$ will eventually exceed $g(x)$ or $h(x)$.

- As a and b increase, the average rate of change between $x = a$ and $x = b$ of an increasing quadratic function $y = g(x)$ will eventually exceed the average rate of change between $x = a$ and $x = b$ of an increasing linear function $y = h(x)$. So, as x increases, $g(x)$ will eventually exceed $h(x)$.

STUDY TIP

You can explore these concepts using a graphing calculator.

EXAMPLE 6 Comparing Different Function Types

Let x represent the number of years since 1900. The function $C(x) = 12x^2 + 12x + 100$ represents the population of Cedar Ridge. In 1900, Pine Valley had a population of 50 people. Pine Valley's population increased by 9% each year.

a. From 1900 to 1950, which town's population had a greater average rate of change?

b. Which town will eventually have a greater population? Explain.

SOLUTION

a. Write the function that represents the population of Cedar Ridge and a function to model the population of Pine Valley.

Cedar Ridge: $C(x) = 12x^2 + 12x + 100$ Quadratic function

Pine Valley: $P(x) = 50(1.09)^x$ Exponential function

Find the average rate of change from 1900 to 1950 for the population of each town.

Cedar Ridge	Pine Valley
$\dfrac{C(50) - C(0)}{50 - 0} = 612$	$\dfrac{P(50) - P(0)}{50 - 0} \approx 73$

▶ From 1900 to 1950, the average rate of change of Cedar Ridge's population was greater.

b. Because Pine Valley's population is given by an increasing exponential function and Cedar Ridge's population is given by an increasing quadratic function, Pine Valley will eventually have a greater population. Using a graphing calculator, you can see that Pine Valley's population caught up to and exceeded Cedar Ridge's population between $x = 87$ and $x = 88$, which corresponds to 1987.

	Pine Valley	Cedar Ridge
X	Y1	Y2
87	90173	91972
87.1	90953	92182
87.2	91740	92392
87.3	92534	92603
87.4	93335	92814
87.5	94143	93025
87.6	94958	93236
X=87		

Monitoring Progress Help in English and Spanish at *BigIdeasMath.com*

8. From 1950 to 2000, which town's population had a greater average rate of change?

Vocabulary and Core Concept Check

1. **WRITING** Name three types of functions that you can use to model data. Describe the equation and graph of each type of function.

2. **WRITING** How can you decide whether to use a linear, an exponential, or a quadratic function to model a data set?

3. **VOCABULARY** Describe how to find the average rate of change of a function $y = f(x)$ between $x = a$ and $x = b$.

4. **WHICH ONE DOESN'T BELONG?** Which graph does *not* belong with the other three? Explain your reasoning.

   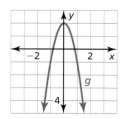

Monitoring Progress and Modeling with Mathematics

In Exercises 5–8, tell whether the points appear to represent a *linear*, an *exponential*, or a *quadratic* function.

5.

6.

7.

8.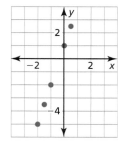

In Exercises 9–14, plot the points. Tell whether the points appear to represent a *linear*, an *exponential*, or a *quadratic* function. *(See Example 1.)*

9. $(-2, -1), (-1, 0), (1, 2), (2, 3), (0, 1)$

10. $\left(0, \frac{1}{4}\right), (1, 1), (2, 4), (3, 16), \left(-1, \frac{1}{16}\right)$

11. $(0, -3), (1, 0), (2, 9), (-2, 9), (-1, 0)$

12. $(-1, -3), (-3, 5), (0, -1), (1, 5), (2, 15)$

13. $(-4, -4), (-2, -3.4), (0, -3), (2, -2.6), (4, -2)$

14. $(0, 8), (-4, 0.25), (-3, 0.4), (-2, 1), (-1, 3)$

In Exercises 15–18, tell whether the table of values represents a *linear*, an *exponential*, or a *quadratic* function. *(See Example 2.)*

15.

x	−2	−1	0	1	2
y	0	0.5	1	1.5	2

16.

x	−1	0	1	2	3
y	0.2	1	5	25	125

17.

x	2	3	4	5	6
y	2	6	18	54	162

18.

x	−3	−2	−1	0	1
y	2	4.5	8	12.5	18

19. MODELING WITH MATHEMATICS A student takes a subway to a public library. The table shows the distances *d* (in miles) the student travels in *t* minutes. Let the time *t* represent the independent variable. Tell whether the data can be modeled by a *linear*, an *exponential*, or a *quadratic* function. Explain.

Time, *t*	0.5	1	3	5
Distance, *d*	0.335	0.67	2.01	3.35

20. MODELING WITH MATHEMATICS A store sells custom circular rugs. The table shows the costs *c* (in dollars) of rugs that have diameters of *d* feet. Let the diameter *d* represent the independent variable. Tell whether the data can be modeled by a *linear*, an *exponential*, or a *quadratic* function. Explain.

Diameter, *d*	3	4	5	6
Cost, *c*	63.90	113.60	177.50	255.60

In Exercises 21–26, tell whether the data represent a *linear*, an *exponential*, or a *quadratic* function. Then write the function. *(See Example 3.)*

21. $(-2, 8), (-1, 0), (0, -4), (1, -4), (2, 0), (3, 8)$

22. $(-3, 8), (-2, 4), (-1, 2), (0, 1), (1, 0.5)$

23.

x	−2	−1	0	1	2
y	4	1	−2	−5	−8

24.

x	−1	0	1	2	3
y	2.5	5	10	20	40

25.

26.
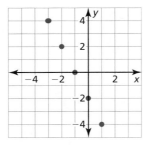

In Exercises 27 and 28, write a recursive rule for the function represented by the table of values.
(See Example 4.)

27.

x	0	1	2	3	4
f(x)	2	1	2	5	10

28.

x	0	1	2	3	4
f(x)	3	6	12	24	48

29. ERROR ANALYSIS Describe and correct the error in determining whether the table represents a linear, an exponential, or a quadratic function.

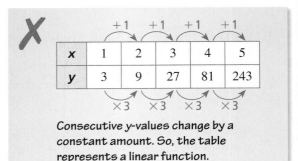

30. ERROR ANALYSIS Describe and correct the error in writing the function represented by the table.

31. REASONING The table shows the numbers of people attending the first five football games at a high school.

Game, *g*	1	2	3	4	5
People, *p*	252	325	270	249	310

a. Plot the points. Let the game *g* represent the independent variable.

b. Can a linear, an exponential, or a quadratic function represent this situation? Explain.

32. MODELING WITH MATHEMATICS The table shows the breathing rates y (in liters of air per minute) of a cyclist traveling at different speeds x (in miles per hour).

Speed, x	20	21	22	23	24
Breathing rate, y	51.4	57.1	63.3	70.3	78.0

a. Plot the points. Let the speed x represent the independent variable. Then determine the type of function that best represents this situation.

b. Write a function that models the data.

c. Find the breathing rate of a cyclist traveling 18 miles per hour. Round your answer to the nearest tenth.

33. ANALYZING RATES OF CHANGE The function $f(t) = -16t^2 + 48t + 3$ represents the height (in feet) of a volleyball t seconds after it is hit into the air.

a. Copy and complete the table.

t	0	0.5	1	1.5	2	2.5	3
$f(t)$							

b. Plot the ordered pairs and draw a smooth curve through the points.

c. Describe where the function is increasing and decreasing.

d. Find the average rate of change for each 0.5-second interval in the table. What do you notice about the average rates of change when the function is increasing? decreasing?

34. ANALYZING RELATIONSHIPS The population of Species A in 2010 was 100. The population of Species A increased by 6% every year. Let x represent the number of years since 2010. The graph shows the population of Species B. Compare the populations of the species by calculating and interpreting the average rates of change from 2010 to 2016. *(See Example 5.)*

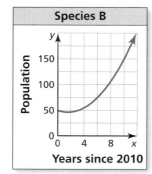

35. ANALYZING RELATIONSHIPS Three charities are holding telethons. Charity A begins with one pledge, and the number of pledges triples each hour. The table shows the numbers of pledges received by Charity B. The graph shows the numbers of pledges received by Charity C.

Time (hours), t	Number of pledges, y
0	12
1	24
2	36
3	48
4	60
5	72
6	84

a. What type of function represents the numbers of pledges received by Charity A? B? C?

b. Find the average rates of change of each function for each 1-hour interval from $t = 0$ to $t = 6$.

c. For which function does the average rate of change increase most quickly? What does this tell you about the numbers of pledges received by the three charities?

36. COMPARING FUNCTIONS Let x represent the number of years since 1900. The function

$$H(x) = 10x^2 + 10x + 500$$

represents the population of Oak Hill. In 1900, Poplar Grove had a population of 200 people. Poplar Grove's population increased by 8% each year. *(See Example 6.)*

a. From 1900 to 1950, which town's population had a greater average rate of change?

b. Which town will eventually have a greater population? Explain.

37. COMPARING FUNCTIONS Let x represent the number of years since 2000. The function

$$R(x) = 0.01x^2 + 0.22x + 1.08$$

represents the revenue (in millions of dollars) of Company A. In 2000, Company B had a revenue of $2.12 million. Company B's revenue increased by $0.32 million each year.

a. From 2000 to 2015, which company's revenue had a greater average rate of change?

b. Which company will eventually have a greater revenue? Explain.

38. HOW DO YOU SEE IT? Match each graph with its function. Explain your reasoning.

a.

b.

c.

d.

A. $y = 2x^2 - 4$

B. $y = 2^x - 1$

C. $y = 2x - 1$

D. $y = -2x^2 + 4$

39. REASONING Explain why the average rate of change of a linear function is constant and the average rate of change of a quadratic or exponential function is not constant.

40. CRITICAL THINKING In the ordered pairs below, the y-values are given in terms of n. Tell whether the ordered pairs represent a *linear*, an *exponential*, or a *quadratic* function. Explain.

$(1, 3n - 1), (2, 10n + 2), (3, 26n),$
$(4, 51n - 7), (5, 85n - 19)$

41. USING STRUCTURE Write a function that has constant second differences of 3.

42. CRITICAL THINKING Is the graph of a set of points enough to determine whether the points represent a linear, an exponential, or a quadratic function? Justify your answer.

43. MAKING AN ARGUMENT Function p is an exponential function and function q is a quadratic function. Your friend says that after about $x = 3$, function q will always have a greater y-value than function p. Is your friend correct? Explain.

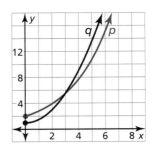

44. THOUGHT PROVOKING Find three different patterns in the figure. Determine whether each pattern represents a *linear*, an *exponential*, or a *quadratic* function. Write a model for each pattern.

$n = 1$ $n = 2$ $n = 3$ $n = 4$

45. USING TOOLS The table shows the amount a (in billions of dollars) United States residents spent on pets or pet-related products and services each year for a 5-year period. Let the year x represent the independent variable. Using technology, find a function that models the data. How did you choose the model? Predict how much residents will spend on pets or pet-related products and services in Year 7.

Year, x	1	2	3	4	5
Amount, a	53.1	56.9	61.8	65.7	67.1

Maintaining Mathematical Proficiency
Reviewing what you learned in previous grades and lessons

Evaluate the expression. *(Section 1.5)*

46. $\sqrt{121}$

47. $\sqrt[3]{125}$

48. $\sqrt[3]{512}$

49. $\sqrt[5]{243}$

Find the product. *(Section 2.3)*

50. $(x + 6)(x - 6)$

51. $(2y + 5)(2y - 5)$

52. $(4c - 3d)(4c + 3d)$

53. $(-3s + 8t)(-3s - 8t)$

Core Vocabulary

even function, *p. 146*
odd function, *p. 146*

vertex form (of a quadratic
  function), *p. 148*

intercept form, *p. 154*
focus, *p. 162*
directrix, *p. 162*

Core Concepts

Section 3.4

Even and Odd Functions, *p. 146*
Graphing $f(x) = a(x - h)^2$, *p. 147*
Graphing $f(x) = a(x - h)^2 + k$, *p. 148*

Writing Quadratic Functions of the Form
  $f(x) = a(x - h)^2 + k$, *p. 149*

Section 3.5

Graphing $f(x) = a(x - p)(x - q)$, *p. 154*
Factors and Zeros, *p. 156*

Using Characteristics to Graph and Write Quadratic
  Functions, *p. 156*

Section 3.6

Standard Equations of a Parabola with Vertex at the
  Origin, *p. 163*

Standard Equations of a Parabola with Vertex at (h, k),
  p. 164

Section 3.7

Linear, Exponential, and Quadratic Functions, *p. 170*
Differences and Ratios of Functions, *p. 171*

Writing Functions to Model Data, *p. 172*
Comparing Functions Using Average Rates of Change,
  p. 173

Mathematical Practices

1. How can you use technology to confirm your answer in Exercise 64 on page 152?

2. How did you use the structure of the equation in Exercise 65 on page 159 to solve the problem?

3. Describe why your answer makes sense considering the context of the data in Exercise 20 on page 176.

Performance Task:

Solar Energy

There are many factors that influence the design of a product, such as aesthetics, available space, and special properties. What are the special properties of a parabola that contribute to its use? How do parabolas help create power from solar energy?

To explore the answers to these questions and more, check out the Performance Task and Real-Life STEM video at *BigIdeasMath.com*.

3.1 Graphing $f(x) = ax^2$ *(pp. 123–128)*

Graph $g(x) = -4x^2$. Compare the graph to the graph of $f(x) = x^2$.

Step 1 Make a table of values.

x	−2	−1	0	1	2
g(x)	−16	−4	0	−4	−16

Step 2 Plot the ordered pairs.

Step 3 Draw a smooth curve through the points.

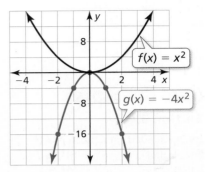

▶ The graphs have the same vertex, (0, 0), and the same axis of symmetry, $x = 0$, but the graph of g opens down and is narrower than the graph of f. So, the graph of g is a vertical stretch by a factor of 4 and a reflection in the x-axis of the graph of f.

Graph the function. Compare the graph to the graph of $f(x) = x^2$.

1. $p(x) = 7x^2$
2. $q(x) = \frac{1}{2}x^2$
3. $g(x) = -\frac{3}{4}x^2$
4. $h(x) = -6x^2$

5. Identify characteristics of the quadratic function and its graph.

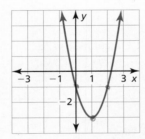

3.2 Graphing $f(x) = ax^2 + c$ *(pp. 129–134)*

Graph $g(x) = 2x^2 + 3$. Compare the graph to the graph of $f(x) = x^2$.

Step 1 Make a table of values.

x	−2	−1	0	1	2
g(x)	11	5	3	5	11

Step 2 Plot the ordered pairs.

Step 3 Draw a smooth curve through the points.

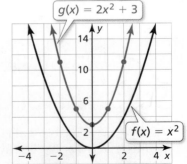

▶ Both graphs open up and have the same axis of symmetry, $x = 0$.
The graph of g is narrower, and its vertex, (0, 3), is above the vertex of the graph of f, (0, 0). So, the graph of g is a vertical stretch by a factor of 2 and a vertical translation 3 units up of the graph of f.

Graph the function. Compare the graph to the graph of $f(x) = x^2$.

6. $g(x) = x^2 + 5$
7. $h(x) = -x^2 - 4$
8. $m(x) = -2x^2 + 6$
9. $n(x) = \frac{1}{3}x^2 - 5$

3.3 Graphing $f(x) = ax^2 + bx + c$ (pp. 135–142)

Graph $f(x) = 4x^2 + 8x - 1$. Describe the domain and range.

Step 1 Find and graph the axis of symmetry: $x = -\dfrac{b}{2a} = -\dfrac{8}{2(4)} = -1$.

Step 2 Find and plot the vertex. The axis of symmetry is $x = -1$. So, the x-coordinate of the vertex is -1. The y-coordinate of the vertex is $f(-1) = 4(-1)^2 + 8(-1) - 1 = -5$. So, the vertex is $(-1, -5)$.

Step 3 Use the y-intercept to find two more points on the graph. Because $c = -1$, the y-intercept is -1. So, $(0, -1)$ lies on the graph. Because the axis of symmetry is $x = -1$, the point $(-2, -1)$ also lies on the graph.

Step 4 Draw a smooth curve through the points.

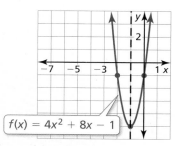

$f(x) = 4x^2 + 8x - 1$

▶ The domain is all real numbers. The range is $y \geq -5$.

Graph the function. Describe the domain and range.

10. $y = x^2 - 2x + 7$

11. $f(x) = -3x^2 + 3x - 4$

12. $y = \frac{1}{2}x^2 - 6x + 10$

13. The function $f(t) = -16t^2 + 88t + 12$ represents the height (in feet) of a pumpkin t seconds after it is launched from a catapult. When does the pumpkin reach its maximum height? What is the maximum height of the pumpkin?

3.4 Graphing $f(x) = a(x - h)^2 + k$ (pp. 145–152)

Determine whether $f(x) = 2x^2 + 4$ is *even*, *odd*, or *neither*.

$f(x) = 2x^2 + 4$ Write the original function.

$f(-x) = 2(-x)^2 + 4$ Substitute $-x$ for x.

$= 2x^2 + 4$ Simplify.

$= f(x)$ Substitute $f(x)$ for $2x^2 + 4$.

▶ Because $f(-x) = f(x)$, the function is even.

Determine whether the function is *even*, *odd*, or *neither*.

14. $w(x) = 5^x$

15. $r(x) = -8x$

16. $h(x) = 3x^2 - 2x$

Graph the function. Compare the graph to the graph of $f(x) = x^2$.

17. $h(x) = 2(x - 4)^2$

18. $g(x) = \frac{1}{2}(x - 1)^2 + 1$

19. $q(x) = -(x + 4)^2 + 7$

20. Consider the function $g(x) = -3(x + 2)^2 - 4$. Graph $h(x) = g(x - 1)$.

21. Write a quadratic function whose graph has a vertex of $(3, 2)$ and passes through the point $(4, 7)$.

3.5 Graphing $f(x) = a(x - p)(x - q)$ (pp. 153–160)

a. Graph $f(x) = -(x + 4)(x - 2)$. Describe the domain and range.

Step 1 Identify the x-intercepts. Because the x-intercepts are $p = -4$ and $q = 2$, plot $(-4, 0)$ and $(2, 0)$.

Step 2 Find and graph the axis of symmetry.

$$x = \frac{p + q}{2} = \frac{-4 + 2}{2} = -1$$

Step 3 Find and plot the vertex.

The x-coordinate of the vertex is -1. To find the y-coordinate of the vertex, substitute -1 for x and simplify.

$$f(-1) = -(-1 + 4)(-1 - 2) = 9$$

So, the vertex is $(-1, 9)$.

Step 4 Draw a parabola through the vertex and the points where the x-intercepts occur.

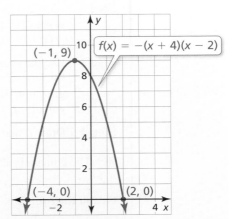

▶ The domain is all real numbers. The range is $y \le 9$.

b. Use zeros to graph $h(x) = x^2 - 7x + 6$.

The function is in standard form. The parabola opens up ($a > 0$), and the y-intercept is 6. So, plot $(0, 6)$.

The polynomial that defines the function is factorable. So, write the function in intercept form and identify the zeros.

$$h(x) = x^2 - 7x + 6 \qquad \text{Write the function.}$$
$$= (x - 6)(x - 1) \qquad \text{Factor the trinomial.}$$

The zeros of the function are 1 and 6. So, plot $(1, 0)$ and $(6, 0)$. Draw a parabola through the points.

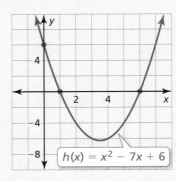

Graph the quadratic function. Label the vertex, axis of symmetry, and x-intercepts. Describe the domain and range of the function.

22. $y = (x - 4)(x + 2)$

23. $f(x) = -3(x + 3)(x + 1)$

24. $y = x^2 - 8x + 15$

Use zeros to graph the function.

25. $y = -2x^2 + 6x + 8$

26. $f(x) = x^2 + x - 2$

27. $f(x) = 2x^2 - 18$

28. Write a quadratic function in standard form whose graph passes through $(4, 0)$ and $(6, 0)$.

3.6 **Focus of a Parabola** *(pp. 161–168)*

a. **Identify the focus, directrix, and axis of symmetry of $8x = y^2$. Graph the equation.**

Step 1 Rewrite the equation in standard form.

$8x = y^2$ Write the original equation.

$x = \dfrac{1}{8}y^2$ Divide each side by 8.

Step 2 Identify the focus, directrix, and axis of symmetry. The equation has the form $x = \dfrac{1}{4p}y^2$, where $p = 2$. The focus is $(p, 0)$, or $(2, 0)$. The directrix is $x = -p$, or $x = -2$. Because y is squared, the axis of symmetry is the x-axis.

Step 3 Use a table of values to graph the equation. Notice that it is easier to substitute y-values and solve for x.

y	0	±2	±4	±6
x	0	0.5	2	4.5

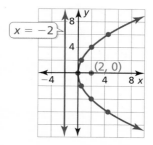

b. **Write an equation of the parabola shown.**

Because the vertex is not at the origin and the axis of symmetry is vertical, the equation has the form $y = \dfrac{1}{4p}(x - h)^2 + k$. The vertex (h, k) is $(2, 3)$ and the focus $(h, k + p)$ is $(2, 4)$, so $h = 2$, $k = 3$, and $p = 1$. Substitute these values to write an equation of the parabola.

$$y = \frac{1}{4(1)}(x - 2)^2 + 3 = \frac{1}{4}(x - 2)^2 + 3$$

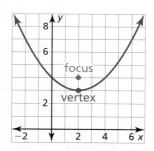

▶ An equation of the parabola is $y = \dfrac{1}{4}(x - 2)^2 + 3$.

29. You can make a solar hot-dog cooker by shaping foil-lined cardboard into a parabolic trough and passing a wire through the focus of each end piece. For the trough shown, how far from the bottom should the wire be placed?

30. Graph the equation $36y = x^2$. Identify the focus, directrix, and axis of symmetry.

Write an equation of the parabola with the given characteristics.

31. vertex: $(0, 0)$
    directrix: $x = 2$

32. focus: $(2, 2)$
    vertex: $(2, 6)$

Tell whether the data represent a *linear*, an *exponential*, or a *quadratic* function.

a. $(-4, 1), (-3, -2), (-2, -3)$
$(-1, -2), (0, 1)$

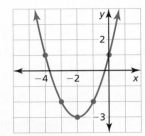

▶ The points appear to represent
a quadratic function.

b. $(-2, 16), (-1, 8), (0, 4)$
$(1, 2), (2, 1)$

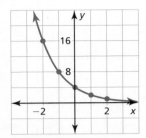

▶ The points appear to represent
an exponential function.

c.

x	−1	0	1	2	3
y	15	8	1	−6	−13

▶ The first differences are constant. So,
the table represents a linear function.

d.

x	0	1	2	3	4
y	1	5	6	4	−1

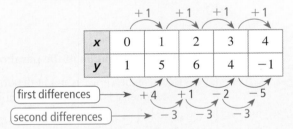

▶ The second differences are constant.
So, the table represents a quadratic
function.

33. Tell whether the table of values represents a *linear*, an *exponential*, or a *quadratic* function.
Then write the function.

x	−1	0	1	2	3
y	512	128	32	8	2

34. Write a recursive rule for the function represented by the table of values.

x	0	1	2	3	4
f(x)	5	6	11	20	33

35. The balance y (in dollars) of your savings account after t years is represented by $y = 200(1.1)^t$.
The beginning balance of your friend's account is $250, and the balance increases by
$20 each year. Compare the account balances by calculating and interpreting the average rates
of change from $t = 2$ to $t = 7$.

Graph the function. Compare the graph to the graph of $f(x) = x^2$.

1. $h(x) = 2x^2 - 3$

2. $g(x) = -\frac{1}{2}x^2$

3. $p(x) = \frac{1}{2}(x + 1)^2 - 1$

4. Consider the graph of the function f.

    a. Find the domain, range, and zeros of the function.

    b. Write the function f in standard form.

    c. Compare the graph of f to the graph of $g(x) = x^2$.

    d. Graph $h(x) = f(x - 6)$.

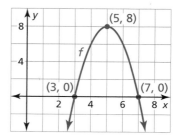

Use zeros to graph the function. Describe the domain and range of the function.

5. $f(x) = 2x^2 - 8x + 8$

6. $y = -(x + 5)(x - 1)$

7. $h(x) = 16x^2 - 4$

8. Identify an focus, directrix, and axis of symmetry of $x = 2y^2$. Graph the equation.

Write an equation of the parabola. Justify your answer.

9.

10.

11.

Tell whether the table of values represents a *linear*, an *exponential*, or a *quadratic* function. Explain your reasoning. Then write the function.

12.

x	−1	0	1	2	3
y	4	8	16	32	64

13.

x	−2	−1	0	1	2
y	−8	−2	0	−2	−8

14. You are playing tennis with a friend. The path of the tennis ball after you return a serve can be modeled by the function $y = -0.005x^2 + 0.17x + 3$, where x is the horizontal distance (in feet) from where you hit the ball and y is the height (in feet) of the ball.

    a. What is the maximum height of the tennis ball?

    b. You are standing 30 feet from the net, which is 3 feet high. Will the ball clear the net? Explain your reasoning.

15. Find values of a, b, and c so that the function $f(x) = ax^2 + bx + c$ is (a) even, (b) odd, and (c) neither even nor odd.

16. Consider the function $f(x) = x^2 + 4$. Find the average rate of change from $x = 0$ to $x = 1$, from $x = 1$ to $x = 2$, and from $x = 2$ to $x = 3$. What do you notice about the average rates of change when the function is increasing?

1. Which function is represented by the graph?

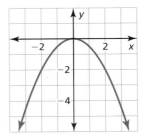

   Ⓐ $y = \frac{1}{2}x^2$

   Ⓑ $y = 2x^2$

   Ⓒ $y = -\frac{1}{2}x^2$

   Ⓓ $y = -2x^2$

2. A linear function f has the following values at $x = 2$ and $x = 5$.

$$f(2) = 6, \ f(5) = 3$$

   What is the value of the inverse of f at $x = 4$?

3. The function $f(t) = -16t^2 + v_0 t + s_0$ represents the height (in feet) of a ball t seconds after it is thrown from an initial height s_0 (in feet) with an initial vertical velocity v_0 (in feet per second). The ball reaches its maximum height after $\frac{7}{8}$ second when it is thrown with an initial vertical velocity of _____ feet per second.

4. Order the following parabolas from widest to narrowest.

   A. focus: $(0, -3)$; directrix: $y = 3$

   B. $y = \frac{1}{16}x^2 + 4$

   C. $x = \frac{1}{8}y^2$

   D. $y = \frac{1}{4}(x - 2)^2 + 3$

5. Which polynomial represents the area (in square feet) of the shaded region of the figure?

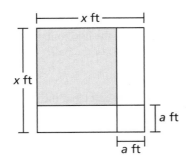

   Ⓐ $a^2 - x^2$

   Ⓑ $x^2 - a^2$

   Ⓒ $x^2 - 2ax + a^2$

   Ⓓ $x^2 + 2ax + a^2$

6. Consider the functions represented by the tables.

x	0	1	2	3
p(x)	−4	−16	−28	−40

x	1	2	3	4
r(x)	0	15	40	75

x	1	2	3	4
s(x)	72	36	18	9

x	1	3	5	7
t(x)	3	−5	−21	−45

   a. Classify each function as *linear*, *exponential*, or *quadratic*.

   b. Order the functions from least to greatest according to the average rates of change between $x = 1$ and $x = 3$.

7. Which expressions are equivalent to $14x - 15 + 8x^2$?

$(4x + 3)(2x - 5)$	$(4x - 3)(2x + 5)$
$(4x + 3)(2x + 5)$	$(4x - 3)(2x - 5)$
$8x^2 - 14x - 15$	$8x^2 + 14x - 15$

8. Complete each function using the symbols $+$ or $-$, so that the graph of the quadratic function satisfies the given conditions.

   a. $f(x) = 5(x \quad 3)^2 \quad 4$; vertex: $(-3, 4)$

   b. $g(x) = -(x \quad 2)(x \quad 8)$; x-intercepts: -8 and 2

   c. $h(x) = \quad 3x^2 \quad 6$; range: $y \geq -6$

   d. $j(x) = \quad 4(x \quad 1)(x \quad 1)$; range: $y \leq 4$

9. Which expressions are equivalent to $(b^{-5})^{-4}$?

b^{-20}	$b^{-6}b^{-14}$	$(b^{-4})^{-5}$	b^{-9}	$(b^{-2})^{-7}$
$b^{-5}b^{-4}$	$(b^{10})^2$	b^{20}	$(b^{-12})^3$	$b^{12}b^8$

4 Solving Quadratic Equations

Robot-Building Competition *(p. 265)*

Feeding Gannet *(p. 250)*

Electrical Circuits *(p. 240)*

Half-pipe *(p. 223)*

SEE the Big Idea

Parthenon *(p. 195)*

Maintaining Mathematical Proficiency

Factoring Perfect Square Trinomials

Example 1 **Factor $x^2 + 14x + 49$.**

$$x^2 + 14x + 49 = x^2 + 2(x)(7) + 7^2 \qquad \text{Write as } a^2 + 2ab + b^2.$$
$$= (x + 7)^2 \qquad \text{Perfect square trinomial pattern}$$

Factor the trinomial.

1. $x^2 + 10x + 25$

2. $x^2 - 20x + 100$

3. $x^2 + 12x + 36$

4. $x^2 - 18x + 81$

5. $x^2 + 16x + 64$

6. $x^2 - 30x + 225$

Solving Systems of Linear Equations by Graphing

Example 2 **Solve the system of linear equations by graphing.**

$$y = 2x + 1 \qquad \text{Equation 1}$$

$$y = -\frac{1}{3}x + 8 \qquad \text{Equation 2}$$

Step 1 Graph each equation.

Step 2 Estimate the point of intersection.
The graphs appear to intersect at $(3, 7)$.

Step 3 Check your point from Step 2.

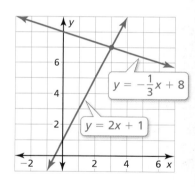

Equation 1   Equation 2

$$y = 2x + 1 \qquad y = -\frac{1}{3}x + 8$$

$$7 \overset{?}{=} 2(3) + 1 \qquad 7 \overset{?}{=} -\frac{1}{3}(3) + 8$$

$$7 = 7 \checkmark \qquad 7 = 7 \checkmark$$

▶ The solution is $(3, 7)$.

Solve the system of linear equations by graphing.

7. $y = -5x + 3$
$\quad\; y = 2x - 4$

8. $y = \frac{3}{2}x - 2$
$\quad\; y = -\frac{1}{4}x + 5$

9. $y = \frac{1}{2}x + 4$
$\quad\; y = -3x - 3$

10. ABSTRACT REASONING What value of c makes $x^2 + bx + c$ a perfect square trinomial?

Mathematical Practices

Mathematically proficient students monitor their work and change course as needed.

Problem-Solving Strategies

Core Concept

Guess, Check, and Revise

When solving a problem in mathematics, it is often helpful to estimate a solution and then observe how close that solution is to being correct. For instance, you can use the guess, check, and revise strategy to find a decimal approximation of the square root of 2.

	Guess	Check	How to revise
1.	1.4	$1.4^2 = 1.96$	Increase guess.
2.	1.41	$1.41^2 = 1.9881$	Increase guess.
3.	1.415	$1.415^2 = 2.002225$	Decrease guess.

By continuing this process, you can determine that the square root of 2 is approximately 1.4142.

EXAMPLE 1 Approximating a Solution of an Equation

The graph of $y = x^2 + x - 1$ is shown. Approximate the positive solution of the equation $x^2 + x - 1 = 0$ to the nearest thousandth.

SOLUTION

Using the graph, you can make an initial estimate of the positive solution to be $x = 0.65$.

	Guess	Check	How to revise
1.	0.65	$0.65^2 + 0.65 - 1 = 0.0725$	Decrease guess.
2.	0.62	$0.62^2 + 0.62 - 1 = 0.0044$	Decrease guess.
3.	0.618	$0.618^2 + 0.618 - 1 = -0.000076$	Increase guess.
4.	0.6181	$0.6181^2 + 0.6181 - 1 \approx 0.00015$	The solution is between 0.618 and 0.6181.

▶ So, to the nearest thousandth, the positive solution of the equation is $x = 0.618$.

Monitoring Progress

1. Use the graph in Example 1 to approximate the negative solution of the equation $x^2 + x - 1 = 0$ to the nearest thousandth.

2. The graph of $y = x^2 + x - 3$ is shown. Approximate both solutions of the equation $x^2 + x - 3 = 0$ to the nearest thousandth.

4.1 Properties of Radicals

Essential Question How can you multiply and divide square roots?

EXPLORATION 1   Operations with Square Roots

Work with a partner. For each operation with square roots, compare the results obtained using the two indicated orders of operations. What can you conclude?

a. Square Roots and Addition

Is $\sqrt{36} + \sqrt{64}$ equal to $\sqrt{36 + 64}$?

In general, is $\sqrt{a} + \sqrt{b}$ equal to $\sqrt{a + b}$? Explain your reasoning.

b. Square Roots and Multiplication

Is $\sqrt{4} \cdot \sqrt{9}$ equal to $\sqrt{4 \cdot 9}$?

In general, is $\sqrt{a} \cdot \sqrt{b}$ equal to $\sqrt{a \cdot b}$? Explain your reasoning.

c. Square Roots and Subtraction

Is $\sqrt{64} - \sqrt{36}$ equal to $\sqrt{64 - 36}$?

In general, is $\sqrt{a} - \sqrt{b}$ equal to $\sqrt{a - b}$? Explain your reasoning.

d. Square Roots and Division

Is $\dfrac{\sqrt{100}}{\sqrt{4}}$ equal to $\sqrt{\dfrac{100}{4}}$?

In general, is $\dfrac{\sqrt{a}}{\sqrt{b}}$ equal to $\sqrt{\dfrac{a}{b}}$? Explain your reasoning.

REASONING ABSTRACTLY

To be proficient in math, you need to recognize and use counterexamples.

EXPLORATION 2   Writing Counterexamples

Work with a partner. A **counterexample** is an example that proves that a general statement is *not* true. For each general statement in Exploration 1 that is not true, write a counterexample different from the example given.

Communicate Your Answer

3. How can you multiply and divide square roots?

4. Give an example of multiplying square roots and an example of dividing square roots that are different from the examples in Exploration 1.

5. Write an algebraic rule for each operation.

   a. the product of square roots

   b. the quotient of square roots

What You Will Learn

▶ Use properties of radicals to simplify expressions.

▶ Simplify expressions by rationalizing the denominator.

▶ Perform operations with radicals.

Using Properties of Radicals

A **radical expression** is an expression that contains a radical. An expression involving a radical with index n is in **simplest form** when these three conditions are met.

• No radicands have perfect nth powers as factors other than 1.

• No radicands contain fractions.

• No radicals appear in the denominator of a fraction.

You can use the property below to simplify radical expressions involving square roots.

Core Concept

Product Property of Square Roots

Words The square root of a product equals the product of the square roots of the factors.

Numbers $\sqrt{9 \cdot 5} = \sqrt{9} \cdot \sqrt{5} = 3\sqrt{5}$

Algebra $\sqrt{ab} = \sqrt{a} \cdot \sqrt{b}$, where $a, b \geq 0$

STUDY TIP

There can be more than one way to factor a radicand. An efficient method is to find the greatest perfect square factor.

EXAMPLE 1 **Using the Product Property of Square Roots**

a. $\sqrt{108} = \sqrt{36 \cdot 3}$ Factor using the greatest perfect square factor.

     $= \sqrt{36} \cdot \sqrt{3}$ Product Property of Square Roots

     $= 6\sqrt{3}$ Simplify.

b. $\sqrt{9x^3} = \sqrt{9 \cdot x^2 \cdot x}$ Factor using the greatest perfect square factor.

     $= \sqrt{9} \cdot \sqrt{x^2} \cdot \sqrt{x}$ Product Property of Square Roots

     $= 3x\sqrt{x}$ Simplify.

STUDY TIP

In this course, whenever a variable appears in the radicand, assume that it has only *nonnegative* values.

Monitoring Progress Help in English and Spanish at *BigIdeasMath.com*

Simplify the expression.

  1. $\sqrt{24}$ **2.** $-\sqrt{80}$ **3.** $\sqrt{49x^3}$ **4.** $\sqrt{75n^5}$

Core Concept

Quotient Property of Square Roots

Words The square root of a quotient equals the quotient of the square roots of the numerator and denominator.

Numbers $\sqrt{\dfrac{3}{4}} = \dfrac{\sqrt{3}}{\sqrt{4}} = \dfrac{\sqrt{3}}{2}$ **Algebra** $\sqrt{\dfrac{a}{b}} = \dfrac{\sqrt{a}}{\sqrt{b}}$, where $a \geq 0$ and $b > 0$

EXAMPLE 2 **Using the Quotient Property of Square Roots**

a. $\sqrt{\dfrac{15}{64}} = \dfrac{\sqrt{15}}{\sqrt{64}}$ Quotient Property of Square Roots

     $= \dfrac{\sqrt{15}}{8}$ Simplify.

b. $\sqrt{\dfrac{81}{x^2}} = \dfrac{\sqrt{81}}{\sqrt{x^2}}$ Quotient Property of Square Roots

     $= \dfrac{9}{x}$ Simplify.

You can extend the Product and Quotient Properties of Square Roots to other radicals, such as cube roots. When using these *properties of cube roots*, the radicands may contain negative numbers.

EXAMPLE 3 **Using Properties of Cube Roots**

a. $\sqrt[3]{-128} = \sqrt[3]{-64 \cdot 2}$ Factor using the greatest perfect cube factor.

     $= \sqrt[3]{-64} \cdot \sqrt[3]{2}$ Product Property of Cube Roots

     $= -4\sqrt[3]{2}$ Simplify.

b. $\sqrt[3]{125x^7} = \sqrt[3]{125 \cdot x^6 \cdot x}$ Factor using the greatest perfect cube factors.

     $= \sqrt[3]{125} \cdot \sqrt[3]{x^6} \cdot \sqrt[3]{x}$ Product Property of Cube Roots

     $= 5x^2\sqrt[3]{x}$ Simplify.

c. $\sqrt[3]{\dfrac{y}{216}} = \dfrac{\sqrt[3]{y}}{\sqrt[3]{216}}$ Quotient Property of Cube Roots

     $= \dfrac{\sqrt[3]{y}}{6}$ Simplify.

d. $\sqrt[3]{\dfrac{8x^4}{27y^3}} = \dfrac{\sqrt[3]{8x^4}}{\sqrt[3]{27y^3}}$ Quotient Property of Cube Roots

     $= \dfrac{\sqrt[3]{8 \cdot x^3 \cdot x}}{\sqrt[3]{27 \cdot y^3}}$ Factor using the greatest perfect cube factors.

     $= \dfrac{\sqrt[3]{8} \cdot \sqrt[3]{x^3} \cdot \sqrt[3]{x}}{\sqrt[3]{27} \cdot \sqrt[3]{y^3}}$ Product Property of Cube Roots

     $= \dfrac{2x\sqrt[3]{x}}{3y}$ Simplify.

STUDY TIP

To write a cube root in simplest form, find factors of the radicand that are perfect cubes.

Monitoring Progress Help in English and Spanish at *BigIdeasMath.com*

Simplify the expression.

5. $\sqrt{\dfrac{23}{9}}$ **6.** $-\sqrt{\dfrac{17}{100}}$ **7.** $\sqrt{\dfrac{36}{z^2}}$ **8.** $\sqrt{\dfrac{4x^2}{64}}$

9. $\sqrt[3]{54}$ **10.** $\sqrt[3]{16x^4}$ **11.** $\sqrt[3]{\dfrac{a}{-27}}$ **12.** $\sqrt[3]{\dfrac{25c^7d^3}{64}}$

Rationalizing the Denominator

When a radical is in the denominator of a fraction, you can multiply the fraction by an appropriate form of 1 to eliminate the radical from the denominator. This process is called **rationalizing the denominator**.

EXAMPLE 4 Rationalizing the Denominator

STUDY TIP

Rationalizing the denominator works because you multiply the numerator and denominator by the same nonzero number a, which is the same as multiplying by $\frac{a}{a}$, or 1.

a. $\dfrac{\sqrt{5}}{\sqrt{3n}} = \dfrac{\sqrt{5}}{\sqrt{3n}} \cdot \dfrac{\sqrt{3n}}{\sqrt{3n}}$　　　Multiply by $\dfrac{\sqrt{3n}}{\sqrt{3n}}$.

$\qquad\quad = \dfrac{\sqrt{15n}}{\sqrt{9n^2}}$　　　Product Property of Square Roots

$\qquad\quad = \dfrac{\sqrt{15n}}{\sqrt{9} \cdot \sqrt{n^2}}$　　　Product Property of Square Roots

$\qquad\quad = \dfrac{\sqrt{15n}}{3n}$　　　Simplify.

b. $\dfrac{2}{\sqrt[3]{9}} = \dfrac{2}{\sqrt[3]{9}} \cdot \dfrac{\sqrt[3]{3}}{\sqrt[3]{3}}$　　　Multiply by $\dfrac{\sqrt[3]{3}}{\sqrt[3]{3}}$.

$\qquad\quad = \dfrac{2\sqrt[3]{3}}{\sqrt[3]{27}}$　　　Product Property of Cube Roots

$\qquad\quad = \dfrac{2\sqrt[3]{3}}{3}$　　　Simplify.

The binomials $a\sqrt{b} + c\sqrt{d}$ and $a\sqrt{b} - c\sqrt{d}$, where a, b, c, and d are rational numbers, are called **conjugates**. You can use conjugates to simplify radical expressions that contain a sum or difference involving square roots in the denominator.

EXAMPLE 5 Rationalizing the Denominator Using Conjugates

LOOKING FOR STRUCTURE

Notice that the product of two conjugates $a\sqrt{b} + c\sqrt{d}$ and $a\sqrt{b} - c\sqrt{d}$ does not contain a radical and is a *rational* number.

$\left(a\sqrt{b} + c\sqrt{d}\right)\left(a\sqrt{b} - c\sqrt{d}\right)$
$= \left(a\sqrt{b}\right)^2 - \left(c\sqrt{d}\right)^2$
$= a^2 b - c^2 d$

Simplify $\dfrac{7}{2 - \sqrt{3}}$.

SOLUTION

$\dfrac{7}{2 - \sqrt{3}} = \dfrac{7}{2 - \sqrt{3}} \cdot \dfrac{2 + \sqrt{3}}{2 + \sqrt{3}}$　　　The conjugate of $2 - \sqrt{3}$ is $2 + \sqrt{3}$.

$\qquad\quad = \dfrac{7(2 + \sqrt{3})}{2^2 - \left(\sqrt{3}\right)^2}$　　　Sum and difference pattern

$\qquad\quad = \dfrac{14 + 7\sqrt{3}}{1}$　　　Simplify.

$\qquad\quad = 14 + 7\sqrt{3}$　　　Simplify.

Monitoring Progress Help in English and Spanish at *BigIdeasMath.com*

Simplify the expression.

13. $\dfrac{1}{\sqrt{5}}$　　　**14.** $\dfrac{\sqrt{10}}{\sqrt{3}}$　　　**15.** $\dfrac{7}{\sqrt{2x}}$　　　**16.** $\sqrt{\dfrac{2y^2}{3}}$

17. $\dfrac{5}{\sqrt[3]{32}}$　　　**18.** $\dfrac{8}{1 + \sqrt{3}}$　　　**19.** $\dfrac{\sqrt{13}}{\sqrt{5} - 2}$　　　**20.** $\dfrac{12}{\sqrt{2} + \sqrt{7}}$

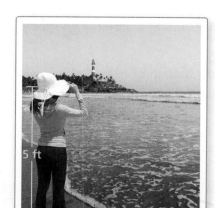

EXAMPLE 6 Solving a Real-Life Problem

The distance d (in miles) that you can see to the horizon with your eye level h feet above the water is given by $d = \sqrt{\dfrac{3h}{2}}$. How far can you see when your eye level is 5 feet above the water?

SOLUTION

$$d = \sqrt{\frac{3(5)}{2}} \qquad \text{Substitute 5 for } h.$$

$$= \frac{\sqrt{15}}{\sqrt{2}} \qquad \text{Quotient Property of Square Roots}$$

$$= \frac{\sqrt{15}}{\sqrt{2}} \cdot \frac{\sqrt{2}}{\sqrt{2}} \qquad \text{Multiply by } \frac{\sqrt{2}}{\sqrt{2}}.$$

$$= \frac{\sqrt{30}}{2} \qquad \text{Simplify.}$$

▶ You can see $\dfrac{\sqrt{30}}{2}$, or about 2.74 miles.

EXAMPLE 7 Modeling with Mathematics

The ratio of the length to the width of a *golden rectangle* is $\left(1 + \sqrt{5}\right) : 2$. The dimensions of the face of the Parthenon in Greece form a golden rectangle. What is the height h of the Parthenon?

SOLUTION

1. **Understand the Problem** Think of the length and height of the Parthenon as the length and width of a golden rectangle. The length of the rectangular face is 31 meters. You know the ratio of the length to the height. Find the height h.

2. **Make a Plan** Use the ratio $\left(1 + \sqrt{5}\right) : 2$ to write a proportion and solve for h.

3. **Solve the Problem**

$$\frac{1 + \sqrt{5}}{2} = \frac{31}{h} \qquad \text{Write a proportion.}$$

$$h\left(1 + \sqrt{5}\right) = 62 \qquad \text{Cross Products Property}$$

$$h = \frac{62}{1 + \sqrt{5}} \qquad \text{Divide each side by } 1 + \sqrt{5}.$$

$$h = \frac{62}{1 + \sqrt{5}} \cdot \frac{1 - \sqrt{5}}{1 - \sqrt{5}} \qquad \begin{array}{l}\text{Multiply the numerator and}\\\text{denominator by the conjugate.}\end{array}$$

$$h = \frac{62 - 62\sqrt{5}}{-4} \qquad \text{Simplify.}$$

$$h \approx 19.16 \qquad \text{Use a calculator.}$$

▶ The height is about 19 meters.

4. **Look Back** $\dfrac{1 + \sqrt{5}}{2} \approx 1.62$ and $\dfrac{31}{19.16} \approx 1.62$. So, your answer is reasonable.

Monitoring Progress Help in English and Spanish at *BigIdeasMath.com*

21. **WHAT IF?** In Example 6, how far can you see when your eye level is 35 feet above the water?

22. The dimensions of a dance floor form a golden rectangle. The shorter side of the dance floor is 50 feet. What is the length of the longer side of the dance floor?

Performing Operations with Radicals

Radicals with the same index and radicand are called **like radicals**. You can add and subtract like radicals the same way you combine like terms by using the Distributive Property.

STUDY TIP

Do not assume that radicals with different radicands cannot be added or subtracted. Always check to see whether you can simplify the radicals. In some cases, the radicals will become like radicals.

EXAMPLE 8   Adding and Subtracting Radicals

a. $5\sqrt{7} + \sqrt{11} - 8\sqrt{7} = 5\sqrt{7} - 8\sqrt{7} + \sqrt{11}$ Commutative Property of Addition

$= (5 - 8)\sqrt{7} + \sqrt{11}$ Distributive Property

$= -3\sqrt{7} + \sqrt{11}$ Subtract.

b. $10\sqrt{5} + \sqrt{20} = 10\sqrt{5} + \sqrt{4 \cdot 5}$ Factor using the greatest perfect square factor.

$= 10\sqrt{5} + \sqrt{4} \cdot \sqrt{5}$ Product Property of Square Roots

$= 10\sqrt{5} + 2\sqrt{5}$ Simplify.

$= (10 + 2)\sqrt{5}$ Distributive Property

$= 12\sqrt{5}$ Add.

c. $6\sqrt[3]{x} + 2\sqrt[3]{x} = (6 + 2)\sqrt[3]{x}$ Distributive Property

$= 8\sqrt[3]{x}$ Add.

EXAMPLE 9   Multiplying Radicals

Simplify $\sqrt{5}(\sqrt{3} - \sqrt{75})$.

SOLUTION

Method 1 $\sqrt{5}(\sqrt{3} - \sqrt{75}) = \sqrt{5} \cdot \sqrt{3} - \sqrt{5} \cdot \sqrt{75}$ Distributive Property

$= \sqrt{15} - \sqrt{375}$ Product Property of Square Roots

$= \sqrt{15} - 5\sqrt{15}$ Simplify.

$= (1 - 5)\sqrt{15}$ Distributive Property

$= -4\sqrt{15}$ Subtract.

Method 2 $\sqrt{5}(\sqrt{3} - \sqrt{75}) = \sqrt{5}(\sqrt{3} - 5\sqrt{3})$ Simplify $\sqrt{75}$.

$= \sqrt{5}[(1 - 5)\sqrt{3}]$ Distributive Property

$= \sqrt{5}(-4\sqrt{3})$ Subtract.

$= -4\sqrt{15}$ Product Property of Square Roots

Monitoring Progress Help in English and Spanish at *BigIdeasMath.com*

Simplify the expression.

23. $3\sqrt{2} - \sqrt{6} + 10\sqrt{2}$

24. $4\sqrt{7} - 6\sqrt{63}$

25. $4\sqrt[3]{5x} - 11\sqrt[3]{5x}$

26. $\sqrt{3}(8\sqrt{2} + 7\sqrt{32})$

27. $(2\sqrt{5} - 4)^2$

28. $\sqrt[3]{-4}(\sqrt[3]{2} - \sqrt[3]{16})$

Vocabulary and Core Concept Check

1. **COMPLETE THE SENTENCE** The process of eliminating a radical from the denominator of a radical expression is called _____.

2. **VOCABULARY** What is the conjugate of the binomial $\sqrt{6} + 4$?

3. **WRITING** Are the expressions $\frac{1}{3}\sqrt{2x}$ and $\sqrt{\frac{2x}{9}}$ equivalent? Explain your reasoning.

4. **WHICH ONE DOESN'T BELONG?** Which expression does *not* belong with the other three? Explain your reasoning.

$$-\frac{1}{3}\sqrt{6} \qquad 6\sqrt{3} \qquad \frac{1}{6}\sqrt{3} \qquad -3\sqrt{3}$$

Monitoring Progress and Modeling with Mathematics

In Exercises 5–12, determine whether the expression is in simplest form. If the expression is not in simplest form, explain why.

5. $\sqrt{19}$

6. $\sqrt{\frac{1}{7}}$

7. $\sqrt{48}$

8. $\sqrt{34}$

9. $\frac{5}{\sqrt{2}}$

10. $\frac{3\sqrt{10}}{4}$

11. $\frac{1}{2 + \sqrt[3]{2}}$

12. $6 - \sqrt[3]{54}$

In Exercises 13–20, simplify the expression.
(See Example 1.)

13. $\sqrt{20}$

14. $\sqrt{32}$

15. $\sqrt{128}$

16. $-\sqrt{72}$

17. $\sqrt{125b}$

18. $\sqrt{4x^2}$

19. $-\sqrt{81m^3}$

20. $\sqrt{48n^5}$

In Exercises 21–28, simplify the expression.
(See Example 2.)

21. $\sqrt{\frac{4}{49}}$

22. $-\sqrt{\frac{7}{81}}$

23. $-\sqrt{\frac{23}{64}}$

24. $\sqrt{\frac{65}{121}}$

25. $\sqrt{\frac{a^3}{49}}$

26. $\sqrt{\frac{144}{k^2}}$

27. $\sqrt{\frac{100}{4x^2}}$

28. $\sqrt{\frac{25v^2}{36}}$

In Exercises 29–36, simplify the expression.
(See Example 3.)

29. $\sqrt[3]{16}$

30. $\sqrt[3]{-108}$

31. $\sqrt[3]{-64x^5}$

32. $-\sqrt[3]{343n^2}$

33. $\sqrt[3]{\frac{6c}{-125}}$

34. $\sqrt[3]{\frac{8h^4}{27}}$

35. $-\sqrt[3]{\frac{81y^2}{1000x^3}}$

36. $\sqrt[3]{\frac{21}{-64a^3b^6}}$

ERROR ANALYSIS In Exercises 37 and 38, describe and correct the error in simplifying the expression.

37.

$$\sqrt{72} = \sqrt{4 \cdot 18}$$
$$= \sqrt{4} \cdot \sqrt{18}$$
$$= 2\sqrt{18}$$

38.
$$\sqrt[3]{\frac{128y^3}{125}} = \frac{\sqrt[3]{128y^3}}{125}$$
$$= \frac{\sqrt[3]{64 \cdot 2 \cdot y^3}}{125}$$
$$= \frac{\sqrt[3]{64} \cdot \sqrt[3]{2} \cdot \sqrt[3]{y^3}}{125}$$
$$= \frac{4y\sqrt[3]{2}}{125}$$

In Exercises 39–44, write a factor that you can use to rationalize the denominator of the expression.

39. $\dfrac{4}{\sqrt{6}}$

40. $\dfrac{1}{\sqrt{13z}}$

41. $\dfrac{2}{\sqrt[3]{x^2}}$

42. $\dfrac{3m}{\sqrt[3]{4}}$

43. $\dfrac{\sqrt{2}}{\sqrt{5}-8}$

44. $\dfrac{5}{\sqrt{3}+\sqrt{7}}$

In Exercises 45–54, simplify the expression. *(See Example 4.)*

45. $\dfrac{2}{\sqrt{2}}$

46. $\dfrac{4}{\sqrt{3}}$

47. $\dfrac{\sqrt{5}}{\sqrt{48}}$

48. $\sqrt{\dfrac{4}{52}}$

49. $\dfrac{3}{\sqrt{a}}$

50. $\dfrac{1}{\sqrt{2x}}$

51. $\sqrt{\dfrac{3d^2}{5}}$

52. $\dfrac{\sqrt{8}}{\sqrt{3n^3}}$

53. $\dfrac{4}{\sqrt[3]{25}}$

54. $\sqrt[3]{\dfrac{1}{108y^2}}$

In Exercises 55–60, simplify the expression. *(See Example 5.)*

55. $\dfrac{1}{\sqrt{7}+1}$

56. $\dfrac{2}{5-\sqrt{3}}$

57. $\dfrac{\sqrt{10}}{7-\sqrt{2}}$

58. $\dfrac{\sqrt{5}}{6+\sqrt{5}}$

59. $\dfrac{3}{\sqrt{5}-\sqrt{2}}$

60. $\dfrac{\sqrt{3}}{\sqrt{7}+\sqrt{3}}$

61. MODELING WITH MATHEMATICS The time t (in seconds) it takes an object to hit the ground is given by $t=\sqrt{\dfrac{h}{16}}$, where h is the height (in feet) from which the object was dropped. *(See Example 6.)*

a. How long does it take an earring to hit the ground when it falls from the roof of the building?

b. How much sooner does the earring hit the ground when it is dropped from two stories (22 feet) below the roof?

55 ft

62. MODELING WITH MATHEMATICS The orbital period of a planet is the time it takes the planet to travel around the Sun. You can find the orbital period P (in Earth years) using the formula $P=\sqrt{d^3}$, where d is the average distance (in astronomical units, abbreviated AU) of the planet from the Sun.

Jupiter

Sun

$d=5.2$ AU

a. Simplify the formula.

b. What is Jupiter's orbital period?

63. MODELING WITH MATHEMATICS The electric current I (in amperes) an appliance uses is given by the formula $I=\sqrt{\dfrac{P}{R}}$, where P is the power (in watts) and R is the resistance (in ohms). Find the current an appliance uses when the power is 147 watts and the resistance is 5 ohms.

64. MODELING WITH MATHEMATICS You can find the average annual interest rate r (in decimal form) of a savings account using the formula $r=\sqrt{\dfrac{V_2}{V_0}}-1$, where V_0 is the initial investment and V_2 is the balance of the account after 2 years. Use the formula to compare the savings accounts. In which account would you invest money? Explain.

Account	Initial investment	Balance after 2 years
1	$275	$293
2	$361	$382
3	$199	$214
4	$254	$272
5	$386	$406

In Exercises 65–68, evaluate the function for the given value of x. Write your answer in simplest form and in decimal form rounded to the nearest hundredth.

65. $h(x) = \sqrt{5x}; x = 10$ **66.** $g(x) = \sqrt{3x}; x = 60$

67. $r(x) = \sqrt{\dfrac{3x}{3x^2 + 6}}; x = 4$

68. $p(x) = \sqrt{\dfrac{x - 1}{5x}}; x = 8$

In Exercises 69–72, evaluate the expression when $a = -2$, $b = 8$, and $c = \frac{1}{2}$. Write your answer in simplest form and in decimal form rounded to the nearest hundredth.

69. $\sqrt{a^2 + bc}$ **70.** $-\sqrt{4c - 6ab}$

71. $-\sqrt{2a^2 + b^2}$ **72.** $\sqrt{b^2 - 4ac}$

73. **MODELING WITH MATHEMATICS** The text in the book shown forms a golden rectangle. What is the width w of the text? *(See Example 7.)*

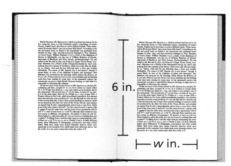

6 in.

$\longmapsto w$ in. $\longmapsto$

74. **MODELING WITH MATHEMATICS** The flag of Togo is approximately the shape of a golden rectangle. What is the width w of the flag?

$\longmapsto$ 42 in. $\longmapsto$

w in.

In Exercises 75–82, simplify the expression. *(See Example 8.)*

75. $\sqrt{3} - 2\sqrt{2} + 6\sqrt{2}$ **76.** $\sqrt{5} - 5\sqrt{13} - 8\sqrt{5}$

77. $2\sqrt{6} - 5\sqrt{54}$ **78.** $9\sqrt{32} + \sqrt{2}$

79. $\sqrt{12} + 6\sqrt{3} + 2\sqrt{6}$ **80.** $3\sqrt{7} - 5\sqrt{14} + 2\sqrt{28}$

81. $\sqrt[3]{-81} + 4\sqrt[3]{3}$ **82.** $6\sqrt[3]{128t} - 2\sqrt[3]{2t}$

In Exercises 83–90, simplify the expression. *(See Example 9.)*

83. $\sqrt{2}(\sqrt{45} + \sqrt{5})$ **84.** $\sqrt{3}(\sqrt{72} - 3\sqrt{2})$

85. $\sqrt{5}(2\sqrt{6x} - \sqrt{96x})$ **86.** $\sqrt{7y}(\sqrt{27y} + 5\sqrt{12y})$

87. $(4\sqrt{2} - \sqrt{98})^2$ **88.** $(\sqrt{3} + \sqrt{48})(\sqrt{20} - \sqrt{5})$

89. $\sqrt[3]{3}(\sqrt[3]{4} + \sqrt[3]{32})$ **90.** $\sqrt[3]{2}(\sqrt[3]{135} - 4\sqrt[3]{5})$

91. **MODELING WITH MATHEMATICS** The circumference C of the art room in a mansion is approximated by the formula $C \approx 2\pi\sqrt{\dfrac{a^2 + b^2}{2}}$. Approximate the circumference of the room.

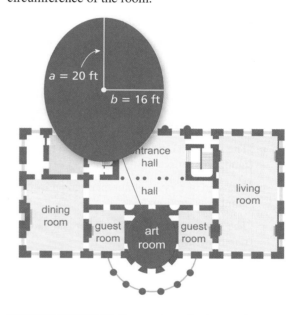

$a = 20$ ft

$b = 16$ ft

entrance hall

hall

living room

dining room

guest room

art room

guest room

92. **CRITICAL THINKING** Determine whether each expression represents a *rational* or an *irrational* number. Justify your answer.

a. $4 + \sqrt{6}$ **b.** $\dfrac{\sqrt{48}}{\sqrt{3}}$

c. $\dfrac{8}{\sqrt{12}}$ **d.** $\sqrt{3} + \sqrt{7}$

e. $\dfrac{a}{\sqrt{10} - \sqrt{2}}$, where a is a positive integer

f. $\dfrac{2 + \sqrt{5}}{2b + \sqrt{5b^2}}$, where b is a positive integer

In Exercises 93–98, simplify the expression.

93. $\sqrt[5]{\dfrac{13}{5x^5}}$ **94.** $\sqrt[4]{\dfrac{10}{81}}$

95. $\sqrt[4]{256y}$ **96.** $\sqrt[5]{160x^6}$

97. $6\sqrt[4]{9} - \sqrt[5]{9} + 3\sqrt[4]{9}$ **98.** $\sqrt[5]{2}(\sqrt[4]{7} + \sqrt[5]{16})$

REASONING In Exercises 99 and 100, use the table shown.

	2	$\frac{1}{4}$	0	$\sqrt{3}$	$-\sqrt{3}$	π
2						
$\frac{1}{4}$						
0						
$\sqrt{3}$						
$-\sqrt{3}$						
π						

99. Copy and complete the table by (a) finding each sum $\left(2 + 2, 2 + \frac{1}{4}, \text{etc.}\right)$ and (b) finding each product $\left(2 \cdot 2, 2 \cdot \frac{1}{4}, \text{etc.}\right)$.

100. Use your answers in Exercise 99 to determine whether each statement is *always*, *sometimes*, or *never* true. Justify your answer.

   a. The sum of a rational number and a rational number is rational.

   b. The sum of a rational number and an irrational number is irrational.

   c. The sum of an irrational number and an irrational number is irrational.

   d. The product of a rational number and a rational number is rational.

   e. The product of a nonzero rational number and an irrational number is irrational.

   f. The product of an irrational number and an irrational number is irrational.

101. **REASONING** Let m be a positive integer. For what values of m will the simplified form of the expression $\sqrt{2^m}$ contain a radical? For what values will it *not* contain a radical? Explain.

102. **HOW DO YOU SEE IT?** The edge length s of a cube is an irrational number, the surface area is an irrational number, and the volume is a rational number. Give a possible value of s.

103. **REASONING** Let a and b be positive numbers. Explain why $\sqrt{ab}$ lies between a and b on a number line. (*Hint:* Let $a < b$ and multiply each side of $a < b$ by a. Then let $a < b$ and multiply each side by b.)

104. **MAKING AN ARGUMENT** Your friend says that you can rationalize the denominator of the expression $\dfrac{2}{4 + \sqrt[3]{5}}$ by multiplying the numerator and denominator by $4 - \sqrt[3]{5}$. Is your friend correct? Explain.

105. **PROBLEM SOLVING** The ratio of consecutive terms $\dfrac{a_n}{a_{n-1}}$ in the Fibonacci sequence gets closer and closer to the golden ratio $\dfrac{1 + \sqrt{5}}{2}$ as n increases. Find the term that precedes 610 in the sequence.

106. **THOUGHT PROVOKING** Use the golden ratio $\dfrac{1 + \sqrt{5}}{2}$ and the golden ratio conjugate $\dfrac{1 - \sqrt{5}}{2}$ for each of the following.

   a. Show that the golden ratio and golden ratio conjugate are both solutions of $x^2 - x - 1 = 0$.

   b. Construct a geometric diagram that has the golden ratio as the length of a part of the diagram.

107. **CRITICAL THINKING** Use the special product pattern $(a + b)(a^2 - ab + b^2) = a^3 + b^3$ to simplify the expression $\dfrac{2}{\sqrt[3]{x} + 1}$. Explain your reasoning.

Maintaining Mathematical Proficiency   Reviewing what you learned in previous grades and lessons

Graph the linear equation. Identify the x-intercept.   (*Skills Review Handbook*)

108. $y = x - 4$ 109. $y = -2x + 6$ 110. $y = -\frac{1}{3}x - 1$ 111. $y = \frac{3}{2}x + 6$

Find the product.   (*Section 2.3*)

112. $(z + 3)^2$ 113. $(3a - 5b)^2$ 114. $(x + 8)(x - 8)$ 115. $(4y + 2)(4y - 2)$

4.2 Solving Quadratic Equations by Graphing

Essential Question How can you use a graph to solve a quadratic equation in one variable?

Based on the definition of an x-intercept of a graph, it follows that the x-intercept of the graph of the linear equation

$$y = ax + b \qquad \text{2 variables}$$

is the same value as the solution of

$$ax + b = 0. \qquad \text{1 variable}$$

You can use similar reasoning to solve *quadratic equations*.

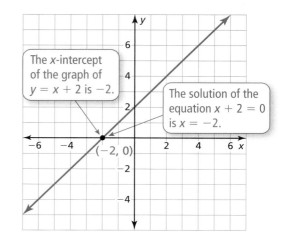

The x-intercept of the graph of $y = x + 2$ is -2.

The solution of the equation $x + 2 = 0$ is $x = -2$.

$(-2, 0)$

EXPLORATION 1 Solving a Quadratic Equation by Graphing

Work with a partner.

a. Sketch the graph of $y = x^2 - 2x$.

b. What is the definition of an x-intercept of a graph? How many x-intercepts does this graph have? What are they?

c. What is the definition of a solution of an equation in x? How many solutions does the equation $x^2 - 2x = 0$ have? What are they?

d. Explain how you can verify the solutions you found in part (c).

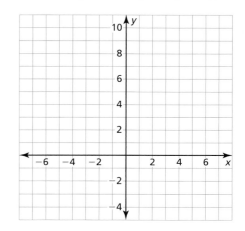

EXPLORATION 2 Solving Quadratic Equations by Graphing

Work with a partner. Solve each equation by graphing.

a. $x^2 - 4 = 0$

b. $x^2 + 3x = 0$

c. $-x^2 + 2x = 0$

d. $x^2 - 2x + 1 = 0$

e. $x^2 - 3x + 5 = 0$

f. $-x^2 + 3x - 6 = 0$

MAKING SENSE OF PROBLEMS

To be proficient in math, you need to check your answers to problems using a different method and continually ask yourself, "Does this make sense?"

Communicate Your Answer

3. How can you use a graph to solve a quadratic equation in one variable?

4. After you find a solution graphically, how can you check your result algebraically? Check your solutions for parts (a)−(d) in Exploration 2 algebraically.

5. How can you determine graphically that a quadratic equation has no solution?

Core Vocabulary

quadratic equation, *p. 202*

Previous
x-intercept
root
zero of a function

What You Will Learn

▶ Solve quadratic equations by graphing.

▶ Use graphs to find and approximate the zeros of functions.

▶ Solve real-life problems using graphs of quadratic functions.

Solving Quadratic Equations by Graphing

A **quadratic equation** is a nonlinear equation that can be written in the standard form $ax^2 + bx + c = 0$, where $a \neq 0$.

In Chapter 2, you solved quadratic equations by factoring. You can also solve quadratic equations by graphing.

⑤ Core Concept

Solving Quadratic Equations by Graphing

Step 1 Write the equation in standard form, $ax^2 + bx + c = 0$.

Step 2 Graph the related function $y = ax^2 + bx + c$.

Step 3 Find the *x*-intercepts, if any.

The solutions, or *roots*, of $ax^2 + bx + c = 0$ are the *x*-intercepts of the graph.

EXAMPLE 1   **Solving a Quadratic Equation: Two Real Solutions**

Solve $x^2 + 2x = 3$ by graphing.

SOLUTION

Step 1 Write the equation in standard form.

$$x^2 + 2x = 3 \qquad \text{Write original equation.}$$

$$x^2 + 2x - 3 = 0 \qquad \text{Subtract 3 from each side.}$$

Step 2 Graph the related function $y = x^2 + 2x - 3$.

Step 3 Find the *x*-intercepts. The *x*-intercepts are -3 and 1.

▶ So, the solutions are $x = -3$ and $x = 1$.

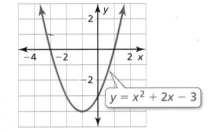

$y = x^2 + 2x - 3$

Check

$x^2 + 2x = 3$	Original equation	$x^2 + 2x = 3$
$(-3)^2 + 2(-3) \overset{?}{=} 3$	Substitute.	$1^2 + 2(1) \overset{?}{=} 3$
$3 = 3$ ✓	Simplify.	$3 = 3$ ✓

Monitoring Progress 🔊 Help in English and Spanish at *BigIdeasMath.com*

Solve the equation by graphing. Check your solutions.

1. $x^2 - x - 2 = 0$ **2.** $x^2 + 7x = -10$ **3.** $x^2 + x = 12$

EXAMPLE 2 **Solving a Quadratic Equation: One Real Solution**

Solve $x^2 - 8x = -16$ by graphing.

SOLUTION

Step 1 Write the equation in standard form.

$$x^2 - 8x = -16 \quad \text{Write original equation.}$$
$$x^2 - 8x + 16 = 0 \quad \text{Add 16 to each side.}$$

Step 2 Graph the related function $y = x^2 - 8x + 16$.

Step 3 Find the x-intercept. The only x-intercept is at the vertex, $(4, 0)$.

▶ So, the solution is $x = 4$.

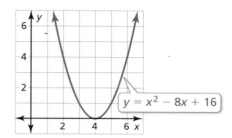

$y = x^2 - 8x + 16$

ANOTHER WAY

You can also solve the equation in Example 2 by factoring.

$$x^2 - 8x + 16 = 0$$
$$(x - 4)(x - 4) = 0$$

So, $x = 4$.

EXAMPLE 3 **Solving a Quadratic Equation: No Real Solutions**

Solve $-x^2 = 2x + 4$ by graphing.

SOLUTION

Method 1 Write the equation in standard form, $x^2 + 2x + 4 = 0$. Then graph the related function $y = x^2 + 2x + 4$, as shown at the left.

▶ There are no x-intercepts. So, $-x^2 = 2x + 4$ has no real solutions.

Method 2 Graph each side of the equation.

$$y = -x^2 \quad \text{Left side}$$
$$y = 2x + 4 \quad \text{Right side}$$

▶ The graphs do not intersect.
So, $-x^2 = 2x + 4$ has no real solutions.

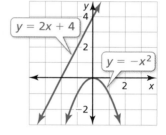

$y = 2x + 4$
$y = -x^2$

$y = x^2 + 2x + 4$

Monitoring Progress Help in English and Spanish at *BigIdeasMath.com*

Solve the equation by graphing.

4. $x^2 + 36 = 12x$ **5.** $x^2 + 4x = 0$ **6.** $x^2 + 10x = -25$

7. $x^2 = 3x - 3$ **8.** $x^2 + 7x = -6$ **9.** $2x + 5 = -x^2$

Concept Summary

Number of Solutions of a Quadratic Equation

A quadratic equation has:

- two real solutions when the graph of its related function has two x-intercepts.
- one real solution when the graph of its related function has one x-intercept.
- no real solutions when the graph of its related function has no x-intercepts.

Finding Zeros of Functions

Recall that a zero of a function is an *x*-intercept of the graph of the function.

EXAMPLE 4 **Finding the Zeros of a Function**

The graph of $f(x) = -x^2 + 2x + 3$ is shown. Find the zeros of f.

SOLUTION

The *x*-intercepts are -1 and 3.

▶ So, the zeros of f are -1 and 3.

Check

$f(-1) = -(-1)^2 + 2(-1) + 3 = 0$ ✔

$f(3) = -3^2 + 2(3) + 3 = 0$ ✔

$f(x) = -x^2 + 2x + 3$

The zeros of a function are not necessarily integers. To approximate zeros, analyze the signs of function values. When two function values have different signs, a zero lies between the *x*-values that correspond to the function values.

EXAMPLE 5 **Approximating the Zeros of a Function**

The graph of $f(x) = x^2 + 4x + 1$ is shown. Approximate the zeros of f to the nearest tenth.

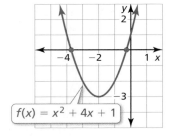

$f(x) = x^2 + 4x + 1$

SOLUTION

There are two *x*-intercepts: one between -4 and -3, and another between -1 and 0.

Make tables using *x*-values between -4 and -3, and between -1 and 0. Use an increment of 0.1. Look for a change in the signs of the function values.

x	-3.9	-3.8	-3.7	-3.6	-3.5	-3.4	-3.3	-3.2	-3.1
f(x)	0.61	0.24	-0.11	-0.44	-0.75	-1.04	-1.31	-1.56	-1.79

change in signs

x	-0.9	-0.8	-0.7	-0.6	-0.5	-0.4	-0.3	-0.2	-0.1
f(x)	-1.79	-1.56	-1.31	-1.04	-0.75	-0.44	-0.11	0.24	0.61

change in signs

ANOTHER WAY

You could approximate one zero using a table and then use the axis of symmetry to find the other zero.

The function values that are closest to 0 correspond to *x*-values that best approximate the zeros of the function.

▶ In each table, the function value closest to 0 is -0.11. So, the zeros of f are about -3.7 and -0.3.

Monitoring Progress Help in English and Spanish at *BigIdeasMath.com*

10. Graph $f(x) = x^2 + x - 6$. Find the zeros of f.

11. Graph $f(x) = -x^2 + 2x + 2$. Approximate the zeros of f to the nearest tenth.

Solving Real-Life Problems

EXAMPLE 6   **Real-Life Application**

A football player kicks a football 2 feet above the ground with an initial vertical velocity of 75 feet per second. The function $h = -16t^2 + 75t + 2$ represents the height h (in feet) of the football after t seconds. (a) Find the height of the football each second after it is kicked. (b) Use the results of part (a) to estimate when the height of the football is 50 feet. (c) Using a graph, after how many seconds is the football 50 feet above the ground?

SOLUTION

a. Make a table of values starting with $t = 0$ seconds using an increment of 1. Continue the table until a function value is negative.

Seconds, t	Height, h
0	2
1	61
2	88
3	83
4	46
5	-23

▶ The height of the football is 61 feet after 1 second, 88 feet after 2 seconds, 83 feet after 3 seconds, and 46 feet after 4 seconds.

b. From part (a), you can estimate that the height of the football is 50 feet between 0 and 1 second and between 3 and 4 seconds.

▶ Based on the function values, it is reasonable to estimate that the height of the football is 50 feet slightly less than 1 second and slightly less than 4 seconds after it is kicked.

c. To determine when the football is 50 feet above the ground, find the t-values for which $h = 50$. So, solve the equation $-16t^2 + 75t + 2 = 50$ by graphing.

Step 1   Write the equation in standard form.

$$-16t^2 + 75t + 2 = 50 \qquad \text{Write the equation.}$$

$$-16t^2 + 75t - 48 = 0 \qquad \text{Subtract 50 from each side.}$$

Step 2   Use a graphing calculator to graph the related function $h = -16t^2 + 75t - 48$.

REMEMBER

Equations have *solutions*, or *roots*. Graphs have *x-intercepts*. Functions have *zeros*.

Step 3   Use the *zero* feature to find the zeros of the function.

▶ The football is 50 feet above the ground after about 0.8 second and about 3.9 seconds, which supports the estimates in part (b).

Monitoring Progress   Help in English and Spanish at *BigIdeasMath.com*

12. WHAT IF? After how many seconds is the football 65 feet above the ground?

Vocabulary and Core Concept Check

1. **VOCABULARY** What is a quadratic equation?

2. **WHICH ONE DOESN'T BELONG?** Which equation does *not* belong with the other three? Explain your reasoning.

$$x^2 + 5x = 20 \qquad x^2 + x - 4 = 0 \qquad x^2 - 6 = 4x \qquad 7x + 12 = x^2$$

3. **WRITING** How can you use a graph to find the number of solutions of a quadratic equation?

4. **WRITING** How are solutions, roots, x-intercepts, and zeros related?

Monitoring Progress and Modeling with Mathematics

In Exercises 5–8, use the graph to solve the equation.

5. $-x^2 + 2x + 3 = 0$

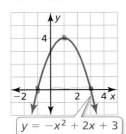

$y = -x^2 + 2x + 3$

6. $x^2 - 6x + 8 = 0$

$y = x^2 - 6x + 8$

7. $x^2 + 8x + 16 = 0$

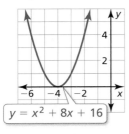

$y = x^2 + 8x + 16$

8. $-x^2 - 4x - 6 = 0$

$y = -x^2 - 4x - 6$

In Exercises 9–12, write the equation in standard form.

9. $4x^2 = 12$

10. $-x^2 = 15$

11. $2x - x^2 = 1$

12. $5 + x = 3x^2$

In Exercises 13–24, solve the equation by graphing. *(See Examples 1, 2, and 3.)*

13. $x^2 - 5x = 0$

14. $x^2 - 4x + 4 = 0$

15. $x^2 - 2x + 5 = 0$

16. $x^2 - 6x - 7 = 0$

17. $x^2 = 6x - 9$

18. $-x^2 = 8x + 20$

19. $x^2 = -1 - 2x$

20. $x^2 = -x - 3$

21. $4x - 12 = -x^2$

22. $5x - 6 = x^2$

23. $x^2 - 2 = -x$

24. $16 + x^2 = -8x$

25. **ERROR ANALYSIS** Describe and correct the error in solving $x^2 + 3x = 18$ by graphing.

$y = x^2 + 3x$

The solutions of the equation
$x^2 + 3x = 18$ are $x = -3$ and $x = 0$.

26. **ERROR ANALYSIS** Describe and correct the error in solving $x^2 + 6x + 9 = 0$ by graphing.

$y = x^2 + 6x + 9$

The solution of the equation
$x^2 + 6x + 9 = 0$ is $x = 9$.

27. MODELING WITH MATHEMATICS The height y (in yards) of a flop shot in golf can be modeled by $y = -x^2 + 5x$, where x is the horizontal distance (in yards).

   a. Interpret the x-intercepts of the graph of the equation.

   b. How far away does the golf ball land?

28. MODELING WITH MATHEMATICS The height h (in feet) of an underhand volleyball serve can be modeled by $h = -16t^2 + 30t + 4$, where t is the time (in seconds).

   a. Do both t-intercepts of the graph of the function have meaning in this situation? Explain.

   b. No one receives the serve. After how many seconds does the volleyball hit the ground?

In Exercises 29–36, solve the equation by using Method 2 from Example 3.

29. $x^2 = 10 - 3x$ **30.** $2x - 3 = x^2$

31. $5x - 7 = x^2$ **32.** $x^2 = 6x - 5$

33. $x^2 + 12x = -20$ **34.** $x^2 + 8x = 9$

35. $-x^2 - 5 = -2x$ **36.** $-x^2 - 4 = -4x$

In Exercises 37–42, find the zero(s) of f. *(See Example 4.)*

37.
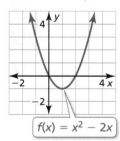
$f(x) = x^2 - 2x$

38.
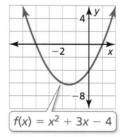
$f(x) = x^2 + 3x - 4$

39.
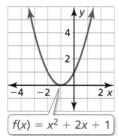
$f(x) = x^2 + 2x + 1$

40.

$f(x) = -x^2 + 6x - 9$

41.
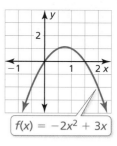
$f(x) = 2x^2 - x - 1$

42.
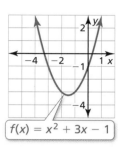
$f(x) = -2x^2 + 3x$

In Exercises 43–46, approximate the zeros of f to the nearest tenth. *(See Example 5.)*

43.

$f(x) = x^2 - 5x + 3$

44.

$f(x) = x^2 + 3x - 1$

45.
$f(x) = -x^2 + 2x + 1$

46.
$f(x) = -x^2 + 6x - 2$

In Exercises 47–52, graph the function. Approximate the zeros of the function to the nearest tenth, if necessary.

47. $f(x) = x^2 + 6x + 1$ **48.** $f(x) = x^2 - 3x + 2$

49. $y = -x^2 + 4x - 2$ **50.** $y = -x^2 + 9x - 6$

51. $f(x) = \frac{1}{2}x^2 + 2x - 5$ **52.** $f(x) = -3x^2 + 4x + 3$

53. MODELING WITH MATHEMATICS At a Civil War reenactment, a cannonball is fired into the air with an initial vertical velocity of 128 feet per second. The release point is 6 feet above the ground. The function $h = -16t^2 + 128t + 6$ represents the height h (in feet) of the cannonball after t seconds. *(See Example 6.)*

   a. Find the height of the cannonball each second after it is fired.

   b. Use the results of part (a) to estimate when the height of the cannonball is 150 feet.

   c. Using a graph, after how many seconds is the cannonball 150 feet above the ground?

54. MODELING WITH MATHEMATICS You throw a softball straight up into the air with an initial vertical velocity of 40 feet per second. The release point is 5 feet above the ground. The function $h = -16t^2 + 40t + 5$ represents the height h (in feet) of the softball after t seconds.

a. Find the height of the softball each second after it is released.

b. Use the results of part (a) to estimate when the height of the softball is 15 feet.

c. Using a graph, after how many seconds is the softball 15 feet above the ground?

MATHEMATICAL CONNECTIONS In Exercises 55 and 56, use the given surface area S of the cylinder to find the radius r to the nearest tenth.

55. $S = 225 \text{ ft}^2$

6 ft

56. $S = 750 \text{ m}^2$

13 m

57. WRITING Explain how to approximate zeros of a function when the zeros are not integers.

58. HOW DO YOU SEE IT? Consider the graph shown.

$y = -3x + 4$

$y = x^2$

a. How many solutions does the quadratic equation $x^2 = -3x + 4$ have? Explain.

b. Without graphing, describe what you know about the graph of $y = x^2 + 3x - 4$.

59. COMPARING METHODS Example 3 shows two methods for solving a quadratic equation. Which method do you prefer? Explain your reasoning.

60. THOUGHT PROVOKING How many different parabolas have -2 and 2 as x-intercepts? Sketch examples of parabolas that have these two x-intercepts.

61. MODELING WITH MATHEMATICS To keep water off a road, the surface of the road is shaped like a parabola. A cross section of the road is shown in the diagram. The surface of the road can be modeled by $y = -0.0017x^2 + 0.041x$, where x and y are measured in feet. Find the width of the road to the nearest tenth of a foot.

62. MAKING AN ARGUMENT A stream of water from a fire hose can be modeled by $y = -0.003x^2 + 0.58x + 3$, where x and y are measured in feet. A firefighter is standing 57 feet from a building and is holding the hose 3 feet above the ground. The bottom of a window of the building is 26 feet above the ground. Your friend claims the stream of water will pass through the window. Is your friend correct? Explain.

REASONING In Exercises 63–65, determine whether the statement is *always*, *sometimes*, or *never* true. Justify your answer.

63. The graph of $y = ax^2 + c$ has two x-intercepts when a is negative.

64. The graph of $y = ax^2 + c$ has no x-intercepts when a and c have the same sign.

65. The graph of $y = ax^2 + bx + c$ has more than two x-intercepts when $a \neq 0$.

Maintaining Mathematical Proficiency
Reviewing what you learned in previous grades and lessons

Show that an exponential model fits the data. Then write a recursive rule that models the data. *(Section 1.6)*

66.

n	0	1	2	3
f(n)	18	3	$\frac{1}{2}$	$\frac{1}{12}$

67.

n	0	1	2	3
f(n)	2	8	32	128

4.3 Solving Quadratic Equations Using Square Roots

Essential Question How can you determine the number of solutions of a quadratic equation of the form $ax^2 + c = 0$?

EXPLORATION 1 | The Number of Solutions of $ax^2 + c = 0$

Work with a partner. Solve each equation by graphing. Explain how the number of solutions of $ax^2 + c = 0$ relates to the graph of $y = ax^2 + c$.

a. $x^2 - 4 = 0$ **b.** $2x^2 + 5 = 0$

c. $x^2 = 0$ **d.** $x^2 - 5 = 0$

EXPLORATION 2 | Estimating Solutions

Work with a partner. Complete each table. Use the completed tables to estimate the solutions of $x^2 - 5 = 0$. Explain your reasoning.

a.

x	$x^2 - 5$
2.21	
2.22	
2.23	
2.24	
2.25	
2.26	

b.

x	$x^2 - 5$
-2.21	
-2.22	
-2.23	
-2.24	
-2.25	
-2.26	

ATTENDING TO PRECISION

To be proficient in math, you need to calculate accurately and express numerical answers with a level of precision appropriate for the problem's context.

EXPLORATION 3 | Using Technology to Estimate Solutions

Work with a partner. Two equations are equivalent when they have the same solutions.

a. Are the equations $x^2 - 5 = 0$ and $x^2 = 5$ equivalent? Explain your reasoning.

b. Use the square root key on a calculator to estimate the solutions of $x^2 - 5 = 0$. Describe the accuracy of your estimates in Exploration 2.

c. Write the exact solutions of $x^2 - 5 = 0$.

Communicate Your Answer

4. How can you determine the number of solutions of a quadratic equation of the form $ax^2 + c = 0$?

5. Write the exact solutions of each equation. Then use a calculator to estimate the solutions.

   a. $x^2 - 2 = 0$

   b. $3x^2 - 18 = 0$

   c. $x^2 = 8$

What You Will Learn

▶ Solve quadratic equations using square roots.

▶ Approximate the solutions of quadratic equations.

Solving Quadratic Equations Using Square Roots

Earlier in this chapter, you studied properties of square roots. Now you will use square roots to solve quadratic equations of the form $ax^2 + c = 0$. First isolate x^2 on one side of the equation to obtain $x^2 = d$. Then solve by taking the square root of each side.

🌀 Core Concept

Solutions of $x^2 = d$

- When $d > 0$, $x^2 = d$ has two real solutions, $x = \pm\sqrt{d}$.
- When $d = 0$, $x^2 = d$ has one real solution, $x = 0$.
- When $d < 0$, $x^2 = d$ has no real solutions.

ANOTHER WAY

You can also solve $3x^2 - 27 = 0$ by factoring.

$$3(x^2 - 9) = 0$$
$$3(x - 3)(x + 3) = 0$$
$$x = 3 \text{ or } x = -3$$

EXAMPLE 1   **Solving Quadratic Equations Using Square Roots**

a. Solve $3x^2 - 27 = 0$ using square roots.

$3x^2 - 27 = 0$	Write the equation.
$3x^2 = 27$	Add 27 to each side.
$x^2 = 9$	Divide each side by 3.
$x = \pm\sqrt{9}$	Take the square root of each side.
$x = \pm 3$	Simplify.

▶ The solutions are $x = 3$ and $x = -3$.

b. Solve $x^2 - 10 = -10$ using square roots.

$x^2 - 10 = -10$	Write the equation.
$x^2 = 0$	Add 10 to each side.
$x = 0$	Take the square root of each side.

▶ The only solution is $x = 0$.

c. Solve $-5x^2 + 11 = 16$ using square roots.

$-5x^2 + 11 = 16$	Write the equation.
$-5x^2 = 5$	Subtract 11 from each side.
$x^2 = -1$	Divide each side by -5.

▶ The square of a real number cannot be negative. So, the equation has no real solutions.

STUDY TIP

Each side of the equation $(x - 1)^2 = 25$ is a square. So, you can still solve by taking the square root of each side.

EXAMPLE 2 Solving a Quadratic Equation Using Square Roots

Solve $(x - 1)^2 = 25$ using square roots.

SOLUTION

$(x - 1)^2 = 25$	Write the equation.
$x - 1 = \pm 5$	Take the square root of each side.
$x = 1 \pm 5$	Add 1 to each side.

 So, the solutions are $x = 1 + 5 = 6$ and $x = 1 - 5 = -4$.

> **Check**
>
> Use a graphing calculator to check your answer. Rewrite the equation as $(x - 1)^2 - 25 = 0$. Graph the related function $f(x) = (x - 1)^2 - 25$ and find the zeros of the function. The zeros are -4 and 6.
>
>

Monitoring Progress 🔊 Help in English and Spanish at *BigIdeasMath.com*

Solve the equation using square roots.

1. $-3x^2 = -75$ **2.** $x^2 + 12 = 10$ **3.** $4x^2 - 15 = -15$

4. $(x + 7)^2 = 0$ **5.** $4(x - 3)^2 = 9$ **6.** $(2x + 1)^2 = 36$

Approximating Solutions of Quadratic Equations

EXAMPLE 3 Approximating Solutions of a Quadratic Equation

Solve $4x^2 - 13 = 15$ using square roots. Round the solutions to the nearest hundredth.

SOLUTION

> **Check**
>
> Graph each side of the equation and find the points of intersection. The x-values of the points of intersection are about -2.65 and 2.65.
>
>

$4x^2 - 13 = 15$	Write the equation.
$4x^2 = 28$	Add 13 to each side.
$x^2 = 7$	Divide each side by 4.
$x = \pm\sqrt{7}$	Take the square root of each side.
$x \approx \pm 2.65$	Use a calculator.

The solutions are $x \approx -2.65$ and $x \approx 2.65$.

Monitoring Progress 🔊 Help in English and Spanish at *BigIdeasMath.com*

Solve the equation using square roots. **Round your solutions to the nearest hundredth.**

7. $x^2 + 8 = 19$ **8.** $5x^2 - 2 = 0$ **9.** $3x^2 - 30 = 4$

EXAMPLE 4 **Solving a Real-Life Problem**

A touch tank has a height of 3 feet. Its length is three times its width. The volume of the tank is 270 cubic feet. Find the length and width of the tank.

3 ft

SOLUTION

The length ℓ is three times the width w, so $\ell = 3w$. Write an equation using the formula for the volume of a rectangular prism.

$V = \ell wh$	Write the formula.
$270 = 3w(w)(3)$	Substitute 270 for V, $3w$ for ℓ, and 3 for h.
$270 = 9w^2$	Multiply.
$30 = w^2$	Divide each side by 9.
$\pm\sqrt{30} = w$	Take the square root of each side.

The solutions are $\sqrt{30}$ and $-\sqrt{30}$. Use the positive solution.

▶ So, the width is $\sqrt{30} \approx 5.5$ feet and the length is $3\sqrt{30} \approx 16.4$ feet.

INTERPRETING MATHEMATICAL RESULTS

Use the positive square root because negative solutions do not make sense in this context. Length and width cannot be negative.

EXAMPLE 5 **Rearranging and Evaluating a Formula**

The area A of an equilateral triangle with side length s is given by the formula $A = \dfrac{\sqrt{3}}{4}s^2$. Solve the formula for s. Then approximate the side length of the traffic sign that has an area of 390 square inches.

YIELD

s

s s

SOLUTION

Step 1 Solve the formula for s.

$A = \dfrac{\sqrt{3}}{4}s^2$	Write the formula.
$\dfrac{4A}{\sqrt{3}} = s^2$	Multiply each side by $\dfrac{4}{\sqrt{3}}$.
$\sqrt{\dfrac{4A}{\sqrt{3}}} = s$	Take the positive square root of each side.

Step 2 Substitute 390 for A in the new formula and evaluate.

$$s = \sqrt{\dfrac{4A}{\sqrt{3}}} = \sqrt{\dfrac{4(390)}{\sqrt{3}}} = \sqrt{\dfrac{1560}{\sqrt{3}}} \approx 30 \qquad \text{Use a calculator.}$$

▶ The side length of the traffic sign is about 30 inches.

ANOTHER WAY

Notice that you can rewrite the formula as $s = \dfrac{2}{3^{1/4}}\sqrt{A}$, or $s \approx 1.52\sqrt{A}$.

This can help you efficiently find the value of s for various values of A.

Monitoring Progress Help in English and Spanish at *BigIdeasMath.com*

10. **WHAT IF?** In Example 4, the volume of the tank is 315 cubic feet. Find the length and width of the tank.

11. The surface area S of a sphere with radius r is given by the formula $S = 4\pi r^2$. Solve the formula for r. Then find the radius of a globe with a surface area of 804 square inches.

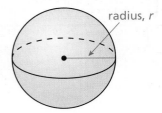

radius, r

Vocabulary and Core Concept Check

1. COMPLETE THE SENTENCE The equation $x^2 = d$ has ____ real solutions when $d > 0$.

2. DIFFERENT WORDS, SAME QUESTION Which is different? Find "both" answers.

Solve $x^2 = 144$ using square roots.	Solve $x^2 - 144 = 0$ using square roots.
Solve $x^2 + 146 = 2$ using square roots.	Solve $x^2 + 2 = 146$ using square roots.

Monitoring Progress and Modeling with Mathematics

In Exercises 3–8, determine the number of real solutions of the equation. Then solve the equation using square roots.

3. $x^2 = 25$ **4.** $x^2 = -36$

5. $x^2 = -21$ **6.** $x^2 = 400$

7. $x^2 = 0$ **8.** $x^2 = 169$

In Exercises 9–18, solve the equation using square roots. *(See Example 1.)*

9. $x^2 - 16 = 0$ **10.** $x^2 + 6 = 0$

11. $3x^2 + 12 = 0$ **12.** $x^2 - 55 = 26$

13. $2x^2 - 98 = 0$ **14.** $-x^2 + 9 = 9$

15. $-3x^2 - 5 = -5$ **16.** $4x^2 - 371 = 29$

17. $4x^2 + 10 = 11$ **18.** $9x^2 - 35 = 14$

In Exercises 19–24, solve the equation using square roots. *(See Example 2.)*

19. $(x + 3)^2 = 0$ **20.** $(x - 1)^2 = 4$

21. $(2x - 1)^2 = 81$ **22.** $(4x + 5)^2 = 9$

23. $9(x + 1)^2 = 16$ **24.** $4(x - 2)^2 = 25$

In Exercises 25–30, solve the equation using square roots. Round your solutions to the nearest hundredth. *(See Example 3.)*

25. $x^2 + 6 = 13$ **26.** $x^2 + 11 = 24$

27. $2x^2 - 9 = 11$ **28.** $5x^2 + 2 = 6$

29. $-21 = 15 - 2x^2$ **30.** $2 = 4x^2 - 5$

31. ERROR ANALYSIS Describe and correct the error in solving the equation $2x^2 - 33 = 39$ using square roots.

$$2x^2 - 33 = 39$$
$$2x^2 = 72$$
$$x^2 = 36$$
$$x = 6$$
The solution is $x = 6$.

32. MODELING WITH MATHEMATICS An in-ground pond has the shape of a rectangular prism. The pond has a depth of 24 inches and a volume of 72,000 cubic inches. The length of the pond is two times its width. Find the length and width of the pond. *(See Example 4.)*

33. MODELING WITH MATHEMATICS A person sitting in the top row of the bleachers at a sporting event drops a pair of sunglasses from a height of 24 feet. The function $h = -16x^2 + 24$ represents the height h (in feet) of the sunglasses after x seconds. How long does it take the sunglasses to hit the ground?

34. MAKING AN ARGUMENT Your friend says that the solution of the equation $x^2 + 4 = 0$ is $x = 0$. Your cousin says that the equation has no real solutions. Who is correct? Explain your reasoning.

35. MODELING WITH MATHEMATICS The design of a square rug for your living room is shown. You want the area of the inner square to be 25% of the total area of the rug. Find the side length x of the inner square.

6 ft

36. MATHEMATICAL CONNECTIONS The area A of a circle with radius r is given by the formula $A = \pi r^2$. *(See Example 5.)*

   a. Solve the formula for r.

   b. Use the formula from part (a) to find the radius of each circle.

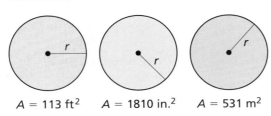

   $A = 113$ ft^2 $A = 1810$ in.^{2} $A = 531$ m^2

   c. Explain why it is beneficial to solve the formula for r before finding the radius.

37. WRITING How can you approximate the roots of a quadratic equation when the roots are not integers?

38. WRITING Given the equation $ax^2 + c = 0$, describe the values of a and c so the equation has the following number of solutions.

   a. two real solutions

   b. one real solution

   c. no real solutions

39. REASONING Without graphing, where do the graphs of $y = x^2$ and $y = 9$ intersect? Explain.

40. HOW DO YOU SEE IT? The graph represents the function $f(x) = (x - 1)^2$. How many solutions does the equation $(x - 1)^2 = 0$ have? Explain.

41. REASONING Solve $x^2 = 1.44$ without using a calculator. Explain your reasoning.

42. THOUGHT PROVOKING The quadratic equation

$$ax^2 + bx + c = 0$$

can be rewritten in the following form.

$$\left(x + \frac{b}{2a}\right)^2 = \frac{b^2 - 4ac}{4a^2}$$

Use this form to write the solutions of the equation.

43. REASONING An equation of the graph shown is $y = \frac{1}{2}(x - 2)^2 + 1$. Two points on the parabola have y-coordinates of 9. Find the x-coordinates of these points.

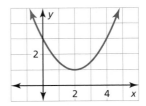

44. CRITICAL THINKING Solve each equation without graphing.

   a. $x^2 - 12x + 36 = 64$

   b. $x^2 + 14x + 49 = 16$

Maintaining Mathematical Proficiency

Reviewing what you learned in previous grades and lessons

Factor the polynomial. *(Section 2.7)*

45. $x^2 + 8x + 16$ **46.** $x^2 - 4x + 4$ **47.** $x^2 - 14x + 49$

48. $x^2 + 18x + 81$ **49.** $x^2 + 12x + 36$ **50.** $x^2 - 22x + 121$

4.4 Solving Quadratic Equations by Completing the Square

Essential Question How can you use "completing the square" to solve a quadratic equation?

EXPLORATION 1 Solving by Completing the Square

Work with a partner.

a. Write the equation modeled by the algebra tiles. This is the equation to be solved.

b. Four algebra tiles are added to the left side to "complete the square." Why are four algebra tiles also added to the right side?

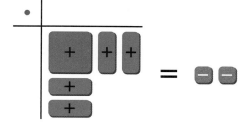

c. Use algebra tiles to label the dimensions of the square on the left side and simplify on the right side.

d. Write the equation modeled by the algebra tiles so that the left side is the square of a binomial. Solve the equation using square roots.

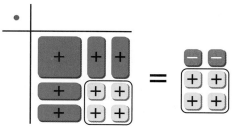

MAKING SENSE OF PROBLEMS

To be proficient in math, you need to explain to yourself the meaning of a problem. After that, you need to look for entry points to its solution.

EXPLORATION 2 Solving by Completing the Square

Work with a partner.

a. Write the equation modeled by the algebra tiles.

b. Use algebra tiles to "complete the square."

c. Write the solutions of the equation.

d. Check each solution in the original equation.

Communicate Your Answer

3. How can you use "completing the square" to solve a quadratic equation?

4. Solve each quadratic equation by completing the square.

a. $x^2 - 2x = 1$ b. $x^2 - 4x = -1$ c. $x^2 + 4x = -3$

What You Will Learn

▶ Complete the square for expressions of the form $x^2 + bx$.

▶ Solve quadratic equations by completing the square.

▶ Find and use maximum and minimum values.

▶ Solve real-life problems by completing the square.

Core Vocabulary

completing the square, *p. 216*

Previous
perfect square trinomial
coefficient
maximum value
minimum value
vertex form of a quadratic
    function

Completing the Square

For an expression of the form $x^2 + bx$, you can add a constant c to the expression so that $x^2 + bx + c$ is a perfect square trinomial. This process is called **completing the square**.

🌀 Core Concept

Completing the Square

Words   To complete the square for an expression of the form $x^2 + bx$, follow these steps.

   Step 1   Find one-half of b, the coefficient of x.

   Step 2   Square the result from Step 1.

   Step 3   Add the result from Step 2 to $x^2 + bx$.

   Factor the resulting expression as the square of a binomial.

Algebra $x^2 + bx + \left(\dfrac{b}{2}\right)^2 = \left(x + \dfrac{b}{2}\right)^2$

JUSTIFYING STEPS

In each diagram below, the combined area of the shaded regions is $x^2 + bx$.

Adding $\left(\dfrac{b}{2}\right)^2$ completes the square in the second diagram.

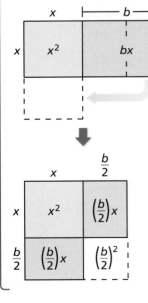

EXAMPLE 1   **Completing the Square**

Complete the square for each expression. Then factor the trinomial.

a. $x^2 + 6x$ $\qquad\qquad\qquad$ **b.** $x^2 - 9x$

SOLUTION

a. **Step 1**   Find one-half of b. $\qquad\qquad\qquad\qquad$ $\dfrac{b}{2} = \dfrac{6}{2} = 3$

$\quad$ **Step 2**   Square the result from Step 1. $\qquad\qquad$ $3^2 = 9$

$\quad$ **Step 3**   Add the result from Step 2 to $x^2 + bx$. $\quad$ $x^2 + 6x + 9$

▶ $x^2 + 6x + 9 = (x + 3)^2$

b. **Step 1**   Find one-half of b. $\qquad\qquad\qquad\qquad$ $\dfrac{b}{2} = \dfrac{-9}{2}$

$\quad$ **Step 2**   Square the result from Step 1. $\qquad\qquad$ $\left(\dfrac{-9}{2}\right)^2 = \dfrac{81}{4}$

$\quad$ **Step 3**   Add the result from Step 2 to $x^2 + bx$. $\quad$ $x^2 - 9x + \dfrac{81}{4}$

▶ $x^2 - 9x + \dfrac{81}{4} = \left(x - \dfrac{9}{2}\right)^2$

Monitoring Progress Help in English and Spanish at *BigIdeasMath.com*

Complete the square for the expression. Then factor the trinomial.

$\quad$ **1.** $x^2 + 10x$ $\qquad\qquad$ **2.** $x^2 - 4x$ $\qquad\qquad$ **3.** $x^2 + 7x$

Solving Quadratic Equations by Completing the Square

The method of completing the square can be used to solve any quadratic equation. To solve a quadratic equation by completing the square, you must write the equation in the form $x^2 + bx = d$.

EXAMPLE 2   Solving a Quadratic Equation: $x^2 + bx = d$

Solve $x^2 - 16x = -15$ by completing the square.

SOLUTION

$x^2 - 16x = -15$	Write the equation.
$x^2 - 16x + (-8)^2 = -15 + (-8)^2$	Complete the square by adding $\left(\frac{-16}{2}\right)^2$, or $(-8)^2$, to each side.
$(x - 8)^2 = 49$	Write the left side as the square of a binomial.
$x - 8 = \pm 7$	Take the square root of each side.
$x = 8 \pm 7$	Add 8 to each side.

▶ The solutions are $x = 8 + 7 = 15$ and $x = 8 - 7 = 1$.

Check

$x^2 - 16x = -15$	Original equation	$x^2 - 16x = -15$
$15^2 - 16(15) \overset{?}{=} -15$	Substitute.	$1^2 - 16(1) \overset{?}{=} -15$
$-15 = -15$ ✓	Simplify.	$-15 = -15$ ✓

EXAMPLE 3   Solving a Quadratic Equation: $ax^2 + bx + c = 0$

Solve $2x^2 + 20x - 8 = 0$ by completing the square.

SOLUTION

$2x^2 + 20x - 8 = 0$	Write the equation.
$2x^2 + 20x = 8$	Add 8 to each side.
$x^2 + 10x = 4$	Divide each side by 2.
$x^2 + 10x + 5^2 = 4 + 5^2$	Complete the square by adding $\left(\frac{10}{2}\right)^2$, or 5^2, to each side.
$(x + 5)^2 = 29$	Write the left side as the square of a binomial.
$x + 5 = \pm\sqrt{29}$	Take the square root of each side.
$x = -5 \pm \sqrt{29}$	Subtract 5 from each side.

▶ The solutions are $x = -5 + \sqrt{29} \approx 0.39$ and $x = -5 - \sqrt{29} \approx -10.39$.

Monitoring Progress Help in English and Spanish at *BigIdeasMath.com*

Solve the equation by completing the square. Round your solutions to the nearest hundredth, if necessary.

4. $x^2 - 2x = 3$ **5.** $m^2 + 12m = -8$ **6.** $3g^2 - 24g + 27 = 0$

Finding and Using Maximum and Minimum Values

One way to find the maximum or minimum value of a quadratic function is to write the function in vertex form by completing the square. Recall that the vertex form of a quadratic function is $y = a(x - h)^2 + k$, where $a \neq 0$. The vertex of the graph is (h, k).

EXAMPLE 4 Finding a Minimum Value

Find the minimum value of $y = x^2 + 4x - 1$.

SOLUTION

Write the function in vertex form.

$y = x^2 + 4x - 1$ Write the function.

$y + 1 = x^2 + 4x$ Add 1 to each side.

$y + 1 + 4 = x^2 + 4x + 4$ Complete the square for $x^2 + 4x$.

$y + 5 = x^2 + 4x + 4$ Simplify the left side.

$y + 5 = (x + 2)^2$ Write the right side as the square of a binomial.

$y = (x + 2)^2 - 5$ Write in vertex form.

The vertex is $(-2, -5)$. Because a is positive ($a = 1$), the parabola opens up and the y-coordinate of the vertex is the minimum value.

Check

▶ So, the function has a minimum value of -5.

EXAMPLE 5 Finding a Maximum Value

Find the maximum value of $y = -x^2 + 2x + 7$.

SOLUTION

Write the function in vertex form.

$y = -x^2 + 2x + 7$ Write the function.

$y - 7 = -x^2 + 2x$ Subtract 7 from each side.

$y - 7 = -(x^2 - 2x)$ Factor out -1.

$y - 7 - 1 = -(x^2 - 2x + 1)$ Complete the square for $x^2 - 2x$.

$y - 8 = -(x^2 - 2x + 1)$ Simplify the left side.

$y - 8 = -(x - 1)^2$ Write $x^2 - 2x + 1$ as the square of a binomial.

$y = -(x - 1)^2 + 8$ Write in vertex form.

STUDY TIP

Adding 1 inside the parentheses results in subtracting 1 from the right side of the equation.

The vertex is $(1, 8)$. Because a is negative ($a = -1$), the parabola opens down and the y-coordinate of the vertex is the maximum value.

▶ So, the function has a maximum value of 8.

Monitoring Progress Help in English and Spanish at *BigIdeasMath.com*

Determine whether the quadratic function has a maximum or minimum value. Then find the value.

7. $y = -x^2 - 4x + 4$ **8.** $y = x^2 + 12x + 40$ **9.** $y = x^2 - 2x - 2$

EXAMPLE 6   Interpreting Forms of Quadratic Functions

Which of the functions could be represented by the graph? Explain.

SOLUTION

You do not know the scale of either axis. To eliminate functions, consider the characteristics of the graph and information provided by the form of each function. The graph appears to be a parabola that opens down, which means the function has a maximum value. The vertex of the graph is in the first quadrant. Both x-intercepts are positive.

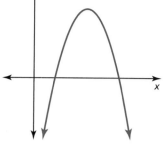

$f(x) = -\frac{1}{2}(x + 4)^2 + 8$

$g(x) = -(x - 5)^2 + 9$

$m(x) = (x - 3)(x - 12)$

$p(x) = -(x - 2)(x - 8)$

- The graph of f opens down because $a < 0$, which means f has a maximum value. However, the vertex $(-4, 8)$ of the graph of f is in the second quadrant. So, the graph does not represent f.

- The graph of g opens down because $a < 0$, which means g has a maximum value. The vertex $(5, 9)$ of the graph of g is in the first quadrant. By solving $0 = -(x - 5)^2 + 9$, you see that the x-intercepts of the graph of g are 2 and 8. So, the graph could represent g.

- The graph of m has two positive x-intercepts. However, its graph opens up because $a > 0$, which means m has a minimum value. So, the graph does not represent m.

- The graph of p has two positive x-intercepts, and its graph opens down because $a < 0$. This means that p has a maximum value and the vertex must be in the first quadrant. So, the graph could represent p.

▶ The graph could represent function g or function p.

EXAMPLE 7   Real-Life Application

The function $y = -16x^2 + 96x$ represents the height y (in feet) of a model rocket x seconds after it is launched. (a) Find the maximum height of the rocket. (b) Find and interpret the axis of symmetry.

SOLUTION

a. To find the maximum height, identify the maximum value of the function.

$y = -16x^2 + 96x$	Write the function.
$y = -16(x^2 - 6x)$	Factor out -16.
$y - 144 = -16(x^2 - 6x + 9)$	Complete the square for $x^2 - 6x$.
$y = -16(x - 3)^2 + 144$	Write in vertex form.

> **STUDY TIP**
>
> Adding 9 inside the parentheses results in subtracting 144 from the right side of the equation.

▶ Because the maximum value is 144, the model rocket reaches a maximum height of 144 feet.

b. The vertex is $(3, 144)$. So, the axis of symmetry is $x = 3$. On the left side of $x = 3$, the height increases as time increases. On the right side of $x = 3$, the height decreases as time increases.

Monitoring Progress Help in English and Spanish at *BigIdeasMath.com*

Determine whether the function could be represented by the graph in Example 6. Explain.

10. $h(x) = (x - 8)^2 + 10$

11. $n(x) = -2(x - 5)(x - 20)$

12. WHAT IF? Repeat Example 7 when the function is $y = -16x^2 + 128x$.

Solving Real-Life Problems

EXAMPLE 8 **Modeling with Mathematics**

You decide to use chalkboard paint to create a chalkboard on a door. You want the chalkboard to cover 6 square feet and to have a uniform border, as shown. Find the width of the border to the nearest inch.

SOLUTION

1. **Understand the Problem** You know the dimensions (in feet) of the door from the diagram. You also know the area (in square feet) of the chalkboard and that it will have a uniform border. You are asked to find the width of the border to the nearest inch.

2. **Make a Plan** Use a verbal model to write an equation that represents the area of the chalkboard. Then solve the equation.

3. **Solve the Problem**

   Let x be the width (in feet) of the border, as shown in the diagram.

Area of chalkboard (square feet)	=	Length of chalkboard (feet)	•	Width of chalkboard (feet)
6	=	$(7 - 2x)$	•	$(3 - 2x)$

$6 = (7 - 2x)(3 - 2x)$	Write the equation.
$6 = 21 - 20x + 4x^2$	Multiply the binomials.
$-15 = 4x^2 - 20x$	Subtract 21 from each side.
$-\dfrac{15}{4} = x^2 - 5x$	Divide each side by 4.
$-\dfrac{15}{4} + \dfrac{25}{4} = x^2 - 5x + \dfrac{25}{4}$	Complete the square for $x^2 - 5x$.
$\dfrac{5}{2} = x^2 - 5x + \dfrac{25}{4}$	Simplify the left side.
$\dfrac{5}{2} = \left(x - \dfrac{5}{2}\right)^2$	Write the right side as the square of a binomial.
$\pm\sqrt{\dfrac{5}{2}} = x - \dfrac{5}{2}$	Take the square root of each side.
$\dfrac{5}{2} \pm \sqrt{\dfrac{5}{2}} = x$	Add $\dfrac{5}{2}$ to each side.

   The solutions of the equation are $x = \dfrac{5}{2} + \sqrt{\dfrac{5}{2}} \approx 4.08$ and $x = \dfrac{5}{2} - \sqrt{\dfrac{5}{2}} \approx 0.92$.

   It is not possible for the width of the border to be 4.08 feet because the width of the door is 3 feet. So, the width of the border is about 0.92 foot.

   $$0.92 \text{ ft} \cdot \frac{12 \text{ in.}}{1 \text{ ft}} = 11.04 \text{ in.} \qquad \text{Convert 0.92 foot to inches.}$$

   ▶ The width of the border should be about 11 inches.

4. **Look Back** When the width of the border is slightly less than 1 foot, the length of the chalkboard is slightly more than 5 feet and the width of the chalkboard is slightly more than 1 foot. Multiplying these dimensions gives an area close to 6 square feet. So, an 11-inch border is reasonable.

Monitoring Progress Help in English and Spanish at *BigIdeasMath.com*

13. **WHAT IF?** You want the chalkboard to cover 4 square feet. Find the width of the border to the nearest inch.

Vocabulary and Core Concept Check

1. **COMPLETE THE SENTENCE** The process of adding a constant c to the expression $x^2 + bx$ so that $x^2 + bx + c$ is a perfect square trinomial is called _____.

2. **VOCABULARY** Explain how to complete the square for an expression of the form $x^2 + bx$.

3. **WRITING** Is it more convenient to complete the square for $x^2 + bx$ when b is odd or when b is even? Explain.

4. **WRITING** Describe how you can use the process of completing the square to find the maximum or minimum value of a quadratic function.

Monitoring Progress and Modeling with Mathematics

In Exercises 5–10, find the value of c that completes the square.

5. $x^2 - 8x + c$

6. $x^2 - 2x + c$

7. $x^2 + 4x + c$

8. $x^2 + 12x + c$

9. $x^2 - 15x + c$

10. $x^2 + 9x + c$

In Exercises 11–16, complete the square for the expression. Then factor the trinomial. *(See Example 1.)*

11. $x^2 - 10x$

12. $x^2 - 40x$

13. $x^2 + 16x$

14. $x^2 + 22x$

15. $x^2 + 5x$

16. $x^2 - 3x$

In Exercises 17–22, solve the equation by completing the square. Round your solutions to the nearest hundredth, if necessary. *(See Example 2.)*

17. $x^2 + 14x = 15$

18. $x^2 - 6x = 16$

19. $x^2 - 4x = -2$

20. $x^2 + 2x = 5$

21. $x^2 - 5x = 8$

22. $x^2 + 11x = -10$

23. **MODELING WITH MATHEMATICS** The area of the patio is 216 square feet.

    a. Write an equation that represents the area of the patio.

    b. Find the dimensions of the patio by completing the square.

(x + 6) ft

x ft

24. **MODELING WITH MATHEMATICS** Some sand art contains sand and water sealed in a glass case, similar to the one shown. When the art is turned upside down, the sand and water fall to create a new picture. The glass case has a depth of 1 centimeter and a volume of 768 cubic centimeters.

(x − 8) cm

x cm

    a. Write an equation that represents the volume of the glass case.

    b. Find the dimensions of the glass case by completing the square.

In Exercises 25–32, solve the equation by completing the square. Round your solutions to the nearest hundredth, if necessary. *(See Example 3.)*

25. $x^2 - 8x + 15 = 0$

26. $x^2 + 4x - 21 = 0$

27. $2x^2 + 20x + 44 = 0$

28. $3x^2 - 18x + 12 = 0$

29. $-3x^2 - 24x + 17 = -40$

30. $-5x^2 - 20x + 35 = 30$

31. $2x^2 - 14x + 10 = 26$

32. $4x^2 + 12x - 15 = 5$

33. ERROR ANALYSIS Describe and correct the error in solving $x^2 + 8x = 10$ by completing the square.

$$\begin{aligned}
x^2 + 8x &= 10 \\
x^2 + 8x + 16 &= 10 \\
(x + 4)^2 &= 10 \\
x + 4 &= \pm\sqrt{10} \\
x &= -4 \pm \sqrt{10}
\end{aligned}$$

34. ERROR ANALYSIS Describe and correct the error in the first two steps of solving $2x^2 - 2x - 4 = 0$ by completing the square.

$$\begin{aligned}
2x^2 - 2x - 4 &= 0 \\
2x^2 - 2x &= 4 \\
2x^2 - 2x + 1 &= 4 + 1
\end{aligned}$$

35. NUMBER SENSE Find all values of b for which $x^2 + bx + 25$ is a perfect square trinomial. Explain how you found your answer.

36. REASONING You are completing the square to solve $3x^2 + 6x = 12$. What is the first step?

In Exercises 37–40, write the function in vertex form by completing the square. Then match the function with its graph.

37. $y = x^2 + 6x + 3$

38. $y = -x^2 + 8x - 12$

39. $y = -x^2 - 4x - 2$

40. $y = x^2 - 2x + 4$

A.

B.

C.

D.
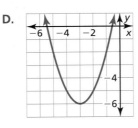

In Exercises 41–46, determine whether the quadratic function has a maximum or minimum value. Then find the value. *(See Examples 4 and 5.)*

41. $y = x^2 - 4x - 2$

42. $y = x^2 + 6x + 10$

43. $y = -x^2 - 10x - 30$

44. $y = -x^2 + 14x - 34$

45. $f(x) = -3x^2 - 6x - 9$

46. $f(x) = 4x^2 - 28x + 32$

In Exercises 47–50, determine whether the graph could represent the function. Explain.

47. $y = -(x + 8)(x + 3)$

48. $y = (x - 5)^2$

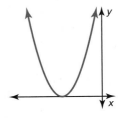

49. $y = \frac{1}{4}(x + 2)^2 - 4$

50. $y = -2(x - 1)(x + 2)$

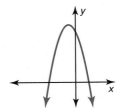

In Exercises 51 and 52, determine which of the functions could be represented by the graph. Explain. *(See Example 6.)*

51.
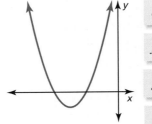

$h(x) = (x + 2)^2 + 3$

$f(x) = 2(x + 3)^2 - 2$

$g(x) = -\frac{1}{2}(x - 8)(x - 4)$

$m(x) = (x + 2)(x + 4)$

52.
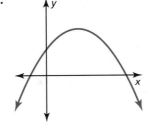

$r(x) = -\frac{1}{3}(x - 5)(x + 1)$

$p(x) = -2(x - 2)(x - 6)$

$q(x) = (x + 1)^2 + 4$

$n(x) = -(x - 2)^2 + 9$

53. MODELING WITH MATHEMATICS The function $h = -16t^2 + 48t$ represents the height h (in feet) of a kickball t seconds after it is kicked from the ground. *(See Example 7.)*

   a. Find the maximum height of the kickball.

   b. Find and interpret the axis of symmetry.

54. MODELING WITH MATHEMATICS
You throw a stone from a height of 16 feet with an initial vertical velocity of 32 feet per second. The function $h = -16t^2 + 32t + 16$ represents the height h (in feet) of the stone after t seconds.

16 ft

a. Find the maximum height of the stone.

b. Find and interpret the axis of symmetry.

55. MODELING WITH MATHEMATICS You are building a rectangular brick patio surrounded by a crushed stone border with a uniform width, as shown. You purchase patio bricks to cover 140 square feet. Find the width of the border. *(See Example 8.)*

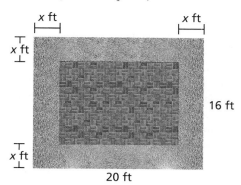

x ft   x ft
x ft
16 ft
x ft
20 ft

56. MODELING WITH MATHEMATICS
You are making a poster that will have a uniform border, as shown. The total area of the poster is 722 square inches. Find the width of the border to the nearest inch.

x in.
22 in.
x in.
28 in.

MATHEMATICAL CONNECTIONS In Exercises 57 and 58, find the value of x. Round your answer to the nearest hundredth, if necessary.

57. $A = 108 \text{ m}^2$

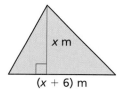

x m
(x + 6) m

58. $A = 288 \text{ in.}^2$

3x in.
(2x + 10) in.

In Exercises 59–62, solve the equation by completing the square. Round your solutions to the nearest hundredth, if necessary.

59. $0.5x^2 + x - 2 = 0$

60. $0.75x^2 + 1.5x = 4$

61. $\frac{8}{3}x - \frac{2}{3}x^2 = -\frac{5}{6}$

62. $\frac{1}{4}x^2 + \frac{1}{2}x - \frac{5}{4} = 0$

63. PROBLEM SOLVING The distance d (in feet) that it takes a car to come to a complete stop can be modeled by $d = 0.05s^2 + 2.2s$, where s is the speed of the car (in miles per hour). A car has 168 feet to come to a complete stop. Find the maximum speed at which the car can travel.

64. PROBLEM SOLVING During a "big air" competition, snowboarders launch themselves from a half-pipe, perform tricks in the air, and land back in the half-pipe. The height h (in feet) of a snowboarder above the bottom of the half-pipe can be modeled by $h = -16t^2 + 24t + 16.4$, where t is the time (in seconds) after the snowboarder launches into the air. The snowboarder lands 3.2 feet lower than the height of the launch. How long is the snowboarder in the air? Round your answer to the nearest tenth of a second.

Initial vertical
velocity = 24 ft/sec
16.4 ft
Cross section of a half-pipe

65. PROBLEM SOLVING You have 80 feet of fencing to make a rectangular horse pasture that covers 750 square feet. A barn will be used as one side of the pasture, as shown.

w   w
ℓ

a. Write equations for the amount of fencing to be used and the area enclosed by the fencing.

b. Use substitution to solve the system of equations from part (a). What are the possible dimensions of the pasture?

66. HOW DO YOU SEE IT? The graph represents the quadratic function $y = x^2 - 4x + 6$.

a. Use the graph to estimate the x-values for which $y = 3$.

b. Explain how you can use the method of completing the square to check your estimates in part (a).

67. COMPARING METHODS Consider the quadratic equation $x^2 + 12x + 2 = 12$.

a. Solve the equation by graphing.

b. Solve the equation by completing the square.

c. Compare the two methods. Which do you prefer? Explain.

68. THOUGHT PROVOKING Sketch the graph of the equation $x^2 - 2xy + y^2 - x - y = 0$. Identify the graph.

69. REASONING The product of two consecutive even integers that are positive is 48. Write and solve an equation to find the integers.

70. REASONING The product of two consecutive odd integers that are negative is 195. Write and solve an equation to find the integers.

71. MAKING AN ARGUMENT You purchase stock for $16 per share. You sell the stock 30 days later for $23.50 per share. The price y (in dollars) of a share during the 30-day period can be modeled by $y = -0.025x^2 + x + 16$, where x is the number of days after the stock is purchased. Your friend says you could have sold the stock earlier for $23.50 per share. Is your friend correct? Explain.

72. REASONING You are solving the equation $x^2 + 9x = 18$. What are the advantages of solving the equation by completing the square instead of using other methods you have learned?

73. PROBLEM SOLVING You are knitting a rectangular scarf. The pattern results in a scarf that is 60 inches long and 4 inches wide. However, you have enough yarn to knit 396 square inches. You decide to increase the dimensions of the scarf so that you will use all your yarn. The increase in the length is three times the increase in the width. What are the dimensions of your scarf?

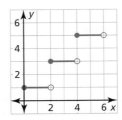

74. WRITING How many solutions does $x^2 + bx = c$ have when $c < -\left(\dfrac{b}{2}\right)^2$? Explain.

Maintaining Mathematical Proficiency
Reviewing what you learned in previous grades and lessons

Write a piecewise function for the graph. *(Section 1.2)*

75.

76.

77.

Simplify the expression $\sqrt{b^2 - 4ac}$ for the given values. *(Section 4.1)*

78. $a = 3, b = -6, c = 2$

79. $a = -2, b = 4, c = 7$

80. $a = 1, b = 6, c = 4$

Essential Question How can you derive a formula that can be used to write the solutions of any quadratic equation in standard form?

EXPLORATION 1 Deriving the Quadratic Formula

Work with a partner. The following steps show a method of solving $ax^2 + bx + c = 0$. Explain what was done in each step.

$$ax^2 + bx + c = 0$$ ← 1. Write the equation.

$$4a^2x^2 + 4abx + 4ac = 0$$ ← 2. What was done?

$$4a^2x^2 + 4abx + 4ac + b^2 = b^2$$ ← 3. What was done?

$$4a^2x^2 + 4abx + b^2 = b^2 - 4ac$$ ← 4. What was done?

$$(2ax + b)^2 = b^2 - 4ac$$ ← 5. What was done?

$$2ax + b = \pm\sqrt{b^2 - 4ac}$$ ← 6. What was done?

$$2ax = -b \pm \sqrt{b^2 - 4ac}$$ ← 7. What was done?

Quadratic Formula: $x = \dfrac{-b \pm \sqrt{b^2 - 4ac}}{2a}$ ← 8. What was done?

EXPLORATION 2 Deriving the Quadratic Formula by Completing the Square

Work with a partner.

a. Solve $ax^2 + bx + c = 0$ by completing the square. (*Hint:* Subtract c from each side, divide each side by a, and then proceed by completing the square.)

b. Compare this method with the method in Exploration 1. Explain why you think $4a$ and b^2 were chosen in Steps 2 and 3 of Exploration 1.

Communicate Your Answer

USING TOOLS STRATEGICALLY

To be proficient in math, you need to identify relevant external mathematical resources.

3. How can you derive a formula that can be used to write the solutions of any quadratic equation in standard form?

4. Use the Quadratic Formula to solve each quadratic equation.

    a. $x^2 + 2x - 3 = 0$ **b.** $x^2 - 4x + 4 = 0$ **c.** $x^2 + 4x + 5 = 0$

5. Use the Internet to research *imaginary numbers*. How are they related to quadratic equations?

What You Will Learn

▶ Solve quadratic equations using the Quadratic Formula.
▶ Interpret the discriminant.
▶ Choose efficient methods for solving quadratic equations.

Using the Quadratic Formula

By completing the square for the quadratic equation $ax^2 + bx + c = 0$, you can develop a formula that gives the solutions of any quadratic equation in standard form. This formula is called the **Quadratic Formula**.

Core Concept

Quadratic Formula

The real solutions of the quadratic equation $ax^2 + bx + c = 0$ are

$$x = \frac{-b \pm \sqrt{b^2 - 4ac}}{2a} \qquad \text{Quadratic Formula}$$

where $a \neq 0$ and $b^2 - 4ac \geq 0$.

EXAMPLE 1 **Using the Quadratic Formula**

Solve $2x^2 - 5x + 3 = 0$ using the Quadratic Formula.

SOLUTION

STUDY TIP

You can use the roots of a quadratic equation to factor the related expression. In Example 1, you can use 1 and $\frac{3}{2}$ to factor $2x^2 - 5x + 3$ as $(x - 1)(2x - 3)$.

$$x = \frac{-b \pm \sqrt{b^2 - 4ac}}{2a} \qquad \text{Quadratic Formula}$$

$$= \frac{-(-5) \pm \sqrt{(-5)^2 - 4(2)(3)}}{2(2)} \qquad \text{Substitute 2 for } a, -5 \text{ for } b, \text{ and 3 for } c.$$

$$= \frac{5 \pm \sqrt{1}}{4} \qquad \text{Simplify.}$$

$$= \frac{5 \pm 1}{4} \qquad \text{Evaluate the square root.}$$

▶ So, the solutions are $x = \frac{5 + 1}{4} = \frac{3}{2}$ and $x = \frac{5 - 1}{4} = 1$.

Check

$2x^2 - 5x + 3 = 0$	Original equation	$2x^2 - 5x + 3 = 0$
$2\left(\frac{3}{2}\right)^2 - 5\left(\frac{3}{2}\right) + 3 \stackrel{?}{=} 0$	Substitute.	$2(1)^2 - 5(1) + 3 \stackrel{?}{=} 0$
$\frac{9}{2} - \frac{15}{2} + 3 \stackrel{?}{=} 0$	Simplify.	$2 - 5 + 3 \stackrel{?}{=} 0$
$0 = 0$ ✔	Simplify.	$0 = 0$ ✔

Monitoring Progress Help in English and Spanish at *BigIdeasMath.com*

Solve the equation using the Quadratic Formula. Round your solutions to the nearest tenth, if necessary.

1. $x^2 - 6x + 5 = 0$

2. $\frac{1}{2}x^2 + x - 10 = 0$

3. $-3x^2 + 2x + 7 = 0$

4. $4x^2 - 4x = -1$

EXAMPLE 2 **Modeling With Mathematics**

The number y of Northern Rocky Mountain wolf breeding pairs x years since 1990 can be modeled by the function $y = 0.20x^2 + 1.8x - 3$. When were there about 35 breeding pairs?

Wolf Breeding Pairs

$y = 0.20x^2 + 1.8x - 3$

Number of breeding pairs (y-axis): 0, 15, 30, 45, 60, 75, 90, 105, 120

Years since 1990 (x-axis): 0, 3, 6, 9, 12, 15, 18

SOLUTION

1. **Understand the Problem** You are given a quadratic function that represents the number of wolf breeding pairs for years after 1990. You need to use the model to determine when there were 35 wolf breeding pairs.

2. **Make a Plan** To determine when there were 35 wolf breeding pairs, find the x-values for which $y = 35$. So, solve the equation $35 = 0.20x^2 + 1.8x - 3$.

3. **Solve the Problem**

$35 = 0.20x^2 + 1.8x - 3$ Write the equation.

$0 = 0.20x^2 + 1.8x - 38$ Write in standard form.

$x = \dfrac{-b \pm \sqrt{b^2 - 4ac}}{2a}$ Quadratic Formula

$= \dfrac{-1.8 \pm \sqrt{1.8^2 - 4(0.2)(-38)}}{2(0.2)}$ Substitute 0.2 for a, 1.8 for b, and -38 for c.

$= \dfrac{-1.8 \pm \sqrt{33.64}}{0.4}$ Simplify.

$= \dfrac{-1.8 \pm 5.8}{0.4}$ Simplify.

The solutions are $x = \dfrac{-1.8 + 5.8}{0.4} = 10$ and $x = \dfrac{-1.8 - 5.8}{0.4} = -19$.

INTERPRETING MATHEMATICAL RESULTS

You can ignore the solution $x = -19$ because -19 represents the year 1971, which is not in the given time period.

▶ Because x represents the number of years since 1990, x is greater than or equal to zero. So, there were about 35 breeding pairs 10 years after 1990, in 2000.

4. **Look Back** Use a graphing calculator to graph the equations $y = 0.20x^2 + 1.8x - 3$ and $y = 35$. Then use the *intersect* feature to find the point of intersection. The graphs intersect at (10, 35).

$y = 35$ 50

-30 20

Intersection
X=10   Y=35 $y = 0.20x^2 + 1.8x - 3$

-20

Monitoring Progress Help in English and Spanish at *BigIdeasMath.com*

5. **WHAT IF?** When were there about 60 wolf breeding pairs?

6. The number y of bald eagle nesting pairs in a state x years since 2000 can be modeled by the function $y = 0.34x^2 + 13.1x + 51$.

   a. When were there about 160 bald eagle nesting pairs?

   b. How many bald eagle nesting pairs were there in 2000?

Interpreting the Discriminant

The expression $b^2 - 4ac$ in the Quadratic Formula is called the **discriminant**.

$$x = \frac{-b \pm \sqrt{b^2 - 4ac}}{2a} \quad \longleftarrow \quad \boxed{\text{discriminant}}$$

Because the discriminant is under the radical symbol, you can use the value of the discriminant to determine the number of real solutions of a quadratic equation and the number of x-intercepts of the graph of the related function.

Core Concept

Interpreting the Discriminant

$b^2 - 4ac > 0$	$b^2 - 4ac = 0$	$b^2 - 4ac < 0$
		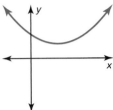
• two real solutions	• one real solution	• no real solutions
• two x-intercepts	• one x-intercept	• no x-intercepts

EXAMPLE 3 **Determining the Number of Real Solutions**

a. Determine the number of real solutions of $x^2 + 8x - 3 = 0$.

$b^2 - 4ac = 8^2 - 4(1)(-3)$ *Substitute 1 for a, 8 for b, and −3 for c.*

$\quad\quad\quad = 64 + 12$ *Simplify.*

$\quad\quad\quad = 76$ *Add.*

▶ The discriminant is greater than 0. So, the equation has two real solutions.

b. Determine the number of real solutions of $9x^2 + 1 = 6x$.

Write the equation in standard form: $9x^2 - 6x + 1 = 0$.

$b^2 - 4ac = (-6)^2 - 4(9)(1)$ *Substitute 9 for a, −6 for b, and 1 for c.*

$\quad\quad\quad = 36 - 36$ *Simplify.*

$\quad\quad\quad = 0$ *Subtract.*

▶ The discriminant is 0. So, the equation has one real solution.

Monitoring Progress Help in English and Spanish at *BigIdeasMath.com*

Determine the number of real solutions of the equation.

7. $-x^2 + 4x - 4 = 0$

8. $6x^2 + 2x = -1$

9. $\frac{1}{2}x^2 = 7x - 1$

EXAMPLE 4   **Finding the Number of *x*-Intercepts of a Parabola**

Find the number of *x*-intercepts of the graph of $y = 2x^2 + 3x + 9$.

SOLUTION

Determine the number of real solutions of $0 = 2x^2 + 3x + 9$.

$b^2 - 4ac = 3^2 - 4(2)(9)$ Substitute 2 for *a*, 3 for *b*, and 9 for *c*.

$\qquad = 9 - 72$ Simplify.

$\qquad = -63$ Subtract.

Because the discriminant is less than 0, the equation has no real solutions.

▶ So, the graph of $y = 2x^2 + 3x + 9$ has no *x*-intercepts.

Check
Use a graphing calculator to check your answer. Notice that the graph of $y = 2x^2 + 3x + 9$ has no *x*-intercepts.

Monitoring Progress Help in English and Spanish at *BigIdeasMath.com*

Find the number of *x*-intercepts of the graph of the function.

10. $y = -x^2 + x - 6$ **11.** $y = x^2 - x$ **12.** $f(x) = x^2 + 12x + 36$

Choosing an Efficient Method

The table shows five methods for solving quadratic equations. For a given equation, it may be more efficient to use one method instead of another. Some advantages and disadvantages of each method are shown.

Core Concept

Methods for Solving Quadratic Equations

Method	Advantages	Disadvantages
Factoring *(Lessons 2.5–2.8)*	• Straightforward when the equation can be factored easily	• Some equations are not factorable.
Graphing *(Lesson 4.2)*	• Can easily see the number of solutions • Use when approximate solutions are sufficient. • Can use a graphing calculator	• May not give exact solutions
Using Square Roots *(Lesson 4.3)*	• Use to solve equations of the form $x^2 = d$.	• Can only be used for certain equations
Completing the Square *(Lesson 4.4)*	• Best used when $a = 1$ and *b* is even	• May involve difficult calculations
Quadratic Formula *(Lesson 4.5)*	• Can be used for any quadratic equation • Gives exact solutions	• Takes time to do calculations

EXAMPLE 5 **Choosing a Method**

Solve the equation using any method. Explain your choice of method.

a. $x^2 - 10x = 1$ **b.** $2x^2 - 13x - 24 = 0$ **c.** $x^2 + 8x + 12 = 0$

SOLUTION

a. The coefficient of the x^2-term is 1, and the coefficient of the x-term is an even number. So, solve by completing the square.

$x^2 - 10x = 1$	Write the equation.
$x^2 - 10x + 25 = 1 + 25$	Complete the square for $x^2 - 10x$.
$(x - 5)^2 = 26$	Write the left side as the square of a binomial.
$x - 5 = \pm\sqrt{26}$	Take the square root of each side.
$x = 5 \pm \sqrt{26}$	Add 5 to each side.

▶ So, the solutions are $x = 5 + \sqrt{26} \approx 10.1$ and $x = 5 - \sqrt{26} \approx -0.1$.

b. The equation is not easily factorable, and the numbers are somewhat large. So, solve using the Quadratic Formula.

$x = \dfrac{-b \pm \sqrt{b^2 - 4ac}}{2a}$	Quadratic Formula
$= \dfrac{-(-13) \pm \sqrt{(-13)^2 - 4(2)(-24)}}{2(2)}$	Substitute 2 for a, -13 for b, and -24 for c.
$= \dfrac{13 \pm \sqrt{361}}{4}$	Simplify.
$= \dfrac{13 \pm 19}{4}$	Evaluate the square root.

Check

Graph the related function $f(x) = x^2 + 8x + 12$ and find the zeros. The zeros are -6 and -2.

▶ So, the solutions are $x = \dfrac{13 + 19}{4} = 8$ and $x = \dfrac{13 - 19}{4} = -\dfrac{3}{2}$.

c. The equation is easily factorable. So, solve by factoring.

$x^2 + 8x + 12 = 0$	Write the equation.
$(x + 2)(x + 6) = 0$	Factor the polynomial.
$x + 2 = 0 \quad$ or $\quad x + 6 = 0$	Zero-Product Property
$x = -2 \quad$ or $\quad x = -6$	Solve for x.

▶ The solutions are $x = -2$ and $x = -6$.

Monitoring Progress ◀)) Help in English and Spanish at *BigIdeasMath.com*

Solve the equation using any method. Explain your choice of method.

13. $x^2 + 11x - 12 = 0$

14. $9x^2 - 5 = 4$

15. $5x^2 - x - 1 = 0$

16. $x^2 = 2x - 5$

Vocabulary and Core Concept Check

1. **VOCABULARY** What formula can you use to solve any quadratic equation? Write the formula.

2. **VOCABULARY** In the Quadratic Formula, what is the discriminant? What does the value of the discriminant determine?

Monitoring Progress and Modeling with Mathematics

In Exercises 3–8, write the equation in standard form. Then identify the values of a, b, and c that you would use to solve the equation using the Quadratic Formula.

3. $x^2 = 7x$

4. $x^2 - 4x = -12$

5. $-2x^2 + 1 = 5x$

6. $3x + 2 = 4x^2$

7. $4 - 3x = -x^2 + 3x$

8. $-8x - 1 = 3x^2 + 2$

In Exercises 9–22, solve the equation using the Quadratic Formula. Round your solutions to the nearest tenth, if necessary. *(See Example 1.)*

9. $x^2 - 12x + 36 = 0$

10. $x^2 + 7x + 16 = 0$

11. $x^2 - 10x - 11 = 0$

12. $2x^2 - x - 1 = 0$

13. $2x^2 - 6x + 5 = 0$

14. $9x^2 - 6x + 1 = 0$

15. $6x^2 - 13x = -6$

16. $-3x^2 + 6x = 4$

17. $1 - 8x = -16x^2$

18. $x^2 - 5x + 3 = 0$

19. $x^2 + 2x = 9$

20. $5x^2 - 2 = 4x$

21. $2x^2 + 9x + 7 = 3$

22. $8x^2 + 8 = 6 - 9x$

23. **MODELING WITH MATHEMATICS** A dolphin jumps out of the water, as shown in the diagram. The function $h = -16t^2 + 26t$ models the height h (in feet) of the dolphin after t seconds. After how many seconds is the dolphin at a height of 5 feet? *(See Example 2.)*

24. **MODELING WITH MATHEMATICS** The amount of trout y (in tons) caught in a lake from 1995 to 2014 can be modeled by the equation $y = -0.08x^2 + 1.6x + 10$, where x is the number of years since 1995.

   a. When were about 15 tons of trout caught in the lake?

   b. Do you think this model can be used to determine the amounts of trout caught in future years? Explain your reasoning.

In Exercises 25–30, determine the number of real solutions of the equation. *(See Example 3.)*

25. $x^2 - 6x + 10 = 0$

26. $x^2 - 5x - 3 = 0$

27. $2x^2 - 12x = -18$

28. $4x^2 = 4x - 1$

29. $-\frac{1}{4}x^2 + 4x = -2$

30. $-5x^2 + 8x = 9$

In Exercises 31–36, find the number of x-intercepts of the graph of the function. *(See Example 4.)*

31. $y = x^2 + 5x - 1$

32. $y = 4x^2 + 4x + 1$

33. $y = -6x^2 + 3x - 4$

34. $y = -x^2 + 5x + 13$

35. $f(x) = 4x^2 + 3x - 6$

36. $f(x) = 2x^2 + 8x + 8$

In Exercises 37–44, solve the equation using any method. Explain your choice of method. *(See Example 5.)*

37. $-10x^2 + 13x = 4$

38. $x^2 - 3x - 40 = 0$

39. $x^2 + 6x = 5$

40. $-5x^2 = -25$

41. $x^2 + x - 12 = 0$

42. $x^2 - 4x + 1 = 0$

43. $4x^2 - x = 17$

44. $x^2 + 6x + 9 = 16$

45. ERROR ANALYSIS Describe and correct the error in solving the equation $3x^2 - 7x - 6 = 0$ using the Quadratic Formula.

> ✗
> $$x = \frac{-7 \pm \sqrt{(-7)^2 - 4(3)(-6)}}{2(3)}$$
> $$= \frac{-7 \pm \sqrt{121}}{6}$$
> $$x = \frac{2}{3} \text{ and } x = -3$$

46. ERROR ANALYSIS Describe and correct the error in solving the equation $-2x^2 + 9x = 4$ using the Quadratic Formula.

> ✗
> $$x = \frac{-9 \pm \sqrt{9^2 - 4(-2)(4)}}{2(-2)}$$
> $$= \frac{-9 \pm \sqrt{113}}{-4}$$
> $$x \approx -0.41 \text{ and } x \approx 4.91$$

47. MODELING WITH MATHEMATICS A fountain shoots a water arc that can be modeled by the graph of the equation $y = -0.006x^2 + 1.2x + 10$, where x is the horizontal distance (in feet) from the river's north shore and y is the height (in feet) above the river. Does the water arc reach a height of 50 feet? If so, about how far from the north shore is the water arc 50 feet above the water?

48. MODELING WITH MATHEMATICS Between the months of April and September, the number y of hours of daylight per day in Seattle, Washington, can be modeled by $y = -0.00046x^2 + 0.076x + 13$, where x is the number of days since April 1.

   a. Do any of the days between April and September in Seattle have 17 hours of daylight? If so, how many?

   b. Do any of the days between April and September in Seattle have 14 hours of daylight? If so, how many?

49. MAKING AN ARGUMENT Your friend uses the discriminant of the equation $2x^2 - 5x - 2 = -11$ and determines that the equation has two real solutions. Is your friend correct? Explain your reasoning.

50. MODELING WITH MATHEMATICS The frame of the tent shown is defined by a rectangular base and two parabolic arches that connect the opposite corners of the base. The graph of $y = -0.18x^2 + 1.6x$ models the height y (in feet) of one of the arches x feet along the diagonal of the base. Can a child who is 4 feet tall walk under one of the arches without having to bend over? Explain.

MATHEMATICAL CONNECTIONS In Exercises 51 and 52, use the given area A of the rectangle to find the value of x. Then give the dimensions of the rectangle.

51. $A = 91$ m^2

$(x + 2)$ m

$(2x + 3)$ m

52. $A = 209$ ft^2

$(4x - 5)$ ft

$(4x + 3)$ ft

COMPARING METHODS In Exercises 53 and 54, solve the equation by (a) graphing, (b) factoring, and (c) using the Quadratic Formula. Which method do you prefer? Explain your reasoning.

53. $x^2 + 4x + 4 = 0$ **54.** $3x^2 + 11x + 6 = 0$

55. REASONING How many solutions does the equation $ax^2 + bx + c = 0$ have when a and c have different signs? Explain your reasoning.

56. REASONING When the discriminant is a perfect square, are the solutions of $ax^2 + bx + c = 0$ rational or irrational? (Assume a, b, and c are integers.) Explain your reasoning.

REASONING In Exercises 57–59, give a value of c for which the equation has (a) two solutions, (b) one solution, and (c) no solutions.

57. $x^2 - 2x + c = 0$

58. $x^2 - 8x + c = 0$

59. $4x^2 + 12x + c = 0$

60. REPEATED REASONING You use the Quadratic Formula to solve an equation.

   a. You obtain solutions that are integers. Could you have used factoring to solve the equation? Explain your reasoning.

   b. You obtain solutions that are fractions. Could you have used factoring to solve the equation? Explain your reasoning.

   c. Make a generalization about quadratic equations with rational solutions.

61. MODELING WITH MATHEMATICS The fuel economy y (in miles per gallon) of a car can be modeled by the equation $y = -0.013x^2 + 1.25x + 5.6$, where $5 \le x \le 75$ and x is the speed (in miles per hour) of the car. Find the speed(s) at which you can travel and have a fuel economy of 32 miles per gallon.

62. MODELING WITH MATHEMATICS The depth d (in feet) of a river can be modeled by the equation $d = -0.25t^2 + 1.7t + 3.5$, where $0 \le t \le 7$ and t is the time (in hours) after a heavy rain begins. When is the river 6 feet deep?

ANALYZING EQUATIONS In Exercises 63–68, tell whether the vertex of the graph of the function lies above, below, or on the x-axis. Explain your reasoning without using a graph.

63. $y = x^2 - 3x + 2$ **64.** $y = 3x^2 - 6x + 3$

65. $y = 6x^2 - 2x + 4$ **66.** $y = -15x^2 + 10x - 25$

67. $f(x) = -3x^2 - 4x + 8$

68. $f(x) = 9x^2 - 24x + 16$

69. REASONING NASA creates a weightless environment by flying a plane in a series of parabolic paths. The height h (in feet) of a plane after t seconds in a parabolic flight path can be modeled by $h = -11t^2 + 700t + 21,000$. The passengers experience a weightless environment when the height of the plane is greater than or equal to 30,800 feet. For approximately how many seconds do passengers experience weightlessness on such a flight? Explain.

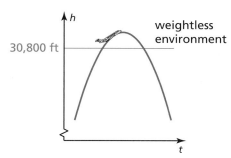

70. WRITING EQUATIONS Use the numbers to create a quadratic equation with the solutions $x = -1$ and $x = -\frac{1}{4}$.

$$\underline{\quad}x^2 + \underline{\quad}x + \underline{\quad} = 0$$

−5	−4	−3	−2	−1
1	2	3	4	5

71. PROBLEM SOLVING A rancher constructs two rectangular horse pastures that share a side, as shown. The pastures are enclosed by 1050 feet of fencing. Each pasture has an area of 15,000 square feet.

   a. Show that $y = 350 - \frac{4}{3}x$.

   b. Find the possible lengths and widths of each pasture.

72. PROBLEM SOLVING A kicker punts a football from a height of 2.5 feet above the ground with an initial vertical velocity of 45 feet per second.

Not drawn to scale

   a. Write an equation that models this situation using the function $h = -16t^2 + v_0t + s_0$, where h is the height (in feet) of the football, t is the time (in seconds) after the football is punted, v_0 is the initial vertical velocity (in feet per second), and s_0 is the initial height (in feet).

   b. The football is caught 5.5 feet above the ground, as shown in the diagram. Find the amount of time that the football is in the air.

73. CRITICAL THINKING The solutions of the quadratic equation $ax^2 + bx + c = 0$ are $x = \dfrac{-b + \sqrt{b^2 - 4ac}}{2a}$ and $x = \dfrac{-b - \sqrt{b^2 - 4ac}}{2a}$. Find the mean of the solutions. How is the mean of the solutions related to the graph of $y = ax^2 + bx + c$? Explain.

74. HOW DO YOU SEE IT? Match each graph with its discriminant. Explain your reasoning.

A.

B.

C.
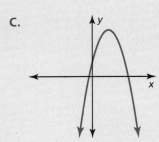

a. $b^2 - 4ac > 0$

b. $b^2 - 4ac = 0$

c. $b^2 - 4ac < 0$

75. CRITICAL THINKING You are trying to hang a tire swing. To get the rope over a tree branch that is 15 feet high, you tie the rope to a weight and throw it over the branch. You release the weight at a height s_0 of 5.5 feet. What is the minimum initial vertical velocity v_0 needed to reach the branch? (*Hint:* Use the equation $h = -16t^2 + v_0t + s_0$.)

76. THOUGHT PROVOKING Consider the graph of the standard form of a quadratic function $y = ax^2 + bx + c$. Then consider the Quadratic Formula as given by

$$x = -\frac{b}{2a} \pm \frac{\sqrt{b^2 - 4ac}}{2a}.$$

Write a graphical interpretation of the two parts of this formula.

77. ANALYZING RELATIONSHIPS Find the sum and product of $\dfrac{-b + \sqrt{b^2 - 4ac}}{2a}$ and $\dfrac{-b - \sqrt{b^2 - 4ac}}{2a}$. Then write a quadratic equation whose solutions have a sum of 2 and a product of $\dfrac{1}{2}$.

78. WRITING A FORMULA Derive a formula that can be used to find solutions of equations that have the form $ax^2 + x + c = 0$. Use your formula to solve $-2x^2 + x + 8 = 0$.

79. MULTIPLE REPRESENTATIONS If p is a solution of a quadratic equation $ax^2 + bx + c = 0$, then $(x - p)$ is a factor of $ax^2 + bx + c$.

a. Copy and complete the table for each pair of solutions.

Solutions	Factors	Quadratic equation
3, 4	$(x - 3), (x - 4)$	$x^2 - 7x + 12 = 0$
$-1, 6$		
0, 2		
$-\frac{1}{2}, 5$		

b. Graph the related function for each equation. Identify the zeros of the function.

CRITICAL THINKING In Exercises 80–82, find all values of k for which the equation has (a) two solutions, (b) one solution, and (c) no solutions.

80. $2x^2 + x + 3k = 0$ **81.** $x^2 - 4kx + 36 = 0$

82. $kx^2 + 5x - 16 = 0$

Maintaining Mathematical Proficiency
Reviewing what you learned in previous grades and lessons

Find the sum or difference. *(Section 2.1)*

83. $(x^2 + 2) + (2x^2 - x)$

84. $(x^3 + x^2 - 4) + (3x^2 + 10)$

85. $(-2x + 1) - (-3x^2 + x)$

86. $(-3x^3 + x^2 - 12x) - (-6x^2 + 3x - 9)$

Find the product. *(Section 2.2 and Section 2.3)*

87. $(x + 2)(x - 2)$

88. $2x(3 - x + 5x^2)$

89. $(7 - x)(x - 1)$

Core Vocabulary

counterexample, *p. 191*
radical expression, *p. 192*
simplest form of a radical, *p. 192*
rationalizing the denominator,
   p. 194

conjugates, *p. 194*
like radicals, *p. 196*
quadratic equation, *p. 202*
completing the square, *p. 216*

Quadratic Formula, *p. 226*
discriminant, *p. 228*

Core Concepts

Section 4.1

Product Property of Square Roots, *p. 192*
Quotient Property of Square Roots, *p. 192*

Rationalizing the Denominator, *p. 194*
Performing Operations with Radicals, *p. 196*

Section 4.2

Solving Quadratic Equations by Graphing, *p. 202*
Number of Solutions of a Quadratic Equation, *p. 203*

Finding Zeros of Functions, *p. 204*

Section 4.3

Solutions of $x^2 = d$, *p. 210*

Approximating Solutions of Quadratic Equations,
   p. 211

Section 4.4

Completing the Square, *p. 216*

Finding and Using Maximum and Minimum Values,
   p. 218

Section 4.5

Quadratic Formula, *p. 226*

Interpreting the Discriminant, *p. 228*

Mathematical Practices

1. For each part of Exercise 100 on page 200 that is *sometimes* true, list all examples and
   counterexamples from the table that represent the sum or product being described.

2. Describe how solving a simpler equation can help you solve the equation in Exercise 41
   on page 214.

Keeping a Positive Attitude

Do you ever feel frustrated or overwhelmed by
math? You're not alone. Just take a deep breath
and assess the situation. Try to find a productive
study environment, review your notes and the
examples in the textbook, and ask your teacher
or friends for help.

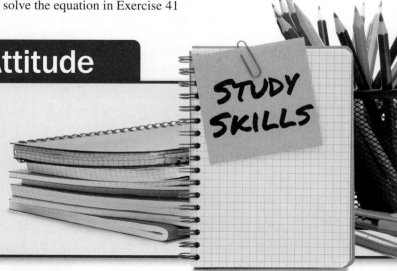

STUDY
SKILLS

Simplify the expression. *(Section 4.1)*

1. $\sqrt{112x^3}$

2. $\sqrt{\dfrac{18}{81}}$

3. $\sqrt[3]{-625}$

4. $\dfrac{4}{\sqrt{11}}$

5. $\sqrt[3]{\dfrac{54x^4}{343y^6}}$

6. $\dfrac{6}{5 + \sqrt{3}}$

7. $2\sqrt{5} + 7\sqrt{10} - 3\sqrt{20}$

8. $\sqrt{6}\left(7\sqrt{12} - 4\sqrt{3}\right)$

Use the graph to solve the equation. *(Section 4.2)*

9. $x^2 - 2x - 3 = 0$

10. $x^2 - 2x + 3 = 0$

11. $x^2 + 10x + 25 = 0$

$y = x^2 - 2x - 3$

$y = x^2 - 2x + 3$

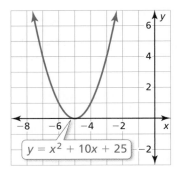

$y = x^2 + 10x + 25$

Solve the equation using square roots. *(Section 4.3)*

12. $4x^2 = 64$

13. $-3x^2 + 6 = 10$

14. $(x - 8)^2 = 1$

Solve the equation by completing the square. Round your solutions to the nearest hundredth, if necessary. *(Section 4.4)*

15. $x^2 - 6x + 8 = 0$

16. $x^2 + 12x + 4 = 0$

17. $4x(x + 6) = -40$

Solve the equation using the Quadratic Formula. Round your solutions to the nearest tenth, if necessary. *(Section 4.5)*

18. $x^2 + 9x + 14 = 0$

19. $x^2 + 4x = 1$

20. $-2x^2 + 7 = 3x$

21. Which method would you use to solve $2x^2 + 3x + 1 = 0$? Explain your reasoning. *(Section 4.5)*

22. The length of a rectangular prism is four times its width. The volume of the prism is 380 cubic meters. Find the length and width of the prism. *(Section 4.3)*

5 m

23. You cast a fishing lure into the water from a height of 4 feet above the water. The height h (in feet) of the fishing lure after t seconds can be modeled by the equation $h = -16t^2 + 24t + 4$. *(Section 4.5)*

   a. After how many seconds does the fishing lure reach a height of 12 feet?

   b. After how many seconds does the fishing lure hit the water?

Essential Question   What are the subsets of the set of complex numbers?

In your study of mathematics, you have probably worked with only *real numbers*, which can be represented graphically on the real number line. In this lesson, the system of numbers is expanded to include *imaginary numbers*. The real numbers and imaginary numbers compose the set of *complex numbers*.

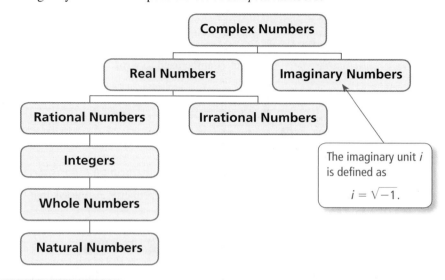

The imaginary unit i is defined as

$$i = \sqrt{-1}.$$

EXPLORATION 1   Classifying Numbers

Work with a partner. Determine which subsets of the set of complex numbers contain each number.

a. $\sqrt{9}$ **b.** $\sqrt{0}$ **c.** $-\sqrt{4}$

d. $\sqrt{\dfrac{4}{9}}$ **e.** $\sqrt{2}$ **f.** $\sqrt{-1}$

EXPLORATION 2   Simplifying i^2

ATTENDING TO PRECISION

To be proficient in math, you need to use clear definitions in your reasoning and discussions with others.

Work with a partner. Justify each step in the simplification of i^2.

Algebraic Step	Justification
$i^2 = (\sqrt{-1})^2$	
$= -1$	

Communicate Your Answer

3. What are the subsets of the set of complex numbers? Give an example of a number in each subset.

4. Is it possible for a number to be both whole and natural? natural and rational? rational and irrational? real and imaginary? Explain your reasoning.

5. Your friend claims that the conclusion in Exploration 2 is incorrect because $i^2 = i \cdot i = \sqrt{-1} \cdot \sqrt{-1} = \sqrt{-1(-1)} = \sqrt{1} = 1$. Is your friend correct? Explain.

What You Will Learn

▶ Define and use the imaginary unit i.

▶ Add and subtract complex numbers.

▶ Multiply complex numbers.

Core Vocabulary

imaginary unit *i*, *p. 238*
complex number, *p. 238*
imaginary number, *p. 238*
pure imaginary number, *p. 238*
complex conjugates, *p. 241*

The Imaginary Unit *i*

Not all quadratic equations have real-number solutions. For example, $x^2 = -3$ has no real-number solutions because the square of any real number is never a negative number.

To overcome this problem, mathematicians created an expanded system of numbers using the **imaginary unit *i***, defined as $i = \sqrt{-1}$. Note that $i^2 = -1$. The imaginary unit i can be used to write the square root of *any* negative number.

🔄 Core Concept

The Square Root of a Negative Number

Property	Example
1. If r is a positive real number, then $\sqrt{-r} = i\sqrt{r}$.	$\sqrt{-3} = i\sqrt{3}$
2. By the first property, it follows that $(i\sqrt{r})^2 = -r$.	$(i\sqrt{3})^2 = i^2 \cdot 3 = -3$

EXAMPLE 1 **Finding Square Roots of Negative Numbers**

Find the square root of each number.

a. $\sqrt{-25}$ **b.** $\sqrt{-72}$ **c.** $-5\sqrt{-9}$

SOLUTION

a. $\sqrt{-25} = \sqrt{25} \cdot \sqrt{-1} = 5i$

b. $\sqrt{-72} = \sqrt{72} \cdot \sqrt{-1} = \sqrt{36} \cdot \sqrt{2} \cdot i = 6\sqrt{2}\,i = 6i\sqrt{2}$

c. $-5\sqrt{-9} = -5\sqrt{9} \cdot \sqrt{-1} = -5 \cdot 3 \cdot i = -15i$

Monitoring Progress   Help in English and Spanish at *BigIdeasMath.com*

Find the square root of the number.

1. $\sqrt{-4}$ **2.** $\sqrt{-12}$ **3.** $-\sqrt{-36}$ **4.** $2\sqrt{-54}$

A **complex number** written in *standard form* is a number $a + bi$ where a and b are real numbers. The number a is the *real part*, and the number bi is the *imaginary part*.

$$a + bi$$

If $b \neq 0$, then $a + bi$ is an **imaginary number**. If $a = 0$ and $b \neq 0$, then $a + bi$ is a **pure imaginary number**. The diagram shows how different types of complex numbers are related.

Complex Numbers ($a + bi$)

Real Numbers ($a + 0i$)	Imaginary Numbers ($a + bi, b \neq 0$)
-1 $\frac{5}{3}$ π $\sqrt{2}$	$2 + 3i$ $9 - 5i$ **Pure Imaginary Numbers** ($0 + bi, b \neq 0$) $-4i$ $6i$

Two complex numbers $a + bi$ and $c + di$ are equal if and only if $a = c$ and $b = d$.

EXAMPLE 2 **Equality of Two Complex Numbers**

Find the values of x and y that satisfy the equation $2x - 7i = 10 + yi$.

SOLUTION

Set the real parts equal to each other and the imaginary parts equal to each other.

$2x = 10$	Equate the real parts.	$-7i = yi$	Equate the imaginary parts.
$x = 5$	Solve for x.	$-7 = y$	Solve for y.

▶ So, $x = 5$ and $y = -7$.

Monitoring Progress Help in English and Spanish at *BigIdeasMath.com*

Find the values of x and y that satisfy the equation.

5. $x + 3i = 9 - yi$

6. $9 + 4yi = -2x + 3i$

Adding and Subtracting Complex Numbers

Core Concept

Sums and Differences of Complex Numbers

To add (or subtract) two complex numbers, add (or subtract) their real parts and their imaginary parts separately.

Sum of complex numbers: $(a + bi) + (c + di) = (a + c) + (b + d)i$

Difference of complex numbers: $(a + bi) - (c + di) = (a - c) + (b - d)i$

EXAMPLE 3 **Adding and Subtracting Complex Numbers**

Add or subtract. Write the answer in standard form.

a. $(8 - i) + (5 + 4i)$

b. $(7 - 6i) - (3 - 6i)$

c. $13 - (2 + 7i) + 5i$

SOLUTION

a. $(8 - i) + (5 + 4i) = (8 + 5) + (-1 + 4)i$ Definition of complex addition

$= 13 + 3i$ Write in standard form.

b. $(7 - 6i) - (3 - 6i) = (7 - 3) + (-6 + 6)i$ Definition of complex subtraction

$= 4 + 0i$ Simplify.

$= 4$ Write in standard form.

c. $13 - (2 + 7i) + 5i = [(13 - 2) - 7i] + 5i$ Definition of complex subtraction

$= (11 - 7i) + 5i$ Simplify.

$= 11 + (-7 + 5)i$ Definition of complex addition

$= 11 - 2i$ Write in standard form.

EXAMPLE 4   Solving a Real-Life Problem

Electrical circuit components, such as resistors, inductors, and capacitors, all oppose the flow of current. This opposition is called *resistance* for resistors and *reactance* for inductors and capacitors. Each of these quantities is measured in ohms. The symbol used for ohms is Ω, the uppercase Greek letter omega.

Component and symbol	Resistor —\/\/\—	Inductor —⎍⎍⎍—	Capacitor —⊣⊢—
Resistance or reactance (in ohms)	R	L	C
Impedance (in ohms)	R	Li	$-Ci$

Alternating current source

The table shows the relationship between a component's resistance or reactance and its contribution to impedance. A *series circuit* is also shown with the resistance or reactance of each component labeled. The impedance for a series circuit is the sum of the impedances for the individual components. Find the impedance of the circuit.

SOLUTION

The resistor has a resistance of 5 ohms, so its impedance is 5 ohms. The inductor has a reactance of 3 ohms, so its impedance is $3i$ ohms. The capacitor has a reactance of 4 ohms, so its impedance is $-4i$ ohms.

$$\text{Impedance of circuit} = 5 + 3i + (-4i) = 5 - i$$

▶ The impedance of the circuit is $(5 - i)$ ohms.

Monitoring Progress   Help in English and Spanish at *BigIdeasMath.com*

Add or subtract. Write the answer in standard form.

7. $(9 - i) + (-6 + 7i)$ **8.** $(3 + 7i) - (8 - 2i)$

9. $-4 - (1 + i) - (5 + 9i)$ **10.** $5 + (-9 + 3i) + 6i$

11. WHAT IF? In Example 4, what is the impedance of the circuit when the capacitor is replaced with one having a reactance of 7 ohms?

Multiplying Complex Numbers

Many properties of real numbers are also valid for complex numbers, such as those used below to multiply two complex numbers.

$(a + bi)(c + di) = a(c + di) + bi(c + di)$	Distributive Property
$= ac + (ad)i + (bc)i + (bd)i^2$	Distributive Property
$= ac + (ad)i + (bc)i + (bd)(-1)$	Use $i^2 = -1$.
$= ac - bd + (ad)i + (bc)i$	Commutative Property
$= (ac - bd) + (ad + bc)i$	Associative Property

This result shows a pattern that you could use to multiply two complex numbers. However, it is often more practical to use the Distributive Property or the FOIL Method, just as you do when multiplying real numbers or algebraic expressions.

EXAMPLE 5 Multiplying Complex Numbers

Multiply. Write the answer in standard form.

a. $4i(-6 + i)$ **b.** $(9 - 2i)(-4 + 7i)$

SOLUTION

> **STUDY TIP**
>
> When simplifying an expression that involves complex numbers, be sure to simplify i^2 as -1.

a.
$$4i(-6 + i) = -24i + 4i^2 \qquad \text{Distributive Property}$$
$$= -24i + 4(-1) \qquad \text{Use } i^2 = -1.$$
$$= -4 - 24i \qquad \text{Write in standard form.}$$

b.
$$(9 - 2i)(-4 + 7i) = -36 + 63i + 8i - 14i^2 \qquad \text{Multiply using FOIL.}$$
$$= -36 + 71i - 14(-1) \qquad \text{Simplify and use } i^2 = -1.$$
$$= -36 + 71i + 14 \qquad \text{Simplify.}$$
$$= -22 + 71i \qquad \text{Write in standard form.}$$

Monitoring Progress Help in English and Spanish at *BigIdeasMath.com*

Multiply. Write the answer in standard form.

12. $(-3i)(10i)$ **13.** $i(8 - i)$ **14.** $(3 + i)(5 - i)$

Pairs of complex numbers of the forms $a + bi$ and $a - bi$, where $b \neq 0$, are called **complex conjugates**. Consider the product of complex conjugates below.

$$(a + bi)(a - bi) = a^2 - (ab)i + (ab)i - b^2i^2 \qquad \text{Multiply using FOIL.}$$
$$= a^2 - b^2(-1) \qquad \text{Simplify and use } i^2 = -1.$$
$$= a^2 + b^2 \qquad \text{Simplify.}$$

Because a and b are real numbers, $a^2 + b^2$ is a real number. So, the product of complex conjugates is a real number.

EXAMPLE 6 Multiplying Complex Conjugates

Multiply $5 + 2i$ by its complex conjugate.

SOLUTION

> **LOOKING FOR STRUCTURE**
>
> You can use the pattern $(a + bi)(a - bi) = a^2 + b^2$, where $a = 5$ and $b = 2$, to find the product in Example 6.
>
> $(5 + 2i)(5 - 2i) = 5^2 + 2^2$
> $= 25 + 4$
> $= 29$

The complex conjugate of $5 + 2i$ is $5 - 2i$.
$$(5 + 2i)(5 - 2i) = 25 - 10i + 10i - 4i^2 \qquad \text{Multiply using FOIL.}$$
$$= 25 - 4(-1) \qquad \text{Simplify and use } i^2 = -1.$$
$$= 29 \qquad \text{Simplify.}$$

Monitoring Progress Help in English and Spanish at *BigIdeasMath.com*

Multiply the complex number by its complex conjugate.

15. $1 + i$ **16.** $4 - 7i$ **17.** $-3 - 2i$

Vocabulary and Core Concept Check

1. **VOCABULARY** What is the imaginary unit i defined as and how can you use i?

2. **COMPLETE THE SENTENCE** For the complex number $5 + 2i$, the imaginary part is _____ and the real part is _____.

3. **WRITING** Describe how to add complex numbers.

4. **WHICH ONE DOESN'T BELONG?** Which number does *not* belong with the other three? Explain your reasoning.

$$3 + 0i \qquad 2 + 5i \qquad \sqrt{3} + 6i \qquad 0 - 7i$$

Monitoring Progress and Modeling with Mathematics

In Exercises 5–12, find the square root of the number.
(See Example 1.)

5. $\sqrt{-36}$

6. $\sqrt{-64}$

7. $\sqrt{-18}$

8. $\sqrt{-24}$

9. $2\sqrt{-16}$

10. $-3\sqrt{-49}$

11. $-4\sqrt{-32}$

12. $6\sqrt{-63}$

In Exercises 13–20, find the values of x and y that satisfy the equation. *(See Example 2.)*

13. $4x + 2i = 8 + yi$

14. $3x + 6i = 27 + yi$

15. $-10x + 12i = 20 + 3yi$

16. $9x - 18i = -36 + 6yi$

17. $2x - yi = 14 + 12i$

18. $-12x + yi = 60 - 13i$

19. $54 - \frac{1}{7}yi = 9x - 4i$

20. $15 - 3yi = \frac{1}{2}x + 2i$

In Exercises 21–30, add or subtract. Write the answer in standard form. *(See Example 3.)*

21. $(6 - i) + (7 + 3i)$

22. $(9 + 5i) + (11 + 2i)$

23. $(12 + 4i) - (3 - 7i)$

24. $(2 - 15i) - (4 + 5i)$

25. $(12 - 3i) + (7 + 3i)$

26. $(16 - 9i) - (2 - 9i)$

27. $7 - (3 + 4i) + 6i$

28. $16 - (2 - 3i) - i$

29. $-10 + (6 - 5i) - 9i$

30. $-3 + (8 + 2i) + 7i$

31. **USING STRUCTURE** Write each expression as a complex number in standard form.

    a. $\sqrt{-9} + \sqrt{-4} - \sqrt{16}$

    b. $\sqrt{-16} + \sqrt{8} + \sqrt{-36}$

32. **REASONING** The additive inverse of a complex number z is a complex number z_a such that $z + z_a = 0$. Find the additive inverse of each complex number.

    a. $z = 1 + i$ b. $z = 3 - i$ c. $z = -2 + 8i$

In Exercises 33–36, find the impedance of the series circuit. *(See Example 4.)*

33.

34.

35.

36.

In Exercises 37–44, multiply. Write the answer in standard form. *(See Example 5.)*

37. $3i(-5 + i)$

38. $2i(7 - i)$

39. $(3 - 2i)(4 + i)$

40. $(7 + 5i)(8 - 6i)$

41. $(5 - 2i)(-2 - 3i)$

42. $(-1 + 8i)(9 + 3i)$

43. $(3 - 6i)^2$

44. $(8 + 3i)^2$

JUSTIFYING STEPS **In Exercises 45 and 46, justify each step in performing the operation.**

45. $11 - (4 + 3i) + 5i$

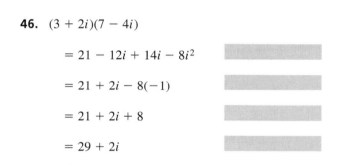

$= [(11 - 4) - 3i] + 5i$

$= (7 - 3i) + 5i$

$= 7 + (-3 + 5)i$

$= 7 + 2i$

46. $(3 + 2i)(7 - 4i)$

$= 21 - 12i + 14i - 8i^2$

$= 21 + 2i - 8(-1)$

$= 21 + 2i + 8$

$= 29 + 2i$

REASONING **In Exercises 47 and 48, place the tiles in the expression to make a true statement.**

47. $(\underline{} - \underline{}i) - (\underline{} - \underline{}i) = 2 - 4i$

| 7 | 4 | 3 | 6 |

48. $\underline{}i(\underline{} + \underline{}i) = -18 - 10i$

| −5 | 9 | 2 |

In Exercises 49–54, multiply the complex number by its complex conjugate. *(See Example 6.)*

49. $1 - i$

50. $8 + i$

51. $4 + 2i$

52. $5 - 6i$

53. $-2 + 2i$

54. $-1 - 9i$

55. **OPEN-ENDED** Write a pair of imaginary numbers whose product is 80.

56. **NUMBER SENSE** Write the complex conjugate of $1 - \sqrt{-12}$. Then find the product of the complex conjugates.

57. **USING STRUCTURE** Expand $(a - bi)^2$ and write the result in standard form. Use your result to check your answer in Exercise 43.

58. **USING STRUCTURE** Expand $(a + bi)^2$ and write the result in standard form. Use your result to check your answer in Exercise 44.

ERROR ANALYSIS **In Exercises 59 and 60, describe and correct the error in performing the operation and writing the answer in standard form.**

59.

✗ $(3 + 2i)(5 - i) = 15 - 3i + 10i - 2i^2$

$= 15 + 7i - 2i^2$

$= -2i^2 + 7i + 15$

60.

✗ $(4 + 6i)^2 = (4)^2 + (6i)^2$

$= 16 + 36i^2$

$= 16 + (36)(-1)$

$= -20$

61. **NUMBER SENSE** Simplify each expression. Then classify your results in the table below.

   a. $(-4 + 7i) + (-4 - 7i)$

   b. $(2 - 6i) - (-10 + 4i)$

   c. $(25 + 15i) - (25 - 6i)$

   d. $(5 + i)(8 - i)$

   e. $(17 - 3i) + (-17 - 6i)$

   f. $(-1 + 2i)(11 - i)$

   g. $(7 + 5i) + (7 - 5i)$

   h. $(-3 + 6i) - (-3 - 8i)$

Real numbers	Imaginary numbers	Pure imaginary numbers

62. **MAKING AN ARGUMENT** The Product Property of Square Roots states $\sqrt{a} \cdot \sqrt{b} = \sqrt{ab}$. Your friend concludes $\sqrt{-4} \cdot \sqrt{-9} = \sqrt{36} = 6$. Is your friend correct? Explain.

63. FINDING A PATTERN Make a table that shows the powers of i from i^1 to i^8 in the first row and the simplified forms of these powers in the second row. Describe the pattern you observe in the table. Verify the pattern continues by evaluating the next four powers of i.

64. HOW DO YOU SEE IT? The coordinate system shown below is called the *complex plane*. In the complex plane, the point that corresponds to the complex number $a + bi$ is (a, b). Match each complex number with its corresponding point.

a. 2

b. $2i$

c. $4 - 2i$

d. $3 + 3i$

e. $-2 + 4i$

f. $-3 - 3i$

In Exercises 65–70, write the expression as a complex number in standard form.

65. $(3 + 4i) - (7 - 5i) + 2i(9 + 12i)$

66. $3i(2 + 5i) + (6 - 7i) - (9 + i)$

67. $(3 + 5i)(2 - 7i^4)$

68. $2i^3(5 - 12i)$

69. $(2 + 4i^5) + (1 - 9i^6) - (3 + i^7)$

70. $(8 - 2i^4) + (3 - 7i^8) - (4 + i^9)$

71. NUMBER SENSE Write a pair of complex numbers whose sum is -4 and whose product is 53.

72. COMPARING METHODS Describe the two different methods shown for writing the complex expression in standard form. Which method do you prefer? Explain.

> **Method 1**
> $$4i(2 - 3i) + 4i(1 - 2i) = 8i - 12i^2 + 4i - 8i^2$$
> $$= 8i - 12(-1) + 4i - 8(-1)$$
> $$= 20 + 12i$$

> **Method 2**
> $$4i(2 - 3i) + 4i(1 - 2i) = 4i[(2 - 3i) + (1 - 2i)]$$
> $$= 4i[3 - 5i]$$
> $$= 12i - 20i^2$$
> $$= 12i - 20(-1)$$
> $$= 20 + 12i$$

73. CRITICAL THINKING Determine whether each statement is *true* or *false*. If it is true, give an example. If it is false, give a counterexample.

a. The sum of two imaginary numbers is an imaginary number.

b. The product of two pure imaginary numbers is a real number.

c. A pure imaginary number is an imaginary number.

d. A complex number is a real number.

74. THOUGHT PROVOKING Create a circuit that has an impedance of $14 - 3i$.

Maintaining Mathematical Proficiency Reviewing what you learned in previous grades and lessons

Write a quadratic function in vertex form whose graph is shown. *(Section 3.4)*

75.

76.

77.
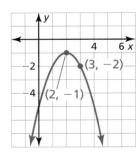

Find the value of c that completes the square. *(Section 4.4)*

78. $x^2 + 8x + c$

79. $x^2 - 20x + c$

80. $x^2 - 7x + c$

Essential Question How can you determine whether a quadratic equation has real solutions or imaginary solutions?

EXPLORATION 1   **Using Graphs to Solve Quadratic Equations**

Work with a partner. Use the discriminant of $f(x) = 0$ and the sign of the leading coefficient of $f(x)$ to match each quadratic function with its graph. Explain your reasoning. Then find the real solution(s) (if any) of each quadratic equation $f(x) = 0$.

a. $f(x) = x^2 - 2x$ **b.** $f(x) = x^2 - 2x + 1$ **c.** $f(x) = x^2 - 2x + 2$

d. $f(x) = -x^2 + 2x$ **e.** $f(x) = -x^2 + 2x - 1$ **f.** $f(x) = -x^2 + 2x - 2$

A.

B.

C.

D.

E.

F.

EXPLORATION 2   **Finding Imaginary Solutions**

MAKING SENSE OF PROBLEMS

To be proficient in math, you need to make conjectures about the form and meaning of solutions.

Work with a partner. What do you know about the discriminants of quadratic equations that have no real solutions? Use the Quadratic Formula and what you learned about the imaginary unit i to find the *imaginary* solutions of each equation in Exploration 1 that has no real solutions. Use substitution to check your answers.

Communicate Your Answer

3. How can you determine whether a quadratic equation has real solutions or imaginary solutions?

4. Describe the number and type of solutions of $x^2 + 2x + 3 = 0$. How do you know? What are the solutions?

What You Will Learn

▶ Solve quadratic equations and find zeros of quadratic functions.

▶ Use the discriminant.

Finding Solutions and Zeros

Previously, you learned that you can use the discriminant of a quadratic equation to determine whether the equation has two real solutions, one real solution, or no real solutions. When the discriminant is negative, you can use the imaginary unit i to write two *imaginary* solutions of the equation. So, all quadratic equations have complex number solutions.

You have solved quadratic equations with real solutions. Now you will solve quadratic equations with *imaginary* solutions.

> **STUDY TIP**
>
> In general, every polynomial equation has complex number solutions. This is implied by the *Fundamental Theorem of Algebra*. You will learn more about this theorem in a future course.

EXAMPLE 1   Solving Quadratic Equations

Solve each equation.

a. $x^2 + 9 = 0$ **b.** $x^2 + 4x + 5 = 0$ **c.** $5x^2 - 4x + 1 = 0$

SOLUTION

a. The equation does not have an x-term. So, solve using square roots.

$x^2 + 9 = 0$	Write the equation.
$x^2 = -9$	Subtract 9 from each side.
$x = \pm\sqrt{-9}$	Take the square root of each side.
$x = \pm 3i$	Write in terms of i.

> **LOOKING FOR STRUCTURE**
>
> You can use the pattern $(a + bi)(a - bi) = a^2 + b^2$ to rewrite $x^2 + 9 = 0$ as $(x + 3i)(x - 3i) = 0$. So, $x = \pm 3i$.

b. The coefficient of the x^2-term is 1, and the coefficient of the x-term is an even number. So, solve by completing the square.

$$x^2 + 4x + 5 = 0$$
$$x^2 + 4x = -5$$
$$x^2 + 4x + 4 = -5 + 4$$
$$(x + 2)^2 = -1$$
$$x + 2 = \pm\sqrt{-1}$$
$$x = -2 \pm \sqrt{-1}$$
$$x = -2 \pm i$$

> **Check** You can check imaginary solutions algebraically. The check for one of the imaginary solutions, $-2 + i$, is shown.
>
> $$(-2 + i)^2 + 4(-2 + i) + 5 \overset{?}{=} 0$$
> $$3 - 4i - 8 + 4i + 5 \overset{?}{=} 0$$
> $$0 = 0 ✓$$

c. The equation is not factorable, and completing the square would result in fractions. So, solve using the Quadratic Formula.

$x = \dfrac{-(-4) \pm \sqrt{(-4)^2 - 4(5)(1)}}{2(5)}$	Substitute 5 for a, -4 for b, and 1 for c.
$x = \dfrac{4 \pm \sqrt{-4}}{10}$	Simplify.
$x = \dfrac{4 \pm 2i}{10}$	Write in terms of i.
$x = \dfrac{2 \pm i}{5}$	Simplify.

EXAMPLE 2 Finding Zeros of a Quadratic Function

Find the zeros of $f(x) = 4x^2 + 20$.

SOLUTION

$4x^2 + 20 = 0$	Set $f(x)$ equal to 0.
$4x^2 = -20$	Subtract 20 from each side.
$x^2 = -5$	Divide each side by 4.
$x = \pm\sqrt{-5}$	Take the square root of each side.
$x = \pm i\sqrt{5}$	Write in terms of i.

▶ So, the zeros of f are $i\sqrt{5}$ and $-i\sqrt{5}$.

Check

$f(i\sqrt{5}) = 4(i\sqrt{5})^2 + 20$
$= 4(-5) + 20$
$= 0$ ✓

$f(-i\sqrt{5}) = 4(-i\sqrt{5})^2 + 20$
$= 4(-5) + 20$
$= 0$ ✓

Monitoring Progress Help in English and Spanish at *BigIdeasMath.com*

Solve the equation using any method. Explain your choice of method.

1. $-x^2 - 25 = 0$ **2.** $x^2 - 4x + 8 = 0$ **3.** $8x^2 + 5 = 12x$

Find the zeros of the function.

4. $f(x) = -2x^2 - 18$ **5.** $f(x) = 9x^2 + 1$ **6.** $f(x) = x^2 - 6x + 10$

Using the Discriminant

EXAMPLE 3 Writing an Equation

Find a possible pair of integer values for a and c so that the equation $ax^2 - 4x + c = 0$ has two imaginary solutions. Then write the equation.

SOLUTION

For the equation to have two imaginary solutions, the discriminant must be less than zero.

$b^2 - 4ac < 0$	Write the discriminant.	**Check** The graph of
$(-4)^2 - 4ac < 0$	Substitute -4 for b.	$y = 2x^2 - 4x + 3$
$16 - 4ac < 0$	Evaluate the power.	does not have
$-4ac < -16$	Subtract 16 from each side.	any x-intercepts. ✓
$ac > 4$	Divide each side by -4. Reverse inequality symbol.	

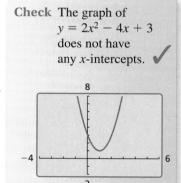

ANOTHER WAY

Another possible equation in Example 3 is $3x^2 - 4x + 2 = 0$. You can obtain this equation by letting $a = 3$ and $c = 2$.

Because $ac > 4$, choose two integers whose product is greater than 4, such as $a = 2$ and $c = 3$.

▶ So, one possible equation is $2x^2 - 4x + 3 = 0$.

Monitoring Progress Help in English and Spanish at *BigIdeasMath.com*

7. Find a possible pair of integer values for a and c so that the equation $ax^2 + 3x + c = 0$ has two imaginary solutions. Then write the equation.

The function $h = -16t^2 + s_0$ is used to model the height of a *dropped* object, where h is the height (in feet), t is the time in motion (in seconds), and s_0 is the initial height (in feet). For an object that is *launched* or *thrown*, an extra term v_0t must be added to the model to account for the object's initial vertical velocity v_0 (in feet per second).

$$h = -16t^2 + s_0 \qquad \text{Object is dropped.}$$

$$h = -16t^2 + v_0t + s_0 \qquad \text{Object is launched or thrown.}$$

As shown below, the value of v_0 can be positive, negative, or zero depending on whether the object is launched upward, downward, or parallel to the ground.

$v_0 > 0$

$v_0 < 0$

$v_0 = 0$

EXAMPLE 4 Modeling a Launched Object

A juggler tosses a ball into the air. The ball leaves the juggler's hand 4 feet above the ground and has an initial vertical velocity of 30 feet per second. Does the ball reach a height of 25 feet? 10 feet? Explain your reasoning.

SOLUTION

Because the ball is *thrown*, use the model $h = -16t^2 + v_0t + s_0$ to write a function that represents the height of the ball.

$$h = -16t^2 + v_0t + s_0 \qquad \text{Write the height model.}$$

$$h = -16t^2 + 30t + 4 \qquad \text{Substitute 30 for } v_0 \text{ and 4 for } s_0.$$

To determine whether the ball reaches each height, substitute each height for h to create two equations. Then solve each equation using the Quadratic Formula.

$$25 = -16t^2 + 30t + 4 \qquad\qquad 10 = -16t^2 + 30t + 4$$

$$0 = -16t^2 + 30t - 21 \qquad\qquad 0 = -16t^2 + 30t - 6$$

$$t = \frac{-30 \pm \sqrt{30^2 - 4(-16)(-21)}}{2(-16)} \qquad t = \frac{-30 \pm \sqrt{30^2 - 4(-16)(-6)}}{2(-16)}$$

$$t = \frac{-30 \pm \sqrt{-444}}{-32} \qquad\qquad t = \frac{-30 \pm \sqrt{516}}{-32}$$

When $h = 25$, the equation has two imaginary solutions because the discriminant is negative. When $h = 10$, the equation has two real solutions, $t \approx 0.23$ and $t \approx 1.65$.

▶ So, the ball reaches a height of 10 feet, but it does not reach a height of 25 feet.

Check The graph shows that the ball reaches a height of 10 feet but not 25 feet. ✔

30

y = 25

y = 10

Maximum
X=.93750131 Y=18.0625   2.5
0
0

Monitoring Progress Help in English and Spanish at *BigIdeasMath.com*

8. The ball leaves the juggler's hand with an initial vertical velocity of 40 feet per second. Does the ball reach a height of 30 feet? 20 feet? Explain.

Vocabulary and Core Concept Check

1. **COMPLETE THE SENTENCE** When the graph of a quadratic function $y = f(x)$ has no x-intercepts, the equation $f(x) = 0$ has two _____ solutions.

2. **WRITING** Can a quadratic equation with real coefficients have one imaginary solution? Explain.

Monitoring Progress and Modeling with Mathematics

ANALYZING EQUATIONS In Exercises 3–6, use the discriminant to match the quadratic equation with the graph of the related function. Then describe the number and type of solutions of the equation.

3. $x^2 - 6x + 25 = 0$ 4. $2x^2 - 20x + 50 = 0$

5. $3x^2 + 6x - 9 = 0$ 6. $5x^2 - 10x - 35 = 0$

A.   B.

C.   D.

In Exercises 7–20, solve the equation using any method. Explain your choice of method. *(See Example 1.)*

7. $x^2 + 49 = 0$ 8. $2x^2 - 7 = -3$

9. $x^2 - 4x + 3 = 0$ 10. $3x^2 + 6x + 3 = 0$

11. $x^2 + 6x + 15 = 0$ 12. $6x^2 - 2x + 1 = 0$

13. $9x^2 + 17 = 24x$ 14. $-3x = 2x^2 - 4$

15. $-10x = -25 - x^2$ 16. $-2x^2 - 5 = -2x$

17. $-4x^2 + 3x = -5$ 18. $3x^2 + 87 = 30x$

19. $-z^2 = -12z + 6$ 20. $-7w + 6 = -4w^2$

21. **ERROR ANALYSIS** Describe and correct the error in solving the equation.

$$x^2 + 10x + 74 = 0$$

$$x = \frac{-10 \pm \sqrt{10^2 - 4(1)(74)}}{2(1)}$$

$$= \frac{-10 \pm \sqrt{-196}}{2}$$

$$= \frac{-10 \pm 14}{2}$$

$$= -12 \text{ or } 2$$

22. **REASONING** Write a quadratic equation in the form $ax^2 + bx + c = 0$ that has the solutions $x = 1 \pm i$.

In Exercises 23–28, find the zeros of the function. *(See Example 2.)*

23. $f(x) = 5x^2 + 35$ 24. $g(x) = -3x^2 + 24$

25. $h(x) = x^2 + 8x - 13$ 26. $r(x) = 8x^2 + 4x + 5$

27. $m(x) = -5x^2 + 50x - 135$

28. $r(x) = 4x^2 + 9x + 3$

OPEN-ENDED In Exercises 29–32, find a possible pair of integer values for a and c so that the quadratic equation has the given solution(s). Then write the equation. *(See Example 3.)*

29. $ax^2 + 4x + c = 0$; two imaginary solutions

30. $ax^2 - 8x + c = 0$; two real solutions

31. $ax^2 + 10x = c$; one real solution

32. $-4x + c = -ax^2$; two imaginary solutions

MODELING WITH MATHEMATICS In Exercises 33 and 34, write a function that represents the situation.

33. A gannet is a bird that feeds on fish by diving into the water. A gannet spots a fish on the surface of the water and dives 100 feet to catch it. The bird plunges toward the water with an initial vertical velocity of -88 feet per second.

34. An archer is shooting at targets. The height of the arrow is 5 feet above the ground. Due to safety rules, the archer must aim the arrow parallel to the ground.

35. **MODELING WITH MATHEMATICS** A lacrosse player throws a ball in the air from an initial height of 7 feet. The ball has an initial vertical velocity of 35 feet per second. Does the ball reach a height of 30 feet? 26 feet? Explain your reasoning. *(See Example 4.)*

36. **PROBLEM SOLVING** A rocketry club is launching model rockets. The launching pad is 30 feet above the ground. Your model rocket has an initial vertical velocity of 105 feet per second. Your friend's model rocket has an initial vertical velocity of 100 feet per second.

    a. Does your rocket reach a height of 200 feet? Does your friend's rocket? Explain your reasoning.

    b. Which rocket is in the air longer? How much longer?

37. **CRITICAL THINKING** When a quadratic equation with real coefficients has imaginary solutions, why are the solutions complex conjugates? As part of your explanation, show that there is no such equation with solutions of $3i$ and $-2i$.

38. **HOW DO YOU SEE IT?** The graphs of three functions are shown. Which function(s) has real zeros? imaginary zeros? Explain your reasoning.

39. **USING STRUCTURE** Use the Quadratic Formula to write a quadratic equation that has the solutions $x = \dfrac{-8 \pm \sqrt{-176}}{-10}$.

40. **THOUGHT PROVOKING** Describe a real-life story that could be modeled by $h = -16t^2 + v_0t + s_0$. Write the height model for your story and determine how long your object is in the air.

41. **MODELING WITH MATHEMATICS** The Stratosphere Tower in Las Vegas is 921 feet tall and has a "needle" at its top that extends even higher into the air. A thrill ride called Big Shot catapults riders 160 feet up the needle and then lets them fall back to the launching pad.

    a. The height h (in feet) of a rider on the Big Shot can be modeled by $h = -16t^2 + v_0t + 921$, where t is the elapsed time (in seconds) after launch and v_0 is the initial vertical velocity (in feet per second). Find v_0 using the fact that the maximum value of h is $921 + 160 = 1081$ feet.

    b. A brochure for the Big Shot states that the ride up the needle takes 2 seconds. Compare this time to the time given by the model $h = -16t^2 + v_0t + 921$, where v_0 is the value you found in part (a). Discuss the accuracy of the model.

Maintaining Mathematical Proficiency
Reviewing what you learned in previous grades and lessons

Solve the system of linear equations using any method. Explain why you chose the method.
(Skills Review Handbook)

42. $y = -x + 4$
    $y = 2x - 8$

43. $x = 16 - 4y$
    $3x + 4y = 8$

44. $2x - y = 7$
    $2x + 7y = 31$

45. $3x - 2y = -20$
    $x + 1.2y = 6.4$

Find (a) the axis of symmetry and (b) the vertex of the graph of the function. *(Section 3.3)*

46. $y = -x^2 + 2x + 1$

47. $y = 2x^2 - x + 3$

48. $f(x) = 0.5x^2 + 2x + 5$

4.8 Solving Nonlinear Systems of Equations

Essential Question How can you solve a system of two equations when one is linear and the other is quadratic?

EXPLORATION 1   Solving a System of Equations

Work with a partner. Solve the system of equations by graphing each equation and finding the points of intersection.

System of Equations

$y = x + 2$ Linear

$y = x^2 + 2x$ Quadratic

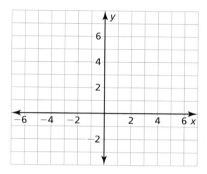

EXPLORATION 2   Analyzing Systems of Equations

Work with a partner. Match each system of equations with its graph. Then solve the system of equations.

a. $y = x^2 - 4$
    $y = -x - 2$

b. $y = x^2 - 2x + 2$
    $y = 2x - 2$

c. $y = x^2 + 1$
    $y = x - 1$

d. $y = x^2 - x - 6$
    $y = 2x - 2$

A.

B.

C.

D.

MAKING SENSE OF PROBLEMS

To be proficient in math, you need to analyze givens, relationships, and goals.

Communicate Your Answer

3. How can you solve a system of two equations when one is linear and the other is quadratic?

4. Write a system of equations (one linear and one quadratic) that has (a) no solutions, (b) one solution, and (c) two solutions. Your systems should be different from those in Explorations 1 and 2.

What You Will Learn

▶ Solve systems of nonlinear equations by graphing.

▶ Solve systems of nonlinear equations algebraically.

▶ Approximate solutions of nonlinear systems and equations.

Solving Nonlinear Systems by Graphing

The methods for solving systems of linear equations can also be used to solve *systems of nonlinear equations*. A **system of nonlinear equations** is a system in which at least one of the equations is nonlinear.

When a nonlinear system consists of a linear equation and a quadratic equation, the graphs can intersect in zero, one, or two points. So, the system can have zero, one, or two solutions, as shown.

STUDY TIP

In this section, *solutions* of a nonlinear system refer to the *real* solutions of the system.

No solutions   **One solution**   **Two solutions**

EXAMPLE 1   **Solving a Nonlinear System by Graphing**

Solve the system by graphing.

$$y = 2x^2 + 5x - 1 \qquad \text{Equation 1}$$

$$y = x - 3 \qquad \text{Equation 2}$$

SOLUTION

Step 1 Graph each equation.

Step 2 Estimate the point of intersection. The graphs appear to intersect at $(-1, -4)$.

Step 3 Check the point from Step 2 by substituting the coordinates into each of the original equations.

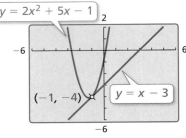

Equation 1

$$y = 2x^2 + 5x - 1$$
$$-4 \overset{?}{=} 2(-1)^2 + 5(-1) - 1$$
$$-4 = -4 \checkmark$$

Equation 2

$$y = x - 3$$
$$-4 \overset{?}{=} -1 - 3$$
$$-4 = -4 \checkmark$$

▶ The solution is $(-1, -4)$.

Monitoring Progress   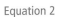 Help in English and Spanish at *BigIdeasMath.com*

Solve the system by graphing.

1. $y = x^2 + 4x - 4$
   $y = 2x - 5$

2. $y = -x + 6$
   $y = -2x^2 - x + 3$

3. $y = 3x - 15$
   $y = \frac{1}{2}x^2 - 2x - 7$

Solving Nonlinear Systems Algebraically

EXAMPLE 2 **Solving a Nonlinear System by Substitution**

Solve the system by substitution.

$$y = x^2 + x - 1 \qquad \text{Equation 1}$$
$$y = -2x + 3 \qquad \text{Equation 2}$$

SOLUTION

Step 1 The equations are already solved for y.

Step 2 Substitute $-2x + 3$ for y in Equation 1 and solve for x.

$-2x + 3 = x^2 + x - 1$	Substitute $-2x + 3$ for y in Equation 1.
$3 = x^2 + 3x - 1$	Add $2x$ to each side.
$0 = x^2 + 3x - 4$	Subtract 3 from each side.
$0 = (x + 4)(x - 1)$	Factor the polynomial.
$x + 4 = 0 \quad$ or $\quad x - 1 = 0$	Zero-Product Property
$x = -4 \quad$ or $\quad x = 1$	Solve for x.

Step 3 Substitute -4 and 1 for x in Equation 2 and solve for y.

$$y = -2(-4) + 3 \qquad \text{Substitute for } x \text{ in Equation 2.} \qquad y = -2(1) + 3$$
$$= 11 \qquad\qquad\qquad \text{Simplify.} \qquad\qquad\qquad\qquad = 1$$

▶ So, the solutions are $(-4, 11)$ and $(1, 1)$.

EXAMPLE 3 **Solving a Nonlinear System by Elimination**

Solve the system by elimination.

$$y = x^2 - 3x - 2 \qquad \text{Equation 1}$$
$$y = -3x - 8 \qquad \text{Equation 2}$$

SOLUTION

Step 1 Because the coefficients of the y-terms are the same, you do not need to multiply either equation by a constant.

Step 2 Subtract Equation 2 from Equation 1.

$y = x^2 - 3x - 2$	Equation 1
$y = -3x - 8$	Equation 2
$0 = x^2 + 6$	Subtract the equations.

Step 3 Solve for x.

$0 = x^2 + 6$	Resulting equation from Step 2
$-6 = x^2$	Subtract 6 from each side.

▶ The square of a real number cannot be negative. So, the system has no real solutions.

Solve the system by substitution.

4. $y = x^2 + 9$
$y = 9$

5. $y = -5x$
$y = x^2 - 3x - 3$

6. $y = -3x^2 + 2x + 1$
$y = 5 - 3x$

Solve the system by elimination.

7. $y = x^2 + x$
$y = x + 5$

8. $y = 9x^2 + 8x - 6$
$y = 5x - 4$

9. $y = 2x + 5$
$y = -3x^2 + x - 4$

Approximating Solutions

When you cannot find the exact solution(s) of a system of equations, you can analyze output values to approximate the solution(s).

EXAMPLE 4 **Approximating Solutions of a Nonlinear System**

Approximate the solution(s) of the system to the nearest thousandth.

$y = \frac{1}{2}x^2 + 3$ Equation 1

$y = 3^x$ Equation 2

SOLUTION

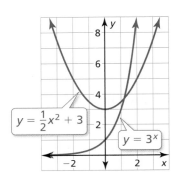

Sketch a graph of the system. You can see that the system has one solution between $x = 1$ and $x = 2$.

Substitute 3^x for y in Equation 1 and rewrite the equation.

$$3^x = \frac{1}{2}x^2 + 3 \quad\quad \text{Substitute } 3^x \text{ for } y \text{ in Equation 1.}$$

$$3^x - \frac{1}{2}x^2 - 3 = 0 \quad\quad \text{Rewrite the equation.}$$

Because you do not know how to solve this equation algebraically, let $f(x) = 3^x - \frac{1}{2}x^2 - 3$. Then evaluate the function for x-values between 1 and 2.

$\left.\begin{array}{l} f(1.1) \approx -0.26 \\ f(1.2) \approx 0.02 \end{array}\right\}$ Because $f(1.1) < 0$ and $f(1.2) > 0$, the zero is between 1.1 and 1.2.

> **REMEMBER**
> The function values that are closest to 0 correspond to x-values that best approximate the zeros of the function.

$f(1.2)$ is closer to 0 than $f(1.1)$, so decrease your guess and evaluate $f(1.19)$.

$f(1.19) \approx -0.012$ Because $f(1.19) < 0$ and $f(1.2) > 0$, the zero is between 1.19 and 1.2. So, increase guess.

$f(1.191) \approx -0.009$ Result is negative. Increase guess.

$f(1.192) \approx -0.006$ Result is negative. Increase guess.

$f(1.193) \approx -0.003$ Result is negative. Increase guess.

$f(1.194) \approx -0.0002$ Result is negative. Increase guess.

$f(1.195) \approx 0.003$ Result is positive.

Because $f(1.194)$ is closest to 0, $x \approx 1.194$.

Substitute $x = 1.194$ into one of the original equations and solve for y.

$$y = \frac{1}{2}x^2 + 3 = \frac{1}{2}(1.194)^2 + 3 \approx 3.713$$

▶ So, the solution of the system is about $(1.194, 3.713)$.

When entering the equations, be sure to use an appropriate viewing window that shows all the points of intersection. For this system, an appropriate viewing window is $-4 \leq x \leq 4$ and $-4 \leq y \leq 4$.

Recall that you can use systems of equations to solve equations with variables on both sides. To solve $f(x) = g(x)$, graph the system of equations $y = f(x)$ and $y = g(x)$. The x-value of each solution of the system is a solution of $f(x) = g(x)$.

EXAMPLE 5 **Approximating Solutions of an Equation**

Solve $-2(4)^x + 3 = 0.5x^2 - 2x$.

SOLUTION

You do not know how to solve this equation algebraically. So, use each side of the equation to write the system $y = -2(4)^x + 3$ and $y = 0.5x^2 - 2x$.

Method 1 Use a graphing calculator to graph the system. Then use the *intersect* feature to find the coordinates of each point of intersection.

One point of intersection is $(-1, 2.5)$.

The other point of intersection is about $(0.47, -0.83)$.

▶ So, the solutions of the equation are $x = -1$ and $x \approx 0.47$.

Method 2 Use the *table* feature to create a table of values for the equations. Find the x-values for which the corresponding y-values are approximately equal.

You can use the differences between the corresponding y-values to determine the best approximation of a solution.

X	Y₁	Y₂
-1.03	2.5204	2.5905
-1.02	2.5137	2.5602
-1.01	2.5069	2.5301
-1	2.5	2.5
-.99	2.493	2.4701
-.98	2.4859	2.4402
-.97	2.4788	2.4105
X=-1		

X	Y₁	Y₂
.44	-.6808	-.7832
.45	-.7321	-.7988
.46	-.7842	-.8142
.47	-.8371	-.8296
.48	-.8906	-.8448
.49	-.9449	-.86
.50	-1	-.875
X=.47		

When $x = -1$, the corresponding y-values are 2.5.

When $x = 0.47$, the corresponding y-values are approximately -0.83.

▶ So, the solutions of the equation are $x = -1$ and $x \approx 0.47$.

Monitoring Progress Help in English and Spanish at *BigIdeasMath.com*

Use the method in Example 4 to approximate the solution(s) of the system to the nearest thousandth.

10. $y = 4^x$
$y = x^2 + x + 3$

11. $y = 4x^2 - 1$
$y = -2(3)^x + 4$

12. $y = x^2 + 3x$
$y = -x^2 + x + 10$

Solve the equation. Round your solution(s) to the nearest hundredth.

13. $3^x - 1 = x^2 - 2x + 5$

14. $4x^2 + x = -2\left(\frac{1}{2}\right)^x + 5$

Vocabulary and Core Concept Check

1. **VOCABULARY** Describe how to use substitution to solve a system of nonlinear equations.

2. **WRITING** How is solving a system of nonlinear equations similar to solving a system of linear equations? How is it different?

Monitoring Progress and Modeling with Mathematics

In Exercises 3–6, match the system of equations with its graph. Then solve the system.

3. $y = x^2 - 2x + 1$
$y = x + 1$

4. $y = x^2 + 3x + 2$
$y = -x - 3$

5. $y = x - 1$
$y = -x^2 + x - 1$

6. $y = -x + 3$
$y = -x^2 - 2x + 5$

A.

B.

C.

D.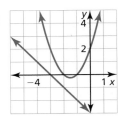

In Exercises 7–12, solve the system by graphing.
(See Example 1.)

7. $y = 3x^2 - 2x + 1$
$y = x + 7$

8. $y = x^2 + 2x + 5$
$y = -2x - 5$

9. $y = -2x^2 - 4x$
$y = 2$

10. $y = \frac{1}{2}x^2 - 3x + 4$
$y = x - 2$

11. $y = \frac{1}{3}x^2 + 2x - 3$
$y = 2x$

12. $y = 4x^2 + 5x - 7$
$y = -3x + 5$

In Exercises 13–18, solve the system by substitution.
(See Example 2.)

13. $y = x - 5$
$y = x^2 + 4x - 5$

14. $y = -3x^2$
$y = 6x + 3$

15. $y = -x + 7$
$y = -x^2 - 2x - 1$

16. $y = -x^2 + 7$
$y = 2x + 4$

17. $y - 5 = -x^2$
$y = 5$

18. $y = 2x^2 + 3x - 4$
$y - 4x = 2$

In Exercises 19–26, solve the system by elimination.
(See Example 3.)

19. $y = x^2 - 5x - 7$
$y = -5x + 9$

20. $y = -3x^2 + x + 2$
$y = x + 4$

21. $y = -x^2 - 2x + 2$
$y = 4x + 2$

22. $y = -2x^2 + x - 3$
$y = 2x - 2$

23. $y = 2x - 1$
$y = x^2$

24. $y = x^2 + x + 1$
$y = -x - 2$

25. $y + 2x = 0$
$y = x^2 + 4x - 6$

26. $y = 2x - 7$
$y + 5x = x^2 - 2$

27. **ERROR ANALYSIS** Describe and correct the error in solving the system of equations by graphing.

$y = x^2 - 3x + 4$
$y = 2x + 4$

The only solution of the system is $(0, 4)$.

28. ERROR ANALYSIS Describe and correct the error in solving for one of the variables in the system.

> ✗
> $y = 3x^2 - 6x + 4$
> $y = 4$
>
> $y = 3(4)^2 - 6(4) + 4$ Substitute.
> $y = 28$ Simplify.

In Exercises 29–32, use the table to describe the locations of the zeros of the quadratic function f.

29.

x	−4	−3	−2	−1	0	1
f(x)	−2	2	4	4	2	−2

30.

x	−1	0	1	2	3	4
f(x)	11	5	1	−1	−1	1

31.

x	−4	−3	−2	−1	0	1
f(x)	3	−1	−1	3	11	23

32.

x	1	2	3	4	5	6
f(x)	−25	−9	1	5	3	−5

In Exercises 33–38, use the method in Example 4 to approximate the solution(s) of the system to the nearest thousandth. *(See Example 4.)*

33. $y = x^2 + 2x + 3$
$y = 3^x$

34. $y = 2^x + 5$
$y = x^2 - 3x + 1$

35. $y = 2(4)^x - 1$
$y = 3x^2 + 8x$

36. $y = -x^2 - 4x - 4$
$y = -5^x - 2$

37. $y = -x^2 - x + 5$
$y = 2x^2 + 6x - 3$

38. $y = 2x^2 + x - 8$
$y = x^2 - 5$

In Exercises 39–46, solve the equation. Round your solution(s) to the nearest hundredth. *(See Example 5.)*

39. $3x + 1 = x^2 + 7x - 1$

40. $-x^2 + 2x = -2x + 5$

41. $x^2 - 6x + 4 = -x^2 - 2x$

42. $2x^2 + 8x + 10 = -x^2 - 2x + 5$

43. $-4\left(\frac{1}{2}\right)^x = -x^2 - 5$ **44.** $1.5(2)^x - 3 = -x^2 + 4x$

45. $8^{x-2} + 3 = 2\left(\frac{3}{2}\right)^x$ **46.** $-0.5(4)^x = 5^x - 6$

47. COMPARING METHODS Solve the system in Exercise 37 using substitution. Compare the exact solutions to the approximated solutions.

48. COMPARING METHODS Solve the system in Exercise 38 using elimination. Compare the exact solutions to the approximated solutions.

49. MODELING WITH MATHEMATICS The attendances y for two movies can be modeled by the following equations, where x is the number of days since the movies opened.

$y = -x^2 + 35x + 100$ Movie A

$y = -5x + 275$ Movie B

When is the attendance for each movie the same?

50. MODELING WITH MATHEMATICS You and a friend are driving boats on the same lake. Your path can be modeled by the equation $y = -x^2 - 4x - 1$, and your friend's path can be modeled by the equation $y = 2x + 8$. Do your paths cross each other? If so, what are the coordinates of the point(s) where the paths meet?

51. MODELING WITH MATHEMATICS The arch of a bridge can be modeled by $y = -0.002x^2 + 1.06x$, where x is the distance (in meters) from the left pylons and y is the height (in meters) of the arch above the water. The road can be modeled by the equation $y = 52$. To the nearest meter, how far from the left pylons are the two points where the road intersects the arch of the bridge?

52. MAKING AN ARGUMENT Your friend says that a system of equations consisting of a linear equation and a quadratic equation can have zero, one, two, or infinitely many solutions. Is your friend correct? Explain.

COMPARING METHODS In Exercises 53 and 54, solve the system of equations by (a) graphing, (b) substitution, and (c) elimination. Which method do you prefer? Explain your reasoning.

53. $y = 4x + 3$
    $y = x^2 + 4x - 1$

54. $y = x^2 - 5$
    $y = -x + 7$

55. **MODELING WITH MATHEMATICS** The function $y = -x^2 + 65x + 256$ models the number y of subscribers to a website, where x is the number of days since the website launched. The number of subscribers to a competitor's website can be modeled by a linear function. The websites have the same number of subscribers on Days 1 and 34.

   a. Write a linear function that models the number of subscribers to the competitor's website.

   b. Solve the system to verify the function from part (a).

56. **HOW DO YOU SEE IT?** The diagram shows the graphs of two equations in a system that has one solution.

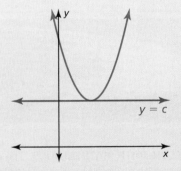

   a. How many solutions will the system have when you change the linear equation to $y = c + 2$?

   b. How many solutions will the system have when you change the linear equation to $y = c - 2$?

57. **WRITING** A system of equations consists of a quadratic equation whose graph opens up and a quadratic equation whose graph opens down. Describe the possible numbers of solutions of the system. Sketch examples to justify your answer.

58. **PROBLEM SOLVING** The population of a country is 2 million people and increases by 3% each year. The country's food supply is sufficient to feed 3 million people and increases at a constant rate that feeds 0.25 million additional people each year.

   a. When will the country first experience a food shortage?

   b. The country doubles the rate at which its food supply increases. Will food shortages still occur? If so, in what year?

59. **ANALYZING GRAPHS** Use the graphs of the linear and quadratic functions.

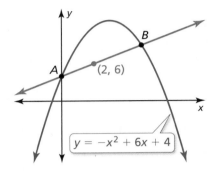

$y = -x^2 + 6x + 4$

   a. Find the coordinates of point A.

   b. Find the coordinates of point B.

60. **THOUGHT PROVOKING** Is it possible for a system of two quadratic equations to have exactly three solutions? exactly four solutions? Explain your reasoning.

61. **PROBLEM SOLVING** Solve the system of three equations shown.

   $y = 2x - 8$
   $y = x^2 - 4x - 3$
   $y = -3(2)^x$

62. **PROBLEM SOLVING** Find the point(s) of intersection, if any, of the line $y = -x - 1$ and the circle $x^2 + y^2 = 41$.

Maintaining Mathematical Proficiency
Reviewing what you learned in previous grades and lessons

Graph the inequality in a coordinate plane. *(Skills Review Handbook)*

63. $y \leq 4x - 1$

64. $y > -\frac{1}{2}x + 3$

65. $4y - 12 \geq 8x$

66. $3y + 3 < x$

Graph the function. Describe the domain and range. *(Section 3.3)*

67. $y = 3x^2 + 2$

68. $y = -x^2 - 6x$

69. $y = -2x^2 + 12x - 7$

70. $y = 5x^2 + 10x - 3$

4.9 Quadratic Inequalities

Essential Question How can you solve a quadratic inequality?

EXPLORATION 1 Solving a Quadratic Inequality

Work with a partner. The graphing calculator screen shows the graph of

$$f(x) = x^2 + 2x - 3.$$

Explain how you can use the graph to solve the inequality

$$x^2 + 2x - 3 \le 0.$$

Then solve the inequality.

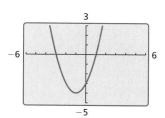

EXPLORATION 2 Solving Quadratic Inequalities

Work with a partner. Match each inequality with the graph of its related quadratic function. Then use the graph to solve the inequality.

a. $x^2 - 3x + 2 > 0$ **b.** $x^2 - 4x + 3 \le 0$ **c.** $x^2 - 2x - 3 < 0$

d. $x^2 + x - 2 \ge 0$ **e.** $x^2 - x - 2 < 0$ **f.** $x^2 - 4 > 0$

A.

B.

C.

D.

E.

F.
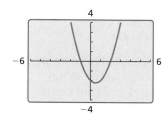

Communicate Your Answer

3. How can you solve a quadratic inequality?

4. Explain how you can use the graph in Exploration 1 to solve each inequality. Then solve each inequality.

     a. $x^2 + 2x - 3 > 0$ **b.** $x^2 + 2x - 3 < 0$ **c.** $x^2 + 2x - 3 \ge 0$

What You Will Learn

▶ Graph quadratic inequalities in two variables.

▶ Solve quadratic inequalities in one variable.

Core Vocabulary

quadratic inequality in
  two variables, *p. 260*
quadratic inequality in
  one variable, *p. 262*

Previous
linear inequality in
  two variables

Graphing Quadratic Inequalities in Two Variables

A **quadratic inequality in two variables** can be written in one of the following forms, where a, b, and c are real numbers and $a \neq 0$.

$$y < ax^2 + bx + c \qquad\qquad y > ax^2 + bx + c$$
$$y \leq ax^2 + bx + c \qquad\qquad y \geq ax^2 + bx + c$$

The graph of any such inequality consists of all solutions (x, y) of the inequality.

Previously, you graphed linear inequalities in two variables. You can use a similar procedure to graph quadratic inequalities in two variables.

🔄 Core Concept

Graphing a Quadratic Inequality in Two Variables

To graph a quadratic inequality in one of the forms above, follow these steps.

Step 1 Graph the parabola with the equation $y = ax^2 + bx + c$. Make the parabola *dashed* for inequalities with $<$ or $>$ and *solid* for inequalities with $\leq$ or $\geq$.

Step 2 Test a point (x, y) inside the parabola to determine whether the point is a solution of the inequality.

Step 3 Shade the region inside the parabola if the point from Step 2 is a solution. Shade the region outside the parabola if it is not a solution.

EXAMPLE 1 **Graphing a Quadratic Inequality in Two Variables**

Graph $y < -x^2 - 2x - 1$.

SOLUTION

Step 1 Graph $y = -x^2 - 2x - 1$. Because the inequality symbol is $<$, make the parabola dashed.

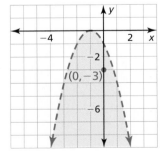

LOOKING FOR STRUCTURE

Notice that testing a point is less complicated when the x-value is 0 (the point is on the y-axis).

Step 2 Test a point inside the parabola, such as $(0, -3)$.

$$y < -x^2 - 2x - 1$$
$$-3 \overset{?}{<} -0^2 - 2(0) - 1$$
$$-3 < -1 \quad ✓$$

So, $(0, -3)$ is a solution of the inequality.

Step 3 Shade the region inside the parabola.

EXAMPLE 2   Using a Quadratic Inequality in Real Life

A manila rope used for rappelling down a cliff can safely support a weight W (in pounds) provided

$$W \le 1480d^2$$

where d is the diameter (in inches) of the rope. Graph the inequality and interpret the solution.

SOLUTION

Graph $W = 1480d^2$ for nonnegative values of d. Because the inequality symbol is $\le$, make the parabola solid. Test a point inside the parabola, such as $(1, 3000)$.

$$W \le 1480d^2$$

$$3000 \overset{?}{\le} 1480(1)^2$$

$$3000 \nleq 1480$$

▶ Because $(1, 3000)$ is not a solution, shade the region outside the parabola. The shaded region represents weights that can be supported by ropes with various diameters.

Graphing a *system* of quadratic inequalities is similar to graphing a system of linear inequalities. First graph each inequality in the system. Then identify the region in the coordinate plane common to all of the graphs. This region is called the *graph of the system*.

EXAMPLE 3   Graphing a System of Quadratic Inequalities

Graph the system of quadratic inequalities.

$$y < -x^2 + 3 \qquad \text{Inequality 1}$$
$$y \ge x^2 + 2x - 3 \qquad \text{Inequality 2}$$

SOLUTION

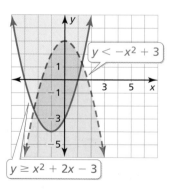

Step 1 Graph $y < -x^2 + 3$. The graph is the red region inside (but not including) the parabola $y = -x^2 + 3$.

Step 2 Graph $y \ge x^2 + 2x - 3$. The graph is the blue region inside and including the parabola $y = x^2 + 2x - 3$.

Step 3 Identify the purple region where the two graphs overlap. This region is the graph of the system.

Check

Check that a point in the solution region, such as $(0, 0)$, is a solution of the system.

$$y < -x^2 + 3$$
$$0 \overset{?}{<} -0^2 + 3$$
$$0 < 3 ✓$$

$$y \ge x^2 + 2x - 3$$
$$0 \overset{?}{\ge} 0^2 + 2(0) - 3$$
$$0 \ge -3 ✓$$

Monitoring Progress   Help in English and Spanish at *BigIdeasMath.com*

Graph the inequality.

1. $y \ge x^2 + 2x - 8$ **2.** $y \le 2x^2 - x - 1$ **3.** $y > -x^2 + 2x + 4$

4. Graph the system of inequalities consisting of $y \le -x^2$ and $y > x^2 - 3$.

Solving Quadratic Inequalities in One Variable

A **quadratic inequality in one variable** can be written in one of the following forms, where a, b, and c are real numbers and $a \neq 0$.

$$ax^2 + bx + c < 0 \qquad ax^2 + bx + c > 0 \qquad ax^2 + bx + c \leq 0 \qquad ax^2 + bx + c \geq 0$$

You can solve quadratic inequalities using algebraic methods or graphs.

EXAMPLE 4 — Solving a Quadratic Inequality Algebraically

Solve $x^2 - 3x - 4 < 0$ algebraically.

SOLUTION

First, write and solve the equation obtained by replacing $<$ with $=$.

$x^2 - 3x - 4 = 0$	Write the related equation.
$(x - 4)(x + 1) = 0$	Factor.
$x = 4 \quad \text{or} \quad x = -1$	Zero-Product Property

The numbers -1 and 4 are the *critical values* of the original inequality. Plot -1 and 4 on a number line, using open dots because the values do not satisfy the inequality. The critical x-values partition the number line into three intervals. Test an x-value in each interval to determine whether it satisfies the inequality.

Test $x = -2$.   Test $x = 0$.   Test $x = 5$.

$$(-2)^2 - 3(-2) - 4 = 6 \not< 0 \qquad 0^2 - 3(0) - 4 = -4 < 0 \checkmark \qquad 5^2 - 3(5) - 4 = 6 \not< 0$$

▶ So, the solution is $-1 < x < 4$.

Another way to solve $ax^2 + bx + c < 0$ is to first graph the related function $y = ax^2 + bx + c$. Then, because the inequality symbol is $<$, identify the x-values for which the graph lies *below* the x-axis. You can use a similar procedure to solve quadratic inequalities that involve $\leq$, $>$, or $\geq$.

EXAMPLE 5 — Solving a Quadratic Inequality by Graphing

Solve $3x^2 - x - 5 \geq 0$ by graphing.

SOLUTION

The solution consists of the x-values for which the graph of $y = 3x^2 - x - 5$ lies on or above the x-axis. Find the x-intercepts of the graph by letting $y = 0$ and using the Quadratic Formula to solve $0 = 3x^2 - x - 5$ for x.

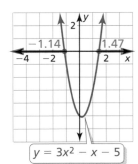

$y = 3x^2 - x - 5$

$$x = \frac{-(-1) \pm \sqrt{(-1)^2 - 4(3)(-5)}}{2(3)} \qquad a = 3, b = -1, c = -5$$

$$x = \frac{1 \pm \sqrt{61}}{6} \qquad \text{Simplify.}$$

The solutions are $x \approx -1.14$ and $x \approx 1.47$. Sketch a parabola that opens up and has -1.14 and 1.47 as x-intercepts. The graph lies on or above the x-axis to the left of (and including) $x = -1.14$ and to the right of (and including) $x = 1.47$.

▶ The solution of the inequality is approximately $x \leq -1.14$ or $x \geq 1.47$.

EXAMPLE 6 Modeling with Mathematics

A rectangular parking lot must have a perimeter of 440 feet and an area of at least 8000 square feet. Describe the possible lengths of the parking lot.

SOLUTION

1. **Understand the Problem** You are given the perimeter and the minimum area of a parking lot. You are asked to determine the possible lengths of the parking lot.

2. **Make a Plan** Use the perimeter and area formulas to write a quadratic inequality describing the possible lengths of the parking lot. Then solve the inequality.

3. **Solve the Problem** Let ℓ represent the length (in feet) and let w represent the width (in feet) of the parking lot.

ANOTHER WAY

You can graph each side of $220\ell - \ell^2 = 8000$ and use the intersection points to determine when $220\ell - \ell^2$ is greater than or equal to 8000.

$$\text{Perimeter} = 440 \qquad \text{Area} \geq 8000$$
$$2\ell + 2w = 440 \qquad \ell w \geq 8000$$

Solve the perimeter equation for w to obtain $w = 220 - \ell$. Substitute this into the area inequality to obtain a quadratic inequality in one variable.

$\ell w \geq 8000$	Write the area inequality.
$\ell(220 - \ell) \geq 8000$	Substitute $220 - \ell$ for w.
$220\ell - \ell^2 \geq 8000$	Distributive Property
$-\ell^2 + 220\ell - 8000 \geq 0$	Write in standard form.

Use a graphing calculator to find the ℓ-intercepts of $y = -\ell^2 + 220\ell - 8000$.

USING TECHNOLOGY

Variables displayed when using technology may not match the variables used in applications. In the graphs shown, the length ℓ corresponds to the independent variable x.

The ℓ-intercepts are $\ell \approx 45.97$ and $\ell \approx 174.03$. The solution consists of the ℓ-values for which the graph lies on or above the ℓ-axis. The graph lies on or above the ℓ-axis when $45.97 \leq \ell \leq 174.03$.

▶ So, the approximate length of the parking lot is at least 46 feet and at most 174 feet.

4. **Look Back** Choose a length in the solution region, such as $\ell = 100$, and find the width. Then check that the dimensions satisfy the original area inequality.

$$2\ell + 2w = 440 \qquad\qquad \ell w \geq 8000$$
$$2(100) + 2w = 440 \qquad 100(120) \overset{?}{\geq} 8000$$
$$w = 120 \qquad\qquad 12{,}000 \geq 8000 \checkmark$$

Monitoring Progress Help in English and Spanish at *BigIdeasMath.com*

Solve the inequality.

5. $2x^2 + 3x \leq 2$ **6.** $-3x^2 - 4x + 1 < 0$ **7.** $2x^2 + 2 > -5x$

8. WHAT IF? In Example 6, the area must be at least 8500 square feet. Describe the possible lengths of the parking lot.

Vocabulary and Core Concept Check

1. **WRITING** Compare the graph of a quadratic inequality in one variable to the graph of a quadratic inequality in two variables.

2. **WRITING** Explain how to solve $x^2 + 6x - 8 < 0$ using algebraic methods and using graphs.

Monitoring Progress and Modeling with Mathematics

In Exercises 3–6, match the inequality with its graph. Explain your reasoning.

3. $y \le x^2 + 4x + 3$ 4. $y > -x^2 + 4x - 3$

5. $y < x^2 - 4x + 3$ 6. $y \ge x^2 + 4x + 3$

A.

B.

C.

D.
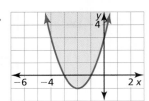

In Exercises 7–14, graph the inequality. *(See Example 1.)*

7. $y < -x^2$ 8. $y \ge 4x^2$

9. $y > x^2 - 9$ 10. $y < x^2 + 5$

11. $y \le x^2 + 5x$ 12. $y \ge -2x^2 + 9x - 4$

13. $y > 2(x + 3)^2 - 1$ 14. $y \le \left(x - \frac{1}{2}\right)^2 + \frac{5}{2}$

ANALYZING RELATIONSHIPS In Exercises 15 and 16, use the graph to write an inequality in terms of $f(x)$ so point P is a solution.

15.

16.
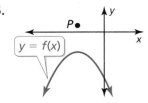

ERROR ANALYSIS In Exercises 17 and 18, describe and correct the error in graphing $y \ge x^2 + 2$.

17.

18.
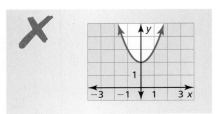

19. **MODELING WITH MATHEMATICS** A hardwood shelf in a wooden bookcase can safely support a weight W (in pounds) provided $W \le 115x^2$, where x is the thickness (in inches) of the shelf. Graph the inequality and interpret the solution. *(See Example 2.)*

20. **MODELING WITH MATHEMATICS** A wire rope can safely support a weight W (in pounds) provided $W \le 8000d^2$, where d is the diameter (in inches) of the rope. Graph the inequality and interpret the solution.

In Exercises 21–26, graph the system of quadratic inequalities. *(See Example 3.)*

21. $y \ge 2x^2$
    $y < -x^2 + 1$

22. $y > -5x^2$
    $y > 3x^2 - 2$

23. $y \le -x^2 + 4x - 4$
    $y < x^2 + 2x - 8$

24. $y \ge x^2 - 4$
    $y \le -2x^2 + 7x + 4$

25. $y \ge 2x^2 + x - 5$
    $y < -x^2 + 5x + 10$

26. $y \ge x^2 - 3x - 6$
    $y \ge x^2 + 7x + 6$

In Exercises 27–34, solve the inequality algebraically. *(See Example 4.)*

27. $4x^2 < 25$

28. $x^2 + 10x + 9 < 0$

29. $x^2 - 11x \geq -28$

30. $3x^2 - 13x > -10$

31. $2x^2 - 5x - 3 \leq 0$

32. $4x^2 + 8x - 21 \geq 0$

33. $\frac{1}{2}x^2 - x > 4$

34. $-\frac{1}{2}x^2 + 4x \leq 1$

In Exercises 35–42, solve the inequality by graphing. *(See Example 5.)*

35. $x^2 - 3x + 1 < 0$

36. $x^2 - 4x + 2 > 0$

37. $x^2 + 8x > -7$

38. $x^2 + 6x < -3$

39. $3x^2 - 8 \leq -2x$

40. $3x^2 + 5x - 3 < 1$

41. $\frac{1}{3}x^2 + 2x \geq 2$

42. $\frac{3}{4}x^2 + 4x \geq 3$

43. **DRAWING CONCLUSIONS** Consider the graph of the function $f(x) = ax^2 + bx + c$.

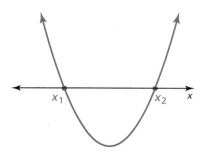

   a. What are the solutions of $ax^2 + bx + c < 0$?

   b. What are the solutions of $ax^2 + bx + c > 0$?

   c. The graph of g represents a reflection in the x-axis of the graph of f. For which values of x is $g(x)$ positive?

44. **MODELING WITH MATHEMATICS** A rectangular fountain display has a perimeter of 400 feet and an area of at least 9100 feet. Describe the possible widths of the fountain. *(See Example 6.)*

45. **MODELING WITH MATHEMATICS** The arch of the Sydney Harbor Bridge in Sydney, Australia, can be modeled by $y = -0.00211x^2 + 1.06x$, where x is the distance (in meters) from the left pylons and y is the height (in meters) of the arch above the water. For what distances x is the arch above the road?

pylon

52 m

46. **PROBLEM SOLVING** The number T of teams that have participated in a robot-building competition for high-school students over a recent period of time x (in years) can be modeled by

$$T(x) = 17.155x^2 + 193.68x + 235.81, \ 0 \leq x \leq 6.$$

After how many years is the number of teams greater than 1000? Justify your answer.

47. **PROBLEM SOLVING** A study found that a driver's reaction time $A(x)$ to audio stimuli and his or her reaction time $V(x)$ to visual stimuli (both in milliseconds) can be modeled by

$$A(x) = 0.0051x^2 - 0.319x + 15, \ 16 \leq x \leq 70$$
$$V(x) = 0.005x^2 - 0.23x + 22, \ 16 \leq x \leq 70$$

where x is the age (in years) of the driver.

   a. Write an inequality that you can use to find the x-values for which $A(x)$ is less than $V(x)$.

   b. Use a graphing calculator to solve the inequality $A(x) < V(x)$. Describe how you used the domain $16 \leq x \leq 70$ to determine a reasonable solution.

   c. Based on your results from parts (a) and (b), do you think a driver would react more quickly to a traffic light changing from green to yellow or to the siren of an approaching ambulance? Explain.

48. HOW DO YOU SEE IT? The graph shows a system of quadratic inequalities.

a. Identify two solutions of the system.

b. Are the points $(1, -2)$ and $(5, 6)$ solutions of the system? Explain.

c. Is it possible to change the inequality symbol(s) so that one, but not both of the points in part (b), is a solution of the system? Explain.

49. MODELING WITH MATHEMATICS The length L (in millimeters) of the larvae of the black porgy fish can be modeled by

$$L(x) = 0.00170x^2 + 0.145x + 2.35, \ 0 \le x \le 40$$

where x is the age (in days) of the larvae. Write and solve an inequality to find at what ages a larva's length tends to be greater than 10 millimeters. Explain how the given domain affects the solution.

50. MAKING AN ARGUMENT You claim the system of inequalities below, where a and b are real numbers, has no solution. Your friend claims the system will always have at least one solution. Who is correct? Explain.

$$y < (x + a)^2$$
$$y < (x + b)^2$$

51. MATHEMATICAL CONNECTIONS The area A of the region bounded by a parabola and a horizontal line can be modeled by $A = \frac{2}{3}bh$, where b and h are as defined in the diagram. Find the area of the region determined by each pair of inequalities.

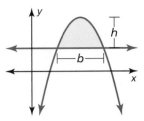

a. $y \le -x^2 + 4x$
   $y \ge 0$

b. $y \ge x^2 - 4x - 5$
   $y \le 7$

52. THOUGHT PROVOKING Draw a company logo that is created by the intersection of two quadratic inequalities. Justify your answer.

53. REASONING A truck that is 11 feet tall and 7 feet wide is traveling under an arch. The arch can be modeled by $y = -0.0625x^2 + 1.25x + 5.75$, where x and y are measured in feet.

a. Will the truck fit under the arch? Explain.

b. What is the maximum width that a truck 11 feet tall can have and still make it under the arch?

c. What is the maximum height that a truck 7 feet wide can have and still make it under the arch?

Maintaining Mathematical Proficiency   Reviewing what you learned in previous grades and lessons

Tell whether the function has a minimum value or maximum value. Then find the value.
(Section 3.3)

54. $f(x) = -x^2 - 6x - 10$

55. $f(x) = -x^2 - 4x + 21$

56. $h(x) = \frac{1}{2}x^2 + 2x + 2$

57. $h(x) = x^2 + 3x - 18$

Find the zeros of the function. *(Section 3.5)*

58. $f(x) = (x + 7)(x - 9)$

59. $g(x) = x^2 - 4x$

60. $h(x) = -x^2 + 5x - 6$

Core Vocabulary

Core Concepts

Section 4.6

Section 4.7

Section 4.8

Section 4.9

Mathematical Practices

1. How can you use technology to determine whose rocket lands first in part (b) of Exercise 36 on page 250?

2. Compare the methods used to solve Exercise 53 on page 258. Discuss the similarities and differences among the methods.

3. Explain your plan to find the possible widths of the fountain in Exercise 44 on page 265.

Performance Task:

The Golden Ratio

The golden ratio is one of the most famous numbers in history. It can be seen in the simplicity of a seashell as well as in the grandeur of the Greek Parthenon. What is this number and how can it help you decorate your room?

To explore the answers to these questions and more, check out the Performance Task and Real-Life STEM video at *BigIdeasMath.com*.

4 Chapter Review

Dynamic Solutions available at *BigIdeasMath.com*

4.1 Properties of Radicals *(pp. 191–200)*

a. Simplify $\sqrt[3]{27x^{10}}$.

$$\sqrt[3]{27x^{10}} = \sqrt[3]{27 \cdot x^9 \cdot x}$$ Factor using the greatest perfect cube factors.

$$= \sqrt[3]{27} \cdot \sqrt[3]{x^9} \cdot \sqrt[3]{x}$$ Product Property of Cube Roots

$$= 3x^3\sqrt[3]{x}$$ Simplify.

b. Simplify $\dfrac{12}{3 + \sqrt{5}}$.

$$\frac{12}{3 + \sqrt{5}} = \frac{12}{3 + \sqrt{5}} \cdot \frac{3 - \sqrt{5}}{3 - \sqrt{5}}$$ The conjugate of $3 + \sqrt{5}$ is $3 - \sqrt{5}$.

$$= \frac{12(3 - \sqrt{5})}{3^2 - (\sqrt{5})^2}$$ Sum and difference pattern

$$= \frac{36 - 12\sqrt{5}}{4}$$ Simplify.

$$= 9 - 3\sqrt{5}$$ Simplify.

Simplify the expression.

1. $\sqrt{72p^7}$

2. $\sqrt{\dfrac{45}{7y}}$

3. $\sqrt[3]{\dfrac{125x^{11}}{4}}$

4. $\dfrac{8}{\sqrt{6} + 2}$

5. $4\sqrt{3} + 5\sqrt{12}$

6. $15\sqrt[3]{2} - 2\sqrt[3]{54}$

7. $(3\sqrt{7} + 5)^2$

8. $\sqrt{6}(\sqrt{18} + \sqrt{8})$

4.2 Solving Quadratic Equations by Graphing *(pp. 201–208)*

Solve $x^2 + 3x = 4$ by graphing.

Step 1   Write the equation in standard form.

$$x^2 + 3x = 4$$ Write original equation.

$$x^2 + 3x - 4 = 0$$ Subtract 4 from each side.

Step 2   Graph the related function $y = x^2 + 3x - 4$.

Step 3   Find the x-intercepts. The x-intercepts are -4 and 1.

▶   So, the solutions are $x = -4$ and $x = 1$.

$y = x^2 + 3x - 4$

Solve the equation by graphing.

9. $x^2 - 9x + 18 = 0$

10. $x^2 - 2x = -4$

11. $-8x - 16 = x^2$

12. The graph of $f(x) = x^2 + 7x + 10$ is shown. Find the zeros of f.

13. Graph $f(x) = x^2 + 2x - 5$. Approximate the zeros of f to the nearest tenth.

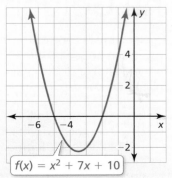

$f(x) = x^2 + 7x + 10$

4.3 Solving Quadratic Equations Using Square Roots *(pp. 209–214)*

A sprinkler sprays water that covers a circular region of 90π square feet. Find the diameter of the circle.

Write an equation using the formula for the area of a circle.

$A = \pi r^2$	Write the formula.
$90\pi = \pi r^2$	Substitute 90π for A.
$90 = r^2$	Divide each side by π.
$\pm\sqrt{90} = r$	Take the square root of each side.
$\pm 3\sqrt{10} = r$	Simplify.

A diameter cannot be negative, so use the positive square root. The diameter is twice the radius. So, the diameter is $6\sqrt{10}$.

▶ The diameter of the circle is $6\sqrt{10} \approx 19$ feet.

Solve the equation using square roots. Round your solutions to the nearest hundredth, if necessary.

14. $x^2 + 5 = 17$ **15.** $x^2 - 14 = -14$ **16.** $(x + 2)^2 = 64$

17. $4x^2 + 25 = 75$ **18.** $(x - 1)^2 = 0$ **19.** $19 = 30 - 5x^2$

4.4 Solving Quadratic Equations by Completing the Square *(pp. 215–224)*

Solve $x^2 - 6x + 4 = 11$ by completing the square.

$x^2 - 6x + 4 = 11$	Write the equation.
$x^2 - 6x = 7$	Subtract 4 from each side.
$x^2 - 6x + (-3)^2 = 7 + (-3)^2$	Complete the square by adding $\left(\frac{-6}{2}\right)^2$, or $(-3)^2$, to each side.
$(x - 3)^2 = 16$	Write the left side as the square of a binomial.
$x - 3 = \pm 4$	Take the square root of each side.
$x = 3 \pm 4$	Add 3 to each side.

▶ The solutions are $x = 3 + 4 = 7$ and $x = 3 - 4 = -1$.

Solve the equation by completing the square. Round your solutions to the nearest hundredth, if necessary.

20. $x^2 + 6x - 40 = 0$ **21.** $x^2 + 2x + 5 = 4$ **22.** $2x^2 - 4x = 10$

Determine whether the quadratic function has a maximum or minimum value. Then find the value.

23. $y = -x^2 + 6x - 1$ **24.** $f(x) = x^2 + 4x + 11$ **25.** $y = 3x^2 - 24x + 15$

26. The width w of a credit card is 3 centimeters shorter than the length ℓ. The area is 46.75 square centimeters. Find the perimeter.

4.5 Solving Quadratic Equations Using the Quadratic Formula (pp. 225–234)

Solve $-3x^2 + x = -8$ using the Quadratic Formula.

$$-3x^2 + x = -8 \qquad \text{Write the equation.}$$

$$-3x^2 + x + 8 = 0 \qquad \text{Write in standard form.}$$

$$x = \frac{-b \pm \sqrt{b^2 - 4ac}}{2a} \qquad \text{Quadratic Formula}$$

$$x = \frac{-1 \pm \sqrt{1^2 - 4(-3)(8)}}{2(-3)} \qquad \text{Substitute } -3 \text{ for } a, 1 \text{ for } b, \text{ and } 8 \text{ for } c.$$

$$x = \frac{-1 \pm \sqrt{97}}{-6} \qquad \text{Simplify.}$$

▶ So, the solutions are $x = \dfrac{-1 + \sqrt{97}}{-6} \approx -1.5$ and $x = \dfrac{-1 - \sqrt{97}}{-6} \approx 1.8$.

Solve the equation using the Quadratic Formula. Round your solutions to the nearest tenth, if necessary.

27. $x^2 + 2x - 15 = 0$ **28.** $2x^2 - x + 8 = 16$ **29.** $-5x^2 + 10x = 5$

Find the number of x-intercepts of the graph of the function.

30. $y = -x^2 + 6x - 9$ **31.** $y = 2x^2 + 4x + 8$ **32.** $y = -\frac{1}{2}x^2 + 2x$

4.6 Complex Numbers (pp. 237–244)

Perform each operation. Write the answer in standard form.

a. $(3 - 6i) - (7 + 2i) = (3 - 7) + (-6 - 2)i \qquad$ Definition of complex subtraction

$$= -4 - 8i \qquad \text{Write in standard form.}$$

b. $5i(4 + 5i) = 20i + 25i^2 \qquad$ Distributive Property

$$= 20i + 25(-1) \qquad \text{Use } i^2 = -1.$$

$$= -25 + 20i \qquad \text{Write in standard form.}$$

c. $(2 + 5i)(1 - 3i) = 2 - 6i + 5i - 15i^2 \qquad$ Multiply using FOIL.

$$= 2 - i - 15(-1) \qquad \text{Simplify and use } i^2 = -1.$$

$$= 2 - i + 15 \qquad \text{Simplify.}$$

$$= 17 - i \qquad \text{Write in standard form.}$$

33. Find the values of x and y that satisfy the equation $36 - yi = 4x + 3i$.

Perform the operation. Write the answer in standard form.

34. $(-2 + 3i) + (7 - 6i)$ **35.** $(9 + 3i) - (-2 - 7i)$ **36.** $(5 + 6i)(-4 + 7i)$

37. Multiply $8 - 2i$ by its complex conjugate.

Solving Quadratic Equations with Complex Solutions *(pp. 245–250)*

Solve each equation.

a. $x^2 - 14x + 53 = 0$

The coefficient of the x^2-term is 1, and the coefficient of the x-term is an even number. So, solve by completing the square.

$x^2 - 14x + 53 = 0$	Write the equation.
$x^2 - 14x = -53$	Subtract 53 from each side.
$x^2 - 14x + 49 = -53 + 49$	Complete the square for $x^2 - 14x$.
$(x - 7)^2 = -4$	Write the left side as the square of a binomial.
$x - 7 = \pm\sqrt{-4}$	Take the square root of each side.
$x = 7 \pm \sqrt{-4}$	Add 7 to each side.
$x = 7 \pm 2i$	Simplify the radical.

▶ The solutions are $7 + 2i$ and $7 - 2i$.

b. $9x^2 - 6x + 5 = 0$

The equation is not factorable, and completing the square would result in fractions. So, solve using the Quadratic Formula.

$x = \dfrac{-(-6) \pm \sqrt{(-6)^2 - 4(9)(5)}}{2(9)}$	Substitute 9 for a, -6 for b, and 5 for c.
$x = \dfrac{6 \pm \sqrt{-144}}{18}$	Simplify.
$x = \dfrac{6 \pm 12i}{18}$	Write in terms of i.
$x = \dfrac{1 \pm 2i}{3}$	Simplify.

▶ The solutions are $\dfrac{1 + 2i}{3}$ and $\dfrac{1 - 2i}{3}$.

Solve the equation using any method. Explain your choice of method.

38. $-x^2 - 100 = 0$ **39.** $4x^2 + 53 = -11$ **40.** $x^2 + 16x - 17 = 0$

41. $-2x^2 + 12x = 36$ **42.** $2x^2 + 5x = 4$ **43.** $3x^2 - 7x + 13 = 0$

Find the zeros of the function.

44. $f(x) = x^2 + 81$ **45.** $f(x) = x^2 - 2x + 9$ **46.** $f(x) = -8x^2 + 4x - 1$

47. While marching, a drum major tosses a baton into the air from an initial height of 6 feet. The baton has an initial vertical velocity of 32 feet per second. Does the baton reach a height of 25 feet? 20 feet? Explain your reasoning.

4.8 **Solving Nonlinear Systems of Equations** *(pp. 251–258)*

Solve the system by substitution.

$$y = x^2 - 5 \qquad \text{Equation 1}$$
$$y = -x + 1 \qquad \text{Equation 2}$$

Step 1 The equations are already solved for y.

Step 2 Substitute $-x + 1$ for y in Equation 1 and solve for x.

$-x + 1 = x^2 - 5$	Substitute $-x + 1$ for y in Equation 1.
$1 = x^2 + x - 5$	Add x to each side.
$0 = x^2 + x - 6$	Subtract 1 from each side.
$0 = (x + 3)(x - 2)$	Factor the polynomial.
$x + 3 = 0 \quad$ or $\quad x - 2 = 0$	Zero-Product Property
$x = -3 \quad$ or $\quad x = 2$	Solve for x.

Step 3 Substitute -3 and 2 for x in Equation 2 and solve for y.

$$y = -(-3) + 1 \qquad \text{Substitute for } x \text{ in Equation 2.} \qquad y = -2 + 1$$
$$= 4 \qquad \qquad \text{Simplify.} \qquad \qquad\qquad = -1$$

▶ So, the solutions are $(-3, 4)$ and $(2, -1)$.

Solve the system using any method.

48. $y = x^2 - 2x - 4$
$\ y = -5$

49. $y = x^2 - 9$
$\ y = 2x + 5$

50. $y = 2\left(\frac{1}{2}\right)^x - 5$
$\ y = -x^2 - x + 4$

4.9 **Quadratic Inequalities** *(pp. 259–266)*

Graph the system of quadratic inequalities.

$$y > x^2 - 2 \qquad \text{Inequality 1}$$
$$y \le -x^2 - 3x + 4 \qquad \text{Inequality 2}$$

Step 1 Graph $y > x^2 - 2$. The graph is the red region inside (but not including) the parabola $y = x^2 - 2$.

Step 2 Graph $y \le -x^2 - 3x + 4$. The graph is the blue region inside and including the parabola $y = -x^2 - 3x + 4$.

Step 3 Identify the purple region where the two graphs overlap. This region is the graph of the system.

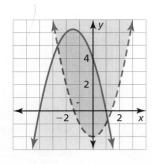

Graph the inequality.

51. $y > x^2 + 8x + 16$

52. $y \ge x^2 + 6x + 8$

53. $x^2 + y \le 7x - 12$

Graph the system of quadratic inequalities.

54. $x^2 - 4x + 8 > y$
$\ -x^2 + 4x + 2 \le y$

55. $2x^2 - x \ge y - 5$
$\ 0.5x^2 > y - 2x - 1$

56. $-3x^2 - 2x \le y + 1$
$\ -2x^2 + x - 5 > -y$

57. Solve (a) $3x^2 + 2 \le 5x$ and (b) $-x^2 - 10x < 21$.

Solve the equation using any method. Explain your choice of method.

1. $x^2 + 121 = 0$

2. $x^2 - 6x = -58$

3. $-2x^2 + 3x + 7 = 0$

4. $x^2 - 7x + 12 = 0$

5. $5x^2 + x + 4 = 0$

6. $(4x + 3)^2 = 16$

Perform the operation. Write the answer in standard form.

7. $(2 + 5i) + (-4 + 3i)$

8. $(3 + 9i) - (1 - 7i)$

9. $(2 + 4i)(-3 - 5i)$

Solve the system using any method.

10. $y = x^2 - 4x - 2$
$y = -4x + 2$

11. $y = -5x^2 + x - 1$
$y = -7$

12. $y = \frac{1}{2}(4)^x + 1$
$y = x^2 - 2x + 4$

13. Graph the system of inequalities consisting of $y \geq 2x^2 - 3$ and $y < -x^2 + x + 4$.

14. Write an expression involving radicals in which a conjugate can be used to simplify the expression. Then simplify the expression.

15. Describe the value(s) of c for which $x^2 + 4x = c$ has (a) two real solutions, (b) one real solution, and (c) two imaginary solutions.

16. Simplify the expression $\sqrt{30x^7} \cdot \dfrac{36}{\sqrt{3}}$.

17. A skier leaves an 8-foot-tall ramp with an initial vertical velocity of 28 feet per second. The skier has a perfect landing. How many points does the skier earn?

Criteria	Scoring
Maximum height	1 point per foot
Time in air	5 points per second
Perfect landing	25 points

18. You are playing a game of horseshoes. One of your tosses is modeled in the diagram, where x is the horseshoe's horizontal position (in feet) and y is the corresponding height (in feet). Does the horseshoe reach a height of 8 feet? 4 feet? Explain your reasoning.

$y = -0.01x^2 + 0.3x + 2$

19. The numbers y of two types of bacteria after x hours are represented by the models below.

$y = 3x^2 + 8x + 20$ Type A
$y = 27x + 60$ Type B

a. When are there 400 Type A bacteria?

b. When are the number of Type A and Type B bacteria the same?

c. When are there more Type A bacteria than Type B? When are there more Type B bacteria than Type A? Use a graph to support your answer.

1. The graphs of four quadratic functions are shown. Determine whether the discriminants of the equations $f(x) = 0$, $g(x) = 0$, $h(x) = 0$, and $j(x) = 0$ are positive, negative, or zero.

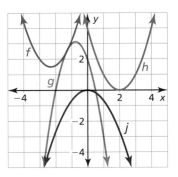

2. Your friend claims to be able to find the radius r of each figure, given the surface area S. Do you support your friend's claim? Justify your answer.

   a.

   $S = 2\pi r^2 + 2\pi rh$

   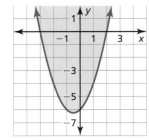

   b.

   $S = 4\pi r^2$

3. Choose values for the constants h and k in the equation $x = \frac{1}{4}(y - k)^2 + h$ so that each statement is true.

   a. The graph of $x = \frac{1}{4}\left(y - \boxed{}\right)^2 + \boxed{}$ is a parabola with its vertex in the second quadrant.

   b. The graph of $x = \frac{1}{4}\left(y - \boxed{}\right)^2 + \boxed{}$ is a parabola with its focus in the first quadrant.

   c. The graph of $x = \frac{1}{4}\left(y - \boxed{}\right)^2 + \boxed{}$ is a parabola with its focus in the third quadrant.

4. The graph of which inequality is shown?

   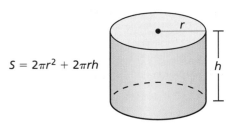

   (A) $y > x^2 + x - 6$

   (B) $y \geq x^2 + x - 6$

   (C) $y > x^2 - x - 6$

   (D) $y \geq x^2 - x - 6$

5. Use the graphs of the functions to answer each question.

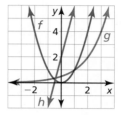

   a. Are there any values of x greater than 0 where $f(x) > h(x)$? Explain.

   b. Are there any values of x greater than 1 where $g(x) > f(x)$? Explain.

   c. Are there any values of x greater than 0 where $g(x) > h(x)$? Explain.

6. Which statement best describes the solution(s) of the system of equations?

$$y = x^2 + 2x - 8$$
$$y = 5x + 2$$

   (A) The graphs intersect at one point, $(-2, -8)$. So, there is one solution.

   (B) The graphs intersect at two points, $(-2, -8)$ and $(5, 27)$. So, there are two solutions.

   (C) The graphs do not intersect. So, there is no solution.

   (D) The graph of $y = x^2 + 2x - 8$ has two x-intercepts. So, there are two solutions.

7. Which expressions are in simplest form?

8. You are making a tabletop with a tiled center and a uniform mosaic border.

   a. Write the polynomial in standard form that represents the perimeter of the tabletop.

   b. Write the polynomial in standard form that represents the area of the tabletop.

   c. The perimeter of the tabletop is less than 80 inches, and the area of tabletop is at least 252 square inches. Select all the possible values of x.

0.5	1	1.5	2	2.5	3	3.5	4

9. Let $f(x) = 2x - 5$. Solve $y = f(x)$ for x. Then find the input when the output is -4.

5 Probability

Class Ring (p. 323)

Horse Racing (p. 313)

SEE the Big Idea

Tree Growth (p. 310)

Jogging (p. 299)

Coaching (p. 294)

Maintaining Mathematical Proficiency

Finding a Percent

Example 1 **What percent of 12 is 9?**

$$\frac{a}{w} = \frac{p}{100}$$ Write the percent proportion.

$$\frac{9}{12} = \frac{p}{100}$$ Substitute 9 for a and 12 for w.

$$100 \cdot \frac{9}{12} = 100 \cdot \frac{p}{100}$$ Multiplication Property of Equality.

$$75 = p$$ Simplify.

▶ So, 9 is 75% of 12.

Write and solve a proportion to answer the question.

1. What percent of 30 is 6?   **2.** What number is 68% of 25?   **3.** 34.4 is what percent of 86?

Making a Histogram

Example 2 **The frequency table shows the ages of people at a gym. Display the data in a histogram.**

Age	Frequency
10–19	7
20–29	12
30–39	6
40–49	4
50–59	0
60–69	3

Step 1 Draw and label the axes.

Step 2 Draw a bar to represent the frequency of each interval.

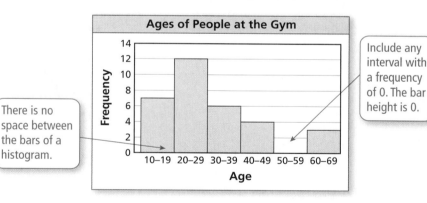

There is no space between the bars of a histogram.

Include any interval with a frequency of 0. The bar height is 0.

Display the data in a histogram.

4.

Movies Watched per Week			
Movies	0–1	2–3	4–5
Frequency	35	11	6

5. ABSTRACT REASONING You want to purchase either a sofa or an arm chair at a furniture store. Each item has the same retail price. The sofa is 20% off. The arm chair is 10% off, and you have a coupon to get an additional 10% off the discounted price of the chair. Are the items equally priced after the discounts are applied? Explain.

Mathematical Practices

Mathematically proficient students apply the mathematics they know to solve real-life problems.

Modeling with Mathematics

Core Concept

Likelihoods and Probabilities

The **probability of an event** is a measure of the likelihood that the event will occur. Probability is a number from 0 to 1, including 0 and 1. The diagram relates *likelihoods* (described in words) and probabilities.

Words	Impossible	Unlikely	Equally likely to happen or not happen	Likely	Certain
Fraction	0	$\frac{1}{4}$	$\frac{1}{2}$	$\frac{3}{4}$	1
Decimal	0	0.25	0.5	0.75	1
Percent	0%	25%	50%	75%	100%

EXAMPLE 1   Describing Likelihoods

Describe the likelihood of each event.

Probability of an Asteroid or a Meteoroid Hitting Earth			
Name	Diameter	Probability of impact	Flyby date
a. Meteoroid	6 in.	0.75	Any day
b. Apophis	886 ft	0	2029
c. 2000 SG344	121 ft	$\frac{1}{435}$	2068–2110

SOLUTION

a. On any given day, it is *likely* that a meteoroid of this size will enter Earth's atmosphere. If you have ever seen a "shooting star," then you have seen a meteoroid.

b. A probability of 0 means this event is *impossible*.

c. With a probability of $\frac{1}{435} \approx 0.23\%$, this event is very *unlikely*. Of 435 identical asteroids, you would expect only one of them to hit Earth.

Monitoring Progress

In Exercises 1 and 2, describe the event as unlikely, equally likely to happen or not happen, or likely. Explain your reasoning.

1. The oldest child in a family is a girl.

2. The two oldest children in a family with three children are girls.

3. Give an example of an event that is certain to occur.

Essential Question   How can you list the possible outcomes in the sample space of an experiment?

The **sample space** of an experiment is the set of all possible outcomes for that experiment.

EXPLORATION 1   Finding the Sample Space of an Experiment

Work with a partner. In an experiment, three coins are flipped. List the possible outcomes in the sample space of the experiment.

EXPLORATION 2   Finding the Sample Space of an Experiment

Work with a partner. List the possible outcomes in the sample space of the experiment.

a. One six-sided die is rolled.

b. Two six-sided dice are rolled.

EXPLORATION 3   Finding the Sample Space of an Experiment

Work with a partner. In an experiment, a spinner is spun.

a. How many ways can you spin a 1? 2? 3? 4? 5?

b. List the sample space.

c. What is the total number of outcomes?

EXPLORATION 4   Finding the Sample Space of an Experiment

Work with a partner. In an experiment, a bag contains 2 blue marbles and 5 red marbles. Two marbles are drawn from the bag.

a. How many ways can you choose two blue? a red then blue? a blue then red? two red?

b. List the sample space.

c. What is the total number of outcomes?

LOOKING FOR A PATTERN

To be proficient in math, you need to look closely to discern a pattern or structure.

Communicate Your Answer

5. How can you list the possible outcomes in the sample space of an experiment?

6. For Exploration 3, find the ratio of the number of each possible outcome to the total number of outcomes. Then find the sum of these ratios. Repeat for Exploration 4. What do you observe?

What You Will Learn

▶ Find sample spaces.
▶ Find theoretical probabilities.
▶ Find experimental probabilities.
▶ Find odds.

Sample Spaces

A **probability experiment** is an action, or trial, that has varying results. The possible results of a probability experiment are **outcomes**. For instance, when you roll a six-sided die, there are 6 possible outcomes: 1, 2, 3, 4, 5, or 6. A collection of one or more outcomes is an **event**, such as rolling an odd number. The set of all possible outcomes is called a **sample space**.

EXAMPLE 1 Finding a Sample Space

You flip a coin and roll a six-sided die. How many possible outcomes are in the sample space? List the possible outcomes.

SOLUTION

Use a tree diagram to find the outcomes in the sample space.

ANOTHER WAY

Using H for "heads" and T for "tails," you can list the outcomes as shown below.

H1 H2 H3 H4 H5 H6
T1 T2 T3 T4 T5 T6

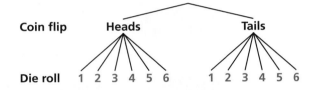

▶ The sample space has 12 possible outcomes. They are listed below.

Heads, 1   Heads, 2   Heads, 3   Heads, 4   Heads, 5   Heads, 6

Tails, 1   Tails, 2   Tails, 3   Tails, 4   Tails, 5   Tails, 6

Monitoring Progress Help in English and Spanish at *BigIdeasMath.com*

Find the number of possible outcomes in the sample space. Then list the possible outcomes.

1. You flip two coins.   **2.** You flip two coins and roll a six-sided die.

Theoretical Probabilities

The **probability of an event** is a measure of the likelihood, or chance, that the event will occur. Probability is a number from 0 to 1, including 0 and 1, and can be expressed as a decimal, fraction, or percent.

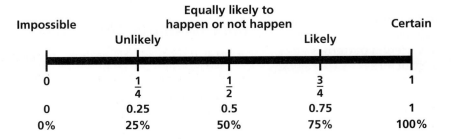

The outcomes for a specified event are called *favorable outcomes*. When all outcomes are equally likely, the **theoretical probability** of the event can be found using the following.

$$\text{Theoretical probability} = \frac{\text{Number of favorable outcomes}}{\text{Total number of outcomes}}$$

The probability of event A is written as $P(A)$.

EXAMPLE 2 Finding a Theoretical Probability

A student taking a quiz randomly guesses the answers to four true-false questions. What is the probability of the student guessing exactly two correct answers?

SOLUTION

Step 1 Find the outcomes in the sample space. Let C represent a correct answer and I represent an incorrect answer. The possible outcomes are:

Number correct	Outcome
0	IIII
1	CIII ICII IICI IIIC
2	IICC ICIC ICCI CIIC CICI CCII
3	ICCC CICC CCIC CCCI
4	CCCC

exactly two correct → 2

Step 2 Identify the number of favorable outcomes and the total number of outcomes. There are 6 favorable outcomes with exactly two correct answers and the total number of outcomes is 16.

Step 3 Find the probability of the student guessing exactly two correct answers. Because the student is randomly guessing, the outcomes should be equally likely. So, use the theoretical probability formula.

$$P(\text{exactly two correct answers}) = \frac{\text{Number of favorable outcomes}}{\text{Total number of outcomes}}$$

$$= \frac{6}{16}$$

$$= \frac{3}{8}$$

▶ The probability of the student guessing exactly two correct answers is $\frac{3}{8}$, or 37.5%.

The sum of the probabilities of all outcomes in a sample space is 1. So, when you know the probability of event A, you can find the probability of the *complement* of event A. The *complement* of event A consists of all outcomes that are not in A and is denoted by $\overline{A}$. The notation $\overline{A}$ is read as "A bar." You can use the following formula to find $P(\overline{A})$.

Core Concept

Probability of the Complement of an Event

The probability of the complement of event A is

$$P(\overline{A}) = 1 - P(A).$$

EXAMPLE 3   Finding Probabilities of Complements

You roll two six-sided dice. Find the probability of each event.

a. The sum is not 6.

b. The sum is less than or equal to 9.

SOLUTION

Find the outcomes in the sample space, as shown. There are 36 possible outcomes.

a. $P(\text{sum is not } 6) = 1 - P(\text{sum is } 6) = 1 - \frac{5}{36} = \frac{31}{36} \approx 0.861$

b. $P(\text{sum} \le 9) = 1 - P(\text{sum} > 9) = 1 - \frac{6}{36} = \frac{30}{36} = \frac{5}{6} \approx 0.833$

Monitoring Progress Help in English and Spanish at *BigIdeasMath.com*

3. You flip a coin and roll a six-sided die. What is the probability that the coin shows tails and the die shows 4?

Find $P(\overline{A})$.

4. $P(A) = 0.45$ **5.** $P(A) = \frac{1}{4}$ **6.** $P(A) = 1$ **7.** $P(A) = 0.03$

Experimental Probabilities

An **experimental probability** is based on repeated *trials* of a probability experiment. The number of trials is the number of times the probability experiment is performed. Each trial in which a favorable outcome occurs is called a *success*. The experimental probability can be found using the following.

$$\text{Experimental probability} = \frac{\text{Number of successes}}{\text{Number of trials}}$$

EXAMPLE 4   Finding an Experimental Probability

Spinner Results			
red	**green**	**blue**	**yellow**
5	9	3	3

Each section of the spinner shown has the same area. The spinner was spun 20 times. The table shows the results. For which color is the experimental probability of stopping on the color the same as the theoretical probability?

SOLUTION

The theoretical probability of stopping on each of the four colors is $\frac{1}{4}$. Use the outcomes in the table to find the experimental probabilities.

$P(\text{red}) = \frac{5}{20} = \frac{1}{4}$ $P(\text{green}) = \frac{9}{20}$ $P(\text{blue}) = \frac{3}{20}$ $P(\text{yellow}) = \frac{3}{20}$

▶ The experimental probability of stopping on red is the same as the theoretical probability.

Monitoring Progress Help in English and Spanish at *BigIdeasMath.com*

8. For which color is the experimental probability of stopping on the color greater than the theoretical probability?

EXAMPLE 5   Solving a Real-Life Problem

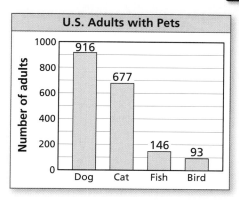

U.S. Adults with Pets

Number of adults: 916 (Dog), 677 (Cat), 146 (Fish), 93 (Bird)

In the United States, a survey of 2184 adults ages 18 and over found that 1328 of them have at least one pet. The types of pets these adults have are shown in the figure. What is the probability that a pet-owning adult chosen at random has a dog?

SOLUTION

The number of trials is the number of pet-owning adults, 1328. A success is a pet-owning adult who has a dog. From the graph, there are 916 adults who have a dog.

$$P(\text{pet-owning adult has a dog}) = \frac{916}{1328} = \frac{229}{332} \approx 0.690$$

▶ The probability that a pet-owning adult chosen at random has a dog is about 69%.

Monitoring Progress Help in English and Spanish at *BigIdeasMath.com*

9. What is the probability that a pet-owning adult chosen at random owns a fish?

Odds

The **odds** of an event compare the number of favorable and unfavorable outcomes when all outcomes are equally likely.

$$\text{Odds } in\ favor = \frac{\text{Number of favorable outcomes}}{\text{Number of unfavorable outcomes}} \qquad \text{Odds } against = \frac{\text{Number of unfavorable outcomes}}{\text{Number of favorable outcomes}}$$

EXAMPLE 6   Finding Odds

In Example 4, find the odds in favor of stopping on yellow.

READING

Odds are read as the ratio of one number to another.

SOLUTION

The 4 possible outcomes are all equally likely. Yellow is the 1 favorable outcome and the other 3 colors are unfavorable outcomes.

$$\text{Odds in favor of yellow} = \frac{\text{Number of favorable outcomes}}{\text{Number of unfavorable outcomes}} = \frac{1}{3}, \text{ or } 1:3$$

EXAMPLE 7   Making a Decision

The probability of winning a balloon dart game is 0.2. The odds of winning a ring toss game are $1:5$. Which game gives you a better chance of winning?

STUDY TIP

Using the given odds, there is 1 favorable outcome and 5 unfavorable outcomes. So, the total number of outcomes is 6.

SOLUTION

Find the probability of winning the ring toss game. Then compare the probabilities.

$$P(\text{winning ring toss game}) = \frac{\text{Number of favorable outcomes}}{\text{Total number of outcomes}} = \frac{1}{6} \approx 0.17$$

▶ Because $0.2 > 0.17$, the balloon dart game gives you a better chance of winning.

Monitoring Progress Help in English and Spanish at *BigIdeasMath.com*

10. In Example 4, find the odds against stopping on red.

11. **WHAT IF?** The odds of winning the ring toss game are $2:7$. Does this change your answer in Example 7? Explain your reasoning.

Vocabulary and Core Concept Check

1. **WRITING** Describe the difference between theoretical probability and experimental probability.

2. **WRITING** Explain how the probability of an event differs from the odds in favor of the event when all outcomes are equally likely.

Monitoring Progress and Modeling with Mathematics

In Exercises 3–6, find the number of possible outcomes in the sample space. Then list the possible outcomes. *(See Example 1.)*

3. You roll a die and flip three coins.

4. You flip a coin and draw a marble at random from a bag containing two purple marbles and one white marble.

5. A bag contains four red cards numbered 1 through 4, four white cards numbered 1 through 4, and four black cards numbered 1 through 4. You choose a card at random.

6. You draw two marbles without replacement from a bag containing three green marbles and four black marbles.

7. **PROBLEM SOLVING** A game show airs on television five days per week. Each day, a prize is randomly placed behind one of two doors. The contestant wins the prize by selecting the correct door. What is the probability that exactly two of the five contestants win a prize during a week? *(See Example 2.)*

8. **PROBLEM SOLVING** Your friend has two standard decks of 52 playing cards and asks you to randomly draw one card from each deck. What is the probability that you will draw two spades?

9. **PROBLEM SOLVING** You roll two six-sided dice. Find the probability that (a) the sum is not 4 and (b) the sum is greater than 5. *(See Example 3.)*

10. **PROBLEM SOLVING** The age distribution of a population is shown. Find the probability of each event.

Age Distribution

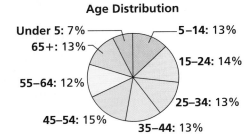

Under 5: 7%
65+: 13%
5–14: 13%
15–24: 14%
25–34: 13%
35–44: 13%
45–54: 15%
55–64: 12%

a. A person chosen at random is at least 15 years old.

b. A person chosen at random is from 25 to 44 years old.

11. **ERROR ANALYSIS** A student randomly guesses the answers to two true-false questions. Describe and correct the error in finding the probability of the student guessing both answers correctly.

> The student can either guess two incorrect answers, two correct answers, or one of each. So the probability of guessing both answers correctly is $\frac{1}{3}$.

12. **ERROR ANALYSIS** A student randomly draws a number between 1 and 30. Describe and correct the error in finding the probability that the number drawn is greater than 4.

> The probability that the number is less than 4 is $\frac{3}{30}$, or $\frac{1}{10}$. So, the probability that the number is greater than 4 is $1 - \frac{1}{10}$, or $\frac{9}{10}$.

13. **DRAWING CONCLUSIONS** You roll a six-sided die 60 times. The table shows the results. For which number is the experimental probability of rolling the number the same as the theoretical probability? *(See Example 4.)*

Six-sided Die Results					
11	14	7	10	6	12

14. **DRAWING CONCLUSIONS** A bag contains 5 marbles that are each a different color. A marble is drawn, its color is recorded, and then the marble is placed back in the bag. This process is repeated until 30 marbles have been drawn. The table shows the results. For which marble is the experimental probability of drawing the marble the same as the theoretical probability?

Drawing Results				
white	black	red	green	blue
5	6	8	2	9

15. **REASONING** Refer to the spinner shown. The spinner is divided into sections with the same area.

a. What is the theoretical probability that the spinner stops on a multiple of 3?

b. You spin the spinner 30 times. It stops on a multiple of 3 twenty times. What is the experimental probability of stopping on a multiple of 3?

c. Explain why the probability you found in part (b) is different than the probability you found in part(a).

d. You spin the spinner 60 times. It stops on a multiple of 10 six times. How does the experimental probability of stopping on a multiple of 10 compare to the theoretical probability that the spinner stops on a multiple of 10?

16. **OPEN-ENDED** Describe a real-life event that has a probability of 0. Then describe a real-life event that has a probability of 1.

17. **DRAWING CONCLUSIONS** A survey of 2237 adults ages 18 and over asked which sport is their favorite. The results are shown in the figure. What is the probability that an adult chosen at random prefers auto racing? *(See Example 5.)*

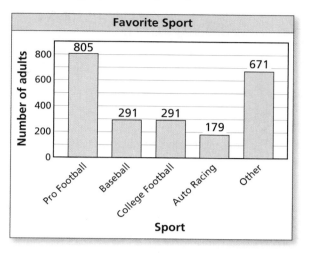

18. **DRAWING CONCLUSIONS** A survey of 2392 adults ages 18 and over asked what type of food they would be most likely to choose at a restaurant. The results are shown in the figure. What is the probability that an adult chosen at random prefers Italian food?

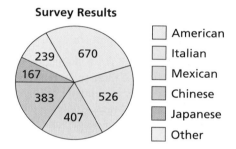

In Exercises 19–22, use the spinner in Exercise 15 to find the given odds. *(See Example 6.)*

19. in favor of stopping on a multiple of 6

20. in favor of stopping on a number greater than 10

21. against stopping on a number less than 9

22. against stopping on a number that is divisible by 7

23. **PROBLEM SOLVING** The odds of winning a lottery game are 3 : 5. The probability of winning a bingo game is 35%. Which game gives you a better chance of winning? Explain. *(See Example 7.)*

24. **PROBLEM SOLVING** The probability of winning a carnival game is $\frac{1}{4}$. The odds of winning a raffle are 1 : 3. For which do you have a better chance of winning? Explain.

25. REASONING Use the spinner in Exercise 15 to give an example of an event whose odds are 1 : 1.

26. ANALYZING RELATIONSHIPS Refer to the chart below.

Four-Day Forecast			
Friday	Saturday	Sunday	Monday
Chance of Rain **5%**	Chance of Rain **30%**	Chance of Rain **80%**	Chance of Rain **90%**

  a. Order the following events from least likely to most likely.

   A. It rains on Sunday.

   B. It does not rain on Saturday.

   C. It rains on Monday.

   D. It does not rain on Friday.

  b. Find the odds in favor of rain for each day.

27. USING TOOLS Use the figure in Example 3 to answer each question.

  a. List the possible sums that result from rolling two six-sided dice.

  b. Find the theoretical probability of rolling each sum.

  c. The table below shows a simulation of rolling two six-sided dice three times. Use a random number generator to simulate rolling two six-sided dice 50 times. Compare the experimental probabilities of rolling each sum with the theoretical probabilities.

	A	B	C
1	**First Die**	**Second Die**	**Sum**
2	4	6	10
3	3	5	8
4	1	6	7
5			

28. MAKING AN ARGUMENT You flip a coin three times. It lands on heads twice and on tails once. Your friend concludes that the theoretical probability of the coin landing heads up is $P(\text{heads up}) = \frac{2}{3}$. Is your friend correct? Explain your reasoning.

29. CRITICAL THINKING You randomly draw a marble from a bag containing red, white, and blue marbles. The odds against drawing a white marble are 47 : 3.

  a. There are less than 100 marbles in the bag. How many marbles are in the bag? Justify your answer.

  b. The probability of drawing a red marble is 0.5. What is the probability of drawing a blue marble? Explain your reasoning.

30. HOW DO YOU SEE IT?
Consider the graph of f shown. What is the probability that the graph of $y = f(x) + c$ intersects the x-axis when c is a randomly chosen integer from 1 to 6? Explain.

31. DRAWING CONCLUSIONS A manufacturer tests 1200 computers and finds that 9 of them have defects. Find the probability that a computer chosen at random has a defect. Predict the number of computers with defects in a shipment of 15,000 computers. Explain your reasoning.

32. THOUGHT PROVOKING The tree diagram shows a sample space. Write a probability problem that can be represented by the sample space. Then write the answer(s) to the problem.

Box A	Box B	Outcomes	Sum	Product
1	1	(1, 1)	2	1
	2	(1, 2)	3	2
2	1	(2, 1)	3	2
	2	(2, 2)	4	4
3	1	(3, 1)	4	3
	2	(3, 2)	5	6

Maintaining Mathematical Proficiency Reviewing what you learned in previous grades and lessons

Factor the polynomial. *(Section 2.6)*

33. $3x^2 + 12x - 36$

34. $2x^2 - 11x + 9$

35. $4x^2 + 7x - 15$

Solve the equation using square roots. *(Section 4.3)*

36. $x^2 - 36 = 0$

37. $5x^2 - 20 = 0$

38. $(x + 4)^2 = 81$

39. $25(x - 2)^2 = 9$

Essential Question How can you determine whether two events are independent or dependent?

Two events are **independent events** when the occurrence of one event does not affect the occurrence of the other event. Two events are **dependent events** when the occurrence of one event *does* affect the occurrence of the other event.

EXPLORATION 1 **Identifying Independent and Dependent Events**

REASONING ABSTRACTLY

To be proficient in math, you need to make sense of quantities and their relationships in problem situations.

Work with a partner. Determine whether the events are independent or dependent. Explain your reasoning.

a. Two six-sided dice are rolled.

b. Six pieces of paper, numbered 1 through 6, are in a bag. Two pieces of paper are selected one at a time without replacement.

EXPLORATION 2 **Finding Experimental Probabilities**

Work with a partner.

a. In Exploration 1(a), experimentally estimate the probability that the sum of the two numbers rolled is 7. Describe your experiment.

b. In Exploration 1(b), experimentally estimate the probability that the sum of the two numbers selected is 7. Describe your experiment.

EXPLORATION 3 **Finding Theoretical Probabilities**

Work with a partner.

a. In Exploration 1(a), find the theoretical probability that the sum of the two numbers rolled is 7. Then compare your answer with the experimental probability you found in Exploration 2(a).

b. In Exploration 1(b), find the theoretical probability that the sum of the two numbers selected is 7. Then compare your answer with the experimental probability you found in Exploration 2(b).

c. Compare the probabilities you obtained in parts (a) and (b).

Communicate Your Answer

4. How can you determine whether two events are independent or dependent?

5. Determine whether the events are independent or dependent. Explain your reasoning.

    a. You roll a 4 on a six-sided die and spin red on a spinner.

    b. Your teacher chooses a student to lead a group, chooses another student to lead a second group, and chooses a third student to lead a third group.

What You Will Learn

▶ Determine whether events are independent events.

▶ Find probabilities of independent and dependent events.

▶ Find conditional probabilities.

Determining Whether Events Are Independent

Two events are **independent events** when the occurrence of one event does not affect the occurrence of the other event.

🌀 Core Concept

Probability of Independent Events

Words Two events A and B are independent events if and only if the probability that both events occur is the product of the probabilities of the events.

Symbols $P(A \text{ and } B) = P(A) \cdot P(B)$

EXAMPLE 1 **Determining Whether Events Are Independent**

A student taking a quiz randomly guesses the answers to four true-false questions. Use a sample space to determine whether guessing Question 1 correctly and guessing Question 2 correctly are independent events.

SOLUTION

Using the sample space in Example 2 on page 281:

$P(\text{correct on Question 1}) = \frac{8}{16} = \frac{1}{2}$ $P(\text{correct on Question 2}) = \frac{8}{16} = \frac{1}{2}$

$P(\text{correct on Question 1 and correct on Question 2}) = \frac{4}{16} = \frac{1}{4}$

▶ Because $\frac{1}{2} \cdot \frac{1}{2} = \frac{1}{4}$, the events are independent.

EXAMPLE 2 **Determining Whether Events Are Independent**

A group of four students includes one boy and three girls. The teacher randomly selects one of the students to be the speaker and a different student to be the recorder. Use a sample space to determine whether randomly selecting a girl first and randomly selecting a girl second are independent events.

SOLUTION

Let B represent the boy. Let G_1, G_2, and G_3 represent the three girls. Use a table to list the outcomes in the sample space.

Number of girls	Outcome	
1	G_1B	BG_1
1	G_2B	BG_2
1	G_3B	BG_3
2	G_1G_2	G_2G_1
2	G_1G_3	G_3G_1
2	G_2G_3	G_3G_2

Using the sample space:

$P(\text{girl first}) = \frac{9}{12} = \frac{3}{4}$ $P(\text{girl second}) = \frac{9}{12} = \frac{3}{4}$

$P(\text{girl first and girl second}) = \frac{6}{12} = \frac{1}{2}$

▶ Because $\frac{3}{4} \cdot \frac{3}{4} \neq \frac{1}{2}$, the events are not independent.

Monitoring Progress 🔊 Help in English and Spanish at *BigIdeasMath.com*

1. In Example 1, determine whether guessing Question 1 incorrectly and guessing Question 2 correctly are independent events.

2. In Example 2, determine whether randomly selecting a girl first and randomly selecting a boy second are independent events.

Finding Probabilities of Events

In Example 1, it makes sense that the events are independent because the second guess should not be affected by the first guess. In Example 2, however, the selection of the second person *depends* on the selection of the first person because the same person cannot be selected twice. These events are *dependent*. Two events are **dependent events** when the occurrence of one event *does* affect the occurrence of the other event.

The probability that event B occurs given that event A has occurred is called the **conditional probability** of B given A and is written as $P(B|A)$.

MAKING SENSE OF PROBLEMS

One way that you can find $P(\text{girl second}|\text{girl first})$ is to list the 9 outcomes in which a girl is chosen first and then find the fraction of these outcomes in which a girl is chosen second:

$$G_1B \quad G_2B \quad G_3B$$
$$\overline{G_1G_2 \quad G_2G_1 \quad G_3G_1}$$
$$G_1G_3 \quad G_2G_3 \quad G_3G_2$$

⤳

🌀 Core Concept

Probability of Dependent Events

Words If two events A and B are dependent events, then the probability that both events occur is the product of the probability of the first event and the conditional probability of the second event given the first event.

Symbols $P(A \text{ and } B) = P(A) \cdot P(B|A)$

Example Using the information in Example 2:

$$P(\text{girl first and girl second}) = P(\text{girl first}) \cdot P(\text{girl second}|\text{girl first})$$
$$= \frac{9}{12} \cdot \frac{6}{9} = \frac{1}{2}$$

EXAMPLE 3 **Finding the Probability of Independent Events**

As part of a board game, you need to spin the spinner, which is divided into equal parts. Find the probability that you get a 5 on your first spin and a number greater than 3 on your second spin.

SOLUTION

Let event A be "5 on first spin" and let event B be "greater than 3 on second spin."

The events are independent because the outcome of your second spin is not affected by the outcome of your first spin. Find the probability of each event and then multiply the probabilities.

$$P(A) = \frac{1}{8} \qquad \text{1 of the 8 sections is a "5."}$$

$$P(B) = \frac{5}{8} \qquad \text{5 of the 8 sections (4, 5, 6, 7, 8) are greater than 3.}$$

$$P(A \text{ and } B) = P(A) \cdot P(B) = \frac{1}{8} \cdot \frac{5}{8} = \frac{5}{64} \approx 0.078$$

▶ So, the probability that you get a 5 on your first spin and a number greater than 3 on your second spin is about 7.8%.

EXAMPLE 4   Finding the Probability of Dependent Events

A bag contains twenty $1 bills and five $100 bills. You randomly draw a bill from the bag, set it aside, and then randomly draw another bill from the bag. Find the probability that both events A and B will occur.

Event A: The first bill is $100.   **Event B:** The second bill is $100.

SOLUTION

The events are dependent because there is one less bill in the bag on your second draw than on your first draw. Find $P(A)$ and $P(B|A)$. Then multiply the probabilities.

$P(A) = \frac{5}{25}$ 5 of the 25 bills are $100 bills.

$P(B|A) = \frac{4}{24}$ 4 of the remaining 24 bills are $100 bills.

$P(A \text{ and } B) = P(A) \cdot P(B|A) = \frac{5}{25} \cdot \frac{4}{24} = \frac{1}{5} \cdot \frac{1}{6} = \frac{1}{30} \approx 0.033.$

▶ So, the probability that you draw two $100 bills is about 3.3%.

EXAMPLE 5   Comparing Independent and Dependent Events

You randomly select 3 cards from a standard deck of 52 playing cards. What is the probability that all 3 cards are hearts when (a) you replace each card before selecting the next card, and (b) you do not replace each card before selecting the next card? Compare the probabilities.

SOLUTION

Let event A be "first card is a heart," event B be "second card is a heart," and event C be "third card is a heart."

a. Because you replace each card before you select the next card, the events are independent. So, the probability is

$$P(A \text{ and } B \text{ and } C) = P(A) \cdot P(B) \cdot P(C) = \frac{13}{52} \cdot \frac{13}{52} \cdot \frac{13}{52} = \frac{1}{64} \approx 0.016.$$

b. Because you do not replace each card before you select the next card, the events are dependent. So, the probability is

$$P(A \text{ and } B \text{ and } C) = P(A) \cdot P(B|A) \cdot P(C|A \text{ and } B)$$

$$= \frac{13}{52} \cdot \frac{12}{51} \cdot \frac{11}{50} = \frac{11}{850} \approx 0.013.$$

▶ So, you are $\frac{1}{64} \div \frac{11}{850} \approx 1.2$ times more likely to select 3 hearts when you replace each card before you select the next card.

> **STUDY TIP**
> The formulas for finding probabilities of independent and dependent events can be extended to three or more events.

Monitoring Progress   ◀)) Help in English and Spanish at *BigIdeasMath.com*

3. In Example 3, what is the probability that you spin an even number and then an odd number?

4. In Example 4, what is the probability that both bills are $1 bills?

5. In Example 5, what is the probability that none of the cards drawn are hearts when (a) you replace each card, and (b) you do not replace each card? Compare the probabilities.

Finding Conditional Probabilities

EXAMPLE 6 **Using a Table to Find Conditional Probabilities**

A quality-control inspector checks for defective parts. The table shows the results of the inspector's work. Find (a) the probability that a defective part "passes," and (b) the probability that a non-defective part "fails."

	Pass	Fail
Defective	3	36
Non-defective	450	11

SOLUTION

a. $P(\text{pass} \mid \text{defective}) = \dfrac{\text{Number of defective parts "passed"}}{\text{Total number of defective parts}}$

$$= \frac{3}{3 + 36} = \frac{3}{39} = \frac{1}{13} \approx 0.077, \text{ or about } 7.7\%$$

b. $P(\text{fail} \mid \text{non-defective}) = \dfrac{\text{Number of non-defective parts "failed"}}{\text{Total number of non-defective parts}}$

$$= \frac{11}{450 + 11} = \frac{11}{461} \approx 0.024, \text{ or about } 2.4\%$$

STUDY TIP

Note that when A and B are independent, this rule still applies because $P(B) = P(B \mid A)$.

You can rewrite the formula for the probability of dependent events to write a rule for finding conditional probabilities.

$$P(A) \cdot P(B \mid A) = P(A \text{ and } B) \qquad \text{Write formula.}$$

$$P(B \mid A) = \frac{P(A \text{ and } B)}{P(A)} \qquad \text{Divide each side by } P(A).$$

EXAMPLE 7 **Finding a Conditional Probability**

At a school, 60% of students buy a school lunch. Only 10% of students buy lunch and dessert. What is the probability that a student who buys lunch also buys dessert?

SOLUTION

Let event A be "buys lunch" and let event B be "buys dessert." You are given $P(A) = 0.6$ and $P(A \text{ and } B) = 0.1$. Use the formula to find $P(B \mid A)$.

$$P(B \mid A) = \frac{P(A \text{ and } B)}{P(A)} \qquad \text{Write formula for conditional probability.}$$

$$= \frac{0.1}{0.6} \qquad \text{Substitute 0.1 for } P(A \text{ and } B) \text{ and 0.6 for } P(A).$$

$$= \frac{1}{6} \approx 0.167 \qquad \text{Simplify.}$$

▶ So, the probability that a student who buys lunch also buys dessert is about 16.7%.

Monitoring Progress ◀))) Help in English and Spanish at *BigIdeasMath.com*

6. In Example 6, find (a) the probability that a non-defective part "passes," and (b) the probability that a defective part "fails."

7. At a coffee shop, 80% of customers order coffee. Only 15% of customers order coffee and a bagel. What is the probability that a customer who orders coffee also orders a bagel?

Vocabulary and Core Concept Check

1. **WRITING** Explain the difference between dependent events and independent events, and give an example of each.

2. **COMPLETE THE SENTENCE** The probability that event *B* will occur given that event *A* has occurred is called the _____ of *B* given *A* and is written as _____ .

Monitoring Progress and Modeling with Mathematics

In Exercises 3–6, tell whether the events are independent or dependent. Explain your reasoning.

3. A box of granola bars contains an assortment of flavors. You randomly choose a granola bar and eat it. Then you randomly choose another bar.

   Event A: You choose a coconut almond bar first.

   Event B: You choose a cranberry almond bar second.

4. You roll a six-sided die and flip a coin.

   Event A: You get a 4 when rolling the die.

   Event B: You get tails when flipping the coin.

5. Your MP3 player contains hip-hop and rock songs. You randomly choose a song. Then you randomly choose another song without repeating song choices.

   Event A: You choose a hip-hop song first.

   Event B: You choose a rock song second.

6. There are 22 novels of various genres on a shelf. You randomly choose a novel and put it back. Then you randomly choose another novel.

   Event A: You choose a mystery novel.

   Event B: You choose a science fiction novel.

In Exercises 7–10, determine whether the events are independent. *(See Examples 1 and 2.)*

7. You play a game that involves spinning a wheel. Each section of the wheel shown has the same area. Use a sample space to determine whether randomly spinning blue and then green are independent events.

8. You have one red apple and three green apples in a bowl. You randomly select one apple to eat now and another apple for your lunch. Use a sample space to determine whether randomly selecting a green apple first and randomly selecting a green apple second are independent events.

9. A student is taking a multiple-choice test where each question has four choices. The student randomly guesses the answers to the five-question test. Use a sample space to determine whether guessing Question 1 correctly and Question 2 correctly are independent events.

10. A vase contains four white roses and one red rose. You randomly select two roses to take home. Use a sample space to determine whether randomly selecting a white rose first and randomly selecting a white rose second are independent events.

11. **PROBLEM SOLVING** You play a game that involves spinning the money wheel shown. You spin the wheel twice. Find the probability that you get more than $500 on your first spin and then go bankrupt on your second spin. *(See Example 3.)*

12. **PROBLEM SOLVING** You play a game that involves drawing two numbers from a hat. There are 25 pieces of paper numbered from 1 to 25 in the hat. Each number is replaced after it is drawn. Find the probability that you will draw the 3 on your first draw and a number greater than 10 on your second draw.

13. **PROBLEM SOLVING** A drawer contains 12 white socks and 8 black socks. You randomly choose 1 sock and do not replace it. Then you randomly choose another sock. Find the probability that both events A and B will occur. *(See Example 4.)*

    Event A: The first sock is white.

    Event B: The second sock is white.

14. **PROBLEM SOLVING** A word game has 100 tiles, 98 of which are letters and 2 of which are blank. The numbers of tiles of each letter are shown. You randomly draw 1 tile, set it aside, and then randomly draw another tile. Find the probability that both events A and B will occur.

    Event A: The first tile is a consonant.

    Event B: The second tile is a vowel.

    A – 9 H – 2 O – 8 V – 2
    B – 2 I – 9 P – 2 W – 2
    C – 2 J – 1 Q – 1 X – 1
    D – 4 K – 1 R – 6 Y – 2
    E – 12 L – 4 S – 4 Z – 1
    F – 2 M – 2 T – 6   – 2
    G – 3 N – 6 U – 4 Blank

15. **ERROR ANALYSIS** Events A and B are independent. Describe and correct the error in finding $P(A \text{ and } B)$.

    $$P(A) = 0.6 \qquad P(B) = 0.2$$
    $$P(A \text{ and } B) = 0.6 + 0.2 = 0.8$$

16. **ERROR ANALYSIS** A shelf contains 3 fashion magazines and 4 health magazines. You randomly choose one to read, set it aside, and randomly choose another for your friend to read. Describe and correct the error in finding the probability that both events A and B occur.

    Event A: The first magazine is fashion.

    Event B: The second magazine is health.

    $$P(A) = \frac{3}{7} \qquad P(B \mid A) = \frac{4}{7}$$
    $$P(A \text{ and } B) = \frac{3}{7} \cdot \frac{4}{7} = \frac{12}{49} \approx 0.245$$

17. **NUMBER SENSE** Events A and B are independent. Suppose $P(B) = 0.4$ and $P(A \text{ and } B) = 0.13$. Find $P(A)$.

18. **NUMBER SENSE** Events A and B are dependent. Suppose $P(B \mid A) = 0.6$ and $P(A \text{ and } B) = 0.15$. Find $P(A)$.

19. **ANALYZING RELATIONSHIPS** You randomly select three cards from a standard deck of 52 playing cards. What is the probability that all three cards are face cards when (a) you replace each card before selecting the next card, and (b) you do not replace each card before selecting the next card? Compare the probabilities. *(See Example 5.)*

20. **ANALYZING RELATIONSHIPS** A bag contains 9 red marbles, 4 blue marbles, and 7 yellow marbles. You randomly select three marbles from the bag. What is the probability that all three marbles are red when (a) you replace each marble before selecting the next marble, and (b) you do not replace each marble before selecting the next marble? Compare the probabilities.

21. **ATTEND TO PRECISION** The table shows the number of species in the United States listed as endangered and threatened. Find (a) the probability that a randomly selected endangered species is a bird, and (b) the probability that a randomly selected mammal is endangered. *(See Example 6.)*

	Endangered	Threatened
Mammals	70	16
Birds	80	16
Other	318	142

22. **ATTEND TO PRECISION** The table shows the number of tropical cyclones that formed during the hurricane seasons over a 12-year period. Find (a) the probability to predict whether a future tropical cyclone in the Northern Hemisphere is a hurricane, and (b) the probability to predict whether a hurricane is in the Southern Hemisphere.

Type of Tropical Cyclone	Northern Hemisphere	Southern Hemisphere
tropical depression	100	107
tropical storm	342	487
hurricane	379	525

23. **PROBLEM SOLVING** At a school, 43% of students attend the homecoming football game. Only 23% of students go to the game and the homecoming dance. What is the probability that a student who attends the football game also attends the dance? *(See Example 7.)*

24. PROBLEM SOLVING At a gas station, 84% of customers buy gasoline. Only 5% of customers buy gasoline and a beverage. What is the probability that a customer who buys gasoline also buys a beverage?

25. PROBLEM SOLVING You and 19 other students volunteer to present the "Best Teacher" award at a school banquet. One student volunteer will be chosen to present the award. Each student worked at least 1 hour in preparation for the banquet. You worked for 4 hours, and the group worked a combined total of 45 hours. For each situation, describe a process that gives you a "fair" chance to be chosen, and find the probability that you are chosen.

   a. "Fair" means equally likely.

   b. "Fair" means proportional to the number of hours each student worked in preparation.

26. HOW DO YOU SEE IT? A bag contains one red marble and one blue marble. The diagrams show the possible outcomes of randomly choosing two marbles using different methods. For each method, determine whether the marbles were selected with or without replacement.

   a.   1st   2nd   **b.**   1st   2nd

       Draw   Draw   Draw   Draw

27. MAKING AN ARGUMENT A meteorologist claims that there is a 70% chance of rain. When it rains, there is a 75% chance that your softball game will be rescheduled. Your friend believes the game is more likely to be rescheduled than played. Is your friend correct? Explain your reasoning.

28. THOUGHT PROVOKING Two six-sided dice are rolled once. Events A and B are represented by the diagram. Describe each event. Are the two events dependent or independent? Justify your reasoning.

29. MODELING WITH MATHEMATICS A football team is losing by 14 points near the end of a game. The team scores two touchdowns (worth 6 points each) before the end of the game. After each touchdown, the coach must decide whether to go for 1 point with a kick (which is successful 99% of the time) or 2 points with a run or pass (which is successful 45% of the time).

   a. If the team goes for 1 point after each touchdown, what is the probability that the team wins? loses? ties?

   b. If the team goes for 2 points after each touchdown, what is the probability that the team wins? loses? ties?

   c. Can you develop a strategy so that the coach's team has a probability of winning the game that is greater than the probability of losing? If so, explain your strategy and calculate the probabilities of winning and losing the game.

30. ABSTRACT REASONING Assume that A and B are independent events.

   a. Explain why $P(B) = P(B|A)$ and $P(A) = P(A|B)$.

   b. Can $P(A \text{ and } B)$ also be defined as $P(B) \cdot P(A|B)$? Justify your reasoning.

Maintaining Mathematical Proficiency   Reviewing what you learned in previous grades and lessons

Solve the equation. Check your solution.   *(Skills Review Handbook)*

31. $\frac{9}{10}x = 0.18$ **32.** $\frac{1}{4}x + 0.5x = 1.5$ **33.** $0.3x - \frac{3}{5}x + 1.6 = 1.555$

Essential Question How can you construct and interpret a two-way table?

EXPLORATION 1 **Completing and Using a Two-Way Table**

Work with a partner. A *two-way table* displays the same information as a Venn diagram. In a two-way table, one category is represented by the rows and the other category is represented by the columns.

The Venn diagram shows the results of a survey in which 80 students were asked whether they play a musical instrument and whether they speak a foreign language. Use the Venn diagram to complete the two-way table. Then use the two-way table to answer each question.

Survey of 80 Students

	Play an Instrument	Do Not Play an Instrument	Total
Speak a Foreign Language			
Do Not Speak a Foreign Language			
Total			

a. How many students play an instrument?

b. How many students speak a foreign language?

c. How many students play an instrument and speak a foreign language?

d. How many students do not play an instrument and do not speak a foreign language?

e. How many students play an instrument and do not speak a foreign language?

EXPLORATION 2 **Two-Way Tables and Probability**

Work with a partner. In Exploration 1, one student is selected at random from the 80 students who took the survey. Find the probability that the student

a. plays an instrument.

b. speaks a foreign language.

c. plays an instrument and speaks a foreign language.

d. does not play an instrument and does not speak a foreign language.

e. plays an instrument and does not speak a foreign language.

MODELING WITH MATHEMATICS

To be proficient in math, you need to identify important quantities in a practical situation and map their relationships using such tools as diagrams and two-way tables.

EXPLORATION 3 **Conducting a Survey**

Work with your class. Conduct a survey of the students in your class. Choose two categories that are different from those given in Explorations 1 and 2. Then summarize the results in both a Venn diagram and a two-way table. Discuss the results.

Communicate Your Answer

4. How can you construct and interpret a two-way table?

5. How can you use a two-way table to determine probabilities?

5.3 Lesson

Core Vocabulary

two-way table, *p. 296*
joint frequency, *p. 296*
marginal frequency, *p. 296*
joint relative frequency,
    p. 297
marginal relative frequency,
    p. 297
conditional relative frequency,
    p. 297
Previous
conditional probability

READING

A two-way table is also
called a *contingency table*,
or a *two-way frequency
table*.

What You Will Learn

▶ Make two-way tables.

▶ Find relative and conditional relative frequencies.

▶ Use conditional relative frequencies to find conditional probabilities.

Making Two-Way Tables

A **two-way table** is a frequency table that displays data collected from one source that belong to two different categories. One category of data is represented by rows and the other is represented by columns. Suppose you randomly survey freshmen and sophomores about whether they are attending a school concert. A two-way table is one way to organize your results.

Each entry in the table is called a **joint frequency**. The sums of the rows and columns are called **marginal frequencies**, which you will find in Example 1.

		Attendance	
		Attending	**Not Attending**
Class	**Freshman**	25	44
	Sophomore	80	32

joint frequency

EXAMPLE 1   Making a Two-Way Table

In another survey similar to the one above, 106 juniors and 114 seniors respond. Of those, 42 juniors and 77 seniors plan on attending. Organize these results in a two-way table. Then find and interpret the marginal frequencies.

SOLUTION

Step 1   Find the joint frequencies. Because 42 of the 106 juniors are attending, $106 - 42 = 64$ juniors are not attending. Because 77 of the 114 seniors are attending, $114 - 77 = 37$ seniors are not attending. Place each joint frequency in its corresponding cell.

Step 2   Find the marginal frequencies. Create a new column and row for the sums. Then add the entries and interpret the results.

		Attendance		
		Attending	**Not Attending**	**Total**
Class	**Junior**	42	64	106	← 106 juniors responded.
	Senior	77	37	114	← 114 seniors responded.
	Total	119	101	220	← 220 students were surveyed.

119 students are attending.   101 students are not attending.

Step 3   Find the sums of the marginal frequencies. Notice the sums $106 + 114 = 220$ and $119 + 101 = 220$ are equal. Place this value at the bottom right.

Monitoring Progress Help in English and Spanish at *BigIdeasMath.com*

1. You randomly survey students about whether they are in favor of planting a community garden at school. Of 96 boys surveyed, 61 are in favor. Of 88 girls surveyed, 17 are against. Organize the results in a two-way table. Then find and interpret the marginal frequencies.

Finding Relative and Conditional Relative Frequencies

You can display values in a two-way table as frequency counts (as in Example 1) or as *relative frequencies*.

 Core Concept

Relative and Conditional Relative Frequencies

A **joint relative frequency** is the ratio of a frequency that is not in the total row or the total column to the total number of values or observations.

A **marginal relative frequency** is the sum of the joint relative frequencies in a row or a column.

A **conditional relative frequency** is the ratio of a joint relative frequency to the marginal relative frequency. You can find a conditional relative frequency using a row total or a column total of a two-way table.

> **STUDY TIP**
>
> Two-way tables can display relative frequencies based on the total number of observations, the row totals, or the column totals.

EXAMPLE 2 Finding Joint and Marginal Relative Frequencies

Use the survey results in Example 1 to make a two-way table that shows the joint and marginal relative frequencies.

SOLUTION

To find the joint relative frequencies, divide each frequency by the total number of students in the survey. Then find the sum of each row and each column to find the marginal relative frequencies.

> **INTERPRETING MATHEMATICAL RESULTS**
>
> Relative frequencies can be interpreted as probabilities. The probability that a randomly selected student is a junior and is *not* attending the concert is 29.1%.

		Attendance		
		Attending	**Not Attending**	**Total**
Class	**Junior**	$\frac{42}{220} \approx 0.191$	$\frac{64}{220} \approx 0.291$	0.482
	Senior	$\frac{77}{220} = 0.35$	$\frac{37}{220} \approx 0.168$	0.518
	Total	0.541	0.459	1

About 29.1% of the students in the survey are juniors and are *not* attending the concert.

About 51.8% of the students in the survey are seniors.

EXAMPLE 3 Finding Conditional Relative Frequencies

Use the survey results in Example 1 to make a two-way table that shows the conditional relative frequencies based on the row totals.

SOLUTION

Use the marginal relative frequency of each *row* to calculate the conditional relative frequencies.

		Attendance	
		Attending	**Not Attending**
Class	**Junior**	$\frac{0.191}{0.482} \approx 0.396$	$\frac{0.291}{0.482} \approx 0.604$
	Senior	$\frac{0.35}{0.518} \approx 0.676$	$\frac{0.168}{0.518} \approx 0.324$

Given that a student is a senior, the conditional relative frequency that he or she is *not* attending the concert is about 32.4%.

2. Use the survey results in Monitoring Progress Question 1 to make a two-way table that shows the joint and marginal relative frequencies.

3. Use the survey results in Example 1 to make a two-way table that shows the conditional relative frequencies based on the column totals. Interpret the conditional relative frequencies in the context of the problem.

4. Use the survey results in Monitoring Progress Question 1 to make a two-way table that shows the conditional relative frequencies based on the row totals. Interpret the conditional relative frequencies in the context of the problem.

Finding Conditional Probabilities

You can use conditional relative frequencies to find conditional probabilities.

EXAMPLE 4   **Finding Conditional Probabilities**

A satellite TV provider surveys customers in three cities. The survey asks whether they would recommend the TV provider to a friend. The results, given as joint relative frequencies, are shown in the two-way table.

<table>
<tr><th rowspan="2">Response</th><th colspan="3">Location</th></tr>
<tr><th>Glendale</th><th>Santa Monica</th><th>Long Beach</th></tr>
<tr><th>Yes</th><td>0.29</td><td>0.27</td><td>0.32</td></tr>
<tr><th>No</th><td>0.05</td><td>0.03</td><td>0.04</td></tr>
</table>

a. What is the probability that a randomly selected customer who is located in Glendale will recommend the provider?

b. What is the probability that a randomly selected customer who will not recommend the provider is located in Long Beach?

c. Determine whether recommending the provider to a friend and living in Long Beach are independent events.

SOLUTION

INTERPRETING MATHEMATICAL RESULTS

The probability 0.853 is a conditional relative frequency based on a column total. The condition is that the customer lives in Glendale.

a. $P(\text{yes} \mid \text{Glendale}) = \dfrac{P(\text{Glendale and yes})}{P(\text{Glendale})} = \dfrac{0.29}{0.29 + 0.05} \approx 0.853$

▶ So, the probability that a customer who is located in Glendale will recommend the provider is about 85.3%.

b. $P(\text{Long Beach} \mid \text{no}) = \dfrac{P(\text{no and Long Beach})}{P(\text{no})} = \dfrac{0.04}{0.05 + 0.03 + 0.04} \approx 0.333$

▶ So, the probability that a customer who will not recommend the provider is located in Long Beach is about 33.3%.

c. Use the formula $P(B) = P(B \mid A)$ and compare $P(\text{Long Beach})$ and $P(\text{Long Beach} \mid \text{yes})$.

$P(\text{Long Beach}) = 0.32 + 0.04 = 0.36$

$P(\text{Long Beach} \mid \text{yes}) = \dfrac{P(\text{Yes and Long Beach})}{P(\text{yes})} = \dfrac{0.32}{0.29 + 0.27 + 0.32} \approx 0.36$

▶ Because $P(\text{Long Beach}) \approx P(\text{Long Beach} \mid \text{yes})$, the two events are independent.

5. In Example 4, what is the probability that a randomly selected customer who is located in Santa Monica will not recommend the provider to a friend?

6. In Example 4, determine whether recommending the provider to a friend and living in Santa Monica are independent events. Explain your reasoning.

EXAMPLE 5 **Comparing Conditional Probabilities**

A jogger wants to burn a certain number of calories during his workout. He maps out three possible jogging routes. Before each workout, he randomly selects a route, and then determines the number of calories he burns and whether he reaches his goal. The table shows his findings. Which route should he use?

	Reaches Goal	Does Not Reach Goal
Route A	JHT JHT I	JHT I
Route B	JHT JHT I	IIII
Route C	JHT JHT II	JHT I

SOLUTION

Step 1 Use the findings to make a two-way table that shows the joint and marginal relative frequencies. There are a total of 50 observations in the table.

Result

Route	Reaches Goal	Does Not Reach Goal	Total
A	0.22	0.12	0.34
B	0.22	0.08	0.30
C	0.24	0.12	0.36
Total	0.68	0.32	1

Step 2 Find the conditional probabilities by dividing each joint relative frequency in the "Reaches Goal" column by the marginal relative frequency in its corresponding row.

$$P(\text{reaches goal} \mid \text{Route A}) = \frac{P(\text{Route A and reaches goal})}{P(\text{Route A})} = \frac{0.22}{0.34} \approx 0.647$$

$$P(\text{reaches goal} \mid \text{Route B}) = \frac{P(\text{Route B and reaches goal})}{P(\text{Route B})} = \frac{0.22}{0.30} \approx 0.733$$

$$P(\text{reaches goal} \mid \text{Route C}) = \frac{P(\text{Route C and reaches goal})}{P(\text{Route C})} = \frac{0.24}{0.36} \approx 0.667$$

▶ Based on the sample, the probability that he reaches his goal is greatest when he uses Route B. So, he should use Route B.

Monitoring Progress Help in English and Spanish at *BigIdeasMath.com*

7. A manager is assessing three employees in order to offer one of them a promotion. Over a period of time, the manager records whether the employees meet or exceed expectations on their assigned tasks. The table shows the manager's results. Which employee should be offered the promotion? Explain.

	Exceed Expectations	Meet Expectations
Joy	JHT IIII	JHT I
Elena	JHT JHT II	JHT III
Sam	JHT JHT I	JHT II

Vocabulary and Core Concept Check

1. **COMPLETE THE SENTENCE** A(n) _____ displays data collected from the same source that belongs to two different categories.

2. **WRITING** Compare the definitions of joint relative frequency, marginal relative frequency, and conditional relative frequency.

Monitoring Progress and Modeling with Mathematics

In Exercises 3 and 4, complete the two-way table.

3.

		Preparation		
		Studied	Did Not Study	Total
Grade	Pass		6	
	Fail			10
	Total	38		50

4.

		Response		
		Yes	No	Total
Role	Student	56		
	Teacher		7	10
	Total		49	

5. **MODELING WITH MATHEMATICS** You survey 171 males and 180 females at Grand Central Station in New York City. Of those, 132 males and 151 females wash their hands after using the public rest rooms. Organize these results in a two-way table. Then find and interpret the marginal frequencies. *(See Example 1.)*

6. **MODELING WITH MATHEMATICS** A survey asks 60 teachers and 48 parents whether school uniforms reduce distractions in school. Of those, 49 teachers and 18 parents say uniforms reduce distractions in school. Organize these results in a two-way table. Then find and interpret the marginal frequencies.

USING STRUCTURE In Exercises 7 and 8, use the two-way table to create a two-way table that shows the joint and marginal relative frequencies.

7.

		Dominant Hand		
		Left	Right	Total
Gender	Female	11	104	115
	Male	24	92	116
	Total	35	196	231

8.

		Gender		
		Male	Female	Total
Experience	Expert	62	6	68
	Average	275	24	299
	Novice	40	3	43
	Total	377	33	410

9. **MODELING WITH MATHEMATICS** Use the survey results from Exercise 5 to make a two-way table that shows the joint and marginal relative frequencies. *(See Example 2.)*

10. **MODELING WITH MATHEMATICS** In a survey, 49 people received a flu vaccine before the flu season and 63 people did not receive the vaccine. Of those who receive the flu vaccine, 16 people got the flu. Of those who did not receive the vaccine, 17 got the flu. Make a two-way table that shows the joint and marginal relative frequencies.

11. MODELING WITH MATHEMATICS A survey finds that 110 people ate breakfast and 30 people skipped breakfast. Of those who ate breakfast, 10 people felt tired. Of those who skipped breakfast, 10 people felt tired. Make a two-way table that shows the conditional relative frequencies based on the breakfast totals. *(See Example 3.)*

12. MODELING WITH MATHEMATICS Use the survey results from Exercise 10 to make a two-way table that shows the conditional relative frequencies based on the flu vaccine totals.

13. PROBLEM SOLVING Three different local hospitals in New York surveyed their patients. The survey asked whether the patient's physician communicated efficiently. The results, given as joint relative frequencies, are shown in the two-way table. *(See Example 4.)*

		Location		
		Glens Falls	Saratoga	Albany
Response	Yes	0.123	0.288	0.338
	No	0.042	0.077	0.131

a. What is the probability that a randomly selected patient located in Saratoga was satisfied with the communication of the physician?

b. What is the probability that a randomly selected patient who was not satisfied with the physician's communication is located in Glens Falls?

c. Determine whether being satisfied with the communication of the physician and living in Saratoga are independent events.

14. PROBLEM SOLVING A researcher surveys a random sample of high school students in seven states. The survey asks whether students plan to stay in their home state after graduation. The results, given as joint relative frequencies, are shown in the two-way table.

		Location		
		Nebraska	North Carolina	Other States
Response	Yes	0.044	0.051	0.056
	No	0.400	0.193	0.256

a. What is the probability that a randomly selected student who lives in Nebraska plans to stay in his or her home state after graduation?

b. What is the probability that a randomly selected student who does not plan to stay in his or her home state after graduation lives in North Carolina?

c. Determine whether planning to stay in their home state and living in Nebraska are independent events.

ERROR ANALYSIS In Exercises 15 and 16, describe and correct the error in finding the given conditional probability.

		City			
		Tokyo	London	Washington, D.C.	Total
Response	Yes	0.049	0.136	0.171	0.356
	No	0.341	0.112	0.191	0.644
	Total	0.39	0.248	0.362	1

15. $P(\text{yes} \mid \text{Tokyo})$

$$\times \quad P(\text{yes} \mid \text{Tokyo}) = \frac{P(\text{Tokyo and yes})}{P(\text{Tokyo})}$$
$$= \frac{0.049}{0.356} \approx 0.138$$

16. $P(\text{London} \mid \text{no})$

$$\times \quad P(\text{London} \mid \text{no}) = \frac{P(\text{no and London})}{P(\text{London})}$$
$$= \frac{0.112}{0.248} \approx 0.452$$

17. PROBLEM SOLVING You want to find the quickest route to school. You map out three routes. Before school, you randomly select a route and record whether you are late or on time. The table shows your findings. Assuming you leave at the same time each morning, which route should you use? Explain. *(See Example 5.)*

	On Time	Late
Route A	JHT II	IIII
Route B	JHT JHT I	III
Route C	JHT JHT II	IIII

18. PROBLEM SOLVING A teacher is assessing three groups of students in order to offer one group a prize. Over a period of time, the teacher records whether the groups meet or exceed expectations on their assigned tasks. The table shows the teacher's results. Which group should be awarded the prize? Explain.

	Exceed Expectations	Meet Expectations
Group 1	JHT JHT II	IIII
Group 2	JHT III	JHT
Group 3	JHT IIII	JHT I

19. OPEN-ENDED Create and conduct a survey in your class. Organize the results in a two-way table. Then create a two-way table that shows the joint and marginal frequencies.

20. HOW DO YOU SEE IT? A research group surveys parents and coaches of high school students about whether competitive sports are important in school. The two-way table shows the results of the survey.

	Role		
	Parent	**Coach**	**Total**
Yes	880	456	1336
No	120	45	165
Total	1000	501	1501

(row label at left: Important)

a. What does 120 represent?

b. What does 1336 represent?

c. What does 1501 represent?

21. MAKING AN ARGUMENT Your friend uses the table below to determine which workout routine is the best. Your friend decides that Routine B is the best option because it has the fewest tally marks in the "Does Not Reach Goal" column. Is your friend correct? Explain your reasoning.

	Reached Goal	**Does Not Reach Goal**
Routine A |卌	|||
Routine B	||||	||
Routine C	卌 ||	||||

22. MODELING WITH MATHEMATICS A survey asks students whether they prefer math class or science class. Of the 150 male students surveyed, 62% prefer math class over science class. Of the female students surveyed, 74% prefer math. Construct a two-way table to show the number of students in each category if 350 students were surveyed.

23. MULTIPLE REPRESENTATIONS Use the Venn diagram to construct a two-way table. Then use your table to answer the questions.

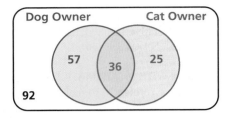

a. What is the probability that a randomly selected person does not own either pet?

b. What is the probability that a randomly selected person who owns a dog also owns a cat?

24. WRITING Compare two-way tables and Venn diagrams. Then describe the advantages and disadvantages of each.

25. PROBLEM SOLVING A company creates a new snack, N, and tests it against its current leader, L. The table shows the results.

	Prefer L	**Prefer N**
Current L Consumer	72	46
Not Current L Consumer	52	114

The company is deciding whether it should try to improve the snack before marketing it, and to whom the snack should be marketed. Use probability to explain the decisions the company should make when the total size of the snack's market is expected to (a) change very little, and (b) expand very rapidly.

26. THOUGHT PROVOKING Bayes' Theorem is given by

$$P(A \mid B) = \frac{P(B \mid A) \cdot P(A)}{P(B)}.$$

Use a two-way table to write an example of Bayes' Theorem.

Maintaining Mathematical Proficiency   *Reviewing what you learned in previous grades and lessons*

Draw a Venn diagram of the sets described.   *(Skills Review Handbook)*

27. Of the positive integers less than 15, set *A* consists of the factors of 15 and set *B* consists of all odd numbers.

28. Of the positive integers less than 14, set *A* consists of all prime numbers and set *B* consists of all even numbers.

29. Of the positive integers less than 24, set *A* consists of the multiples of 2 and set *B* consists of all the multiples of 3.

Core Vocabulary

probability experiment, *p. 280*
outcome, *p. 280*
event, *p. 280*
sample space, *p. 280*
probability of an event, *p. 280*
theoretical probability, *p. 281*

experimental probability, *p. 282*
odds, *p. 283*
independent events, *p. 288*
dependent events, *p. 289*
conditional probability, *p. 289*
two-way table, *p. 296*

joint frequency, *p. 296*
marginal frequency, *p. 296*
joint relative frequency, *p. 297*
marginal relative frequency, *p. 297*
conditional relative frequency,
      p. 297

Core Concepts

Section 5.1

Theoretical Probabilities, *p. 280*
Probability of the Complement of an Event, *p. 281*
Experimental Probabilities, *p. 282*
Odds, *p. 283*

Section 5.2

Probability of Independent Events, *p. 288*
Probability of Dependent Events, *p. 289*
Finding Conditional Probabilities, *p. 291*

Section 5.3

Making Two-Way Tables, *p. 296*
Relative and Conditional Relative Frequencies, *p. 297*

Mathematical Practices

1. How can you use a number line to analyze the error in Exercise 12 on page 284?

2. Explain how you used probability to correct the flawed logic of your friend in Exercise 21 on page 302.

Making a Mental Cheat Sheet

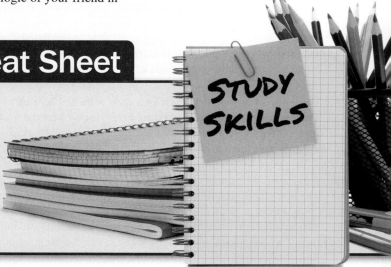

STUDY SKILLS

- Write down important information on note cards.

- Memorize the information on the note cards, placing the ones containing information you know in one stack and the ones containing information you do not know in another stack. Keep working on the information you do not know.

1. You randomly draw a marble out of a bag containing 8 green marbles, 4 blue marbles, 12 yellow marbles, and 10 red marbles. Find the probability of drawing a marble that is not yellow. *(Section 5.1)*

Find $P(\overline{A})$. *(Section 5.1)*

2. $P(A) = 0.32$

3. $P(A) = \frac{8}{9}$

4. $P(A) = 0.01$

5. You roll a six-sided die 30 times. A 5 is rolled 8 times. What is the theoretical probability of rolling a 5? What is the experimental probability of rolling a 5? *(Section 5.1)*

6. You randomly draw one card from a standard deck of 52 playing cards. *(Section 5.1)*

   a. What are the odds that it is a diamond?

   b. What are the odds that it is a 7?

7. Events A and B are independent. Find the missing probability. *(Section 5.2)*

   $P(A) = 0.25$

   $P(B) = $ _____

   $P(A \text{ and } B) = 0.05$

8. Events A and B are dependent. Find the missing probability. *(Section 5.2)*

   $P(A) = 0.6$

   $P(B|A) = 0.2$

   $P(A \text{ and } B) = $ _____

You roll a red six-sided die and a blue six-sided die. Find the probability. *(Section 5.2)*

9. $P(\text{red odd and blue odd})$

10. $P(\text{red and blue both less than 3})$

11. $P(\text{red 2 and blue greater than 1})$

12. A survey asks 13-year-old and 15-year-old students about their eating habits. Four hundred students are surveyed, 100 male students and 100 female students from each age group. The bar graph shows the number of students who said they eat fruit every day. *(Section 5.2)*

    a. Find the probability that a female student, chosen at random from the students surveyed, eats fruit every day.

    b. Find the probability that a 15-year-old student, chosen at random from the students surveyed, eats fruit every day.

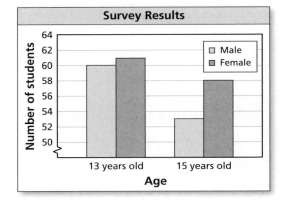

13. At school, 55% of students use public transportation. Twenty-five percent of students use public transportation and participate in an extracurricular activity after school. What is the probability that a student who uses public transportation also participates in an extracurricular activity after school? *(Section 5.2)*

14. There are 14 boys and 18 girls in a class. The teacher allows the students to vote whether they want to take a test on Friday or on Monday. A total of 6 boys and 10 girls vote to take the test on Friday. Organize the information in a two-way table. Then find and interpret the marginal frequencies. *(Section 5.3)*

15. Three schools compete in a cross country invitational. Of the 15 athletes on your team, 9 achieve their goal times. Of the 20 athletes on the home team, 6 achieve their goal times. On your rival's team, 8 of the 13 athletes achieve their goal times. Organize the information in a two-way table. Then determine the probability that a randomly selected runner who achieves his or her goal time is from your school. *(Section 5.3)*

5.4 Probability of Disjoint and Overlapping Events

Essential Question How can you find probabilities of disjoint and overlapping events?

Two events are **disjoint**, or **mutually exclusive**, when they have no outcomes in common. Two events are **overlapping** when they have one or more outcomes in common.

MODELING WITH MATHEMATICS

To be proficient in math, you need to map the relationships between important quantities in a practical situation using such tools as diagrams.

EXPLORATION 1   **Disjoint Events and Overlapping Events**

Work with a partner. A six-sided die is rolled. Draw a Venn diagram that relates the two events. Then decide whether the events are disjoint or overlapping.

a. Event A: The result is an even number.
Event B: The result is a prime number.

b. Event A: The result is 2 or 4.
Event B: The result is an odd number.

EXPLORATION 2   **Finding the Probability that Two Events Occur**

Work with a partner. A six-sided die is rolled. For each pair of events, find (a) $P(A)$, (b) $P(B)$, (c) $P(A \text{ and } B)$, and (d) $P(A \text{ or } B)$.

a. Event A: The result is an even number.
Event B: The result is a prime number.

b. Event A: The result is 2 or 4.
Event B: The result is an odd number.

EXPLORATION 3   **Discovering Probability Formulas**

Work with a partner.

a. In general, if event A and event B are disjoint, then what is the probability that event A or event B will occur? Use a Venn diagram to justify your conclusion.

b. In general, if event A and event B are overlapping, then what is the probability that event A or event B will occur? Use a Venn diagram to justify your conclusion.

c. Conduct an experiment using a six-sided die. Roll the die 50 times and record the results. Then use the results to find the probabilities described in Exploration 2. How closely do your experimental probabilities compare to the theoretical probabilities you found in Exploration 2?

Communicate Your Answer

4. How can you find probabilities of disjoint and overlapping events?

5. Give examples of disjoint events and overlapping events that do not involve dice.

5.4 Lesson

What You Will Learn

▶ Find probabilities of compound events.

▶ Use more than one probability rule to solve real-life problems.

Core Vocabulary

compound event, *p. 306*
overlapping events, *p. 306*
disjoint or mutually exclusive
  events, *p. 306*

Previous
Venn diagram

Compound Events

When you consider all the outcomes for either of two events A and B, you form the *union* of A and B, as shown in the first diagram. When you consider only the outcomes shared by both A and B, you form the *intersection* of A and B, as shown in the second diagram. The union or intersection of two events is called a **compound event**.

  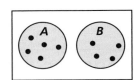

| Union of A and B | Intersection of A and B | Intersection of A and B is empty. |

To find $P(A$ or $B)$ you must consider what outcomes, if any, are in the intersection of A and B. Two events are **overlapping** when they have one or more outcomes in common, as shown in the first two diagrams. Two events are **disjoint**, or **mutually exclusive**, when they have no outcomes in common, as shown in the third diagram.

STUDY TIP

If two events A and B are overlapping, then the outcomes in the intersection of A and B are counted *twice* when $P(A)$ and $P(B)$ are added. So, $P(A$ and $B)$ must be subtracted from the sum.

Core Concept

Probability of Compound Events

If A and B are any two events, then the probability of A or B is

$$P(A \text{ or } B) = P(A) + P(B) - P(A \text{ and } B).$$

If A and B are disjoint events, then the probability of A or B is

$$P(A \text{ or } B) = P(A) + P(B).$$

EXAMPLE 1 **Finding the Probability of Disjoint Events**

A card is randomly selected from a standard deck of 52 playing cards. What is the probability that it is a 10 *or* a face card?

SOLUTION

Let event A be selecting a 10 and event B be selecting a face card. From the diagram, A has 4 outcomes and B has 12 outcomes. Because A and B are disjoint, the probability is

$P(A \text{ or } B) = P(A) + P(B)$	Write disjoint probability formula.
$= \dfrac{4}{52} + \dfrac{12}{52}$	Substitute known probabilities.
$= \dfrac{16}{52}$	Add.
$= \dfrac{4}{13}$	Simplify.
$\approx 0.308.$	Use a calculator.

EXAMPLE 2 **Finding the Probability of Overlapping Events**

A card is randomly selected from a standard deck of 52 playing cards. What is the probability that it is a face card *or* a spade?

SOLUTION

Let event *A* be selecting a face card and event *B* be selecting a spade. From the diagram, *A* has 12 outcomes and *B* has 13 outcomes. Of these, 3 outcomes are common to *A* and *B*. So, the probability of selecting a face card or a spade is

$$P(A \text{ or } B) = P(A) + P(B) - P(A \text{ and } B)$$ Write general formula.

$$= \frac{12}{52} + \frac{13}{52} - \frac{3}{52}$$ Substitute known probabilities.

$$= \frac{22}{52}$$ Add.

$$= \frac{11}{26}$$ Simplify.

$$\approx 0.423.$$ Use a calculator.

EXAMPLE 3 **Using a Formula to Find *P*(*A* and *B*)**

Out of 200 students in a senior class, 113 students are either varsity athletes or on the honor roll. There are 74 seniors who are varsity athletes and 51 seniors who are on the honor roll. What is the probability that a randomly selected senior is both a varsity athlete *and* on the honor roll?

SOLUTION

Let event *A* be selecting a senior who is a varsity athlete and event *B* be selecting a senior on the honor roll. From the given information, you know that $P(A) = \frac{74}{200}$, $P(B) = \frac{51}{200}$, and $P(A \text{ or } B) = \frac{113}{200}$. The probability that a randomly selected senior is both a varsity athlete *and* on the honor roll is *P*(*A* and *B*).

$$P(A \text{ or } B) = P(A) + P(B) - P(A \text{ and } B)$$ Write general formula.

$$\frac{113}{200} = \frac{74}{200} + \frac{51}{200} - P(A \text{ and } B)$$ Substitute known probabilities.

$$P(A \text{ and } B) = \frac{74}{200} + \frac{51}{200} - \frac{113}{200}$$ Solve for *P*(*A* and *B*).

$$P(A \text{ and } B) = \frac{12}{200}$$ Simplify.

$$P(A \text{ and } B) = \frac{3}{50}, \text{ or } 0.06$$ Simplify.

Monitoring Progress Help in English and Spanish at *BigIdeasMath.com*

A card is randomly selected from a standard deck of 52 playing cards. Find the probability of the event.

1. selecting an ace *or* an 8

2. selecting a 10 *or* a diamond

3. WHAT IF? In Example 3, suppose 32 seniors are in the band and 64 seniors are in the band or on the honor roll. What is the probability that a randomly selected senior is both in the band and on the honor roll?

Using More Than One Probability Rule

In the first four sections of this chapter, you have learned several probability rules. The solution to some real-life problems may require the use of two or more of these probability rules, as shown in the next example.

EXAMPLE 4   Solving a Real-Life Problem

The American Diabetes Association estimates that 8.3% of people in the United States have diabetes. Suppose that a medical lab has developed a simple diagnostic test for diabetes that is 98% accurate for people who have the disease and 95% accurate for people who do not have it. The medical lab gives the test to a randomly selected person. What is the probability that the diagnosis is correct?

SOLUTION

Let event A be "person has diabetes" and event B be "correct diagnosis." Notice that the probability of B depends on the occurrence of A, so the events are dependent. When A occurs, $P(B) = 0.98$. When A does not occur, $P(B) = 0.95$.

A probability tree diagram, where the probabilities are given along the branches, can help you see the different ways to obtain a correct diagnosis. Use the complements of events A and B to complete the diagram, where $\overline{A}$ is "person does not have diabetes" and $\overline{B}$ is "incorrect diagnosis." Notice that the probabilities for all branches from the same point must sum to 1.

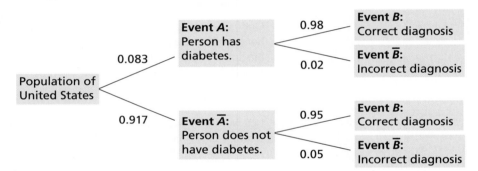

To find the probability that the diagnosis is correct, follow the branches leading to event B.

$$P(B) = P(A \text{ and } B) + P(\overline{A} \text{ and } B) \qquad \text{Use tree diagram.}$$

$$= P(A) \cdot P(B|A) + P(\overline{A}) \cdot P(B|\overline{A}) \qquad \text{Probability of dependent events}$$

$$= (0.083)(0.98) + (0.917)(0.95) \qquad \text{Substitute.}$$

$$\approx 0.952 \qquad \text{Use a calculator.}$$

▶ The probability that the diagnosis is correct is about 0.952, or 95.2%.

Monitoring Progress   🔊 Help in English and Spanish at *BigIdeasMath.com*

4. In Example 4, what is the probability that the diagnosis is *incorrect*?

5. A high school basketball team leads at halftime in 60% of the games in a season. The team wins 80% of the time when they have the halftime lead, but only 10% of the time when they do not. What is the probability that the team wins a particular game during the season?

Vocabulary and Core Concept Check

1. **WRITING** Are the events A and $\overline{A}$ disjoint? Explain. Then give an example of a real-life event and its complement.

2. **DIFFERENT WORDS, SAME QUESTION** Which is different? Find "both" answers.

   How many outcomes are in the intersection of A and B?

   How many outcomes are shared by both A and B?

   How many outcomes are in the union of A and B?

   How many outcomes in B are also in A?

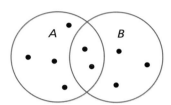

Monitoring Progress and Modeling with Mathematics

In Exercises 3–6, events A and B are disjoint. Find $P(A \text{ or } B)$.

3. $P(A) = 0.3$, $P(B) = 0.1$

4. $P(A) = 0.55$, $P(B) = 0.2$

5. $P(A) = \frac{1}{3}$, $P(B) = \frac{1}{4}$

6. $P(A) = \frac{2}{3}$, $P(B) = \frac{1}{5}$

7. **PROBLEM SOLVING** Your dart is equally likely to hit any point inside the board shown. You throw a dart and pop a balloon. What is the probability that the balloon is red or blue? *(See Example 1.)*

8. **PROBLEM SOLVING** You and your friend are among several candidates running for class president. You estimate that there is a 45% chance you will win and a 25% chance your friend will win. What is the probability that you or your friend win the election?

9. **PROBLEM SOLVING** You are performing an experiment to determine how well plants grow under different light sources. Of the 30 plants in the experiment, 12 receive visible light, 15 receive ultraviolet light, and 6 receive both visible and ultraviolet light. What is the probability that a plant in the experiment receives visible or ultraviolet light? *(See Example 2.)*

10. **PROBLEM SOLVING** Of 162 students honored at an academic awards banquet, 48 won awards for mathematics and 78 won awards for English. There are 14 students who won awards for both mathematics and English. A newspaper chooses a student at random for an interview. What is the probability that the student interviewed won an award for English or mathematics?

ERROR ANALYSIS In Exercises 11 and 12, describe and correct the error in finding the probability of randomly drawing the given card from a standard deck of 52 playing cards.

11.

$P(\text{heart or face card})$
$= P(\text{heart}) + P(\text{face card})$
$= \frac{13}{52} + \frac{12}{52} = \frac{25}{52}$

12.

$P(\text{club or 9})$
$= P(\text{club}) + P(9) + P(\text{club and 9})$
$= \frac{13}{52} + \frac{4}{52} + \frac{1}{52} = \frac{9}{26}$

In Exercises 13 and 14, you roll a six-sided die. Find $P(A \text{ or } B)$.

13. Event A: Roll a 6.
    Event B: Roll a prime number.

14. Event A: Roll an odd number.
    Event B: Roll a number less than 5.

15. **DRAWING CONCLUSIONS** A group of 40 trees in a forest are not growing properly. A botanist determines that 34 of the trees have a disease or are being damaged by insects, with 18 trees having a disease and 20 being damaged by insects. What is the probability that a randomly selected tree has both a disease and is being damaged by insects? *(See Example 3.)*

16. **DRAWING CONCLUSIONS** A company paid overtime wages or hired temporary help during 9 months of the year. Overtime wages were paid during 7 months, and temporary help was hired during 4 months. At the end of the year, an auditor examines the accounting records and randomly selects one month to check the payroll. What is the probability that the auditor will select a month in which the company paid overtime wages and hired temporary help?

17. **DRAWING CONCLUSIONS** A company is focus testing a new type of fruit drink. The focus group is 47% male. Of the responses, 40% of the males and 54% of the females said they would buy the fruit drink. What is the probability that a randomly selected person would buy the fruit drink? *(See Example 4.)*

18. **DRAWING CONCLUSIONS** The Redbirds trail the Bluebirds by one goal with 1 minute left in the hockey game. The Redbirds' coach must decide whether to remove the goalie and add a frontline player. The probabilities of each team scoring are shown in the table.

	Goalie	No goalie
Redbirds score	0.1	0.3
Bluebirds score	0.1	0.6

a. Find the probability that the Redbirds score and the Bluebirds do not score when the coach leaves the goalie in.

b. Find the probability that the Redbirds score and the Bluebirds do not score when the coach takes the goalie out.

c. Based on parts (a) and (b), what should the coach do?

19. **PROBLEM SOLVING** You can win concert tickets from a radio station if you are the first person to call when the song of the day is played, or if you are the first person to correctly answer the trivia question. The song of the day is announced at a random time between 7:00 and 7:30 A.M. The trivia question is asked at a random time between 7:15 and 7:45 A.M. You begin listening to the radio station at 7:20. Find the probability that you miss the announcement of the song of the day or the trivia question.

20. **HOW DO YOU SEE IT?** Are events A and B disjoint events? Explain your reasoning.

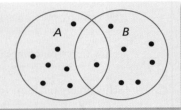

21. **PROBLEM SOLVING** You take a bus from your neighborhood to your school. The express bus arrives at your neighborhood at a random time between 7:30 and 7:36 A.M. The local bus arrives at your neighborhood at a random time between 7:30 and 7:40 A.M. You arrive at the bus stop at 7:33 A.M. Find the probability that you missed both the express bus and the local bus.

22. **THOUGHT PROVOKING** Write a general rule for finding $P(A \text{ or } B \text{ or } C)$ for (a) disjoint and (b) overlapping events A, B, and C.

23. **MAKING AN ARGUMENT** A bag contains 40 cards numbered 1 through 40 that are either red or blue. A card is drawn at random and placed back in the bag. This is done four times. Two red cards are drawn, numbered 31 and 19, and two blue cards are drawn, numbered 22 and 7. Your friend concludes that red cards and even numbers must be mutually exclusive. Is your friend correct? Explain.

Maintaining Mathematical Proficiency
Reviewing what you learned in previous grades and lessons

Graph the function. Compare the graph to the graph of $f(x) = x^2$. *(Section 3.1)*

24. $r(x) = 3x^2$

25. $g(x) = \frac{3}{4}x^2$

26. $h(x) = -5x^2$

Essential Question   How can a tree diagram help you visualize the number of ways in which two or more events can occur?

EXPLORATION 1   **Reading a Tree Diagram**

Work with a partner. Two coins are flipped and the spinner is spun. The tree diagram shows the possible outcomes.

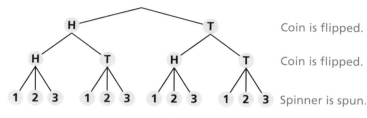

Coin is flipped.

Coin is flipped.

Spinner is spun.

a. How many outcomes are possible?

b. List the possible outcomes.

EXPLORATION 2   **Reading a Tree Diagram**

Work with a partner. Consider the tree diagram below.

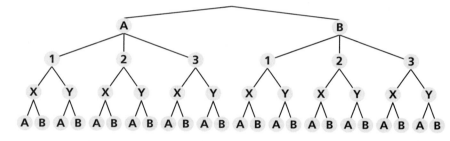

a. How many events are shown?   **b.** What outcomes are possible for each event?

c. How many outcomes are possible?   **d.** List the possible outcomes.

CONSTRUCTING VIABLE ARGUMENTS

To be proficient in math, you need to make conjectures and build a logical progression of statements to explore the truth of your conjectures.

EXPLORATION 3   **Writing a Conjecture**

Work with a partner.

a. Consider the following general problem: Event 1 can occur in *m* ways and event 2 can occur in *n* ways. Write a conjecture about the number of ways the two events can occur. Explain your reasoning.

b. Use the conjecture you wrote in part (a) to write a conjecture about the number of ways *more than* two events can occur. Explain your reasoning.

c. Use the results of Explorations 1(a) and 2(c) to verify your conjectures.

Communicate Your Answer

4. How can a tree diagram help you visualize the number of ways in which two or more events can occur?

5. In Exploration 1, the spinner is spun a second time. How many outcomes are possible?

What You Will Learn

▷ Use the formula for the number of permutations.

▷ Use the formula for the number of combinations.

Core Vocabulary

permutation, *p. 312*
n factorial, *p. 312*
combination, *p. 314*

Previous
Fundamental Counting
 Principle

Permutations

A **permutation** is an arrangement of objects in which order is important. For instance, the 6 possible permutations of the letters A, B, and C are shown.

ABC   ACB   BAC   BCA   CAB   CBA

EXAMPLE 1   Counting Permutations

Consider the number of permutations of the letters in the word JULY. In how many ways can you arrange (a) all of the letters and (b) 2 of the letters?

SOLUTION

a. Use the Fundamental Counting Principle to find the number of permutations of the letters in the word JULY.

$$\text{Number of permutations} = \left(\begin{array}{c}\text{Choices for}\\ \text{1st letter}\end{array}\right)\left(\begin{array}{c}\text{Choices for}\\ \text{2nd letter}\end{array}\right)\left(\begin{array}{c}\text{Choices for}\\ \text{3rd letter}\end{array}\right)\left(\begin{array}{c}\text{Choices for}\\ \text{4th letter}\end{array}\right)$$

$$= 4 \cdot 3 \cdot 2 \cdot 1$$

$$= 24$$

▷ There are 24 ways you can arrange all of the letters in the word JULY.

b. When arranging 2 letters of the word JULY, you have 4 choices for the first letter and 3 choices for the second letter.

$$\text{Number of permutations} = \left(\begin{array}{c}\text{Choices for}\\ \text{1st letter}\end{array}\right)\left(\begin{array}{c}\text{Choices for}\\ \text{2nd letter}\end{array}\right)$$

$$= 4 \cdot 3$$

$$= 12$$

▷ There are 12 ways you can arrange 2 of the letters in the word JULY.

Monitoring Progress   Help in English and Spanish at *BigIdeasMath.com*

1. In how many ways can you arrange the letters in the word HOUSE?

2. In how many ways can you arrange 3 of the letters in the word MARCH?

In Example 1(a), you evaluated the expression 4 • 3 • 2 • 1. This expression can be written as 4! and is read "4 *factorial.*" For any positive integer *n*, the product of the integers from 1 to *n* is called **n factorial** and is written as

$$n! = n \cdot (n - 1) \cdot (n - 2) \cdot \cdots \cdot 3 \cdot 2 \cdot 1.$$

As a special case, the value of 0! is defined to be 1.

In Example 1(b), you found the permutations of 4 objects taken 2 at a time. You can find the number of permutations using the formulas on the next page.

REMEMBER

Fundamental Counting Principle: If one event can occur in *m* ways and another event can occur in *n* ways, then the number of ways that both events can occur is *m • n*. The Fundamental Counting Principle can be extended to three or more events.

Core Concept

Permutations

Formulas	Examples

Formulas

The number of permutations of n objects is given by

$$_nP_n = n!.$$

The number of permutations of n objects taken r at a time, where $r \leq n$, is given by

$$_nP_r = \frac{n!}{(n-r)!}.$$

Examples

The number of permutations of 4 objects is

$$_4P_4 = 4! = 4 \cdot 3 \cdot 2 \cdot 1 = 24.$$

The number of permutations of 4 objects taken 2 at a time is

$$_4P_2 = \frac{4!}{(4-2)!} = \frac{4 \cdot 3 \cdot 2!}{2!} = 12.$$

EXAMPLE 2   Using a Permutations Formula

Ten horses are running in a race. In how many different ways can the horses finish first, second, and third? (Assume there are no ties.)

SOLUTION

To find the number of permutations of 3 horses chosen from 10, find $_{10}P_3$.

$$_{10}P_3 = \frac{10!}{(10-3)!} \qquad \text{Permutations formula}$$

$$= \frac{10!}{7!} \qquad \text{Subtract.}$$

$$= \frac{10 \cdot 9 \cdot 8 \cdot 7!}{7!} \qquad \text{Expand factorial. Divide out common factor, 7!.}$$

$$= 720 \qquad \text{Simplify.}$$

> There are 720 ways for the horses to finish first, second, and third.

STUDY TIP

When you divide out common factors, remember that 7! is a factor of 10!.

EXAMPLE 3   Finding a Probability Using Permutations

For a town parade, you will ride on a float with your soccer team. There are 12 floats in the parade, and their order is chosen at random. Find the probability that your float is first and the float with the school chorus is second.

SOLUTION

Step 1 Write the number of possible outcomes as the number of permutations of the 12 floats in the parade. This is $_{12}P_{12} = 12!$.

Step 2 Write the number of favorable outcomes as the number of permutations of the other floats, given that the soccer team is first and the chorus is second. This is $_{10}P_{10} = 10!$.

Step 3 Find the probability.

$$P(\text{soccer team is 1st, chorus is 2nd}) = \frac{10!}{12!} \qquad \text{Form a ratio of favorable to possible outcomes.}$$

$$= \frac{10!}{12 \cdot 11 \cdot 10!} \qquad \text{Expand factorial. Divide out common factor, 10!.}$$

$$= \frac{1}{132} \qquad \text{Simplify.}$$

3. **WHAT IF?** In Example 2, suppose there are 8 horses in the race. In how many different ways can the horses finish first, second, and third? (Assume there are no ties.)

4. **WHAT IF?** In Example 3, suppose there are 14 floats in the parade. Find the probability that the soccer team is first and the chorus is second.

Combinations

A **combination** is a selection of objects in which order is *not* important. For instance, in a drawing for 3 identical prizes, you would use combinations, because the order of the winners would not matter. If the prizes were different, then you would use permutations, because the order would matter.

| EXAMPLE 4 | **Counting Combinations** |

Count the possible combinations of 2 letters chosen from the list A, B, C, D.

SOLUTION

List all of the permutations of 2 letters from the list A, B, C, D. Because order is not important in a combination, cross out any duplicate pairs.

AB   AC   AD   B̶A̶   BC   BD   BD and DB are the same pair.

C̶A̶   C̶B̶   CD   D̶A̶   D̶B̶   D̶C̶

▶ There are 6 possible combinations of 2 letters from the list A, B, C, D.

Monitoring Progress Help in English and Spanish at *BigIdeasMath.com*

5. Count the possible combinations of 3 letters chosen from the list A, B, C, D, E.

In Example 4, you found the number of combinations of objects by making an organized list. You can also find the number of combinations using the following formula.

USING A GRAPHING CALCULATOR

Most graphing calculators can calculate combinations.

Core Concept

Combinations

Formula The number of combinations of n objects taken r at a time, where $r \leq n$, is given by

$$_nC_r = \frac{n!}{(n-r)! \cdot r!}.$$

Example The number of combinations of 4 objects taken 2 at a time is

$$_4C_2 = \frac{4!}{(4-2)! \cdot 2!} = \frac{4 \cdot 3 \cdot 2!}{2! \cdot (2 \cdot 1)} = 6.$$

EXAMPLE 5 Using the Combinations Formula

You order a sandwich at a restaurant. You can choose 2 side dishes from a list of 8. How many combinations of side dishes are possible?

SOLUTION

The order in which you choose the side dishes is not important. So, to find the number of combinations of 8 side dishes taken 2 at a time, find $_8C_2$.

Check

```
8  nCr  2
                    28
```

$$_8C_2 = \frac{8!}{(8-2)! \cdot 2!}$$ Combinations formula

$$= \frac{8!}{6! \cdot 2!}$$ Subtract.

$$= \frac{8 \cdot 7 \cdot \cancel{6!}}{\cancel{6!} \cdot (2 \cdot 1)}$$ Expand factorials. Divide out common factor, 6!.

$$= 28$$ Multiply.

▶ There are 28 different combinations of side dishes you can order.

EXAMPLE 6 Finding a Probability Using Combinations

A yearbook editor has selected 14 photos, including one of you and one of your friend, to use in a collage for the yearbook. The photos are placed at random. There is room for 2 photos at the top of the page. What is the probability that your photo and your friend's photo are the 2 placed at the top of the page?

SOLUTION

Step 1 Write the number of possible outcomes as the number of combinations of 14 photos taken 2 at a time, or $_{14}C_2$, because the order in which the photos are chosen is not important.

$$_{14}C_2 = \frac{14!}{(14-2)! \cdot 2!}$$ Combinations formula

$$= \frac{14!}{12! \cdot 2!}$$ Subtract.

$$= \frac{14 \cdot 13 \cdot \cancel{12!}}{\cancel{12!} \cdot (2 \cdot 1)}$$ Expand factorials. Divide out common factor, 12!.

$$= 91$$ Multiply.

Step 2 Find the number of favorable outcomes. Only one of the possible combinations includes your photo and your friend's photo.

Step 3 Find the probability.

$$P(\text{your photo and your friend's photos are chosen}) = \frac{1}{91}$$

Monitoring Progress Help in English and Spanish at *BigIdeasMath.com*

6. **WHAT IF?** In Example 5, suppose you can choose 3 side dishes out of the list of 8 side dishes. How many combinations are possible?

7. **WHAT IF?** In Example 6, suppose there are 20 photos in the collage. Find the probability that your photo and your friend's photo are the 2 placed at the top of the page.

Vocabulary and Core Concept Check

1. **COMPLETE THE SENTENCE** An arrangement of objects in which order is important is called a(n) _____.

2. **WHICH ONE DOESN'T BELONG?** Which expression does *not* belong with the other three? Explain your reasoning.

$$\frac{7!}{2! \cdot 5!}$$ $${}_7C_5$$ $${}_7C_2$$ $$\frac{7!}{(7-2)!}$$

Monitoring Progress and Modeling with Mathematics

In Exercises 3–8, find the number of ways you can arrange (a) all of the letters and (b) 2 of the letters in the given word. *(See Example 1.)*

3. AT

4. TRY

5. ROCK

6. WATER

7. FAMILY

8. FLOWERS

In Exercises 9–16, evaluate the expression.

9. $${}_5P_2$$

10. $${}_7P_3$$

11. $${}_9P_1$$

12. $${}_6P_5$$

13. $${}_8P_6$$

14. $${}_{12}P_0$$

15. $${}_{30}P_2$$

16. $${}_{25}P_5$$

17. **PROBLEM SOLVING** Eleven students are competing in an art contest. In how many different ways can the students finish first, second, and third? *(See Example 2.)*

18. **PROBLEM SOLVING** Six friends go to a movie theater. In how many different ways can they sit together in a row of 6 empty seats?

19. **PROBLEM SOLVING** You and your friend are 2 of 8 servers working a shift in a restaurant. At the beginning of the shift, the manager randomly assigns one section to each server. Find the probability that you are assigned Section 1 and your friend is assigned Section 2. *(See Example 3.)*

20. **PROBLEM SOLVING** You make 6 posters to hold up at a basketball game. Each poster has a letter of the word TIGERS. You and 5 friends sit next to each other in a row. The posters are distributed at random. Find the probability that TIGERS is spelled correctly when you hold up the posters.

In Exercises 21–24, count the possible combinations of *r* letters chosen from the given list. *(See Example 4.)*

21. A, B, C, D; $r = 3$

22. L, M, N, O; $r = 2$

23. U, V, W, X, Y, Z; $r = 3$

24. D, E, F, G, H; $r = 4$

In Exercises 25–32, evaluate the expression.

25. $${}_5C_1$$

26. $${}_8C_5$$

27. $${}_9C_9$$

28. $${}_8C_6$$

29. $${}_{12}C_3$$

30. $${}_{11}C_4$$

31. $${}_{15}C_8$$

32. $${}_{20}C_5$$

33. **PROBLEM SOLVING** Each year, 64 golfers participate in a golf tournament. The golfers play in groups of 4. How many groups of 4 golfers are possible? *(See Example 5.)*

34. PROBLEM SOLVING You want to purchase vegetable dip for a party. A grocery store sells 7 different flavors of vegetable dip. You have enough money to purchase 2 flavors. How many combinations of 2 flavors of vegetable dip are possible?

ERROR ANALYSIS In Exercises 35 and 36, describe and correct the error in evaluating the expression.

35.
$$\times \quad {}_{11}P_7 = \frac{11!}{(11-7)} = \frac{11!}{4} = 9{,}979{,}200$$

36.
$$\times \quad {}_9C_4 = \frac{9!}{(9-4)!} = \frac{9!}{5!} = 3024$$

REASONING In Exercises 37–40, tell whether the question can be answered using *permutations* or *combinations*. Explain your reasoning. Then answer the question.

37. To complete an exam, you must answer 8 questions from a list of 10 questions. In how many ways can you complete the exam?

38. Ten students are auditioning for 3 different roles in a play. In how many ways can the 3 roles be filled?

39. Fifty-two athletes are competing in a bicycle race. In how many orders can the bicyclists finish first, second, and third? (Assume there are no ties.)

40. An employee at a pet store needs to catch 5 tetras in an aquarium containing 27 tetras. In how many groupings can the employee capture 5 tetras?

41. CRITICAL THINKING Compare the quantities ${}_{50}C_9$ and ${}_{50}C_{41}$ without performing any calculations. Explain your reasoning.

42. CRITICAL THINKING Show that each identity is true for any whole numbers r and n, where $0 \le r \le n$.

    a. ${}_nC_n = 1$ **b.** ${}_nC_r = {}_nC_{n-r}$

    c. ${}_{n+1}C_r = {}_nC_r + {}_nC_{r-1}$

43. REASONING Complete the table for each given value of r. Then write an inequality relating ${}_nP_r$ and ${}_nC_r$. Explain your reasoning.

	$r = 0$	$r = 1$	$r = 2$	$r = 3$
${}_3P_r$				
${}_3C_r$				

44. REASONING Write an equation that relates ${}_nP_r$ and ${}_nC_r$. Then use your equation to find and interpret the value of $\dfrac{{}_{182}P_4}{{}_{182}C_4}$.

45. PROBLEM SOLVING You and your friend are in the studio audience on a television game show. From an audience of 300 people, 2 people are randomly selected as contestants. What is the probability that you and your friend are chosen? *(See Example 6.)*

46. PROBLEM SOLVING You work 5 evenings each week at a bookstore. Your supervisor assigns you 5 evenings at random from the 7 possibilities. What is the probability that your schedule does not include working on the weekend?

REASONING In Exercises 47 and 48, find the probability of winning a lottery using the given rules. Assume that lottery numbers are selected at random.

47. You must correctly select 6 numbers, each an integer from 0 to 49. The order is not important.

48. You must correctly select 4 numbers, each an integer from 0 to 9. The order is important.

49. MATHEMATICAL CONNECTIONS
A polygon is convex when no line that contains a side of the polygon contains a point in the interior of the polygon. Consider a convex polygon with n sides.

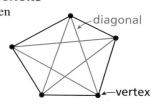

    a. Use the combinations formula to write an expression for the number of diagonals in an n-sided polygon.

    b. Use your result from part (a) to write a formula for the number of diagonals of an n-sided convex polygon.

50. PROBLEM SOLVING You are ordering a burrito with 2 main ingredients and 3 toppings. The menu below shows the possible choices. How many different burritos are possible?

51. PROBLEM SOLVING You want to purchase 2 different types of contemporary music CDs and 1 classical music CD from the music collection shown. How many different sets of music types can you choose for your purchase?

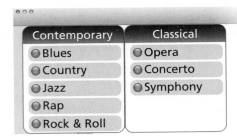

Contemporary
- Blues
- Country
- Jazz
- Rap
- Rock & Roll

Classical
- Opera
- Concerto
- Symphony

52. HOW DO YOU SEE IT? A bag contains one green marble, one red marble, and one blue marble. The diagram shows the possible outcomes of randomly drawing three marbles from the bag without replacement.

1st Draw   2nd Draw   3rd Draw

a. How many combinations of three marbles can be drawn from the bag? Explain.

b. How many permutations of three marbles can be drawn from the bag? Explain.

53. PROBLEM SOLVING Every student in your history class is required to present a project in front of the class. Each day, 4 students make their presentations in an order chosen at random by the teacher. You make your presentation on the first day.

a. What is the probability that you are chosen to be the first or second presenter on the first day?

b. What is the probability that you are chosen to be the second or third presenter on the first day? Compare your answer with that in part (a).

54. PROBLEM SOLVING The organizer of a cast party for a drama club asks each of the 6 cast members to bring 1 food item from a list of 10 items. Assuming each member randomly chooses a food item to bring, what is the probability that at least 2 of the 6 cast members bring the same item?

55. PROBLEM SOLVING You are one of 10 students performing in a school talent show. The order of the performances is determined at random. The first 5 performers go on stage before the intermission.

a. What is the probability that you are the last performer before the intermission and your rival performs immediately before you?

b. What is the probability that you are *not* the first performer?

56. THOUGHT PROVOKING How many integers, greater than 999 but not greater than 4000, can be formed with the digits 0, 1, 2, 3, and 4? Repetition of digits is allowed.

57. PROBLEM SOLVING There are 30 students in your class. Your science teacher chooses 5 students at random to complete a group project. Find the probability that you and your 2 best friends in the science class are chosen to work in the group. Explain how you found your answer.

58. PROBLEM SOLVING Follow the steps below to explore a famous probability problem called the *birthday problem*. (Assume there are 365 equally likely birthdays possible.)

a. What is the probability that at least 2 people share the same birthday in a group of 6 randomly chosen people? in a group of 10 randomly chosen people?

b. Generalize the results from part (a) by writing a formula for the probability $P(n)$ that at least 2 people in a group of n people share the same birthday. (*Hint:* Use $_nP_r$ notation in your formula.)

c. Enter the formula from part (b) into a graphing calculator. Use the *table* feature to make a table of values. For what group size does the probability that at least 2 people share the same birthday first exceed 50%?

Maintaining Mathematical Proficiency
Reviewing what you learned in previous grades and lessons

59. A bag contains 12 white marbles and 3 black marbles. You pick 1 marble at random. What is the probability that you pick a black marble? *(Section 5.1)*

60. The table shows the results of flipping two coins 12 times. For what outcome is the experimental probability the same as the theoretical probability? *(Section 5.1)*

HH	HT	TH	TT
2	6	3	1

5.6 Binomial Distributions

Essential Question How can you determine the frequency of each outcome of an event?

EXPLORATION 1 **Analyzing Histograms**

Work with a partner. The histograms show the results when *n* coins are flipped.

STUDY TIP

When 4 coins are flipped (*n* = 4), the possible outcomes are

TTTT TTTH TTHT TTHH

THTT THTH THHT THHH

HTTT HTTH HTHT HTHH

HHTT HHTH HHHT HHHH.

The histogram shows the numbers of outcomes having 0, 1, 2, 3, and 4 heads.

Number of Heads ($n = 1$)

Number of Heads ($n = 2$)

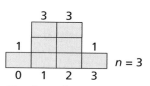

Number of Heads ($n = 3$)

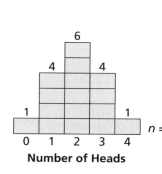

Number of Heads ($n = 4$)

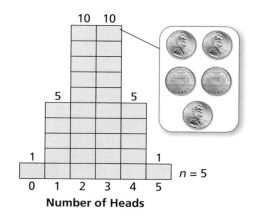

Number of Heads ($n = 5$)

a. In how many ways can 3 heads occur when 5 coins are flipped?

b. Draw a histogram that shows the numbers of heads that can occur when 6 coins are flipped.

c. In how many ways can 3 heads occur when 6 coins are flipped?

EXPLORATION 2 **Determining the Number of Occurrences**

Work with a partner.

a. Complete the table showing the numbers of ways in which 2 heads can occur when *n* coins are flipped.

LOOKING FOR A PATTERN

To be proficient in math, you need to look closely to discern a pattern or structure.

n	3	4	5	6	7
Occurrences of 2 heads					

b. Determine the pattern shown in the table. Use your result to find the number of ways in which 2 heads can occur when 8 coins are flipped.

Communicate Your Answer

3. How can you determine the frequency of each outcome of an event?

4. How can you use a histogram to find the probability of an event?

What You Will Learn

▶ Construct and interpret probability distributions.

▶ Construct and interpret binomial distributions.

Probability Distributions

A **random variable** is a variable whose value is determined by the outcomes of a probability experiment. For example, when you roll a six-sided die, you can define a random variable x that represents the number showing on the die. So, the possible values of x are 1, 2, 3, 4, 5, and 6. For every random variable, a *probability distribution* can be defined.

Core Concept

Probability Distributions

A **probability distribution** is a function that gives the probability of each possible value of a random variable. The sum of all the probabilities in a probability distribution must equal 1.

Probability Distribution for Rolling a Six-Sided Die						
x	1	2	3	4	5	6
$P(x)$	$\frac{1}{6}$	$\frac{1}{6}$	$\frac{1}{6}$	$\frac{1}{6}$	$\frac{1}{6}$	$\frac{1}{6}$

EXAMPLE 1 Constructing a Probability Distribution

Let x be a random variable that represents the sum when two six-sided dice are rolled. Make a table and draw a histogram showing the probability distribution for x.

SOLUTION

Step 1 Make a table. The possible values of x are the integers from 2 to 12. The table shows how many outcomes of rolling two dice produce each value of x. Divide the number of outcomes for x by 36 to find $P(x)$.

x (sum)	2	3	4	5	6	7	8	9	10	11	12
Outcomes	1	2	3	4	5	6	5	4	3	2	1
$P(x)$	$\frac{1}{36}$	$\frac{1}{18}$	$\frac{1}{12}$	$\frac{1}{9}$	$\frac{5}{36}$	$\frac{1}{6}$	$\frac{5}{36}$	$\frac{1}{9}$	$\frac{1}{12}$	$\frac{1}{18}$	$\frac{1}{36}$

STUDY TIP

Recall that there are 36 possible outcomes when rolling two six-sided dice. These are listed in Example 3 on page 282.

Step 2 Draw a histogram where the intervals are given by x and the frequencies are given by $P(x)$.

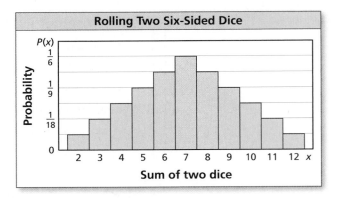

EXAMPLE 2   **Interpreting a Probability Distribution**

Use the probability distribution in Example 1 to answer each question.

a. What is the most likely sum when rolling two six-sided dice?

b. What is the probability that the sum of the two dice is at least 10?

SOLUTION

a. The most likely sum when rolling two six-sided dice is the value of x for which $P(x)$ is greatest. This probability is greatest for $x = 7$. So, when rolling the two dice, the most likely sum is 7.

b. The probability that the sum of the two dice is at least 10 is

$$P(x \geq 10) = P(x = 10) + P(x = 11) + P(x = 12)$$

$$= \tfrac{3}{36} + \tfrac{2}{36} + \tfrac{1}{36}$$

$$= \tfrac{6}{36}$$

$$= \tfrac{1}{6}$$

$$\approx 0.167.$$

▶ The probability is about 16.7%.

Monitoring Progress Help in English and Spanish at *BigIdeasMath.com*

An octahedral die has eight sides numbered 1 through 8. Let x be a random variable that represents the sum when two such dice are rolled.

1. Make a table and draw a histogram showing the probability distribution for x.

2. What is the most likely sum when rolling the two dice?

3. What is the probability that the sum of the two dice is at most 3?

Binomial Distributions

One type of probability distribution is a **binomial distribution**. A binomial distribution shows the probabilities of the outcomes of a *binomial experiment*.

 Core Concept

Binomial Experiments

A **binomial experiment** meets the following conditions.

- There are n independent trials.

- Each trial has only two possible outcomes: success and failure.

- The probability of success is the same for each trial. This probability is denoted by p. The probability of failure is $1 - p$.

For a binomial experiment, the probability of exactly k successes in n trials is

$$P(k \text{ successes}) = {}_nC_k p^k (1 - p)^{n-k}.$$

EXAMPLE 3 Constructing a Binomial Distribution

According to a survey, about 33% of people ages 16 and older in the U.S. own an electronic book reading device, or e-reader. You ask 6 randomly chosen people (ages 16 and older) whether they own an e-reader. Draw a histogram of the binomial distribution for your survey.

SOLUTION

The probability that a randomly selected person has an e-reader is $p = 0.33$. Because you survey 6 people, $n = 6$.

$P(k = 0) = {_6}C_0(0.33)^0(0.67)^6 \approx 0.090$

$P(k = 1) = {_6}C_1(0.33)^1(0.67)^5 \approx 0.267$

$P(k = 2) = {_6}C_2(0.33)^2(0.67)^4 \approx 0.329$

$P(k = 3) = {_6}C_3(0.33)^3(0.67)^3 \approx 0.216$

$P(k = 4) = {_6}C_4(0.33)^4(0.67)^2 \approx 0.080$

$P(k = 5) = {_6}C_5(0.33)^5(0.67)^1 \approx 0.016$

$P(k = 6) = {_6}C_6(0.33)^6(0.67)^0 \approx 0.001$

ATTENDING TO PRECISION

When probabilities are rounded, the sum of the probabilities may differ slightly from 1.

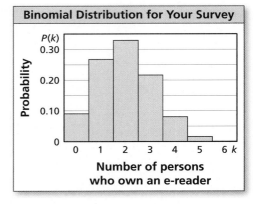

A histogram of the distribution is shown.

EXAMPLE 4 Interpreting a Binomial Distribution

Use the binomial distribution in Example 3 to answer each question.

a. What is the most likely outcome of the survey?

b. What is the probability that at most 2 people have an e-reader?

SOLUTION

a. The most likely outcome of the survey is the value of k for which $P(k)$ is greatest. This probability is greatest for $k = 2$. The most likely outcome is that 2 of the 6 people own an e-reader.

b. The probability that at most 2 people have an e-reader is

$$P(k \leq 2) = P(k = 0) + P(k = 1) + P(k = 2)$$

$$\approx 0.090 + 0.267 + 0.329$$

$$\approx 0.686.$$

▶ The probability is about 68.6%.

COMMON ERROR

Because a person may not have an e-reader, be sure you include $P(k = 0)$ when finding the probability that at most 2 people have an e-reader.

Monitoring Progress Help in English and Spanish at *BigIdeasMath.com*

According to a survey, about 85% of people ages 18 and older in the U.S. use the Internet or e-mail. You ask 4 randomly chosen people (ages 18 and older) whether they use the Internet or e-mail.

4. Draw a histogram of the binomial distribution for your survey.

5. What is the most likely outcome of your survey?

6. What is the probability that at most 2 people you survey use the Internet or e-mail?

Vocabulary and Core Concept Check

1. **VOCABULARY** What is a random variable?

2. **WRITING** Give an example of a binomial experiment and describe how it meets the conditions of a binomial experiment.

Monitoring Progress and Modeling with Mathematics

In Exercises 3–6, make a table and draw a histogram showing the probability distribution for the random variable. *(See Example 1.)*

3. x = the number on a table tennis ball randomly chosen from a bag that contains 5 balls labeled "1," 3 balls labeled "2," and 2 balls labeled "3."

4. $c = 1$ when a randomly chosen card out of a standard deck of 52 playing cards is a heart and $c = 2$ otherwise.

5. $w = 1$ when a randomly chosen letter from the English alphabet is a vowel and $w = 2$ otherwise.

6. n = the number of digits in a random integer from 0 through 999.

In Exercises 7 and 8, use the probability distribution to determine (a) the number that is most likely to be spun on a spinner, and (b) the probability of spinning an even number. *(See Example 2.)*

7.

8.

USING EQUATIONS In Exercises 9–12, calculate the probability of flipping a coin 20 times and getting the given number of heads.

9. 1

10. 4

11. 18

12. 20

13. **MODELING WITH MATHEMATICS** According to a survey, 27% of high school students in the United States buy a class ring. You ask 6 randomly chosen high school students whether they own a class ring. *(See Examples 3 and 4.)*

a. Draw a histogram of the binomial distribution for your survey.

b. What is the most likely outcome of your survey?

c. What is the probability that at most 2 people have a class ring?

14. **MODELING WITH MATHEMATICS** According to a survey, 48% of adults in the United States believe that Unidentified Flying Objects (UFOs) are observing our planet. You ask 8 randomly chosen adults whether they believe UFOs are watching Earth.

a. Draw a histogram of the binomial distribution for your survey.

b. What is the most likely outcome of your survey?

c. What is the probability that at most 3 people believe UFOs are watching Earth?

ERROR ANALYSIS In Exercises 15 and 16, describe and correct the error in calculating the probability of rolling a 1 exactly 3 times in 5 rolls of a six-sided die.

15.

✗ $P(k = 3) = {}_5C_3\left(\frac{1}{6}\right)^{5-3}\left(\frac{5}{6}\right)^3$

  ≈ 0.161

16.

✗ $P(k = 3) = \left(\frac{1}{6}\right)^3\left(\frac{5}{6}\right)^{5-3}$

  ≈ 0.003

17. MATHEMATICAL CONNECTIONS At most 7 gopher holes appear each week on the farm shown. Let x represent how many of the gopher holes appear in the carrot patch. Assume that a gopher hole has an equal chance of appearing at any point on the farm.

0.8 mi

0.5 mi

0.3 mi   0.3 mi

  a. Find $P(x)$ for $x = 0, 1, 2, \ldots, 7$. (*Note:* The probability of a gopher hole appearing in the carrot patch is equal to the ratio of the area of the carrot patch to the area of the entire farm.)

  b. Make a table showing the probability distribution for x.

  c. Make a histogram showing the probability distribution for x.

18. HOW DO YOU SEE IT? Complete the probability distribution for the random variable x. What is the probability the value of x is greater than 2?

x	1	2	3	4
P(x)	0.1	0.3	0.4	

19. MAKING AN ARGUMENT The binomial distribution shows the results of a binomial experiment. Your friend claims that the probability p of a success must be greater than the probability $1 - p$ of a failure. Is your friend correct? Explain your reasoning.

20. THOUGHT PROVOKING There are 100 coins in a bag. Only one of them has a date of 2010. You choose a coin at random, check the date, and then put the coin back in the bag. You repeat this 100 times. Are you certain of choosing the 2010 coin at least once? Explain your reasoning.

21. MODELING WITH MATHEMATICS Assume that having a male and having a female child are independent events, and that the probability of each is 0.5.

  a. A couple has 4 male children. Evaluate the validity of this statement: "The first 4 kids were all boys, so the next one will probably be a girl."

  b. What is the probability of having 4 male children and then a female child?

  c. Let x be a random variable that represents the number of children a couple already has when they have their first female child. Draw a histogram of the distribution of $P(x)$ for $0 \le x \le 10$. Describe the shape of the histogram.

22. CRITICAL THINKING An entertainment system has n speakers. Each speaker will function properly with probability p, independent of whether the other speakers are functioning. The system will operate effectively when at least 50% of its speakers are functioning. For what values of p is a 5-speaker system more likely to operate than a 3-speaker system?

Maintaining Mathematical Proficiency   Reviewing what you learned in previous grades and lessons

List the possible outcomes for the situation.   (*Section 5.1*)

23. guessing the gender of three children

24. picking one of two doors and one of three curtains

Core Vocabulary

compound event, *p. 306*
overlapping events, *p. 306*
disjoint events, *p. 306*
mutually exclusive events, *p. 306*

permutation, *p. 312*
n factorial, *p. 312*
combination, *p. 314*
random variable, *p. 320*

probability distribution, *p. 320*
binomial distribution, *p. 321*
binomial experiment, *p. 321*

Core Concepts

Section 5.4

Probability of Compound Events, *p. 306*

Section 5.5

Permutations, *p. 313*
Combinations, *p. 314*

Section 5.6

Probability Distributions, *p. 320*
Binomial Experiments, *p. 321*

Mathematical Practices

1. How can you use diagrams to understand the situation in Exercise 22 on page 310?

2. Describe a relationship between the results in part (a) and part (b) in Exercise 52 on page 318.

3. Explain how you were able to break the situation into cases to evaluate the validity of the statement in part (a) of Exercise 21 on page 324.

Performance Task:

Risk Analysis

An arborist performs an extensive risk analysis to help identify and treat tree diseases. How can this process be applied to other things?

To explore the answer to this question and more, check out the Performance Task and Real-Life STEM video at *BigIdeasMath.com*.

5.1 Sample Spaces and Probability *(pp. 279–286)*

Spinner Results	
green	4
orange	6
red	9
blue	8
yellow	3

Each section of the spinner shown has the same area. The spinner was spun 30 times. The table shows the results. For which color is the experimental probability of stopping on the color the same as the theoretical probability?

The theoretical probability of stopping on each of the five colors is $\frac{1}{5}$. Use the outcomes in the table to find the experimental probabilities.

$$P(\text{green}) = \frac{4}{30} = \frac{2}{15} \quad P(\text{orange}) = \frac{6}{30} = \frac{1}{5} \quad P(\text{red}) = \frac{9}{30} = \frac{3}{10} \quad P(\text{blue}) = \frac{8}{30} = \frac{4}{15} \quad P(\text{yellow}) = \frac{3}{30} = \frac{1}{10}$$

▶ The experimental probability of stopping on orange is the same as the theoretical probability.

1. You record a person's gender and whether they respond *yes*, *no*, or *maybe* to a survey question. How many possible outcomes are in the sample space? List the possible outcomes.

2. A bag contains 9 tiles, one for each letter in the word HAPPINESS. You choose a tile at random. What is the probability that you choose a tile with the letter S? What is the probability that you choose a tile with a letter other than P?

3. Using the spinner above, what are the odds in favor of stopping on yellow? What are the odds against stopping on blue?

5.2 Independent and Dependent Events *(pp. 287–294)*

You randomly select 2 cards from a standard deck of 52 playing cards. What is the probability that both cards are jacks when (a) you replace the first card before selecting the second, and (b) you do not replace the first card. Compare the probabilities.

Let event *A* be "first card is a jack" and event *B* be "second card is a jack."

a. Because you replace the first card before you select the second card, the events are independent. So, the probability is

$$P(A \text{ and } B) = P(A) \cdot P(B) = \frac{4}{52} \cdot \frac{4}{52} = \frac{16}{2704} = \frac{1}{169} \approx 0.006.$$

b. Because you do not replace the first card before you select the second card, the events are dependent. So, the probability is

$$P(A \text{ and } B) = P(A) \cdot P(B \mid A) = \frac{4}{52} \cdot \frac{3}{51} = \frac{12}{2652} = \frac{1}{221} \approx 0.005.$$

▶ So, you are $\frac{1}{169} \div \frac{1}{221} \approx 1.3$ times more likely to select 2 jacks when you replace the first card before you select the second card.

Find the probability of randomly selecting the given marbles from a bag of 5 red, 8 green, and 3 blue marbles when (a) you replace the first marble before drawing the second, and (b) you do not replace the first marble. Compare the probabilities.

4. red, then green

5. blue, then red

6. green, then green

Two-Way Tables and Probability (pp. 295–302)

A survey asks residents of the east and west sides of a city whether they support the construction of a bridge. The results, given as joint relative frequencies, are shown in the two-way table. What is the probability that a randomly selected resident from the east side will support the project?

		Location	
		East Side	West Side
Response	Yes	0.47	0.36
	No	0.08	0.09

Find the joint and marginal relative frequencies. Then use these values to find the conditional probability.

$$P(\text{yes}\,|\,\text{east side}) = \frac{P(\text{east side and yes})}{P(\text{east side})} = \frac{0.47}{0.47 + 0.08} \approx 0.855$$

▶ So, the probability that a resident of the east side of the city will support the project is about 85.5%.

7. What is the probability that a randomly selected resident who does not support the project in the example above is from the west side?

8. After a conference, 220 men and 270 women respond to a survey. Of those, 200 men and 230 women say the conference was impactful. Organize these results in a two-way table. Then find and interpret the marginal frequencies.

Probability of Disjoint and Overlapping Events (pp. 305–310)

Let A and B be events such that $P(A) = \frac{2}{3}$, $P(B) = \frac{1}{2}$, and $P(A \text{ and } B) = \frac{1}{3}$. Find $P(A \text{ or } B)$.

$P(A \text{ or } B) = P(A) + P(B) - P(A \text{ and } B)$	Write general formula.
$\quad = \frac{2}{3} + \frac{1}{2} - \frac{1}{3}$	Substitute known probabilities.
$\quad = \frac{5}{6}$	Simplify.
$\quad \approx 0.833$	Use a calculator.

9. Let A and B be events such that $P(A) = 0.32$, $P(B) = 0.48$, and $P(A \text{ and } B) = 0.12$. Find $P(A \text{ or } B)$.

10. Out of 100 employees at a company, 92 employees either work part time or work 5 days each week. There are 14 employees who work part time and 80 employees who work 5 days each week. What is the probability that a randomly selected employee works both part time and 5 days each week?

5.5 Permutations and Combinations (pp. 311–318)

A 5-digit code consists of 5 different integers from 0 to 9. How many different codes are possible?

To find the number of permutations of 5 integers chosen from 10, find $_{10}P_5$.

$$_{10}P_5 = \frac{10!}{(10-5)!} \qquad \text{Permutations formula}$$

$$= \frac{10!}{5!} \qquad \text{Subtract.}$$

$$= \frac{10 \cdot 9 \cdot 8 \cdot 7 \cdot 6 \cdot \cancel{5!}}{\cancel{5!}} \qquad \text{Expand factorials. Divide out common factor, 5!.}$$

$$= 30{,}240 \qquad \text{Simplify.}$$

▶ There are 30,240 possible codes.

Evaluate the expression.

11. $_7P_6$ **12.** $_{13}P_{10}$ **13.** $_6C_2$ **14.** $_8C_4$

15. In how many ways can you arrange (a) all of the letters and (b) 3 of the letters in the word UNCLE?

16. A random drawing will determine which 3 people in a group of 9 will win concert tickets. What is the probability that you and your 2 friends will win the tickets?

5.6 Binomial Distributions (pp. 319–324)

According to a survey, about 21% of adults in the U.S. visited an art museum last year. You ask 4 randomly chosen adults whether they visited an art museum last year. Draw a histogram of the binomial distribution for your survey.

The probability that a randomly selected person visited an art museum is $p = 0.21$. Because you survey 4 people, $n = 4$.

$$P(k = 0) = {_4}C_0(0.21)^0(0.79)^4 \approx 0.390$$

$$P(k = 1) = {_4}C_1(0.21)^1(0.79)^3 \approx 0.414$$

$$P(k = 2) = {_4}C_2(0.21)^2(0.79)^2 \approx 0.165$$

$$P(k = 3) = {_4}C_3(0.21)^3(0.79)^1 \approx 0.029$$

$$P(k = 4) = {_4}C_4(0.21)^4(0.79)^0 \approx 0.002$$

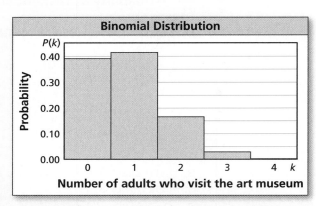

17. Find the probability of flipping a coin 12 times and getting exactly 4 heads.

18. A basketball player makes a free throw 82.6% of the time. The player attempts 5 free throws. Draw a histogram of the binomial distribution of the number of successful free throws. What is the most likely outcome?

You roll a six-sided die. Find the probability of the event described. Explain your reasoning.

1. You roll a number less than 5.

2. You roll a multiple of 3.

Evaluate the expression.

3. $_7P_2$

4. $_8P_3$

5. $_6C_3$

6. $_{12}C_7$

7. The odds in favor of an event are $2:9$. What are the odds against the event?

8. You find the probability $P(A \text{ or } B)$ by using the equation $P(A \text{ or } B) = P(A) + P(B) - P(A \text{ and } B)$. Describe why it is necessary to subtract $P(A \text{ and } B)$ when the events A and B are overlapping. Then describe why it is *not* necessary to subtract $P(A \text{ and } B)$ when the events A and B are disjoint.

9. Is it possible to use the formula $P(A \text{ and } B) = P(A) \cdot P(B|A)$ when events A and B are independent? Explain your reasoning.

10. According to a survey, about 58% of families sit down for a family dinner at least four times per week. You ask 5 randomly chosen families whether they have a family dinner at least four times per week.

   a. Draw a histogram of the binomial distribution for the survey.

   b. What is the most likely outcome of the survey?

   c. What is the probability that at least 3 families have a family dinner four times per week?

11. You are choosing a cell phone company to sign with for the next 2 years. The three plans you consider are equally priced. You ask several of your neighbors whether they are satisfied with their current cell phone company. The table shows the results. According to this survey, which company should you choose?

	Satisfied	Not Satisfied
Company A	IIII	II
Company B	IIII	III
Company C	ⅢＩ I	ⅢＩ

12. Out of 10,500 people that attend a math conference, 7315 people are either college professors or female. There are 4680 college professors and 5140 females. What is the probability that a randomly selected person is both a college professor and female?

13. Consider a bag that contains all the chess pieces in a set, as shown in the diagram.

	King	Queen	Bishop	Rook	Knight	Pawn
Black	1	1	2	2	2	8
White	1	1	2	2	2	8

   a. You choose one piece at random. Find the probability that you choose a black piece or a queen.

   b. You choose one piece at random, do not replace it, then choose a second piece at random. Find the probability that you choose a king, then a pawn.

14. Three volunteers are chosen at random from a group of 12 to help at a summer camp.

   a. What is the probability that you, your brother, and your friend are chosen?

   b. The first person chosen will be a counselor, the second will be a lifeguard, and the third will be a cook. What is the probability that you are the cook, your brother is the lifeguard, and your friend is the counselor?

1. According to a survey, 63% of Americans consider themselves sports fans. You randomly select 14 Americans to survey.

   a. Draw a histogram of the binomial distribution of your survey.

   b. What is the most likely number of Americans who consider themselves sports fans?

   c. What is the probability at least 7 Americans consider themselves sports fans?

2. Place each function into one of the three categories.

No zeros	One zero	Two zeros
$f(x) = 3x^2 + 4x + 2$ $f(x) = -x^2 + 2x$	$f(x) = 4x^2 - 8x + 4$ $f(x) = x^2 - 3x - 21$	$f(x) = 7x^2$ $f(x) = -6x^2 - 5$

3. You order a fruit smoothie made with 2 liquid ingredients and 3 fruit ingredients from the menu shown. How many different fruit smoothies can you order?

Liquids
- Water   • Tea
- Coconut Water
- Almond Milk
- Apple Juice
- Orange Juice

Fruits
- Orange
- Banana
- Pineapple
- Cantaloupe
- Strawberry

- Watermelon
- Kiwi
- Peach
- Blueberry
- Pomegranate

4. Select all the numbers that are in the range of the function shown.

$$y = \begin{cases} x^2 + 4x + 7, & \text{if } x \le -1 \\ \frac{1}{2}x + 2, & \text{if } x > -1 \end{cases}$$

| 0 | $\frac{1}{2}$ | 1 | $1\frac{1}{2}$ | 2 | $2\frac{1}{2}$ | 3 | $3\frac{1}{2}$ | 4 |

5. Complete the equation so that the solutions of the system of equations are $(-2, 4)$ and $(1, -5)$.

$$y = \boxed{}\, x + \boxed{}$$
$$y = 2x^2 - x - 6$$

6. Use the diagram to explain why the equation is true.

$$P(A) + P(B) = P(A \text{ or } B) + P(A \text{ and } B)$$

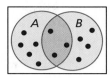

7. Which polynomial represents the product of $2x - 4$ and $x^2 + 6x - 2$?

Ⓐ $2x^3 + 8x^2 - 4x + 8$

Ⓑ $2x^3 + 8x^2 - 28x + 8$

Ⓒ $2x^3 + 8$

Ⓓ $2x^3 - 24x - 2$

8. A survey asked male and female students about whether they prefer to take gym class or choir. The table shows the results of the survey.

		Class		
		Gym	**Choir**	**Total**
Gender	**Male**			50
	Female	23		
	Total		49	106

    a. Complete the two-way table.

    b. What is the probability that a randomly selected student is female and prefers choir?

    c. What is the probability that a randomly selected male student prefers gym class?

9. The owner of a lawn-mowing business has three mowers. As long as one of the mowers is working, the owner can stay productive. One of the mowers is unusable 10% of the time, one is unusable 8% of the time, and one is unusable 18% of the time.

    a. Find the probability that all three mowers are unusable on a given day.

    b. Find the probability that at least one of the mowers is unusable on a given day.

    c. Suppose the least-reliable mower stops working completely. How does this affect the probability that the lawn-mowing business can be productive on a given day?

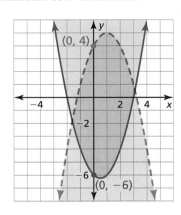

10. Write a system of quadratic inequalities whose solution is represented in the graph.

6 Relationships Within Triangles

Biking (p. 388)

Montana (p. 383)

SEE the Big Idea

Roof Truss (p. 373)

Windmill (p. 360)

Bridge (p. 345)

Maintaining Mathematical Proficiency

Writing an Equation of a Perpendicular Line (Math I)

Example 1 Write the equation of a line passing through the point $(-2, 0)$ that is perpendicular to the line $y = 2x + 8$.

    Step 1 Find the slope m of the perpendicular line. The line $y = 2x + 8$ has a slope of 2. Use the Slopes of Perpendicular Lines Theorem.

$$2 \cdot m = -1 \qquad \text{The product of the slopes of } \perp \text{ lines is } -1.$$

$$m = -\tfrac{1}{2} \qquad \text{Divide each side by 2.}$$

    Step 2 Find the y-intercept b by using $m = -\tfrac{1}{2}$ and $(x, y) = (-2, 0)$.

$$y = mx + b \qquad \text{Use the slope-intercept form.}$$

$$0 = -\tfrac{1}{2}(-2) + b \qquad \text{Substitute for } m, x, \text{ and } y.$$

$$-1 = b \qquad \text{Solve for } b.$$

▶ Because $m = -\tfrac{1}{2}$ and $b = -1$, an equation of the line is $y = -\tfrac{1}{2}x - 1$.

Write an equation of the line passing through point P that is perpendicular to the given line.

1. $P(3, 1)$, $y = \tfrac{1}{3}x - 5$ **2.** $P(4, -3)$, $y = -x - 5$ **3.** $P(-1, -2)$, $y = -4x + 13$

Writing Compound Inequalities (Math I)

Example 2 Write each sentence as an inequality.

    a. A number x is greater than or equal to -1 and less than 6.

      A number x is greater than or equal to -1 and less than 6.

$$x \geq -1 \qquad \qquad and \qquad x < 6$$

    ▶ An inequality is $-1 \leq x < 6$.

    b. A number y is at most 4 or at least 9.

      A number y is at most 4 or at least 9.

$$y \leq 4 \qquad \qquad or \qquad y \geq 9$$

    ▶ An inequality is $y \leq 4$ or $y \geq 9$.

Write the sentence as an inequality.

4. A number w is at least -3 and no more than 8.   **5.** A number m is more than 0 and less than 11.

6. A number s is less than or equal to 5 or greater than 2.   **7.** A number d is fewer than 12 or no less than -7.

8. ABSTRACT REASONING Is it possible for the solution of a compound inequality to be all real numbers? Explain your reasoning.

Mathematical Practices

Mathematically proficient students use technological tools to explore concepts.

Lines, Rays, and Segments in Triangles

⑤ Core Concept

Lines, Rays, and Segments in Triangles

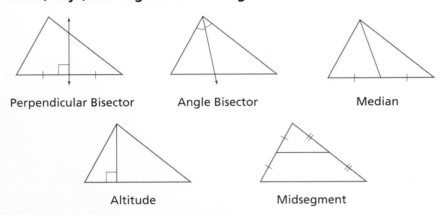

Perpendicular Bisector   Angle Bisector   Median

Altitude   Midsegment

EXAMPLE 1   Drawing a Perpendicular Bisector

Use dynamic geometry software to construct the perpendicular bisector of one of the sides of the triangle with vertices $A(-1, 2)$, $B(5, 4)$, and $C(4, -1)$. Find the lengths of the two segments of the bisected side.

SOLUTION

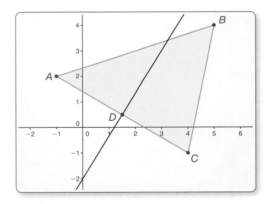

Sample

Points
$A(-1, 2)$
$B(5, 4)$
$C(4, -1)$

Line
$-5x + 3y = -6$

Segments
$AD = 2.92$
$CD = 2.92$

▶   The two segments of the bisected side have the same length, $AD = CD = 2.92$ units.

Monitoring Progress

Refer to the figures at the top of the page to describe each type of line, ray, or segment in a triangle.

1. perpendicular bisector   **2.** angle bisector   **3.** median

4. altitude   **5.** midsegment

6.1 Proving Geometric Relationships

Essential Question   How can you prove a mathematical statement?

A **proof** is a logical argument that uses deductive reasoning to show that a statement is true.

EXPLORATION 1   Writing Reasons in a Proof

Work with a partner. Four steps of a proof are shown. Write the reasons for each statement.

Given $AD = AB + AC$

Prove $CD = AB$

REASONING ABSTRACTLY

To be proficient in math, you need to know and be able to use algebraic properties.

STATEMENTS	REASONS
1. $AD = AB + AC$	**1.** Given
2. $AC + CD = AD$	**2.**
3. $AC + CD = AB + AC$	**3.**
4. $CD = AB$	**4.**

EXPLORATION 2   Writing Steps in a Proof

Work with a partner. Five steps of a proof are shown. Complete the statements that correspond to each reason.

Given $m\angle ABD = m\angle CBE$

Prove $m\angle 1 = m\angle 3$

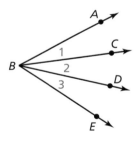

STATEMENTS	REASONS
1. $m\angle ABD = m\angle 1 + m\angle 2$	**1.** Angle Addition Postulate
2. $m\angle CBE = $	**2.** Angle Addition Postulate
3.	**3.** Given
4. $m\angle 1 + m\angle 2 = m\angle 2 + m\angle 3$	**4.** Substitution Property of Equality
5.	**5.** Subtraction Property of Equality

Communicate Your Answer

3. How can you prove a mathematical statement?

4. In Exploration 2, can you prove that $m\angle 1 = m\angle 2$? Explain your reasoning.

Core Vocabulary
proof, *p. 336*
two-column proof, *p. 336*
paragraph proof, *p. 337*
flowchart proof, or flow proof,
   p. 338
coordinate proof, *p. 339*

What You Will Learn

▶ Write two-column proofs to prove geometric relationships.
▶ Write paragraph proofs to prove geometric relationships.
▶ Write flowchart proofs to prove geometric relationships.
▶ Write coordinate proofs to prove geometric relationships.

Writing Two-Column Proofs

A **proof** is a logical argument that uses deductive reasoning to show that a statement is true. There are several formats for proofs. A **two-column proof** has numbered statements and corresponding reasons that show an argument in a logical order.

In a two-column proof, each statement in the left-hand column is either given information or the result of applying a known property or fact to statements already made. Each reason in the right-hand column is the explanation for the corresponding statement.

EXAMPLE 1   Writing a Two-Column Proof

Write a two-column proof of the
Vertical Angles Congruence Theorem.

Given $\angle 1$ and $\angle 3$ are vertical angles.

Prove $\angle 1 \cong \angle 3$

STATEMENTS	REASONS
1. $\angle 1$ and $\angle 3$ are vertical angles.	1. Given
2. $\angle 1$ and $\angle 2$ are a linear pair. $\angle 2$ and $\angle 3$ are a linear pair.	2. Definition of linear pair, as shown in the diagram
3. $\angle 1$ and $\angle 2$ are supplementary. $\angle 2$ and $\angle 3$ are supplementary.	3. Linear Pair Postulate
4. $\angle 1 \cong \angle 3$	4. Congruent Supplements Theorem

Monitoring Progress Help in English and Spanish at *BigIdeasMath.com*

1. Six steps of a two-column proof are shown. Copy and complete the proof.

Given B is the midpoint of $\overline{AC}$.

Prove $x = 7$

A   6x   B   4x + 14   C

STATEMENTS	REASONS
1. B is the midpoint of $\overline{AC}$.	1. _____
2. $\overline{AB} \cong \overline{BC}$	2. Definition of midpoint
3. $AB = BC$	3. Definition of congruent segments
4. $6x = 4x + 14$	4. _____
5. _____	5. Subtraction Property of Equality
6. $x = 7$	6. _____

Writing Paragraph Proofs

Another proof format is a **paragraph proof**, which presents the statements and reasons of a proof as sentences in a paragraph. It uses words to explain the logical flow of the argument.

EXAMPLE 2 **Writing a Paragraph Proof**

Use the given paragraph proof to write a two-column proof of the Corresponding Angles Theorem.

Given $\overleftrightarrow{AB} \parallel \overleftrightarrow{CD}$

Prove $\angle 1 \cong \angle 2$

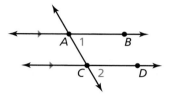

Paragraph Proof

Because $\overleftrightarrow{AB} \parallel \overleftrightarrow{CD}$ and translations map lines to parallel lines, a translation along $\overrightarrow{AC}$ maps $\overleftrightarrow{AB}$ to $\overleftrightarrow{CD}$. Because translations are rigid motions, angle measures are preserved, which means the angles formed by $\overleftrightarrow{AB}$ and $\overleftrightarrow{AC}$ are congruent to the corresponding angles formed by $\overleftrightarrow{CD}$ and $\overleftrightarrow{AC}$. So, $\angle 1 \cong \angle 2$.

Two-Column Proof

STATEMENTS	REASONS
1. $\overleftrightarrow{AB} \parallel \overleftrightarrow{CD}$	**1.** Given
2. A translation along $\overrightarrow{AC}$ maps $\overleftrightarrow{AB}$ to $\overleftrightarrow{CD}$.	**2.** Translations map lines to parallel lines.
3. Angles formed by $\overleftrightarrow{AB}$ and $\overleftrightarrow{AC}$ are congruent to the corresponding angles formed by $\overleftrightarrow{CD}$ and $\overleftrightarrow{AC}$.	**3.** Translations are rigid motions.
4. $\angle 1 \cong \angle 2$	**4.** $\angle 1$ and $\angle 2$ are corresponding angles.

Monitoring Progress Help in English and Spanish at *BigIdeasMath.com*

2. Copy and complete the paragraph proof of the Alternate Interior Angles Theorem. Then write a two-column proof.

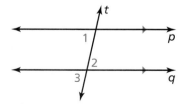

Given $p \parallel q$

Prove $\angle 1 \cong \angle 2$

$\angle 1 \cong \angle 3$ by the _____. $\angle 3 \cong \angle 2$ by the Vertical Angles Congruence Theorem. $\angle 1 \cong \angle 2$ by the _____.

Writing Flowchart Proofs

Another proof format is a **flowchart proof**, or **flow proof**, which uses boxes and arrows to show the flow of a logical argument. Each reason is below the statement it justifies.

EXAMPLE 3 Writing a Flowchart Proof

Use the given flowchart proof to write a two-column proof of the Triangle Sum Theorem.

Given $\triangle ABC$

Prove $m\angle 1 + m\angle 2 + m\angle 3 = 180°$

Flowchart Proof

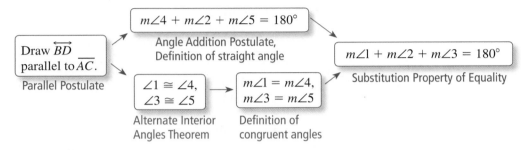

Two-Column Proof

STATEMENTS	REASONS
1. Draw $\overleftrightarrow{BD}$ parallel to $\overline{AC}$.	**1.** Parallel Postulate
2. $m\angle 4 + m\angle 2 + m\angle 5 = 180°$	**2.** Angle Addition Postulate and definition of straight angle
3. $\angle 1 \cong \angle 4, \angle 3 \cong \angle 5$	**3.** Alternate Interior Angles Theorem
4. $m\angle 1 = m\angle 4, m\angle 3 = m\angle 5$	**4.** Definition of congruent angles
5. $m\angle 1 + m\angle 2 + m\angle 3 = 180°$	**5.** Substitution Property of Equality

Monitoring Progress Help in English and Spanish at *BigIdeasMath.com*

3. Copy and complete the flowchart proof of the Base Angles Theorem. Then write a two-column proof.

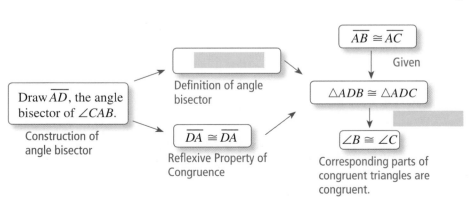

Writing Coordinate Proofs

A **coordinate proof** involves placing geometric figures in a coordinate plane. When you use variables to represent the coordinates of a figure in a coordinate proof, the results are true for all figures of that type.

EXAMPLE 4 **Writing a Coordinate Proof**

Write a coordinate proof.

Given $P(0, k)$, $Q(h, 0)$, $R(-h, 0)$

Prove $\triangle PQR$ is isosceles.

By the Distance Formula, $PR = \sqrt{h^2 + k^2}$ and $PQ = \sqrt{h^2 + k^2}$. So, $\triangle PQR$ is isosceles by definition.

Monitoring Progress Help in English and Spanish at *BigIdeasMath.com*

4. Write a coordinate proof.

   Given $T(m, 0)$, $U(0, -m)$, $V(-m, 0)$, $W(0, m)$

   Prove $\triangle TUV \cong \triangle VWT$

Concept Summary

Types of Proofs

Symmetric Property of Angle Congruence

> **Given** $\angle 1 \cong \angle 2$
>
> **Prove** $\angle 2 \cong \angle 1$

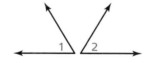

Two-Column Proof

STATEMENTS	REASONS
1. $\angle 1 \cong \angle 2$	**1.** Given
2. $m\angle 1 = m\angle 2$	**2.** Definition of congruent angles
3. $m\angle 2 = m\angle 1$	**3.** Symmetric Property of Equality
4. $\angle 2 \cong \angle 1$	**4.** Definition of congruent angles

Flowchart Proof

$\boxed{\angle 1 \cong \angle 2} \rightarrow \boxed{m\angle 1 = m\angle 2} \rightarrow \boxed{m\angle 2 = m\angle 1} \rightarrow \boxed{\angle 2 \cong \angle 1}$

Given   Definition of   Symmetric Property   Definition of
           congruent angles   of Equality   congruent angles

Paragraph Proof

$\angle 1$ is congruent to $\angle 2$. By the definition of congruent angles, the measure of $\angle 1$ is equal to the measure of $\angle 2$. The measure of $\angle 2$ is equal to the measure of $\angle 1$ by the Symmetric Property of Equality. Then by the definition of congruent angles, $\angle 2$ is congruent to $\angle 1$.

Vocabulary and Core Concept Check

1. **WRITING** Describe how paragraph proofs and flowchart proofs differ in how they present the reason for each step.

2. **COMPLETE THE SENTENCE** In a two-column proof, the _____ are on the left and the _____ are on the right.

Monitoring Progress and Modeling with Mathematics

PROOF In Exercises 3–6, copy and complete the proof. *(See Example 1.)*

3. Right Angles Congruence Theorem
   Given ∠1 and ∠2 are right angles.
   Prove ∠1 ≅ ∠2

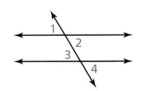

STATEMENTS	REASONS
1. ∠1 and ∠2 are right angles.	1. _____
2. $m\angle 1 = 90°$, $m\angle 2 = 90°$	2. Definition of right angle
3. _____	3. Transitive Property of Equality
4. ∠1 ≅ ∠2	4. Definition of congruent angles

4. Statement about congruent angles
   Given ∠1 ≅ ∠4
   Prove ∠2 ≅ ∠3

STATEMENTS	REASONS
1. ∠1 ≅ ∠4	1. Given
2. ∠1 ≅ ∠2, ∠3 ≅ ∠4	2. Vertical Angles Congruence Theorem
3. _____	3. Transitive Property of Congruence
4. ∠2 ≅ ∠3	4. _____

5. Statement about congruent angles
   Given ∠1 ≅ ∠3
   Prove ∠2 ≅ ∠4

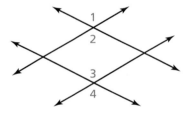

STATEMENTS	REASONS
1. ∠1 ≅ ∠3	1. Given
2. ∠1 ≅ ∠2, ∠3 ≅ ∠4	2. _____
3. _____	3. Transitive Property of Congruence
4. ∠2 ≅ ∠4	4. Transitive Property of Congruence

6. Alternate Exterior Angles Theorem
   Given $p \parallel q$
   Prove ∠1 ≅ ∠2

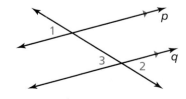

STATEMENTS	REASONS
1. $p \parallel q$	1. Given
2. _____	2. Corresponding Angles Theorem
3. ∠3 ≅ ∠2	3. _____
4. ∠1 ≅ ∠2	4. Transitive Property of Congruence

PROVING A THEOREM In Exercises 7 and 8, copy and complete the paragraph proof. Then write a two-column proof. *(See Example 2.)*

7. Consecutive Interior Angles Theorem

    Given $n \parallel p$

    Prove $\angle 1$ and $\angle 2$ are supplementary.

    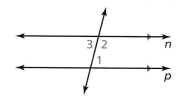

    Line n and line p are parallel. By the _____, $\angle 1 \cong \angle 3$. By the definition of congruent angles, $m\angle 1 = m\angle 3$. By the Linear Pair Postulate, _____. By the definition of supplementary angles, _____ = 180°. By substitution, $m\angle 2 + m\angle 1 = 180°$. So, $\angle 1$ and $\angle 2$ are supplementary by the definition of supplementary angles.

8. Perpendicular Transversal Theorem

    Given $h \parallel k, j \perp h$

    Prove $j \perp k$

    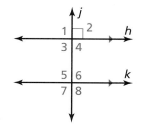

    Line h and line k are parallel, and line j and line h are perpendicular. By the definition of perpendicular lines, $m\angle 2 =$ _____. By the _____, $\angle 2 \cong \angle 6$. By the definition of congruent angles, _____. By the Transitive Property of Equality, _____ = 90°. By the _____, $j \perp k$.

PROVING A THEOREM In Exercises 9 and 10, copy and complete the flowchart proof. Then write a two-column proof. *(See Example 3.)*

9. Corresponding Angles Converse

    Given $\angle ABD \cong \angle CDE$

    Prove $\overleftrightarrow{AB} \parallel \overleftrightarrow{CD}$

10. Alternate Interior Angles Converse

    Given $\angle 4 \cong \angle 5$

    Prove $g \parallel h$

PROOF In Exercises 11 and 12, write a coordinate proof. *(See Example 4.)*

11. Given Coordinates of vertices of $\triangle OBC$ and $\triangle ODC$
Prove $\triangle OBC$ and $\triangle ODC$ are isosceles triangles.

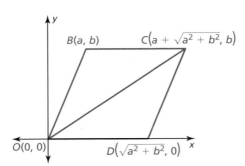

12. Given X is the midpoint of $\overline{YW}$.
Prove $\triangle XYZ \cong \triangle XWO$

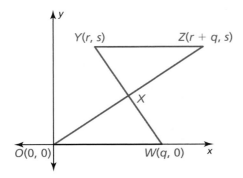

13. ERROR ANALYSIS In the diagram, $\overline{AE} \cong \overline{DE}$ and $\overline{AE} \cong \overline{BE}$. Describe and correct the error in the reasoning.

Because $\overline{AE} \cong \overline{DE}$ and $\overline{AE} \cong \overline{BE}$, then $\overline{DE} \cong \overline{BE}$ by the Symmetric Property of Congruence.

14. HOW DO YOU SEE IT? Use the figure to write each proof.

a. Alternate Exterior Angles Converse

Given $\angle 2 \cong \angle 7$

Prove $m \parallel n$

b. Consecutive Interior Angles Converse

Given $\angle 3$ and $\angle 5$ are supplementary.

Prove $m \parallel n$

15. MAKING AN ARGUMENT Your friend says that there is enough information to prove that $\angle ABC$ and $\angle DBE$ are vertical angles. Is your friend correct? Explain your reasoning.

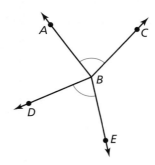

16. THOUGHT PROVOKING Describe convenient ways in which you can place a figure in a coordinate plane to complete a coordinate proof. Then place an equilateral triangle in a coordinate plane and label the vertices.

Maintaining Mathematical Proficiency
Reviewing what you learned in previous grades and lessons

$\overrightarrow{BD}$ bisects $\angle ABC$ such that $m\angle ABD = (4x - 5)°$ and $m\angle DBC = (3x + 2)°$. *(Skills Review Handbook)*

17. Find the value of x.

18. Find $m\angle ABC$.

19. Point M is the midpoint of $\overline{AB}$. Find the length of $\overline{AB}$. *(Skills Review Handbook)*

6.2 Perpendicular and Angle Bisectors

Essential Question What conjectures can you make about a point on the perpendicular bisector of a segment and a point on the bisector of an angle?

EXPLORATION 1 Points on a Perpendicular Bisector

Work with a partner. Use dynamic geometry software.

a. Draw any segment and label it $\overline{AB}$. Construct the perpendicular bisector of $\overline{AB}$.

b. Label a point C that is on the perpendicular bisector of $\overline{AB}$ but is not on $\overline{AB}$.

c. Draw $\overline{CA}$ and $\overline{CB}$ and find their lengths. Then move point C to other locations on the perpendicular bisector and note the lengths of $\overline{CA}$ and $\overline{CB}$.

d. Repeat parts (a)–(c) with other segments. Describe any relationship(s) you notice.

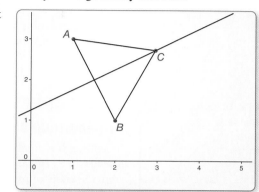

Sample
Points
$A(1, 3)$
$B(2, 1)$
$C(2.95, 2.73)$
Segments
$AB = 2.24$
$CA = ?$
$CB = ?$
Line
$-x + 2y = 2.5$

USING TOOLS STRATEGICALLY

To be proficient in math, you need to visualize the results of varying assumptions, explore consequences, and compare predictions with data.

EXPLORATION 2 Points on an Angle Bisector

Work with a partner. Use dynamic geometry software.

a. Draw two rays $\overrightarrow{AB}$ and $\overrightarrow{AC}$ to form $\angle BAC$. Construct the bisector of $\angle BAC$.

b. Label a point D on the bisector of $\angle BAC$.

c. Construct and find the lengths of the perpendicular segments from D to the sides of $\angle BAC$. Move point D along the angle bisector and note how the lengths change.

d. Repeat parts (a)–(c) with other angles. Describe any relationship(s) you notice.

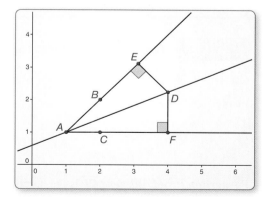

Sample
Points
$A(1, 1)$
$B(2, 2)$
$C(2, 1)$
$D(4, 2.24)$
Rays
$AB = -x + y = 0$
$AC = y = 1$
Line
$-0.38x + 0.92y = 0.54$

Communicate Your Answer

3. What conjectures can you make about a point on the perpendicular bisector of a segment and a point on the bisector of an angle?

4. In Exploration 2, what is the distance from point D to $\overrightarrow{AB}$ when the distance from D to $\overrightarrow{AC}$ is 5 units? Justify your answer.

What You Will Learn

▶ Use perpendicular bisectors to find measures.

▶ Use angle bisectors to find measures and distance relationships.

▶ Write equations for perpendicular bisectors.

Using Perpendicular Bisectors

Previously, you learned that a *perpendicular bisector* of a line segment is the line that is perpendicular to the segment at its midpoint.

A point is **equidistant** from two figures when the point is the *same distance* from each figure.

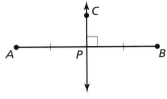

$\overleftrightarrow{CP}$ is a ⊥ bisector of $\overline{AB}$.

STUDY TIP

A perpendicular bisector can be a segment, a ray, a line, or a plane.

⟳ Theorems

Perpendicular Bisector Theorem

In a plane, if a point lies on the perpendicular bisector of a segment, then it is equidistant from the endpoints of the segment.

If $\overleftrightarrow{CP}$ is the ⊥ bisector of $\overline{AB}$, then $CA = CB$.

Proof p. 344

Converse of the Perpendicular Bisector Theorem

In a plane, if a point is equidistant from the endpoints of a segment, then it lies on the perpendicular bisector of the segment.

If $DA = DB$, then point D lies on the ⊥ bisector of $\overline{AB}$.

Proof Ex. 32, p. 350

PROOF   **Perpendicular Bisector Theorem**

Given $\overleftrightarrow{CP}$ is the perpendicular bisector of $\overline{AB}$.

Prove $CA = CB$

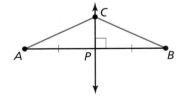

Paragraph Proof Because $\overleftrightarrow{CP}$ is the perpendicular bisector of $\overline{AB}$, $\overleftrightarrow{CP}$ is perpendicular to $\overline{AB}$ and point P is the midpoint of $\overline{AB}$. By the definition of midpoint, $AP = BP$, and by the definition of perpendicular lines, $m\angle CPA = m\angle CPB = 90°$. Then by the definition of segment congruence, $\overline{AP} \cong \overline{BP}$, and by the definition of angle congruence, $\angle CPA \cong \angle CPB$. By the Reflexive Property of Congruence, $\overline{CP} \cong \overline{CP}$. So, $\triangle CPA \cong \triangle CPB$ by the SAS Congruence Theorem, and $\overline{CA} \cong \overline{CB}$ because corresponding parts of congruent triangles are congruent. So, $CA = CB$ by the definition of segment congruence.

EXAMPLE 1 Using the Perpendicular Bisector Theorems

Find each measure.

a. *RS*

From the figure, $\overleftrightarrow{SQ}$ is the perpendicular bisector of $\overline{PR}$. By the Perpendicular Bisector Theorem, $PS = RS$.

▶ So, $RS = PS = 6.8$.

b. *EG*

Because $EH = GH$ and $\overleftrightarrow{HF} \perp \overline{EG}$, $\overleftrightarrow{HF}$ is the perpendicular bisector of $\overline{EG}$ by the Converse of the Perpendicular Bisector Theorem. By the definition of segment bisector, $EG = 2GF$.

▶ So, $EG = 2(9.5) = 19$.

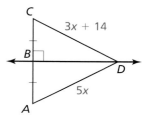

c. *AD*

From the figure, $\overleftrightarrow{BD}$ is the perpendicular bisector of $\overline{AC}$.

$AD = CD$	Perpendicular Bisector Theorem
$5x = 3x + 14$	Substitute.
$x = 7$	Solve for x.

▶ So, $AD = 5x = 5(7) = 35$.

EXAMPLE 2 Solving a Real-Life Problem

Is there enough information in the diagram to conclude that point N lies on the perpendicular bisector of $\overline{KM}$?

SOLUTION

It is given that $\overline{KL} \cong \overline{ML}$. So, $\overline{LN}$ is a segment bisector of $\overline{KM}$. You do not know whether $\overline{LN}$ is perpendicular to $\overline{KM}$ because it is not indicated in the diagram.

▶ So, you cannot conclude that point N lies on the perpendicular bisector of $\overline{KM}$.

Monitoring Progress Help in English and Spanish at *BigIdeasMath.com*

Use the diagram and the given information to find the indicated measure.

1. $\overleftrightarrow{ZX}$ is the perpendicular bisector of $\overline{WY}$, and $YZ = 13.75$. Find WZ.

2. $\overleftrightarrow{ZX}$ is the perpendicular bisector of $\overline{WY}$, $WZ = 4n - 13$, and $YZ = n + 17$. Find YZ.

3. Find WX when $WZ = 20.5$, $WY = 14.8$, and $YZ = 20.5$.

Using Angle Bisectors

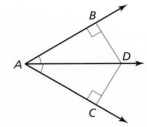

Previously, you learned that an *angle bisector* is a ray that divides an angle into two congruent adjacent angles. You also know that the *distance from a point to a line* is the length of the perpendicular segment from the point to the line. So, in the figure, $\overrightarrow{AD}$ is the bisector of $\angle BAC$, and the distance from point D to $\overrightarrow{AB}$ is DB, where $\overline{DB} \perp \overrightarrow{AB}$.

🌀 Theorems

Angle Bisector Theorem

If a point lies on the bisector of an angle, then it is equidistant from the two sides of the angle.

If $\overrightarrow{AD}$ bisects $\angle BAC$ and $\overline{DB} \perp \overrightarrow{AB}$ and $\overline{DC} \perp \overrightarrow{AC}$, then $DB = DC$.

Proof Ex. 33(a), p. 350

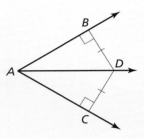

Converse of the Angle Bisector Theorem

If a point is in the interior of an angle and is equidistant from the two sides of the angle, then it lies on the bisector of the angle.

If $\overline{DB} \perp \overrightarrow{AB}$ and $\overline{DC} \perp \overrightarrow{AC}$ and $DB = DC$, then $\overrightarrow{AD}$ bisects $\angle BAC$.

Proof Ex. 33(b), p. 350

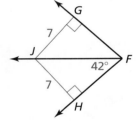

EXAMPLE 3 **Using the Angle Bisector Theorems**

Find each measure.

a. $m\angle GFJ$

Because $\overline{JG} \perp \overrightarrow{FG}$ and $\overline{JH} \perp \overrightarrow{FH}$ and $JG = JH = 7$, $\overrightarrow{FJ}$ bisects $\angle GFH$ by the Converse of the Angle Bisector Theorem.

▶ So, $m\angle GFJ = m\angle HFJ = 42°$.

b. RS

$PS = RS$	Angle Bisector Theorem
$5x = 6x - 5$	Substitute.
$5 = x$	Solve for x.

▶ So, $RS = 6x - 5 = 6(5) - 5 = 25$.

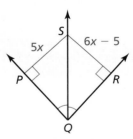

Monitoring Progress 🔊 Help in English and Spanish at *BigIdeasMath.com*

Use the diagram and the given information to find the indicated measure.

4. $\overrightarrow{BD}$ bisects $\angle ABC$, and $DC = 6.9$. Find DA.

5. $\overrightarrow{BD}$ bisects $\angle ABC$, $AD = 3z + 7$, and $CD = 2z + 11$. Find CD.

6. Find $m\angle ABC$ when $AD = 3.2$, $CD = 3.2$, and $m\angle DBC = 39°$.

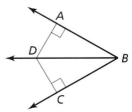

EXAMPLE 4   Solving a Real-Life Problem

A soccer goalie's position relative to the ball and goalposts forms congruent angles, as shown. Will the goalie have to move farther to block a shot toward the right goalpost R or the left goalpost L?

SOLUTION

The congruent angles tell you that the goalie is on the bisector of $\angle LBR$. By the Angle Bisector Theorem, the goalie is equidistant from $\overrightarrow{BR}$ and $\overrightarrow{BL}$.

▶ So, the goalie must move the same distance to block either shot.

Writing Equations for Perpendicular Bisectors

EXAMPLE 5   Writing an Equation for a Bisector

Write an equation of the perpendicular bisector of the segment with endpoints $P(-2, 3)$ and $Q(4, 1)$.

SOLUTION

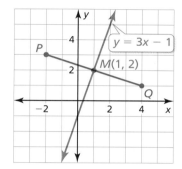

Step 1   Graph $\overline{PQ}$. By definition, the perpendicular bisector of $\overline{PQ}$ is perpendicular to $\overline{PQ}$ at its midpoint.

Step 2   Find the midpoint M of $\overline{PQ}$.

$$M\left(\frac{-2 + 4}{2}, \frac{3 + 1}{2}\right) = M\left(\frac{2}{2}, \frac{4}{2}\right) = M(1, 2)$$

Step 3   Find the slope of the perpendicular bisector.

$$\text{slope of } \overline{PQ} = \frac{1 - 3}{4 - (-2)} = \frac{-2}{6} = -\frac{1}{3}$$

Because the slopes of perpendicular lines are negative reciprocals, the slope of the perpendicular bisector is 3.

Step 4   Write an equation. The bisector of $\overline{PQ}$ has slope 3 and passes through $(1, 2)$.

$y = mx + b$	Use slope-intercept form.
$2 = 3(1) + b$	Substitute for m, x, and y.
$-1 = b$	Solve for b.

▶ So, an equation of the perpendicular bisector of $\overline{PQ}$ is $y = 3x - 1$.

Monitoring Progress   Help in English and Spanish at *BigIdeasMath.com*

7. Do you have enough information to conclude that $\overrightarrow{QS}$ bisects $\angle PQR$? Explain.

8. Write an equation of the perpendicular bisector of the segment with endpoints $(-1, -5)$ and $(3, -1)$.

Vocabulary and Core Concept Check

1. **COMPLETE THE SENTENCE** Point *C* is in the interior of ∠*DEF*. If ∠*DEC* and ∠*CEF* are congruent, then $\overrightarrow{EC}$ is the _____ of ∠*DEF*.

2. **DIFFERENT WORDS, SAME QUESTION** Which is different? Find "both" answers.

Is point *B* the same distance from both *X* and *Z*?

Is point *B* equidistant from *X* and *Z*?

Is point *B* collinear with *X* and *Z*?

Is point *B* on the perpendicular bisector of $\overline{XZ}$?

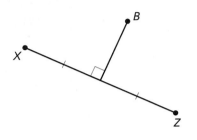

Monitoring Progress and Modeling with Mathematics

In Exercises 3–6, find the indicated measure. Explain your reasoning. *(See Example 1.)*

3. *GH*

4. *QR*

5. *AB*

6. *UW*

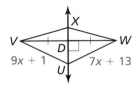

In Exercises 7–10, tell whether the information in the diagram allows you to conclude that point *P* lies on the perpendicular bisector of $\overline{LM}$. Explain your reasoning. *(See Example 2.)*

7.

8.

9.

10.

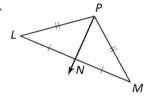

In Exercises 11–14, find the indicated measure. Explain your reasoning. *(See Example 3.)*

11. *m∠ABD*

12. *PS*

13. *m∠KJL*

14. *FG*

In Exercises 15 and 16, tell whether the information in the diagram allows you to conclude that $\overrightarrow{EH}$ bisects $\angle FEG$. Explain your reasoning. *(See Example 4.)*

15.

16.

In Exercises 17 and 18, tell whether the information in the diagram allows you to conclude that $DB = DC$. Explain your reasoning.

17.

18.

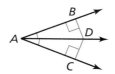

In Exercises 19–22, write an equation of the perpendicular bisector of the segment with the given endpoints. *(See Example 5.)*

19. $M(1, 5), N(7, -1)$

20. $Q(-2, 0), R(6, 12)$

21. $U(-3, 4), V(9, 8)$

22. $Y(10, -7), Z(-4, 1)$

ERROR ANALYSIS In Exercises 23 and 24, describe and correct the error in the student's reasoning.

23.

Because $AD = AE$, $\overrightarrow{AB}$ will pass through point C.

24.

By the Angle Bisector Theorem, $x = 5$.

25. MODELING MATHEMATICS In the photo, the road is perpendicular to the support beam and $\overline{AB} \cong \overline{CB}$. Which theorem allows you to conclude that $\overline{AD} \cong \overline{CD}$?

26. MODELING WITH MATHEMATICS The diagram shows the position of the goalie and the puck during a hockey game. The goalie is at point G, and the puck is at point P.

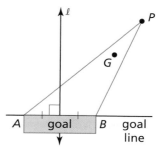

a. What should be the relationship between $\overrightarrow{PG}$ and $\angle APB$ to give the goalie equal distances to travel on each side of $\overrightarrow{PG}$?

b. How does $m\angle APB$ change as the puck gets closer to the goal? Does this change make it easier or more difficult for the goalie to defend the goal? Explain your reasoning.

27. CONSTRUCTION Use a compass and straightedge to construct a copy of $\overline{XY}$. Construct a perpendicular bisector and plot a point Z on the bisector so that the distance between point Z and $\overline{XY}$ is 3 centimeters. Measure $\overline{XZ}$ and $\overline{YZ}$. Which theorem does this construction demonstrate?

28. WRITING Explain how the Converse of the Perpendicular Bisector Theorem is related to the construction of a perpendicular bisector.

29. REASONING What is the value of x in the diagram?

(A) 13

(B) 18

(C) 33

(D) not enough information

30. REASONING Which point lies on the perpendicular bisector of the segment with endpoints $M(7, 5)$ and $N(-1, 5)$?

(A) $(2, 0)$ (B) $(3, 9)$

(C) $(4, 1)$ (D) $(1, 3)$

31. MAKING AN ARGUMENT Your friend says it is impossible for an angle bisector of a triangle to be the same line as the perpendicular bisector of the opposite side. Is your friend correct? Explain your reasoning.

32. PROVING A THEOREM Prove the Converse of the Perpendicular Bisector Theorem. (*Hint:* Construct a line through point C perpendicular to $\overline{AB}$ at point P.)

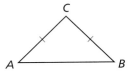

Given $CA = CB$

Prove Point C lies on the perpendicular bisector of $\overline{AB}$.

33. PROVING A THEOREM Use a congruence theorem to prove each theorem.

a. Angle Bisector Theorem

b. Converse of the Angle Bisector Theorem

34. HOW DO YOU SEE IT? The figure shows a map of a city. The city is arranged so each block north to south is the same length and each block east to west is the same length.

a. Which school is approximately equidistant from both hospitals? Explain your reasoning.

b. Is the museum approximately equidistant from Wilson School and Roosevelt School? Explain your reasoning.

35. MATHEMATICAL CONNECTIONS Write an equation whose graph consists of all the points in the given quadrants that are equidistant from the x- and y-axes.

a. I and III   b. II and IV   c. I and II

36. THOUGHT PROVOKING The postulates and theorems you have learned represent Euclidean geometry. In spherical geometry, all points are on the surface of a sphere. A line is a circle on the sphere whose diameter is equal to the diameter of the sphere. In spherical geometry, is it possible for two lines to be perpendicular but not bisect each other? Explain your reasoning.

37. PROOF Use the information in the diagram to prove that $\overline{AB} \cong \overline{CB}$ if and only if points D, E, and B are collinear.

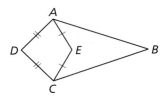

38. PROOF Prove the statements in parts (a)–(c).

Given Plane P is a perpendicular bisector of $\overline{XZ}$ at point Y.

Prove a. $\overline{XW} \cong \overline{ZW}$

b. $\overline{XV} \cong \overline{ZV}$

c. $\angle VXW \cong \angle VZW$

Maintaining Mathematical Proficiency

Reviewing what you learned in previous grades and lessons

Classify the triangle by its sides. (*Skills Review Handbook*)

39.

40.

41.

Classify the triangle by its angles. (*Skills Review Handbook*)

42.

43.

44.

6.3 Bisectors of Triangles

Essential Question What conjectures can you make about the perpendicular bisectors and the angle bisectors of a triangle?

EXPLORATION 1   Properties of the Perpendicular Bisectors of a Triangle

Work with a partner. Use dynamic geometry software. Draw any △ABC.

a. Construct the perpendicular bisectors of all three sides of △ABC. Then drag the vertices to change △ABC. What do you notice about the perpendicular bisectors?

b. Label a point D at the intersection of the perpendicular bisectors.

c. Draw the circle with center D through vertex A of △ABC. Then drag the vertices to change △ABC. What do you notice?

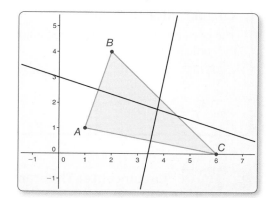

Sample
Points
$A(1, 1)$
$B(2, 4)$
$C(6, 0)$
Segments
$BC = 5.66$
$AC = 5.10$
$AB = 3.16$
Lines
$x + 3y = 9$
$-5x + y = -17$

LOOKING FOR STRUCTURE

To be proficient in math, you need to see complicated things as single objects or as being composed of several objects.

EXPLORATION 2   Properties of the Angle Bisectors of a Triangle

Work with a partner. Use dynamic geometry software. Draw any △ABC.

a. Construct the angle bisectors of all three angles of △ABC. Then drag the vertices to change △ABC. What do you notice about the angle bisectors?

b. Label a point D at the intersection of the angle bisectors.

c. Find the distance between D and $\overline{AB}$. Draw the circle with center D and this distance as a radius. Then drag the vertices to change △ABC. What do you notice?

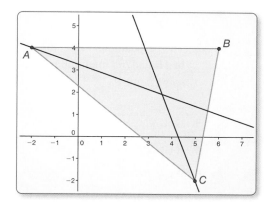

Sample
Points
$A(-2, 4)$
$B(6, 4)$
$C(5, -2)$
Segments
$BC = 6.08$
$AC = 9.22$
$AB = 8$
Lines
$0.35x + 0.94y = 3.06$
$-0.94x - 0.34y = -4.02$

Communicate Your Answer

3. What conjectures can you make about the perpendicular bisectors and the angle bisectors of a triangle?

6.3 Lesson

What You Will Learn

▶ Use and find the circumcenter of a triangle.
▶ Use and find the incenter of a triangle.

Core Vocabulary

concurrent, *p. 352*
point of concurrency, *p. 352*
circumcenter, *p. 352*
incenter, *p. 355*

Previous
perpendicular bisector
angle bisector

Using the Circumcenter of a Triangle

When three or more lines, rays, or segments intersect in the same point, they are called **concurrent** lines, rays, or segments. The point of intersection of the lines, rays, or segments is called the **point of concurrency**.

In a triangle, the three perpendicular bisectors are concurrent. The point of concurrency is the **circumcenter** of the triangle.

⑤ Theorems

Circumcenter Theorem

The circumcenter of a triangle is equidistant from the vertices of the triangle.

If $\overline{PD}$, $\overline{PE}$, and $\overline{PF}$ are perpendicular bisectors, then $PA = PB = PC$.

Proof p. 352

PROOF   **Circumcenter Theorem**

Given $\triangle ABC$; the perpendicular bisectors of $\overline{AB}$, $\overline{BC}$, and $\overline{AC}$

Prove   The perpendicular bisectors intersect in a point; that point is equidistant from A, B, and C.

Plan for Proof   Show that P, the point of intersection of the perpendicular bisectors of $\overline{AB}$ and $\overline{BC}$, also lies on the perpendicular bisector of $\overline{AC}$. Then show that point P is equidistant from the vertices of the triangle.

STUDY TIP

Use diagrams like the one below to help visualize your proof.

Plan in Action	STATEMENTS	REASONS
	1. $\triangle ABC$; the perpendicular bisectors of $\overline{AB}$, $\overline{BC}$, and $\overline{AC}$	1. Given
	2. The perpendicular bisectors of $\overline{AB}$ and $\overline{BC}$ intersect at some point P.	2. Because the sides of a triangle cannot be parallel, these perpendicular bisectors must intersect in some point. Call it P.
	3. Draw $\overline{PA}$, $\overline{PB}$, and $\overline{PC}$.	3. Two Point Postulate
	4. $PA = PB$, $PB = PC$	4. Perpendicular Bisector Theorem
	5. $PA = PC$	5. Transitive Property of Equality
	6. P is on the perpendicular bisector of $\overline{AC}$.	6. Converse of the Perpendicular Bisector Theorem
	7. $PA = PB = PC$. So, P is equidistant from the vertices of the triangle.	7. From the results of Steps 4 and 5 and the definition of equidistant

EXAMPLE 1   **Solving a Real-Life Problem**

Three snack carts sell frozen yogurt from points A, B, and C outside a city. Each of the three carts is the same distance from the frozen yogurt distributor.

Find the location of the distributor.

SOLUTION

The distributor is equidistant from the three snack carts. The Circumcenter Theorem shows that you can find a point equidistant from three points by using the perpendicular bisectors of the triangle formed by those points.

Copy the positions of points A, B, and C and connect the points to draw $\triangle ABC$. Then use a ruler and protractor to draw the three perpendicular bisectors of $\triangle ABC$. The circumcenter D is the location of the distributor.

Monitoring Progress 🔊) Help in English and Spanish at *BigIdeasMath.com*

1. Three snack carts sell hot pretzels from points A, B, and E. What is the location of the pretzel distributor if it is equidistant from the three carts? Sketch the triangle and show the location.

  B •

  A •   • E

READING

The prefix *circum-* means "around" or "about," as in *circumference* (distance around a circle).

The circumcenter P is equidistant from the three vertices, so P is the center of a circle that passes through all three vertices. As shown below, the location of P depends on the type of triangle. The circle with center P is said to be *circumscribed* about the triangle.

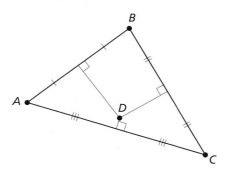

Acute triangle   Right triangle   Obtuse triangle
P is inside triangle. P is on triangle. P is outside triangle.

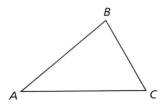

CONSTRUCTION **Circumscribing a Circle About a Triangle**

Use a compass and straightedge to construct a circle that is circumscribed about △ABC.

SOLUTION

Step 1	Step 2	Step 3
		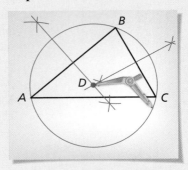

Draw a bisector Draw the perpendicular bisector of $\overline{AB}$.

Draw a bisector Draw the perpendicular bisector of $\overline{BC}$. Label the intersection of the bisectors *D*. This is the circumcenter.

Draw a circle Place the compass at *D*. Set the width by using any vertex of the triangle. This is the radius of the *circumcircle*. Draw the circle. It should pass through all three vertices *A*, *B*, and *C*.

STUDY TIP

Note that you only need to find the equations for *two* perpendicular bisectors. You can use the perpendicular bisector of the third side to verify your result.

MAKING SENSE OF PROBLEMS

Because △*ABC* is a right triangle, the circumcenter lies on the triangle.

EXAMPLE 2 **Finding the Circumcenter of a Triangle**

Find the coordinates of the circumcenter of △*ABC* with vertices *A*(0, 3), *B*(0, −1), and *C*(6, −1).

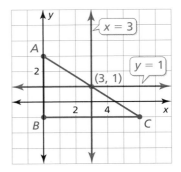

SOLUTION

Step 1 Graph △*ABC*.

Step 2 Find equations for two perpendicular bisectors. Use the Slopes of Perpendicular Lines Theorem, which states that horizontal lines are perpendicular to vertical lines.

The midpoint of $\overline{AB}$ is (0, 1). The line through (0, 1) that is perpendicular to $\overline{AB}$ is $y = 1$.

The midpoint of $\overline{BC}$ is (3, −1). The line through (3, −1) that is perpendicular to $\overline{BC}$ is $x = 3$.

Step 3 Find the point where $x = 3$ and $y = 1$ intersect. They intersect at (3, 1).

▶ So, the coordinates of the circumcenter are (3, 1).

Monitoring Progress Help in English and Spanish at *BigIdeasMath.com*

Find the coordinates of the circumcenter of the triangle with the given vertices.

2. *R*(−2, 5), *S*(−6, 5), *T*(−2, −1)   **3.** *W*(−1, 4), *X*(1, 4), *Y*(1, −6)

Using the Incenter of a Triangle

Just as a triangle has three perpendicular bisectors, it also has three angle bisectors. The angle bisectors of a triangle are also concurrent. This point of concurrency is the **incenter** of the triangle. For any triangle, the incenter always lies inside the triangle.

⟲ Theorem

Incenter Theorem

The incenter of a triangle is equidistant from the sides of the triangle.

If $\overline{AP}, \overline{BP}$, and $\overline{CP}$ are angle bisectors of $\triangle ABC$, then $PD = PE = PF$.

Proof Ex. 38, p. 359

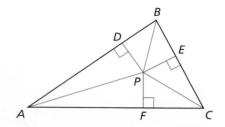

EXAMPLE 3 **Using the Incenter of a Triangle**

In the figure shown, $ND = 5x - 1$ and $NE = 2x + 11$.

a. Find NF.

b. Can NG be equal to 18? Explain your reasoning.

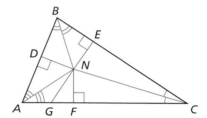

SOLUTION

a. N is the incenter of $\triangle ABC$ because it is the point of concurrency of the three angle bisectors. So, by the Incenter Theorem, $ND = NE = NF$.

Step 1 Solve for x.

$ND = NE$	Incenter Theorem
$5x - 1 = 2x + 11$	Substitute.
$x = 4$	Solve for x.

Step 2 Find ND (or NE).

$$ND = 5x - 1 = 5(4) - 1 = 19$$

▶ So, because $ND = NF$, $NF = 19$.

b. Recall that the shortest distance between a point and a line is a perpendicular segment. In this case, the perpendicular segment is $\overline{NF}$, which has a length of 19. Because $18 < 19$, NG cannot be equal to 18.

Monitoring Progress Help in English and Spanish at *BigIdeasMath.com*

4. In the figure shown, $QM = 3x + 8$ and $QN = 7x + 2$. Find QP.

Because the incenter *P* is equidistant from the three sides of the triangle, a circle drawn using *P* as the center and the distance to one side of the triangle as the radius will just touch the other two sides of the triangle. The circle is said to be *inscribed* within the triangle.

CONSTRUCTION   Inscribing a Circle Within a Triangle

Use a compass and straightedge to construct a circle that is inscribed within △*ABC*.

SOLUTION

Step 1

Draw a bisector Draw the angle bisector of ∠*A*.

Step 2

Draw a bisector Draw the angle bisector of ∠*C*. Label the intersection of the bisectors *D*. This is the incenter.

Step 3

Draw a perpendicular line Draw the perpendicular line from *D* to $\overline{AB}$. Label the point where it intersects $\overline{AB}$ as *E*.

Step 4

Draw a circle Place the compass at *D*. Set the width to *E*. This is the radius of the *incircle*. Draw the circle. It should touch each side of the triangle.

EXAMPLE 4   Solving a Real-Life Problem

ATTENDING TO PRECISION

Pay close attention to how a problem is stated. The city wants the lamppost to be the *same distance* from the three streets, not from where the streets intersect.

A city wants to place a lamppost on the boulevard shown so that the lamppost is the same distance from all three streets. Should the location of the lamppost be at the *circumcenter* or *incenter* of the triangular boulevard? Explain.

SOLUTION

Because the shape of the boulevard is an obtuse triangle, its circumcenter lies outside the triangle. So, the location of the lamppost cannot be at the circumcenter. The city wants the lamppost to be the same distance from all three streets. By the Incenter Theorem, the incenter of a triangle is equidistant from the sides of a triangle.

▶   So, the location of the lamppost should be at the incenter of the boulevard.

Monitoring Progress   🔊 Help in English and Spanish at *BigIdeasMath.com*

5. Draw a sketch to show the location *L* of the lamppost in Example 4.

Vocabulary and Core Concept Check

1. **VOCABULARY** When three or more lines, rays, or segments intersect in the same point, they are called _____ lines, rays, or segments.

2. **WHICH ONE DOESN'T BELONG?** Which triangle does *not* belong with the other three? Explain your reasoning.

Monitoring Progress and Modeling with Mathematics

In Exercises 3 and 4, the perpendicular bisectors of △ABC intersect at point G and are shown in blue. Find the indicated measure.

3. Find BG.

4. Find GA.

 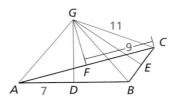

In Exercises 5 and 6, the angle bisectors of △XYZ intersect at point P and are shown in red. Find the indicated measure.

5. Find PB.

6. Find HP.

 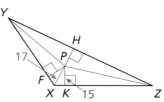

In Exercises 7–10, find the coordinates of the circumcenter of the triangle with the given vertices. (See Example 2.)

7. $A(2, 6)$, $B(8, 6)$, $C(8, 10)$

8. $D(-7, -1)$, $E(-1, -1)$, $F(-7, -9)$

9. $H(-10, 7)$, $J(-6, 3)$, $K(-2, 3)$

10. $L(3, -6)$, $M(5, -3)$, $N(8, -6)$

In Exercises 11–14, N is the incenter of △ABC. Use the given information to find the indicated measure. (See Example 3.)

11. $ND = 6x - 2$
    $NE = 3x + 7$
    Find NF.

12. $NG = x + 3$
    $NH = 2x - 3$
    Find NJ.

 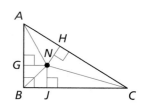

13. $NK = 2x - 2$
    $NL = -x + 10$
    Find NM.

14. $NQ = 2x$
    $NR = 3x - 2$
    Find NS.

15. P is the circumcenter of △XYZ. Use the given information to find PZ.

    $PX = 3x + 2$
    $PY = 4x - 8$

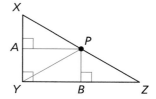

16. P is the circumcenter of $\triangle XYZ$. Use the given information to find PY.

$PX = 4x + 3$
$PZ = 6x - 11$

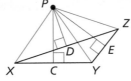

CONSTRUCTION In Exercises 17–20, draw a triangle of the given type. Find the circumcenter. Then construct the circumscribed circle.

17. right

18. obtuse

19. acute isosceles

20. equilateral

CONSTRUCTION In Exercises 21–24, copy the triangle with the given angle measures. Find the incenter. Then construct the inscribed circle.

21.

22.

23.

24.

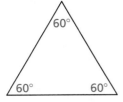

ERROR ANALYSIS In Exercises 25 and 26, describe and correct the error in identifying equal distances inside the triangle.

25.

26.

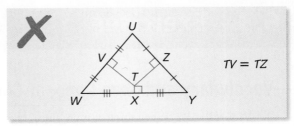

27. MODELING WITH MATHEMATICS You and two friends plan to meet to walk your dogs together. You want the meeting place to be the same distance from each person's house. Explain how you can use the diagram to locate the meeting place. *(See Example 1.)*

28. MODELING WITH MATHEMATICS You are placing a fountain in a triangular koi pond. You want the fountain to be the same distance from each edge of the pond. Where should you place the fountain? Explain your reasoning. Use a sketch to support your answer. *(See Example 4.)*

CRITICAL THINKING In Exercises 29–32, complete the statement with *always*, *sometimes*, or *never*. Explain your reasoning.

29. The circumcenter of a scalene triangle is _____ inside the triangle.

30. If the perpendicular bisector of one side of a triangle intersects the opposite vertex, then the triangle is _____ isosceles.

31. The perpendicular bisectors of a triangle intersect at a point that is _____ equidistant from the midpoints of the sides of the triangle.

32. The angle bisectors of a triangle intersect at a point that is _____ equidistant from the sides of the triangle.

CRITICAL THINKING In Exercises 33 and 34, find the coordinates of the circumcenter of the triangle with the given vertices.

33. $A(2, 5)$, $B(6, 6)$, $C(12, 3)$

34. $D(-9, -5)$, $E(-5, -9)$, $F(-2, -2)$

MATHEMATICAL CONNECTIONS In Exercises 35 and 36, find the value of x that makes N the incenter of the triangle.

35.

36.

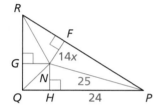

37. PROOF Where is the circumcenter located in any right triangle? Write a coordinate proof of this result.

38. PROVING A THEOREM Write a proof of the Incenter Theorem.

Given $\triangle ABC$, $\overline{AD}$ bisects $\angle CAB$, $\overline{BD}$ bisects $\angle CBA$, $\overline{DE} \perp \overline{AB}$, $\overline{DF} \perp \overline{BC}$, and $\overline{DG} \perp \overline{CA}$

Prove The angle bisectors intersect at D, which is equidistant from $\overline{AB}$, $\overline{BC}$, and $\overline{CA}$.

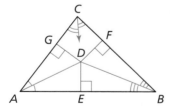

39. WRITING Explain the difference between the circumcenter and the incenter of a triangle.

40. REASONING Is the incenter of a triangle ever located outside the triangle? Explain your reasoning.

41. MODELING WITH MATHEMATICS You are installing a circular pool in the triangular courtyard shown. You want to have the largest pool possible on the site without extending into the walkway.

a. Copy the triangle and show how to install the pool so that it just touches each edge. Then explain how you can be sure that you could not fit a larger pool on the site.

b. You want to have the largest pool possible while leaving at least 1 foot of space around the pool. Would the center of the pool be in the same position as in part (a)? Justify your answer.

42. MODELING WITH MATHEMATICS Archaeologists find three stones. They believe that the stones were once part of a circle of stones with a community fire pit at its center. They mark the locations of stones A, B, and C on a graph, where distances are measured in feet.

a. Explain how archaeologists can use a sketch to estimate the center of the circle of stones.

b. Copy the diagram and find the approximate coordinates of the point at which the archaeologists should look for the fire pit.

43. REASONING Point P is inside $\triangle ABC$ and is equidistant from points A and B. On which of the following segments must P be located?

   Ⓐ $\overline{AB}$

   Ⓑ the perpendicular bisector of $\overline{AB}$

   Ⓒ $\overline{AC}$

   Ⓓ the perpendicular bisector of $\overline{AC}$

44. CRITICAL THINKING A high school is being built for the four towns shown on the map. Each town agrees that the school should be an equal distance from each of the four towns. Is there a single point where they could agree to build the school? If so, find it. If not, explain why not. Justify your answer with a diagram.

45. MAKING AN ARGUMENT Your friend says that the circumcenter of an equilateral triangle is also the incenter of the triangle. Is your friend correct? Explain your reasoning.

46. HOW DO YOU SEE IT? The arms of the windmill are the angle bisectors of the red triangle. What point of concurrency is the point that connects the three arms?

47. ABSTRACT REASONING You are asked to draw a triangle and all its perpendicular bisectors and angle bisectors.

   a. For which type of triangle would you need the fewest segments? What is the minimum number of segments you would need? Explain.

   b. For which type of triangle would you need the most segments? What is the maximum number of segments you would need? Explain.

48. THOUGHT PROVOKING The diagram shows an official hockey rink used by the National Hockey League. Create a triangle using hockey players as vertices in which the center circle is inscribed in the triangle. The center dot should be the incenter of your triangle. Sketch a drawing of the locations of your hockey players. Then label the actual lengths of the sides and the angle measures in your triangle.

COMPARING METHODS In Exercises 49 and 50, state whether you would use *perpendicular bisectors* or *angle bisectors*. Then solve the problem.

49. You need to cut the largest circle possible from an isosceles triangle made of paper whose sides are 8 inches, 12 inches, and 12 inches. Find the radius of the circle.

50. On a map of a camp, you need to create a circular walking path that connects the pool at (10, 20), the nature center at (16, 2), and the tennis court at (2, 4). Find the coordinates of the center of the circle and the radius of the circle.

51. CRITICAL THINKING Point D is the incenter of $\triangle ABC$. Write an expression for the length x in terms of the three side lengths AB, AC, and BC.

Maintaining Mathematical Proficiency   Reviewing what you learned in previous grades and lessons

The endpoints of $\overline{AB}$ are given. Find the coordinates of the midpoint M. Then find AB.
(Skills Review Handbook)

52. $A(-3, 5), B(3, 5)$ **53.** $A(2, -1), B(10, 7)$

54. $A(-5, 1), B(4, -5)$ **55.** $A(-7, 5), B(5, 9)$

Write an equation of the line passing through point P that is perpendicular to the given line. Graph the equations of the lines to check that they are perpendicular. *(Skills Review Handbook)*

56. $P(2, 8), y = 2x + 1$ **57.** $P(6, -3), y = -5$

58. $P(-8, -6), 2x + 3y = 18$ **59.** $P(-4, 1), y + 3 = -4(x + 3)$

Essential Question What conjectures can you make about the medians and altitudes of a triangle?

> ## EXPLORATION 1   Finding Properties of the Medians of a Triangle

Work with a partner. Use dynamic geometry software. Draw any △ABC.

a. Plot the midpoint of $\overline{BC}$ and label it D. Draw $\overline{AD}$, which is a *median* of △ABC. Construct the medians to the other two sides of △ABC.

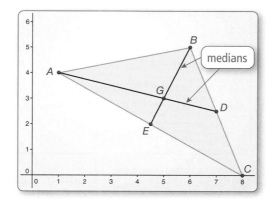

Sample
Points
A(1, 4)
B(6, 5)
C(8, 0)
D(7, 2.5)
E(4.5, 2)
G(5, 3)

b. What do you notice about the medians? Drag the vertices to change △ABC. Use your observations to write a conjecture about the medians of a triangle.

c. In the figure above, point G divides each median into a shorter segment and a longer segment. Find the ratio of the length of each longer segment to the length of the whole median. Is this ratio always the same? Justify your answer.

> ## EXPLORATION 2   Finding Properties of the Altitudes of a Triangle

Work with a partner. Use dynamic geometry software. Draw any △ABC.

LOOKING FOR STRUCTURE

To be proficient in math, you need to look closely to discern a pattern or structure.

a. Construct the perpendicular segment from vertex A to $\overline{BC}$. Label the endpoint D. $\overline{AD}$ is an *altitude* of △ABC.

b. Construct the altitudes to the other two sides of △ABC. What do you notice?

c. Write a conjecture about the altitudes of a triangle. Test your conjecture by dragging the vertices to change △ABC.

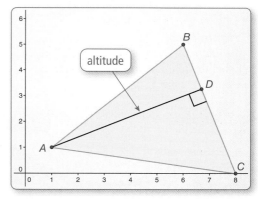

Communicate Your Answer

3. What conjectures can you make about the medians and altitudes of a triangle?

4. The length of median $\overline{RU}$ in △RST is 3 inches. The point of concurrency of the three medians of △RST divides $\overline{RU}$ into two segments. What are the lengths of these two segments?

What You Will Learn

▶ Use medians and find the centroids of triangles.

▶ Use altitudes and find the orthocenters of triangles.

Using the Median of a Triangle

A **median of a triangle** is a segment from a vertex to the midpoint of the opposite side. The three medians of a triangle are concurrent. The point of concurrency, called the **centroid**, is inside the triangle.

⟳ Theorem

Centroid Theorem

The centroid of a triangle is two-thirds of the distance from each vertex to the midpoint of the opposite side.

The medians of △*ABC* meet at point *P*, and $AP = \frac{2}{3}AE$, $BP = \frac{2}{3}BF$, and $CP = \frac{2}{3}CD$.

Proof   BigIdeasMath.com

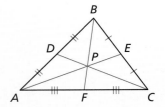

CONSTRUCTION   **Finding the Centroid of a Triangle**

Use a compass and straightedge to construct the medians of △*ABC*.

SOLUTION

Step 1	Step 2	Step 3
Find midpoints Draw △*ABC*. Find the midpoints of $\overline{AB}, \overline{BC}$, and $\overline{AC}$. Label the midpoints of the sides *D*, *E*, and *F*, respectively.	**Draw medians** Draw $\overline{AE}, \overline{BF}$, and $\overline{CD}$. These are the three medians of △*ABC*.	**Label a point** Label the point where $\overline{AE}, \overline{BF}$, and $\overline{CD}$ intersect as *P*. This is the centroid.

EXAMPLE 1   **Using the Centroid of a Triangle**

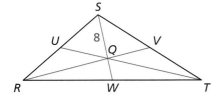

In △*RST*, point *Q* is the centroid, and *SQ* = 8. Find *QW* and *SW*.

SOLUTION

$$SQ = \frac{2}{3}SW \qquad \text{Centroid Theorem}$$

$$8 = \frac{2}{3}SW \qquad \text{Substitute 8 for } SQ.$$

$$12 = SW \qquad \text{Multiply each side by the reciprocal, } \frac{3}{2}.$$

Then *QW* = *SW* − *SQ* = 12 − 8 = 4.

▶ So, *QW* = 4 and *SW* = 12.

EXAMPLE 2 Finding the Centroid of a Triangle

Find the coordinates of the centroid of $\triangle RST$ with vertices $R(2, 1)$, $S(5, 8)$, and $T(8, 3)$.

SOLUTION

Step 1 Graph $\triangle RST$.

Step 2 Use the Midpoint Formula to find the midpoint V of $\overline{RT}$ and sketch median $\overline{SV}$.

$$V\left(\frac{2+8}{2}, \frac{1+3}{2}\right) = (5, 2)$$

Step 3 Find the centroid. It is two-thirds of the distance from each vertex to the midpoint of the opposite side.

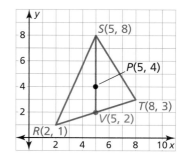

The distance from vertex $S(5, 8)$ to $V(5, 2)$ is $8 - 2 = 6$ units. So, the centroid is $\frac{2}{3}(6) = 4$ units down from vertex S on $\overline{SV}$.

▶ So, the coordinates of the centroid P are $(5, 8 - 4)$, or $(5, 4)$.

Monitoring Progress Help in English and Spanish at *BigIdeasMath.com*

There are three paths through a triangular park. Each path goes from the midpoint of one edge to the opposite corner. The paths meet at point P.

1. Find PS and PC when $SC = 2100$ feet.

2. Find TC and BC when $BT = 1000$ feet.

3. Find PA and TA when $PT = 800$ feet.

Find the coordinates of the centroid of the triangle with the given vertices.

4. $F(2, 5)$, $G(4, 9)$, $H(6, 1)$

5. $X(-3, 3)$, $Y(1, 5)$, $Z(-1, -2)$

Using the Altitude of a Triangle

An **altitude of a triangle** is the perpendicular segment from a vertex to the opposite side or to the line that contains the opposite side.

altitude from Q to $\overleftrightarrow{PR}$

Core Concept

Orthocenter

The lines containing the altitudes of a triangle are concurrent. This point of concurrency is the **orthocenter** of the triangle.

The lines containing $\overline{AF}$, $\overline{BD}$, and $\overline{CE}$ meet at the orthocenter G of $\triangle ABC$.

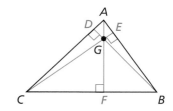

As shown below, the location of the orthocenter P of a triangle depends on the type of triangle.

Acute triangle
P is inside triangle.

Right triangle
P is on triangle.

Obtuse triangle
P is outside triangle.

READING
The altitudes are shown in red. Notice that in the right triangle, the legs are also altitudes. The altitudes of the obtuse triangle are extended to find the orthocenter.

EXAMPLE 3   **Finding the Orthocenter of a Triangle**

Find the coordinates of the orthocenter of $\triangle XYZ$ with vertices $X(-5, -1)$, $Y(-2, 4)$, and $Z(3, -1)$.

SOLUTION

Step 1 Graph $\triangle XYZ$.

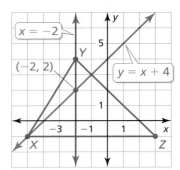

Step 2 Find an equation of the line that contains the altitude from Y to $\overline{XZ}$. Because $\overline{XZ}$ is horizontal, the altitude is vertical. The line that contains the altitude passes through $Y(-2, 4)$. So, the equation of the line is $x = -2$.

Step 3 Find an equation of the line that contains the altitude from X to $\overline{YZ}$.

$$\text{slope of } \overleftrightarrow{YZ} = \frac{-1-4}{3-(-2)} = -1$$

Because the product of the slopes of two perpendicular lines is -1, the slope of a line perpendicular to $\overleftrightarrow{YZ}$ is 1. The line passes through $X(-5, -1)$.

$y = mx + b$ Use slope-intercept form.

$-1 = 1(-5) + b$ Substitute -1 for y, 1 for m, and -5 for x.

$4 = b$ Solve for b.

So, the equation of the line is $y = x + 4$.

Step 4 Find the point of intersection of the graphs of the equations $x = -2$ and $y = x + 4$.

Substitute -2 for x in the equation $y = x + 4$. Then solve for y.

$y = x + 4$ Write equation.

$y = -2 + 4$ Substitute -2 for x.

$y = 2$ Solve for y.

▶ So, the coordinates of the orthocenter are $(-2, 2)$.

Monitoring Progress   Help in English and Spanish at *BigIdeasMath.com*

Tell whether the orthocenter of the triangle with the given vertices is *inside*, *on*, or *outside* the triangle. Then find the coordinates of the orthocenter.

6. $A(0, 3)$, $B(0, -2)$, $C(6, -3)$ **7.** $J(-3, -4)$, $K(-3, 4)$, $L(5, 4)$

In an isosceles triangle, the perpendicular bisector, angle bisector, median, and altitude from the vertex angle to the base are all the same segment. In an equilateral triangle, this is true for any vertex.

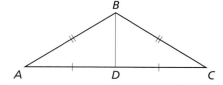

EXAMPLE 4   **Proving a Property of Isosceles Triangles**

Prove that the median from the vertex angle to the base of an isosceles triangle is an altitude.

SOLUTION

Given $\triangle ABC$ is isosceles, with base $\overline{AC}$.
$\overline{BD}$ is the median to base $\overline{AC}$.

Prove $\overline{BD}$ is an altitude of $\triangle ABC$.

Paragraph Proof Legs $\overline{AB}$ and $\overline{BC}$ of isosceles $\triangle ABC$ are congruent. $\overline{CD} \cong \overline{AD}$ because $\overline{BD}$ is the median to $\overline{AC}$. Also, $\overline{BD} \cong \overline{BD}$ by the Reflexive Property of Congruence. So, $\triangle ABD \cong \triangle CBD$ by the SSS Congruence Theorem. $\angle ADB \cong \angle CDB$ because corresponding parts of congruent triangles are congruent. Also, $\angle ADB$ and $\angle CDB$ are a linear pair. $\overline{BD}$ and $\overline{AC}$ intersect to form a linear pair of congruent angles, so $\overline{BD} \perp \overline{AC}$ and $\overline{BD}$ is an altitude of $\triangle ABC$.

Monitoring Progress   ))) Help in English and Spanish at *BigIdeasMath.com*

8. **WHAT IF?** In Example 4, you want to show that median $\overline{BD}$ is also an angle bisector. How would your proof be different?

Concept Summary

Segments, Lines, Rays, and Points in Triangles

	Example	Point of Concurrency	Property	Example
perpendicular bisector		circumcenter	The circumcenter P of a triangle is equidistant from the vertices of the triangle.	
angle bisector		incenter	The incenter I of a triangle is equidistant from the sides of the triangle.	
median		centroid	The centroid R of a triangle is two thirds of the distance from each vertex to the midpoint of the opposite side.	
altitude		orthocenter	The lines containing the altitudes of a triangle are concurrent at the orthocenter O.	

Vocabulary and Core Concept Check

1. **VOCABULARY** Name the four types of points of concurrency. Which lines intersect to form each of the points?

2. **COMPLETE THE SENTENCE** The length of a segment from a vertex to the centroid is _____ the length of the median from that vertex.

Monitoring Progress and Modeling with Mathematics

In Exercises 3–6, point *P* is the centroid of △*LMN*. Find *PN* and *QP*. *(See Example 1.)*

3. *QN* = 9

4. *QN* = 21

5. *QN* = 30

6. *QN* = 42

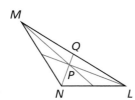

In Exercises 7–10, point *D* is the centroid of △*ABC*. Find *CD* and *CE*.

7. *DE* = 5

8. *DE* = 11

9. *DE* = 9

10. *DE* = 15

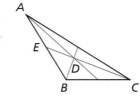

In Exercises 11–14, point *G* is the centroid of △*ABC*. *BG* = 6, *AF* = 12, and *AE* = 15. Find the length of the segment.

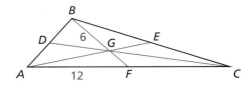

11. $\overline{FC}$

12. $\overline{BF}$

13. $\overline{AG}$

14. $\overline{GE}$

In Exercises 15–18, find the coordinates of the centroid of the triangle with the given vertices. *(See Example 2.)*

15. *A*(2, 3), *B*(8, 1), *C*(5, 7)

16. *F*(1, 5), *G*(−2, 7), *H*(−6, 3)

17. *S*(5, 5), *T*(11, −3), *U*(−1, 1)

18. *X*(1, 4), *Y*(7, 2), *Z*(2, 3)

In Exercises 19–22, tell whether the orthocenter is *inside*, *on*, or *outside* the triangle. Then find the coordinates of the orthocenter. *(See Example 3.)*

19. *L*(0, 5), *M*(3, 1), *N*(8, 1)

20. *X*(−3, 2), *Y*(5, 2), *Z*(−3, 6)

21. *A*(−4, 0), *B*(1, 0), *C*(−1, 3)

22. *T*(−2, 1), *U*(2, 1), *V*(0, 4)

CONSTRUCTION In Exercises 23–26, draw the indicated triangle and find its centroid and orthocenter.

23. isosceles right triangle   24. obtuse scalene triangle

25. right scalene triangle   26. acute isosceles triangle

ERROR ANALYSIS In Exercises 27 and 28, describe and correct the error in finding *DE*. Point *D* is the centroid of △*ABC*.

27.
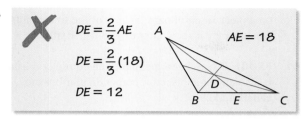

$$DE = \frac{2}{3}AE$$

$$DE = \frac{2}{3}(18)$$

$$DE = 12$$

$$AE = 18$$

28.

$$DE = \frac{2}{3}AD$$

$$DE = \frac{2}{3}(24)$$

$$DE = 16$$

$$AD = 24$$

PROOF In Exercises 29 and 30, write a proof of the statement. *(See Example 4.)*

29. The angle bisector from the vertex angle to the base of an isosceles triangle is also a median.

30. The altitude from the vertex angle to the base of an isosceles triangle is also a perpendicular bisector.

CRITICAL THINKING In Exercises 31–36, complete the statement with *always*, *sometimes*, or *never*. Explain your reasoning.

31. The centroid is _____ on the triangle.

32. The orthocenter is _____ outside the triangle.

33. A median is _____ the same line segment as a perpendicular bisector.

34. An altitude is _____ the same line segment as an angle bisector.

35. The centroid and orthocenter are _____ the same point.

36. The centroid is _____ formed by the intersection of the three medians.

37. **WRITING** Compare an altitude of a triangle with a perpendicular bisector of a triangle.

38. **WRITING** Compare a median, an altitude, and an angle bisector of a triangle.

39. **MODELING WITH MATHEMATICS** Find the area of the triangular part of the paper airplane wing that is outlined in red. Which special segment of the triangle did you use?

9 in.

3 in.

40. **ANALYZING RELATIONSHIPS** Copy and complete the statement for △*DEF* with centroid *K* and medians $\overline{DH}, \overline{EJ}$, and $\overline{FG}$.

   a. $EJ = $ _____ KJ b. $DK = $ _____ KH

   c. $FG = $ _____ KF d. $KG = $ _____ FG

MATHEMATICAL CONNECTIONS In Exercises 41–44, point *D* is the centroid of △*ABC*. Use the given information to find the value of *x*.

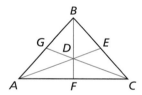

41. $BD = 4x + 5$ and $BF = 9x$

42. $GD = 2x - 8$ and $GC = 3x + 3$

43. $AD = 5x$ and $DE = 3x - 2$

44. $DF = 4x - 1$ and $BD = 6x + 4$

45. **MATHEMATICAL CONNECTIONS** Graph the lines on the same coordinate plane. Find the centroid of the triangle formed by their intersections.

$$y_1 = 3x - 4$$

$$y_2 = \frac{3}{4}x + 5$$

$$y_3 = -\frac{3}{2}x - 4$$

46. **CRITICAL THINKING** In what type(s) of triangles can a vertex be one of the points of concurrency of the triangle? Explain your reasoning.

47. WRITING EQUATIONS Use the numbers and symbols to write three different equations for *PE*.

| PE | AE | AP | + | − |

| = | $\dfrac{1}{4}$ | $\dfrac{1}{3}$ | $\dfrac{1}{2}$ | $\dfrac{2}{3}$ |

48. HOW DO YOU SEE IT? Use the figure.

a. What type of segment is $\overline{KM}$? Which point of concurrency lies on $\overline{KM}$?

b. What type of segment is $\overline{KN}$? Which point of concurrency lies on $\overline{KN}$?

c. Compare the areas of $\triangle JKM$ and $\triangle KLM$. Do you think the areas of the triangles formed by the median of any triangle will always compare this way? Explain your reasoning.

49. MAKING AN ARGUMENT Your friend claims that it is possible for the circumcenter, incenter, centroid, and orthocenter to all be the same point. Do you agree? Explain your reasoning.

50. DRAWING CONCLUSIONS The center of gravity of a triangle, the point where a triangle can balance on the tip of a pencil, is one of the four points of concurrency. Draw and cut out a large scalene triangle on a piece of cardboard. Which of the four points of concurrency is the center of gravity? Explain.

51. PROOF Prove that a median of an equilateral triangle is also an angle bisector, perpendicular bisector, and altitude.

52. THOUGHT PROVOKING Construct an acute scalene triangle. Find the orthocenter, centroid, and circumcenter. What can you conclude about the three points of concurrency?

53. CONSTRUCTION Follow the steps to construct a nine-point circle. Why is it called a nine-point circle?

Step 1 Construct a large acute scalene triangle.

Step 2 Find the orthocenter and circumcenter of the triangle.

Step 3 Find the midpoint between the orthocenter and circumcenter.

Step 4 Find the midpoint between each vertex and the orthocenter.

Step 5 Construct a circle. Use the midpoint in Step 3 as the center of the circle, and the distance from the center to the midpoint of a side of the triangle as the radius.

54. PROOF Prove the statements in parts (a)−(c).

Given $\overline{LP}$ and $\overline{MQ}$ are medians of scalene $\triangle LMN$. Point R is on $\overrightarrow{LP}$ such that $\overline{LP} \cong \overline{PR}$. Point S is on $\overrightarrow{MQ}$ such that $\overline{MQ} \cong \overline{QS}$.

Prove   a. $\overline{NS} \cong \overline{NR}$
       b. $\overline{NS}$ and $\overline{NR}$ are both parallel to $\overline{LM}$.
       c. R, N, and S are collinear.

Maintaining Mathematical Proficiency
Reviewing what you learned in previous grades and lessons

Determine whether $\overline{AB}$ is parallel to $\overline{CD}$.   *(Skills Review Handbook)*

55. $A(5, 6)$, $B(-1, 3)$, $C(-4, 9)$, $D(-16, 3)$

56. $A(-3, 6)$, $B(5, 4)$, $C(-14, -10)$, $D(-2, -7)$

57. $A(6, -3)$, $B(5, 2)$, $C(-4, -4)$, $D(-5, 2)$

58. $A(-5, 6)$, $B(-7, 2)$, $C(7, 1)$, $D(4, -5)$

6.1–6.4 What Did You Learn?

Core Vocabulary

proof, *p. 336*
two-column proof, *p. 336*
paragraph proof, *p. 337*
flowchart proof, or flow proof,
  p. 338

coordinate proof, *p. 339*
equidistant, *p. 344*
concurrent, *p. 352*
point of concurrency, *p. 352*
circumcenter, *p. 352*

incenter, *p. 355*
median of a triangle, *p. 362*
centroid, *p. 362*
altitude of a triangle, *p. 363*
orthocenter, *p. 363*

Core Concepts

Section 6.1

Writing Two-Column Proofs, *p. 336*
Writing Paragraph Proofs, *p. 337*

Writing Flowchart Proofs, *p. 338*
Writing Coordinate Proofs, *p. 339*

Section 6.2

Perpendicular Bisector Theorem, *p. 344*
Converse of the Perpendicular Bisector Theorem,
  p. 344

Angle Bisector Theorem, *p. 346*
Converse of the Angle Bisector Theorem, *p. 346*

Section 6.3

Circumcenter Theorem, *p. 352*

Incenter Theorem, *p. 355*

Section 6.4

Centroid Theorem, *p. 362*
Orthocenter, *p. 363*

Segments, Lines, Rays, and Points in Triangles, *p. 365*

Mathematical Practices

1. Did you make a plan before completing your proof in Exercise 37 on page 350? Describe your thought process.

2. What tools did you use to complete Exercises 17–20 on page 358? Describe how you could use technological tools to complete these exercises.

Rework Your Notes

A good way to reinforce concepts and put them into your long-term memory is to rework your notes. When you take notes, leave extra space on the pages. You can go back after class and fill in

*   important definitions and rules,
*   additional examples, and
*   questions you have about the material.

STUDY SKILLS

Find the indicated measure. Explain your reasoning. *(Section 6.2)*

1. *UV*

2. *QP*

3. *m∠GJK*

Find the coordinates of the circumcenter of the triangle with the given vertices.
(Section 6.3)

4. $A(-4, 2), B(-4, -4), C(0, -4)$

5. $D(3, 5), E(7, 9), F(11, 5)$

The incenter of △ABC is point N. Use the given information to find the indicated measure. *(Section 6.3)*

6. $NQ = 2x + 1, NR = 4x - 9$
Find *NS*.

7. $NU = -3x + 6, NV = -5x$
Find *NT*.

8. $NZ = 4x - 10, NY = 3x - 1$
Find *NW*.

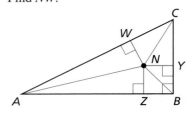

Find the coordinates of the centroid of the triangle with the given vertices. *(Section 6.4)*

9. $J(-1, 2), K(5, 6), L(5, -2)$

10. $M(-8, -6), N(-4, -2), P(0, -4)$

Tell whether the orthocenter is *inside*, *on*, or *outside* the triangle. Then find its coordinates.
(Section 6.4)

11. $T(-2, 5), U(0, 1), V(2, 5)$

12. $X(-1, -4), Y(7, -4), Z(7, 4)$

13. A woodworker is cutting the largest wheel possible from a triangular
scrap of wood. The wheel just touches each side of the triangle, as shown.
(Section 6.1 and Section 6.3)

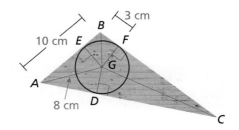

  a. Which point of concurrency is the center of the circle? What type
  of segments are $\overline{BG}, \overline{CG},$ and $\overline{AG}$?

  b. Prove that $△BGF \cong △BGE$.

  c. Find the radius of the wheel to the nearest tenth of a centimeter. Justify
  your answer.

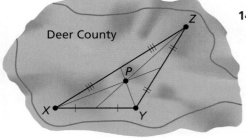

14. The Deer County Parks Committee plans to build a park at point *P*,
equidistant from the three largest cities labeled *X*, *Y*, and *Z*. The map
shown was created by the committee. *(Section 6.3 and Section 6.4)*

  a. Which point of concurrency did the committee use as the location
  of the park?

  b. Did the committee use the best point of concurrency for the location
  of the park? If not, which point would be better to use? Explain.

6.5   The Triangle Midsegment Theorem

Essential Question   How are the midsegments of a triangle related to the sides of the triangle?

EXPLORATION 1   Midsegments of a Triangle

Work with a partner. Use dynamic geometry software. Draw any △ABC.

a. Plot midpoint D of $\overline{AB}$ and midpoint E of $\overline{BC}$. Draw $\overline{DE}$, which is a *midsegment* of △ABC.

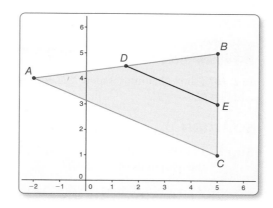

Sample
Points
A(−2, 4)
B(5, 5)
C(5, 1)
D(1.5, 4.5)
E(5, 3)
Segments
BC = 4
AC = 7.62
AB = 7.07
DE = ?

b. Compare the slope and length of $\overline{DE}$ with the slope and length of $\overline{AC}$.

c. Write a conjecture about the relationships between the midsegments and sides of a triangle. Test your conjecture by drawing the other midsegments of △ABC, dragging vertices to change △ABC, and noting whether the relationships hold.

CONSTRUCTING VIABLE ARGUMENTS

To be proficient in math, you need to make conjectures and build a logical progression of statements to explore the truth of your conjectures.

EXPLORATION 2   Midsegments of a Triangle

Work with a partner. Use dynamic geometry software. Draw any △ABC.

a. Draw all three midsegments of △ABC.

b. Use the drawing to write a conjecture about the triangle formed by the midsegments of the original triangle.

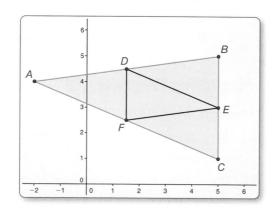

Sample

Points	Segments
A(−2, 4)	BC = 4
B(5, 5)	AC = 7.62
C(5, 1)	AB = 7.07
D(1.5, 4.5)	DE = ?
E(5, 3)	DF = ?
	EF = ?

Communicate Your Answer

3. How are the midsegments of a triangle related to the sides of the triangle?

4. In △RST, $\overline{UV}$ is the midsegment connecting the midpoints of $\overline{RS}$ and $\overline{ST}$. Given UV = 12, find RT.

What You Will Learn

▶ Use midsegments of triangles in the coordinate plane.

▶ Use the Triangle Midsegment Theorem to find distances.

Core Vocabulary

midsegment of a triangle,
  p. 372
Previous
midpoint
parallel
slope
coordinate proof

Using the Midsegment of a Triangle

A **midsegment of a triangle** is a segment that connects the midpoints of two sides of the triangle. Every triangle has three midsegments, which form the *midsegment triangle*.

The midsegments of $\triangle ABC$ at the right are $\overline{MP}$, $\overline{MN}$, and $\overline{NP}$. The *midsegment triangle* is $\triangle MNP$.

EXAMPLE 1   Using Midsegments in the Coordinate Plane

In $\triangle JKL$, show that midsegment $\overline{MN}$ is parallel to $\overline{JL}$ and that $MN = \frac{1}{2}JL$.

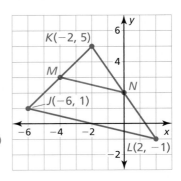

> **READING**
>
> In the figure for Example 1, midsegment $\overline{MN}$ can be called "the midsegment opposite $\overline{JL}$."

SOLUTION

Step 1 Find the coordinates of M and N by finding the midpoints of $\overline{JK}$ and $\overline{KL}$.

$$M\left(\frac{-6 + (-2)}{2}, \frac{1 + 5}{2}\right) = M\left(\frac{-8}{2}, \frac{6}{2}\right) = M(-4, 3)$$

$$N\left(\frac{-2 + 2}{2}, \frac{5 + (-1)}{2}\right) = N\left(\frac{0}{2}, \frac{4}{2}\right) = N(0, 2)$$

Step 2 Find and compare the slopes of $\overline{MN}$ and $\overline{JL}$.

$$\text{slope of } \overline{MN} = \frac{2 - 3}{0 - (-4)} = -\frac{1}{4} \qquad \text{slope of } \overline{JL} = \frac{-1 - 1}{2 - (-6)} = -\frac{2}{8} = -\frac{1}{4}$$

▶ Because the slopes are the same, $\overline{MN}$ is parallel to $\overline{JL}$.

Step 3 Find and compare the lengths of $\overline{MN}$ and $\overline{JL}$.

$$MN = \sqrt{[0 - (-4)]^2 + (2 - 3)^2} = \sqrt{16 + 1} = \sqrt{17}$$

$$JL = \sqrt{[2 - (-6)]^2 + (-1 - 1)^2} = \sqrt{64 + 4} = \sqrt{68} = 2\sqrt{17}$$

▶ Because $\sqrt{17} = \frac{1}{2}\left(2\sqrt{17}\right)$, $MN = \frac{1}{2}JL$.

Monitoring Progress Help in English and Spanish at *BigIdeasMath.com*

Use the graph of $\triangle ABC$.

1. In $\triangle ABC$, show that midsegment $\overline{DE}$ is parallel to $\overline{AC}$ and that $DE = \frac{1}{2}AC$.

2. Find the coordinates of the endpoints of midsegment $\overline{EF}$, which is opposite $\overline{AB}$. Show that $\overline{EF}$ is parallel to $\overline{AB}$ and that $EF = \frac{1}{2}AB$.

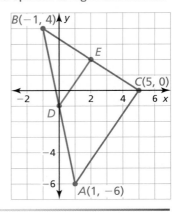

Using the Triangle Midsegment Theorem

⟳ Theorem

Triangle Midsegment Theorem

The segment connecting the midpoints of two sides of
a triangle is parallel to the third side and is half as
long as that side.

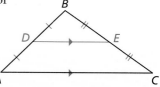

$\overline{DE}$ is a midsegment of $\triangle ABC$, $\overline{DE} \parallel \overline{AC}$,
and $DE = \frac{1}{2}AC$.

Proof Example 2, p. 373; Monitoring Progress Question 3, p. 373; Ex. 22, p. 376

EXAMPLE 2 **Proving the Triangle Midsegment Theorem**

Write a coordinate proof of the Triangle
Midsegment Theorem for one midsegment.

Given $\overline{DE}$ is a midsegment of $\triangle OBC$.

Prove $\overline{DE} \parallel \overline{OC}$ and $DE = \frac{1}{2}OC$

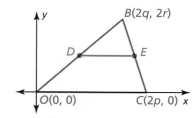

SOLUTION

STUDY TIP

When assigning
coordinates, try to choose
coordinates that make
some of the computations
easier. In Example 2, you
can avoid fractions by using
$2p$, $2q$, and $2r$.

Step 1 Place $\triangle OBC$ in a coordinate plane and assign coordinates. Because you are
finding midpoints, use $2p$, $2q$, and $2r$. Then find the coordinates of D and E.

$$D\left(\frac{2q + 0}{2}, \frac{2r + 0}{2}\right) = D(q, r) \qquad E\left(\frac{2q + 2p}{2}, \frac{2r + 0}{2}\right) = E(q + p, r)$$

Step 2 Prove $\overline{DE} \parallel \overline{OC}$. The y-coordinates of D and E are the same, so $\overline{DE}$ has a slope
of 0. $\overline{OC}$ is on the x-axis, so its slope is 0.

▶ Because their slopes are the same, $\overline{DE} \parallel \overline{OC}$.

Step 3 Prove $DE = \frac{1}{2}OC$. Use the Ruler Postulate to find DE and OC.

$$DE = |(q + p) - q| = p \qquad OC = |2p - 0| = 2p$$

▶ Because $p = \frac{1}{2}(2p)$, $DE = \frac{1}{2}OC$.

Monitoring Progress 🔊 Help in English and Spanish at *BigIdeasMath.com*

3. In Example 2, find the coordinates of F, the midpoint of $\overline{OC}$. Show that $\overline{FE} \parallel \overline{OB}$
and $FE = \frac{1}{2}OB$.

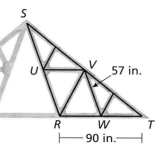

EXAMPLE 3 **Using the Triangle Midsegment Theorem**

Triangles are used for strength in roof trusses. In the
diagram, $\overline{UV}$ and $\overline{VW}$ are midsegments of $\triangle RST$.
Find UV and RS.

SOLUTION

$$UV = \frac{1}{2} \cdot RT = \frac{1}{2}(90 \text{ in.}) = 45 \text{ in.}$$

$$RS = 2 \cdot VW = 2(57 \text{ in.}) = 114 \text{ in.}$$

EXAMPLE 4 **Using the Triangle Midsegment Theorem**

In the kaleidoscope image, $\overline{AE} \cong \overline{BE}$ and $\overline{AD} \cong \overline{CD}$. Show that $\overline{CB} \parallel \overline{DE}$.

SOLUTION

Because $\overline{AE} \cong \overline{BE}$ and $\overline{AD} \cong \overline{CD}$, E is the midpoint of $\overline{AB}$ and D is the midpoint of $\overline{AC}$ by definition. Then $\overline{DE}$ is a midsegment of $\triangle ABC$ by definition and $\overline{CB} \parallel \overline{DE}$ by the Triangle Midsegment Theorem.

EXAMPLE 5 **Modeling with Mathematics**

Pear Street intersects Cherry Street and Peach Street at their midpoints. Your home is at point P. You leave your home and jog down Cherry Street to Plum Street, over Plum Street to Peach Street, up Peach Street to Pear Street, over Pear Street to Cherry Street, and then back home up Cherry Street. About how many miles do you jog?

SOLUTION

1. **Understand the Problem** You know the distances from your home to Plum Street along Peach Street, from Peach Street to Cherry Street along Plum Street, and from Pear Street to your home along Cherry Street. You need to find the other distances on your route, then find the total number of miles you jog.

2. **Make a Plan** By definition, you know that Pear Street is a midsegment of the triangle formed by the other three streets. Use the Triangle Midsegment Theorem to find the length of Pear Street and the definition of midsegment to find the length of Cherry Street. Then add the distances along your route.

3. **Solve the Problem**

   length of Pear Street $= \frac{1}{2} \cdot$ (length of Plum St.) $= \frac{1}{2}(1.4 \text{ mi}) = 0.7 \text{ mi}$

   length of Cherry Street $= 2 \cdot$ (length from P to Pear St.) $= 2(1.3 \text{ mi}) = 2.6 \text{ mi}$

   distance along your route: $2.6 + 1.4 + \frac{1}{2}(2.25) + 0.7 + 1.3 = 7.125$

   ▶ So, you jog about 7 miles.

4. **Look Back** Use compatible numbers to check that your answer is reasonable.

   total distance:

   $$2.6 + 1.4 + \tfrac{1}{2}(2.25) + 0.7 + 1.3 \approx 2.5 + 1.5 + 1 + 0.5 + 1.5 = 7 \checkmark$$

Monitoring Progress Help in English and Spanish at *BigIdeasMath.com*

4. Copy the diagram in Example 3. Draw and name the third midsegment. Then find the length of $\overline{VS}$ when the length of the third midsegment is 81 inches.

5. In Example 4, if F is the midpoint of $\overline{CB}$, what do you know about $\overline{DF}$?

6. **WHAT IF?** In Example 5, you jog down Peach Street to Plum Street, over Plum Street to Cherry Street, up Cherry Street to Pear Street, over Pear Street to Peach Street, and then back home up Peach Street. Do you jog more miles in Example 5? Explain.

Vocabulary and Core Concept Check

1. **VOCABULARY** The _____ of a triangle is a segment that connects the midpoints of two sides of the triangle.

2. **COMPLETE THE SENTENCE** If $\overline{DE}$ is the midsegment opposite $\overline{AC}$ in $\triangle ABC$, then $\overline{DE} \parallel \overline{AC}$ and $DE = \underline{\quad} AC$ by the Triangle Midsegment Theorem.

Monitoring Progress and Modeling with Mathematics

In Exercises 3–6, use the graph of $\triangle ABC$ with midsegments $\overline{DE}, \overline{EF}$, and $\overline{DF}$. *(See Example 1.)*

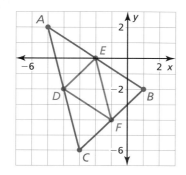

3. Find the coordinates of points D, E, and F.

4. Show that $\overline{DE}$ is parallel to $\overline{CB}$ and that $DE = \frac{1}{2}CB$.

5. Show that $\overline{EF}$ is parallel to $\overline{AC}$ and that $EF = \frac{1}{2}AC$.

6. Show that $\overline{DF}$ is parallel to $\overline{AB}$ and that $DF = \frac{1}{2}AB$.

In Exercises 7–10, $\overline{DE}$ is a midsegment of $\triangle ABC$. Find the value of x. *(See Example 3.)*

7.

8.

9.

10.
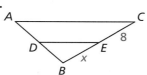

In Exercises 11–16, $\overline{XJ} \cong \overline{JY}, \overline{YL} \cong \overline{LZ}$, and $\overline{XK} \cong \overline{KZ}$. Copy and complete the statement. *(See Example 4.)*

11. $\overline{JK} \parallel$ ____

12. $\overline{JL} \parallel$ ____

13. $\overline{XY} \parallel$ ____

14. $\overline{JY} \cong$ ____ $\cong$ ____

15. $\overline{JL} \cong$ ____ $\cong$ ____

16. $\overline{JK} \cong$ ____ $\cong$ ____

MATHEMATICAL CONNECTIONS In Exercises 17–19, use $\triangle GHJ$, where A, B, and C are midpoints of the sides.

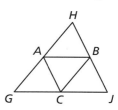

17. When $AB = 3x + 8$ and $GJ = 2x + 24$, what is AB?

18. When $AC = 3y - 5$ and $HJ = 4y + 2$, what is HB?

19. When $GH = 7z - 1$ and $CB = 4z - 3$, what is GA?

20. **ERROR ANALYSIS** Describe and correct the error.

21. MODELING WITH MATHEMATICS The distance between consecutive bases on a baseball field is 90 feet. A second baseman stands halfway between first base and second base, a shortstop stands halfway between second base and third base, and a pitcher stands halfway between first base and third base. Find the distance between the shortstop and the pitcher. *(See Example 5.)*

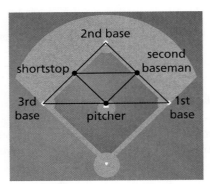

22. PROVING A THEOREM Use the figure from Example 2 to prove the Triangle Midsegment Theorem for midsegment $\overline{DF}$, where F is the midpoint of $\overline{OC}$. *(See Example 2.)*

23. CRITICAL THINKING $\overline{XY}$ is a midsegment of $\triangle LMN$. Suppose $\overline{DE}$ is called a "quarter segment" of $\triangle LMN$. What do you think an "eighth segment" would be? Make conjectures about the properties of a quarter segment and an eighth segment. Use variable coordinates to verify your conjectures.

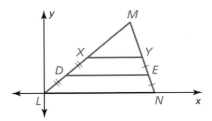

24. THOUGHT PROVOKING Find a real-life object that uses midsegments as part of its structure. Print a photograph of the object and identify the midsegments of one of the triangles in the structure.

25. ABSTRACT REASONING To create the design shown, shade the triangle formed by the three midsegments of the triangle. Then repeat the process for each unshaded triangle.

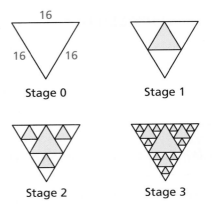

Stage 0   Stage 1

Stage 2   Stage 3

a. What is the perimeter of the shaded triangle in Stage 1?

b. What is the total perimeter of all the shaded triangles in Stage 2?

c. What is the total perimeter of all the shaded triangles in Stage 3?

26. HOW DO YOU SEE IT? Explain how you know that the yellow triangle is the midsegment triangle of the red triangle in the pattern of floor tiles shown.

27. ATTENDING TO PRECISION The points $P(2, 1)$, $Q(4, 5)$, and $R(7, 4)$ are the midpoints of the sides of a triangle. Graph the three midsegments. Then show how to use your graph and the properties of midsegments to draw the original triangle. Give the coordinates of each vertex.

Maintaining Mathematical Proficiency
Reviewing what you learned in previous grades and lessons

Find a counterexample to show that the conjecture is false. *(Skills Review Handbook)*

28. The difference of two numbers is always less than the greater number.

29. An isosceles triangle is always equilateral.

6.6 Indirect Proof and Inequalities in One Triangle

Essential Question How are the sides related to the angles of a triangle? How are any two sides of a triangle related to the third side?

Work with a partner. Use dynamic geometry software. Draw any scalene △*ABC*.

a. Find the side lengths and angle measures of the triangle.

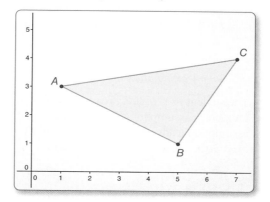

Sample

Points	Angles
$A(1, 3)$	$m\angle A = ?$
$B(5, 1)$	$m\angle B = ?$
$C(7, 4)$	$m\angle C = ?$

Segments
$BC = ?$
$AC = ?$
$AB = ?$

ATTENDING TO PRECISION

To be proficient in math, you need to express numerical answers with a degree of precision appropriate for the content.

b. Order the side lengths. Order the angle measures. What do you observe?

c. Drag the vertices of △*ABC* to form new triangles. Record the side lengths and angle measures in a table. Write a conjecture about your findings.

Work with a partner. Use dynamic geometry software. Draw any △*ABC*.

a. Find the side lengths of the triangle.

b. Compare each side length with the sum of the other two side lengths.

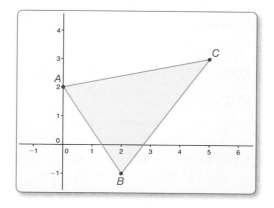

Sample

Points
$A(0, 2)$
$B(2, -1)$
$C(5, 3)$
Segments
$BC = ?$
$AC = ?$
$AB = ?$

c. Drag the vertices of △*ABC* to form new triangles and repeat parts (a) and (b). Organize your results in a table. Write a conjecture about your findings.

Communicate Your Answer

3. How are the sides related to the angles of a triangle? How are any two sides of a triangle related to the third side?

4. Is it possible for a triangle to have side lengths of 3, 4, and 10? Explain.

6.6 Lesson

Core Vocabulary

indirect proof, *p. 378*

Previous
proof
inequality

What You Will Learn

▶ Write indirect proofs.

▶ List sides and angles of a triangle in order by size.

▶ Use the Triangle Inequality Theorem to find possible side lengths of triangles.

Writing an Indirect Proof

Suppose a student looks around the cafeteria, concludes that hamburgers are not being served, and explains as follows.

> *At first, I assumed that we are having hamburgers because today is Tuesday, and Tuesday is usually hamburger day.*
>
> *There is always ketchup on the table when we have hamburgers, so I looked for the ketchup, but I didn't see any.*
>
> *So, my assumption that we are having hamburgers must be false.*

The student uses *indirect* reasoning. In an **indirect proof**, you start by making the temporary assumption that the desired conclusion is false. By then showing that this assumption leads to a logical impossibility, you prove the original statement true *by contradiction*.

🔄 Core Concept

How to Write an Indirect Proof (Proof by Contradiction)

Step 1 Identify the statement you want to prove. Assume temporarily that this statement is false by assuming that its opposite is true.

Step 2 Reason logically until you reach a contradiction.

Step 3 Point out that the desired conclusion must be true because the contradiction proves the temporary assumption false.

EXAMPLE 1   Writing an Indirect Proof

Write an indirect proof that in a given triangle, there can be at most one right angle.

Given $\triangle ABC$

Prove $\triangle ABC$ can have at most one right angle.

SOLUTION

READING

You have reached a *contradiction* when you have two statements that cannot both be true at the same time.

Step 1 Assume temporarily that $\triangle ABC$ has two right angles. Then assume $\angle A$ and $\angle B$ are right angles.

Step 2 By the definition of right angle, $m\angle A = m\angle B = 90°$. By the Triangle Sum Theorem, $m\angle A + m\angle B + m\angle C = 180°$. Using the Substitution Property of Equality, $90° + 90° + m\angle C = 180°$. So, $m\angle C = 0°$ by the Subtraction Property of Equality. A triangle cannot have an angle measure of $0°$. So, this contradicts the given information.

Step 3 So, the assumption that $\triangle ABC$ has two right angles must be false, which proves that $\triangle ABC$ can have at most one right angle.

Monitoring Progress Help in English and Spanish at *BigIdeasMath.com*

1. Write an indirect proof that a scalene triangle cannot have two congruent angles.

Relating Sides and Angles of a Triangle

EXAMPLE 2   Relating Side Length and Angle Measure

Draw an obtuse scalene triangle. Find the largest angle and longest side and mark them in red. Find the smallest angle and shortest side and mark them in blue. What do you notice?

SOLUTION

The longest side and largest angle are opposite each other.

The shortest side and smallest angle are opposite each other.

The relationships in Example 2 are true for all triangles, as stated in the two theorems below. These relationships can help you decide whether a particular arrangement of side lengths and angle measures in a triangle may be possible.

COMMON ERROR

Be careful not to confuse the symbol ∠ meaning *angle* with the symbol < meaning *is less than*. Notice that the bottom edge of the angle symbol is horizontal.

🌀 Theorems

Triangle Longer Side Theorem

If one side of a triangle is longer than another side, then the angle opposite the longer side is larger than the angle opposite the shorter side.

Proof Ex. 43, p. 384

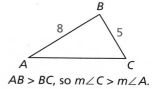

$AB > BC$, so $m\angle C > m\angle A$.

Triangle Larger Angle Theorem

If one angle of a triangle is larger than another angle, then the side opposite the larger angle is longer than the side opposite the smaller angle.

Proof p. 379

$m\angle A > m\angle C$, so $BC > AB$.

PROOF   Triangle Larger Angle Theorem

COMMON ERROR

Be sure to consider all cases when assuming the opposite is true.

Given $m\angle A > m\angle C$

Prove $BC > AB$

Indirect Proof

Step 1   Assume temporarily that $BC \not> AB$. Then it follows that either $BC < AB$ or $BC = AB$.

Step 2   If $BC < AB$, then $m\angle A < m\angle C$ by the Triangle Longer Side Theorem. If $BC = AB$, then $m\angle A = m\angle C$ by the Base Angles Theorem.

Step 3   Both conclusions contradict the given statement that $m\angle A > m\angle C$. So, the temporary assumption that $BC \not> AB$ cannot be true. This proves that $BC > AB$.

EXAMPLE 3 Ordering Angle Measures of a Triangle

You are constructing a stage prop that shows a large triangular mountain. The bottom edge of the mountain is about 32 feet long, the left slope is about 24 feet long, and the right slope is about 26 feet long. List the angles of △JKL in order from smallest to largest.

SOLUTION

Draw the triangle that represents the mountain. Label the side lengths.

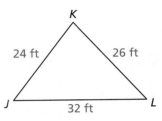

The sides from shortest to longest are $\overline{JK}$, $\overline{KL}$, and $\overline{JL}$. The angles opposite these sides are ∠L, ∠J, and ∠K, respectively.

▶ So, by the Triangle Longer Side Theorem, the angles from smallest to largest are ∠L, ∠J, and ∠K.

EXAMPLE 4 Ordering Side Lengths of a Triangle

List the sides of △DEF in order from shortest to longest.

SOLUTION

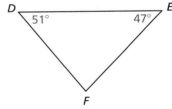

First, find $m\angle F$ using the Triangle Sum Theorem.

$$m\angle D + m\angle E + m\angle F = 180°$$
$$51° + 47° + m\angle F = 180°$$
$$m\angle F = 82°$$

The angles from smallest to largest are ∠E, ∠D, and ∠F. The sides opposite these angles are $\overline{DF}$, $\overline{EF}$, and $\overline{DE}$, respectively.

▶ So, by the Triangle Larger Angle Theorem, the sides from shortest to longest are $\overline{DF}$, $\overline{EF}$, and $\overline{DE}$.

Monitoring Progress Help in English and Spanish at *BigIdeasMath.com*

2. List the angles of △PQR in order from smallest to largest.

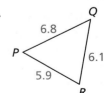

3. List the sides of △RST in order from shortest to longest.

Using the Triangle Inequality Theorem

Not every group of three segments can be used to form a triangle. The lengths of the segments must fit a certain relationship. For example, three attempted triangle constructions using segments with given lengths are shown below. Only the first group of segments forms a triangle.

  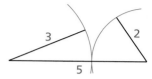

When you start with the longest side and attach the other two sides at its endpoints, you can see that the other two sides are not long enough to form a triangle in the second and third figures. This leads to the *Triangle Inequality Theorem*.

Theorem

Triangle Inequality Theorem

The sum of the lengths of any two sides of a triangle is greater than the length of the third side.

$$AB + BC > AC \qquad AC + BC > AB \qquad AB + AC > BC$$

Proof Ex. 47, p. 384

EXAMPLE 5 **Finding Possible Side Lengths**

A triangle has one side of length 14 and another side of length 9. Describe the possible lengths of the third side.

SOLUTION

Let x represent the length of the third side. Draw diagrams to help visualize the small and large values of x. Then use the Triangle Inequality Theorem to write and solve inequalities.

Small values of x   **Large values of x**

    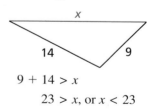

$$x + 9 > 14 \qquad\qquad 9 + 14 > x$$
$$x > 5 \qquad\qquad 23 > x, \text{ or } x < 23$$

▶ The length of the third side must be greater than 5 and less than 23.

CONNECTIONS TO ALGEBRA

You can combine the two inequalities, $x > 5$ and $x < 23$, to write the compound inequality $5 < x < 23$. This can be read as *x is between 5 and 23.*

Monitoring Progress Help in English and Spanish at *BigIdeasMath.com*

4. A triangle has one side of length 12 inches and another side of length 20 inches. Describe the possible lengths of the third side.

Decide whether it is possible to construct a triangle with the given side lengths. Explain your reasoning.

5. 4 ft, 9 ft, 10 ft   6. 8 m, 9 m, 18 m   7. 5 cm, 7 cm, 12 cm

---

Vocabulary and Core Concept Check

1. **VOCABULARY** Why is an indirect proof also called a *proof by contradiction*?

2. **WRITING** How can you tell which side of a triangle is the longest from the angle measures of the triangle? How can you tell which side is the shortest?

Monitoring Progress and Modeling with Mathematics

In Exercises 3–6, write the first step in an indirect proof of the statement. *(See Example 1.)*

3. If $WV + VU \neq 12$ inches and $VU = 5$ inches, then $WV \neq 7$ inches.

4. If x and y are odd integers, then xy is odd.

5. In $\triangle ABC$, if $m\angle A = 100°$, then $\angle B$ is not a right angle.

6. In $\triangle JKL$, if M is the midpoint of $\overline{KL}$, then $\overline{JM}$ is a median.

In Exercises 7 and 8, determine which two statements contradict each other. Explain your reasoning.

7. (A) $\triangle LMN$ is a right triangle.

    (B) $\angle L \cong \angle N$

    (C) $\triangle LMN$ is equilateral.

8. (A) Both $\angle X$ and $\angle Y$ have measures greater than 20°.

    (B) Both $\angle X$ and $\angle Y$ have measures less than 30°.

    (C) $m\angle X + m\angle Y = 62°$

In Exercises 9 and 10, use a ruler and protractor to draw the given type of triangle. Mark the largest angle and longest side in red and the smallest angle and shortest side in blue. What do you notice? *(See Example 2.)*

9. acute scalene

10. right scalene

In Exercises 11 and 12, list the angles of the given triangle from smallest to largest. *(See Example 3.)*

11.

12.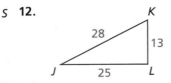

In Exercises 13–16, list the sides of the given triangle from shortest to longest. *(See Example 4.)*

13.

14.

15.

16.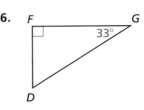

In Exercises 17–20, describe the possible lengths of the third side of the triangle given the lengths of the other two sides. *(See Example 5.)*

17. 5 inches, 12 inches

18. 12 feet, 18 feet

19. 2 feet, 40 inches

20. 25 meters, 25 meters

In Exercises 21–24, is it possible to construct a triangle with the given side lengths? If not, explain why not.

21. 6, 7, 11

22. 3, 6, 9

23. 28, 17, 46

24. 35, 120, 125

25. **ERROR ANALYSIS** Describe and correct the error in writing the first step of an indirect proof.

> ✗ Show that $\angle A$ is obtuse.
>
> **Step 1** Assume temporarily that $\angle A$ is acute.

26. ERROR ANALYSIS Describe and correct the error in labeling the side lengths 1, 2, and $\sqrt{3}$ on the triangle.

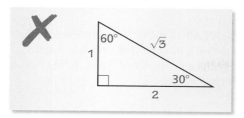

27. REASONING You are a lawyer representing a client who has been accused of a crime. The crime took place in Los Angeles, California. Security footage shows your client in New York at the time of the crime. Explain how to use indirect reasoning to prove your client is innocent.

28. REASONING Your class has fewer than 30 students. The teacher divides your class into two groups. The first group has 15 students. Use indirect reasoning to show that the second group must have fewer than 15 students.

29. PROBLEM SOLVING Which statement about $\triangle TUV$ is false?

(A) $UV > TU$

(B) $UV + TV > TU$

(C) $UV < TV$

(D) $\triangle TUV$ is isosceles.

30. PROBLEM SOLVING In $\triangle RST$, which is a possible side length for ST? Select all that apply.

(A) 7

(B) 8

(C) 9

(D) 10

31. PROOF Write an indirect proof that an odd number is not divisible by 4.

32. PROOF Write an indirect proof of the statement "In $\triangle QRS$, if $m\angle Q + m\angle R = 90°$, then $m\angle S = 90°$."

33. WRITING Explain why the hypotenuse of a right triangle must always be longer than either leg.

34. CRITICAL THINKING Is it possible to decide if three side lengths form a triangle without checking all three inequalities shown in the Triangle Inequality Theorem? Explain your reasoning.

35. MODELING WITH MATHEMATICS You can estimate the width of the river from point A to the tree at point B by measuring the angle to the tree at several locations along the riverbank. The diagram shows the results for locations C and D.

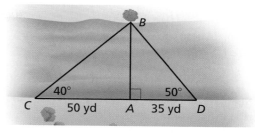

a. Using $\triangle BCA$ and $\triangle BDA$, determine the possible widths of the river. Explain your reasoning.

b. What could you do if you wanted a closer estimate?

36. MODELING WITH MATHEMATICS You travel from Fort Peck Lake to Glacier National Park and from Glacier National Park to Granite Peak.

a. Write two inequalities to represent the possible distances from Granite Peak back to Fort Peck Lake.

b. How is your answer to part (a) affected if you know that $m\angle 2 < m\angle 1$ and $m\angle 2 < m\angle 3$?

37. REASONING In the figure, $\overline{XY}$ bisects $\angle WYZ$. List all six angles of $\triangle XYZ$ and $\triangle WXY$ in order from smallest to largest. Explain your reasoning.

38. MATHEMATICAL CONNECTIONS In $\triangle DEF$, $m\angle D = (x + 25)°$, $m\angle E = (2x - 4)°$, and $m\angle F = 63°$. List the side lengths and angle measures of the triangle in order from least to greatest.

39. ANALYZING RELATIONSHIPS Another triangle inequality relationship is given by the Exterior Angle Inequality Theorem. It states:

The measure of an exterior angle of a triangle is greater than the measure of either of the nonadjacent interior angles.

Explain how you know that $m\angle 1 > m\angle A$ and $m\angle 1 > m\angle B$ in $\triangle ABC$ with exterior angle $\angle 1$.

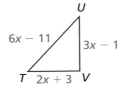

MATHEMATICAL CONNECTIONS In Exercises 40 and 41, describe the possible values of x.

40.

41.

42. HOW DO YOU SEE IT? Your house is on the corner of Hill Street and Eighth Street. The library is on the corner of View Street and Seventh Street. What is the shortest route to get from your house to the library? Explain your reasoning.

43. PROVING A THEOREM Use the diagram to prove the Triangle Longer Side Theorem.

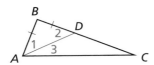

Given $BC > AB$, $BD = BA$

Prove $m\angle BAC > m\angle C$

44. USING STRUCTURE The length of the base of an isosceles triangle is ℓ. Describe the possible lengths for each leg. Explain your reasoning.

45. MAKING AN ARGUMENT Your classmate claims to have drawn a triangle with one side length of 13 inches and a perimeter of 2 feet. Is this possible? Explain your reasoning.

46. THOUGHT PROVOKING Cut two pieces of string that are each 24 centimeters long. Construct an isosceles triangle out of one string and a scalene triangle out of the other. Measure and record the side lengths. Then classify each triangle by its angles.

47. PROVING A THEOREM Prove the Triangle Inequality Theorem.

Given $\triangle ABC$

Prove $AB + BC > AC$, $AC + BC > AB$, and $AB + AC > BC$

48. ATTENDING TO PRECISION The perimeter of $\triangle HGF$ must be between what two integers? Explain your reasoning.

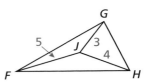

49. PROOF Write an indirect proof that a perpendicular segment is the shortest segment from a point to a plane.

Given $\overline{PC} \perp$ plane M

Prove $\overline{PC}$ is the shortest segment from P to plane M.

Maintaining Mathematical Proficiency
Reviewing what you learned in previous grades and lessons

Name the included angle between the pair of sides given. *(Skills Review Handbook)*

50. $\overline{AE}$ and $\overline{BE}$

51. $\overline{AC}$ and $\overline{DC}$

52. $\overline{AD}$ and $\overline{DC}$

53. $\overline{CE}$ and $\overline{BE}$

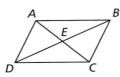

6.7 Inequalities in Two Triangles

Essential Question If two sides of one triangle are congruent to two sides of another triangle, what can you say about the third sides of the triangles?

EXPLORATION 1 Comparing Measures in Triangles

Work with a partner. Use dynamic geometry software.

a. Draw △*ABC*, as shown below.

b. Draw the circle with center *C*(3, 3) through the point *A*(1, 3).

c. Draw △*DBC* so that *D* is a point on the circle.

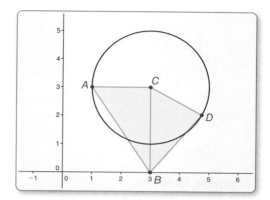

Sample
Points
A(1, 3)
B(3, 0)
C(3, 3)
D(4.75, 2.03)
Segments
BC = 3
AC = 2
DC = 2
AB = 3.61
DB = 2.68

d. Which two sides of △*ABC* are congruent to two sides of △*DBC*? Justify your answer.

e. Compare the lengths of $\overline{AB}$ and $\overline{DB}$. Then compare the measures of ∠*ACB* and ∠*DCB*. Are the results what you expected? Explain.

f. Drag point *D* to several locations on the circle. At each location, repeat part (e). Copy and record your results in the table below.

	D	*AC*	*BC*	*AB*	*BD*	*m∠ACB*	*m∠BCD*
1.	(4.75, 2.03)	2	3				
2.		2	3				
3.		2	3				
4.		2	3				
5.		2	3				

CONSTRUCTING VIABLE ARGUMENTS

To be proficient in math, you need to make conjectures and build a logical progression of statements to explore the truth of your conjectures.

g. Look for a pattern of the measures in your table. Then write a conjecture that summarizes your observations.

Communicate Your Answer

2. If two sides of one triangle are congruent to two sides of another triangle, what can you say about the third sides of the triangles?

3. Explain how you can use the hinge shown at the left to model the concept described in Question 2.

Previous
indirect proof
inequality

What You Will Learn

▶ Compare measures in triangles.

▶ Solve real-life problems using the Hinge Theorem.

Comparing Measures in Triangles

Imagine a gate between fence posts A and B that has hinges at A and swings open at B.

As the gate swings open, you can think of $\triangle ABC$, with side $\overline{AC}$ formed by the gate itself, side $\overline{AB}$ representing the distance between the fence posts, and side $\overline{BC}$ representing the opening between post B and the outer edge of the gate.

Notice that as the gate opens wider, both the measure of $\angle A$ and the distance BC increase. This suggests the *Hinge Theorem*.

⭕ Theorems

Hinge Theorem

If two sides of one triangle are congruent to two sides of another triangle, and the included angle of the first is larger than the included angle of the second, then the third side of the first is longer than the third side of the second.

Proof BigIdeasMath.com

$WX > ST$

Converse of the Hinge Theorem

If two sides of one triangle are congruent to two sides of another triangle, and the third side of the first is longer than the third side of the second, then the included angle of the first is larger than the included angle of the second.

Proof Example 3, p. 387

$m\angle C > m\angle F$

EXAMPLE 1   Using the Converse of the Hinge Theorem

Given that $\overline{ST} \cong \overline{PR}$, how does $m\angle PST$ compare to $m\angle SPR$?

SOLUTION

You are given that $\overline{ST} \cong \overline{PR}$, and you know that $\overline{PS} \cong \overline{PS}$ by the Reflexive Property of Congruence. Because 24 inches > 23 inches, $PT > SR$. So, two sides of $\triangle STP$ are congruent to two sides of $\triangle PRS$ and the third side of $\triangle STP$ is longer.

▶ By the Converse of the Hinge Theorem, $m\angle PST > m\angle SPR$.

EXAMPLE 2 Using the Hinge Theorem

Given that $\overline{JK} \cong \overline{LK}$, how does JM compare to LM?

SOLUTION

You are given that $\overline{JK} \cong \overline{LK}$, and you know that $\overline{KM} \cong \overline{KM}$ by the Reflexive Property of Congruence. Because $64° > 61°$, $m\angle JKM > m\angle LKM$. So, two sides of $\triangle JKM$ are congruent to two sides of $\triangle LKM$, and the included angle in $\triangle JKM$ is larger.

▶ By the Hinge Theorem, $JM > LM$.

Monitoring Progress Help in English and Spanish at *BigIdeasMath.com*

Use the diagram.

1. If $PR = PS$ and $m\angle QPR > m\angle QPS$, which is longer, $\overline{SQ}$ or $\overline{RQ}$?

2. If $PR = PS$ and $RQ < SQ$, which is larger, $\angle RPQ$ or $\angle SPQ$?

EXAMPLE 3 Proving the Converse of the Hinge Theorem

Write an indirect proof of the Converse of the Hinge Theorem.

Given $\overline{AB} \cong \overline{DE}, \overline{BC} \cong \overline{EF}, AC > DF$

Prove $m\angle B > m\angle E$

Indirect Proof

Step 1 Assume temporarily that $m\angle B \not> m\angle E$. Then it follows that either $m\angle B < m\angle E$ or $m\angle B = m\angle E$.

Step 2 If $m\angle B < m\angle E$, then $AC < DF$ by the Hinge Theorem.

If $m\angle B = m\angle E$, then $\angle B \cong \angle E$. So, $\triangle ABC \cong \triangle DEF$ by the SAS Congruence Theorem and $AC = DF$.

Step 3 Both conclusions contradict the given statement that $AC > DF$. So, the temporary assumption that $m\angle B \not> m\angle E$ cannot be true. This proves that $m\angle B > m\angle E$.

EXAMPLE 4 Proving Triangle Relationships

Write a paragraph proof.

Given $\angle XWY \cong \angle XYW, WZ > YZ$

Prove $m\angle WXZ > m\angle YXZ$

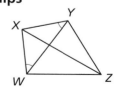

Paragraph Proof Because $\angle XWY \cong \angle XYW$, $\overline{XY} \cong \overline{XW}$ by the Converse of the Base Angles Theorem. By the Reflexive Property of Congruence, $\overline{XZ} \cong \overline{XZ}$. Because $WZ > YZ$, $m\angle WXZ > m\angle YXZ$ by the Converse of the Hinge Theorem.

Monitoring Progress Help in English and Spanish at *BigIdeasMath.com*

3. Write a temporary assumption you can make to prove the Hinge Theorem indirectly. What two cases does that assumption lead to?

Solving Real-Life Problems

EXAMPLE 5 **Solving a Real-Life Problem**

Two groups of bikers leave the same camp heading in opposite directions. Each group travels 2 miles, then changes direction and travels 1.2 miles. Group A starts due east and then turns 45° toward north. Group B starts due west and then turns 30° toward south. Which group is farther from camp? Explain your reasoning.

SOLUTION

1. **Understand the Problem** You know the distances and directions that the groups of bikers travel. You need to determine which group is farther from camp. You can interpret a turn of 45° toward north, as shown.

2. **Make a Plan** Draw a diagram that represents the situation and mark the given measures. The distances that the groups bike and the distances back to camp form two triangles. The triangles have two congruent side lengths of 2 miles and 1.2 miles. Include the third side of each triangle in the diagram.

3. **Solve the Problem** Use linear pairs to find the included angles for the paths that the groups take.

   Group A: 180° − 45° = 135°   **Group B:** 180° − 30° = 150°

   The included angles are 135° and 150°.

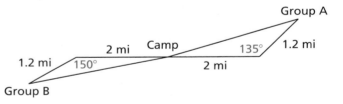

   Because 150° > 135°, the distance Group B is from camp is greater than the distance Group A is from camp by the Hinge Theorem.

   ▶ So, Group B is farther from camp.

4. **Look Back** Because the included angle for Group A is 15° less than the included angle for Group B, you can reason that Group A would be closer to camp than Group B. So, Group B is farther from camp.

Monitoring Progress Help in English and Spanish at *BigIdeasMath.com*

4. **WHAT IF?** In Example 5, Group C leaves camp and travels 2 miles due north, then turns 40° toward east and travels 1.2 miles. Compare the distances from camp for all three groups.

Vocabulary and Core Concept Check

1. **WRITING** Explain why the Hinge Theorem has that name.

2. **COMPLETE THE SENTENCE** In $\triangle ABC$ and $\triangle DEF$, $\overline{AB} \cong \overline{DE}$, $\overline{BC} \cong \overline{EF}$, and $AC < DF$. So $m\angle$____ $> m\angle$____ by the Converse of the Hinge Theorem.

Monitoring Progress and Modeling with Mathematics

In Exercises 3–6, copy and complete the statement with <, >, or =. Explain your reasoning. *(See Example 1.)*

3. $m\angle 1$ ____ $m\angle 2$

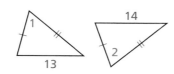

4. $m\angle 1$ ____ $m\angle 2$

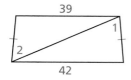

5. $m\angle 1$ ____ $m\angle 2$

6. $m\angle 1$ ____ $m\angle 2$

In Exercises 7–10, copy and complete the statement with <, >, or =. Explain your reasoning. *(See Example 2.)*

7. AD ____ CD

8. MN ____ LK

9. TR ____ UR

10. AC ____ DC

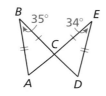

PROOF In Exercises 11 and 12, write a proof. *(See Example 4.)*

11. **Given** $\overline{XY} \cong \overline{YZ}$, $m\angle WYZ > m\angle WYX$

    Prove $WZ > WX$

12. **Given** $\overline{BC} \cong \overline{DA}$, $DC < AB$

    Prove $m\angle BCA > m\angle DAC$

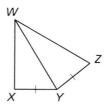

In Exercises 13 and 14, you and your friend leave on different flights from the same airport. Determine which flight is farther from the airport. Explain your reasoning. *(See Example 5.)*

13. **Your flight:** Flies 100 miles due west, then turns 20° toward north and flies 50 miles.

    Friend's flight: Flies 100 miles due north, then turns 30° toward east and flies 50 miles.

14. **Your flight:** Flies 210 miles due south, then turns 70° toward west and flies 80 miles.

    Friend's flight: Flies 80 miles due north, then turns 50° toward east and flies 210 miles.

15. ERROR ANALYSIS Describe and correct the error in using the Hinge Theorem.

By the Hinge Theorem, PQ < SR.

16. REPEATED REASONING Which is a possible measure for ∠JKM? Select all that apply.

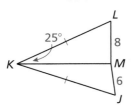

(A) 15°   (B) 22°   (C) 25°   (D) 35°

17. DRAWING CONCLUSIONS The path from E to F is longer than the path from E to D. The path from G to D is the same length as the path from G to F. What can you conclude about the angles of the paths? Explain your reasoning.

18. ABSTRACT REASONING In △EFG, the bisector of ∠F intersects the bisector of ∠G at point H. Explain why $\overline{FG}$ must be longer than $\overline{FH}$ or $\overline{HG}$.

19. ABSTRACT REASONING $\overline{NR}$ is a median of △NPQ, and NQ > NP. Explain why ∠NRQ is obtuse.

MATHEMATICAL CONNECTIONS In Exercises 20 and 21, write and solve an inequality for the possible values of x.

20.

21.

22. HOW DO YOU SEE IT? In the diagram, triangles are formed by the locations of the players on the basketball court. The dashed lines represent the possible paths of the basketball as the players pass. How does m∠ACB compare with m∠ACD?

23. CRITICAL THINKING In △ABC, the altitudes from B and C meet at point D, and m∠BAC > m∠BDC. What is true about △ABC? Justify your answer.

24. THOUGHT PROVOKING The postulates and theorems you have learned represent Euclidean geometry. In spherical geometry, all points are on the surface of a sphere. A line is a circle on the sphere whose diameter is equal to the diameter of the sphere. In spherical geometry, state an inequality involving the sum of the angles of a triangle. Find a formula for the area of a triangle in spherical geometry.

Maintaining Mathematical Proficiency

Reviewing what you learned in previous grades and lessons

Find the value of x. *(Skills Review Handbook)*

25.

26.

27.

28.

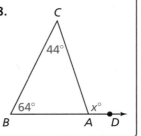

Core Vocabulary

midsegment of a triangle, *p. 372*
indirect proof, *p. 378*

Core Concepts

Section 6.5

Using the Midsegment of a Triangle, *p. 372*
Triangle Midsegment Theorem, *p. 373*

Section 6.6

How to Write an Indirect Proof (Proof by Contradiction), *p. 378*
Triangle Longer Side Theorem, *p. 379*
Triangle Larger Angle Theorem, *p. 379*
Triangle Inequality Theorem, *p. 381*

Section 6.7

Hinge Theorem, *p. 386*
Converse of the Hinge Theorem, *p. 386*

Mathematical Practices

1. In Exercise 25 on page 376, analyze the relationship between the stage and the total perimeter of all the shaded triangles at that stage. Then predict the total perimeter of all the shaded triangles in Stage 4.

2. In Exercise 17 on page 382, write all three inequalities using the Triangle Inequality Theorem. Determine the reasonableness of each one. Why do you only need to use two of the three inequalities?

3. In Exercise 23 on page 390, try all three cases of triangles (acute, right, obtuse) to gain insight into the solution.

Performance Task:

Building a Roof Truss

The simple roof truss is also called a planar truss because all its components lie in a two-dimensional plane. How can this structure be extended to three-dimensional space? What applications would this type of structure be used for?

To explore the answers to these questions and more, check out the Performance Task and Real-Life STEM video at *BigIdeasMath.com*.

6.1 Proving Geometric Relationships (pp. 335–342)

a. **Rewrite the two-column proof into a paragraph proof.**

Given $\angle 6 \cong \angle 7$

Prove $\angle 7 \cong \angle 2$

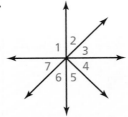

Two-Column Proof

STATEMENTS	REASONS
1. $\angle 6 \cong \angle 7$	**1.** Given
2. $\angle 6 \cong \angle 2$	**2.** Vertical Angles Congruence Theorem
3. $\angle 7 \cong \angle 2$	**3.** Transitive Property of Congruence

Paragraph Proof

$\angle 6$ and $\angle 7$ are congruent. By the Vertical Angles Congruence Theorem, $\angle 6 \cong \angle 2$. So, by the Transitive Property of Congruence, $\angle 7 \cong \angle 2$.

b. **Write a coordinate proof.**

Given Coordinates of vertices of $\triangle OAC$ and $\triangle BAC$

Prove $\triangle OAC \cong \triangle BAC$

Segments $\overline{OA}$ and $\overline{BA}$ have the same length, so $\overline{OA} \cong \overline{BA}$.

$$OA = \left| \frac{c}{2} - 0 \right| = \frac{c}{2}$$

$$BA = \left| c - \frac{c}{2} \right| = \frac{c}{2}$$

Segments $\overline{OC}$ and $\overline{BC}$ have the same length, so $\overline{OC} \cong \overline{BC}$.

$$OC = \sqrt{\left(0 - \frac{c}{2}\right)^2 + (0 - c)^2} = \sqrt{\left(-\frac{c}{2}\right)^2 + (-c)^2} = \sqrt{\frac{5c^2}{4}} = \frac{1}{2}c\sqrt{5}$$

$$BC = \sqrt{\left(c - \frac{c}{2}\right)^2 + (0 - c)^2} = \sqrt{\left(\frac{c}{2}\right)^2 + (-c)^2} = \sqrt{\frac{5c^2}{4}} = \frac{1}{2}c\sqrt{5}$$

By the Reflexive Property of Congruence, $\overline{AC} \cong \overline{AC}$.

▶ So, you can apply the SSS Congruence Theorem to conclude that $\triangle OAC \cong \triangle BAC$.

1. Use the figure in part (a). Write a proof using any format.

   Given $\angle 5$ and $\angle 6$ are complementary.
   $m\angle 5 + m\angle 7 = 90°$

   Prove $\angle 6 \cong \angle 7$

2. Use the figure at the right. Write a coordinate proof.

   Given Coordinates of vertices of $\triangle OBC$

   Prove $\triangle OBC$ is isosceles.

Perpendicular and Angle Bisectors *(pp. 343–350)*

Find each measure.

a. *AD*

From the figure, $\overleftrightarrow{AC}$ is the perpendicular bisector of $\overline{BD}$.

$AB = AD$	Perpendicular Bisector Theorem
$4x + 3 = 6x - 9$	Substitute.
$x = 6$	Solve for *x*.

▶ So, $AD = 6(6) - 9 = 27$.

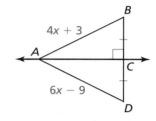

b. *FG*

Because $EH = GH$ and $\overleftrightarrow{HF} \perp \overline{EG}$, $\overleftrightarrow{HF}$ is the perpendicular bisector of $\overline{EG}$ by the Converse of the Perpendicular Bisector Theorem. By the definition of segment bisector, $EF = FG$.

▶ So, $FG = EF = 6$.

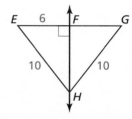

c. *LM*

$JM = LM$	Angle Bisector Theorem
$8x - 15 = 3x$	Substitute.
$x = 3$	Solve for *x*.

▶ So, $LM = 3x = 3(3) = 9$.

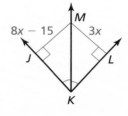

d. $m\angle XWZ$

Because $\overrightarrow{ZX} \perp \overrightarrow{WX}$ and $\overrightarrow{ZY} \perp \overrightarrow{WY}$ and $ZX = ZY = 8$, $\overrightarrow{WZ}$ bisects $\angle XWY$ by the Converse of the Angle Bisector Theorem.

▶ So, $m\angle XWZ = m\angle YWZ = 46°$.

Find the indicated measure. Explain your reasoning.

3. *DC*

4. *RS*

5. $m\angle JFH$

6.3   **Bisectors of Triangles**   *(pp. 351–360)*

a. Find the coordinates of the circumcenter of △QRS with vertices Q(3, 3), R(5, 7), and S(9, 3).

Step 1   Graph △QRS.

Step 2   Find equations for two perpendicular bisectors.

The midpoint of $\overline{QS}$ is (6, 3). The line through (6, 3) that is perpendicular to $\overline{QS}$ is $x = 6$.

The midpoint of $\overline{QR}$ is (4, 5). The line through (4, 5) that is perpendicular to $\overline{QR}$ is $y = -\frac{1}{2}x + 7$.

Step 3   Find the point where $x = 6$ and $y = -\frac{1}{2}x + 7$ intersect. They intersect at (6, 4).

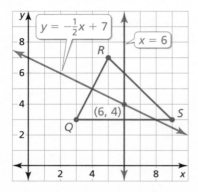

▶   So, the coordinates of the circumcenter are (6, 4).

b. Point N is the incenter of △ABC. In the figure shown, ND = 4x + 7 and NE = 3x + 9. Find NF.

Step 1   Solve for x.

$ND = NE$ Incenter Theorem

$4x + 7 = 3x + 9$ Substitute.

$x = 2$ Solve for x.

Step 2   Find ND (or NE).

$ND = 4x + 7 = 4(2) + 7 = 15$

▶   So, because $ND = NF$, $NF = 15$.

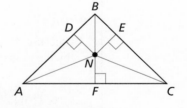

Find the coordinates of the circumcenter of the triangle with the given vertices.

6. $T(-6, -5)$, $U(0, -1)$, $V(0, -5)$

7. $X(-2, 1)$, $Y(2, -3)$, $Z(6, -3)$

8.   Point D is the incenter of △LMN. Find the value of x.

6.4 Medians and Altitudes of Triangles (pp. 361–368)

Find the coordinates of the centroid of $\triangle TUV$ with vertices $T(1, -8)$, $U(4, -1)$, and $V(7, -6)$.

Step 1 Graph $\triangle TUV$.

Step 2 Use the Midpoint Formula to find the midpoint W of $\overline{TV}$. Sketch median $\overline{UW}$.

$$W\left(\frac{1+7}{2}, \frac{-8+(-6)}{2}\right) = (4, -7)$$

Step 3 Find the centroid. It is two-thirds of the distance from each vertex to the midpoint of the opposite side.

The distance from vertex $U(4, -1)$ to $W(4, -7)$ is $-1 - (-7) = 6$ units.

So, the centroid is $\frac{2}{3}(6) = 4$ units down from vertex U on $\overline{UW}$.

▶ So, the coordinates of the centroid P are $(4, -1 - 4)$, or $(4, -5)$.

Find the coordinates of the centroid of the triangle with the given vertices.

9. $A(-10, 3)$, $B(-4, 5)$, $C(-4, 1)$ **10.** $D(2, -8)$, $E(2, -2)$, $F(8, -2)$

Tell whether the orthocenter of the triangle with the given vertices is *inside*, *on*, or *outside* the triangle. Then find the coordinates of the orthocenter.

11. $G(1, 6)$, $H(5, 6)$, $J(3, 1)$ **12.** $K(-8, 5)$, $L(-6, 3)$, $M(0, 5)$

6.5 The Triangle Midsegment Theorem (pp. 371–376)

In $\triangle JKL$, show that midsegment $\overline{MN}$ is parallel to $\overline{JL}$ and that $MN = \frac{1}{2}JL$.

Step 1 Find the coordinates of M and N by finding the midpoints of $\overline{JK}$ and $\overline{KL}$.

$$M\left(\frac{-8+(-4)}{2}, \frac{1+7}{2}\right) = M\left(\frac{-12}{2}, \frac{8}{2}\right) = M(-6, 4)$$

$$N\left(\frac{-4+(-2)}{2}, \frac{7+3}{2}\right) = N\left(\frac{-6}{2}, \frac{10}{2}\right) = N(-3, 5)$$

Step 2 Find and compare the slopes of $\overline{MN}$ and $\overline{JL}$.

$$\text{slope of } \overline{MN} = \frac{5-4}{-3-(-6)} = \frac{1}{3}$$

$$\text{slope of } \overline{JL} = \frac{3-1}{-2-(-8)} = \frac{2}{6} = \frac{1}{3}$$

▶ Because the slopes are the same, $\overline{MN}$ is parallel to $\overline{JL}$.

Step 3 Find and compare the lengths of $\overline{MN}$ and $\overline{JL}$.

$$MN = \sqrt{[-3-(-6)]^2 + (5-4)^2} = \sqrt{9+1} = \sqrt{10}$$

$$JL = \sqrt{[-2-(-8)]^2 + (3-1)^2} = \sqrt{36+4} = \sqrt{40} = 2\sqrt{10}$$

▶ Because $\sqrt{10} = \frac{1}{2}(2\sqrt{10})$, $MN = \frac{1}{2}JL$.

Find the coordinates of the vertices of the midsegment triangle for the triangle with the given vertices.

13. $A(-6, 8)$, $B(-6, 4)$, $C(0, 4)$ **14.** $D(-3, 1)$, $E(3, 5)$, $F(1, -5)$

6.6 Indirect Proof and Inequalities in One Triangle *(pp. 377–384)*

a. List the sides of △*ABC* in order from shortest to longest.

First, find $m\angle C$ using the Triangle Sum Theorem.

$$m\angle A + m\angle B + m\angle C = 180°$$
$$35° + 95° + m\angle C = 180°$$
$$m\angle C = 50°$$

The angles from smallest to largest are $\angle A$, $\angle C$, and $\angle B$. The sides opposite these angles are $\overline{BC}$, $\overline{AB}$, and $\overline{AC}$, respectively.

▶ So, by the Triangle Larger Angle Theorem, the sides from shortest to longest are $\overline{BC}$, $\overline{AB}$, and $\overline{AC}$.

b. List the angles of △*DEF* in order from smallest to largest.

The sides from shortest to longest are $\overline{DF}$, $\overline{EF}$, and $\overline{DE}$. The angles opposite these sides are $\angle E$, $\angle D$, and $\angle F$, respectively.

▶ So, by the Triangle Longer Side Theorem, the angles from smallest to largest are $\angle E$, $\angle D$, and $\angle F$.

Describe the possible lengths of the third side of the triangle given the lengths of the other two sides.

15. 4 inches, 8 inches   **16.** 6 meters, 9 meters   **17.** 11 feet, 18 feet

18. Write an indirect proof of the statement "In △*XYZ*, if $XY = 4$ and $XZ = 8$, then $YZ > 4$."

6.7 Inequalities in Two Triangles *(pp. 385–390)*

Given that $\overline{WZ} \cong \overline{YZ}$, how does *XY* compare to *XW*?

You are given that $\overline{WZ} \cong \overline{YZ}$, and you know that $\overline{XZ} \cong \overline{XZ}$ by the Reflexive Property of Congruence.

Because $90° > 80°$, $m\angle XZY > m\angle XZW$. So, two sides of △*XZY* are congruent to two sides of △*XZW* and the included angle in △*XZY* is larger.

▶ By the Hinge Theorem, $XY > XW$.

Use the diagram.

19. If $RQ = RS$ and $m\angle QRT > m\angle SRT$, then how does $\overline{QT}$ compare to $\overline{ST}$?

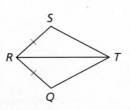

20. If $RQ = RS$ and $QT > ST$, then how does $\angle QRT$ compare to $\angle SRT$?

In Exercises 1 and 2, $\overline{MN}$ is a midsegment of $\triangle JKL$. Find the value of x.

1.

2.

Find the indicated measure. Identify the theorem you use.

3. ST

4. WY

5. BW

Copy and complete the statement with <, >, or =.

6. AB __ CB

7. $m\angle 1$ ___ $m\angle 2$

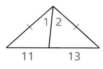

8. $m\angle MNP$ ___ $m\angle NPM$

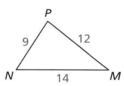

9. Find the coordinates of the circumcenter, orthocenter, and centroid of the triangle with vertices $A(0, -2)$, $B(4, -2)$, and $C(0, 6)$.

10. Write an indirect proof of the Corollary to the Base Angles Theorem: If $\triangle PQR$ is equilateral, then it is equiangular.

11. $\triangle DEF$ is a right triangle with area A. Use the area for $\triangle DEF$ to write an expression for the area of $\triangle GEH$. Justify your answer.

12. Prove the Corollary to the Triangle Sum Theorem using any format.

Given $\triangle ABC$ is a right triangle.

Prove $\angle A$ and $\angle B$ are complementary.

In Exercises 13–15, use the map.

13. Describe the possible lengths of Pine Avenue.

14. You ride your bike along a trail that represents the shortest distance from the beach to Main Street. You end up exactly halfway between your house and the movie theatre. How long is Pine Avenue? Explain.

15. A market is the same distance from your house, the movie theater, and the beach. Copy the map and locate the market.

1. Which definition(s) and/or theorem(s) do you need to use to prove the Converse of the Perpendicular Bisector Theorem? Select all that apply.

   Given $CA = CB$

   Prove Point C lies on the perpendicular bisector of $\overline{AB}$.

   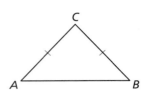

definition of perpendicular bisector	definition of angle bisector
definition of segment congruence	definition of angle congruence
Base Angles Theorem	Converse of the Base Angles Theorem
ASA Congruence Theorem	AAS Congruence Theorem

2. Which of the following values are x-coordinates of the solutions of the system?

   $$y = x^2 - 3x + 3$$

   $$y = 3x - 5$$

-7	-4	-3	-2	-1
1	2	3	4	7

3. What are the coordinates of the centroid of $\triangle LMN$?

   (A) (2, 5)

   (B) (3, 5)

   (C) (4, 5)

   (D) (5, 5)

4. Use the steps in the construction to explain how you know that the circle is circumscribed about $\triangle ABC$.

   Step 1

   Step 2

   Step 3

   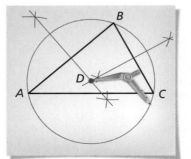

5. According to a survey, 58% of voting-age citizens in a town are planning to vote in an upcoming election. You randomly select 10 citizens to survey.

    a. What is the probability that less than 4 citizens are planning to vote?

    b. What is the probability that exactly 4 citizens are planning to vote?

    c. What is the probability that more than 4 citizens are planning to vote?

6. What are the solutions of $2x^2 + 18 = -6$?

    Ⓐ $i\sqrt{6}$ and $-i\sqrt{6}$

    Ⓑ $2i\sqrt{3}$ and $-2i\sqrt{3}$

    Ⓒ $i\sqrt{15}$ and $-i\sqrt{15}$

    Ⓓ $-i\sqrt{21}$ and $i\sqrt{21}$

7. Use the graph of $\triangle QRS$.

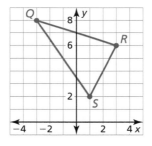

    a. Find the coordinates of the vertices of the midsegment triangle. Label the vertices T, U, and V.

    b. Show that each midsegment joining the midpoints of two sides is parallel to the third side and is equal to half the length of the third side.

8. The graph of which inequality is shown?

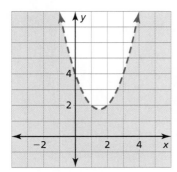

    Ⓐ $y > x^2 - 3x + 4$

    Ⓑ $y \geq x^2 - 3x + 4$

    Ⓒ $y < x^2 - 3x + 4$

    Ⓓ $y \leq x^2 - 3x + 4$

7 Quadrilaterals and Other Polygons

SEE the Big Idea

Diamond *(p. 450)*

Window *(p. 439)*

Amusement Park Ride *(p. 421)*

Arrow *(p. 417)*

Gazebo *(p. 409)*

Maintaining Mathematical Proficiency

Using Structure to Solve a Multi-Step Equation

Example 1 Solve $3(2 + x) = -9$ by interpreting the expression $2 + x$ as a single quantity.

$$3(2 + x) = -9$$ Write the equation.

$$\frac{3(2 + x)}{3} = \frac{-9}{3}$$ Divide each side by 3.

$$2 + x = -3$$ Simplify.

$$\underline{-2 \qquad -2}$$ Subtract 2 from each side.

$$x = -5$$ Simplify.

Solve the equation by interpreting the expression in parentheses as a single quantity.

1. $4(7 - x) = 16$ **2.** $7(1 - x) + 2 = -19$ **3.** $3(x - 5) + 8(x - 5) = 22$

Identifying Parallel and Perpendicular Lines

Example 2 Determine which of the lines are parallel and which are perpendicular.

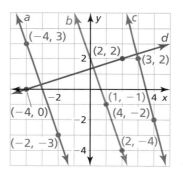

Find the slope of each line.

Line a: $m = \dfrac{3 - (-3)}{-4 - (-2)} = -3$

Line b: $m = \dfrac{-1 - (-4)}{1 - 2} = -3$

Line c: $m = \dfrac{2 - (-2)}{3 - 4} = -4$

Line d: $m = \dfrac{2 - 0}{2 - (-4)} = \dfrac{1}{3}$

Because lines a and b have the same slope, lines a and b are parallel. Because $\frac{1}{3}(-3) = -1$, lines a and d are perpendicular and lines b and d are perpendicular.

Determine which lines are parallel and which are perpendicular.

4.   **5.**   **6.**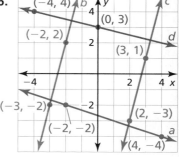

7. ABSTRACT REASONING Explain why interpreting an expression as a single quantity does not contradict the order of operations.

Mathematical Practices

Mathematically proficient students understand and use previously established results.

Proving by Mathematical Induction

🔗 Core Concept

Mathematical Induction

Mathematical induction is a technique that you can use to prove statements involving natural numbers. A proof by mathematical induction has two steps.

Base Case: Show that the statement P_n is true for the first case, usually $n = 1$.

Inductive Step: Assume that P_n is true for a natural number $n = k$. This assumption is called the *inductive hypothesis*. Use the inductive hypothesis to prove that P_n is true for the next natural number, $n = k + 1$.

EXAMPLE 1   Proving by Mathematical Induction

Prove that $1 + 2 + 3 + \cdots + n = \dfrac{n(n + 1)}{2}$ for all natural numbers $n \geq 1$.

SOLUTION

Base Case: Let $n = 1$. Show that the statement is true.

$$1 \stackrel{?}{=} \frac{1(1 + 1)}{2}$$

$$1 = 1 \ \checkmark$$

So, the statement is true for $n = 1$.

Inductive Step: Assume that $1 + 2 + 3 + \cdots + k = \dfrac{k(k + 1)}{2}$ for a natural number $k \geq 1$.

Prove that $1 + 2 + 3 + \cdots + k + (k + 1) = \dfrac{(k + 1)[(k + 1) + 1]}{2}$, or $\dfrac{(k + 1)(k + 2)}{2}$.

$1 + 2 + 3 + \cdots + k + (k + 1) = (1 + 2 + 3 + \cdots + k) + (k + 1)$		Assoc. Prop. of Addition
$= \dfrac{k(k + 1)}{2} + (k + 1)$		Inductive hypothesis
$= \dfrac{k(k + 1)}{2} + \dfrac{2(k + 1)}{2}$		Rewrite using LCD.
$= \dfrac{k(k + 1) + 2(k + 1)}{2}$		Add.
$= \dfrac{(k + 1)(k + 2)}{2}$		Factor.

So, if the statement is true for a natural number $k \geq 1$, then it is true for $k + 1$.

▶ So, you can conclude that the statement is true for all natural numbers $n \geq 1$.

Monitoring Progress

Use mathematical induction to prove the statement.

1. $1^2 + 2^2 + 3^2 + \cdots + n^2 = \dfrac{n(n + 1)(2n + 1)}{6}$

2. $1^3 + 2^3 + 3^3 + \cdots + n^3 = \dfrac{n^2(n + 1)^2}{4}$

Essential Question What is the sum of the measures of the interior angles of a polygon?

EXPLORATION 1 **The Sum of the Angle Measures of a Polygon**

Work with a partner. Use dynamic geometry software.

a. Draw a quadrilateral and a pentagon. Find the sum of the measures of the interior angles of each polygon.

Sample

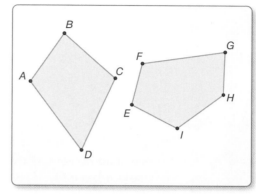

b. Draw other polygons and find the sums of the measures of their interior angles. Record your results in the table below.

Number of sides, n	3	4	5	6	7	8	9
Sum of angle measures, S							

c. Plot the data from your table in a coordinate plane.

d. Write a function that fits the data. Explain what the function represents.

CONSTRUCTING VIABLE ARGUMENTS

To be proficient in math, you need to reason inductively about data.

EXPLORATION 2 **Measure of One Angle in a Regular Polygon**

Work with a partner.

a. Use the function you found in Exploration 1 to write a new function that gives the measure of one interior angle in a regular polygon with n sides.

b. Use the function in part (a) to find the measure of one interior angle of a regular pentagon. Use dynamic geometry software to check your result by constructing a regular pentagon and finding the measure of one of its interior angles.

c. Copy your table from Exploration 1 and add a row for the measure of one interior angle in a regular polygon with n sides. Complete the table. Use dynamic geometry software to check your results.

Communicate Your Answer

3. What is the sum of the measures of the interior angles of a polygon?

4. Find the measure of one interior angle in a regular dodecagon (a polygon with 12 sides).

What You Will Learn

▶ Use the interior angle measures of polygons.

▶ Use the exterior angle measures of polygons.

Using Interior Angle Measures of Polygons

In a polygon, two vertices that are endpoints of the same side are called *consecutive vertices*. A **diagonal** of a polygon is a segment that joins two nonconsecutive vertices.

Polygon *ABCDE*

diagonals

A and *B* are consecutive vertices.
Vertex *B* has two diagonals, $\overline{BD}$ and $\overline{BE}$.

As you can see, the diagonals from one vertex divide a polygon into triangles. Dividing a polygon with *n* sides into (*n* − 2) triangles shows that the sum of the measures of the interior angles of a polygon is a multiple of 180°.

REMEMBER

A polygon is *convex* when no line that contains a side of the polygon contains a point in the interior of the polygon.

⑤ Theorem

Polygon Interior Angles Theorem

The sum of the measures of the interior angles of a convex *n*-gon is (*n* − 2) • 180°.

$$m\angle 1 + m\angle 2 + \cdots + m\angle n = (n - 2) \cdot 180°$$

Proof Ex. 42, p. 409

n = 6

EXAMPLE 1   **Finding the Sum of Angle Measures in a Polygon**

Find the sum of the measures of the interior angles of the figure.

SOLUTION

The figure is a convex octagon. It has 8 sides. Use the Polygon Interior Angles Theorem.

$(n - 2) \cdot 180° = (8 - 2) \cdot 180°$ Substitute 8 for *n*.

$= 6 \cdot 180°$ Subtract.

$= 1080°$ Multiply.

▶ The sum of the measures of the interior angles of the figure is 1080°.

Monitoring Progress Help in English and Spanish at *BigIdeasMath.com*

1. The coin shown is in the shape of an 11-gon. Find the sum of the measures of the interior angles.

EXAMPLE 2   **Finding the Number of Sides of a Polygon**

The sum of the measures of the interior angles of a convex polygon is 900°. Classify the polygon by the number of sides.

SOLUTION

Use the Polygon Interior Angles Theorem to write an equation involving the number of sides n. Then solve the equation to find the number of sides.

$(n - 2) \cdot 180° = 900°$	Polygon Interior Angles Theorem
$n - 2 = 5$	Divide each side by 180°.
$n = 7$	Add 2 to each side.

▶ The polygon has 7 sides. It is a heptagon.

Corollary

Corollary to the Polygon Interior Angles Theorem

The sum of the measures of the interior angles of a quadrilateral is 360°.

Proof Ex. 43, p. 410

EXAMPLE 3   **Finding an Unknown Interior Angle Measure**

Find the value of x in the diagram.

SOLUTION

The polygon is a quadrilateral. Use the Corollary to the Polygon Interior Angles Theorem to write an equation involving x. Then solve the equation.

$x° + 108° + 121° + 59° = 360°$	Corollary to the Polygon Interior Angles Theorem
$x + 288 = 360$	Combine like terms.
$x = 72$	Subtract 288 from each side.

▶ The value of x is 72.

Monitoring Progress Help in English and Spanish at *BigIdeasMath.com*

2. The sum of the measures of the interior angles of a convex polygon is 1440°. Classify the polygon by the number of sides.

3. The measures of the interior angles of a quadrilateral are $x°$, $3x°$, $5x°$, and $7x°$. Find the measures of all the interior angles.

In an **equilateral polygon**, all sides are congruent.

In an **equiangular polygon**, all angles in the interior of the polygon are congruent.

A **regular polygon** is a convex polygon that is both equilateral and equiangular.

EXAMPLE 4 **Finding Angle Measures in Polygons**

A home plate for a baseball field is shown.

a. Is the polygon regular? Explain your reasoning.

b. Find the measures of ∠C and ∠E.

SOLUTION

a. The polygon is not equilateral or equiangular. So, the polygon is not regular.

b. Find the sum of the measures of the interior angles.

$$(n - 2) \cdot 180° = (5 - 2) \cdot 180° = 540°$$ Polygon Interior Angles Theorem

Then write an equation involving x and solve the equation.

$$x° + x° + 90° + 90° + 90° = 540°$$ Write an equation.

$$2x + 270 = 540$$ Combine like terms.

$$x = 135$$ Solve for x.

▶ So, $m\angle C = m\angle E = 135°$.

Monitoring Progress   🔊 Help in English and Spanish at *BigIdeasMath.com*

4. Find $m\angle S$ and $m\angle T$ in the diagram.

5. Sketch a pentagon that is equilateral but not equiangular.

Using Exterior Angle Measures of Polygons

Unlike the sum of the interior angle measures of a convex polygon, the sum of the exterior angle measures does *not* depend on the number of sides of the polygon. The diagrams suggest that the sum of the measures of the exterior angles, one angle at each vertex, of a pentagon is 360°. In general, this sum is 360° for any convex polygon.

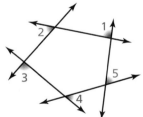

JUSTIFYING STEPS

To help justify this conclusion, you can visualize a circle containing two straight angles. So, there are 180° + 180°, or 360°, in a circle.

Step 1 Shade one exterior angle at each vertex.

Step 2 Cut out the exterior angles.

Step 3 Arrange the exterior angles to form 360°.

🌀 Theorem

Polygon Exterior Angles Theorem

The sum of the measures of the exterior angles of a convex polygon, one angle at each vertex, is 360°.

$$m\angle 1 + m\angle 2 + \cdots + m\angle n = 360°$$

Proof Ex. 51, p. 410

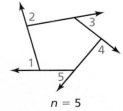

EXAMPLE 5　Finding an Unknown Exterior Angle Measure

Find the value of x in the diagram.

SOLUTION

Use the Polygon Exterior Angles Theorem to write and solve an equation.

$x° + 2x° + 89° + 67° = 360°$　　Polygon Exterior Angles Theorem

$3x + 156 = 360$　　Combine like terms.

$x = 68$　　Solve for x.

▶ The value of x is 68.

EXAMPLE 6　Finding Angle Measures in Regular Polygons

The trampoline shown is shaped like a regular dodecagon.

a. Find the measure of each interior angle.

b. Find the measure of each exterior angle.

SOLUTION

a. Use the Polygon Interior Angles Theorem to find the sum of the measures of the interior angles.

$(n − 2) \cdot 180° = (12 − 2) \cdot 180°$

$= 1800°$

Then find the measure of one interior angle. A regular dodecagon has 12 congruent interior angles. Divide 1800° by 12.

$\dfrac{1800°}{12} = 150°$

▶ The measure of each interior angle in the dodecagon is 150°.

b. By the Polygon Exterior Angles Theorem, the sum of the measures of the exterior angles, one angle at each vertex, is 360°. Divide 360° by 12 to find the measure of one of the 12 congruent exterior angles.

$\dfrac{360°}{12} = 30°$

▶ The measure of each exterior angle in the dodecagon is 30°.

Monitoring Progress　 Help in English and Spanish at *BigIdeasMath.com*

6. A convex hexagon has exterior angles with measures 34°, 49°, 58°, 67°, and 75°. What is the measure of an exterior angle at the sixth vertex?

7. An interior angle and an adjacent exterior angle of a polygon form a linear pair. How can you use this fact as another method to find the measure of each exterior angle in Example 6?

Vocabulary and Core Concept Check

1. **VOCABULARY** Why do vertices connected by a diagonal of a polygon have to be nonconsecutive?

2. **WHICH ONE DOESN'T BELONG?** Which sum does *not* belong with the other three? Explain your reasoning.

the sum of the measures of the interior angles of a quadrilateral	the sum of the measures of the exterior angles of a quadrilateral
the sum of the measures of the interior angles of a pentagon	the sum of the measures of the exterior angles of a pentagon

Monitoring Progress and Modeling with Mathematics

In Exercises 3–6, find the sum of the measures of the interior angles of the indicated convex polygon. *(See Example 1.)*

3. nonagon

4. 14-gon

5. 16-gon

6. 20-gon

In Exercises 7–10, the sum of the measures of the interior angles of a convex polygon is given. Classify the polygon by the number of sides. *(See Example 2.)*

7. 720°

8. 1080°

9. 2520°

10. 3240°

In Exercises 11–14, find the value of *x*. *(See Example 3.)*

11.

12.

13.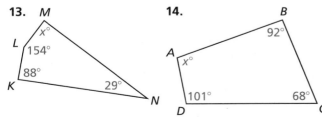

14.

In Exercises 15–18, find the value of *x*.

15.

16.

17.

18.

In Exercises 19–22, find the measures of ∠*X* and ∠*Y*. *(See Example 4.)*

19.

20.

21.

22.

In Exercises 23–26, find the value of *x*. *(See Example 5.)*

23.

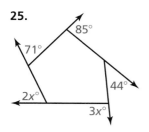

65°
x°
106°
78°

24.

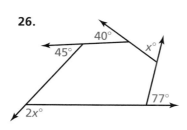

50° 48°
39° 59°
58° *x*°
x°

25.

85°
71°
2*x*°
44°
3*x*°

26.

40°
45° *x*°
2*x*° 77°

In Exercises 27–30, find the measure of each interior angle and each exterior angle of the indicated regular polygon. *(See Example 6.)*

27. pentagon

28. 18-gon

29. 45-gon

30. 90-gon

ERROR ANALYSIS **In Exercises 31 and 32, describe and correct the error in finding the measure of one exterior angle of a regular pentagon.**

31.

$(n - 2) \cdot 180° = (5 - 2) \cdot 180°$
$= 3 \cdot 180°$
$= 540°$

The sum of the measures of the angles is 540°. There are five angles, so the measure of one exterior angle is $\dfrac{540°}{5} = 108°$.

32.

There are a total of 10 exterior angles, two at each vertex, so the measure of one exterior angle is $\dfrac{360°}{10} = 36°$.

33. **MODELING WITH MATHEMATICS** The base of a jewelry box is shaped like a regular hexagon. What is the measure of each interior angle of the jewelry box base?

34. **MODELING WITH MATHEMATICS** The floor of the gazebo shown is shaped like a regular decagon. Find the measure of each interior angle of the regular decagon. Then find the measure of each exterior angle.

35. **WRITING A FORMULA** Write a formula to find the number of sides *n* in a regular polygon given that the measure of one interior angle is *x*°.

36. **WRITING A FORMULA** Write a formula to find the number of sides *n* in a regular polygon given that the measure of one exterior angle is *x*°.

REASONING **In Exercises 37–40, find the number of sides for the regular polygon described.**

37. Each interior angle has a measure of 156°.

38. Each interior angle has a measure of 165°.

39. Each exterior angle has a measure of 9°.

40. Each exterior angle has a measure of 6°.

41. **DRAWING CONCLUSIONS** Which of the following angle measures are possible interior angle measures of a regular polygon? Explain your reasoning. Select all that apply.

(**A**) 162°   (**B**) 171°   (**C**) 75°   (**D**) 40°

42. **PROVING A THEOREM** The Polygon Interior Angles Theorem states that the sum of the measures of the interior angles of a convex *n*-gon is $(n - 2) \cdot 180°$.

a. Write a paragraph proof of this theorem for the case when *n* = 5.

b. You proved statements using mathematical induction on page 402. Prove this theorem for $n \geq 3$ using mathematical induction and the figure shown.

A_1
A_{k+1}
A_2
A_k
A_3
A_{k-1}

43. PROVING A COROLLARY Write a paragraph proof of the Corollary to the Polygon Interior Angles Theorem.

44. MAKING AN ARGUMENT Your friend claims that to find the interior angle measures of a regular polygon, you do not have to use the Polygon Interior Angles Theorem. You instead can use the Polygon Exterior Angles Theorem and then the Linear Pair Postulate. Is your friend correct? Explain your reasoning.

45. MATHEMATICAL CONNECTIONS In an equilateral hexagon, four of the exterior angles each have a measure of $x°$. The other two exterior angles each have a measure of twice the sum of x and 48. Find the measure of each exterior angle.

46. THOUGHT PROVOKING For a concave polygon, is it true that at least one of the interior angle measures must be greater than 180°? If not, give an example. If so, explain your reasoning.

47. WRITING EXPRESSIONS Write an expression to find the sum of the measures of the interior angles for a concave polygon. Explain your reasoning.

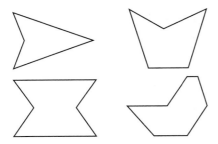

48. ANALYZING RELATIONSHIPS Polygon *ABCDEFGH* is a regular octagon. Suppose sides $\overline{AB}$ and $\overline{CD}$ are extended to meet at a point *P*. Find $m\angle BPC$. Explain your reasoning. Include a diagram with your answer.

49. MULTIPLE REPRESENTATIONS The formula for the measure of each interior angle in a regular polygon can be written in function notation.

   a. Write a function $h(n)$, where n is the number of sides in a regular polygon and $h(n)$ is the measure of any interior angle in the regular polygon.

   b. Use the function to find $h(9)$.

   c. Use the function to find n when $h(n) = 150°$.

   d. Plot the points for $n = 3, 4, 5, 6, 7$, and 8. What happens to the value of $h(n)$ as n gets larger?

50. HOW DO YOU SEE IT? Is the hexagon a regular hexagon? Explain your reasoning.

51. PROVING A THEOREM Write a paragraph proof of the Polygon Exterior Angles Theorem. *(Hint: In a convex n-gon, the sum of the measures of an interior angle and an adjacent exterior angle at any vertex is 180°.)*

52. ABSTRACT REASONING You are given a convex polygon. You are asked to draw a new polygon by increasing the sum of the interior angle measures by 540°. How many more sides does your new polygon have? Explain your reasoning.

Maintaining Mathematical Proficiency
Reviewing what you learned in previous grades and lessons

Find the value of x. *(Skills Review Handbook)*

53.

$x°$
$79°$

54.

$113°$
$x°$

55.

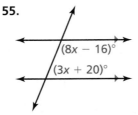

$(8x − 16)°$
$(3x + 20)°$

56.

$(6x − 19)°$
$(3x + 10)°$

7.2 Properties of Parallelograms

Essential Question   What are the properties of parallelograms?

> **EXPLORATION 1**   **Discovering Properties of Parallelograms**

Work with a partner. Use dynamic geometry software.

a. Construct any parallelogram and label it *ABCD*. Explain your process.

Sample

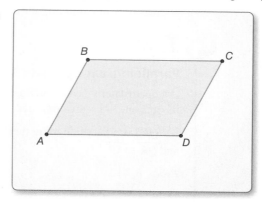

b. Find the angle measures of the parallelogram. What do you observe?

c. Find the side lengths of the parallelogram. What do you observe?

d. Repeat parts (a)–(c) for several other parallelograms. Use your results to write conjectures about the angle measures and side lengths of a parallelogram.

> **EXPLORATION 2**   **Discovering a Property of Parallelograms**

Work with a partner. Use dynamic geometry software.

a. Construct any parallelogram and label it *ABCD*.

b. Draw the two diagonals of the parallelogram. Label the point of intersection *E*.

Sample

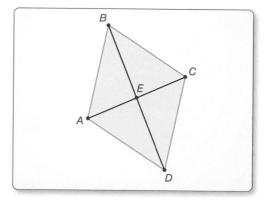

MAKING SENSE OF PROBLEMS

To be proficient in math, you need to analyze givens, constraints, relationships, and goals.

c. Find the segment lengths *AE*, *BE*, *CE*, and *DE*. What do you observe?

d. Repeat parts (a)–(c) for several other parallelograms. Use your results to write a conjecture about the diagonals of a parallelogram.

Communicate Your Answer

3. What are the properties of parallelograms?

What You Will Learn

▶ Use properties to find side lengths and angles of parallelograms.

▶ Use parallelograms in the coordinate plane.

Core Vocabulary

parallelogram, *p. 412*

Previous
quadrilateral
diagonal
interior angles
segment bisector

Using Properties of Parallelograms

A **parallelogram** is a quadrilateral with both pairs of opposite sides parallel. In □*PQRS*, $\overline{PQ} \parallel \overline{RS}$ and $\overline{QR} \parallel \overline{PS}$ by definition. The theorems below describe other properties of parallelograms.

🔄 Theorems

Parallelogram Opposite Sides Theorem

If a quadrilateral is a parallelogram, then its opposite sides are congruent.

If *PQRS* is a parallelogram, then $\overline{PQ} \cong \overline{RS}$ and $\overline{QR} \cong \overline{SP}$.

Proof p. 412

Parallelogram Opposite Angles Theorem

If a quadrilateral is a parallelogram, then its opposite angles are congruent.

If *PQRS* is a parallelogram, then $\angle P \cong \angle R$ and $\angle Q \cong \angle S$.

Proof Ex. 37, p. 417

PROOF   **Parallelogram Opposite Sides Theorem**

Given *PQRS* is a parallelogram.

Prove $\overline{PQ} \cong \overline{RS}, \overline{QR} \cong \overline{SP}$

Plan for Proof
a. Draw diagonal $\overline{QS}$ to form △*PQS* and △*RSQ*.

b. Use the ASA Congruence Theorem to show that △*PQS* ≅ △*RSQ*.

c. Use congruent triangles to show that $\overline{PQ} \cong \overline{RS}$ and $\overline{QR} \cong \overline{SP}$.

Plan in Action

STATEMENTS	REASONS
1. *PQRS* is a parallelogram.	**1.** Given
a. **2.** Draw $\overline{QS}$.	**2.** Through any two points, there exists exactly one line.
3. $\overline{PQ} \parallel \overline{RS}, \overline{QR} \parallel \overline{PS}$	**3.** Definition of parallelogram
b. **4.** $\angle PQS \cong \angle RSQ,$ $\angle PSQ \cong \angle RQS$	**4.** Alternate Interior Angles Theorem
5. $\overline{QS} \cong \overline{SQ}$	**5.** Reflexive Property of Congruence
6. △*PQS* ≅ △*RSQ*	**6.** ASA Congruence Theorem
c. **7.** $\overline{PQ} \cong \overline{RS}, \overline{QR} \cong \overline{SP}$	**7.** Corresponding parts of congruent triangles are congruent.

EXAMPLE 1 **Using Properties of Parallelograms**

Find the values of x and y.

SOLUTION

ABCD is a parallelogram by the definition of a parallelogram. Use the Parallelogram Opposite Sides Theorem to find the value of x.

$AB = CD$ Opposite sides of a parallelogram are congruent.

$x + 4 = 12$ Substitute $x + 4$ for *AB* and 12 for *CD*.

$x = 8$ Subtract 4 from each side.

By the Parallelogram Opposite Angles Theorem, $\angle A \cong \angle C$, or $m\angle A = m\angle C$. So, $y° = 65°$.

▶ In $\square ABCD$, $x = 8$ and $y = 65$.

Monitoring Progress ◀)) Help in English and Spanish at *BigIdeasMath.com*

1. Find *FG* and $m\angle G$.

2. Find the values of x and y.

The Consecutive Interior Angles Theorem states that if two parallel lines are cut by a transversal, then the pairs of consecutive interior angles formed are supplementary.

A pair of consecutive angles in a parallelogram is like a pair of consecutive interior angles between parallel lines. This similarity suggests the Parallelogram Consecutive Angles Theorem.

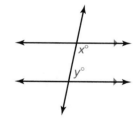

⑤ Theorems

Parallelogram Consecutive Angles Theorem

If a quadrilateral is a parallelogram, then its consecutive angles are supplementary.

If *PQRS* is a parallelogram, then $x° + y° = 180°$.

Proof Ex. 38, p. 417

Parallelogram Diagonals Theorem

If a quadrilateral is a parallelogram, then its diagonals bisect each other.

If *PQRS* is a parallelogram, then $\overline{QM} \cong \overline{SM}$ and $\overline{PM} \cong \overline{RM}$.

Proof p. 414

PROOF Parallelogram Diagonals Theorem

Given *PQRS* is a parallelogram. Diagonals $\overline{PR}$ and $\overline{QS}$ intersect at point *M*.

Prove *M* bisects $\overline{QS}$ and $\overline{PR}$.

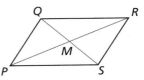

STATEMENTS	REASONS
1. *PQRS* is a parallelogram.	1. Given
2. $\overline{PQ} \parallel \overline{RS}$	2. Definition of a parallelogram
3. $\angle QPR \cong \angle SRP$, $\angle PQS \cong \angle RSQ$	3. Alternate Interior Angles Theorem
4. $\overline{PQ} \cong \overline{RS}$	4. Parallelogram Opposite Sides Theorem
5. $\triangle PMQ \cong \triangle RMS$	5. ASA Congruence Theorem
6. $\overline{QM} \cong \overline{SM}$, $\overline{PM} \cong \overline{RM}$	6. Corresponding parts of congruent triangles are congruent.
7. *M* bisects $\overline{QS}$ and $\overline{PR}$.	7. Definition of segment bisector

EXAMPLE 2 Using Properties of a Parallelogram

As shown, part of the extending arm of a desk lamp is a parallelogram. The angles of the parallelogram change as the lamp is raised and lowered. Find $m\angle BCD$ when $m\angle ADC = 110°$.

SOLUTION

By the Parallelogram Consecutive Angles Theorem, the consecutive angle pairs in $\square ABCD$ are supplementary. So, $m\angle ADC + m\angle BCD = 180°$. Because $m\angle ADC = 110°$, $m\angle BCD = 180° - 110° = 70°$.

EXAMPLE 3 Writing a Two-Column Proof

Write a two-column proof.

Given *ABCD* and *GDEF* are parallelograms.

Prove $\angle B \cong \angle F$

STATEMENTS	REASONS
1. *ABCD* and *GDEF* are parallelograms.	1. Given
2. $\angle CDA \cong \angle B$, $\angle EDG \cong \angle F$	2. If a quadrilateral is a parallelogram, then its opposite angles are congruent.
3. $\angle CDA \cong \angle EDG$	3. Vertical Angles Congruence Theorem
4. $\angle B \cong \angle F$	4. Transitive Property of Congruence

Monitoring Progress   Help in English and Spanish at *BigIdeasMath.com*

3. **WHAT IF?** In Example 2, find $m\angle BCD$ when $m\angle ADC$ is twice the measure of $\angle BCD$.

4. Using the figure and the given statement in Example 3, prove that $\angle C$ and $\angle F$ are supplementary angles.

Using Parallelograms in the Coordinate Plane

JUSTIFYING STEPS

In Example 4, you can use either diagonal to find the coordinates of the intersection. Using diagonal $\overline{OM}$ helps simplify the calculation because one endpoint is (0, 0).

EXAMPLE 4   Using Parallelograms in the Coordinate Plane

Find the coordinates of the intersection of the diagonals of $\square LMNO$ with vertices $L(1, 4)$, $M(7, 4)$, $N(6, 0)$, and $O(0, 0)$.

SOLUTION

By the Parallelogram Diagonals Theorem, the diagonals of a parallelogram bisect each other. So, the coordinates of the intersection are the midpoints of diagonals $\overline{LN}$ and $\overline{OM}$.

coordinates of midpoint of $\overline{OM} = \left(\dfrac{7 + 0}{2}, \dfrac{4 + 0}{2}\right) = \left(\dfrac{7}{2}, 2\right)$ Midpoint Formula

▶ The coordinates of the intersection of the diagonals are $\left(\dfrac{7}{2}, 2\right)$. You can check your answer by graphing $\square LMNO$ and drawing the diagonals. The point of intersection appears to be correct.

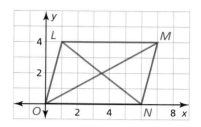

EXAMPLE 5   Using Parallelograms in the Coordinate Plane

Three vertices of $\square WXYZ$ are $W(-1, -3)$, $X(-3, 2)$, and $Z(4, -4)$. Find the coordinates of vertex Y.

REMEMBER

When graphing a polygon in the coordinate plane, the name of the polygon gives the order of the vertices.

SOLUTION

Step 1   Graph the vertices W, X, and Z.

Step 2   Find the slope of $\overline{WX}$.

slope of $\overline{WX} = \dfrac{2 - (-3)}{-3 - (-1)} = \dfrac{5}{-2} = -\dfrac{5}{2}$

Step 3   Start at $Z(4, -4)$. Use the rise and run from Step 2 to find vertex Y.

A rise of 5 represents a change of 5 units up. A run of -2 represents a change of 2 units left.

So, plot the point that is 5 units up and 2 units left from $Z(4, -4)$. The point is $(2, 1)$. Label it as vertex Y.

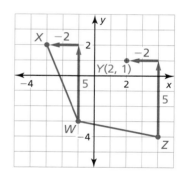

Step 4   Find the slopes of $\overline{XY}$ and $\overline{WZ}$ to verify that they are parallel.

slope of $\overline{XY} = \dfrac{1 - 2}{2 - (-3)} = \dfrac{-1}{5} = -\dfrac{1}{5}$ slope of $\overline{WZ} = \dfrac{-4 - (-3)}{4 - (-1)} = \dfrac{-1}{5} = -\dfrac{1}{5}$

▶ So, the coordinates of vertex Y are $(2, 1)$.

Monitoring Progress Help in English and Spanish at *BigIdeasMath.com*

5. Find the coordinates of the intersection of the diagonals of $\square STUV$ with vertices $S(-2, 3)$, $T(1, 5)$, $U(6, 3)$, and $V(3, 1)$.

6. Three vertices of $\square ABCD$ are $A(2, 4)$, $B(5, 2)$, and $C(3, -1)$. Find the coordinates of vertex D.

Vocabulary and Core Concept Check

1. **VOCABULARY** Why is a parallelogram always a quadrilateral, but a quadrilateral is only sometimes a parallelogram?

2. **WRITING** You are given one angle measure of a parallelogram. Explain how you can find the other angle measures of the parallelogram.

Monitoring Progress and Modeling with Mathematics

In Exercises 3–6, find the value of each variable in the parallelogram. (*See Example 1.*)

3.

4.

5.

6.

In Exercises 7 and 8, find the measure of the indicated angle in the parallelogram. (*See Example 2.*)

7. Find $m\angle B$.

8. Find $m\angle N$.

In Exercises 9–16, find the indicated measure in □*LMNQ*. Explain your reasoning.

9. *LM*

10. *LP*

11. *LQ*

12. *MQ*

13. $m\angle LMN$

14. $m\angle NQL$

15. $m\angle MNQ$

16. $m\angle LMQ$

In Exercises 17–20, find the value of each variable in the parallelogram.

17.

18.

19.

20.

ERROR ANALYSIS In Exercises 21 and 22, describe and correct the error in using properties of parallelograms.

21.

Because quadrilateral *STUV* is a parallelogram, $\angle S \cong \angle V$. So, $m\angle V = 50°$.

22.

Because quadrilateral *GHJK* is a parallelogram, $\overline{GF} \cong \overline{FH}$.

PROOF In Exercises 23 and 24, write a two-column proof. *(See Example 3.)*

23. **Given** *ABCD* and *CEFD* are parallelograms.

Prove $\overline{AB} \cong \overline{FE}$

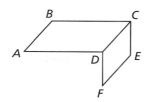

24. **Given** *ABCD*, *EBGF,* and *HJKD* are parallelograms.

Prove $\angle 2 \cong \angle 3$

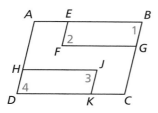

In Exercises 25 and 26, find the coordinates of the intersection of the diagonals of the parallelogram with the given vertices. *(See Example 4.)*

25. $W(-2, 5), X(2, 5), Y(4, 0), Z(0, 0)$

26. $Q(-1, 3), R(5, 2), S(1, -2), T(-5, -1)$

In Exercises 27–30, three vertices of □*DEFG* are given. Find the coordinates of the remaining vertex. *(See Example 5.)*

27. $D(0, 2), E(-1, 5), G(4, 0)$

28. $D(-2, -4), F(0, 7), G(1, 0)$

29. $D(-4, -2), E(-3, 1), F(3, 3)$

30. $E(-1, 4), F(5, 6), G(8, 0)$

MATHEMATICAL CONNECTIONS In Exercises 31 and 32, find the measure of each angle.

31. The measure of one interior angle of a parallelogram is 0.25 times the measure of another angle.

32. The measure of one interior angle of a parallelogram is 50 degrees more than 4 times the measure of another angle.

33. **MAKING AN ARGUMENT** In quadrilateral *ABCD*, $m\angle B = 124°$, $m\angle A = 56°$, and $m\angle C = 124°$. Your friend claims quadrilateral *ABCD* could be a parallelogram. Is your friend correct? Explain your reasoning.

34. **ATTENDING TO PRECISION** $\angle J$ and $\angle K$ are consecutive angles in a parallelogram, $m\angle J = (3x + 7)°$, and $m\angle K = (5x - 11)°$. Find the measure of each angle.

35. **CONSTRUCTION** Construct any parallelogram and label it *ABCD*. Draw diagonals $\overline{AC}$ and $\overline{BD}$. Explain how to use paper folding to verify the Parallelogram Diagonals Theorem for □*ABCD*.

36. **MODELING WITH MATHEMATICS** The feathers on an arrow form two congruent parallelograms. The parallelograms are reflections of each other over the line that contains their shared side. Show that $m\angle 2 = 2m\angle 1$.

37. **PROVING A THEOREM** Use the diagram to write a two-column proof of the Parallelogram Opposite Angles Theorem.

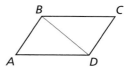

Given *ABCD* is a parallelogram.

Prove $\angle A \cong \angle C, \angle B \cong \angle D$

38. **PROVING A THEOREM** Use the diagram to write a two-column proof of the Parallelogram Consecutive Angles Theorem.

Given *PQRS* is a parallelogram.

Prove $x° + y° = 180°$

39. **PROBLEM SOLVING** The sides of □*MNPQ* are represented by the expressions below. Sketch □*MNPQ* and find its perimeter.

$$MQ = -2x + 37 \qquad QP = y + 14$$
$$NP = x - 5 \qquad MN = 4y + 5$$

40. **PROBLEM SOLVING** In □*LMNP*, the ratio of *LM* to *MN* is 4 : 3. Find *LM* when the perimeter of □*LMNP* is 28.

41. ABSTRACT REASONING Can you prove that two parallelograms are congruent by proving that all their corresponding sides are congruent? Explain your reasoning.

42. HOW DO YOU SEE IT? The mirror shown is attached to the wall by an arm that can extend away from the wall. In the figure, points P, Q, R, and S are the vertices of a parallelogram. This parallelogram is one of several that change shape as the mirror is extended.

a. What happens to $m\angle P$ as $m\angle Q$ increases? Explain.

b. What happens to QS as $m\angle Q$ decreases? Explain.

c. What happens to the overall distance between the mirror and the wall when $m\angle Q$ decreases? Explain.

43. MATHEMATICAL CONNECTIONS In $\square STUV$, $m\angle TSU = 32°$, $m\angle USV = (x^2)°$, $m\angle TUV = 12x°$, and $\angle TUV$ is an acute angle. Find $m\angle USV$.

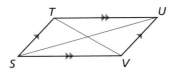

44. THOUGHT PROVOKING Is it possible that any triangle can be partitioned into four congruent triangles that can be rearranged to form a parallelogram? Explain your reasoning.

45. CRITICAL THINKING Points $W(1, 2)$, $X(3, 6)$, and $Y(6, 4)$ are three vertices of a parallelogram. How many parallelograms can be created using these three vertices? Find the coordinates of each point that could be the fourth vertex.

46. PROOF In the diagram, $\overline{EK}$ bisects $\angle FEH$, and $\overline{FJ}$ bisects $\angle EFG$. Prove that $\overline{EK} \perp \overline{FJ}$. (*Hint:* Write equations using the angle measures of the triangles and quadrilaterals formed.)

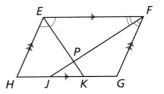

47. PROOF Prove the *Congruent Parts of Parallel Lines Corollary*: If three or more parallel lines cut off congruent segments on one transversal, then they cut off congruent segments on every transversal.

Given $\overleftrightarrow{GH} \parallel \overleftrightarrow{JK} \parallel \overleftrightarrow{LM}, \overline{GJ} \cong \overline{JL}$

Prove $\overline{HK} \cong \overline{KM}$

(*Hint:* Draw $\overline{KP}$ and $\overline{MQ}$ such that quadrilateral $GPKJ$ and quadrilateral $JQML$ are parallelograms.)

Maintaining Mathematical Proficiency
Reviewing what you learned in previous grades and lessons

Determine whether lines ℓ and m are parallel. Explain your reasoning. (*Skills Review Handbook*)

48.

49.

50.

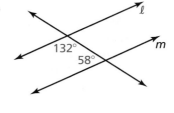

7.3 Proving That a Quadrilateral Is a Parallelogram

Essential Question How can you prove that a quadrilateral is a parallelogram?

EXPLORATION 1 Proving That a Quadrilateral Is a Parallelogram

Work with a partner.
Use dynamic geometry software.

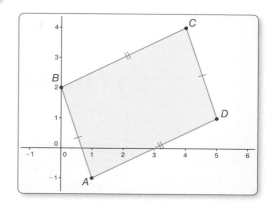

Sample

Points
$A(1, -1)$
$B(0, 2)$
$C(4, 4)$
$D(5, 1)$
Segments
$AB = 3.16$
$BC = 4.47$
$CD = 3.16$
$DA = 4.47$

REASONING ABSTRACTLY

To be proficient in math, you need to know and flexibly use different properties of objects.

a. Construct any quadrilateral *ABCD* whose opposite sides are congruent.

b. Is the quadrilateral a parallelogram? Justify your answer.

c. Repeat parts (a) and (b) for several other quadrilaterals. Then write a conjecture based on your results.

d. Write the converse of your conjecture. Is the converse true? Explain.

EXPLORATION 2 Proving That a Quadrilateral Is a Parallelogram

Work with a partner. Use dynamic geometry software.

a. Construct any quadrilateral *ABCD* whose opposite angles are congruent.

b. Is the quadrilateral a parallelogram? Justify your answer.

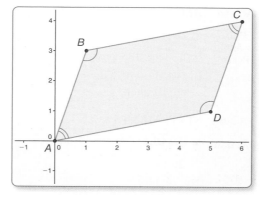

Sample

Points
$A(0, 0)$
$B(1, 3)$
$C(6, 4)$
$D(5, 1)$
Angles
$\angle A = 60.26°$
$\angle B = 119.74°$
$\angle C = 60.26°$
$\angle D = 119.74°$

c. Repeat parts (a) and (b) for several other quadrilaterals. Then write a conjecture based on your results.

d. Write the converse of your conjecture. Is the converse true? Explain.

Communicate Your Answer

3. How can you prove that a quadrilateral is a parallelogram?

4. Is the quadrilateral at the left a parallelogram? Explain your reasoning.

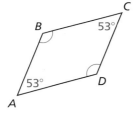

What You Will Learn

▶ Identify and verify parallelograms.

▶ Show that a quadrilateral is a parallelogram in the coordinate plane.

Identifying and Verifying Parallelograms

Given a parallelogram, you can use the Parallelogram Opposite Sides Theorem and the Parallelogram Opposite Angles Theorem to prove statements about the sides and angles of the parallelogram. The converses of the theorems are stated below. You can use these and other theorems in this lesson to prove that a quadrilateral with certain properties is a parallelogram.

🌀 Theorems

Parallelogram Opposite Sides Converse

If both pairs of opposite sides of a quadrilateral are congruent, then the quadrilateral is a parallelogram.

If $\overline{AB} \cong \overline{CD}$ and $\overline{BC} \cong \overline{DA}$, then $ABCD$ is a parallelogram.

Parallelogram Opposite Angles Converse

If both pairs of opposite angles of a quadrilateral are congruent, then the quadrilateral is a parallelogram.

If $\angle A \cong \angle C$ and $\angle B \cong \angle D$, then $ABCD$ is a parallelogram.

Proof Ex. 39, p. 427

PROOF **Parallelogram Opposite Sides Converse**

Given $\overline{AB} \cong \overline{CD}, \overline{BC} \cong \overline{DA}$

Prove $ABCD$ is a parallelogram.

Plan for Proof

a. Draw diagonal $\overline{AC}$ to form $\triangle ABC$ and $\triangle CDA$.

b. Use the SSS Congruence Theorem to show that $\triangle ABC \cong \triangle CDA$.

c. Use the Alternate Interior Angles Converse to show that opposite sides are parallel.

Plan in Action	STATEMENTS	REASONS
a.	**1.** $\overline{AB} \cong \overline{CD}, \overline{BC} \cong \overline{DA}$	**1.** Given
	2. Draw $\overline{AC}$.	**2.** Through any two points, there exists exactly one line.
	3. $\overline{AC} \cong \overline{CA}$	**3.** Reflexive Property of Congruence
b.	**4.** $\triangle ABC \cong \triangle CDA$	**4.** SSS Congruence Theorem
c.	**5.** $\angle BAC \cong \angle DCA$, $\angle BCA \cong \angle DAC$	**5.** Corresponding parts of congruent triangles are congruent.
	6. $\overline{AB} \parallel \overline{CD}, \overline{BC} \parallel \overline{DA}$	**6.** Alternate Interior Angles Converse
	7. $ABCD$ is a parallelogram.	**7.** Definition of parallelogram

EXAMPLE 1 Identifying a Parallelogram

An amusement park ride has a moving platform attached to four swinging arms. The platform swings back and forth, higher and higher, until it goes over the top and around in a circular motion. In the diagram below, $\overline{AD}$ and $\overline{BC}$ represent two of the swinging arms, and $\overline{DC}$ is parallel to the ground (line ℓ). Explain why the moving platform $\overline{AB}$ is always parallel to the ground.

SOLUTION

The shape of quadrilateral $ABCD$ changes as the moving platform swings around, but its side lengths do not change. Both pairs of opposite sides are congruent, so $ABCD$ is a parallelogram by the Parallelogram Opposite Sides Converse.

By the definition of a parallelogram, $\overline{AB} \parallel \overline{DC}$. Because $\overline{DC}$ is parallel to line ℓ, $\overline{AB}$ is also parallel to line ℓ by the Transitive Property of Parallel Lines. So, the moving platform is parallel to the ground.

Monitoring Progress   Help in English and Spanish at *BigIdeasMath.com*

1. In quadrilateral $WXYZ$, $m\angle W = 42°$, $m\angle X = 138°$, and $m\angle Y = 42°$. Find $m\angle Z$. Is $WXYZ$ a parallelogram? Explain your reasoning.

EXAMPLE 2 Finding Side Lengths of a Parallelogram

For what values of x and y is quadrilateral $PQRS$ a parallelogram?

SOLUTION

By the Parallelogram Opposite Sides Converse, if both pairs of opposite sides of a quadrilateral are congruent, then the quadrilateral is a parallelogram. Find x so that $\overline{PQ} \cong \overline{SR}$.

$PQ = SR$	Set the segment lengths equal.
$x + 9 = 2x - 1$	Substitute $x + 9$ for PQ and $2x - 1$ for SR.
$10 = x$	Solve for x.

When $x = 10$, $PQ = 10 + 9 = 19$ and $SR = 2(10) - 1 = 19$. Find y so that $\overline{PS} \cong \overline{QR}$.

$PS = QR$	Set the segment lengths equal.
$y = x + 7$	Substitute y for PS and $x + 7$ for QR.
$y = 10 + 7$	Substitute 10 for x.
$y = 17$	Add.

When $x = 10$ and $y = 17$, $PS = 17$ and $QR = 10 + 7 = 17$.

▶ Quadrilateral $PQRS$ is a parallelogram when $x = 10$ and $y = 17$.

⟳ Theorems

Opposite Sides Parallel and Congruent Theorem

If one pair of opposite sides of a quadrilateral are congruent and parallel, then the quadrilateral is a parallelogram.

If $\overline{BC} \parallel \overline{AD}$ and $\overline{BC} \cong \overline{AD}$, then $ABCD$ is a parallelogram.

Proof Ex. 40, p. 427

Parallelogram Diagonals Converse

If the diagonals of a quadrilateral bisect each other, then the quadrilateral is a parallelogram.

If $\overline{BD}$ and $\overline{AC}$ bisect each other, then $ABCD$ is a parallelogram.

Proof Ex. 41, p. 427

EXAMPLE 3   Identifying a Parallelogram

The doorway shown is part of a building in England. Over time, the building has leaned sideways. Explain how you know that $SV = TU$.

SOLUTION

In the photograph, $\overline{ST} \parallel \overline{UV}$ and $\overline{ST} \cong \overline{UV}$. By the Opposite Sides Parallel and Congruent Theorem, quadrilateral $STUV$ is a parallelogram. By the Parallelogram Opposite Sides Theorem, you know that opposite sides of a parallelogram are congruent. So, $SV = TU$.

EXAMPLE 4   Finding Diagonal Lengths of a Parallelogram

For what value of x is quadrilateral $CDEF$ a parallelogram?

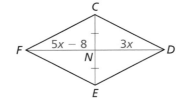

SOLUTION

By the Parallelogram Diagonals Converse, if the diagonals of $CDEF$ bisect each other, then it is a parallelogram. You are given that $\overline{CN} \cong \overline{EN}$. Find x so that $\overline{FN} \cong \overline{DN}$.

$FN = DN$	Set the segment lengths equal.
$5x - 8 = 3x$	Substitute $5x - 8$ for FN and $3x$ for DN.
$2x - 8 = 0$	Subtract $3x$ from each side.
$2x = 8$	Add 8 to each side.
$x = 4$	Divide each side by 2.

When $x = 4$, $FN = 5(4) - 8 = 12$ and $DN = 3(4) = 12$.

▶ Quadrilateral $CDEF$ is a parallelogram when $x = 4$.

2. For what values of *x* and *y* is quadrilateral *ABCD* a parallelogram? Explain your reasoning.

State the theorem you can use to show that the quadrilateral is a parallelogram.

3.

30 m

30 m

4.

7 in.

5 in.   5 in.

7 in.

5.

65°   115°

115°   65°

6. For what value of *x* is quadrilateral *MNPQ* a parallelogram? Explain your reasoning.

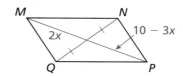

M   N

2x   10 − 3x

Q   P

Concept Summary

Ways to Prove a Quadrilateral Is a Parallelogram

1. Show that both pairs of opposite sides are parallel. *(Definition)*	
2. Show that both pairs of opposite sides are congruent. *(Parallelogram Opposite Sides Converse)*	
3. Show that both pairs of opposite angles are congruent. *(Parallelogram Opposite Angles Converse)*	
4. Show that one pair of opposite sides are congruent and parallel. *(Opposite Sides Parallel and Congruent Theorem)*	
5. Show that the diagonals bisect each other. *(Parallelogram Diagonals Converse)*	

Using Coordinate Geometry

EXAMPLE 5 **Identifying a Parallelogram in the Coordinate Plane**

Show that quadrilateral $ABCD$ is a parallelogram.

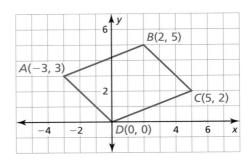

SOLUTION

Method 1   Show that a pair of sides are congruent and parallel. Then apply the Opposite Sides Parallel and Congruent Theorem.

First, use the Distance Formula to show that $\overline{AB}$ and $\overline{CD}$ are congruent.

$$AB = \sqrt{[2 - (-3)]^2 + (5 - 3)^2} = \sqrt{29}$$
$$CD = \sqrt{(5 - 0)^2 + (2 - 0)^2} = \sqrt{29}$$

Because $AB = CD = \sqrt{29}$, $\overline{AB} \cong \overline{CD}$.

Then, use the slope formula to show that $\overline{AB} \parallel \overline{CD}$.

$$\text{slope of } \overline{AB} = \frac{5 - 3}{2 - (-3)} = \frac{2}{5}$$

$$\text{slope of } \overline{CD} = \frac{2 - 0}{5 - 0} = \frac{2}{5}$$

Because $\overline{AB}$ and $\overline{CD}$ have the same slope, they are parallel.

▶ $\overline{AB}$ and $\overline{CD}$ are congruent and parallel. So, $ABCD$ is a parallelogram by the Opposite Sides Parallel and Congruent Theorem.

Method 2   Show that opposite sides are congruent. Then apply the Parallelogram Opposite Sides Converse. In Method 1, you already have shown that because $AB = CD = \sqrt{29}$, $\overline{AB} \cong \overline{CD}$. Now find AD and BC.

$$AD = \sqrt{(-3 - 0)^2 + (3 - 0)^2} = 3\sqrt{2}$$
$$BC = \sqrt{(2 - 5)^2 + (5 - 2)^2} = 3\sqrt{2}$$

Because $AD = BC = 3\sqrt{2}$, $\overline{AD} \cong \overline{BC}$.

▶ $\overline{AB} \cong \overline{CD}$ and $\overline{AD} \cong \overline{BC}$. So, $ABCD$ is a parallelogram by the Parallelogram Opposite Sides Converse.

Monitoring Progress   Help in English and Spanish at *BigIdeasMath.com*

7. Show that quadrilateral $JKLM$ is a parallelogram.

8. Refer to the Concept Summary on page 423. Explain two other methods you can use to show that quadrilateral $ABCD$ in Example 5 is a parallelogram.

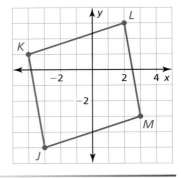

Vocabulary and Core Concept Check

1. **WRITING** A quadrilateral has four congruent sides. Is the quadrilateral a parallelogram? Justify your answer.

2. **DIFFERENT WORDS, SAME QUESTION** Which is different? Find "both" answers.

Construct a quadrilateral with opposite sides congruent.	Construct a quadrilateral with one pair of parallel sides.
Construct a quadrilateral with opposite angles congruent.	Construct a quadrilateral with one pair of opposite sides congruent and parallel.

Monitoring Progress and Modeling with Mathematics

In Exercises 3–8, state which theorem you can use to show that the quadrilateral is a parallelogram. *(See Examples 1 and 3.)*

3.

4.

5.

6.

7.

8.

In Exercises 9–12, find the values of x and y that make the quadrilateral a parallelogram. *(See Example 2.)*

9.

10.

11.

12.

In Exercises 13–16, find the value of x that makes the quadrilateral a parallelogram. *(See Example 4.)*

13.

14.

15.

16.
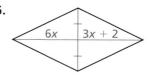

In Exercises 17–20, graph the quadrilateral with the given vertices in a coordinate plane. Then show that the quadrilateral is a parallelogram. *(See Example 5.)*

17. $A(0, 1)$, $B(4, 4)$, $C(12, 4)$, $D(8, 1)$

18. $E(-3, 0)$, $F(-3, 4)$, $G(3, -1)$, $H(3, -5)$

19. $J(-2, 3)$, $K(-5, 7)$, $L(3, 6)$, $M(6, 2)$

20. $N(-5, 0)$, $P(0, 4)$, $Q(3, 0)$, $R(-2, -4)$

ERROR ANALYSIS In Exercises 21 and 22, describe and correct the error in identifying a parallelogram.

21.

DEFG is a parallelogram by the Parallelogram Opposite Sides Converse.

22.

JKLM is a parallelogram by the Opposite Sides Parallel and Congruent Theorem.

23. **MATHEMATICAL CONNECTIONS** What value of x makes the quadrilateral a parallelogram? Explain how you found your answer.

24. **MAKING AN ARGUMENT** Your friend says you can show that quadrilateral $WXYZ$ is a parallelogram by using the Consecutive Interior Angles Converse and the Opposite Sides Parallel and Congruent Theorem. Is your friend correct? Explain your reasoning.

ANALYZING RELATIONSHIPS In Exercises 25–27, write the indicated theorems as a biconditional statement.

25. Parallelogram Opposite Sides Theorem and Parallelogram Opposite Sides Converse

26. Parallelogram Opposite Angles Theorem and Parallelogram Opposite Angles Converse

27. Parallelogram Diagonals Theorem and Parallelogram Diagonals Converse

28. **CONSTRUCTION** Describe a method that uses the Opposite Sides Parallel and Congruent Theorem to construct a parallelogram. Then construct a parallelogram using your method.

29. **REASONING** Follow the steps below to construct a parallelogram. Explain why this method works. State a theorem to support your answer.

Step 1 Use a ruler to draw two segments that intersect at their midpoints.

Step 2 Connect the endpoints of the segments to form a parallelogram.

30. **MAKING AN ARGUMENT** Your brother says to show that quadrilateral $QRST$ is a parallelogram, you must show that $\overline{QR} \parallel \overline{TS}$ and $\overline{QT} \parallel \overline{RS}$. Your sister says that you must show that $\overline{QR} \cong \overline{TS}$ and $\overline{QT} \cong \overline{RS}$. Who is correct? Explain your reasoning.

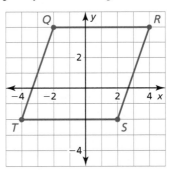

REASONING In Exercises 31 and 32, your classmate incorrectly claims that the marked information can be used to show that the figure is a parallelogram. Draw a quadrilateral with the same marked properties that is clearly *not* a parallelogram.

31.   32.

33. MODELING WITH MATHEMATICS You shoot a pool ball, and it rolls back to where it started, as shown in the diagram. The ball bounces off each wall at the same angle at which it hits the wall.

a. The ball hits the first wall at an angle of 63°. So $m\angle AEF = m\angle BEH = 63°$. What is $m\angle AFE$? Explain your reasoning.

b. Explain why $m\angle FGD = 63°$.

c. What is $m\angle GHC$? $m\angle EHB$?

d. Is quadrilateral *EFGH* a parallelogram? Explain your reasoning.

34. MODELING WITH MATHEMATICS In the diagram of the parking lot shown, $m\angle JKL = 60°$, $JK = LM = 21$ feet, and $KL = JM = 9$ feet.

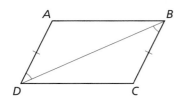

a. Explain how to show that parking space *JKLM* is a parallelogram.

b. Find $m\angle JML$, $m\angle KJM$, and $m\angle KLM$.

c. $\overline{LM} \parallel \overline{NO}$ and $\overline{NO} \parallel \overline{PQ}$. Which theorem could you use to show that $\overline{JK} \parallel \overline{PQ}$?

REASONING In Exercises 35–37, describe how to prove that *ABCD* is a parallelogram.

35.

36.

37.

38. REASONING Quadrilateral *JKLM* is a parallelogram. Describe how to prove that $\triangle MGJ \cong \triangle KHL$.

39. PROVING A THEOREM Prove the Parallelogram Opposite Angles Converse. (*Hint*: Let $x°$ represent $m\angle A$ and $m\angle C$. Let $y°$ represent $m\angle B$ and $m\angle D$. Write and simplify an equation involving x and y.)

Given $\angle A \cong \angle C$, $\angle B \cong \angle D$

Prove *ABCD* is a parallelogram.

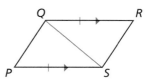

40. PROVING A THEOREM Use the diagram of *PQRS* with the auxiliary line segment drawn to prove the Opposite Sides Parallel and Congruent Theorem.

Given $\overline{QR} \parallel \overline{PS}$, $\overline{QR} \cong \overline{PS}$

Prove *PQRS* is a parallelogram.

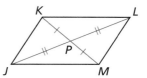

41. PROVING A THEOREM Prove the Parallelogram Diagonals Converse.

Given Diagonals $\overline{JL}$ and $\overline{KM}$ bisect each other.

Prove *JKLM* is a parallelogram.

42. PROOF Write a proof.

   Given *DEBF* is a parallelogram.
   AE = *CF*

   Prove *ABCD* is a parallelogram.

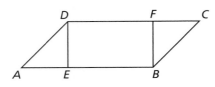

43. REASONING Three interior angle measures of a quadrilateral are 67°, 67°, and 113°. Is this enough information to conclude that the quadrilateral is a parallelogram? Explain your reasoning.

44. HOW DO YOU SEE IT? A music stand can be folded up, as shown. In the diagrams, *AEFD* and *EBCF* are parallelograms. Which labeled segments remain parallel as the stand is folded?

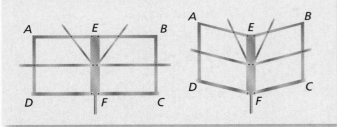

45. CRITICAL THINKING In the diagram, *ABCD* is a parallelogram, *BF* = *DE* = 12, and *CF* = 8. Find *AE*. Explain your reasoning.

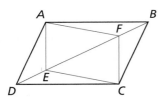

46. THOUGHT PROVOKING Create a regular hexagon using congruent parallelograms.

47. WRITING The Parallelogram Consecutive Angles Theorem says that if a quadrilateral is a parallelogram, then its consecutive angles are supplementary. Write the converse of this theorem. Then write a plan for proving the converse. Include a diagram.

48. PROOF Write a proof.

   Given *ABCD* is a parallelogram.
   ∠*A* is a right angle.

   Prove ∠*B*, ∠*C*, and ∠*D* are right angles.

49. ABSTRACT REASONING The midpoints of the sides of a quadrilateral have been joined to form what looks like a parallelogram. Show that a quadrilateral formed by connecting the midpoints of the sides of any quadrilateral is always a parallelogram. (*Hint:* Draw a diagram. Include a diagonal of the larger quadrilateral. Show how two sides of the smaller quadrilateral relate to the diagonal.)

50. CRITICAL THINKING Show that if *ABCD* is a parallelogram with its diagonals intersecting at *E*, then you can connect the midpoints *F*, *G*, *H*, and *J* of $\overline{AE}, \overline{BE}, \overline{CE},$ and $\overline{DE}$, respectively, to form another parallelogram, *FGHJ*.

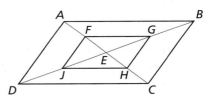

Maintaining Mathematical Proficiency

Reviewing what you learned in previous grades and lessons

Classify the quadrilateral. *(Skills Review Handbook)*

51.

52.

53.

54.

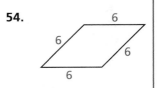

Core Vocabulary

diagonal, *p. 404*   equiangular polygon, *p. 405*   parallelogram, *p. 412*
equilateral polygon, *p. 405*   regular polygon, *p. 405*

Core Concepts

Section 7.1

Polygon Interior Angles Theorem, *p. 404*
Corollary to the Polygon Interior Angles Theorem, *p. 405*
Polygon Exterior Angles Theorem, *p. 406*

Section 7.2

Parallelogram Opposite Sides Theorem, *p. 412*
Parallelogram Opposite Angles Theorem, *p. 412*
Parallelogram Consecutive Angles Theorem, *p. 413*
Parallelogram Diagonals Theorem, *p. 413*
Using Parallelograms in the Coordinate Plane, *p. 415*

Section 7.3

Parallelogram Opposite Sides Converse, *p. 420*
Parallelogram Opposite Angles Converse, *p. 420*
Opposite Sides Parallel and Congruent Theorem, *p. 422*
Parallelogram Diagonals Converse, *p. 422*
Ways to Prove a Quadrilateral is a Parallelogram, *p. 423*
Showing That a Quadrilateral Is a Parallelogram in the Coordinate Plane, *p. 424*

Mathematical Practices

1. In Exercise 52 on page 410, what is the relationship between the 540° increase and the answer?

2. Explain why the process you used works every time in Exercise 25 on page 417. Is there another way to do it?

3. In Exercise 23 on page 426, explain how you started the problem. Why did you start that way? Could you have started another way? Explain.

Keeping Your Mind Focused during Class

STUDY SKILLS

- When you sit down at your desk, get all other issues out of your mind by reviewing your notes from the last class and focusing on just math.

- Repeat in your mind what you are writing in your notes.

- When the math is particularly difficult, ask your teacher for another example.

Find the value of x. *(Section 7.1)*

1.

2.

3.

Find the measure of each interior angle and each exterior angle of the indicated regular polygon. *(Section 7.1)*

4. decagon   **5.** 15-gon   **6.** 24-gon   **7.** 60-gon

Find the indicated measure in □ABCD. Explain your reasoning. *(Section 7.2)*

8. *CD*   **9.** *AD*

10. *AE*   **11.** *BD*

12. *m∠BCD*   **13.** *m∠ABC*

14. *m∠ADC*   **15.** *m∠DBC*

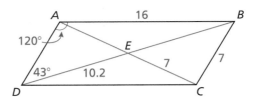

State which theorem you can use to show that the quadrilateral is a parallelogram. *(Section 7.3)*

16.

17.

18.

Graph the quadrilateral with the given vertices in a coordinate plane. Then show that the quadrilateral is a parallelogram. *(Section 7.3)*

19. $Q(-5, -2)$, $R(3, -2)$, $S(1, -6)$, $T(-7, -6)$ **20.** $W(-3, 7)$, $X(3, 3)$, $Y(1, -3)$, $Z(-5, 1)$

21. A stop sign is a regular polygon. *(Section 7.1)*

    a. Classify the stop sign by its number of sides.

    b. Find the measure of each interior angle and each exterior angle of the stop sign.

22. In the diagram of the staircase shown, *JKLM* is a parallelogram, $\overline{QT} \parallel \overline{RS}$, $QT = RS = 9$ feet, $QR = 3$ feet, and $m\angle QRS = 123°$. *(Section 7.2 and Section 7.3)*

    a. List all congruent sides and angles in □*JKLM*. Explain your reasoning.

    b. Which theorem could you use to show that *QRST* is a parallelogram?

    c. Find *ST*, *m∠QTS*, *m∠TQR*, and *m∠TSR*. Explain your reasoning.

Essential Question What are the properties of the diagonals of rectangles, rhombuses, and squares?

Recall the three types of parallelograms shown below.

Rhombus

Rectangle

Square

EXPLORATION 1   Identifying Special Quadrilaterals

Work with a partner. Use dynamic geometry software.

a. Draw a circle with center *A*.

b. Draw two diameters of the circle. Label the endpoints *B*, *C*, *D*, and *E*.

c. Draw quadrilateral *BDCE*.

d. Is *BDCE* a parallelogram? rectangle? rhombus? square? Explain your reasoning.

e. Repeat parts (a)–(d) for several other circles. Write a conjecture based on your results.

Sample

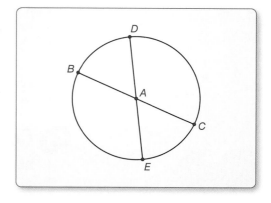

EXPLORATION 2   Identifying Special Quadrilaterals

Work with a partner. Use dynamic geometry software.

CONSTRUCTING VIABLE ARGUMENTS

To be proficient in math, you need to make conjectures and build a logical progression of statements to explore the truth of your conjectures.

a. Construct two segments that are perpendicular bisectors of each other. Label the endpoints *A*, *B*, *D*, and *E*. Label the intersection *C*.

b. Draw quadrilateral *AEBD*.

c. Is *AEBD* a parallelogram? rectangle? rhombus? square? Explain your reasoning.

d. Repeat parts (a)–(c) for several other segments. Write a conjecture based on your results.

Sample

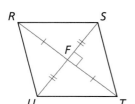

Communicate Your Answer

3. What are the properties of the diagonals of rectangles, rhombuses, and squares?

4. Is *RSTU* a parallelogram? rectangle? rhombus? square? Explain your reasoning.

5. What type of quadrilateral has congruent diagonals that bisect each other?

What You Will Learn

▶ Use properties of special parallelograms.

▶ Use properties of diagonals of special parallelograms.

▶ Use coordinate geometry to identify special types of parallelograms.

Using Properties of Special Parallelograms

In this lesson, you will learn about three special types of parallelograms: *rhombuses*, *rectangles*, and *squares*.

Core Concept

Rhombuses, Rectangles, and Squares

A **rhombus** is a parallelogram with four congruent sides.

A **rectangle** is a parallelogram with four right angles.

A **square** is a parallelogram with four congruent sides and four right angles.

You can use the corollaries below to prove that a quadrilateral is a rhombus, rectangle, or square, without first proving that the quadrilateral is a parallelogram.

Corollaries

Rhombus Corollary

A quadrilateral is a rhombus if and only if it has four congruent sides.

$ABCD$ is a rhombus if and only if $\overline{AB} \cong \overline{BC} \cong \overline{CD} \cong \overline{AD}$.

Proof Ex. 81, p. 440

Rectangle Corollary

A quadrilateral is a rectangle if and only if it has four right angles.

$ABCD$ is a rectangle if and only if $\angle A$, $\angle B$, $\angle C$, and $\angle D$ are right angles.

Proof Ex. 82, p. 440

Square Corollary

A quadrilateral is a square if and only if it is a rhombus and a rectangle.

$ABCD$ is a square if and only if $\overline{AB} \cong \overline{BC} \cong \overline{CD} \cong \overline{AD}$ and $\angle A$, $\angle B$, $\angle C$, and $\angle D$ are right angles.

Proof Ex. 83, p. 440

The Venn diagram below illustrates some important relationships among parallelograms, rhombuses, rectangles, and squares. For example, you can see that a square is a rhombus because it is a parallelogram with four congruent sides. Because it has four right angles, a square is also a rectangle.

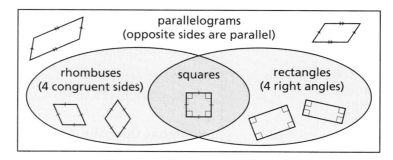

EXAMPLE 1   **Using Properties of Special Quadrilaterals**

For any rhombus *QRST*, decide whether the statement is *always* or *sometimes* true. Draw a diagram and explain your reasoning.

a. $\angle Q \cong \angle S$ **b.** $\angle Q \cong \angle R$

SOLUTION

a. By definition, a rhombus is a parallelogram with four congruent sides. By the Parallelogram Opposite Angles Theorem, opposite angles of a parallelogram are congruent. So, $\angle Q \cong \angle S$. The statement is *always* true.

b. If rhombus *QRST* is a square, then all four angles are congruent right angles. So, $\angle Q \cong \angle R$ when *QRST* is a square. Because not all rhombuses are also squares, the statement is *sometimes* true.

EXAMPLE 2   **Classifying Special Quadrilaterals**

Classify the special quadrilateral. Explain your reasoning.

SOLUTION

The quadrilateral has four congruent sides. By the Rhombus Corollary, the quadrilateral is a rhombus. Because one of the angles is not a right angle, the rhombus cannot be a square.

Monitoring Progress Help in English and Spanish at *BigIdeasMath.com*

1. For any square *JKLM*, is it *always* or *sometimes* true that $\overline{JK} \perp \overline{KL}$? Explain your reasoning.

2. For any rectangle *EFGH*, is it *always* or *sometimes* true that $\overline{FG} \cong \overline{GH}$? Explain your reasoning.

3. A quadrilateral has four congruent sides and four congruent angles. Sketch the quadrilateral and classify it.

Using Properties of Diagonals

🌀 Theorems

Rhombus Diagonals Theorem

A parallelogram is a rhombus if and only if its diagonals are perpendicular.

$\square ABCD$ is a rhombus if and only if $\overline{AC} \perp \overline{BD}$.

Proof p. 434; Ex. 72, p. 439

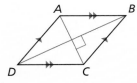

Rhombus Opposite Angles Theorem

A parallelogram is a rhombus if and only if each diagonal bisects a pair of opposite angles.

$\square ABCD$ is a rhombus if and only if $\overline{AC}$ bisects $\angle BCD$ and $\angle BAD$, and $\overline{BD}$ bisects $\angle ABC$ and $\angle ADC$.

Proof Exs. 73 and 74, p. 439

READING

Recall that biconditionals, such as the Rhombus Diagonals Theorem, can be rewritten as two parts. To prove a biconditional, you must prove both parts.

PROOF **Part of Rhombus Diagonals Theorem**

Given $ABCD$ is a rhombus.

Prove $\overline{AC} \perp \overline{BD}$

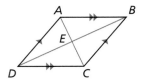

$ABCD$ is a rhombus. By the definition of a rhombus, $\overline{AB} \cong \overline{BC}$. Because a rhombus is a parallelogram and the diagonals of a parallelogram bisect each other, $\overline{BD}$ bisects $\overline{AC}$ at E. So, $\overline{AE} \cong \overline{EC}$. $\overline{BE} \cong \overline{BE}$ by the Reflexive Property of Congruence. So, $\triangle AEB \cong \triangle CEB$ by the SSS Congruence Theorem. $\angle AEB \cong \angle CEB$ because corresponding parts of congruent triangles are congruent. Then by the Linear Pair Postulate, $\angle AEB$ and $\angle CEB$ are supplementary. Two congruent angles that form a linear pair are right angles, so $m\angle AEB = m\angle CEB = 90°$ by the definition of a right angle. So, $\overline{AC} \perp \overline{BD}$ by the definition of perpendicular lines.

EXAMPLE 3 **Finding Angle Measures in a Rhombus**

Find the measures of the numbered angles in rhombus $ABCD$.

SOLUTION

Use the Rhombus Diagonals Theorem and the Rhombus Opposite Angles Theorem to find the angle measures.

$m\angle 1 = 90°$	The diagonals of a rhombus are perpendicular.
$m\angle 2 = 61°$	Alternate Interior Angles Theorem
$m\angle 3 = 61°$	Each diagonal of a rhombus bisects a pair of opposite angles, and $m\angle 2 = 61°$.
$m\angle 1 + m\angle 3 + m\angle 4 = 180°$	Triangle Sum Theorem
$90° + 61° + m\angle 4 = 180°$	Substitute 90° for $m\angle 1$ and 61° for $m\angle 3$.
$m\angle 4 = 29°$	Solve for $m\angle 4$.

▶ So, $m\angle 1 = 90°$, $m\angle 2 = 61°$, $m\angle 3 = 61°$, and $m\angle 4 = 29°$.

4. In Example 3, what is $m\angle ADC$ and $m\angle BCD$?

5. Find the measures of the numbered angles in rhombus *DEFG*.

⟳ Theorem

Rectangle Diagonals Theorem

A parallelogram is a rectangle if and only if its diagonals are congruent.

▱*ABCD* is a rectangle if and only if $\overline{AC} \cong \overline{BD}$.

Proof Exs. 87 and 88, p. 440

EXAMPLE 4 **Identifying a Rectangle**

You are building a frame for a window. The window will be installed in the opening shown in the diagram.

a. The opening must be a rectangle. Given the measurements in the diagram, can you assume that it is? Explain.

b. You measure the diagonals of the opening. The diagonals are 54.8 inches and 55.3 inches. What can you conclude about the shape of the opening?

SOLUTION

a. No, you cannot. The boards on opposite sides are the same length, so they form a parallelogram. But you do not know whether the angles are right angles.

b. By the Rectangle Diagonals Theorem, the diagonals of a rectangle are congruent. The diagonals of the quadrilateral formed by the boards are not congruent, so the boards do not form a rectangle.

EXAMPLE 5 **Finding Diagonal Lengths in a Rectangle**

In rectangle *QRST*, $QS = 5x - 31$ and $RT = 2x + 11$. Find the lengths of the diagonals of *QRST*.

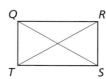

SOLUTION

By the Rectangle Diagonals Theorem, the diagonals of a rectangle are congruent. Find x so that $\overline{QS} \cong \overline{RT}$.

$QS = RT$	Set the diagonal lengths equal.
$5x - 31 = 2x + 11$	Substitute $5x - 31$ for *QS* and $2x + 11$ for *RT*.
$3x - 31 = 11$	Subtract $2x$ from each side.
$3x = 42$	Add 31 to each side.
$x = 14$	Divide each side by 3.

When $x = 14$, $QS = 5(14) - 31 = 39$ and $RT = 2(14) + 11 = 39$.

▶ Each diagonal has a length of 39 units.

6. Suppose you measure only the diagonals of the window opening in Example 4 and they have the same measure. Can you conclude that the opening is a rectangle? Explain.

7. **WHAT IF?** In Example 5, $QS = 4x - 15$ and $RT = 3x + 8$. Find the lengths of the diagonals of $QRST$.

Using Coordinate Geometry

EXAMPLE 6   **Identifying a Parallelogram in the Coordinate Plane**

Decide whether $\square ABCD$ with vertices $A(-2, 6)$, $B(6, 8)$, $C(4, 0)$, and $D(-4, -2)$ is a *rectangle*, a *rhombus*, or a *square*. Give all names that apply.

SOLUTION

1. **Understand the Problem** You know the vertices of $\square ABCD$. You need to identify the type of parallelogram.

2. **Make a Plan** Begin by graphing the vertices. From the graph, it appears that all four sides are congruent and there are no right angles.

   Check the lengths and slopes of the diagonals of $\square ABCD$. If the diagonals are congruent, then $\square ABCD$ is a rectangle. If the diagonals are perpendicular, then $\square ABCD$ is a rhombus. If they are both congruent and perpendicular, then $\square ABCD$ is a rectangle, a rhombus, and a square.

3. **Solve the Problem** Use the Distance Formula to find AC and BD.

$$AC = \sqrt{(-2 - 4)^2 + (6 - 0)^2} = \sqrt{72} = 6\sqrt{2}$$

$$BD = \sqrt{[6 - (-4)]^2 + [8 - (-2)]^2} = \sqrt{200} = 10\sqrt{2}$$

Because $6\sqrt{2} \neq 10\sqrt{2}$, the diagonals are not congruent. So, $\square ABCD$ is not a rectangle. Because it is not a rectangle, it also cannot be a square.

Use the slope formula to find the slopes of the diagonals $\overline{AC}$ and $\overline{BD}$.

$$\text{slope of } \overline{AC} = \frac{6 - 0}{-2 - 4} = \frac{6}{-6} = -1 \qquad \text{slope of } \overline{BD} = \frac{8 - (-2)}{6 - (-4)} = \frac{10}{10} = 1$$

Because the product of the slopes of the diagonals is -1, the diagonals are perpendicular.

▶ So, $\square ABCD$ is a rhombus.

4. **Look Back** Check the side lengths of $\square ABCD$. Each side has a length of $2\sqrt{17}$ units, so $\square ABCD$ is a rhombus. Check the slopes of two consecutive sides.

$$\text{slope of } \overline{AB} = \frac{8 - 6}{6 - (-2)} = \frac{2}{8} = \frac{1}{4} \qquad \text{slope of } \overline{BC} = \frac{8 - 0}{6 - 4} = \frac{8}{2} = 4$$

Because the product of these slopes is not -1, $\overline{AB}$ is not perpendicular to $\overline{BC}$.

So, $\angle ABC$ is not a right angle, and $\square ABCD$ cannot be a rectangle or a square. ✓

8. Decide whether $\square PQRS$ with vertices $P(-5, 2)$, $Q(0, 4)$, $R(2, -1)$, and $S(-3, -3)$ is a *rectangle*, a *rhombus*, or a *square*. Give all names that apply.

Vocabulary and Core Concept Check

1. **VOCABULARY** What is another name for an equilateral rectangle?

2. **WRITING** What should you look for in a parallelogram to know if the parallelogram is also a rhombus?

Monitoring Progress and Modeling with Mathematics

In Exercises 3–8, for any rhombus *JKLM*, decide whether the statement is *always* or *sometimes* true. Draw a diagram and explain your reasoning. *(See Example 1.)*

3. $\angle L \cong \angle M$

4. $\angle K \cong \angle M$

5. $\overline{JM} \cong \overline{KL}$

6. $\overline{JK} \cong \overline{KL}$

7. $\overline{JL} \cong \overline{KM}$

8. $\angle JKM \cong \angle LKM$

In Exercises 9–12, classify the quadrilateral. Explain your reasoning. *(See Example 2.)*

9.

10.

11.

12.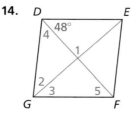

In Exercises 13–16, find the measures of the numbered angles in rhombus *DEFG*. *(See Example 3.)*

13.

14.

15.

16.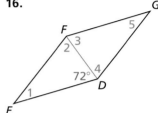

In Exercises 17–22, for any rectangle *WXYZ*, decide whether the statement is *always* or *sometimes* true. Draw a diagram and explain your reasoning.

17. $\angle W \cong \angle X$

18. $\overline{WX} \cong \overline{YZ}$

19. $\overline{WX} \cong \overline{XY}$

20. $\overline{WY} \cong \overline{XZ}$

21. $\overline{WY} \perp \overline{XZ}$

22. $\angle WXZ \cong \angle YXZ$

In Exercises 23 and 24, determine whether the quadrilateral is a rectangle. *(See Example 4.)*

23.

24.

In Exercises 25–28, find the lengths of the diagonals of rectangle *WXYZ*. *(See Example 5.)*

25. $WY = 6x - 7$
    $XZ = 3x + 2$

26. $WY = 14x + 10$
    $XZ = 11x + 22$

27. $WY = 24x - 8$
    $XZ = -18x + 13$

28. $WY = 16x + 2$
    $XZ = 36x - 6$

In Exercises 29–34, name each quadrilateral— *parallelogram*, *rectangle*, *rhombus*, **or** *square*—**for which the statement is always true.**

29. It is equiangular.

30. It is equiangular and equilateral.

31. The diagonals are perpendicular.

32. Opposite sides are congruent.

33. The diagonals bisect each other.

34. The diagonals bisect opposite angles.

35. **ERROR ANALYSIS** Quadrilateral *PQRS* is a rectangle. Describe and correct the error in finding the value of *x*.

$$m\angle QSR = m\angle QSP$$
$$x° = 58°$$
$$x = 58$$

36. **ERROR ANALYSIS** Quadrilateral *PQRS* is a rhombus. Describe and correct the error in finding the value of *x*.

$$m\angle QRP = m\angle SQR$$
$$x° = 37°$$
$$x = 37$$

In Exercises 37–42, the diagonals of rhombus *ABCD* intersect at *E*. Given that *m∠BAC* = 53°, *DE* = 8, and *EC* = 6, find the indicated measure.

37. *m∠DAC*

38. *m∠AED*

39. *m∠ADC*

40. *DB*

41. *AE*

42. *AC*

In Exercises 43–48, the diagonals of rectangle *QRST* intersect at *P*. Given that *m∠PTS* = 34° and *QS* = 10, find the indicated measure.

43. *m∠QTR*

44. *m∠QRT*

45. *m∠SRT*

46. *QP*

47. *RT*

48. *RP*

In Exercises 49–54, the diagonals of square *LMNP* intersect at *K*. Given that *LK* = 1, find the indicated measure.

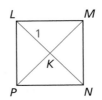

49. *m∠MKN*

50. *m∠LMK*

51. *m∠LPK*

52. *KN*

53. *LN*

54. *MP*

In Exercises 55–60, decide whether □*JKLM* is a rectangle, a rhombus, or a square. Give all names that apply. Explain your reasoning. *(See Example 6.)*

55. *J*(−4, 2), *K*(0, 3), *L*(1, −1), *M*(−3, −2)

56. *J*(−2, 7), *K*(7, 2), *L*(−2, −3), *M*(−11, 2)

57. *J*(3, 1), *K*(3, −3), *L*(−2, −3), *M*(−2, 1)

58. *J*(−1, 4), *K*(−3, 2), *L*(2, −3), *M*(4, −1)

59. *J*(5, 2), *K*(1, 9), *L*(−3, 2), *M*(1, −5)

60. *J*(5, 2), *K*(2, 5), *L*(−1, 2), *M*(2, −1)

MATHEMATICAL CONNECTIONS In Exercises 61 and 62, classify the quadrilateral. Explain your reasoning. Then find the values of *x* and *y*.

61.

62.

63. DRAWING CONCLUSIONS In the window, $\overline{BD} \cong \overline{DF} \cong \overline{BH} \cong \overline{HF}$. Also, $\angle HAB$, $\angle BCD$, $\angle DEF$, and $\angle FGH$ are right angles.

a. Classify *HBDF* and *ACEG*. Explain your reasoning.

b. What can you conclude about the lengths of the diagonals $\overline{AE}$ and $\overline{GC}$? Given that these diagonals intersect at *J*, what can you conclude about the lengths of $\overline{AJ}, \overline{JE}, \overline{CJ}$, and $\overline{JG}$? Explain.

64. ABSTRACT REASONING Order the terms in a diagram so that each term builds off the previous term(s). Explain why each figure is in the location you chose.

quadrilateral	square
rectangle	rhombus
parallelogram	

CRITICAL THINKING In Exercises 65–70, complete each statement with *always*, *sometimes*, or *never*. Explain your reasoning.

65. A square is _____ a rhombus.

66. A rectangle is _____ a square.

67. A rectangle _____ has congruent diagonals.

68. The diagonals of a square _____ bisect its angles.

69. A rhombus _____ has four congruent angles.

70. A rectangle _____ has perpendicular diagonals.

71. USING TOOLS You want to mark off a square region for a garden at school. You use a tape measure to mark off a quadrilateral on the ground. Each side of the quadrilateral is 2.5 meters long. Explain how you can use the tape measure to make sure that the quadrilateral is a square.

72. PROVING A THEOREM Use the plan for proof below to write a paragraph proof for one part of the Rhombus Diagonals Theorem.

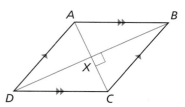

Given *ABCD* is a parallelogram.
$\overline{AC} \perp \overline{BD}$

Prove *ABCD* is a rhombus.

Plan for Proof Because *ABCD* is a parallelogram, its diagonals bisect each other at *X*. Use $\overline{AC} \perp \overline{BD}$ to show that $\triangle BXC \cong \triangle DXC$. Then show that $\overline{BC} \cong \overline{DC}$. Use the properties of a parallelogram to show that *ABCD* is a rhombus.

PROVING A THEOREM In Exercises 73 and 74, write a proof for part of the Rhombus Opposite Angles Theorem.

73. Given *PQRS* is a parallelogram.
$\overline{PR}$ bisects $\angle SPQ$ and $\angle QRS$.
$\overline{SQ}$ bisects $\angle PSR$ and $\angle RQP$.

Prove *PQRS* is a rhombus.

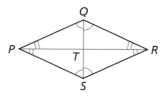

74. Given *WXYZ* is a rhombus.

Prove $\overline{WY}$ bisects $\angle ZWX$ and $\angle XYZ$.
$\overline{ZX}$ bisects $\angle WZY$ and $\angle YXW$.

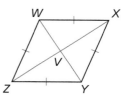

75. **ABSTRACT REASONING** Will a diagonal of a square ever divide the square into two equilateral triangles? Explain your reasoning.

76. **ABSTRACT REASONING** Will a diagonal of a rhombus ever divide the rhombus into two equilateral triangles? Explain your reasoning.

77. **CRITICAL THINKING** Which quadrilateral could be called a regular quadrilateral? Explain your reasoning.

78. **HOW DO YOU SEE IT?** What other information do you need to determine whether the figure is a rectangle?

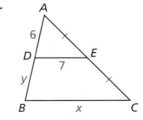

79. **REASONING** Are all rhombuses similar? Are all squares similar? Explain your reasoning.

80. **THOUGHT PROVOKING** Use the Rhombus Diagonals Theorem to explain why every rhombus has at least two lines of symmetry.

PROVING A COROLLARY In Exercises 81–83, write the corollary as a conditional statement and its converse. Then explain why each statement is true.

81. Rhombus Corollary

82. Rectangle Corollary

83. Square Corollary

84. **MAKING AN ARGUMENT** Your friend claims a rhombus will never have congruent diagonals because it would have to be a rectangle. Is your friend correct? Explain your reasoning.

85. **PROOF** Write a proof in the style of your choice.

   Given $\triangle XYZ \cong \triangle XWZ$, $\angle XYW \cong \angle ZWY$

   Prove $WXYZ$ is a rhombus.

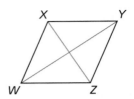

86. **PROOF** Write a proof in the style of your choice.

   Given $\overline{BC} \cong \overline{AD}$, $\overline{BC} \perp \overline{DC}$, $\overline{AD} \perp \overline{DC}$

   Prove $ABCD$ is a rectangle.

PROVING A THEOREM In Exercises 87 and 88, write a proof for part of the Rectangle Diagonals Theorem.

87. **Given** $PQRS$ is a rectangle.

   Prove $\overline{PR} \cong \overline{SQ}$

88. **Given** $PQRS$ is a parallelogram.
   $\overline{PR} \cong \overline{SQ}$

   Prove $PQRS$ is a rectangle.

Maintaining Mathematical Proficiency
Reviewing what you learned in previous grades and lessons

$\overline{DE}$ is a midsegment of $\triangle ABC$. Find the values of x and y. *(Section 6.5)*

89.

90.

91.
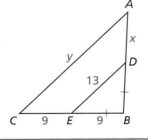

Essential Question   What are some properties of trapezoids and kites?

Recall the types of quadrilaterals shown below.

Trapezoid   Isosceles Trapezoid   Kite

PERSEVERE IN SOLVING PROBLEMS

To be proficient in math, you need to draw diagrams of important features and relationships, and search for regularity or trends.

EXPLORATION 1   **Making a Conjecture about Trapezoids**

Work with a partner. Use dynamic geometry software.

a. Construct a trapezoid whose base angles are congruent. Explain your process.

b. Is the trapezoid isosceles? Justify your answer.

c. Repeat parts (a) and (b) for several other trapezoids. Write a conjecture based on your results.

Sample

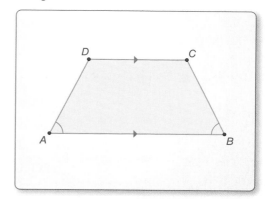

EXPLORATION 2   **Discovering a Property of Kites**

Work with a partner. Use dynamic geometry software.

a. Construct a kite. Explain your process.

b. Measure the angles of the kite. What do you observe?

c. Repeat parts (a) and (b) for several other kites. Write a conjecture based on your results.

Sample

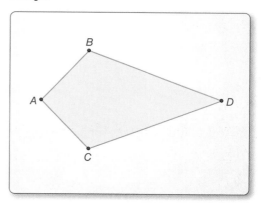

Communicate Your Answer

3. What are some properties of trapezoids and kites?

4. Is the trapezoid at the left isosceles? Explain.

5. A quadrilateral has angle measures of 70°, 70°, 110°, and 110°. Is the quadrilateral a kite? Explain.

What You Will Learn

▶ Use properties of trapezoids.

▶ Use the Trapezoid Midsegment Theorem to find distances.

▶ Use properties of kites.

▶ Identify quadrilaterals.

Core Vocabulary

trapezoid, *p. 442*
bases, *p. 442*
base angles, *p. 442*
legs, *p. 442*
isosceles trapezoid, *p. 442*
midsegment of a trapezoid,
   p. 444
kite, *p. 445*

Previous
diagonal
parallelogram

Using Properties of Trapezoids

A **trapezoid** is a quadrilateral with exactly one pair of parallel sides. The parallel sides are the **bases**.

Base angles of a trapezoid are two consecutive angles whose common side is a base. A trapezoid has two pairs of base angles. For example, in trapezoid *ABCD*, $\angle A$ and $\angle D$ are one pair of base angles, and $\angle B$ and $\angle C$ are the second pair. The nonparallel sides are the **legs** of the trapezoid.

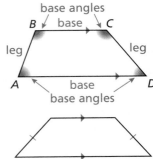

If the legs of a trapezoid are congruent, then the trapezoid is an **isosceles trapezoid**.

Isosceles trapezoid

EXAMPLE 1   **Identifying a Trapezoid in the Coordinate Plane**

Show that *ORST* is a trapezoid. Then decide whether it is isosceles.

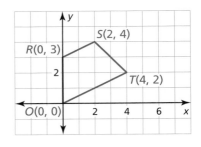

SOLUTION

Step 1   Compare the slopes of opposite sides.

$$\text{slope of } \overline{RS} = \frac{4-3}{2-0} = \frac{1}{2}$$

$$\text{slope of } \overline{OT} = \frac{2-0}{4-0} = \frac{2}{4} = \frac{1}{2}$$

The slopes of $\overline{RS}$ and $\overline{OT}$ are the same, so $\overline{RS} \parallel \overline{OT}$.

$$\text{slope of } \overline{ST} = \frac{2-4}{4-2} = \frac{-2}{2} = -1 \quad \text{slope of } \overline{RO} = \frac{3-0}{0-0} = \frac{3}{0} \quad \text{Undefined}$$

The slopes of $\overline{ST}$ and $\overline{RO}$ are not the same, so $\overline{ST}$ is not parallel to $\overline{OR}$.

▶ Because *ORST* has exactly one pair of parallel sides, it is a trapezoid.

Step 2   Compare the lengths of legs $\overline{RO}$ and $\overline{ST}$.

$$RO = |3 - 0| = 3 \qquad ST = \sqrt{(2-4)^2 + (4-2)^2} = \sqrt{8} = 2\sqrt{2}$$

Because $RO \neq ST$, legs $\overline{RO}$ and $\overline{ST}$ are *not* congruent.

▶ So, *ORST* is not an isosceles trapezoid.

Monitoring Progress Help in English and Spanish at *BigIdeasMath.com*

1. The points $A(-5, 6)$, $B(4, 9)$, $C(4, 4)$, and $D(-2, 2)$ form the vertices of a quadrilateral. Show that *ABCD* is a trapezoid. Then decide whether it is isosceles.

Theorems

Isosceles Trapezoid Base Angles Theorem

If a trapezoid is isosceles, then each pair of base angles is congruent.

If trapezoid *ABCD* is isosceles, then $\angle A \cong \angle D$ and $\angle B \cong \angle C$.

Proof Ex. 39, p. 449

Isosceles Trapezoid Base Angles Converse

If a trapezoid has a pair of congruent base angles, then it is an isosceles trapezoid.

If $\angle A \cong \angle D$ (or if $\angle B \cong \angle C$), then trapezoid *ABCD* is isosceles.

Proof Ex. 40, p. 449

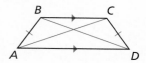

Isosceles Trapezoid Diagonals Theorem

A trapezoid is isosceles if and only if its diagonals are congruent.

Trapezoid *ABCD* is isosceles if and only if $\overline{AC} \cong \overline{BD}$.

Proof Ex. 51, p. 450

EXAMPLE 2   **Using Properties of Isosceles Trapezoids**

The stone above the arch in the diagram is an isosceles trapezoid. Find $m\angle K$, $m\angle M$, and $m\angle J$.

SOLUTION

Step 1   Find $m\angle K$. *JKLM* is an isosceles trapezoid. So, $\angle K$ and $\angle L$ are congruent base angles, and $m\angle K = m\angle L = 85°$.

Step 2   Find $m\angle M$. Because $\angle L$ and $\angle M$ are consecutive interior angles formed by $\overleftrightarrow{LM}$ intersecting two parallel lines, they are supplementary. So, $m\angle M = 180° - 85° = 95°$.

Step 3   Find $m\angle J$. Because $\angle J$ and $\angle M$ are a pair of base angles, they are congruent, and $m\angle J = m\angle M = 95°$.

▶   So, $m\angle K = 85°$, $m\angle M = 95°$, and $m\angle J = 95°$.

Monitoring Progress Help in English and Spanish at *BigIdeasMath.com*

In Exercises 2 and 3, use trapezoid *EFGH*.

2. If $EG = FH$, is trapezoid *EFGH* isosceles? Explain.

3. If $m\angle HEF = 70°$ and $m\angle FGH = 110°$, is trapezoid *EFGH* isosceles? Explain.

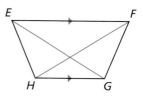

Using the Trapezoid Midsegment Theorem

Recall that a midsegment of a triangle is a segment that connects the midpoints of two sides of the triangle. The **midsegment of a trapezoid** is the segment that connects the midpoints of its legs. The theorem below is similar to the Triangle Midsegment Theorem.

READING

The midsegment of a trapezoid is sometimes called the *median* of the trapezoid.

↻ Theorem

Trapezoid Midsegment Theorem

The midsegment of a trapezoid is parallel to each base, and its length is one-half the sum of the lengths of the bases.

If $\overline{MN}$ is the midsegment of trapezoid $ABCD$, then $\overline{MN} \parallel \overline{AB}$, $\overline{MN} \parallel \overline{DC}$, and $MN = \frac{1}{2}(AB + CD)$.

Proof Ex. 49, p. 450

EXAMPLE 3   Using the Midsegment of a Trapezoid

In the diagram, $\overline{MN}$ is the midsegment of trapezoid $PQRS$. Find MN.

SOLUTION

$MN = \frac{1}{2}(PQ + SR)$ Trapezoid Midsegment Theorem

$\quad\;\; = \frac{1}{2}(12 + 28)$ Substitute 12 for PQ and 28 for SR.

$\quad\;\; = 20$ Simplify.

▶ The length of $\overline{MN}$ is 20 inches.

EXAMPLE 4   Using a Midsegment in the Coordinate Plane

Find the length of midsegment $\overline{YZ}$ in trapezoid $STUV$.

SOLUTION

Step 1 Find the lengths of $\overline{SV}$ and $\overline{TU}$.

$SV = \sqrt{(0-2)^2 + (6-2)^2} = \sqrt{20} = 2\sqrt{5}$

$TU = \sqrt{(8-12)^2 + (10-2)^2} = \sqrt{80} = 4\sqrt{5}$

Step 2 Multiply the sum of SV and TU by $\frac{1}{2}$.

$YZ = \frac{1}{2}(2\sqrt{5} + 4\sqrt{5}) = \frac{1}{2}(6\sqrt{5}) = 3\sqrt{5}$

▶ So, the length of $\overline{YZ}$ is $3\sqrt{5}$ units.

Monitoring Progress Help in English and Spanish at *BigIdeasMath.com*

4. In trapezoid $JKLM$, $\angle J$ and $\angle M$ are right angles, and $JK = 9$ centimeters. The length of midsegment $\overline{NP}$ of trapezoid $JKLM$ is 12 centimeters. Sketch trapezoid $JKLM$ and its midsegment. Find ML. Explain your reasoning.

5. Explain another method you can use to find the length of $\overline{YZ}$ in Example 4.

Using Properties of Kites

A **kite** is a quadrilateral that has two pairs of consecutive congruent sides, but opposite sides are not congruent.

⑤ Theorems

Kite Diagonals Theorem

If a quadrilateral is a kite, then its diagonals are perpendicular.

If quadrilateral *ABCD* is a kite, then $\overline{AC} \perp \overline{BD}$.

Proof p. 445

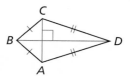

Kite Opposite Angles Theorem

If a quadrilateral is a kite, then exactly one pair of opposite angles are congruent.

If quadrilateral *ABCD* is a kite and $\overline{BC} \cong \overline{BA}$, then $\angle A \cong \angle C$ and $\angle B \not\cong \angle D$.

Proof Ex. 47, p. 450

STUDY TIP

The congruent angles of a kite are formed by the noncongruent adjacent sides.

PROOF **Kite Diagonals Theorem**

Given *ABCD* is a kite, $\overline{BC} \cong \overline{BA}$, and $\overline{DC} \cong \overline{DA}$.
Prove $\overline{AC} \perp \overline{BD}$

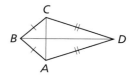

STATEMENTS	REASONS
1. *ABCD* is a kite with $\overline{BC} \cong \overline{BA}$ and $\overline{DC} \cong \overline{DA}$.	**1.** Given
2. *B* and *D* lie on the ⊥ bisector of $\overline{AC}$.	**2.** Converse of the ⊥ Bisector Theorem
3. $\overline{BD}$ is the ⊥ bisector of $\overline{AC}$.	**3.** Through any two points, there exists exactly one line.
4. $\overline{AC} \perp \overline{BD}$	**4.** Definition of ⊥ bisector

EXAMPLE 5 **Finding Angle Measures in a Kite**

Find *m∠D* in the kite shown.

SOLUTION

By the Kite Opposite Angles Theorem, *DEFG* has exactly one pair of congruent opposite angles. Because $\angle E \not\cong \angle G$, $\angle D$ and $\angle F$ must be congruent. So, $m\angle D = m\angle F$. Write and solve an equation to find *m∠D*.

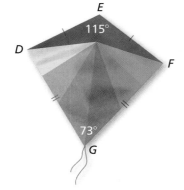

$m\angle D + m\angle F + 115° + 73° = 360°$ Corollary to the Polygon Interior Angles Theorem

$m\angle D + m\angle D + 115° + 73° = 360°$ Substitute *m∠D* for *m∠F*.

$2m\angle D + 188° = 360°$ Combine like terms.

$m\angle D = 86°$ Solve for *m∠D*.

6. In a kite, the measures of the angles are $3x°$, 75°, 90°, and 120°. Find the value of x. What are the measures of the angles that are congruent?

Identifying Special Quadrilaterals

The diagram shows relationships among the special quadrilaterals you have studied in this chapter. Each shape in the diagram has the properties of the shapes linked above it. For example, a rhombus has the properties of a parallelogram and a quadrilateral.

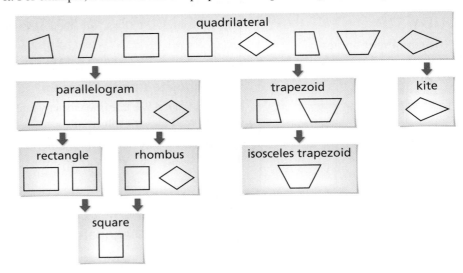

EXAMPLE 6   **Identifying a Quadrilateral**

What is the most specific name for quadrilateral *ABCD*?

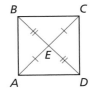

SOLUTION

The diagram shows $\overline{AE} \cong \overline{CE}$ and $\overline{BE} \cong \overline{DE}$. So, the diagonals bisect each other. By the Parallelogram Diagonals Converse, *ABCD* is a parallelogram.

Rectangles, rhombuses, and squares are also parallelograms. However, there is no information given about the side lengths or angle measures of *ABCD*. So, you cannot determine whether it is a rectangle, a rhombus, or a square.

▶ So, the most specific name for *ABCD* is a parallelogram.

Monitoring Progress Help in English and Spanish at *BigIdeasMath.com*

7. Quadrilateral *DEFG* has at least one pair of opposite sides congruent. What types of quadrilaterals meet this condition?

Give the most specific name for the quadrilateral. Explain your reasoning.

8.

9.

10.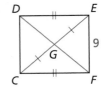

Vocabulary and Core Concept Check

1. **WRITING** Describe the differences between a trapezoid and a kite.

2. **DIFFERENT WORDS, SAME QUESTION** Which is different? Find "both" answers.

Is there enough information to prove that trapezoid *ABCD* is isosceles?

Is there enough information to prove that $\overline{AB} \cong \overline{DC}$?

Is there enough information to prove that the non-parallel sides of trapezoid *ABCD* are congruent?

Is there enough information to prove that the legs of trapezoid *ABCD* are congruent?

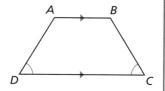

Monitoring Progress and Modeling with Mathematics

In Exercises 3–6, show that the quadrilateral with the given vertices is a trapezoid. Then decide whether it is isosceles. *(See Example 1.)*

3. $W(1, 4), X(1, 8), Y(-3, 9), Z(-3, 3)$

4. $D(-3, 3), E(-1, 1), F(1, -4), G(-3, 0)$

5. $M(-2, 0), N(0, 4), P(5, 4), Q(8, 0)$

6. $H(1, 9), J(4, 2), K(5, 2), L(8, 9)$

In Exercises 7 and 8, find the measure of each angle in the isosceles trapezoid. *(See Example 2.)*

7.

8.

In Exercises 9 and 10, find the length of the midsegment of the trapezoid. *(See Example 3.)*

9.

10.

In Exercises 11 and 12, find *AB*.

11.

12.

In Exercises 13 and 14, find the length of the midsegment of the trapezoid with the given vertices. *(See Example 4.)*

13. $A(2, 0), B(8, -4), C(12, 2), D(0, 10)$

14. $S(-2, 4), T(-2, -4), U(3, -2), V(13, 10)$

In Exercises 15–18, find $m\angle G$. *(See Example 5.)*

15.

16.

17.

18.

19. **ERROR ANALYSIS** Describe and correct the error in finding *DC*.

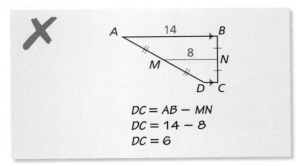

DC = AB − MN
DC = 14 − 8
DC = 6

20. **ERROR ANALYSIS** Describe and correct the error in finding *m∠A*.

Opposite angles of a kite are congruent, so *m∠A* = 50°.

In Exercises 21–24, give the most specific name for the quadrilateral. Explain your reasoning. *(See Example 6.)*

21.

22.

23.

24.

REASONING In Exercises 25 and 26, tell whether enough information is given in the diagram to classify the quadrilateral by the indicated name. Explain.

25. rhombus

26. square

MATHEMATICAL CONNECTIONS In Exercises 27 and 28, find the value of *x*.

27.

28.

29. **MODELING WITH MATHEMATICS** In the diagram, *NP* = 8 inches, and *LR* = 20 inches. What is the diameter of the bottom layer of the cake?

30. **PROBLEM SOLVING** You and a friend are building a kite. You need a stick to place from *X* to *W* and a stick to place from *W* to *Z* to finish constructing the frame. You want the kite to have the geometric shape of a kite. How long does each stick need to be? Explain your reasoning.

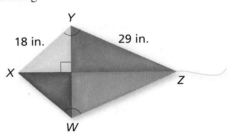

REASONING In Exercises 31–34, determine which pairs of segments or angles must be congruent so that you can prove that *ABCD* is the indicated quadrilateral. Explain your reasoning. (There may be more than one right answer.)

31. isosceles trapezoid

32. kite

33. parallelogram

34. square

35. PROOF Write a proof.

Given $\overline{JL} \cong \overline{LN}$, $\overline{KM}$ is a midsegment of $\triangle JLN$.

Prove Quadrilateral $JKMN$ is an isosceles trapezoid.

36. PROOF Write a proof.

Given $ABCD$ is a kite.
$\overline{AB} \cong \overline{CB}$, $\overline{AD} \cong \overline{CD}$

Prove $\overline{CE} \cong \overline{AE}$

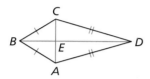

37. ABSTRACT REASONING Point U lies on the perpendicular bisector of $\overline{RT}$. Describe the set of points S for which $RSTU$ is a kite.

38. REASONING Determine whether the points $A(4, 5)$, $B(-3, 3)$, $C(-6, -13)$, and $D(6, -2)$ are the vertices of a kite. Explain your reasoning.

PROVING A THEOREM In Exercises 39 and 40, use the diagram to prove the given theorem. In the diagram, $\overline{EC}$ is drawn parallel to $\overline{AB}$.

39. Isosceles Trapezoid Base Angles Theorem

Given $ABCD$ is an isosceles trapezoid.
$\overline{BC} \parallel \overline{AD}$

Prove $\angle A \cong \angle D$, $\angle B \cong \angle BCD$

40. Isosceles Trapezoid Base Angles Converse

Given $ABCD$ is a trapezoid.
$\angle A \cong \angle D$, $\overline{BC} \parallel \overline{AD}$

Prove $ABCD$ is an isosceles trapezoid.

41. MAKING AN ARGUMENT Your cousin claims there is enough information to prove that $JKLM$ is an isosceles trapezoid. Is your cousin correct? Explain.

42. MATHEMATICAL CONNECTIONS The bases of a trapezoid lie on the lines $y = 2x + 7$ and $y = 2x - 5$. Write the equation of the line that contains the midsegment of the trapezoid.

43. CONSTRUCTION $\overline{AC}$ and $\overline{BD}$ bisect each other.

a. Construct quadrilateral $ABCD$ so that $\overline{AC}$ and $\overline{BD}$ are congruent, but not perpendicular. Classify the quadrilateral. Justify your answer.

b. Construct quadrilateral $ABCD$ so that $\overline{AC}$ and $\overline{BD}$ are perpendicular, but not congruent. Classify the quadrilateral. Justify your answer.

44. PROOF Write a proof.

Given $QRST$ is an isosceles trapezoid.

Prove $\angle TQS \cong \angle SRT$

45. MODELING WITH MATHEMATICS A plastic spiderweb is made in the shape of a regular dodecagon (12-sided polygon). $\overline{AB} \parallel \overline{PQ}$, and X is equidistant from the vertices of the dodecagon.

a. Are you given enough information to prove that $ABPQ$ is an isosceles trapezoid?

b. What is the measure of each interior angle of $ABPQ$?

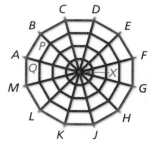

46. ATTENDING TO PRECISION In trapezoid $PQRS$, $\overline{PQ} \parallel \overline{RS}$ and $\overline{MN}$ is the midsegment of $PQRS$. If $RS = 5 \cdot PQ$, what is the ratio of MN to RS?

  Ⓐ 3 : 5   Ⓑ 5 : 3

  Ⓒ 1 : 2   Ⓓ 3 : 1

47. PROVING A THEOREM Use the plan for proof below to write a paragraph proof of the Kite Opposite Angles Theorem.

Given *EFGH* is a kite.
$\overline{EF} \cong \overline{FG}, \overline{EH} \cong \overline{GH}$

Prove $\angle E \cong \angle G, \angle F \not\cong \angle H$

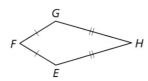

Plan for Proof First show that $\angle E \cong \angle G$. Then use an indirect argument to show that $\angle F \not\cong \angle H$.

48. HOW DO YOU SEE IT? One of the earliest shapes used for cut diamonds is called the *table cut*, as shown in the figure. Each face of a cut gem is called a *facet*.

a. $\overline{BC} \parallel \overline{AD}$, and $\overline{AB}$ and $\overline{DC}$ are not parallel. What shape is the facet labeled *ABCD*?

b. $\overline{DE} \parallel \overline{GF}$, and $\overline{DG}$ and $\overline{EF}$ are congruent but not parallel. What shape is the facet labeled *DEFG*?

49. PROVING A THEOREM In the diagram below, $\overline{BG}$ is the midsegment of $\triangle ACD$, and $\overline{GE}$ is the midsegment of $\triangle ADF$. Use the diagram to prove the Trapezoid Midsegment Theorem.

50. THOUGHT PROVOKING Is SSASS a valid congruence theorem for kites? Justify your answer.

51. PROVING A THEOREM To prove the biconditional statement in the Isosceles Trapezoid Diagonals Theorem, you must prove both parts separately.

a. Prove part of the Isosceles Trapezoid Diagonals Theorem.

Given *JKLM* is an isosceles trapezoid.
$\overline{KL} \parallel \overline{JM}, \overline{JK} \cong \overline{LM}$

Prove $\overline{JL} \cong \overline{KM}$

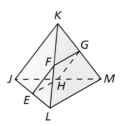

b. Write the other part of the Isosceles Trapezoid Diagonals Theorem as a conditional. Then prove the statement is true.

52. PROOF What special type of quadrilateral is *EFGH*? Write a proof to show that your answer is correct.

Given In the three-dimensional figure, $\overline{JK} \cong \overline{LM}$. *E*, *F*, *G*, and *H* are the midpoints of $\overline{JL}$, $\overline{KL}$, $\overline{KM}$, and $\overline{JM}$, respectively.

Prove *EFGH* is a _____.

Maintaining Mathematical Proficiency
Reviewing what you learned in previous grades and lessons

Graph $\triangle PQR$ with vertices $P(-3, 2)$, $Q(2, 3)$, and $R(4, -2)$ and its image after the translation.
(Skills Review Handbook)

53. $(x, y) \rightarrow (x + 5, y + 8)$

54. $(x, y) \rightarrow (x + 6, y - 3)$

55. $(x, y) \rightarrow (x - 4, y - 7)$

Tell whether the two figures are similar. Explain your reasoning. *(Skills Review Handbook)*

56.

57.

58.

Core Vocabulary

rhombus, *p. 432*
rectangle, *p. 432*
square, *p. 432*
trapezoid, *p. 442*
bases (of a trapezoid), *p. 442*

base angles (of a trapezoid), *p. 442*
legs (of a trapezoid), *p. 442*
isosceles trapezoid, *p. 442*
midsegment of a trapezoid, *p. 444*
kite, *p. 445*

Core Concepts

Section 7.4

Rhombus Corollary, *p. 432*
Rectangle Corollary, *p. 432*
Square Corollary, *p. 432*
Relationships between Special Parallelograms, *p. 433*
Rhombus Diagonals Theorem, *p. 434*

Rhombus Opposite Angles Theorem, *p. 434*
Rectangle Diagonals Theorem, *p. 435*
Identifying Special Parallelograms in the Coordinate
   Plane, *p. 436*

Section 7.5

Showing That a Quadrilateral Is a Trapezoid in the
   Coordinate Plane, *p. 442*
Isosceles Trapezoid Base Angles Theorem, *p. 443*
Isosceles Trapezoid Base Angles Converse, *p. 443*
Isosceles Trapezoid Diagonals Theorem, *p. 443*

Trapezoid Midsegment Theorem, *p. 444*
Kite Diagonals Theorem, *p. 445*
Kite Opposite Angles Theorem, *p. 445*
Identifying Special Quadrilaterals, *p. 446*

Mathematical Practices

1. In Exercise 14 on page 437, one reason $m\angle 4$, $m\angle 5$, and $m\angle DFE$ are all 48° is because diagonals of a rhombus bisect each other. What is another reason they are equal?

2. Explain how the diagram you created in Exercise 64 on page 439 can help you answer questions like Exercises 65–70.

3. In Exercise 29 on page 448, describe a pattern you can use to find the measure of a base of a trapezoid when given the length of the midsegment and the other base.

Performance Task:

Diamonds

Have you ever heard someone say, "Diamonds are a girl's best friend"? What are the properties of diamonds that make them shine? In what ways does mathematics contribute to the brilliance of a diamond?

To explore the answers to these questions and more, check out the Performance Task and Real-Life STEM video at *BigIdeasMath.com*.

7.1 Angles of Polygons *(pp. 403–410)*

Find the sum of the measures of the interior angles of the figure.

The figure is a convex hexagon. It has 6 sides. Use the Polygon Interior Angles Theorem.

$(n - 2) \cdot 180° = (6 - 2) \cdot 180°$ Substitute 6 for *n*.

$\qquad\qquad\quad = 4 \cdot 180°$ Subtract.

$\qquad\qquad\quad = 720°$ Multiply.

▶ The sum of the measures of the interior angles of the figure is 720°.

1. Find the sum of the measures of the interior angles of a regular 30-gon. Then find the measure of each interior angle and each exterior angle.

Find the value of *x*.

2.

120°
97°
x°
130°
150°

3.

2*x*° 125°
160°
110°
x°
147° 112°

4.

7*x*°
49°
83°
6*x*°
33°

7.2 Properties of Parallelograms *(pp. 411–418)*

Find the values of *x* and *y*.

ABCD is a parallelogram by the definition of a parallelogram. Use the Parallelogram Opposite Sides Theorem to find the value of *x*.

$AD = BC$ Opposite sides of a parallelogram are congruent.

$x + 6 = 9$ Substitute $x + 6$ for *AD* and 9 for *BC*.

$x = 3$ Subtract 6 from each side.

By the Parallelogram Opposite Angles Theorem, $\angle D \cong \angle B$, or $m\angle D = m\angle B$. So, $y° = 66°$.

▶ In □*ABCD*, $x = 3$ and $y = 66$.

Find the value of each variable in the parallelogram.

5.

a°   *b*°
101°

6.
18
(*b* + 16)°
103°
a − 10

7.

11   14
c + 5
d + 4

8. Find the coordinates of the intersection of the diagonals of □*QRST* with vertices $Q(-8, 1)$, $R(2, 1)$, $S(4, -3)$, and $T(-6, -3)$.

9. Three vertices of □*JKLM* are $J(1, 4)$, $K(5, 3)$, and $L(6, -3)$. Find the coordinates of vertex *M*.

7.3 Proving That a Quadrilateral Is a Parallelogram (pp. 419–428)

For what value of x is quadrilateral DEFG a parallelogram?

By the Opposite Sides Parallel and Congruent Theorem, if one pair of opposite sides are congruent and parallel, then *DEFG* is a parallelogram. You are given that $\overline{DE} \parallel \overline{FG}$. Find *x* so that $\overline{DE} \cong \overline{FG}$.

$DE = FG$	Set the segment lengths equal.
$3x + 1 = 2x + 7$	Substitute $3x + 1$ for *DE* and $2x + 7$ for *FG*.
$x + 1 = 7$	Subtract 2*x* from each side.
$x = 6$	Subtract 1 from each side.

When $x = 6$, $DE = 3(6) + 1 = 19$ and $FG = 2(6) + 7 = 19$.

▶ Quadrilateral *DEFG* is a parallelogram when $x = 6$.

State which theorem you can use to show that the quadrilateral is a parallelogram.

10.

11.

12.

13. Find the values of *x* and *y* that make the quadrilateral a parallelogram.

14. Find the value of *x* that makes the quadrilateral a parallelogram.

15. Show that quadrilateral *WXYZ* with vertices $W(-1, 6)$, $X(2, 8)$, $Y(1, 0)$, and $Z(-2, -2)$ is a parallelogram.

7.4 Properties of Special Parallelograms (pp. 431–440)

Classify the special quadrilateral. Explain your reasoning.

The quadrilateral has four right angles. By the Rectangle Corollary, the quadrilateral is a rectangle. Because the four sides are not marked as congruent, you cannot conclude that the rectangle is a square.

Classify the special quadrilateral. Explain your reasoning.

16.

17.

18.

19. Find the lengths of the diagonals of rectangle *WXYZ* where $WY = -2x + 34$ and $XZ = 3x - 26$.

20. Decide whether ▱*JKLM* with vertices $J(5, 8)$, $K(9, 6)$, $L(7, 2)$, and $M(3, 4)$ is a rectangle, a rhombus, or a square. Give all names that apply. Explain.

7.5 **Properties of Trapezoids and Kites** *(pp. 441–450)*

Find the length of midsegment $\overline{EF}$ **in trapezoid** *ABCD*.

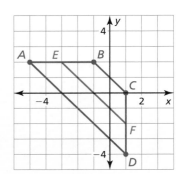

Step 1 Find the lengths of $\overline{AD}$ and $\overline{BC}$.

$$AD = \sqrt{[1 - (-5)]^2 + (-4 - 2)^2}$$
$$= \sqrt{72} = 6\sqrt{2}$$
$$BC = \sqrt{[1 - (-1)]^2 + (0 - 2)^2}$$
$$= \sqrt{8} = 2\sqrt{2}$$

Step 2 Multiply the sum of *AD* and *BC* by $\frac{1}{2}$.

$$EF = \tfrac{1}{2}\left(6\sqrt{2} + 2\sqrt{2}\right) = \tfrac{1}{2}\left(8\sqrt{2}\right) = 4\sqrt{2}$$

▶ So, the length of $\overline{EF}$ is $4\sqrt{2}$ units.

21. Find the measure of each angle in the isosceles trapezoid *WXYZ*.

22. Find the length of the midsegment of trapezoid *ABCD*.

23. Find the length of the midsegment of trapezoid *JKLM* with vertices $J(6, 10)$, $K(10, 6)$, $L(8, 2)$, and $M(2, 2)$.

24. A kite has angle measures of $7x°$, $65°$, $85°$, and $105°$. Find the value of *x*. What are the measures of the angles that are congruent?

25. Quadrilateral *WXYZ* is a trapezoid with one pair of congruent base angles. Is *WXYZ* an isosceles trapezoid? Explain your reasoning.

Give the most specific name for the quadrilateral. Explain your reasoning.

26.

27.

28.

7 Chapter Test

Find the value of each variable in the parallelogram.

1.

2.

3.

Give the most specific name for the quadrilateral. Explain your reasoning.

4.

5.

6.

7. In a convex octagon, three of the exterior angles each have a measure of $x°$. The other five exterior angles each have a measure of $(2x + 7)°$. Find the measure of each exterior angle.

8. Quadrilateral $PQRS$ has vertices $P(5, 1)$, $Q(9, 6)$, $R(5, 11)$, and $S(1, 6)$. Classify quadrilateral $PQRS$ using the most specific name.

Determine whether enough information is given to show that the quadrilateral is a parallelogram. Explain your reasoning.

9.

10.

11.

12. Explain why a parallelogram with one right angle must be a rectangle.

13. Summarize the ways you can prove that a quadrilateral is a square.

14. Three vertices of $\square JKLM$ are $J(-2, -1)$, $K(0, 2)$, and $L(4, 3)$.

    a. Find the coordinates of vertex M.

    b. Find the coordinates of the intersection of the diagonals of $\square JKLM$.

15. You are building a plant stand with three equally-spaced circular shelves. The diagram shows a vertical cross section of the plant stand. What is the diameter of the middle shelf?

16. The Pentagon in Washington, D.C., is shaped like a regular pentagon. Find the measure of each interior angle.

17. You are designing a binocular mount. If $\overline{BC}$ is always vertical, the binoculars will point in the same direction while they are raised and lowered for different viewers. How can you design the mount so $\overline{BC}$ is always vertical? Justify your answer.

18. The measure of one angle of a kite is 90°. The measure of another angle in the kite is 30°. Sketch a kite that matches this description.

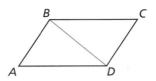

1. Copy and complete the flowchart proof of the Parallelogram Opposite Angles Theorem.

   Given *ABCD* is a parallelogram.

   Prove $\angle A \cong \angle C$, $\angle B \cong \angle D$

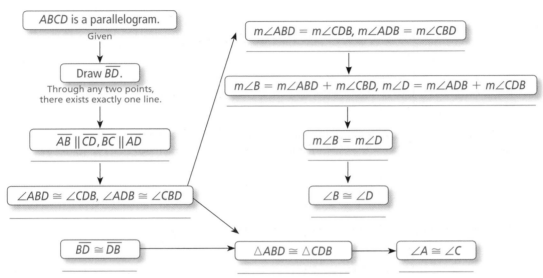

2. Which function is represented by the graph?

   Ⓐ $y = -\dfrac{1}{4}x^2$

   Ⓑ $y = \dfrac{1}{4}x^2$

   Ⓒ $y = -4x^2$

   Ⓓ $y = 4x^2$

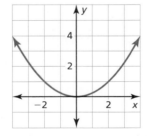

3. Account A has an initial balance of $1000 and increases by $50 each year. Account B has an initial balance of $500 and increases by 10% each year. Will Account A always have a greater balance than Account B? Explain.

4. Your friend claims that he can prove the Parallelogram Opposite Sides Theorem using the SSS Congruence Theorem and the Parallelogram Opposite Sides Theorem. Is your friend correct? Explain your reasoning.

5. You randomly select a vertex of polygon *QRSTUV*. What is the probability that the *x*-coordinate is greater than −3 or the *y*-coordinate is less than 4?

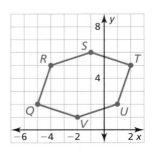

6. Choose the correct symbols to complete the proof of the Converse of the Hinge Theorem.

Given $\overline{AB} \cong \overline{DE}, \overline{BC} \cong \overline{EF}, AC > DF$

Prove $m\angle B > m\angle E$

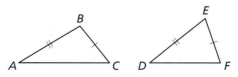

Indirect Proof

Step 1 Assume temporarily that $m\angle B \not> m\angle E$. Then it follows that either $m\angle B$ ___ $m\angle E$ or $m\angle B$ ___ $m\angle E$.

Step 2 If $m\angle B$ ___ $m\angle E$, then AC ___ DF by the Hinge Theorem.
If $m\angle B$ ___ $m\angle E$, then $\angle B$ ___ $\angle E$. So, $\triangle ABC$ ___ $\triangle DEF$ by the SAS Congruence Theorem and AC ___ DF.

Step 3 Both conclusions contradict the given statement that AC ___ DF. So, the temporary assumption that $m\angle B \not> m\angle E$ cannot be true. This proves that $m\angle B$ ___ $m\angle E$.

7. Use the Isosceles Trapezoid Base Angles Converse to prove that $ABCD$ is an isosceles trapezoid.

Given $\overline{BC} \parallel \overline{AD}, \angle EBC \cong \angle ECB, \angle ABE \cong \angle DCE$

Prove $ABCD$ is an isosceles trapezoid.

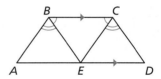

8. One part of the Rectangle Diagonals Theorem says, "If the diagonals of a parallelogram are congruent, then it is a rectangle." Using the reasons given, there are multiple ways to prove this part of the theorem. Provide a statement for each reason to form one possible proof of this part of the theorem.

Given $QRST$ is a parallelogram.
$\overline{QS} \cong \overline{RT}$

Prove $QRST$ is a rectangle.

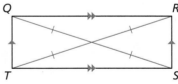

STATEMENTS	REASONS
1. $\overline{QS} \cong \overline{RT}$	**1.** Given
2. _____	**2.** Parallelogram Opposite Sides Theorem
3. _____	**3.** SSS Congruence Theorem
4. _____	**4.** Corresponding parts of congruent triangles are congruent.
5. _____	**5.** Parallelogram Consecutive Angles Theorem
6. _____	**6.** Congruent supplementary angles have the same measure.
7. _____	**7.** Parallelogram Consecutive Angles Theorem
8. _____	**8.** Subtraction Property of Equality
9. _____	**9.** Definition of a right angle
10. _____	**10.** Definition of a rectangle

8 Similarity

Ferris Wheel *(p. 498)*

Tennis Court *(p. 483)*

SEE the Big Idea

Olympic-Size Swimming Pool *(p. 478)*

Magnification *(p. 467)*

Photo Stickers *(p. 465)*

Maintaining Mathematical Proficiency

Determining Whether Ratios Form a Proportion

Example 1 Tell whether $\frac{2}{8}$ and $\frac{3}{12}$ form a proportion.

Compare the ratios in simplest form.

$$\frac{2}{8} = \frac{2 \div 2}{8 \div 2} = \frac{1}{4} \qquad\qquad \frac{3}{12} = \frac{3 \div 3}{12 \div 3} = \frac{1}{4}$$

The ratios are equivalent.

▶ So, $\frac{2}{8}$ and $\frac{3}{12}$ form a proportion.

Tell whether the ratios form a proportion.

1. $\frac{5}{3}, \frac{35}{21}$

2. $\frac{9}{24}, \frac{24}{64}$

3. $\frac{8}{56}, \frac{6}{28}$

4. $\frac{18}{4}, \frac{27}{9}$

5. $\frac{15}{21}, \frac{55}{77}$

6. $\frac{26}{8}, \frac{39}{12}$

Identifying Similar Figures

Example 2 Which rectangle is similar to Rectangle A?

Rectangle A
8
4

Rectangle B
4
1

Rectangle C
6
3

Each figure is a rectangle, so corresponding angles are congruent.
Check to see whether corresponding side lengths are proportional.

Rectangle A and Rectangle B

$\dfrac{\text{Length of A}}{\text{Length of B}} = \dfrac{8}{4} = 2 \qquad \dfrac{\text{Width of A}}{\text{Width of B}} = \dfrac{4}{1} = 4$

not proportional

Rectangle A and Rectangle C

$\dfrac{\text{Length of A}}{\text{Length of C}} = \dfrac{8}{6} = \dfrac{4}{3} \qquad \dfrac{\text{Width of A}}{\text{Width of C}} = \dfrac{4}{3}$

proportional

▶ So, Rectangle C is similar to Rectangle A.

Tell whether the two figures are similar. Explain your reasoning.

7.

5
12

14
7

8.

8
10
6

9
15
12

9.

10
6

5
3

10. **ABSTRACT REASONING** Can you draw two squares that are not similar? Explain your reasoning.

Mathematical Practices

Mathematically proficient students look for and make use of a pattern or structure.

Discerning a Pattern or Structure

Core Concept

Dilations, Perimeter, Area, and Volume

Consider a figure that is dilated by a scale factor of k.

1. The perimeter of the image is k times the perimeter of the original figure.

2. The area of the image is k^2 times the area of the original figure.

3. If the original figure is three dimensional, then the volume of the image is k^3 times the volume of the original figure.

Scale factor: k

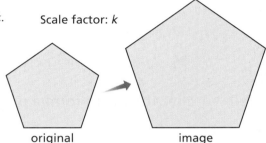

original   image

EXAMPLE 1   Finding Perimeter and Area after a Dilation

The triangle shown has side lengths of 3 inches, 4 inches, and 5 inches. Find the perimeter and area of the image when the triangle is dilated by a scale factor of (a) 2, (b) 3, and (c) 4.

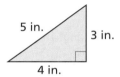

5 in.   3 in.

4 in.

SOLUTION

Perimeter: $P = 5 + 3 + 4 = 12$ in.   Area: $A = \frac{1}{2}(4)(3) = 6$ in.^{2}

	Scale factor: k	Perimeter: kP	Area: k^2A
a.	2	$2(12) = 24$ in.	$(2^2)(6) = 24$ in.^{2}
b.	3	$3(12) = 36$ in.	$(3^2)(6) = 54$ in.^{2}
c.	4	$4(12) = 48$ in.	$(4^2)(6) = 96$ in.^{2}

Monitoring Progress

1. Find the perimeter and area of the image when the trapezoid is dilated by a scale factor of (a) 2, (b) 3, and (c) 4.

2 cm

3 cm   5 cm

6 cm

2. Find the perimeter and area of the image when the parallelogram is dilated by a scale factor of (a) 2, (b) 3, and (c) $\frac{1}{2}$.

5 ft   4 ft

2 ft

3. A rectangular prism is 3 inches wide, 4 inches long, and 5 inches tall. Find the surface area and volume of the image of the prism when it is dilated by a scale factor of (a) 2, (b) 3, and (c) 4.

8.1 Dilations

Essential Question What does it mean to dilate a figure?

EXPLORATION 1 **Dilating a Triangle in a Coordinate Plane**

Work with a partner. Use dynamic geometry software to draw any triangle and label it △*ABC*.

a. *Dilate* △*ABC* using a *scale factor* of 2 and a *center of dilation* at the origin to form △*A′B′C′*. Compare the coordinates, side lengths, and angle measures of △*ABC* and △*A′B′C′*.

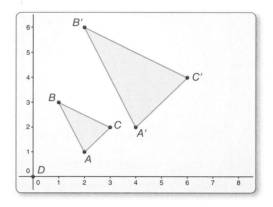

Sample

Points
A(2, 1)
B(1, 3)
C(3, 2)
Segments
$AB = 2.24$
$BC = 2.24$
$AC = 1.41$
Angles
$m\angle A = 71.57°$
$m\angle B = 36.87°$
$m\angle C = 71.57°$

LOOKING FOR STRUCTURE

To be proficient in math, you need to look closely to discern a pattern or structure.

b. Repeat part (a) using a *scale factor* of $\frac{1}{2}$.

c. What do the results of parts (a) and (b) suggest about the coordinates, side lengths, and angle measures of the image of △*ABC* after a dilation with a scale factor of *k*?

EXPLORATION 2 **Dilating Lines in a Coordinate Plane**

Work with a partner. Use dynamic geometry software to draw $\overleftrightarrow{AB}$ that passes through the origin and $\overleftrightarrow{AC}$ that does not pass through the origin.

a. *Dilate* $\overleftrightarrow{AB}$ using a *scale factor* of 3 and a *center of dilation* at the origin. Describe the image.

b. *Dilate* $\overleftrightarrow{AC}$ using a *scale factor* of 3 and a *center of dilation* at the origin. Describe the image.

c. Repeat parts (a) and (b) using a scale factor of $\frac{1}{4}$.

d. What do you notice about dilations of lines passing through the center of dilation and dilations of lines not passing through the center of dilation?

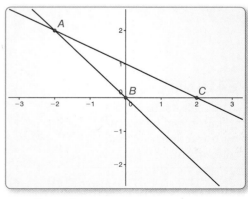

Sample

Points	Lines
A(−2, 2)	$x + y = 0$
B(0, 0)	$x + 2y = 2$
C(2, 0)	

Communicate Your Answer

3. What does it mean to dilate a figure?

4. Repeat Exploration 1 using a center of dilation at a point other than the origin.

Core Vocabulary

dilation, *p. 462*
center of dilation, *p. 462*
scale factor, *p. 462*
enlargement, *p. 462*
reduction, *p. 462*

What You Will Learn

▶ Identify and perform dilations.

▶ Solve real-life problems involving scale factors and dilations.

Identifying and Performing Dilations

⑤ Core Concept

Dilations

A **dilation** is a transformation in which a figure is enlarged or reduced with respect to a fixed point C called the **center of dilation** and a **scale factor** k, which is the ratio of the lengths of the corresponding sides of the image and the preimage.

A dilation with center of dilation C and scale factor k maps every point P in a figure to a point P' so that the following are true.

• If P is the center point C, then $P = P'$.

• If P is not the center point C, then the image point P' lies on $\overrightarrow{CP}$. The scale factor k is a positive number such that $k = \dfrac{CP'}{CP}$.

• Angle measures are preserved.

A dilation does not change any line that passes through the center of dilation. A dilation maps a line that does not pass through the center of dilation to a parallel line. In the figure above, $\overleftrightarrow{PR} \parallel \overleftrightarrow{P'R'}$, $\overleftrightarrow{PQ} \parallel \overleftrightarrow{P'Q'}$, and $\overleftrightarrow{QR} \parallel \overleftrightarrow{Q'R'}$.

When the scale factor $k > 1$, a dilation is an **enlargement**. When $0 < k < 1$, a dilation is a **reduction**.

EXAMPLE 1   **Identifying Dilations**

Find the scale factor of the dilation. Then tell whether the dilation is a *reduction* or an *enlargement*.

a.

b.

READING

The scale factor of a dilation can be written as a fraction, decimal, or percent.

SOLUTION

a. Because $\dfrac{CP'}{CP} = \dfrac{12}{8}$, the scale factor is $k = \dfrac{3}{2}$. So, the dilation is an enlargement.

b. Because $\dfrac{CP'}{CP} = \dfrac{18}{30}$, the scale factor is $k = \dfrac{3}{5}$. So, the dilation is a reduction.

Monitoring Progress Help in English and Spanish at *BigIdeasMath.com*

1. In a dilation, $CP' = 3$ and $CP = 12$. Find the scale factor. Then tell whether the dilation is a *reduction* or an *enlargement*.

Core Concept

Coordinate Rule for Dilations

If $P(x, y)$ is the preimage of a point, then its image after a dilation centered at the origin $(0, 0)$ with scale factor k is the point $P'(kx, ky)$.

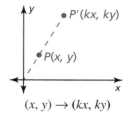

$$(x, y) \rightarrow (kx, ky)$$

READING DIAGRAMS

In this chapter, for all of the dilations in the coordinate plane, the center of dilation is the origin unless otherwise noted.

EXAMPLE 2   Dilating a Figure in the Coordinate Plane

Graph $\triangle ABC$ with vertices $A(2, 1)$, $B(4, 1)$, and $C(4, -1)$ and its image after a dilation with a scale factor of 2.

SOLUTION

Use the coordinate rule for a dilation with $k = 2$ to find the coordinates of the vertices of the image. Then graph $\triangle ABC$ and its image.

$$(x, y) \rightarrow (2x, 2y)$$
$$A(2, 1) \rightarrow A'(4, 2)$$
$$B(4, 1) \rightarrow B'(8, 2)$$
$$C(4, -1) \rightarrow C'(8, -2)$$

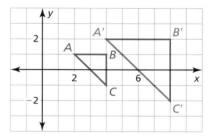

Notice the relationships between the lengths and slopes of the sides of the triangles in Example 2. Each side length of $\triangle A'B'C'$ is longer than its corresponding side by the scale factor. The corresponding sides are parallel because their slopes are the same.

EXAMPLE 3   Dilating a Figure in the Coordinate Plane

Graph quadrilateral $KLMN$ with vertices $K(-3, 6)$, $L(0, 6)$, $M(3, 3)$, and $N(-3, -3)$ and its image after a dilation with a scale factor of $\frac{1}{3}$.

SOLUTION

Use the coordinate rule for a dilation with $k = \frac{1}{3}$ to find the coordinates of the vertices of the image. Then graph quadrilateral $KLMN$ and its image.

$$(x, y) \rightarrow \left(\tfrac{1}{3}x, \tfrac{1}{3}y\right)$$
$$K(-3, 6) \rightarrow K'(-1, 2)$$
$$L(0, 6) \rightarrow L'(0, 2)$$
$$M(3, 3) \rightarrow M'(1, 1)$$
$$N(-3, -3) \rightarrow N'(-1, -1)$$

Monitoring Progress   Help in English and Spanish at *BigIdeasMath.com*

Graph $\triangle PQR$ and its image after a dilation with scale factor k.

  2. $P(-2, -1)$, $Q(-1, 0)$, $R(0, -1)$; $k = 4$

  3. $P(5, -5)$, $Q(10, -5)$, $R(10, 5)$; $k = 0.4$

CONSTRUCTION   Constructing a Dilation

Use a compass and straightedge to construct a dilation of $\triangle PQR$ with a scale factor of 2. Use a point C outside the triangle as the center of dilation.

SOLUTION

Step 1	**Step 2**	**Step 3**
		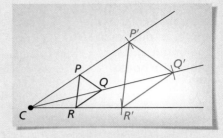
Draw a triangle Draw $\triangle PQR$ and choose the center of the dilation C outside the triangle. Draw rays from C through the vertices of the triangle.	**Use a compass** Use a compass to locate P' on $\overrightarrow{CP}$ so that $CP' = 2(CP)$. Locate Q' and R' using the same method.	**Connect points** Connect points P', Q', and R' to form $\triangle P'Q'R'$.

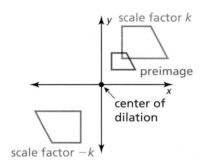

In the coordinate plane, you can have scale factors that are negative numbers. When this occurs, the figure rotates 180°. So, when $k > 0$, a dilation with a scale factor of $-k$ is the same as the composition of a dilation with a scale factor of k followed by a rotation of 180° about the center of dilation. Using the coordinate rules for a dilation and a rotation of 180°, you can think of the notation as

$$(x, y) \rightarrow (kx, ky) \rightarrow (-kx, -ky).$$

EXAMPLE 4   Using a Negative Scale Factor

Graph $\triangle FGH$ with vertices $F(-4, -2)$, $G(-2, 4)$, and $H(-2, -2)$ and its image after a dilation with a scale factor of $-\frac{1}{2}$.

SOLUTION

Use the coordinate rule for a dilation with $k = -\frac{1}{2}$ to find the coordinates of the vertices of the image. Then graph $\triangle FGH$ and its image.

$$(x, y) \rightarrow \left(-\frac{1}{2}x, -\frac{1}{2}y\right)$$

$$F(-4, -2) \rightarrow F'(2, 1)$$
$$G(-2, 4) \rightarrow G'(1, -2)$$
$$H(-2, -2) \rightarrow H'(1, 1)$$

Monitoring Progress   Help in English and Spanish at *BigIdeasMath.com*

4. Graph $\triangle PQR$ with vertices $P(1, 2)$, $Q(3, 1)$, and $R(1, -3)$ and its image after a dilation with a scale factor of -2.

5. Suppose a figure containing the origin is dilated. Explain why the corresponding point in the image of the figure is also the origin.

Solving Real-Life Problems

EXAMPLE 5 **Finding a Scale Factor**

4 in.

You are making your own photo stickers. Your photo is 4 inches by 4 inches. The image on the stickers is 1.1 inches by 1.1 inches. What is the scale factor of this dilation?

SOLUTION

The scale factor is the ratio of a side length of the sticker image to a side length of the original photo, or $\dfrac{1.1 \text{ in.}}{4 \text{ in.}}$.

1.1 in.

▶ So, in simplest form, the scale factor is $\dfrac{11}{40}$.

EXAMPLE 6 **Finding the Length of an Image**

You are using a magnifying glass that shows the image of an object that is six times the object's actual size. Determine the length of the image of the spider seen through the magnifying glass.

1.5 cm

SOLUTION

$$\frac{\text{image length}}{\text{actual length}} = k$$

$$\frac{x}{1.5} = 6$$

$$x = 9$$

▶ So, the image length through the magnifying glass is 9 centimeters.

Monitoring Progress Help in English and Spanish at *BigIdeasMath.com*

6. An optometrist dilates the pupils of a patient's eyes to get a better look at the back of the eyes. A pupil dilates from 4.5 millimeters to 8 millimeters. What is the scale factor of this dilation?

7. The image of a spider seen through the magnifying glass in Example 6 is shown at the left. Find the actual length of the spider.

12.6 cm

When a transformation, such as a dilation, changes the shape or size of a figure, the transformation is *nonrigid*. In addition to dilations, there are many possible nonrigid transformations. Two examples are shown below. It is important to pay close attention to whether a nonrigid transformation preserves lengths and angle measures.

Horizontal Stretch   **Vertical Stretch**

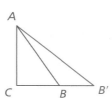

READING

Scale factors are written so that the units in the numerator and denominator divide out.

Vocabulary and Core Concept Check

1. **COMPLETE THE SENTENCE** If $P(x, y)$ is the preimage of a point, then its image after a dilation centered at the origin $(0, 0)$ with scale factor k is the point _____.

2. **WHICH ONE DOESN'T BELONG?** Which scale factor does *not* belong with the other three? Explain your reasoning.

| $\frac{5}{4}$ | 60% | 115% | 2 |

Monitoring Progress and Modeling with Mathematics

In Exercises 3–6, find the scale factor of the dilation. Then tell whether the dilation is a *reduction* or an *enlargement.* *(See Example 1.)*

3.

4.

5.

6.

CONSTRUCTION In Exercises 7–10, copy the diagram. Then use a compass and straightedge to construct a dilation of $\triangle LMN$ with the given center and scale factor k.

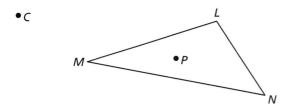

7. Center C, $k = 2$

8. Center P, $k = 3$

9. Center M, $k = \frac{1}{2}$

10. Center C, $k = 25\%$

CONSTRUCTION In Exercises 11–14, copy the diagram. Then use a compass and straightedge to construct a dilation of quadrilateral $RSTU$ with the given center and scale factor k.

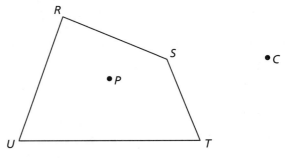

11. Center C, $k = 3$

12. Center P, $k = 2$

13. Center R, $k = 0.25$

14. Center C, $k = 75\%$

In Exercises 15–18, graph the polygon and its image after a dilation with scale factor k. *(See Examples 2 and 3.)*

15. $X(6, -1)$, $Y(-2, -4)$, $Z(1, 2)$; $k = 3$

16. $A(0, 5)$, $B(-10, -5)$, $C(5, -5)$; $k = 120\%$

17. $T(9, -3)$, $U(6, 0)$, $V(3, 9)$, $W(0, 0)$; $k = \frac{2}{3}$

18. $J(4, 0)$, $K(-8, 4)$, $L(0, -4)$, $M(12, -8)$; $k = 0.25$

In Exercises 19–22, graph the polygon and its image after a dilation with scale factor k. *(See Example 4.)*

19. $B(-5, -10)$, $C(-10, 15)$, $D(0, 5)$; $k = -\frac{1}{5}$

20. $L(0, 0)$, $M(-4, 1)$, $N(-3, -6)$; $k = -3$

21. $R(-7, -1)$, $S(2, 5)$, $T(-2, -3)$, $U(-3, -3)$; $k = -4$

22. $W(8, -2)$, $X(6, 0)$, $Y(-6, 4)$, $Z(-2, 2)$; $k = -0.5$

ERROR ANALYSIS In Exercises 23 and 24, describe and correct the error in finding the scale factor of the dilation.

23.
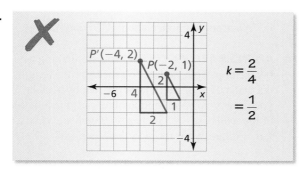
$$k = \frac{12}{3}$$
$$= 4$$

24.

$$k = \frac{2}{4}$$
$$= \frac{1}{2}$$

In Exercises 25–28, the red figure is the image of the blue figure after a dilation with center *C*. Find the scale factor of the dilation. Then find the value of the variable.

25.

26.

27.

28.
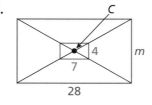

29. **FINDING A SCALE FACTOR** You receive wallet-sized photos of your school picture. The photo is 2.5 inches by 3.5 inches. You decide to dilate the photo to 5 inches by 7 inches at the store. What is the scale factor of this dilation? *(See Example 5.)*

30. **FINDING A SCALE FACTOR** Your visually impaired friend asked you to enlarge your notes from class so he can study. You took notes on 8.5-inch by 11-inch paper. The enlarged copy has a smaller side with a length of 10 inches. What is the scale factor of this dilation?

In Exercises 31–34, you are using a magnifying glass. Use the length of the insect and the magnification level to determine the length of the image seen through the magnifying glass. *(See Example 6.)*

31. emperor moth
Magnification: 5×

60 mm

32. ladybug
Magnification: 10×

4.5 mm

33. dragonfly
Magnification: 20×

47 mm

34. carpenter ant
Magnification: 15×

12 mm

35. **ANALYZING RELATIONSHIPS** Use the given actual and magnified lengths to determine which of the following insects were looked at using the same magnifying glass. Explain your reasoning.

grasshopper
Actual: 2 in.
Magnified: 15 in.

black beetle
Actual: 0.6 in.
Magnified: 4.2 in.

honeybee
Actual: $\frac{5}{8}$ in.
Magnified: $\frac{75}{16}$ in.

monarch butterfly
Actual: 3.9 in.
Magnified: 29.25 in.

36. **THOUGHT PROVOKING** Draw $\triangle ABC$ and $\triangle A'B'C'$ so that $\triangle A'B'C'$ is a dilation of $\triangle ABC$. Find the center of dilation and explain how you found it.

37. **REASONING** Your friend prints a 4-inch by 6-inch photo for you from the school dance. All you have is an 8-inch by 10-inch frame. Can you dilate the photo to fit the frame? Explain your reasoning.

38. HOW DO YOU SEE IT? Point C is the center of dilation of the images. The scale factor is $\frac{1}{3}$. Which figure is the original figure? Which figure is the dilated figure? Explain your reasoning.

39. MATHEMATICAL CONNECTIONS The larger triangle is a dilation of the smaller triangle. Find the values of x and y.

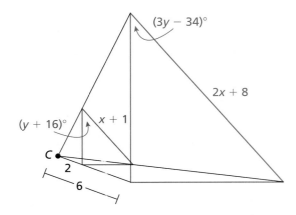

40. WRITING Explain why a scale factor of 2 is the same as 200%.

In Exercises 41–44, determine whether the dilated figure or the original figure is closer to the center of dilation. Use the given location of the center of dilation and scale factor k.

41. Center of dilation: inside the figure; $k = 3$

42. Center of dilation: inside the figure; $k = \frac{1}{2}$

43. Center of dilation: outside the figure; $k = 120\%$

44. Center of dilation: outside the figure; $k = 0.1$

45. ANALYZING RELATIONSHIPS Dilate the line through $O(0, 0)$ and $A(1, 2)$ using a scale factor of 2.

    a. What do you notice about the lengths of $\overline{O'A'}$ and $\overline{OA}$?

    b. What do you notice about $\overleftrightarrow{O'A'}$ and $\overleftrightarrow{OA}$?

46. ANALYZING RELATIONSHIPS Dilate the line through $A(0, 1)$ and $B(1, 2)$ using a scale factor of $\frac{1}{2}$.

    a. What do you notice about the lengths of $\overline{A'B'}$ and $\overline{AB}$?

    b. What do you notice about $\overleftrightarrow{A'B'}$ and $\overleftrightarrow{AB}$?

47. ATTENDING TO PRECISION You are making a blueprint of your house. You measure the lengths of the walls of your room to be 11 feet by 12 feet. When you draw your room on the blueprint, the lengths of the walls are 8.25 inches by 9 inches. What scale factor dilates your room to the blueprint?

48. MAKING AN ARGUMENT Your friend claims that dilating a figure by 1 is the same as dilating a figure by -1 because the original figure will not be enlarged or reduced. Is your friend correct? Explain your reasoning.

49. USING STRUCTURE Rectangle $WXYZ$ has vertices $W(-3, -1)$, $X(-3, 3)$, $Y(5, 3)$, and $Z(5, -1)$.

    a. Find the perimeter and area of the rectangle.

    b. Dilate the rectangle using a scale factor of 3. Find the perimeter and area of the dilated rectangle. Compare with the original rectangle. What do you notice?

    c. Repeat part (b) using a scale factor of $\frac{1}{4}$.

    d. Make a conjecture for how the perimeter and area change when a figure is dilated.

50. REASONING You put a reduction of a page on the original page. Explain why there is a point that is in the same place on both pages.

51. REASONING $\triangle ABC$ has vertices $A(4, 2)$, $B(4, 6)$, and $C(7, 2)$. Find the coordinates of the vertices of the image after a dilation with center $(4, 0)$ and a scale factor of 2.

Maintaining Mathematical Proficiency   <small>Reviewing what you learned in previous grades and lessons</small>

The vertices of $\triangle ABC$ are $A(2, -1)$, $B(0, 4)$, and $C(-3, 5)$. Find the coordinates of the vertices of the image after the translation. *(Skills Review Handbook)*

52. $(x, y) \rightarrow (x, y - 4)$ **53.** $(x, y) \rightarrow (x - 1, y + 3)$ **54.** $(x, y) \rightarrow (x + 3, y - 1)$

55. $(x, y) \rightarrow (x - 2, y)$ **56.** $(x, y) \rightarrow (x + 1, y - 2)$ **57.** $(x, y) \rightarrow (x - 3, y + 1)$

8.2 Similarity and Transformations

Essential Question When a figure is translated, reflected, rotated, or dilated in the plane, is the image always similar to the original figure?

Two figures are *similar figures* when they have the same shape but not necessarily the same size.

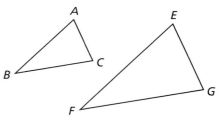

Similar Triangles

ATTENDING TO PRECISION

To be proficient in math, you need to use clear definitions in discussions with others and in your own reasoning.

EXPLORATION 1 **Dilations and Similarity**

Work with a partner.

a. Use dynamic geometry software to draw any triangle and label it △*ABC*.

b. Dilate the triangle using a scale factor of 3. Is the image similar to the original triangle? Justify your answer.

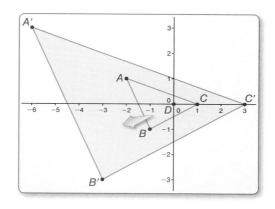

Sample

Points
$A(-2, 1)$
$B(-1, -1)$
$C(1, 0)$
$D(0, 0)$

Segments
$AB = 2.24$
$BC = 2.24$
$AC = 3.16$

Angles
$m\angle A = 45°$
$m\angle B = 90°$
$m\angle C = 45°$

EXPLORATION 2 **Rigid Motions and Similarity**

Work with a partner.

a. Use dynamic geometry software to draw any triangle.

b. Copy the triangle and translate it 3 units left and 4 units up. Is the image similar to the original triangle? Justify your answer.

c. Reflect the triangle in the *y*-axis. Is the image similar to the original triangle? Justify your answer.

d. Rotate the original triangle 90° counterclockwise about the origin. Is the image similar to the original triangle? Justify your answer.

Communicate Your Answer

3. When a figure is translated, reflected, rotated, or dilated in the plane, is the image always similar to the original figure? Explain your reasoning.

4. A figure undergoes a composition of transformations, which includes translations, reflections, rotations, and dilations. Is the image similar to the original figure? Explain your reasoning.

What You Will Learn

▶ Perform similarity transformations.

▶ Describe similarity transformations.

▶ Prove that figures are similar.

Performing Similarity Transformations

A dilation is a transformation that preserves shape but not size. So, a dilation is a nonrigid motion. A **similarity transformation** is a dilation or a composition of rigid motions and dilations. Two geometric figures are **similar figures** if and only if there is a similarity transformation that maps one of the figures onto the other. Similar figures have the same shape but not necessarily the same size.

Congruence transformations preserve length and angle measure. When the scale factor of the dilation(s) is not equal to 1 or −1, similarity transformations preserve angle measure only.

EXAMPLE 1   Performing a Similarity Transformation

Graph $\triangle ABC$ with vertices $A(-4, 1)$, $B(-2, 2)$, and $C(-2, 1)$ and its image after the similarity transformation.

Translation: $(x, y) \rightarrow (x + 5, y + 1)$

Dilation: $(x, y) \rightarrow (2x, 2y)$

SOLUTION

Step 1   Graph $\triangle ABC$.

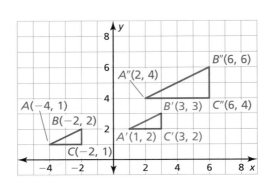

Step 2   Translate $\triangle ABC$ 5 units right and 1 unit up. $\triangle A'B'C'$ has vertices $A'(1, 2)$, $B'(3, 3)$, and $C'(3, 2)$.

Step 3   Dilate $\triangle A'B'C'$ using a scale factor of 2. $\triangle A''B''C''$ has vertices $A''(2, 4)$, $B''(6, 6)$, and $C''(6, 4)$.

Monitoring Progress Help in English and Spanish at *BigIdeasMath.com*

1. Graph $\overline{CD}$ with endpoints $C(-2, 2)$ and $D(2, 2)$ and its image after the similarity transformation.

   Rotation: 90° about the origin

   Dilation: $(x, y) \rightarrow \left(\frac{1}{2}x, \frac{1}{2}y\right)$

2. Graph $\triangle FGH$ with vertices $F(1, 2)$, $G(4, 4)$, and $H(2, 0)$ and its image after the similarity transformation.

   Reflection: in the x-axis

   Dilation: $(x, y) \rightarrow (1.5x, 1.5y)$

STUDY TIP

In this chapter, all rotations are counterclockwise unless otherwise noted.

Describing Similarity Transformations

EXAMPLE 2 **Describing a Similarity Transformation**

Describe a similarity transformation that maps trapezoid *PQRS* to trapezoid *WXYZ*.

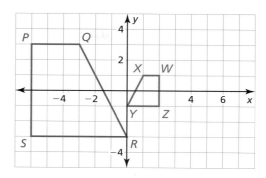

SOLUTION

$\overline{QR}$ falls from left to right, and $\overline{XY}$ rises from left to right. If you reflect trapezoid *PQRS* in the *y*-axis as shown, then the image, trapezoid $P'Q'R'S'$, will have the same orientation as trapezoid *WXYZ*.

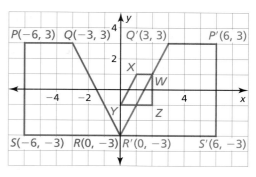

Trapezoid *WXYZ* appears to be about one-third as large as trapezoid $P'Q'R'S'$. Dilate trapezoid $P'Q'R'S'$ using a scale factor of $\frac{1}{3}$.

$$(x, y) \rightarrow \left(\tfrac{1}{3}x, \tfrac{1}{3}y\right)$$

$$P'(6, 3) \rightarrow P''(2, 1)$$

$$Q'(3, 3) \rightarrow Q''(1, 1)$$

$$R'(0, -3) \rightarrow R''(0, -1)$$

$$S'(6, -3) \rightarrow S''(2, -1)$$

The vertices of trapezoid $P''Q''R''S''$ match the vertices of trapezoid *WXYZ*.

▶ So, a similarity transformation that maps trapezoid *PQRS* to trapezoid *WXYZ* is a reflection in the *y*-axis followed by a dilation with a scale factor of $\frac{1}{3}$.

Monitoring Progress Help in English and Spanish at *BigIdeasMath.com*

3. In Example 2, describe another similarity transformation that maps trapezoid *PQRS* to trapezoid *WXYZ*.

4. Describe a similarity transformation that maps quadrilateral *DEFG* to quadrilateral *STUV*.

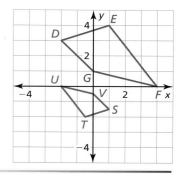

Proving Figures Are Similar

To prove that two figures are similar, you must prove that a similarity transformation maps one of the figures onto the other.

EXAMPLE 3 **Proving That Two Squares Are Similar**

Prove that square *ABCD* is similar to square *EFGH*.

Given Square *ABCD* with side length *r*,
square *EFGH* with side length *s*,
$\overline{AD} \parallel \overline{EH}$

Prove Square *ABCD* is similar to
square *EFGH*.

SOLUTION

Translate square *ABCD* so that point *A* maps to point *E*. Because translations map segments to parallel segments and $\overline{AD} \parallel \overline{EH}$, the image of $\overline{AD}$ lies on $\overline{EH}$.

Because translations preserve length and angle measure, the image of *ABCD*, *EB'C'D'*, is a square with side length *r*. Because all the interior angles of a square are right angles, $\angle B'ED' \cong \angle FEH$. When $\overrightarrow{ED'}$ coincides with $\overrightarrow{EH}$, $\overrightarrow{EB'}$ coincides with $\overrightarrow{EF}$. So, $\overline{EB'}$ lies on $\overline{EF}$. Next, dilate square *EB'C'D'* using center of dilation *E*. Choose the scale factor to be the ratio of the side lengths of *EFGH* and *EB'C'D'*, which is $\frac{s}{r}$.

This dilation maps $\overline{ED'}$ to $\overline{EH}$ and $\overline{EB'}$ to $\overline{EF}$ because the images of $\overline{ED'}$ and $\overline{EB'}$ have side length $\frac{s}{r}(r) = s$ and the segments $\overline{ED'}$ and $\overline{EB'}$ lie on lines passing through the center of dilation. So, the dilation maps *B'* to *F* and *D'* to *H*. The image of *C'* lies $\frac{s}{r}(r) = s$ units to the right of the image of *B'* and $\frac{s}{r}(r) = s$ units above the image of *D'*. So, the image of *C'* is *G*.

▶ A similarity transformation maps square *ABCD* to square *EFGH*. So, square *ABCD* is similar to square *EFGH*.

Monitoring Progress Help in English and Spanish at *BigIdeasMath.com*

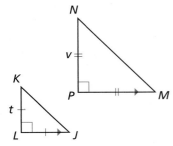

5. Prove that △*JKL* is similar to △*MNP*.

  Given Right isosceles △*JKL* with leg length *t*, right isosceles △*MNP* with leg length *v*, $\overline{LJ} \parallel \overline{PM}$

  Prove △*JKL* is similar to △*MNP*.

Vocabulary and Core Concept Check

1. **VOCABULARY** What is the difference between *similar figures* and *congruent figures*?

2. **COMPLETE THE SENTENCE** A transformation that produces a similar figure, such as a dilation, is called a _____.

Monitoring Progress and Modeling with Mathematics

In Exercises 3–6, graph △*FGH* with vertices *F*(−2, 2), *G*(−2, −4), and *H*(−4, −4) and its image after the similarity transformation. *(See Example 1.)*

3. **Translation:** $(x, y) \rightarrow (x + 3, y + 1)$
   Dilation: $(x, y) \rightarrow (2x, 2y)$

4. **Dilation:** $(x, y) \rightarrow \left(\frac{1}{2}x, \frac{1}{2}y\right)$
   Reflection: in the *y*-axis

5. **Rotation:** 90° about the origin
   Dilation: $(x, y) \rightarrow (3x, 3y)$

6. **Dilation:** $(x, y) \rightarrow \left(\frac{3}{4}x, \frac{3}{4}y\right)$
   Reflection: in the *x*-axis

In Exercises 7 and 8, describe a similarity transformation that maps the blue preimage to the green image. *(See Example 2.)*

7.

8.

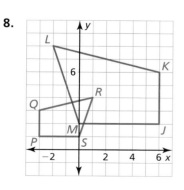

In Exercises 9–12, determine whether the polygons with the given vertices are similar. Use transformations to explain your reasoning.

9. *A*(6, 0), *B*(9, 6), *C*(12, 6) and *D*(0, 3), *E*(1, 5), *F*(2, 5)

10. *Q*(−1, 0), *R*(−2, 2), *S*(1, 3), *T*(2, 1) and *W*(0, 2), *X*(4, 4), *Y*(6, −2), *Z*(2, −4)

11. *G*(−2, 3), *H*(4, 3), *I*(4, 0) and *J*(1, 0), *K*(6, −2), *L*(1, −2)

12. *D*(−4, 3), *E*(−2, 3), *F*(−1, 1), *G*(−4, 1) and *L*(1, −1), *M*(3, −1), *N*(6, −3), *P*(1, −3)

In Exercises 13 and 14, prove that the figures are similar. *(See Example 3.)*

13. **Given** Right isosceles △*ABC* with leg length *j*, right isosceles △*RST* with leg length *k*, $\overline{CA} \parallel \overline{RT}$

    Prove △*ABC* is similar to △*RST*.

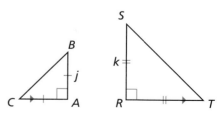

14. **Given** Rectangle *JKLM* with side lengths *x* and *y*, rectangle *QRST* with side lengths 2*x* and 2*y*

    Prove Rectangle *JKLM* is similar to rectangle *QRST*.

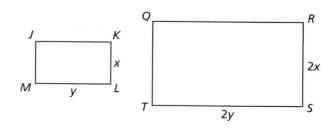

15. **MODELING WITH MATHEMATICS** Determine whether the regular-sized stop sign and the stop sign sticker are similar. Use transformations to explain your reasoning.

12.6 in.

4 in.

16. **ERROR ANALYSIS** Describe and correct the error in comparing the figures.

Figure A is similar to Figure B.

17. **MAKING AN ARGUMENT** A member of the homecoming decorating committee gives a printing company a banner that is 3 inches by 14 inches to enlarge. The committee member claims the banner she receives is distorted. Do you think the printing company distorted the image she gave it? Explain.

← 84 in. →

18 in.

18. **HOW DO YOU SEE IT?** Determine whether each pair of figures is similar. Explain your reasoning.

a.   b.

19. **ANALYZING RELATIONSHIPS** Graph a polygon in a coordinate plane. Use a similarity transformation involving a dilation (where k is a whole number) and a translation to graph a second polygon. Then describe a similarity transformation that maps the second polygon onto the first.

20. **THOUGHT PROVOKING** Is the composition of a rotation and a dilation commutative? (In other words, do you obtain the same image regardless of the order in which you perform the transformations?) Justify your answer.

21. **MATHEMATICAL CONNECTIONS** Quadrilateral $JKLM$ is mapped to quadrilateral $J'K'L'M'$ using the dilation $(x, y) \rightarrow \left(\frac{3}{2}x, \frac{3}{2}y\right)$. Then quadrilateral $J'K'L'M'$ is mapped to quadrilateral $J''K''L''M''$ using the translation $(x, y) \rightarrow (x + 3, y - 4)$. The vertices of quadrilateral $J'K'L'M'$ are $J'(-12, 0)$, $K'(-12, 18)$, $L'(-6, 18)$, and $M'(-6, 0)$. Find the coordinates of the vertices of quadrilateral $JKLM$ and quadrilateral $J''K''L''M''$. Are quadrilateral $JKLM$ and quadrilateral $J''K''L''M''$ similar? Explain.

22. **REPEATED REASONING** Use the diagram.

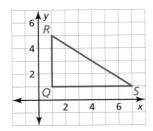

a. Connect the midpoints of the sides of $\triangle QRS$ to make another triangle. Is this triangle similar to $\triangle QRS$? Use transformations to support your answer.

b. Repeat part (a) for two other triangles. What conjecture can you make?

Maintaining Mathematical Proficiency
Reviewing what you learned in previous grades and lessons

Classify the angle as *acute*, *obtuse*, *right*, or *straight*. *(Skills Review Handbook)*

23.
113°

24.

25.
82°

26.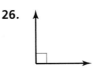

8.3　Similar Polygons

Essential Question　How are similar polygons related?

EXPLORATION 1　Comparing Triangles after a Dilation

Work with a partner. Use dynamic geometry software to draw any △*ABC*. Dilate △*ABC* to form a similar △*A'B'C'* using any scale factor *k* and any center of dilation.

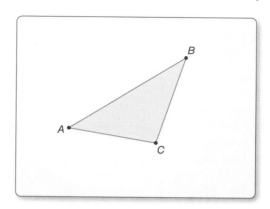

a. Compare the corresponding angles of △*A'B'C'* and △*ABC*.

b. Find the ratios of the lengths of the sides of △*A'B'C'* to the lengths of the corresponding sides of △*ABC*. What do you observe?

c. Repeat parts (a) and (b) for several other triangles, scale factors, and centers of dilation. Do you obtain similar results?

EXPLORATION 2　Comparing Triangles after a Dilation

Work with a partner. Use dynamic geometry software to draw any △*ABC*. Dilate △*ABC* to form a similar △*A'B'C'* using any scale factor *k* and any center of dilation.

LOOKING FOR STRUCTURE

To be proficient in math, you need to look closely to discern a pattern or structure.

a. Compare the perimeters of △*A'B'C'* and △*ABC*. What do you observe?

b. Compare the areas of △*A'B'C'* and △*ABC*. What do you observe?

c. Repeat parts (a) and (b) for several other triangles, scale factors, and centers of dilation. Do you obtain similar results?

Communicate Your Answer

3. How are similar polygons related?

4. A △*RST* is dilated by a scale factor of 3 to form △*R'S'T'*. The area of △*RST* is 1 square inch. What is the area of △*R'S'T'*?

What You Will Learn

▶ Use similarity statements.

▶ Find corresponding lengths in similar polygons.

▶ Find perimeters and areas of similar polygons.

▶ Decide whether polygons are similar.

Using Similarity Statements

⟳ Core Concept

Corresponding Parts of Similar Polygons

In the diagram below, $\triangle ABC$ is similar to $\triangle DEF$. You can write "$\triangle ABC$ is similar to $\triangle DEF$" as $\triangle ABC \sim \triangle DEF$. A similarity transformation preserves angle measure. So, corresponding angles are congruent. A similarity transformation also enlarges or reduces side lengths by a scale factor k. So, corresponding side lengths are proportional.

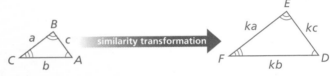

Corresponding angles

$\angle A \cong \angle D, \angle B \cong \angle E, \angle C \cong \angle F$

Ratios of corresponding side lengths

$\dfrac{DE}{AB} = \dfrac{EF}{BC} = \dfrac{FD}{CA} = k$

LOOKING FOR STRUCTURE

Notice that any two congruent figures are also similar. In $\triangle LMN$ and $\triangle WXY$ below, the scale factor is $\frac{5}{5} = \frac{6}{6} = \frac{7}{7} = 1$. So, you can write $\triangle LMN \sim \triangle WXY$ and $\triangle LMN \cong \triangle WXY$.

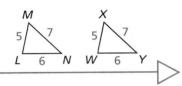

EXAMPLE 1   **Using Similarity Statements**

In the diagram, $\triangle RST \sim \triangle XYZ$.

a. Find the scale factor from $\triangle RST$ to $\triangle XYZ$.

b. List all pairs of congruent angles.

c. Write the ratios of the corresponding side lengths in a *statement of proportionality*.

READING

In a *statement of proportionality*, any pair of ratios forms a true proportion.

SOLUTION

a. $\dfrac{XY}{RS} = \dfrac{12}{20} = \dfrac{3}{5}$ $\dfrac{YZ}{ST} = \dfrac{18}{30} = \dfrac{3}{5}$ $\dfrac{ZX}{TR} = \dfrac{15}{25} = \dfrac{3}{5}$

So, the scale factor is $\dfrac{3}{5}$.

b. $\angle R \cong \angle X$, $\angle S \cong \angle Y$, and $\angle T \cong \angle Z$.

c. Because the ratios in part (a) are equal, $\dfrac{XY}{RS} = \dfrac{YZ}{ST} = \dfrac{ZX}{TR}$.

Monitoring Progress Help in English and Spanish at *BigIdeasMath.com*

1. In the diagram, $\triangle JKL \sim \triangle PQR$. Find the scale factor from $\triangle JKL$ to $\triangle PQR$. Then list all pairs of congruent angles and write the ratios of the corresponding side lengths in a statement of proportionality.

Finding Corresponding Lengths in Similar Polygons

READING

Corresponding lengths in similar triangles include side lengths, altitudes, medians, and midsegments.

Core Concept

Corresponding Lengths in Similar Polygons

If two polygons are similar, then the ratio of any two corresponding lengths in the polygons is equal to the scale factor of the similar polygons.

EXAMPLE 2 Finding a Corresponding Length

In the diagram, $\triangle DEF \sim \triangle MNP$. Find the value of x.

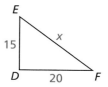

SOLUTION

The triangles are similar, so the corresponding side lengths are proportional.

$\dfrac{MN}{DE} = \dfrac{NP}{EF}$ Write proportion.

$\dfrac{18}{15} = \dfrac{30}{x}$ Substitute.

$18x = 450$ Cross Products Property

$x = 25$ Solve for x.

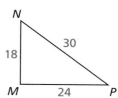

▶ The value of x is 25.

FINDING AN ENTRY POINT

There are several ways to write the proportion. For example, you could write $\dfrac{DF}{MP} = \dfrac{EF}{NP}$.

EXAMPLE 3 Finding a Corresponding Length

In the diagram, $\triangle TPR \sim \triangle XPZ$. Find the length of the altitude $\overline{PS}$.

SOLUTION

First, find the scale factor from $\triangle XPZ$ to $\triangle TPR$.

$\dfrac{TR}{XZ} = \dfrac{6+6}{8+8} = \dfrac{12}{16} = \dfrac{3}{4}$

Because the ratio of the lengths of the altitudes in similar triangles is equal to the scale factor, you can write the following proportion.

$\dfrac{PS}{PY} = \dfrac{3}{4}$ Write proportion.

$\dfrac{PS}{20} = \dfrac{3}{4}$ Substitute 20 for PY.

$PS = 15$ Multiply each side by 20 and simplify.

▶ The length of the altitude $\overline{PS}$ is 15.

Monitoring Progress Help in English and Spanish at *BigIdeasMath.com*

2. Find the value of x.

3. Find KM.

$ABCD \sim QRST$

$\triangle JKL \sim \triangle EFG$

Finding Perimeters and Areas of Similar Polygons

⟳ Theorem

Perimeters of Similar Polygons

If two polygons are similar, then the ratio of their perimeters is equal to the ratios of their corresponding side lengths.

ANALYZING RELATIONSHIPS

When two similar polygons have a scale factor of k, the ratio of their perimeters is equal to k.

If $KLMN \sim PQRS$, then $\dfrac{PQ + QR + RS + SP}{KL + LM + MN + NK} = \dfrac{PQ}{KL} = \dfrac{QR}{LM} = \dfrac{RS}{MN} = \dfrac{SP}{NK}$.

Proof Ex. 52, p. 484; *BigIdeasMath.com*

EXAMPLE 4   Modeling with Mathematics

A town plans to build a new swimming pool. An Olympic pool is rectangular with a length of 50 meters and a width of 25 meters. The new pool will be similar in shape to an Olympic pool but will have a length of 40 meters. Find the perimeters of an Olympic pool and the new pool.

SOLUTION

1. **Understand the Problem** You are given the length and width of a rectangle and the length of a similar rectangle. You need to find the perimeters of both rectangles.

2. **Make a Plan** Find the scale factor of the similar rectangles and find the perimeter of an Olympic pool. Then use the Perimeters of Similar Polygons Theorem to write and solve a proportion to find the perimeter of the new pool.

3. **Solve the Problem** Because the new pool will be similar to an Olympic pool, the scale factor is the ratio of the lengths, $\frac{40}{50} = \frac{4}{5}$. The perimeter of an Olympic pool is $2(50) + 2(25) = 150$ meters. Write and solve a proportion to find the perimeter x of the new pool.

STUDY TIP

You can also write the scale factor as a decimal. In Example 4, you can write the scale factor as 0.8 and multiply by 150 to get $x = 0.8(150) = 120$.

$$\frac{x}{150} = \frac{4}{5} \qquad \text{Perimeters of Similar Polygons Theorem}$$

$$x = 120 \qquad \text{Multiply each side by 150 and simplify.}$$

▶ So, the perimeter of an Olympic pool is 150 meters, and the perimeter of the new pool is 120 meters.

4. **Look Back** Check that the ratio of the perimeters is equal to the scale factor.

$$\frac{120}{150} = \frac{4}{5} \ ✓$$

Monitoring Progress 🔊 Help in English and Spanish at *BigIdeasMath.com*

4. The two gazebos shown are similar pentagons. Find the perimeter of Gazebo A.

Areas of Similar Polygons

ANALYZING RELATIONSHIPS

When two similar polygons have a scale factor of k, the ratio of their areas is equal to k^2.

If two polygons are similar, then the ratio of their areas is equal to the squares of the ratios of their corresponding side lengths.

If $KLMN \sim PQRS$, then $\dfrac{\text{Area of } PQRS}{\text{Area of } KLMN} = \left(\dfrac{PQ}{KL}\right)^2 = \left(\dfrac{QR}{LM}\right)^2 = \left(\dfrac{RS}{MN}\right)^2 = \left(\dfrac{SP}{NK}\right)^2$.

Proof Ex. 53, p. 484; *BigIdeasMath.com*

EXAMPLE 5 **Finding Areas of Similar Polygons**

In the diagram, $\triangle ABC \sim \triangle DEF$. Find the area of $\triangle DEF$.

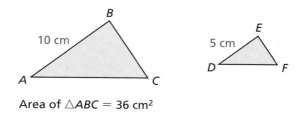

Area of $\triangle ABC = 36 \text{ cm}^2$

SOLUTION

Because the triangles are similar, the ratio of the area of $\triangle ABC$ to the area of $\triangle DEF$ is equal to the square of the ratio of AB to DE. Write and solve a proportion to find the area of $\triangle DEF$. Let A represent the area of $\triangle DEF$.

$\dfrac{\text{Area of } \triangle ABC}{\text{Area of } \triangle DEF} = \left(\dfrac{AB}{DE}\right)^2$	Areas of Similar Polygons Theorem
$\dfrac{36}{A} = \left(\dfrac{10}{5}\right)^2$	Substitute.
$\dfrac{36}{A} = \dfrac{100}{25}$	Square the right side of the equation.
$36 \cdot 25 = 100 \cdot A$	Cross Products Property
$900 = 100A$	Simplify.
$9 = A$	Solve for A.

▶ The area of $\triangle DEF$ is 9 square centimeters.

Monitoring Progress Help in English and Spanish at *BigIdeasMath.com*

5. In the diagram, $GHJK \sim LMNP$. Find the area of $LMNP$.

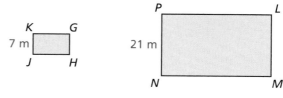

Area of $GHJK = 84 \text{ m}^2$

Deciding Whether Polygons Are Similar

EXAMPLE 6 **Deciding Whether Polygons Are Similar**

Decide whether *ABCDE* and *KLQRP* are similar. Explain your reasoning.

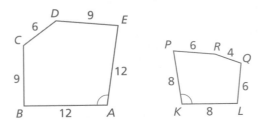

SOLUTION

Corresponding sides of the pentagons are proportional with a scale factor of $\frac{2}{3}$. However, this does not necessarily mean the pentagons are similar. A dilation with center *A* and scale factor $\frac{2}{3}$ moves *ABCDE* onto *AFGHJ*. Then a reflection moves *AFGHJ* onto *KLMNP*.

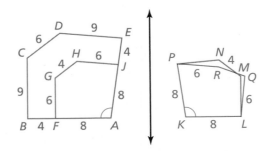

KLMNP does not exactly coincide with *KLQRP*, because not all the corresponding angles are congruent. (Only ∠*A* and ∠*K* are congruent.)

▶ Because angle measure is not preserved, the two pentagons are not similar.

Monitoring Progress Help in English and Spanish at *BigIdeasMath.com*

Refer to the floor tile designs below. In each design, the red shape is a regular hexagon.

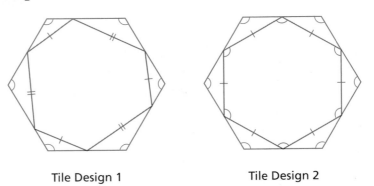

Tile Design 1   Tile Design 2

6. Decide whether the hexagons in Tile Design 1 are similar. Explain.

7. Decide whether the hexagons in Tile Design 2 are similar. Explain.

Vocabulary and Core Concept Check

1. **COMPLETE THE SENTENCE** For two figures to be similar, the corresponding angles must be _____, and the corresponding side lengths must be _____.

2. **DIFFERENT WORDS, SAME QUESTION** Which is different? Find "both" answers.

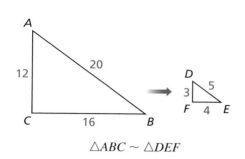

△ABC ~ △DEF

What is the scale factor?

What is the ratio of their areas?

What is the ratio of their corresponding side lengths?

What is the ratio of their perimeters?

Monitoring Progress and Modeling with Mathematics

In Exercises 3 and 4, find the scale factor. Then list all pairs of congruent angles and write the ratios of the corresponding side lengths in a statement of proportionality. *(See Example 1.)*

3. △ABC ~ △LMN

4. DEFG ~ PQRS

In Exercises 5–8, the polygons are similar. Find the value of *x*. *(See Example 2.)*

5.

6.

7.

8.

In Exercises 9 and 10, the black triangles are similar. Identify the type of segment shown in blue and find the value of the variable. *(See Example 3.)*

9.

10.
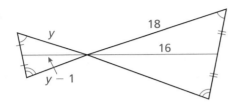

In Exercises 11 and 12, *RSTU ~ ABCD*. Find the ratio of their perimeters.

11.

12.
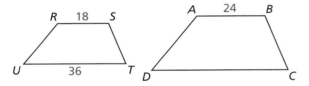

In Exercises 13–16, two polygons are similar. The perimeter of one polygon and the ratio of the corresponding side lengths are given. Find the perimeter of the other polygon.

13. perimeter of smaller polygon: 48 cm; ratio: $\frac{2}{3}$

14. perimeter of smaller polygon: 66 ft; ratio: $\frac{3}{4}$

15. perimeter of larger polygon: 120 yd; ratio: $\frac{1}{6}$

16. perimeter of larger polygon: 85 m; ratio: $\frac{2}{5}$

17. **MODELING WITH MATHEMATICS** A school gymnasium is being remodeled. The basketball court will be similar to an NCAA basketball court, which has a length of 94 feet and a width of 50 feet. The school plans to make the width of the new court 45 feet. Find the perimeters of an NCAA court and of the new court in the school. *(See Example 4.)*

18. **MODELING WITH MATHEMATICS** Your family has decided to put a rectangular patio in your backyard, similar to the shape of your backyard. Your backyard has a length of 45 feet and a width of 20 feet. The length of your new patio is 18 feet. Find the perimeters of your backyard and of the patio.

In Exercises 19–22, the polygons are similar. The area of one polygon is given. Find the area of the other polygon. *(See Example 5.)*

19.

20.

21.

22.

23. **ERROR ANALYSIS** Describe and correct the error in finding the perimeter of triangle B. The triangles are similar.

24. **ERROR ANALYSIS** Describe and correct the error in finding the area of rectangle B. The rectangles are similar.

In Exercises 25 and 26, decide whether the red and blue polygons are similar. *(See Example 6.)*

25.

26.
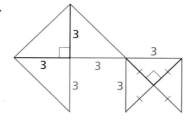

27. REASONING Triangles *ABC* and *DEF* are similar. Which statement is correct? Select all that apply.

(A) $\dfrac{BC}{EF} = \dfrac{AC}{DF}$ (B) $\dfrac{AB}{DE} = \dfrac{CA}{FE}$

(C) $\dfrac{AB}{EF} = \dfrac{BC}{DE}$ (D) $\dfrac{CA}{FD} = \dfrac{BC}{EF}$

ANALYZING RELATIONSHIPS In Exercises 28–34,
JKLM ~ EFGH.

28. Find the scale factor of *JKLM* to *EFGH*.

29. Find the scale factor of *EFGH* to *JKLM*.

30. Find the values of *x*, *y*, and *z*.

31. Find the perimeter of each polygon.

32. Find the ratio of the perimeters of *JKLM* to *EFGH*.

33. Find the area of each polygon.

34. Find the ratio of the areas of *JKLM* to *EFGH*.

35. USING STRUCTURE Rectangle A is similar to rectangle B. Rectangle A has side lengths of 6 and 12. Rectangle B has a side length of 18. What are the possible values for the length of the other side of rectangle B? Select all that apply.

(A) 6   (B) 9   (C) 24   (D) 36

36. DRAWING CONCLUSIONS In table tennis, the table is a rectangle 9 feet long and 5 feet wide. A tennis court is a rectangle 78 feet long and 36 feet wide. Are the two surfaces similar? Explain. If so, find the scale factor of the tennis court to the table.

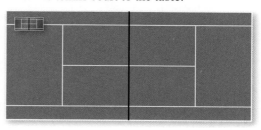

MATHEMATICAL CONNECTIONS In Exercises 37 and 38, the two polygons are similar. Find the values of *x* and *y*.

37.

38.
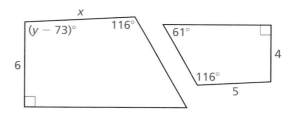

ATTENDING TO PRECISION In Exercises 39–42, the figures are similar. Find the missing corresponding side length.

39. Figure A has a perimeter of 72 meters and one of the side lengths is 18 meters. Figure B has a perimeter of 120 meters.

40. Figure A has a perimeter of 24 inches. Figure B has a perimeter of 36 inches and one of the side lengths is 12 inches.

41. Figure A has an area of 48 square feet and one of the side lengths is 6 feet. Figure B has an area of 75 square feet.

42. Figure A has an area of 18 square feet. Figure B has an area of 98 square feet and one of the side lengths is 14 feet.

CRITICAL THINKING In Exercises 43–48, tell whether the polygons are *always, sometimes,* or *never* similar.

43. two isosceles triangles   44. two isosceles trapezoids

45. two rhombuses   46. two squares

47. two regular polygons

48. a right triangle and an equilateral triangle

49. **MAKING AN ARGUMENT** Your sister claims that when the side lengths of two rectangles are proportional, the two rectangles must be similar. Is she correct? Explain your reasoning.

50. **HOW DO YOU SEE IT?** You shine a flashlight directly on an object to project its image onto a parallel screen. Will the object and the image be similar? Explain your reasoning.

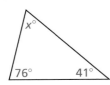

51. **MODELING WITH MATHEMATICS** During a total eclipse of the Sun, the moon is directly in line with the Sun and blocks the Sun's rays. The distance *DA* between Earth and the Sun is 93,000,000 miles, the distance *DE* between Earth and the moon is 240,000 miles, and the radius *AB* of the Sun is 432,500 miles. Use the diagram and the given measurements to estimate the radius *EC* of the moon.

△*DEC* ~ △*DAB*   *Not drawn to scale*

52. **PROVING A THEOREM** Prove the Perimeters of Similar Polygons Theorem for similar rectangles. Include a diagram in your proof.

53. **PROVING A THEOREM** Prove the Areas of Similar Polygons Theorem for similar rectangles. Include a diagram in your proof.

54. **THOUGHT PROVOKING** The postulates and theorems you have learned represent Euclidean geometry. In spherical geometry, all points are points on the surface of a sphere. A line is a circle on the sphere whose diameter is equal to the diameter of the sphere. A plane is the surface of the sphere. In spherical geometry, is it possible that two triangles are similar but not congruent? Explain your reasoning.

55. **CRITICAL THINKING** In the diagram, *PQRS* is a square, and *PLMS* ~ *LMRQ*. Find the exact value of *x*. This value is called the *golden ratio*. Golden rectangles have their length and width in this ratio. Show that the similar rectangles in the diagram are golden rectangles.

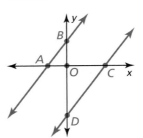

56. **MATHEMATICAL CONNECTIONS** The equations of the lines shown are $y = \frac{4}{3}x + 4$ and $y = \frac{4}{3}x - 8$. Show that △*AOB* ~ △*COD*.

Maintaining Mathematical Proficiency
Reviewing what you learned in previous grades and lessons

Find the value of x. *(Section 7.1)*

57.

58.

59.

60.

Essential Question What can you conclude about two triangles when you know that two pairs of corresponding angles are congruent?

EXPLORATION 1
Comparing Triangles

Work with a partner. Use dynamic geometry software.

a. Construct △ABC and △DEF so that $m\angle A = m\angle D = 106°$, $m\angle B = m\angle E = 31°$, and △DEF is not congruent to △ABC.

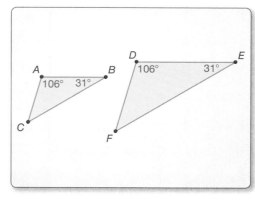

b. Find the third angle measure and the side lengths of each triangle. Copy the table below and record your results in column 1.

	1.	2.	3.	4.	5.	6.
$m\angle A, m\angle D$	106°	88°	40°			
$m\angle B, m\angle E$	31°	42°	65°			
$m\angle C$						
$m\angle F$						
AB						
DE						
BC						
EF						
AC						
DF						

CONSTRUCTING VIABLE ARGUMENTS

To be proficient in math, you need to understand and use stated assumptions, definitions, and previously established results in constructing arguments.

c. Are the two triangles similar? Explain.

d. Repeat parts (a)–(c) to complete columns 2 and 3 of the table for the given angle measures.

e. Complete each remaining column of the table using your own choice of two pairs of equal corresponding angle measures. Can you construct two triangles in this way that are *not* similar?

f. Make a conjecture about any two triangles with two pairs of congruent corresponding angles.

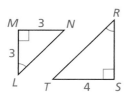

Communicate Your Answer

2. What can you conclude about two triangles when you know that two pairs of corresponding angles are congruent?

3. Find *RS* in the figure at the left.

What You Will Learn

▶ Use the Angle-Angle Similarity Theorem.

▶ Solve real-life problems.

Using the Angle-Angle Similarity Theorem

🔄 Theorem

Angle-Angle (AA) Similarity Theorem

If two angles of one triangle are congruent to two angles of another triangle, then the two triangles are similar.

If $\angle A \cong \angle D$ and $\angle B \cong \angle E$, then $\triangle ABC \sim \triangle DEF$.

Proof p. 486

PROOF Angle-Angle (AA) Similarity Theorem

Given $\angle A \cong \angle D$, $\angle B \cong \angle E$

Prove $\triangle ABC \sim \triangle DEF$

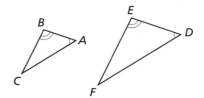

Dilate $\triangle ABC$ using a scale factor of $k = \dfrac{DE}{AB}$ and center A. The image of $\triangle ABC$ is $\triangle AB'C'$.

Because a dilation is a similarity transformation, $\triangle ABC \sim \triangle AB'C'$. Because the ratio of corresponding lengths of similar polygons equals the scale factor, $\dfrac{AB'}{AB} = \dfrac{DE}{AB}$. Multiplying each side by AB yields $AB' = DE$. By the definition of congruent segments, $\overline{AB'} \cong \overline{DE}$.

By the Reflexive Property of Congruence, $\angle A \cong \angle A$. Because corresponding angles of similar polygons are congruent, $\angle B' \cong \angle B$. Because $\angle B' \cong \angle B$ and $\angle B \cong \angle E$, $\angle B' \cong \angle E$ by the Transitive Property of Congruence.

Because $\angle A \cong \angle D$, $\angle B' \cong \angle E$, and $\overline{AB'} \cong \overline{DE}$, $\triangle AB'C' \cong \triangle DEF$ by the ASA Congruence Theorem. So, a composition of rigid motions maps $\triangle AB'C'$ to $\triangle DEF$.

Because a dilation followed by a composition of rigid motions maps $\triangle ABC$ to $\triangle DEF$, $\triangle ABC \sim \triangle DEF$.

EXAMPLE 1 **Using the AA Similarity Theorem**

Determine whether the triangles are similar. If they are, write a similarity statement. Explain your reasoning.

SOLUTION

Because they are both right angles, ∠D and ∠G are congruent.

By the Triangle Sum Theorem, 26° + 90° + m∠E = 180°, so m∠E = 64°. So, ∠E and ∠H are congruent.

▶ So, △CDE ~ △KGH by the AA Similarity Theorem.

EXAMPLE 2 **Using the AA Similarity Theorem**

Show that the two triangles are similar.

a. △ABE ~ △ACD

b. △SVR ~ △UVT

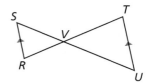

SOLUTION

a. Because m∠ABE and m∠C both equal 52°, ∠ABE ≅ ∠C. By the Reflexive Property of Congruence, ∠A ≅ ∠A.

▶ So, △ABE ~ △ACD by the AA Similarity Theorem.

b. You know ∠SVR ≅ ∠UVT by the Vertical Angles Congruence Theorem. The diagram shows $\overline{RS} \parallel \overline{UT}$, so ∠S ≅ ∠U by the Alternate Interior Angles Theorem.

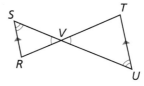

▶ So, △SVR ~ △UVT by the AA Similarity Theorem.

Monitoring Progress ◄)) Help in English and Spanish at *BigIdeasMath.com*

Show that the triangles are similar. Write a similarity statement.

1. △FGH and △RQS

2. △CDF and △DEF

3. WHAT IF? Suppose that $\overline{SR} \nparallel \overline{TU}$ in Example 2 part (b). Could the triangles still be similar? Explain.

VISUAL REASONING

Use colored pencils to show congruent angles. This will help you write similarity statements.

VISUAL REASONING

You may find it helpful to redraw the triangles separately.

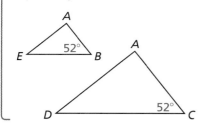

Solving Real-Life Problems

Previously, you learned a way to use congruent triangles to find measurements indirectly. Another useful way to find measurements indirectly is by using similar triangles.

EXAMPLE 3   **Modeling with Mathematics**

A flagpole casts a shadow that is 50 feet long. At the same time, a woman standing nearby who is 5 feet 4 inches tall casts a shadow that is 40 inches long. How tall is the flagpole to the nearest foot?

Not drawn to scale

SOLUTION

1. **Understand the Problem** You are given the length of a flagpole's shadow, the height of a woman, and the length of the woman's shadow. You need to find the height of the flagpole.

2. **Make a Plan** Use similar triangles to write a proportion and solve for the height of the flagpole.

3. **Solve the Problem** The flagpole and the woman form sides of two right triangles with the ground. The Sun's rays hit the flagpole and the woman at the same angle. You have two pairs of congruent angles, so the triangles are similar by the AA Similarity Theorem.

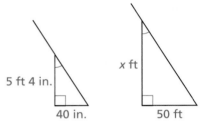

You can use a proportion to find the height *x*. Write 5 feet 4 inches as 64 inches so that you can form two ratios of feet to inches.

$$\frac{x \text{ ft}}{64 \text{ in.}} = \frac{50 \text{ ft}}{40 \text{ in.}}$$ Write proportion of side lengths.

$$40x = 3200$$ Cross Products Property

$$x = 80$$ Solve for *x*.

▶ The flagpole is 80 feet tall.

4. **Look Back** Attend to precision by checking that your answer has the correct units. The problem asks for the height of the flagpole to the nearest *foot*. Because your answer is 80 feet, the units match.

Also, check that your answer is reasonable in the context of the problem. A height of 80 feet makes sense for a flagpole. You can estimate that an eight-story building would be about 8(10 feet) = 80 feet, so it is reasonable that a flagpole could be that tall.

Monitoring Progress   Help in English and Spanish at *BigIdeasMath.com*

4. **WHAT IF?** A child who is 58 inches tall is standing next to the woman in Example 3. How long is the child's shadow?

5. You are standing outside, and you measure the lengths of the shadows cast by both you and a tree. Write a proportion showing how you could find the height of the tree.

Vocabulary and Core Concept Check

1. **COMPLETE THE SENTENCE** If two angles of one triangle are congruent to two angles of another triangle, then the triangles are _____.

2. **WRITING** Can you assume that corresponding sides and corresponding angles of any two similar triangles are congruent? Explain.

Monitoring Progress and Modeling with Mathematics

In Exercises 3–6, determine whether the triangles are similar. If they are, write a similarity statement. Explain your reasoning. *(See Example 1.)*

3.

4.

5.

6.
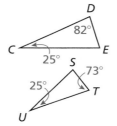

In Exercises 7–10, show that the two triangles are similar. *(See Example 2.)*

7.

8.

9.

10.

In Exercises 11–18, use the diagram to copy and complete the statement.

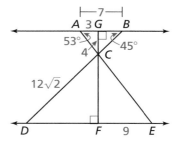

11. $\triangle CAG \sim$ ▢

12. $\triangle DCF \sim$ ▢

13. $\triangle ACB \sim$ ▢

14. $m\angle ECF =$ ▢

15. $m\angle ECD =$ ▢

16. $CF =$ ▢

17. $BC =$ ▢

18. $DE =$ ▢

19. **ERROR ANALYSIS** Describe and correct the error in using the AA Similarity Theorem.

Quadrilateral *ABCD* ~ quadrilateral *EFGH* by the AA Similarity Theorem.

20. **ERROR ANALYSIS** Describe and correct the error in finding the value of *x*.

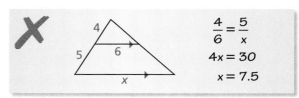

$$\frac{4}{6} = \frac{5}{x}$$

$$4x = 30$$

$$x = 7.5$$

21. MODELING WITH MATHEMATICS You can measure the width of the lake using a surveying technique, as shown in the diagram. Find the width of the lake, *WX*. Justify your answer. *(See Example 3.)*

Not drawn to scale

22. MAKING AN ARGUMENT You and your cousin are trying to determine the height of a telephone pole. Your cousin tells you to stand in the pole's shadow so that the tip of your shadow coincides with the tip of the pole's shadow. Your cousin claims to be able to use the distance between the tips of the shadows and you, the distance between you and the pole, and your height to estimate the height of the telephone pole. Is this possible? Explain. Include a diagram in your answer.

REASONING In Exercises 23–26, is it possible for △*JKL* and △*XYZ* to be similar? Explain your reasoning.

23. $m\angle J = 71°$, $m\angle K = 52°$, $m\angle X = 71°$, and $m\angle Z = 57°$

24. △*JKL* is a right triangle and $m\angle X + m\angle Y = 150°$.

25. $m\angle L = 87°$ and $m\angle Y = 94°$

26. $m\angle J + m\angle K = 85°$ and $m\angle Y + m\angle Z = 80°$

27. MATHEMATICAL CONNECTIONS Explain how you can use similar triangles to show that any two points on a line can be used to find its slope.

28. HOW DO YOU SEE IT? In the diagram, which triangles would you use to find the distance *x* between the shoreline and the buoy? Explain your reasoning.

29. WRITING Explain why all equilateral triangles are similar.

30. THOUGHT PROVOKING Decide whether each is a valid method of showing that two quadrilaterals are similar. Justify your answer.

 a. AAA   **b.** AAAA

31. PROOF Without using corresponding lengths in similar polygons, prove that the ratio of two corresponding angle bisectors in similar triangles is equal to the scale factor.

32. PROOF Prove that if the lengths of two sides of a triangle are *a* and *b*, respectively, then the lengths of the corresponding altitudes to those sides are in the ratio $\frac{b}{a}$.

33. MODELING WITH MATHEMATICS A portion of an amusement park ride is shown. Find *EF*. Justify your answer.

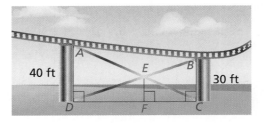

Maintaining Mathematical Proficiency
Reviewing what you learned in previous grades and lessons

Determine whether there is enough information to prove that the triangles are congruent. Explain your reasoning. *(Skills Review Handbook)*

34.

35.

36.
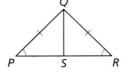

Core Vocabulary

dilation, *p. 462*

center of dilation, *p. 462*

scale factor, *p. 462*

enlargement, *p. 462*

reduction, *p. 462*

similarity transformation, *p. 470*

similar figures, *p. 470*

Core Concepts

Section 8.1

Dilations and Scale Factor, *p. 462*

Coordinate Rule for Dilations, *p. 463*

Negative Scale Factors, *p. 464*

Section 8.2

Similarity Transformations, *p. 470*

Section 8.3

Corresponding Parts of Similar Polygons, *p. 476*

Corresponding Lengths in Similar Polygons, *p. 477*

Perimeters of Similar Polygons, *p. 478*

Areas of Similar Polygons, *p. 479*

Section 8.4

Angle-Angle (AA) Similarity Theorem, *p. 486*

Mathematical Practices

1. In Exercise 35 on page 483, why is there more than one correct answer for the length of the other side?

2. In Exercise 50 on page 484, how could you find the scale factor of the similar figures? Describe any tools that might be helpful.

3. In Exercise 21 on page 490, explain why the surveyor needs V, X, and Y to be collinear and Z, X, and W to be collinear.

Analyzing Your Errors

STUDY SKILLS

Misreading Directions

• **What Happens:** You incorrectly read or do not understand directions.

• **How to Avoid This Error:** Read the instructions for exercises at least twice and make sure you understand what they mean. Make this a habit and use it when taking tests.

Graph the triangle and its image after a dilation with scale factor k. *(Section 8.1)*

1. $A(3, 6)$, $B(3, 9)$, $C(6, 3)$; $k = \frac{2}{3}$

2. $D(-2, -1)$, $E(3, 1)$, $F(1, -3)$; $k = -2$

3. $M(-4, -2)$, $N(8, 6)$, $P(4, -4)$; $k = 0.5$

4. $Q(-3, -2)$, $R(-4, 3)$, $S(2, -4)$; $k = 300\%$

Describe a similarity transformation that maps $\triangle JKL$ to $\triangle MNP$. *(Section 8.2)*

5. $J(2, 1)$, $K(-3, -2)$, $L(1, -3)$ and $M(6, 4)$, $N(-4, -2)$, $P(4, -4)$

6. $J(6, 2)$, $K(-4, 2)$, $L(-6, 4)$ and $M(-3, 1)$, $N(2, 1)$, $P(3, 2)$

List all pairs of congruent angles. Then write the ratios of the corresponding side lengths in a statement of proportionality. *(Section 8.3)*

7. $\triangle BDG \sim \triangle MPQ$

8. $DEFG \sim HJKL$

The polygons are similar. Find the value of x. *(Section 8.3)*

9.

10.

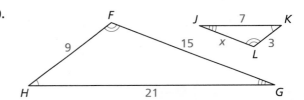

Show that the two triangles are similar. *(Section 8.4)*

11.

12.

13.

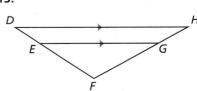

14. The dimensions of an official hockey rink used by the National Hockey League (NHL) are 200 feet by 85 feet. The dimensions of an air hockey table are 96 inches by 40.8 inches. Assume corresponding angles are congruent. *(Section 8.3)*

   a. Determine whether the two surfaces are similar.

   b. If the surfaces are similar, find the ratio of their perimeters and the ratio of their areas. If not, find the dimensions of an air hockey table that are similar to an NHL hockey rink.

15. You and a friend buy camping tents made by the same company but in different sizes and colors. Use the information given in the diagram to decide whether the triangular faces of the tents are similar. Explain your reasoning. *(Section 8.4)*

Proving Triangle Similarity by SSS and SAS

Essential Question What are two ways to use corresponding sides of two triangles to determine that the triangles are similar?

EXPLORATION 1 Deciding Whether Triangles Are Similar

Work with a partner. Use dynamic geometry software.

a. Construct △ABC and △DEF with the side lengths given in column 1 of the table below.

	1.	2.	3.	4.	5.	6.	7.
AB	5	5	6	15	9	24	
BC	8	8	8	20	12	18	
AC	10	10	10	10	8	16	
DE	10	15	9	12	12	8	
EF	16	24	12	16	15	6	
DF	20	30	15	8	10	8	
m∠A							
m∠B							
m∠C							
m∠D							
m∠E							
m∠F							

CONSTRUCTING VIABLE ARGUMENTS

To be proficient in math, you need to analyze situations by breaking them into cases and recognize and use counterexamples.

b. Copy the table and complete column 1.

c. Are the triangles similar? Explain your reasoning.

d. Repeat parts (a)–(c) for columns 2–6 in the table.

e. How are the corresponding side lengths related in each pair of triangles that are similar? Is this true for each pair of triangles that are not similar?

f. Make a conjecture about the similarity of two triangles based on their corresponding side lengths.

g. Use your conjecture to write another set of side lengths of two similar triangles. Use the side lengths to complete column 7 of the table.

EXPLORATION 2 Deciding Whether Triangles Are Similar

Work with a partner. Use dynamic geometry software. Construct any △ABC.

a. Find AB, AC, and m∠A. Choose any positive rational number k and construct △DEF so that DE = k • AB, DF = k • AC, and m∠D = m∠A.

b. Is △DEF similar to △ABC? Explain your reasoning.

c. Repeat parts (a) and (b) several times by changing △ABC and k. Describe your results.

Communicate Your Answer

3. What are two ways to use corresponding sides of two triangles to determine that the triangles are similar?

What You Will Learn

▶ Use the Side-Side-Side Similarity Theorem.
▶ Use the Side-Angle-Side Similarity Theorem.

Using the Side-Side-Side Similarity Theorem

In addition to using congruent corresponding angles to show that two triangles are similar, you can use proportional corresponding side lengths.

🌀 Theorem

Side-Side-Side (SSS) Similarity Theorem

If the corresponding side lengths of two triangles are proportional, then the triangles are similar.

If $\dfrac{AB}{RS} = \dfrac{BC}{ST} = \dfrac{CA}{TR}$, then $\triangle ABC \sim \triangle RST$.

Proof p. 495

EXAMPLE 1 Using the SSS Similarity Theorem

Is either $\triangle DEF$ or $\triangle GHJ$ similar to $\triangle ABC$?

FINDING AN
ENTRY POINT

When using the SSS Similarity Theorem, compare the shortest sides, the longest sides, and then the remaining sides.

SOLUTION

Compare $\triangle ABC$ and $\triangle DEF$ by finding ratios of corresponding side lengths.

Shortest sides	Longest sides	Remaining sides
$\dfrac{AB}{DE} = \dfrac{8}{6}$	$\dfrac{CA}{FD} = \dfrac{16}{12}$	$\dfrac{BC}{EF} = \dfrac{12}{9}$
$= \dfrac{4}{3}$	$= \dfrac{4}{3}$	$= \dfrac{4}{3}$

▶ All the ratios are equal, so $\triangle ABC \sim \triangle DEF$.

Compare $\triangle ABC$ and $\triangle GHJ$ by finding ratios of corresponding side lengths.

Shortest sides	Longest sides	Remaining sides
$\dfrac{AB}{GH} = \dfrac{8}{8}$	$\dfrac{CA}{JG} = \dfrac{16}{16}$	$\dfrac{BC}{HJ} = \dfrac{12}{10}$
$= 1$	$= 1$	$= \dfrac{6}{5}$

▶ The ratios are not all equal, so $\triangle ABC$ and $\triangle GHJ$ are not similar.

PROOF **SSS Similarity Theorem**

Given $\dfrac{RS}{JK} = \dfrac{ST}{KL} = \dfrac{TR}{LJ}$

Prove $\triangle RST \sim \triangle JKL$

JUSTIFYING STEPS

The Parallel Postulate allows you to draw an auxiliary line $\overleftrightarrow{PQ}$ in $\triangle RST$. There is only one line through point P parallel to $\overleftrightarrow{RT}$, so you are able to draw it.

Locate P on $\overline{RS}$ so that $PS = JK$. Draw $\overline{PQ}$ so that $\overline{PQ} \parallel \overline{RT}$. Then $\triangle RST \sim \triangle PSQ$ by the AA Similarity Theorem, and $\dfrac{RS}{PS} = \dfrac{ST}{SQ} = \dfrac{TR}{QP}$. You can use the given proportion and the fact that $PS = JK$ to deduce that $SQ = KL$ and $QP = LJ$. By the SSS Congruence Theorem, it follows that $\triangle PSQ \cong \triangle JKL$. Finally, use the definition of congruent triangles and the AA Similarity Theorem to conclude that $\triangle RST \sim \triangle JKL$.

EXAMPLE 2 **Using the SSS Similarity Theorem**

Find the value of x that makes $\triangle ABC \sim \triangle DEF$.

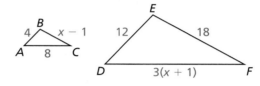

FINDING AN ENTRY POINT

You can use either $\dfrac{AB}{DE} = \dfrac{BC}{EF}$ or $\dfrac{AB}{DE} = \dfrac{AC}{DF}$ in Step 1.

SOLUTION

Step 1 Find the value of x that makes corresponding side lengths proportional.

$\dfrac{AB}{DE} = \dfrac{BC}{EF}$ Write proportion.

$\dfrac{4}{12} = \dfrac{x-1}{18}$ Substitute.

$4 \cdot 18 = 12(x - 1)$ Cross Products Property

$72 = 12x - 12$ Simplify.

$7 = x$ Solve for x.

Step 2 Check that the side lengths are proportional when $x = 7$.

$BC = x - 1 = 6$ $DF = 3(x + 1) = 24$

$\dfrac{AB}{DE} \overset{?}{=} \dfrac{BC}{EF} \implies \dfrac{4}{12} = \dfrac{6}{18}$ ✓ $\dfrac{AB}{DE} \overset{?}{=} \dfrac{AC}{DF} \implies \dfrac{4}{12} = \dfrac{8}{24}$ ✓

▶ When $x = 7$, the triangles are similar by the SSS Similarity Theorem.

Monitoring Progress Help in English and Spanish at *BigIdeasMath.com*

Use the diagram.

1. Which of the three triangles are similar? Write a similarity statement.

2. The shortest side of a triangle similar to $\triangle RST$ is 12 units long. Find the other side lengths of the triangle.

Using the Side-Angle-Side Similarity Theorem

Theorem

Side-Angle-Side (SAS) Similarity Theorem

If an angle of one triangle is congruent to an angle of a second triangle and the lengths of the sides including these angles are proportional, then the triangles are similar.

If $\angle X \cong \angle M$ and $\dfrac{ZX}{PM} = \dfrac{XY}{MN}$, then $\triangle XYZ \sim \triangle MNP$.

Proof Ex. 19, p. 498

EXAMPLE 3 Using the SAS Similarity Theorem

You are building a lean-to shelter starting from a tree branch, as shown. Can you construct the right end so it is similar to the left end using the angle measure and lengths shown?

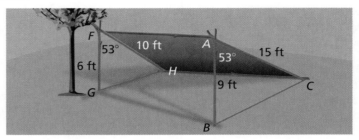

SOLUTION

Both $m\angle A$ and $m\angle F$ equal 53°, so $\angle A \cong \angle F$. Next, compare the ratios of the lengths of the sides that include $\angle A$ and $\angle F$.

Shorter sides	Longer sides
$\dfrac{AB}{FG} = \dfrac{9}{6}$	$\dfrac{AC}{FH} = \dfrac{15}{10}$
$= \dfrac{3}{2}$	$= \dfrac{3}{2}$

The lengths of the sides that include $\angle A$ and $\angle F$ are proportional. So, by the SAS Similarity Theorem, $\triangle ABC \sim \triangle FGH$.

▶ Yes, you can make the right end similar to the left end of the shelter.

Monitoring Progress Help in English and Spanish at *BigIdeasMath.com*

Explain how to show that the indicated triangles are similar.

3. $\triangle SRT \sim \triangle PNQ$

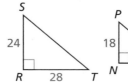

4. $\triangle XZW \sim \triangle YZX$

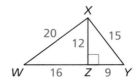

---

496 **Chapter 8** Similarity

Vocabulary and Core Concept Check

1. **COMPLETE THE SENTENCE** You plan to show that $\triangle QRS$ is similar to $\triangle XYZ$ by the SSS Similarity Theorem.

   Copy and complete the proportion that you will use: $\dfrac{QR}{} = \dfrac{}{YZ} = \dfrac{QS}{}$.

2. **WHICH ONE DOESN'T BELONG?** Which triangle does *not* belong with the other three? Explain your reasoning.

   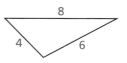

Monitoring Progress and Modeling with Mathematics

In Exercises 3 and 4, determine whether $\triangle JKL$ or $\triangle RST$ is similar to $\triangle ABC$. *(See Example 1.)*

3.

4.

In Exercises 5 and 6, find the value of x that makes $\triangle DEF \sim \triangle XYZ$. *(See Example 2.)*

5.

6.

In Exercises 7 and 8, verify that $\triangle ABC \sim \triangle DEF$. Find the scale factor of $\triangle ABC$ to $\triangle DEF$.

7. $\triangle ABC$: $BC = 18$, $AB = 15$, $AC = 12$
   $\triangle DEF$: $EF = 12$, $DE = 10$, $DF = 8$

8. $\triangle ABC$: $AB = 10$, $BC = 16$, $CA = 20$
   $\triangle DEF$: $DE = 25$, $EF = 40$, $FD = 50$

In Exercises 9 and 10, determine whether the two triangles are similar. If they are similar, write a similarity statement and find the scale factor of triangle B to triangle A. *(See Example 3.)*

9.

10.

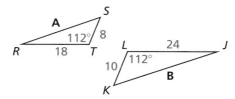

In Exercises 11 and 12, sketch the triangles using the given description. Then determine whether the two triangles can be similar.

11. In $\triangle RST$, $RS = 20$, $ST = 32$, and $m\angle S = 16°$. In $\triangle FGH$, $GH = 30$, $HF = 48$, and $m\angle H = 24°$.

12. The side lengths of $\triangle ABC$ are 24, $8x$, and 48, and the side lengths of $\triangle DEF$ are 15, 25, and $6x$.

13. ERROR ANALYSIS Describe and correct the error in writing a similarity statement.

△ABC ~ △PQR by the SAS Similarity Theorem.

14. MATHEMATICAL CONNECTIONS Find the value of n that makes △DEF ~ △XYZ when $DE = 4$, $EF = 5$, $XY = 4(n + 1)$, $YZ = 7n - 1$, and $\angle E \cong \angle Y$. Include a sketch.

15. MAKING AN ARGUMENT Your friend claims that △JKL ~ △MNO by the SAS Similarity Theorem when $JK = 18$, $m\angle K = 130°$, $KL = 16$, $MN = 9$, $m\angle N = 65°$, and $NO = 8$. Do you support your friend's claim? Explain your reasoning.

16. ANALYZING RELATIONSHIPS Certain sections of stained glass are sold in triangular, beveled pieces. Which of the three beveled pieces, if any, are similar?

17. ATTENDING TO PRECISION In the diagram, $\dfrac{MN}{MR} = \dfrac{MP}{MQ}$. Which of the statements must be true? Select all that apply. Explain your reasoning.

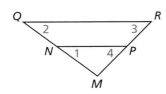

Ⓐ $\angle 1 \cong \angle 2$ Ⓑ $\overline{QR} \parallel \overline{NP}$

Ⓒ $\angle 1 \cong \angle 4$ Ⓓ △MNP ~ △MRQ

18. WRITING Are any two right triangles similar? Explain.

19. PROVING A THEOREM Write a two-column proof of the SAS Similarity Theorem.

Given $\angle A \cong \angle D$, $\dfrac{AB}{DE} = \dfrac{AC}{DF}$

Prove △ABC ~ △DEF

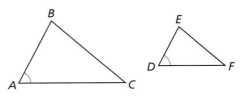

20. HOW DO YOU SEE IT? Which theorem could you use to show that △OPQ ~ △OMN in the portion of the Ferris wheel shown when $PM = QN = 5$ feet and $MO = NO = 10$ feet?

21. DRAWING CONCLUSIONS Explain why it is not necessary to have an Angle-Side-Angle Similarity Theorem.

22. THOUGHT PROVOKING Decide whether each is a valid method of showing that two quadrilaterals are similar. Justify your answer.

a. SASA b. SASAS c. SSSS d. SASSS

23. WRITING Can two triangles have all three ratios of corresponding angle measures equal to a value greater than 1? less than 1? Explain.

24. MULTIPLE REPRESENTATIONS Use a diagram to show why there is no Side-Side-Angle Similarity Theorem.

Maintaining Mathematical Proficiency Reviewing what you learned in previous grades and lessons

Find the slope of the line that passes through the given points. (*Skills Review Handbook*)

25. $(-3, 6)$, $(2, 1)$ **26.** $(-3, -5)$, $(9, -1)$ **27.** $(1, -2)$, $(8, 12)$

Essential Question What proportionality relationships exist in a triangle intersected by an angle bisector or by a line parallel to one of the sides?

Discovering a Proportionality Relationship

Work with a partner. Use dynamic geometry software to draw any △ABC.

a. Construct $\overline{DE}$ parallel to $\overline{BC}$ with endpoints on $\overline{AB}$ and $\overline{AC}$, respectively.

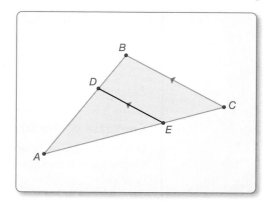

LOOKING FOR STRUCTURE

To be proficient in math, you need to look closely to discern a pattern or structure.

b. Compare the ratios of AD to BD and AE to CE.

c. Move $\overline{DE}$ to other locations parallel to $\overline{BC}$ with endpoints on $\overline{AB}$ and $\overline{AC}$, and repeat part (b).

d. Change △ABC and repeat parts (a)–(c) several times. Write a conjecture that summarizes your results.

Discovering a Proportionality Relationship

Work with a partner. Use dynamic geometry software to draw any △ABC.

a. Bisect ∠B and plot point D at the intersection of the angle bisector and $\overline{AC}$.

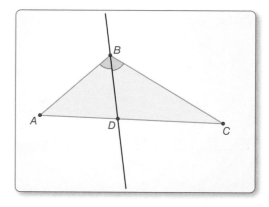

b. Compare the ratios of AD to DC and BA to BC.

c. Change △ABC and repeat parts (a) and (b) several times. Write a conjecture that summarizes your results.

Communicate Your Answer

3. What proportionality relationships exist in a triangle intersected by an angle bisector or by a line parallel to one of the sides?

4. Use the figure at the right to write a proportion.

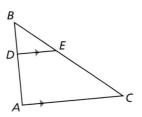

What You Will Learn

▶ Use proportionality theorems.

▶ Partition directed line segments.

Core Vocabulary

directed line segment, *p. 502*

Previous
corresponding angles
ratio
proportion

Using Proportionality Theorems

⟳ Theorems

Triangle Proportionality Theorem

If a line parallel to one side of a triangle intersects the other two sides, then it divides the two sides proportionally.

If $\overline{TU} \parallel \overline{QS}$, then $\dfrac{RT}{TQ} = \dfrac{RU}{US}$.

Proof Ex. 27, p. 505

Converse of the Triangle Proportionality Theorem

If a line divides two sides of a triangle proportionally, then it is parallel to the third side.

If $\dfrac{RT}{TQ} = \dfrac{RU}{US}$, then $\overline{TU} \parallel \overline{QS}$.

Proof Ex. 28, p. 505

EXAMPLE 1   Finding the Length of a Segment

In the diagram, $\overline{QS} \parallel \overline{UT}$, $RS = 4$, $ST = 6$, and $QU = 9$. What is the length of $\overline{RQ}$?

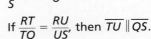

SOLUTION

$\dfrac{RQ}{QU} = \dfrac{RS}{ST}$ Triangle Proportionality Theorem

$\dfrac{RQ}{9} = \dfrac{4}{6}$ Substitute.

$RQ = 6$ Multiply each side by 9 and simplify.

▶ The length of $\overline{RQ}$ is 6 units.

Monitoring Progress   ◀)) Help in English and Spanish at *BigIdeasMath.com*

1. Find the length of $\overline{YZ}$.

The theorems above also imply the following:

Contrapositive of the Triangle Proportionality Theorem	**Inverse of the Triangle Proportionality Theorem**
If $\dfrac{RT}{TQ} \neq \dfrac{RU}{US}$, then $\overline{TU} \nparallel \overline{QS}$.	If $\overline{TU} \nparallel \overline{QS}$, then $\dfrac{RT}{TQ} \neq \dfrac{RU}{US}$.

EXAMPLE 2 **Solving a Real-Life Problem**

On the shoe rack shown, $BA = 33$ centimeters, $CB = 27$ centimeters, $CD = 44$ centimeters, and $DE = 25$ centimeters. Explain why the shelf is not parallel to the floor.

SOLUTION

Find and simplify the ratios of the lengths.

$$\frac{CD}{DE} = \frac{44}{25} \qquad\qquad \frac{CB}{BA} = \frac{27}{33} = \frac{9}{11}$$

▶ Because $\frac{44}{25} \neq \frac{9}{11}$, $\overline{BD}$ is not parallel to $\overline{AE}$. So, the shelf is not parallel to the floor.

Monitoring Progress Help in English and Spanish at *BigIdeasMath.com*

2. Determine whether $\overline{PS} \parallel \overline{QR}$.

🌀 Theorem

Three Parallel Lines Theorem

If three parallel lines intersect two transversals, then they divide the transversals proportionally.

Proof Ex. 32, p. 505

$$\frac{UW}{WY} = \frac{VX}{XZ}$$

EXAMPLE 3 **Using the Three Parallel Lines Theorem**

In the diagram, $\angle 1$, $\angle 2$, and $\angle 3$ are all congruent, $GF = 120$ yards, $DE = 150$ yards, and $CD = 300$ yards. Find the distance HF between Main Street and South Main Street.

SOLUTION

Corresponding angles are congruent, so $\overleftrightarrow{FE}$, $\overleftrightarrow{GD}$, and $\overleftrightarrow{HC}$ are parallel.

Use the Three Parallel Lines Theorem to set up a proportion.

$$\frac{HG}{GF} = \frac{CD}{DE} \qquad \text{Three Parallel Lines Theorem}$$

$$\frac{HG}{120} = \frac{300}{150} \qquad \text{Substitute.}$$

$$HG = 240 \qquad \text{Multiply each side by 120 and simplify.}$$

By the Segment Addition Postulate, $HF = HG + GF = 240 + 120 = 360$.

▶ The distance between Main Street and South Main Street is 360 yards.

Theorem

Triangle Angle Bisector Theorem

If a ray bisects an angle of a triangle, then it divides the opposite side into segments whose lengths are proportional to the lengths of the other two sides.

Proof Ex. 35, p. 506

$$\frac{AD}{DB} = \frac{CA}{CB}$$

EXAMPLE 4 **Using the Triangle Angle Bisector Theorem**

In the diagram, $\angle QPR \cong \angle RPS$. Use the given side lengths to find the length of $\overline{RS}$.

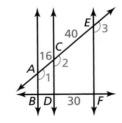

SOLUTION

Because $\overrightarrow{PR}$ is an angle bisector of $\angle QPS$, you can apply the Triangle Angle Bisector Theorem. Let $RS = x$. Then $RQ = 15 - x$.

$\dfrac{RQ}{RS} = \dfrac{PQ}{PS}$	Triangle Angle Bisector Theorem
$\dfrac{15 - x}{x} = \dfrac{7}{13}$	Substitute.
$195 - 13x = 7x$	Cross Products Property
$9.75 = x$	Solve for x.

▶ The length of $\overline{RS}$ is 9.75 units.

Monitoring Progress
Help in English and Spanish at *BigIdeasMath.com*

Find the length of the given line segment.

3. $\overline{BD}$

4. $\overline{JM}$

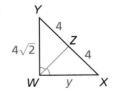

Find the value of the variable.

5.

6.

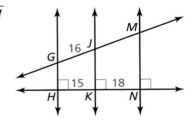

Partitioning a Directed Line Segment

A **directed line segment** AB is a segment that represents moving from point A to point B. The following example shows how to use slope to find a point on a directed line segment that partitions the segment in a given ratio.

EXAMPLE 5   **Partitioning a Directed Line Segment**

Find the coordinates of point P along the directed line segment AB so that the ratio of AP to PB is 3 to 2.

SOLUTION

In order to divide the segment in the ratio 3 to 2, think of dividing, or *partitioning*, the segment into $3 + 2$, or 5 congruent pieces. Point P is the point that is $\frac{3}{5}$ of the way from point A to point B.

Find the rise and run from point A to point B. Leave the slope in terms of rise and run and do not simplify.

$$\text{slope of } \overline{AB}:\ m = \frac{8-2}{6-3} = \frac{6}{3} = \frac{\text{rise}}{\text{run}}$$

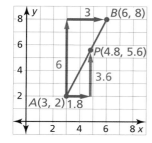

To find the coordinates of point P, add $\frac{3}{5}$ of the run to the x-coordinate of A, and add $\frac{3}{5}$ of the rise to the y-coordinate of A.

$$\text{run: } \frac{3}{5} \text{ of } 3 = \frac{3}{5} \cdot 3 = 1.8 \qquad \text{rise: } \frac{3}{5} \text{ of } 6 = \frac{3}{5} \cdot 6 = 3.6$$

So, the coordinates of P are $(3 + 1.8, 2 + 3.6) = (4.8, 5.6)$. The ratio of AP to PB is 3 to 2.

Monitoring Progress Help in English and Spanish at *BigIdeasMath.com*

Find the coordinates of point P along the directed line segment AB so that AP to PB is the given ratio.

7. $A(1, 3)$, $B(8, 4)$; 4 to 1

8. $A(-2, 1)$, $B(4, 5)$; 3 to 7

You can apply the Triangle Proportionality Theorem to construct a point along a directed line segment that partitions the segment in a given ratio.

CONSTRUCTION   **Constructing a Point along a Directed Line Segment**

Construct the point L on $\overline{AB}$ so that the ratio of AL to LB is 3 to 1.

SOLUTION

Step 1	Step 2	Step 3
		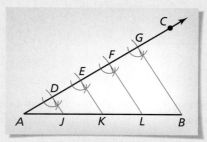
Draw a segment and a ray Draw $\overleftrightarrow{AB}$ of any length. Choose any point C not on $\overleftrightarrow{AB}$. Draw $\overrightarrow{AC}$.	**Draw arcs** Place the point of a compass at A and make an arc of any radius intersecting $\overrightarrow{AC}$. Label the point of intersection D. Using the same compass setting, make three more arcs on $\overrightarrow{AC}$, as shown. Label the points of intersection E, F, and G and note that $AD = DE = EF = FG$.	**Draw a segment** Draw $\overline{GB}$. Copy $\angle AGB$ and construct congruent angles at D, E, and F with sides that intersect $\overline{AB}$ at J, K, and L. Sides $\overline{DJ}$, $\overline{EK}$, and $\overline{FL}$ are all parallel, and they divide $\overline{AB}$ equally. So, $AJ = JK = KL = LB$. Point L divides directed line segment AB in the ratio 3 to 1.

Vocabulary and Core Concept Check

1. **COMPLETE THE STATEMENT** If a line divides two sides of a triangle proportionally, then it is _____ to the third side. This theorem is known as the _____.

2. **VOCABULARY** In $\triangle ABC$, point R lies on $\overline{BC}$ and $\overrightarrow{AR}$ bisects $\angle CAB$. Write the proportionality statement for the triangle that is based on the Triangle Angle Bisector Theorem.

Monitoring Progress and Modeling with Mathematics

In Exercises 3 and 4, find the length of $\overline{AB}$. *(See Example 1.)*

3.

4.
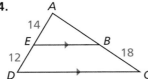

In Exercises 5–8, determine whether $\overline{KM} \parallel \overline{JN}$. *(See Example 2.)*

5.

6.

7.

8.

In Exercises 9 and 10, use the diagram to complete the proportion.

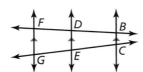

9. $\dfrac{BD}{BF} = \dfrac{\rule{0.6cm}{0.3cm}}{CG}$

10. $\dfrac{CG}{\rule{0.6cm}{0.3cm}} = \dfrac{BF}{DF}$

In Exercises 11 and 12, find the length of the indicated line segment. *(See Example 3.)*

11. $\overline{VX}$

12. $\overline{SU}$

In Exercises 13–16, find the value of the variable. *(See Example 4.)*

13.

14.

15.

16.

In Exercises 17–20, find the coordinates of point P along the directed line segment AB so that AP to PB is the given ratio. *(See Example 5.)*

17. $A(8, 0)$, $B(3, -2)$; 1 to 4

18. $A(-2, -4)$, $B(6, 1)$; 3 to 2

19. $A(1, 6)$, $B(-2, -3)$; 5 to 1

20. $A(-3, 2)$, $B(5, -4)$; 2 to 6

CONSTRUCTION In Exercises 21 and 22, draw a segment with the given length. Construct the point that divides the segment in the given ratio.

21. 3 in.; 1 to 4

22. 2 in.; 2 to 3

23. ERROR ANALYSIS Describe and correct the error in solving for x.

$$\frac{AB}{BC} = \frac{CD}{AD} \Rightarrow \frac{10}{16} = \frac{14}{x}$$
$$10x = 224$$
$$x = 22.4$$

24. ERROR ANALYSIS Describe and correct the error in the student's reasoning.

Because $\dfrac{BD}{CD} = \dfrac{AB}{AC}$ and $BD = CD$, it follows that $AB = AC$.

MATHEMATICAL CONNECTIONS In Exercises 25 and 26, find the value of x for which $\overline{PQ} \parallel \overline{RS}$.

25.

26.

27. PROVING A THEOREM Prove the Triangle Proportionality Theorem.

Given $\overline{QS} \parallel \overline{TU}$

Prove $\dfrac{QT}{TR} = \dfrac{SU}{UR}$

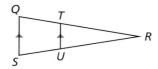

28. PROVING A THEOREM Prove the Converse of the Triangle Proportionality Theorem.

Given $\dfrac{ZY}{YW} = \dfrac{ZX}{XV}$

Prove $\overline{YX} \parallel \overline{WV}$

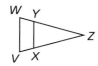

29. MODELING WITH MATHEMATICS The real estate term *lake frontage* refers to the distance along the edge of a piece of property that touches a lake.

a. Find the lake frontage (to the nearest tenth) of each lot shown.

b. In general, the more lake frontage a lot has, the higher its selling price. Which lot(s) should be listed for the highest price?

c. Suppose that lot prices are in the same ratio as lake frontages. If the least expensive lot is $250,000, what are the prices of the other lots? Explain your reasoning.

30. MODELING WITH MATHEMATICS Your school lies directly between your house and the movie theater. The distance from your house to the school is one-fourth of the distance from the school to the movie theater. What point on the graph represents your school?

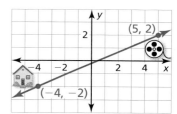

31. REASONING In the construction on page 503, explain why you can apply the Triangle Proportionality Theorem in Step 3.

32. PROVING A THEOREM Use the diagram with the auxiliary line drawn to write a paragraph proof of the Three Parallel Lines Theorem.

Given $k_1 \parallel k_2 \parallel k_3$

Prove $\dfrac{CB}{BA} = \dfrac{DE}{EF}$

33. CRITICAL THINKING In $\triangle LMN$, the angle bisector of $\angle M$ also bisects $\overline{LN}$. Classify $\triangle LMN$ as specifically as possible. Justify your answer.

34. HOW DO YOU SEE IT? During a football game, the quarterback throws the ball to the receiver. The receiver is between two defensive players, as shown. If Player 1 is closer to the quarterback when the ball is thrown and both defensive players move at the same speed, which player will reach the receiver first? Explain your reasoning.

35. PROVING A THEOREM Use the diagram with the auxiliary lines drawn to write a paragraph proof of the Triangle Angle Bisector Theorem.

Given $\angle YXW \cong \angle WXZ$

Prove $\dfrac{YW}{WZ} = \dfrac{XY}{XZ}$

auxiliary lines

36. THOUGHT PROVOKING Write the converse of the Triangle Angle Bisector Theorem. Is the converse true? Justify your answer.

37. REASONING How is the Triangle Midsegment Theorem related to the Triangle Proportionality Theorem? Explain your reasoning.

38. MAKING AN ARGUMENT Two people leave points A and B at the same time. They intend to meet at point C at the same time. The person who leaves point A walks at a speed of 3 miles per hour. You and a friend are trying to determine how fast the person who leaves point B must walk. Your friend claims you need to know the length of $\overline{AC}$. Is your friend correct? Explain your reasoning.

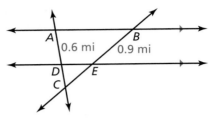

39. CONSTRUCTION Given segments with lengths r, s, and t, construct a segment of length x, such that $\dfrac{r}{s} = \dfrac{t}{x}$.

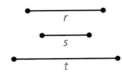

40. PROOF Prove *Ceva's Theorem*: If P is any point inside $\triangle ABC$, then $\dfrac{AY}{YC} \cdot \dfrac{CX}{XB} \cdot \dfrac{BZ}{ZA} = 1$.

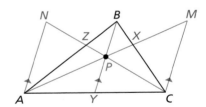

(*Hint*: Draw segments parallel to $\overline{BY}$ through A and C, as shown. Apply the Triangle Proportionality Theorem to $\triangle ACM$. Show that $\triangle APN \sim \triangle MPC$, $\triangle CXM \sim \triangle BXP$, and $\triangle BZP \sim \triangle AZN$.)

Maintaining Mathematical Proficiency
Reviewing what you learned in previous grades and lessons

Use the triangle. *(Skills Review Handbook)*

41. Which sides are the legs?

42. Which side is the hypotenuse?

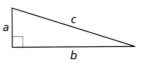

Solve the equation. *(Section 4.3)*

43. $x^2 = 121$

44. $x^2 + 16 = 25$

45. $36 + x^2 = 85$

Core Vocabulary

directed line segment, *p. 502*

Core Concepts

Section 8.5

Side-Side-Side (SSS) Similarity Theorem, *p. 494*
Side-Angle-Side (SAS) Similarity Theorem, *p. 496*

Section 8.6

Triangle Proportionality Theorem, *p. 500*
Converse of the Triangle Proportionality Theorem, *p. 500*
Three Parallel Lines Theorem, *p. 501*
Triangle Angle Bisector Theorem, *p. 502*
Partitioning a Directed Line Segment, *p. 503*

Mathematical Practices

1. In Exercise 16 on page 498, why do you only need to find two ratios instead of three to compare the side lengths of a pair of triangles?

2. In Exercise 4 on page 504, is it better to use $\frac{7}{6}$ or 1.17 as your ratio of the lengths when finding the length of $\overline{AB}$? Explain your reasoning.

3. In Exercise 30 on page 505, a classmate tells you that your answer is incorrect because you should have divided the segment into four congruent pieces. Respond to your classmate's argument by justifying your original answer.

Performance Task:

Pool Maintenance

Your pool service company has been very successful at maintaining rectangular pools designed for regulation competitions. Now you want to expand your services to owners of private, recreational pools. How will your experience transfer to pools of various shapes and sizes?

To explore the answer to this question and more, check out the Performance Task and Real-Life STEM video at *BigIdeasMath.com*.

8.1 Dilations *(pp. 461–468)*

Graph trapezoid *ABCD* with vertices *A*(1, 1), *B*(1, 3), *C*(3, 2), and *D*(3, 1) and its image after a dilation with a scale factor of 2.

Use the coordinate rule for a dilation with $k = 2$ to find the coordinates of the vertices of the image. Then graph trapezoid *ABCD* and its image.

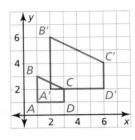

$$(x, y) \rightarrow (2x, 2y)$$

$A(1, 1) \rightarrow A'(2, 2)$

$B(1, 3) \rightarrow B'(2, 6)$

$C(3, 2) \rightarrow C'(6, 4)$

$D(3, 1) \rightarrow D'(6, 2)$

Graph the triangle and its image after a dilation with scale factor *k*.

1. $P(2, 2), Q(4, 4), R(8, 2); k = \frac{1}{2}$

2. $X(-3, 2), Y(2, 3), Z(1, -1); k = -3$

3. You are using a magnifying glass that shows the image of an object that is eight times the object's actual size. The image length is 15.2 centimeters. Find the actual length of the object.

8.2 Similarity and Transformations *(pp. 469–474)*

Describe a similarity transformation that maps △*FGH* to △*LMN*, as shown at the right.

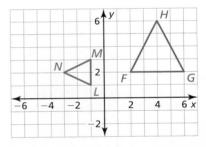

$\overline{FG}$ is horizontal, and $\overline{LM}$ is vertical. If you rotate △*FGH* 90° about the origin as shown at the bottom right, then the image, △*F'G'H'*, will have the same orientation as △*LMN*. △*LMN* appears to be half as large as △*F'G'H'*. Dilate △*F'G'H'* using a scale factor of $\frac{1}{2}$.

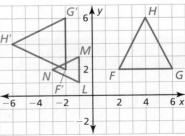

$$(x, y) \rightarrow \left(\tfrac{1}{2}x, \tfrac{1}{2}y\right)$$

$F'(-2, 2) \rightarrow F''(-1, 1)$

$G'(-2, 6) \rightarrow G''(-1, 3)$

$H'(-6, 4) \rightarrow H''(-3, 2)$

The vertices of △*F''G''H''* match the vertices of △*LMN*.

▶ So, a similarity transformation that maps △*FGH* to △*LMN* is a rotation of 90° about the origin followed by a dilation with a scale factor of $\frac{1}{2}$.

Describe a similarity transformation that maps △*ABC* to △*RST*.

4. $A(1, 0), B(-2, -1), C(-1, -2)$ and $R(-3, 0), S(6, -3), T(3, -6)$

5. $A(6, 4), B(-2, 0), C(-4, 2)$ and $R(2, 3), S(0, -1), T(1, -2)$

6. $A(3, -2), B(0, 4), C(-1, -3)$ and $R(-4, -6), S(8, 0), T(-6, 2)$

8.3 **Similar Polygons** *(pp. 475–484)*

In the diagram, *EHGF* ~ *KLMN*. Find the scale factor from *EHGF* to *KLMN*. Then list all pairs of congruent angles and write the ratios of the corresponding side lengths in a statement of proportionality.

From the diagram, you can see that $\overline{EH}$ and $\overline{KL}$ are corresponding sides. So, the scale factor of *EHGF* to *KLMN* is $\dfrac{KL}{EH} = \dfrac{18}{12} = \dfrac{3}{2}$.

$\angle E \cong \angle K$, $\angle H \cong \angle L$, $\angle G \cong \angle M$, and $\angle F \cong \angle N$.

$$\frac{KL}{EH} = \frac{LM}{HG} = \frac{MN}{GF} = \frac{NK}{FE}$$

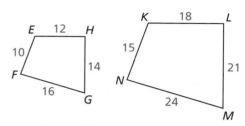

Find the scale factor. Then list all pairs of congruent angles and write the ratios of the corresponding side lengths in a statement of proportionality.

7. *ABCD* ~ *EFGH*

8. △*XYZ* ~ △*RPQ*

9. Two similar triangles have a scale factor of 3 : 5. The altitude of the larger triangle is 24 inches. What is the altitude of the smaller triangle?

10. Two similar triangles have a pair of corresponding sides of length 12 meters and 8 meters. The larger triangle has a perimeter of 48 meters and an area of 180 square meters. Find the perimeter and area of the smaller triangle.

8.4 **Proving Triangle Similarity by AA** *(pp. 485–490)*

Determine whether the triangles are similar. If they are, write a similarity statement. Explain your reasoning.

Because they are both right angles, $\angle F$ and $\angle B$ are congruent. By the Triangle Sum Theorem, $61° + 90° + m\angle E = 180°$, so $m\angle E = 29°$. So, $\angle E$ and $\angle A$ are congruent. So, △*DFE* ~ △*CBA* by the AA Similarity Theorem.

Show that the triangles are similar. Write a similarity statement.

11.

12.

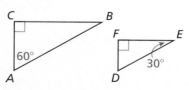

13. A cellular telephone tower casts a shadow that is 72 feet long, while a nearby tree that is 27 feet tall casts a shadow that is 6 feet long. How tall is the tower?

8.5 Proving Triangle Similarity by SSS and SAS   *(pp. 493–498)*

Show that the triangles are similar.

Compare △*ABC* and △*DEF* by finding ratios of corresponding side lengths.

Shortest sides	**Longest sides**	**Remaining sides**
$\dfrac{AB}{DE} = \dfrac{14}{6} = \dfrac{7}{3}$	$\dfrac{AC}{DF} = \dfrac{35}{15} = \dfrac{7}{3}$	$\dfrac{BC}{EF} = \dfrac{28}{12} = \dfrac{7}{3}$

▶ All the ratios are equal, so △*ABC* ~ △*DEF* by the SSS Similarity Theorem.

Use the SSS Similarity Theorem or the SAS Similarity Theorem to show that the triangles are similar.

14.

15.

8.6 Proportionality Theorems   *(pp. 499–506)*

In the diagram, $\overline{AD}$ bisects ∠*CAB*. Find the length of $\overline{DB}$.

Because $\overline{AD}$ is an angle bisector of ∠*CAB*, you can apply the Triangle Angle Bisector Theorem.

$$\frac{DB}{DC} = \frac{AB}{AC}$$ Triangle Angle Bisector Theorem

$$\frac{x}{5} = \frac{15}{8}$$ Substitute.

$$8x = 75$$ Cross Products Property

$$9.375 = x$$ Solve for *x*.

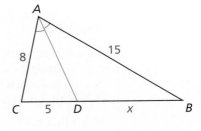

▶ The length of $\overline{DB}$ is 9.375 units.

Find the length of $\overline{AB}$.

16.

17.
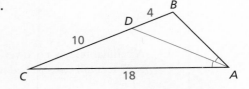

Determine whether the triangles are similar. If they are, write a similarity statement. Explain your reasoning.

1.

2.

3.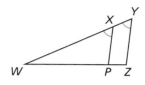

Find the value of the variable.

4.

5.

6.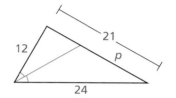

7. Given $\triangle QRS \sim \triangle MNP$, list all pairs of congruent angles. Then write the ratios of the corresponding side lengths in a statement of proportionality.

8. There is one slice of a large pizza and one slice of a small pizza in the box.

   a. Describe a similarity transformation that maps pizza slice *ABC* to pizza slice *DEF*.

   b. What is one possible scale factor for a medium slice of pizza? Explain your reasoning. (Use a dilation on the large slice of pizza.)

9. The original photograph shown is 4 inches by 6 inches.

   a. What transfomations can you use to produce the new photograph?

   b. You dilate the original photograph by a scale factor of $\frac{1}{2}$. What are the dimensions of the new photograph?

   c. You have a frame that holds photos that are 8.5 inches by 11 inches. Can you dilate the original photograph to fit the frame? Explain your reasoning.

original

new

10. In a *perspective drawing*, lines that are parallel in real life must meet at a vanishing point on the horizon. To make the train cars in the drawing appear equal in length, they are drawn so that the lines connecting the opposite corners of each car are parallel. Find the length of the bottom edge of the drawing of Car 2.

1. Use the graph of quadrilaterals *ABCD* and *QRST*.

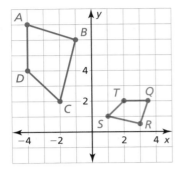

   a. Write a composition of transformations that maps quadrilateral *ABCD* to quadrilateral *QRST*.

   b. Are the quadrilaterals similar? Explain your reasoning.

2. In the diagram, *ABCD* is a parallelogram. Which congruence theorem(s) could you use to show that $\triangle AED \cong \triangle CEB$? Select all that apply.

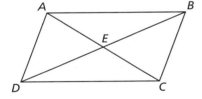

SAS Congruence Theorem
SSS Congruence Theorem
HL Congruence Theorem
ASA Congruence Theorem
AAS Congruence Theorem

3. Which expression is *not* equivalent to $20x^2 + 27x - 14$?

   A $27x + 20x^2 - 14$

   B $(5x - 2)(4x + 7)$

   C $(5x + 2)(4x - 7)$

   D $(4x + 7)(5x - 2)$

4. A bag contains six tiles with a letter on each tile. The letters are A, B, C, D, E, and F. You randomly draw two tiles from the bag. Which expression represents the probability that you draw the A tile and the B tile?

$$\dfrac{2!}{6!} \qquad \dfrac{1}{_6P_2} \qquad {_6P_2} \qquad \dfrac{1}{_6C_2} \qquad {_6C_2} \qquad \dfrac{_6C_2}{_6C_4}$$

5. Enter a statement or reason in each blank to complete the two-column proof.

Given $\dfrac{KJ}{KL} = \dfrac{KH}{KM}$

Prove $\angle LMN \cong \angle JHG$

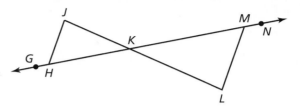

STATEMENTS	REASONS
1. $\dfrac{KJ}{KL} = \dfrac{KH}{KM}$	**1.** Given
2. $\angle JKH \cong \angle LKM$	**2.** _____
3. $\triangle JKH \sim \triangle LKM$	**3.** _____
4. $\angle KHJ \cong \angle KML$	**4.** _____
5. _____	**5.** Definition of congruent angles
6. $m\angle KHJ + m\angle JHG = 180°$	**6.** Linear Pair Postulate
7. $m\angle JHG = 180° - m\angle KHJ$	**7.** _____
8. $m\angle KML + m\angle LMN = 180°$	**8.** _____
9. _____	**9.** Subtraction Property of Equality
10. $m\angle LMN = 180° - m\angle KHJ$	**10.** _____
11. _____	**11.** Transitive Property of Equality
12. $\angle LMN \cong \angle JHG$	**12.** _____

6. The coordinates of the vertices of $\triangle DEF$ are $D(-8, 5)$, $E(-5, 8)$, and $F(-1, 4)$. The coordinates of the vertices of $\triangle JKL$ are $J(16, -10)$, $K(10, -16)$, and $L(2, -8)$. $\angle D \cong \angle J$. Can you show that $\triangle DEF \sim \triangle JKL$ by using the AA Similarity Theorem? If so, do so by listing the congruent corresponding angles and writing a similarity transformation that maps $\triangle DEF$ to $\triangle JKL$. If not, explain why not.

7. Classify the quadrilateral using the most specific name.

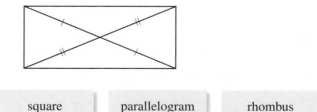

rectangle   square   parallelogram   rhombus

8. Your friend makes the statement "Quadrilateral $PQRS$ is similar to quadrilateral $WXYZ$." Describe the relationships between corresponding angles and between corresponding sides that make this statement true.

9 Right Triangles and Trigonometry

Footbridge (p. 561)

Skiing (p. 551)

Washington Monument (p. 545)

SEE the Big Idea

Rock Wall (p. 535)

Fire Escape (p. 523)

Maintaining Mathematical Proficiency

Using Properties of Radicals

Example 1 Simplify $\sqrt{128}$.

$$\sqrt{128} = \sqrt{64 \cdot 2}$$ Factor using the greatest perfect square factor.

$$= \sqrt{64} \cdot \sqrt{2}$$ Product Property of Square Roots

$$= 8\sqrt{2}$$ Simplify.

Example 2 Simplify $\dfrac{4}{\sqrt{5}}$.

$$\frac{4}{\sqrt{5}} = \frac{4}{\sqrt{5}} \cdot \frac{\sqrt{5}}{\sqrt{5}}$$ Multiply by $\dfrac{\sqrt{5}}{\sqrt{5}}$.

$$= \frac{4\sqrt{5}}{\sqrt{25}}$$ Product Property of Square Roots

$$= \frac{4\sqrt{5}}{5}$$ Simplify.

Simplify the expression.

1. $\sqrt{75}$ **2.** $\sqrt{270}$ **3.** $\sqrt{135}$

4. $\dfrac{2}{\sqrt{7}}$ **5.** $\dfrac{5}{\sqrt{2}}$ **6.** $\dfrac{12}{\sqrt{6}}$

Solving Proportions

Example 3 Solve $\dfrac{x}{10} = \dfrac{3}{2}$.

$$\frac{x}{10} = \frac{3}{2}$$ Write the proportion.

$$x \cdot 2 = 10 \cdot 3$$ Cross Products Property

$$2x = 30$$ Multiply.

$$\frac{2x}{2} = \frac{30}{2}$$ Divide each side by 2.

$$x = 15$$ Simplify.

Solve the proportion.

7. $\dfrac{x}{12} = \dfrac{3}{4}$ **8.** $\dfrac{x}{3} = \dfrac{5}{2}$ **9.** $\dfrac{4}{x} = \dfrac{7}{56}$

10. $\dfrac{10}{23} = \dfrac{4}{x}$ **11.** $\dfrac{x + 1}{2} = \dfrac{21}{14}$ **12.** $\dfrac{9}{3x - 15} = \dfrac{3}{12}$

13. **ABSTRACT REASONING** The Product Property of Square Roots allows you to simplify the square root of a product. Are you able to simplify the square root of a sum? of a difference? Explain.

Mathematical Practices

Mathematically proficient students express numerical answers precisely.

Attending to Precision

Core Concept

Standard Position for a Right Triangle

In *unit circle trigonometry*, a right triangle is in **standard position** when:

1. The hypotenuse is a radius of the circle of radius 1 with center at the origin.

2. One leg of the right triangle lies on the *x*-axis.

3. The other leg of the right triangle is perpendicular to the *x*-axis.

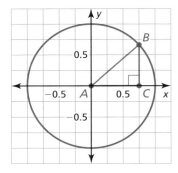

EXAMPLE 1   Drawing an Isosceles Right Triangle in Standard Position

Use dynamic geometry software to construct an isosceles right triangle in standard position. What are the exact coordinates of its vertices?

SOLUTION

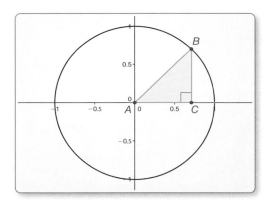

Sample

Points
$A(0, 0)$
$B(0.71, 0.71)$
$C(0.71, 0)$
Segments
$AB = 1$
$BC = 0.71$
$AC = 0.71$
Angle
$m\angle A = 45°$

To determine the exact coordinates of the vertices, label the length of each leg *x*. By the Pythagorean Theorem, which you will study in Section 9.1, $x^2 + x^2 = 1$. Solving this equation yields

$$x = \frac{1}{\sqrt{2}}, \text{ or } \frac{\sqrt{2}}{2}.$$

▶ So, the exact coordinates of the vertices are $A(0, 0)$, $B\left(\dfrac{\sqrt{2}}{2}, \dfrac{\sqrt{2}}{2}\right)$, and $C\left(\dfrac{\sqrt{2}}{2}, 0\right)$.

Monitoring Progress

1. Use dynamic geometry software to construct a right triangle with acute angle measures of 30° and 60° in standard position. What are the exact coordinates of its vertices?

2. Use dynamic geometry software to construct a right triangle with acute angle measures of 20° and 70° in standard position. What are the approximate coordinates of its vertices?

9.1 The Pythagorean Theorem

Essential Question How can you prove the Pythagorean Theorem?

EXPLORATION 1 **Proving the Pythagorean Theorem without Words**

Work with a partner.

a. Draw and cut out a right triangle with legs a and b, and hypotenuse c.

b. Make three copies of your right triangle. Arrange all four triangles to form a large square, as shown.

c. Find the area of the large square in terms of a, b, and c by summing the areas of the triangles and the small square.

d. Copy the large square. Divide it into two smaller squares and two equally-sized rectangles, as shown.

e. Find the area of the large square in terms of a and b by summing the areas of the rectangles and the smaller squares.

f. Compare your answers to parts (c) and (e). Explain how this proves the Pythagorean Theorem.

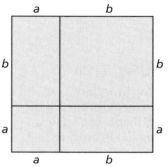

EXPLORATION 2 **Proving the Pythagorean Theorem**

Work with a partner.

a. Draw a right triangle with legs a and b, and hypotenuse c, as shown. Draw the altitude from C to $\overline{AB}$. Label the lengths, as shown.

REASONING ABSTRACTLY

To be proficient in math, you need to know and flexibly use different properties of operations and objects.

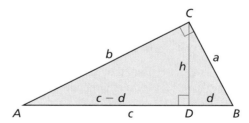

b. Explain why $\triangle ABC$, $\triangle ACD$, and $\triangle CBD$ are similar.

c. Write a two-column proof using the similar triangles in part (b) to prove that $a^2 + b^2 = c^2$.

Communicate Your Answer

3. How can you prove the Pythagorean Theorem?

4. Use the Internet or some other resource to find a way to prove the Pythagorean Theorem that is different from Explorations 1 and 2.

What You Will Learn

▶ Use the Pythagorean Theorem.

▶ Use the Converse of the Pythagorean Theorem.

▶ Classify triangles.

Core Vocabulary

Pythagorean triple, *p. 518*

Previous
right triangle
legs of a right triangle
hypotenuse

Using the Pythagorean Theorem

One of the most famous theorems in mathematics is the Pythagorean Theorem, named for the ancient Greek mathematician Pythagoras. This theorem describes the relationship between the side lengths of a right triangle.

🌀 Theorem

Pythagorean Theorem

In a right triangle, the square of the length of the hypotenuse is equal to the sum of the squares of the lengths of the legs.

Proof Explorations 1 and 2, p. 517; Ex. 39, p. 538

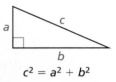

$$c^2 = a^2 + b^2$$

A **Pythagorean triple** is a set of three positive integers a, b, and c that satisfy the equation $c^2 = a^2 + b^2$.

STUDY TIP

You may find it helpful to memorize the basic Pythagorean triples, shown in **bold**, for standardized tests.

🌀 Core Concept

Common Pythagorean Triples and Some of Their Multiples

3, 4, 5	**5, 12, 13**	**8, 15, 17**	**7, 24, 25**
6, 8, 10	10, 24, 26	16, 30, 34	14, 48, 50
9, 12, 15	15, 36, 39	24, 45, 51	21, 72, 75
$3x, 4x, 5x$	$5x, 12x, 13x$	$8x, 15x, 17x$	$7x, 24x, 25x$

The most common Pythagorean triples are in bold. The other triples are the result of multiplying each integer in a bold-faced triple by the same factor.

EXAMPLE 1 Using the Pythagorean Theorem

Find the value of x. Then tell whether the side lengths form a Pythagorean triple.

SOLUTION

$c^2 = a^2 + b^2$	Pythagorean Theorem
$x^2 = 5^2 + 12^2$	Substitute.
$x^2 = 25 + 144$	Multiply.
$x^2 = 169$	Add.
$x = 13$	Find the positive square root.

▶ The value of x is 13. Because the side lengths 5, 12, and 13 are integers that satisfy the equation $c^2 = a^2 + b^2$, they form a Pythagorean triple.

EXAMPLE 2 Using the Pythagorean Theorem

Find the value of x. Then tell whether the side lengths form a Pythagorean triple.

SOLUTION

$$c^2 = a^2 + b^2$$ Pythagorean Theorem

$$14^2 = 7^2 + x^2$$ Substitute.

$$196 = 49 + x^2$$ Multiply.

$$147 = x^2$$ Subtract 49 from each side.

$$\sqrt{147} = x$$ Find the positive square root.

$$\sqrt{49} \cdot \sqrt{3} = x$$ Product Property of Square Roots

$$7\sqrt{3} = x$$ Simplify.

The Product Property of Square Roots on page 192 states that the square root of a product equals the product of the square roots of the factors.

CONNECTIONS TO ALGEBRA

▶ The value of x is $7\sqrt{3}$. Because $7\sqrt{3}$ is not an integer, the side lengths do not form a Pythagorean triple.

EXAMPLE 3 Solving a Real-Life Problem

The skyscrapers shown are connected by a skywalk with support beams. Use the Pythagorean Theorem to approximate the length of each support beam.

SOLUTION

Each support beam forms the hypotenuse of a right triangle. The right triangles are congruent, so the support beams are the same length.

$$x^2 = (23.26)^2 + (47.57)^2$$ Pythagorean Theorem

$$x = \sqrt{(23.26)^2 + (47.57)^2}$$ Find the positive square root.

$$x \approx 52.95$$ Use a calculator to approximate.

▶ The length of each support beam is about 52.95 meters.

Monitoring Progress Help in English and Spanish at *BigIdeasMath.com*

Find the value of x. Then tell whether the side lengths form a Pythagorean triple.

1.

2.

3. An anemometer is a device used to measure wind speed. The anemometer shown is attached to the top of a pole. Support wires are attached to the pole 5 feet above the ground. Each support wire is 6 feet long. How far from the base of the pole is each wire attached to the ground?

Using the Converse of the Pythagorean Theorem

The converse of the Pythagorean Theorem is also true. You can use it to determine whether a triangle with given side lengths is a right triangle.

> ### ⟳ Theorem
>
> **Converse of the Pythagorean Theorem**
>
> If the square of the length of the longest side of a triangle is equal to the sum of the squares of the lengths of the other two sides, then the triangle is a right triangle.
>
> If $c^2 = a^2 + b^2$, then $\triangle ABC$ is a right triangle.
>
>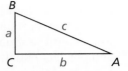
>
> *Proof* Ex. 39, p. 524

EXAMPLE 4   **Verifying Right Triangles**

Tell whether each triangle is a right triangle.

a.

b.

USING TOOLS STRATEGICALLY

Use a calculator to determine that $\sqrt{113} \approx 10.630$ is the length of the longest side in part (a).

SOLUTION

Let c represent the length of the longest side of the triangle. Check to see whether the side lengths satisfy the equation $c^2 = a^2 + b^2$.

a. $\left(\sqrt{113}\right)^2 \overset{?}{=} 7^2 + 8^2$

       $113 \overset{?}{=} 49 + 64$

       $113 = 113$ ✔

▶ The triangle is a right triangle.

b. $\left(4\sqrt{95}\right)^2 \overset{?}{=} 15^2 + 36^2$

   $4^2 \cdot \left(\sqrt{95}\right)^2 \overset{?}{=} 15^2 + 36^2$

      $16 \cdot 95 \overset{?}{=} 225 + 1296$

       $1520 \neq 1521$ ✗

▶ The triangle is *not* a right triangle.

Monitoring Progress Help in English and Spanish at *BigIdeasMath.com*

Tell whether the triangle is a right triangle.

4.

5.

Classifying Triangles

The Converse of the Pythagorean Theorem is used to determine whether a triangle is a right triangle. You can use the theorem below to determine whether a triangle is acute or obtuse.

 Theorem

Pythagorean Inequalities Theorem

For any $\triangle ABC$, where c is the length of the longest side, the following statements are true.

If $c^2 < a^2 + b^2$, then $\triangle ABC$ is acute.   If $c^2 > a^2 + b^2$, then $\triangle ABC$ is obtuse.

$c^2 < a^2 + b^2$ $c^2 > a^2 + b^2$

Proof Exs. 42 and 43, p. 524

REMEMBER

The Triangle Inequality Theorem on page 381 states that the sum of the lengths of any two sides of a triangle is greater than the length of the third side.

EXAMPLE 5   **Classifying Triangles**

Verify that segments with lengths of 4.3 feet, 5.2 feet, and 6.1 feet form a triangle. Is the triangle *acute*, *right*, or *obtuse*?

SOLUTION

Step 1   Use the Triangle Inequality Theorem to verify that the segments form a triangle.

$$4.3 + 5.2 \overset{?}{>} 6.1 \qquad 4.3 + 6.1 \overset{?}{>} 5.2 \qquad 5.2 + 6.1 \overset{?}{>} 4.3$$

$$9.5 > 6.1 ✓ \qquad\qquad 10.4 > 5.2 ✓ \qquad\qquad 11.3 > 4.3 ✓$$

▶   The segments with lengths of 4.3 feet, 5.2 feet, and 6.1 feet form a triangle.

Step 2   Classify the triangle by comparing the square of the length of the longest side with the sum of the squares of the lengths of the other two sides.

c^2		$a^2 + b^2$	Compare c^2 with $a^2 + b^2$.
6.1^2		$4.3^2 + 5.2^2$	Substitute.
37.21		$18.49 + 27.04$	Simplify.
37.21	$<$	45.53	c^2 is less than $a^2 + b^2$.

▶   The segments with lengths of 4.3 feet, 5.2 feet, and 6.1 feet form an acute triangle.

Monitoring Progress   Help in English and Spanish at *BigIdeasMath.com*

6. Verify that segments with lengths of 3, 4, and 6 form a triangle. Is the triangle *acute*, *right*, or *obtuse*?

7. Verify that segments with lengths of 2.1, 2.8, and 3.5 form a triangle. Is the triangle *acute*, *right*, or *obtuse*?

Vocabulary and Core Concept Check

1. **VOCABULARY** What is a Pythagorean triple?

2. **DIFFERENT WORDS, SAME QUESTION** Which is different? Find "both" answers.

Find the length of the longest side.

Find the length of the hypotenuse.

Find the length of the longest leg.

Find the length of the side opposite the right angle.

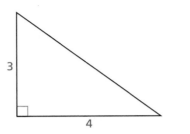

Monitoring Progress and Modeling with Mathematics

In Exercises 3–6, find the value of *x*. Then tell whether the side lengths form a Pythagorean triple. *(See Example 1.)*

3.

4.

5.

6.
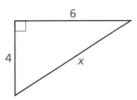

In Exercises 7–10, find the value of *x*. Then tell whether the side lengths form a Pythagorean triple. *(See Example 2.)*

7.

8.

9.

10.
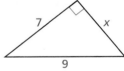

ERROR ANALYSIS In Exercises 11 and 12, describe and correct the error in using the Pythagorean Theorem.

11.

$$c^2 = a^2 + b^2$$
$$x^2 = 7^2 + 24^2$$
$$x^2 = (7 + 24)^2$$
$$x^2 = 31^2$$
$$x = 31$$

12.
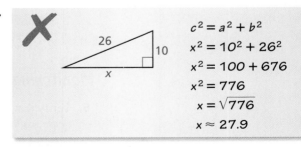

$$c^2 = a^2 + b^2$$
$$x^2 = 10^2 + 26^2$$
$$x^2 = 100 + 676$$
$$x^2 = 776$$
$$x = \sqrt{776}$$
$$x \approx 27.9$$

13. MODELING WITH MATHEMATICS The fire escape forms a right triangle, as shown. Use the Pythagorean Theorem to approximate the distance between the two platforms. *(See Example 3.)*

16.7 ft
x
8.9 ft

14. MODELING WITH MATHEMATICS The backboard of the basketball hoop forms a right triangle with the supporting rods, as shown. Use the Pythagorean Theorem to approximate the distance between the rods where they meet the backboard.

x
13.4 in.
9.8 in.

In Exercises 15–20, tell whether the triangle is a right triangle. *(See Example 4.)*

15.

97
65
72

16.

21.2
11.4
23

17.

4√19
14
10

18.

√26
5
1

19.

2
6
3√5

20.

89
80
39

In Exercises 21–28, verify that the segment lengths form a triangle. Is the triangle *acute*, *right*, or *obtuse*? *(See Example 5.)*

21. 10, 11, and 14

22. 6, 8, and 10

23. 12, 16, and 20

24. 15, 20, and 26

25. 5.3, 6.7, and 7.8

26. 4.1, 8.2, and 12.2

27. 24, 30, and $6\sqrt{43}$

28. 10, 15, and $5\sqrt{13}$

29. MODELING WITH MATHEMATICS In baseball, the lengths of the paths between consecutive bases are 90 feet, and the paths form right angles. The player on first base tries to steal second base. How far does the ball need to travel from home plate to second base to get the player out?

30. REASONING You are making a canvas frame for a painting using stretcher bars. The rectangular painting will be 10 inches long and 8 inches wide. Using a ruler, how can you be certain that the corners of the frame are 90°?

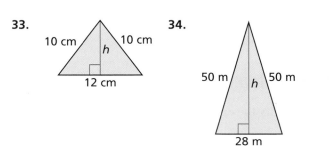

In Exercises 31–34, find the area of the isosceles triangle.

31.

17 m
h
17 m
16 m

32.

20 ft
h
20 ft
32 ft

33.

10 cm
h
10 cm
12 cm

34.

50 m
h
50 m
28 m

35. ANALYZING RELATIONSHIPS Justify the Distance Formula using the Pythagorean Theorem.

36. HOW DO YOU SEE IT? How do you know $\angle C$ is a right angle?

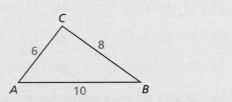

37. PROBLEM SOLVING You are making a kite and need to figure out how much binding to buy. You need the binding for the perimeter of the kite. The binding comes in packages of two yards. How many packages should you buy?

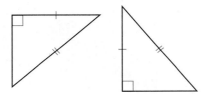

15 in.

12 in.

12 in.

20 in.

38. PROVING A THEOREM Use the Pythagorean Theorem to prove the Hypotenuse-Leg (HL) Congruence Theorem.

39. PROVING A THEOREM Prove the Converse of the Pythagorean Theorem. (*Hint*: Draw $\triangle ABC$ with side lengths a, b, and c, where c is the length of the longest side. Then draw a right triangle with side lengths a, b, and x, where x is the length of the hypotenuse. Compare lengths c and x.)

40. THOUGHT PROVOKING Consider two positive integers m and n, where $m > n$. Do the following expressions produce a Pythagorean triple? If yes, prove your answer. If no, give a counterexample.

$$2mn, \quad m^2 - n^2, \quad m^2 + n^2$$

41. MAKING AN ARGUMENT Your friend claims 72 and 75 cannot be part of a Pythagorean triple because $72^2 + 75^2$ does not equal a positive integer squared. Is your friend correct? Explain your reasoning.

42. PROVING A THEOREM Copy and complete the proof of the Pythagorean Inequalities Theorem when $c^2 < a^2 + b^2$.

Given In $\triangle ABC$, $c^2 < a^2 + b^2$, where c is the length of the longest side. $\triangle PQR$ has side lengths a, b, and x, where x is the length of the hypotenuse, and $\angle R$ is a right angle.

Prove $\triangle ABC$ is an acute triangle.

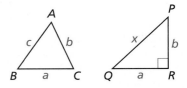

STATEMENTS	REASONS
1. In $\triangle ABC$, $c^2 < a^2 + b^2$, where c is the length of the longest side. $\triangle PQR$ has side lengths a, b, and x, where x is the length of the hypotenuse, and $\angle R$ is a right angle.	**1.** _____
2. $a^2 + b^2 = x^2$	**2.** _____
3. $c^2 < x^2$	**3.** _____
4. $c < x$	**4.** Take the positive square root of each side.
5. $m\angle R = 90°$	**5.** _____
6. $m\angle C < m\angle R$	**6.** Converse of the Hinge Theorem
7. $m\angle C < 90°$	**7.** _____
8. $\angle C$ is an acute angle.	**8.** _____
9. $\triangle ABC$ is an acute triangle.	**9.** _____

43. PROVING A THEOREM Prove the Pythagorean Inequalities Theorem when $c^2 > a^2 + b^2$. (*Hint*: Look back at Exercise 42.)

Maintaining Mathematical Proficiency

Reviewing what you learned in previous grades and lessons

Simplify the expression by rationalizing the denominator. *(Section 4.1)*

44. $\dfrac{7}{\sqrt{2}}$

45. $\dfrac{14}{\sqrt{3}}$

46. $\dfrac{8}{\sqrt{2}}$

47. $\dfrac{12}{\sqrt{3}}$

9.2 Special Right Triangles

Essential Question What is the relationship among the side lengths of 45°-45°-90° triangles? 30°-60°-90° triangles?

EXPLORATION 1 Side Ratios of an Isosceles Right Triangle

Work with a partner.

a. Use dynamic geometry software to construct an isosceles right triangle with a leg length of 4 units.

b. Find the acute angle measures. Explain why this triangle is called a 45°-45°-90° triangle.

ATTENDING TO PRECISION

To be proficient in math, you need to express numerical answers with a degree of precision appropriate for the problem context.

c. Find the exact ratios of the side lengths (using square roots).

$$\frac{AB}{AC} = \rule{1.5cm}{0.4cm}$$

$$\frac{AB}{BC} = \rule{1.5cm}{0.4cm}$$

$$\frac{AC}{BC} = \rule{1.5cm}{0.4cm}$$

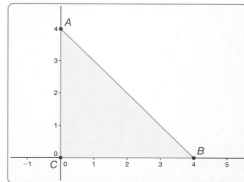

Sample

Points
$A(0, 4)$
$B(4, 0)$
$C(0, 0)$
Segments
$AB = 5.66$
$BC = 4$
$AC = 4$
Angles
$m\angle A = 45°$
$m\angle B = 45°$

d. Repeat parts (a) and (c) for several other isosceles right triangles. Use your results to write a conjecture about the ratios of the side lengths of an isosceles right triangle.

EXPLORATION 2 Side Ratios of a 30°-60°-90° Triangle

Work with a partner.

a. Use dynamic geometry software to construct a right triangle with acute angle measures of 30° and 60° (a 30°-60°-90° triangle), where the shorter leg length is 3 units.

b. Find the exact ratios of the side lengths (using square roots).

$$\frac{AB}{AC} = \rule{1.5cm}{0.4cm}$$

$$\frac{AB}{BC} = \rule{1.5cm}{0.4cm}$$

$$\frac{AC}{BC} = \rule{1.5cm}{0.4cm}$$

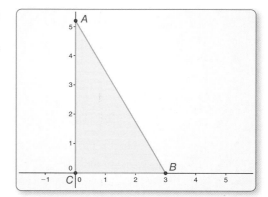

Sample

Points
$A(0, 5.20)$
$B(3, 0)$
$C(0, 0)$
Segments
$AB = 6$
$BC = 3$
$AC = 5.20$
Angles
$m\angle A = 30°$
$m\angle B = 60°$

c. Repeat parts (a) and (b) for several other 30°-60°-90° triangles. Use your results to write a conjecture about the ratios of the side lengths of a 30°-60°-90° triangle.

Communicate Your Answer

3. What is the relationship among the side lengths of 45°-45°-90° triangles? 30°-60°-90° triangles?

What You Will Learn

▶ Find side lengths in special right triangles.
▶ Solve real-life problems involving special right triangles.

Finding Side Lengths in Special Right Triangles

A 45°-45°-90° triangle is an *isosceles right triangle* that can be formed by cutting a square in half diagonally.

⟳ Theorem

REMEMBER

An expression involving a radical with index 2 is in simplest form when no radicands have perfect squares as factors other than 1, no radicands contain fractions, and no radicals appear in the denominator of a fraction.

45°-45°-90° Triangle Theorem

In a 45°-45°-90° triangle, the hypotenuse is $\sqrt{2}$ times as long as each leg.

hypotenuse = leg • $\sqrt{2}$

Proof Ex. 19, p. 530

EXAMPLE 1   Finding Side Lengths in 45°-45°-90° Triangles

Find the value of x. Write your answer in simplest form.

a.

b.

SOLUTION

a. By the Triangle Sum Theorem, the measure of the third angle must be 45°, so the triangle is a 45°-45°-90° triangle.

hypotenuse = leg • $\sqrt{2}$	45°-45°-90° Triangle Theorem
$x = 8 • \sqrt{2}$	Substitute.
$x = 8\sqrt{2}$	Simplify.

▶ The value of x is $8\sqrt{2}$.

b. By the Base Angles Theorem and the Corollary to the Triangle Sum Theorem, the triangle is a 45°-45°-90° triangle.

hypotenuse = leg • $\sqrt{2}$	45°-45°-90° Triangle Theorem
$5\sqrt{2} = x • \sqrt{2}$	Substitute.
$\dfrac{5\sqrt{2}}{\sqrt{2}} = \dfrac{x\sqrt{2}}{\sqrt{2}}$	Divide each side by $\sqrt{2}$.
$5 = x$	Simplify.

▶ The value of x is 5.

⟳ Theorem

30°-60°-90° Triangle Theorem

In a 30°-60°-90° triangle, the hypotenuse is twice as long as the shorter leg, and the longer leg is $\sqrt{3}$ times as long as the shorter leg.

hypotenuse = shorter leg · 2
longer leg = shorter leg · $\sqrt{3}$

Proof Ex. 21, p. 530

REMEMBER

Because the angle opposite 9 is larger than the angle opposite x, the leg with length 9 is longer than the leg with length x by the Triangle Larger Angle Theorem.

⊳

EXAMPLE 2   **Finding Side Lengths in a 30°-60°-90° Triangle**

Find the values of x and y. Write your answer in simplest form.

SOLUTION

Step 1 Find the value of x.

longer leg = shorter leg · $\sqrt{3}$	30°-60°-90° Triangle Theorem
$9 = x \cdot \sqrt{3}$	Substitute.
$\dfrac{9}{\sqrt{3}} = x$	Divide each side by $\sqrt{3}$.
$\dfrac{9}{\sqrt{3}} \cdot \dfrac{\sqrt{3}}{\sqrt{3}} = x$	Multiply by $\dfrac{\sqrt{3}}{\sqrt{3}}$.
$\dfrac{9\sqrt{3}}{3} = x$	Multiply fractions.
$3\sqrt{3} = x$	Simplify.

▶ The value of x is $3\sqrt{3}$.

Step 2 Find the value of y.

hypotenuse = shorter leg · 2	30°-60°-90° Triangle Theorem
$y = 3\sqrt{3} \cdot 2$	Substitute.
$y = 6\sqrt{3}$	Simplify.

▶ The value of y is $6\sqrt{3}$.

Monitoring Progress 🔊 Help in English and Spanish at *BigIdeasMath.com*

Find the value of the variable. Write your answer in simplest form.

1.

2.

3.

4.

Solving Real-Life Problems

EXAMPLE 3 Modeling with Mathematics

The road sign is shaped like an equilateral triangle. Estimate the area of the sign by finding the area of the equilateral triangle.

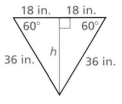

SOLUTION

First find the height h of the triangle by dividing it into two 30°-60°-90° triangles. The length of the longer leg of one of these triangles is h. The length of the shorter leg is 18 inches.

$h = 18 \cdot \sqrt{3} = 18\sqrt{3}$ 30°-60°-90° Triangle Theorem

Use $h = 18\sqrt{3}$ to find the area of the equilateral triangle.

$$\text{Area} = \tfrac{1}{2}bh = \tfrac{1}{2}(36)\left(18\sqrt{3}\right) \approx 561.18$$

▶ The area of the sign is about 561 square inches.

EXAMPLE 4 Finding the Height of a Ramp

A tipping platform is a ramp used to unload trucks. How high is the end of an 80-foot ramp when the tipping angle is 30°? 45°?

SOLUTION

When the tipping angle is 30°, the height h of the ramp is the length of the shorter leg of a 30°-60°-90° triangle. The length of the hypotenuse is 80 feet.

$80 = 2h$ 30°-60°-90° Triangle Theorem

$40 = h$ Divide each side by 2.

When the tipping angle is 45°, the height h of the ramp is the length of a leg of a 45°-45°-90° triangle. The length of the hypotenuse is 80 feet.

$80 = h \cdot \sqrt{2}$ 45°-45°-90° Triangle Theorem

$\dfrac{80}{\sqrt{2}} = h$ Divide each side by $\sqrt{2}$.

$56.6 \approx h$ Use a calculator.

▶ When the tipping angle is 30°, the ramp height is 40 feet. When the tipping angle is 45°, the ramp height is about 56 feet 7 inches.

Monitoring Progress Help in English and Spanish at *BigIdeasMath.com*

5. The logo on a recycling bin resembles an equilateral triangle with side lengths of 6 centimeters. Approximate the area of the logo.

6. The body of a dump truck is raised to empty a load of sand. How high is the 14-foot-long body from the frame when it is tipped upward by a 60° angle?

Vocabulary and Core Concept Check

1. **VOCABULARY** Name two special right triangles by their angle measures.

2. **WRITING** Explain why the acute angles in an isosceles right triangle always measure 45°.

Monitoring Progress and Modeling with Mathematics

In Exercises 3–6, find the value of *x*. Write your answer in simplest form. *(See Example 1.)*

3.

4.

5.

6.

In Exercises 7–10, find the values of *x* and *y*. Write your answers in simplest form. *(See Example 2.)*

7.

8.

9.

10.

ERROR ANALYSIS In Exercises 11 and 12, describe and correct the error in finding the length of the hypotenuse.

11.

By the Triangle Sum Theorem, the measure of the third angle must be 60°. So, the triangle is a 30°-60°-90° triangle.

hypotenuse = shorter leg • $\sqrt{3}$ = $7\sqrt{3}$

So, the length of the hypotenuse is $7\sqrt{3}$ units.

12.

By the Triangle Sum Theorem, the measure of the third angle must be 45°. So, the triangle is a 45°-45°-90° triangle.

hypotenuse = leg • leg • $\sqrt{2}$ = $5\sqrt{2}$

So, the length of the hypotenuse is $5\sqrt{2}$ units.

In Exercises 13 and 14, sketch the figure that is described. Find the indicated length. Round decimal answers to the nearest tenth.

13. The side length of an equilateral triangle is 5 centimeters. Find the length of an altitude.

14. The perimeter of a square is 36 inches. Find the length of a diagonal.

In Exercises 15 and 16, find the area of the figure. Round decimal answers to the nearest tenth. *(See Example 3.)*

15.

16.

17. **PROBLEM SOLVING** Each half of the drawbridge is about 284 feet long. How high does the drawbridge rise when *x* is 30°? 45°? 60°? *(See Example 4.)*

18. MODELING WITH MATHEMATICS A nut is shaped like a regular hexagon with side lengths of 1 centimeter. Find the value of *x*. (*Hint*: A regular hexagon can be divided into six congruent triangles.)

1 cm

x

19. PROVING A THEOREM Write a paragraph proof of the 45°-45°-90° Triangle Theorem.

Given △*DEF* is a 45°-45°-90° triangle.

Prove The hypotenuse is √2 times as long as each leg.

20. HOW DO YOU SEE IT? The diagram shows part of the *Wheel of Theodorus*.

a. Which triangles, if any, are 45°-45°-90° triangles?

b. Which triangles, if any, are 30°-60°-90° triangles?

21. PROVING A THEOREM Write a paragraph proof of the 30°-60°-90° Triangle Theorem. (*Hint*: Construct △*JML* congruent to △*JKL*.)

Given △*JKL* is a 30°-60°-90° triangle.

Prove The hypotenuse is twice as long as the shorter leg, and the longer leg is √3 times as long as the shorter leg.

22. THOUGHT PROVOKING The diagram below is called the *Ailles rectangle*. Each triangle in the diagram has rational angle measures and each side length contains at most one square root. Label the sides and angles in the diagram. Describe the triangles.

23. WRITING Describe two ways to show that all isosceles right triangles are similar to each other.

24. MAKING AN ARGUMENT Each triangle in the diagram is a 45°-45°-90° triangle. At Stage 0, the legs of the triangle are each 1 unit long. Your brother claims the lengths of the legs of the triangles added are halved at each stage. So, the length of a leg of a triangle added in Stage 8 will be $\frac{1}{256}$ unit. Is your brother correct? Explain your reasoning.

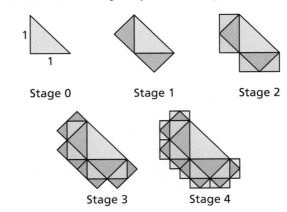

Stage 0   Stage 1   Stage 2

Stage 3   Stage 4

25. USING STRUCTURE △*TUV* is a 30°-60°-90° triangle, where two vertices are *U*(3, −1) and *V*(−3, −1), $\overline{UV}$ is the hypotenuse, and point *T* is in Quadrant I. Find the coordinates of *T*.

Maintaining Mathematical Proficiency

Reviewing what you learned in previous grades and lessons

Find the value of *x*. (*Section 8.3*)

26. △*DEF* ~ △*LMN*

27. △*ABC* ~ △*QRS*

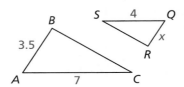

9.3 Similar Right Triangles

Essential Question How are altitudes and geometric means of right triangles related?

EXPLORATION 1 **Writing a Conjecture**

Work with a partner.

a. Use dynamic geometry software to construct right $\triangle ABC$, as shown. Draw $\overline{CD}$ so that it is an altitude from the right angle to the hypotenuse of $\triangle ABC$.

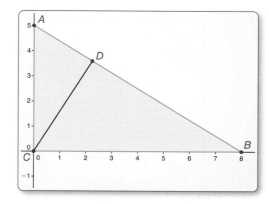

Points
$A(0, 5)$
$B(8, 0)$
$C(0, 0)$
$D(2.25, 3.6)$
Segments
$AB = 9.43$
$BC = 8$
$AC = 5$

CONSTRUCTING VIABLE ARGUMENTS

To be proficient in math, you need to understand and use stated assumptions, definitions, and previously established results in constructing arguments.

b. The **geometric mean** of two positive numbers a and b is the positive number x that satisfies

$$\frac{a}{x} = \frac{x}{b}.$$ x is the geometric mean of a and b.

Write a proportion involving the side lengths of $\triangle CBD$ and $\triangle ACD$ so that CD is the geometric mean of two of the other side lengths. Use similar triangles to justify your steps.

c. Use the proportion you wrote in part (b) to find CD.

d. Generalize the proportion you wrote in part (b). Then write a conjecture about how the geometric mean is related to the altitude from the right angle to the hypotenuse of a right triangle.

EXPLORATION 2 **Comparing Geometric and Arithmetic Means**

Work with a partner. Use a spreadsheet to find the arithmetic mean and the geometric mean of several pairs of positive numbers. Compare the two means. What do you notice?

	A	B	C	D
1	a	b	Arithmetic Mean	Geometric Mean
2	3	4	3.5	3.464
3	4	5		
4	6	7		
5	0.5	0.5		
6	0.4	0.8		
7	2	5		
8	1	4		
9	9	16		
10	10	100		
11				

Communicate Your Answer

3. How are altitudes and geometric means of right triangles related?

What You Will Learn

▶ Identify similar triangles.

▶ Solve real-life problems involving similar triangles.

▶ Use geometric means.

Identifying Similar Triangles

When the altitude is drawn to the hypotenuse of a right triangle, the two smaller triangles are similar to the original triangle and to each other.

🌀 Theorem

Right Triangle Similarity Theorem

If the altitude is drawn to the hypotenuse of a right triangle, then the two triangles formed are similar to the original triangle and to each other.

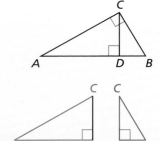

$\triangle CBD \sim \triangle ABC$, $\triangle ACD \sim \triangle ABC$, and $\triangle CBD \sim \triangle ACD$.

Proof Ex. 45, p. 538

EXAMPLE 1   **Identifying Similar Triangles**

Identify the similar triangles in the diagram.

SOLUTION

Sketch the three similar right triangles so that the corresponding angles and sides have the same orientation.

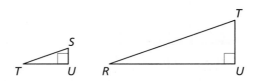

▶ $\triangle TSU \sim \triangle RTU \sim \triangle RST$

Monitoring Progress 🔊 Help in English and Spanish at *BigIdeasMath.com*

Identify the similar triangles.

1.

2.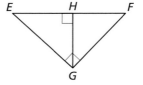

Solving Real-Life Problems

EXAMPLE 2 **Modeling with Mathematics**

A roof has a cross section that is a right triangle. The diagram shows the approximate dimensions of this cross section. Find the height h of the roof.

SOLUTION

1. **Understand the Problem** You are given the side lengths of a right triangle. You need to find the height of the roof, which is the altitude drawn to the hypotenuse.

2. **Make a Plan** Identify any similar triangles. Then use the similar triangles to write a proportion involving the height and solve for h.

3. **Solve the Problem** Identify the similar triangles and sketch them.

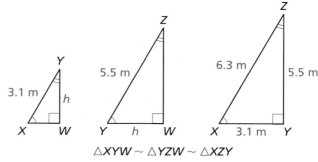

$$\triangle XYW \sim \triangle YZW \sim \triangle XZY$$

COMMON ERROR

Notice that if you tried to write a proportion using $\triangle XYW$ and $\triangle YZW$, then there would be two unknowns, so you would not be able to solve for h.

Because $\triangle XYW \sim \triangle XZY$, you can write a proportion.

$\dfrac{YW}{ZY} = \dfrac{XY}{XZ}$ Corresponding side lengths of similar triangles are proportional.

$\dfrac{h}{5.5} = \dfrac{3.1}{6.3}$ Substitute.

$h \approx 2.7$ Multiply each side by 5.5.

▶   The height of the roof is about 2.7 meters.

4. **Look Back** Because the height of the roof is a leg of right $\triangle YZW$ and right $\triangle XYW$, it should be shorter than each of their hypotenuses. The lengths of the two hypotenuses are $YZ = 5.5$ and $XY = 3.1$. Because $2.7 < 3.1$, the answer seems reasonable.

Monitoring Progress 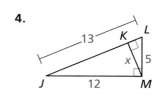 Help in English and Spanish at *BigIdeasMath.com*

Find the value of x.

3.

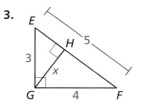

4.

Using a Geometric Mean

Geometric Mean

The **geometric mean** of two positive numbers a and b is the positive number x that satisfies $\dfrac{a}{x} = \dfrac{x}{b}$. So, $x^2 = ab$ and $x = \sqrt{ab}$.

EXAMPLE 3   **Finding a Geometric Mean**

Find the geometric mean of 24 and 48.

SOLUTION

$x^2 = ab$	Definition of geometric mean
$x^2 = 24 \cdot 48$	Substitute 24 for a and 48 for b.
$x = \sqrt{24 \cdot 48}$	Take the positive square root of each side.
$x = \sqrt{24 \cdot 24 \cdot 2}$	Factor.
$x = 24\sqrt{2}$	Simplify.

▶ The geometric mean of 24 and 48 is $24\sqrt{2} \approx 33.9$.

In right $\triangle ABC$, altitude $\overline{CD}$ is drawn to the hypotenuse, forming two smaller right triangles that are similar to $\triangle ABC$. From the Right Triangle Similarity Theorem, you know that $\triangle CBD \sim \triangle ACD \sim \triangle ABC$. Because the triangles are similar, you can write and simplify the following proportions involving geometric means.

$$\frac{CD}{AD} = \frac{BD}{CD} \qquad\qquad \frac{CB}{DB} = \frac{AB}{CB} \qquad\qquad \frac{AC}{AD} = \frac{AB}{AC}$$

$$CD^2 = AD \cdot BD \qquad\quad CB^2 = DB \cdot AB \qquad\quad AC^2 = AD \cdot AB$$

Theorems

Geometric Mean (Altitude) Theorem

In a right triangle, the altitude from the right angle to the hypotenuse divides the hypotenuse into two segments.

The length of the altitude is the geometric mean of the lengths of the two segments of the hypotenuse.

Proof Ex. 41, p. 538

$CD^2 = AD \cdot BD$

Geometric Mean (Leg) Theorem

In a right triangle, the altitude from the right angle to the hypotenuse divides the hypotenuse into two segments.

The length of each leg of the right triangle is the geometric mean of the lengths of the hypotenuse and the segment of the hypotenuse that is adjacent to the leg.

Proof Ex. 42, p. 538

$CB^2 = DB \cdot AB$
$AC^2 = AD \cdot AB$

Using a Geometric Mean

Find the value of each variable.

a.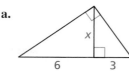

b.

COMMON ERROR

In Example 4(b), the Geometric Mean (Leg) Theorem gives
$y^2 = 2 \cdot (5 + 2)$, not
$y^2 = 5 \cdot (5 + 2)$, because the side with length y is adjacent to the segment with length 2.

SOLUTION

a. Apply the Geometric Mean (Altitude) Theorem.

$$x^2 = 6 \cdot 3$$
$$x^2 = 18$$
$$x = \sqrt{18}$$
$$x = \sqrt{9} \cdot \sqrt{2}$$
$$x = 3\sqrt{2}$$

▶ The value of x is $3\sqrt{2}$.

b. Apply the Geometric Mean (Leg) Theorem.

$$y^2 = 2 \cdot (5 + 2)$$
$$y^2 = 2 \cdot 7$$
$$y^2 = 14$$
$$y = \sqrt{14}$$

▶ The value of y is $\sqrt{14}$.

EXAMPLE 5 **Using Indirect Measurement**

To find the cost of installing a rock wall in your school gymnasium, you need to find the height of the gym wall. You use a cardboard square to line up the top and bottom of the gym wall. Your friend measures the vertical distance from the ground to your eye and the horizontal distance from you to the gym wall. Approximate the height of the gym wall.

SOLUTION

By the Geometric Mean (Altitude) Theorem, you know that 8.5 is the geometric mean of w and 5.

$8.5^2 = w \cdot 5$	Geometric Mean (Altitude) Theorem
$72.25 = 5w$	Square 8.5.
$14.45 = w$	Divide each side by 5.

▶ The height of the wall is $5 + w = 5 + 14.45 = 19.45$ feet.

Monitoring Progress Help in English and Spanish at *BigIdeasMath.com*

Find the geometric mean of the two numbers.

5. 12 and 27   **6.** 18 and 54   **7.** 16 and 18

8. Find the value of x in the triangle at the left.

9. WHAT IF? In Example 5, the vertical distance from the ground to your eye is 5.5 feet and the distance from you to the gym wall is 9 feet. Approximate the height of the gym wall.

Vocabulary and Core Concept Check

1. **COMPLETE THE SENTENCE** If the altitude is drawn to the hypotenuse of a right triangle, then the two triangles formed are similar to the original triangle and _____.

2. **WRITING** In your own words, explain *geometric mean*.

Monitoring Progress and Modeling with Mathematics

In Exercises 3 and 4, identify the similar triangles.
(See Example 1.)

3.

4.

In Exercises 5–10, find the value of *x*. *(See Example 2.)*

5.

6.

7.

8.

9.

10.

In Exercises 11–18, find the geometric mean of the two numbers. *(See Example 3.)*

11. 8 and 32   12. 9 and 16

13. 14 and 20   14. 25 and 35

15. 16 and 25   16. 8 and 28

17. 17 and 36   18. 24 and 45

In Exercises 19–26, find the value of the variable.
(See Example 4.)

19.   20.

21.   22.

23.   24.

25.

26.

ERROR ANALYSIS In Exercises 27 and 28, describe and correct the error in writing an equation for the given diagram.

27.

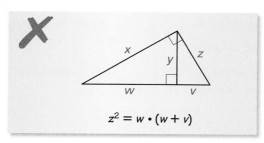

$$z^2 = w \cdot (w + v)$$

28.

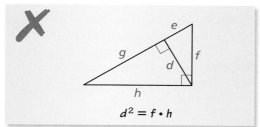

$$d^2 = f \cdot h$$

MODELING WITH MATHEMATICS In Exercises 29 and 30, use the diagram. *(See Example 5.)*

Ex. 29   Ex. 30

29. You want to determine the height of a monument at a local park. You use a cardboard square to line up the top and bottom of the monument, as shown at the above left. Your friend measures the vertical distance from the ground to your eye and the horizontal distance from you to the monument. Approximate the height of the monument.

30. Your classmate is standing on the other side of the monument. She has a piece of rope staked at the base of the monument. She extends the rope to the cardboard square she is holding lined up to the top and bottom of the monument. Use the information in the diagram above to approximate the height of the monument. Do you get the same answer as in Exercise 29? Explain your reasoning.

MATHEMATICAL CONNECTIONS In Exercises 31–34, find the value(s) of the variable(s).

31.

32.

33.

34.

35. **REASONING** Use the diagram. Decide which proportions are true. Select all that apply.

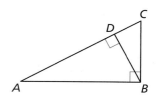

(A) $\dfrac{DB}{DC} = \dfrac{DA}{DB}$

(B) $\dfrac{BA}{CB} = \dfrac{CB}{BD}$

(C) $\dfrac{CA}{BA} = \dfrac{BA}{CA}$

(D) $\dfrac{DB}{BC} = \dfrac{DA}{BA}$

36. **ANALYZING RELATIONSHIPS** You are designing a diamond-shaped kite. You know that $AD = 44.8$ centimeters, $DC = 72$ centimeters, and $AC = 84.8$ centimeters. You want to use a straight crossbar $\overline{BD}$. About how long should it be? Explain your reasoning.

37. **ANALYZING RELATIONSHIPS** Use both of the Geometric Mean Theorems to find AC and BD.

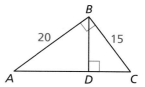

38. HOW DO YOU SEE IT? In which of the following triangles does the Geometric Mean (Altitude) Theorem apply?

(A)

(B)

(C)

(D)

39. PROVING A THEOREM Use the diagram of $\triangle ABC$. Copy and complete the proof of the Pythagorean Theorem.

Given In $\triangle ABC$, $\angle BCA$ is a right angle.

Prove $c^2 = a^2 + b^2$

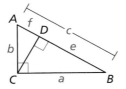

STATEMENTS	REASONS
1. In $\triangle ABC$, $\angle BCA$ is a right angle.	**1.** _____
2. Draw a perpendicular segment (altitude) from C to $\overline{AB}$.	**2.** Perpendicular Postulate
3. $ce = a^2$ and $cf = b^2$	**3.** _____
4. $ce + b^2 =$ ____ $+ b^2$	**4.** Addition Property of Equality
5. $ce + cf = a^2 + b^2$	**5.** _____
6. $c(e + f) = a^2 + b^2$	**6.** _____
7. $e + f =$ ____	**7.** Segment Addition Postulate
8. $c \cdot c = a^2 + b^2$	**8.** _____
9. $c^2 = a^2 + b^2$	**9.** Simplify.

40. MAKING AN ARGUMENT Your friend claims the geometric mean of 4 and 9 is 6, and then labels the triangle, as shown. Is your friend correct? Explain your reasoning.

In Exercises 41 and 42, use the given statements to prove the theorem.

Given $\triangle ABC$ is a right triangle.
Altitude $\overline{CD}$ is drawn to hypotenuse $\overline{AB}$.

41. PROVING A THEOREM Prove the Geometric Mean (Altitude) Theorem by showing that $CD^2 = AD \cdot BD$.

42. PROVING A THEOREM Prove the Geometric Mean (Leg) Theorem by showing that $CB^2 = DB \cdot AB$ and $AC^2 = AD \cdot AB$.

43. CRITICAL THINKING Draw a right isosceles triangle and label the two leg lengths x. Then draw the altitude to the hypotenuse and label its length y. Now, use the Right Triangle Similarity Theorem to draw the three similar triangles from the image and label any side length that is equal to either x or y. What can you conclude about the relationship between the two smaller triangles? Explain your reasoning.

44. THOUGHT PROVOKING The arithmetic mean and geometric mean of two nonnegative numbers x and y are shown.

$$\text{arithmetic mean} = \frac{x + y}{2}$$

$$\text{geometric mean} = \sqrt{xy}$$

Write an inequality that relates these two means. Justify your answer.

45. PROVING A THEOREM Prove the Right Triangle Similarity Theorem by proving three similarity statements.

Given $\triangle ABC$ is a right triangle.
Altitude $\overline{CD}$ is drawn to hypotenuse $\overline{AB}$.

Prove $\triangle CBD \sim \triangle ABC$, $\triangle ACD \sim \triangle ABC$, $\triangle CBD \sim \triangle ACD$

Maintaining Mathematical Proficiency Reviewing what you learned in previous grades and lessons

Solve the equation for x. *(Skills Review Handbook)*

46. $13 = \dfrac{x}{5}$ **47.** $29 = \dfrac{x}{4}$ **48.** $9 = \dfrac{78}{x}$ **49.** $30 = \dfrac{115}{x}$

Core Vocabulary

Pythagorean triple, *p. 518*   geometric mean, *p. 534*

Core Concepts

Section 9.1

Pythagorean Theorem, *p. 518*
Common Pythagorean Triples and Some of Their Multiples, *p. 518*
Converse of the Pythagorean Theorem, *p. 520*
Pythagorean Inequalities Theorem, *p. 521*

Section 9.2

45°-45°-90° Triangle Theorem, *p. 526*
30°-60°-90° Triangle Theorem, *p. 527*

Section 9.3

Right Triangle Similarity Theorem, *p. 532*
Geometric Mean (Altitude) Theorem, *p. 534*
Geometric Mean (Leg) Theorem, *p. 534*

Mathematical Practices

1. In Exercise 31 on page 523, describe the steps you took to find the area of the triangle.

2. In Exercise 23 on page 530, can one of the ways be used to show that all 30°-60°-90° triangles are similar? Explain.

3. Explain why the Geometric Mean (Altitude) Theorem does not apply to three of the triangles in Exercise 38 on page 538.

Form a Weekly Study Group, Set Up Rules

Consider using the following rules.
- Members must attend regularly, be on time, and participate.
- The sessions will focus on the key math concepts, not on the needs of one student.
- Students who skip classes will not be allowed to participate in the study group.
- Students who keep the group from being productive will be asked to leave the group.

STUDY SKILLS

Find the value of *x*. Tell whether the side lengths form a Pythagorean triple.
(Section 9.1)

1.

2.

3.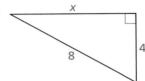

Verify that the segment lengths form a triangle. Is the triangle *acute*, *right*, or *obtuse*?
(Section 9.1)

4. 24, 32, and 40

5. 7, 9, and 13

6. 12, 15, and $10\sqrt{3}$

Find the values of *x* and *y*. Write your answers in simplest form. *(Section 9.2)*

7.

8.

9.

Find the geometric mean of the two numbers. *(Section 9.3)*

10. 6 and 12

11. 15 and 20

12. 18 and 26

Identify the similar right triangles. Then find the value of the variable. *(Section 9.3)*

13.

14.

15.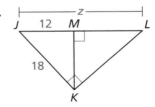

16. Television sizes are measured by the length of their diagonal. You want to purchase a television that is at least 40 inches. Should you purchase the television shown? Explain your reasoning. *(Section 9.1)*

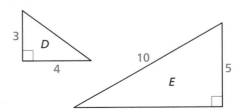

17. Each triangle shown below is a right triangle. *(Sections 9.1–9.3)*

   a. Are any of the triangles special right triangles? Explain your reasoning.

   b. List all similar triangles, if any.

   c. Find the lengths of the altitudes of triangles *B* and *C*.

9.4 The Tangent Ratio

Essential Question How is a right triangle used to find the tangent of an acute angle? Is there a unique right triangle that must be used?

Let △*ABC* be a right triangle with acute ∠*A*. The *tangent* of ∠*A* (written as tan *A*) is defined as follows.

$$\tan A = \frac{\text{length of leg opposite } \angle A}{\text{length of leg adjacent to } \angle A} = \frac{BC}{AC}$$

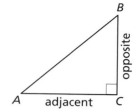

EXPLORATION 1 **Calculating a Tangent Ratio**

Work with a partner. Use dynamic geometry software.

a. Construct △*ABC*, as shown. Construct segments perpendicular to $\overline{AC}$ to form right triangles that share vertex *A* and are similar to △*ABC* with vertices, as shown.

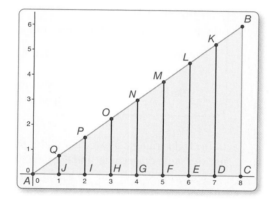

Sample
Points
A(0, 0)
B(8, 6)
C(8, 0)
Angle
$m\angle BAC = 36.87°$

b. Calculate each given ratio to complete the table for the decimal value of tan *A* for each right triangle. What can you conclude?

Ratio	$\frac{BC}{AC}$	$\frac{KD}{AD}$	$\frac{LE}{AE}$	$\frac{MF}{AF}$	$\frac{NG}{AG}$	$\frac{OH}{AH}$	$\frac{PI}{AI}$	$\frac{QJ}{AJ}$
tan *A*								

ATTENDING TO PRECISION

To be proficient in math, you need to express numerical answers with a degree of precision appropriate for the problem context.

EXPLORATION 2 **Using a Calculator**

Work with a partner. Use a calculator that has a tangent key to calculate the tangent of 36.87°. Do you get the same result as in Exploration 1? Explain.

Communicate Your Answer

3. Repeat Exploration 1 for △*ABC* with vertices *A*(0, 0), *B*(8, 5), and *C*(8, 0). Construct the seven perpendicular segments so that not all of them intersect $\overline{AC}$ at integer values of *x*. Discuss your results.

4. How is a right triangle used to find the tangent of an acute angle? Is there a unique right triangle that must be used?

What You Will Learn

▶ Use the tangent ratio.

▶ Solve real-life problems involving the tangent ratio.

Using the Tangent Ratio

A **trigonometric ratio** is a ratio of the lengths of two sides in a right triangle. All right triangles with a given acute angle are similar by the AA Similarity Theorem. So, $\triangle JKL \sim \triangle XYZ$, and you can write $\dfrac{KL}{YZ} = \dfrac{JL}{XZ}$. This can be rewritten as $\dfrac{KL}{JL} = \dfrac{YZ}{XZ}$, which is a trigonometric ratio. So, trigonometric ratios are constant for a given angle measure.

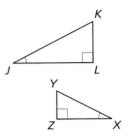

The **tangent** ratio is a trigonometric ratio for acute angles that involves the lengths of the legs of a right triangle.

READING

Remember the following abbreviations.

tangent → tan
opposite → opp.
adjacent → adj.

Core Concept

Tangent Ratio

Let $\triangle ABC$ be a right triangle with acute $\angle A$.

The tangent of $\angle A$ (written as tan A) is defined as follows.

$$\tan A = \frac{\text{length of leg opposite } \angle A}{\text{length of leg adjacent to } \angle A} = \frac{BC}{AC}$$

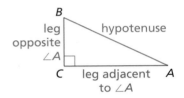

In the right triangle above, $\angle A$ and $\angle B$ are complementary. So, $\angle B$ is acute. You can use the same diagram to find the tangent of $\angle B$. Notice that the leg adjacent to $\angle A$ is the leg *opposite* $\angle B$ and the leg opposite $\angle A$ is the leg *adjacent* to $\angle B$.

ATTENDING TO PRECISION

Unless told otherwise, you should round the values of trigonometric ratios to four decimal places and round lengths to the nearest tenth.

EXAMPLE 1   Finding Tangent Ratios

Find tan S and tan R. Write each answer as a fraction and as a decimal rounded to four places.

SOLUTION

$$\tan S = \frac{\text{opp. } \angle S}{\text{adj. to } \angle S} = \frac{RT}{ST} = \frac{80}{18} = \frac{40}{9} \approx 4.4444$$

$$\tan R = \frac{\text{opp. } \angle R}{\text{adj. to } \angle R} = \frac{ST}{RT} = \frac{18}{80} = \frac{9}{40} = 0.2250$$

Monitoring Progress Help in English and Spanish at *BigIdeasMath.com*

Find tan *J* and tan *K*. Write each answer as a fraction and as a decimal rounded to four places.

1.

2.

EXAMPLE 2 **Finding a Leg Length**

Find the value of x. Round your answer to the nearest tenth.

SOLUTION

Use the tangent of an acute angle to find a leg length.

$$\tan 32° = \frac{\text{opp.}}{\text{adj.}}$$ Write ratio for tangent of 32°.

$$\tan 32° = \frac{11}{x}$$ Substitute.

$$x \cdot \tan 32° = 11$$ Multiply each side by x.

$$x = \frac{11}{\tan 32°}$$ Divide each side by tan 32°.

$$x \approx 17.6$$ Use a calculator.

▶   The value of x is about 17.6.

> **USING TOOLS STRATEGICALLY**
>
> You can also use the Table of Trigonometric Ratios available at *BigIdeasMath.com* to find the decimal approximations of trigonometric ratios.

You can find the tangent of an acute angle measuring 30°, 45°, or 60° by applying what you know about special right triangles.

EXAMPLE 3 **Using a Special Right Triangle to Find a Tangent**

Use a special right triangle to find the tangent of a 60° angle.

SOLUTION

Step 1 Because all 30°-60°-90° triangles are similar, you can simplify your calculations by choosing 1 as the length of the shorter leg. Use the 30°-60°-90° Triangle Theorem to find the length of the longer leg.

longer leg = shorter leg $\cdot \sqrt{3}$ 30°-60°-90° Triangle Theorem

          = $1 \cdot \sqrt{3}$ Substitute.

          = $\sqrt{3}$ Simplify.

Step 2 Find tan 60°.

$$\tan 60° = \frac{\text{opp.}}{\text{adj.}}$$ Write ratio for tangent of 60°.

$$\tan 60° = \frac{\sqrt{3}}{1}$$ Substitute.

$$\tan 60° = \sqrt{3}$$ Simplify.

▶   The tangent of any 60° angle is $\sqrt{3} \approx 1.7321$.

> **STUDY TIP**
>
> The tangents of all 60° angles are the same constant ratio. Any right triangle with a 60° angle can be used to determine this value.

Monitoring Progress Help in English and Spanish at *BigIdeasMath.com*

Find the value of x. Round your answer to the nearest tenth.

3.

4.

5. **WHAT IF?** In Example 3, the length of the shorter leg is 5 instead of 1. Show that the tangent of 60° is still equal to $\sqrt{3}$.

Solving Real-Life Problems

The angle that an upward line of sight makes with a horizontal line is called the **angle of elevation**.

EXAMPLE 4 **Modeling with Mathematics**

You are measuring the height of a spruce tree. You stand 45 feet from the base of the tree. You measure the angle of elevation from the ground to the top of the tree to be 59°. Find the height h of the tree to the nearest foot.

SOLUTION

1. **Understand the Problem** You are given the angle of elevation and the distance from the tree. You need to find the height of the tree to the nearest foot.

2. **Make a Plan** Write a trigonometric ratio for the tangent of the angle of elevation involving the height h. Then solve for h.

3. **Solve the Problem**

   $\tan 59° = \dfrac{\text{opp.}}{\text{adj.}}$ Write ratio for tangent of 59°.

   $\tan 59° = \dfrac{h}{45}$ Substitute.

   $45 \cdot \tan 59° = h$ Multiply each side by 45.

   $74.9 \approx h$ Use a calculator.

   ▶ The tree is about 75 feet tall.

4. **Look Back** Check your answer. Because 59° is close to 60°, the value of h should be close to the length of the longer leg of a 30°-60°-90° triangle, where the length of the shorter leg is 45 feet.

   $\text{longer leg} = \text{shorter leg} \cdot \sqrt{3}$ 30°-60°-90° Triangle Theorem

   $= 45 \cdot \sqrt{3}$ Substitute.

   ≈ 77.9 Use a calculator.

   The value of 77.9 feet is close to the value of h. ✔

Monitoring Progress Help in English and Spanish at *BigIdeasMath.com*

6. You are measuring the height of a lamppost. You stand 40 inches from the base of the lamppost. You measure the angle of elevation from the ground to the top of the lamppost to be 70°. Find the height h of the lamppost to the nearest inch.

Vocabulary and Core Concept Check

1. **COMPLETE THE SENTENCE** The tangent ratio compares the length of _____ to the length of _____.

2. **WRITING** Explain how you know the tangent ratio is constant for a given angle measure.

Monitoring Progress and Modeling with Mathematics

In Exercises 3–6, find the tangents of the acute angles in the right triangle. Write each answer as a fraction and as a decimal rounded to four decimal places. *(See Example 1.)*

3.

4.

5.

6.

In Exercises 7–10, find the value of *x*. Round your answer to the nearest tenth. *(See Example 2.)*

7.

8.

9.

10.

ERROR ANALYSIS In Exercises 11 and 12, describe the error in the statement of the tangent ratio. Correct the error if possible. Otherwise, write not possible.

11.

$$\tan D = \frac{35}{37}$$

12.

$$\tan 55° = \frac{18}{11.0}$$

In Exercises 13 and 14, use a special right triangle to find the tangent of the given angle measure. *(See Example 3.)*

13. 45°

14. 30°

15. **MODELING WITH MATHEMATICS** A surveyor is standing 118 feet from the base of the Washington Monument. The surveyor measures the angle of elevation from the ground to the top of the monument to be 78°. Find the height *h* of the Washington Monument to the nearest foot. *(See Example 4.)*

16. **MODELING WITH MATHEMATICS** Scientists can measure the depths of craters on the moon by looking at photos of shadows. The length of the shadow cast by the edge of a crater is 500 meters. The angle of elevation of the rays of the Sun is 55°. Estimate the depth *d* of the crater.

17. **USING STRUCTURE** Find the tangent of the smaller acute angle in a right triangle with side lengths 5, 12, and 13.

18. **USING STRUCTURE** Find the tangent of the larger acute angle in a right triangle with side lengths 3, 4, and 5.

19. **REASONING** How does the tangent of an acute angle in a right triangle change as the angle measure increases? Justify your answer.

20. **CRITICAL THINKING** For what angle measure(s) is the tangent of an acute angle in a right triangle equal to 1? greater than 1? less than 1? Justify your answer.

21. **MAKING AN ARGUMENT** Your family room has a sliding-glass door. You want to buy an awning for the door that will be just long enough to keep the Sun out when it is at its highest point in the sky. The angle of elevation of the rays of the Sun at this point is 70°, and the height of the door is 8 feet. Your sister claims you can determine how far the overhang should extend by multiplying 8 by tan 70°. Is your sister correct? Explain.

22. **HOW DO YOU SEE IT?** Write expressions for the tangent of each acute angle in the right triangle. Explain how the tangent of one acute angle is related to the tangent of the other acute angle. What kind of angle pair is ∠A and ∠B?

23. **REASONING** Explain why it is not possible to find the tangent of a right angle or an obtuse angle.

24. **THOUGHT PROVOKING** To create the diagram below, you begin with an isosceles right triangle with legs 1 unit long. Then the hypotenuse of the first triangle becomes the leg of a second triangle, whose remaining leg is 1 unit long. Continue the diagram until you have constructed an angle whose tangent is $\dfrac{1}{\sqrt{6}}$. Approximate the measure of this angle.

25. **PROBLEM SOLVING** Your class is having a class picture taken on the lawn. The photographer is positioned 14 feet away from the center of the class. The photographer turns 50° to look at either end of the class.

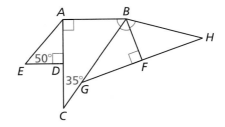

   a. What is the distance between the ends of the class?

   b. The photographer turns another 10° either way to see the end of the camera range. If each student needs 2 feet of space, about how many more students can fit at the end of each row? Explain.

26. **PROBLEM SOLVING** Find the perimeter of the figure, where $AC = 26$, $AD = BF$, and D is the midpoint of $\overline{AC}$.

───Maintaining Mathematical Proficiency── Reviewing what you learned in previous grades and lessons

Find the value of x. *(Section 9.2)*

27.

28.

29.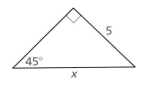

9.5 The Sine and Cosine Ratios

Essential Question How is a right triangle used to find the sine and cosine of an acute angle? Is there a unique right triangle that must be used?

Let △ABC be a right triangle with acute ∠A. The *sine* of ∠A and *cosine* of ∠A (written as sin A and cos A, respectively) are defined as follows.

$$\sin A = \frac{\text{length of leg opposite } \angle A}{\text{length of hypotenuse}} = \frac{BC}{AB}$$

$$\cos A = \frac{\text{length of leg adjacent to } \angle A}{\text{length of hypotenuse}} = \frac{AC}{AB}$$

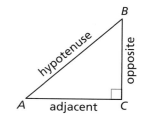

EXPLORATION 1 Calculating Sine and Cosine Ratios

Work with a partner. Use dynamic geometry software.

a. Construct △ABC, as shown. Construct segments perpendicular to $\overline{AC}$ to form right triangles that share vertex A and are similar to △ABC with vertices, as shown.

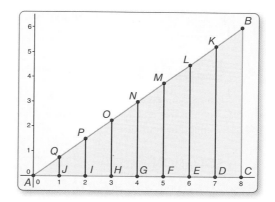

Sample
Points
A(0, 0)
B(8, 6)
C(8, 0)
Angle
m∠BAC = 36.87°

b. Calculate each given ratio to complete the table for the decimal values of sin A and cos A for each right triangle. What can you conclude?

Sine ratio	$\frac{BC}{AB}$	$\frac{KD}{AK}$	$\frac{LE}{AL}$	$\frac{MF}{AM}$	$\frac{NG}{AN}$	$\frac{OH}{AO}$	$\frac{PI}{AP}$	$\frac{QJ}{AQ}$
sin A								
Cosine ratio	$\frac{AC}{AB}$	$\frac{AD}{AK}$	$\frac{AE}{AL}$	$\frac{AF}{AM}$	$\frac{AG}{AN}$	$\frac{AH}{AO}$	$\frac{AI}{AP}$	$\frac{AJ}{AQ}$
cos A								

LOOKING FOR STRUCTURE

To be proficient in math, you need to look closely to discern a pattern or structure.

Communicate Your Answer

2. How is a right triangle used to find the sine and cosine of an acute angle? Is there a unique right triangle that must be used?

3. In Exploration 1, what is the relationship between ∠A and ∠B in terms of their measures? Find sin B and cos B. How are these two values related to sin A and cos A? Explain why these relationships exist.

9.5 Lesson

Core Vocabulary

sine, *p. 548*
cosine, *p. 548*
angle of depression, *p. 551*

What You Will Learn

▶ Use the sine and cosine ratios.
▶ Find the sine and cosine of angle measures in special right triangles.
▶ Solve real-life problems involving sine and cosine ratios.
▶ Use a trigonometric identity.

Using the Sine and Cosine Ratios

The **sine** and **cosine** ratios are trigonometric ratios for acute angles that involve the lengths of a leg and the hypotenuse of a right triangle.

Core Concept

Sine and Cosine Ratios

Let $\triangle ABC$ be a right triangle with acute $\angle A$. The sine of $\angle A$ and cosine of $\angle A$ (written as sin A and cos A) are defined as follows.

$$\sin A = \frac{\text{length of leg opposite } \angle A}{\text{length of hypotenuse}} = \frac{BC}{AB}$$

$$\cos A = \frac{\text{length of leg adjacent to } \angle A}{\text{length of hypotenuse}} = \frac{AC}{AB}$$

EXAMPLE 1   Finding Sine and Cosine Ratios

Find sin S, sin R, cos S, and cos R. Write each answer as a fraction and as a decimal rounded to four places.

SOLUTION

$$\sin S = \frac{\text{opp. } \angle S}{\text{hyp.}} = \frac{RT}{SR} = \frac{63}{65} \approx 0.9692 \qquad \sin R = \frac{\text{opp. } \angle R}{\text{hyp.}} = \frac{ST}{SR} = \frac{16}{65} \approx 0.2462$$

$$\cos S = \frac{\text{adj. to } \angle S}{\text{hyp.}} = \frac{ST}{SR} = \frac{16}{65} \approx 0.2462 \qquad \cos R = \frac{\text{adj. to } \angle R}{\text{hyp.}} = \frac{RT}{SR} = \frac{63}{65} \approx 0.9692$$

In Example 1, notice that sin S = cos R and sin R = cos S. This is true because the side opposite $\angle S$ is adjacent to $\angle R$ and the side opposite $\angle R$ is adjacent to $\angle S$. The relationship between the sine and cosine of $\angle S$ and $\angle R$ is true for all complementary angles.

Core Concept

Sine and Cosine of Complementary Angles

The sine of an acute angle is equal to the cosine of its complement. The cosine of an acute angle is equal to the sine of its complement.

Let A and B be complementary angles. Then the following statements are true.

$$\sin A = \cos(90° - A) = \cos B \qquad \sin B = \cos(90° - B) = \cos A$$

$$\cos A = \sin(90° - A) = \sin B \qquad \cos B = \sin(90° - B) = \sin A$$

EXAMPLE 2   Rewriting Trigonometric Expressions

Write sin 56° in terms of cosine.

SOLUTION

Use the fact that the sine of an acute angle is equal to the cosine of its complement.

$$\sin 56° = \cos(90° - 56°) = \cos 34°$$

▶   The sine of 56° is the same as the cosine of 34°.

You can use the sine and cosine ratios to find unknown measures in right triangles.

EXAMPLE 3   Finding Leg Lengths

Find the values of x and y using sine and cosine.
Round your answers to the nearest tenth.

SOLUTION

Step 1   Use a sine ratio to find the value of x.

$$\sin 26° = \frac{\text{opp.}}{\text{hyp.}}$$ Write ratio for sine of 26°.

$$\sin 26° = \frac{x}{14}$$ Substitute.

$$14 \cdot \sin 26° = x$$ Multiply each side by 14.

$$6.1 \approx x$$ Use a calculator.

▶   The value of x is about 6.1.

Step 2   Use a cosine ratio to find the value of y.

$$\cos 26° = \frac{\text{adj.}}{\text{hyp.}}$$ Write ratio for cosine of 26°.

$$\cos 26° = \frac{y}{14}$$ Substitute.

$$14 \cdot \cos 26° = y$$ Multiply each side by 14.

$$12.6 \approx y$$ Use a calculator.

▶   The value of y is about 12.6.

Monitoring Progress   Help in English and Spanish at *BigIdeasMath.com*

1. Find sin D, sin F, cos D, and cos F. Write each answer as a fraction and as a decimal rounded to four places.

2. Write cos 23° in terms of sine.

3. Find the values of u and t using sine and cosine. Round your answers to the nearest tenth.

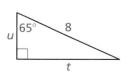

Finding Sine and Cosine in Special Right Triangles

EXAMPLE 4 **Finding the Sine and Cosine of 45°**

Find the sine and cosine of a 45° angle.

SOLUTION

Begin by sketching a 45°-45°-90° triangle. Because all such triangles are similar, you can simplify your calculations by choosing 1 as the length of each leg. Using the 45°-45°-90° Triangle Theorem, the length of the hypotenuse is $\sqrt{2}$.

STUDY TIP

Notice that

$\sin 45° = \cos(90 - 45)°$

$\qquad = \cos 45°.$

$$\sin 45° = \frac{\text{opp.}}{\text{hyp.}} \qquad\qquad \cos 45° = \frac{\text{adj.}}{\text{hyp.}}$$

$$= \frac{1}{\sqrt{2}} \qquad\qquad\qquad = \frac{1}{\sqrt{2}}$$

$$= \frac{\sqrt{2}}{2} \qquad\qquad\qquad = \frac{\sqrt{2}}{2}$$

$$\approx 0.7071 \qquad\qquad\qquad \approx 0.7071$$

EXAMPLE 5 **Finding the Sine and Cosine of 30°**

Find the sine and cosine of a 30° angle.

SOLUTION

Begin by sketching a 30°-60°-90° triangle. Because all such triangles are similar, you can simplify your calculations by choosing 1 as the length of the shorter leg. Using the 30°-60°-90° Triangle Theorem, the length of the longer leg is $\sqrt{3}$ and the length of the hypotenuse is 2.

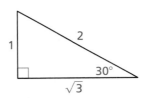

$$\sin 30° = \frac{\text{opp.}}{\text{hyp.}} \qquad\qquad \cos 30° = \frac{\text{adj.}}{\text{hyp.}}$$

$$= \frac{1}{2} \qquad\qquad\qquad = \frac{\sqrt{3}}{2}$$

$$= 0.5000 \qquad\qquad\qquad \approx 0.8660$$

Monitoring Progress Help in English and Spanish at *BigIdeasMath.com*

4. Find the sine and cosine of a 60° angle.

Solving Real-Life Problems

Recall from the previous lesson that the angle an upward line of sight makes with a horizontal line is called the *angle of elevation*. The angle that a downward line of sight makes with a horizontal line is called the **angle of depression**.

EXAMPLE 6   **Modeling with Mathematics**

You are skiing on a mountain with an altitude of 1200 feet. The angle of depression is 21°. Find the distance x you ski down the mountain to the nearest foot.

21°

x ft

1200 ft

Not drawn to scale

SOLUTION

1. **Understand the Problem** You are given the angle of depression and the altitude of the mountain. You need to find the distance that you ski down the mountain.

2. **Make a Plan** Write a trigonometric ratio for the sine of the angle of depression involving the distance x. Then solve for x.

3. **Solve the Problem**

$$\sin 21° = \frac{\text{opp.}}{\text{hyp.}} \qquad \text{Write ratio for sine of } 21°.$$

$$\sin 21° = \frac{1200}{x} \qquad \text{Substitute.}$$

$$x \cdot \sin 21° = 1200 \qquad \text{Multiply each side by } x.$$

$$x = \frac{1200}{\sin 21°} \qquad \text{Divide each side by } \sin 21°.$$

$$x \approx 3348.5 \qquad \text{Use a calculator.}$$

▶ You ski about 3349 feet down the mountain.

4. **Look Back** Check your answer. The value of $\sin 21°$ is about 0.3584. Substitute for x in the sine ratio and compare the values.

$$\frac{1200}{x} \approx \frac{1200}{3348.5}$$

$$\approx 0.3584$$

This value is approximately the same as the value of $\sin 21°$. ✓

Monitoring Progress Help in English and Spanish at *BigIdeasMath.com*

5. **WHAT IF?** In Example 6, the angle of depression is 28°. Find the distance x you ski down the mountain to the nearest foot.

Using a Trigonometric Identity

In the figure, the point (x, y) is on a circle of radius 1 with center at the origin. Consider an angle θ (the Greek letter *theta*) with its vertex at the origin. You know that $x = \cos \theta$ and $y = \sin \theta$. By the Pythagorean Theorem,

$$x^2 + y^2 = 1.$$

So,

$$\cos^2 \theta + \sin^2 \theta = 1.$$

STUDY TIP

Note that $\sin^2 \theta$ represents $(\sin \theta)^2$ and $\cos^2 \theta$ represents $(\cos \theta)^2$.

The equation $\cos^2 \theta + \sin^2 \theta = 1$ is true for any value of θ. In this section, θ will always be an acute angle. A trigonometric equation that is true for all values of the variable for which both sides of the equation are defined is called a *trigonometric identity*. Because of its derivation above, $\cos^2 \theta + \sin^2 \theta = 1$ is also referred to as a *Pythagorean identity*.

EXAMPLE 7 Finding Trigonometric Values

Given that $\cos \theta = \dfrac{3}{5}$, find $\sin \theta$ and $\tan \theta$.

SOLUTION

Step 1 Find $\sin \theta$.

$\sin^2 \theta + \cos^2 \theta = 1$	Write Pythagorean identity.
$\sin^2 \theta + \left(\dfrac{3}{5}\right)^2 = 1$	Substitute $\dfrac{3}{5}$ for $\cos \theta$.
$\sin^2 \theta + \dfrac{9}{25} = 1$	Evaluate power.
$\sin^2 \theta = 1 - \dfrac{9}{25}$	Subtract $\dfrac{9}{25}$ from each side.
$\sin^2 \theta = \dfrac{16}{25}$	Subtract.
$\sin \theta = \dfrac{4}{5}$	Take the positive square root of each side.

STUDY TIP

Using the diagram above, you can write

$$\tan \theta = \frac{y}{x} = \frac{\sin \theta}{\cos \theta}.$$

Step 2 Find $\tan \theta$ using $\sin \theta$ and $\cos \theta$.

$$\tan \theta = \frac{\sin \theta}{\cos \theta} = \frac{\dfrac{4}{5}}{\dfrac{3}{5}} = \frac{4}{3}$$

Monitoring Progress Help in English and Spanish at *BigIdeasMath.com*

6. Given that $\sin \theta = \dfrac{5}{13}$, find $\cos \theta$ and $\tan \theta$.

Vocabulary and Core Concept Check

1. **VOCABULARY** The sine ratio compares the length of _____ to the length of _____.

2. **VOCABULARY** The _____ ratio compares the length of the adjacent leg to the length of the hypotenuse.

3. **WRITING** How are angles of elevation and angles of depression similar? How are they different?

4. **WHICH ONE DOESN'T BELONG?** Which ratio does *not* belong with the other three? Explain your reasoning.

| sin B | cos C | tan B | $\dfrac{AC}{BC}$ |

Monitoring Progress and Modeling with Mathematics

In Exercises 5–10, find sin *D*, sin *E*, cos *D*, and cos *E*. Write each answer as a fraction and as a decimal rounded to four places. *(See Example 1.)*

5.

6.

7.

8.

9.

10.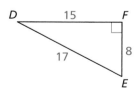

In Exercises 11–14, write the expression in terms of cosine. *(See Example 2.)*

11. sin 37°

12. sin 81°

13. sin 29°

14. sin 64°

In Exercises 15–18, write the expression in terms of sine.

15. cos 59°

16. cos 42°

17. cos 73°

18. cos 18°

In Exercises 19–24, find the value of each variable using sine and cosine. Round your answers to the nearest tenth. *(See Example 3.)*

19.

20.

21.

22.

23.

24.

25. REASONING Which ratios are equal? Select all that apply. *(See Example 4.)*

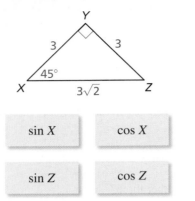

sin X	cos X

sin Z	cos Z

26. REASONING Which ratios are equal to $\frac{1}{2}$? Select all that apply. *(See Example 5.)*

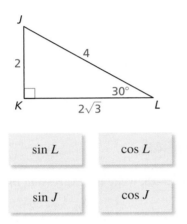

sin L	cos L

sin J	cos J

27. REASONING Write the trigonometric ratios that have a value of $\frac{\sqrt{3}}{2}$.

28. REASONING Write the trigonometric ratios that have a value of $\frac{1}{2}$.

29. WRITING Explain how to tell which side of a right triangle is adjacent to an angle and which side is the hypotenuse.

30. ERROR ANALYSIS Describe and correct the error in finding sin A.

31. MODELING WITH MATHEMATICS The top of the slide is 12 feet from the ground and has an angle of depression of 53°. What is the length of the slide? *(See Example 6.)*

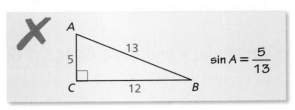

32. MODELING WITH MATHEMATICS Find the horizontal distance *x* the escalator covers.

In Exercises 33–38, find sin θ and tan θ.
(See Example 7.)

33. $\cos \theta = \frac{2}{5}$ **34.** $\cos \theta = \frac{3}{7}$

35. $\cos \theta = \frac{5}{9}$ **36.** $\cos \theta = \frac{8}{11}$

37. $\cos \theta = \frac{7}{8}$ **38.** $\cos \theta = \frac{9}{10}$

In Exercises 39–44, find cos θ and tan θ.

39. $\sin \theta = \frac{1}{2}$ **40.** $\sin \theta = \frac{2}{3}$

41. $\sin \theta = \frac{5}{8}$ **42.** $\sin \theta = \frac{7}{10}$

43. $\sin \theta = \frac{2}{9}$ **44.** $\sin \theta = \frac{6}{7}$

45. ERROR ANALYSIS Describe and correct the error in finding $\cos \theta$ when $\sin \theta = \frac{8}{9}$.

$$\cos^2 \theta - \sin^2 \theta = 1$$
$$\cos^2 \theta - \left(\frac{8}{9}\right)^2 = 1$$
$$\cos^2 \theta - \frac{64}{81} = 1$$
$$\cos^2 \theta = 1 + \frac{64}{81}$$
$$\cos^2 \theta = \frac{145}{81}$$
$$\cos \theta = \frac{\sqrt{145}}{9}$$

46. ERROR ANALYSIS Describe and correct the error in finding $\sin \theta$ when $\cos \theta = \frac{18}{25}$.

$$\sin^2 \theta + \cos^2 \theta = 1$$
$$\sin^2 \theta + \frac{18}{25} = 1$$
$$\sin^2 \theta = 1 - \frac{18}{25}$$
$$\sin^2 \theta = \frac{7}{25}$$
$$\sin \theta = \frac{\sqrt{7}}{5}$$

47. PROBLEM SOLVING You are flying a kite with 20 feet of string extended. The angle of elevation from the spool of string to the kite is 67°.

a. Draw and label a diagram that represents the situation.

b. How far off the ground is the kite if you hold the spool 5 feet off the ground? Describe how the height where you hold the spool affects the height of the kite.

48. MAKING AN ARGUMENT Your friend uses the equation $\sin 49° = \frac{x}{16}$ to find BC. Your cousin uses the equation $\cos 41° = \frac{x}{16}$ to find BC. Who is correct? Explain your reasoning.

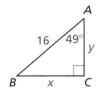

49. MODELING WITH MATHEMATICS Planes that fly at high speeds and low elevations have radar systems that can determine the range of an obstacle and the angle of elevation to the top of the obstacle. The radar of a plane flying at an altitude of 20,000 feet detects a tower that is 25,000 feet away, with an angle of elevation of 1°.

a. How many feet must the plane rise to pass over the tower?

b. Planes cannot come closer than 1000 feet vertically to any object. At what altitude must the plane fly in order to pass over the tower?

50. WRITING Describe what you must know about a triangle in order to use the sine ratio and what you must know about a triangle in order to use the cosine ratio.

51. MATHEMATICAL CONNECTIONS If $\triangle EQU$ is equilateral and $\triangle RGT$ is a right triangle with $RG = 2$, $RT = 1$, and $m\angle T = 90°$, show that $\sin E = \cos G$.

52. MODELING WITH MATHEMATICS Submarines use sonar systems, which are similar to radar systems, to detect obstacles. Sonar systems use sound to detect objects under water.

a. You are traveling underwater in a submarine. The sonar system detects an iceberg 4000 meters ahead, with an angle of depression of 34° to the bottom of the iceberg. How many meters must the submarine lower to pass under the iceberg?

b. The sonar system then detects a sunken ship 1500 meters ahead, with an angle of elevation of 19° to the highest part of the sunken ship. How many meters must the submarine rise to pass over the sunken ship?

53. REASONING Use $\sin A = \dfrac{\text{opp.}}{\text{hyp.}}$ and $\cos A = \dfrac{\text{adj.}}{\text{hyp.}}$ to show that $\tan A = \dfrac{\sin A}{\cos A}$.

54. HOW DO YOU SEE IT? Using only the given information, would you use a sine ratio or a cosine ratio to find the length of the hypotenuse? Explain your reasoning.

55. MULTIPLE REPRESENTATIONS You are standing on a cliff above an ocean. You see a sailboat from your vantage point 30 feet above the ocean.

   a. Draw and label a diagram of the situation.

   b. Make a table showing the angle of depression and the length of your line of sight. Use the angles 40°, 50°, 60°, 70°, and 80°.

   c. Graph the values you found in part (b), with the angle measures on the x-axis.

   d. Predict the length of the line of sight when the angle of depression is 30°.

56. THOUGHT PROVOKING One of the following infinite series represents $\sin x$ and the other one represents $\cos x$ (where x is measured in radians). Which is which? Justify your answer. Then use each series to approximate the sine and cosine of $\dfrac{\pi}{6}$. (*Hints*: $\pi = 180°$; $5! = 5 \cdot 4 \cdot 3 \cdot 2 \cdot 1$; Find the values that the sine and cosine ratios approach as the angle measure approaches zero.)

   a. $x - \dfrac{x^3}{3!} + \dfrac{x^5}{5!} - \dfrac{x^7}{7!} + \cdots$

   b. $1 - \dfrac{x^2}{2!} + \dfrac{x^4}{4!} - \dfrac{x^6}{6!} + \cdots$

57. ABSTRACT REASONING Make a conjecture about how you could use trigonometric ratios to find angle measures in a triangle.

58. CRITICAL THINKING Explain why the area of $\triangle ABC$ in the diagram can be found using the formula Area $= \frac{1}{2}ab \sin C$. Then calculate the area when $a = 4$, $b = 7$, and $m\angle C = 40°$.

Maintaining Mathematical Proficiency
Reviewing what you learned in previous grades and lessons

Find the value of x. Tell whether the side lengths form a Pythagorean triple. *(Section 9.1)*

59.

60.

61.

62.
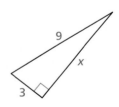

63. Use the two-way table to create a two-way table that shows the joint and marginal relative frequencies. *(Section 5.3)*

		Gender		
		Male	**Female**	**Total**
Class	**Sophomore**	26	54	80
	Junior	32	48	80
	Senior	50	55	105
	Total	108	157	265

9.6 Solving Right Triangles

Essential Question When you know the lengths of the sides of a right triangle, how can you find the measures of the two acute angles?

EXPLORATION 1 Solving Special Right Triangles

Work with a partner. Use the figures to find the values of the sine and cosine of ∠A and ∠B. Use these values to find the measures of ∠A and ∠B. Use dynamic geometry software to verify your answers.

a.

b.

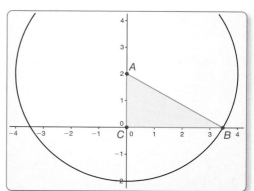

EXPLORATION 2 Solving Right Triangles

Work with a partner. You can use a calculator to find the measure of an angle when you know the value of the sine, cosine, or tangent of the angle. Use the inverse sine, inverse cosine, or inverse tangent feature of your calculator to approximate the measures of ∠A and ∠B to the nearest tenth of a degree. Then use dynamic geometry software to verify your answers.

a.

b.

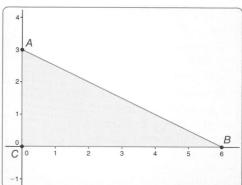

ATTENDING TO PRECISION

To be proficient in math, you need to calculate accurately and efficiently, expressing numerical answers with a degree of precision appropriate for the problem context.

Communicate Your Answer

3. When you know the lengths of the sides of a right triangle, how can you find the measures of the two acute angles?

4. A ladder leaning against a building forms a right triangle with the building and the ground. The legs of the right triangle (in meters) form a 5-12-13 Pythagorean triple. Find the measures of the two acute angles to the nearest tenth of a degree.

Core Vocabulary

inverse tangent, *p. 558*
inverse sine, *p. 558*
inverse cosine, *p. 558*
solve a right triangle, *p. 559*

What You Will Learn

▶ Use inverse trigonometric ratios.
▶ Solve right triangles.

Using Inverse Trigonometric Ratios

EXAMPLE 1   **Identifying Angles from Trigonometric Ratios**

Determine which of the two acute angles has a cosine of 0.5.

SOLUTION

Find the cosine of each acute angle.

$$\cos A = \frac{\text{adj. to } \angle A}{\text{hyp.}} = \frac{\sqrt{3}}{2} \approx 0.8660 \qquad \cos B = \frac{\text{adj. to } \angle B}{\text{hyp.}} = \frac{1}{2} = 0.5$$

▶ The acute angle that has a cosine of 0.5 is $\angle B$.

If the measure of an acute angle is 60°, then its cosine is 0.5. The converse is also true. If the cosine of an acute angle is 0.5, then the measure of the angle is 60°. So, in Example 1, the measure of $\angle B$ must be 60° because its cosine is 0.5.

🌀 Core Concept

Inverse Trigonometric Ratios

Let $\angle A$ be an acute angle.

Inverse Tangent   If $\tan A = x$, then $\tan^{-1} x = m\angle A$. $\tan^{-1} \dfrac{BC}{AC} = m\angle A$

Inverse Sine   If $\sin A = y$, then $\sin^{-1} y = m\angle A$. $\sin^{-1} \dfrac{BC}{AB} = m\angle A$

Inverse Cosine   If $\cos A = z$, then $\cos^{-1} z = m\angle A$. $\cos^{-1} \dfrac{AC}{AB} = m\angle A$

EXAMPLE 2   **Finding Angle Measures**

Let $\angle A$, $\angle B$, and $\angle C$ be acute angles. Use a calculator to approximate the measures of $\angle A$, $\angle B$, and $\angle C$ to the nearest tenth of a degree.

a. $\tan A = 0.75$ **b.** $\sin B = 0.87$ **c.** $\cos C = 0.15$

SOLUTION

a. $m\angle A = \tan^{-1} 0.75 \approx 36.9°$

b. $m\angle B = \sin^{-1} 0.87 \approx 60.5°$

c. $m\angle C = \cos^{-1} 0.15 \approx 81.4°$

Monitoring Progress Help in English and Spanish at *BigIdeasMath.com*

Determine which of the two acute angles has the given trigonometric ratio.

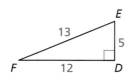

1. The sine of the angle is $\frac{12}{13}$.   **2.** The tangent of the angle is $\frac{5}{12}$.

Monitoring Progress Help in English and Spanish at *BigIdeasMath.com*

Let $\angle G$, $\angle H$, and $\angle K$ be acute angles. Use a calculator to approximate the measures of $\angle G$, $\angle H$, and $\angle K$ to the nearest tenth of a degree.

3. $\tan G = 0.43$ **4.** $\sin H = 0.68$ **5.** $\cos K = 0.94$

Solving Right Triangles

Core Concept

Solving a Right Triangle

To **solve a right triangle** means to find all unknown side lengths and angle measures. You can solve a right triangle when you know either of the following.

- two side lengths
- one side length and the measure of one acute angle

EXAMPLE 3   **Solving a Right Triangle**

Solve the right triangle. Round decimal answers to the nearest tenth.

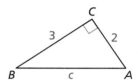

SOLUTION

Step 1 Use the Pythagorean Theorem to find the length of the hypotenuse.

$c^2 = a^2 + b^2$	Pythagorean Theorem
$c^2 = 3^2 + 2^2$	Substitute.
$c^2 = 13$	Simplify.
$c = \sqrt{13}$	Find the positive square root.
$c \approx 3.6$	Use a calculator.

ANOTHER WAY

You could also have found $m\angle A$ first by finding $\tan^{-1}\dfrac{3}{2} \approx 56.3°$.

Step 2 Find $m\angle B$.

$$m\angle B = \tan^{-1}\frac{2}{3} \approx 33.7°$$ Use a calculator.

Step 3 Find $m\angle A$.

Because $\angle A$ and $\angle B$ are complements, you can write

$$m\angle A = 90° - m\angle B$$
$$\approx 90° - 33.7°$$
$$= 56.3°.$$

▶ In $\triangle ABC$, $c \approx 3.6$, $m\angle B \approx 33.7°$, and $m\angle A \approx 56.3°$.

Monitoring Progress Help in English and Spanish at *BigIdeasMath.com*

Solve the right triangle. Round decimal answers to the nearest tenth.

6.   **7.**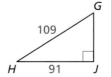

EXAMPLE 4 Solving a Right Triangle

Solve the right triangle. Round decimal answers to the nearest tenth.

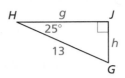

SOLUTION

Use trigonometric ratios to find the values of g and h.

$$\sin H = \frac{\text{opp.}}{\text{hyp.}} \qquad\qquad \cos H = \frac{\text{adj.}}{\text{hyp.}}$$

$$\sin 25° = \frac{h}{13} \qquad\qquad \cos 25° = \frac{g}{13}$$

$$13 \cdot \sin 25° = h \qquad\qquad 13 \cdot \cos 25° = g$$

$$5.5 \approx h \qquad\qquad 11.8 \approx g$$

Because $\angle H$ and $\angle G$ are complements, you can write

$$m\angle G = 90° - m\angle H = 90° - 25° = 65°.$$

▶ In $\triangle GHJ$, $h \approx 5.5$, $g \approx 11.8$, and $m\angle G = 65°$.

READING

A *raked stage* slants upward from front to back to give the audience a better view.

EXAMPLE 5 Solving a Real-Life Problem

Your school is building a *raked stage*. The stage will be 30 feet long from front to back, with a total rise of 2 feet. You want the rake (angle of elevation) to be 5° or less for safety. Is the raked stage within your desired range?

SOLUTION

Use the inverse sine ratio to find the degree measure x of the rake.

$$x \approx \sin^{-1}\frac{2}{30} \approx 3.8$$

▶ The rake is about 3.8°, so it is within your desired range of 5° or less.

Monitoring Progress Help in English and Spanish at *BigIdeasMath.com*

8. Solve the right triangle. Round decimal answers to the nearest tenth.

9. **WHAT IF?** In Example 5, suppose another raked stage is 20 feet long from front to back with a total rise of 2 feet. Is the raked stage within your desired range?

Vocabulary and Core Concept Check

1. **COMPLETE THE SENTENCE** To solve a right triangle means to find the measures of all its _____ and _____.

2. **WRITING** Explain when you can use a trigonometric ratio to find a side length of a right triangle and when you can use the Pythagorean Theorem.

Monitoring Progress and Modeling with Mathematics

In Exercises 3–6, determine which of the two acute angles has the given trigonometric ratio. *(See Example 1.)*

3. The cosine of the angle is $\frac{4}{5}$.

4. The sine of the angle is $\frac{5}{11}$.

5. The sine of the angle is 0.96.

6. The tangent of the angle is 1.5.

In Exercises 7–12, let $\angle D$ be an acute angle. Use a calculator to approximate the measure of $\angle D$ to the nearest tenth of a degree. *(See Example 2.)*

7. $\sin D = 0.75$

8. $\sin D = 0.19$

9. $\cos D = 0.33$

10. $\cos D = 0.64$

11. $\tan D = 0.28$

12. $\tan D = 0.72$

In Exercises 13–18, solve the right triangle. Round decimal answers to the nearest tenth. *(See Examples 3 and 4.)*

13.

14.

15.

16.

17.

18.

19. **ERROR ANALYSIS** Describe and correct the error in using an inverse trigonometric ratio.

20. **PROBLEM SOLVING** In order to unload clay easily, the body of a dump truck must be elevated to at least 45°. The body of a dump truck that is 14 feet long has been raised 8 feet. Will the clay pour out easily? Explain your reasoning. *(See Example 5.)*

21. **PROBLEM SOLVING** You are standing on a footbridge that is 12 feet above a lake. You look down and see a duck in the water. The duck is 7 feet away from the footbridge. What is the angle of elevation from the duck to you?

22. HOW DO YOU SEE IT? Write three expressions that can be used to approximate the measure of ∠A. Which expression would you choose? Explain your choice.

23. MODELING WITH MATHEMATICS The Uniform Federal Accessibility Standards specify that a wheelchair ramp may not have an incline greater than 4.76°. You want to build a ramp with a vertical rise of 8 inches. You want to minimize the horizontal distance taken up by the ramp. Draw a diagram showing the approximate dimensions of your ramp.

24. MODELING WITH MATHEMATICS The horizontal part of a step is called the *tread*. The vertical part is called the *riser*. The recommended riser-to-tread ratio is 7 inches : 11 inches.

a. Find the value of x for stairs built using the recommended riser-to-tread ratio.

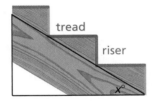

b. You want to build stairs that are less steep than the stairs in part (a). Give an example of a riser-to-tread ratio that you could use. Find the value of x for your stairs.

25. USING TOOLS Find the measure of ∠R without using a protractor. Justify your technique.

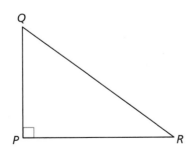

26. MAKING AN ARGUMENT Your friend claims that $\tan^{-1} x = \dfrac{1}{\tan x}$. Is your friend correct? Explain your reasoning.

USING STRUCTURE In Exercises 27 and 28, solve each triangle.

27. △JKM and △LKM

28. △TUS and △VTW

29. MATHEMATICAL CONNECTIONS Write an expression that can be used to find the measure of the acute angle formed by each line and the x-axis. Then approximate the angle measure to the nearest tenth of a degree.

a. $y = 3x$

b. $y = \dfrac{4}{3}x + 4$

30. THOUGHT PROVOKING Simplify each expression. Justify your answer.

a. $\sin^{-1}(\sin x)$

b. $\tan(\tan^{-1} y)$

c. $\cos(\cos^{-1} z)$

31. REASONING Explain why the expression $\sin^{-1}(1.2)$ does not make sense.

32. USING STRUCTURE The perimeter of rectangle *ABCD* is 16 centimeters, and the ratio of its width to its length is 1 : 3. Segment *BD* divides the rectangle into two congruent triangles. Find the side lengths and angle measures of these two triangles.

Maintaining Mathematical Proficiency Reviewing what you learned in previous grades and lessons

Solve the equation. *(Skills Review Handbook)*

33. $\dfrac{12}{x} = \dfrac{3}{2}$

34. $\dfrac{13}{9} = \dfrac{x}{18}$

35. $\dfrac{x}{2.1} = \dfrac{4.1}{3.5}$

36. $\dfrac{5.6}{12.7} = \dfrac{4.9}{x}$

Core Vocabulary

trigonometric ratio, *p. 542*   cosine, *p. 548*   inverse cosine, *p. 558*
tangent, *p. 542*   angle of depression, *p. 551*   solve a right triangle, *p. 559*
angle of elevation, *p. 544*   inverse tangent, *p. 558*
sine, *p. 548*   inverse sine, *p. 558*

Core Concepts

Section 9.4

Tangent Ratio, *p. 542*

Section 9.5

Sine and Cosine Ratios, *p. 548*
Sine and Cosine of Complementary Angles, *p. 548*
Using a Trigonometric Identity, *p. 552*

Section 9.6

Inverse Trigonometric Ratios, *p. 558*
Solving a Right Triangle, *p. 559*

Mathematical Practices

1. In Exercise 21 on page 546, your brother claims that you could determine how far the
    overhang should extend by dividing 8 by tan 70°. Justify his conclusion and explain why
    it works.

2. In Exercise 47 on page 555, explain the flaw in the argument that the kite is 18.4 feet high.

Performance Task:

Challenging the Rock Wall

There are multiple ways to use indirect measurement when
you cannot measure directly. When you look at a rock wall,
do you wonder about its height before you attempt to climb
it? What other situations require you to calculate a height
using trigonometry and indirect measurement?

To explore the answers to these questions and
more, check out the Performance Task and
Real-Life STEM video at *BigIdeasMath.com*.

9.1 The Pythagorean Theorem *(pp. 517–524)*

Find the value of *x*. Then tell whether the side lengths form a Pythagorean triple.

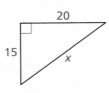

$$c^2 = a^2 + b^2 \qquad \text{Pythagorean Theorem}$$
$$x^2 = 15^2 + 20^2 \qquad \text{Substitute.}$$
$$x^2 = 225 + 400 \qquad \text{Multiply.}$$
$$x^2 = 625 \qquad \text{Add.}$$
$$x = 25 \qquad \text{Find the positive square root.}$$

▶ The value of *x* is 25. Because the side lengths 15, 20, and 25 are integers that satisfy the equation $c^2 = a^2 + b^2$, they form a Pythagorean triple.

Find the value of *x*. Then tell whether the side lengths form a Pythagorean triple.

1.

2.

3.

Verify that the segment lengths form a triangle. Is the triangle *acute*, *right*, or *obtuse*?

4. 6, 8, and 9

5. $10, 2\sqrt{2},$ and $6\sqrt{3}$

6. $13, 18,$ and $3\sqrt{55}$

9.2 Special Right Triangles *(pp. 525–530)*

Find the value of *x*. Write your answer in simplest form.

By the Triangle Sum Theorem, the measure of the third angle must be 45°, so the triangle is a 45°-45°-90° triangle.

$$\text{hypotenuse} = \text{leg} \cdot \sqrt{2} \qquad \text{45°-45°-90° Triangle Theorem}$$
$$x = 10 \cdot \sqrt{2} \qquad \text{Substitute.}$$
$$x = 10\sqrt{2} \qquad \text{Simplify.}$$

▶ The value of *x* is $10\sqrt{2}$.

Find the value of *x*. Write your answer in simplest form.

7.

8.

9.

9.3 Similar Right Triangles   *(pp. 531–538)*

Identify the similar triangles. Then find the value of x.

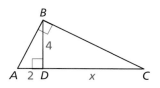

Sketch the three similar right triangles so that the corresponding angles and sides have the same orientation.

▶ $\triangle DBA \sim \triangle DCB \sim \triangle BCA$

By the Geometric Mean (Altitude) Theorem, you know that 4 is the geometric mean of 2 and *x*.

$4^2 = 2 \cdot x$	Geometric Mean (Altitude) Theorem
$16 = 2x$	Square 4.
$8 = x$	Divide each side by 2.

▶ The value of *x* is 8.

Identify the similar triangles. Then find the value of x.

10.

11.

12.

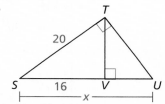

9.4 The Tangent Ratio   *(pp. 541–546)*

Find tan M and tan N. Write each answer as a fraction and as a decimal rounded to four places.

$$\tan M = \frac{\text{opp. } \angle M}{\text{adj. to } \angle M} = \frac{LN}{LM} = \frac{6}{8} = \frac{3}{4} = 0.7500$$

$$\tan N = \frac{\text{opp. } \angle N}{\text{adj. to } \angle N} = \frac{LM}{LN} = \frac{8}{6} = \frac{4}{3} \approx 1.3333$$

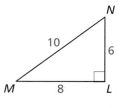

13. Find tan *J* and tan *L*. Write each answer as a fraction and as a decimal rounded to four decimal places.

14. The angle between the bottom of a fence and the top of a tree is 75°. The tree is 4 feet from the fence. How tall is the tree? Round your answer to the nearest foot.

9.5   **The Sine and Cosine Ratios**   *(pp. 547–556)*

Find sin A, sin B, cos A, and cos B. Write each answer as a fraction and as a decimal rounded to four places.

$$\sin A = \frac{\text{opp. } \angle A}{\text{hyp.}} = \frac{BC}{AB} = \frac{30}{34} = \frac{15}{17} \approx 0.8824$$

$$\sin B = \frac{\text{opp. } \angle B}{\text{hyp.}} = \frac{AC}{AB} = \frac{16}{34} = \frac{8}{17} \approx 0.4706$$

$$\cos A = \frac{\text{adj. to } \angle A}{\text{hyp.}} = \frac{AC}{AB} = \frac{16}{34} = \frac{8}{17} \approx 0.4706 \qquad \cos B = \frac{\text{adj. to } \angle B}{\text{hyp.}} = \frac{BC}{AB} = \frac{30}{34} = \frac{15}{17} \approx 0.8824$$

15.   Find sin X, sin Z, cos X, and cos Z. Write each answer as a fraction and as a decimal rounded to four decimal places.

Find the value of each variable using sine and cosine. Round your answers to the nearest tenth.

16.   **17.**   **18.**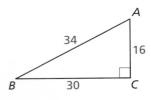

19.   Write sin 72° in terms of cosine.   **20.**   Given that $\sin \theta = \frac{24}{25}$, find $\cos \theta$ and $\tan \theta$.

9.6   **Solving Right Triangles**   *(pp. 557–562)*

Solve the right triangle. Round decimal answers to the nearest tenth.

Step 1   Use the Pythagorean Theorem to find the length of the hypotenuse.

$$c^2 = a^2 + b^2 \qquad \text{Pythagorean Theorem}$$
$$c^2 = 19^2 + 12^2 \qquad \text{Substitute.}$$
$$c^2 = 505 \qquad \text{Simplify.}$$
$$c = \sqrt{505} \qquad \text{Find the positive square root.}$$
$$c \approx 22.5 \qquad \text{Use a calculator.}$$

Step 2   Find $m\angle B$.

$$m\angle B = \tan^{-1} \frac{12}{19} \approx 32.3° \qquad \text{Use a calculator.}$$

Step 3   Find $m\angle A$. Because $\angle A$ and $\angle B$ are complements, you can write $m\angle A = 90° - m\angle B \approx 90° - 32.3° = 57.7°$.

▶   In $\triangle ABC$, $c \approx 22.5$, $m\angle B \approx 32.3°$, and $m\angle A \approx 57.7°$.

Solve the right triangle. Round decimal answers to the nearest tenth.

21.   **22.**   **23.**

Find the value of each variable. Round your answers to the nearest tenth.

1.

2.

3.

Verify that the segment lengths form a triangle. Is the triangle *acute*, *right*, or *obtuse*?

4. 16, 30, and 34

5. 4, $\sqrt{67}$, and 9

6. $\sqrt{5}$, 5, and 5.5

Solve △ABC. Round decimal answers to the nearest tenth.

7.

8.

9.

10. Find the geometric mean of 9 and 25.

11. Write cos 53° in terms of sine.

Find the value of each variable. Write your answers in simplest form.

12.

13.

14.

15. Given that $\cos \theta = \dfrac{5}{7}$, find sin θ and tan θ.

16. You are given the measures of both acute angles of a right triangle. Can you determine the side lengths? Explain.

17. You are at a parade looking up at a large balloon floating directly above the street. You are 60 feet from a point on the street directly beneath the balloon. To see the top of the balloon, you look up at an angle of 53°. To see the bottom of the balloon, you look up at an angle of 29°. Estimate the height *h* of the balloon.

viewing angle

18. You want to take a picture of a statue on Easter Island, called a *moai*. The moai is about 13 feet tall. Your camera is on a tripod that is 5 feet tall. The vertical viewing angle of your camera is set at 90°. How far from the moai should you stand so that the entire height of the moai is perfectly framed in the photo?

1. The size of a laptop screen is measured by the length of its diagonal. You want to purchase a laptop with the largest screen possible. Which laptop should you buy?

Ⓐ 12 in. 9 in.

Ⓑ 20 in. 11.25 in.

Ⓒ 12 in. 6.75 in.

Ⓓ 8 in. 6 in.

2. In $\triangle PQR$ and $\triangle SQT$, S is between P and Q, T is between R and Q, and $\dfrac{QS}{SP} = \dfrac{QT}{TR}$. What must be true about $\overline{ST}$ and $\overline{PR}$? Select all that apply.

$\overline{ST} \perp \overline{PR}$ $\overline{ST} \parallel \overline{PR}$ $ST = PR$ $ST = \dfrac{1}{2}PR$

3. In the diagram, $\triangle JKL \sim \triangle QRS$. Choose the symbol that makes each statement true.

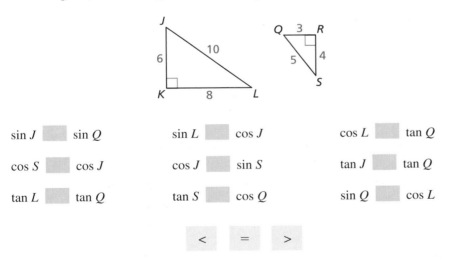

sin J ▭ sin Q   sin L ▭ cos J   cos L ▭ tan Q

cos S ▭ cos J   cos J ▭ sin S   tan J ▭ tan Q

tan L ▭ tan Q   tan S ▭ cos Q   sin Q ▭ cos L

$<$ $=$ $>$

4. Out of 60 students, 46 like fiction novels, 30 like nonfiction novels, and 22 like both. What is the probability that a randomly selected student likes fiction or nonfiction novels?

5. Create as many true equations as possible.

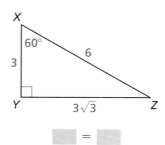

$$\boxed{} = \boxed{}$$

$\sin X$	$\cos X$	$\tan X$	$\dfrac{XY}{XZ}$	$\dfrac{YZ}{XZ}$
$\sin Z$	$\cos Z$	$\tan Z$	$\dfrac{XY}{YZ}$	$\dfrac{YZ}{XY}$

6. Prove that quadrilateral $DEFG$ is a kite.

Given $\overline{HE} \cong \overline{HG}, \overline{EG} \perp \overline{DF}$

Prove $\overline{FE} \cong \overline{FG}, \overline{DE} \cong \overline{DG}$

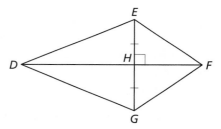

7. The area of the triangle is 42 square inches. Find the value of x.

8. Classify the solution(s) of each equation as real numbers, imaginary numbers, or pure imaginary numbers. Justify your answers.

a. $x + \sqrt{-16} = 0$

b. $(11 - 2i) - (-3i + 6) = 8 + x$

c. $3x^2 - 14 = -20$

d. $x^2 + 2x = -3$

e. $x^2 = 16$

f. $x^2 - 5x - 8 = 0$

9. The Red Pyramid in Egypt has a square base. Each side of the base measures 722 feet. The height of the pyramid is 343 feet.

a. Use the side length of the base, the height of the pyramid, and the Pythagorean Theorem to find the *slant height*, AB, of the pyramid.

b. Find AC.

c. Name three possible ways of finding $m\angle 1$. Then, find $m\angle 1$.

SEE the Big Idea

Seismograph *(p. 622)*

Saturn *(p. 617)*

Car *(p. 594)*

Dartboard *(p. 587)*

Bicycle Chain *(p. 579)*

Maintaining Mathematical Proficiency

Multiplying Binomials

Example 1 Find the product $(x + 3)(2x - 1)$.

$$
\underset{\text{First}\quad\text{Outer}\quad\text{Inner}\quad\text{Last}}{(x + 3)(2x - 1) = x(2x) + x(-1) + 3(2x) + (3)(-1)} \qquad \text{FOIL Method}
$$

$$
= 2x^2 + (-x) + 6x + (-3) \qquad \text{Multiply.}
$$

$$
= 2x^2 + 5x - 3 \qquad \text{Simplify.}
$$

▶ The product is $2x^2 + 5x - 3$.

Find the product.

1. $(x + 7)(x + 4)$

2. $(a + 1)(a - 5)$

3. $(q - 9)(3q - 4)$

4. $(2v - 7)(5v + 1)$

5. $(4h + 3)(2 + h)$

6. $(8 - 6b)(5 - 3b)$

Solving Quadratic Equations by Completing the Square

Example 2 Solve $x^2 + 8x - 3 = 0$ by completing the square.

$$
x^2 + 8x - 3 = 0 \qquad \text{Write original equation.}
$$

$$
x^2 + 8x = 3 \qquad \text{Add 3 to each side.}
$$

$$
x^2 + 8x + 4^2 = 3 + 4^2 \qquad \text{Complete the square by adding } \left(\tfrac{8}{2}\right)^2, \text{ or } 4^2, \text{ to each side.}
$$

$$
(x + 4)^2 = 19 \qquad \text{Write the left side as a square of a binomial.}
$$

$$
x + 4 = \pm\sqrt{19} \qquad \text{Take the square root of each side.}
$$

$$
x = -4 \pm\sqrt{19} \qquad \text{Subtract 4 from each side.}
$$

▶ The solutions are $x = -4 + \sqrt{19} \approx 0.36$ and $x = -4 - \sqrt{19} \approx -8.36$.

Solve the equation by completing the square. Round your answer to the nearest hundredth, if necessary.

7. $x^2 - 2x = 5$

8. $r^2 + 10r = -7$

9. $w^2 - 8w = 9$

10. $p^2 + 10p - 4 = 0$

11. $k^2 - 4k - 7 = 0$

12. $-z^2 + 2z = 1$

13. **ABSTRACT REASONING** Write an expression that represents the product of two consecutive positive odd integers. Explain your reasoning.

Mathematical Practices

Mathematically proficient students make sense of problems and do not give up when faced with challenges.

Analyzing Relationships of Circles

Core Concept

Circles and Tangent Circles

A **circle** is the set of all points in a plane that are equidistant from a given point called the **center** of the circle. A circle with center D is called "circle D" and can be written as $\odot D$.

circle D, or $\odot D$

Coplanar circles that intersect in one point are called **tangent circles**.

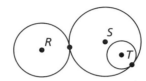

$\odot R$ and $\odot S$ are tangent circles.
$\odot S$ and $\odot T$ are tangent circles.

EXAMPLE 1 Relationships of Circles and Tangent Circles

a. Each circle at the right consists of points that are 3 units from the center. What is the greatest distance from any point on $\odot A$ to any point on $\odot B$?

b. Three circles, $\odot C$, $\odot D$, and $\odot E$, consist of points that are 3 units from their centers. The centers C, D, and E of the circles are collinear, $\odot C$ is tangent to $\odot D$, and $\odot D$ is tangent to $\odot E$. What is the distance from $\odot C$ to $\odot E$?

SOLUTION

a. Because the points on each circle are 3 units from the center, the greatest distance from any point on $\odot A$ to any point on $\odot B$ is $3 + 3 + 3 = 9$ units.

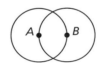

b. Because C, D, and E are collinear, $\odot C$ is tangent to $\odot D$, and $\odot D$ is tangent to $\odot E$, the circles are as shown. So, the distance from $\odot C$ to $\odot E$ is $3 + 3 = 6$ units.

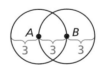

Monitoring Progress

Let $\odot A$, $\odot B$, and $\odot C$ consist of points that are 3 units from the centers.

1. Draw $\odot C$ so that it passes through points A and B in the figure at the right. Explain your reasoning.

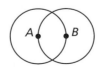

2. Draw $\odot A$, $\odot B$, and $\odot C$ so that each is tangent to the other two. Draw a larger circle, $\odot D$, that is tangent to each of the other three circles. Is the distance from point D to a point on $\odot D$ *less than*, *greater than*, or *equal to* 6? Explain.

10.1 Lines and Segments That Intersect Circles

Essential Question
What are the definitions of the lines and segments that intersect a circle?

EXPLORATION 1 **Lines and Line Segments That Intersect Circles**

Work with a partner. The drawing at the right shows five lines or segments that intersect a circle. Use the relationships shown to write a definition for each type of line or segment. Then use the Internet or some other resource to verify your definitions.

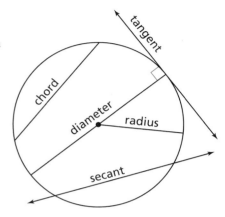

Chord: _____

Secant: _____

Tangent: _____

Radius: _____

Diameter: _____

EXPLORATION 2 **Using String to Draw a Circle**

Work with a partner. Use two pencils, a piece of string, and a piece of paper.

a. Tie the two ends of the piece of string loosely around the two pencils.

b. Anchor one pencil on the paper at the center of the circle. Use the other pencil to draw a circle around the anchor point while using slight pressure to keep the string taut. Do not let the string wind around either pencil.

REASONING ABSTRACTLY

To be proficient in math, you need to know and flexibly use different properties of operations and objects.

c. Explain how the distance between the two pencil points as you draw the circle is related to two of the lines or line segments you defined in Exploration 1.

Communicate Your Answer

3. What are the definitions of the lines and segments that intersect a circle?

4. Of the five types of lines and segments in Exploration 1, which one is a subset of another? Explain.

5. Explain how to draw a circle with a diameter of 8 inches.

Core Vocabulary

circle, *p. 574*
center, *p. 574*
radius, *p. 574*
chord, *p. 574*
diameter, *p. 574*
secant, *p. 574*
tangent, *p. 574*
point of tangency, *p. 574*
tangent circles, *p. 575*
concentric circles, *p. 575*
common tangent, *p. 575*

> **READING**
>
> The words "radius" and "diameter" refer to lengths as well as segments. For a given circle, think of *a* radius and *a* diameter as segments and *the* radius and *the* diameter as lengths.

> **STUDY TIP**
>
> In this book, assume that all segments, rays, or lines that appear to be tangent to a circle are tangents.

What You Will Learn

▶ Identify special segments and lines.
▶ Draw and identify common tangents.
▶ Use properties of tangents.

Identifying Special Segments and Lines

A **circle** is the set of all points in a plane that are equidistant from a given point called the **center** of the circle. A circle with center P is called "circle P" and can be written as $\odot P$.

circle *P*, or $\odot P$

🌀 Core Concept

Lines and Segments That Intersect Circles

A segment whose endpoints are the center and any point on a circle is a **radius**.

A **chord** is a segment whose endpoints are on a circle. A **diameter** is a chord that contains the center of the circle.

A **secant** is a line that intersects a circle in two points.

A **tangent** is a line in the plane of a circle that intersects the circle in exactly one point, the **point of tangency**. The *tangent ray* $\overrightarrow{AB}$ and the *tangent segment* $\overline{AB}$ are also called tangents.

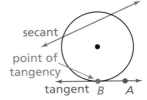

EXAMPLE 1 **Identifying Special Segments and Lines**

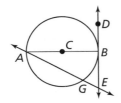

Tell whether the line, ray, or segment is best described as a *radius*, *chord*, *diameter*, *secant*, or *tangent* of $\odot C$.

a. $\overline{AC}$ b. $\overline{AB}$

c. $\overrightarrow{DE}$ d. $\overleftrightarrow{AE}$

SOLUTION

a. $\overline{AC}$ is a radius because C is the center and A is a point on the circle.

b. $\overline{AB}$ is a diameter because it is a chord that contains the center C.

c. $\overrightarrow{DE}$ is a tangent ray because it is contained in a line that intersects the circle in exactly one point.

d. $\overleftrightarrow{AE}$ is a secant because it is a line that intersects the circle in two points.

Monitoring Progress 🔊 Help in English and Spanish at *BigIdeasMath.com*

1. In Example 1, what word best describes $\overline{AG}$? $\overline{CB}$?

2. In Example 1, name a tangent and a tangent segment.

Drawing and Identifying Common Tangents

Core Concept

Coplanar Circles and Common Tangents

In a plane, two circles can intersect in two points, one point, or no points. Coplanar circles that intersect in one point are called **tangent circles**. Coplanar circles that have a common center are called **concentric circles**.

2 points of intersection

1 point of intersection (tangent circles)

no points of intersection

concentric circles

A line or segment that is tangent to two coplanar circles is called a **common tangent**. A *common internal tangent* intersects the segment that joins the centers of the two circles. A *common external tangent* does not intersect the segment that joins the centers of the two circles.

EXAMPLE 2   Drawing and Identifying Common Tangents

Tell how many common tangents the circles have and draw them. Use blue to indicate common external tangents and red to indicate common internal tangents.

a.   b.   c.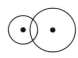

SOLUTION

Draw the segment that joins the centers of the two circles. Then draw the common tangents. Use blue to indicate lines that do not intersect the segment joining the centers and red to indicate lines that intersect the segment joining the centers.

a. 4 common tangents   **b.** 3 common tangents   **c.** 2 common tangents

---

Monitoring Progress   Help in English and Spanish at *BigIdeasMath.com*

Tell how many common tangents the circles have and draw them. State whether the tangents are external tangents or internal tangents.

3.   4.   5.

Using Properties of Tangents

🔄 Theorems

Tangent Line to Circle Theorem

In a plane, a line is tangent to a circle if and only if the line is perpendicular to a radius of the circle at its endpoint on the circle.

Proof Ex. 47, p. 580

Line m is tangent to $\odot Q$ if and only if $m \perp \overline{QP}$.

External Tangent Congruence Theorem

Tangent segments from a common external point are congruent.

Proof Ex. 46, p. 580

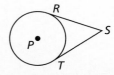

If $\overline{SR}$ and $\overline{ST}$ are tangent segments, then $\overline{SR} \cong \overline{ST}$.

EXAMPLE 3   **Verifying a Tangent to a Circle**

Is $\overline{ST}$ tangent to $\odot P$?

SOLUTION

Use the Converse of the Pythagorean Theorem. Because $12^2 + 35^2 = 37^2$, $\triangle PTS$ is a right triangle and $\overline{ST} \perp \overline{PT}$. So, $\overline{ST}$ is perpendicular to a radius of $\odot P$ at its endpoint on $\odot P$.

▶ By the Tangent Line to Circle Theorem, $\overline{ST}$ is tangent to $\odot P$.

EXAMPLE 4   **Finding the Radius of a Circle**

In the diagram, point B is a point of tangency. Find the radius r of $\odot C$.

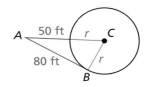

SOLUTION

You know from the Tangent Line to Circle Theorem that $\overline{AB} \perp \overline{BC}$, so $\triangle ABC$ is a right triangle. You can use the Pythagorean Theorem.

$AC^2 = BC^2 + AB^2$	Pythagorean Theorem
$(r + 50)^2 = r^2 + 80^2$	Substitute.
$r^2 + 100r + 2500 = r^2 + 6400$	Multiply.
$100r = 3900$	Subtract r^2 and 2500 from each side.
$r = 39$	Divide each side by 100.

▶ The radius is 39 feet.

CONSTRUCTION Constructing a Tangent to a Circle

Given $\odot C$ and point A, construct a line tangent to $\odot C$ that passes through A. Use a compass and straightedge.

SOLUTION

Step 1

Find a midpoint
Draw $\overline{AC}$. Construct the bisector of the segment and label the midpoint M.

Step 2

Draw a circle
Construct $\odot M$ with radius MA. Label one of the points where $\odot M$ intersects $\odot C$ as point B.

Step 3

Construct a tangent line
Draw $\overleftrightarrow{AB}$. It is a tangent to $\odot C$ that passes through A.

EXAMPLE 5 Using Properties of Tangents

$\overline{RS}$ is tangent to $\odot C$ at S, and $\overline{RT}$ is tangent to $\odot C$ at T. Find the value of x.

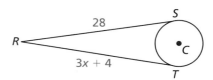

SOLUTION

$RS = RT$	External Tangent Congruence Theorem
$28 = 3x + 4$	Substitute.
$8 = x$	Solve for x.

▶ The value of x is 8.

Monitoring Progress Help in English and Spanish at *BigIdeasMath.com*

6. Is $\overline{DE}$ tangent to $\odot C$?

7. $\overline{ST}$ is tangent to $\odot Q$. Find the radius of $\odot Q$.

8. Points M and N are points of tangency. Find the value(s) of x.

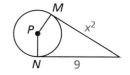

Vocabulary and Core Concept Check

1. **WRITING** How are chords and secants alike? How are they different?

2. **WRITING** Explain how you can determine from the context whether the words *radius* and *diameter* are referring to segments or lengths.

3. **COMPLETE THE SENTENCE** Coplanar circles that have a common center are called _____.

4. **WHICH ONE DOESN'T BELONG?** Which segment does *not* belong with the other three? Explain your reasoning.

| chord | radius | tangent | diameter |

Monitoring Progress and Modeling with Mathematics

In Exercises 5–10, use the diagram. *(See Example 1.)*

5. Name the circle.

6. Name two radii.

7. Name two chords.

8. Name a diameter.

9. Name a secant.

10. Name a tangent and a point of tangency.

In Exercises 11–14, copy the diagram. Tell how many common tangents the circles have and draw them. *(See Example 2.)*

11.   12.

13.   14.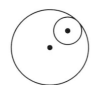

In Exercises 15–18, tell whether the common tangent is *internal* or *external*.

15.   16.

17.   18.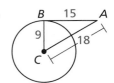

In Exercises 19–22, tell whether $\overline{AB}$ is tangent to $\odot C$. Explain your reasoning. *(See Example 3.)*

19.   20.

21.   22.

In Exercises 23–26, point *B* is a point of tangency. Find the radius *r* of $\odot C$. *(See Example 4.)*

23.   24.

25.   26.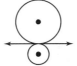

CONSTRUCTION In Exercises 27 and 28, construct ⊙C with the given radius and point A outside of ⊙C. Then construct a line tangent to ⊙C that passes through A.

27. $r = 2$ in.   **28.** $r = 4.5$ cm

In Exercises 29–32, points B and D are points of tangency. Find the value(s) of x. *(See Example 5.)*

29.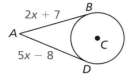

2x + 7
5x − 8

30.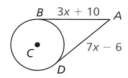

B   3x + 10   A
7x − 6

31.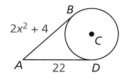

2x² + 4
A   22   D

32.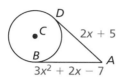

2x + 5
3x² + 2x − 7

33. ERROR ANALYSIS Describe and correct the error in determining whether $\overline{XY}$ is tangent to ⊙Z.

Because $11^2 + 60^2 = 61^2$, △XYZ is a right triangle. So, $\overline{XY}$ is tangent to ⊙Z.

34. ERROR ANALYSIS Describe and correct the error in finding the radius of ⊙T.

$39^2 - 36^2 = 15^2$
So, the radius is 15.

35. ABSTRACT REASONING For a point outside of a circle, how many lines exist tangent to the circle that pass through the point? How many such lines exist for a point on the circle? inside the circle? Explain your reasoning.

36. CRITICAL THINKING When will two lines tangent to the same circle not intersect? Justify your answer.

37. USING STRUCTURE Each side of quadrilateral TVWX is tangent to ⊙Y. Find the perimeter of the quadrilateral.

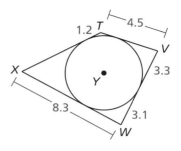

38. LOGIC In ⊙C, radii $\overline{CA}$ and $\overline{CB}$ are perpendicular. $\overleftrightarrow{BD}$ and $\overleftrightarrow{AD}$ are tangent to ⊙C.

a. Sketch ⊙C, $\overline{CA}$, $\overline{CB}$, $\overleftrightarrow{BD}$, and $\overleftrightarrow{AD}$.

b. What type of quadrilateral is CADB? Explain your reasoning.

39. MAKING AN ARGUMENT Two bike paths are tangent to an approximately circular pond. Your class is building a nature trail that begins at the intersection B of the bike paths and runs between the bike paths and over a bridge through the center P of the pond. Your classmate uses the Converse of the Angle Bisector Theorem to conclude that the trail must bisect the angle formed by the bike paths. Is your classmate correct? Explain your reasoning.

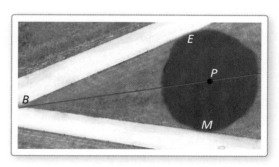

40. MODELING WITH MATHEMATICS A bicycle chain is pulled tightly so that $\overline{MN}$ is a common tangent of the gears. Find the distance between the centers of the gears.

41. WRITING Explain why the diameter of a circle is the longest chord of the circle.

42. HOW DO YOU SEE IT? In the figure, $\overrightarrow{PA}$ is tangent to the dime, $\overrightarrow{PC}$ is tangent to the quarter, and $\overrightarrow{PB}$ is a common internal tangent. How do you know that $\overline{PA} \cong \overline{PB} \cong \overline{PC}$?

43. PROOF In the diagram, $\overline{RS}$ is a common internal tangent to $\odot A$ and $\odot B$. Prove that $\dfrac{AC}{BC} = \dfrac{RC}{SC}$.

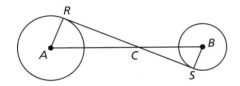

44. THOUGHT PROVOKING A polygon is *circumscribed* about a circle when every side of the polygon is tangent to the circle. In the diagram, quadrilateral $ABCD$ is circumscribed about $\odot Q$. Is it always true that $AB + CD = AD + BC$? Justify your answer.

45. MATHEMATICAL CONNECTIONS Find the values of x and y. Justify your answer.

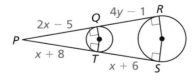

46. PROVING A THEOREM Prove the External Tangent Congruence Theorem.

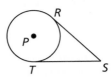

Given $\overline{SR}$ and $\overline{ST}$ are tangent to $\odot P$.
Prove $\overline{SR} \cong \overline{ST}$

47. PROVING A THEOREM Use the diagram to prove each part of the biconditional in the Tangent Line to Circle Theorem.

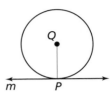

a. Prove indirectly that if a line is tangent to a circle, then it is perpendicular to a radius. (*Hint*: If you assume line m is not perpendicular to $\overline{QP}$, then the perpendicular segment from point Q to line m must intersect line m at some other point R.)

   Given Line m is tangent to $\odot Q$ at point P.
   Prove $m \perp \overline{QP}$

b. Prove indirectly that if a line is perpendicular to a radius at its endpoint, then the line is tangent to the circle.

   Given $m \perp \overline{QP}$
   Prove Line m is tangent to $\odot Q$.

48. REASONING In the diagram, $AB = AC = 12$, $BC = 8$, and all three segments are tangent to $\odot P$. What is the radius of $\odot P$? Justify your answer.

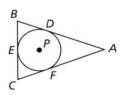

Maintaining Mathematical Proficiency
Reviewing what you learned in previous grades and lessons

Determine whether the events are independent. *(Section 5.2)*

49. A pouch contains three blue marbles and two red marbles. You randomly select one marble from the pouch, set it aside, then randomly select another marble from the pouch. Use a sample space to determine whether selecting a blue marble first and selecting a red marble second are independent events.

50. One-half of a spinner is blue and the other half is red. Use a sample space to determine whether randomly spinning blue and then red are independent events.

10.2 Finding Arc Measures

Essential Question How are circular arcs measured?

A **central angle** of a circle is an angle whose vertex is the center of the circle. A *circular arc* is a portion of a circle, as shown below. The measure of a circular arc is the measure of its central angle.

If $m\angle AOB < 180°$, then the circular arc is called a **minor arc** and is denoted by $\overset{\frown}{AB}$.

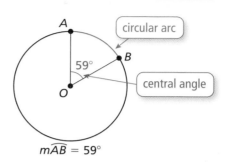

$m\overset{\frown}{AB} = 59°$

EXPLORATION 1 Measuring Circular Arcs

Work with a partner. Use dynamic geometry software to find the measure of $\overset{\frown}{BC}$. Verify your answers using trigonometry.

a.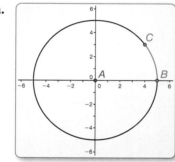

Points
$A(0, 0)$
$B(5, 0)$
$C(4, 3)$

b.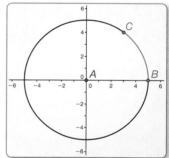

Points
$A(0, 0)$
$B(5, 0)$
$C(3, 4)$

c.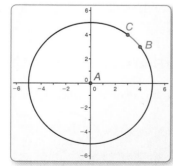

Points
$A(0, 0)$
$B(4, 3)$
$C(3, 4)$

d.

Points
$A(0, 0)$
$B(4, 3)$
$C(-4, 3)$

USING TOOLS STRATEGICALLY

To be proficient in math, you need to use technological tools to explore and deepen your understanding of concepts.

Communicate Your Answer

2. How are circular arcs measured?

3. Use dynamic geometry software to draw a circular arc with the given measure.

    a. 30°   **b.** 45°

    c. 60°   **d.** 90°

What You Will Learn

▶ Find arc measures.

▶ Identify congruent arcs.

▶ Prove circles are similar.

Finding Arc Measures

A **central angle** of a circle is an angle whose vertex is the center of the circle. In the diagram, $\angle ACB$ is a central angle of $\odot C$.

If $m\angle ACB$ is less than $180°$, then the points on $\odot C$ that lie in the interior of $\angle ACB$ form a **minor arc** with endpoints A and B. The points on $\odot C$ that do not lie on the minor arc AB form a **major arc** with endpoints A and B. A **semicircle** is an arc with endpoints that are the endpoints of a diameter.

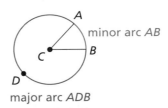

minor arc *AB*

major arc *ADB*

Minor arcs are named by their endpoints. The minor arc associated with $\angle ACB$ is named $\overset{\frown}{AB}$. Major arcs and semicircles are named by their endpoints and a point on the arc. The major arc associated with $\angle ACB$ can be named $\overset{\frown}{ADB}$.

STUDY TIP

The measure of a minor arc is less than 180°. The measure of a major arc is greater than 180°.

Core Concept

Measuring Arcs

The **measure of a minor arc** is the measure of its central angle. The expression $m\overset{\frown}{AB}$ is read as "the measure of arc AB."

The measure of the entire circle is $360°$. The **measure of a major arc** is the difference of $360°$ and the measure of the related minor arc. The measure of a semicircle is $180°$.

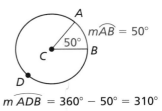

$m\overset{\frown}{AB} = 50°$

$m\overset{\frown}{ADB} = 360° - 50° = 310°$

EXAMPLE 1 **Finding Measures of Arcs**

Find the measure of each arc of $\odot P$, where $\overline{RT}$ is a diameter.

a. $\overset{\frown}{RS}$

b. $\overset{\frown}{RTS}$

c. $\overset{\frown}{RST}$

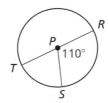

SOLUTION

a. $\overset{\frown}{RS}$ is a minor arc, so $m\overset{\frown}{RS} = m\angle RPS = 110°$.

b. $\overset{\frown}{RTS}$ is a major arc, so $m\overset{\frown}{RTS} = 360° - 110° = 250°$.

c. $\overline{RT}$ is a diameter, so $\overset{\frown}{RST}$ is a semicircle, and $m\overset{\frown}{RST} = 180°$.

Two arcs of the same circle are **adjacent arcs** when they intersect at exactly one point. You can add the measures of two adjacent arcs.

Postulate

Arc Addition Postulate

The measure of an arc formed by two adjacent arcs is the sum of the measures of the two arcs.

$$m\overset{\frown}{ABC} = m\overset{\frown}{AB} + m\overset{\frown}{BC}$$

EXAMPLE 2   Using the Arc Addition Postulate

Find the measure of each arc.

a. $\overset{\frown}{GE}$ b. $\overset{\frown}{GEF}$ c. $\overset{\frown}{GF}$

SOLUTION

a. $m\overset{\frown}{GE} = m\overset{\frown}{GH} + m\overset{\frown}{HE} = 40° + 80° = 120°$

b. $m\overset{\frown}{GEF} = m\overset{\frown}{GE} + m\overset{\frown}{EF} = 120° + 110° = 230°$

c. $m\overset{\frown}{GF} = 360° - m\overset{\frown}{GEF} = 360° - 230° = 130°$

EXAMPLE 3   Finding Measures of Arcs

A recent survey asked teenagers whether they would rather meet a famous musician, athlete, actor, inventor, or other person. The circle graph shows the results. Find the indicated arc measures.

a. $m\overset{\frown}{AC}$ b. $m\overset{\frown}{ACD}$

c. $m\overset{\frown}{ADC}$ d. $m\overset{\frown}{EBD}$

Whom Would You Rather Meet?

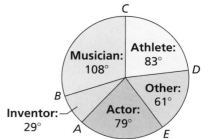

SOLUTION

a. $m\overset{\frown}{AC} = m\overset{\frown}{AB} + m\overset{\frown}{BC}$
   $= 29° + 108°$
   $= 137°$

c. $m\overset{\frown}{ADC} = 360° - m\overset{\frown}{AC}$
   $= 360° - 137°$
   $= 223°$

b. $m\overset{\frown}{ACD} = m\overset{\frown}{AC} + m\overset{\frown}{CD}$
   $= 137° + 83°$
   $= 220°$

d. $m\overset{\frown}{EBD} = 360° - m\overset{\frown}{ED}$
   $= 360° - 61°$
   $= 299°$

Monitoring Progress   Help in English and Spanish at *BigIdeasMath.com*

Identify the given arc as a *major arc*, *minor arc*, or *semicircle*. Then find the measure of the arc.

1. $\overset{\frown}{TQ}$ 2. $\overset{\frown}{QRT}$ 3. $\overset{\frown}{TQR}$

4. $\overset{\frown}{QS}$ 5. $\overset{\frown}{TS}$ 6. $\overset{\frown}{RST}$

Identifying Congruent Arcs

Two circles are **congruent circles** if and only if a rigid motion or a composition of rigid motions maps one circle onto the other. This statement is equivalent to the Congruent Circles Theorem below.

Theorem

Congruent Circles Theorem

Two circles are congruent circles if and only if they have the same radius.

Proof Ex. 35, p. 588

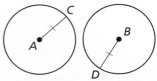

⊙A ≅ ⊙B if and only if $\overline{AC} \cong \overline{BD}$.

Two arcs are **congruent arcs** if and only if they have the same measure and they are arcs of the same circle or of congruent circles.

Theorem

Congruent Central Angles Theorem

In the same circle, or in congruent circles, two minor arcs are congruent if and only if their corresponding central angles are congruent.

Proof Ex. 37, p. 588

$\overset{\frown}{BC} \cong \overset{\frown}{DE}$ if and only if ∠BAC ≅ ∠DAE.

EXAMPLE 4   **Identifying Congruent Arcs**

Tell whether the red arcs are congruent. Explain why or why not.

a.   **b.**   **c.**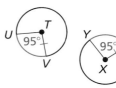

STUDY TIP

The two circles in part (c) are congruent by the Congruent Circles Theorem because they have the same radius.

SOLUTION

a. $\overset{\frown}{CD} \cong \overset{\frown}{EF}$ by the Congruent Central Angles Theorem because they are arcs of the same circle and they have congruent central angles, ∠CBD ≅ ∠FBE.

b. $\overset{\frown}{RS}$ and $\overset{\frown}{TU}$ have the same measure, but are not congruent because they are arcs of circles that are not congruent.

c. $\overset{\frown}{UV} \cong \overset{\frown}{YZ}$ by the Congruent Central Angles Theorem because they are arcs of congruent circles and they have congruent central angles, ∠UTV ≅ ∠YXZ.

Tell whether the red arcs are congruent. Explain why or why not.

7.

8.

Proving Circles Are Similar

 Theorem

Similar Circles Theorem

All circles are similar.

Proof p. 585; Ex. 33, p. 588

PROOF **Similar Circles Theorem**

All circles are similar.

Given $\odot C$ with center C and radius r,
$\odot D$ with center D and radius s

Prove $\odot C \sim \odot D$

First, translate $\odot C$ so that point C maps to point D. The image of $\odot C$ is $\odot C'$ with center D. So, $\odot C'$ and $\odot D$ are concentric circles.

  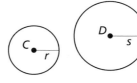

$\odot C'$ is the set of all points that are r units from point D. Dilate $\odot C'$ using center of dilation D and scale factor $\dfrac{s}{r}$.

 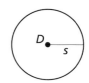

This dilation maps the set of all the points that are r units from point D to the set of all points that are $\dfrac{s}{r}(r) = s$ units from point D. $\odot D$ is the set of all points that are s units from point D. So, this dilation maps $\odot C'$ to $\odot D$.

Because a similarity transformation maps $\odot C$ to $\odot D$, $\odot C \sim \odot D$.

Two arcs are **similar arcs** if and only if they have the same measure. All congruent arcs are similar, but not all similar arcs are congruent. For instance, in Example 4, the pairs of arcs in parts (a), (b), and (c) are similar but only the pairs of arcs in parts (a) and (c) are congruent.

Vocabulary and Core Concept Check

1. **VOCABULARY** Copy and complete: If ∠ACB and ∠DCE are congruent central angles of ⊙C, then $\overset{\frown}{AB}$ and $\overset{\frown}{DE}$ are _____.

2. **WHICH ONE DOESN'T BELONG?** Which circle does *not* belong with the other three? Explain your reasoning.

6 in.

1 ft

12 in.

6 in.

Monitoring Progress and Modeling with Mathematics

In Exercises 3–6, name the red minor arc and find its measure. Then name the blue major arc and find its measure.

3.

4.

5.

6.

In Exercises 7–14, identify the given arc as a *major arc*, *minor arc*, or *semicircle*. Then find the measure of the arc. *(See Example 1.)*

7. $\overset{\frown}{BC}$ 8. $\overset{\frown}{DC}$

9. $\overset{\frown}{ED}$ 10. $\overset{\frown}{AE}$

11. $\overset{\frown}{EAB}$

12. $\overset{\frown}{ABC}$

13. $\overset{\frown}{BAC}$

14. $\overset{\frown}{EBD}$

In Exercises 15 and 16, find the measure of each arc. *(See Example 2.)*

15. a. $\overset{\frown}{JL}$
    b. $\overset{\frown}{KM}$
    c. $\overset{\frown}{JLM}$
    d. $\overset{\frown}{JM}$

16. a. $\overset{\frown}{RS}$
    b. $\overset{\frown}{QRS}$
    c. $\overset{\frown}{QST}$
    d. $\overset{\frown}{QT}$

17. **MODELING WITH MATHEMATICS** A recent survey asked high school students their favorite type of music. The results are shown in the circle graph. Find each indicated arc measure. *(See Example 3.)*

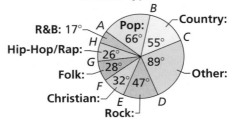

Favorite Type of Music

a. $m\overset{\frown}{AE}$ b. $m\overset{\frown}{ACE}$ c. $m\overset{\frown}{GDC}$

d. $m\overset{\frown}{BHC}$ e. $m\overset{\frown}{FD}$ f. $m\overset{\frown}{FBD}$

18. ABSTRACT REASONING The circle graph shows the percentages of students enrolled in fall sports at a high school. Is it possible to find the measure of each minor arc? If so, find the measure of the arc for each category shown. If not, explain why it is not possible.

High School Fall Sports

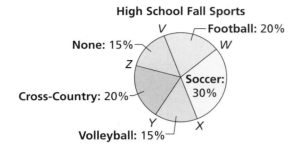

In Exercises 19–22, tell whether the red arcs are congruent. Explain why or why not. *(See Example 4.)*

19.

20.

21.

22.

MATHEMATICAL CONNECTIONS In Exercises 23 and 24, find the value of *x*. Then find the measure of the red arc.

23.

24.

25. MAKING AN ARGUMENT Your friend claims that any two arcs with the same measure are similar. Your cousin claims that any two arcs with the same measure are congruent. Who is correct? Explain.

26. MAKING AN ARGUMENT Your friend claims that there is not enough information given to find the value of *x*. Is your friend correct? Explain your reasoning.

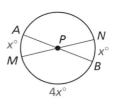

27. ERROR ANALYSIS Describe and correct the error in naming the red arc.

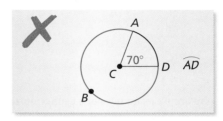

28. ERROR ANALYSIS Describe and correct the error in naming congruent arcs.

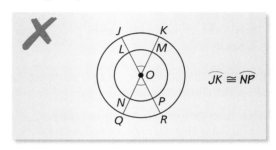

29. ATTENDING TO PRECISION Two diameters of ⊙*P* are $\overline{AB}$ and $\overline{CD}$. Find $m\widehat{ACD}$ and $m\widehat{AC}$ when $m\widehat{AD} = 20°$.

30. REASONING In ⊙*R*, $m\widehat{AB} = 60°$, $m\widehat{BC} = 25°$, $m\widehat{CD} = 70°$, and $m\widehat{DE} = 20°$. Find two possible measures of $\widehat{AE}$.

31. MODELING WITH MATHEMATICS On a regulation dartboard, the outermost circle is divided into twenty congruent sections. What is the measure of each arc in this circle?

32. MODELING WITH MATHEMATICS You can use the time zone wheel to find the time in different locations across the world. For example, to find the time in Tokyo when it is 4 P.M. in San Francisco, rotate the small wheel until 4 P.M. and San Francisco line up, as shown. Then look at Tokyo to see that it is 9 A.M. there.

a. What is the arc measure between each time zone on the wheel?

b. What is the measure of the minor arc from the Tokyo zone to the Anchorage zone?

c. If two locations differ by 180° on the wheel, then it is 3 P.M. at one location when it is _____ at the other location.

33. PROVING A THEOREM Write a coordinate proof of the Similar Circles Theorem.

Given ⊙O with center $O(0, 0)$ and radius r,
⊙A with center $A(a, 0)$ and radius s

Prove ⊙O ~ ⊙A

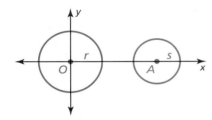

34. ABSTRACT REASONING Is there enough information to tell whether ⊙C ≅ ⊙D? Explain your reasoning.

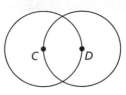

35. PROVING A THEOREM Use the diagram on page 584 to prove each part of the biconditional in the Congruent Circles Theorem.

a. **Given** $\overline{AC} \cong \overline{BD}$
   Prove ⊙A ≅ ⊙B

b. **Given** ⊙A ≅ ⊙B
   Prove $\overline{AC} \cong \overline{BD}$

36. HOW DO YOU SEE IT? Are the circles on the target *similar* or *congruent*? Explain your reasoning.

37. PROVING A THEOREM Use the diagram to prove each part of the biconditional in the Congruent Central Angles Theorem.

a. **Given** ∠BAC ≅ ∠DAE
   Prove $\overset{\frown}{BC} \cong \overset{\frown}{DE}$

b. **Given** $\overset{\frown}{BC} \cong \overset{\frown}{DE}$
   Prove ∠BAC ≅ ∠DAE

38. THOUGHT PROVOKING Write a formula for the length of a circular arc. Justify your answer.

Maintaining Mathematical Proficiency Reviewing what you learned in previous grades and lessons

Find the value of x. Tell whether the side lengths form a Pythagorean triple. *(Section 9.1)*

39.

40.

41.

42.
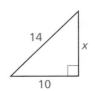

10.3 Using Chords

Essential Question
What are two ways to determine when a chord is a diameter of a circle?

LOOKING FOR STRUCTURE

To be proficient in math, you need to look closely to discern a pattern or structure.

EXPLORATION 1 Drawing Diameters

Work with a partner. Use dynamic geometry software to construct a circle of radius 5 with center at the origin. Draw a diameter that has the given point as an endpoint. Explain how you know that the chord you drew is a diameter.

a. $(4, 3)$ **b.** $(0, 5)$ **c.** $(-3, 4)$ **d.** $(-5, 0)$

EXPLORATION 2 Writing a Conjecture about Chords

Work with a partner. Use dynamic geometry software to construct a chord $\overline{BC}$ of a circle A. Construct a chord on the perpendicular bisector of $\overline{BC}$. What do you notice? Change the original chord and the circle several times. Are your results always the same? Use your results to write a conjecture.

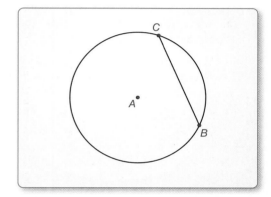

EXPLORATION 3 A Chord Perpendicular to a Diameter

Work with a partner. Use dynamic geometry software to construct a diameter $\overline{BC}$ of a circle A. Then construct a chord $\overline{DE}$ perpendicular to $\overline{BC}$ at point F. Find the lengths DF and EF. What do you notice? Change the chord perpendicular to $\overline{BC}$ and the circle several times. Do you always get the same results? Write a conjecture about a chord that is perpendicular to a diameter of a circle.

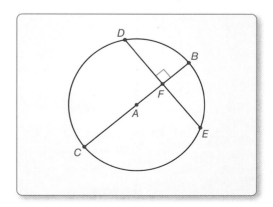

Communicate Your Answer

4. What are two ways to determine when a chord is a diameter of a circle?

10.3 Lesson

What You Will Learn

▶ Use chords of circles to find lengths and arc measures.

Core Vocabulary

Previous
chord
arc
diameter

Using Chords of Circles

Recall that a *chord* is a segment with endpoints on a circle. Because its endpoints lie on the circle, any chord divides the circle into two arcs. A diameter divides a circle into two semicircles. Any other chord divides a circle into a minor arc and a major arc.

semicircle

major arc

diameter

chord

semicircle

minor arc

READING

If $\overset{\frown}{GD} \cong \overset{\frown}{GF}$, then the point G, and any line, segment, or ray that contains G, bisects $\overset{\frown}{FD}$.

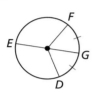

$\overline{EG}$ bisects $\overset{\frown}{FD}$.

⟲ Theorems

Congruent Corresponding Chords Theorem

In the same circle, or in congruent circles, two minor arcs are congruent if and only if their corresponding chords are congruent.

Proof Ex. 19, p. 594

$\overset{\frown}{AB} \cong \overset{\frown}{CD}$ if and only if $\overline{AB} \cong \overline{CD}$.

Perpendicular Chord Bisector Theorem

If a diameter of a circle is perpendicular to a chord, then the diameter bisects the chord and its arc.

Proof Ex. 22, p. 594

If $\overline{EG}$ is a diameter and $\overline{EG} \perp \overline{DF}$, then $\overline{HD} \cong \overline{HF}$ and $\overset{\frown}{GD} \cong \overset{\frown}{GF}$.

Perpendicular Chord Bisector Converse

If one chord of a circle is a perpendicular bisector of another chord, then the first chord is a diameter.

Proof Ex. 23, p. 594

If $\overline{QS}$ is a perpendicular bisector of $\overline{TR}$, then $\overline{QS}$ is a diameter of the circle.

EXAMPLE 1 Using Congruent Chords to Find an Arc Measure

In the diagram, $\odot P \cong \odot Q$, $\overline{FG} \cong \overline{JK}$, and $m\overset{\frown}{JK} = 80°$. Find $m\overset{\frown}{FG}$.

SOLUTION

Because $\overline{FG}$ and $\overline{JK}$ are congruent chords in congruent circles, the corresponding minor arcs $\overset{\frown}{FG}$ and $\overset{\frown}{JK}$ are congruent by the Congruent Corresponding Chords Theorem.

▶ So, $m\overset{\frown}{FG} = m\overset{\frown}{JK} = 80°$.

590   **Chapter 10**   Circles

EXAMPLE 2 Using a Diameter

a. Find *HK*. **b.** Find $m\widehat{HK}$.

SOLUTION

a. Diameter $\overline{JL}$ is perpendicular to $\overline{HK}$. So, by the Perpendicular Chord Bisector Theorem, $\overline{JL}$ bisects $\overline{HK}$, and $HN = NK$.

▶ So, $HK = 2(NK) = 2(7) = 14$.

b. Diameter $\overline{JL}$ is perpendicular to $\overline{HK}$. So, by the Perpendicular Chord Bisector Theorem, $\overline{JL}$ bisects $\widehat{HK}$, and $m\widehat{HJ} = m\widehat{JK}$.

$m\widehat{HJ} = m\widehat{JK}$	Perpendicular Chord Bisector Theorem
$11x° = (70 + x)°$	Substitute.
$10x = 70$	Subtract *x* from each side.
$x = 7$	Divide each side by 10.

▶ So, $m\widehat{HJ} = m\widehat{JK} = (70 + x)° = (70 + 7)° = 77°$, and $m\widehat{HK} = 2(m\widehat{HJ}) = 2(77°) = 154°$.

EXAMPLE 3 Using Perpendicular Bisectors

Three bushes are arranged in a garden, as shown. Where should you place a sprinkler so that it is the same distance from each bush?

SOLUTION

Step 1

Label the bushes *A*, *B*, and *C*, as shown. Draw segments $\overline{AB}$ and $\overline{BC}$.

Step 2

Draw the perpendicular bisectors of $\overline{AB}$ and $\overline{BC}$. By the Perpendicular Chord Bisector Converse, these lie on diameters of the circle containing *A*, *B*, and *C*.

Step 3

Find the point where the perpendicular bisectors intersect. This is the center of the circle, which is equidistant from points *A*, *B*, and *C*.

Monitoring Progress Help in English and Spanish at *BigIdeasMath.com*

In Exercises 1 and 2, use the diagram of ⊙*D*.

1. If $m\widehat{AB} = 110°$, find $m\widehat{BC}$.

2. If $m\widehat{AC} = 150°$, find $m\widehat{AB}$.

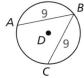

In Exercises 3 and 4, find the indicated length or arc measure.

3. *CE*

4. $m\widehat{CE}$

⟳ Theorem

Equidistant Chords Theorem

In the same circle, or in congruent circles, two chords are congruent if and only if they are equidistant from the center.

Proof Ex. 25, p. 594

$\overline{AB} \cong \overline{CD}$ if and only if $EF = EG$.

EXAMPLE 4   **Using Congruent Chords to Find a Circle's Radius**

In the diagram, $QR = ST = 16$, $CU = 2x$, and $CV = 5x - 9$. Find the radius of $\odot C$.

SOLUTION

Because $\overline{CQ}$ is a segment whose endpoints are the center and a point on the circle, it is a radius of $\odot C$. Because $\overline{CU} \perp \overline{QR}$, $\triangle QUC$ is a right triangle. Apply properties of chords to find the lengths of the legs of $\triangle QUC$.

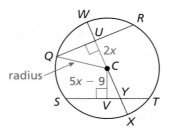

Step 1   Find CU.

Because $\overline{QR}$ and $\overline{ST}$ are congruent chords, $\overline{QR}$ and $\overline{ST}$ are equidistant from C by the Equidistant Chords Theorem. So, $CU = CV$.

$$CU = CV \qquad \text{Equidistant Chords Theorem}$$
$$2x = 5x - 9 \qquad \text{Substitute.}$$
$$x = 3 \qquad \text{Solve for } x.$$

So, $CU = 2x = 2(3) = 6$.

Step 2   Find QU.

Because diameter $\overline{WX} \perp \overline{QR}$, $\overline{WX}$ bisects $\overline{QR}$ by the Perpendicular Chord Bisector Theorem.

So, $QU = \frac{1}{2}(16) = 8$.

Step 3   Find CQ.

Because the lengths of the legs are $CU = 6$ and $QU = 8$, $\triangle QUC$ is a right triangle with the Pythagorean triple 6, 8, 10. So, $CQ = 10$.

▶ So, the radius of $\odot C$ is 10 units.

Monitoring Progress   🔊 Help in English and Spanish at *BigIdeasMath.com*

5. In the diagram, $JK = LM = 24$, $NP = 3x$, and $NQ = 7x - 12$. Find the radius of $\odot N$.

Vocabulary and Core Concept Check

1. **WRITING** Describe what it means to bisect a chord.

2. **WRITING** Two chords of a circle are perpendicular and congruent. Does one of them have to be a diameter? Explain your reasoning.

Monitoring Progress and Modeling with Mathematics

In Exercises 3–6, find the measure of the red arc or chord in ⊙C. *(See Example 1.)*

3.

4.

5.

6.

In Exercises 7–10, find the value of x. *(See Example 2.)*

7.

8.

9.

10.

11. **ERROR ANALYSIS** Describe and correct the error in reasoning.

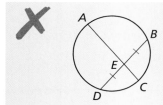

Because $\overline{AC}$ bisects $\overline{DB}$, $\overset{\frown}{BC} \cong \overset{\frown}{CD}$.

12. **PROBLEM SOLVING** In the cross section of the submarine shown, the control panels are parallel and the same length. Describe a method you can use to find the center of the cross section. Justify your method. *(See Example 3.)*

In Exercises 13 and 14, determine whether $\overline{AB}$ is a diameter of the circle. Explain your reasoning.

13.

14.

In Exercises 15 and 16, find the radius of ⊙Q. *(See Example 4.)*

15.

16.

17. **PROBLEM SOLVING** An archaeologist finds part of a circular plate. What was the diameter of the plate to the nearest tenth of an inch? Justify your answer.

18. HOW DO YOU SEE IT? What can you conclude from each diagram? Name a theorem that justifies your answer.

a.

b.

c.

d.

19. PROVING A THEOREM Use the diagram to prove each part of the biconditional in the Congruent Corresponding Chords Theorem.

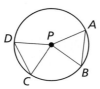

a. **Given** $\overline{AB}$ and $\overline{CD}$ are congruent chords.
   Prove $\overset{\frown}{AB} \cong \overset{\frown}{CD}$

b. **Given** $\overset{\frown}{AB} \cong \overset{\frown}{CD}$
   Prove $\overline{AB} \cong \overline{CD}$

20. MATHEMATICAL CONNECTIONS In ⊙P, all the arcs shown have integer measures. Show that x must be even.

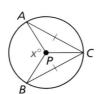

21. REASONING In ⊙P, the lengths of the parallel chords are 20, 16, and 12. Find $m\overset{\frown}{AB}$. Explain your reasoning.

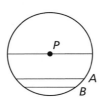

22. PROVING A THEOREM Use congruent triangles to prove the Perpendicular Chord Bisector Theorem.

Given $\overline{EG}$ is a diameter of ⊙L.
$\overline{EG} \perp \overline{DF}$

Prove $\overline{DC} \cong \overline{FC}, \overset{\frown}{DG} \cong \overset{\frown}{FG}$

23. PROVING A THEOREM Write a proof of the Perpendicular Chord Bisector Converse.

Given $\overline{QS}$ is a perpendicular bisector of $\overline{RT}$.

Prove $\overline{QS}$ is a diameter of the circle L.

(*Hint*: Plot the center L and draw $\triangle LPT$ and $\triangle LPR$.)

24. THOUGHT PROVOKING Consider two chords that intersect at point P. Do you think that $\dfrac{AP}{BP} = \dfrac{CP}{DP}$? Justify your answer.

25. PROVING A THEOREM Use the diagram with the Equidistant Chords Theorem on page 592 to prove both parts of the biconditional of this theorem.

26. MAKING AN ARGUMENT A car is designed so that the rear wheel is only partially visible below the body of the car. The bottom edge of the panel is parallel to the ground. Your friend claims that the point where the tire touches the ground bisects $\overset{\frown}{AB}$. Is your friend correct? Explain your reasoning.

Maintaining Mathematical Proficiency   Reviewing what you learned in previous grades and lessons

Find the missing interior angle measure. (*Section 7.1*)

27. Quadrilateral *JKLM* has angle measures $m\angle J = 32°$, $m\angle K = 25°$, and $m\angle L = 44°$. Find $m\angle M$.

28. Pentagon *PQRST* has angle measures $m\angle P = 85°$, $m\angle Q = 134°$, $m\angle R = 97°$, and $m\angle S = 102°$. Find $m\angle T$.

Core Vocabulary

circle, *p. 574*
center, *p. 574*
radius, *p. 574*
chord, *p. 574*
diameter, *p. 574*
secant, *p. 574*
tangent, *p. 574*

point of tangency, *p. 574*
tangent circles, *p. 575*
concentric circles, *p. 575*
common tangent, *p. 575*
central angle, *p. 582*
minor arc, *p. 582*
major arc, *p. 582*

semicircle, *p. 582*
measure of a minor arc, *p. 582*
measure of a major arc, *p. 582*
adjacent arcs, *p. 583*
congruent circles, *p. 584*
congruent arcs, *p. 584*
similar arcs, *p. 585*

Core Concepts

Section 10.1

Lines and Segments That Intersect Circles, *p. 574*
Coplanar Circles and Common Tangents, *p. 575*

Tangent Line to Circle Theorem, *p. 576*
External Tangent Congruence Theorem, *p. 576*

Section 10.2

Measuring Arcs, *p. 582*
Arc Addition Postulate, *p. 583*
Congruent Circles Theorem, *p. 584*

Congruent Central Angles Theorem, *p. 584*
Similar Circles Theorem, *p. 585*

Section 10.3

Congruent Corresponding Chords Theorem, *p. 590*
Perpendicular Chord Bisector Theorem, *p. 590*

Perpendicular Chord Bisector Converse, *p. 590*
Equidistant Chords Theorem, *p. 592*

Mathematical Practices

1. Explain how separating quadrilateral *TVWX* into several segments helped you solve Exercise 37 on page 579.

2. In Exercise 30 on page 587, what two cases did you consider to reach your answers? Are there any other cases? Explain your reasoning.

3. Explain how you used inductive reasoning to solve Exercise 24 on page 594.

Keeping Your Mind Focused While Completing Homework

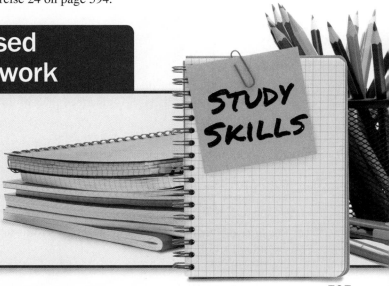

STUDY SKILLS

- Before doing homework, review the Concept boxes and Examples. Talk through the Examples out loud.

- Complete homework as though you were also preparing for a quiz. Memorize the different types of problems, formulas, rules, and so on.

In Exercises 1–6, use the diagram. *(Section 10.1)*

1. Name the circle.

2. Name a radius.

3. Name a diameter.

4. Name a chord.

5. Name a secant.

6. Name a tangent.

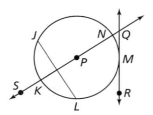

Find the value of x. *(Section 10.1)*

7.

8.

Identify the given arc as a *major arc*, *minor arc*, or *semicircle*. Then find the measure of the arc. *(Section 10.2)*

9. $\overset{\frown}{AE}$

10. $\overset{\frown}{BC}$

11. $\overset{\frown}{AC}$

12. $\overset{\frown}{ACD}$

13. $\overset{\frown}{ACE}$

14. $\overset{\frown}{BEC}$

Tell whether the red arcs are congruent. Explain why or why not. *(Section 10.2)*

15.

16.

17. Find the measure of the red arc in ⊙Q. *(Section 10.3)*

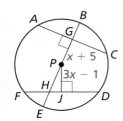

18. In the diagram, $AC = FD = 30$, $PG = x + 5$, and $PJ = 3x - 1$. Find the radius of ⊙P. *(Section 10.3)*

19. A circular clock can be divided into 12 congruent sections. *(Section 10.2)*

   a. Find the measure of each arc in this circle.

   b. Find the measure of the minor arc formed by the hour and minute hands when the time is 7:00.

   c. Find a time at which the hour and minute hands form an arc that is congruent to the arc in part (b).

10.4 Inscribed Angles and Polygons

Essential Question How are inscribed angles related to their intercepted arcs? How are the angles of an inscribed quadrilateral related to each other?

An **inscribed angle** is an angle whose vertex is on a circle and whose sides contain chords of the circle. An arc that lies between two lines, rays, or segments is called an **intercepted arc**. Recall that a polygon is an inscribed polygon when all its vertices lie on a circle.

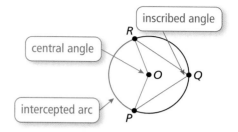

EXPLORATION 1 Inscribed Angles and Central Angles

Work with a partner. Use dynamic geometry software.

a. Construct an inscribed angle in a circle. Then construct the corresponding central angle.

b. Measure both angles. How is the inscribed angle related to its intercepted arc?

c. Repeat parts (a) and (b) several times. Record your results in a table. Write a conjecture about how an inscribed angle is related to its intercepted arc.

Sample

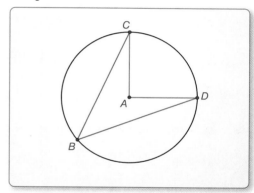

ATTENDING TO PRECISION

To be proficient in math, you need to communicate precisely with others.

EXPLORATION 2 A Quadrilateral with Inscribed Angles

Work with a partner. Use dynamic geometry software.

a. Construct a quadrilateral with each vertex on a circle.

b. Measure all four angles. What relationships do you notice?

c. Repeat parts (a) and (b) several times. Record your results in a table. Then write a conjecture that summarizes the data.

Sample

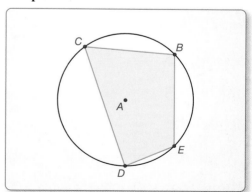

Communicate Your Answer

3. How are inscribed angles related to their intercepted arcs? How are the angles of an inscribed quadrilateral related to each other?

4. Quadrilateral *EFGH* is inscribed in ⊙*C*, and *m*∠*E* = 80°. What is *m*∠*G*? Explain.

What You Will Learn

▶ Use inscribed angles.

▶ Use inscribed polygons.

Core Vocabulary

inscribed angle, *p. 598*
intercepted arc, *p. 598*
subtend, *p. 598*

Previous
inscribed polygon
circumscribed circle

Using Inscribed Angles

Core Concept

Inscribed Angle and Intercepted Arc

An **inscribed angle** is an angle whose vertex is on a circle and whose sides contain chords of the circle. An arc that lies between two lines, rays, or segments is called an **intercepted arc**. If the endpoints of a chord or arc lie on the sides of an inscribed angle, then the chord or arc is said to **subtend** the angle.

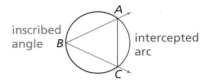

$\angle B$ intercepts $\overset{\frown}{AC}$.
$\overset{\frown}{AC}$ subtends $\angle B$.
$\overline{AC}$ subtends $\angle B$.

Theorem

Measure of an Inscribed Angle Theorem

The measure of an inscribed angle is one-half the measure of its intercepted arc.

$m\angle ADB = \frac{1}{2}m\overset{\frown}{AB}$

Proof Ex. 35, p. 604

The proof of the Measure of an Inscribed Angle Theorem involves three cases.

Case 1 Center *C* is on a side of the inscribed angle.

Case 2 Center *C* is inside the inscribed angle.

Case 3 Center *C* is outside the inscribed angle.

EXAMPLE 1 Using Inscribed Angles

Find the indicated measure.

a. $m\angle T$

b. $m\overset{\frown}{QR}$

SOLUTION

a. $m\angle T = \frac{1}{2}m\overset{\frown}{RS} = \frac{1}{2}(48°) = 24°$

b. $m\overset{\frown}{TQ} = 2m\angle R = 2 \cdot 50° = 100°$
Because $\overset{\frown}{TQR}$ is a semicircle, $m\overset{\frown}{QR} = 180° - m\overset{\frown}{TQ} = 180° - 100° = 80°$.

EXAMPLE 2   **Finding the Measure of an Intercepted Arc**

Find $m\overset{\frown}{RS}$ and $m\angle STR$. What do you notice
about $\angle STR$ and $\angle RUS$?

SOLUTION

From the Measure of an Inscribed Angle Theorem, you know that
$m\overset{\frown}{RS} = 2m\angle RUS = 2(31°) = 62°$.

Also, $m\angle STR = \frac{1}{2}m\overset{\frown}{RS} = \frac{1}{2}(62°) = 31°$.

▶   So, $\angle STR \cong \angle RUS$.

Example 2 suggests the Inscribed Angles of a Circle Theorem.

🔄 Theorem

Inscribed Angles of a Circle Theorem

If two inscribed angles of a circle intercept
the same arc, then the angles are congruent.

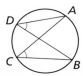

Proof Ex. 36, p. 604

$\angle ADB \cong \angle ACB$

EXAMPLE 3   **Finding the Measure of an Angle**

Given $m\angle E = 75°$, find $m\angle F$.

SOLUTION

Both $\angle E$ and $\angle F$ intercept $\overset{\frown}{GH}$. So, $\angle E \cong \angle F$ by the Inscribed Angles of a
Circle Theorem.

▶   So, $m\angle F = m\angle E = 75°$.

Monitoring Progress Help in English and Spanish at *BigIdeasMath.com*

Find the measure of the red arc or angle.

1.

2.

3.

Using Inscribed Polygons

Recall that a polygon is an inscribed polygon when all its vertices lie on a circle. The circle that contains the vertices is a circumscribed circle.

Theorems

Inscribed Right Triangle Theorem

If a right triangle is inscribed in a circle, then the hypotenuse is a diameter of the circle. Conversely, if one side of an inscribed triangle is a diameter of the circle, then the triangle is a right triangle and the angle opposite the diameter is the right angle.

$m\angle ABC = 90°$ if and only if $\overline{AC}$ is a diameter of the circle.

Proof Ex. 37, p. 604

Inscribed Quadrilateral Theorem

A quadrilateral can be inscribed in a circle if and only if its opposite angles are supplementary.

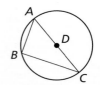

D, E, F, and G lie on $\odot C$ if and only if $m\angle D + m\angle F = m\angle E + m\angle G = 180°$.

Proof Ex. 38, p. 604; *BigIdeasMath.com*

> **EXAMPLE 4**   Using Inscribed Polygons

Find the value of each variable.

a.

b.

SOLUTION

a. $\overline{AB}$ is a diameter. So, $\angle C$ is a right angle, and $m\angle C = 90°$ by the Inscribed Right Triangle Theorem.

$$2x° = 90°$$

$$x = 45$$

▶ The value of x is 45.

b. *DEFG* is inscribed in a circle, so opposite angles are supplementary by the Inscribed Quadrilateral Theorem.

$$m\angle D + m\angle F = 180° \qquad\qquad m\angle E + m\angle G = 180°$$

$$z + 80 = 180 \qquad\qquad\qquad 120 + y = 180$$

$$z = 100 \qquad\qquad\qquad\qquad y = 60$$

▶ The value of z is 100 and the value of y is 60.

EXAMPLE 5   Using a Circumscribed Circle

Your camera has a 90° field of vision, and you want to photograph the front of a statue. You stand at a location in which the front of the statue is all that appears in your camera's field of vision, as shown. You want to change your location. Where else can you stand so that the front of the statue is all that appears in your camera's field of vision?

SOLUTION

From the Inscribed Right Triangle Theorem, you know that if a right triangle is inscribed in a circle, then the hypotenuse of the triangle is a diameter of the circle. So, draw the circle that has the front of the statue as a diameter.

▶ The statue fits perfectly within your camera's 90° field of vision from any point on the semicircle in front of the statue.

Monitoring Progress   🔊 Help in English and Spanish at *BigIdeasMath.com*

Find the value of each variable.

4.

5.

6.

7.

8. In Example 5, explain how to find locations where the left side of the statue is all that appears in your camera's field of vision.

Vocabulary and Core Concept Check

1. **VOCABULARY** An arc that lies between two lines, rays, or segments is called a(n) _____.

2. **DIFFERENT WORDS, SAME QUESTION** Which is different?
Find "both" answers.

Find $m\angle ABC$.

Find $m\angle AGC$.

Find $m\angle AEC$.

Find $m\angle ADC$.

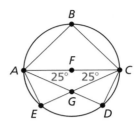

Monitoring Progress and Modeling with Mathematics

In Exercises 3–8, find the indicated measure.
(See Examples 1 and 2.)

3. $m\angle A$

4. $m\angle G$

5. $m\angle N$

6. $m\widehat{RS}$

7. $m\widehat{VU}$

8. $m\widehat{WX}$

In Exercises 9 and 10, name two pairs of congruent angles.

9.

10.

In Exercises 11 and 12, find the measure of the red arc or angle. *(See Example 3.)*

11.

12.

In Exercises 13–16, find the value of each variable.
(See Example 4.)

13.

14.

15.

16.

17. **ERROR ANALYSIS** Describe and correct the error in finding $m\widehat{BC}$.

$m\widehat{BC} = 53°$

18. MODELING WITH MATHEMATICS A *carpenter's square* is an L-shaped tool used to draw right angles. You need to cut a circular piece of wood into two semicircles. How can you use the carpenter's square to draw a diameter on the circular piece of wood? *(See Example 5.)*

MATHEMATICAL CONNECTIONS In Exercises 19–21, find the values of *x* and *y*. Then find the measures of the interior angles of the polygon.

19.

20.

21.

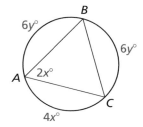

22. MAKING AN ARGUMENT Your friend claims that ∠*PTQ* ≅ ∠*PSQ* ≅ ∠*PRQ*. Is your friend correct? Explain your reasoning.

REASONING In Exercises 23–28, determine whether a quadrilateral of the given type can always be inscribed inside a circle. Explain your reasoning.

23. square

24. rectangle

25. parallelogram

26. kite

27. rhombus

28. isosceles trapezoid

29. MODELING WITH MATHEMATICS Three moons, A, B, and C, are in the same circular orbit 100,000 kilometers above the surface of a planet. The planet is 20,000 kilometers in diameter and *m*∠*ABC* = 90°. Draw a diagram of the situation. How far is moon A from moon C?

30. MODELING WITH MATHEMATICS At the movie theater, you want to choose a seat that has the best *viewing angle*, so that you can be close to the screen and still see the whole screen without moving your eyes. You previously decided that seat F7 has the best viewing angle, but this time someone else is already sitting there. Where else can you sit so that your seat has the same viewing angle as seat F7? Explain.

31. WRITING A right triangle is inscribed in a circle, and the radius of the circle is given. Explain how to find the length of the hypotenuse.

32. HOW DO YOU SEE IT? Let point *Y* represent your location on the soccer field below. What type of angle is ∠*AYB* if you stand anywhere on the circle except at point *A* or point *B*?

33. WRITING Explain why the diagonals of a rectangle inscribed in a circle are diameters of the circle.

34. THOUGHT PROVOKING The figure shows a circle that is circumscribed about △*ABC*. Is it possible to circumscribe a circle about any triangle? Justify your answer.

35. PROVING A THEOREM If an angle is inscribed in ⊙*Q*, the center *Q* can be on a side of the inscribed angle, inside the inscribed angle, or outside the inscribed angle. Prove each case of the Measure of an Inscribed Angle Theorem.

   a. Case 1

      Given ∠*ABC* is inscribed in ⊙*Q*.
      Let $m\angle B = x°$.
      Center *Q* lies on $\overline{BC}$.

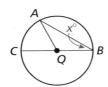

      Prove $m\angle ABC = \frac{1}{2}\,m\widehat{AC}$

      (*Hint*: Show that △*AQB* is isosceles. Then write $m\widehat{AC}$ in terms of *x*.)

   b. Case 2 Use the diagram and auxiliary line to write **Given** and **Prove** statements for Case 2. Then write a proof.

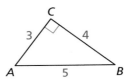

   c. Case 3 Use the diagram and auxiliary line to write **Given** and **Prove** statements for Case 3. Then write a proof.

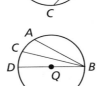

36. PROVING A THEOREM Write a paragraph proof of the Inscribed Angles of a Circle Theorem. First, draw a diagram and write **Given** and **Prove** statements.

37. PROVING A THEOREM The Inscribed Right Triangle Theorem is written as a conditional statement and its converse. Write a plan for proof for each statement.

38. PROVING A THEOREM Copy and complete the paragraph proof for one part of the Inscribed Quadrilateral Theorem.

   Given ⊙*C* with inscribed quadrilateral *DEFG*

   Prove $m\angle D + m\angle F = 180°$,
        $m\angle E + m\angle G = 180°$

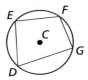

   By the Arc Addition Postulate,
   $m\widehat{EFG}$ + _____ = 360° and $m\widehat{FGD} + m\widehat{DEF} = 360°$.
   Using the _____ Theorem, $m\widehat{EDG} = 2m\angle F$,
   $m\widehat{EFG} = 2m\angle D$, $m\widehat{DEF} = 2m\angle G$, and
   $m\widehat{FGD} = 2m\angle E$. By the Substitution Property
   of Equality, $2m\angle D +$ ___ = 360°, so ___.
   Similarly, ____.

39. CRITICAL THINKING In the diagram, ∠*C* is a right angle. If you draw the smallest possible circle through *C* tangent to $\overline{AB}$, the circle will intersect $\overline{AC}$ at *J* and $\overline{BC}$ at *K*. Find the exact length of $\overline{JK}$.

40. CRITICAL THINKING You are making a circular cutting board. To begin, you glue eight 1-inch boards together, as shown. Then you draw and cut a circle with an 8-inch diameter from the boards.

   a. $\overline{FH}$ is a diameter of the circular cutting board. Write a proportion relating *GJ* and *JH*. State a theorem to justify your answer.

   b. Find *FJ*, *JH*, and *GJ*. What is the length of the cutting board seam labeled $\overline{GK}$?

Maintaining Mathematical Proficiency
                       Reviewing what you learned in previous grades and lessons

Solve the equation. Check your solution. *(Skills Review Handbook)*

41. $3x = 145$

42. $\frac{1}{2}x = 63$

43. $240 = 2x$

44. $75 = \frac{1}{2}(x - 30)$

Essential Question When a chord intersects a tangent line or another chord, what relationships exist among the angles and arcs formed?

EXPLORATION 1 Angles Formed by a Chord and Tangent Line

Work with a partner. Use dynamic geometry software.

a. Construct a chord in a circle. At one of the endpoints of the chord, construct a tangent line to the circle.

b. Find the measures of the two angles formed by the chord and the tangent line.

c. Find the measures of the two circular arcs determined by the chord.

d. Repeat parts (a)–(c) several times. Record your results in a table. Then write a conjecture that summarizes the data.

Sample

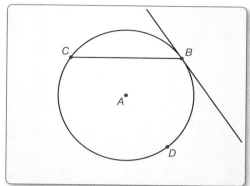

EXPLORATION 2 Angles Formed by Intersecting Chords

Work with a partner. Use dynamic geometry software.

CONSTRUCTING VIABLE ARGUMENTS

To be proficient in math, you need to understand and use stated assumptions, definitions, and previously established results.

a. Construct two chords that intersect inside a circle.

b. Find the measure of one of the angles formed by the intersecting chords.

c. Find the measures of the arcs intercepted by the angle in part (b) and its vertical angle. What do you observe?

d. Repeat parts (a)–(c) several times. Record your results in a table. Then write a conjecture that summarizes the data.

Sample

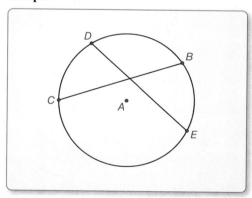

Communicate Your Answer

3. When a chord intersects a tangent line or another chord, what relationships exist among the angles and arcs formed?

4. Line *m* is tangent to the circle in the figure at the left. Find the measure of ∠1.

5. Two chords intersect inside a circle to form a pair of vertical angles with measures of 55°. Find the sum of the measures of the arcs intercepted by the two angles.

What You Will Learn

Core Vocabulary

circumscribed angle, *p. 608*

Previous
tangent
chord
secant

▶ Find angle and arc measures.
▶ Use circumscribed angles.

Finding Angle and Arc Measures

⟳ Theorem

Tangent and Intersected Chord Theorem

If a tangent and a chord intersect at a point on a circle, then the measure of each angle formed is one-half the measure of its intercepted arc.

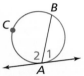

Proof Ex. 33, p. 612

$$m\angle 1 = \frac{1}{2}m\overset{\frown}{AB} \quad m\angle 2 = \frac{1}{2}m\overset{\frown}{BCA}$$

EXAMPLE 1 **Finding Angle and Arc Measures**

Line *m* is tangent to the circle. Find the measure of the red angle or arc.

a.

b.

SOLUTION

a. $m\angle 1 = \frac{1}{2}(130°) = 65°$

b. $m\overset{\frown}{KJL} = 2(125°) = 250°$

Monitoring Progress 🔊 Help in English and Spanish at *BigIdeasMath.com*

Line *m* is tangent to the circle. Find the indicated measure.

1. $m\angle 1$

2. $m\overset{\frown}{RST}$

3. $m\overset{\frown}{XY}$

⟳ Core Concept

Intersecting Lines and Circles

If two nonparallel lines intersect a circle, there are three places where the lines can intersect.

on the circle   inside the circle   outside the circle

Theorems

Angles Inside the Circle Theorem

If two chords intersect *inside* a circle, then the measure of each angle is one-half the *sum* of the measures of the arcs intercepted by the angle and its vertical angle.

Proof Ex. 35, p. 612

$$m\angle 1 = \tfrac{1}{2}(m\widehat{DC} + m\widehat{AB}),$$
$$m\angle 2 = \tfrac{1}{2}(m\widehat{AD} + m\widehat{BC})$$

Angles Outside the Circle Theorem

If a tangent and a secant, two tangents, or two secants intersect *outside* a circle, then the measure of the angle formed is one-half the *difference* of the measures of the intercepted arcs.

$$m\angle 1 = \tfrac{1}{2}(m\widehat{BC} - m\widehat{AC}) \quad m\angle 2 = \tfrac{1}{2}(m\widehat{PQR} - m\widehat{PR}) \quad m\angle 3 = \tfrac{1}{2}(m\widehat{XY} - m\widehat{WZ})$$

Proof Ex. 37, p. 612

EXAMPLE 2 Finding an Angle Measure

Find the value of *x*.

a.

b.

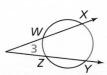

SOLUTION

a. The chords $\overline{JL}$ and $\overline{KM}$ intersect inside the circle. Use the Angles Inside the Circle Theorem.

$$x° = \tfrac{1}{2}(m\widehat{JM} + m\widehat{LK})$$

$$x° = \tfrac{1}{2}(130° + 156°)$$

$$x = 143$$

▶ So, the value of *x* is 143.

b. The tangent $\overrightarrow{CD}$ and the secant $\overrightarrow{CB}$ intersect outside the circle. Use the Angles Outside the Circle Theorem.

$$m\angle BCD = \tfrac{1}{2}(m\widehat{AD} - m\widehat{BD})$$

$$x° = \tfrac{1}{2}(178° - 76°)$$

$$x = 51$$

▶ So, the value of *x* is 51.

Monitoring Progress 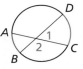 Help in English and Spanish at *BigIdeasMath.com*

Find the value of the variable.

4.

5.

Using Circumscribed Angles

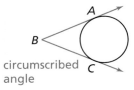 Core Concept

Circumscribed Angle

A **circumscribed angle** is an angle whose sides are tangent to a circle.

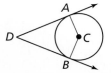

Theorem

Circumscribed Angle Theorem

The measure of a circumscribed angle is equal to 180° minus the measure of the central angle that intercepts the same arc.

Proof Ex. 38, p. 612

$m\angle ADB = 180° - m\angle ACB$

EXAMPLE 3   **Finding Angle Measures**

Find the value of x.

a.

b.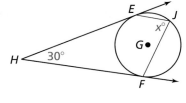

SOLUTION

a. Use the Circumscribed Angle Theorem to find $m\angle ADB$.

$m\angle ADB = 180° - m\angle ACB$	Circumscribed Angle Theorem
$x° = 180° - 135°$	Substitute.
$x = 45$	Subtract.

▶ So, the value of x is 45.

b. Use the Measure of an Inscribed Angle Theorem and the Circumscribed Angle Theorem to find $m\angle EJF$.

$m\angle EJF = \frac{1}{2}m\widehat{EF}$	Measure of an Inscribed Angle Theorem
$m\angle EJF = \frac{1}{2}m\angle EGF$	Definition of minor arc
$m\angle EJF = \frac{1}{2}(180° - m\angle EHF)$	Circumscribed Angle Theorem
$m\angle EJF = \frac{1}{2}(180° - 30°)$	Substitute.
$x = \frac{1}{2}(180 - 30)$	Substitute.
$x = 75$	Simplify.

▶ So, the value of x is 75.

EXAMPLE 4 **Modeling with Mathematics**

The northern lights are bright flashes of colored light between 50 and 200 miles above Earth. A flash occurs 150 miles above Earth at point C. What is the measure of $\overset{\frown}{BD}$, the portion of Earth from which the flash is visible? (Earth's radius is approximately 4000 miles.)

4150 mi — 4000 mi

Not drawn to scale

SOLUTION

1. **Understand the Problem** You are given the approximate radius of Earth and the distance above Earth that the flash occurs. You need to find the measure of the arc that represents the portion of Earth from which the flash is visible.

2. **Make a Plan** Use properties of tangents, triangle congruence, and angles outside a circle to find the arc measure.

3. **Solve the Problem** Because $\overline{CB}$ and $\overline{CD}$ are tangents, $\overline{CB} \perp \overline{AB}$ and $\overline{CD} \perp \overline{AD}$ by the Tangent Line to Circle Theorem. Also, $\overline{BC} \cong \overline{DC}$ by the External Tangent Congruence Theorem, and $\overline{CA} \cong \overline{CA}$ by the Reflexive Property of Congruence. So, $\triangle ABC \cong \triangle ADC$ by the Hypotenuse-Leg Congruence Theorem. Because corresponding parts of congruent triangles are congruent, $\angle BCA \cong \angle DCA$. Solve right $\triangle CBA$ to find that $m\angle BCA \approx 74.5°$. So, $m\angle BCD \approx 2(74.5°) = 149°$.

COMMON ERROR

Because the value for $m\angle BCD$ is an approximation, use the symbol $\approx$ instead of $=$.

$m\angle BCD = 180° - m\angle BAD$	Circumscribed Angle Theorem
$m\angle BCD = 180° - m\overset{\frown}{BD}$	Definition of minor arc
$149° \approx 180° - m\overset{\frown}{BD}$	Substitute.
$31° \approx m\overset{\frown}{BD}$	Solve for $m\overset{\frown}{BD}$.

▶ The measure of the arc from which the flash is visible is about 31°.

4. **Look Back** You can use inverse trigonometric ratios to find $m\angle BAC$ and $m\angle DAC$.

$$m\angle BAC = \cos^{-1}\left(\frac{4000}{4150}\right) \approx 15.5°$$

$$m\angle DAC = \cos^{-1}\left(\frac{4000}{4150}\right) \approx 15.5°$$

So, $m\angle BAD \approx 15.5° + 15.5° = 31°$, and therefore $m\overset{\frown}{BD} \approx 31°$.

Monitoring Progress Help in English and Spanish at *BigIdeasMath.com*

Find the value of x.

6.

7.

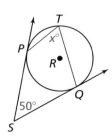

8. You are on top of Mount Rainier on a clear day. You are about 2.73 miles above sea level at point B. Find $m\overset{\frown}{CD}$, which represents the part of Earth that you can see.

4002.73 mi — 4000 mi

Not drawn to scale

Vocabulary and Core Concept Check

1. **COMPLETE THE SENTENCE** Points A, B, C, and D are on a circle, and $\overleftrightarrow{AB}$ intersects $\overleftrightarrow{CD}$ at point P. If $m\angle APC = \frac{1}{2}(m\widehat{BD} - m\widehat{AC})$, then point P is _____ the circle.

2. **WRITING** Explain how to find the measure of a circumscribed angle.

Monitoring Progress and Modeling with Mathematics

In Exercises 3–6, line t is tangent to the circle. Find the indicated measure. *(See Example 1.)*

3. $m\widehat{AB}$

4. $m\widehat{DEF}$

5. $m\angle 1$

6. $m\angle 3$

In Exercises 7–14, find the value of x.
(See Examples 2 and 3.)

7.

8.

9.

10.

11.

12.

13.

14.

ERROR ANALYSIS In Exercises 15 and 16, describe and correct the error in finding the angle measure.

15.

16.

In Exercises 17–22, find the indicated angle measure. Justify your answer.

17. $m\angle 1$

18. $m\angle 2$

19. $m\angle 3$

20. $m\angle 4$

21. $m\angle 5$

22. $m\angle 6$

23. PROBLEM SOLVING You are flying in a hot air balloon about 1.2 miles above the ground. Find the measure of the arc that represents the part of Earth you can see. The radius of Earth is about 4000 miles. *(See Example 4.)*

4001.2 mi   4000 mi

Not drawn to scale

24. PROBLEM SOLVING You are watching fireworks over San Diego Bay S as you sail away in a boat. The highest point the fireworks reach F is about 0.2 mile above the bay. Your eyes E are about 0.01 mile above the water. At point B you can no longer see the fireworks because of the curvature of Earth. The radius of Earth is about 4000 miles, and $\overline{FE}$ is tangent to Earth at point T. Find $m\overset{\frown}{SB}$. Round your answer to the nearest tenth.

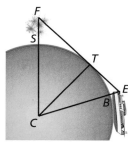

Not drawn to scale

25. MATHEMATICAL CONNECTIONS In the diagram, $\overrightarrow{BA}$ is tangent to $\odot E$. Write an algebraic expression for $m\overset{\frown}{CD}$ in terms of x. Then find $m\overset{\frown}{CD}$.

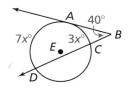

26. MATHEMATICAL CONNECTIONS The circles in the diagram are concentric. Write an algebraic expression for c in terms of a and b.

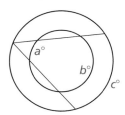

27. ABSTRACT REASONING In the diagram, $\overrightarrow{PL}$ is tangent to the circle, and $\overline{KJ}$ is a diameter. What is the range of possible angle measures of $\angle LPJ$? Explain your reasoning.

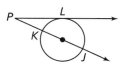

28. ABSTRACT REASONING In the diagram, $\overline{AB}$ is any chord that is not a diameter of the circle. Line m is tangent to the circle at point A. What is the range of possible values of x? Explain your reasoning. (The diagram is not drawn to scale.)

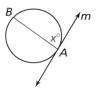

29. PROOF In the diagram, $\overleftrightarrow{JL}$ and $\overleftrightarrow{NL}$ are secant lines that intersect at point L. Prove that $m\angle JPN > m\angle JLN$.

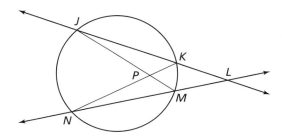

30. MAKING AN ARGUMENT Your friend claims that it is possible for a circumscribed angle to have the same measure as its intercepted arc. Is your friend correct? Explain your reasoning.

31. REASONING Points A and B are on a circle, and t is a tangent line containing A and another point C.

   a. Draw two diagrams that illustrate this situation.

   b. Write an equation for $m\overset{\frown}{AB}$ in terms of $m\angle BAC$ for each diagram.

   c. For what measure of $\angle BAC$ can you use either equation to find $m\overset{\frown}{AB}$? Explain.

32. REASONING $\triangle XYZ$ is an equilateral triangle inscribed in $\odot P$. $\overline{AB}$ is tangent to $\odot P$ at point X, $\overline{BC}$ is tangent to $\odot P$ at point Y, and $\overline{AC}$ is tangent to $\odot P$ at point Z. Draw a diagram that illustrates this situation. Then classify $\triangle ABC$ by its angles and sides. Justify your answer.

33. PROVING A THEOREM To prove the Tangent and Intersected Chord Theorem, you must prove three cases.

a. The diagram shows the case where $\overline{AB}$ contains the center of the circle. Use the Tangent Line to Circle Theorem to write a paragraph proof for this case.

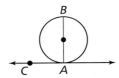

b. Draw a diagram and write a proof for the case where the center of the circle is in the interior of $\angle CAB$.

c. Draw a diagram and write a proof for the case where the center of the circle is in the exterior of $\angle CAB$.

34. HOW DO YOU SEE IT? In the diagram, television cameras are positioned at A and B to record what happens on stage. The stage is an arc of $\odot A$. You would like the camera at B to have a 30° view of the stage. Should you move the camera closer or farther away? Explain your reasoning.

35. PROVING A THEOREM Write a proof of the Angles Inside the Circle Theorem.

Given Chords $\overline{AC}$ and $\overline{BD}$ intersect inside a circle.

Prove $m\angle 1 = \frac{1}{2}(m\widehat{DC} + m\widehat{AB})$

36. THOUGHT PROVOKING In the figure, $\overleftrightarrow{BP}$ and $\overleftrightarrow{CP}$ are tangent to the circle. Point A is any point on the major arc formed by the endpoints of the chord $\overline{BC}$. Label all congruent angles in the figure. Justify your reasoning.

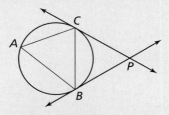

37. PROVING A THEOREM Use the diagram below to prove the Angles Outside the Circle Theorem for the case of a tangent and a secant. Then copy the diagrams for the other two cases on page 607 and draw appropriate auxiliary segments. Use your diagrams to prove each case.

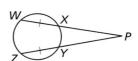

38. PROVING A THEOREM Prove that the Circumscribed Angle Theorem follows from the Angles Outside the Circle Theorem.

In Exercises 39 and 40, find the indicated measure(s). Justify your answer.

39. Find $m\angle P$ when $m\widehat{WZY} = 200°$.

40. Find $m\widehat{AB}$ and $m\widehat{ED}$.

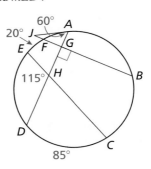

Maintaining Mathematical Proficiency
Reviewing what you learned in previous grades and lessons

Solve the equation using the Quadratic Formula. *(Section 4.5)*

41. $x^2 + x = 12$

42. $x^2 = 12x + 35$

43. $-3 = x^2 + 4x$

Essential Question What relationships exist among the segments formed by two intersecting chords or among segments of two secants that intersect outside a circle?

| EXPLORATION 1 | **Segments Formed by Two Intersecting Chords** |

Work with a partner. Use dynamic geometry software.

a. Construct two chords $\overline{BC}$ and $\overline{DE}$ that intersect in the interior of a circle at a point F.

Sample

b. Find the segment lengths BF, CF, DF, and EF and complete the table. What do you observe?

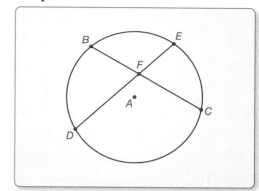

BF	CF	BF · CF

DF	EF	DF · EF

REASONING ABSTRACTLY

To be proficient in math, you need to make sense of quantities and their relationships in problem situations.

c. Repeat parts (a) and (b) several times. Write a conjecture about your results.

| EXPLORATION 2 | **Secants Intersecting Outside a Circle** |

Work with a partner. Use dynamic geometry software.

a. Construct two secants $\overleftrightarrow{BC}$ and $\overleftrightarrow{BD}$ that intersect at a point B outside a circle, as shown.

Sample

b. Find the segment lengths BE, BC, BF, and BD, and complete the table. What do you observe?

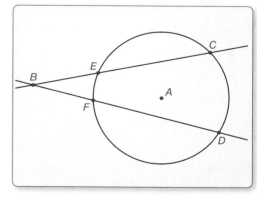

BE	BC	BE · BC

BF	BD	BF · BD

c. Repeat parts (a) and (b) several times. Write a conjecture about your results.

Communicate Your Answer

3. What relationships exist among the segments formed by two intersecting chords or among segments of two secants that intersect outside a circle?

4. Find the segment length AF in the figure at the left.

What You Will Learn

▶ Use segments of chords, tangents, and secants.

Core Vocabulary

segments of a chord, *p. 614*
tangent segment, *p. 615*
secant segment, *p. 615*
external segment, *p. 615*

Using Segments of Chords, Tangents, and Secants

When two chords intersect in the interior of a circle, each chord is divided into two segments that are called **segments of the chord**.

🌀 Theorem

Segments of Chords Theorem

If two chords intersect in the interior of a circle, then the product of the lengths of the segments of one chord is equal to the product of the lengths of the segments of the other chord.

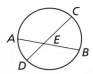

Proof Ex. 19, p. 618

$EA \cdot EB = EC \cdot ED$

EXAMPLE 1   **Using Segments of Chords**

Find *ML* and *JK*.

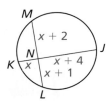

SOLUTION

$$NK \cdot NJ = NL \cdot NM$$ Segments of Chords Theorem

$$x \cdot (x + 4) = (x + 1) \cdot (x + 2)$$ Substitute.

$$x^2 + 4x = x^2 + 3x + 2$$ Simplify.

$$4x = 3x + 2$$ Subtract x^2 from each side.

$$x = 2$$ Subtract $3x$ from each side.

Find *ML* and *JK* by substitution.

$$ML = (x + 2) + (x + 1) \qquad\qquad JK = x + (x + 4)$$
$$= 2 + 2 + 2 + 1 \qquad\qquad\qquad = 2 + 2 + 4$$
$$= 7 \qquad\qquad\qquad\qquad\qquad = 8$$

▶ So, $ML = 7$ and $JK = 8$.

Monitoring Progress 🔊 Help in English and Spanish at *BigIdeasMath.com*

Find the value of *x*.

1.

2.

Core Concept

Tangent Segment and Secant Segment

A **tangent segment** is a segment that is tangent to a circle at an endpoint. A **secant segment** is a segment that contains a chord of a circle and has exactly one endpoint outside the circle. The part of a secant segment that is outside the circle is called an **external segment**.

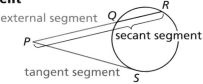

$\overline{PS}$ is a tangent segment.
$\overline{PR}$ is a secant segment.
$\overline{PQ}$ is the external segment of $\overline{PR}$.

Theorem

Segments of Secants Theorem

If two secant segments share the same endpoint outside a circle, then the product of the lengths of one secant segment and its external segment equals the product of the lengths of the other secant segment and its external segment.

Proof Ex. 20, p. 618

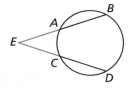

$EA \cdot EB = EC \cdot ED$

EXAMPLE 2   **Using Segments of Secants**

Find the value of x.

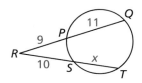

SOLUTION

$$RP \cdot RQ = RS \cdot RT \qquad \text{Segments of Secants Theorem}$$
$$9 \cdot (11 + 9) = 10 \cdot (x + 10) \qquad \text{Substitute.}$$
$$180 = 10x + 100 \qquad \text{Simplify.}$$
$$80 = 10x \qquad \text{Subtract 100 from each side.}$$
$$8 = x \qquad \text{Divide each side by 10.}$$

▶ The value of x is 8.

Monitoring Progress Help in English and Spanish at *BigIdeasMath.com*

Find the value of x.

3.

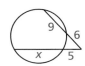

4.

⟲ Theorem

Segments of Secants and Tangents Theorem

If a secant segment and a tangent segment share an endpoint outside a circle, then the product of the lengths of the secant segment and its external segment equals the square of the length of the tangent segment.

Proof Exs. 21 and 22, p. 618

$EA^2 = EC \cdot ED$

EXAMPLE 3 **Using Segments of Secants and Tangents**

Find *RS*.

SOLUTION

$RQ^2 = RS \cdot RT$ Segments of Secants and Tangents Theorem

$16^2 = x \cdot (x + 8)$ Substitute.

$256 = x^2 + 8x$ Simplify.

$0 = x^2 + 8x - 256$ Write in standard form.

$x = \dfrac{-8 \pm \sqrt{8^2 - 4(1)(-256)}}{2(1)}$ Use Quadratic Formula.

$x = -4 \pm 4\sqrt{17}$ Simplify.

Use the positive solution because lengths cannot be negative.

▶ So, $x = -4 + 4\sqrt{17} \approx 12.49$, and $RS \approx 12.49$.

ANOTHER WAY

In Example 3, you can draw segments $\overline{QS}$ and $\overline{QT}$.

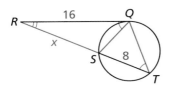

Because $\angle RQS$ and $\angle RTQ$ intercept the same arc, they are congruent. By the Reflexive Property of Congruence, $\angle QRS \cong \angle TRQ$. So, $\triangle RSQ \sim \triangle RQT$ by the AA Similarity Theorem. You can use this fact to write and solve a proportion to find x.

EXAMPLE 4 **Finding the Radius of a Circle**

Find the radius of the aquarium tank.

SOLUTION

$CB^2 = CE \cdot CD$ Segments of Secants and Tangents Theorem

$20^2 = 8 \cdot (2r + 8)$ Substitute.

$400 = 16r + 64$ Simplify.

$336 = 16r$ Subtract 64 from each side.

$21 = r$ Divide each side by 16.

▶ So, the radius of the tank is 21 feet.

Monitoring Progress 🔊 Help in English and Spanish at *BigIdeasMath.com*

Find the value of *x*.

5.

6.

7.

8. WHAT IF? In Example 4, $CB = 35$ feet and $CE = 14$ feet. Find the radius of the tank.

Vocabulary and Core Concept Check

1. **VOCABULARY** The part of the secant segment that is outside the circle is called a(n) _____.

2. **WRITING** Explain the difference between a tangent segment and a secant segment.

Monitoring Progress and Modeling with Mathematics

In Exercises 3–6, find the value of x. (*See Example 1.*)

3.

4.

5.

6.

In Exercises 7–10, find the value of x. (*See Example 2.*)

7.

8.

9.

10.

In Exercises 11–14, find the value of x. (*See Example 3.*)

11.

12.

13.

14.

15. **ERROR ANALYSIS** Describe and correct the error in finding CD.

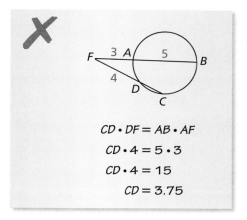

$$CD \cdot DF = AB \cdot AF$$
$$CD \cdot 4 = 5 \cdot 3$$
$$CD \cdot 4 = 15$$
$$CD = 3.75$$

16. **MODELING WITH MATHEMATICS** The Cassini spacecraft is on a mission in orbit around Saturn until September 2017. Three of Saturn's moons, Tethys, Calypso, and Telesto, have nearly circular orbits of radius 295,000 kilometers. The diagram shows the positions of the moons and the spacecraft on one of Cassini's missions. Find the distance DB from Cassini to Tethys when $\overline{AD}$ is tangent to the circular orbit. (*See Example 4.*)

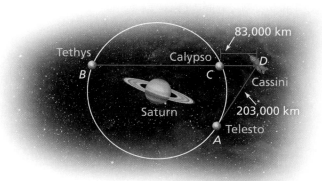

17. **MODELING WITH MATHEMATICS** The circular stone mound in Ireland called Newgrange has a diameter of 250 feet. A passage 62 feet long leads toward the center of the mound. Find the perpendicular distance x from the end of the passage to either side of the mound.

18. **MODELING WITH MATHEMATICS** You are designing an animated logo for your website. Sparkles leave point C and move to the outer circle along the segments shown so that all of the sparkles reach the outer circle at the same time. Sparkles travel from point C to point D at 2 centimeters per second. How fast should sparkles move from point C to point N? Explain.

19. **PROVING A THEOREM** Write a two-column proof of the Segments of Chords Theorem.

Plan for Proof Use the diagram from page 614. Draw $\overline{AC}$ and $\overline{DB}$. Show that $\triangle EAC$ and $\triangle EDB$ are similar. Use the fact that corresponding side lengths in similar triangles are proportional.

20. **PROVING A THEOREM** Prove the Segments of Secants Theorem. (*Hint:* Draw a diagram and add auxiliary line segments to form similar triangles.)

21. **PROVING A THEOREM** Use the Tangent Line to Circle Theorem to prove the Segments of Secants and Tangents Theorem for the special case when the secant segment contains the center of the circle.

22. **PROVING A THEOREM** Prove the Segments of Secants and Tangents Theorem. (*Hint:* Draw a diagram and add auxiliary line segments to form similar triangles.)

23. **WRITING EQUATIONS** In the diagram of the water well, AB, AD, and DE are known. Write an equation for BC using these three measurements.

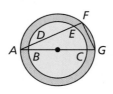

24. **HOW DO YOU SEE IT?** Which two theorems would you need to use to find PQ? Explain your reasoning.

25. **CRITICAL THINKING** In the figure, $AB = 12$, $BC = 8$, $DE = 6$, $PD = 4$, and A is a point of tangency. Find the radius of $\odot P$.

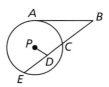

26. **THOUGHT PROVOKING** Circumscribe a triangle about a circle. Then, using the points of tangency, inscribe a triangle in the circle. Must it be true that the two triangles are similar? Explain your reasoning.

Maintaining Mathematical Proficiency Reviewing what you learned in previous grades and lessons

Solve the equation by completing the square. (*Section 4.4*)

27. $x^2 + 4x = 45$

28. $x^2 - 2x - 1 = 8$

29. $2x^2 + 12x + 20 = 34$

30. $-4x^2 + 8x + 44 = 16$

10.7 Circles in the Coordinate Plane

Essential Question What is the equation of a circle with center (h, k) and radius r in the coordinate plane?

EXPLORATION 1 **The Equation of a Circle with Center at the Origin**

Work with a partner. Use dynamic geometry software to construct and determine the equations of circles centered at $(0, 0)$ in the coordinate plane, as described below.

a. Complete the first two rows of the table for circles with the given radii. Complete the other rows for circles with radii of your choice.

b. Write an equation of a circle with center $(0, 0)$ and radius r.

Radius	Equation of circle
1	
2	

EXPLORATION 2 **The Equation of a Circle with Center (h, k)**

Work with a partner. Use dynamic geometry software to construct and determine the equations of circles of radius 2 in the coordinate plane, as described below.

a. Complete the first two rows of the table for circles with the given centers. Complete the other rows for circles with centers of your choice.

b. Write an equation of a circle with center (h, k) and radius 2.

c. Write an equation of a circle with center (h, k) and radius r.

Center	Equation of circle
$(0, 0)$	
$(2, 0)$	

EXPLORATION 3 **Deriving the Standard Equation of a Circle**

MAKING SENSE OF PROBLEMS

To be proficient in math, you need to explain correspondences between equations and graphs.

Work with a partner. Consider a circle with radius r and center (h, k).

Write the Distance Formula to represent the distance d between a point (x, y) on the circle and the center (h, k) of the circle. Then square each side of the Distance Formula equation.

How does your result compare with the equation you wrote in part (c) of Exploration 2?

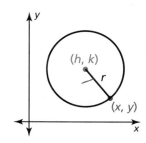

Communicate Your Answer

4. What is the equation of a circle with center (h, k) and radius r in the coordinate plane?

5. Write an equation of the circle with center $(4, -1)$ and radius 3.

10.7 Lesson

Core Vocabulary

standard equation of a circle,
p. 620

Previous
completing the square

What You Will Learn

▶ Write and graph equations of circles.

▶ Write coordinate proofs involving circles.

▶ Solve real-life problems using graphs of circles.

▶ Solve nonlinear systems.

Writing and Graphing Equations of Circles

Let (x, y) represent any point on a circle with center at the origin and radius r. By the Pythagorean Theorem,

$$x^2 + y^2 = r^2.$$

This is the equation of a circle with center at the origin and radius r.

Core Concept

Standard Equation of a Circle

Let (x, y) represent any point on a circle with center (h, k) and radius r. By the Pythagorean Theorem,

$$(x - h)^2 + (y - k)^2 = r^2.$$

This is the **standard equation of a circle** with center (h, k) and radius r.

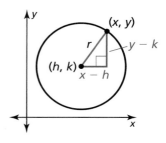

EXAMPLE 1   **Writing the Standard Equation of a Circle**

Write the standard equation of each circle.

a. the circle shown at the left

b. a circle with center $(0, -9)$ and radius 4.2

SOLUTION

a. The radius is 3, and the center is at the origin.

$$(x - h)^2 + (y - k)^2 = r^2 \quad \text{Standard equation of a circle}$$

$$(x - 0)^2 + (y - 0)^2 = 3^2 \quad \text{Substitute.}$$

$$x^2 + y^2 = 9 \quad \text{Simplify.}$$

▶ The standard equation of the circle is $x^2 + y^2 = 9$.

b. The radius is 4.2, and the center is at $(0, -9)$.

$$(x - h)^2 + (y - k)^2 = r^2$$

$$(x - 0)^2 + [y - (-9)]^2 = 4.2^2$$

$$x^2 + (y + 9)^2 = 17.64$$

▶ The standard equation of the circle is $x^2 + (y + 9)^2 = 17.64$.

Monitoring Progress Help in English and Spanish at *BigIdeasMath.com*

Write the standard equation of the circle with the given center and radius.

1. center: $(0, 0)$, radius: 2.5

2. center: $(-2, 5)$, radius: 7

EXAMPLE 2 Writing the Standard Equation of a Circle

The point $(-5, 6)$ is on a circle with center $(-1, 3)$. Write the standard equation of the circle.

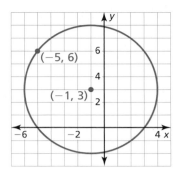

SOLUTION

To write the standard equation, you need to know the values of h, k, and r. To find r, find the distance between the center and the point $(-5, 6)$ on the circle.

$$r = \sqrt{[-5 - (-1)]^2 + (6 - 3)^2}$$ Distance Formula

$$= \sqrt{(-4)^2 + 3^2}$$ Simplify.

$$= 5$$ Simplify.

Substitute the values for the center and the radius into the standard equation of a circle.

$$(x - h)^2 + (y - k)^2 = r^2$$ Standard equation of a circle

$$[x - (-1)]^2 + (y - 3)^2 = 5^2$$ Substitute $(h, k) = (-1, 3)$ and $r = 5$.

$$(x + 1)^2 + (y - 3)^2 = 25$$ Simplify.

▶ The standard equation of the circle is $(x + 1)^2 + (y - 3)^2 = 25$.

EXAMPLE 3 Graphing a Circle

The equation of a circle is $x^2 + y^2 - 8x + 4y - 16 = 0$. Find the center and the radius of the circle. Then graph the circle.

SOLUTION

You can write the equation in standard form by completing the square on the x-terms and the y-terms.

$$x^2 + y^2 - 8x + 4y - 16 = 0$$ Equation of circle

$$x^2 - 8x + y^2 + 4y = 16$$ Isolate constant. Group terms.

$$x^2 - 8x + 16 + y^2 + 4y + 4 = 16 + 16 + 4$$ Complete the square twice.

$$(x - 4)^2 + (y + 2)^2 = 36$$ Factor left side. Simplify right side.

$$(x - 4)^2 + [y - (-2)]^2 = 6^2$$ Rewrite the equation to find the center and the radius.

▶ The center is $(4, -2)$, and the radius is 6. Use a compass to graph the circle.

CONNECTIONS TO ALGEBRA

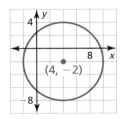

Recall from Section 4.4 that to complete the square for the expression $x^2 + bx$, you add the square of half the coefficient of the term bx.

$$x^2 + bx + \left(\frac{b}{2}\right)^2 = \left(x + \frac{b}{2}\right)^2$$

Monitoring Progress Help in English and Spanish at *BigIdeasMath.com*

3. The point $(3, 4)$ is on a circle with center $(1, 4)$. Write the standard equation of the circle.

4. The equation of a circle is $x^2 + y^2 - 8x + 6y + 9 = 0$. Find the center and the radius of the circle. Then graph the circle.

Writing Coordinate Proofs Involving Circles

EXAMPLE 4 Writing a Coordinate Proof Involving a Circle

Prove or disprove that the point $(\sqrt{2}, \sqrt{2})$ lies on the circle centered at the origin and containing the point $(2, 0)$.

SOLUTION

The circle centered at the origin and containing the point $(2, 0)$ has the following radius.

$$r = \sqrt{(x - h)^2 + (y - k)^2} = \sqrt{(2 - 0)^2 + (0 - 0)^2} = 2$$

So, a point lies on the circle if and only if the distance from that point to the origin is 2. The distance from $(\sqrt{2}, \sqrt{2})$ to $(0, 0)$ is

$$d = \sqrt{(\sqrt{2} - 0)^2 + (\sqrt{2} - 0)^2} = 2.$$

▶ So, the point $(\sqrt{2}, \sqrt{2})$ lies on the circle centered at the origin and containing the point $(2, 0)$.

Monitoring Progress Help in English and Spanish at *BigIdeasMath.com*

5. Prove or disprove that the point $(1, \sqrt{5})$ lies on the circle centered at the origin and containing the point $(0, 1)$.

Solving Real-Life Problems

EXAMPLE 5 Using Graphs of Circles

The epicenter of an earthquake is the point on Earth's surface directly above the earthquake's origin. A seismograph can be used to determine the distance to the epicenter of an earthquake. Seismographs are needed in three different places to locate an earthquake's epicenter.

Use the seismograph readings from locations A, B, and C to find the epicenter of an earthquake.

- The epicenter is 7 miles away from $A(-2, 2.5)$.
- The epicenter is 4 miles away from $B(4, 6)$.
- The epicenter is 5 miles away from $C(3, -2.5)$.

SOLUTION

The set of all points equidistant from a given point is a circle, so the epicenter is located on each of the following circles.

⊙A with center $(-2, 2.5)$ and radius 7

⊙B with center $(4, 6)$ and radius 4

⊙C with center $(3, -2.5)$ and radius 5

To find the epicenter, graph the circles on a coordinate plane where each unit corresponds to one mile. Find the point of intersection of the three circles.

▶ The epicenter is at about $(5, 2)$.

Monitoring Progress Help in English and Spanish at *BigIdeasMath.com*

6. Why are three seismographs needed to locate an earthquake's epicenter?

Solving Nonlinear Systems

In Section 4.8, you solved systems involving parabolas and lines. Now you can solve systems involving circles and lines.

EXAMPLE 6 Solving a Nonlinear System

Solve the system.

$$x^2 + y^2 = 1 \qquad \text{Equation 1}$$

$$y = \frac{x + 1}{2} \qquad \text{Equation 2}$$

SOLUTION

Step 1 Equation 2 is already solved for y.

Step 2 Substitute $\dfrac{x + 1}{2}$ for y in Equation 1 and solve for x.

$$x^2 + y^2 = 1 \qquad\qquad \text{Equation 1}$$

$$x^2 + \left(\frac{x + 1}{2}\right)^2 = 1 \qquad\qquad \text{Substitute } \frac{x + 1}{2} \text{ for } y.$$

$$x^2 + \frac{(x + 1)^2}{4} = 1 \qquad\qquad \text{Power of a Quotient Property}$$

$$4x^2 + (x + 1)^2 = 4 \qquad\qquad \text{Multiply each side by 4.}$$

$$5x^2 + 2x - 3 = 0 \qquad\qquad \text{Write in standard form.}$$

$$x = \frac{-2 \pm \sqrt{2^2 - 4(5)(-3)}}{2(5)} \qquad \text{Use the Quadratic Formula.}$$

$$x = \frac{-2 \pm \sqrt{64}}{10} \qquad\qquad \text{Simplify.}$$

$$x = \frac{-2 \pm 8}{10} \qquad\qquad \text{Evaluate the square root.}$$

$$x = \frac{-1 \pm 4}{5} \qquad\qquad \text{Simplify.}$$

So, $x = \dfrac{-1 + 4}{5} = \dfrac{3}{5}$ and $x = \dfrac{-1 - 4}{5} = -1$.

Step 3 Substitute $\dfrac{3}{5}$ and -1 for x in Equation 2 and solve for y.

$$y = \frac{\frac{3}{5} + 1}{2} \qquad \text{Substitute for } x \text{ in Equation 2.} \qquad y = \frac{-1 + 1}{2}$$

$$= \frac{4}{5} \qquad\qquad\qquad \text{Simplify.} \qquad\qquad\qquad = 0$$

▶ So, the solutions are $\left(\dfrac{3}{5}, \dfrac{4}{5}\right)$ and $(-1, 0)$.

Check

Graph the equations in a coordinate plane to check your answer.

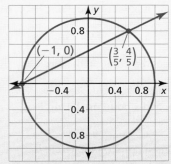

Help in English and Spanish at *BigIdeasMath.com*

Monitoring Progress

Solve the system.

7. $x^2 + y^2 = 1$

$y = x$

8. $x^2 + y^2 = 2$

$y = -x + 2$

9. $(x - 1)^2 + y^2 = 4$

$y = \dfrac{x + 6}{2}$

Vocabulary and Core Concept Check

1. **VOCABULARY** What is the standard equation of a circle?

2. **WRITING** Explain why knowing the location of the center and one point on a circle is enough to graph the circle.

Monitoring Progress and Modeling with Mathematics

In Exercises 3–8, find the center and radius of the circle.

3.

4.

5.

6.

7.

8.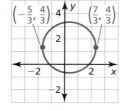

In Exercises 9–20, write the standard equation of the circle. *(See Example 1.)*

9.

10.

11.

12.

13.

14.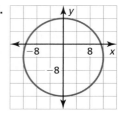

15. a circle with center (0, 0) and radius 7

16. a circle with center (4, 1) and radius 5

17. a circle with center (−3, 4) and radius 1

18. a circle with center (3, −5) and radius 7

19. a circle with center (−2, −6) and radius 1.1

20. a circle with center (−10, −8) and radius 3.2

In Exercises 21–26, use the given information to write the standard equation of the circle. *(See Example 2.)*

21. The center is (0, 0), and a point on the circle is (0, 6).

22. The center is (1, 2), and a point on the circle is (4, 2).

23. The center is (7, −9), and a point on the circle is (3, −6).

24. The center is (−4, 3), and a point on the circle is (−10, −5).

25. The center is (0, 0), and a point on the circle is (3, −7).

26. The center is (−1, −3), and a point on the circle is (−5, 8).

27. **ERROR ANALYSIS** Describe and correct the error in writing the standard equation of the circle.

> The standard equation of the circle
> with center (−3, −5) and radius 3
> is $(x - 3)^2 + (y - 5)^2 = 9$.

28. ERROR ANALYSIS Describe and correct the error in writing the standard equation of the circle.

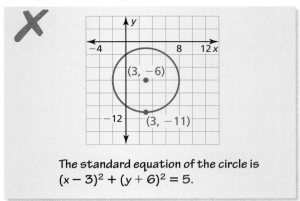

The standard equation of the circle is
$(x - 3)^2 + (y + 6)^2 = 5.$

In Exercises 29–38, find the center and radius of the circle. Then graph the circle. *(See Example 3.)*

29. $x^2 + y^2 = 49$ **30.** $x^2 + y^2 = 64$

31. $(x + 5)^2 + (y - 3)^2 = 9$

32. $(x - 6)^2 + (y + 2)^2 = 36$

33. $x^2 + y^2 - 6x = 7$

34. $x^2 + y^2 + 4y = 32$

35. $x^2 + y^2 - 8x - 2y = -16$

36. $x^2 + y^2 + 4x + 12y = -15$

37. $x^2 + y^2 + 8x - 4y + 4 = 0$

38. $x^2 + y^2 + 12x - 8y + 16 = 0$

In Exercises 39–44, prove or disprove the statement. *(See Example 4.)*

39. The point $(2, 3)$ lies on the circle centered at the origin with radius 8.

40. The point $(4, \sqrt{5})$ lies on the circle centered at the origin with radius 3.

41. The point $(\sqrt{6}, 2)$ lies on the circle centered at the origin and containing the point $(3, -1)$.

42. The point $(\sqrt{7}, 5)$ lies on the circle centered at the origin and containing the point $(5, 2)$.

43. The point $(4, 4)$ lies on the circle centered at $(1, 0)$ and containing the point $(5, -3)$.

44. The point $(2.4, 4)$ lies on the circle centered at $(-3, 2)$ and containing the point $(-11, 8)$.

45. MODELING WITH MATHEMATICS A city's commuter system has three zones. Zone 1 serves people living within 3 miles of the city's center. Zone 2 serves those between 3 and 7 miles from the center. Zone 3 serves those over 7 miles from the center. *(See Example 5.)*

a. Graph this situation on a coordinate plane where each unit corresponds to 1 mile. Locate the city's center at the origin.

b. Determine which zone serves people whose homes are represented by the points $(3, 4)$, $(6, 5)$, $(1, 2)$, $(0, 3)$, and $(1, 6)$.

46. MODELING WITH MATHEMATICS Telecommunication towers can be used to transmit cellular phone calls. A graph with units measured in kilometers shows towers at points $(0, 0)$, $(0, 5)$, and $(6, 3)$. These towers have a range of about 3 kilometers.

a. Sketch a graph and locate the towers. Are there any locations that may receive calls from more than one tower? Explain your reasoning.

b. The center of City A is located at $(-2, 2.5)$, and the center of City B is located at $(5, 4)$. Each city has a radius of 1.5 kilometers. Which city seems to have better cell phone coverage? Explain your reasoning.

In Exercises 47–56, solve the system. *(See Example 6.)*

47. $x^2 + y^2 = 4$ **48.** $x^2 + y^2 = 1$
$\quad\ y = 1$ $\quad\ y = -5$

49. $x^2 + y^2 = 64$ **50.** $x^2 + y^2 = 2$
$\quad\ y = x - 10$ $\quad\ y = x + 2$

51. $x^2 + y^2 = 16$ **52.** $x^2 + y^2 = 9$
$\quad\ y = x + 16$ $\quad\ y = x + 3$

53. $x^2 + y^2 = 1$ **54.** $x^2 + y^2 = 1$
$\quad\ y = \dfrac{-x + 1}{2}$ $\quad\ y = \dfrac{-5x + 13}{12}$

55. $(x - 3)^2 + (y + 1)^2 = 1$ **56.** $(x + 2)^2 + (y - 6)^2 = 25$
$\quad\ y = 2x - 6$ $\quad\ y = -2x - 23$

57. REASONING Consider the graph shown.

a. Explain how you can use the given points to form Pythagorean triples.

b. Identify another point on the circle that you can use to form the Pythagorean triple 3, 4, 5.

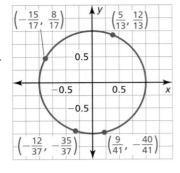

$\left(-\frac{15}{17}, \frac{8}{17}\right)$ $\left(\frac{5}{13}, \frac{12}{13}\right)$

$\left(-\frac{12}{37}, -\frac{35}{37}\right)$ $\left(\frac{9}{41}, -\frac{40}{41}\right)$

58. HOW DO YOU SEE IT? Match each graph with its equation.

a.

b.

c.

d.

A. $x^2 + (y + 3)^2 = 4$ **B.** $(x - 3)^2 + y^2 = 4$

C. $(x + 3)^2 + y^2 = 4$ **D.** $x^2 + (y - 3)^2 = 4$

59. REASONING Sketch the graph of the circle whose equation is $x^2 + y^2 = 16$. Then sketch the graph of the circle after the translation $(x, y) \rightarrow (x - 2, y - 4)$. What is the equation of the image? Make a conjecture about the equation of the image of a circle centered at the origin after a translation m units to the left and n units down.

60. THOUGHT PROVOKING A circle has center (h, k) and contains point (a, b). Write the equation of the line tangent to the circle at point (a, b).

61. USING STRUCTURE The vertices of $\triangle XYZ$ are $X(4, 5)$, $Y(4, 13)$, and $Z(8, 9)$. Find the equation of the circle circumscribed about $\triangle XYZ$. Justify your answer.

62. MAKING AN ARGUMENT Your friend claims that the equation of a circle passing through the points $(-1, 0)$ and $(1, 0)$ is $x^2 - 2yk + y^2 = 1$ with center $(0, k)$. Is your friend correct? Explain your reasoning.

MATHEMATICAL CONNECTIONS In Exercises 63–66, use the equations to determine whether the line is *a tangent*, *a secant*, *a secant that contains the diameter*, or *none of these*. Explain your reasoning.

63. Circle: $(x - 4)^2 + (y - 3)^2 = 9$
Line: $y = 6$

64. Circle: $(x + 2)^2 + (y - 2)^2 = 16$
Line: $y = 2x - 4$

65. Circle: $(x - 5)^2 + (y + 1)^2 = 4$
Line: $y = \frac{1}{5}x - 3$

66. Circle: $(x + 3)^2 + (y - 6)^2 = 25$
Line: $y = -\frac{4}{3}x + 2$

67. REASONING Four tangent circles are centered on the x-axis. The radius of $\odot A$ is twice the radius of $\odot O$. The radius of $\odot B$ is three times the radius of $\odot O$. The radius of $\odot C$ is four times the radius of $\odot O$. All circles have integer radii, and the point $(63, 16)$ is on $\odot C$. What is the equation of $\odot A$? Explain your reasoning.

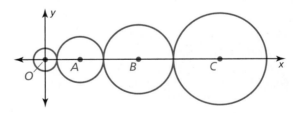

Maintaining Mathematical Proficiency   Reviewing what you learned in previous grades and lessons

Identify the arc as a *major arc*, *minor arc*, or *semicircle*. Then find the measure of the arc. *(Section 10.2)*

68. $\overarc{RS}$ **69.** $\overarc{PR}$

70. $\overarc{PRT}$ **71.** $\overarc{ST}$

72. $\overarc{RST}$ **73.** $\overarc{QS}$

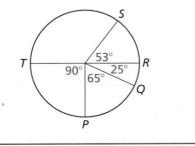

Core Vocabulary

inscribed angle, *p. 598*
intercepted arc, *p. 598*
subtend, *p. 598*

circumscribed angle, *p. 608*
segments of a chord, *p. 614*
tangent segment, *p. 615*

secant segment, *p. 615*
external segment, *p. 615*
standard equation of a circle, *p. 620*

Core Concepts

Section 10.4

Inscribed Angle and Intercepted Arc, *p. 598*
Measure of an Inscribed Angle Theorem, *p. 598*
Inscribed Angles of a Circle Theorem, *p. 599*

Inscribed Right Triangle Theorem, *p. 600*
Inscribed Quadrilateral Theorem, *p. 600*

Section 10.5

Tangent and Intersected Chord Theorem, *p. 606*
Intersecting Lines and Circles, *p. 606*
Angles Inside the Circle Theorem, *p. 607*

Angles Outside the Circle Theorem, *p. 607*
Circumscribed Angle, *p. 608*
Circumscribed Angle Theorem, *p. 608*

Section 10.6

Segments of Chords Theorem, *p. 614*
Tangent Segment and Secant Segment, *p. 615*

Segments of Secants Theorem, *p. 615*
Segments of Secants and Tangents Theorem, *p. 616*

Section 10.7

Standard Equation of a Circle, *p. 620*
Writing Coordinate Proofs Involving Circles, *p. 622*

Solving Nonlinear Systems, *p. 623*

Mathematical Practices

1. What other tools could you use to complete the task in Exercise 18 on page 603?

2. You have a classmate who is confused about why two diagrams are needed in part (a) of
    Exercise 31 on page 611. Explain to your classmate why two diagrams are needed.

Performance Task:

Finding Locations

Scientists use seismographs to locate the epicenter of an
earthquake. They use distance data taken from the instruments
to create three circles. The intersection of these circles determines
the precise location of the epicenter. This process, which is called
trilateration, is also used by the Global Positioning System (GPS)
to determine a person's location. How does it work?

To explore the answer to this question and
more, check out the Performance Task and
Real-Life STEM video at *BigIdeasMath.com*.

10.1 **Lines and Segments That Intersect Circles** *(pp. 573–580)*

In the diagram, $\overline{AB}$ is tangent to $\odot C$ at B and $\overline{AD}$ is tangent to $\odot C$ at D. Find the value of x.

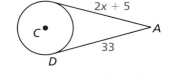

$AB = AD$	External Tangent Congruence Theorem
$2x + 5 = 33$	Substitute.
$x = 14$	Solve for x.

▶ The value of x is 14.

Tell whether the line, ray, or segment is best described as a *radius*, *chord*, *diameter*, *secant*, or *tangent* of $\odot P$.

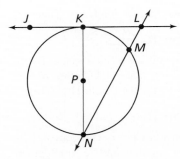

1. $\overline{PK}$ 2. $\overline{NM}$

3. $\overrightarrow{JL}$ 4. $\overline{KN}$

5. $\overleftrightarrow{NL}$ 6. $\overline{PN}$

Tell whether the common tangent is *internal* or *external*.

7.

8.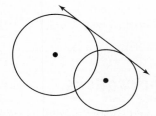

Points Y and Z are points of tangency. Find the value of the variable.

9.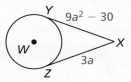

$9a^2 - 30$

$3a$

10.

$2c^2 + 9c + 6$

$9c + 14$

11.

12. Tell whether $\overline{AB}$ is tangent to $\odot C$. Explain.

10.2 Finding Arc Measures *(pp. 581–588)*

Find the measure of each arc of ⊙P, where $\overline{LN}$ is a diameter.

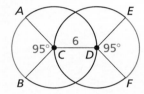

a. $\widehat{MN}$

▶ $\widehat{MN}$ is a minor arc, so $m\widehat{MN} = m\angle MPN = 120°$.

b. $\widehat{NLM}$

▶ $\widehat{NLM}$ is a major arc, so $m\widehat{NLM} = 360° - 120° = 240°$.

c. $\widehat{NML}$

▶ $\overline{NL}$ is a diameter, so $\widehat{NML}$ is a semicircle, and $m\widehat{NML} = 180°$.

Use the diagram above to find the measure of the indicated arc.

13. $\widehat{KL}$ **14.** $\widehat{LM}$ **15.** $\widehat{KM}$ **16.** $\widehat{KN}$

Tell whether the red arcs are congruent. Explain why or why not.

17.

18.

10.3 Using Chords *(pp. 589–594)*

In the diagram, $⊙A ≅ ⊙B$, $\overline{CD} ≅ \overline{FE}$, and $m\widehat{FE} = 75°$. Find $m\widehat{CD}$.

Because $\overline{CD}$ and $\overline{FE}$ are congruent chords in congruent circles, the corresponding minor arcs $\widehat{CD}$ and $\widehat{FE}$ are congruent by the Congruent Corresponding Chords Theorem.

▶ So, $m\widehat{CD} = m\widehat{FE} = 75°$.

Find the measure of $\widehat{AB}$.

19.

20.

21.

22. In the diagram, $QN = QP = 10$, $JK = 4x$, and $LM = 6x - 24$. Find the radius of ⊙Q.

Find the value of each variable.

LMNP is inscribed in a circle, so opposite angles are supplementary by the Inscribed Quadrilateral Theorem.

$$m\angle L + m\angle N = 180° \qquad\qquad m\angle P + m\angle M = 180°$$
$$3a° + 3a° = 180° \qquad\qquad\quad b° + 50° = 180°$$
$$6a = 180 \qquad\qquad\qquad\quad b = 130$$
$$a = 30$$

▶   The value of *a* is 30, and the value of *b* is 130.

Find the value(s) of the variable(s).

23.

24.

25.

26.

27.

28.

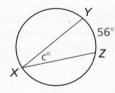

Find the value of *y*.

The tangent $\overrightarrow{RQ}$ and secant $\overrightarrow{RT}$ intersect outside the circle, so you can use the Angles Outside the Circle Theorem.

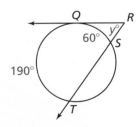

$$y° = \tfrac{1}{2}(m\widehat{QT} - m\widehat{SQ}) \qquad \text{Angles Outside the Circle Theorem}$$
$$y° = \tfrac{1}{2}(190° - 60°) \qquad\quad \text{Substitute.}$$
$$y = 65 \qquad\qquad\qquad\quad \text{Simplify.}$$

▶   The value of *y* is 65.

Find the value of x.

29.

250°   x°

30.

152°   x°   60°

31.

40°   x°   96°

32. Line ℓ is tangent to the circle. Find $m\widehat{XYZ}$.

Y   X
120°
Z ℓ

10.6 **Segment Relationships in Circles** *(pp. 613–618)*

Find the value of x.

The chords $\overline{EG}$ and $\overline{FH}$ intersect inside the circle, so you can use the Segments of Chords Theorem.

$EP \cdot PG = FP \cdot PH$ Segments of Chords Theorem

$x \cdot 2 = 3 \cdot 6$ Substitute.

$x = 9$ Simplify.

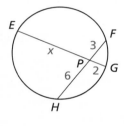
E   F
x   3
P   G
6   2
H

▶ The value of x is 9.

Find the value of x.

33.
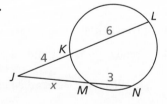
L
6
K
4
J
x   M   3   N

34.
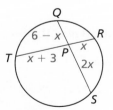
Q
6 − x   R
T   x + 3   P   x
2x
S

35.
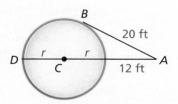
W   12   X
8
Y
x
Z

36. A local park has a circular ice skating rink. You are standing at point *A*, about 12 feet from the edge of the rink. The distance from you to a point of tangency on the rink is about 20 feet. Estimate the radius of the rink.

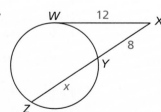
B
20 ft
D   r   r   A
C   12 ft

Write the standard equation of the circle shown.

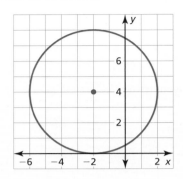

The radius is 4, and the center is $(-2, 4)$.

$$(x - h)^2 + (y - k)^2 = r^2 \qquad \text{Standard equation of a circle}$$
$$[x - (-2)]^2 + (y - 4)^2 = 4^2 \qquad \text{Substitute.}$$
$$(x + 2)^2 + (y - 4)^2 = 16 \qquad \text{Simplify.}$$

▶ The standard equation of the circle is $(x + 2)^2 + (y - 4)^2 = 16$.

Write the standard equation of the circle shown.

37.

38.

39.
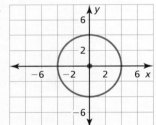

Write the standard equation of the circle with the given center and radius.

40. center: $(0, 0)$, radius: 9

41. center: $(-5, 2)$, radius: 1.3

42. The point $(-7, 1)$ is on a circle with center $(-7, 6)$. Write the standard equation of the circle.

43. The equation of a circle is $x^2 + y^2 - 12x + 8y + 48 = 0$. Find the center and the radius of the circle. Then graph the circle.

44. Prove or disprove that the point $(4, -3)$ lies on the circle centered at the origin and containing the point $(-5, 0)$.

Solve the system.

45. $x^2 + y^2 = 25$

$y = -6$

46. $x^2 + (y + 2)^2 = 1$

$y = 2x - 3$

Find the measure of each numbered angle in ⊙*P*. Justify your answer.

1.
   145°

2.

3.
   36°
   38°
   96°

4.
   77° 48°
   215°

Use the diagram.

5. $AG = 2$, $GD = 9$, and $BG = 3$. Find GF.

6. $CF = 12$, $CB = 3$, and $CD = 9$. Find CE.

7. Solve the system. $x^2 + y^2 = 225$

   $y = x + 3$

8. Sketch a pentagon inscribed in a circle. Label the pentagon *ABCDE*. Describe the relationship between each pair of angles. Explain your reasoning.

   a. ∠*CDE* and ∠*CAE*   b. ∠*CBE* and ∠*CAE*

Find the value of the variable. Justify your answer.

9.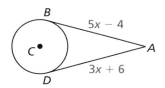
   B
   $5x - 4$
   C   *A*
   $3x + 6$
   D

10.
    A 6 *B* *r* *C*
    12   *r*
    D

11. Prove or disprove that the point $\left(2\sqrt{2}, -1\right)$ lies on the circle centered at $(0, 2)$ and containing the point $(-1, 4)$.

Prove the given statement.

12. $\overset{\frown}{ST} \cong \overset{\frown}{RQ}$

13. $\overset{\frown}{JM} \cong \overset{\frown}{LM}$

14. $\overset{\frown}{DG} \cong \overset{\frown}{FG}$

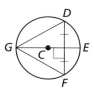

15. A bank of lighting hangs over a stage. Each light illuminates a circular region on the stage. A coordinate plane is used to arrange the lights, using a corner of the stage as the origin. The equation $(x - 13)^2 + (y - 4)^2 = 16$ represents the boundary of the region illuminated by one of the lights. Three actors stand at the points $A(11, 4)$, $B(8, 5)$, and $C(15, 5)$. Graph the given equation. Then determine which actors are illuminated by the light.

16. If a car goes around a turn too quickly, it can leave tracks that form an arc of a circle. By finding the radius of the circle, accident investigators can estimate the speed of the car.

    a. To find the radius, accident investigators choose points *A* and *B* on the tire marks. Then the investigators find the midpoint *C* of $\overline{AB}$. Use the diagram to find the radius *r* of the circle. Explain why this method works.

    b. The formula $S = 3.87\sqrt{fr}$ can be used to estimate a car's speed in miles per hour, where *f* is the *coefficient of friction* and *r* is the radius of the circle in feet. If $f = 0.7$, estimate the car's speed in part (a).

D   160 ft   *B*
80 ft
r ft
160 ft   *C*
$(r - 80)$ ft
A
r ft   *Not drawn to scale*

1. Classify each segment as specifically as possible.

   a. $\overline{BG}$ **b.** $\overline{CD}$

   c. $\overline{AD}$ **d.** $\overline{FE}$

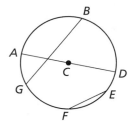

2. Copy and complete the paragraph proof.

   Given Circle C with center $(2, 1)$ and radius 1,
   Circle D with center $(0, 3)$ and radius 4

   Prove Circle C is similar to Circle D.

   Map Circle C to Circle C' by using the _____ $(x, y) \rightarrow$ _____
   so that Circle C' and Circle D have the same center at (__, __). Dilate
   Circle C' using a center of dilation (__, __) and a scale factor of ___.
   Because there is a _____ transformation that maps Circle C to Circle D,
   Circle C is _____ Circle D.

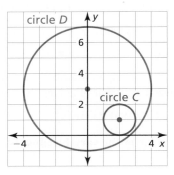

3. Use the diagram to write a proof.

   Given $\triangle JPL \cong \triangle NPL$
   $\overline{PK}$ is an altitude of $\triangle JPL$.
   $\overline{PM}$ is an altitude of $\triangle NPL$.

   Prove $\triangle PKL \sim \triangle NMP$

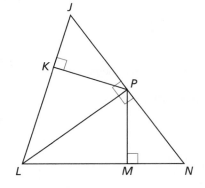

4. The equation of a circle is $x^2 + y^2 + 14x - 16y + 77 = 0$.
   What are the center and radius of the circle?

   A center: $(14, -16)$, radius: 8.8

   B center: $(-7, 8)$, radius: 6

   C center: $(-14, 16)$, radius: 8.8

   D center: $(7, -8)$, radius: 5.2

5. Which expression is *not* equivalent to the others?

   A $\dfrac{x^{1/2} \cdot x^{5/4} \cdot \sqrt[4]{x}}{x^{-3} \cdot x^3}$ **B** $\dfrac{x^{-9} \cdot (x^{7/3})^3}{x^{-4}}$

   C $\dfrac{x^5 \cdot x^3}{x^{-6}}$ **D** $\dfrac{\sqrt[3]{x} \cdot x^{-4/3}}{x^{-3}}$

6. Which angles have the same measure as ∠ACB? Select all that apply.

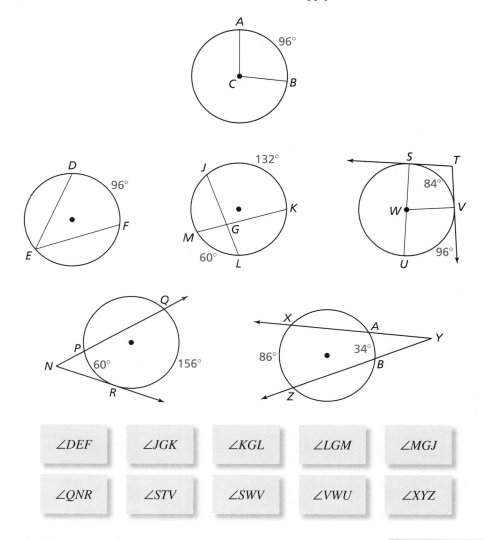

| ∠DEF | ∠JGK | ∠KGL | ∠LGM | ∠MGJ |

| ∠QNR | ∠STV | ∠SWV | ∠VWU | ∠XYZ |

7. A survey asked freshman and sophomore students about whether they think the new school mascot should be a tiger or a lion. The table shows the results of the survey.

a. Complete the two-way table.

b. What is the probability that a randomly selected student is a freshman and prefers a tiger?

c. What is the probability that a randomly selected sophomore prefers a tiger?

		New Mascot		
		Tiger	Lion	Total
Class	Freshman			100
	Sophomore		48	
	Total	110		212

8. Your friend claims that the quadrilateral shown can be inscribed in a circle. Is your friend correct? Explain your reasoning.

70° 110°
110° 70°

11 Circumference, Area, and Volume

Khafre's Pyramid (p. 675)

Basaltic Columns (p. 661)

SEE the Big Idea

Ceramic Tiles (p. 659)

Irrigation System (p. 647)

London Eye (p. 645)

Maintaining Mathematical Proficiency

Finding Surface Area

Example 1 Find the surface area of the prism.

$S = 2\ell w + 2\ell h + 2wh$ Write formula for surface area of a rectangular prism.

$= 2(2)(4) + 2(2)(6) + 2(4)(6)$ Substitute 2 for ℓ, 4 for w, and 6 for h.

$= 16 + 24 + 48$ Multiply.

$= 88$ Add.

▶ The surface area is 88 square inches.

Find the surface area of the prism.

1.

2.

3.

Finding a Missing Dimension

Example 2 A rectangle has a perimeter of 10 meters and a length of 3 meters. What is the width of the rectangle?

$P = 2\ell + 2w$ Write formula for perimeter of a rectangle.

$10 = 2(3) + 2w$ Substitute 10 for P and 3 for ℓ.

$10 = 6 + 2w$ Multiply 2 and 3.

$4 = 2w$ Subtract 6 from each side.

$2 = w$ Divide each side by 2.

▶ The width is 2 meters.

Find the missing dimension.

4. A rectangle has a perimeter of 28 inches and a width of 5 inches. What is the length of the rectangle?

5. A triangle has an area of 12 square centimeters and a height of 12 centimeters. What is the base of the triangle?

6. A rectangle has an area of 84 square feet and a width of 7 feet. What is the length of the rectangle?

7. **ABSTRACT REASONING** Write an equation for the surface area of a prism with a length, width, and height of x inches. What solid figure does the prism represent?

Mathematical Practices

Mathematically proficient students create valid representations of problems.

Creating a Valid Representation

Core Concept

Nets for Three-Dimensional Figures

A **net** for a three-dimensional figure is a two-dimensional pattern that can be folded to form the three-dimensional figure.

	ℓ		
	base	w	
w		w	ℓ
lateral face	lateral face	lateral face	lateral face
	base		

h

h

w

ℓ

EXAMPLE 1 **Drawing a Net for a Pyramid**

Draw a net of the pyramid.

20 in.

19 in.

19 in.

SOLUTION

The pyramid has a square base. Its four lateral faces are congruent isosceles triangles.

19 in.

19 in.

20 in.

Monitoring Progress

Draw a net of the three-dimensional figure. Label the dimensions.

1.

4 ft

4 ft

2 ft

2.

5 m

12 m

8 m

3.

15 in.

10 in.

10 in.

11.1 Circumference and Arc Length

Essential Question How can you find the length of a circular arc?

EXPLORATION 1 **Finding the Length of a Circular Arc**

Work with a partner. Find the length of each red circular arc.

a. entire circle

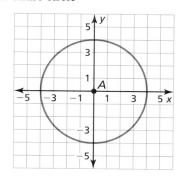

b. one-fourth of a circle

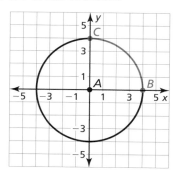

c. one-third of a circle

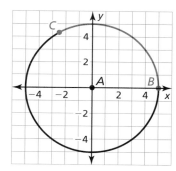

d. five-eighths of a circle

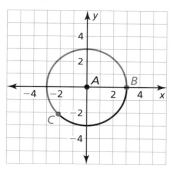

EXPLORATION 2 **Using Arc Length**

Work with a partner. The rider is attempting to stop with the front tire of the motorcycle in the painted rectangular box for a skills test. The front tire makes exactly one-half additional revolution before stopping. The diameter of the tire is 25 inches. Is the front tire still in contact with the painted box? Explain.

├── 3 ft ──┤

LOOKING FOR REGULARITY IN REPEATED REASONING

To be proficient in math, you need to notice if calculations are repeated and look both for general methods and for shortcuts.

Communicate Your Answer

3. How can you find the length of a circular arc?

4. A motorcycle tire has a diameter of 24 inches. Approximately how many inches does the motorcycle travel when its front tire makes three-fourths of a revolution?

What You Will Learn

▶ Use the formula for circumference.

▶ Use arc lengths to find measures.

▶ Solve real-life problems.

▶ Measure angles in radians.

Core Vocabulary

circumference, *p. 640*
arc length, *p. 641*
radian, *p. 643*

Previous
circle
diameter
radius

Using the Formula for Circumference

The **circumference** of a circle is the distance around the circle. Consider a regular polygon inscribed in a circle. As the number of sides increases, the polygon approximates the circle and the ratio of the perimeter of the polygon to the diameter of the circle approaches $\pi \approx 3.14159. . ..$

For all circles, the ratio of the circumference C to the diameter d is the same. This ratio is $\dfrac{C}{d} = \pi$. Solving for C yields the formula for the circumference of a circle, $C = \pi d$. Because $d = 2r$, you can also write the formula as $C = \pi(2r) = 2\pi r$.

 Core Concept

Circumference of a Circle

The circumference C of a circle is $C = \pi d$ or $C = 2\pi r$, where d is the diameter of the circle and r is the radius of the circle.

$$C = \pi d = 2\pi r$$

EXAMPLE 1   **Using the Formula for Circumference**

Find each indicated measure.

a. circumference of a circle with a radius of 9 centimeters

b. radius of a circle with a circumference of 26 meters

SOLUTION

a. $C = 2\pi r$

$\quad\; = 2 \cdot \pi \cdot 9$

$\quad\; = 18\pi$

$\quad\; \approx 56.55$

▶ The circumference is about 56.55 centimeters.

b. $C = 2\pi r$

$26 = 2\pi r$

$\dfrac{26}{2\pi} = r$

$4.14 \approx r$

▶ The radius is about 4.14 meters.

ATTENDING TO PRECISION

You have sometimes used 3.14 to approximate the value of π. Throughout this chapter, you should use the π key on a calculator, then round to the hundredths place unless instructed otherwise.

Monitoring Progress Help in English and Spanish at *BigIdeasMath.com*

1. Find the circumference of a circle with a diameter of 5 inches.

2. Find the diameter of a circle with a circumference of 17 feet.

Using Arc Lengths to Find Measures

An **arc length** is a portion of the circumference of a circle. You can use the measure of the arc (in degrees) to find its length (in linear units).

 Core Concept

Arc Length

In a circle, the ratio of the length of a given arc to the circumference is equal to the ratio of the measure of the arc to 360°.

$$\frac{\text{Arc length of } \overarc{AB}}{2\pi r} = \frac{m\overarc{AB}}{360°}, \text{ or}$$

$$\text{Arc length of } \overarc{AB} = \frac{m\overarc{AB}}{360°} \cdot 2\pi r$$

EXAMPLE 2 **Using Arc Lengths to Find Measures**

Find each indicated measure.

a. arc length of $\overarc{AB}$

b. circumference of $\odot Z$

c. $m\overarc{RS}$

SOLUTION

a. Arc length of $\overarc{AB} = \dfrac{60°}{360°} \cdot 2\pi(8)$

≈ 8.38 cm

b. $\dfrac{\text{Arc length of } \overarc{XY}}{C} = \dfrac{m\overarc{XY}}{360°}$

$\dfrac{4.19}{C} = \dfrac{40°}{360°}$

$\dfrac{4.19}{C} = \dfrac{1}{9}$

$37.71 \text{ in.} = C$

c. $\dfrac{\text{Arc length of } \overarc{RS}}{2\pi r} = \dfrac{m\overarc{RS}}{360°}$

$\dfrac{44}{2\pi(15.28)} = \dfrac{m\overarc{RS}}{360°}$

$360° \cdot \dfrac{44}{2\pi(15.28)} = m\overarc{RS}$

$165° \approx m\overarc{RS}$

Monitoring Progress Help in English and Spanish at *BigIdeasMath.com*

Find the indicated measure.

3. arc length of $\overarc{PQ}$ **4.** circumference of $\odot N$ **5.** radius of $\odot G$

Solving Real-Life Problems

EXAMPLE 3 **Using Circumference to Find Distance Traveled**

The dimensions of a car tire are shown. To the nearest foot, how far does the tire travel when it makes 15 revolutions?

5.5 in.

15 in.

5.5 in.

SOLUTION

Step 1 Find the diameter of the tire.
$$d = 15 + 2(5.5) = 26 \text{ in.}$$

Step 2 Find the circumference of the tire.
$$C = \pi d = \pi \cdot 26 = 26\pi \text{ in.}$$

Step 3 Find the distance the tire travels in 15 revolutions. In one revolution, the tire travels a distance equal to its circumference. In 15 revolutions, the tire travels a distance equal to 15 times its circumference.

$$\boxed{\begin{array}{c} \text{Distance} \\ \text{traveled} \end{array}} = \boxed{\begin{array}{c} \text{Number of} \\ \text{revolutions} \end{array}} \cdot \boxed{\text{Circumference}}$$

$$= 15 \cdot 26\pi \approx 1225.2 \text{ in.}$$

> **COMMON ERROR**
>
> Always pay attention to units. In Example 3, you need to convert units to get a correct answer.

Step 4 Use unit analysis. Change 1225.2 inches to feet.

$$1225.2 \text{ in.} \cdot \frac{1 \text{ ft}}{12 \text{ in.}} = 102.1 \text{ ft}$$

▶ The tire travels approximately 102 feet.

EXAMPLE 4 **Using Arc Length to Find Distances**

The curves at the ends of the track shown are 180° arcs of circles. The radius of the arc for a runner on the red path shown is 36.8 meters. About how far does this runner travel to go once around the track? Round to the nearest tenth of a meter.

44.02 m

36.8 m

├──84.39 m──┤

SOLUTION

The path of the runner on the red path is made of two straight sections and two semicircles. To find the total distance, find the sum of the lengths of each part.

$$\boxed{\text{Distance}} = \boxed{\begin{array}{c} 2 \cdot \text{Length of each} \\ \text{straight section} \end{array}} + \boxed{\begin{array}{c} 2 \cdot \text{Length of} \\ \text{each semicircle} \end{array}}$$

$$= 2(84.39) + 2\left(\tfrac{1}{2} \cdot 2\pi \cdot 36.8\right)$$

$$\approx 400.0$$

▶ The runner on the red path travels about 400.0 meters.

Monitoring Progress 🔊 Help in English and Spanish at *BigIdeasMath.com*

6. A car tire has a diameter of 28 inches. How many revolutions does the tire make while traveling 500 feet?

7. In Example 4, the radius of the arc for a runner on the blue path is 44.02 meters, as shown in the diagram. About how far does this runner travel to go once around the track? Round to the nearest tenth of a meter.

Measuring Angles in Radians

Recall that in a circle, the ratio of the length of a given arc to the circumference is equal to the ratio of the measure of the arc to 360°. To see why, consider the diagram.

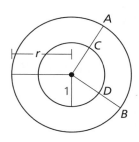

A circle of radius 1 has circumference 2π, so the arc length of $\overset{\frown}{CD}$ is $\dfrac{m\overset{\frown}{CD}}{360°} \cdot 2\pi$.

Recall that all circles are similar and corresponding lengths of similar figures are proportional. Because $m\overset{\frown}{AB} = m\overset{\frown}{CD}$, $\overset{\frown}{AB}$ and $\overset{\frown}{CD}$ are corresponding arcs. So, you can write the following proportion.

$$\frac{\text{Arc length of } \overset{\frown}{AB}}{\text{Arc length of } \overset{\frown}{CD}} = \frac{r}{1}$$

$$\text{Arc length of } \overset{\frown}{AB} = r \cdot \text{Arc length of } \overset{\frown}{CD}$$

$$\text{Arc length of } \overset{\frown}{AB} = r \cdot \frac{m\overset{\frown}{CD}}{360°} \cdot 2\pi$$

This form of the equation shows that the arc length associated with a central angle is *proportional to the radius* of the circle. The constant of proportionality, $\dfrac{m\overset{\frown}{CD}}{360°} \cdot 2\pi$, is defined to be the **radian** measure of the central angle associated with the arc.

In a circle of radius 1, the radian measure of a given central angle can be thought of as the length of the arc associated with the angle. The radian measure of a complete circle (360°) is exactly 2π radians, because the circumference of a circle of radius 1 is exactly 2π. You can use this fact to convert from degree measure to radian measure and vice versa.

Core Concept

Converting between Degrees and Radians

Degrees to radians

Multiply degree measure by

$$\frac{2\pi \text{ radians}}{360°}, \text{ or } \frac{\pi \text{ radians}}{180°}.$$

Radians to degrees

Multiply radian measure by

$$\frac{360°}{2\pi \text{ radians}}, \text{ or } \frac{180°}{\pi \text{ radians}}.$$

EXAMPLE 5   Converting between Degree and Radian Measure

a. Convert 45° to radians.

b. Convert $\dfrac{3\pi}{2}$ radians to degrees.

SOLUTION

a. $45° \cdot \dfrac{\pi \text{ radians}}{180°} = \dfrac{\pi}{4}$ radian

▶ So, $45° = \dfrac{\pi}{4}$ radian.

b. $\dfrac{3\pi}{2}$ radians $\cdot \dfrac{180°}{\pi \text{ radians}} = 270°$

▶ So, $\dfrac{3\pi}{2}$ radians $= 270°$.

Monitoring Progress Help in English and Spanish at *BigIdeasMath.com*

8. Convert 15° to radians.

9. Convert $\dfrac{4\pi}{3}$ radians to degrees.

Vocabulary and Core Concept Check

1. **COMPLETE THE SENTENCE** The circumference of a circle with diameter *d* is *C* = _____.

2. **WRITING** Describe the difference between an arc measure and an arc length.

Monitoring Progress and Modeling with Mathematics

In Exercises 3–10, find the indicated measure.
(See Examples 1 and 2.)

3. circumference of a circle with a radius of 6 inches

4. diameter of a circle with a circumference of 63 feet

5. radius of a circle with a circumference of 28π

6. exact circumference of a circle with a diameter of 5 inches

7. arc length of $\overarc{AB}$

8. $m\overarc{DE}$

9. circumference of $\odot C$

10. radius of $\odot R$

11. **ERROR ANALYSIS** Describe and correct the error in finding the circumference of $\odot C$.

$$C = 2\pi r$$
$$= 2\pi(9)$$
$$= 18\pi \text{ in.}$$

12. **ERROR ANALYSIS** Describe and correct the error in finding the length of $\overarc{GH}$.

Arc length of $\overarc{GH}$
$$= m\overarc{GH} \cdot 2\pi r$$
$$= 75 \cdot 2\pi(5)$$
$$= 750\pi \text{ cm}$$

13. **PROBLEM SOLVING** A measuring wheel is used to calculate the length of a path. The diameter of the wheel is 8 inches. The wheel makes 87 complete revolutions along the length of the path. To the nearest foot, how long is the path? *(See Example 3.)*

14. **PROBLEM SOLVING** You ride your bicycle 40 meters. How many complete revolutions does the front wheel make?

32.5 cm

In Exercises 15–18, find the perimeter of the shaded region. *(See Example 4.)*

15.

13

6

16.

6   3

3   6

17.

18.

In Exercises 19–22, convert the angle measure.
(See Example 5.)

19. Convert 70° to radians.

20. Convert 300° to radians.

21. Convert $\dfrac{11\pi}{12}$ radians to degrees.

22. Convert $\dfrac{\pi}{8}$ radian to degrees.

23. PROBLEM SOLVING The London Eye is a Ferris wheel in London, England, that travels at a speed of 0.26 meter per second. How many minutes does it take the London Eye to complete one full revolution?

67.5 m

24. PROBLEM SOLVING You are planning to plant a circular garden adjacent to one of the corners of a building, as shown. You can use up to 38 feet of fence to make a border around the garden. What radius (in feet) can the garden have? Choose all that apply. Explain your reasoning.

(A) 7 (B) 8 (C) 9 (D) 10

In Exercises 25 and 26, find the circumference of the circle with the given equation. Write the circumference in terms of π.

25. $x^2 + y^2 = 16$

26. $(x + 2)^2 + (y - 3)^2 = 9$

27. USING STRUCTURE A semicircle has endpoints $(-2, 5)$ and $(2, 8)$. Find the arc length of the semicircle.

28. REASONING $\widehat{EF}$ is an arc on a circle with radius r. Let $x°$ be the measure of $\widehat{EF}$. Describe the effect on the length of $\widehat{EF}$ if you (a) double the radius of the circle, and (b) double the measure of $\widehat{EF}$.

29. MAKING AN ARGUMENT Your friend claims that it is possible for two arcs with the same measure to have different arc lengths. Is your friend correct? Explain your reasoning.

30. PROBLEM SOLVING Over 2000 years ago, the Greek scholar Eratosthenes estimated Earth's circumference by assuming that the Sun's rays were parallel. He chose a day when the Sun shone straight down into a well in the city of Syene. At noon, he measured the angle the Sun's rays made with a vertical stick in the city of Alexandria. Eratosthenes assumed that the distance from Syene to Alexandria was equal to about 575 miles. Explain how Eratosthenes was able to use this information to estimate Earth's circumference. Then estimate Earth's circumference.

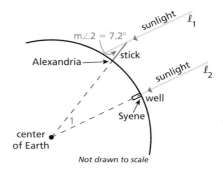

31. ANALYZING RELATIONSHIPS In $\odot C$, the ratio of the length of $\widehat{PQ}$ to the length of $\widehat{RS}$ is 2 to 1. What is the ratio of $m\angle PCQ$ to $m\angle RCS$?

(A) 4 to 1 (B) 2 to 1

(C) 1 to 4 (D) 1 to 2

32. ANALYZING RELATIONSHIPS A 45° arc in $\odot C$ and a 30° arc in $\odot P$ have the same length. What is the ratio of the radius r_1 of $\odot C$ to the radius r_2 of $\odot P$? Explain your reasoning.

33. PROBLEM SOLVING How many revolutions does the smaller gear complete during a single revolution of the larger gear?

34. USING STRUCTURE Find the circumference of each circle.

   a. a circle circumscribed about a right triangle whose legs are 12 inches and 16 inches long

   b. a circle circumscribed about a square with a side length of 6 centimeters

   c. a circle inscribed in an equilateral triangle with a side length of 9 inches

35. REWRITING A FORMULA Write a formula in terms of the measure θ of the central angle (in radians) that can be used to find the length of an arc of a circle. Then use this formula to find the length of an arc of a circle with a radius of 4 inches and a central angle of $\frac{3\pi}{4}$ radians.

36. HOW DO YOU SEE IT?
Compare the circumference of $\odot P$ to the length of $\overset{\frown}{DE}$. Explain your reasoning.

37. MAKING AN ARGUMENT In the diagram, the measure of the red shaded angle is 30°. The arc length a is 2. Your classmate claims that it is possible to find the circumference of the blue circle without finding the radius of either circle. Is your classmate correct? Explain your reasoning.

38. MODELING WITH MATHEMATICS What is the measure (in radians) of the angle formed by the hands of a clock at each time? Explain your reasoning.

   a. 1:30 P.M.   **b.** 3:15 P.M.

39. MATHEMATICAL CONNECTIONS The sum of the circumferences of circles A, B, and C is 63π. Find AC.

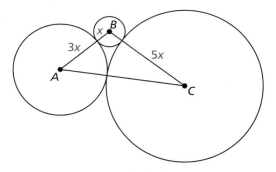

40. THOUGHT PROVOKING Is π a rational number? Compare the rational number $\frac{355}{113}$ to π. Find a different rational number that is even closer to π.

41. PROOF The circles in the diagram are concentric and $\overline{FG} \cong \overline{GH}$. Prove that $\overset{\frown}{JK}$ and $\overset{\frown}{NG}$ have the same length.

42. REPEATED REASONING $\overline{AB}$ is divided into four congruent segments, and semicircles with radius r are drawn.

   a. What is the sum of the four arc lengths?

   b. What would the sum of the arc lengths be if $\overline{AB}$ was divided into 8 congruent segments? 16 congruent segments? n congruent segments? Explain your reasoning.

Maintaining Mathematical Proficiency
Reviewing what you learned in previous grades and lessons

Find the area of the polygon with the given vertices. *(Skills Review Handbook)*

43. $X(2, 4)$, $Y(8, -1)$, $Z(2, -1)$

44. $L(-3, 1)$, $M(4, 1)$, $N(4, -5)$, $P(-3, -5)$

11.2 Areas of Circles and Sectors

Essential Question How can you find the area of a sector of a circle?

EXPLORATION 1   Finding the Area of a Sector of a Circle

Work with a partner. A **sector of a circle** is the region bounded by two radii of the circle and their intercepted arc. Find the area of each shaded circle or sector of a circle.

a. entire circle

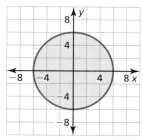

b. one-fourth of a circle

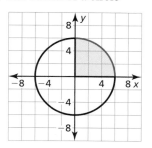

c. seven-eighths of a circle

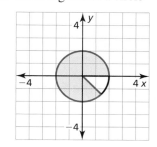

d. two-thirds of a circle

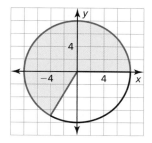

REASONING ABSTRACTLY

To be proficient in math, you need to explain to yourself the meaning of a problem and look for entry points to its solution.

EXPLORATION 2   Finding the Area of a Circular Sector

Work with a partner. A center pivot irrigation system consists of 400 meters of sprinkler equipment that rotates around a central pivot point at a rate of once every 3 days to irrigate a circular region with a diameter of 800 meters. Find the area of the sector that is irrigated by this system in one day.

Communicate Your Answer

3. How can you find the area of a sector of a circle?

4. In Exploration 2, find the area of the sector that is irrigated in 2 hours.

What You Will Learn

▶ Use the formula for the area of a circle.

▶ Find areas of sectors.

▶ Use areas of sectors.

Using the Formula for the Area of a Circle

You can divide a circle into congruent sections and rearrange the sections to form a figure that approximates a parallelogram. Increasing the number of congruent sections increases the figure's resemblance to a parallelogram.

The base of the parallelogram that the figure approaches is half of the circumference, so $b = \frac{1}{2}C = \frac{1}{2}(2\pi r) = \pi r$. The height is the radius, so $h = r$. So, the area of the parallelogram is $A = bh = (\pi r)(r) = \pi r^2$.

Core Concept

Area of a Circle

The area of a circle is

$$A = \pi r^2$$

where r is the radius of the circle.

EXAMPLE 1 **Using the Formula for the Area of a Circle**

Find each indicated measure.

a. area of a circle with a radius of 2.5 centimeters

b. diameter of a circle with an area of 113.1 square centimeters

SOLUTION

a. $A = \pi r^2$ Formula for area of a circle

$\quad = \pi \cdot (2.5)^2$ Substitute 2.5 for r.

$\quad = 6.25\pi$ Simplify.

$\quad \approx 19.63$ Use a calculator.

▶ The area of the circle is about 19.63 square centimeters.

b. $\quad A = \pi r^2$ Formula for area of a circle

$\quad 113.1 = \pi r^2$ Substitute 113.1 for A.

$\quad \dfrac{113.1}{\pi} = r^2$ Divide each side by π.

$\quad\quad 6 \approx r$ Find the positive square root of each side.

▶ The radius is about 6 centimeters, so the diameter is about 12 centimeters.

Monitoring Progress Help in English and Spanish at *BigIdeasMath.com*

1. Find the area of a circle with a radius of 4.5 meters.

2. Find the radius of a circle with an area of 176.7 square feet.

Probabilities found by calculating a ratio of two lengths, areas, or volumes are called **geometric probabilities**.

EXAMPLE 2 **Using Area to Find Probability**

You throw a dart at the board shown. Your dart is equally likely to hit any point inside the square board. Are you more likely to get 10 points or 0 points?

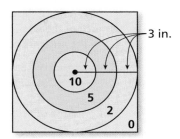

SOLUTION

The probability of getting 10 points is

$$P(10 \text{ points}) = \frac{\text{Area of smallest circle}}{\text{Area of entire board}}$$

$$= \frac{\pi \cdot 3^2}{18^2}$$

$$= \frac{9\pi}{324}$$

$$= \frac{\pi}{36}$$

$$\approx 0.0873.$$

The probability of getting 0 points is

$$P(0 \text{ points}) = \frac{\text{Area outside largest circle}}{\text{Area of entire board}}$$

$$= \frac{18^2 - (\pi \cdot 9^2)}{18^2}$$

$$= \frac{324 - 81\pi}{324}$$

$$= \frac{4 - \pi}{4}$$

$$\approx 0.215.$$

 You are more likely to get 0 points.

Monitoring Progress 🔊 Help in English and Spanish at *BigIdeasMath.com*

Use the diagram in Example 2.

3. Are you more likely to get 10 points or 5 points?

4. Are you more likely to get 2 points or 0 points?

5. Are you more likely to get 5 or more points or 2 or less points?

6. Are you more likely to score points (10, 5, or 2) or get 0 points?

Finding Areas of Sectors

A **sector of a circle** is the region bounded by two radii of the circle and their intercepted arc. In the diagram below, sector APB is bounded by $\overline{AP}$, $\overline{BP}$, and $\overset{\frown}{AB}$.

ANALYZING RELATIONSHIPS

The area of a sector is a fractional part of the area of a circle. The area of a sector formed by a 45° arc is $\frac{45°}{360°}$, or $\frac{1}{8}$ of the area of the circle.

 Core Concept

Area of a Sector

The ratio of the area of a sector of a circle to the area of the whole circle (πr^2) is equal to the ratio of the measure of the intercepted arc to 360°.

$$\frac{\text{Area of sector } APB}{\pi r^2} = \frac{m\overset{\frown}{AB}}{360°}, \text{ or}$$

$$\text{Area of sector } APB = \frac{m\overset{\frown}{AB}}{360°} \cdot \pi r^2$$

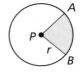

EXAMPLE 3 Finding Areas of Sectors

Find the areas of the sectors formed by $\angle UTV$.

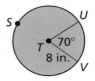

SOLUTION

Step 1 Find the measures of the minor and major arcs.

Because $m\angle UTV = 70°$, $m\overset{\frown}{UV} = 70°$ and $m\overset{\frown}{USV} = 360° - 70° = 290°$.

Step 2 Find the areas of the small and large sectors.

$\text{Area of small sector} = \dfrac{m\overset{\frown}{UV}}{360°} \cdot \pi r^2$	Formula for area of a sector
$= \dfrac{70°}{360°} \cdot \pi \cdot 8^2$	Substitute.
≈ 39.10	Use a calculator.
$\text{Area of large sector} = \dfrac{m\overset{\frown}{USV}}{360°} \cdot \pi r^2$	Formula for area of a sector
$= \dfrac{290°}{360°} \cdot \pi \cdot 8^2$	Substitute.
≈ 161.97	Use a calculator.

▶ The areas of the small and large sectors are about 39.10 square inches and about 161.97 square inches, respectively.

Monitoring Progress Help in English and Spanish at *BigIdeasMath.com*

Find the indicated measure.

7. area of red sector

8. area of blue sector

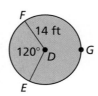

Using Areas of Sectors

EXAMPLE 4 Using the Area of a Sector

Find the area of $\odot V$.

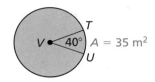

SOLUTION

$$\text{Area of sector } TVU = \frac{m\widehat{TU}}{360°} \cdot \text{Area of } \odot V \qquad \text{Formula for area of a sector}$$

$$35 = \frac{40°}{360°} \cdot \text{Area of } \odot V \qquad \text{Substitute.}$$

$$315 = \text{Area of } \odot V \qquad \text{Solve for area of } \odot V.$$

▶ The area of $\odot V$ is 315 square meters.

EXAMPLE 5 Finding the Area of a Region

A rectangular wall has an entrance cut into it. You want to paint the wall. To the nearest square foot, what is the area of the region you need to paint?

SOLUTION

COMMON ERROR

Use the radius (8 feet), not the diameter (16 feet), when you calculate the area of the semicircle.

The area you need to paint is the area of the rectangle minus the area of the entrance. The entrance can be divided into a semicircle and a square.

| Area of wall | = | Area of rectangle | − | (Area of semicircle + Area of square) |

$$= 36(26) - \left[\frac{180°}{360°} \cdot (\pi \cdot 8^2) + 16^2\right]$$

$$= 936 - (32\pi + 256)$$

$$\approx 579.47$$

▶ The area you need to paint is about 579 square feet.

Monitoring Progress ◀)) Help in English and Spanish at *BigIdeasMath.com*

9. Find the area of $\odot H$.

$A = 214.37 \text{ cm}^2$

10. Find the area of the figure.

11. If you know the area and radius of a sector of a circle, can you find the measure of the intercepted arc? Explain.

Vocabulary and Core Concept Check

1. **VOCABULARY** A(n) _____ of a circle is the region bounded by two radii of the circle and their intercepted arc.

2. **WRITING** The arc measure of a sector in a given circle is doubled. Will the area of the sector also be doubled? Explain your reasoning.

Monitoring Progress and Modeling with Mathematics

In Exercises 3–10, find the indicated measure. *(See Example 1.)*

3. area of ⊙C

4. area of ⊙C

5. area of a circle with a radius of 5 inches

6. area of a circle with a diameter of 16 feet

7. radius of a circle with an area of 89 square feet

8. radius of a circle with an area of 380 square inches

9. diameter of a circle with an area of 12.6 square inches

10. diameter of a circle with an area of 676π square centimeters

In Exercises 11–18, you throw a dart at the board shown. Your dart is equally likely to hit any point inside the square board. Find the probability that your dart lands in the indicated region. *(See Example 2.)*

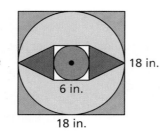

11. red

12. blue

13. white

14. yellow

15. yellow or red

16. yellow or green

17. not blue

18. not yellow

In Exercises 19–22, find the areas of the sectors formed by ∠DFE. *(See Example 3.)*

19.

20.

21.

22.

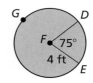

23. **ERROR ANALYSIS** Describe and correct the error in finding the area of the circle.

$$A = \pi(12)^2$$
$$= 144\pi$$
$$\approx 452.39 \text{ ft}^2$$

24. **ERROR ANALYSIS** Describe and correct the error in finding the area of sector *XZY* when the area of ⊙Z is 255 square feet.

Let *n* be the area of sector XZY.

$$\frac{n}{360} = \frac{115}{255}$$

$$n \approx 162.35 \text{ ft}^2$$

In Exercises 25 and 26, the area of the shaded sector is shown. Find the indicated measure. *(See Example 4.)*

25. area of ⊙M

26. radius of ⊙M

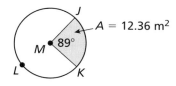

In Exercises 27–32, find the area of the shaded region. *(See Example 5.)*

27.

28.

29.

30.

31.

32.

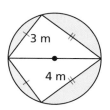

33. PROBLEM SOLVING The diagram shows the shape of a putting green at a miniature golf course. One part of the green is a sector of a circle. Find the area of the putting green.

34. MAKING AN ARGUMENT Your friend claims that if the radius of a circle is doubled, then its area doubles. Is your friend correct? Explain your reasoning.

35. MODELING WITH MATHEMATICS The diagram shows the area of a lawn covered by a water sprinkler.

a. What is the area of the lawn that is covered by the sprinkler?

b. The water pressure is weakened so that the radius is 12 feet. What is the area of the lawn that will be covered?

36. MODELING WITH MATHEMATICS The diagram shows a projected beam of light from a lighthouse.

a. What is the area of water that can be covered by the light from the lighthouse?

b. What is the area of land that can be covered by the light from the lighthouse?

37. ANALYZING RELATIONSHIPS Look back at the Perimeters of Similar Polygons Theorem and the Areas of Similar Polygons Theorem in Section 8.3. How would you rewrite these theorems to apply to circles? Explain your reasoning.

38. ANALYZING RELATIONSHIPS A square is inscribed in a circle. The same square is also circumscribed about a smaller circle. Draw a diagram that represents this situation. Then find the ratio of the area of the larger circle to the area of the smaller circle.

39. CONSTRUCTION The table shows how students get to school.

Method	Percent of students
bus	65%
walk	25%
other	10%

a. Explain why a circle graph is appropriate for the data.

b. You will represent each method by a sector of a circle graph. Find the central angle to use for each sector. Then construct the graph using a radius of 2 inches.

c. Find the area of each sector in your graph.

40. HOW DO YOU SEE IT? The outermost edges of the pattern shown form a square. If you know the dimensions of the outer square, is it possible to compute the total colored area? Explain.

41. ABSTRACT REASONING A circular pizza with a 12-inch diameter is enough for you and 2 friends. You want to buy pizzas for yourself and 7 friends. A 10-inch diameter pizza with one topping costs $6.99 and a 14-inch diameter pizza with one topping costs $12.99. How many 10-inch and 14-inch pizzas should you buy in each situation? Explain.

a. You want to spend as little money as possible.

b. You want to have three pizzas, each with a different topping, and spend as little money as possible.

c. You want to have as much of the thick outer crust as possible.

42. THOUGHT PROVOKING You know that the area of a circle is πr^2. Find the formula for the area of an *ellipse*, shown below.

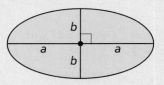

43. MULTIPLE REPRESENTATIONS Consider a circle with a radius of 3 inches.

a. Complete the table, where x is the measure of the arc and y is the area of the corresponding sector. Round your answers to the nearest tenth.

x	30°	60°	90°	120°	150°	180°
y						

b. Graph the data in the table.

c. Is the relationship between x and y linear? Explain.

d. If parts (a)–(c) were repeated using a circle with a radius of 5 inches, would the areas in the table change? Would your answer to part (c) change? Explain your reasoning.

44. CRITICAL THINKING Find the area between the three congruent tangent circles. The radius of each circle is 6 inches.

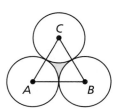

45. PROOF Semicircles with diameters equal to three sides of a right triangle are drawn, as shown. Prove that the sum of the areas of the two shaded crescents equals the area of the triangle.

Maintaining Mathematical Proficiency
Reviewing what you learned in previous grades and lessons

Find the area of the figure. *(Skills Review Handbook)*

46.

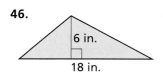

6 in.
18 in.

47.

4 ft
7 ft
10 ft

48.

13 in.
9 in.

49.

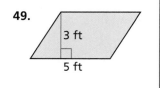

3 ft
5 ft

Essential Question How can you find the area of a regular polygon?

The **center of a regular polygon** is the center of its circumscribed circle.

The distance from the center to any side of a regular polygon is called the **apothem of a regular polygon**.

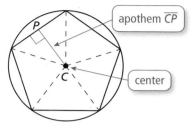

apothem $\overline{CP}$

center

EXPLORATION 1 **Finding the Area of a Regular Polygon**

Work with a partner. Use dynamic geometry software to construct each regular polygon with side lengths of 4, as shown. Find the apothem and use it to find the area of the polygon. Describe the steps that you used.

a.

b.

c.

d.

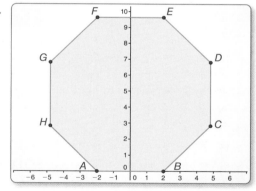

EXPLORATION 2 **Writing a Formula for Area**

Work with a partner. Generalize the steps you used in Exploration 1 to develop a formula for the area of a regular polygon.

REASONING ABSTRACTLY

To be proficient in math, you need to know and flexibly use different properties of operations and objects.

Communicate Your Answer

3. How can you find the area of a regular polygon?

4. Regular pentagon *ABCDE* has side lengths of 6 meters and an apothem of approximately 4.13 meters. Find the area of *ABCDE*.

What You Will Learn

▶ Find areas of rhombuses and kites.

▶ Find angle measures in regular polygons.

▶ Find areas of regular polygons.

Core Vocabulary

center of a regular polygon,
  p. 657
radius of a regular polygon,
  p. 657
apothem of a regular polygon,
  p. 657
central angle of a regular
  polygon, p. 657

Previous
rhombus
kite

Finding Areas of Rhombuses and Kites

You can divide a rhombus or kite with diagonals d_1 and d_2 into two congruent triangles with base d_1, height $\frac{1}{2}d_2$, and area $\frac{1}{2}d_1\left(\frac{1}{2}d_2\right) = \frac{1}{4}d_1d_2$. So, the area of a rhombus or kite is $2\left(\frac{1}{4}d_1d_2\right) = \frac{1}{2}d_1d_2$.

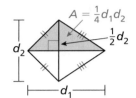

Core Concept

Area of a Rhombus or Kite

The area of a rhombus or kite with diagonals d_1 and d_2 is $\frac{1}{2}d_1d_2$.

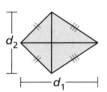

EXAMPLE 1   Finding the Area of a Rhombus or Kite

Find the area of each rhombus or kite.

a.

b.

SOLUTION

a. $A = \frac{1}{2}d_1d_2$

  $= \frac{1}{2}(6)(8)$

  $= 24$

  ▶ So, the area is 24 square meters.

b. $A = \frac{1}{2}d_1d_2$

  $= \frac{1}{2}(10)(7)$

  $= 35$

  ▶ So, the area is
    35 square centimeters.

Monitoring Progress 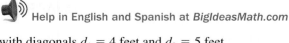 Help in English and Spanish at *BigIdeasMath.com*

1. Find the area of a rhombus with diagonals $d_1 = 4$ feet and $d_2 = 5$ feet.

2. Find the area of a kite with diagonals $d_1 = 12$ inches and $d_2 = 9$ inches.

Finding Angle Measures in Regular Polygons

The diagram shows a regular polygon inscribed in a circle. The **center of a regular polygon** and the **radius of a regular polygon** are the center and the radius of its circumscribed circle.

The distance from the center to any side of a regular polygon is called the **apothem of a regular polygon**. The apothem is the height to the base of an isosceles triangle that has two radii as legs. The word "apothem" refers to a segment as well as a length. For a given regular polygon, think of *an* apothem as a segment and *the* apothem as a length.

∠MPN is a central angle.

A **central angle of a regular polygon** is an angle formed by two radii drawn to consecutive vertices of the polygon. To find the measure of each central angle, divide 360° by the number of sides.

EXAMPLE 2   **Finding Angle Measures in a Regular Polygon**

In the diagram, *ABCDE* is a regular pentagon inscribed in ⊙*F*. Find each angle measure.

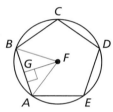

a. $m\angle AFB$ **b.** $m\angle AFG$ **c.** $m\angle GAF$

ANALYZING RELATIONSHIPS

$\overline{FG}$ is an altitude of an isosceles triangle, so it is also a median and angle bisector of the isosceles triangle.

SOLUTION

a. ∠*AFB* is a central angle, so $m\angle AFB = \dfrac{360°}{5} = 72°$.

b. $\overline{FG}$ is an apothem, which makes it an altitude of isosceles △*AFB*.

So, $\overline{FG}$ bisects ∠*AFB* and $m\angle AFG = \dfrac{1}{2}m\angle AFB = 36°$.

c. By the Triangle Sum Theorem, the sum of the angle measures of right △*GAF* is 180°.

$$m\angle GAF = 180° - 90° - 36°$$
$$= 54°$$

So, $m\angle GAF = 54°$.

Monitoring Progress 🔊 Help in English and Spanish at *BigIdeasMath.com*

In the diagram, *WXYZ* is a square inscribed in ⊙*P*.

3. Identify the center, a radius, an apothem, and a central angle of the polygon.

4. Find $m\angle XPY$, $m\angle XPQ$, and $m\angle PXQ$.

Finding Areas of Regular Polygons

You can find the area of any regular n-gon by dividing it into congruent triangles.

$$A = \text{Area of one triangle} \cdot \text{Number of triangles}$$

$$= \left(\tfrac{1}{2} \cdot s \cdot a\right) \cdot n \qquad \text{Base of triangle is } s \text{ and height of triangle is } a. \text{ Number of triangles is } n.$$

$$= \tfrac{1}{2} \cdot a \cdot (n \cdot s) \qquad \text{Commutative and Associative Properties of Multiplication}$$

$$= \tfrac{1}{2} a \cdot P \qquad \text{There are } n \text{ congruent sides of length } s, \text{ so perimeter } P \text{ is } n \cdot s.$$

🌀 Core Concept

Area of a Regular Polygon

The area of a regular n-gon with side length s is one-half the product of the apothem a and the perimeter P.

$$A = \tfrac{1}{2}aP, \text{ or } A = \tfrac{1}{2}a \cdot ns$$

EXAMPLE 3 **Finding the Area of a Regular Polygon**

A regular nonagon is inscribed in a circle with a radius of 4 units. Find the area of the nonagon.

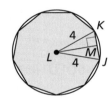

SOLUTION

The measure of central $\angle JLK$ is $\frac{360°}{9}$, or $40°$. Apothem $\overline{LM}$ bisects the central angle, so $m\angle KLM$ is $20°$. To find the lengths of the legs, use trigonometric ratios for right $\triangle KLM$.

$$\sin 20° = \frac{MK}{LK} \qquad\qquad \cos 20° = \frac{LM}{LK}$$

$$\sin 20° = \frac{MK}{4} \qquad\qquad \cos 20° = \frac{LM}{4}$$

$$4 \sin 20° = MK \qquad\qquad 4 \cos 20° = LM$$

The regular nonagon has side length $s = 2(MK) = 2(4 \sin 20°) = 8 \sin 20°$, and apothem $a = LM = 4 \cos 20°$.

▶ So, the area is $A = \tfrac{1}{2}a \cdot ns = \tfrac{1}{2}(4 \cos 20°) \cdot (9)(8 \sin 20°) \approx 46.3$ square units.

READING DIAGRAMS

In this book, a point shown inside a regular polygon marks the center of the circle that can be circumscribed about the polygon.

EXAMPLE 4 **Finding the Area of a Regular Polygon**

You are decorating the top of a table by covering it with small ceramic tiles. The tabletop is a regular octagon with 15-inch sides and a radius of about 19.6 inches. What is the area you are covering?

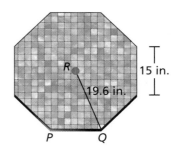

15 in.

19.6 in.

SOLUTION

Step 1 Find the perimeter P of the tabletop.
An octagon has 8 sides, so $P = 8(15) = 120$ inches.

Step 2 Find the apothem a. The apothem is height RS of $\triangle PQR$.

Because $\triangle PQR$ is isosceles, altitude $\overline{RS}$ bisects $\overline{QP}$.

So, $QS = \frac{1}{2}(QP) = \frac{1}{2}(15) = 7.5$ inches.

19.6 in.

7.5 in.

To find RS, use the Pythagorean Theorem for $\triangle RQS$.

$$a = RS = \sqrt{19.6^2 - 7.5^2} = \sqrt{327.91} \approx 18.108$$

Step 3 Find the area A of the tabletop.

$A = \frac{1}{2}aP$ Formula for area of a regular polygon

$\quad = \frac{1}{2}(\sqrt{327.91})(120)$ Substitute.

$\quad \approx 1086.5$ Simplify.

▶ The area you are covering with tiles is about 1086.5 square inches.

Monitoring Progress Help in English and Spanish at *BigIdeasMath.com*

Find the area of the regular polygon.

5.

6.5   8

6.

7

Vocabulary and Core Concept Check

1. **WRITING** Explain how to find the measure of a central angle of a regular polygon.

2. **DIFFERENT WORDS, SAME QUESTION** Which is different? Find "both" answers.

Find the radius of ⊙F.	Find the apothem of polygon ABCDE.
Find AF.	Find the radius of polygon ABCDE.

Monitoring Progress and Modeling with Mathematics

In Exercises 3–6, find the area of the kite or rhombus. (*See Example 1.*)

3.

4.

5.

6.

In Exercises 7–10, use the diagram.

7. Identify the center of polygon *JKLMN*.

8. Identify a central angle of polygon *JKLMN*.

9. What is the radius of polygon *JKLMN?*

10. What is the apothem of polygon *JKLMN?*

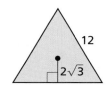

In Exercises 11–14, find the measure of a central angle of a regular polygon with the given number of sides. Round answers to the nearest tenth of a degree, if necessary.

11. 10 sides

12. 18 sides

13. 24 sides

14. 7 sides

In Exercises 15–18, find the given angle measure for regular octagon *ABCDEFGH*. (*See Example 2.*)

15. $m\angle GJH$

16. $m\angle GJK$

17. $m\angle KGJ$

18. $m\angle EJH$

In Exercises 19–24, find the area of the regular polygon. (*See Examples 3 and 4.*)

19.

20.

21.

22.

23. an octagon with a radius of 11 units

24. a pentagon with an apothem of 5 units

25. **ERROR ANALYSIS** Describe and correct the error in finding the area of the kite.

$$A = \frac{1}{2}(3.6)(5.4)$$
$$= 9.72$$

So, the area of the kite is 9.72 square units.

26. ERROR ANALYSIS Describe and correct the error in finding the area of the regular hexagon.

$$s = \sqrt{15^2 - 13^2} \approx 7.5$$
$$A = \frac{1}{2}a \cdot ns$$
$$\approx \frac{1}{2}(13)(6)(7.5)$$
$$= 292.5$$

So, the area of the hexagon is about 292.5 square units.

In Exercises 27–30, you throw a dart at the region shown. Your dart is equally likely to hit any point inside the region. Find the probability that your dart lands in the shaded region.

27.

12 in.

28.

14 in.

29.

8 in.

30.

$2\sqrt{3}$ in. 60°

31. MODELING WITH MATHEMATICS Basaltic columns are geological formations that result from rapidly cooling lava. Giant's Causeway in Ireland contains many hexagonal basaltic columns. Suppose the top of one of the columns is in the shape of a regular hexagon with a radius of 8 inches. Find the area of the top of the column to the nearest square inch.

32. MODELING WITH MATHEMATICS A watch has a circular surface on a background that is a regular octagon. Find the area of the octagon. Then find the area of the silver border around the circular face.

0.2 cm   1 cm

CRITICAL THINKING In Exercises 33–35, tell whether the statement is *true* or *false*. Explain your reasoning.

33. The area of a regular n-gon of a fixed radius r increases as n increases.

34. The apothem of a regular polygon is always less than the radius.

35. The radius of a regular polygon is always less than the side length.

36. REASONING Predict which figure has the greatest area and which has the least area. Explain your reasoning. Check by finding the area of each figure.

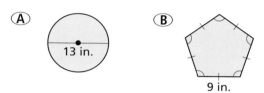

Ⓐ 13 in.   Ⓑ 9 in.

Ⓒ
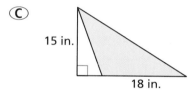
15 in.   18 in.

37. USING EQUATIONS Find the area of a regular pentagon inscribed in a circle whose equation is given by $(x - 4)^2 + (y + 2)^2 = 25$.

38. REASONING What happens to the area of a kite if you double the length of one of the diagonals? if you double the length of both diagonals? Justify your answer.

MATHEMATICAL CONNECTIONS In Exercises 39 and 40, write and solve an equation to find the indicated lengths. Round decimal answers to the nearest tenth.

39. The area of a kite is 324 square inches. One diagonal is twice as long as the other diagonal. Find the length of each diagonal.

40. One diagonal of a rhombus is four times the length of the other diagonal. The area of the rhombus is 98 square feet. Find the length of each diagonal.

41. REASONING The perimeter of a regular nonagon, or 9-gon, is 18 inches. Is this enough information to find the area? If so, find the area and explain your reasoning. If not, explain why not.

42. **MAKING AN ARGUMENT** Your friend claims that it is possible to find the area of any rhombus if you only know the perimeter of the rhombus. Is your friend correct? Explain your reasoning.

43. **PROOF** Prove that the area of any quadrilateral with perpendicular diagonals is $A = \frac{1}{2}d_1d_2$, where d_1 and d_2 are the lengths of the diagonals.

44. **HOW DO YOU SEE IT?** Explain how to find the area of the regular hexagon by dividing the hexagon into equilateral triangles.

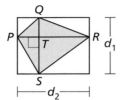

45. **REWRITING A FORMULA** Rewrite the formula for the area of a rhombus for the special case of a square with side length s. Show that this is the same as the formula for the area of a square, $A = s^2$.

46. **REWRITING A FORMULA** Use the formula for the area of a regular polygon to show that the area of an equilateral triangle can be found by using the formula $A = \frac{1}{4}s^2\sqrt{3}$, where s is the side length.

47. **CRITICAL THINKING** The area of a regular pentagon is 72 square centimeters. Find the length of one side.

48. **CRITICAL THINKING** The area of a dodecagon, or 12-gon, is 140 square inches. Find the apothem of the polygon.

49. **USING STRUCTURE** In the figure, an equilateral triangle lies inside a square inside a regular pentagon inside a regular hexagon. Find the approximate area of the entire shaded region to the nearest whole number.

50. **THOUGHT PROVOKING** The area of a regular n-gon is given by $A = \frac{1}{2}aP$. As n approaches infinity, what does the n-gon approach? What does P approach? What does a approach? What can you conclude from your three answers? Explain your reasoning.

51. **COMPARING METHODS** Find the area of regular pentagon $ABCDE$ by using the formula $A = \frac{1}{2}aP$, or $A = \frac{1}{2}a \cdot ns$. Then find the area by adding the areas of smaller polygons. Check that both methods yield the same area. Which method do you prefer? Explain your reasoning.

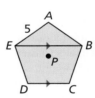

52. **USING STRUCTURE** Two regular polygons both have n sides. One of the polygons is inscribed in, and the other is circumscribed about, a circle of radius r. Find the area between the two polygons in terms of n and r.

Maintaining Mathematical Proficiency
Reviewing what you learned in previous grades and lessons

Complete the two-way table. *(Section 5.3)*

53.

		Response		
		Yes	No	Total
Gender	Male		52	
	Female	48		110
	Total	65		

54.

		Response		
		Yes	No	Total
Class	Junior	65		105
	Senior		12	
	Total	116		

Core Vocabulary

circumference, *p. 640*
arc length, *p. 641*
radian, *p. 643*
geometric probability, *p. 649*
sector of a circle, *p. 650*

center of a regular polygon, *p. 657*
radius of a regular polygon, *p. 657*
apothem of a regular polygon, *p. 657*
central angle of a regular polygon, *p. 657*

Core Concepts

Section 11.1

Circumference of a Circle, *p. 640*
Arc Length, *p. 641*

Converting between Degrees and Radians, *p. 643*

Section 11.2

Area of a Circle, *p. 648*

Area of a Sector, *p. 650*

Section 11.3

Area of a Rhombus or Kite, *p. 656*

Area of a Regular Polygon, *p. 658*

Mathematical Practices

1. In Exercise 13 on page 644, why does it matter how many revolutions the wheel makes?

2. Your friend is confused with Exercise 23 on page 652. What question(s) could you ask your friend to help them figure it out?

3. In Exercise 38 on page 661, write a proof to support your answer.

Kinesthetic Learners

STUDY SKILLS

Incorporate physical activity.

- Act out a word problem as much as possible. Use props when you can.

- Solve a word problem on a large whiteboard. The physical action of writing is more kinesthetic when the writing is larger and you can move around while doing it.

- Make a review card.

Find the indicated measure. *(Section 11.1)*

1. $m\widehat{EF}$

13.7 m

E

F

7 m

G

2. arc length of $\widehat{QS}$

Q

S

4 cm 83°

R

3. circumference of $\odot N$

L   8 in.

M

48°

N

Convert the angle measure. *(Section 11.1)*

4. Convert 26° to radians.

5. Convert $\dfrac{5\pi}{9}$ radians to degrees.

Use the figure to find the indicated measure. *(Section 11.2)*

6. area of red sector

7. area of blue sector

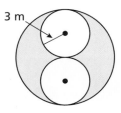

H

100°

K

J   12 yd

L

In the diagram, *RSTUVWXY* **is a regular octagon inscribed in** $\odot C$. *(Section 11.3)*

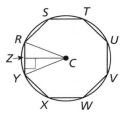

S   T

R   U

Z→

C

Y   V

X   W

8. Identify the center, a radius, an apothem, and a central angle of the polygon.

9. Find $m\angle RCY$, $m\angle RCZ$, and $m\angle ZRC$.

10. The radius of the circle is 8 units. Find the area of the octagon.

11. The two white congruent circles just fit into the blue circle. What is the area of the blue region? *(Section 11.2)*

3 m

12. Find the area of each rhombus tile. Then find the area of the pattern. *(Section 11.3)*

15.7 mm

11.4 mm

18.5 mm

6 mm

11.4 Volumes of Prisms and Cylinders

Essential Question How can you find the volume of a prism or cylinder that is not a right prism or right cylinder?

Recall that the volume V of a right prism or a right cylinder is equal to the product of the area of a base B and the height h.

$$V = Bh$$

right prisms   right cylinder

EXPLORATION 1 Finding Volume

Work with a partner. Consider a stack of square papers that is in the form of a right prism.

a. What is the volume of the prism?

b. When you twist the stack of papers, as shown at the right, do you change the volume? Explain your reasoning.

c. Write a carefully worded conjecture that describes the conclusion you reached in part (b).

d. Use your conjecture to find the volume of the twisted stack of papers.

ATTENDING TO PRECISION

To be proficient in math, you need to communicate precisely to others.

8 in.

2 in. 2 in.

EXPLORATION 2 Finding Volume

Work with a partner. Use the conjecture you wrote in Exploration 1 to find the volume of the cylinder.

a.

2 in.

3 in.

b.

5 cm

15 cm

Communicate Your Answer

3. How can you find the volume of a prism or cylinder that is not a right prism or right cylinder?

4. In Exploration 1, would the conjecture you wrote change if the papers in each stack were not squares? Explain your reasoning.

What You Will Learn

▶ Classify solids.

▶ Find volumes of prisms and cylinders.

Core Vocabulary

polyhedron, *p. 666*
face, *p. 666*
edge, *p. 666*
vertex, *p. 666*
volume, *p. 667*
Cavalieri's Principle, *p. 667*
similar solids, *p. 669*

Previous
solid
prism
pyramid
cylinder
cone
sphere
base
composite solid

Classifying Solids

A three-dimensional figure, or solid, is bounded by flat or curved surfaces that enclose a single region of space. A **polyhedron** is a solid that is bounded by polygons, called **faces**. An **edge** of a polyhedron is a line segment formed by the intersection of two faces. A **vertex** of a polyhedron is a point where three or more edges meet. The plural of polyhedron is *polyhedra* or *polyhedrons*.

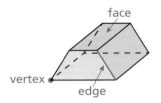

Core Concept

Types of Solids

Polyhedra

prism

Not Polyhedra

cylinder   cone

pyramid

sphere

Pentagonal prism

Bases are pentagons.

Triangular pyramid

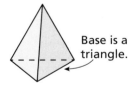

Base is a triangle.

To name a prism or a pyramid, use the shape of the *base*. The two bases of a prism are congruent polygons in parallel planes. For example, the bases of a pentagonal prism are pentagons. The base of a pyramid is a polygon. For example, the base of a triangular pyramid is a triangle.

EXAMPLE 1 Classifying Solids

Tell whether each solid is a polyhedron. If it is, name the polyhedron.

a.

b.

c.

SOLUTION

a. The solid is formed by polygons, so it is a polyhedron. The two bases are congruent rectangles, so it is a rectangular prism.

b. The solid is formed by polygons, so it is a polyhedron. The base is a hexagon, so it is a hexagonal pyramid.

c. The cone has a curved surface, so it is not a polyhedron.

Tell whether the solid is a polyhedron. If it is, name the polyhedron.

1.

2.

3.

Finding Volumes of Prisms and Cylinders

The **volume** of a solid is the number of cubic units contained in its interior. Volume is measured in cubic units, such as cubic centimeters (cm^3). **Cavalieri's Principle**, named after Bonaventura Cavalieri (1598–1647), states that if two solids have the same height and the same cross-sectional area at every level, then they have the same volume. The prisms below have equal heights h and equal cross-sectional areas B at every level. By Cavalieri's Principle, the prisms have the same volume.

🌀 Core Concept

Volume of a Prism

The volume V of a prism is

$$V = Bh$$

where B is the area of a base and h is the height.

EXAMPLE 2   **Finding Volumes of Prisms**

Find the volume of each prism.

a.

b.

SOLUTION

a. The area of a base is $B = \frac{1}{2}(3)(4) = 6$ cm² and the height is $h = 2$ cm.

$$V = Bh = 6(2) = 12$$

▶ The volume is 12 cubic centimeters.

b. The area of a base is $B = \frac{1}{2}(3)(6 + 14) = 30$ cm² and the height is $h = 5$ cm.

$$V = Bh = 30(5) = 150$$

▶ The volume is 150 cubic centimeters.

Consider a cylinder with height h and base radius r and a rectangular prism with the same height that has a square base with sides of length $r\sqrt{\pi}$.

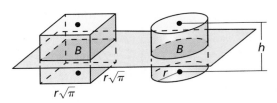

The cylinder and the prism have the same cross-sectional area, πr^2, at every level and the same height. By Cavalieri's Principle, the prism and the cylinder have the same volume. The volume of the prism is $V = Bh = \pi r^2 h$, so the volume of the cylinder is also $V = Bh = \pi r^2 h$.

Core Concept

Volume of a Cylinder

The volume V of a cylinder is

$$V = Bh = \pi r^2 h$$

where B is the area of a base, h is the height, and r is the radius of a base.

EXAMPLE 3   **Finding Volumes of Cylinders**

Find the volume of each cylinder.

a.

9 ft

6 ft

b.

4 cm

7 cm

SOLUTION

a. The dimensions of the cylinder are $r = 9$ ft and $h = 6$ ft.

$$V = \pi r^2 h = \pi(9)^2(6) = 486\pi \approx 1526.81$$

▶ The volume is 486π, or about 1526.81 cubic feet.

b. The dimensions of the cylinder are $r = 4$ cm and $h = 7$ cm.

$$V = \pi r^2 h = \pi(4)^2(7) = 112\pi \approx 351.86$$

▶ The volume is 112π, or about 351.86 cubic centimeters.

Monitoring Progress Help in English and Spanish at *BigIdeasMath.com*

Find the volume of the solid.

4.

8 m

9 m   5 m

5.

8 ft

14 ft

Core Concept

Similar Solids

Two solids of the same type with equal ratios of corresponding linear measures, such as heights or radii, are called **similar solids**. The ratio of the corresponding linear measures of two similar solids is called the *scale factor*. If two similar solids have a scale factor of k, then the ratio of their volumes is equal to k^3.

EXAMPLE 4 Finding the Volume of a Similar Solid

Cylinder A and cylinder B are similar. Find the volume of cylinder B.

Cylinder A
3 cm
$V = 45\pi$ cm³

Cylinder B
6 cm

SOLUTION

The scale factor is $k = \dfrac{\text{Radius of cylinder B}}{\text{Radius of cylinder A}}$

$= \dfrac{6}{3} = 2.$

COMMON ERROR

Be sure to write the ratio of the volumes in the same order you wrote the ratio of the radii.

Use the scale factor to find the volume of cylinder B.

$\dfrac{\text{Volume of cylinder B}}{\text{Volume of cylinder A}} = k^3$ The ratio of the volumes is k^3.

$\dfrac{\text{Volume of cylinder B}}{45\pi} = 2^3$ Substitute.

Volume of cylinder B $= 360\pi$ Solve for volume of cylinder B.

▶ The volume of cylinder B is 360π cubic centimeters.

Prism C

$V = 1536$ m³

Prism D

3 m

Monitoring Progress Help in English and Spanish at *BigIdeasMath.com*

6. Prism C and prism D are similar. Find the volume of prism D.

EXAMPLE 5 Finding the Volume of a Composite Solid

Find the volume of the concrete block.

0.33 ft   0.39 ft   0.33 ft
0.66 ft
0.66 ft
1.31 ft

SOLUTION

To find the area of the base, subtract two times the area of the small rectangle from the large rectangle.

$B = \boxed{\text{Area of large rectangle}} - 2 \cdot \boxed{\text{Area of small rectangle}}$

$= 1.31(0.66) - 2(0.33)(0.39)$

$= 0.6072$

Using the formula for the volume of a prism, the volume is

$V = Bh = 0.6072(0.66) \approx 0.40.$

▶ The volume is about 0.40 cubic foot.

Monitoring Progress Help in English and Spanish at *BigIdeasMath.com*

3 ft
6 ft
10 ft

7. Find the volume of the composite solid.

Vocabulary and Core Concept Check

1. **VOCABULARY** In what type of units is the volume of a solid measured?

2. **WHICH ONE DOESN'T BELONG?** Which solid does *not* belong with the other three? Explain your reasoning.

Monitoring Progress and Modeling with Mathematics

In Exercises 3–6, match the polyhedron with its name.

3.

4.

5.

6.
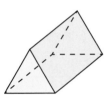

A. triangular prism

B. rectangular pyramid

C. hexagonal pyramid

D. pentagonal prism

In Exercises 7–10, tell whether the solid is a polyhedron. If it is, name the polyhedron. *(See Example 1.)*

7.

8.

9.

10.

In Exercises 11–14, find the volume of the prism. *(See Example 2.)*

11.
1.2 cm
1.8 cm
2 cm
2.3 cm

12.
1.5 m
2 m
4 m

13.
7 in.
10 in.
5 in.

14.
14 m
11 m
6 m

In Exercises 15–18, find the volume of the cylinder. *(See Example 3.)*

15.
3 ft
10.2 ft

16.
26.8 cm
9.8 cm

17.
5 ft
8 ft

18.
12 m
18 m
60°

In Exercises 19 and 20, make a sketch of the solid and find its volume. Round your answer to the nearest hundredth.

19. A prism has a height of 11.2 centimeters and an equilateral triangle for a base, where each base edge is 8 centimeters.

20. A pentagonal prism has a height of 9 feet and each base edge is 3 feet.

21. ERROR ANALYSIS Describe and correct the error in identifying the solid.

The solid is a rectangular pyramid.

22. ERROR ANALYSIS Describe and correct the error in finding the volume of the cylinder.

$V = 2\pi rh$
$= 2\pi(4)(3)$
$= 24\pi$
So, the volume of the cylinder is 24π cubic feet.

In Exercises 23–28, find the missing dimension of the prism or cylinder.

23. Volume = 560 ft³

24. Volume = 2700 yd³

25. Volume = 80 cm³

26. Volume = 72.66 in.³

27. Volume = 3000 ft³

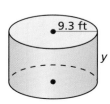

28. Volume = 1696.5 m³

In Exercises 29 and 30, the solids are similar. Find the volume of solid B. *(See Example 4.)*

29.

Prism A
9 cm
$V = 2673$ cm³
Prism B
3 cm

30.

Cylinder A
12 in.
Cylinder B
15 in.
$V = 4608\pi$ in.³

In Exercises 31–34, find the volume of the composite solid. *(See Example 5.)*

31.

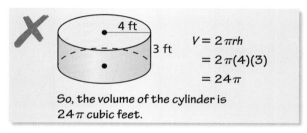
5 ft
2 ft
3 ft
2 ft
6 ft
10 ft

32.

4 in.
4 in.
4 in.

33.

3 in.
8 in.
11 in.

34.

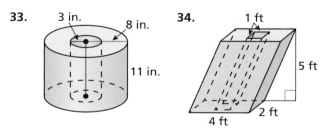
1 ft
5 ft
4 ft
2 ft

35. MODELING WITH MATHEMATICS The Great Blue Hole is a cylindrical trench located off the coast of Belize. It is approximately 1000 feet wide and 400 feet deep. About how many gallons of water does the Great Blue Hole contain? (1 ft³ ≈ 7.48 gallons)

36. COMPARING METHODS The *Volume Addition Postulate* states that the volume of a solid is the sum of the volumes of all its nonoverlapping parts. Use this postulate to find the volume of the block of concrete in Example 5 by subtracting the volume of each hole from the volume of the large rectangular prism. Which method do you prefer? Explain your reasoning.

37. WRITING Both of the figures shown are made up of the same number of congruent rectangles. Explain how Cavalieri's Principle can be adapted to compare the areas of these figures.

38. HOW DO YOU SEE IT? Each stack of memo papers contains 500 equally-sized sheets of paper. Compare their volumes. Explain your reasoning.

39. OPEN-ENDED Sketch two rectangular prisms that have volumes of 100 cubic inches but different surface areas. Include dimensions in your sketches.

40. MAKING AN ARGUMENT Your friend says that the polyhedron shown is a triangular prism. Your cousin says that it is a triangular pyramid. Who is correct? Explain your reasoning.

41. MAKING AN ARGUMENT A prism and a cylinder have the same height and different cross-sectional areas. Your friend claims that the two solids have the same volume by Cavalieri's Principle. Is your friend correct? Explain your reasoning.

42. THOUGHT PROVOKING Cavalieri's Principle states that the two solids shown below have the same volume. Do they also have the same surface area? Explain your reasoning.

43. PROBLEM SOLVING A barn is in the shape of a pentagonal prism with the dimensions shown. The volume of the barn is 9072 cubic feet. Find the dimensions of each half of the roof.

Not drawn to scale

44. PROBLEM SOLVING A wooden box is in the shape of a regular pentagonal prism. The sides, top, and bottom of the box are 1 centimeter thick. Approximate the volume of wood used to construct the box. Round your answer to the nearest tenth.

Maintaining Mathematical Proficiency
Reviewing what you learned in previous grades and lessons

Find the surface area of the regular pyramid. *(Skills Review Handbook)*

45.

3 m, 2 m

46.

10 cm, 8 cm, Area of base is 166.3 cm².

47.

20 in., 18 in., 15.6 in.

11.5 Volumes of Pyramids

Essential Question How can you find the volume of a pyramid?

EXPLORATION 1 Finding the Volume of a Pyramid

Work with a partner. The pyramid and the prism have the same height and the same square base.

When the pyramid is filled with sand and poured into the prism, it takes three pyramids to fill the prism.

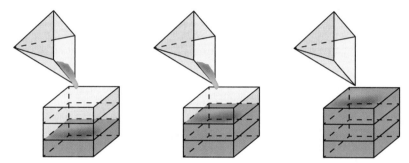

LOOKING FOR STRUCTURE

To be proficient in math, you need to look closely to discern a pattern or structure.

Use this information to write a formula for the volume V of a pyramid.

EXPLORATION 2 Finding the Volume of a Pyramid

Work with a partner. Use the formula you wrote in Exploration 1 to find the volume of the hexagonal pyramid.

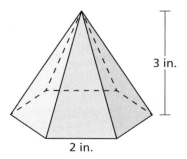

3 in.

2 in.

Communicate Your Answer

3. How can you find the volume of a pyramid?

4. In Section 11.6, you will study volumes of cones. How do you think you could use a method similar to the one presented in Exploration 1 to write a formula for the volume of a cone? Explain your reasoning.

What You Will Learn

▶ Find volumes of pyramids.

▶ Use volumes of pyramids.

Finding Volumes of Pyramids

Consider a triangular prism with parallel, congruent bases $\triangle JKL$ and $\triangle MNP$. You can divide this triangular prism into three triangular pyramids.

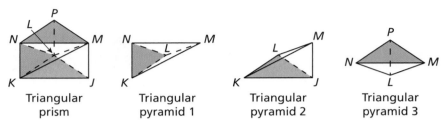

Triangular   Triangular   Triangular   Triangular
prism   pyramid 1   pyramid 2   pyramid 3

Pyramid Q

Pyramid R

You can combine triangular pyramids 1 and 2 to form a pyramid with a base that is a parallelogram, as shown at the left. Name this pyramid Q. Similarly, you can combine triangular pyramids 1 and 3 to form pyramid R with a base that is a parallelogram.

In pyramid Q, diagonal $\overline{KM}$ divides $\square JKNM$ into two congruent triangles, so the bases of triangular pyramids 1 and 2 are congruent. Similarly, you can divide any cross section parallel to $\square JKNM$ into two congruent triangles that are the cross sections of triangular pyramids 1 and 2.

By Cavalieri's Principle, triangular pyramids 1 and 2 have the same volume. Similarly, using pyramid R, you can show that triangular pyramids 1 and 3 have the same volume. By the Transitive Property of Equality, triangular pyramids 2 and 3 have the same volume.

The volume of each pyramid must be one-third the volume of the prism, or $V = \frac{1}{3}Bh$. You can generalize this formula to say that the volume of any pyramid with any base is equal to $\frac{1}{3}$ the volume of a prism with the same base and height because you can divide any polygon into triangles and any pyramid into triangular pyramids.

🌀 Core Concept

Volume of a Pyramid

The volume V of a pyramid is

$$V = \frac{1}{3}Bh$$

where B is the area of the base and h is the height.

EXAMPLE 1   Finding the Volume of a Pyramid

Find the volume of the pyramid.

SOLUTION

$V = \frac{1}{3}Bh$ Formula for volume of a pyramid

$= \frac{1}{3}\left(\frac{1}{2} \cdot 4 \cdot 6\right)(9)$ Substitute.

$= 36$ Simplify.

▶ The volume is 36 cubic meters.

Find the volume of the pyramid.

1.

12 cm

10 cm

2.

20 cm

12 cm

Using Volumes of Pyramids

EXAMPLE 2 **Using the Volume of a Pyramid**

Originally, Khafre's Pyramid had a height of about 144 meters and a volume of about 2,218,800 cubic meters. Find the side length of the square base.

SOLUTION

$V = \frac{1}{3}Bh$	Formula for volume of a pyramid
$2{,}218{,}800 \approx \frac{1}{3}x^2(144)$	Substitute.
$6{,}656{,}400 \approx 144x^2$	Multiply each side by 3.
$46{,}225 \approx x^2$	Divide each side by 144.
$215 \approx x$	Find the positive square root.

Khafre's Pyramid, Egypt

▶ Originally, the side length of the square base was about 215 meters.

EXAMPLE 3 **Using the Volume of a Pyramid**

Find the height of the triangular pyramid.

$V = 14$ ft³

h

3 ft

4 ft

SOLUTION

The area of the base is $B = \frac{1}{2}(3)(4) = 6$ ft² and the volume is $V = 14$ ft³.

$V = \frac{1}{3}Bh$	Formula for volume of a pyramid
$14 = \frac{1}{3}(6)h$	Substitute.
$7 = h$	Solve for h.

▶ The height is 7 feet.

$V = 24$ m³

h

3 m

6 m

Monitoring Progress Help in English and Spanish at *BigIdeasMath.com*

3. The volume of a square pyramid is 75 cubic meters and the height is 9 meters. Find the side length of the square base.

4. Find the height of the triangular pyramid at the left.

EXAMPLE 4 **Finding the Volume of a Similar Solid**

Pyramid A and pyramid B are similar.
Find the volume of pyramid B.

Pyramid A   **Pyramid B**

8 m

6 m

$V = 96 \text{ m}^3$

SOLUTION

The scale factor is $k = \dfrac{\text{Height of pyramid B}}{\text{Height of pyramid A}} = \dfrac{6}{8} = \dfrac{3}{4}$.

Use the scale factor to find the volume of pyramid B.

$\dfrac{\text{Volume of pyramid B}}{\text{Volume of pyramid A}} = k^3$ The ratio of the volumes is k^3.

$\dfrac{\text{Volume of pyramid B}}{96} = \left(\dfrac{3}{4}\right)^3$ Substitute.

Volume of pyramid B $= 40.5$ Solve for volume of pyramid B.

▶ The volume of pyramid B is 40.5 cubic meters.

Monitoring Progress Help in English and Spanish at *BigIdeasMath.com*

5. Pyramid C and pyramid D are similar. Find the volume of pyramid D.

Pyramid C   **Pyramid D**

$V = 324 \text{ m}^3$

9 m

3 m

EXAMPLE 5 **Finding the Volume of a Composite Solid**

Find the volume of the composite solid.

SOLUTION

6 m

6 m

6 m

6 m

Volume of solid	=	Volume of cube	+	Volume of pyramid

$= s^3 + \dfrac{1}{3}Bh$ Write formulas.

$= 6^3 + \dfrac{1}{3}(6)^2 \cdot 6$ Substitute.

$= 216 + 72$ Simplify.

$= 288$ Add.

▶ The volume is 288 cubic meters.

Monitoring Progress Help in English and Spanish at *BigIdeasMath.com*

6. Find the volume of the composite solid.

3 ft

5 ft

4 ft   8 ft

Vocabulary and Core Concept Check

1. **VOCABULARY** Explain the difference between a triangular prism and a triangular pyramid.

2. **REASONING** A square pyramid and a cube have the same base and height. Compare the volume of the square pyramid to the volume of the cube.

Monitoring Progress and Modeling with Mathematics

In Exercises 3 and 4, find the volume of the pyramid.
(See Example 1.)

3.

7 m
16 m
12 m

4.

3 in.
4 in.
3 in.

In Exercises 5–8, find the indicated measure.
(See Example 2.)

5. A pyramid with a square base has a volume of 120 cubic meters and a height of 10 meters. Find the side length of the square base.

6. A pyramid with a square base has a volume of 912 cubic feet and a height of 19 feet. Find the side length of the square base.

7. A pyramid with a rectangular base has a volume of 480 cubic inches and a height of 10 inches. The width of the rectangular base is 9 inches. Find the length of the rectangular base.

8. A pyramid with a rectangular base has a volume of 105 cubic centimeters and a height of 15 centimeters. The length of the rectangular base is 7 centimeters. Find the width of the rectangular base.

9. **ERROR ANALYSIS** Describe and correct the error in finding the volume of the pyramid.

5 ft
6 ft
$V = \frac{1}{3}(6)(5)$
$= \frac{1}{3}(30)$
$= 10\,\text{ft}^3$

10. **OPEN-ENDED** Give an example of a pyramid and a prism that have the same base and the same volume. Explain your reasoning.

In Exercises 11–14, find the height of the pyramid.
(See Example 3.)

11. Volume = 15 ft³

3 ft
3 ft

12. Volume = 224 in.³

12 in.
8 in.

13. Volume = 198 yd³

9 yd
11 yd

14. Volume = 392 cm³

14 cm
7 cm

In Exercises 15 and 16, the pyramids are similar. Find the volume of pyramid B. *(See Example 4.)*

15. Pyramid A   Pyramid B

12 ft
$V = 256\,\text{ft}^3$
3 ft

16. Pyramid A   Pyramid B

3 in.
$V = 10\,\text{in.}^3$
6 in.

In Exercises 17–20, find the volume of the composite solid. *(See Example 5.)*

17.
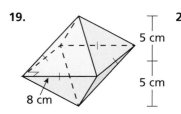
3 in.
2 in.
4 in.
6 in.

18.

7 cm
10 cm
9 cm
12 cm

19.
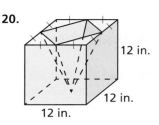
8 cm

20.
5 cm
5 cm
12 in.
12 in.
12 in.

21. ABSTRACT REASONING A pyramid has a height of 8 feet and a square base with a side length of 6 feet.

   a. How does the volume of the pyramid change when the base stays the same and the height is doubled?

   b. How does the volume of the pyramid change when the height stays the same and the side length of the base is doubled?

   c. Are your answers to parts (a) and (b) true for any square pyramid? Explain your reasoning.

22. HOW DO YOU SEE IT? The cube shown is formed by three pyramids, each with the same square base and the same height. How could you use this to verify the formula for the volume of a pyramid?

23. CRITICAL THINKING Find the volume of the regular pentagonal pyramid. Round your answer to the nearest hundredth. In the diagram, $m\angle ABC = 35°$.

A
C
B
3 ft

24. THOUGHT PROVOKING A *frustum* of a pyramid is the part of the pyramid that lies between the base and a plane parallel to the base, as shown. Write a formula for the volume of the frustum of a square pyramid in terms of a, b, and h. (*Hint*: Consider the "missing" top of the pyramid and use similar triangles.)

b
b
h
a
a

25. MODELING WITH MATHEMATICS Nautical deck prisms were used as a safe way to illuminate decks on ships. The deck prism shown here is composed of the following three solids: a regular hexagonal prism with an edge length of 3.5 inches and a height of 1.5 inches, a regular hexagonal prism with an edge length of 3.25 inches and a height of 0.25 inch, and a regular hexagonal pyramid with an edge length of 3 inches and a height of 3 inches. Find the volume of the deck prism.

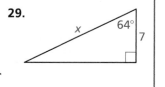

Maintaining Mathematical Proficiency   Reviewing what you learned in previous grades and lessons

Find the value of x. Round your answer to the nearest tenth. *(Section 9.4 and Section 9.5)*

26.
35°
x
9

27.
57°
15
x

28.
x
30°
10

29.
x
64°
7

Essential Question How can you find the surface area and the volume of a cone?

EXPLORATION 1 **Finding the Surface Area of a Cone**

Work with a partner. Construct a circle with a radius of 3 inches. Mark the circumference of the circle into six equal parts, and label the length of each part. Then cut out one sector of the circle and make a cone.

a. Explain why the base of the cone is a circle. What are the circumference and radius of the base?

b. What is the area of the original circle? What is the area with one sector missing?

c. Describe the surface area of the cone, including the base. Use your description to find the surface area.

EXPLORATION 2 **Finding the Volume of a Cone**

Work with a partner. The cone and the cylinder have the same height and the same circular base.

When the cone is filled with sand and poured into the cylinder, it takes three cones to fill the cylinder.

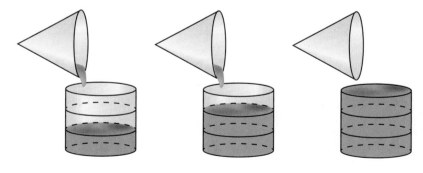

CONSTRUCTING VIABLE ARGUMENTS

To be proficient in math, you need to understand and use stated assumptions, definitions, and previously established results in constructing arguments.

Use this information to write a formula for the volume V of a cone.

Communicate Your Answer

3. How can you find the surface area and the volume of a cone?

4. In Exploration 1, cut another sector from the circle and make a cone. Find the radius of the base and the surface area of the cone. Repeat this three times, recording your results in a table. Describe the pattern.

What You Will Learn

▶ Find surface areas of right cones.

▶ Find volumes of cones.

▶ Use volumes of cones.

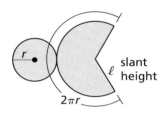

Finding Surface Areas of Right Cones

Recall that a *circular cone*, or *cone*, has a circular *base* and a *vertex* that is not in the same plane as the base. The *altitude*, or *height*, is the perpendicular distance between the vertex and the base. In a *right cone*, the height meets the base at its center and the *slant height* is the distance between the vertex and a point on the base edge.

The **lateral surface of a cone** consists of all segments that connect the vertex with points on the base edge. When you cut along the slant height and lay the right cone flat, you get the net shown at the left. In the net, the circular base has an area of πr^2 and the lateral surface is a sector of a circle. You can find the area of this sector by using a proportion, as shown below.

$$\frac{\text{Area of sector}}{\text{Area of circle}} = \frac{\text{Arc length}}{\text{Circumference of circle}} \qquad \text{Set up proportion.}$$

$$\frac{\text{Area of sector}}{\pi \ell^2} = \frac{2\pi r}{2\pi \ell} \qquad \text{Substitute.}$$

$$\text{Area of sector} = \pi \ell^2 \cdot \frac{2\pi r}{2\pi \ell} \qquad \text{Multiply each side by } \pi \ell^2.$$

$$\text{Area of sector} = \pi r \ell \qquad \text{Simplify.}$$

The surface area of a right cone is the sum of the base area and the lateral area, $\pi r \ell$.

Core Concept

Surface Area of a Right Cone

The surface area S of a right cone is

$$S = \pi r^2 + \pi r \ell$$

where r is the radius of the base and ℓ is the slant height.

EXAMPLE 1   **Finding Surface Areas of Right Cones**

Find the surface area of the right cone.

SOLUTION

$$S = \pi r^2 + \pi r \ell = \pi \cdot 4^2 + \pi(4)(6) = 40\pi \approx 125.66$$

▶ The surface area is 40π, or about 125.66 square inches.

Monitoring Progress Help in English and Spanish at *BigIdeasMath.com*

1. Find the surface area of the right cone.

Finding Volumes of Cones

Consider a cone with a regular polygon inscribed in the base. The pyramid with the same vertex as the cone has volume $V = \frac{1}{3}Bh$. As you increase the number of sides of the polygon, it approaches the base of the cone and the pyramid approaches the cone. The volume approaches $\frac{1}{3}\pi r^2 h$ as the base area B approaches πr^2.

Core Concept

Volume of a Cone

The volume V of a cone is

$$V = \frac{1}{3}Bh = \frac{1}{3}\pi r^2 h$$

where B is the area of the base, h is the height, and r is the radius of the base.

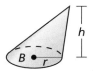

EXAMPLE 2   Finding the Volume of a Cone

Find the volume of the cone.

4.5 cm

2.2 cm

SOLUTION

$V = \frac{1}{3}\pi r^2 h$ Formula for volume of a cone

$\quad = \frac{1}{3}\pi \cdot (2.2)^2 \cdot 4.5$ Substitute.

$\quad = 7.26\pi$ Simplify.

$\quad \approx 22.81$ Use a calculator.

▶ The volume is 7.26π, or about 22.81 cubic centimeters.

Monitoring Progress Help in English and Spanish at *BigIdeasMath.com*

Find the volume of the cone.

2.

13 in.

7 in.

3.
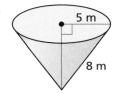

5 m

8 m

Using Volumes of Cones

EXAMPLE 3 **Finding the Volume of a Similar Solid**

Cone A and cone B are similar. Find the volume of cone B.

Cone A

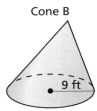

$V = 15\pi$ ft³

Cone B

9 ft

SOLUTION

The scale factor is $k = \dfrac{\text{Radius of cone B}}{\text{Radius of cone A}} = \dfrac{9}{3} = 3$.

Use the scale factor to find the volume of cone B.

$\dfrac{\text{Volume of cone B}}{\text{Volume of cone A}} = k^3$ The ratio of the volumes is k^3.

$\dfrac{\text{Volume of cone B}}{15\pi} = 3^3$ Substitute.

$\text{Volume of cone B} = 405\pi$ Solve for volume of cone B.

▶ The volume of cone B is 405π cubic feet.

Cone C

8 cm

$V = 384\pi$ cm³

Cone D

2 cm

Monitoring Progress 🔊 Help in English and Spanish at *BigIdeasMath.com*

4. Cone C and cone D are similar. Find the volume of cone D.

EXAMPLE 4 **Finding the Volume of a Composite Solid**

Find the volume of the composite solid.

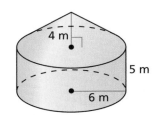

4 m

5 m

6 m

SOLUTION

Let h_1 be the height of the cylinder and let h_2 be the height of the cone.

Volume of solid	=	Volume of cylinder	+	Volume of cone

$= \pi r^2 h_1 + \dfrac{1}{3}\pi r^2 h_2$ Write formulas.

$= \pi \cdot 6^2 \cdot 5 + \dfrac{1}{3}\pi \cdot 6^2 \cdot 4$ Substitute.

$= 180\pi + 48\pi$ Simplify.

$= 228\pi$ Add.

≈ 716.28 Use a calculator.

▶ The volume is 228π, or about 716.28 cubic meters.

5 cm

10 cm

3 cm

Monitoring Progress 🔊 Help in English and Spanish at *BigIdeasMath.com*

5. Find the volume of the composite solid.

Vocabulary and Core Concept Check

1. **WRITING** Describe the differences between pyramids and cones. Describe their similarities.

2. **COMPLETE THE SENTENCE** The volume of a cone with radius r and height h is $\frac{1}{3}$ the volume of a(n) _____ with radius r and height h.

Monitoring Progress and Modeling with Mathematics

In Exercises 3–6, find the surface area of the right cone. *(See Example 1.)*

3.

16 in.
8 in.

4.

7.2 cm
11 cm

5. A right cone has a radius of 9 inches and a height of 12 inches.

6. A right cone has a diameter of 11.2 feet and a height of 9.2 feet.

In Exercises 7–10, find the volume of the cone. *(See Example 2.)*

7.

13 mm
10 mm

8.
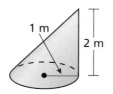
1 m
2 m

9. A cone has a diameter of 11.5 inches and a height of 15.2 inches.

10. A right cone has a radius of 3 feet and a slant height of 6 feet.

In Exercises 11 and 12, find the missing dimension(s).

11. Surface area = 75.4 cm²

h ℓ
3 cm

12. Volume = 216π in.³

18 in.
r

In Exercises 13 and 14, the cones are similar. Find the volume of cone B. *(See Example 3.)*

13.
Cone A

8 ft
$V = 32\pi$ ft³

Cone B

16 ft

14.
Cone A

10 m
$V = 120\pi$ m³

Cone B
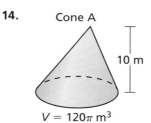
4 m

In Exercises 15 and 16, find the volume of the composite solid. *(See Example 4.)*

15.

3 cm
3 cm
10 cm

16.
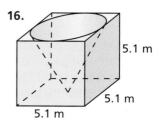
5.1 m
5.1 m
5.1 m

17. **ANALYZING RELATIONSHIPS** A cone has height h and a base with radius r. You want to change the cone so its volume is doubled. What is the new height if you change only the height? What is the new radius if you change only the radius? Explain.

18. HOW DO YOU SEE IT A snack stand serves a small order of popcorn in a cone-shaped container and a large order of popcorn in a cylindrical container. Do not perform any calculations.

3 in.   3 in.

8 in.   8 in.

$1.25 $2.50

a. How many small containers of popcorn do you have to buy to equal the amount of popcorn in a large container? Explain.

b. Which container gives you more popcorn for your money? Explain.

In Exercises 19 and 20, find the volume of the right cone.

19.

22 ft   60°

20.

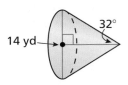

14 yd   32°

21. MODELING WITH MATHEMATICS
A cat eats half a cup of food, twice per day. Will the automatic pet feeder hold enough food for 10 days? Explain your reasoning. (1 cup ≈ 14.4 in.^{3})

2.5 in.

7.5 in.

4 in.

22. MODELING WITH MATHEMATICS During a chemistry lab, you use a funnel to pour a solvent into a flask. The radius of the funnel is 5 centimeters and its height is 10 centimeters. You pour the solvent into the funnel at a rate of 80 milliliters per second and the solvent flows out of the funnel at a rate of 65 milliliters per second. How long will it be before the funnel overflows? (1 mL = 1 cm^3)

23. REASONING To make a paper drinking cup, start with a circular piece of paper that has a 3-inch radius, then follow the given steps. How does the surface area of the cup compare to the original paper circle? Find $m\angle ABC$.

3 in.   fold   fold   A C
                        B
                        open cup

24. THOUGHT PROVOKING A *frustum* of a cone is the part of the cone that lies between the base and a plane parallel to the base, as shown. Write a formula for the volume of the frustum of a cone in terms of a, b, and h. (*Hint*: Consider the "missing" top of the cone and use similar triangles.)

a
h
b

25. MAKING AN ARGUMENT In the figure, the two cylinders are congruent. The combined height of the two smaller cones equals the height of the larger cone. Your friend claims that this means the total volume of the two smaller cones is equal to the volume of the larger cone. Is your friend correct? Justify your answer.

26. MODELING WITH MATHEMATICS Water flows into a reservoir shaped like a right cone at a rate of 1.8 cubic meters per minute. The height and diameter of the reservoir are equal.

a. Show that $V = \dfrac{\pi h^3}{12}$.

b. Make a table showing the heights h of the water after 1, 2, 3, 4, and 5 minutes.

c. Is there a linear relationship between the height of the water and time? Explain.

Maintaining Mathematical Proficiency
Reviewing what you learned in previous grades and lessons

Find the indicated measure. *(Section 11.2)*

27. area of a circle with a radius of 7 feet

28. area of a circle with a diameter of 22 centimeters

29. diameter of a circle with an area of 256π square meters

30. radius of a circle with an area of 529π square inches

Essential Question How can you find the surface area and the volume of a sphere?

EXPLORATION 1 **Finding the Surface Area of a Sphere**

Work with a partner. Remove the covering from a baseball or softball.

USING TOOLS STRATEGICALLY

To be proficient in math, you need to identify relevant external mathematical resources, such as content located on a website.

You will end up with two "figure 8" pieces of material, as shown above. From the amount of material it takes to cover the ball, what would you estimate the surface area S of the ball to be? Express your answer in terms of the radius r of the ball.

$S = $ ⬚   Surface area of a sphere

Use the Internet or some other resource to confirm that the formula you wrote for the surface area of a sphere is correct.

EXPLORATION 2 **Finding the Volume of a Sphere**

Work with a partner. A cylinder is circumscribed about a sphere, as shown. Write a formula for the volume V of the cylinder in terms of the radius r.

$V = $ ⬚   Volume of cylinder

When half of the sphere (a *hemisphere*) is filled with sand and poured into the cylinder, it takes three hemispheres to fill the cylinder. Use this information to write a formula for the volume V of a sphere in terms of the radius r.

$V = $ ⬚   Volume of a sphere

Communicate Your Answer

3. How can you find the surface area and the volume of a sphere?

4. Use the results of Explorations 1 and 2 to find the surface area and the volume of a sphere with a radius of (a) 3 inches and (b) 2 centimeters.

What You Will Learn

▶ Find surface areas of spheres.

▶ Find volumes of spheres.

Finding Surface Areas of Spheres

A *sphere* is the set of all points in space equidistant from a given point. This point is called the *center* of the sphere. A *radius* of a sphere is a segment from the center to a point on the sphere. A **chord of a sphere** is a segment whose endpoints are on the sphere. A *diameter* of a sphere is a chord that contains the center.

As with circles, the terms radius and diameter also represent distances, and the diameter is twice the radius.

If a plane intersects a sphere, then the intersection is either a single point or a circle. If the plane contains the center of the sphere, then the intersection is a **great circle** of the sphere. The circumference of a great circle is the circumference of the sphere. Every great circle of a sphere separates the sphere into two congruent halves called *hemispheres*.

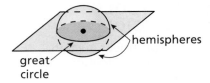

🌀 Core Concept

Surface Area of a Sphere

The surface area S of a sphere is

$$S = 4\pi r^2$$

where r is the radius of the sphere.

$S = 4\pi r^2$

To understand the formula for the surface area of a sphere, think of a baseball. The surface area of a baseball is sewn from two congruent shapes, each of which resembles two joined circles.

So, the entire covering of the baseball consists of four circles, each with radius r. The area A of a circle with radius r is $A = \pi r^2$. So, the area of the covering can be approximated by $4\pi r^2$. This is the formula for the surface area of a sphere.

leather covering

EXAMPLE 1 **Finding the Surface Areas of Spheres**

Find the surface area of each sphere.

a.

b.

SOLUTION

a. $S = 4\pi r^2$ Formula for surface area of a sphere

    $= 4\pi(8)^2$ Substitute 8 for r.

    $= 256\pi$ Simplify.

    ≈ 804.25 Use a calculator.

▶   The surface area is 256π, or about 804.25 square inches.

b. The circumference of the sphere is 12π, so the radius of the sphere is $\dfrac{12\pi}{2\pi} = 6$ feet.

     $S = 4\pi r^2$ Formula for surface area of a sphere

      $= 4\pi(6)^2$ Substitute 6 for r.

      $= 144\pi$ Simplify.

      ≈ 452.39 Use a calculator.

▶   The surface area is 144π, or about 452.39 square feet.

EXAMPLE 2 **Finding the Diameter of a Sphere**

Find the diameter of the sphere.

SOLUTION

       $S = 4\pi r^2$ Formula for surface area of a sphere

  $20.25\pi = 4\pi r^2$ Substitute 20.25π for S.

    $5.0625 = r^2$ Divide each side by 4π.

      $2.25 = r$ Find the positive square root.

COMMON ERROR

Be sure to multiply the value of r by 2 to find the diameter.

▶   The diameter is $2r = 2 \cdot 2.25 = 4.5$ centimeters.

Monitoring Progress Help in English and Spanish at *BigIdeasMath.com*

Find the surface area of the sphere.

1.

2.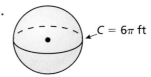

3. Find the radius of the sphere.

Finding Volumes of Spheres

The figure shows a hemisphere and a cylinder with a cone removed. A plane parallel to their bases intersects the solids z units above their bases.

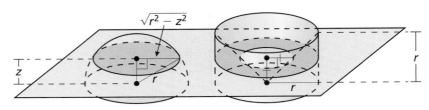

Using the AA Similarity Theorem, you can show that the radius of the cross section of the cone at height z is z. The area of the cross section formed by the plane is $\pi(r^2 - z^2)$ for both solids. Because the solids have the same height and the same cross-sectional area at every level, they have the same volume by Cavalieri's Principle.

$$V_{\text{hemisphere}} = V_{\text{cylinder}} - V_{\text{cone}}$$

$$= \pi r^2(r) - \tfrac{1}{3}\pi r^2(r)$$

$$= \tfrac{2}{3}\pi r^3$$

So, the volume of a sphere of radius r is

$$2 \cdot V_{\text{hemisphere}} = 2 \cdot \tfrac{2}{3}\pi r^3 = \tfrac{4}{3}\pi r^3.$$

🌀 Core Concept

Volume of a Sphere

The volume V of a sphere is

$$V = \frac{4}{3}\pi r^3$$

where r is the radius of the sphere.

$V = \tfrac{4}{3}\pi r^3$

EXAMPLE 3   **Finding the Volume of a Sphere**

Find the volume of the soccer ball.

4.5 in.

SOLUTION

$$V = \tfrac{4}{3}\pi r^3 \qquad \text{Formula for volume of a sphere}$$

$$= \tfrac{4}{3}\pi(4.5)^3 \qquad \text{Substitute 4.5 for } r.$$

$$= 121.5\pi \qquad \text{Simplify.}$$

$$\approx 381.70 \qquad \text{Use a calculator.}$$

▶ The volume of the soccer ball is 121.5π, or about 381.70 cubic inches.

EXAMPLE 4   **Finding the Volume of a Sphere**

The surface area of a sphere is 324π square centimeters. Find the volume of the sphere.

SOLUTION

Step 1 Use the surface area to find the radius.

$$S = 4\pi r^2 \qquad \text{Formula for surface area of a sphere}$$

$$324\pi = 4\pi r^2 \qquad \text{Substitute } 324\pi \text{ for } S.$$

$$81 = r^2 \qquad \text{Divide each side by } 4\pi.$$

$$9 = r \qquad \text{Find the positive square root.}$$

The radius is 9 centimeters.

Step 2 Use the radius to find the volume.

$$V = \tfrac{4}{3}\pi r^3 \qquad \text{Formula for volume of a sphere}$$

$$= \tfrac{4}{3}\pi(9)^3 \qquad \text{Substitute 9 for } r.$$

$$= 972\pi \qquad \text{Simplify.}$$

$$\approx 3053.63 \qquad \text{Use a calculator.}$$

▶ The volume is 972π, or about 3053.63 cubic centimeters.

EXAMPLE 5   **Finding the Volume of a Composite Solid**

Find the volume of the composite solid.

2 in.

2 in.

SOLUTION

Volume of solid	=	Volume of cylinder	−	Volume of hemisphere

$$= \pi r^2 h - \tfrac{1}{2}\left(\tfrac{4}{3}\pi r^3\right) \qquad \text{Write formulas.}$$

$$= \pi(2)^2(2) - \tfrac{2}{3}\pi(2)^3 \qquad \text{Substitute.}$$

$$= 8\pi - \tfrac{16}{3}\pi \qquad \text{Multiply.}$$

$$= \tfrac{24}{3}\pi - \tfrac{16}{3}\pi \qquad \begin{array}{l}\text{Rewrite fractions using least} \\ \text{common denominator.}\end{array}$$

$$= \tfrac{8}{3}\pi \qquad \text{Subtract.}$$

$$\approx 8.38 \qquad \text{Use a calculator.}$$

▶ The volume is $\tfrac{8}{3}\pi$, or about 8.38 cubic inches.

Monitoring Progress Help in English and Spanish at *BigIdeasMath.com*

4. The radius of a sphere is 5 yards. Find the volume of the sphere.

5. The diameter of a sphere is 36 inches. Find the volume of the sphere.

6. The surface area of a sphere is 576π square centimeters. Find the volume of the sphere.

7. Find the volume of the composite solid at the left.

1 m

5 m

Vocabulary and Core Concept Check

1. **VOCABULARY** When a plane intersects a sphere, what must be true for the intersection to be a great circle?

2. **WRITING** Explain the difference between a sphere and a hemisphere.

Monitoring Progress and Modeling with Mathematics

In Exercises 3–6, find the surface area of the sphere. *(See Example 1.)*

3.

4 ft

4.

7.5 cm

5.

18.3 m

6.
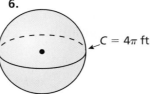
$C = 4\pi$ ft

In Exercises 7–10, find the indicated measure. *(See Example 2.)*

7. Find the radius of a sphere with a surface area of 4π square feet.

8. Find the radius of a sphere with a surface area of 1024π square inches.

9. Find the diameter of a sphere with a surface area of 900π square meters.

10. Find the diameter of a sphere with a surface area of 196π square centimeters.

In Exercises 11 and 12, find the surface area of the hemisphere.

11.

5 m

12.

12 in.

In Exercises 13–18, find the volume of the sphere. *(See Example 3.)*

13.

8 m

14.

4 ft

15.

22 yd

16.

14 ft

17.

$C = 20\pi$ cm

18.
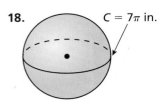
$C = 7\pi$ in.

In Exercises 19 and 20, find the volume of the sphere with the given surface area. *(See Example 4.)*

19. Surface area $= 16\pi$ ft²

20. Surface area $= 484\pi$ cm²

21. **ERROR ANALYSIS** Describe and correct the error in finding the volume of the sphere.

6 ft

$V = \frac{4}{3}\pi(6)^2$

$= 48\pi$

≈ 150.80 ft³

22. ERROR ANALYSIS Describe and correct the error in finding the volume of the sphere.

$$V = \frac{4}{3}\pi(3)^3$$
3 in.
$$= 36\pi$$
$$\approx 113.10 \text{ in.}^3$$

In Exercises 23–26, find the volume of the composite solid. *(See Example 5.)*

23.

9 in.
5 in.

24.

6 ft
12 ft

25.

18 cm
10 cm

26.

14 m
6 m

In Exercises 27–32, find the surface area and volume of the ball.

27. bowling ball

$d = 8.5$ in.

28. basketball

$C = 29.5$ in.

29. softball

$C = 12$ in.

30. golf ball

$d = 1.7$ in.

31. volleyball

$C = 26$ in.

32. baseball

$C = 9$ in.

33. MAKING AN ARGUMENT You friend claims that if the radius of a sphere is doubled, then the surface area of the sphere will also be doubled. Is your friend correct? Explain your reasoning.

34. MODELING WITH MATHEMATICS The circumference of Earth is about 24,900 miles. Find the surface area of the Western Hemisphere of Earth.

35. MODELING WITH MATHEMATICS A silo has the dimensions shown. The top of the silo is a hemispherical shape. Find the volume of the silo.

60 ft
20 ft

36. MODELING WITH MATHEMATICS Three tennis balls are stored in a cylindrical container with a height of 8 inches and a radius of 1.43 inches. The circumference of a tennis ball is 8 inches.

  a. Find the volume of a tennis ball.

  b. Find the amount of space within the cylinder not taken up by the tennis balls.

37. ANALYZING RELATIONSHIPS Use the table shown for a sphere.

Radius	Surface area	Volume
3 in.	36π in.^{2}	36π in.^{3}
6 in.		
9 in.		
12 in.		

  a. Copy and complete the table. Leave your answers in terms of π.

  b. What happens to the surface area of the sphere when the radius is doubled? tripled? quadrupled?

  c. What happens to the volume of the sphere when the radius is doubled? tripled? quadrupled?

38. MATHEMATICAL CONNECTIONS A sphere has a diameter of $4(x + 3)$ centimeters and a surface area of 784π square centimeters. Find the value of x.

39. MODELING WITH MATHEMATICS The radius of Earth is about 3960 miles. The radius of the moon is about 1080 miles.

   a. Find the surface area of Earth and the moon.

   b. Compare the surface areas of Earth and the moon.

   c. About 70% of the surface of Earth is water. How many square miles of water are on Earth's surface?

40. MODELING WITH MATHEMATICS The Torrid Zone on Earth is the area between the Tropic of Cancer and the Tropic of Capricorn. The distance between these two tropics is about 3250 miles. You can estimate the distance as the height of a cylindrical belt around Earth at the equator.

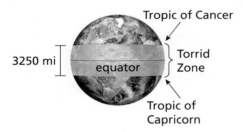

   a. Estimate the surface area of the Torrid Zone. (The radius of Earth is about 3960 miles.)

   b. A meteorite is equally likely to hit anywhere on Earth. Estimate the probability that a meteorite will land in the Torrid Zone.

41. ABSTRACT REASONING A sphere is inscribed in a cube with a volume of 64 cubic inches. What is the surface area of the sphere? Explain your reasoning.

42. HOW DO YOU SEE IT? The formula for the volume of a hemisphere and a cone are shown. If each solid has the same radius and $r = h$, which solid will have a greater volume? Explain your reasoning.

$$V = \tfrac{2}{3}\pi r^3 \qquad\qquad V = \tfrac{1}{3}\pi r^2 h$$

43. CRITICAL THINKING Let V be the volume of a sphere, S be the surface area of the sphere, and r be the radius of the sphere. Write an equation for V in terms of r and S. $\left(\text{Hint: Start with the ratio } \dfrac{V}{S}.\right)$

44. THOUGHT PROVOKING A *spherical lune* is the region between two great circles of a sphere. Find the formula for the area of a lune.

45. CRITICAL THINKING The volume of a right cylinder is the same as the volume of a sphere. The radius of the sphere is 1 inch. Give three possibilities for the dimensions of the cylinder.

46. PROBLEM SOLVING A *spherical cap* is a portion of a sphere cut off by a plane. The formula for the volume of a spherical cap is $V = \dfrac{\pi h}{6}(3a^2 + h^2)$, where a is the radius of the base of the cap and h is the height of the cap. Use the diagram and given information to find the volume of each spherical cap.

   a. $r = 5$ ft, $a = 4$ ft

   b. $r = 34$ cm, $a = 30$ cm

   c. $r = 13$ m, $h = 8$ m

   d. $r = 75$ in., $h = 54$ in.

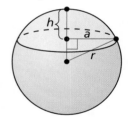

47. CRITICAL THINKING A sphere with a radius of 2 inches is inscribed in a right cone with a height of 6 inches. Find the surface area and the volume of the cone.

Maintaining Mathematical Proficiency
Reviewing what you learned in previous grades and lessons

Events A and B are disjoint. Find $P(A \text{ or } B)$. *(Section 5.4)*

48. $P(A) = 0.4$, $P(B) = 0.2$

49. $P(A) = 0.75$, $P(B) = 0.05$

50. $P(A) = \tfrac{1}{8}$, $P(B) = \tfrac{3}{4}$

51. $P(A) = \tfrac{2}{5}$, $P(B) = \tfrac{3}{10}$

Core Vocabulary

polyhedron, *p. 666*

face, *p. 666*

edge, *p. 666*

vertex, *p. 666*

volume, *p. 667*

Cavalieri's Principle, *p. 667*

similar solids, *p. 669*

lateral surface of a cone, *p. 680*

chord of a sphere, *p. 686*

great circle, *p. 686*

Core Concepts

Section 11.4

Types of Solids, *p. 666*

Cavalieri's Principle, *p. 667*

Volume of a Prism, *p. 667*

Volume of a Cylinder, *p. 668*

Similar Solids, *p. 669*

Section 11.5

Volume of a Pyramid, *p. 674*

Section 11.6

Surface Area of a Right Cone, *p. 680*

Volume of a Cone, *p. 681*

Section 11.7

Surface Area of a Sphere, *p. 686*

Volume of a Sphere, *p. 688*

Mathematical Practices

1. In Exercise 15 on page 677, explain why the volume changed by a factor of $\frac{1}{64}$.

2. In Exercise 38 on page 691, explain the steps you used to find the value of x.

Performance Task:

Tabletop Tiling

A Penrose tiling has a variety of properties that make it attractive. How do the concepts of area and circumference contribute to the visual appeal of a tabletop tiled in this type of pattern?

To explore the answer to this question and more, check out the Performance Task and Real-Life STEM video at *BigIdeasMath.com*.

11.1 Circumference and Arc Length *(pp. 639–646)*

The arc length of $\overset{\frown}{QR}$ is 6.54 feet. Find the radius of $\odot P$.

$$\frac{\text{Arc length of } \overset{\frown}{QR}}{2\pi r} = \frac{m\overset{\frown}{QR}}{360°}$$ Formula for arc length

$$\frac{6.54}{2\pi r} = \frac{75°}{360°}$$ Substitute.

$$6.54(360) = 75(2\pi r)$$ Cross Products Property

$$5.00 \approx r$$ Solve for r.

▶ The radius of $\odot P$ is about 5 feet.

Find the indicated measure.

1. diameter of $\odot P$

$C = 94.24$ ft

2. circumference of $\odot F$

$35°$ 5.5 cm

3. arc length of $\overset{\frown}{AB}$

$115°$ 13 in.

4. A mountain bike tire has a diameter of 26 inches. To the nearest foot, how far does the tire travel when it makes 32 revolutions?

11.2 Areas of Circles and Sectors *(pp. 647–654)*

Find the area of sector ADB.

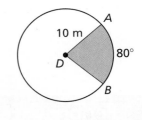

$$\text{Area of sector } ADB = \frac{m\overset{\frown}{AB}}{360°} \cdot \pi r^2$$ Formula for area of a sector

$$= \frac{80°}{360°} \cdot \pi \cdot 10^2$$ Substitute.

$$\approx 69.81$$ Use a calculator.

▶ The area of sector ADB is about 69.81 square meters.

Find the area of the blue shaded region.

5.

$240°$ 9 in.

6.

4 in.

6 in.

7.

$50°$ $A = 27.93$ ft²

A regular hexagon is inscribed in ⊙H. Find (a) $m\angle EHG$, **and (b) the area of the hexagon.**

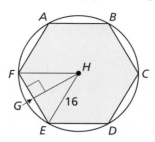

a. $\angle FHE$ is a central angle, so $m\angle FHE = \dfrac{360°}{6} = 60°$.

Apothem $\overline{GH}$ bisects $\angle FHE$.

▶ So, $m\angle EHG = 30°$.

b. Because $\triangle EHG$ is a 30°-60°-90° triangle, $GE = \dfrac{1}{2} \cdot HE = 8$
and $GH = \sqrt{3} \cdot GE = 8\sqrt{3}$. So, $s = 2(GE) = 16$ and $a = GH = 8\sqrt{3}$.

$$A = \frac{1}{2}a \cdot ns \qquad\qquad \text{Formula for area of a regular polygon}$$

$$= \frac{1}{2}\left(8\sqrt{3}\right)(6)(16) \qquad \text{Substitute.}$$

$$\approx 665.1 \qquad\qquad\qquad \text{Simplify.}$$

▶ The area is about 665.1 square units.

Find the area of the kite or rhombus.

8.

9.

10.

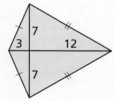

Find the area of the regular polygon.

11.

12.

13.

14. A platter is in the shape of a regular octagon with an apothem of 6 inches. Find the area of the platter.

11.4 **Volumes of Prisms and Cylinders** *(pp. 665–672)*

a. Tell whether the solid is a polyhedron. If it is, name the polyhedron.

▶ The solid is formed by polygons, so it is a polyhedron. The two bases are congruent octagons, so it is an octagonal prism.

b. Find the volume of the triangular prism.

6 in.   8 in.   5 in.

The area of a base is $B = \frac{1}{2}(6)(8) = 24$ in.^{2} and the height is $h = 5$ in.

$V = Bh$ Formula for volume of a prism

$= 24(5)$ Substitute.

$= 120$ Simplify.

▶ The volume is 120 cubic inches.

Tell whether the solid is a polyhedron. If it is, name the polyhedron.

15.

16.

17.

Find the volume of the solid.

18.
3.6 m   2.1 m   1.5 m

19.
8 mm   2 mm

20.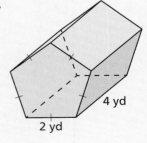
4 yd   2 yd

11.5 **Volumes of Pyramids** *(pp. 673–678)*

Find the volume of the pyramid.

$V = \frac{1}{3}Bh$ Formula for volume of a pyramid

$= \frac{1}{3}\left(\frac{1}{2} \cdot 5 \cdot 8\right)(12)$ Substitute.

$= 80$ Simplify.

▶ The volume is 80 cubic meters.

Find the volume of the pyramid.

21.

22.

23.

24. The volume of a square pyramid is 60 cubic inches and the height is 15 inches. Find the side length of the square base.

25. The volume of a square pyramid is 1024 cubic inches. The base has a side length of 16 inches. Find the height of the pyramid.

11.6 **Surface Areas and Volumes of Cones** *(pp. 679–684)*

Find the (a) surface area and (b) volume of the cone.

a. $S = \pi r^2 + \pi r \ell$ Formula for surface area of a cone

$= \pi \cdot 5^2 + \pi(5)(13)$ Substitute.

$= 90\pi$ Simplify.

≈ 282.74 Use a calculator.

▶ The surface area is 90π, or about 282.74 square centimeters.

b. $V = \frac{1}{3}\pi r^2 h$ Formula for volume of a cone

$= \frac{1}{3}\pi \cdot 5^2 \cdot 12$ Substitute.

$= 100\pi$ Simplify.

≈ 314.16 Use a calculator.

▶ The volume is 100π, or about 314.16 cubic centimeters.

Find the surface area and the volume of the cone.

26.

27.

28.

29. A cone with a diameter of 16 centimeters has a volume of 320π cubic centimeters. Find the height of the cone.

11.7   Surface Areas and Volumes of Spheres   *(pp. 685–692)*

Find the (a) surface area and (b) volume of the sphere.

a. $S = 4\pi r^2$ Formula for surface area of a sphere

$ = 4\pi(18)^2$ Substitute 18 for r.

$ = 1296\pi$ Simplify.

$ \approx 4071.50$ Use a calculator.

▶ The surface area is 1296π, or about 4071.50 square inches.

b. $V = \frac{4}{3}\pi r^3$ Formula for volume of a sphere

$ = \frac{4}{3}\pi(18)^3$ Substitute 18 for r.

$ = 7776\pi$ Simplify.

$ \approx 24{,}429.02$ Use a calculator.

▶ The volume is 7776π, or about 24,429.02 cubic inches.

Find the surface area and the volume of the sphere.

30.

31.

32.

33. The shape of Mercury can be approximated by a sphere with a diameter of 4880 kilometers. Find the surface area and the volume of Mercury.

34. A solid is composed of a cube with a side length of 6 meters and a hemisphere with a diameter of 6 meters. Find the volume of the composite solid.

Tell whether the solid is a polyhedron. If it is, name the polyhedron.

1.

2.

3.

Find the volume of the solid.

4.
15.5 m
8 m

5.
3.2 ft

6.
3 m 4 m
6 m
3 m 4 m

7.
4 ft
8 ft
5 ft 2 ft

Find the indicated measure.

8. circumference of ⊙F

64 in.
210°
D
F
E

9. $m\overset{\frown}{GH}$

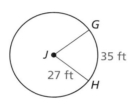
G
J
35 ft
27 ft
H

10. area of shaded sector

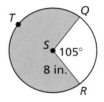
T Q
S 105°
8 in.
R

11. Find the surface area of a right cone with a diameter of 10 feet and a height of 12 feet.

12. You have a funnel with the dimensions shown.

6 cm
10 cm

  a. Find the approximate volume of the funnel.

  b. You use the funnel to put oil in a car. Oil flows out of the funnel at a rate of 45 milliliters per second. How long will it take to empty the funnel when it is full of oil? (1 mL = 1 cm³)

  c. How long would it take to empty a funnel with a radius of 10 centimeters and a height of 6 centimeters if oil flows out of the funnel at a rate of 45 milliliters per second?

  d. Explain why you can claim that the time calculated in part (c) is greater than the time calculated in part (b) without doing any calculations.

13. A water bottle in the shape of a cylinder has a volume of 500 cubic centimeters. The diameter of a base is 7.5 centimeters. What is the height of the bottle? Justify your answer.

14. Find the area of a dodecagon (12 sides) with a side length of 9 inches.

15. In general, a cardboard fan with a greater area does a better job of moving air and cooling you. The fan shown is a sector of a cardboard circle. Another fan has a radius of 6 centimeters and an intercepted arc of 150°. Which fan does a better job of cooling you?

120°
9 cm

1. The directed line segment RS is shown. Point Q is located along $\overrightarrow{RS}$ so that the ratio of RQ to QS is 2 to 3. What are the coordinates of point Q?

   (A) $Q(1.2, 3)$ (B) $Q(4, 2)$

   (C) $Q(2, 3)$ (D) $Q(-6, 7)$

2. In the diagram, $\overleftrightarrow{RS}$ is tangent to $\odot P$ at Q and $\overline{PQ}$ is a radius of $\odot P$. What must be true about $\overleftrightarrow{RS}$ and $\overline{PQ}$? Select all that apply.

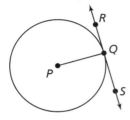

$PQ = \frac{1}{2}RS$	$PQ = RS$	$\overline{PQ}$ is tangent to $\odot P$.	$\overline{PQ} \perp \overleftrightarrow{RS}$

3. A crayon can be approximated by a composite solid made from a cylinder and a cone. A crayon box is a rectangular prism. The dimensions of a crayon and a crayon box containing 24 crayons are shown.

   a. Find the volume of a crayon.

   b. Find the amount of space within the crayon box not taken up by the crayons.

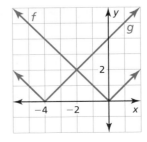

4. The graphs of $f(x) = |x|$ and $g(x) = |x + k|$ are shown. Find the value of k.

5. The top of the Washington Monument in Washington, D.C., is a square pyramid, called a *pyramidion*. What is the volume of the pyramidion?

55.5 ft

34.5 ft

A 22,019.63 ft³

B 172,006.91 ft³

C 66,058.88 ft³

D 207,530.08 ft³

6. Prove or disprove that the point $\left(1, \sqrt{3}\right)$ lies on the circle centered at the origin and containing the point (0, 2).

7. Enter the missing reasons in the proof of the Base Angles Theorem.

Given $\overline{AB} \cong \overline{AC}$

Prove $\angle B \cong \angle C$

STATEMENTS		REASONS	
1.	Draw $\overline{AD}$, the angle bisector of $\angle CAB$.	**1.**	Construction of angle bisector
2.	$\angle CAD \cong \angle BAD$	**2.**	_____
3.	$\overline{AB} \cong \overline{AC}$	**3.**	_____
4.	$\overline{DA} \cong \overline{DA}$	**4.**	_____
5.	$\triangle ADB \cong \triangle ADC$	**5.**	_____
6.	$\angle B \cong \angle C$	**6.**	_____

8. The diagram shows a square pyramid and a cone. Both solids have the same height, h, and the base of the cone has radius r. According to Cavalieri's Principle, the solids will have the same volume if the square base has sides of length _____.

9. A triangle has vertices $X(-2, 2)$, $Y(1, 4)$, and $Z(2, -2)$. Your friend claims that a translation of $(x, y) \rightarrow (x + 2, y - 3)$ and a dilation by a scale factor of 3 will produce a similarity transformation. Do you support your friend's claim? Explain your reasoning.

Selected Answers

Chapter 1

Chapter 1 Maintaining Mathematical Proficiency (p. 1)

1.

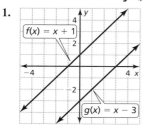

The graph of g is a horizontal translation 4 units right of the graph of f.

2.

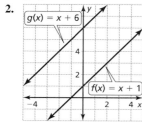

The graph of g is a vertical translation 5 units up of the graph of f.

3.

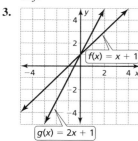

The graph of g is a horizontal shrink of the graph of f by a factor of $\frac{1}{2}$.

4.

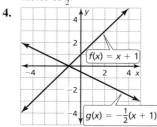

The graph of g is a vertical shrink by a factor of $\frac{1}{2}$ and a reflection in the x-axis of the graph of f.

5.

6.

7.

8.

9. *Sample answer:* $\overline{AB}$ with endpoints $A(-1, 2)$ and $B(2, -1)$

10. The possible inputs for f are all real numbers and the output is a. The input for its reflection is a and the possible outputs are all real numbers.

1.1 Vocabulary and Core Concept Check (p. 8)

1. vertex

3. *Sample answer:* $g(x) = a|x|$ is a vertical stretch or shrink, $g(x) = |x - h|$ is a horizontal translation, and $g(x) = |x| + k$ is a vertical translation.

1.1 Monitoring Progress and Modeling with Mathematics (pp. 8–10)

5.

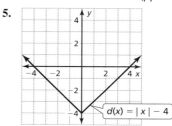

The graph of d is a vertical translation 4 units down of the graph of f; domain: all real numbers; range: $y \geq -4$

7.

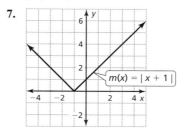

The graph of m is a horizontal translation 1 unit left of the graph of f; domain: all real numbers; range: $y \geq 0$

9.

The graph of p is a vertical shrink of the graph of f by a factor of $\frac{1}{3}$; domain: all real numbers; range: $y \ge 0$

11.

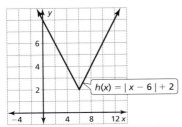

The graph of a is a vertical stretch of the graph of f by a factor of 5 and a reflection in the x-axis; domain: all real numbers; range: $y \le 0$

13.

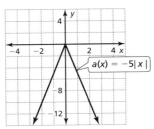

The graph of h is a vertical translation 2 units up of the graph of f.

15.

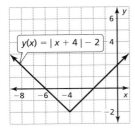

The graph of k is a vertical stretch of the graph of f by a factor of 3 and a reflection in the x-axis.

17.

The graph of y is a horizontal translation 1 unit left of the graph of f.

19. The graph of g is a vertical translation 3 units down of the graph of f; $k = -3$

21. The graph of p is a vertical stretch of the graph of f by a factor of 3 and a reflection in the x-axis; $a = -3$

23. $h(x) = |x| - 7$ **25.** $h(x) = \frac{1}{4}|x|$

27.

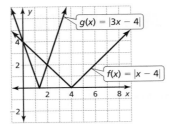

The graph of g is a horizontal shrink of the graph of f by a factor of $\frac{1}{3}$.

29.

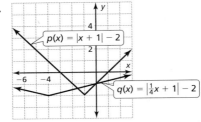

The graph of q is a horizontal stretch of the graph of p by a factor of 4.

31.

The graph of b is a horizontal shrink of the graph of a by a factor of $\frac{1}{4}$ and a reflection in the y-axis.

33. The transformations are a horizontal translation 2 units left then a vertical translation 6 units down.

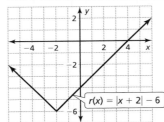

35. The transformations are a horizontal translation 3 units right, then a reflection in the x-axis, then a vertical translation 5 units up.

37. The transformations are a horizontal translation 4 units left, then a vertical shrink by a factor of $\frac{1}{2}$, then a vertical translation 1 unit down.

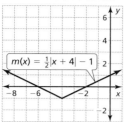

39. The transformations are a horizontal translation 1 unit left, then a reflection in the y-axis, then a vertical translation 5 units down.

41. a.

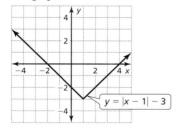

b. 50,000 pairs of shoes

43. a. $A'\left(-\frac{1}{2}, -2\right)$; $B'(1, -5)$; $C'(-4, -7)$

b. $A'\left(\frac{5}{2}, 3\right)$; $B'(4, 0)$; $C'(-1, -2)$

c. $A'\left(-\frac{1}{2}, -3\right)$; $B'(1, 0)$; $C'(-4, 2)$

d. $A'\left(-\frac{1}{2}, 12\right)$; $B'(1, 0)$; $C'(-4, -8)$

45. The graph should have a horizontal shift right, not left.

47. *Sample answer:* $f(x) = -|x| + 2$

49. The graph of p is a horizontal translation 6 units right of the graph of $f(x) = |x|$. The graph of q is a vertical translation 6 units down of the graph of $f(x) = |x|$.

51.

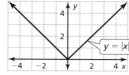

$y = -x$; $y = x$

53.

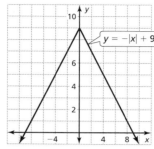

$y = x + 9$; $y = -x + 9$

55.

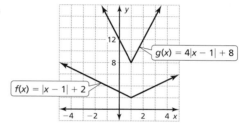

The graph of g is a vertical stretch by a factor of 4 of the graph of f.

57.

The graph of w is a vertical stretch of the graph of v by a factor of $\frac{3}{2}$ and a reflection in the x-axis.

59. The transformations are a vertical translation 4 units down, then a reflection in the x-axis, then a vertical shrink by a factor of $\frac{1}{2}$, then a horizontal translation 1 unit right; *Sample answer:* Determine the transformations from h to g, then perform the opposite transformations in reverse order.

61.

$x = 0$, $x = -4$

63. $\left(\frac{h}{a}, k\right)$

1.1 Maintaining Mathematical Proficiency (p. 10)

65. $w = \dfrac{P - 2\ell}{2}$ or $w = \dfrac{1}{2}P - \ell$

67. $y = -2x + 6$ **69.** $y = -x + 1$

1.2 Vocabulary and Core Concept Check (p. 16)

1. A piecewise function is a function defined by two or more equations. A step function is a special piecewise function defined by a constant value over each part of its domain.

1.2 Monitoring Progress and Modeling with Mathematics (pp. 16–18)

3. -16

5. 3

7. 8

9. 3

11. -1

13. 240 mi

15.
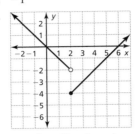
domain: all real numbers;
range: $y \geq -4$

17.
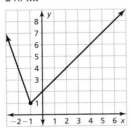
domain: all real numbers;
range: $y \geq 1$

19.
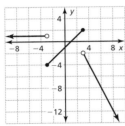
domain: all real numbers; range: $y \leq 2$

21. The wrong expression was used to evaluate the function; $f(5) = 5 + 8 = 13$

23. $f(x) = \begin{cases} x + 2, & \text{if } x < 0 \\ 2, & \text{if } x \geq 0 \end{cases}$

25. $f(x) = \begin{cases} -x, & \text{if } x < 4 \\ -x + 1, & \text{if } x \geq 4 \end{cases}$

27. $f(x) = \begin{cases} 1, & \text{if } x \leq -2 \\ 2x, & \text{if } -2 < x \leq 0 \\ -\frac{1}{2}x + 2, & \text{if } x > 0 \end{cases}$

29. $f(x) = \begin{cases} -5, & \text{if } -5 \leq x < -3 \\ -3, & \text{if } -3 \leq x < -1 \\ -1, & \text{if } -1 \leq x < 1 \end{cases}$

31.

domain: $0 \leq x < 8$;
range: 3, 4, 5, 6

33.

domain: $1 < x \leq 12$;
range: 1, 5, 6, 9

35. $C(p) = \begin{cases} 180, & \text{if } 0 < p \leq 5 \\ 210, & \text{if } 5 < p \leq 6 \\ 240, & \text{if } 6 < p \leq 7 \\ 270, & \text{if } 7 < p \leq 8 \\ 300, & \text{if } 8 < p \leq 9 \end{cases}$

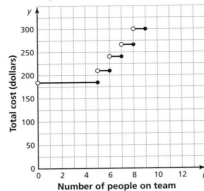

37. $y = \begin{cases} -x + 1, & \text{if } x < 0 \\ x + 1, & \text{if } x \geq 0 \end{cases}$

39. $y = \begin{cases} -x + 2, & \text{if } x < 2 \\ x - 2, & \text{if } x \geq 2 \end{cases}$

41. $y = \begin{cases} -2x - 6, & \text{if } x < -3 \\ 2x + 6, & \text{if } x \geq -3 \end{cases}$

43. $y = \begin{cases} 5x - 40, & \text{if } x < 8 \\ -5x + 40, & \text{if } x \geq 8 \end{cases}$

45. $y = \begin{cases} x - 1, & \text{if } x < 3 \\ -x + 5, & \text{if } x \geq 3 \end{cases}$

47. a. $f(x) = 2|x - 3|$ **b.** $f(x) = \begin{cases} -2x + 6, & \text{if } x < 3 \\ 2x - 6, & \text{if } x \geq 3 \end{cases}$

49. a. -4 **b.** 6

51.
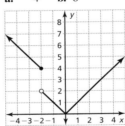
domain: all real numbers; range: $y \geq 0$

53.
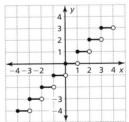
yes; yes; It is a function defined by two or more equations and it is defined by a constant value over each part of its domain.

55. a. $f(x) = \begin{cases} x, & \text{if } 0 \leq x \leq 2 \\ 2x - 2, & \text{if } 2 < x \leq 8 \\ x + 6, & \text{if } 8 < x \leq 9 \end{cases}$

b. no; The total accumulation is 15 inches.

1.2 Maintaining Mathematical Proficiency *(p. 18)*

57. $t \leq 4$ or $t \geq 18$

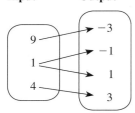

59. The transformations are a vertical stretch by a factor of 2.5 then a reflection in *x*-axis.

61. The transformations are a horizontal translation 3 units left then a vertical stretch by a factor of 4.

1.3 Vocabulary and Core Concept Check *(p. 23)*

1. inverse relation

1.3 Monitoring Progress and Modeling with Mathematics *(pp. 23–24)*

3. $(0, 1), (-8, 3), (-3, 4), (-5, 7), (-1, 9)$

5.

Input	8	6	0	6	8
Output	-5	-5	0	5	10

7. Input   Output

9. $x = y - 5; -3$ **11.** $x = 4y + 4; 12$

13.

domain of inverse: all real numbers; range of inverse: all real numbers

15. $g(x) = \frac{1}{3}x$

17. $g(x) = \frac{x + 1}{4}$

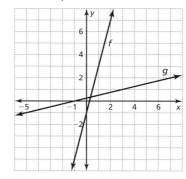

19. $g(x) = -\frac{x + 2}{3}$

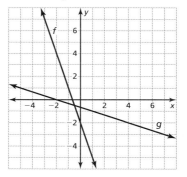

21. $g(x) = 3x - 24$

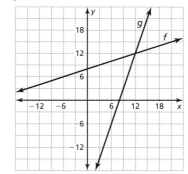

23. *x* and *y* were not switched in the equation; The inverse of *f* is $g(x) = \frac{x - 5}{3}$ or $g(x) = \frac{x}{3} - \frac{5}{3}$.

25. $D = 1.33899E$; about 334.75 U.S. dollars

27. *Sample answer:* $f(x) = \frac{1}{4}x$

29. **a.**

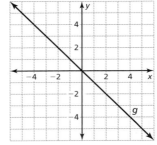

For each point $(a, -a)$ that is on the graph of $g(x) = -x$, the point $(-a, a)$ is also on the graph.

b.

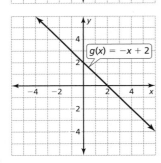

c. The linear function $f(x) = mx + b$ is its own inverse when $m = -1$ and b is any real number or when $m = 1$ and $b = 0$.

31. The inverse of $f(x) = mx + b$, where $b \neq 0$, is

$g(x) = \dfrac{x - b}{m} = \dfrac{1}{m}x - \dfrac{b}{m}$, which is a linear function. The

graph of the inverse function g has a slope of $\dfrac{1}{m}$ and a

y-intercept of $-\dfrac{b}{m}$.

1.3 Maintaining Mathematical Proficiency (p. 24)

33. -1331

35. $-\dfrac{1}{729}$

37. 9.44×10^{-3}

39. 8.2×10^{-8}

1.4 Vocabulary and Core Concept Check (p. 32)

1. Product of Powers Property, Power of a Power Property, definition of negative exponents; Use the Product of Powers Property to simplify the expression inside the parentheses to 4^4. Then, use the Power of a Power Property to simplify the entire expression to 4^{-8}. Then, use the definition of negative exponents to produce the final answer, $\dfrac{1}{4^8} = \dfrac{1}{65{,}536}$.

3. The Quotient of Powers Property is used when dividing powers that have the same base. The answer is the common base raised to the difference of the exponents of the numerator and denominator.

1.4 Monitoring Progress and Modeling with Mathematics (pp. 32–34)

5. 1

7. $\dfrac{1}{625}$

9. $\dfrac{1}{16}$

11. $-\dfrac{4}{3}$

13. $\dfrac{1}{x^7}$

15. $\dfrac{9}{y^3}$

17. $\dfrac{1}{4m^3}$

19. $\dfrac{b^7}{64}$

21. $\dfrac{32x^7}{y^6}$

23. 625

25. 6561

27. p^{24}

29. $\dfrac{1}{216}$

31. x^2

33. 10^{-2} m

35. The product has a base of 2, not $2 \cdot 2$; $2^4 \cdot 2^5 = 2^9$

37. $-125z^3$

39. $\dfrac{n^2}{36}$

41. $\dfrac{1}{243s^{40}}$

43. $\dfrac{36}{w^6}$

45. B, C, D; These expressions simplify to be the volume of the sphere, which is $\dfrac{32\pi s^6}{3}$.

47. $\dfrac{16y^{28}}{81x^{12}}$

49. $\dfrac{n^{10}}{144m^4}$

51. 4.5×10^{-3}; 0.0045

53. 4×10^2; 400

55. about 4.113×10^4 lb/acre; about 41,130 lb/acre

57. **a.** Power of a Product Property

b. Express $\dfrac{(6x)^3}{(2x)^3}$ as $\left(\dfrac{6x}{2x}\right)^3$. Simplify the expression inside the parentheses to produce $(3)^3$, so the volume is 27 times greater.

59. $(2ab)^3$

61. $(2w^3z^2)^6$

63. **a.** $\left(\dfrac{1}{6}\right)^n$ **b.** $\dfrac{1}{1296}$

c. $\dfrac{1}{32}$; The probability of flipping heads once is $\dfrac{1}{2}$, and $\left(\dfrac{1}{2}\right)^5$ is $\dfrac{1}{32}$.

65. $x = 8, y = -1$; Using the Quotient of Powers Property, you can conclude from the first equation that $x - y = 9$. Using the Product of Powers Property and the Quotient of Powers Property, you can conclude from the second equation that $x + 2 - 3y = 13$. Use these equations to solve a system of linear equations.

67. no; The mass of the seed from the double coconut palm is 10 kilograms.

69. **a.** When $a > 1$ and $n < 0$, $a^n < a^{-n}$ because a^n will be less than 1 and a^{-n} will be greater than 1. When $a > 1$ and $n = 0$, $a^n = a^{-n} = 1$, because any number to the zero power is 1. When $a > 1$ and $n > 0$, $a^n > a^{-n}$ because a^n will be greater than 1 and a^{-n} will be less than 1.

b. When $0 < a < 1$ and $n < 0$, $a^n > a^{-n}$, because a^n will be greater than 1 and a^{-n} will be less than 1. When $0 < a < 1$ and $n = 0$, $a^n = a^{-n} = 1$, because any number to the zero power is 1. When $0 < a < 1$ and $n > 0$, $a^n < a^{-n}$ because a^n will be less than 1 and a^{-n} will be greater than 1.

1.4 Maintaining Mathematical Proficiency (p. 34)

71. -10

73. natural number, whole number, integer, rational number, real number

75. irrational number, real number

1.5 Vocabulary and Core Concept Check (p. 39)

1. Find the fourth root of 81, or what real number multiplied by itself four times produces 81.

1.5 Monitoring Progress and Modeling with Mathematics (pp. 39–40)

3. $10^{1/2}$

5. $\sqrt[3]{15}$

7. ± 6

9. 10

11. $s = 4$ in.

13. 4

15. -7

17. 2

19. $8^{4/5}$

21. $\left(\sqrt[7]{-4}\right)^2$

23. 8

25. not a real number

27. -32

29. The numerator and denominator are reversed; $\left(\sqrt[3]{2}\right)^4 = 2^{4/3}$

31. $\frac{1}{10}$

33. $\frac{1}{9}$

35. 6 ft^2

37. about 1 in.

39. Write the radicand, a, as the base and write the exponent as a fraction with the power, m, as the numerator and the index, n, as the denominator.

41. about 5.5%

43. -1, 0, and 1

45. $(xy)^{1/2}$

47. $2xy^2$

49. about 1.38 ft

51. always; Power of a Power Property

53. always; definition of rational exponent

55. sometimes; false when $x = 0$ because division by 0 is undefined

1.5 Maintaining Mathematical Proficiency (p. 40)

57. $f(-3) = -16; f(0) = -10; f(8) = 6$

59. $h(-3) = 16; h(0) = 13; h(8) = 5$

1.6 Vocabulary and Core Concept Check (p. 47)

1. The initial amount is 2.4, the growth factor is 1.5, and the percent increase is 0.5 or 50%.

1.6 Monitoring Progress and Modeling with Mathematics (pp. 47–50)

3. **a.** $\frac{1}{4}$
   b. 8

5. **a.** $\frac{8}{9}$
   b. 216

7. **a.** $\frac{46}{9}$
   b. 32

9. exponential growth

11. exponential decay

13. exponential growth

15. exponential growth

17. exponential decay

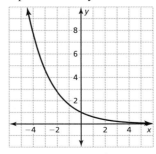

19. $b = 3$

21. a. $y = 494(1.03)^t$; about 664; The population of Austin was about 664,000 at the end of the decade.

    b. about 6 years after the start of the decade

23. The percent decrease needs to be subtracted from 1 to produce the decay factor.

$$y = \left(\begin{matrix}\text{Initial}\\\text{amount}\end{matrix}\right)\left(\begin{matrix}\text{Decay}\\\text{factor}\end{matrix}\right)^t;$$
$$y = 500(1 - 0.02)^t; y = 500(0.98)^t$$

25. $f(0) = 3, f(n) = 7 \cdot f(n - 1)$

27. $f(0) = 12, f(n) = 0.5 \cdot f(n - 1)$

29. $f(0) = 0.5, f(n) = 3 \cdot f(n - 1)$

31. $f(0) = 4, f(n) = \frac{1}{6} \cdot f(n - 1)$

33. The inputs are equally spaced and the common ratio is 2; $f(0) = 0.75, f(n) = 2 \cdot f(n - 1)$

35. The inputs are equally spaced and the common ratio is $\frac{1}{2}$; $f(0) = 96, f(n) = \frac{1}{2} \cdot f(n - 1)$

37. $f(x) = 24(0.1)^x$

39. *Sample answer:* The number of bacteria in a dish after n hours; $f(0) = 1, f(n) = 2 \cdot f(n - 1)$; 64; There are 64 bacteria after 6 hours.

41. exponential decay; 40%   **43.** exponential growth; $33\frac{1}{3}\%$

45. a. The website had 2500 referrals at the beginning of the 10-year period and the number of referrals increased by a factor of 1.50 each year.

    b. 50%; $1 + r = 1.50$, so $r = 0.50$ or 50%

47. Power of a Power Property; Evaluate power; Rewrite in form $y = a(1 + r)^t$.

49. $y \approx 1.52(0.9)^t$; exponential decay; 10%

51. $y \approx 2(1.69)^t$; exponential growth; about 69%

53. $x(t) \approx (1.20)^t$; exponential growth; about 20%

55. $b(t) \approx 0.67(0.55)^t$; exponential decay; 45%

57. $y = a(1 + 0.26)^t$; 26% growth

59. $y = a(1 - 0.04)^t$; 4% decay

61. $y = a(1 + 255)^t$; 25,500% growth

63. about 0.01%

65. a. $y = 25,000(1.055)^t$ **b.** about 0.45%

    c.

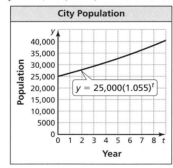

City Population

$y = 25,000(1.055)^t$

about 30,971 people

67. no; $f(x) = 2^x$ eventually increases at a faster rate than $g(x) = 4x$, but not for all $x \geq 0$.

69. a. $y \approx 325(0.9943)^{60t} = 325(0.9943^{60})^t \approx 325(0.7097)^t$;
$y \approx 325(0.843)^{2t} = 325(0.843^2)^t \approx 325(0.7106)^t$

    b. The initial amount of ibuprofen is 325 milligrams in each function. The percent decrease in the first function is about 0.57% each minute. The percent decrease in the second function is about 15.7% each half hour.

71. a. $\dfrac{f(x + 1)}{f(x)} = \dfrac{ab^{x + 1}}{ab^x} = \dfrac{b^{x + 1}}{b^x} = b^{(x + 1) - x} = b^1 = b$

    b. The equation shows that when a value of the function is divided by the previous value, the answer is the constant b. Dividing the y-values in the table by the previous value does not always produce the same number.

73. a. The decay factor is 0.9978. The percent decrease is 0.22%.

    b.

Eggs Produced by Leghorn

    c. about 134 eggs per year

    d. Replace $\dfrac{w}{52}$ with y, where y represents the age of the chicken in years.

1.6 Maintaining Mathematical Proficiency *(p. 50)*

75. $4x$ **77.** $5z + 9$

79. $\dfrac{1}{x^7}$ **81.** $36x^2$

Chapter 1 Review *(pp. 52–54)*

1.

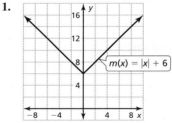

$m(x) = |x| + 6$

The graph of m is a vertical translation 6 units up of the graph of f; domain: all real numbers; range: $y \geq 6$

2.

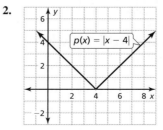

$p(x) = |x - 4|$

The graph of p is a horizontal translation 4 units right of the graph of f; domain: all real numbers; range: $y \geq 0$

3.

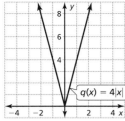

The graph of q is a vertical stretch of the graph of f by a factor of 4; domain: all real numbers; range: $y \geq 0$

4.

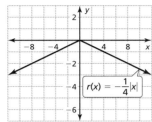

The graph of r is a vertical shrink of the graph of f by a factor of $\frac{1}{4}$ and a reflection in the x-axis; domain: all real numbers; range: $y \leq 0$

5.

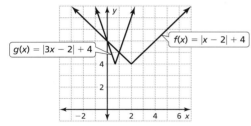

The graph of g is a horizontal shrink of the graph of f by a factor of $\frac{1}{3}$.

6. *Sample answer:* Identify and plot the vertex $(-1, 2)$. Plot another point such as $(0, -1)$ and use symmetry to plot a third point, $(-2, -1)$. Then draw the V-shaped graph.

7. a. The transformations are a horizontal translation 1 unit right, then a vertical shrink by a factor of $\frac{1}{3}$, then a vertical translation 2 units down.

b.

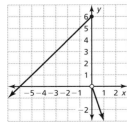

8. a. 3 **b.** -10

9.

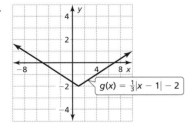

domain: all real numbers; range: $y \leq 6$

10.

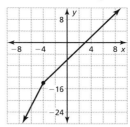

domain: all real numbers; range: all real numbers

11. $y = \begin{cases} -x + 15, & \text{if } x < 0 \\ x + 15, & \text{if } x \geq 0 \end{cases}$

12. $y = \begin{cases} -4x - 20, & \text{if } x < -5 \\ 4x + 20, & \text{if } x \geq -5 \end{cases}$

13. $y = \begin{cases} -2x - 7, & \text{if } x < -2 \\ 2x + 1, & \text{if } x \geq -2 \end{cases}$

14. $f(x) = \begin{cases} 65, & \text{if } 0 < x \leq 1 \\ 100, & \text{if } 1 < x \leq 2 \\ 135, & \text{if } 2 < x \leq 3 \end{cases}$

15. $(-10, 1), (-4, 3), (4, 5), (14, 7), (26, 9)$

16. $g(x) = \frac{4}{3}x$

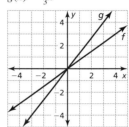

17. $g(x) = \dfrac{10 - x}{5}$

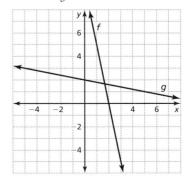

18. $g(x) = -\frac{5}{2}x + 15$

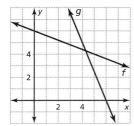

19. $a = 210 - 1.25h$; 175   **20.** $\dfrac{1}{y^2}$

21. $\dfrac{1}{x^3}$ **22.** y^6

23. $\dfrac{25y^8}{4x^4}$ **24.** 2

25. -3 **26.** 125

27. not a real number

28. exponential decay; 66.67%

29. exponential growth; 400%

30. exponential decay; 80%

31. $f(t) \approx 7.81(1.25)^t$, exponential growth; 25%
32. $y \approx 1.59^t$, exponential growth, about 59%
33. $f(t) \approx 12.05(0.84)^t$, exponential decay; 16%

Chapter 2

Chapter 2 Maintaining Mathematical Proficiency *(p. 59)*

1. $5x - 7$ **2.** $-5r + 5$
3. $2t - 1$ **4.** $3s + 2$
5. $9m - 21$ **6.** $3h + 26$
7. 4   **8.** 21
9. 27   **10.** 12
11. 4   **12.** 1
13. no; The number 1 is a factor of every integer.

2.1 Vocabulary and Core Concept Check *(p. 66)*

1. when the exponents of the terms decrease from left to right
3. Determine if performing the operation on any two numbers in the set always results in a number that is also in the set.

2.1 Monitoring Progress and Modeling with Mathematics *(pp. 66–68)*

5. 1   **7.** 2
9. 9   **11.** 11
13. $2c^4 + 6c^2 - c$; 4; 2; trinomial
15. $3p^2 + 7$; 2; 3; binomial
17. $3t^8$; 8; 3; monomial
19. $-\frac{5}{7}r^8 + 2r^5 + \pi r^2$; 8; $-\frac{5}{7}$; trinomial
21. It is the product of a number, $\frac{4}{3}\pi$, and a variable with a whole number exponent, r^3; 3
23. $3y + 10$ **25.** $n^2 - 8n + 5$
27. $6g^2 - 9g + 4$ **29.** $a^3 - 5a^2 + 4a + 5$
31. $-2d - 8$ **33.** $-2y^2 + 2y + 18$
35. $k^3 - k^2 - 7k + 14$ **37.** $t^4 + 8t^2 + 8t - 12$
39. When writing the subtraction as addition, the last term of the polynomial was not multiplied by -1;
$= (x^2 + x) + (-2x^2 + 3x) = (x^2 - 2x^2) + (x + 3x)$
$= -x^2 + 4x$
41. $3b + 2$ **43.** $s^2 - 12st$
45. $2c^2 - 2cd - 4d^2$
47. always; A polynomial is a monomial or a sum of monomials, and each monomial is a term of the polynomial.
49. sometimes; The two terms in the binomial can be of any degree.
51. $-16t^2 - 45t + 200$; 139 ft
53. **a.** $-46t + 92$
   b. The constant term 92 indicates that the distance between the two balls is 92 feet when they begin. The coefficient of the linear term -46 indicates that the two balls become 46 feet closer to each other each second.
55. $12x - 3$
57. yes; Addition is commutative and associative, so you can add in any order.
59. **a.** no; The product of two negative integers is always a positive integer.
   b. yes; The sum of two whole numbers is always a whole number.
61. **a.** $19x^2 - 12x$ **b.** $14,310

2.1 Maintaining Mathematical Proficiency *(p. 68)*

63. $34y - 34$

2.2 Vocabulary and Core Concept Check (p. 73)

1. *Sample answer:* Distribute one of the binomials over each term in the other binomial and simplify; Write each binomial as a sum of terms and make a table of products.

2.2 Monitoring Progress and Modeling with Mathematics (pp. 73–74)

3. $x^2 + 4x + 3$ **5.** $z^2 - 2z - 15$

7. $g^2 - 9g + 14$ **9.** $3m^2 + 28m + 9$

11. $x^2 + 5x + 6$ **13.** $h^2 - 17h + 72$

15. $12k^2 + 23k - 9$ **17.** $8j^2 - 26j + 21$

19. t also should be multiplied by $t + 5$; $= t(t + 5) - 2(t + 5)$ $= t^2 + 5t - 2t - 10 = t^2 + 3t - 10$

21. $b^2 + 10b + 21$ **23.** $k^2 + 4k - 5$

25. $q^2 - \frac{1}{2}q - \frac{3}{16}$ **27.** $3r^2 - 29r + 18$

29. $w^3 + 8w^2 + 15w$ **31.** $2x^2 + x - 45$

33. $\frac{1}{2}x^2 + \frac{11}{2}x + 15$ **35.** $x^3 + 7x^2 + 14x + 8$

37. $y^3 + 11y^2 + 22y - 6$

39. $-5b^3 + 15b^2 + 24b - 16$

41. $18e^3 - 27e^2 + 37e + 7$

43. a. $(40x^2 + 240x + 200)$ ft^2 **b.** 57,600 ft^2

45. The degree of the product is the sum of the degrees of each binomial.

47. no; FOIL would leave out the products that include the middle terms of the two trinomials.

49. yes; You are both multiplying the same binomials, and neither the order in which you multiply nor the method used will make a difference.

51. a. They have the same signs.
b. They have opposite signs.

2.2 Maintaining Mathematical Proficiency (p. 74)

53. $y = \begin{cases} -6x + 18, & \text{if } x < 3 \\ 6x - 18, & \text{if } x \geq 3 \end{cases}$

55. 10^{11} **57.** $\frac{1}{27z^{18}}$

2.3 Vocabulary and Core Concept Check (p. 79)

1. Substitute the first term of the binomial for a and the second term of the binomial for b in the square of a binomial pattern, then simplify.

2.3 Monitoring Progress and Modeling with Mathematics (pp. 79–80)

3. $x^2 + 16x + 64$ **5.** $4f^2 - 4f + 1$

7. $49t^2 - 56t + 16$ **9.** $4a^2 + 4ab + b^2$

11. $x^2 + 8x + 16$ **13.** $49n^2 - 70n + 25$

15. $t^2 - 49$ **17.** $16x^2 - 1$

19. $64 - 9a^2$ **21.** $p^2 - 100q^2$

23. $y^2 - 16$ **25.** 384

27. 1764 **29.** 930.25

31. The middle term in the square of a binomial pattern was not included; $= k^2 + 2(k)(4) + 4^2 = k^2 + 8k + 16$

33. a. $(x^2 + 100x + 2500)$ ft^2 **b.** 4225 ft^2; 1725 ft^2

35. a. 25%
b. $(0.5N + 0.5a)^2 = 0.25N^2 + 0.5Na + 0.25a^2$

37. $(x + 11)(x - 11)$; $x^2 - 121$ fits the product side of the sum and difference pattern, so working backwards, a and b are the square roots of a^2 and b^2.

39. $x^4 - 1$ **41.** $4m^4 - 20m^2n^2 + 25n^4$

43. no; $\left(4\frac{1}{3}\right)^2$ can be written as $\left(4 + \frac{1}{3}\right)^2$, however using the square of a binomial pattern results in $16 + \frac{8}{3} + \frac{1}{9}$, which is $18\frac{7}{9}$, not $16\frac{1}{9}$.

45. $k = 64$

47. *Sample answer:* $a = 3, b = 4$

2.3 Maintaining Mathematical Proficiency (p. 80)

49. $9(r + 3)$ **51.** $5(3x - 2y)$

2.4 Vocabulary and Core Concept Check (p. 85)

1. Set $3x = 0$ and $x - 6 = 0$, then solve both of the equations to get the solutions $x = 0$ and $x = 6$.

2.4 Monitoring Progress and Modeling with Mathematics (pp. 85–86)

3. $x = 0, x = -7$ **5.** $t = 0, t = 5$

7. $s = 9, s = 1$ **9.** $a = 3, a = -5$

11. $m = -\frac{4}{5}$ **13.** $g = \frac{3}{2}, g = 7$

15. $z = 0, z = -2, z = 1$ **17.** $r = 4, r = -8$

19. $c = 3, c = -1, c = 6$ **21.** $x = 8, x = -8$

23. $x = 14, x = 5$ **25.** $5z(z + 9)$

27. $3y^2(y - 3)$ **29.** $n^5(5n + 2)$

31. $p = 0, p = \frac{1}{4}$ **33.** $c = 0, c = -\frac{5}{2}$

35. $n = 0, n = 3$

37. also need to set $6x = 0$ and solve; $6x = 0$ or $x + 5 = 0$; $x = 0$ or $x = -5$; The roots are $x = 0$ and $x = -5$.

39. 20 ft

41. $x = 0, x = 0.3$ sec; The roots represent the times when the penguin is at water level. $x = 0$ is when it leaves the water, and $x = 0.3$ sec is when it returns to the water after the leap.

43. 2; x-intercepts occur when $y = 0$ and the equation has 2 roots when $y = 0$.

45. no; Roots will occur if $x^2 + 3 = 0$ or $x^4 + 1 = 0$. However, solving these equations results in $x^2 = -3$ or $x^4 = -1$, and even powers of any number cannot be negative.

47. a. $x = -y, x = \frac{1}{2}y$ **b.** $x = \pm y, x = -4y$

2.4 Maintaining Mathematical Proficiency (p. 86)

49. 1, 10; 2, 5 **51.** 1, 30; 2, 15; 3, 10; 5, 6

2.5 Vocabulary and Core Concept Check (p. 93)

1. They have opposite signs; When factoring $x^2 + bx + c = (x + p)(x + q)$, if c is negative, p and q must have opposite signs.

2.5 Monitoring Progress and Modeling with Mathematics (pp. 93–94)

3. $(x + 1)(x + 7)$ **5.** $(n + 4)(n + 5)$

7. $(h + 2)(h + 9)$ **9.** $(v - 1)(v - 4)$

11. $(d - 2)(d - 3)$ **13.** $(w - 8)(w - 9)$

15. $(x - 1)(x + 4)$ **17.** $(n - 2)(n + 6)$

19. $(y - 6)(y + 8)$ **21.** $(x + 4)(x - 5)$

23. $(t + 2)(t - 8)$

25. a. $(x - 5)$ ft **b.** 16 ft

27. $4 + 12$ is not 14; $= (x + 6)(x + 8)$

29. $m = -1, m = -2$ **31.** $x = 2, x = -7$

33. $t = -3, t = -12$ **35.** $a = 5, a = -10$

37. $m = 4, m = 11$ **39.** 100 in.^{2}

41. yes; p and q must be factors of -12 that have a sum of b, and -12 has 6 sets of integer factors, -1 and 12, -2 and 6, -3 and 4, -4 and 3, -6 and 2, and -12 and 1.

43. length: 11 ft, width: 4 ft

45. $x^2 - 2x - 24 = 0$; Multiply $(x + 4)(x - 6)$.

47. a. $-x^2 + 38x$ **b.** $-x^2 + 38x = 280$; 10 m

49. $(r + 3s)(r + 4s)$ **51.** $(x + 5y)(x - 7y)$

2.5 Maintaining Mathematical Proficiency (p. 94)

53. $z = -17$ **55.** $k = 0$

2.6 Vocabulary and Core Concept Check (p. 99)

1. 3

2.6 Monitoring Progress and Modeling with Mathematics (pp. 99–100)

3. $3(x - 1)(x + 2)$ **5.** $4(k + 3)(k + 4)$

7. $7(b - 4)(b - 5)$ **9.** $(3h + 2)(h + 3)$

11. $(2x - 1)(3x - 1)$ **13.** $(n + 2)(3n - 1)$

15. $2(g - 2)(4g + 3)$ **17.** $-(t - 3)(3t - 2)$

19. $-(c - 5)(4c + 1)$ **21.** $-(3w - 4)(5w + 7)$

23. need to factor 2 out of every term;
    $= 2(x^2 - x - 12) = 2(x + 3)(x - 4)$

25. $x = -2, x = 3$ **27.** $n = -\frac{5}{3}, n = \frac{3}{4}$

29. $x = -\frac{7}{2}, x = 5$ **31.** $x = -1, x = \frac{5}{7}$

33. a. $(5x - 2)$ ft

   b. Substitute 3 for x into the expression for the area $15x^2 - x - 2$, then simplify; Substitute 3 for x into the expressions for the length $(5x - 2)$ and width $(3x + 1)$, simplify each, then multiply these two numbers.

35. length: 70 m, width: 31 m

37. *Sample answer:* $6x^2 + 3x$

39. when no combination of factors of a and c produce the correct middle term; *Sample answer:* $2x^2 + x + 1$

41. $\pm9, \pm12, \pm21$ **43.** 3.5 in.

45. $(k + 2j)(4k - j)$ **47.** $-(a - 2b)(6a - 7b)$

2.6 Maintaining Mathematical Proficiency (p. 100)

49.

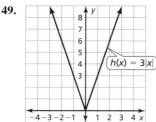

The graph of h is a vertical stretch of the graph of f by a factor of 3; domain: all real numbers; range: $y \geq 0$

51.

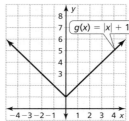

The graph of g is a vertical translation 1 unit up of the graph of f; domain: all real numbers; range: $y \geq 1$

53. -6 **55.** 32

2.7 Vocabulary and Core Concept Check (p. 105)

1. yes; The square roots of the first and last terms are y and 8, and the middle term is $2 \cdot y \cdot 8$, so it fits the pattern.

2.7 Monitoring Progress and Modeling with Mathematics (pp. 105–106)

3. $(m + 7)(m - 7)$ **5.** $(8 + 9d)(8 - 9d)$

7. $9(5a + 2b)(5a - 2b)$ **9.** 63

11. 900   **13.** 600

15. $(h + 6)^2$ **17.** $(y - 11)^2$

19. $(a - 14)^2$ **21.** $(5n + 2)^2$

23. should follow the difference of two squares pattern;
    $= (n + 8)(n - 8)$

25. a. $(d + 4)$ cm   **b.** $(4d + 16)$ cm

27. $z = -2, z = 2$ **29.** $k = 8$

31. $n = 3$ **33.** $y = -\frac{1}{4}$

35. $3(z + 3)(z - 3)$ **37.** $4(y - 2)^2$

39. $2(5y + 6)^2$ **41.** 1.25 sec

43. a. no; $w^2 + 18w + 81$ **b.** no; $y^2 - 10y + 25$

45. Square each binomial, then combine like terms; Use the difference of two squares pattern with each binomial as one of the terms, then simplify; *Sample answer:* The difference of two squares pattern; You do not need to square any binomials.

47. a. $(9x^2 - 144)$ in.^{2}

   b. 5 in.; Setting the polynomial in part (a) equal to 81 and solving results in $x = -5$ or $x = 5$. Length cannot be negative, so 5 is the solution.

2.7 Maintaining Mathematical Proficiency (p. 106)

49. $2 \cdot 5^2$ **51.** $5 \cdot 17$

53. $g(x) = x + 3$ **55.** $g(x) = 2x + 2$

   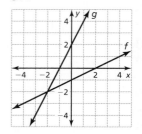

2.8 Vocabulary and Core Concept Check (p. 111)

1. It is written as a product of unfactorable polynomials with integer coefficients.

2.8 Monitoring Progress and Modeling with Mathematics (pp. 111–112)

3. $(x + 1)(x^2 + 2)$
5. $(z - 4)(3z^2 + 2)$
7. $(x + y)(x + 8)$
9. $(m - 3)(m + n)$
11. $2x(x + 1)(x - 1)$
13. unfactorable
15. $6g(g - 2)^2$
17. $3r^3(r + 6)(r - 5)$
19. $-4c^2(c^2 - 2c + 7)$
21. $(b - 5)(b + 2)(b - 2)$
23. $n = 0, n = 2, n = 4$
25. $x = -1, x = -2, x = 2$
27. $s = 0, s = 2, s = -2$
29. $x = 0, x = -9, x = 9$
31. $x = 0, x = 4$
33. In the second group, factor out -6 instead of 6;
$= a^2(a + 8) - 6(a + 8) = (a + 8)(a^2 - 6)$
35. a. $(4w^2 + 16w)$ in.^{3}
 b. length: 4 in., width: 4 in., height: 8 in.
37. $(x + 2y)(x + 1)(x - 1)$ **39.** $(4s - 1)(s + 3t)$
41. no; The factors of the polynomial are $x^2 + 3$ and $x + 2$. Using the Zero-Product Property, $x + 2 = 0$ will give 1 real solution, but $x^2 + 3 = 0$ has no real solutions.
43. a. *Sample answer:* $x^3 + x^2 + x + 2$
 b. *Sample answer:* $x^3 + x^2 + x + 1$
45. $3z, 2z + 3, 2z - 3$ **47.** radius: 5, height: 8
49. a. *Sample answer:* $w = 40$; When $w = 40$, factoring out $5x$ will leave a perfect square trinomial, so there will be 2 factors.
 b. *Sample answer:* $w = 50$; When $w = 50$, factoring out $5x$ will leave a factorable trinomial that is not a perfect square, so there will be 3 factors.

2.8 Maintaining Mathematical Proficiency (p. 112)

51. $(2, 3)$ **53.** $(-6, -2)$
55. exponential decay   **57.** exponential growth

Chapter 2 Review (pp. 114–116)

1. $2x^2 + 6$; 2; 2; binomial
2. $5p^6 - 3p^3 - 4$; 6; 5; trinomial
3. $9x^7 + 13x^5 - 6x^2$; 7; 9; trinomial
4. $8y^3 - 12y$; 3; 8; binomial   **5.** $4a + 6$
6. $3x^2 + 6x + 10$ **7.** $-2y^2 + 6y + 4$
8. $-6p^2 - 12p + 7$ **9.** $x^2 + 2x - 24$
10. $3y^2 - 7y - 40$ **11.** $x^3 + 11x^2 + 28x$
12. $-12y^3 + 7y^2 + 20y - 7$ **13.** $x^2 - 81$
14. $4y^2 - 16$ **15.** $p^2 + 8p + 16$
16. $4d^2 - 4d + 1$ **17.** $x = 0, x = -5$
18. $z = -3, z = 7$ **19.** $b = -13$
20. $y = 0, y = 9, y = -4$ **21.** $(p + 7)(p - 5)$
22. $(b + 8)(b + 10)$ **23.** $(z + 3)(z - 7)$
24. $(x - 7)(x - 4)$ **25.** $(t + 6)(3t - 2)$
26. $-(y + 4)(5y + 2)$ **27.** $(2x + 1)(3x + 7)$
28. $-(y - 2)(2y - 3)$ **29.** $(z + 9)(3z - 1)$
30. $(2a - 3)(5a + 1)$ **31.** $(x + 3)(x - 3)$
32. $(y + 10)(y - 10)$ **33.** $(z - 3)^2$
34. $(m + 8)^2$ **35.** $n(n + 3)(n - 3)$
36. $(x - 3)(x + 4a)$ **37.** $2x^2(x^2 + x - 10)$
38. $x = 0, x = 6, x = -3$ **39.** $x = -\frac{3}{2}, x = \frac{3}{2}$
40. $z = -3, z = 5, z = -5$
41. length: 12 ft, width: 4 ft, height: 2 ft

Chapter 3 Maintaining Mathematical Proficiency (p. 121)

1.
2.
3.
4.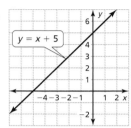

5. 11   **6.** 8
7. -11 **8.** -7
9. 3   **10.** -26
11. $a, 4a, 9a, 16a, 25a$; *Sample answer:* The coefficient of each difference is the next consecutive odd integer; $36a$

3.1 Vocabulary and Core Concept Check (p. 127)

1. parabola

3.1 Monitoring Progress and Modeling with Mathematics (pp. 127–128)

3. The vertex is $(1, -1)$. The axis of symmetry is $x = 1$. The domain is all real numbers. The range is $y \leq -1$. When $x < 1$, y increases as x increases. When $x > 1$, y increases as x decreases.

5.

The graph of g is a vertical stretch by a factor of 6 of the graph of f.

7.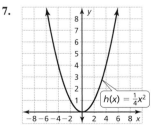

The graph of h is a vertical shrink by a factor of $\frac{1}{4}$ of the graph of f.

9.

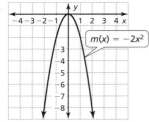

The graph of *m* is a vertical stretch by a factor of 2 and a reflection in the *x*-axis of the graph of *f*.

11.

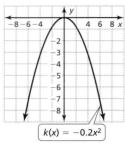

The graph of *k* is a vertical shrink by a factor of 0.2 and a reflection in the *x*-axis of the graph of *f*.

13.

The graph of $y = 4x^2$ is a reflection in the *x*-axis of the graph of $y = -4x^2$.

15.

The graph of $y = -0.04x^2$ is a vertical shrink by a factor of $\frac{1}{100}$ of the graph of $y = -4x^2$.

17. The graph of $y = 0.5x^2$ should be wider than the graph of $y = x^2$;

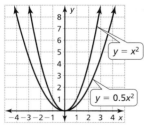

The graphs have the same vertex and the same axis of symmetry. The graph of $y = 0.5x^2$ is wider than the graph of $y = x^2$.

19. a. domain: $d \geq 0$, range: $z \geq 0$

b.

c. no; *Sample answer:* The relationship is quadratic, so a rope with 4 times the diameter will have $4^2 = 16$ times the breaking strength.

21. *f* is increasing when $x > 0$. *g* is increasing when $x < 0$.

23. *f*; $a = \frac{3}{4}$

25. *Sample answer:* The vertex of a parabola that opens up is the minimum point, so its *y*-coordinate is the minimum value of *y*. The graph passes through $(6, -3)$, so 2 is not the minimum value of *y*.

27. always; *Sample answer:* When $|a| > 1$, the graph of *f* will be a vertical stretch of the graph of *g*, so it will be narrower.

29. never; *Sample answer:* When $|a| > |d|$, the graph of *f* will be a vertical stretch of the graph of *g*, so it will be narrower, not wider.

31. a. 8 cm

b. no; *Sample answer:* A faster rotational speed would increase the depth. The diagram shown has a depth of 3.2 centimeters. A model of $y = 0.1x^2$ would only have a depth of 1.6 centimeters, so it would have a slower rotational speed.

3.1 Maintaining Mathematical Proficiency *(p. 128)*

33. 3   **35.** 11

3.2 Vocabulary and Core Concept Check *(p. 133)*

1. $(0, c)$, $x = 0$

3.2 Monitoring Progress and Modeling with Mathematics *(pp. 133–134)*

3.

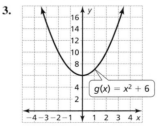

The graph of *g* is a vertical translation 6 units up of the graph of *f*.

5.

The graph of *p* is a vertical translation 3 units down of the graph of *f*.

7.

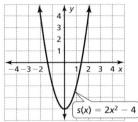

The graph of g is a reflection in the x-axis, and a vertical translation 3 units up of the graph of f.

9.

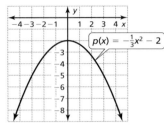

The graph of s is a vertical stretch by a factor of 2 and a vertical translation 4 units down of the graph of f.

11.

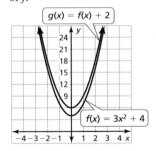

The graph of p is a vertical shrink by a factor of $\frac{1}{3}$, a reflection in the x-axis, and a vertical translation 2 units down of the graph of f.

13. The graph of g is a vertical translation 2 units up of the graph of f.

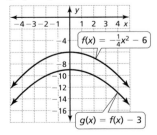

$g(x) = 3x^2 + 6$

15. The graph of g is a vertical translation 3 units down of the graph of f.

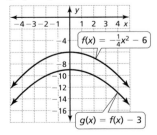

$g(x) = -\frac{1}{4}x^2 - 9$

17. The graph of $y = 3x^2 + 2$ is narrower, so it should be a stretch, not a shrink; The graph of $y = 3x^2 + 2$ is a vertical stretch by a factor of 3 and a translation 2 units up of the graph of $y = x^2$.

19. $x = 1, x = -1$

21. $x = 5, x = -5$

23. $x = 2, x = -2$

25. $x = \frac{1}{2}, x = -\frac{1}{2}$

27. **a.** the height of the balloon after t seconds **b.** 3 sec

c. When $k > 0$, the water balloon will take more than 3 seconds to hit the ground. When $k < 0$, the water balloon will take less than 3 seconds to hit the ground.

29. *Sample answer:*

31. *Sample answer:*

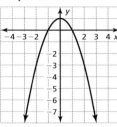

33. **a.** $T(x) = -44$; the distance between the balls

b. 44 ft

35. 12 ft by 12 ft

37. Graph the function and determine the x-intercepts; Set the function equal to 0, factor $-16t^2 + 400$, and apply the Zero-Product Property.

39. **a.** $h = -16t^2 + 45$; $h = -16t^2 + 32$

b. The graph of $h = -16t^2 + 32$ is a vertical translation 13 units down of the graph of $h = -16t^2 + 45$.

41. $(0, 5.8)$; *Sample answer:* The outer edges are located 40 feet from the center. Substituting this into $y = 0.012x^2$ indicates they are 19.2 feet above the x-axis. To be 25 feet above the x-axis, they must be vertically translated up 5.8 feet.

3.2 Maintaining Mathematical Proficiency *(p. 134)*

43. $\frac{3}{8}$

45. $\frac{5}{12}$

3.3 Vocabulary and Core Concept Check (p. 140)

1. *Sample answer:* If the leading coefficient is positive, the graph has a minimum value. If the leading coefficient is negative, the graph has a maximum value.

3.3 Monitoring Progress and Modeling with Mathematics (pp. 140–142)

3. $(2, -1); x = 2; 1$

5. $(-2, 0); x = -2; -3$

7. a. $x = 1$
   b. $(1, -2)$

9. a. $x = -1$
   b. $(-1, 8)$

11. a. $x = 5$
   b. $(5, 4)$

13.

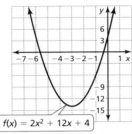

$f(x) = 2x^2 + 12x + 4$

domain: all real numbers, range: $y \geq -14$

15.

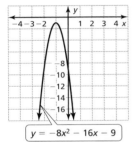

$y = -8x^2 - 16x - 9$

domain: all real numbers, range: $y \leq -1$

17.

$y = \frac{2}{3}x^2 - 6x + 5$

domain: all real numbers, range: $y \geq -\frac{17}{2}$

19. There should be two negatives in the substitution, one from the formula and one because b is -12;

$x = -\dfrac{b}{2a} = -\dfrac{-12}{2(3)} = 2$; The axis of symmetry is $x = 2$.

21. minimum value; -12

23. maximum value; -1

25. maximum value; $66\frac{1}{2}$

27. a. 4 sec   **b.** 256 ft

29. a. 200 ft   **b.** 50 ft
   c. domain: $0 \leq x \leq 400$, range: $50 \leq y \leq 150$

31. $(0, 8)$; *Sample answer:* Because the axis of symmetry is $x = 3$, the point $(0, 8)$ would also lie on the graph.

33. $(-1.41, -4)$

35. $(0.48, 0.72)$

37. a. second aircraft hangar   **b.** first aircraft hangar

39. a. $x = 4.5$ **b.** 20.25 in.^{2}

41. The graph of g is a reflection in the y-axis of the graph of h.

43. down; *Sample answer:* Because $(3, 2)$ and $(9, 2)$ have the same y-coordinate, any point with an x-coordinate between 3 and 9 lies on the part of the parabola between these two points that passes through the vertex. Because 7 is greater than 2, the vertex must be above these 2 points, so the parabola opens down.

45. $y = -2x^2 + 8x$

47. 14 ft

49. $\dfrac{k^2}{8}$ ft^2

3.3 Maintaining Mathematical Proficiency (p. 142)

51. The graph of h is a vertical shrink by a factor of 0.5 and a reflection in the x-axis of the graph of f.

53. The graph of p is a vertical stretch by a factor of 3 and a horizontal translation 1 unit left of the graph of f.

3.4 Vocabulary and Core Concept Check (p. 150)

1. *Sample answer:* The graph of an even function is symmetric about the y-axis. The graph of an odd function is symmetric about the origin.

3. The graph of g is a horizontal translation h units right if h is positive or $|h|$ units left if h is negative, and a vertical translation k units up if k is positive or $|k|$ units down if k is negative of the graph of f.

3.4 Monitoring Progress and Modeling with Mathematics (pp. 150–152)

5. neither

7. neither

9. even

11. neither

13. even

15. neither

17. odd

19. $(-1, 0); x = -1$

21. $(4, 0); x = 4$

23.

$g(x) = 2(x + 3)^2$

The graph of g is a horizontal translation 3 units left and a vertical stretch by a factor of 2 of the graph of f.

25.

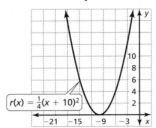

$r(x) = \frac{1}{4}(x + 10)^2$

The graph of r is a horizontal translation 10 units left and a vertical shrink by a factor of $\frac{1}{4}$ of the graph of f.

27.

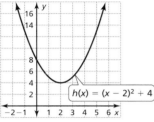

The graph of d is a horizontal translation 5 units right and a vertical shrink by a factor of $\frac{1}{5}$ of the graph of f.

29. If $f(-x) = f(x)$ the function is even; So, $f(x)$ is an even function.

31. $(-4, -3)$; $x = -4$ **33.** $(-3, 1)$; $x = -3$

35. C   **36.** A

37. D   **38.** B

39.

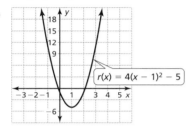

The graph of h is a translation 2 units right and 4 units up of the graph of f.

41.

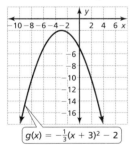

The graph of r is a vertical stretch by a factor of 4, and a translation 1 unit right and 5 units down of the graph of f.

43.

The graph of g is a vertical shrink by a factor of $\frac{1}{3}$, a reflection in the x-axis, and a translation 3 units left and 2 units down of the graph of f.

45. A   **46.** C

47. B   **48.** D

49.

51.

53.

55. a.

b.

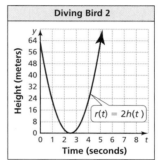

c. The graph of r is a vertical stretch by a factor of 2 of the graph of h; the second bird; *Sample answer:* Because $r(t)$ is twice $h(t)$, the second bird starts at a height twice as high as the first bird.

57. $f(x) = 2(x - 1)^2 + 2$ **59.** $f(x) = -2(x + 2)^2 - 4$

61. $f(x) = \frac{1}{2}(x - 5)^2 - 2$

63. $f(x) = -\frac{18}{125}(x - 25)^2 + 90$

Roller Coaster Track

$f(x) = -\frac{18}{125}(x - 25)^2 + 90$

65. $y = 2(x - 2)^2 - 4$ **67.** $f(x) = -5(x - 1)^2 + 8$

69. no; *Sample answer:* The graph would not pass the Vertical Line Test.

71. The graph of h is a vertical translation 4 units up of the graph of f; $h(x) = -(x + 1)^2 + 2$

73. The graph of h is a vertical stretch by a factor of 2 of the graph of f; $h(x) = 8(x - 2)^2 + 6$

75. $y = (x - 2)^2 - 5; y = x^2 - 4x - 1;$ *Sample answer:* The vertex, $(2, -5)$, can be quickly determined from the vertex form; The y-intercept, -1, can be quickly determined from the standard form.

77. a. the second birdbath; *Sample answer:* The first birdbath has a depth of 4 inches and the second birdbath has a depth of 6 inches.

   b. the first birdbath; *Sample answer:* The first birdbath has a width of 36 inches and the second birdbath has a width of 30 inches.

79. no; *Sample answer:* If the absolute value function includes a horizontal translation, it will not be symmetric about the y-axis.

3.4 Maintaining Mathematical Proficiency (p. 152)

81. $x = -3, x = 8$

3.5 Vocabulary and Core Concept Check (p. 158)

1. x-intercepts

3.5 Monitoring Progress and Modeling with Mathematics (pp. 158–160)

3. $-3, 1; x = -1$　　　　**5.** $-7, 5; x = -1$

7.

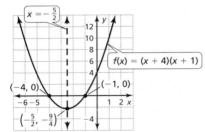

domain: all real numbers, range: $y \geq -\frac{9}{4}$

9.

domain: all real numbers, range: $y \leq 25$

11.

domain: all real numbers, range: $y \geq -\frac{5}{4}$

13.

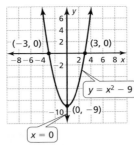

domain: all real numbers, range: $y \geq -9$

15.

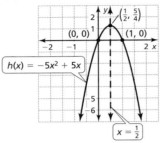

domain: all real numbers, range: $y \leq \frac{5}{4}$

17.

domain: all real numbers, range: $y \geq -\frac{25}{4}$

19.

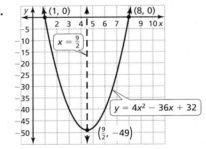

domain: all real numbers, range: $y \geq -49$

21. 2, 10　　　　　　　**23.** $-2, 2$

25. $-8, 3$　　　　　　 **27.** $-2, 7$

29. D　　　　　　　　**30.** F

31. C　　　　　　　　**32.** B

33. A　　　　　　　　**34.** E

35.

37.

39.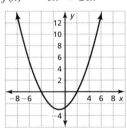

41. The factors need to be set equal to 0 and solved to find the zeros; $x + 3 = 0$ or $x - 2 = 0$; $x = -3$ or $x = 2$; The zeros of the function are -3 and 2.

43. *Sample answer:* $f(x) = x^2 - 14x + 46$

45. *Sample answer:* $f(x) = x^2 - 10x + 9$

47. $f(x) = 3x^2 + 3x - 36$

49. *Sample answer:* $f(x) = x^2 - 7x$

51. *Sample answer:* $f(x) = x^2 + 10x + 25$

53. *Sample answer:* $f(x) = x^2 - 3$

55. $f(x) = 2x^2 + 2x - 12$

57. $f(x) = -4x^2 + 8x + 32$

59. $f(x) = -3x^2 + 21x$

61.

63. *Sample answer:*

65. **a.** 4 ft   **b.** $\frac{1}{2}$ ft   **c.** $y = \frac{1}{6}(x^2 - 9)$

67. D   **68.** A

69. B   **70.** C

71. not possible; *Sample answer:* Because -5 and 1 are the x-intercepts, the axis of symmetry is $x = -2$. The points $(-3, 12)$ and $(-1, 4)$ are the same horizontal distance from the axis of symmetry, so for both of them to lie on the parabola they would have to have the same y-coordinate.

73. **a.** $f(x) = -3(x + 4)(x - 2)$

b.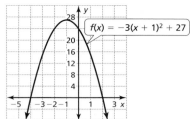

Sample answer: Plot the vertex $(-1, 27)$, which can be determined from the vertex form. Then plot the x-intercepts $(-4, 0)$ and $(2, 0)$, which can be determined from the intercept form. Draw a smooth curve through these points.

75. yes; *Sample answer:* Let p and q be real zeros of a quadratic function. When $p = q$, the function has exactly one real zero and can be written as $y = a(x - p)(x - p)$.

77. $-k, 2k$

79. *Sample answer:* $y = (x + 4)(x - 2)$, $y = 2(x + 4)(x - 2)$; The two given points are x-intercepts, so the graphs of any two quadratic functions having these two intercepts would intersect at these points.

3.5 Maintaining Mathematical Proficiency *(p. 160)*

81. $\sqrt{2}$, or about 1.41   **83.** $\sqrt{5}$, or about 2.24

3.6 Vocabulary and Core Concept Check *(p. 166)*

1. focus; directrix

3.6 Monitoring Progress and Modeling with Mathematics *(pp. 166–168)*

3. $y = \frac{1}{4}x^2$ **5.** $y = -\frac{1}{8}x^2$

7. $y = \frac{1}{24}x^2$ **9.** $y = -\frac{1}{40}x^2$

11. A, B, and D; Each has a value for p that is negative.

Substituting in a negative value for p in $y = \dfrac{1}{4p}x^2$ results in a parabola that has been reflected across the x-axis.

13. The focus is $(0, 2)$. The directrix is $y = -2$. The axis of symmetry is the y-axis.

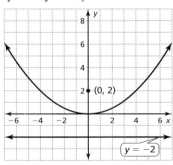

15. The focus is $(-5, 0)$. The directrix is $x = 5$. The axis of symmetry is the x-axis.

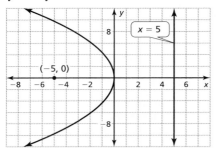

17. The focus is $(4, 0)$. The directrix is $x = -4$. The axis of symmetry is the x-axis.

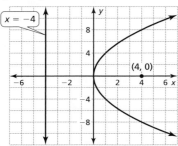

19. The focus is $\left(0, -\frac{1}{8}\right)$. The directrix is $y = \frac{1}{8}$. The axis of symmetry is the y-axis.

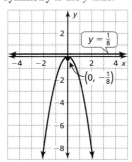

21. Instead of a vertical axis of symmetry, the graph should have a horizontal axis of symmetry.

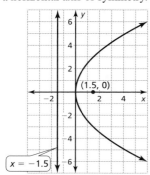

23. 9.5 in.; The receiver should be placed at the focus. The distance from the vertex to the focus is $p = \frac{38}{4} = 9.5$ in.

25. $y = \frac{1}{32}x^2$ **27.** $x = -\frac{1}{10}y^2$

29. $x = \frac{1}{12}y^2$ **31.** $x = \frac{1}{40}y^2$

33. $y = -\frac{3}{20}x^2$ **35.** $y = \frac{7}{24}x^2$

37. $x = -\frac{1}{16}y^2 - 4$ **39.** $y = \frac{1}{6}x^2 + 1$

41. The vertex is $(3, 2)$. The focus is $(3, 4)$. The directrix is $y = 0$. The axis of symmetry is $x = 3$. The graph is a vertical shrink by a factor of $\frac{1}{2}$ followed by a translation 3 units right and 2 units up.

43. The vertex is $(1, 3)$. The focus is $(5, 3)$. The directrix is $x = -3$. The axis of symmetry is $y = 3$. The graph is a horizontal shrink by a factor of $\frac{1}{4}$ followed by a translation 1 unit right and 3 units up.

45. The vertex is $(2, -4)$. The focus is $\left(\frac{23}{12}, -4\right)$. The directrix is $x = \frac{25}{12}$. The axis of symmetry is $y = -4$. The graph is a horizontal stretch by a factor of 12 followed by a reflection in the y-axis and a translation 2 units right and 4 units down.

47. $x = \frac{1}{5.2}y^2$; about 3.08 in.

49. As $|p|$ increases, the graph gets wider; As $|p|$ increases, the constant in the function gets smaller, which results in a vertical shrink, making the graph wider.

51. $y = \frac{1}{4}x^2$ **53.** $x = \frac{1}{4p}y^2$

3.6 Maintaining Mathematical Proficiency *(p. 168)*

55. The inputs are equally spaced and the common ratio is 2; $f(0) = 0.25, f(n) = 2 \cdot f(n - 1)$

57. The inputs are equally spaced and the common ratio is $\frac{1}{2}$; $f(0) = 144, f(n) = \frac{1}{2} \cdot f(n - 1)$

3.7 Vocabulary and Core Concept Check *(p. 175)*

1. linear, exponential, quadratic; $y = mx + b$, $y = ab^x$, $y = ax^2 + bx + c$; a straight line, a continuously increasing or decreasing curve, a parabola

3. Find the slope of the line through $(a, f(a))$ and $(b, f(b))$.

3.7 Monitoring Progress and Modeling with Mathematics *(pp. 175–178)*

5. quadratic   **7.** exponential

9.

linear

11.

quadratic

13.

linear

15. linear   **17.** exponential

19. linear; The first differences are constant.

21. quadratic; $y = 2x^2 - 2x - 4$

23. linear; $y = -3x - 2$ **25.** quadratic; $y = -3x^2$

27. $f(0) = 2, f(n) = f(n - 1) + 2n - 3$

29. Consecutive *y*-values have a constant ratio. They do not change by a constant amount; Consecutive *y*-values change by a constant ratio. So, the table represents an exponential function.

31. a.

b. no; The points do not appear to follow the shape of any of these types of functions.

33. a. 3, 23, 35, 39, 35, 23, 3

b.

c. The function is increasing between 0 and 1.5 seconds, and the function is decreasing between 1.5 seconds and about 3 seconds.

d. 40, 24, 8, −8, −24, −40; The average rate of change decreases when the function is increasing, and the average rate of change increases in the negative direction when the function is decreasing.

35. a. exponential; linear; quadratic

b. Charity A: 2, 6, 18, 54, 162, 486; Charity B: 12, 12, 12, 12, 12, 12; Charity C: 4, 12, 20, 28, 36, 44

c. Charity A; Charity A will have the most pledges followed by Charity C, then Charity B.

37. a. Company A

b. Company A; Company B's revenue can be modeled by an increasing linear function.

39. The average rate of change of a linear function is constant because the dependent variable of a linear function increases by the same amount for each constant change in the independent variable. The average rate of change of a quadratic or exponential function is not constant because the dependent variable of a quadratic or exponential function changes by a different amount for each constant change in the independent variable.

41. *Sample answer:* $y = 1.5x^2$

43. no; The graph of an exponential growth function will always eventually have greater *y*-values than the graph of a quadratic function.

45. *Sample answer:* $y = -0.414x^2 + 6.17x + 47.0$; Compare the linear, quadratic, and exponential models obtained using the regression features of a graphing utility; about $69.9 billion

3.7 Maintaining Mathematical Proficiency *(p. 178)*

47. 5

49. 3

51. $4y^2 - 25$

53. $9s^2 - 64t^2$

Chapter 3 Review *(pp. 180–184)*

1.

The graph of *p* is a vertical stretch by a factor of 7 of the graph of *f*.

2.

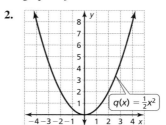

The graph of *q* is a vertical shrink by a factor of $\frac{1}{2}$ of the graph of *f*.

3.

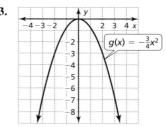

The graph of *g* is a vertical shrink by a factor of $\frac{3}{4}$ and a reflection in the *x*-axis of the graph of *f*.

4.

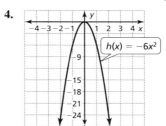

The graph of *h* is a vertical stretch by a factor of 6 and a reflection in the *x*-axis of the graph of *f*.

5. The vertex is (1, −3). The axis of symmetry is $x = 1$. The domain is all real numbers. The range is $y \geq -3$. When $x < 1$, *y* increases as *x* decreases. When $x > 1$, *y* increases as *x* increases.

6.

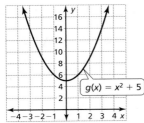

The graph of g is a vertical translation 5 units up of the graph of f.

7.

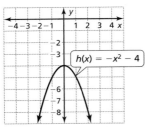

The graph of h is a reflection in the x-axis, and a vertical translation 4 units down of the graph of f.

8.

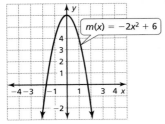

The graph of m is a vertical stretch by a factor of 2, a reflection in the x-axis, and a vertical translation 6 units up of the graph of f.

9.

The graph of n is a vertical shrink by a factor of $\frac{1}{3}$ and a vertical translation 5 units down of the graph of f.

10.

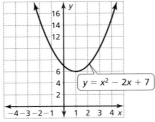

domain: all real numbers, range: $y \geq 6$

11.

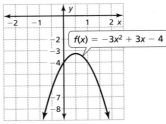

domain: all real numbers, range: $y \leq -\frac{13}{4}$

12.

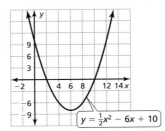

domain: all real numbers, range: $y \geq -8$

13. 2.75 sec; 133 ft   **14.** neither

15. odd   **16.** neither

17.

The graph of h is a vertical stretch by a factor of 2 and a horizontal translation 4 units right of the graph of f.

18.

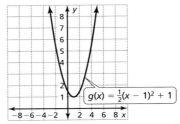

The graph of g is a vertical shrink by a factor of $\frac{1}{2}$, and a translation 1 unit right and 1 unit up of the graph of f.

19.

The graph of q is a reflection in the x-axis, and a translation 4 units left and 7 units up of the graph of f.

20.

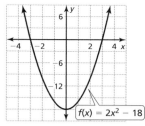

21. $f(x) = 5(x - 3)^2 + 2$

22.

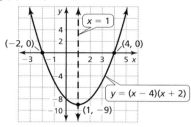

domain: all real numbers, range: $y \geq -9$

23.

domain: all real numbers, range: $y \leq 3$

24.

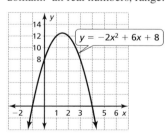

domain: all real numbers, range: $y \geq -1$

25.

26.

27.

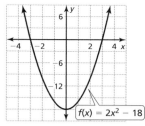

28. *Sample answer:* $x^2 - 10x + 24$

29. 2.25 in.

30. The focus is $(0, 9)$, the directrix is $y = -9$, and the axis of symmetry is $x = 0$.

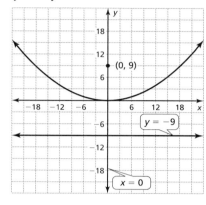

31. $x = -\frac{1}{8}y^2$ **32.** $y = -\frac{1}{16}(x - 2)^2 + 6$

33. exponential; $y = 128\left(\frac{1}{4}\right)^x$

34. $f(0) = 5, f(n) = f(n - 1) + 4n - 3$

35. From year 2 to year 7, your account increased at an average rate of about $29.55 per year and your friend's account increased at an average rate of $20 per year. So, your account is growing faster.

Chapter 4

Chapter 4 Maintaining Mathematical Proficiency *(p. 189)*

1. $(x + 5)^2$ **2.** $(x - 10)^2$

3. $(x + 6)^2$ **4.** $(x - 9)^2$

5. $(x + 8)^2$ **6.** $(x - 15)^2$

7. $(1, -2)$ **8.** $(4, 4)$

9. $(-2, 3)$ **10.** $\left(\frac{b}{2}\right)^2$

4.1 Vocabulary and Core Concept Check *(p. 197)*

1. rationalizing the denominator

3. yes; $\sqrt{\dfrac{2x}{9}} = \sqrt{\dfrac{1}{9} \cdot 2x} = \sqrt{\dfrac{1}{9}} \cdot \sqrt{2x} = \dfrac{1}{3}\sqrt{2x}$

4.1 Monitoring Progress and Modeling with Mathematics *(pp. 197–200)*

5. yes

7. no; The radicand has a perfect square factor of 16.

9. no; A radical appears in the denominator of a fraction.

11. no; A radical appears in the denominator of a fraction.

13. $2\sqrt{5}$ **15.** $8\sqrt{2}$

17. $5\sqrt{5b}$ **19.** $-9m\sqrt{m}$

21. $\dfrac{2}{7}$

23. $-\dfrac{\sqrt{23}}{8}$

25. $\dfrac{a\sqrt{a}}{7}$

27. $\dfrac{5}{x}$

29. $2\sqrt[3]{2}$

31. $-4x\sqrt[3]{x^2}$

33. $-\dfrac{\sqrt[3]{6c}}{5}$

35. $-\dfrac{3\sqrt[3]{3y^2}}{10x}$

37. The radicand 18 has a perfect square factor of 9;
$\sqrt{72} = \sqrt{36 \cdot 2} = 6\sqrt{2}$

39. $\dfrac{\sqrt{6}}{\sqrt{6}}$

41. $\dfrac{\sqrt[3]{x}}{\sqrt[3]{x}}$

43. $\dfrac{\sqrt{5} + 8}{\sqrt{5} + 8}$

45. $\sqrt{2}$

47. $\dfrac{\sqrt{15}}{12}$

49. $\dfrac{3\sqrt{a}}{a}$

51. $\dfrac{d\sqrt{15}}{5}$

53. $\dfrac{4\sqrt[3]{5}}{5}$

55. $\dfrac{\sqrt{7} - 1}{6}$

57. $\dfrac{7\sqrt{10} + 2\sqrt{5}}{47}$

59. $\sqrt{5} + \sqrt{2}$

61. a. about 1.85 sec   **b.** about 0.41 sec

63. about 5.42 amperes

65. $5\sqrt{2}$, about 7.07

67. $\dfrac{\sqrt{2}}{3}$, about 0.47

69. $2\sqrt{2}$, about 2.83

71. $-6\sqrt{2}$, about -8.49

73. about 3.71 in.

75. $\sqrt{3} + 4\sqrt{2}$

77. $-13\sqrt{6}$

79. $8\sqrt{3} + 2\sqrt{6}$

81. $\sqrt[3]{3}$

83. $4\sqrt{10}$

85. $-2\sqrt{30x}$

87. 18

89. $3\sqrt[3]{12}$

91. about 114 ft

93. $\dfrac{\sqrt[5]{8125}}{5x}$

95. $4\sqrt[4]{y}$

97. $9\sqrt[4]{9} - \sqrt[5]{9}$

99. a. $4, 2\frac{1}{4}, 2, 2 + \sqrt{3}, 2 - \sqrt{3}, 2 + \pi;$

$2\frac{1}{4}, \frac{1}{2}, \frac{1}{4}, \frac{1}{4} + \sqrt{3}, \frac{1}{4} - \sqrt{3}, \frac{1}{4} + \pi;$

$2, \frac{1}{4}, 0, \sqrt{3}, -\sqrt{3}, \pi;$

$2 + \sqrt{3}, \frac{1}{4} + \sqrt{3}, \sqrt{3}, 2\sqrt{3}, 0, \pi + \sqrt{3};$

$2 - \sqrt{3}, \frac{1}{4} - \sqrt{3}, -\sqrt{3}, 0, -2\sqrt{3}, \pi - \sqrt{3};$

$2 + \pi, \frac{1}{4} + \pi, \pi, \pi + \sqrt{3}, \pi - \sqrt{3}, 2\pi$

b. $4, \frac{1}{2}, 0, 2\sqrt{3}, -2\sqrt{3}, 2\pi;$

$\frac{1}{2}, \frac{1}{16}, 0, \frac{\sqrt{3}}{4}, -\frac{\sqrt{3}}{4}, \frac{\pi}{4};$

$0, 0, 0, 0, 0, 0;$

$2\sqrt{3}, \frac{\sqrt{3}}{4}, 0, 3, -3, \pi\sqrt{3};$

$-2\sqrt{3}, -\frac{\sqrt{3}}{4}, 0, -3, 3, -\pi\sqrt{3};$

$2\pi, \frac{\pi}{4}, 0, \pi\sqrt{3}, -\pi\sqrt{3}, \pi^2$

101. odd; even; When m is even, 2^m is a perfect square.

103. $a^2 < ab < b^2$ when $a < b$.   **105.** 377

107. $\dfrac{2\sqrt[3]{x^2} - 2\sqrt[3]{x} + 2}{x + 1}$; Multiplying the numerator and denominator

by $\sqrt[3]{x^2} - \sqrt[3]{x} + 1$ rationalizes the denominator.

4.1 Maintaining Mathematical Proficiency (p. 200)

109.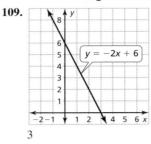

$y = -2x + 6$

3

111.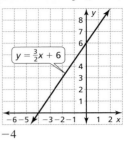

$y = \frac{3}{2}x + 6$

-4

113. $9a^2 - 30ab + 25b^2$ **115.** $16y^2 - 4$

4.2 Vocabulary and Core Concept Check (p. 206)

1. an equation that can be written in the standard form
$ax^2 + bx + c = 0$, where $a \neq 0$

3. The number of x-intercepts is the number of solutions.

4.2 Monitoring Progress and Modeling with Mathematics (pp. 206–208)

5. $x = 3, x = -1$

7. $x = -4$

9. $4x^2 - 12 = 0$ or $-4x^2 + 12 = 0$

11. $x^2 - 2x + 1 = 0$ or $-x^2 + 2x - 1 = 0$

13. $x = 0, x = 5$ **15.** no solution

17. $x = 3$ **19.** $x = -1$

21. $x = -6, x = 2$ **23.** $x = -2, x = 1$

25. The equation needs to be in standard form;
$x^2 + 3x - 18 = 0$

$y = x^2 + 3x - 18$

The solutions are $x = -6$ and $x = 3$.

27. a. The x-intercepts are the distances at which the height is
0 yards.

b. 5 yd

29. $x = -5, x = 2$ **31.** no solution

33. $x = -10, x = -2$ **35.** no solution

37. 0, 2   **39.** -1

41. $-\frac{1}{2}, 1$ **43.** about 4.3, about 0.7

45. about 2.4, about -0.4

47.

$f(x) = x^2 + 6x + 1$

about -0.2, about -5.8

49.

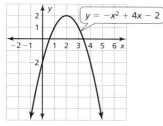

$y = -x^2 + 4x - 2$

about 3.4, about 0.6

51.

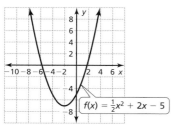

$f(x) = \frac{1}{2}x^2 + 2x - 5$

about 1.7, about -5.7

53. a. 118 ft, 198 ft, 246 ft, 262 ft, 246 ft, 198 ft, 118 ft, 6 ft

    b. about 1.5 sec, about 6.5 sec

    c. about 1.4 sec, about 6.6 sec

55. about 3.7 ft

57. Graph the function to determine which integers the solutions are between. Then make tables using x-values between the integers with an interval of 0.1. Look for a change of sign in the function values, then select the value closest to zero.

59. *Sample answer:* Method 1; Only one graph needs to be drawn.

61. about 24.1 ft

63. sometimes; $y = -2x^2 + 1$ has two x-intercepts, but $y = -2x^2 + (-1)$ has no x-intercepts.

65. never; The graph of $y = ax^2 + bx + c$ has at most two x-intercepts.

4.2 Maintaining Mathematical Proficiency *(p. 208)*

67. The inputs are equally spaced and the common ratio is 4; $f(0) = 2, f(n) = 4 \cdot f(n - 1)$

4.3 Vocabulary and Core Concept Check *(p. 213)*

1. two

4.3 Monitoring Progress and Modeling with Mathematics *(pp. 213–214)*

3. 2; $x = 5, x = -5$ **5.** 0; no real solutions

7. 1; $x = 0$ **9.** $x = 4, x = -4$

11. no real solutions   **13.** $x = 7, x = -7$

15. $x = 0$ **17.** $x = \frac{1}{2}, x = -\frac{1}{2}$

19. $x = -3$ **21.** $x = 5, x = -4$

23. $x = \frac{1}{3}, x = -\frac{7}{3}$ **25.** $x \approx 2.65, x \approx -2.65$

27. $x \approx 3.16, x \approx -3.16$ **29.** $x \approx 4.24, x \approx -4.24$

31. The number 36 has both a positive and negative square root; $x = \pm 6$

33. about 1.2 sec   **35.** 3 ft

37. *Sample answer:* Use a calculator.

39. $(3, 9), (-3, 9)$; When $y = 9, x = \pm 3$.

41. $x = 1.2, x = -1.2; 1.2^2 = 1.44$

43. $x = 6, x = -2$

4.3 Maintaining Mathematical Proficiency *(p. 214)*

45. $(x + 4)^2$ **47.** $(x - 7)^2$

49. $(x + 6)^2$

4.4 Vocabulary and Core Concept Check *(p. 221)*

1. completing the square

3. even; When b is even, $\frac{b}{2}$ is an integer.

4.4 Monitoring Progress and Modeling with Mathematics *(pp. 221–224)*

5. 16   **7.** 4

9. $\frac{225}{4}$ **11.** $x^2 - 10x + 25; (x - 5)^2$

13. $x^2 + 16x + 64; (x + 8)^2$ **15.** $x^2 + 5x + \frac{25}{4}; \left(x + \frac{5}{2}\right)^2$

17. $x = 1, x = -15$ **19.** $x \approx 3.41, x \approx 0.59$

21. $x \approx 6.27, x \approx -1.27$

23. a. $x^2 + 6x = 216$

    b. width: 12 ft, length: 18 ft

25. $x = 5, x = 3$ **27.** $x \approx -3.27, x \approx -6.73$

29. $x \approx 1.92, x \approx -9.92$ **31.** $x = 8, x = -1$

33. The number 16 should be added to each side of the equation; $x^2 + 8x + 16 = 10 + 16; x = -4 \pm\sqrt{26}$

35. $b = 10, b = -10$; In a perfect square trinomial $c = \left(\frac{b}{2}\right)^2$, so $b = \pm 2\sqrt{c}$.

37. $y = (x + 3)^2 - 6$; D   **38.** $y = -(x - 4)^2 + 4$; A

39. $y = -(x + 2)^2 + 2$; B   **40.** $y = (x - 1)^2 + 3$; C

41. minimum value; -6 **43.** maximum value; -5

45. maximum value; -6

47. yes; The graph has two negative x-intercepts and it opens down.

49. no; The x-intercepts are both positive.

51. f, m; The graph has two negative x-intercepts and it opens up.

53. a. 36 ft

    b. $x = \frac{3}{2}$; On the left side of $x = \frac{3}{2}$, the height increases as time increases. On the right side of $x = \frac{3}{2}$, the height decreases as time increases.

55. 3 ft   **57.** 12

59. $x \approx 1.24, x \approx -3.24$ **61.** $x \approx 4.29, x \approx -0.29$

63. 40 mi/h

65. a. $\ell + 2w = 80, \ell w = 750$

    b. length: 30 ft, width: 25 ft; length: 50 ft, width: 15 ft

67. a. $x \approx 0.8, x \approx -12.8$ **b.** $x \approx 0.78, x \approx -12.78$

    c. *Sample answer:* completing the square; The result is more accurate.

69. $x(x + 2) = 48, 6$ and 8

71. yes; Substituting 23.50 for y in the model, the stock is worth $23.50 ten days and thirty days after the stock is purchased.

73. length: 66 in., width: 6 in.

4.4 Maintaining Mathematical Proficiency *(p. 224)*

75. $y = \begin{cases} -x + 1, & \text{if } x < 0 \\ 1, & \text{if } x \geq 0 \end{cases}$ **77.** $y = \begin{cases} 1, & \text{if } 0 \leq x < 2 \\ 3, & \text{if } 2 \leq x < 4 \\ 5, & \text{if } 4 \leq x < 6 \end{cases}$

79. $6\sqrt{2}$

4.5 Vocabulary and Core Concept Check (p. 231)

1. the quadratic formula; $x = \dfrac{-b \pm \sqrt{b^2 - 4ac}}{2a}$

4.5 Monitoring Progress and Modeling with Mathematics (pp. 231–234)

3. $x^2 - 7x = 0$; $a = 1, b = -7, c = 0$ or $-x^2 + 7x = 0$; $a = -1, b = 7, c = 0$

5. $-2x^2 - 5x + 1 = 0$; $a = -2, b = -5, c = 1$ or $2x^2 + 5x - 1 = 0$; $a = 2, b = 5, c = -1$

7. $x^2 - 6x + 4 = 0$; $a = 1, b = -6, c = 4$ or $-x^2 + 6x - 4 = 0$; $a = -1, b = 6, c = -4$

9. $x = 6$

11. $x = 11, x = -1$

13. no real solutions

15. $x = \frac{3}{2}, x = \frac{2}{3}$

17. $x = \frac{1}{4}$

19. $x \approx 2.2, x \approx -4.2$

21. $x = -\frac{1}{2}, x = -4$

23. about 0.2 sec, about 1.4 sec

25. no real solutions

27. one real solution

29. two real solutions

31. two x-intercepts

33. no x-intercepts

35. two x-intercepts

37. $x = \frac{1}{2}, x = \frac{4}{5}$; *Sample answer:* The equation is not easily factorable and $a \neq 1$, so solve using the Quadratic Formula.

39. $x \approx 0.74, x \approx -6.74$; *Sample answer:* $a = 1$ and b is even, so solve by completing the square.

41. $x = -4, x = 3$; *Sample answer:* The equation is easily factorable, so solve by factoring.

43. $x \approx 2.19, x \approx -1.94$; *Sample answer:* The equation cannot be factored and $a \neq 1$, so solve using the Quadratic Formula.

45. $-b$ should be $-(-7)$, not -7;
$x = \dfrac{-(-7) \pm \sqrt{(-7)^2 - 4(3)(-6)}}{2(3)}$; $x = 3$ and $x = -\dfrac{2}{3}$

47. yes; about 42 ft, about 158 ft

49. no; The discriminant is -47, so the equation has no real solutions.

51. 5; length: 13 m, width: 7 m

53. **a–c.** $x = -2$
Sample answer: factoring; The equation is easily factorable.

55. 2; When a and c have different signs, ac is negative, so the discriminant is positive.

57. **a.** *Sample answer:* $\frac{1}{2}$ **b.** 1
c. *Sample answer:* 2

59. **a.** *Sample answer:* 1   **b.** 9
c. *Sample answer:* 10

61. about 31 mi/h, about 65 mi/h

63. below the x-axis; The discriminant is positive and $a > 0$.

65. above the x-axis; The discriminant is negative and $a > 0$.

67. above the x-axis; The discriminant is positive and $a < 0$.

69. about 22 sec; The height is 30,800 feet after about 20.8 seconds and after about 42.8 seconds.

71. **a.** $4x + 3y = 1050$; $3y = 1050 - 4x$; $y = 350 - \frac{4}{3}x$
b. length: about 54 ft, width: about 278 ft; length: about 209 ft, width: about 72 ft

73. $-\dfrac{b}{2a}$; The mean of the solutions is the x-coordinate of the vertex; The mean of the solutions is equal to the graph's axis of symmetry, which is where the vertex lies.

75. about 24.7 ft/sec

77. $\dfrac{-b}{a}; \dfrac{c}{a}$; *Sample answer:* $2x^2 - 4x + 1 = 0$

79. **a.** $(x + 1), (x - 6)$; $x^2 - 5x - 6 = 0$;
$x, (x - 2)$; $x^2 - 2x = 0$;
$\left(x + \frac{1}{2}\right), (x - 5)$; $x^2 - \frac{9}{2}x - \frac{5}{2} = 0$

b.

3, 4

$-1, 6$

0, 2

$-\frac{1}{2}, 5$

81. **a.** $k < -3$ or $k > 3$ **b.** $k = -3$ or $k = 3$
c. $-3 < k < 3$

4.5 Maintaining Mathematical Proficiency (p. 234)

83. $3x^2 - x + 2$

85. $3x^2 - 3x + 1$

87. $x^2 - 4$

89. $-x^2 + 8x - 7$

4.6 Vocabulary and Core Concept Check (p. 242)

1. $i = \sqrt{-1}$ and is used to write the square root of any negative number.

3. Add the real parts and the imaginary parts separately.

4.6 Monitoring Progress and Modeling with Mathematics (pp. 242–244)

5. $6i$

7. $3i\sqrt{2}$

9. $8i$

11. $-16i\sqrt{2}$

13. $x = 2$ and $y = 2$

15. $x = -2$ and $y = 4$

17. $x = 7$ and $y = -12$

19. $x = 6$ and $y = 28$

21. $13 + 2i$

23. $9 + 11i$

25. 19

27. $4 + 2i$

29. $-4 - 14i$

31. **a.** $-4 + 5i$ **b.** $2\sqrt{2} + 10i$

33. $(12 + 2i)$ ohms

35. $(8 + i)$ ohms

37. $-3 - 15i$

39. $14 - 5i$

41. $-16 - 11i$

43. $-27 - 36i$

45. Distributive Property; Simplify; Definition of complex addition; Write in standard form.

47. $(6 - 7i) - (4 - 3i) = 2 - 4i$

49. 2 **51.** 20

53. 8

55. *Sample answer:* $8 + 4i, 8 - 4i$

57. $a^2 - b^2 - 2abi$

59. i^2 can be simplified; $15 - 3i + 10i - 2i^2 = 15 + 7i + 2 = 17 + 7i$

61. **a.** -8 **b.** $12 - 10i$ **c.** $21i$ **d.** $41 + 3i$
e. $-9i$ **f.** $-9 + 23i$ **g.** 14 **h.** $14i$

Real numbers	Imaginary numbers	Pure imaginary numbers
-8	$12 - 10i$	$21i$
14	$14 + 3i$	$-9i$
	$-9 + 23i$	$14i$

63.

Powers of i	i^1	i^2	i^3	i^4	i^5	i^6	i^7	i^8	i^9	i^{10}	i^{11}	i^{12}
Simplified form	i	-1	$-i$	1	i	-1	$-i$	1	i	-1	$-i$	1

The results of i^n alternate in the pattern i, -1, $-i$, and 1.

65. $-28 + 27i$

67. $-15 - 25i$

69. $9 + 5i$

71. $-2 - 7i, -2 + 7i$

73. **a.** false; *Sample answer:* $(3 - 5i) + (4 + 5i) = 7$
b. true; *Sample answer:* $(3i)(2i) = 6i^2 = -6$
c. true; *Sample answer:* $3i = 0 + 3i$
d. false; *Sample answer:* $1 + 8i$

4.6 Maintaining Mathematical Proficiency (p. 244)

75. $y = (x - 1)^2 + 2$ **77.** $y = -(x - 2)^2 - 1$

79. 100

4.7 Vocabulary and Core Concept Check (p. 249)

1. imaginary

4.7 Monitoring Progress and Modeling with Mathematics (pp. 249–250)

3. C; two imaginary solutions   **4.** D; one real solution

5. A; two real solutions   **6.** B; two real solutions

7. $x = \pm 7i$; *Sample answer:* The equation does not have an x-term, so solve using square roots.

9. $x = 3$ and $x = 1$; *Sample answer:* The equation is factorable, so solve by factoring.

11. $x = -3 \pm i\sqrt{6}$; *Sample answer:* $a = 1$ and b is even, so solve by completing the square.

13. $x = \dfrac{4 \pm i}{3}$; *Sample answer:* The equation is not easily factorable and $a \neq 1$, so solve using the Quadratic Formula.

15. $x = 5$; *Sample answer:* The equation is factorable, so solve by factoring.

17. $x = \dfrac{3 \pm \sqrt{89}}{8}$; *Sample answer:* The equation is not easily factorable and $a \neq 1$, so solve using the Quadratic Formula.

19. $z = 6 \pm \sqrt{30}$; *Sample answer:* $a = 1$ and b is even, so solve by completing the square.

21. The i was left out after taking the square root;
$x = \dfrac{-10 \pm \sqrt{-196}}{2} = \dfrac{-10 \pm 14i}{2} = -5 \pm 7i$

23. $\pm\sqrt{7}i$ **25.** $-4 \pm \sqrt{29}$

27. $5 \pm \sqrt{2}i$

29. *Sample answer:* $a = 1$ and $c = 5$; $x^2 + 4x + 5 = 0$

31. *Sample answer:* $a = 5$ and $c = -5$; $5x^2 + 10x + 5 = 0$

33. $h = -16t^2 - 88t + 100$

35. no; yes; *Sample answer:* When $h = 30$, the equation has two imaginary solutions. When $h = 26$, $t = 1$ and $t \approx 1.19$.

37. *Sample answer:* Using the Quadratic Formula, the solutions are $x = \dfrac{-b \pm \sqrt{b^2 - 4ac}}{2a} = \dfrac{-b}{2a} \pm \dfrac{\sqrt{b^2 - 4ac}}{2a}$, so when $b^2 - 4ac < 0$, the solutions are complex conjugates; Because $3i$ and $-2i$ are not complex conjugates, they cannot both be solutions of the same quadratic equation with real coefficients.

39. $-5x^2 + 8x - 12 = 0$

41. **a.** $v_0 = 32\sqrt{10} \approx 101.19$ ft/sec
b. about 3.2 sec; At $t = 2$, $h \approx 140$, so the rider is near the top and the graph is accurate.

4.7 Maintaining Mathematical Proficiency (p. 250)

43. $(-4, 5)$; *Sample answer:* substitution because one equation is solved for x

45. $(-2, 7)$; *Sample answer:* substitution because one of the variables has a coefficient of 1

47. **a.** $x = 0.25$
b. $(0.25, 2.875)$

4.8 Vocabulary and Core Concept Check (p. 256)

1. Solve one of the equations for one of the variables and substitute into the other equation and solve.

4.8 Monitoring Progress and Modeling with Mathematics (pp. 256–258)

3. B; $(0, 1), (3, 4)$ **4.** D; no solutions

5. A; $(0, -1)$ **6.** C; $(-2, 5), (1, 2)$

7. $(2, 9), (-1, 6)$ **9.** $(-1, 2)$

11. $(3, 6), (-3, -6)$ **13.** $(0, -5), (-3, -8)$

15. no solutions   **17.** $(0, 5)$

19. $(4, -11), (-4, 29)$ **21.** $(0, 2), (-6, -22)$

23. $(1, 1)$

25. about $(0.87, -1.74)$, about $(-6.87, 13.74)$

27. The graph does not show both solutions.

The solutions are $(0, 4)$ and $(5, 14)$.

29. between -4 and -3, between 0 and 1

31. between -4 and -3, between -2 and -1

33. about $(2.350, 13.225)$

35. about $(-2.543, -0.941)$, about $(0.185, 1.586)$, about $(1.854, 25.152)$

37. about $(0.840, 3.454)$, about $(-3.174, -1.898)$

39. $x \approx 0.45$, $x \approx -4.45$ **41.** no solutions

43. $x \approx -0.36$ **45.** $x \approx 1.13$, $x \approx 2.40$

47. $\left(\dfrac{-7 + \sqrt{145}}{6}, \dfrac{7 + 2\sqrt{145}}{9}\right)$, $\left(\dfrac{-7 - \sqrt{145}}{6}, \dfrac{7 - 5\sqrt{145}}{9}\right)$;

They are about the same.

49. 5 days and 35 days after the movie opened

51. about 55 m, about 475 m

53. **a–c.** $(2, 11)$, $(-2, -5)$

Sample answer: elimination; The resulting equation can be written in the form $x^2 = d$.

55. **a.** $y = 30x + 290$ **b.** $(1, 320)$, $(34, 1310)$

57. The possible number of solutions is 0, 1, or 2.

59. **a.** $(0, 4)$ **b.** $(5, 9)$

61. $(1, -6)$

4.8 Maintaining Mathematical Proficiency *(p. 258)*

63.

65.

67.

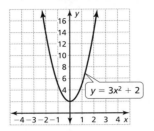

domain: all real numbers; range: $y \geq 2$

69.

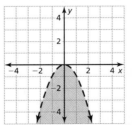

domain: all real numbers; range: $y \leq 11$

4.9 Vocabulary and Core Concept *(p. 264)*

1. The graph of a quadratic inequality in one variable consists of a number line, but the graph of a quadratic inequality in two variables consists of both the x- and y-axis.

4.9 Monitoring Progress and Modeling with Mathematics *(pp. 264–266)*

3. C; The x-intercepts are $x = -1$ and $x = -3$. The test point $(-2, 5)$ does not satisfy the inequality.

5. B; The x-intercepts are $x = 1$ and $x = 3$. The test point $(2, 5)$ does not satisfy the inequality.

7.

9.

11.

13.

15. $y > f(x)$

17. The graph should be solid, not dashed.

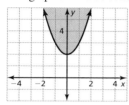

19. The solution represents weights that can be supported by shelves with various thicknesses.

21.

23.

25.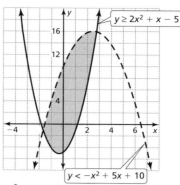

27. $-\frac{5}{2} < x < \frac{5}{2}$ **29.** $x \le 4$ or $x \ge 7$

31. $-0.5 \le x \le 3$ **33.** $x < -2$ or $x > 4$

35. about $0.38 < x < 2.62$ **37.** $x < -7$ or $x > -1$

39. $-2 \le x \le \frac{4}{3}$

41. about $x \le -6.87$ or $x \ge 0.87$

43. a. $x_1 < x < x_2$ **b.** $x < x_1$ or $x > x_2$ **c.** $x_1 < x < x_2$

45. about 55 m from the left pylon to about 447 m from the left pylon

47. a. $0.0051x^2 - 0.319x + 15 < 0.005x^2 - 0.23x + 22$, $16 \le x \le 70$

  b. $A(x) < V(x)$ for $16 \le x \le 70$; Graph the inequalities only on $16 \le x \le 70$. $A(x)$ is always less than $V(x)$.

  c. The driver would react more quickly to the siren of an approaching ambulance; The reaction time to audio stimuli is always less.

49. $0.00170x^2 + 0.145x + 2.35 > 10$, $0 \le x \le 40$; after about 37 days; Because $L(x)$ is a parabola, $L(x) = 10$ has two solutions. Because the x-value must be positive, the domain requires that the negative solution be rejected.

51. a. $\frac{32}{3} \approx 10.67$ square units   **b.** $\frac{256}{3} \approx 85.33$ square units

53. a. yes; The points on the parabola that are exactly 11 feet high are (6, 11) and (14, 11). Because these points are 8 feet apart, there is enough room for a 7-foot wide truck.

  b. 8 ft   **c.** about 11.2 ft

4.9 Maintaining Mathematical Proficiency *(p. 266)*

55. maximum value; 25   **57.** minimum value; $-\frac{81}{4}$

59. 0, 4

Chapter 4 Review *(pp. 268–272)*

1. $6p^3\sqrt{2p}$ **2.** $\dfrac{3\sqrt{35y}}{7y}$

3. $\dfrac{5x^3\sqrt[3]{2x^2}}{2}$ **4.** $4\sqrt{6} - 8$

5. $14\sqrt{3}$ **6.** $9\sqrt[3]{2}$

7. $88 + 30\sqrt{7}$ **8.** $10\sqrt{3}$

9. $x = 6, x = 3$ **10.** no real solutions

11. $x = -4$ **12.** $-5, -2$

13.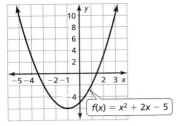

−3.4, 1.4

14. $x \approx 3.46, x \approx -3.46$
15. $x = 0$
16. $x = 6, x = -10$
17. $x \approx 3.54, x \approx -3.54$
18. $x = 1$
19. $x \approx 1.48, x \approx -1.48$
20. $x = 4, x = -10$
21. $x = -1$
22. $x \approx 3.45, x \approx -1.45$
23. maximum value; 8
24. minimum value; 7
25. minimum value; -33
26. 28 cm
27. $x = 3, x = -5$
28. $x \approx 2.3, x \approx -1.8$
29. $x = 1$
30. one x-intercept
31. no x-intercepts
32. two x-intercepts
33. $x = 9$ and $y = -3$
34. $5 - 3i$
35. $11 + 10i$
36. $-62 + 11i$
37. 68
38. $x = \pm 10i$; *Sample answer:* The equation does not have an x-term, so solve using square roots.
39. $x = \pm 4i$; *Sample answer:* The equation does not have an x-term, so solve using square roots.
40. $x = -17, 1$; *Sample answer:* The equation is factorable, so solve by factoring.
41. $x = 3 \pm 3i$; *Sample answer:* The equation is not easily factorable and $a \neq 1$, so solve using the Quadratic Formula.
42. $x = \dfrac{-5 \pm \sqrt{57}}{4}$; *Sample answer:* The equation is not easily factorable and $a \neq 1$, so solve using the Quadratic Formula.
43. $x = \dfrac{7 \pm \sqrt{107}i}{6}$; *Sample answer:* The equation is not easily factorable and $a \neq 1$, so solve using the Quadratic Formula.
44. $\pm 9i$
45. $1 \pm 2\sqrt{2}i$
46. $\dfrac{1 \pm i}{4}$
47. no; yes; *Sample answer:* When $h = 25$, the equation has two imaginary solutions. When $h = 20$, $t \approx 0.65$ and $t \approx 1.35$.
48. $(1, -5)$
49. about $(4.87, 14.75)$, about $(-2.87, -0.75)$
50. about $(-1.88, 2.35)$, about $(2.48, -4.64)$
51.

52.

53.

54.

55.

56.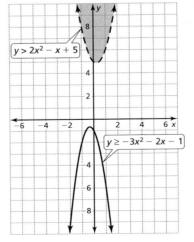

57. a. $\frac{2}{3} \le x \le 1$ **b.** $x < -7$ or $x > -3$

Chapter 5

Chapter 5 Maintaining Mathematical Proficiency *(p. 277)*

1. $\frac{6}{30} = \frac{p}{100}$, 20%   **2.** $\frac{a}{25} = \frac{68}{100}$, 17

3. $\frac{34.4}{86} = \frac{p}{100}$, 40%

4.

5. no; The sofa will cost 80% of the retail price and the arm chair will cost 81% of the retail price.

5.1 Vocabulary and Core Concept Check *(p. 284)*

1. Theoretical probability is based on the number of outcomes and experimental probability is based on repeated trials.

5.1 Monitoring Progress and Modeling with Mathematics *(pp. 284–286)*

3. 48; 1HHH, 1HHT, 1HTH, 1THH, 1HTT, 1THT, 1TTH, 1TTT, 2HHH, 2HHT, 2HTH, 2THH, 2HTT, 2THT, 2TTH, 2TTT, 3HHH, 3HHT, 3HTH, 3THH, 3HTT, 3THT, 3TTH, 3TTT, 4HHH, 4HHT, 4HTH, 4THH, 4HTT, 4THT, 4TTH, 4TTT, 5HHH, 5HHT, 5HTH, 5THH, 5HTT, 5THT, 5TTH, 5TTT, 6HHH, 6HHT, 6HTH, 6THH, 6HTT, 6THT, 6TTH, 6TTT

5. 12; R1, R2, R3, R4, W1, W2, W3, W4, B1, B2, B3, B4

7. $\frac{5}{16}$, or about 31.25%

9. a. $\frac{11}{12}$, or about 92%   **b.** $\frac{13}{18}$, or about 72%

11. There are 4 outcomes, not 3; The probability is $\frac{1}{4}$.

13. 4

15. a. $\frac{9}{10}$, or 90%   **b.** $\frac{2}{3}$, or about 67%

   c. The probability in part (b) is based on trials, not possible outcomes.

   d. They are both $\frac{1}{10}$.

17. about 0.08, or about 8%   **19.** 1 : 1

21. 4 : 1   **23.** lottery game; $\frac{3}{8} > 0.35$

25. *Sample answer:* the odds of stopping on a number less than 16

27. a. 2, 3, 4, 5, 6, 7, 8, 9, 10, 11, 12

   b. 2: $\frac{1}{36}$, 3: $\frac{1}{18}$, 4: $\frac{1}{12}$, 5: $\frac{1}{9}$, 6: $\frac{5}{36}$, 7: $\frac{1}{6}$, 8: $\frac{5}{36}$, 9: $\frac{1}{9}$, 10: $\frac{1}{12}$, 11: $\frac{1}{18}$, 12: $\frac{1}{36}$

   c. *Sample answer:* The probabilities are similar.

29. a. 50; 47 + 3 = 50

   b. 0.44; The probability of not drawing a white marble is $\frac{47}{50} = 0.94$ and $0.94 - 0.5 = 0.44$

31. $\frac{3}{400}$, or 0.75%; about 113; (0.0075)15,000 = 112.5

5.1 Maintaining Mathematical Proficiency *(p. 286)*

33. $3(x + 6)(x - 2)$ **35.** $(x + 3)(4x - 5)$

37. $x = -2, x = 2$ **39.** $x = \frac{7}{5}, x = \frac{13}{5}$

5.2 Vocabulary and Core Concept Check *(p. 292)*

1. When two events are dependent, the occurrence of one event affects the other. When two events are independent, the occurrence of one event does not affect the other. *Sample answer:* choosing two marbles from a bag without replacement; rolling two dice

5.2 Monitoring Progress and Modeling with Mathematics *(pp. 292–294)*

3. dependent; The occurrence of event A affects the occurrence of event B.

5. dependent; The occurrence of event A affects the occurrence of event B.

7. yes   **9.** yes

11. about 2.8%   **13.** about 34.7%

15. The probabilities were added instead of multiplied; $P(A \text{ and } B) = (0.6)(0.2) = 0.12$

17. 0.325

19. a. about 1.2%

   b. about 1.0%

   You are about 1.2 times more likely to select 3 face cards when you replace each card before you select the next card.

21. a. about 17.1%   **b.** about 81.4%

23. about 53.5%

25. a. *Sample answer:* Put 20 pieces of paper with each of the 20 students' names in a hat and pick one; 5%

   b. *Sample answer:* Put 45 pieces of paper in a hat with each student's name appearing once for each hour the student worked. Pick one piece; about 8.9%

27. yes; The chance that it will be rescheduled is $(0.7)(0.75) = 0.525$, which is greater than a 50% chance.

29. a. wins: 0%; loses: 1.99%; ties: 98.01%

   b. wins: 20.25%; loses: 30.25%; ties: 49.5%

   c. yes; Go for 2 points after the first touchdown, and then go for 1 point if they were successful the first time or 2 points if they were unsuccessful the first time; winning: 44.55%; losing: 30.25%

5.2 Maintaining Mathematical Proficiency *(p. 294)*

31. $x = 0.2$ **33.** $x = 0.15$

5.3 Vocabulary and Core Concept Check *(p. 300)*

1. two-way table

5.3 Monitoring Progress and Modeling with Mathematics *(pp. 300–302)*

3. 34; 40; 4; 6; 12

5.

		Gender		
		Male	Female	Total
Response	Yes	132	151	283
	No	39	29	68
	Total	171	180	351

351 people were surveyed, 171 males were surveyed, 180 females were surveyed, 283 people said yes, 68 people said no.

7.

		Dominant Hand		
		Left	Right	Total
Gender	Female	0.048	0.450	0.498
	Male	0.104	0.398	0.502
	Total	0.152	0.848	1

9.

		Gender		
		Male	Female	Total
Response	Yes	0.376	0.430	0.806
	No	0.111	0.083	0.194
	Total	0.487	0.513	1

11.

		Breakfast	
		Ate	Did Not Eat
Feeling	Tired	0.091	0.333
	Not Tired	0.909	0.667

13. a. about 0.789   **b.** 0.168

  c. The events are independent.

15. The value for $P(\text{yes})$ was used in the denominator instead of the value for $P(\text{Tokyo})$;

$$\frac{0.049}{0.39} \approx 0.126$$

17. Route B; It has the best probability of getting to school on time.

19. *Sample answer:*

		Transportation to School			
		Rides Bus	Walks	Car	Total
Gender	Male	6	9	4	19
	Female	5	2	4	11
	Total	11	11	8	30

		Transportation to School			
		Rides Bus	Walks	Car	Total
Gender	Male	0.2	0.3	0.133	0.633
	Female	0.167	0.067	0.133	0.367
	Total	0.367	0.367	0.266	1

21. Routine B is the best option, but your friend's reasoning of why is incorrect; Routine B is the best choice because there is a 66.7% chance of reaching the goal, which is higher than the chances of Routine A (62.5%) and Routine C (63.6%).

23. a. about 0.438   **b.** about 0.387

25. a. More of the current consumers prefer the leader, so they should improve the new snack before marketing it.

b. More of the new consumers prefer the new snack than the leading snack, so there is no need to improve the snack.

5.3 Maintaining Mathematical Proficiency (p. 302)

27.   **29.**

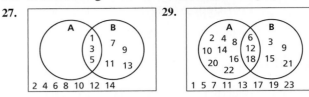

5.4 Vocabulary and Core Concept Check (p. 309)

1. yes; $\overline{A}$ is everything not in A; *Sample answer:* event A: you win the game, event $\overline{A}$: you do not win the game

5.4 Monitoring Progress and Modeling with Mathematics (pp. 309–310)

3. 0.4   **5.** $\frac{7}{12}$, or about 0.58

7. $\frac{9}{20}$, or 0.45   **9.** $\frac{7}{10}$, or 0.7

11. forgot to subtract $P(\text{heart and face card})$;
  $P(\text{heart}) + P(\text{face card}) - P(\text{heart and face card}) = \frac{11}{26}$

13. $\frac{2}{3}$ **15.** 10%

17. 0.4742, or 47.42%   **19.** $\frac{13}{18}$

21. $\frac{3}{20}$

23. no; Until all cards, numbers, and colors are known, the conclusion cannot be made.

5.4 Maintaining Mathematical Proficiency (p. 310)

25.

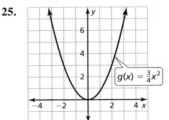

Both graphs open up and have the same vertex, $(0, 0)$, and the same axis of symmetry, $x = 0$. The graph of g is wider than the graph of f because the graph of g is a vertical shrink by a factor of $\frac{3}{4}$ of the graph of f.

5.5 Vocabulary and Core Concept Check (p. 316)

1. permutation

5.5 Monitoring Progress and Modeling with Mathematics (pp. 316–318)

3. a. 2   **5. a.** 24

  b. 2   **b.** 12

7. a. 720

  b. 30

9. 20   **11.** 9

13. 20,160   **15.** 870

17. 990   **19.** $\frac{1}{56}$

21. 4   **23.** 20

25. 5   **27.** 1

29. 220   **31.** 6435

33. 635,376

35. The factorial in the denominator was left out;

$$_{11}P_7 = \frac{11!}{(11-7)!} = 1{,}663{,}200$$

37. combinations; The order is not important; 45

39. permutations; The order is important; 132,600

41. $_{50}C_9 = {}_{50}C_{41}$; For each combination of 9 objects, there is a corresponding combination of the 41 remaining objects.

43.

	$r = 0$	$r = 1$	$r = 2$	$r = 3$
$_3P_r$	1	3	6	6
$_3C_r$	1	3	3	1

$_nP_r \geq {}_nC_r$; Because $_nP_r = \dfrac{n!}{(n-r)!}$ and $_nC_r = \dfrac{n!}{(n-r)! \cdot r!}$,

$_nP_r > {}_nC_r$ when $r > 1$ and $_nP_r = {}_nC_r$ when $r = 0$ or $r = 1$.

45. $\dfrac{1}{44{,}850}$ **47.** $\dfrac{1}{15{,}890{,}700}$

49. a. $_nC_{n-2} - n$ **b.** $\dfrac{n(n-3)}{2}$

51. 30

53. a. $\frac{1}{2}$ **b.** $\frac{1}{2}$; The probabilities are the same.

55. a. $\frac{1}{90}$ **b.** $\frac{9}{10}$

57. $\frac{1}{406}$; There are $_{30}C_5$ possible groups. The number of groups that will have you and your two best friends is $_{27}C_2$.

5.5 Maintaining Mathematical Proficiency *(p. 318)*

59. $\frac{1}{5}$

5.6 Vocabulary and Core Concept Check *(p. 323)*

1. a variable whose value is determined by the outcomes of a probability experiment

5.6 Monitoring Progress and Modeling with Mathematics *(pp. 323–324)*

3.

x (value)	1	2	3
Outcomes	5	3	2
P(x)	$\frac{1}{2}$	$\frac{3}{10}$	$\frac{1}{5}$

5.

w (value)	1	2
Outcomes	5	21
P(w)	$\frac{5}{26}$	$\frac{21}{26}$

7. a. 2
   b. $\frac{5}{8}$

9. about 0.00002   **11.** about 0.00018

13. a.

b. The most likely outcome is that 1 of the 6 students owns a ring.

c. about 0.798

15. The exponents are switched;

$$P(k = 3) = {}_5C_3\left(\frac{1}{6}\right)^3\left(\frac{5}{6}\right)^{5-3} \approx 0.032$$

17. a. $P(0) \approx 0.099$, $P(1) \approx 0.271$, $P(2) \approx 0.319$,
   $P(3) \approx 0.208$, $P(4) \approx 0.081$, $P(5) \approx 0.019$,
   $P(6) \approx 0.0025$, $P(7) \approx 0.00014$

b.

x	0	1	2	3	4
P(x)	0.099	0.271	0.319	0.208	0.081

x	5	6	7
P(x)	0.019	0.0025	0.00014

c.

19. no; The data is skewed right, so the probability of failure is greater.

21. a. The statement is not valid, because having a male and having a female are independent events.

b. 0.03125

c.

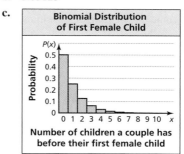

skewed right

5.6 Maintaining Mathematical Proficiency *(p. 324)*

23. FFF, FFM FMF, FMM, MMM, MMF, MFM, MFF

Chapter 5 Review *(pp. 326–328)*

1. 6; FY, FN, FM, MY, MN, MM

2. $\frac{2}{9}$; $\frac{7}{9}$ **3.** 1 : 4; 4 : 1

4. a. 0.15625

b. about 0.1667

You are about 1.07 times more likely to pick a red then a green if you do not replace the first marble.

5. a. about 0.0586

b. 0.0625

You are about 1.07 times more likely to pick a blue then a red if you do not replace the first marble.

6. a. 0.25

b. about 0.2333

You are about 1.07 times more likely to pick a green and then another green if you replace the first marble.

7. about 0.529

8.

		Gender		
		Men	Women	Total
Response	Yes	200	230	430
	No	20	40	60
	Total	220	270	490

About 44.9% of responders were men, about 55.1% of responders were women, about 87.8% of responders thought it was impactful, about 12.2% of responders thought it was not impactful.

9. 0.68

10. 0.02

11. 5040

12. 1,037,836,800

13. 15

14. 70

15. a. 120   **b.** 60

16. $\frac{1}{84}$

17. about 0.12

18.

Binomial Distribution for Made Free Throws

The most likely outcome is that 4 of the 5 free throw shots will be made.

Chapter 6

Chapter 6 Maintaining Mathematical Proficiency (p. 333)

1. $y = -3x + 10$

2. $y = x - 7$

3. $y = \frac{1}{4}x - \frac{7}{4}$

4. $-3 \leq w \leq 8$

5. $0 < m < 11$

6. $s \leq 5 \ or \ s > 2$

7. $d < 12 \ or \ d \geq -7$

8. yes; As with Exercises 6 and 7, if the graphs of the two inequalities overlap going in opposite directions and the variable only has to make one or the other true, then every number on the number line makes the compound inequality true.

6.1 Vocabulary and Core Concept Check (p. 340)

1. Paragraph proofs present reasons as sentences. Flow chart proofs present reasons below the statements they justify.

6.1 Monitoring Progress and Modeling with Mathematics (pp. 340–342)

3. Given; $m\angle 1 = m\angle 2$

5. Vertical Angles Congruence Theorem; $\angle 2 \cong \angle 3$

7. Alternate Interior Angles Theorem; $\angle 2$ and $\angle 3$ are supplementary; $m\angle 2 + m\angle 3$

STATEMENTS	REASONS
1. $n \parallel p$	1. Given
2. $\angle 1 \cong \angle 3$	2. Alternate Interior Angles Theorem
3. $m\angle 1 = m\angle 3$	3. Definition of congruent angles
4. $\angle 2$ and $\angle 3$ are supplementary	4. Linear Pair Postulate
5. $m\angle 2 + m\angle 3 = 180°$	5. Definition of supplementary angles
6. $m\angle 2 + m\angle 1 = 180°$	6. Substitution Property of Equality
7. $\angle 1$ and $\angle 2$ are supplementary	7. Definition of supplementary angles

9. Translations are rigid motions; $\overleftrightarrow{AB} \parallel \overleftrightarrow{CD}$

STATEMENTS	REASONS
1. $\angle ABD \cong \angle CDE$	1. Given
2. A translation along $\overline{BD}$ maps $\angle ABD$ onto $\angle CDE$	2. Translations are rigid motions
3. $\overleftrightarrow{AB} \parallel \overleftrightarrow{CD}$	3. Translations map lines to parallel lines

11. By the Distance Formula, $OB = \sqrt{a^2 + b^2}$, $BC = \sqrt{a^2 + b^2}$, $OD = \sqrt{a^2 + b^2}$, and $DC = \sqrt{a^2 + b^2}$. So, $\triangle OBC$ and $\triangle ODC$ are isosceles by definition.

13. The wrong property is stated; $\overline{DE} \cong \overline{BE}$ by the Transitive Property of Congruence.

15. no; *Sample answer:* $\overrightarrow{BA}$ and $\overrightarrow{BE}$ are not opposite rays, so the angles are not vertical.

6.1 Maintaining Mathematical Proficiency (p. 342)

17. $x = 7$

19. 142

6.2 Vocabulary and Core Concept Check (p. 348)

1. bisector

6.2 Monitoring Progress and Modeling with Mathematics (pp. 348–350)

3. 4.6; Because $GK = KJ$ and $\overline{HK} \perp \overrightarrow{GJ}$, point H is on the perpendicular bisector of $\overrightarrow{GJ}$. So, by the Perpendicular Bisector Theorem, $GH = HJ = 4.6$.

5. 15; Because $\overleftrightarrow{DB} \perp \overrightarrow{AC}$ and point D is equidistant from A and C, point D is on the perpendicular bisector of $\overline{AC}$ by the Converse of the Perpendicular Bisector Theorem. By definition of segment bisector, $AB = BC$. So, $5x = 4x + 3$, and the solution is $x = 3$. So, $AB = 5x = 5(3) = 15$.

7. yes; Because point N is equidistant from L and M, point N is on the perpendicular bisector of $\overline{LM}$ by the Converse of the Perpendicular Bisector Theorem. Because only one line can be perpendicular to $\overline{LM}$ at point K, $\overrightarrow{NK}$ must be the perpendicular bisector of $\overline{LM}$, and P is on $\overrightarrow{NK}$.

9. no; You would need to know that $\overleftrightarrow{PN} \perp \overleftrightarrow{ML}$.

11. $20°$; Because D is equidistant from $\overrightarrow{BC}$ and $\overrightarrow{BA}$, $\overrightarrow{BD}$ bisects $\angle ABC$ by the Converse of the Angle Bisector Theorem. So, $m\angle ABD = m\angle CBD = 20°$.

13. $28°$; Because L is equidistant from $\overrightarrow{JK}$ and $\overrightarrow{JM}$, $\overrightarrow{JL}$ bisects $\angle KJM$ by the Angle Bisector Theorem. This means that $7x = 3x + 16$, and the solution is $x = 4$. So, $m\angle KJL = 7x = 7(4) = 28°$.

15. yes; Because H is equidistant from $\overrightarrow{EF}$ and $\overrightarrow{EG}$, $\overrightarrow{EH}$ bisects $\angle FEG$ by the Angle Bisector Theorem.

17. no; Because neither $\overline{BD}$ nor $\overline{DC}$ are marked as perpendicular to $\overrightarrow{AB}$ or $\overrightarrow{AC}$ respectively, you cannot conclude that $DB = DC$.

19. $y = x - 2$ **21.** $y = -3x + 15$

23. Because $\overline{DC}$ is not necessarily congruent to $\overline{EC}$, $\overleftrightarrow{AB}$ will not necessarily pass through point C; Because $AD = AE$, and $\overleftrightarrow{AB} \perp \overline{DE}$, $\overleftrightarrow{AB}$ is the perpendicular bisector of $\overline{DE}$.

25. Perpendicular Bisector Theorem

27.

Perpendicular Bisector Theorem

29. B

31. no; If the triangle is an isosceles triangle, then the angle bisector of the vertex angle will also be the perpendicular bisector of the base.

33. a.

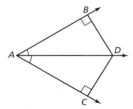

If $\overrightarrow{AD}$ bisects $\angle BAC$, then by definition of angle bisector, $\angle BAD \cong \angle CAD$. Also, because $\overline{DB} \perp \overrightarrow{AB}$ and $\overline{DC} \perp \overrightarrow{AC}$, by definition of perpendicular lines, $\angle ABD$ and $\angle ACD$ are right angles, and congruent to each other by the Right Angles Congruence Theorem. Also, $\overline{AD} \cong \overline{AD}$ by the Reflexive Property of Congruence. So, by the AAS Congruence Theorem, $\triangle ADB \cong \triangle ADC$. Because corresponding parts of congruent triangles are congruent, $DB = DC$. This means that point D is equidistant from each side of $\angle BAC$.

b.

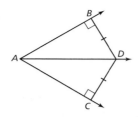

STATEMENTS	REASONS
1. $\overline{DC} \perp \overrightarrow{AC}$, $\overline{DB} \perp \overrightarrow{AB}$, $BD = CD$	**1.** Given
2. $\angle ABD$ and $\angle ACD$ are right angles.	**2.** Definition of perpendicular lines
3. $\triangle ABD$ and $\triangle ACD$ are right triangles.	**3.** Definition of a right triangle
4. $\overline{BD} \cong \overline{CD}$	**4.** Definition of congruent segments
5. $\overline{AD} \cong \overline{AD}$	**5.** Reflexive Property of Congruence
6. $\triangle ABD \cong \triangle ACD$	**6.** HL Congruence Theorem
7. $\angle BAD \cong \angle CAD$	**7.** Corresponding parts of congruent triangles are congruent.
8. $\overrightarrow{AD}$ bisects $\angle BAC$.	**8.** Definition of angle bisector

35. a. $y = x$ **b.** $y = -x$ **c.** $y = |x|$

37. Because $\overline{AD} \cong \overline{CD}$ and $\overline{AE} \cong \overline{CE}$, by the Converse of the Perpendicular Bisector Theorem, both points D and E are on the perpendicular bisector of $\overline{AC}$. So, $\overleftrightarrow{DE}$ is the perpendicular bisector of $\overline{AC}$. So, if $\overline{AB} \cong \overline{CB}$, then by the Converse of the Perpendicular Bisector Theorem, point B is also on $\overleftrightarrow{DE}$. So, points D, E, and B are collinear. Conversely, if points D, E, and B are collinear, then by the Perpendicular Bisector Theorem, point B is also on the perpendicular bisector of $\overline{AC}$. So, $\overline{AB} \cong \overline{CB}$.

6.2 Maintaining Mathematical Proficiency *(p. 350)*

39. isosceles   **41.** equilateral

43. right

6.3 Vocabulary and Core Concept Check *(p. 357)*

1. concurrent

6.3 Monitoring Progress and Modeling with Mathematics *(pp. 357–360)*

3. 9   **5.** 9

7. $(5, 8)$ **9.** $(-4, 9)$

11. 16   **13.** 6

15. 32

17. *Sample answer:*

19. *Sample answer:*

21. *Sample answer:*

23. *Sample answer:*

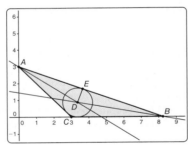

25. Because point G is the intersection of the angle bisectors, it is the incenter. But, because $\overline{GD}$ and $\overline{GF}$ are not necessarily perpendicular to a side of the triangle, there is not sufficient evidence to conclude that $\overline{GD}$ and $\overline{GF}$ are congruent; Point G is equidistant from the sides of the triangle.

27. You could copy the positions of the three houses, and connect the points to draw a triangle. Then draw the three perpendicular bisectors of the triangle. The point where the perpendicular bisectors meet, the circumcenter, should be the location of the meeting place.

29. sometimes; If the scalene triangle is obtuse or right, then the circumcenter is outside or on the triangle, respectively. However, if the scalene triangle is acute, then the circumcenter is inside the triangle.

31. sometimes; This only happens when the triangle is equilateral.

33. $\left(\frac{35}{6}, -\frac{11}{6}\right)$ **35.** $x = 6$

37. The circumcenter of any right triangle is located at the midpoint of the hypotenuse of the triangle. Let $A(0, 2b)$, $B(0, 0)$, and $C(2a, 0)$ represent the vertices of a right triangle where $\angle B$ is the right angle. The midpoint of $\overline{AB}$ is $M_{\overline{AB}}(0, b)$. The midpoint of $\overline{BC}$ is $M_{\overline{BC}}(a, 0)$. The midpoint of $\overline{AC}$ is $M_{\overline{AC}}(a, b)$. Because $\overline{AB}$ is vertical, its perpendicular bisector is horizontal. So, the equation of the horizontal line passing through $M_{\overline{AB}}(0, b)$ is $y = b$. Because $\overline{BC}$ is horizontal, its perpendicular bisector is vertical. So, the equation of the vertical line passing through $M_{\overline{BC}}(a, 0)$ is $x = a$. The circumcenter of $\triangle ABC$ is the intersection of perpendicular bisectors, $y = b$ and $x = a$, which is (a, b). This point is also the midpoint of $\overline{AC}$.

39. The circumcenter is the point of intersection of the perpendicular bisectors of the sides of a triangle, and it is equidistant from the vertices of the triangle. In contrast, the incenter is the point of intersection of the angle bisectors of a triangle, and it is equidistant from the sides of the triangle.

41. a.

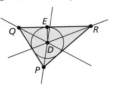

Because this circle is inscribed in the triangle, it is the largest circle that fits inside the triangle without extending into the boundaries.

b. yes; You would keep the center of the pool as the incenter of the triangle, but you would make the radius of the pool at least 1 foot shorter.

43. B

45. yes; In an equilateral triangle, each perpendicular bisector passes through the opposite vertex and divides the triangle into two congruent triangles. So, it is also an angle bisector.

47. a. equilateral; 3; In an equilateral triangle, each perpendicular bisector also bisects the opposite angle.

b. scalene; 6; In a scalene triangle, none of the perpendicular bisectors will also bisect an angle.

49. angle bisectors; about 2.83 in.

51. $x = \dfrac{AB + AC - BC}{2}$ or $x = \dfrac{AB \cdot AC}{AB + AC + BC}$

6.3 Maintaining Mathematical Proficiency (p. 360)

53. $M(6, 3)$; $AB \approx 11.3$ **55.** $M(-1, 7)$; $AB \approx 12.6$

57. $x = 6$

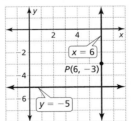

59. $y = \frac{1}{4}x + 2$

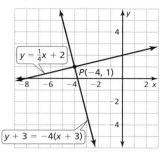

6.4 Vocabulary and Core Concept Check (p. 366)

1. circumcenter, incenter, centroid, orthocenter; Perpendicular bisectors form the circumcenter, angle bisectors form the incenter, medians form the centroid, and altitudes form the orthocenter.

6.4 Monitoring Progress and Modeling with Mathematics (pp. 366–368)

3. 6, 3

5. 20, 10

7. 10, 15

9. 18, 27

11. 12

13. 10

15. $\left(5, \frac{11}{3}\right)$

17. $(5, 1)$

19. outside; $(0, -5)$

21. inside; $(-1, 2)$

23.

25. *Sample answer:*

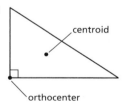

27. The length of $\overline{DE}$ should be $\frac{1}{3}$ of the length of $\overline{AE}$ because it is the shorter segment from the centroid to the side;
$DE = \frac{1}{3}AE$
$DE = \frac{1}{3}(18)$
$DE = 6$

29.

Legs $\overline{AB}$ and $\overline{BC}$ of isosceles $\triangle ABC$ are congruent. $\angle ABD \cong \angle CBD$ because $\overline{BD}$ is an angle bisector of vertex angle $\angle ABC$. Also, $\overline{BD} \cong \overline{BD}$ by the Reflexive Property of Congruence. So, $\triangle ABD \cong \triangle CBD$ by the SAS Congruence Theorem. $\overline{AD} \cong \overline{CD}$ because corresponding parts of congruent triangles are congruent. So, $\overline{BD}$ is a median.

31. never; Because medians are always inside a triangle, and the centroid is the point of concurrency of the medians, it will always be inside the triangle.

33. sometimes; A median is the same line segment as the perpendicular bisector if the triangle is equilateral or if the segment is connecting the vertex angle to the base of an isosceles triangle. Otherwise, the median and the perpendicular bisectors are not the same segment.

35. sometimes; The centroid and the orthocenter are not the same point unless the triangle is equilateral.

37. Both segments are perpendicular to a side of a triangle, and their point of intersection can fall either inside, on, or outside of the triangle. However, the altitude does not necessarily bisect the side, but the perpendicular bisector does. Also, the perpendicular bisector does not necessarily pass through the opposite vertex, but the altitude does.

39. 6.75 in.^{2}; altitude

41. $x = 2.5$

43. $x = 4$

45.

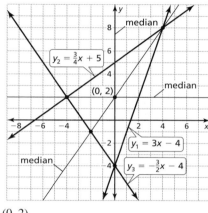

$(0, 2)$

47. $PE = \frac{1}{3}AE$, $PE = \frac{1}{2}AP$, $PE = AE - AP$

49. yes; If the triangle is equilateral, then the perpendicular bisectors, angle bisectors, medians, and altitudes will all be the same three segments.

51.

Sides $\overline{AB}$ and $\overline{BC}$ of equilateral $\triangle ABC$ are congruent. $\overline{AD} \cong \overline{CD}$ because $\overline{BD}$ is the median to $\overline{AC}$. Also, $\overline{BD} \cong \overline{BD}$ by the Reflexive Property of Congruence. So, $\triangle ABD \cong \triangle CBD$ by the SSS Congruence Theorem. $\angle ADB \cong \angle CDB$ and $\angle ABD \cong \angle CBD$ because corresponding parts of congruent triangles are congruent. Also, $\angle ADB$ and $\angle CDB$ are a linear pair. Because $\overline{BD}$ and $\overline{AC}$ intersect to form a linear pair of congruent angles, $\overline{BD} \perp \overline{AC}$. So, median $\overline{BD}$ is also an angle bisector, altitude, and perpendicular bisector of $\triangle ABC$.

53. *Sample answer:*

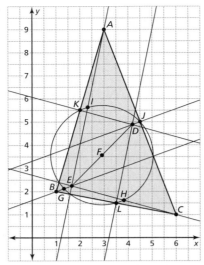

The circle passes through nine significant points of the triangle. They are the midpoints of the sides, the midpoints between each vertex and the orthocenter, and the points of intersection between the sides and the altitudes.

6.4 Maintaining Mathematical Proficiency *(p. 368)*

55. yes   **57.** no

6.5 Vocabulary and Core Concept Check *(p. 375)*

1. midsegment

6.5 Monitoring Progress and Modeling with Mathematics *(pp. 375–376)*

3. $D(-4, -2)$, $E(-2, 0)$, $F(-1, -4)$

5. Because the slopes of $\overline{EF}$ and $\overline{AC}$ are the same (-4), $\overline{EF} \parallel \overline{AC}$. $EF = \sqrt{17}$ and $AC = 2\sqrt{17}$. Because $\sqrt{17} = \frac{1}{2}(2\sqrt{17})$, $EF = \frac{1}{2}AC$.

7. $x = 13$ **9.** $x = 6$

11. $\overline{JK} \parallel \overline{YZ}$ **13.** $\overline{XY} \parallel \overline{KL}$

15. $\overline{JL} \cong \overline{XK} \cong \overline{KZ}$ **17.** 14

19. 17   **21.** 45 ft

23. An eighth segment, $\overline{FG}$, would connect the midpoints of $\overline{DL}$ and $\overline{EN}$; $\overline{DE} \parallel \overline{LN} \parallel \overline{FG}$, $DE = \frac{3}{4}LN$, and $FG = \frac{7}{8}LN$; Because you are finding quarter segments and eighth segments, use $8p$, $8q$, and $8r$: $L(0, 0)$, $M(8q, 8r)$, and $N(8p, 0)$.

Find the coordinates of X, Y, D, E, F, and G.

$X(4q, 4r)$, $Y(4q + 4p, 4r)$, $D(2q, 2r)$, $E(2q + 6p, 2r)$, $F(q, r)$, and $G(q + 7p, r)$.

The y-coordinates of D and E are the same, so $\overline{DE}$ has a slope of 0. The y-coordinates of F and G are also the same, so $\overline{FG}$ also has a slope of 0. $\overline{LN}$ is on the x-axis, so its slope is 0. Because their slopes are the same, $\overline{DE} \parallel \overline{LN} \parallel \overline{FG}$.

Use the Ruler Postulate to find DE, FG, and LN.

$DE = 6p$, $FG = 7p$, and $LN = 8p$.

Because $6p = \frac{3}{4}(8p)$, $DE = \frac{3}{4}LN$. Because $7p = \frac{7}{8}(8p)$, $FG = \frac{7}{8}LN$.

25. a. 24 units   **b.** 60 units   **c.** 114 units

27. After graphing the midsegments, find the slope of each segment. Graph the line parallel to each midsegment passing through the opposite vertex. The intersections of these three lines will be the vertices of the original triangle: $(-1, 2)$, $(9, 8)$, and $(5, 0)$.

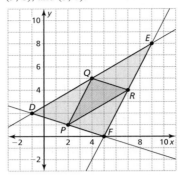

6.5 Maintaining Mathematical Proficiency *(p. 376)*

29. *Sample answer:* An isosceles triangle whose sides are 5 centimeters, 5 centimeters, and 3 centimeters is not equilateral.

6.6 Vocabulary and Core Concept Check *(p. 382)*

1. In an indirect proof, rather than proving a statement directly, you show that when the statement is false, it leads to a contradiction.

6.6 Monitoring Progress and Modeling with Mathematics *(pp. 382–384)*

3. Assume temporarily that $WV = 7$ inches.

5. Assume temporarily that $\angle B$ is a right angle.

7. A and C; The angles of an equilateral triangle are always 60°. So, an equilateral triangle cannot have a 90° angle, and cannot be a right triangle.

9.

The longest side is across from the largest angle, and the shortest side is across from the smallest angle.

11. $\angle S$, $\angle R$, $\angle T$ **13.** $\overline{AB}$, $\overline{BC}$, $\overline{AC}$

15. $\overline{NP}$, $\overline{MN}$, $\overline{MP}$ **17.** 7 in. $< x <$ 17 in.

19. 16 in. $< x <$ 64 in.   **21.** yes

23. no; $28 + 17 \not> 46$

25. An angle that is not obtuse could be acute or right; Assume temporarily that $\angle A$ is not obtuse.

27. Assume temporarily that the client is guilty. Then the client would have been in Los Angeles, California, at the time of the crime. Because the client was in New York at the time of the crime, the assumption must be false, and the client must be innocent.

29. C

31. Assume temporarily that an odd number is divisible by 4. Let the odd number be represented by $2y + 1$ where y is a positive integer. Then, there must be a positive integer x such that $4x = 2y + 1$. However, when you divide each side of the equation by 4, you get $x = \frac{1}{2}y + \frac{1}{4}$, which is not an integer. So, the assumption must be false, and an odd number is not divisible by 4.

33. The right angle of a right triangle must always be the largest angle because the other two will have a sum of 90°. So, according to the Triangle Larger Angle Theorem, because the right angle is larger than either of the other angles, the side opposite the right angle, which is the hypotenuse, will always have to be longer than either of the legs.

35. a. The width of the river must be greater than 35 yards and less than 50 yards. In $\triangle BCA$, the width of the river, $\overline{BA}$, must be less than the length of $\overline{CA}$, which is 50 yards, because the measure of the angle opposite $\overline{BA}$ is less than the measure of the angle opposite $\overline{CA}$, which must be 50°. In $\triangle BDA$, the width of the river, $\overline{BA}$, must be greater than the length of $\overline{DA}$, which is 35 yards, because the measure of the angle opposite $\overline{BA}$ is greater than the measure of the angle opposite $\overline{DA}$, which must be 40°.

b. You could measure from distances that are closer together. In order to do this, you would have to use angle measures that are closer to 45°.

37. $\angle WXY$, $\angle YXZ$, $\angle Z$, $\angle WYX$ and $\angle XYZ$, $\angle W$; In $\triangle WXY$, because $WY < WX < YX$, by the Triangle Longer Side Theorem, $m\angle WXY < m\angle WYX < m\angle W$. Similarly, in $\triangle XYZ$, because $YZ < XY < XZ$, by the Triangle Longer Side Theorem, $m\angle YXZ < m\angle Z < m\angle XYZ$. Because $m\angle WYX = m\angle XYZ$ and $\angle W$ is the only angle greater than either of them, you know that $\angle W$ is the largest angle. Because $\triangle WXY$ has the largest angle and one of the congruent angles, the remaining angle, $\angle WXY$, is the smallest.

39. By the Exterior Angle Theorem, $m\angle 1 = m\angle A + m\angle B$. Then by the Subtraction Property of Equality, $m\angle 1 - m\angle B = m\angle A$. If you assume temporarily that $m\angle 1 \leq m\angle B$, then $m\angle A \leq 0$. Because the measure of any angle in a triangle must be a positive number, the assumption must be false. So, $m\angle 1 > m\angle B$. Similarly, by the Subtraction Property of Equality, $m\angle 1 - m\angle A = m\angle B$. If you assume temporarily that $m\angle 1 \leq m\angle A$, then $m\angle B \leq 0$. Because the measure of any angle in a triangle must be a positive number, the assumption must be false. So, $m\angle 1 > m\angle A$.

41. $2\frac{1}{7} < x < 13$

43. It is given that $BC > AB$ and $BD = BA$. By the Base Angles Theorem, $m\angle 1 = m\angle 2$. By the Angle Addition Postulate, $m\angle BAC = m\angle 1 + m\angle 3$. So, $m\angle BAC > m\angle 1$. Substituting $m\angle 2$ for $m\angle 1$ produces $m\angle BAC > m\angle 2$. By the Exterior Angle Theorem, $m\angle 2 = m\angle 3 + m\angle C$. So, $m\angle 2 > m\angle C$. Finally, because $m\angle BAC > m\angle 2$ and $m\angle 2 > m\angle C$, you can conclude that $m\angle BAC > m\angle C$.

45. no; The sum of the other two sides would be 11 inches, which is less than 13 inches.

47.

Assume $\overline{BC}$ is longer than or the same length as each of the other sides, $\overline{AB}$ and $\overline{AC}$. Then, $AB + BC > AC$ and $AC + BC > AB$. The proof for $AB + AC > BC$ follows.

STATEMENTS	REASONS
1. $\triangle ABC$	1. Given
2. Extend $\overline{AC}$ to D so that $\overline{AB} \cong \overline{AD}$.	2. Ruler Postulate
3. $AB = AD$	3. Definition of segment congruence
4. $AD + AC = DC$	4. Segment Addition Postulate
5. $\angle 1 \cong \angle 2$	5. Base Angles Theorem
6. $m\angle 1 = m\angle 2$	6. Definition of angle congruence
7. $m\angle DBC > m\angle 2$	7. Protractor Postulate
8. $m\angle DBC > m\angle 1$	8. Substitution Property
9. $DC > BC$	9. Triangle Larger Angle Theorem
10. $AD + AC > BC$	10. Substitution Property
11. $AB + AC > BC$	11. Substitution Property

49. Assume temporarily that another segment, $\overline{PA}$, where A is on plane M, is the shortest segment from P to plane M. By definition of the distance between a point and a plane, $\overline{PA} \perp$ plane M. This contradicts the given statement because there cannot be two different segments that share an endpoint and are both perpendicular to the same plane. So, the assumption is false, and because no other segment exists that is the shortest segment from P to plane M, it must be $\overline{PC}$ that is the shortest segment from P to plane M.

6.6 Maintaining Mathematical Proficiency *(p. 384)*

51. $\angle ACD$ **53.** $\angle CEB$

6.7 Vocabulary and Core Concept Check *(p. 389)*

1. The Hinge Theorem refers to two angles with two pairs of sides that have the same measure, just like two hinges whose sides are the same length. Then, the angle whose measure is greater is opposite a longer side, just like the ends of a hinge are farther apart when the hinge is open wider.

6.7 Monitoring Progress and Modeling with Mathematics *(pp. 389–390)*

3. $m\angle 1 > m\angle 2$; By the Converse of the Hinge Theorem, because $\angle 1$ is the included angle in the triangle with the longer third side, its measure is greater than that of $\angle 2$.

5. $m\angle 1 = m\angle 2$; The triangles are congruent by the SSS Congruence Theorem. So, $\angle 1 \cong \angle 2$ because corresponding parts of congruent triangles are congruent.

7. $AD > CD$; By the Hinge Theorem, because $\overline{AD}$ is the third side of the triangle with the larger included angle, it is longer than $\overline{CD}$.

9. $TR < UR$; By the Hinge Theorem, because $\overline{TR}$ is the third side of the triangle with the smaller included angle, it is shorter than $\overline{UR}$.

11. $\overline{XY} \cong \overline{YZ}$ and $m\angle WYZ > m\angle WYX$ are given. By the Reflexive Property of Congruence, $\overline{WY} \cong \overline{WY}$. So, by the Hinge Theorem, $WZ > WX$.

13. your flight; Because $160° > 150°$, the distance you flew is a greater distance than the distance your friend flew by the Hinge Theorem.

15. The measure of the included angle in $\triangle PSQ$ is greater than the measure of the included angle in $\triangle SQR$; By the Hinge Theorem, $PQ > SR$.

17. $m\angle EGF > m\angle DGE$ by the Converse of the Hinge Theorem.

19. Because $\overline{NR}$ is a median, $\overline{PR} \cong \overline{QR}$. $\overline{NR} \cong \overline{NR}$ by the Reflexive Property of Congruence. So, by the Converse of the Hinge Theorem, $\angle NRQ > \angle NRP$. Because $\angle NRQ$ and $\angle NRP$ form a linear pair, they are supplementary. So, $\angle NRQ$ must be obtuse and $\angle NRP$ must be acute.

21. $x > \frac{3}{2}$

23. $\triangle ABC$ is an obtuse triangle; If the altitudes intersect inside the triangle, then $m\angle BAC$ will always be less than $m\angle BDC$ because they both intercept the same segment, $\overline{CD}$. However, because $m\angle BAC > m\angle BDC$, $\angle A$ must be obtuse, and the altitudes must intersect outside of the triangle.

6.7 Maintaining Mathematical Proficiency (p. 390)

25. $x = 38$ 27. $x = 60$

Chapter 6 Review (pp. 392–396)

1.

STATEMENTS	REASONS
1. $\angle 5$ and $\angle 6$ are complementary, $m\angle 5 + m\angle 7 = 90°$	1. Given
2. $\angle 5$ and $\angle 7$ are complementary	2. Definition of complementary angles
3. $\angle 6 \cong \angle 7$	3. Congruent Complements Theorem

2. By the Distance Formula, $OB = \sqrt{a^2 + b^2}$ and $OC = \sqrt{a^2 + b^2}$. So, $\triangle OBC$ is isosceles by the definition of isosceles triangle.

3. 20; Point B is equidistant from A and C, and $\overleftrightarrow{BD} \perp \overline{AC}$. So, by the Converse of the Perpendicular Bisector Theorem, $DC = AD = 20$.

4. 23; $\angle PQS \cong \angle RQS$, $\overline{SR} \perp \overline{QR}$, and $\overline{SP} \perp \overline{QP}$. So, by the Angle Bisector Theorem, $SR = SP$. This means that $6x + 5 = 9x - 4$, and the solution is $x = 3$. So, $RS = 9(3) - 4 = 23$.

5. 47°; Point J is equidistant from $\overrightarrow{FG}$ and $\overrightarrow{FH}$. So, by the Converse of the Angle Bisector Theorem, $m\angle JFH = m\angle JFG = 47°$.

6. $(-3, -3)$ 7. $(4, 3)$

8. $x = 5$ 9. $(-6, 3)$

10. $(4, -4)$ 11. inside; $(3, 5.2)$

12. outside; $(-6, -1)$ 13. $(-6, 6), (-3, 6), (-3, 4)$

14. $(0, 3), (2, 0), (-1, -2)$ 15. 4 in. $< x <$ 12 in.

16. 3 m $< x <$ 15 m 17. 7 ft $< x <$ 29 ft

18. Assume temporarily that $YZ \not> 4$. Then, it follows that either $YZ < 4$ or $YZ = 4$. If $YZ < 4$, then $XY + YZ < XZ$ because $4 + YZ < 8$ when $YZ < 4$. If $YZ = 4$, then $XY + YZ = XZ$ because $4 + 4 = 8$. Both conclusions contradict the Triangle Inequality Theorem, which says that $XY + YZ > XZ$. So, the temporary assumption that $YZ \not> 4$ cannot be true. This proves that in $\triangle XYZ$, if $XY = 4$ and $XZ = 8$, then $YZ > 4$.

19. $QT > ST$ 20. $m\angle QRT > m\angle SRT$

Chapter 7

Chapter 7 Maintaining Mathematical Proficiency (p. 401)

1. $x = 3$ 2. $x = 4$

3. $x = 7$ 4. $a \parallel b, c \perp d$

5. $a \parallel b, c \parallel d, a \perp c, a \perp d, b \perp c, b \perp d$

6. $b \parallel c, b \perp d, c \perp d$

7. You can follow the order of operations with all of the other operations in the equation and treat the operations in the expression separately.

7.1 Vocabulary and Core Concept Check (p. 408)

1. A segment connecting consecutive vertices is a side of the polygon, not a diagonal.

7.1 Monitoring Progress and Modeling with Mathematics (pp. 408–410)

3. $1260°$ 5. $2520°$

7. hexagon 9. 16-gon

11. $x = 64$ 13. $x = 89$

15. $x = 70$ 17. $x = 150$

19. $m\angle X = m\angle Y = 92°$ 21. $m\angle X = m\angle Y = 100.5°$

23. $x = 111$ 25. $x = 32$

27. $108°, 72°$ 29. $172°, 8°$

31. The measure of one interior angle of a regular pentagon was found, but the exterior angle should be found by dividing $360°$ by the number of angles; $\frac{360}{5} = 72°$

33. $120°$ 35. $n = \dfrac{360}{180 - x}$

37. 15 39. 40

41. A, B; Solving the equation found in Exercise 35 for n yields a positive integer greater than or equal to 3 for A and B, but not for C and D.

43. In a quadrilateral, when all the diagonals from one vertex are drawn, the polygon is divided into two triangles. Because the sum of the measures of the interior angles of each triangle is $180°$, the sum of the measures of the interior angles of the quadrilateral is $2 \cdot 180° = 360°$.

45. $21°, 21°, 21°, 21°, 138°, 138°$

47. $(n - 2) \cdot 180°$; When diagonals are drawn from the vertex of the concave angle as shown, the polygon is divided into $n - 2$ triangles whose interior angle measures have the same total as the sum of the interior angle measures of the original polygon.

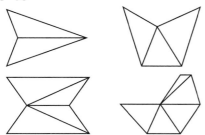

49. **a.** $h(n) = \dfrac{(n - 2) \cdot 180°}{n}$ **b.** $h(9) = 140°$

c. $n = 12$

d.

(graph with points: (8, 135), (7, 128.6), (6, 120), (5, 108), (4, 90), (3, 60))

The values of $h(n)$ increase by lesser amounts as n increases.

51. In a convex n-gon, the sum of the measures of the n interior angles is $(n - 2) \cdot 180°$ using the Polygon Interior Angles Theorem. Because each of the n interior angles forms a linear pair with its corresponding exterior angle, you know that the sum of the measures of the n interior and exterior angles is $180n°$. Subtracting the sum of the interior angle measures from the sum of the measures of the linear pairs gives you $180n° - [(n - 2) \cdot 180°] = 360°$.

7.1 Maintaining Mathematical Proficiency *(p. 410)*

53. $x = 101$ **55.** $x = 16$

7.2 Vocabulary and Core Concept Check *(p. 416)*

1. In order to be a quadrilateral, a polygon must have 4 sides, and parallelograms always have 4 sides. In order to be a parallelogram, a polygon must have 4 sides with opposite sides parallel. Quadrilaterals always have 4 sides, but do not always have opposite sides parallel.

7.2 Monitoring Progress and Modeling with Mathematics *(pp. 416–418)*

3. $x = 9, y = 15$ **5.** $d = 126, z = 28$

7. $129°$

9. 13; By the Parallelogram Opposite Sides Theorem, $LM = QN$.

11. 8; By the Parallelogram Opposite Sides Theorem, $LQ = MN$.

13. $80°$; By the Parallelogram Consecutive Angles Theorem, $\angle QLM$ and $\angle LMN$ are supplementary. So, $m\angle LMN = 180° - 100°$.

15. $100°$; By the Parallelogram Opposite Angles Theorem, $m\angle QLM = m\angle MNQ$.

17. $m = 35, n = 110$ **19.** $k = 7, m = 8$

21. In a parallelogram, consecutive angles are supplementary; Because quadrilateral $STUV$ is a parallelogram, $\angle S$ and $\angle V$ are supplementary. So, $m\angle V = 180° - 50° = 130°$.

23.

STATEMENTS	REASONS
1. $ABCD$ and $CEFD$ are parallelograms.	1. Given
2. $\overline{AB} \cong \overline{DC}, \overline{DC} \cong \overline{FE}$	2. Parallelogram Opposite Sides Theorem
3. $\overline{AB} \cong \overline{FE}$	3. Transitive Property of Congruence

25. $(1, 2.5)$ **27.** $F(3, 3)$

29. $G(2, 0)$ **31.** $36°, 144°$

33. no; *Sample answer:* $\angle A$ and $\angle C$ are opposite angles, but $m\angle A \neq m\angle C$.

35. *Sample Answer:*

(figure: parallelogram with vertices B, C on top, A, D on bottom, with diagonals drawn)

When you fold the parallelogram so that vertex A is on vertex C, the fold will pass through the point where the diagonals intersect, which demonstrates that this point of intersection is also the midpoint of $\overline{AC}$. Similarly, when you fold the parallelogram so that vertex B is on vertex D, the fold will pass through the point where the diagonals intersect, which demonstrates that this point of intersection is also the midpoint of $\overline{BD}$.

37.

STATEMENTS	REASONS
1. $ABCD$ is a parallelogram.	1. Given
2. $\overline{AB} \parallel \overline{DC}, \overline{BC} \parallel \overline{AD}$	2. Definition of parallelogram
3. $\angle BDA \cong \angle DBC$, $\angle DBA \cong \angle BDC$	3. Alternate Interior Angles Theorem (Thm. 3.2)
4. $\overline{BD} \cong \overline{BD}$	4. Reflexive Property of Congruence (Thm. 2.1)
5. $\triangle ABD \cong \triangle CDB$	5. ASA Congruence Theorem (Thm. 5.10)
6. $\angle A \cong \angle C$	6. Corresponding parts of congruent triangles are congruent.
7. $m\angle BDA = m\angle DBC$, $m\angle DBA = m\angle BDC$	7. Definition of congruent angles
8. $m\angle B = m\angle DBC + m\angle DBA, m\angle D = m\angle BDA + m\angle BDC$	8. Angle Addition Postulate
9. $m\angle D = m\angle DBC + m\angle DBA$	9. Substitution Property of Equality
10. $m\angle D = m\angle B$	10. Transitive Property of Equality
11. $\angle D \cong \angle B$	11. Definition of congruent angles

39.

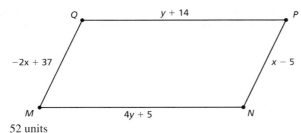

52 units

41. no; Two parallelograms with congruent corresponding sides may or may not have congruent corresponding angles.

43. 16°   **45.** 3; (4, 0), (−2, 4), (8, 8)

47.

STATEMENTS	REASONS
1. $\overleftrightarrow{GH} \parallel \overleftrightarrow{JK} \parallel \overleftrightarrow{LM}, \overline{GJ} \cong \overline{JL}$	1. Given
2. Construct $\overline{PK}$ and $\overline{QM}$ such that $\overline{PK} \parallel \overleftrightarrow{GL} \parallel \overline{QM}$.	2. Construction
3. GPKJ and JQML are parallelograms.	3. Definition of parallelogram
4. $\angle GHK \cong \angle JKM$, $\angle PKQ \cong \angle QML$	4. Corresponding Angles Theorem
5. $\overline{GJ} \cong \overline{PK}, \overline{JL} \cong \overline{QM}$	5. Parallelogram Opposite Sides Theorem
6. $\overline{PK} \cong \overline{QM}$	6. Transitive Property of Congruence
7. $\angle HPK \cong \angle PKQ$, $\angle KQM \cong \angle QML$	7. Alternate Interior Angles Theorem
8. $\angle HPK \cong \angle QML$	8. Transitive Property of Congruence
9. $\angle HPK \cong \angle KQM$	9. Transitive Property of Congruence
10. $\triangle PHK \cong \triangle QKM$	10. AAS Congruence Theorem
11. $\overline{HK} \cong \overline{KM}$	11. Corresponding sides of congruent triangles are congruent.

7.2 Maintaining Mathematical Proficiency *(p. 418)*

49. yes; Alternate Exterior Angles Converse

7.3 Vocabulary and Core Concept Check *(p. 425)*

1. yes; If all four sides are congruent, then both pairs of opposite sides are congruent. So, the quadrilateral is a parallelogram by the Parallelogram Opposite Sides Converse.

7.3 Monitoring Progress and Modeling with Mathematics *(pp. 425–428)*

3. Parallelogram Opposite Angles Converse

5. Parallelogram Diagonals Converse

7. Opposite Sides Parallel and Congruent Theorem

9. $x = 114, y = 66$ **11.** $x = 3, y = 4$

13. $x = 8$ **15.** $x = 7$

17.

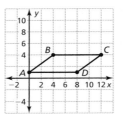

Because $BC = AD = 8, \overline{BC} \cong \overline{AD}$. Because both $\overline{BC}$ and $\overline{AD}$ are horizontal lines, their slope is 0, and they are parallel. $\overline{BC}$ and $\overline{AD}$ are opposite sides that are both congruent and parallel. So, ABCD is a parallelogram by the Opposite Sides Parallel and Congruent Theorem.

19.

Because $JK = LM = 5$ and $KL = JM = \sqrt{65}, \overline{JK} \cong \overline{LM}$ and $\overline{KL} \cong \overline{JM}$. Because both pairs of opposite sides are congruent, quadrilateral JKLM is a parallelogram by the Parallelogram Opposite Sides Converse.

21. In order to be a parallelogram, the quadrilateral must have two pairs of opposite sides that are congruent, not consecutive sides; DEFG is not a parallelogram.

23. $x = 5$; The diagonals must bisect each other so you could solve for x using either $2x + 1 = x + 6$ or $4x − 2 = 3x + 3$. Also, the opposite sides must be congruent, so you could solve for x using either $3x + 1 = 4x − 4$ or $3x + 10 = 5x$.

25. A quadrilateral is a parallelogram if and only if both pairs of opposite sides are congruent.

27. A quadrilateral is a parallelogram if and only if the diagonals bisect each other.

29. Check students' work; Because the diagonals bisect each other, this quadrilateral is a parallelogram by the Parallelogram Diagonals Converse.

31. *Sample answer:*

33. a. 27°; Because $\angle EAF$ is a right angle, the other two angles of $\triangle EAF$ must be complementary. So, $m\angle AFE = 90° − 63° = 27°$.

b. Because $\angle GDF$ is a right angle, the other two angles of $\triangle GDF$ must be complementary. So, $m\angle FGD = 90° − 27° = 63°$.

c. 27°; 27°

d. yes; $\angle HEF \cong \angle HGF$ because they both are adjacent to two congruent angles that together add up to 180°, and $\angle EHG \cong \angle GFE$ for the same reason. So, EFGH is a parallelogram by the Parallelogram Opposite Angles Converse.

35. You can use the Alternate Interior Angles Converse to show that $\overline{AD} \parallel \overline{BC}$. Then, $\overline{AD}$ and $\overline{BC}$ are both congruent and parallel. So, *ABCD* is a parallelogram by the Opposite Sides Parallel and Congruent Theorem.

37. Use the Corresponding Angles Converse to show that $\overline{AD} \parallel \overline{BC}$ and the Alternate Interior Angles Converse to show that $\overline{AB} \parallel \overline{DC}$. So, *ABCD* is a parallelogram by definition.

39.

STATEMENTS	REASONS
1. $\angle A \cong \angle C, \angle B \cong \angle D$	**1.** Given
2. Let $m\angle A = m\angle C = x°$ and $m\angle B = m\angle D = y°$	**2.** Definition of congruent angles
3. $m\angle A + m\angle B + m\angle C + m\angle D = x° + y° + x° + y° = 360°$	**3.** Corollary to the Polygon Interior Angles Theorem
4. $2(x°) + 2(y°) = 360°$	**4.** Simplify
5. $2(x° + y°) = 360°$	**5.** Distributive Property
6. $x° + y° = 180°$	**6.** Division Property of Equality
7. $m\angle A + m\angle B = 180°$, $m\angle A + m\angle D = 180°$	**7.** Substitution Property of Equality
8. $\angle A$ and $\angle B$ are supplementary. $\angle A$ and $\angle D$ are supplementary.	**8.** Definition of supplementary angles
9. $\overline{BC} \parallel \overline{AD}, \overline{AB} \parallel \overline{DC}$	**9.** Consecutive Interior Angles Converse
10. *ABCD* is a parallelogram.	**10.** Definition of parallelogram

41.

STATEMENTS	REASONS
1. Diagonals $\overline{JL}$ and $\overline{KM}$ bisect each other.	**1.** Given
2. $\overline{KP} \cong \overline{MP}, \overline{JP} \cong \overline{LP}$	**2.** Definition of segment bisector
3. $\angle KPL \cong \angle MPJ$	**3.** Vertical Angles Congruence Theorem
4. $\triangle KPL \cong \triangle MPJ$	**4.** SAS Congruence Theorem
5. $\angle MKL \cong \angle KMJ$, $\overline{KL} \cong \overline{MJ}$	**5.** Corresponding parts of congruent triangles are congruent.
6. $\overline{KL} \parallel \overline{MJ}$	**6.** Alternate Interior Angles Converse
7. *JKLM* is a parallelogram.	**7.** Opposite Sides Parallel and Congruent Theorem (Thm. 7.9)

43. no; The fourth angle will be 113° because of the Corollary to the Polygon Interior Angles Theorem, but these could also be the angle measures of an isosceles trapezoid with base angles that are each 67°.

45. 8; By the Parallelogram Opposite Sides Theorem, $\overline{AB} \cong \overline{CD}$. Also, $\angle ABE$ and $\angle CDF$ are congruent alternate interior angles of parallel segments $\overline{AB}$ and $\overline{CD}$. Then, you can use the Segment Addition Postulate, the Substitution Property of Equality, and the Reflexive Property of Congruence to show that $\overline{DF} \cong \overline{BE}$. So, $\triangle ABE \cong \triangle CDF$ by the SAS Congruence Theorem, which means that $AE = CF = 8$ because corresponding parts of congruent triangles are congruent.

47. If every pair of consecutive angles of a quadrilateral is supplementary, then the quadrilateral is a parallelogram; In *ABCD*, you are given that $\angle A$ and $\angle B$ are supplementary, and $\angle B$ and $\angle C$ are supplementary. So, $m\angle A = m\angle C$. Also, $\angle B$ and $\angle C$ are supplementary, and $\angle C$ and $\angle D$ are supplementary. So, $m\angle B = m\angle D$. So, *ABCD* is a parallelogram by the Parallelogram Opposite Angles Converse.

49. Given quadrilateral *ABCD* with midpoints *E*, *F*, *G*, and *H* that are joined to form a quadrilateral, you can construct diagonal $\overline{BD}$. Then $\overline{FG}$ is a midsegment of $\triangle BCD$, and $\overline{EH}$ is a midsegment of $\triangle DAB$. So, by the Triangle Midsegment Theorem, $\overline{FG} \parallel \overline{BD}$, $FG = \frac{1}{2}BD$, $\overline{EH} \parallel \overline{BD}$, and $EH = \frac{1}{2}BD$. So, by the Transitive Property of Parallel Lines, $\overline{EH} \parallel \overline{FG}$ and by the Transitive Property of Equality, $EH = FG$. Because one pair of opposite sides is both congruent and parallel, *EFGH* is a parallelogram by the Opposite Sides Parallel and Congruent Theorem.

7.3 Maintaining Mathematical Proficiency (p. 428)

51. parallelogram   **53.** square

7.4 Vocabulary and Core Concept Check (p. 437)

1. square

7.4 Monitoring Progress and Modeling with Mathematics (pp. 437–440)

3. sometimes; Some rhombuses are squares.

5. always; By definition, a rhombus is a parallelogram, and opposite sides of a parallelogram are congruent.

7. sometimes; Some rhombuses are squares.

9. square; All of the sides are congruent, and all of the angles are congruent.

11. rectangle; Opposite sides are parallel and the angles are 90°.

13. $m\angle 1 = m\angle 2 = m\angle 4 = 27°, m\angle 3 = 90°;$
$m\angle 5 = m\angle 6 = 63°$

15. $m\angle 1 = m\angle 2 = m\angle 3 = m\angle 4 = 37°; m\angle 5 = 106°$

17. always; All angles of a rectangle are congruent.

19. sometimes; Some rectangles are squares.

21. sometimes; Some rectangles are squares.

23. no; All four angles are not congruent.

25. 11   **27.** 4

29. rectangle, square   **31.** rhombus, square

33. parallelogram, rectangle, rhombus, square

35. Diagonals do not necessarily bisect opposite angles of a rectangle;
$m\angle QSR = 90° - m\angle QSP$
$x = 32$

37. 53°   **39.** 74°

41. 6   **43.** 56°

45. 56°   **47.** 10

49. 90°   **51.** 45°

53. 2

55. rectangle, rhombus, square; The diagonals are congruent and perpendicular.

57. rectangle; The sides are perpendicular and not congruent.

59. rhombus; The diagonals are perpendicular and not congruent.

61. rhombus; The sides are congruent; $x = 76; y = 4$

63. a. rhombus; rectangle; *HBDF* has four congruent sides; *ACEG* has four right angles.

   b. $AE = GC; AJ = JE = CJ = JG$; The diagonals of a rectangle are congruent and bisect each other.

65. always; By the Square Corollary, a square is a rhombus.

67. always; The diagonals of a rectangle are congruent by the Rectangle Diagonals Theorem.

69. sometimes; Some rhombuses are squares.

71. Measure the diagonals to see if they are congruent.

73.

STATEMENTS	REASONS
1. *PQRS* is a parallelogram. *PR* bisects $\angle SPQ$ and $\angle QRS$. *SQ* bisects $\angle PSR$ and $\angle RQP$.	1. Given
2. $\angle SRT \cong \angle QRT$, $\angle RQT \cong \angle RST$	2. Definition of angle bisector
3. $\overline{TR} \cong \overline{TR}$	3. Reflexive Property of Congruence
4. $\triangle QRT \cong \triangle SRT$	4. AAS Congruence Theorem
5. $\overline{QR} \cong \overline{SR}$	5. Corresponding parts of congruent triangles are congruent.
6. $\overline{QR} \cong \overline{PS}, \overline{PQ} \cong \overline{SR}$	6. Parallelogram Opposite Sides Theorem
7. $\overline{PS} \cong \overline{QR} \cong \overline{SR} \cong \overline{PQ}$	7. Transitive Property of Congruence
8. *PQRS* is a rhombus.	8. Definition of rhombus

75. no; The diagonals of a square always create two right triangles.

77. square; A square has four congruent sides and four congruent angles.

79. no; yes; Corresponding angles of two rhombuses might not be congruent; Corresponding angles of two squares are congruent.

81. If a quadrilateral is a rhombus, then it has four congruent sides; If a quadrilateral has four congruent sides, then it is a rhombus; The conditional statement is true by the definition of rhombus. The converse is true because if a quadrilateral has four congruent sides, then both pairs of opposite sides are congruent. So, by the Parallelogram Opposite Sides Converse, it is a parallelogram with four congruent sides, which is the definition of a rhombus.

83. If a quadrilateral is a square, then it is a rhombus and a rectangle; If a quadrilateral is a rhombus and a rectangle, then it is a square; The conditional statement is true because if a quadrilateral is a square, then by definition of a square, it has four congruent sides, which makes it a rhombus by the Rhombus Corollary, and it has four right angles, which makes it a rectangle by the Rectangle Corollary; The converse is true because if a quadrilateral is a rhombus and a rectangle, then by the Rhombus Corollary, it has four congruent sides, and by the Rectangle Corollary, it has four right angles. So, by the definition, it is a square.

85.

STATEMENTS	REASONS
1. $\triangle XYZ \cong \triangle XWZ$, $\angle XYW \cong \angle ZWY$	1. Given
2. $\angle YXZ \cong \angle WXZ$, $\angle YZX \cong \angle WZX$, $\overline{XY} \cong \overline{XW}$, $\overline{YZ} \cong \overline{WZ}$	2. Corresponding parts of congruent triangles are congruent.
3. $\overline{XZ}$ bisects $\angle WXY$ and $\angle WZY$.	3. Definition of angle bisector
4. $\angle XWY \cong \angle XYW$, $\angle WYZ \cong \angle ZWY$	4. Base Angles Theorem
5. $\angle XYW \cong \angle WYZ$, $\angle XWY \cong \angle ZWY$	5. Transitive Property of Congruence
6. $\overline{WY}$ bisects $\angle XWZ$ and $\angle XYZ$.	6. Definition of angle bisector
7. $WXYZ$ is a rhombus.	7. Rhombus Opposite Angles Theorem

87.

STATEMENTS	REASONS
1. $PQRS$ is a rectangle.	1. Given
2. $PQRS$ is a parallelogram.	2. Definition of a rectangle
3. $\overline{PS} \cong \overline{QR}$	3. Parallelogram Opposite Side Theorem
4. $\angle PQR$ and $\angle QPS$ are right angles.	4. Definition of a rectangle
5. $\angle PQR \cong \angle QPS$	5. Right Angles Congruence Theorem
6. $\overline{PQ} \cong \overline{PQ}$	6. Reflexive Property of Congruence
7. $\triangle PQR \cong \triangle QPS$	7. SAS Congruence Theorem
8. $\overline{PR} \cong \overline{SQ}$	8. Corresponding parts of congruent triangles are congruent.

7.4 Maintaining Mathematical Proficiency (p. 440)

89. $x = 10, y = 8$ **91.** $x = 9, y = 26$

7.5 Vocabulary and Core Concept Check (p. 447)

1. A trapezoid has exactly one pair of parallel sides, and a kite has two pairs of consecutive congruent sides.

7.5 Monitoring Progress and Modeling with Mathematics (pp. 447–450)

3. slope of $\overline{YZ}$ = slope of $\overline{XW}$ and slope of $\overline{XY} \neq$ slope of $\overline{WZ}$; $XY = WZ$, so $WXYZ$ is isosceles.

5. slope of $\overline{MQ}$ = slope of $\overline{NP}$ and slope of $\overline{MN} \neq$ slope of $\overline{PQ}$; $MN \neq PQ$, so $MNPQ$ is not isosceles.

7. $m\angle L = m\angle M = 62°, m\angle K = m\angle J = 118°$

9. 14   **11.** 4

13. $3\sqrt{13}$ **15.** 110°

17. 80°

19. Because $MN = \frac{1}{2}(AB + DC)$, when you solve for DC, you should get $DC = 2(MN) - AB$; $DC = 2(8) - 14 = 2$.

21. rectangle; $JKLM$ is a quadrilateral with 4 right angles.

23. square; All four sides are congruent and the angles are 90°.

25. no; It could be a kite.   **27.** 3

29. 26 in.

31. $\angle A \cong \angle D$, or $\angle B \cong \angle C$; $\overline{BC} \parallel \overline{AD}$, so base angles need to be congruent.

33. *Sample answer:* $\overline{BE} \cong \overline{DE}$; Then the diagonals bisect each other.

35.

STATEMENTS	REASONS
1. $\overline{JL} \cong \overline{LN}$, $\overline{KM}$ is a midsegment of $\triangle JLN$.	1. Given
2. $\overline{KM} \parallel \overline{JN}$	2. Triangle Midsegment Theorem
3. $JKMN$ is a trapezoid.	3. Definition of trapezoid
4. $\angle LJN \cong \angle LNJ$	4. Base Angles Theorem
5. $JKMN$ is an isosceles trapezoid.	5. Isosceles Trapezoid Base Angles Converse

37. any point on $\overleftrightarrow{UV}$ such that $UV \neq SV$ and $SV \neq 0$

39. Given isosceles trapezoid $ABCD$ with $\overline{BC} \parallel \overline{AD}$, construct $\overline{CE}$ parallel to $\overline{BA}$. Then, $ABCE$ is a parallelogram by definition, so $\overline{AB} \cong \overline{EC}$. Because $\overline{AB} \cong \overline{CD}$ by the definition of an isosceles trapezoid, $\overline{CE} \cong \overline{CD}$ by the Transitive Property of Congruence. So, $\angle CED \cong \angle D$ by the Base Angles Theorem and $\angle A \cong \angle CED$ by the Corresponding Angles Theorem. So, $\angle A \cong \angle D$ by the Transitive Property of Congruence. Next, by the Consecutive Interior Angles Theorem, $\angle B$ and $\angle A$ are supplementary and so are $\angle BCD$ and $\angle D$. So, $\angle B \cong \angle BCD$ by the Congruent Supplements Theorem.

41. no; It could be a square or rectangle.

43. a.

rectangle; The diagonals are congruent, but not perpendicular.

b.

rhombus; The diagonals are perpendicular, but not congruent.

45. a. yes   **b.** 75°, 75°, 105°, 105°

47. Given kite $EFGH$ with $\overline{EF} \cong \overline{FG}$ and $\overline{EH} \cong \overline{GH}$, construct diagonal $\overline{FH}$, which is congruent to itself by the Reflexive Property of Congruence. So, $\triangle FGH \cong \triangle FEH$ by the SSS Congruence Theorem, and $\angle E \cong \angle G$ because corresponding parts of congruent triangles are congruent. Next, assume temporarily that $\angle F \cong \angle H$. Then $EFGH$ is a parallelogram by the Parallelogram Opposite Angles Converse, and opposite sides are congruent. However, this contradicts the definition of a kite, which says that opposite sides cannot be congruent. So, the assumption cannot be true and $\angle F$ is not congruent to $\angle H$.

49. By the Triangle Midsegment Theorem, $\overline{BG} \parallel \overline{CD}$, $BG = \frac{1}{2}CD$, $\overline{GE} \parallel \overline{AF}$, and $GE = \frac{1}{2}AF$. By the Transitive Property of Parallel Lines, $\overline{CD} \parallel \overline{BE} \parallel \overline{AF}$. Also, by the Segment Addition Postulate, $BE = BG + GE$. So, by the Substitution Property of Equality, $BE = \frac{1}{2}CD + \frac{1}{2}AF = \frac{1}{2}(CD + AF)$.

51. a.

STATEMENTS	REASONS
1. $JKLM$ is an isosceles trapezoid, $\overline{KL} \parallel \overline{JM}$, $\overline{JK} \cong \overline{LM}$	1. Given
2. $\angle JKL \cong \angle MLK$	2. Isosceles Trapezoid Base Angles Theorem
3. $\overline{KL} \cong \overline{KL}$	3. Reflexive Property of Congruence
4. $\triangle JKL \cong \triangle MLK$	4. SAS Congruence Theorem
5. $\overline{JL} \cong \overline{KM}$	5. Corresponding parts of congruent triangles are congruent.

b. If the diagonals of a trapezoid are congruent, then the trapezoid is isosceles. Let $JKLM$ be a trapezoid, $\overline{KL} \parallel \overline{JM}$ and $\overline{JL} \cong \overline{KM}$. Construct line segments through K and L perpendicular to $\overline{JM}$ as shown below.

Because $\overline{KL} \parallel \overline{JM}$, $\angle AKL$ and $\angle KLB$ are right angles, so $KLBA$ is a rectangle and $\overline{AK} \cong \overline{BL}$. Then $\triangle JLB \cong \triangle MKA$ by the HL Congruence Theorem. So, $\angle LJB \cong \angle KMA$. $\overline{JM} \cong \overline{JM}$ by the Reflexive Property of Congruence. So, $\triangle KJM \cong \triangle LMJ$ by the SAS Congruence Theorem. Then $\angle KJM \cong \angle LMJ$, and the trapezoid is isosceles by the Isosceles Trapezoid Base Angles Converse.

7.5 Maintaining Mathematical Proficiency (p. 450)

53.

55.
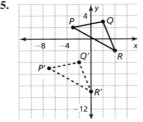

57. no; $\frac{20}{6} \neq \frac{24}{8}$, the side lengths are not proportional.

Chapter 7 Review (pp. 452–454)

1. 5040°; 168°; 12°   **2.** 133
3. 82   **4.** 15
5. $a = 79, b = 101$ **6.** $a = 28, b = 87$
7. $c = 6, d = 10$ **8.** $(-2, -1)$
9. $M(2, -2)$
10. Parallelogram Opposite Sides Converse
11. Parallelogram Diagonals Converse
12. Parallelogram Opposite Angles Converse
13. $x = 1, y = 6$ **14.** 4
15. Because $\overline{WX} = \overline{YZ} = \sqrt{13}$, $\overline{WX} \cong \overline{YZ}$. Because the slopes of $\overline{WX}$ and $\overline{YZ}$ are both $\frac{2}{3}$, they are parallel. $\overline{WX}$ and $\overline{YZ}$ are opposite sides that are both congruent and parallel. So, $WXYZ$ is a parallelogram by the Opposite Sides Parallel and Congruent Theorem.
16. rhombus; There are four congruent sides.
17. parallelogram; There are two pairs of parallel sides.
18. square; There are four congruent sides and the angles are 90°.
19. 10
20. rectangle, rhombus, square; The diagonals are congruent and perpendicular.
21. $m\angle Z = m\angle Y = 58°$, $m\angle W = m\angle X = 122°$
22. 26   **23.** $3\sqrt{5}$
24. $x = 15; 105°$
25. yes; Use the Isosceles Trapezoid Base Angles Converse.
26. trapezoid; There is one pair of parallel sides.
27. rhombus; There are four congruent sides.
28. rectangle; There are four right angles.

Chapter 8

Chapter 8 Maintaining Mathematical Proficiency (p. 459)

1. yes   **2.** yes
3. no   **4.** no
5. yes   **6.** yes
7. no; $\frac{12}{14} = \frac{6}{7} \neq \frac{5}{7}$, The sides are not proportional.
8. yes; The corresponding angles are congruent and the corresponding side lengths are proportional.
9. yes; The corresponding angles are congruent and the corresponding side lengths are proportional.
10. no; Squares have four right angles, so the corresponding angles are always congruent. Because all four sides are congruent, the corresponding sides will always be proportional.

8.1 Vocabulary and Core Concept Check (p. 466)

1. $P'(kx, ky)$

8.1 Monitoring Progress and Modeling with Mathematics (pp. 466–468)

3. $\frac{3}{7}$; reduction   **5.** $\frac{3}{5}$; reduction

7.

Not drawn to scale.

9.

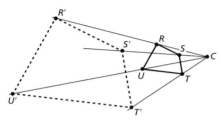

Not drawn to scale.

11.

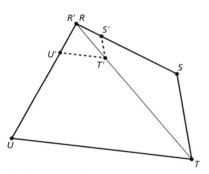

Not drawn to scale.

13.

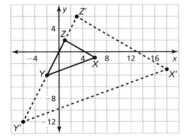

Not drawn to scale.

15.

17.

19.

21.

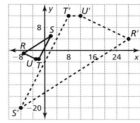

23. The scale factor should be calculated by finding $\dfrac{CP'}{CP}$, not $\dfrac{CP}{CP'}$; $k = \dfrac{3}{12} = \dfrac{1}{4}$

25. $k = \dfrac{5}{3}$; $x = 21$ **27.** $k = \dfrac{2}{3}$; $y = 3$

29. $k = 2$ **31.** 300 mm

33. 940 mm

35. grasshopper, honey bee, and monarch butterfly; The scale factor for these three is $k = \dfrac{15}{2}$. The scale factor for the black beetle is $k = 7$.

37. no; The scale factor for the shorter sides is $\dfrac{8}{4} = 2$, but the scale factor for the longer sides is $\dfrac{10}{6} = \dfrac{5}{3}$. The scale factor for both sides has to be the same or the picture will be distorted.

39. $x = 5$, $y = 25$ **41.** original

43. original

45.

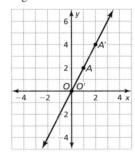

  a. $O'A' = 2(OA)$
  b. $\overleftrightarrow{O'A'}$ coincides with $\overleftrightarrow{OA}$.

47. $k = \dfrac{1}{16}$

49. **a.** $P = 24$ units, $A = 32$ square units

b.

$P = 72$ units, $A = 288$ square units; The perimeter of the dilated rectangle is three times the perimeter of the original rectangle. The area of the dilated rectangle is nine times the area of the original rectangle.

c.

$P = 6$ units, $A = 2$ square units; The perimeter of the dilated rectangle is $\frac{1}{4}$ the perimeter of the original rectangle. The area of the dilated rectangle is $\frac{1}{16}$ the area of the original rectangle.

d. The perimeter changes by a factor of k. The area changes by a factor of k^2.

51. $A'(4, 4)$, $B'(4, 12)$, $C'(10, 4)$

8.1 Maintaining Mathematical Proficiency (p. 468)

53. $A'(1, 2)$, $B'(-1, 7)$, $C'(-4, 8)$

55. $A'(0, -1)$, $B'(-2, 4)$, $C'(-5, 5)$

57. $A'(-1, 0)$, $B'(-3, 5)$, $C'(-6, 6)$

8.2 Vocabulary and Core Concept Check (p. 473)

1. Congruent figures have the same size and shape. Similar figures have the same shape, but not necessarily the same size.

8.2 Monitoring Progress and Modeling with Mathematics (pp. 473–474)

3.

5.

---

7. *Sample answer:* translation 1 unit down and 1 unit right followed by a dilation with center at $E(2, -3)$ and a scale factor of 2

9. yes; $\triangle ABC$ can be mapped to $\triangle DEF$ by a dilation with center at the origin and a scale factor of $\frac{1}{3}$ followed by a translation of 2 units left and 3 units up.

11. no; The scale factor from $\overline{HI}$ to $\overline{JL}$ is $\frac{2}{3}$, but the scale factor from $\overline{GH}$ to $\overline{KL}$ is $\frac{5}{6}$.

13. Reflect $\triangle ABC$ in $\overleftrightarrow{AB}$. Because reflections preserve side lengths and angle measures, the image of $\triangle ABC$, $\triangle ABC'$, is a right isosceles triangle with leg length j. Also because $\overleftrightarrow{AC} \perp \overleftrightarrow{BA}$, point C' is on $\overleftrightarrow{AC}$. So, $\overleftrightarrow{AC'}$ is parallel to $\overrightarrow{RT}$.

Then translate $\triangle ABC'$ so that point A maps to point R. Because translations map segments to parallel segments and $\overline{AC'} \parallel \overline{RT}$, the image of $\overline{AC'}$ lies on $\overline{RT}$.

Because translations preserve side lengths and angle measures, the image of $\triangle ABC'$, $\triangle RB'C''$, is a right isosceles triangle with leg length j. Because $\angle B'RC''$ and $\angle SRT$ are right angles, they are congruent. When $\overrightarrow{RC''}$ coincides with $\overrightarrow{RT}$, $\overrightarrow{RB'}$ coincides with $\overrightarrow{RS}$. So, $\overline{RB'}$ lies on $\overline{RS}$. Next, dilate $\triangle RB'C''$ using center of dilation R. Choose the scale factor to be the ratio of the side lengths of $\triangle RST$ and $\triangle RB'C''$, which is $\frac{k}{j}$.

The dilation maps $\overline{RC''}$ to $\overline{RT}$ and $\overline{RB'}$ to $\overline{RS}$ because the images of $\overline{RC''}$ and $\overline{RB'}$ have side length $\frac{k}{j}(j) = k$ and the segments $\overline{RC''}$ and $\overline{RB'}$ lie on lines passing through the center of dilation. So, the dilation maps C'' to T and B' to S. A similarity transformation maps $\triangle ABC$ to $\triangle RST$. So, $\triangle ABC$ is similar to $\triangle RST$.

15. yes; The stop sign sticker can be mapped to the regular-sized stop sign by translating the sticker to the left until the centers match, and then dilating the sticker with a scale factor of 3.15. Because there is a similarity transformation that maps one stop sign to the other, the sticker is similar to the regular-sized stop sign.

17. no; The scale factor is 6 for both dimensions. So, the enlarged banner is proportional to the smaller one.

19. *Sample answer:*

$\triangle A''B''C''$ can be mapped to $\triangle ABC$ by a translation 3 units right and 2 units up, followed by a dilation with center at the origin and a scale factor of $\frac{1}{2}$.

21. $J(-8, 0)$, $K(-8, 12)$, $L(-4, 12)$, $M(-4, 0)$; $J''(-9, -4)$, $K''(-9, 14)$, $L''(-3, 14)$, $M''(-3, -4)$; yes; A similarity transformation mapped quadrilateral $JKLM$ to quadrilateral $J''K''L''M''$.

8.2 Maintaining Mathematical Proficiency *(p. 474)*

23. obtuse

25. acute

8.3 Vocabulary and Core Concept Check *(p. 481)*

1. congruent; proportional

8.3 Monitoring Progress and Modeling with Mathematics *(pp. 481–484)*

3. $\frac{4}{3}$; $\angle A \cong \angle L$, $\angle B \cong \angle M$, $\angle C \cong \angle N$; $\frac{LM}{AB} = \frac{MN}{BC} = \frac{NL}{CA}$

5. $x = 30$

7. $x = 11$

9. altitude; 24

11. 2 : 3

13. 72 cm

15. 20 yd

17. 288 ft, 259.2 ft

19. 108 ft^2

21. 4 in.^{2}

23. Because the first ratio has a side length of B over a side length of A, the second ratio should have the perimeter of B over the perimeter of A;

$$\frac{5}{10} = \frac{x}{28}$$

$$x = 14$$

25. no; Corresponding angles are not congruent.

27. A, D

29. $\frac{5}{2}$

31. 34, 85

33. 60.5, 378.125

35. B, D

37. $x = 35.25$, $y = 20.25$

39. 30 m

41. 7.5 ft

43. sometimes

45. sometimes

47. sometimes

49. yes; All four angles of each rectangle will always be congruent right angles.

51. about 1116 mi

53.

Let $KLMN$ and $PQRS$ be similar rectangles as shown. The ratio of corresponding side lengths is $\frac{KL}{PQ} = \frac{x}{kx} = \frac{1}{k}$. The area of $KLMN$ is xy and the area of $PQRS$ is $(kx)(ky) = k^2xy$. So, the ratio of the areas is $\frac{xy}{k^2xy} = \frac{1}{k^2} = \left(\frac{1}{k}\right)^2$. Because the ratio of corresponding side lengths is $\frac{1}{k}$, any pair of corresponding side lengths can be substituted for $\frac{1}{k}$. So,

$$\frac{\text{Area of } KLMN}{\text{Area of } PQRS} = \left(\frac{KL}{PQ}\right)^2 = \left(\frac{LM}{QR}\right)^2 = \left(\frac{MN}{RS}\right)^2 = \left(\frac{NK}{SP}\right)^2.$$

55. $x = \frac{1 + \sqrt{5}}{2}$; $x = \frac{1 + \sqrt{5}}{2}$ satisfies the proportion $\frac{1}{x} = \frac{x - 1}{1}$.

8.3 Maintaining Mathematical Proficiency *(p. 484)*

57. $x = 63$

59. $x = 120$

8.4 Vocabulary and Core Concept Check *(p. 489)*

1. similar

8.4 Monitoring Progress and Modeling with Mathematics *(pp. 489–490)*

3. yes; $\angle H \cong \angle J$ and $\angle F \cong \angle K$, so $\triangle FGH \sim \triangle KLJ$.

5. no; $m\angle N = 50°$

7. $\angle N \cong \angle Z$ and $\angle MYN \cong \angle XYZ$, so $\triangle MYN \sim \triangle XYZ$.

9. $\angle Y \cong \angle Y$ and $\angle YZX \cong \angle W$, so $\triangle XYZ \sim \triangle UYW$.

11. $\triangle CAG \sim \triangle CEF$

13. $\triangle ACB \sim \triangle ECD$

15. $m\angle ECD = 82°$

17. $BC = 4\sqrt{2}$

19. The AA Similarity Theorem does not apply to quadrilaterals. There is not enough information to determine whether or not quadrilaterals $ABCD$ and $EFGH$ are similar.

21. 78 m; Corresponding angles are congruent, so the triangles are similar.

23. yes; Corresponding angles are congruent.

25. no; $94° + 87° > 180°$

27. *Sample answer:* Because the triangles are similar, the ratios of the vertical sides to the horizontal sides are equal.

29. The angle measures are 60°.

31.

Let $\triangle ABC \sim \triangle DEF$ with a scale factor of k, and $\overline{AX}$ and $\overline{DY}$ be angle bisectors as shown. Then $\angle C \cong \angle F$, $m\angle CAB = m\angle FDE$, $2m\angle CAX = m\angle CAB$ and $2m\angle FDY = m\angle FDE$. By the Substitution Property of Equality, $2m\angle CAX = 2m\angle FDY$, so $m\angle CAX = m\angle FDY$. Then $\triangle ACX \sim \triangle DFY$ by the AA Similarity Theorem, and because corresponding side lengths are proportional,

$$\frac{AX}{DY} = \frac{AC}{DF} = k.$$

33. about 17.1 ft; $\triangle AED \sim \triangle CEB$, so $\dfrac{DE}{BE} = \dfrac{4}{3}$. $\triangle DEF \sim \triangle DBC$,

so $\dfrac{EF}{30} = \dfrac{DE}{DB} = \dfrac{4}{7}$ and $EF = \dfrac{120}{7}$.

8.4 Maintaining Mathematical Proficiency (p. 490)

35. yes; Use the SSS Congruence Theorem.

8.5 Vocabulary and Core Concept Check (p. 497)

1. $\dfrac{QR}{XY} = \dfrac{RS}{YZ} = \dfrac{QS}{XZ}$

8.5 Monitoring Progress and Modeling with Mathematics (pp. 497–498)

3. $\triangle RST$ **5.** $x = 4$

7. $\dfrac{12}{18} = \dfrac{10}{15} = \dfrac{8}{12} = \dfrac{2}{3}$

9. similar; $\triangle DEF \sim \triangle WXY$; $\dfrac{4}{3}$

11.

no

13. Because $\overline{AB}$ corresponds to $\overline{RQ}$ and $\overline{BC}$ corresponds to $\overline{QP}$, the proportionality statement should be $\triangle ABC \sim \triangle RQP$.

15. no; The included angles are not congruent.

17. D; $\angle M \cong \angle M$, so $\triangle MNP \sim \triangle MRQ$ by the SAS Similarity Theorem.

19.

STATEMENTS	REASONS
1. $\angle A \cong \angle D$, $\dfrac{AB}{DE} = \dfrac{AC}{DF}$	1. Given
2. Draw $\overline{PQ}$ so that P is on $\overline{AB}$, Q is on $\overline{AC}$, $\overline{PQ} \parallel \overline{BC}$, and $AP = DE$.	2. Parallel Postulate
3. $\angle APQ \cong \angle ABC$	3. Corresponding Angles Theorem
4. $\angle A \cong \angle A$	4. Reflexive Property of Congruence
5. $\triangle APQ \sim \triangle ABC$	5. AA Similarity Theorem
6. $\dfrac{AB}{AP} = \dfrac{AC}{AQ} = \dfrac{BC}{PQ}$	6. Corresponding sides of similar figures are proportional.
7. $\dfrac{AB}{DE} = \dfrac{AC}{AQ}$	7. Substitution Property of Equality
8. $AQ \cdot \dfrac{AB}{DE} = AC$, $DF \cdot \dfrac{AB}{DE} = AC$	8. Multiplication Property of Equality
9. $AQ = AC \cdot \dfrac{DE}{AB}$, $DF = AC \cdot \dfrac{DE}{AB}$	9. Multiplication Property of Equality
10. $AQ = DF$	10. Transitive Property of Equality
11. $\overline{AQ} \cong \overline{DF}$, $\overline{AP} \cong \overline{DE}$	11. Definition of congruent segments
12. $\triangle APQ \cong \triangle DEF$	12. SAS Congruence Theorem
13. $\overline{PQ} \cong \overline{EF}$	13. Corresponding parts of congruent triangles are congruent.
14. $PQ = EF$	14. Definition of congruent segments
15. $\dfrac{AB}{DE} = \dfrac{AC}{DF} = \dfrac{BC}{EF}$	15. Substitution Property of Equality
16. $\triangle ABC \sim \triangle DEF$	16. SSS Similarity Theorem

21. If two angles are congruent, then the triangles are similar by the AA Similarity Theorem.

23. no; no; The sum of the angle measures would not be 180°.

8.5 Maintaining Mathematical Proficiency (p. 498)

25. -1 **27.** 2

8.6 Vocabulary and Core Concept Check (p. 504)

1. parallel, Converse of the Triangle Proportionality Theorem

8.6 Monitoring Progress and Modeling with Mathematics (pp. 504–506)

3. 9   **5.** yes

7. no

9. *CE*

11. 6

13. 12

15. 27

17. *P*(7, −0.4)

19. *P*(−1.5, −1.5)

21.

23. The proportion should show that *AD* corresponds with *DC* and *BA* corresponds with *BC*;

$$\frac{AD}{DC} = \frac{BA}{BC}$$

$$\frac{x}{14} = \frac{10}{16}$$

$$x = 8.75$$

25. *x* = 3

27.

STATEMENTS	REASONS
1. $\overline{QS} \parallel \overline{TU}$	1. Given
2. $\angle RQS \cong \angle RTU$, $\angle RSQ \cong \angle RUT$	2. Corresponding Angles Theorem
3. $\triangle RQS \sim \triangle RTU$	3. AA Similarity Theorem
4. $\frac{QR}{TR} = \frac{SR}{UR}$	4. Corresponding side lengths of similar figures are proportional.
5. $QR = QT + TR$, $SR = SU + UR$	5. Segment Addition Postulate
6. $\frac{QT + TR}{TR} = \frac{SU + UR}{UR}$	6. Substitution Property of Equality
7. $\frac{QT}{TR} + \frac{TR}{TR} = \frac{SU}{UR} + \frac{UR}{UR}$	7. Rewrite the proportion.
8. $\frac{QT}{TR} + 1 = \frac{SU}{UR} + 1$	8. Simplify.
9. $\frac{QT}{TR} = \frac{SU}{UR}$	9. Subtraction Property of Equality

29. a. about 50.9 yd, about 58.4 yd, about 64.7 yd

b. Lot C

c. about $287,000, about $318,000; $\frac{50.9}{250,000} \approx \frac{58.4}{287,000}$

and $\frac{50.9}{250,000} \approx \frac{64.7}{318,000}$

31. Because $\overrightarrow{DJ}, \overrightarrow{EK}, \overrightarrow{FL}$, and $\overrightarrow{GB}$ are cut by a transversal $\overrightarrow{AC}$, and $\angle ADJ \cong \angle DEK \cong \angle EFL \cong \angle FGB$ by construction, $\overline{DJ} \parallel \overline{EK} \parallel \overline{FL} \parallel \overline{GB}$ by the Corresponding Angles Converse.

33. isosceles; By the Triangle Angle Bisector Theorem, the ratio of the lengths of the segments of $\overline{LN}$ equals the ratio of the other two side lengths. Because $\overline{LN}$ is bisected, the ratio is 1, and *ML* = *MN*.

35. Because $\overline{WX} \parallel \overline{ZA}$, $\angle XAZ \cong \angle YXW$ by the Corresponding Angles Theorem and $\angle WXZ \cong \angle XZA$ by the Alternate Interior Angles Theorem. So, by the Transitive Property of Congruence, $\angle XAZ \cong \angle XZA$. Then $\overline{XA} \cong \overline{XZ}$ by the Converse of the Base Angles Theorem, and by the Triangle Proportionality Theorem, $\frac{YW}{WZ} = \frac{XY}{XA}$. Because *XA* = *XZ*,

$$\frac{YW}{WZ} = \frac{XY}{XZ}.$$

37. The Triangle Midsegment Theorem is a specific case of the Triangle Proportionality Theorem when the segment parallel to one side of a triangle that connects the other two sides also happens to pass through the midpoints of those two sides.

39.

8.6 Maintaining Mathematical Proficiency *(p. 506)*

41. *a, b*

43. *x* = ±11

45. *x* = ±7

Chapter 8 Review *(pp. 508–510)*

1.

2.

3. 1.9 cm

4. *Sample answer:* reflection in the line *x* = −1 followed by a dilation with center (−3, 0) and *k* = 3

5. *Sample answer:* dilation with center at the origin and $k = \frac{1}{2}$, followed by a reflection in the line *y* = *x*

6. *Sample answer:* 270° rotation about the origin followed by a dilation with center at the origin and *k* = 2

7. $\frac{3}{4}$; $\angle A \cong \angle E$, $\angle B \cong \angle F$, $\angle C \cong \angle G$, $\angle D \cong \angle H$;

$$\frac{EF}{AB} = \frac{FG}{BC} = \frac{GH}{CD} = \frac{EH}{AD}$$

8. $\frac{2}{5}$; $\angle X \cong \angle R$, $\angle Y \cong \angle P$, $\angle Z \cong \angle Q$; $\frac{RP}{XY} = \frac{PQ}{YZ} = \frac{RQ}{XZ}$

9. 14.4 in.

10. *P* = 32 m; *A* = 80 m²

11. $\angle Q \cong \angle T$ and $\angle RSQ \cong \angle UST$, so $\triangle RSQ \sim \triangle UST$.

12. $\angle C \cong \angle F$ and $\angle B \cong \angle E$, so $\triangle ABC \sim \triangle DEF$.

13. 324 ft

14. $\angle C \cong \angle C$ and $\frac{CD}{CE} = \frac{CB}{CA}$, so $\triangle CBD \sim \triangle CAE$.

15. $\frac{QU}{QT} = \frac{QR}{QS} = \frac{UR}{TS}$, so $\triangle QUR \sim \triangle QTS$.

16. 10.5

17. 7.2

Chapter 9

Chapter 9 Maintaining Mathematical Proficiency *(p. 515)*

1. $5\sqrt{3}$

2. $3\sqrt{30}$

3. $3\sqrt{15}$

4. $\frac{2\sqrt{7}}{7}$

5. $\dfrac{5\sqrt{2}}{2}$ **6.** $2\sqrt{6}$

7. $x = 9$ **8.** $x = 7.5$

9. $x = 32$ **10.** $x = 9.2$

11. $x = 217$ **12.** $x = 17$

13. no; no; Because square roots have to do with factors, the rule allows you to simplify with products, not sums and differences.

9.1 Vocabulary and Core Concept Check (p. 522)

1. A Pythagorean triple is a set of three positive integers a, b, and c that satisfy the equation $c^2 = a^2 + b^2$.

9.1 Monitoring Progress and Modeling with Mathematics (pp. 522–524)

3. $x = \sqrt{170} \approx 13.0$; no   **5.** $x = 41$; yes

7. $x = 15$; yes   **9.** $x = 14$; yes

11. Exponents cannot be distributed as shown in the third line; $c^2 = a^2 + b^2$; $x^2 = 7^2 + 24^2$; $x^2 = 49 + 576$; $x^2 = 625$; $x = 25$

13. about 14.1 ft   **15.** yes

17. no   **19.** no

21. yes; acute   **23.** yes; right

25. yes; acute   **27.** yes; obtuse

29. about 127.3 ft   **31.** 120 m²

33. 48 cm²

35. The horizontal distance between any two points is given by $(x_2 - x_1)$, and the vertical distance is given by $(y_2 - y_1)$. The horizontal and vertical segments that represent these distances form a right angle, with the segment between the two points being the hypotenuse. So, you can use the Pythagorean Theorem to say $d^2 = (x_2 - x_1)^2 + (y_2 - y_1)^2$, and when you solve for d, you get the distance formula: $d = \sqrt{(x_2 - x_1)^2 + (y_2 - y_1)^2}$.

37. 2 packages

39.

Let $\triangle ABC$ be any triangle so that the square of the length, c, of the longest side of the triangle is equal to the sum of the squares of the lengths, a and b, of the other two sides: $c^2 = a^2 + b^2$. Let $\triangle DEF$ be any right triangle with leg lengths of a and b. Let x represent the length of its hypotenuse. Because $\triangle DEF$ is a right triangle, by the Pythagorean Theorem, $a^2 + b^2 = x^2$. So, by the Transitive Property, $c^2 = x^2$. By taking the positive square root of each side, you get $c = x$. So, $\triangle ABC \cong \triangle DEF$ by the SSS Congruence Theorem.

41. no; They can be part of a Pythagorean triple if 75 is the hypotenuse: $21^2 + 72^2 = 75^2$

43.

STATEMENTS	REASONS
1. In $\triangle ABC$, $c^2 > a^2 + b^2$, where c is the length of the longest side. $\triangle PQR$ has side lengths a, b, and x, where x is the length of the hypotenuse and $\angle R$ is a right angle.	**1.** Given
2. $a^2 + b^2 = x^2$	**2.** Pythagorean Theorem
3. $c^2 > x^2$	**3.** Substitution Property
4. $c > x$	**4.** Take the positive square root of each side.
5. $m\angle R = 90°$	**5.** Definition of a right angle
6. $m\angle C > m\angle R$	**6.** Converse of the Hinge Theorem
7. $m\angle C > 90°$	**7.** Substitution Property
8. $\angle C$ is an obtuse angle.	**8.** Definition of obtuse angle
9. $\triangle ABC$ is an obtuse triangle.	**9.** Definition of obtuse triangle

9.1 Maintaining Mathematical Proficiency (p. 524)

45. $\dfrac{14\sqrt{3}}{3}$ **47.** $4\sqrt{3}$

9.2 Vocabulary and Core Concept Check (p. 529)

1. 45°-45°-90°, 30°-60°-90°

9.2 Monitoring Progress and Modeling with Mathematics (pp. 529–530)

3. $x = 7\sqrt{2}$ **5.** $x = 3$

7. $x = 9\sqrt{3}$, $y = 18$ **9.** $x = 12\sqrt{3}$, $y = 12$

11. The hypotenuse of a 30°-60°-90° triangle is equal to the shorter leg times 2; hypotenuse = shorter leg • 2 = 7 • 2 = 14; So, the length of the hypotenuse is 14 units.

13.

about 4.3 cm

15. 32 ft²

17. 142 ft; about 200.82 ft; about 245.95 ft

19. Because $\triangle DEF$ is a 45°-45°-90° triangle, by the Converse of the Base Angles Theorem, $\overline{DF} \cong \overline{FE}$. So, let $x = DF = FE$. By the Pythagorean Theorem, $x^2 + x^2 = c^2$, where c is the length of the hypotenuse. So, $2x^2 = c^2$ by the Distributive Property. Take the positive square root of each side to get $x\sqrt{2} = c$. So, the hypotenuse is $\sqrt{2}$ times as long as each leg.

21. Given $\triangle JKL$, which is a 30°-60°-90° triangle, whose shorter leg, $\overline{KL}$, has length x, construct $\triangle JML$, which is congruent and adjacent to $\triangle JKL$. Because corresponding parts of congruent triangles are congruent, $LM = KL = x$, $m\angle M = m\angle K = 60°$, $m\angle MJL = m\angle KJL = 30°$, and $JM = JK$. Also, by the Angle Addition Postulate, $m\angle KJM = m\angle KJL + m\angle MJL$, and by substituting, $m\angle KJM = 30° + 30° = 60°$. So, $\triangle JKM$ has three 60° angles, which means that it is equiangular by definition, and by the Corollary to the Converse of the Base Angles Theorem, it is also equilateral. By the Segment Addition Postulate, $KM = KL + LM$, and by substituting, $KM = x + x = 2x$. So, by the definition of an equilateral triangle, $JM = JK = KM = 2x$. By the Pythagorean Theorem, $(JL)^2 + (KL)^2 = (JK)^2$. By substituting, we get $(JL)^2 + x^2 = (2x)^2$, which is equivalent to $(JL)^2 + x^2 = 4x^2$, when simplified. When the Subtraction Property of Equality is applied, we get $(JL)^2 = 4x^2 - x^2$, which is equivalent to $(JL)^2 = 3x^2$. By taking the positive square root of each side, $JL = x\sqrt{3}$. So, the hypotenuse of the 30°-60°-90° triangle, $\triangle JKL$, is twice as long as the shorter leg, and the longer leg is $\sqrt{3}$ times as long as the shorter leg.

23. *Sample answer:* Because all isosceles right triangles are 45°-45°-90° triangles, they are similar by the AA Similarity Theorem. Because both legs of an isosceles right triangle are congruent, the legs will always be proportional. So, 45°-45°-90° triangles are all similar by the SAS Similarity Theorem also.

25. $T(1.5, 1.5\sqrt{3} - 1)$

9.2 Maintaining Mathematical Proficiency (p. 530)

27. $x = 2$

9.3 Vocabulary and Core Concept Check (p. 536)

1. each other

9.3 Monitoring Progress and Modeling with Mathematics (pp. 536–538)

3. $\triangle HFE \sim \triangle GHE \sim \triangle GFH$ **5.** $x = \frac{168}{25} = 6.72$

7. $x = \frac{180}{13} \approx 13.8$ **9.** about 11.2 ft

11. 16   **13.** $2\sqrt{70} \approx 16.7$

15. 20   **17.** $6\sqrt{17} \approx 24.7$

19. $x = 8$ **21.** $y = 27$

23. $x = 3\sqrt{5} \approx 6.7$ **25.** $z = \frac{729}{16} \approx 45.6$

27. The length of leg z should be the geometric mean of the length of the hypotenuse, $(w + v)$, and the segment of the hypotenuse that is adjacent to z, which is v, not w; $z^2 = v \cdot (w + v)$

29. about 14.9 ft   **31.** $a = 3$

33. $x = 9, y = 15, z = 20$ **35.** A, D

37. $AC = 25, BD = 12$

39. given; Geometric Mean (Leg) Theorem; a^2; Substitution Property of Equality; Distributive Property; c; Substitution Property of Equality

41.

STATEMENTS	REASONS
1. Draw $\triangle ABC$, $\angle BCA$ is a right angle.	1. Given
2. Draw a perpendicular segment (altitude) from C to $\overline{AB}$, and label the new point on $\overline{AB}$ as D.	2. Perpendicular Postulate
3. $\triangle ADC \sim \triangle CDB$	3. Right Triangle Similarity Theorem
4. $\dfrac{BD}{CD} = \dfrac{CD}{AD}$	4. Corresponding sides of similar figures are proportional.
5. $CD^2 = AD \cdot BD$	5. Cross Products Property

43.

The two smaller triangles are congruent; Their corresponding sides lengths are represented by the same variables. So, they are congruent by the SSS Congruence Theorem.

45.

STATEMENTS	REASONS
1. $\triangle ABC$ is a right triangle. Altitude $\overline{CD}$ is drawn to hypotenuse $\overline{AB}$.	1. Given
2. $\angle BCA$ is a right angle.	2. Definition of right triangle
3. $\angle ADC$ and $\angle BDC$ are right angles.	3. Definition of perpendicular lines
4. $\angle BCA \cong \angle ADC \cong \angle BDC$	4. Right Angles Congruence Theorem
5. $\angle A$ and $\angle ACD$ are complementary. $\angle B$ and $\angle BCD$ are complementary.	5. Corollary to the Triangle Sum Theorem
6. $\angle ACD$ and $\angle BCD$ are complementary.	6. Definition of complementary angles
7. $\angle A \cong \angle BCD$, $\angle B \cong \angle ACD$	7. Congruent Complements Theorem
8. $\triangle CBD \sim \triangle ABC$, $\triangle ACD \sim \triangle ABC$, $\triangle CBD \sim \triangle ACD$	8. AA Similarity Theorem

9.3 Maintaining Mathematical Proficiency (p. 538)

47. $x = 116$ **49.** $x = \frac{23}{6} \approx 3.8$

9.4 Vocabulary and Core Concept Check (p. 545)

1. the opposite leg, the adjacent leg

9.4 Monitoring Progress and Modeling with Mathematics (pp. 545–546)

3. $\tan R = \frac{45}{28} \approx 1.6071$, $\tan S = \frac{28}{45} \approx 0.6222$

5. $\tan G = \frac{2}{1} = 2.0000$, $\tan H = \frac{1}{2} = 0.5000$

7. $x \approx 13.8$ **9.** $x \approx 13.7$

11. The tangent ratio should be the length of the leg opposite $\angle D$ to the length of the leg adjacent to $\angle D$, not the length of the hypotenuse; $\tan D = \frac{35}{12}$

13. 1   **15.** about 555 ft

17. $\frac{5}{12} \approx 0.4167$

19. it increases; The opposite side gets longer.

21. no; The Sun's rays form a right triangle with the length of the awning and the height of the door. The tangent of the angle of elevation equals the height of the door divided by the length of the awning, so the length of the awning equals the quotient of the height of the door, 8 feet, and the tangent of the angle of elevation, 70°: $x = \dfrac{8}{\tan 70°} \approx 2.9$ ft

23. You cannot find the tangent of a right angle, because each right angle has two adjacent legs, and the opposite side is the hypotenuse. So, you do not have an opposite leg and an adjacent leg. If a triangle has an obtuse angle, then it cannot be a right triangle, and the tangent ratio only works for right triangles.

25. a. about 33.4 ft

    b. 3 students at each end; The triangle formed by the 60° angle has an opposite leg that is about 7.5 feet longer than the opposite leg of the triangle formed by the 50° angle. Because each student needs 2 feet of space, 3 more students can fit on each end with about 1.5 feet of space left over.

9.4 Maintaining Mathematical Proficiency (p. 546)

27. $x = 2\sqrt{3} \approx 3.5$ **29.** $x = 5\sqrt{2} \approx 7.1$

9.5 Vocabulary and Core Concept Check (p. 553)

1. the opposite leg, the hypotenuse

3. *Sample answer:* Both angles are formed by a horizontal line and a line of sight. An angle of elevation is formed by an upward line of sight and an angle of depression is formed by a downward line of sight.

9.5 Monitoring Progress and Modeling with Mathematics (pp. 553–556)

5. $\sin D = \frac{4}{5} = 0.8000$, $\sin E = \frac{3}{5} = 0.6000$,
$\cos D = \frac{3}{5} = 0.6000$, $\cos E = \frac{4}{5} = 0.8000$

7. $\sin D = \frac{28}{53} \approx 0.5283$, $\sin E = \frac{45}{53} \approx 0.8491$,
$\cos D = \frac{45}{53} \approx 0.8491$, $\cos E = \frac{28}{53} \approx 0.5283$

9. $\sin D = \frac{\sqrt{3}}{2} \approx 0.8660$, $\sin E = \frac{1}{2} = 0.5000$,
$\cos D = \frac{1}{2} = 0.5000$, $\cos E = \frac{\sqrt{3}}{2} \approx 0.8660$

11. $\cos 53°$ **13.** $\cos 61°$

15. $\sin 31°$ **17.** $\sin 17°$

19. $x \approx 9.5$, $y \approx 15.3$ **21.** $v \approx 4.7$, $w \approx 1.6$

23. $a \approx 14.9$, $b \approx 11.1$

25. $\sin X = \cos X = \sin Z = \cos Z$

27. $\sin M$, $\cos N$

29. Any given acute angle in a right triangle is formed by one leg and the hypotenuse. The hypotenuse is across from the right angle, and the leg is called the adjacent leg.

31. about 15 ft

33. $\sin \theta = \dfrac{\sqrt{21}}{5}$; $\tan \theta = \dfrac{\sqrt{21}}{2}$

35. $\sin \theta = \dfrac{2\sqrt{14}}{9}$; $\tan \theta = \dfrac{2\sqrt{14}}{5}$

37. $\sin \theta = \dfrac{\sqrt{15}}{8}$; $\tan \theta = \dfrac{\sqrt{15}}{7}$

39. $\cos \theta = \dfrac{\sqrt{3}}{2}$; $\tan \theta = \dfrac{\sqrt{3}}{3}$

41. $\cos \theta = \dfrac{\sqrt{39}}{8}$; $\tan \theta = \dfrac{5\sqrt{39}}{39}$

43. $\cos \theta = \dfrac{\sqrt{77}}{9}$; $\tan \theta = \dfrac{2\sqrt{77}}{77}$

45. The identity is $\cos^2 \theta + \sin^2 \theta = 1$, not $\cos^2 \theta - \sin^2 \theta = 1$; $\cos \theta = \dfrac{\sqrt{17}}{9}$

47. a.

20 ft
67°

    b. about 23.4 ft; The higher you hold the spool, the farther the kite is from the ground.

49. a. at least 437 ft

    b. at least 21,437 ft

51.

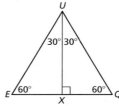

U
30° 30°
E 60° X 60° Q

G
2
T 1 R

Because $\triangle EQU$ is an equilateral triangle, all three angles have a measure of 60°. When an altitude, $\overline{UX}$, is drawn from U to $\overline{EQ}$ as shown, two congruent 30°-60°-90° triangles are formed, where $m\angle E = 60°$. So, $\sin E = \sin 60° = \dfrac{\sqrt{3}}{2}$. Also, in $\triangle RGT$, because the hypotenuse is twice as long as one of the legs, it is also a 30°-60°-90° triangle. Because $\angle G$ is across from the shorter leg, it must have a measure of 30°, which means that $\cos G = \cos 30° = \dfrac{\sqrt{3}}{2}$. So, $\sin E = \cos G$.

53. $\dfrac{\sin A}{\cos A} = \dfrac{\frac{\text{length of side opposite } A}{\text{length of hypotenuse}}}{\frac{\text{length of side adjacent to } A}{\text{length of hypotenuse}}} \cdot \dfrac{\text{length of hypotenuse}}{\text{length of hypotenuse}}$

$= \dfrac{\text{length of side opposite } A}{\text{length of side adjacent to } A}$

$= \tan A$

55. a.

30 ft

b.

Angle of depression	40°	50°	60°	70°	80°
Approximate length of line of sight (feet)	46.7	39.2	34.6	31.9	30.5

c.

View of Sailboat from Cliff

Approximate Length of Line of Sight (feet) vs. Angle of Depression (degrees)

d. 60 ft

57. If you knew how to take the inverse of the trigonometric ratios, you could first find the respective ratio of sides and then take the inverse of the trigonometric ratio to find the measure of the angle.

9.5 Maintaining Mathematical Proficiency (p. 556)

59. $x = 8$; yes   **61.** $x = 45$; yes

63.

		Gender		
		Male	Female	Total
Class	Sophomore	0.10	0.20	0.30
	Junior	0.12	0.18	0.30
	Senior	0.19	0.21	0.40
	Total	0.41	0.59	1

9.6 Vocabulary and Core Concept Check (p. 561)

1. sides, angles

9.6 Monitoring Progress and Modeling with Mathematics (pp. 561–562)

3. $\angle C$ **5.** $\angle A$

7. about 48.6°   **9.** about 70.7°

11. about 15.6°

13. $AB = 15$, $m\angle A \approx 53.1°$, $m\angle B \approx 36.9°$

15. $YZ \approx 8.5$, $m\angle X \approx 70.5°$, $m\angle Z \approx 19.5°$

17. $KL \approx 5.1$, $ML \approx 6.1$, $m\angle K = 50°$

19. The sine ratio should be the length of the opposite side to the length of the hypotenuse, not the adjacent side; $\sin^{-1} \frac{8}{17} = m\angle T$

21. about 59.7°

23.

4.76°   96.4 in.   8 in.   96.1 in.

25. about 36.9°; $PQ = 3$ centimeters and $PR = 4$ centimeters, so $m\angle R = \tan^{-1}\left(\frac{3}{4}\right) \approx 36.9°$.

27. $KM \approx 7.8$ ft, $JK \approx 11.9$ ft, $m\angle JKM = 49°$; $ML \approx 19.5$ ft, $m\angle MKL \approx 68.2°$, $m\angle L \approx 21.8°$

29. a. *Sample answer:* $\tan^{-1}\frac{3}{1}$; about 71.6°

   b. *Sample answer:* $\tan^{-1}\frac{4}{3}$; about 53.1°

31. Because the sine is the ratio of the length of a leg to the length of the hypotenuse, and the hypotenuse is always longer than either of the legs, the sine cannot have a value greater than 1.

9.6 Maintaining Mathematical Proficiency (p. 562)

33. $x = 8$ **35.** $x = 2.46$

Chapter 9 Review (pp. 564–566)

1. $x = 2\sqrt{34} \approx 11.7$; no   **2.** $x = 12$; yes

3. $x = 2\sqrt{30} \approx 11.0$; no   **4.** yes; acute

5. yes; right   **6.** yes; obtuse

7. $x = 6\sqrt{2}$ **8.** $x = 7$

9. $x = 16\sqrt{3}$

10. $\triangle GFH \sim \triangle FEH \sim \triangle GEF$; $x = 13.5$

11. $\triangle KLM \sim \triangle JKM \sim \triangle JLK$; $x = 2\sqrt{6} \approx 4.9$

12. $\triangle TUV \sim \triangle STV \sim \triangle SUT$; $x = 25$

13. $\tan J = \frac{11}{60} \approx 0.1833$, $\tan L = \frac{60}{11} \approx 5.4545$

14. about 15 ft

15. $\sin X = \frac{7\sqrt{149}}{149} \approx 0.5735$, $\sin Z = \frac{10\sqrt{149}}{149} \approx 0.8192$,

   $\cos X = \frac{10\sqrt{149}}{149} \approx 0.8192$, $\cos Z = \frac{7\sqrt{149}}{149} \approx 0.5735$

16. $s \approx 31.3$, $t \approx 13.3$ **17.** $r \approx 4.0$, $s \approx 2.9$

18. $v \approx 9.4$, $w \approx 3.4$ **19.** $\cos 18°$

20. $\cos \theta = \frac{7}{25}$, $\tan \theta = \frac{24}{7}$

21. $m\angle A \approx 48.2°$, $m\angle B \approx 41.8°$, $BC \approx 11.2$

22. $m\angle L = 53°$, $ML \approx 4.5$, $NL \approx 7.5$

23. $m\angle X \approx 46.1°$, $m\angle Z \approx 43.9°$, $XY \approx 17.3$

Chapter 10

Chapter 10 Maintaining Mathematical Proficiency (p. 571)

1. $x^2 + 11x + 28$ **2.** $a^2 - 4a - 5$

3. $3q^2 - 31q + 36$ **4.** $10v^2 - 33v - 7$

5. $4h^2 + 11h + 6$ **6.** $18b^2 - 54b + 40$

7. $x \approx -1.45$; $x \approx 3.45$ **8.** $r \approx -9.24$; $r \approx -0.76$

9. $w = -1$, $w = 9$ **10.** $p \approx -10.39$; $p \approx 0.39$

11. $k \approx -1.32$; $k \approx 5.32$ **12.** $z = 1$

13. *Sample answer:* $(2n + 1)(2n + 3)$; $2n + 1$ is positive and odd when n is a nonnegative integer. The next positive, odd integer is $2n + 3$.

10.1 Vocabulary and Core Concept Check (p. 578)

1. They both intersect the circle in two points; Chords are segments and secants are lines.

3. concentric circles

10.1 Monitoring Progress and Modeling with Mathematics (pp. 578–580)

5. $\odot C$ 7. $\overline{BH}, \overline{AD}$

9. $\overleftrightarrow{KG}$

11. 4

13. 2

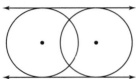

15. external   17. internal

19. yes; $\triangle ABC$ is a right triangle.

21. no; $\triangle ABD$ is not a right triangle.

23. 10   25. 10.5

27. *Sample answer:*

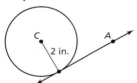

29. 5   31. ±3

33. $\angle Z$ is a right angle, not $\angle YXZ$; $\overline{XY}$ is not tangent to $\odot Z$.

35. 2; 1; 0; *Sample answer:* There are two possible points of tangency from a point outside the circle, one from a point on the circle, and none from a point inside the circle.

37. 25.6 units

39. yes; $\overline{PE}$ and $\overline{PM}$ are radii, so $\overline{PE} \cong \overline{PM}$.

41. *Sample answer:* Every point is the same distance from the center, so the farthest two points can be from each other is opposite sides of the center.

43. $\angle ARC \cong \angle BSC$ and $\angle ACR \cong \angle BCS$, so $\triangle ARC \sim \triangle BSC$ by the AA Similarity Theorem. Because corresponding sides of similar figures are proportional,
$$\frac{AC}{BC} = \frac{RC}{SC}.$$

45. $x = 13$, $y = 5$; $2x - 5 = x + 8$ and $2x + 4y - 6 = 2x + 14$.

47. **a.** Assume m is not perpendicular to $\overline{QP}$. The perpendicular segment from Q to m intersects m at some other point R. Then $QR < QP$, so R must be inside $\odot Q$, and m must be a secant line. This is a contradiction, so m must be perpendicular to $\overline{QP}$.

b. Assume m is not tangent to $\odot Q$. Then m must intersect $\odot Q$ at a second point R. $\overline{QP}$ and $\overline{QR}$ are both radii of $\odot Q$, so $\overline{QP} \cong \overline{QR}$. Because $m \perp \overline{QP}$, $QP < QR$. This is a contradiction, so m must be tangent to $\odot Q$.

10.1 Maintaining Mathematical Proficiency (p. 580)

49. not independent

10.2 Vocabulary and Core Concept Check (p. 586)

1. congruent arcs

10.2 Monitoring Progress and Modeling with Mathematics (pp. 586–588)

3. $\widehat{AB}$, 135°; $\widehat{ADB}$, 225°   5. $\widehat{JL}$, 120°; $\widehat{JKL}$, 240°

7. minor arc; 70°   9. minor arc; 45°

11. semicircle; 180°   13. major arc; 290°

15. **a.** 132°   **b.** 147°
     c. 200°   **d.** 160°

17. **a.** 103°   **b.** 257°
     c. 196°   **d.** 305°
     e. 79°   **f.** 281°

19. congruent; They are in the same circle and $m\widehat{AB} = m\widehat{CD}$.

21. congruent; The circles are congruent and $m\widehat{VW} = m\widehat{XY}$.

23. 70; 110°

25. your friend; The arcs must be in the same circle or congruent circles.

27. $\widehat{AD}$ is the minor arc; $\widehat{ABD}$ 29. 340°; 160°

31. 18°

33. Translate $\odot A$ left a units so that point A maps to point O. The image of $\odot A$ is $\odot A'$ with center O, so $\odot A'$ and $\odot O$ are concentric circles. Dilate $\odot A'$ using center of dilation O and scale factor $\dfrac{r}{s}$, which maps the points s units from point O to the points $\dfrac{r}{s}(s) = r$ units from point O.

So, this dilation maps $\odot A'$ to $\odot O$. Because a similarity transformation maps $\odot A$ to $\odot O$, $\odot O \sim \odot A$.

35. **a.** Translate $\odot B$ so that point B maps to point A. The image of $\odot B$ is $\odot B'$ with center A. Because $\overline{AC} \cong \overline{BD}$, this translation maps $\odot B'$ to $\odot A$. A rigid motion maps $\odot B$ to $\odot A$, so $\odot A \cong \odot B$.

b. Because $\odot A \cong \odot B$, the distance from the center of the circle to a point on the circle is the same for each circle. So, $\overline{AC} \cong \overline{BD}$.

37. **a.** $m\widehat{BC} = m\angle BAC$, $m\widehat{DE} = m\angle DAE$ and $m\angle BAC = m\angle DAE$, so $m\widehat{BC} = m\widehat{DE}$. Because $\widehat{BC}$ and $\widehat{DE}$ are in the same circle, $\widehat{BC} \cong \widehat{DE}$.

b. $m\widehat{BC} = m\angle BAC$ and $m\widehat{DE} = m\angle DAE$. Because $\widehat{BC} \cong \widehat{DE}$, $\angle BAC \cong \angle DAE$.

10.2 Maintaining Mathematical Proficiency (p. 588)

39. 15; yes   41. about 13.04; no

10.3 Vocabulary and Core Concept Check (p. 593)

1. Split the chord into two segments of equal length.

10.3 Monitoring Progress and Modeling with Mathematics (pp. 593–594)

3. 75°   5. 170°

7. 8   9. 5

11. $\overline{AC}$ and $\overline{DB}$ are not perpendicular; $\overline{BC}$ is not congruent to $\overline{CD}$.

13. yes; The triangles are congruent, so $\overline{AB}$ is a perpendicular bisector of $\overline{CD}$.

15. 17

17. about 13.9 in.; The perpendicular bisectors intersect at the center, so the right triangle with legs of 6 inches and 3.5 inches have a hypotenuse equal to the length of the radius.

19. a. Because $PA = PB = PC = PD$, $\triangle PDC \cong \triangle PAB$ by the SSS Congruence Theorem. So, $\angle DPC \cong \angle APB$ and $\overline{AB} \cong \overline{CD}$.

   b. $PA = PB = PC = PD$, and because $\overline{AB} \cong \overline{CD}$, $\angle DPC \cong \angle APB$. By the SAS Congruence Theorem, $\triangle PDC \cong \triangle PAB$, so $\overline{AB} \cong \overline{CD}$.

21. about 16.26°; *Sample answer:* Draw radii $\overline{PA}$ and $\overline{PB}$, and the radius perpendicular to the two chords. Find the angles at P of the right triangles formed and subtract to find $m\angle APB$.

23. $\overline{TP} \cong \overline{PR}$, $\overline{LP} \cong \overline{LP}$, and $\overline{LT} \cong \overline{LR}$, so $\triangle LPR \cong \triangle LPT$ by the SSS Congruence Theorem. Then $\angle LPT \cong \angle LPR$, so $m\angle LPT = m\angle LPR = 90°$. By definition, $\overline{LP}$ is a perpendicular bisector of $\overline{RT}$, so L lies on $\overline{QS}$. Because $\overline{QS}$ contains the center, $\overline{QS}$ is a diameter of $\odot L$.

25. If $\overline{AB} \cong \overline{CD}$, then $\overline{GC} \cong \overline{FA}$. Because $\overline{EC} \cong \overline{EA}$, $\triangle ECG \cong \triangle EAF$ by the HL Congruence Theorem, so $\overline{EF} \cong \overline{EG}$ and $EF = EG$. If $EF = EG$, then because $\overline{EC} \cong \overline{ED} \cong \overline{EA} \cong \overline{EB}$, $\triangle AEF \cong \triangle BEF \cong \triangle DEG \cong \triangle CEG$ by the HL Congruence Theorem. Then $\overline{AF} \cong \overline{BF} \cong \overline{DG} \cong \overline{CG}$, so $\overline{AB} \cong \overline{CD}$.

10.3 Maintaining Mathematical Proficiency (p. 594)

27. 259°

10.4 Vocabulary and Core Concept Check (p. 602)

1. intercepted arc

10.4 Monitoring Progress and Modeling with Mathematics (pp. 602–604)

3. 42°   **5.** 10°

7. 120°

9. $\angle ACB \cong \angle ADB$, $\angle DAC \cong \angle DBC$

11. 51°   **13.** $x = 100$, $y = 85$

15. $a = 20$, $b = 22$

17. The inscribed angle was not doubled; $m\angle BAC = 2(53°) = 106°$

19. $x = 25$, $y = 5$; 130°, 75°, 50°, 105°

21. $x = 30$, $y = 20$; 60°, 60°, 60°

23. yes; Opposite angles are always supplementary.

25. no; Opposite angles are not always supplementary.

27. no; Opposite angles are not always supplementary.

29.

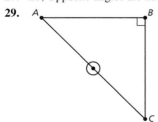

220,000 km

31. double the radius

33. Each diagonal splits the rectangle into two right triangles.

35. a. $\overline{QB} \cong \overline{QA}$, so $\triangle ABC$ is isosceles. By the Base Angles Theorem, $\angle QBA \cong \angle QAB$, so $m\angle BAQ = x°$. By the Exterior Angles Theorem, $m\angle AQC = 2x°$. Then $m\widehat{AC} = 2x°$, so $m\angle ABC = x° = \frac{1}{2}(2x)° = \frac{1}{2}m\widehat{AC}$.

   b. Given: $\angle ABC$ is inscribed in $\odot Q$. $\overline{DB}$ is a diameter; Prove: $m\angle ABC = \frac{1}{2}m\widehat{AC}$; By Case 1, proved in part (a), $m\angle ABD = \frac{1}{2}m\widehat{AD}$ and $m\angle CBD = \frac{1}{2}m\widehat{CD}$. By the Arc Addition Postulate, $m\widehat{AD} + m\widehat{CD} = m\widehat{AC}$. By the Angle Addition Postulate, $m\angle ABD + m\angle CBD = m\angle ABC$. Then $m\angle ABC = \frac{1}{2}m\widehat{AD} + \frac{1}{2}m\widehat{CD}$
$$= \frac{1}{2}\left(m\widehat{AD} + m\widehat{CD}\right)$$
$$= \frac{1}{2}m\widehat{AC}.$$

   c. Given: $\angle ABC$ is inscribed in $\odot Q$. $\overline{DB}$ is a diameter; Prove: $m\angle ABC = \frac{1}{2}m\widehat{AC}$; By Case 1, proved in part (a), $m\angle DBA = \frac{1}{2}m\widehat{AD}$ and $m\angle DBC = \frac{1}{2}m\widehat{CD}$. By the Arc Addition Postulate, $m\widehat{AC} + m\widehat{CD} = m\widehat{AD}$, so $m\widehat{AC} = m\widehat{AD} - m\widehat{CD}$. By the Angle Addition Postulate, $m\angle DBC + m\angle ABC = m\angle DBA$, so $m\angle ABC = m\angle DBA - m\angle DBC$. Then $m\angle ABC = \frac{1}{2}m\widehat{AD} - \frac{1}{2}m\widehat{CD}$
$$= \frac{1}{2}\left(m\widehat{AD} - m\widehat{CD}\right)$$
$$= \frac{1}{2}m\widehat{AC}.$$

37. To prove the conditional, find the measure of the intercepted arc of the right angle and the definition of a semicircle to show the hypotenuse of the right triangle must be the diameter of the circle. To prove the converse, use the definition of a semicircle to find the measure of the angle opposite the diameter.

39. 2.4 units

10.4 Maintaining Mathematical Proficiency (p. 604)

41. $x = \frac{145}{3}$ **43.** $x = 120$

10.5 Vocabulary and Core Concept Check (p. 610)

1. outside

10.5 Monitoring Progress and Modeling with Mathematics (pp. 610–612)

3. 130°   **5.** 130°

7. 115   **9.** 56

11. 40   **13.** 34

15. $\angle SUT$ is not a central angle; $m\angle SUT = \frac{1}{2}\left(m\widehat{QR} + m\widehat{ST}\right) = 41.5°$

17. 60°; When a tangent and a secant intersect outside the circle, the measure of the angle is half of the difference of the measures of the intercepted arcs.

19. 30°; Because the sum of the angles of a triangle always equals 180°, solve the equation $60 + 90 + x = 180$.

21. 30°; This angle is complementary to $\angle 2$, which is 60°.

23. about 2.8°   **25.** $360 - 10x$; 160°

27. $m\angle LPJ < 90$; The difference of $m\widehat{JL}$ and $m\widehat{LK}$ must be less than 180°, so $m\angle LPJ < 90$.

29. By the Angles Inside a Circle Theorem, $m\angle JPN = \frac{1}{2}\left(m\widehat{JN} + m\widehat{KM}\right)$. By the Angles Outside the Circle Theorem, $m\angle JLN = \frac{1}{2}\left(m\widehat{JN} - m\widehat{KM}\right)$. Because the angle measures are positive, $\frac{1}{2}\left(m\widehat{JN} + m\widehat{KM}\right) > \frac{1}{2}m\widehat{JN} > \frac{1}{2}\left(m\widehat{JN} - m\widehat{KM}\right)$, so, $m\angle JPN > m\angle JLN$.

31. a.

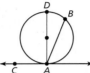

b. $m\overset{\frown}{AB} = 2m\angle BAC$, $m\overset{\frown}{AB} = 360° - 2m\angle BAC$

c. $90°$; $2m\angle BAC = 360° - 2m\angle BAC$ when $m\angle BAC = 90°$.

33. a. By the Tangent Line to Circle Theorem, $m\angle BAC$ is $90°$, which is half the measure of the semicircular arc.

b.

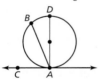

By the Tangent Line to Circle Theorem, $m\angle CAD = 90°$. $m\angle DAB = \frac{1}{2}m\overset{\frown}{DB}$ and by part (a), $m\angle CAD = \frac{1}{2}m\overset{\frown}{AD}$. By the Angle Addition Postulate, $m\angle BAC = m\angle BAD + m\angle CAD$. So, $m\angle BAC = \frac{1}{2}m\overset{\frown}{DB} + \frac{1}{2}m\overset{\frown}{AD} = \frac{1}{2}(m\overset{\frown}{DB} + m\overset{\frown}{AD})$. By the Arc Addition Postulate, $m\overset{\frown}{DB} + m\overset{\frown}{AD} = m\overset{\frown}{ADB}$, so $m\angle BAC = \frac{1}{2}(m\overset{\frown}{ADB})$.

c.

By the Tangent Line to Circle Theorem, $m\angle CAD = 90°$. $m\angle DAB = \frac{1}{2}m\overset{\frown}{DB}$ and by part (a), $m\angle DAC = \frac{1}{2}m\overset{\frown}{ABD}$. By the Angle Addition Postulate, $m\angle BAC = m\angle DAC - m\angle DAB$. So, $m\angle BAC = \frac{1}{2}m\overset{\frown}{ABD} - \frac{1}{2}m\overset{\frown}{DB} = \frac{1}{2}(m\overset{\frown}{ABD} - m\overset{\frown}{DB})$. By the Arc Addition Postulate, $m\overset{\frown}{ABD} - m\overset{\frown}{DB} = m\overset{\frown}{AB}$, so $m\angle BAC = \frac{1}{2}(m\overset{\frown}{AB})$.

35.

STATEMENTS	REASONS
1. Chords $\overline{AC}$ and $\overline{BD}$ intersect.	1. Given
2. $m\angle ACB = \frac{1}{2}m\overset{\frown}{AB}$ and $m\angle DBC = \frac{1}{2}m\overset{\frown}{DC}$	2. Measure of an Inscribed Angle Theorem
3. $m\angle 1 = m\angle DBC + m\angle ACB$	3. Exterior Angle Theorem
4. $m\angle 1 = \frac{1}{2}m\overset{\frown}{DC} + \frac{1}{2}m\overset{\frown}{AB}$	4. Substitution Property of Equality
5. $m\angle 1 = \frac{1}{2}(m\overset{\frown}{DC} + m\overset{\frown}{AB})$	5. Distributive Property

37. By the Exterior Angle Theorem, $m\angle 2 = m\angle 1 + m\angle ABC$, so $m\angle 1 = m\angle 2 - m\angle ABC$. By the Tangent and Intersected Chord Theorem, $m\angle 2 = \frac{1}{2}m\overset{\frown}{BC}$ and by the Measure of an Inscribed Angle Theorem, $m\angle ABC = \frac{1}{2}m\overset{\frown}{AC}$. By the Substitution Property, $m\angle 1 = \frac{1}{2}m\overset{\frown}{BC} - \frac{1}{2}m\overset{\frown}{AC} = \frac{1}{2}(m\overset{\frown}{BC} - m\overset{\frown}{AC})$;

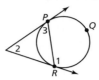

By the Exterior Angle Theorem, $m\angle 1 = m\angle 2 + m\angle 3$, so $m\angle 2 = m\angle 1 - m\angle 3$. By the Tangent and Intersected Chord Theorem, $m\angle 1 = \frac{1}{2}m\overset{\frown}{PQR}$ and $m\angle 3 = \frac{1}{2}m\overset{\frown}{PR}$. By the Substitution Property, $m\angle 2 = \frac{1}{2}m\overset{\frown}{PQR} - \frac{1}{2}m\overset{\frown}{PR} = \frac{1}{2}(m\overset{\frown}{PQR} - m\overset{\frown}{PR})$;

By the Exterior Angle Theorem, $m\angle 1 = m\angle 3 + m\angle WXZ$, so $m\angle 3 = m\angle 1 - m\angle WXZ$. By the Measure of an Inscribed Angle Theorem, $m\angle 1 = \frac{1}{2}m\overset{\frown}{XY}$ and $m\angle WXZ = \frac{1}{2}m\overset{\frown}{WZ}$. By the Substitution Property, $m\angle 3 = \frac{1}{2}m\overset{\frown}{XY} - \frac{1}{2}m\overset{\frown}{WZ} = \frac{1}{2}(m\overset{\frown}{XY} - m\overset{\frown}{WZ})$.

39. $20°$; *Sample answer:* $m\overset{\frown}{WY} = 160°$ and $m\overset{\frown}{WX} = m\overset{\frown}{ZY}$, so
$m\angle P = \frac{1}{2}(m\overset{\frown}{WZ} - m\overset{\frown}{XY})$
$= \frac{1}{2}((200° - m\overset{\frown}{ZY}) - (160° - m\overset{\frown}{WX}))$
$= \frac{1}{2}(40°)$.

10.5 Maintaining Mathematical Proficiency (p. 612)

41. $x = -4, x = 3$ **43.** $x = -3, x = -1$

10.6 Vocabulary and Core Concept Check (p. 617)

1. external segment

10.6 Monitoring Progress and Modeling with Mathematics (pp. 617–618)

3. 5   **5.** 4

7. 4   **9.** 5

11. 12   **13.** 4

15. The chords were used instead of the secant segments; $CF \cdot DF = BF \cdot AF$; $CD = 2$

17. about 124.5 ft

19.

STATEMENTS	REASONS
1. $\overline{AB}$ and $\overline{CD}$ are chords intersecting in the interior of the circle.	1. Given
2. $\angle AEC \cong \angle DEB$	2. Vertical Angles Congruence Theorem
3. $\angle ACD \cong \angle ABD$	3. Inscribed Angles of a Circle Theorem
4. $\triangle AEC \sim \triangle DEB$	4. AA Similarity Theorem
5. $\dfrac{EA}{ED} = \dfrac{EC}{EB}$	5. Corresponding side lengths of similar triangles are proportional.
6. $EB \cdot EA = EC \cdot ED$	6. Cross Products Property

21.

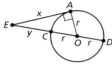

By the Tangent Line to Circle Theorem, $\angle EAO$ is a right angle, which makes $\triangle AEO$ a right triangle. By the Pythagorean Theorem, $(r + y)^2 = r^2 + x^2$. So, $r^2 + 2yr + y^2 = r^2 + x^2$. By the Subtraction Property of Equality, $2yr + y^2 = x^2$. Then $y(2r + y) = x^2$, so $EC \cdot ED = EA^2$.

23. $BC = \dfrac{AD^2 + (AD)(DE) - AB^2}{AB}$

25. $2\sqrt{10}$

10.6 Maintaining Mathematical Proficiency *(p. 618)*

27. $x = -9, x = 5$ **29.** $x = -7, x = 1$

10.7 Vocabulary and Core Concept Check *(p. 624)*

1. $(x - h)^2 + (y - k)^2 = r^2$

10.7 Monitoring Progress and Modeling with Mathematics *(pp. 624–626)*

3. center: $(0, 0)$, radius: 4   **5.** center: $(-3, 3)$, radius: 6

7. center: $(-0.5, 0.5)$, radius: 2

9. $x^2 + y^2 = 4$ **11.** $(x + 3)^2 + (y + 3)^2 = 81$

13. $(x - 4)^2 + y^2 = 64$ **15.** $x^2 + y^2 = 49$

17. $(x + 3)^2 + (y - 4)^2 = 1$ **19.** $(x + 2)^2 + (y + 6)^2 = 1.21$

21. $x^2 + y^2 = 36$ **23.** $(x - 7)^2 + (y + 9)^2 = 25$

25. $x^2 + y^2 = 58$

27. The coordinates of the center should be subtracted; $[x - (-3)]^2 + [y - (-5)]^2 = (x + 3)^2 + (y + 5)^2 = 9$

29. center: $(0, 0)$, radius: 7

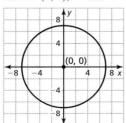

31. center: $(-5, 3)$, radius: 3

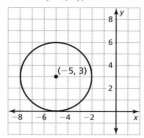

33. center: $(3, 0)$, radius: 4   **35.** center: $(4, 1)$, radius: 1

 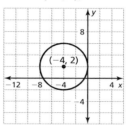

37. center: $(-4, 2)$, radius: 4

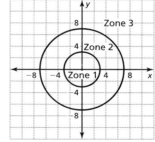

39. The radius of the circle is 8. $\sqrt{(2 - 0)^2 + (3 - 0)^2} = \sqrt{13}$, so $(2, 3)$ does not lie on the circle.

41. The radius of the circle is $\sqrt{10}$.
$\sqrt{\left(\sqrt{6} - 0\right)^2 + (2 - 0)^2} = \sqrt{10}$, so $\left(\sqrt{6}, 2\right)$ does lie on the circle.

43. The radius of the circle is 5. $\sqrt{(4 - 1)^2 + (4 - 0)^2} = 5$, so $(4, 4)$ does lie on the circle.

45. a.

b. zone 2, zone 3, zone 1, zone 1, zone 2

47. $\left(-\sqrt{3}, 1\right), \left(\sqrt{3}, 1\right)$

49. $\left(5 - \sqrt{7}, -5 - \sqrt{7}\right), \left(5 + \sqrt{7}, -5 + \sqrt{7}\right)$

51. no solution   **53.** $\left(-\dfrac{3}{5}, \dfrac{4}{5}\right), (1, 0)$

55. $(2.2, -1.6), (3, 0)$

57. a. *Sample answer:* Write the two numerators and the denominator of the coordinates.

b. *Sample answer:* $\left(\dfrac{3}{5}, \dfrac{4}{5}\right)$

59.

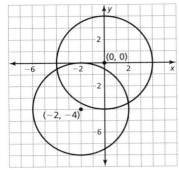

The equation of the image is $(x + 2)^2 + (y + 4)^2 = 16$;
The equation of the image of a circle after a
translation m units to the left and n units down is
$(x + m)^2 + (y + n)^2 = r^2$.

61. $(x - 4)^2 + (y - 9)^2 = 16$; $m\angle Z = 90°$, so $\overline{XY}$ is a diameter.

63. tangent; The system has one solution.

65. secant; The system has two solutions, and $(5, -1)$ is not on the line.

67. $(x - 15)^2 + y^2 = 100$; *Sample answer:* If r is the radius of $\odot O$, C is at $(15r, 0)$, and the distance to $(63, 16)$ is $4r$.

10.7 Maintaining Mathematical Proficiency *(p. 626)*

69. minor arc; 90°   **71.** minor arc, 127°

73. minor arc; 78°

Chapter 10 Review *(pp. 628–632)*

1. radius   **2.** chord

3. tangent   **4.** diameter

5. secant   **6.** radius

7. internal   **8.** external

9. 2   **10.** 2

11. 12   **12.** tangent; $20^2 + 48^2 = 52^2$

13. 100°   **14.** 60°

15. 160°   **16.** 80°

17. not congruent; The circles are not congruent.

18. congruent; The circles are congruent and $m\widehat{AB} = m\widehat{EF}$.

19. 61°   **20.** 65°

21. 91   **22.** 26

23. 80   **24.** $q = 100, r = 20$

25. 5   **26.** $y = 30, z = 10$

27. $m = 44, n = 39$ **28.** 28

29. 70   **30.** 106

31. 16   **32.** 240°

33. 5   **34.** 3

35. 10   **36.** about 10.7 ft

37. $(x - 4)^2 + (y + 1)^2 = 9$ **38.** $(x - 8)^2 + (y - 6)^2 = 36$

39. $x^2 + y^2 = 16$ **40.** $x^2 + y^2 = 81$

41. $(x + 5)^2 + (y - 2)^2 = 1.69$

42. $(x + 7)^2 + (y - 6)^2 = 25$

43. center: $(6, -4)$, radius: 2

44. The radius of the circle is 5. $d = \sqrt{(0 - 4)^2 + (0 + 3)^2} = 5$, so $(4, -3)$ is on the circle.

45. no solution

46. $(0, -3), \left(\frac{4}{5}, -\frac{7}{5}\right)$

Chapter 11

Chapter 11 Maintaining Mathematical Proficiency *(p. 637)*

1. 158 ft²   **2.** 144 m²

3. 184 cm²   **4.** 9 in.

5. 2 cm   **6.** 12 ft

7. $S = 6x^2$; cube

11.1 Vocabulary and Core Concept Check *(p. 644)*

1. πd

11.1 Monitoring Progress and Modeling with Mathematics *(pp. 644–646)*

3. about 37.70 in.   **5.** 14 units

7. about 3.14 ft   **9.** about 35.53 m

11. The diameter was used as the radius; $C = \pi d = 9\pi$ in.

13. 182 ft   **15.** about 44.85 units

17. about 20.57 units   **19.** $\frac{7\pi}{18}$ radian

21. 165°   **23.** about 27.19 min

25. 8π units   **27.** about 7.85 units

29. yes; *Sample answer:* The arc length also depends on the radius.

31. B   **33.** $2\frac{1}{3}$

35. arc length of $\widehat{AB} = r\theta$; about 9.42 in.

37. yes; *Sample answer:* The circumference of the red circle can be found using $2 = \frac{30°}{360°}C$. The circumference of the blue circle is double the circumference of the red circle.

39. 28 units

41. *Sample answer:*

STATEMENTS	REASONS
1. $\overline{FG} \cong \overline{GH}$, $\angle JFK \cong \angle KLF$	1. Given
2. $FG = GH$	2. Definition of congruent segments
3. $FH = FG + GH$	3. Segment Addition Postulate
4. $FH = 2FG$	4. Substitution Property of Equality
5. $m\angle JFK = m\angle KFL$	5. Definition of congruent angles
6. $m\angle JFL$ $= m\angle JFK + m\angle KFL$	6. Angle Addition Postulate
7. $m\angle JFL = 2m\angle JFK$	7. Substitution Property of Equality
8. $\angle NFG \cong \angle JFL$	8. Vertical Angles Congruence Theorem
9. $m\angle NFG = m\angle JFL$	9. Definition of congruent angles
10. $m\angle NFG = 2m\angle JFK$	10. Substitution Property of Equality
11. arc length of $\overset{\frown}{JK}$ $= \dfrac{m\angle JFK}{360°} \cdot 2\pi FH,$ arc length of $\overset{\frown}{NG}$ $= \dfrac{m\angle NFG}{360°} \cdot 2\pi FG$	11. Formula for arc length
12. arc length of $\overset{\frown}{JK}$ $= \dfrac{m\angle JFK}{360°} \cdot 2\pi(2FG),$ arc length of $\overset{\frown}{NG}$ $= \dfrac{2m\angle JFK}{360°} \cdot 2\pi FG$	12. Substitution Property of Equality
13. arc length of $\overset{\frown}{NG}$ $=$ arc length of $\overset{\frown}{JK}$	13. Transitive Property of Equality

11.1 Maintaining Mathematical Proficiency (p. 646)

43. 15 square units

11.2 Vocabulary and Core Concept Check (p. 652)

1. sector

11.2 Monitoring Progress and Modeling with Mathematics (pp. 652–654)

3. about 0.50 cm²
5. about 78.54 in.²
7. about 5.32 ft
9. about 4.00 in.
11. about 0.09, or about 9%
13. about 0.02, or about 2%
15. about 0.65, or about 65%
17. about 0.79, or about 79%
19. about 52.36 in.²; about 261.80 in.²
21. about 937.31 m²; about 1525.70 m²
23. The diameter was substituted in the formula for area as the radius; $A = \pi(6)^2 \approx 113.10$ ft²

25. about 66.04 cm²
27. about 1696.46 m²
29. about 43.98 ft²
31. about 26.77 in.²
33. about 192.48 ft²
35. a. about 285 ft² **b.** about 182 ft²
37. *Sample answer:* change side lengths to radii and perimeter to circumference; Different terms need to be used because a circle is not a polygon.
39. a. *Sample answer:* The total is 100%.
   b. bus 234°; walk 90°; other 36°

How Students Get To School

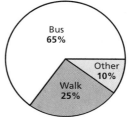

   c. bus: about 8.17 in.²; walk: about 3.14 in.²; other: about 1.26 in.²
41. a. You should buy two 14-inch pizzas; *Sample answer:* The area is 98π square inches and the cost is $25.98.
   b. You should buy two 10-inch pizzas and one 14-inch pizza; *Sample answer:* Buying three 10-inch pizzas is the only cheaper option, and it would not be enough pizza.
   c. You should buy four 10-inch pizzas; *Sample answer:* The total circumference is 20π inches.
43. a. 2.4 in.²; 4.7 in.²; 7.1 in.²; 9.4 in.²; 11.8 in.²; 14.1 in.²
   b.

   c. yes; *Sample answer:* The rate of change is constant.
   d. yes; no; *Sample answer:* The rate of change will still be constant.
45. *Sample answer:* Let $2a$ and $2b$ represent the lengths of the legs of the triangle. The areas of the semicircles are $\frac{1}{2}\pi a^2$, $\frac{1}{2}\pi b^2$, and $\frac{1}{2}\pi(a^2 + b^2)$. $\frac{1}{2}\pi a^2 + \frac{1}{2}\pi b^2 = \frac{1}{2}\pi(a^2 + b^2)$, and subtracting the areas of the unshaded regions from both sides leaves the area of the crescents on the left and the area of the triangle on the right.

11.2 Maintaining Mathematical Proficiency (p. 654)

47. 49 ft²
49. 15 ft²

11.3 Vocabulary and Core Concept Check (p. 660)

1. Divide 360° by the number of sides.

11.3 Monitoring Progress and Modeling with Mathematics (pp. 660–662)

3. 361 square units
5. 70 square units
7. P
9. 5 units
11. 36°
13. 15°

15. 45°   **17.** 67.5°

19. about 62.35 square units

21. about 20.87 square units

23. about 342.24 square units

25. The side lengths were used instead of the diagonals; $A = \frac{1}{2}(8)(4) = 16$

27. about 0.24, or about 24%   **29.** about 0.59, or about 59%

31. about 166 in.²

33. true; *Sample answer:* As the number of sides increases, the polygon fills more of the circle.

35. false; *Sample answer:* The radius can be less than or greater than the side length.

37. about 59.44 square units   **39.** $x^2 = 324$; 18 in.; 36 in.

41. yes; about 24.73 in.²; *Sample answer:* Each side length is 2 inches, and the central angle is 40°.

43. *Sample answer:* Let $QT = x$ and $TS = y$. The area of $PQRS$ is $\frac{1}{2}d_2x + \frac{1}{2}d_2y = \frac{1}{2}d_2(x + y) = \frac{1}{2}d_2d_1$.

45. $A = \frac{1}{2}d^2$; $A = \frac{1}{2}d^2 = \frac{1}{2}(s^2 + s^2) = \frac{1}{2}(2s^2) = s^2$

47. about 6.47 cm   **49.** about 92 square units

51. about 43 square units; *Sample answer:* $A = \frac{1}{2}aP$; There are fewer calculations.

11.3 Maintaining Mathematical Proficiency *(p. 662)*

53.

		Response		
		Yes	No	Total
Gender	Male	17	52	69
	Female	48	62	110
	Total	65	114	179

11.4 Vocabulary and Core Concept Check *(p. 670)*

1. cubic units

11.4 Monitoring Progress and Modeling with Mathematics *(pp. 670–672)*

3. B   **4.** D

5. A   **6.** C

7. yes; pentagonal pyramid   **9.** no

11. 6.3 cm³   **13.** 175 in.³

15. about 288.40 ft³   **17.** about 628.32 ft³

19.

310.38 cm³

21. There are two parallel, congruent bases, so it is a prism, not a pyramid; The solid is a triangular prism.

23. 10 ft   **25.** 4 cm

27. about 11.04 ft   **29.** 99 cm³

31. 150 ft³   **33.** about 1900.66 in.³

35. about 2,350,000,000 gal

37. *Sample answer:* The stacks have the same height and the rectangles have the same lengths, so the stacks have the same area.

39. *Sample answer:*

41. no; The cross-sectional areas must be the same to use Cavalieri's Principle.

43. 36 ft, 15 ft

11.4 Maintaining Mathematical Proficiency *(p. 672)*

45. 16 m²   **47.** 680.4 in.²

11.5 Vocabulary and Core Concept Check *(p. 677)*

1. *Sample answer:* A triangular prism has two parallel bases that are triangles. A triangular pyramid has one base that is a triangle, and the other faces all intersect at a single point.

11.5 Monitoring Progress and Modeling with Mathematics *(pp. 677–678)*

3. 448 m³   **5.** 6 m

7. 16 in.

9. One side length was used in the formula as the base area; $V = \frac{1}{3}(6^2)(5) = 60$ ft³

11. 5 ft   **13.** 12 yd

15. 4 ft³   **17.** 72 in.³

19. about 213.33 cm³

21. **a.** The volume doubles.

    b. The volume is 4 times greater.

    c. yes; *Sample answer:*

    Square pyramid: $V = \frac{1}{3}s^2h$

    Double height: $V = \frac{1}{3}s^2(2h) = 2\left(\frac{1}{3}s^2h\right)$

    Double side length of base: $V = \frac{1}{3}(2s)^2h = 4\left(\frac{1}{3}s^2h\right)$

23. about 9.22 ft³   **25.** about 78 in.³

11.5 Maintaining Mathematical Proficiency *(p. 678)*

27. 12.6   **29.** 16.0

11.6 Vocabulary and Core Concept Check *(p. 683)*

1. *Sample answer:* pyramids have a polygonal base, cones have a circular base; They both have sides that meet at a single vertex.

11.6 Monitoring Progress and Modeling with Mathematics *(pp. 683–684)*

3. about 603.19 in.²   **5.** about 678.58 in.²

7. about 1361.36 mm³   **9.** about 526.27 in.³

11. $\ell \approx 5.00$ cm; $h \approx 4.00$ cm   **13.** 256π ft³

15. about 226.19 cm³

17. $2h$; $r\sqrt{2}$; *Sample answer:* The original volume is $V = \frac{1}{3}\pi r^2h$ and the new volume is $V = \frac{2}{3}\pi r^2h$.

19. about 3716.85 ft³

21. yes; *Sample answer:* The automatic pet feeder holds about 12 cups of food.

23. It is half; about 60°

25. yes; *Sample answer:* The base areas are the same and the total heights are the same.

11.6 Maintaining Mathematical Proficiency *(p. 684)*

27. about 153.94 ft^2 **29.** 32 m

11.7 Vocabulary and Core Concept Check *(p. 690)*

1. The plane must contain the center of the sphere.

11.7 Monitoring Progress and Modeling with Mathematics *(pp. 690–692)*

3. about 201.06 ft^2 **5.** about 1052.09 m^2

7. 1 ft   **9.** 30 m

11. about 157.08 m^2 **13.** about 2144.66 m^3

15. about 5575.28 yd^3 **17.** about 4188.79 cm^3

19. about 33.51 ft^3

21. The radius was squared instead of cubed; $V = \frac{4}{3}\pi(6)^3 \approx 904.78$ ft^3

23. about 445.06 in.^{3} **25.** about 7749.26 cm^3

27. $S \approx 226.98$ in.^{2}; $V \approx 321.56$ in.^{3}

29. $S \approx 45.84$ in.^{2}; $V \approx 29.18$ in.^{3}

31. $S \approx 215.18$ in.^{2}; $V \approx 296.80$ in.^{3}

33. no; The surface area is quadrupled.

35. about 20,944 ft^3

37. a. 144π in.^{2}, 288π in.^{3}; 324π in.^{2}, 972π in.^{3}; 576π in.^{2}, 2304π in.^{3}

   b. It is multiplied by 4; It is multiplied by 9; It is multiplied by 16.

   c. It is multiplied by 8; It is multiplied by 27; It is multiplied by 64.

39. a. Earth: about 197.1 million mi^2; moon: about 14.7 million mi^2

   b. The surface area of the Earth is about 13.4 times greater than the surface area of the moon.

   c. about 137.9 million mi^2

41. about 50.27 in.^{2}; *Sample answer:* The side length of the cube is the diameter of the sphere.

43. $V = \frac{1}{3}rS$

45. *Sample answer:* radius 1 in. and height $\frac{4}{3}$ in.; radius $\frac{1}{3}$ in. and height 12 in.; radius 2 in. and height $\frac{1}{3}$ in.

47. $S \approx 113.10$ in.^{2}, $V \approx 75.40$ in.^{3}

11.7 Maintaining Mathematical Proficiency *(p. 692)*

49. 0.8   **51.** $\frac{7}{10}$

Chapter 11 Review *(pp. 694–698)*

1. about 30.00 ft   **2.** about 56.57 cm

3. about 26.09 in.   **4.** 218 ft

5. about 169.65 in.^{2} **6.** about 17.72 in.^{2}

7. 173.166 ft^2 **8.** 130 square units

9. 96 square units   **10.** 105 square units

11. about 201.20 square units   **12.** about 167.11 square units

13. about 37.30 square units   **14.** about 119.29 in.^{2}

15. yes; square prism   **16.** yes; heptagonal pyramid

17. no   **18.** 11.34 m^3

19. about 100.53 mm^3 **20.** about 27.53 yd^3

21. 189 ft^3 **22.** 400 yd^3

23. 300 m^3 **24.** about 3.46 in.

25. 12 in

26. $S \approx 678.58$ cm^2; $V \approx 1017.88$ cm^3

27. $S \approx 2513.27$ cm^2; $V \approx 8042.48$ cm^3

28. $S \approx 439.82$ m^2; $V \approx 562.10$ m^3

29. 15 cm

30. $S \approx 615.75$ in.^{2}; $V \approx 1436.76$ in.^{3}

31. $S \approx 907.92$ ft^2; $V \approx 2572.44$ ft^3

32. $S \approx 2827.43$ ft^2; $V \approx 14,137.17$ ft^3

33. $S \approx 74.8$ million km^2; $V \approx 60.8$ billion km^3

34. about 272.55 m^3

English-Spanish Glossary

English

Spanish

A

absolute value function *(p. 4)* A function that contains an absolute value expression

función de valor absoluto *(p. 4)* Una función que contiene una expresión de valor absoluto

adjacent arcs *(p. 583)* Arcs of a circle that have exactly one point in common

arcos adyacentes *(p. 583)* Arcos de un círculo que tienen exactamente un punto en común

altitude of a triangle *(p. 363)* The perpendicular segment from a vertex of a triangle to the opposite side or to the line that contains the opposite side

altitud de un triángulo *(p. 363)* El segmento perpendicular desde el vértice de un triángulo al lado opuesto o a la recta que contiene el lado opuesto

angle of depression *(p. 551)* The angle that a downward line of sight makes with a horizontal line

ángulo de depresión *(p. 551)* El ángulo formado entre una recta de vista descendente y una recta horizontal

angle of elevation *(p. 544)* The angle that an upward line of sight makes with a horizontal line

ángulo de elevación *(p. 544)* El ángulo formado entre una recta de vista ascendente y una recta horizontal

apothem of a regular polygon *(p. 657)* The distance from the center to any side of a regular polygon

apotema de un polígono regular *(p. 657)* La distancia desde el centro a cualquier lado de un polígono regular

arc length *(p. 641)* A portion of the circumference of a circle

longitud de arco *(p. 641)* Una porción de la circunferencia de un círculo

asymptote *(p. 42)* A line that a graph approaches more and more closely

asíntota *(p. 42)* Una recta a la que una gráfica se acerca cada vez más

axis of symmetry *(p. 124)* The vertical line that divides a parabola into two symmetric parts

eje de simetría *(p. 124)* La línea vertical que divide una parábola en dos partes simétricas

B

base angles of a trapezoid *(p. 442)* Either pair of consecutive angles whose common side is a base of a trapezoid

ángulos de la base de un trapecio *(p. 442)* Cualquier par de ángulos consecutivos cuyo lado común es la base de un trapezoide

bases of a trapezoid *(p. 442)* The parallel sides of a trapezoid

bases de un trapecio *(p. 442)* Los lados paralelos de un trapezoide

binomial *(p. 63)* A polynomial with two terms

binomio *(p. 63)* Un polinomio con dos términos

binomial distribution *(p. 321)* A type of probability distribution that shows the probabilities of the outcomes of a binomial experiment

distribución del binomio *(p. 321)* Un tipo de distribución de probabilidades que muestra las probabilidades de los resultados posibles de un experimento del binomio

binomial experiment *(p. 321)* An experiment in which there are a fixed number of independent trials, exactly two possible outcomes for each trial, and the probability of success is the same for each trial

experimento del binomio *(p. 321)* Un experimento en el que hay un número fijo de pruebas independientes, exactamente dos resultados posibles para cada prueba, y la probabilidad de éxito es la misma para cada prueba

Cavalieri's Principle *(p. 667)* If two solids have the same height and the same cross-sectional area at every level, then they have the same volume.

Principio de Cavalieri *(p. 667)* Si dos sólidos tienen la misma altura y la misma área transversal en todo nivel, entonces tienen el mismo volumen.

center of a circle *(p. 574)* The point from which all points on a circle are equidistant

centro de un círculo *(p. 574)* El punto desde donde todos los puntos en un círculo son equidistantes

center of dilation *(p. 462)* The fixed point in a dilation

centro de dilatación *(p. 462)* El punto fijo en una dilatación

center of a regular polygon *(p. 657)* The center of a polygon's circumscribed circle

centro de un polígono regular *(p. 657)* El centro del círculo circunscrito de un polígono

central angle of a circle *(p. 582)* An angle whose vertex is the center of a circle

ángulo central de un círculo *(p. 582)* Un ángulo cuyo vértice es el centro de un círculo

central angle of a regular polygon *(p. 657)* An angle formed by two radii drawn to consecutive vertices of a polygon

ángulo central de un polígono regular *(p. 657)* Un ángulo formado por dos radios extendidos a vértices consecutivos de un polígono

centroid *(p. 362)* The point of concurrency of the three medians of a triangle

centroide *(p. 362)* El punto de concurrencia de las tres medianas de un triángulo

chord of a circle *(p. 574)* A segment whose endpoints are on a circle

cuerda de un círculo *(p. 574)* Un segmento cuyos puntos extremos están en un círculo

chord of a sphere *(p. 686)* A segment whose endpoints are on a sphere

cuerda de una esfera *(p. 686)* Un segmento cuyos puntos extremos están en una esfera

circle *(p. 574)* The set of all points in a plane that are equidistant from a given point

círculo *(p. 574)* El conjunto de todos los puntos en un plano que son equidistantes de un punto dado

circumcenter *(p. 352)* The point of concurrency of the three perpendicular bisectors of a triangle

circuncentro *(p. 352)* El punto de concurrencia de las tres bisectrices perpendiculares de un triángulo

circumference *(p. 640)* The distance around a circle

circunferencia *(p. 640)* La distancia alrededor de un círculo

circumscribed angle *(p. 608)* An angle whose sides are tangent to a circle

ángulo circunscrito *(p. 608)* Un ángulo cuyos lados son tangentes a un círculo

closed *(p. 64)* When an operation performed on any two numbers in the set results in a number that is also in the set

operación interna *(p. 64)* Cuando una operación efectuada en dos números cualesquiera del conjunto da como resultado un número que también está en el conjunto

combination *(p. 314)* A selection of objects in which order is not important

combinación *(p. 314)* Una selección de objetos en la que el orden no es importante

common tangent *(p. 575)* A line or segment that is tangent to two coplanar circles

tangente común *(p. 575)* Una recta o segmento que es tangente a dos círculos coplanarios

completing the square *(p. 216)* To add a constant c to an expression of the form $x^2 + bx$ so that $x^2 + bx + c$ is a perfect square trinomial

completando el cuadrado *(p. 216)* Agregar una constante c a una expresión de la forma $x^2 + bx$ para que $x^2 + bx + c$ sea un trinomio de cuadrado perfecto

complex conjugates (p. 241) Pairs of complex numbers of the forms $a + bi$ and $a - bi$, where $b \neq 0$

conjugados complejos (p. 241) Pares de números complejos de las formas $a + bi$ y $a - bi$, donde $b \neq 0$

complex number (p. 238) A number written in the form $a + bi$, where a and b are real numbers

número complejo (p. 238) Un número escrito en la forma $a + bi$, donde a y b son números reales

compound event (p. 306) The union or intersection of two events

evento compuesto (p. 306) La unión o intersección de dos eventos

concentric circles (p. 575) Coplanar circles that have a common center

círculos concéntricos (p. 575) Círculos coplanarios que tienen un centro en común

concurrent (p. 352) Three or more lines, rays, or segments that intersect in the same point

concurrente (p. 352) Tres o más rectas, rayos o segmentos que se intersectan en el mismo punto

conditional probability (p. 289) The probability that event B occurs given that event A has occurred, written as $P(B|A)$

probabilidad condicional (p. 289) La probabilidad de que el evento B ocurra dado que el evento A ha ocurrido, escrito como $P(B|A)$

conditional relative frequency (p. 297) The ratio of a joint relative frequency to the marginal relative frequency in a two-way table

frecuencia relativa condicional (p. 297) La razón de una frecuencia relativa conjunta a la frecuencia relativa marginal en una tabla de doble entrada

congruent arcs (p. 584) Arcs that have the same measure and are of the same circle or of congruent circles

arcos congruentes (p. 584) Arcos que tienen la misma medida y que son del mismo círculo o de círculos congruentes

congruent circles (p. 584) Circles that can be mapped onto each other by a rigid motion or a composition of rigid motions

círculos congruentes (p. 584) Círculos que pueden superponerse sobre sí mismos mediante un movimiento rígido o una composición de movimientos rígidos

conjugates (p. 194) Binomials of the form $a\sqrt{b} + c\sqrt{d}$ and $a\sqrt{b} - c\sqrt{d}$, where a, b, c, and d are rational numbers

conjugados (p. 194) Binomios de la forma $a\sqrt{b} + c\sqrt{d}$ y $a\sqrt{b} - c\sqrt{d}$, donde a, b, c y d son números racionales

coordinate proof (p. 339) A style of proof that involves placing geometric figures in a coordinate plane

prueba de coordenadas (p. 339) Un estilo de prueba que implica colocar figuras geométricas en un plano coordenado

cosine (p. 548) For an acute angle of a right triangle, the ratio of the length of the leg adjacent to the acute angle to the length of the hypotenuse

coseno (p. 548) Para un ángulo agudo de un triángulo rectángulo, la razón de la longitud del cateto adyacente al ángulo agudo a la longitud de la hipotenusa

counterexample (p. 191) An example that proves that a general statement is not true

contraejemplo (p. 191) Un ejemplo que prueba que una afirmación general no es verdadera

---

D

---

decay factor (p. 42) The value of b in an exponential decay function of the form $y = ab^x$, where $a > 0$ and $0 < b < 1$

factor de decaimiento (p. 42) El valor de b en una función de decaimiento exponencial de la forma $y = ab^x$, donde $a > 0$ y $0 < b < 1$

degree of a monomial (p. 62) The sum of the exponents of the variables in the monomial

grado de un monomio (p. 62) La suma de los exponentes de las variables en el monomio

degree of a polynomial (p. 63) The greatest degree of the terms in a polynomial

grado de un polinomio (p. 63) El grado mayor de los términos en un polinomio

dependent events (p. 289) Two events in which the occurrence of one event does affect the occurrence of the other event

eventos dependientes (p. 289) Dos eventos en los que la ocurrencia de un evento afecta la ocurrencia del otro evento

diagonal *(p. 404)* A segment that joins two nonconsecutive vertices of a polygon

diameter *(p. 574)* A chord that contains the center of a circle

dilation *(p. 462)* A transformation in which a figure is enlarged or reduced with respect to a fixed point

directed line segment *(p. 502)* A segment that represents moving from point A to point B is called the directed line segment AB.

directrix *(p. 162)* A fixed line perpendicular to the axis of symmetry, such that the set of all points (x, y) of the parabola are equidistant from the focus and the directrix

discriminant *(p. 228)* The expression $b^2 - 4ac$ in the Quadratic Formula

disjoint events *(p. 306)* Two events that have no outcomes in common

diagonal *(p. 404)* Un segmento que une dos vértices no consecutivos de un polígono

diámetro *(p. 574)* Una cuerda que contiene el centro de un círculo

dilatación *(p. 462)* Una transformación en la cual una figura se agranda o reduce con respecto a un punto fijo

segmento de línea dirigido *(p. 502)* Un segmento que representa el moverse del punto A al punto B se llama el segmento de línea dirigido AB.

directriz *(p. 162)* Una recta fija perpendicular al eje de simetría de modo tal, que el conjunto de todos los puntos (x, y) de la parábola sean equidistantes del foco y la directriz

discriminante *(p. 228)* La expresión $b^2 - 4ac$ en la Fórmula Cuadrática

eventos disjunto *(p. 306)* Dos eventos que no tienen resultados en común

---

E

---

edge *(p. 666)* A line segment formed by the intersection of two faces of a polyhedron

enlargement *(p. 462)* A dilation in which the scale factor is greater than 1

equiangular polygon *(p. 405)* A polygon in which all angles are congruent

equidistant *(p. 344)* A point is equidistant from two figures when it is the same distance from each figure.

equilateral polygon *(p. 405)* A polygon in which all sides are congruent

even function *(p. 146)* A function $y = f(x)$ is even when $f(-x) = f(x)$ for each x in the domain of f.

event *(p. 280)* A collection of one or more outcomes in a probability experiment

experimental probability *(p. 282)* The ratio of the number of successes, or favorable outcomes, to the number of trials in a probability experiment

exponential decay function *(p. 42)* A function of the form $y = a(1 - r)^t$, where $a > 0$ and $0 < r < 1$

exponential function *(p. 42)* A nonlinear function of the form $y = ab^x$, where $a \neq 0$, $b \neq 1$, and $b > 0$

borde *(p. 666)* Un segmento de línea formado por la intersección de dos caras de un poliedro

agrandamiento *(p. 462)* Una dilatación en donde el factor de escala es mayor que 1

polígono equiangular *(p. 405)* Un polígono en donde todos los ángulos son congruentes

equidistante *(p. 344)* Un punto es equidistante desde dos figuras cuando está a la misma distancia de cada figura.

polígono equilátero *(p. 405)* Un polígono en donde todos los lados son congruentes

par función *(p. 146)* Una función $y = f(x)$ es par cuando $f(-x) = f(x)$ para cada x en el dominio de f.

evento *(p. 280)* Una colección de uno o más resultados en un experimento de probabilidades

probabilidad experimental *(p. 282)* La razón del número de éxitos, o resultados favorables, con respecto al número de pruebas en un experimento de probabilidades

función de decaimiento exponencial *(p. 42)* Una función de la forma $y = a(1 - r)^t$, donde $a > 0$ y $0 < r < 1$

función exponencial *(p. 42)* Una función no lineal de la forma $y = ab^x$, donde $a \neq 0$, $b \neq 1$, y $b > 0$

exponential growth function *(p. 42)* A function of the form $y = a(1 + r)^t$, where $a > 0$ and $r > 0$

external segment *(p. 615)* The part of a secant segment that is outside the circle

función de crecimiento exponencial *(p. 42)* Una función de la forma $y = a(1 + r)^t$, donde $a > 0$ y $r > 0$

segmento externo *(p. 615)* La parte de un segmento secante que está fuera del círculo

---

F

---

face *(p. 666)* A flat surface of a polyhedron

cara *(p. 666)* Una superficie plana de un poliedro

factored completely *(p. 108)* A polynomial that is written as a product of unfactorable polynomials with integer coefficients

factorizado completamente *(p. 108)* Un polinomio que se escribe como un producto de polinomios no factorizables con coeficientes de números enteros

factored form *(p. 82)* A polynomial that is written as a product of factors

forma factorizada *(p. 82)* Un polinomio que se escribe como un producto de factores

factoring by grouping *(p. 108)* To use the Distributive Property to factor a polynomial with four terms

factorización por agrupamiento *(p. 108)* Uso de la propiedad distributiva para factorizar un polinomio con cuatro términos

flowchart proof (flow proof) *(p. 338)* A type of proof that uses boxes and arrows to show the flow of a logical argument

prueba de organigrama (prueba de flujo) *(p. 338)* Un tipo de prueba que usa casillas y flechas para mostrar el flujo de un argumento lógico

focus *(p. 162)* A fixed point in the interior of a parabola, such that the set of all points (x, y) of the parabola are equidistant from the focus and the directrix

foco *(p. 162)* Un punto fijo en el interior de una parábola, de tal forma que el conjunto de todos los puntos (x, y) de la parábola sean equidistantes del foco y la directriz

FOIL Method *(p. 71)* A shortcut for multiplying two binomials by finding the sum of the products of the first terms, outer terms, inner terms, and last terms

método FOIL o de multiplicación de binomios *(p. 71)* Un método rápido para multiplicar dos binomios encontrando la suma de los productos de los primeros términos, los segundos términos, los terceros términos y los últimos términos

---

G

---

geometric mean *(p. 534)* The positive number x that satisfies $\dfrac{a}{x} = \dfrac{x}{b}$

So, $x^2 = ab$ and $x = \sqrt{ab}$.

media geométrica *(p. 534)* El número positivo x que satisface $\dfrac{a}{x} = \dfrac{x}{b}$

Entonces, $x^2 = ab$ and $x = \sqrt{ab}$.

geometric probability *(p. 649)* A probability found by calculating a ratio of two lengths, areas, or volumes

probabilidad geométrica *(p. 649)* Una probabilidad hallada al calcular la razón de dos longitudes, áreas o volúmenes

great circle *(p. 686)* The intersection of a plane and a sphere such that the plane contains the center of the sphere

gran círculo *(p. 686)* La intersección de un plano y una esfera, de tal forma que el plano contiene el centro de la esfera

growth factor *(p. 42)* The value of b in an exponential growth function of the form $y = ab^x$, where $a > 0$ and $b > 1$

factor de crecimiento *(p. 42)* El valor de b en una función de crecimiento exponencial de la forma $y = ab^x$, donde $a > 0$ y $b > 1$

I

imaginary number *(p. 238)* A number written in the form $a + bi$, where a and b are real numbers and $b \neq 0$

imaginary unit i *(p. 238)* The square root of -1, denoted $i = \sqrt{-1}$

incenter *(p. 355)* The point of concurrency of the angle bisectors of a triangle

independent events *(p. 288)* Two events in which the occurrence of one event does not affect the occurrence of another event

index of a radical *(p. 36)* The value of n in the radical $\sqrt[n]{a}$

indirect proof *(p. 378)* A style of proof in which you temporarily assume that the desired conclusion is false, then reason logically to a contradiction
This proves that the original statement is true.

inscribed angle *(p. 598)* An angle whose vertex is on a circle and whose sides contain chords of the circle

intercept form *(p. 154)* A quadratic function written in the form $f(x) = a(x - p)(x - q)$, where $a \neq 0$

intercepted arc *(p. 598)* An arc that lies between two lines, rays, or segments

inverse cosine *(p. 558)* An inverse trigonometric ratio, abbreviated as $\cos^{-1}$
For acute angle A, if $\cos A = z$, then $\cos^{-1} z = m\angle A$.

inverse function *(p. 21)* Functions that undo each other

inverse relation *(p. 20)* When the input and output values of the original relation are switched

inverse sine *(p. 558)* An inverse trigonometric ratio, abbreviated as $\sin^{-1}$
For acute angle A, if $\sin A = y$, then $\sin^{-1} y = m\angle A$.

inverse tangent *(p. 558)* An inverse trigonometric ratio, abbreviated as $\tan^{-1}$
For acute angle A, if $\tan A = x$, then $\tan^{-1} x = m\angle A$.

isosceles trapezoid *(p. 442)* A trapezoid with congruent legs

número imaginario *(p. 238)* Un número escrito de la forma $a + bi$, donde a y b son números reales y $b \neq 0$

unidad imaginaria i *(p. 238)* La raíz cuadrada de -1, denotado $i = \sqrt{-1}$

incentro *(p. 355)* El punto de concurrencia de las bisectrices de los ángulos de un triángulo

eventos independientes *(p. 288)* Dos eventos en los que la ocurrencia de un evento no afecta la ocurrencia de otro evento

índice de un radical *(p. 36)* El valor de n en el radical $\sqrt[n]{a}$

prueba indirecta *(p. 378)* Un estilo de prueba en donde uno asume temporalmente que la conclusión deseada es falsa, luego se razona de forma lógica hasta llegar a una contradicción
Esto prueba que el enunciado original es vertdadero.

ángulo inscrito *(p. 598)* Un ángulo cuyo vértice está en un círculo y cuyos lados contienen cuerdas del círculo

forma intersección *(p. 154)* Una ecuación cuadrática escrita en la forma $f(x) = a(x - p)(x - q)$, donde $a \neq 0$

arco interceptado *(p. 598)* Un arco que descansa entre dos rectas, rayos o segmentos

coseno inverso *(p. 558)* Una razón trigonométrica inversa, abreviada como $\cos^{-1}$
Para un ángulo agudo A, si $\cos A = z$, entonces $\cos^{-1} z = m\angle A$.

función inversa *(p. 21)* Funciones que se anulan entre sí

relación inversa *(p. 20)* Cuando los valores y los resultados de la relación original se intercambian

seno inverso *(p. 558)* Una razón trigonométrica inversa, abreviada como $\sin^{-1}$
Para un ángulo agudo A, si $\sin A = y$, entonces $\sin^{-1} y = m\angle A$.

tangente inversa *(p. 558)* Una razón trigonométrica inversa, abreviada como $\tan^{-1}$
Para un ángulo agudo A, si $\tan A = x$, entonces $\tan^{-1} x = m\angle A$.

trapecio isósceles *(p. 442)* Un trapecio con catetos congruentes

J

joint frequency *(p. 296)* Each entry in a two-way table

frecuencia conjunta *(p. 296)* Cada valor en una tabla de doble entrada

joint relative frequency *(p. 297)* The ratio of a frequency that is not in the total row or the total column to the total number of values or observations in a two-way table

frecuencia relativa conjunta *(p. 297)* La razón de una frecuencia que no está en la hilera total o columna total del número total de valores u observaciones en una tabla de doble entrada

K

kite *(p. 445)* A quadrilateral that has two pairs of consecutive congruent sides, but opposite sides are not congruent

papalote *(p. 445)* Un cuadrilátero que tiene dos pares de lados congruentes consecutivos, pero los lados opuestos no son congruentes

L

lateral surface of a cone *(p. 680)* Consists of all segments that connect the vertex with points on the base edge of a cone

superficie lateral de un cono *(p. 680)* Consiste en todos los segmentos que conectan el vértice con puntos en el borde base de un cono

leading coefficient *(p. 63)* The coefficient of the first term of a polynomial written in standard form

coeficiente principal *(p. 63)* El coeficiente del primer término de un polinomio escrito en forma estándar

legs of a trapezoid *(p. 442)* The nonparallel sides of a trapezoid

catetos de un trapecio *(p. 442)* Los lados no paralelos de un trapezoide

like radicals *(p. 196)* Radicals with the same index and radicand

radicales semejantes *(p. 196)* Radicales con el mismo índice y radicando

M

major arc *(p. 582)* An arc with a measure greater than 180°

arco mayor *(p. 582)* Un arco con una medida mayor de 180°

marginal frequency *(p. 296)* The sums of the rows and columns in a two-way table

frecuencia marginal *(p. 296)* Las sumas de las hileras y columnas en una tabla de doble entrada

marginal relative frequency *(p. 297)* The sum of the joint relative frequencies in a row or a column in a two-way table

frecuencia relativa marginal *(p. 297)* La suma de las frecuencias relativas conjuntas en una hilera o columna en una tabla de doble entrada

maximum value *(p. 137)* The y-coordinate of the vertex of the graph of $f(x) = ax^2 + bx + c$, where $a < 0$

valor máximo *(p. 137)* La coordenada y del vértice del gráfico de $f(x) = ax^2 + bx + c$, donde $a < 0$

measure of a major arc *(p. 582)* The measure of a major arc's central angle

medida de arco mayor *(p. 582)* La medida del ángulo central de un arco mayor

measure of a minor arc *(p. 582)* The measure of a minor arc's central angle

medida de arco menor *(p. 582)* La medida del ángulo central de un arco menor

median of a triangle *(p. 362)* A segment from a vertex of a triangle to the midpoint of the opposite side

mediana de un triángulo *(p. 362)* Un segmento desde el vértice de un triángulo hasta el punto medio del lado opuesto

midsegment of a trapezoid *(p. 444)* The segment that connects the midpoints of the legs of a trapezoid

segmento medio de un trapezoide *(p. 444)* El segmento que conecta los puntos medios de los catetos de un trapezoide

midsegment of a triangle *(p. 372)* A segment that connects the midpoints of two sides of a triangle

segmento medio de un triángulo *(p. 372)* Un segmento que conecta los puntos medios de dos lados de un triángulo

minimum value *(p. 137)* The y-coordinate of the vertex of the graph of $f(x) = ax^2 + bx + c$, where $a > 0$

valor mínimo *(p. 137)* La coordenada y del vértice del gráfico de $f(x) = ax^2 + bx + c$, donde $a > 0$

minor arc *(p. 582)* An arc with a measure less than $180°$

arco menor *(p. 582)* Un arco con una medida menor de $180°$

monomial *(p. 62)* A number, a variable, or the product of a number and one or more variables with whole number exponents

monomio *(p. 62)* Un número, una variable o el producto de un número y una o más variables con exponentes en números enteros

mutually exclusive events *(p. 306)* Two events that have no outcomes in common

eventos mutuamente exclusivos *(p. 306)* Dos eventos que no tienen resultados en común

---

N

---

n factorial *(p. 312)* The product of the integers from 1 to n, for any positive integer n

factorial de n *(p. 312)* El producto de los números enteros de 1 a n, para cualquier número entero positivo n

nth root of a *(p. 36)* For an integer n greater than 1, if $b^n = a$, then b is an nth root of a.

raíz de orden n de a *(p. 36)* Para un número entero n mayor que 1, si $b^n = a$, entonces b es una raíz de orden n de a.

O

---

odd function *(p. 146)* A function $y = f(x)$ is odd when $f(-x) = -f(x)$ for each x in the domain of f.

impar funcíon *(p. 146)* Una función $y = f(x)$ es impar cuando $f(-x) = -f(x)$ para cada x en el dominio de f.

odds *(p. 283)* A comparison of the number of favorable and unfavorable outcomes of an event when all outcomes are equally likely

probabilidad de un evento *(p.283)* Una comparación del número de resultados favorables y desfavorables de un evento cuando todos los resultados son igualmente probables

orthocenter *(p. 363)* The point of concurrency of the lines containing the altitudes of a triangle

ortocentro *(p. 363)* El punto de concurrencia de las líneas que contienen las alturas de un triángulo

outcome *(p. 280)* The possible result of a probability experiment

resultado *(p. 280)* El resultado posible de un experimento de probabilidad

overlapping events *(p. 306)* Two events that have one or more outcomes in common

eventos superpuestos *(p. 306)* Dos eventos que tienen uno o más resultados en común

parabola *(p. 124)*   The U-shaped graph of a quadratic function

parágraph proof *(p. 337)*   A style of proof that presents the statements and reasons as sentences in a paragraph, using words to explain the logical flow of an argument

parallelogram *(p. 412)*   A quadrilateral with both pairs of opposite sides parallel

permutation *(p. 312)*   An arrangement of objects in which order is important

piecewise function *(p. 12)*   A function defined by two or more equations

point of concurrency *(p. 352)*   The point of intersection of concurrent lines, rays, or segments

point of tangency *(p. 574)*   The point at which a tangent line intersects a circle

polyhedron *(p. 666)*   A solid that is bounded by polygons

polynomial *(p. 63)*   A monomial or a sum of monomials

probability distribution *(p. 320)*   A function that gives the probability of each possible value of a random variable

probability of an event *(p. 280)*   A measure of the likelihood, or chance, that an event will occur

probability experiment *(p. 280)*   An action, or trial, that has varying results

proof *(p. 336)*   A logical argument that uses deductive reasoning to show that a statement is true

pure imaginary number *(p. 238)*   A number written in the form $a + bi$, where $a = 0$ and $b \neq 0$

Pythagorean triple *(p. 518)*   A set of three positive integers a, b, and c that satisfy the equation $c^2 = a^2 + b^2$

parábola *(p. 124)*   El gráfico en forma de U de una función cuadrática

prueba en forma de párrafo *(p. 337)*   Un estilo de prueba que presenta los enunciados y motivos como oraciones en un párrafo, usando palabras para explicar el flujo lógico de un argumento

paralelogramo *(p. 412)*   Un cuadrilátero con ambos pares de lados opuestos paralelos

permutación *(p. 312)*   Una disposición de objetos en la que el orden es importante

función por tramos *(p. 12)*   Una función definida por dos o más ecuaciones

punto de concurrencia *(p. 352)*   El punto de intersección de rectas, rayos o segmentos concurrentes

punto de tangencia *(p. 574)*   El punto en donde una recta tangente intersecta a un círculo

poliedro *(p. 666)*   Un sólido que está encerrado por polígonos

polinomio *(p. 63)*   Un monomio o una suma de monomios

distribución de probabilidad *(p. 320)*   Una función que da la probabilidad de cada valor posible de una variable aleatoria

probabilidad de un evento *(p. 280)*   Una medida de la probabilidad o posibilidad de que ocurrirá un evento

experimento de probabilidad *(p. 280)*   Una acción o prueba que tiene resultados variables

prueba *(p. 336)*   Un argumento lógico que usa el razonamiento deductivo para mostrar que un enunciado es verdadero

número imaginario puro *(p. 238)*   Un número escrito en la forma $a + bi$, donde $a = 0$ y $b \neq 0$

triple pitagórico *(p. 518)*   Un conjunto de tres números enteros positivos a, b, y c que satisfacen la ecuación $c^2 = a^2 + b^2$

Q

quadratic equation *(p. 202)* A nonlinear equation that can be written in the standard form $ax^2 + bx + c = 0$, where $a \neq 0$

Quadratic Formula *(p. 226)* The real solutions of the quadratic equation $ax^2 + bx + c = 0$ are

$x = \dfrac{-b \pm \sqrt{b^2 - 4ac}}{2a}$, where $a \neq 0$ and $b^2 - 4ac \geq 0$.

quadratic function *(p. 124)* A nonlinear function that can be written in the standard form $y = ax^2 + bx + c$, where $a \neq 0$

quadratic inequality in one variable *(p. 262)* An inequality of the form $ax^2 + bx + c < 0$, $ax^2 + bx + c > 0$, $ax^2 + bx + c \leq 0$, or $ax^2 + bx + c \geq 0$, where a, b, and c are real numbers and $a \neq 0$

quadratic inequality in two variables *(p. 260)* An inequality of the form $y < ax^2 + bx + c$, $y > ax^2 + bx + c$, $y \leq ax^2 + bx + c$, or $y \geq ax^2 + bx + c$, where a, b, and c are real numbers and $a \neq 0$

ecuación cuadrática *(p. 202)* Una ecuación no lineal que puede escribirse en la forma estándar $ax^2 + bx + c = 0$, donde $a \neq 0$

fórmula cuadrática *(p. 226)* Las soluciones reales de la ecuación cuadrática $ax^2 + bx + c = 0$ son

$x = \dfrac{-b \pm \sqrt{b^2 - 4ac}}{2a}$, donde $a \neq 0$ y $b^2 - 4ac \geq 0$.

función cuadrática *(p. 124)* Una ecuación no lineal que puede escribirse en la forma estándar $y = ax^2 + bx + c$, donde $a \neq 0$

desigualdad cuadrática en una variable *(p. 262)* Una desigualdad de la forma $ax^2 + bx + c < 0$, $ax^2 + bx + c > 0$, $ax^2 + bx + c \leq 0$, o $ax^2 + bx + c \geq 0$, donde a, b, y c son números reales y $a \neq 0$

desigualdad cuadrática en dos variables *(p. 260)* Una desigualdad de la forma $y < ax^2 + bx + c$, $y > ax^2 + bx + c$, $y \leq ax^2 + bx + c$, o $y \geq ax^2 + bx + c$, donde a, b, y c son números reales y $a \neq 0$

R

radian *(p. 643)* A unit of measurement for angles

radical *(p. 36)* An expression of the form $\sqrt[n]{a}$

radical expression *(p. 192)* An expression that contains a radical

radius of a circle *(p. 574)* A segment whose endpoints are the center and any point on a circle

radius of a regular polygon *(p. 657)* The radius of a polygon's circumscribed circle

random variable *(p. 320)* A variable whose value is determined by the outcomes of a probability experiment

rationalizing the denominator *(p. 194)* To eliminate a radical from the denominator of a fraction by multiplying by an appropriate form of 1

rectangle *(p. 432)* A parallelogram with four right angles

recursive rule for an exponential function *(p. 44)* A rule that gives the initial value of the function $f(0)$, and a recursive equation that tells how a value $f(n)$ is related to a preceding value $f(n - 1)$

radián *(p. 643)* Una unidad de medida para ángulos

radical *(p. 36)* Una expresión de la forma $\sqrt[n]{a}$

expresión radical *(p. 192)* Una expresión que contiene un radical

radio de un círculo *(p. 574)* Un segmento cuyos puntos extremos son el centro y cualquier punto en un círculo

radio de un polígono regular *(p. 657)* El radio del círculo circunscrito de un polígono

variable aleatoria *(p. 320)* Una variable cuyo valor está determinado por los resultados de un experimento de probabilidad

racionalización del denominador *(p. 194)* Eliminar un radical del denominador de una fracción multiplicando por una forma apropiada de 1

rectángulo *(p. 432)* Un paralelogramo con cuatro ángulos rectos

regla recursiva de una función exponencial *(p. 44)* Una regla que da el valor inicial de la función $f(0)$ y una ecuación recursiva que indica cómo se relaciona un valor $f(n)$ con el valor precedente $f(n - 1)$

reduction *(p. 462)* A dilation in which the scale factor is greater than 0 and less than 1

reducción *(p. 462)* Una dilatación en donde el factor de escala es mayor que 0 y menor que 1

regular polygon *(p. 405)* A convex polygon that is both equilateral and equiangular

polígono regular *(p. 405)* Un polígono convexo que es tanto equilátero como equiángulo

repeated roots *(p. 83)* Two or more roots of an equation that are the same number

raíces repetidas *(p. 83)* Dos o más raíces de una ecuación que son el mismo número

rhombus *(p. 432)* A parallelogram with four congruent sides

rombo *(p. 432)* Un paralelogramo con cuatro lados congruentes

roots *(p. 82)* The solutions of a polynomial equation

raíces *(p. 82)* Las soluciones deuna ecuación de polinomios

S

---

sample space *(p. 280)* The set of all possible outcomes for an experiment

espacio de muestra *(p. 280)* El conjunto de todos los resultados posibles de un experimento

scale factor *(p. 462)* The ratio of the lengths of the corresponding sides of the image and the preimage of a dilation

factor de escala *(p. 462)* La razón de las longitudes de los lados correspondientes de la imagen y la preimagen de una dilatación

secant *(p. 574)* A line that intersects a circle in two points

secante *(p. 574)* Una recta que intersecta a un círculo en dos puntos

secant segment *(p. 615)* A segment that contains a chord of a circle and has exactly one endpoint outside the circle

segmento de secante *(p. 615)* Un segmento que contiene una cuerda de un círculo y que tiene exactamente un punto extremo fuera del círculo

sector of a circle *(p. 650)* The region bounded by two radii of the circle and their intercepted arc

sector de un círculo *(p. 650)* La región encerrada por dos radios del círculo y su arco interceptado

segments of a chord *(p. 614)* The segments formed from two chords that intersect in the interior of a circle

segmentos de una cuerda *(p. 614)* Los segmentos formados a partir de dos cuerdas que se intersectan en el interior de un círculo

semicircle *(p. 582)* An arc with endpoints that are the endpoints of a diameter

semicírculo *(p. 582)* Un arco con puntos extremos que son los puntos extremos de un diámetro

similar arcs *(p. 585)* Arcs that have the same measure

arcos similares *(p. 585)* Arcos que tienen la misma medida

similar figures *(p. 470)* Geometric figures that have the same shape but not necessarily the same size

figuras similares *(p. 470)* Figuras geométricas que tienen la misma forma pero no necesariamente el mismo tamaño

similar solids *(p. 669)* Two solids of the same type with equal ratios of corresponding linear measures

sólidos similares *(p. 669)* Dos sólidos del mismo tipo con razones iguales de medidas lineales correspondientes

similarity transformation *(p. 470)* A dilation or a composition of rigid motions and dilations

transformación de similitud *(p. 470)* Una dilatación o composición de movimientos rígidos y dilataciones

simplest form of a radical *(p. 192)* An expression involving a radical with index n that has no radicands with perfect nth powers as factors other than 1, no radicands that contain fractions, and no radicals that appear in the denominator of a fraction

mínima expresión de un radical *(p. 192)* Una expresión que conlleva un radical con índice n que no tiene radicandos con potencias perfectas de orden n como factores distintos a 1, que no tiene radicandos que contengan fracciones y que no tiene radicales que aparezcan en el denominador de una fracción

sine *(p. 548)* For an acute angle of a right triangle, the ratio of the length of the leg opposite the acute angle to the length of the hypotenuse

solve a right triangle *(p. 559)* To find all unknown side lengths and angle measures of a right triangle

square *(p. 432)* A parallelogram with four congruent sides and four right angles

standard equation of a circle *(p. 620)*
$(x - h)^2 + (y - k)^2 = r^2$, where r is the radius and (h, k) is the center

standard form of a polynomial *(p. 63)* A polynomial in one variable written with the exponents of the terms decreasing from left to right

step function *(p. 14)* A piecewise function defined by a constant value over each part of its domain

subtend *(p. 598)* If the endpoints of a chord or arc lie on the sides of an inscribed angle, the chord or arc is said to subtend the angle.

system of nonlinear equations *(p. 252)* A system in which at least one of the equations is nonlinear

seno *(p. 548)* Para un ángulo agudo de un triángulo rectángulo, la razón de la longitud del cateto enfrente del ángulo agudo a la longitud de la hipotenusa

resolver un triángulo recto *(p. 559)* Para encontrar todas las longitudes de los lados y las medidas de los ángulos desconocidas de un triángulo recto

cuadrado *(p. 432)* Un paralelogramo con cuatro lados congruentes y cuatro ángulos rectos

ecuación estándar de un círculo *(p. 620)*
$(x - h)^2 + (y - k)^2 = r^2$, donde r es el radio y (h, k) es el centro

forma estándar de un polinomio *(p. 63)* Un polinomio en una variable escrita con los exponentes de los términos decreciendo de izquierda a derecha

función escalón *(p. 14)* Una función por tramos definida por un valor constante sobre cada parte de su dominio

subtender *(p. 598)* Si los puntos extremos de una cuerda o arco descansan en los lados de un ángulo inscrito, se dice que la cuerda o arco subtiende el ángulo.

sistema de ecuaciones no lineales *(p. 252)* Un sistema en donde al menos una de las ecuaciones no es lineal

---

T

---

tangent *(p. 542)* For an acute angle of a right triangle, the ratio of the length of the leg opposite the acute angle to the length of the leg adjacent to the acute angle

tangent of a circle *(p. 574)* A line in the plane of a circle that intersects the circle at exactly one point

tangent circles *(p. 575)* Coplanar circles that intersect in one point

tangent segment *(p. 615)* A segment that is tangent to a circle at an endpoint

theoretical probability *(p. 281)* The ratio of the number of favorable outcomes to the total number of outcomes when all outcomes are equally likely

trapezoid *(p. 442)* A quadrilateral with exactly one pair of parallel sides

trigonometric ratio *(p. 542)* A ratio of the lengths of two sides in a right triangle

tangente *(p. 542)* Para un ángulo agudo de un triángulo rectángulo, la razón de la longitud del cateto enfrente del ángulo agudo a la longitud del cateto adyacente al ángulo agudo

tangente de un círculo *(p. 574)* Una recta en el plano de un círculo que intersecta el círculo en exactamente un punto

círculos tangentes *(p. 575)* Círculos coplanarios que se intersectan en un punto

segmento de tangente *(p. 615)* Un segmento que es tangente a un círculo en un punto extremo

probabilidad teórica *(p. 281)* La razón del número de resultados favorables con respecto al número total de resultados cuando todos los resultados son igualmente probables

trapecio *(p. 442)* Un cuadrilátero con exactamente un par de lados paralelos

razón trigonométrica *(p. 542)* Una razón de las longitudes de dos lados en un triángulo recto trinomial *(p. 63)* A polynomial with three terms

two-column proof *(p. 336)* A type of proof that has numbered statements and corresponding reasons that show an argument in a logical order

two-way table *(p. 296)* A frequency table that displays data collected from one source that belong to two different categories

trinomio *(p. 63)* Un polinomio con tres términos

prueba de dos columnas *(p. 336)* Un tipo de prueba que tiene enunciados numerados y motivos correspondientes que muestran un argumento en un orden lógico

tabla de doble entrada *(p. 296)* Una tabla de frecuencia que muestra los datos recogidos de una fuente que pertenece a dos categorías distintas

---

V

---

vertex *(p. 4)* The point where a graph changes direction

vertex form of an absolute value function *(p. 6)* An absolute value function written in the form $f(x) = a|x - h| + k$, where $a \neq 0$

vertex form of a quadratic function *(p. 148)* A quadratic function written in the form $f(x) = a(x - h)^2 + k$, where $a \neq 0$

vertex of a parabola *(p. 124)* The lowest point on a parabola that opens up or the highest point on a parabola that opens down

vertex of a polyhedron *(p. 666)* A point of a polyhedron where three or more edges meet

volume *(p. 667)* The number of cubic units contained in the interior of a solid

vértice *(p. 4)* El punto en donde un gráfico cambia de dirección

forma de vértice de una función de valor absoluto *(p. 6)* Una función de valor absoluto escrita en la forma $f(x) = a|x - h| + k$, donde $a \neq 0$

forma de vértice de una función cuadrática *(p. 148)* Una función cuadrática escrita en la forma $f(x) = a(x - h)^2 + k$, donde $a \neq 0$

vértice de una parábola *(p. 124)* El punto más bajo de una parábola que se abre hacia arriba o el punto más alto de una parábola que se abre hacia abajo

vértice de un poliedro *(p. 666)* Un punto de un poliedro donde se encuentran tres o más bordes

volumen *(p. 667)* El número de unidades cúbicas contenidas en el interior de u sólido

---

Z

---

zero of a function *(p. 132)* An x-value of a function f for which $f(x) = 0$

Zero-Product Property *(p. 82)* If the product of two real numbers is 0, then at least one of the numbers is 0.

cero de una función *(p. 132)* Un valor x de una función f para el cual $f(x) = 0$

propiedad de producto cero *(p. 82)* Si el producto de dos números reales es 0, entonces al menos uno de los números es 0.

Index

of regions, 651
of rhombuses, 656
of semicircles, 651
of trapezoids, 72
using to find probability, 649
Areas of Similar Polygons Theorem, 479
Arithmetic mean, compared to geometric mean, 531
Asymptotes, 42
Average rate of change
comparing functions using, 173–174
defined, 173
using and interpreting, 173
Axis of symmetry
defined, 124
finding, 136–137
and standard equations of parabolas, 163–164

B

Basal area, 48
Base (of cones), 680
Base (of solids), 666
Base (of trapezoids), 442
Base angles (of trapezoids), 442
Bayes' Theorem, 302
Biconditional statements, 434
Binomial(s)
defined, 63
finding factors, 89, 95
multiplying, 69–72, 114, 571
with trinomials, 72
using FOIL Method, 71, 77
square of binomial pattern, 75–76
sum and difference pattern, 75, 77
Binomial distributions, 319–322, 328
constructing, 322
defined, 321
interpreting, 322
Binomial experiments, 321
Birthday problem, 318
Bisecting angles, See Angle bisector
Bisectors of triangles, 351–356, 394
angle (See Angle bisectors)
circumcenter of triangle, 352–354
circumscribing circle about triangle, 353–354
incenter of triangle, 355–356
inscribing circle within triangle, 356
perpendicular (See Perpendicular bisector(s))

C

Calculator, See Graphing calculator
Carpenter's square, 603
Cavalieri, Bonaventura, 667

Cavalieri's Principle, 667–668
Center of circle, 572, 574
Center of dilation, 462
Center of regular polygon, 655, 657
Center of sphere, 686
Central angle of circles
defined, 581, 582
and inscribed angles, 597
Central angle of regular polygon, 657
Centroid of triangle
defined, 362
finding, 362–363
Centroid Theorem, 362
Chords of circles, 589–592, 629
defined, 574, 590
identifying, 574
intersections among, 605, 613–614
intersections with tangents on circles, 605
perpendicular to diameter, 589
using, 589–592, 629
Chords of spheres, 686
Circles, 570
analyzing relationships among, 572
angle relationships in, 605–609, 630–631
finding angle and arc measures, 606–607
using circumscribed angles, 608–609
arc measures of, 581–585, 629
areas of, 647–651, 694
center of, 572, 574
central angle of, 581, 582, 597
chords of (See Chords of circles)
circumference of, 639–643, 694
circumscribed about triangle, 353–354, 601
concentric, 575
congruent, 584
in coordinate plane, 619–623, 632
defined, 572, 574
diameters of, 574, 589, 591
drawing by using string, 573
equations of, 619–621
graphing, 621, 622
inscribed angles in, 597–599, 630
inscribed polygons in, 600–601, 630
lines and segments that intersect, 573–577, 606, 628
polygon circumscribed about, 580
proving similarity in, 585
radius of, 574, 592, 616
segment relationships in, 613–616, 631
tangent, 572, 575
writing coordinate proofs involving, 622

Circular arcs, See Arc(s), circular
Circular cones, 680, See also Cones
Circumcenter of triangles, 352–354
circumscribing circle about triangle, 353–354
defined, 352
finding, 354
Circumcenter Theorem, 352
Circumference of circles, 636
and arc length, 639–643, 694
defined, 640
finding distances using, 642
formula for, 640
Circumscribed Angle Theorem, 608
Circumscribed angles
defined, 608
using, 608–609
Circumscribed circle, 353–354
Closed set of numbers, 64
Coefficient of friction, 633
Coin flip, 279, 280, 311, 319
Combinations, 311–315, 328
counting, 314
defined, 314
finding probability using, 315
formula, 314–315
Common Errors
angle approximation, 609
angle symbol compared to less than symbol, 379
area of semicircle, 651
completing the square, 217
diameter of sphere, 687
falling objects, 132
geometric mean of right triangle, 535
indirect proofs, 379
negative signs, 137
paying attention to units, 642
polynomials, 64
probability
and binomial distribution, 322
overlapping events, 307
proportions, 533
ratio of volumes, 669
Common external tangents, 575
Common internal tangents, 575
Common tangents, 575
Compass, 354
Complementary angles, sine and cosine of, 548
Complements of events, 281–282
Completing the square
defined, 216
deriving Quadratic Formula by, 225
finding maximum and minimum values, 218–219

$f(x) = ax^2 + c$, 129–132, 180
  parent function, 122, 124
  using zeros, 156
  quadratic inequalities, 260–262, 272
    systems of, 261
    in two variables, 260–261
  step functions, 14
  systems of linear equations, 189
  systems of nonlinear equations, 252
Graphing calculator
  combinations, 314
  functions with restricted domain, 2
  intersect feature, 227, 255
  maximum feature, 139, 149
  permutations, 313
  π key, 640
  quadratic functions, 129, 145
  quadratic inequalities, 259
  table feature, 44, 255, 318
  tangent key, 541
  variables displayed, 263
  viewing windows, 255
  zero feature, 149
Great circle, 686
Greatest common factor (GCF)
  factoring out, 96
  factoring polynomials using, 83–84
  finding, 59, 83
Greatest common monomial factor,
    83
Grouping, factoring by, 108
Growth, *See* Exponential growth
Growth factor, 42, *See also*
    Exponential growth function

Hemispheres, 685, 686
Hinge Theorem, 386–388
Hinge Theorem, Converse of,
    386–387
Histograms
  analyzing, 319
  making, 277
Horizontal axis of symmetry, of
    parabolas, 163–164
Horizontal shrinks, of absolute value
    functions, 6
Horizontal stretches, as nonrigid
    transformations, 465
Horizontal translations
  of absolute value functions, 4
  of quadratic functions, 130

Imaginary numbers
  defined, 238
  nth roots as, 36

pure, 238
  and quadratic equations, 225
  in set of complex numbers, 237
Imaginary solutions, of quadratic
    equations, 245–248
Imaginary unit *i*, 238
  defined, 237, 238
  equality of two complex numbers,
    239
  finding square roots of negative
    numbers, 238–239
Incenter of triangle
  defined, 355
  inscribing circle within triangle, 356
  using, 355–356
Incenter Theorem, 355
Independent events, 287–291, 326
  comparing to dependent events, 290
  defined, 287, 288
  determination of, 287, 288–289
  probability of, 288–289
Index of radical, 36
Indirect measurement, using
    geometric mean of right
    triangle, 535
Indirect proofs, 377–381, 396
  defined, 378
  writing, 378
Induction, 402
Inductive hypothesis, 402
Inequalities
  compound, writing, 333, 381
  in one triangle, 377–381, 396
  Pythagorean, 521
  quadratic, 259–263, 272
  in two triangles, 385–388, 396
Inscribed angles, 597–599, 630
  defined, 597, 598
  finding measure of, 599
  using, 598–599
Inscribed Angles of a Circle
    Theorem, 599
Inscribed polygons, 600–601, 630
  defined, 600
  using, 600–601
Inscribed Quadrilateral Theorem,
    600
Inscribed Right Triangle Theorem,
    600
Intercept form, of quadratic functions
  defined, 154
  using to find zeros of functions,
    155–156
Intercepted arcs, 597, 598
Interior angle measures, of polygons,
    404–406
  finding unknown, 405

number of sides of polygon, 405
  sum of angle measures, 404
Intersecting lines
  and circles, 606
  examples of, 606
Intersection of events, 306–307
Inverse cosine, 558
Inverse functions, 21
Inverse of the Triangle
    Proportionality Theorem,
    500
Inverse relation, 20
Inverse sine, 558
Inverse tangent, 558
Inverse trigonometric ratios, 558–559
Inverses of functions, 19–22, 53
  finding algebraically, 22
  formula for input of function, 21
Isosceles right triangles
  defined, 526
  finding sine and cosine of, 550
  side lengths of, 525–526
  in standard position, 516
Isosceles trapezoid(s)
  defined, 442
  properties of, 443
Isosceles Trapezoid Base Angles
    Converse, 443
Isosceles Trapezoid Base Angles
    Theorem, 443
Isosceles Trapezoid Diagonals
    Theorem, 443
Isosceles triangles, *See also* Isosceles
    right triangles
  median and altitude of, 365

Joint frequencies, 296
Joint relative frequencies, 297–298

Kite(s)
  angle measures of, 445
  areas of, 656
  defined, 445
  properties of, 441, 445, 454
Kite Diagonals Theorem, 445
Kite Opposite Angles Theorem, 445

Lake frontage, 505
Lateral surfaces of cones, 680
Latus rectum, 168
Leading coefficient, 63
Legs (of right triangles)
  finding with sine and cosine ratios,
    549
  finding with tangent ratio, 543

Postulates

Integrated Mathematics I

Ruler Postulate (p. 388)

The points on a line can be matched one to one with the real numbers. The real number that corresponds to a point is the coordinate of the point. The distance between points A and B, written as AB, is the absolute value of the difference of the coordinates of A and B.

Segment Addition Postulate (p. 390)

If B is between A and C, then $AB + BC = AC$.
If $AB + BC = AC$, then B is between A and C.

Protractor Postulate (p. 415)

Consider $\overleftrightarrow{OB}$ and a point A on one side of $\overleftrightarrow{OB}$. The rays of the form $\overrightarrow{OA}$ can be matched one to one with the real numbers from 0 to 180. The measure of $\angle AOB$, which can be written as $m\angle AOB$, is equal to the absolute value of the difference between the real numbers matched with $\overrightarrow{OA}$ and $\overrightarrow{OB}$ on a protractor.

Angle Addition Postulate (p. 417)

If P is in the interior of $\angle RST$, then the measure of $\angle RST$ is equal to the sum of the measures of $\angle RSP$ and $\angle PST$.

Two Point Postulate (p. 460)

Through any two points, there exists exactly one line.

Line-Point Postulate (p. 460)

A line contains at least two points.

Line Intersection Postulate (p. 460)

If two lines intersect, then their intersection is exactly one point.

Three Point Postulate (p. 460)

Through any three noncollinear points, there exists exactly one plane.

Plane-Point Postulate (p. 460)

A plane contains at least three noncollinear points.

Plane-Line Postulate (p. 460)

If two points lie in a plane, then the line containing them lies in the plane.

Plane Intersection Postulate (p. 460)

If two planes intersect, then their intersection is a line.

Linear Pair Postulate (p. 480)

If two angles form a linear pair, then they are supplementary.

Parallel Postulate (p. 499)

If there is a line and a point not on the line, then there is exactly one line through the point parallel to the given line.

Perpendicular Postulate (p. 499)

If there is a line and a point not on the line, then there is exactly one line through the point perpendicular to the given line.

Translation Postulate (p. 546)

A translation is a rigid motion.

Reflection Postulate (p. 554)

A reflection is a rigid motion.

Rotation Postulate (p. 564)

A rotation is a rigid motion.

Integrated Mathematics II

Arc Addition Postulate (p. 583)

The measure of an arc formed by two adjacent arcs is the sum of the measures of the two arcs.

Theorems

Integrated Mathematics I

Properties of Segment Congruence (p. 471)

Segment congruence is reflexive, symmetric, and transitive.

Reflexive For any segment AB, $\overline{AB} \cong \overline{AB}$.

Symmetric If $\overline{AB} \cong \overline{CD}$, then $\overline{CD} \cong \overline{AB}$.

Transitive If $\overline{AB} \cong \overline{CD}$ and $\overline{CD} \cong \overline{EF}$, then $\overline{AB} \cong \overline{EF}$.

Properties of Angle Congruence (p. 471)

Angle congruence is reflexive, symmetric, and transitive.

Reflexive For any angle A, $\angle A \cong \angle A$.

Symmetric If $\angle A \cong \angle B$, then $\angle B \cong \angle A$.

Transitive If $\angle A \cong \angle B$ and $\angle B \cong \angle C$, then $\angle A \cong \angle C$.

Right Angles Congruence Theorem (p. 478)

All right angles are congruent.

Congruent Supplements Theorem (p. 479)

If two angles are supplementary to the same angle (or to congruent angles), then they are congruent.

Congruent Complements Theorem (p. 479)

If two angles are complementary to the same angle (or to congruent angles), then they are congruent.

Vertical Angles Congruence Theorem (p. 480)

Vertical angles are congruent.

Corresponding Angles Theorem (p. 504)

If two parallel lines are cut by a transversal, then the pairs of corresponding angles are congruent.

Alternate Interior Angles Theorem (p. 504)

If two parallel lines are cut by a transversal, then the pairs of alternate interior angles are congruent.

Alternate Exterior Angles Theorem (p. 504)

If two parallel lines are cut by a transversal, then the pairs of alternate exterior angles are congruent.

Consecutive Interior Angles Theorem (p. 504)

If two parallel lines are cut by a transversal, then the pairs of consecutive interior angles are supplementary.

Corresponding Angles Converse (p. 510)

If two lines are cut by a transversal so the corresponding angles are congruent, then the lines are parallel.

Alternate Interior Angles Converse (p. 511)

If two lines are cut by a transversal so the alternate interior angles are congruent, then the lines are parallel.

Alternate Exterior Angles Converse (p. 511)

If two lines are cut by a transversal so the alternate exterior angles are congruent, then the lines are parallel.

Consecutive Interior Angles Converse (p. 511)

If two lines are cut by a transversal so the consecutive interior angles are supplementary, then the lines are parallel.

Transitive Property of Parallel Lines (p. 513)

If two lines are parallel to the same line, then they are parallel to each other.

Linear Pair Perpendicular Theorem (p. 522)

If two lines intersect to form a linear pair of congruent angles, then the lines are perpendicular.

Perpendicular Transversal Theorem (p. 522)

In a plane, if a transversal is perpendicular to one of two parallel lines, then it is perpendicular to the other line.

Lines Perpendicular to a Transversal Theorem (p. 522)

In a plane, if two lines are perpendicular to the same line, then they are parallel to each other.

Slopes of Parallel Lines (p. 528)

In a coordinate plane, two distinct nonvertical lines are parallel if and only if they have the same slope. Any two vertical lines are parallel.

Slopes of Perpendicular Lines (p. 528)

In a coordinate plane, two nonvertical lines are perpendicular if and only if the product of their slopes is -1. Horizontal lines are perpendicular to vertical lines.

Composition Theorem (p. 546)

The composition of two (or more) rigid motions is a rigid motion.

Reflections in Parallel Lines Theorem (p. 572)

If lines k and m are parallel, then a reflection in line k followed by a reflection in line m is the same as a translation. If A'' is the image of A, then

1. $\overline{AA''}$ is perpendicular to k and m, and
2. $AA'' = 2d$, where d is the distance between k and m.

Reflections in Intersecting Lines Theorem (p. 573)

If lines k and m intersect at point P, then a reflection in line k followed by a reflection in line m is the same as a rotation about point P. The angle of rotation is $2x°$, where $x°$ is the measure of the acute or right angle formed by lines k and m.

Triangle Sum Theorem (p. 589)

The sum of the measures of the interior angles of a triangle is $180°$.

Exterior Angle Theorem (p. 590)

The measure of an exterior angle of a triangle is equal to the sum of the measures of the two nonadjacent interior angles.

Corollary to the Triangle Sum Theorem (p. 591)

The acute angles of a right triangle are complementary.

Properties of Triangle Congruence (p. 597)

Triangle congruence is reflexive, symmetric, and transitive.

Reflexive   For any triangle $\triangle ABC$, $\triangle ABC \cong \triangle ABC$.

Symmetric   If $\triangle ABC \cong \triangle DEF$, then $\triangle DEF \cong \triangle ABC$.

Transitive   If $\triangle ABC \cong \triangle DEF$ and $\triangle DEF \cong \triangle JKL$, then $\triangle ABC \cong \triangle JKL$.

Third Angles Theorem (p. 598)

If two angles of one triangle are congruent to two angles of another triangle, then the third angles are also congruent.

Side-Angle-Side (SAS) Congruence Theorem (p. 602)

If two sides and the included angle of one triangle are congruent to two sides and the included angle of a second triangle, then the two triangles are congruent.

Base Angles Theorem (p. 608)

If two sides of a triangle are congruent, then the angles opposite them are congruent.

Converse of the Base Angles Theorem (p. 608)

If two angles of a triangle are congruent, then the sides opposite them are congruent.

Corollary to the Base Angles Theorem (p. 609)

If a triangle is equilateral, then it is equiangular.

Corollary to the Converse of the Base Angles Theorem (p. 609)

If a triangle is equiangular, then it is equilateral.

Side-Side-Side (SSS) Congruence Theorem (p. 618)

If three sides of one triangle are congruent to three sides of a second triangle, then the two triangles are congruent.

Hypotenuse-Leg (HL) Congruence Theorem (p. 620)

If the hypotenuse and a leg of a right triangle are congruent to the hypotenuse and a leg of a second right triangle, then the two triangles are congruent.

Angle-Side-Angle (ASA) Congruence Theorem (p. 626)

If two angles and the included side of one triangle are congruent to two angles and the included side of a second triangle, then the two triangles are congruent.

Angle-Angle-Side (AAS) Congruence Theorem (p. 627)

If two angles and a non-included side of one triangle are congruent to two angles and the corresponding non-included side of a second triangle, then the two triangles are congruent.

Integrated Mathematics II

Perpendicular Bisector Theorem (p. 344)

In a plane, if a point lies on the perpendicular bisector of a segment, then it is equidistant from the endpoints of the segment.

Converse of the Perpendicular Bisector Theorem (p. 344)

In a plane, if a point is equidistant from the endpoints of a segment, then it lies on the perpendicular bisector of the segment.

Angle Bisector Theorem (p. 346)

If a point lies on the bisector of an angle, then it is equidistant from the two sides of the angle.

Converse of the Angle Bisector Theorem (p. 346)

If a point is in the interior of an angle and is equidistant from the two sides of the angle, then it lies on the bisector of the angle.

Circumcenter Theorem (p. 352)

The circumcenter of a triangle is equidistant from the vertices of the triangle.

Incenter Theorem (p. 355)

The incenter of a triangle is equidistant from the sides of the triangle.

Centroid Theorem (p. 362)

The centroid of a triangle is two-thirds of the distance from each vertex to the midpoint of the opposite side.

Triangle Midsegment Theorem (p. 373)

The segment connecting the midpoints of two sides of a triangle is parallel to the third side and is half as long as that side.

Triangle Longer Side Theorem (p. 379)

If one side of a triangle is longer than another side, then the angle opposite the longer side is larger than the angle opposite the shorter side.

Triangle Larger Angle Theorem (p. 379)

If one angle of a triangle is larger than another angle, then the side opposite the larger angle is longer than the side opposite the smaller angle.

Triangle Inequality Theorem (p. 381)

The sum of the lengths of any two sides of a triangle is greater than the length of the third side.

Hinge Theorem (p. 386)

If two sides of one triangle are congruent to two sides of another triangle, and the included angle of the first is larger than the included angle of the second, then the third side of the first is longer than the third side of the second.

Converse of the Hinge Theorem (p. 386)

If two sides of one triangle are congruent to two sides of another triangle, and the third side of the first is longer than the third side of the second, then the included angle of the first is larger than the included angle of the second.

Polygon Interior Angles Theorem (p. 404)

The sum of the measures of the interior angles of a convex n-gon is $(n - 2) \cdot 180°$.

Corollary to the Polygon Interior Angles Theorem (p. 405)

The sum of the measures of the interior angles of a quadrilateral is 360°.

Polygon Exterior Angles Theorem (p. 406)

The sum of the measures of the exterior angles of a convex polygon, one angle at each vertex, is 360°.

Parallelogram Opposite Sides Theorem (p. 412)

If a quadrilateral is a parallelogram, then its opposite sides are congruent.

Parallelogram Opposite Angles Theorem (p. 412)

If a quadrilateral is a parallelogram, then its opposite angles are congruent.

Parallelogram Consecutive Angles Theorem (p. 413)

If a quadrilateral is a parallelogram, then its consecutive angles are supplementary.

Parallelogram Diagonals Theorem (p. 413)

If a quadrilateral is a parallelogram, then its diagonals bisect each other.

Parallelogram Opposite Sides Converse (p. 420)

If both pairs of opposite sides of a quadrilateral are congruent, then the quadrilateral is a parallelogram.

Parallelogram Opposite Angles Converse (p. 420)

If both pairs of opposite angles of a quadrilateral are congruent, then the quadrilateral is a parallelogram.

Opposite Sides Parallel and Congruent Theorem (p. 422)

If one pair of opposite sides of a quadrilateral are congruent and parallel, then the quadrilateral is a parallelogram.

Parallelogram Diagonals Converse (p. 422)

If the diagonals of a quadrilateral bisect each other, then the quadrilateral is a parallelogram.

Rhombus Corollary (p. 432)

A quadrilateral is a rhombus if and only if it has four congruent sides.

Rectangle Corollary (p. 432)

A quadrilateral is a rectangle if and only if it has four right angles.

Square Corollary (p. 432)

A quadrilateral is a square if and only if it is a rhombus and a rectangle.

Rhombus Diagonals Theorem (p. 434)

A parallelogram is a rhombus if and only if its diagonals are perpendicular.

Rhombus Opposite Angles Theorem (p. 434)

A parallelogram is a rhombus if and only if each diagonal bisects a pair of opposite angles.

Rectangle Diagonals Theorem (p. 435)

A parallelogram is a rectangle if and only if its diagonals are congruent.

Isosceles Trapezoid Base Angles Theorem (p. 443)

If a trapezoid is isosceles, then each pair of base angles is congruent.

Isosceles Trapezoid Base Angles Converse (p. 443)

If a trapezoid has a pair of congruent base angles, then it is an isosceles trapezoid.

Isosceles Trapezoid Diagonals Theorem (p. 443)

A trapezoid is isosceles if and only if its diagonals are congruent.

Trapezoid Midsegment Theorem (p. 444)

The midsegment of a trapezoid is parallel to each base, and its length is one-half the sum of the lengths of the bases.

Kite Diagonals Theorem (p. 445)

If a quadrilateral is a kite, then its diagonals are perpendicular.

Kite Opposite Angles Theorem (p. 445)

If a quadrilateral is a kite, then exactly one pair of opposite angles are congruent.

Perimeters of Similar Polygons (p. 478)

If two polygons are similar, then the ratio of their perimeters is equal to the ratios of their corresponding side lengths.

Areas of Similar Polygons (p. 479)

If two polygons are similar, then the ratio of their areas is equal to the squares of the ratios of their corresponding side lengths.

Angle-Angle (AA) Similarity Theorem (p. 486)

If two angles of one triangle are congruent to two angles of another triangle, then the two triangles are similar.

Side-Side-Side (SSS) Similarity Theorem (p. 494)

If the corresponding side lengths of two triangles are proportional, then the triangles are similar.

Side-Angle-Side (SAS) Similarity Theorem (p. 496)

If an angle of one triangle is congruent to an angle of a second triangle and the lengths of the sides including these angles are proportional, then the triangles are similar.

Triangle Proportionality Theorem (p. 500)

If a line parallel to one side of a triangle intersects the other two sides, then it divides the two sides proportionally.

Converse of the Triangle Proportionality Theorem (p. 500)

If a line divides two sides of a triangle proportionally, then it is parallel to the third side.

Three Parallel Lines Theorem (p. 501)

If three parallel lines intersect two transversals, then they divide the transversals proportionally.

Triangle Angle Bisector Theorem (p. 502)

If a ray bisects an angle of a triangle, then it divides the opposite side into segments whose lengths are proportional to the lengths of the other two sides.

Pythagorean Theorem (p. 518)

In a right triangle, the square of the length of the hypotenuse is equal to the sum of the squares of the lengths of the legs.

Converse of the Pythagorean Theorem (p. 520)

If the square of the length of the longest side of a triangle is equal to the sum of the squares of the lengths of the other two sides, then the triangle is a right triangle.

Pythagorean Inequalities Theorem (p. 521)

For any $\triangle ABC$, where c is the length of the longest side, the following statements are true.
If $c^2 < a^2 + b^2$, then $\triangle ABC$ is acute.
If $c^2 > a^2 + b^2$, then $\triangle ABC$ is obtuse.

45°-45°-90° Triangle Theorem (p. 526)

In a 45°-45°-90° triangle, the hypotenuse is $\sqrt{2}$ times as long as each leg.

30°-60°-90° Triangle Theorem (p. 527)

In a 30°-60°-90° triangle, the hypotenuse is twice as long as the shorter leg, and the longer leg is $\sqrt{3}$ times as long as the shorter leg.

Right Triangle Similarity Theorem (p. 532)

If the altitude is drawn to the hypotenuse of a right triangle, then the two triangles formed are similar to the original triangle and to each other.

Geometric Mean (Altitude) Theorem (p. 534)

In a right triangle, the altitude from the right angle to the hypotenuse divides the hypotenuse into two segments. The length of the altitude is the geometric mean of the lengths of the two segments of the hypotenuse.

Geometric Mean (Leg) Theorem (p. 534)

In a right triangle, the altitude from the right angle to the hypotenuse divides the hypotenuse into two segments. The length of each leg of the right triangle is the geometric mean of the lengths of the hypotenuse and the segment of the hypotenuse that is adjacent to the leg.

Tangent Line to Circle Theorem (p. 576)

In a plane, a line is tangent to a circle if and only if the line is perpendicular to a radius of the circle at its endpoint on the circle.

External Tangent Congruence Theorem (p. 576)

Tangent segments from a common external point are congruent.

Congruent Circles Theorem *(p. 584)*

Two circles are congruent circles if and only if they have the same radius.

Congruent Central Angles Theorem *(p. 584)*

In the same circle, or in congruent circles, two minor arcs are congruent if and only if their corresponding central angles are congruent.

Similar Circles Theorem *(p. 585)*

All circles are similar.

Congruent Corresponding Chords Theorem *(p. 590)*

In the same circle, or in congruent circles, two minor arcs are congruent if and only if their corresponding chords are congruent.

Perpendicular Chord Bisector Theorem *(p. 590)*

If a diameter of a circle is perpendicular to a chord, then the diameter bisects the chord and its arc.

Perpendicular Chord Bisector Converse *(p. 590)*

If one chord of a circle is a perpendicular bisector of another chord, then the first chord is a diameter.

Equidistant Chords Theorem *(p. 592)*

In the same circle, or in congruent circles, two chords are congruent if and only if they are equidistant from the center.

Measure of an Inscribed Angle Theorem *(p. 598)*

The measure of an inscribed angle is one-half the measure of its intercepted arc.

Inscribed Angles of a Circle Theorem *(p. 599)*

If two inscribed angles of a circle intercept the same arc, then the angles are congruent.

Inscribed Right Triangle Theorem *(p. 600)*

If a right triangle is inscribed in a circle, then the hypotenuse is a diameter of the circle. Conversely, if one side of an inscribed triangle is a diameter of the circle, then the triangle is a right triangle and the angle opposite the diameter is the right angle.

Inscribed Quadrilateral Theorem *(p. 600)*

A quadrilateral can be inscribed in a circle if and only if its opposite angles are supplementary.

Tangent and Intersected Chord Theorem *(p. 606)*

If a tangent and a chord intersect at a point on a circle, then the measure of each angle formed is one-half the measure of its intercepted arc.

Angles Inside the Circle Theorem *(p. 607)*

If two chords intersect inside a circle, then the measure of each angle is one-half the sum of the measures of the arcs intercepted by the angle and its vertical angle.

Angles Outside the Circle Theorem *(p. 607)*

If a tangent and a secant, two tangents, or two secants intersect outside a circle, then the measure of the angle formed is one-half the difference of the measures of the intercepted arcs.

Circumscribed Angle Theorem *(p. 608)*

The measure of a circumscribed angle is equal to 180° minus the measure of the central angle that intercepts the same arc.

Segments of Chords Theorem *(p. 614)*

If two chords intersect in the interior of a circle, then the product of the lengths of the segments of one chord is equal to the product of the lengths of the segments of the other chord.

Segments of Secants Theorem *(p. 615)*

If two secant segments share the same endpoint outside a circle, then the product of the lengths of one secant segment and its external segment equals the product of the lengths of the other secant segment and its external segment.

Segments of Secants and Tangents Theorem *(p. 616)*

If a secant segment and a tangent segment share an endpoint outside a circle, then the product of the lengths of the secant segment and its external segment equals the square of the length of the tangent segment.

Integrated Mathematics III

Law of Sines *(p. 487)*

The Law of Sines can be written in either of the following forms for $\triangle ABC$ with sides of length a, b, and c.

$$\frac{\sin A}{a} = \frac{\sin B}{b} = \frac{\sin C}{c}$$

$$\frac{a}{\sin A} = \frac{b}{\sin B} = \frac{c}{\sin C}$$

Law of Cosines *(p. 494)*

If $\triangle ABC$ has sides of length a, b, and c, then the following are true.

$$a^2 = b^2 + c^2 - 2bc \cos A$$
$$b^2 = a^2 + c^2 - 2ac \cos B$$
$$c^2 = a^2 + b^2 - 2ab \cos C$$

Reference

Properties

Properties of Equality

Let a, b, and c be real numbers.

Addition Property of Equality
If $a = b$, then $a + c = b + c$.

Subtraction Property of Equality
If $a = b$, then $a - c = b - c$.

Multiplication Property of Equality
If $a = b$, then $a \cdot c = b \cdot c$, $c \neq 0$.

Division Property of Equality
If $a = b$, then $a \div c = b \div c$, $c \neq 0$.

Reflexive Property of Equality
$a = a$

Symmetric Property of Equality
If $a = b$, then $b = a$.

Transitive Property of Equality
If $a = b$ and $b = c$, then $a = c$.

Substitution Property of Equality
If $a = b$, then a can be substituted for b (or b for a) in any equation or expression.

Properties of Inequality

Let a, b, and c be real numbers.

Addition Property of Inequality
If $a > b$, then $a + c > b + c$.
If $a < b$, then $a + c < b + c$.

Subtraction Property of Inequality
If $a > b$, then $a - c > b - c$.
If $a < b$, then $a - c < b - c$.

Multiplication Property of Inequality ($c > 0$)
If $a > b$ and $c > 0$, then $ac > bc$.
If $a < b$ and $c > 0$, then $ac < bc$.

Division Property of Inequality ($c > 0$)
If $a > b$ and $c > 0$, then $\dfrac{a}{c} > \dfrac{b}{c}$.

If $a < b$ and $c > 0$, then $\dfrac{a}{c} < \dfrac{b}{c}$.

Multiplication Property of Inequality ($c < 0$)
If $a > b$ and $c < 0$, then $ac < bc$.
If $a < b$ and $c < 0$, then $ac > bc$.

Division Property of Inequality ($c < 0$)
If $a > b$ and $c < 0$, then $\dfrac{a}{c} < \dfrac{b}{c}$.

If $a < b$ and $c < 0$, then $\dfrac{a}{c} > \dfrac{b}{c}$.

* The Properties of Inequality are also true for $\geq$ and $\leq$.

Properties of Exponents

Let a and b be real numbers and let m and n be rational numbers.

Zero Exponent
$a^0 = 1$, where $a \neq 0$

Negative Exponent
$a^{-n} = \dfrac{1}{a^n}$, where $a \neq 0$

Product of Powers Property
$a^m \cdot a^n = a^{m+n}$

Quotient of Powers Property
$\dfrac{a^m}{a^n} = a^{m-n}$, where $a \neq 0$

Power of a Power Property
$(a^m)^n = a^{mn}$

Power of a Product Property
$(ab)^m = a^m b^m$

Power of a Quotient Property
$\left(\dfrac{a}{b}\right)^m = \dfrac{a^m}{b^m}$, where $b \neq 0$

Rational Exponents
$a^{m/n} = (a^{1/n})^m = (\sqrt[n]{a})^m$

Rational Exponents
$a^{-m/n} = \dfrac{1}{a^{m/n}} = \dfrac{1}{(a^{1/n})^m} = \dfrac{1}{(\sqrt[n]{a})^m}$,
where $a \neq 0$

Properties of Absolute Value

Let a and b be real numbers.

$|a| \geq 0$ $\qquad$ $|-a| = |a|$ $\qquad$ $|ab| = |a||b|$ $\qquad$ $\left|\dfrac{a}{b}\right| = \dfrac{|a|}{|b|}$, $b \neq 0$

Properties of Radicals

Let a and b be real numbers and let n be an integer greater than 1.

Product Property of Square Roots
$\sqrt{ab} = \sqrt{a} \cdot \sqrt{b}$, where $a, b \geq 0$

Quotient Property of Square Roots
$\sqrt{\dfrac{a}{b}} = \dfrac{\sqrt{a}}{\sqrt{b}}$, where $a \geq 0$ and $b > 0$

Product Property of Radicals
$\sqrt[n]{ab} = \sqrt[n]{a} \cdot \sqrt[n]{b}$

Quotient Property of Radicals
$\sqrt[n]{\dfrac{a}{b}} = \dfrac{\sqrt[n]{a}}{\sqrt[n]{b}}$, where $b \neq 0$

Square Root of a Negative Number
1. If r is a positive real number, then $\sqrt{-r} = i\sqrt{r}$.
2. By the first property, it follows that $(i\sqrt{r})^2 = -r$.

Properties of Logarithms

Let b, m, and n be positive real numbers with $b \neq 1$.

Product Property
$\log_b mn = \log_b m + \log_b n$

Quotient Property
$\log_b \dfrac{m}{n} = \log_b m - \log_b n$

Power Property
$\log_b m^n = n \log_b m$

Properties of Segment and Angle Congruence

Reflexive Property of Congruence
For any segment AB, $\overline{AB} \cong \overline{AB}$.

For any angle A, $\angle A \cong \angle A$.

Symmetric Property of Congruence
If $\overline{AB} \cong \overline{CD}$, then $\overline{CD} \cong \overline{AB}$.

If $\angle A \cong \angle B$, then $\angle B \cong \angle A$.

Transitive Property of Congruence
If $\overline{AB} \cong \overline{CD}$ and $\overline{CD} \cong \overline{EF}$, then $\overline{AB} \cong \overline{EF}$.

If $\angle A \cong \angle B$ and $\angle B \cong \angle C$, then $\angle A \cong \angle C$.

Other Properties

Property of Equality for Exponential Equations
If $b > 0$ and $b \neq 1$, then $b^x = b^y$ if and only if $x = y$.

Zero-Product Property
If a and b are real numbers and $ab = 0$, then $a = 0$ or $b = 0$.

Property of Equality for Logarithmic Equations
If b, x, and y are positive real numbers with $b \neq 1$, then $\log_b x = \log_b y$ if and only if $x = y$.

Transitive Property of Parallel Lines
If $p \parallel q$ and $q \parallel r$, then $p \parallel r$.

Distributive Property
Sum
$a(b + c) = ab + ac$

Difference
$a(b - c) = ab - ac$

Triangle Inequalities

Triangle Inequality Theorem

$AB + BC > AC$
$AC + BC > AB$
$AB + AC > BC$

Pythagorean Inequalities Theorem

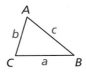

If $c^2 < a^2 + b^2$, then $\triangle ABC$ is acute.

If $c^2 > a^2 + b^2$, then $\triangle ABC$ is obtuse.

Patterns

Square of a Binomial Pattern
$(a + b)^2 = a^2 + 2ab + b^2$
$(a - b)^2 = a^2 - 2ab + b^2$

Sum and Difference Pattern
$(a + b)(a - b) = a^2 - b^2$

Cube of a Binomial Pattern
$(a + b)^3 = a^3 + 3a^2b + 3ab^2 + b^3$
$(a - b)^3 = a^3 - 3a^2b + 3ab^2 - b^3$

Completing the Square
$$x^2 + bx + \left(\frac{b}{2}\right)^2 = \left(x + \frac{b}{2}\right)^2$$

Difference of Two Squares Pattern
$a^2 - b^2 = (a + b)(a - b)$

Perfect Square Trinomial Pattern
$a^2 + 2ab + b^2 = (a + b)^2$
$a^2 - 2ab + b^2 = (a - b)^2$

Sum of Two Cubes Pattern
$a^3 + b^3 = (a + b)(a^2 - ab + b^2)$

Difference of Two Cubes Pattern
$a^3 - b^3 = (a - b)(a^2 + ab + b^2)$

Algebra Theorems

The Remainder Theorem
If a polynomial $f(x)$ is divided by $x - k$, then the remainder is $r = f(k)$.

The Factor Theorem
A polynomial $f(x)$ has a factor $x - k$ if and only if $f(k) = 0$.

The Rational Root Theorem
If $f(x) = a_n x^n + \cdots + a_1 x + a_0$ has *integer* coefficients, then every rational solution of $f(x) = 0$ has the form

$\dfrac{p}{q} = \dfrac{\text{factor of constant term } a_0}{\text{factor of leading coefficient } a_n}$.

The Irrational Conjugates Theorem
Let f be a polynomial function with rational coefficients, and let a and b be rational numbers such that $\sqrt{b}$ is irrational. If $a + \sqrt{b}$ is a zero of f, then $a - \sqrt{b}$ is also a zero of f.

The Fundamental Theorem of Algebra

Theorem   If $f(x)$ is a polynomial of degree n where $n > 0$, then the equation $f(x) = 0$ has at least one solution in the set of complex numbers.

Corollary   If $f(x)$ is a polynomial of degree n where $n > 0$, then the equation $f(x) = 0$ has exactly n solutions provided each solution repeated twice is counted as two solutions, each solution repeated three times is counted as three solutions, and so on.

The Complex Conjugates Theorem
If f is a polynomial function with real coefficients, and $a + bi$ is an imaginary zero of f, then $a - bi$ is also a zero of f.

Descartes's Rule of Signs
Let $f(x) = a_n x^n + a_{n-1} x^{n-1} + \cdots + a_2 x^2 + a_1 x + a_0$ be a polynomial function with real coefficients.

- The number of positive real zeros of f is equal to the number of changes in sign of the coefficients of $f(x)$ or is less than this by an even number.

- The number of negative real zeros of f is equal to the number of changes in sign of the coefficients of $f(-x)$ or is less than this by an even number.

Formulas

Algebra

Slope

$$m = \frac{y_2 - y_1}{x_2 - x_1}$$

Slope-intercept form

$$y = mx + b$$

Point-slope form

$$y - y_1 = m(x - x_1)$$

Standard form of a linear equation

$Ax + By = C$, where A and B are not both 0

Vertex form of an absolute value function

$f(x) = a|x - h| + k$, where $a \neq 0$

Standard form of a quadratic function

$f(x) = ax^2 + bx + c$, where $a \neq 0$

Vertex form of a quadratic function

$f(x) = a(x - h)^2 + k$, where $a \neq 0$

Intercept form of a quadratic function

$f(x) = a(x - p)(x - q)$, where $a \neq 0$

Quadratic Formula

$$x = \frac{-b \pm \sqrt{b^2 - 4ac}}{2a}, \text{ where } a \neq 0$$

Standard equation of a circle

$(x - h)^2 + (y - k)^2 = r^2$

Standard form of a polynomial function

$f(x) = a_n x^n + a_{n-1} x^{n-1} + \cdots + a_1 x + a_0$

Exponential growth function

$y = a(1 + r)^t$, where $a > 0$ and $r > 0$

or

$y = ab^x$, where $a > 0$ and $b > 1$

Exponential decay function

$y = a(1 - r)^t$, where $a > 0$ and $0 < r < 1$

or

$y = ab^x$, where $a > 0$ and $0 < b < 1$

Logarithm of y with base b

$\log_b y = x$ if and only if $b^x = y$

Change-of-base formula

$\log_c a = \dfrac{\log_b a}{\log_b c}$, where a, b, and c are positive real numbers

with $b \neq 1$ and $c \neq 1$.

Explicit rule for an arithmetic sequence

$a_n = a_1 + (n - 1)d$

Explicit rule for a geometric sequence

$a_n = a_1 r^{n-1}$

Recursive equation for an arithmetic sequence

$a_n = a_{n-1} + d$

Recursive equation for a geometric sequence

$a_n = r \cdot a_{n-1}$

Sum of n terms of 1

$$\sum_{i=1}^{n} 1 = n$$

Sum of first n positive integers

$$\sum_{i=1}^{n} i = \frac{n(n+1)}{2}$$

Sum of squares of first n positive integers

$$\sum_{i=1}^{n} i^2 = \frac{n(n+1)(2n+1)}{6}$$

Sum of first n terms of an arithmetic series

$$S_n = n\left(\frac{a_1 + a_n}{2}\right)$$

Sum of first n terms of a geometric series

$$S_n = a_1\left(\frac{1 - r^n}{1 - r}\right), \text{ where } r \neq 1$$

Sum of an infinite geometric series

$$S = \frac{a_1}{1 - r} \text{ provided } |r| < 1$$

Statistics

Sample mean

$$\bar{x} = \frac{\Sigma x}{n}$$

Standard deviation

$$\sigma = \sqrt{\frac{(x_1 - \bar{x})^2 + (x_2 - \bar{x})^2 + \cdots + (x_n - \bar{x})^2}{n}}$$

z-Score

$$z = \frac{x - \mu}{\sigma}$$

Margin of error for sample proportions

$$\pm \frac{1}{\sqrt{n}}$$

Probability and Combinatorics

$$\text{Theoretical Probability} = \frac{\text{Number of favorable outcomes}}{\text{Total number of outcomes}}$$

$$\text{Experimental Probability} = \frac{\text{Number of successes}}{\text{Number of trials}}$$

Probability of the complement of an event
$$P(\overline{A}) = 1 - P(A)$$

Probability of independent events
$$P(A \text{ and } B) = P(A) \cdot P(B)$$

Probability of dependent events
$$P(A \text{ and } B) = P(A) \cdot P(B \mid A)$$

Probability of compound events
$$P(A \text{ or } B) = P(A) + P(B) - P(A \text{ and } B)$$

Odds

$$\text{Odds in favor} = \frac{\text{Number of favorable outcomes}}{\text{Number of unfavorable outcomes}}$$

$$\text{Odds against} = \frac{\text{Number of unfavorable outcomes}}{\text{Number of favorable outcomes}}$$

Permutations
$$_nP_r = \frac{n!}{(n-r)!}$$

Combinations
$$_nC_r = \frac{n!}{(n-r)! \cdot r!}$$

Binomial experiments
$$P(k \text{ successes}) = {}_nC_k p^k (1-p)^{n-k}$$

The Binomial Theorem
$$(a+b)^n = {}_nC_0 a^n b^0 + {}_nC_1 a^{n-1} b^1 + {}_nC_2 a^{n-2} b^2 + \cdots + {}_nC_n a^0 b^n, \text{ where } n \text{ is a positive integer.}$$

Coordinate Geometry

Midpoint Formula
$$\left(\frac{x_1 + x_2}{2}, \frac{y_1 + y_2}{2} \right)$$

Distance Formula
$$d = \sqrt{(x_2 - x_1)^2 + (y_2 - y_1)^2}$$

Right Triangles

Pythagorean Theorem

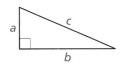

$$a^2 + b^2 = c^2$$

45°-45°-90° Triangles

$$\text{hypotenuse} = \text{leg} \cdot \sqrt{2}$$

30°-60°-90° Triangles

$$\text{hypotenuse} = \text{shorter leg} \cdot 2$$
$$\text{longer leg} = \text{shorter leg} \cdot \sqrt{3}$$

Trigonometric Ratios

$$\sin A = \frac{BC}{AB}$$

$$\cos A = \frac{AC}{AB}$$

$$\tan A = \frac{BC}{AC}$$

$$\sin^{-1} \frac{BC}{AB} = m\angle A$$

$$\cos^{-1} \frac{AC}{AB} = m\angle A$$

$$\tan^{-1} \frac{BC}{AC} = m\angle A$$

Sine and cosine of complementary angles
Let A and B be complementary angles. Then the following statements are true.

$$\sin A = \cos(90° - A) = \cos B$$
$$\cos A = \sin(90° - A) = \sin B$$

$$\sin B = \cos(90° - B) = \cos A$$
$$\cos B = \sin(90° - B) = \sin A$$

Reference

Trigonometry

General definitions of trigonometric functions

Let θ be an angle in standard position, and let (x, y) be the point where the terminal side of θ intersects the circle $x^2 + y^2 = r^2$. The six trigonometric functions of θ are defined as shown.

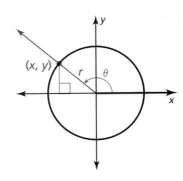

$$\sin \theta = \frac{y}{r} \qquad \cos \theta = \frac{x}{r} \qquad \tan \theta = \frac{y}{x}, x \neq 0$$

$$\csc \theta = \frac{r}{y}, y \neq 0 \qquad \sec \theta = \frac{r}{x}, x \neq 0 \qquad \cot \theta = \frac{x}{y}, y \neq 0$$

Conversion between degrees and radians
$180° = \pi$ radians

Arc length of a sector
$s = r\theta$

Area of a sector
$A = \frac{1}{2}r^2\theta$

Reciprocal Identities

$$\sin \theta = \frac{1}{\csc \theta} \qquad \cos \theta = \frac{1}{\sec \theta} \qquad \tan \theta = \frac{1}{\cot \theta}$$

$$\csc \theta = \frac{1}{\sin \theta} \qquad \sec \theta = \frac{1}{\cos \theta} \qquad \cot \theta = \frac{1}{\tan \theta}$$

Tangent and Cotangent Identities

$$\tan \theta = \frac{\sin \theta}{\cos \theta} \qquad \cot \theta = \frac{\cos \theta}{\sin \theta}$$

Pythagorean Identities
$\sin^2 \theta + \cos^2 \theta = 1$
$1 + \tan^2 \theta = \sec^2 \theta$
$1 + \cot^2 \theta = \csc^2 \theta$

Negative Angle Identities
$\sin(-\theta) = -\sin \theta$
$\cos(-\theta) = \cos \theta$
$\tan(-\theta) = -\tan \theta$
$\csc(-\theta) = -\csc \theta$
$\sec(-\theta) = \sec \theta$
$\cot(-\theta) = -\cot \theta$

Cofunction Identites

$$\sin\left(\frac{\pi}{2} - \theta\right) = \cos \theta \qquad \csc\left(\frac{\pi}{2} - \theta\right) = \sec \theta$$

$$\cos\left(\frac{\pi}{2} - \theta\right) = \sin \theta \qquad \sec\left(\frac{\pi}{2} - \theta\right) = \csc \theta$$

$$\tan\left(\frac{\pi}{2} - \theta\right) = \cot \theta \qquad \cot\left(\frac{\pi}{2} - \theta\right) = \tan \theta$$

Sum Formulas
$\sin(a + b) = \sin a \cos b + \cos a \sin b$
$\cos(a + b) = \cos a \cos b - \sin a \sin b$

$$\tan(a + b) = \frac{\tan a + \tan b}{1 - \tan a \tan b}$$

Difference Formulas
$\sin(a - b) = \sin a \cos b - \cos a \sin b$
$\cos(a - b) = \cos a \cos b + \sin a \sin b$

$$\tan(a - b) = \frac{\tan a - \tan b}{1 + \tan a \tan b}$$

Any Triangle

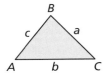

Area

$\text{Area} = \frac{1}{2}bc \sin A$

$\text{Area} = \frac{1}{2}ac \sin B$

$\text{Area} = \frac{1}{2}ab \sin C$

Law of Sines

$$\frac{\sin A}{a} = \frac{\sin B}{b} = \frac{\sin C}{c}$$

$$\frac{a}{\sin A} = \frac{b}{\sin B} = \frac{c}{\sin C}$$

Law of Cosines
$a^2 = b^2 + c^2 - 2bc \cos A$
$b^2 = a^2 + c^2 - 2ac \cos B$
$c^2 = a^2 + b^2 - 2ab \cos C$

Polygons

Triangle Sum Theorem

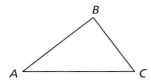

$$m\angle A + m\angle B + m\angle C = 180°$$

Exterior Angle Theorem

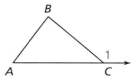

$$m\angle 1 = m\angle A + m\angle B$$

Triangle Midsegment Theorem

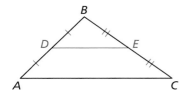

$$\overline{DE} \parallel \overline{AC}$$
$$DE = \tfrac{1}{2}AC$$

Trapezoid Midsegment Theorem

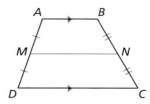

$$\overline{MN} \parallel \overline{AB}$$
$$\overline{MN} \parallel \overline{DC}$$
$$MN = \tfrac{1}{2}(AB + CD)$$

Polygon Interior Angles Theorem

$$n = 6$$

$$m\angle 1 + m\angle 2 + \cdots + m\angle n = (n - 2) \cdot 180°$$

Polygon Exterior Angles Theorem

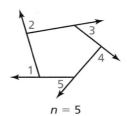

$$n = 5$$

$$m\angle 1 + m\angle 2 + \cdots + m\angle n = 360°$$

Geometric Mean (Altitude) Theorem

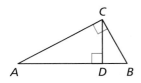

$$CD^2 = AD \cdot BD$$

Geometric Mean (Leg) Theorem

$$CB^2 = DB \cdot AB$$
$$AC^2 = AD \cdot AB$$

Circles

Arc length

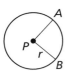

Arc length of $\widehat{AB} = \dfrac{m\widehat{AB}}{360°} \cdot 2\pi r$

Area of a sector

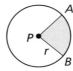

Area of sector $APB = \dfrac{m\widehat{AB}}{360°} \cdot \pi r^2$

Central angles

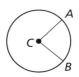

$m\angle ACB = m\widehat{AB}$

Inscribed angles

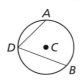

$m\angle ADB = \frac{1}{2}m\widehat{AB}$

Tangent and intersected chord

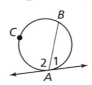

$m\angle 1 = \frac{1}{2}m\widehat{AB}$

$m\angle 2 = \frac{1}{2}m\widehat{BCA}$

Angles and Segments of Circles

Two chords

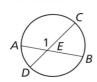

$m\angle 1 = \frac{1}{2}\left(m\widehat{AC} + m\widehat{DB}\right)$

$EA \cdot EB = EC \cdot ED$

Two secants

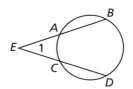

$m\angle 1 = \frac{1}{2}\left(m\widehat{BD} - m\widehat{AC}\right)$

$EA \cdot EB = EC \cdot ED$

Tangent and secant

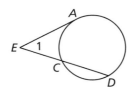

$m\angle 1 = \frac{1}{2}\left(m\widehat{AD} - m\widehat{AC}\right)$

$EA^2 = EC \cdot ED$

Two tangents

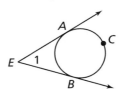

$m\angle 1 = \frac{1}{2}\left(m\widehat{ACB} - m\widehat{AB}\right)$

$EA = EB$

Other Formulas

Simple Interest

$I = Prt$

Compound Interest

$A = P\left(1 + \dfrac{r}{n}\right)^{nt}$

Continuously Compounded Interest

$A = Pe^{rt}$

Distance

$d = rt$

Geometric mean

$x = \sqrt{a \cdot b}$

Density

$\text{Density} = \dfrac{\text{Mass}}{\text{Volume}}$

Similar polygons or similar solids with scale factor k

Ratio of perimeters $= k$

Ratio of areas $= k^2$

Ratio of volumes $= k^3$

Perimeter, Area, and Volume Formulas

Square

$P = 4s$
$A = s^2$

Rectangle

$P = 2\ell + 2w$
$A = \ell w$

Triangle

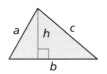

$P = a + b + c$
$A = \frac{1}{2}bh$

Circle

$C = \pi d$ or $C = 2\pi r$
$A = \pi r^2$

Parallelogram

$A = bh$

Trapezoid

$A = \frac{1}{2}h(b_1 + b_2)$

Rhombus/Kite

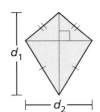

$A = \frac{1}{2}d_1 d_2$

Regular *n*-gon

$A = \frac{1}{2}aP$ or $A = \frac{1}{2}a \cdot ns$

Prism

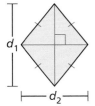

$L = Ph$
$S = 2B + Ph$
$V = Bh$

Cylinder

$L = 2\pi rh$
$S = 2\pi r^2 + 2\pi rh$
$V = \pi r^2 h$

Pyramid

$L = \frac{1}{2}P\ell$
$S = B + \frac{1}{2}P\ell$
$V = \frac{1}{3}Bh$

Cone

$L = \pi r\ell$
$S = \pi r^2 + \pi r\ell$
$V = \frac{1}{3}\pi r^2 h$

Sphere

$S = 4\pi r^2$
$V = \frac{4}{3}\pi r^3$

Conversions

U.S. Customary

1 foot = 12 inches
1 yard = 3 feet
1 mile = 5280 feet
1 mile = 1760 yards
1 acre = 43,560 square feet
1 cup = 8 fluid ounces
1 pint = 2 cups
1 quart = 2 pints
1 gallon = 4 quarts
1 gallon = 231 cubic inches
1 pound = 16 ounces
1 ton = 2000 pounds

U.S. Customary to Metric

1 inch = 2.54 centimeters
1 foot ≈ 0.3 meter
1 mile ≈ 1.61 kilometers
1 quart ≈ 0.95 liter
1 gallon ≈ 3.79 liters
1 cup ≈ 237 milliliters
1 pound ≈ 0.45 kilogram
1 ounce ≈ 28.3 grams
1 gallon ≈ 3785 cubic centimeters

Time

1 minute = 60 seconds
1 hour = 60 minutes
1 hour = 3600 seconds
1 year = 52 weeks

Temperature

$$C = \frac{5}{9}(F - 32)$$

$$F = \frac{9}{5}C + 32$$

Metric

1 centimeter = 10 millimeters
1 meter = 100 centimeters
1 kilometer = 1000 meters
1 liter = 1000 milliliters
1 kiloliter = 1000 liters
1 milliliter = 1 cubic centimeter
1 liter = 1000 cubic centimeters
1 cubic millimeter = 0.001 milliliter
1 gram = 1000 milligrams
1 kilogram = 1000 grams

Metric to U.S. Customary

1 centimeter ≈ 0.39 inch
1 meter ≈ 3.28 feet
1 meter ≈ 39.37 inches
1 kilometer ≈ 0.62 mile
1 liter ≈ 1.06 quarts
1 liter ≈ 0.26 gallon
1 kilogram ≈ 2.2 pounds
1 gram ≈ 0.035 ounce
1 cubic meter ≈ 264 gallons

Credits

Front Matter

i Rainbow-Pic/Shutterstock.com; **vii** ©iStockphoto.com/Christopher Futcher; **viii** Will Rodrigues/Shutterstock.com; **ix** anyaivanova/ Shutterstock.com; **x** J.D.S/Shutterstock.com; **xi** ©iStockphoto.com/ MinistryOfJoy; **xii** Nadiia Gerbish/Shutterstock.com; **xiii** sculpies/ Shutterstock.com; **xiv** FreshPaint/Shutterstock.com; **xv** koh sze kiat/ Shutterstock.com; **xvi** ©iStockphoto.com/Pamela Moore; **xvii** ©iStockphoto.com/-hakusan-; **xviii** Baloncici/Shutterstock.com; **xix** Monkey Business Images/Shutterstock.com

Chapter 1

0 *top left* Olga Kovalenko/Shutterstock.com; *top right* kavram/ Shutterstock.com; *center left* Karyna Che/Shutterstock.com; *bottom right* Pressmaster/Shutterstock.com; *bottom left* Will Rodrigues/Shutterstock.com; **9** Pakhnyushcha/Shutterstock.com; **14** Pressmaster/Shutterstock.com; **16** manish mansinh/Shutterstock.com; **25** Nattika/Shutterstock.com; **26** Pashin Georgiy/Shutterstock.com; **32** *top right* Vitaly Korovin/ Shutterstock.com; *bottom right* Jiri Hera/Shutterstock.com; **33** *center left* Mark III Photonics/Shutterstock.com; *top right* NASA; **38** Glenda M. Powers/Shutterstock.com, siamionau pavel/Shutterstock.com; **40** *top right* ©iStockphoto.com/katkov, ©iStockphoto.com/Andrew Johnson; *center left* Dodecahedron by User:Cyp (*http://commons.wikimedia.org/wiki/ File:Dodecahedron.jpg*), CC-BY-SA 3.0; **46** risteski goce/Shutterstock.com; **48** bornholm/Shutterstock.com, Masalski Maksim/Shutterstock.com; **49** *bottom left* Olga Kovalenko/Shutterstock.com; *top right* Tupungato/ Shutterstock.com; *center right* U.S. Department of Energy; **50** Egon Zitter/ Shutterstock.com **51** tuulijumala/Shutterstock.com, Aleksej Zhagunov/ Shutterstock.com; **55** Africa Studio/Shutterstock.com

Chapter 2

58 *top left* anyaivanova/Shutterstock.com; *top right* jaroslava V/ Shutterstock.com; *center left* luchschen/Shutterstock.com; *bottom right* Rudy Balasko/Shutterstock.com; *bottom left* Andresr/Shutterstock.com; **65** ©iStockphoto.com/edge69; **66** ecco/Shutterstock.com ; **67** *center left* Johanna Goodyear/Shutterstock.com; *exercise 51* ©iStockphoto.com/ edge69; *exercise 52* Matt Antonino/Shutterstock.com; *exercise 53* ©iStockphoto.com/ lumpynoodles; **72** *left* d3images/Shutterstock.com; *right* Fejas/Shutterstock.com; **74** Andresr/Shutterstock.com; **78** Eric Isselee/ Shutterstock.com, Erik Lam/Shutterstock.com; **80** Tamara Kulikova/ Shutterstock.com; **86** Rudy Balasko/Shutterstock.com; **87** Nattika/ Shutterstock.com; **88** *top right* Tuja/Shutterstock.com; *bottom right* ©iStockphoto.com/tirc83; **93** deer boy/Shutterstock.com; **94** *top left* luchschen/Shutterstock.com; *center left* cobalt88/Shutterstock.com; **98** jaroslava V/Shutterstock.com; **107** G Tipene/Shutterstock.com; **105** Mark Stout Photography/Shutterstock.com; **106** *top left* MarijaPiliponyte/Shutterstock.com; *center left* Sergiy Telesh/ Shutterstock.com; **110** Dirk Ercken/Shutterstock.com; **111** Anna Breitenberger/Shutterstock.com; **113** tuulijumala/Shutterstock.com, HERGON/Shutterstock.com

Chapter 3

120 *top left* homydesign/Shutterstock.com; *top right* J.D.S/ Shutterstock.com *center left* Susana Ortega/Shutterstock.com; *bottom right* MishAl/Shutterstock.com; *bottom left* Ron Zmiri/Shutterstock.com; **127** Charles Brutlag/Shutterstock.com; **128** Wolna/Shutterstock.com, ©iStockphoto.com/PLAINVIEW; **132** ©iStockphoto.com/edge69; **134** Ron Zmiri/Shutterstock.com; **141** *top left* James Thew/Shutterstock.com; *bottom right* James Hoenstine/Shutterstock.com; **143** Nattika/Shutterstock.com; **144** Rob Byron/Shutterstock.com; **149** dompr/Shutterstock.com; **151** Paul St. Clair/Shutterstock.com; **152** Susana Ortega/Shutterstock.com; **159** Serg64/Shutterstock.com; **167** inxti/Shutterstock.com; **176** Zarja/ Shutterstock.com; **177** homydesign/Shutterstock.com; **179** tuulijumala/ Shutterstock.com, J.D.S/Shutterstock.com

Chapter 4

188 *top left* Pavel L Photo and Video/Shutterstock.com; *top right* paul cowell/Shutterstock.com; *center left* rickyd/Shutterstock.com; *bottom right* NatalieJean/Shutterstock.com; *bottom left* ©iStockphoto.com/ MinistryOfJoy; **195** *top left* Radovan Spurny/Shutterstock.com, Worldpics/ Shutterstock.com, wong yu liang/Shutterstock.com; *center left* ©iStockphoto.com/MinistryOfJoy **198** Jon Le-Bon/Shutterstock.com; **199** Dan Gerber/Shutterstock.com; **205** Richard Paul Kane/ Shutterstock.com; **207** *top left* Ben Haslam/Haslam Photography/ Shutterstock.com; *bottom right* Don Williamson/Shutterstock.com; **208** Steve Cukrov/Shutterstock.com; **213** Zhukov Oleg/Shutterstock.com; **214** Baker Alhashki/Shutterstock.com; **221** Klaus Bösch Rainbow Vision Sandpicture; **223** *exercise 57* graphixmania/Shutterstock.com; *exercise 58* Petrovic Igor/Shutterstock.com; *center right* © Kaleb Timberlake | Dreamstime.com; **224** *top right* Ermek/Shutterstock.com; *center right* © South12th | Dreamstime.com; **231** © Kjersti Joergensen | Dreamstime.com; **232** *center left* ©iStockphoto.com/edhor; *top right* Vereshchagin Dmitry/Shutterstock.com; **233** bikeriderlondon/ Shutterstock.com, Aspen Photo/Shutterstock.com, Ruth Peterkin/ Shutterstock.com; **235** Nattika/Shutterstock.com; **236** ©iStockphoto.com/ mikdam; **240** rickyd/Shutterstock.com; **248** *top left* © Matthew Apps | Dreamstime.com; *top center* muzsy/Shutterstock.com; *top right* © Vlue | Dreamstime.com; **250** *top left* paul cowell/Shutterstock.com; *center left* Haslam Photography/Shutterstock.com; **257** luigi nifosi/ Shutterstock.com; **265** *bottom left* © Tammygaffney | Dreamstime.com; *top right* Dan Breckwoldt/Shutterstock.com; *center right* Pavel L Photo and Video/Shutterstock.com; **266** *center left* BlueRingMedia/Shutterstock.com; *center right* © Tatjana Keisa | Dreamstime.com; **267** tuulijumala/ Shutterstock.com, barbar34/Shutterstock.com

Chapter 5

276 *top left* Margaret M Stewart/Shutterstock.com; *top right* Mikhail Pogosov/Shutterstock.com; *center left* Nadiia Gerbish/Shutterstock.com; *bottom right* Tyler Olson/Shutterstock.com; *bottom left* bikeriderlondon/ Shutterstock.com; **279** *top* Sascha Burkard/Shutterstock.com; *center* Ruslan Gi/Shutterstock.com; *bottom right* cobalt88/ Shutterstock.com, Sanchai Khudpin/Shutterstock.com; **286** ©iStockphoto.com/hugolacasse; **287** *top right* cTermit/ Shutterstock.com; *top center* Picsfive/Shutterstock.com; **290** ©iStockphoto.com/andriikoval; **292** *center left* Marques/ Shutterstock.com, Laurin Rinder/Shutterstock.com; *bottom left* oliveromg/ Shutterstock.com; **294** *center left* cobalt88/Shutterstock.com; *center right* bikeriderlondon/Shutterstock.com; **299** Tyler Olson/Shutterstock.com; **300** *bottom left* Andrey Bayda/Shutterstock.com; *bottom right* Image Point Fr/Shutterstock.com; **303** Nattika/Shutterstock.com; **305** CrackerClips Stock Media/Shutterstock.com; **309** ©iStockphoto.com/Andy Cook; **310** *top left* Nadiia Gerbish/Shutterstock.com; *center right* bikeriderlondon/ Shutterstock.com; **313** Mikhail Pogosov/Shutterstock.com; **315** *center top* Alan Bailey/Shutterstock.com; *center bottom* ©iStockphoto.com/zorani; **317** Tony Oshlick/Shutterstock.com; **318** Telnov Oleksii/Shutterstock.com; **319** Sascha Burkard/Shutterstock.com; **321** claudiofichera/Shutterstock.com; **323** Margaret M Stewart/Shutterstock.com; **324** ecco/Shutterstock.com; **325** tuulijumala/Shutterstock.com, MARGRIT HIRSCH/Shutterstock.com; **329** Christos Georghiou/Shutterstock.com